WHEREIN LIE THE BEGINNINGS OF SELF-KNOWLEDGE?

PSYCHOLOGY AND YOU
Second Edition

PSYCHOLOGY AND YOU
Second Edition

Judith W. McMahon   Frank B. McMahon   Tony Romano

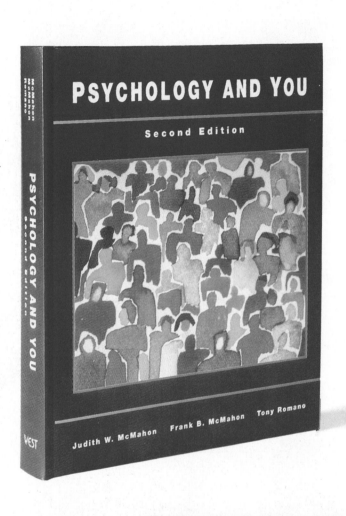

PSYCHOLOGY AND YOU is a high school text that introduces students to the fascinating world of psychology. **PSYCHOLOGY AND YOU** covers the information students need to learn about psychology, themselves, and others.

With this new and expanded edition, students learn more than just the science of psychology. Practical examples and an engaging writing style enable students to become more aware of how psychology applies to their lives.

The text's writing style, combined with examples relevant to students' lives, presents the science of psychology in an exciting and manageable way. Acknowledging the need for a commitment to the study of a complex subject, **PSYCHOLOGY AND YOU** utilizes a friendly writing style that makes the learning process enjoyable and unintimidating. A conversational tone is recognizable through the authors' use of humor, anecdotes, and a straight-forward approach. The text attracts student interest through its discussions of interesting experiments, unusual events and phenomena, and everyday issues and concerns. **PSYCHOLOGY AND YOU** is a text that helps students understand the field of psychology and how it relates to their lives.

THE AUTHORS

- Judith McMahon holds a B.A. degree in psychology from the University of Missouri, St. Louis and a Ph.D. in clinical psychology from Washington University, St. Louis. In twenty-four years of teaching she has covered areas such as personality theory, multicultural issues in psychology, counseling, child and adolescent psychology, and more. She is currently an Associate Professor of Psychology at Webster University, St. Louis.

- Throughout his life, Frank McMahon was committed to the study and teaching of psychology. That his name remains vital to this second edition is a reflection of that commitment. Professor McMahon earned a B.A., M.A., and Ph.D. in psychology from Washington University, St. Louis, and taught at the college level for twenty-six years. His areas of instruction included introductory psychology, history and systems, group dynamics, ethics, and others. At the time of his death in 1990 he was a Professor of Psychology at Southern University, Edwardsville, Illinois.

- A coauthor of the first edition, Tony Romano's articles have appeared in the *Chicago Tribune* and *English Journal*. Holding a B.A. in psychology and an M.A. in literature, Mr. Romano is an award-winning writer and currently teaches psychology at William Fremd High School, Palatine, Illinois. His teaching experience, writing style, and imagination have helped create projects, discussions, and suggestions that will enlighten students and enrich their understanding of psychology.

And because you, the educator, are the key presenter of this text's valuable information, WEST PUBLISHING has provided you with a complete teacher support package that adds impact to your classroom presentation while helping you organize your classes and evaluate student performance.

PSYCHOLOGY AND YOU
The Second Edition

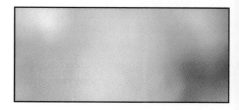

In preparing materials for this second edition, the authors accepted suggestions offered by teachers who used the highly successful first edition of **PSYCHOLOGY AND YOU**. Responding to this valuable input, each chapter has been carefully evaluated and revisions have been made where necessary. The language of the text, its coverage of topics such as the brain, nervous system, and others have been refined and updated.

Wishing to emphasize that psychology does not always focus on the abnormal or dysfunctional, **PSYCHOLOGY AND YOU** contains new material on self-concept and self-esteem. These sections have been added to help students assess the characteristics of the healthy personality. **PSYCHOLOGY AND YOU** also addresses the awareness of multiculturalism that has arisen within the psychology field. While this awareness can be seen throughout the text, a new section on cultural diversity and two chapters on sociocultural influences most clearly reflect the involvement with multicultural concerns. Other new or expanded student-centered sections discuss eating disorders, parenting styles, family issues, gender differences in communication, and defense mechanisms.

And because there are more than **90** new or updated scientific references in **PSYCHOLOGY AND YOU**, the majority from the 1990s, you are assured the information is backed by current studies.

A REFINED AND UPDATED TEXT

PSYCHOLOGY AND YOU
Student Text Features

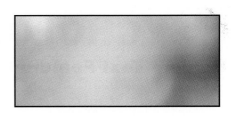

▲ **Chapter Objectives**
Chapter Objectives are listed, providing an excellent introduction to the subject matter and goals of each chapter.

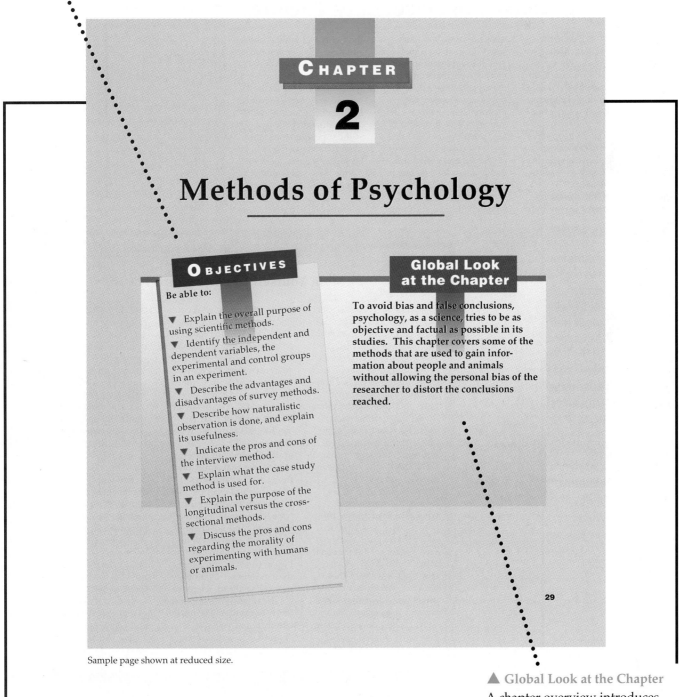

CHAPTER

2

Methods of Psychology

OBJECTIVES

Be able to:

▼ Explain the overall purpose of using scientific methods.

▼ Identify the independent and dependent variables, the experimental and control groups in an experiment.

▼ Describe the advantages and disadvantages of survey methods.

▼ Describe how naturalistic observation is done, and explain its usefulness.

▼ Indicate the pros and cons of the interview method.

▼ Explain what the case study method is used for.

▼ Explain the purpose of the longitudinal versus the cross-sectional methods.

▼ Discuss the pros and cons regarding the morality of experimenting with humans or animals.

Global Look at the Chapter

To avoid bias and false conclusions, psychology, as a science, tries to be as objective and factual as possible in its studies. This chapter covers some of the methods that are used to gain information about people and animals without allowing the personal bias of the researcher to distort the conclusions reached.

29

Sample page shown at reduced size.

▲ **Global Look at the Chapter**
A chapter overview introduces the student to chapter concepts.

PSYCHOLOGY AND YOU
Student Text Features Continued

Finding Yourself in Personality Theories

As we mentioned at the beginning of this chapter, we don't have enough information yet on how accurate different personality theories are. Still, it might be interesting for you to explore some things about yourself, and see if you can find support for the theories discussed. Don't take it all too seriously; we're just doing an "experiment," so to speak.

Start with the Freudian theory. Go back in your mind to the last time you had a secret desire to do something you didn't think proper or moral. Note that you didn't merely go out and do it without caring. Instead, what probably happened was that you felt a very strong internal "push" to go ahead and do it. Next you began to feel concerned and guilty, and you had a sinking feeling in your stomach that you might actually do it. Then you weighed the pros and cons, the rights and wrongs of the situation. Finally, you did or didn't do it. Note how very close this comes to your ego (your*self*) trying to let the id have its way, but also balancing the reality and morality of the situation by listening to the superego. It certainly seems like Freud might have been partly right, doesn't it?

Now the behavioral theory. Pick a habit you have that you're not necessarily *(continued on next page)*

Sample pages shown at reduced size.

Finding Yourself in Personality Theories

(continued from previous page) happy with: biting your fingernails, humming, doing funny things with your fingers, tugging at your socks, or who knows what. Go back in your mind to the last couple of times you did this behavior. You didn't want to do it, but it came automatically. Such habits are very hard to trace in some cases, but here is how they probably get started: sometime in the past you felt a lot of stress and strain. The way the body is constructed, when stress occurs, we prepare to take some kind of action, like running away. That's natural. But we can't actually run away—society won't allow it. So, rather than run, you started doing something—anything—with your body to relieve the tension. Having done *something*, your body relaxed a little; this made you feel better, which reinforced the behav-ior (even though what you did wasn't *really* helpful). Thus, you tend to repeat this something—humming, nail biting, and so on—year after year; each time, the reinforcement adds up so that the drive to do it gets stronger and stronger. The behavior becomes part of you. As you can see, this is the behavioral explanation for how we gradually develop patterns of activities that come to represent our personalities.

For the third example, the humanistic theories, you have to use your "Freudian superego" and not cheat. At a certain point, we will tell you not to read any further. Please don't, or you'll spoil the experiment. Don't even peek a line ahead. Here we go: in private write down the three things that you most admire about yourself. Beneath that, write the three things about yourself that you find obnoxious, gross, or unpleasant. Be *very* honest. Don't read any further until you have finished writing.

Now you need to examine your inner feelings very carefully. Notice how much stress and strain you felt, how physically uncomfortable you were, when you wrote the bad part. Note how you avoided and wanted to get away from it. Why? Could it be that you are basically a good person seeking self-actualization and fulfillment and that you are destined to be good? That these negative things just don't seem to belong to you and should go away? That's what the humanists would say. (Don't forget to destroy what you wrote! And remember that defects are part of all of us, and you're not alone at all in feeling bad about certain aspects of yourself.)

▲ **Psychology in Your Life**
Placed at the end of every chapter, these features apply chapter concepts to students' lives. Some of the issues covered include occupational possibilities within psychology, socialized gender differences, memory, human territoriality, and attitudes and beliefs.

▲ **In Focus** - These study aids, often orientated for visual learners, help students better understand difficult and important chapter concepts. New topics such as Experimental Procedure, Male and Female Communication, Overcoming Substance Abuse, and How to Persuade have been introduced.

IN FOCUS

Size Constancy

If we stand on a railroad tie and look down the track, the railroad ties in the distance actually seem to get smaller. But because of size constancy, we're not fooled for a moment. The *eyes* record the railroad ties in the distance as tiny, but the brain S T R E T C H E S them out to "normal" size.

Are we born with this size constancy ability? Does experience influence it?

▲ End of Chapter Pedagogy

Review Questions and Discussion Questions - These questions help you monitor your students' grasp of key textbook concepts. The discussion questions will stimulate conversations that explore issues from different perspectives.

Vocabulary Review - These review sections help reinforce text material and serve as excellent quick-study sources for students later on.

▲ At the back of the book you'll also find a **Statistics Appendix** and **Spanish Equivalents for Important Psychological Terms in English**.

Activities - Detailed and class-tested activities give students the opportunity to apply chapter concepts by conducting experiments and surveys. Students will learn the scientific methods behind psychology while they learn about others and themselves.

PSYCHOLOGY AND YOU

Student Text Features Continued

Valuable charts and graphs show in clear detail the results of many break-through studies in psychology. Elsewhere in the text, key illustrations provide helpful diagrams of complex psychological and physiological concepts.

▲ *Walking and swimming together — Konrad Lorenz and his imprinted "children."*

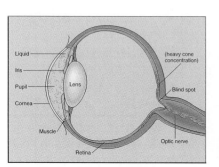

Shown at reduced size.

learning at about four months. Both animals and humans need frequent touching, holding, and rubbing from birth onward, or the results are disastrous (the case of Genie, discussed later, provides more details about this). Finally, a most intriguing critical period occurs for humans: if you want to learn a foreign language with a correct and natural accent, you must start learning it before the age of

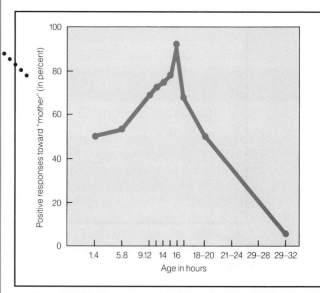

▲ *Figure 10.1* Duck's response to imprinting. Note the critical period at 16 hours.

284

Sample pages shown at reduced size.

VISUALLY STRIKING – EASY TO READ – EASY TO UNDERSTAND

Many new full-color photos, such as the one below, add greater visual diversity to this second edition. Students will find them to be useful visual anchors to key concepts and passages within the text.

Chimpanzees prefer their own babies to ours.

2 years. After that age, you can learn the language, but you will never have speech sounds that match those of the native speakers. There is one exception, though. A few people have a special ability to imitate sounds; these people are said to have an "ear" for languages. They will be able to get much closer to matching the correct accent, but the rule still applies for most of us.

You probably have heard tales about children who supposedly have been reared by animals. They are called **feral** (FER-al) **children,** the term *feral* meaning "wild, untamed." Such children supposedly walk on all fours and swing from trees. There has been one documented case of a boy who was discovered at age 11 or 12 after living in the woods by himself. The young man could not speak, and he did bite as any human child will, but he didn't growl, swing from trees, or act like an animal in other ways. The importance of critical periods and maturation within a social setting did show up. Since they were bypassed, he had almost no "human" skills. The boy eventually learned primitive speech and could print a few words, but he was never able to come close to what others his age could do in either area. He did learn the ways of society, in that he cleaned himself and ate the way we do and was able to accept and give affection as humans do, despite his childhood spent in isolation from other humans (Itard, 1932).

When you read about cases of children being brought up by animals, be careful not to accept them before asking yourself some questions. For instance, chimpanzees will almost automatically "adopt" an orphaned infant chimpanzee if its mother belonged to their group. They have even been known to take in an orphan whose mother was not a member of their group, but that is very, very rare. Chimpanzees

feral children

Children supposedly reared by animals.

▲ Key Terms - Learning the language of psychology can be a demanding process. To help students learn, key vocabulary and new terms are **boldfaced** in the text and supported by definitions in the margins. To reinforce learning, many terms are redefined when used in other chapters. The text also provides pronunciations for difficult words.

PSYCHOLOGY AND YOU
The Teacher's Wraparound Edition

New!

Structured to be the ideal teaching tool for today's high school classroom, the **TEACHER'S WRAPAROUND EDITION**, written by Tony Romano, is stocked with easily accessible and exciting teaching activities and strategies! Chapter opener pages introduce the chapter, provide a stimulating kick-off activity, and help you plan your lessons with a pacing chart. Support material for the chapter, available in the supplemental Teacher Resources, is also listed. A wide variety of activities, experiments, and projects utilizing cooperative learning techniques and critical thinking skills are prominently featured. The Wraparound Edition also contains additional suggestions for student journal writing and discussion questions, and makes connections to other parts of the text. Included as well are many items specifically directed to the instructor, such as teaching hints, reteaching strategies, FYIs, and points to stress. Evaluation strategies, comprehension checks, and answers to the end-of-chapter activities, discussion questions, and In Focus feature questions are also provided. Jim Matiya, a high school teacher in Orland Park, Illinois, has prepared interesting and up-to-date background information. This additional material, located on the unit opener pages, may be used to enhance classroom discussion.

All of the ready-information within the **TEACHER'S WRAPAROUND EDITION** lies at your fingertips! It's an easy-to-use teacher's edition that not only makes sense, but also saves time and assists you in coordinating your resource material, preparing your presentations, and assessing your students' progress.

▲ Journal Topic - These provide excellent opportunities for students to write and review on their own while exploring events or issues within their own lives.

▲ **Activities** - Many types of activities, such as this Discovery, promote understanding of key psychological concepts through active classroom participation. Students learn by experiencing psychology in action.

ACTIVITY ACTIVITY ACTIVITY ACTIVITY ACTIVITY ACTI

DISCOVERY

Complete the preceding **Discovery,** but this time adopt a humanist point of view. Argue that *most* of the behaviors listed are motivated by free will. For instance, a humanist might say that it's preposterous to focus on a single behavior like hair-washing.

We wash our hair so we can concentrate on more important, self-fulfilling aspects of life. So in a sense, even hair-washing is based on free will. To encourage more involvement, you might have students pair up and have each partner adopt a humanist

or behaviorist stance be to select any one lists and to argue wh ior is motivated more by external reinforce

Journal Topic

"Describe a recent argument or disagreement you've had with a parent or friend." Then have students write or discuss how a proponent from each of the six approaches in psychology might view the argument. In other words, how would Freud, Skinner, and others view the argument? The Analyzing Your Neighbor section should be very helpful for this exercise. After students finish their journal writing, they may need to add some details so they have something to analyze.

Discuss the Photo

Rogers believed that many adult problems are the result of trying to live by other people's standards.

Unit 1 APPROACHES TO PSYCHOLOGY

humanistic approach
Believing that people are basically good and capable of helping themselves.

▲ Carl Rogers "When I am closest to my inner, intuitive self, . . . whatever I do seems to be full of healing" (1986).

result of everything that has happened to moment, not an impulse. Another problem is take into account what is going on in you attached to a person who takes drugs or if y that is involved in drugs, the pull you feel t be greater than if you are close to people wh at times, previous learning is not as importa tion. Finally, the most uncomfortable aspect that it sees us as little more than robots, a b accept.

The Humanistic Approach

The **humanistic approach** to human beha the problems we've mentioned about behavi *istic* comes from *humane*. So, this group of psy people are basically good and that our very could reach perfection—if all went right.

To the humanists, each of us is like the pe right amount of water, nutrients, and sunligh we will become a perfect flower. Personal gro individual. We are in control of our destinies our lives worthwhile. Unlike the behaviorists that the environment does not *force* us to beco acts as a background for our internal growt death of a loved one, for instance, is an indiv call on our own internal resources to make the

The most famous humanist is **Carl Rogers** minister for a while before he entered psycho enced his beliefs, because he saw people a with free will and choice (Rogers, 1961, 1986 had the potential to become great in his or he way, with just a little guidance.

Some people find humanism a little too times when we are alone and think about ou the best and most "normal" of us can find inside that are quite removed from anythi flower.

The Psychoanalytic Appro

The best known of all theories, that of Sig our inner selves to be cesspools of forbidde oped a theory that centered around sexual a that are hidden in our unconscious from o impulses live below the surface of consciousn trol our everyday behavior in ways we are n

14

14

ENRICHMENT

Have students read a few case studies on the dismal conditions in some orphanages around the world, and they will acquire an appreciation for Harlow's studies. Harlow showed that infants need to be held and rocked, not simply "maintained."

▲ **Enrichment** - Enrichment Activities help students understand psychological findings in a real-world context.

Points to Stress

Some students may argue that they are intrinsically motivated at school. They enjoy learning; they work hard because they enjoy doing their best. But if these students were told that they would not be receiving diplomas after four years, no matter how hard they worked, would they still work hard or even attend classes? The point is that intrinsic and extrinsic motivation often go hand in hand.

Discussion

On one side of a sheet of paper, have students write down all the ways in which they are intrinsically motivated. The other side should include their extrinsic motivations. Do the lists balance? Remind students that *extrinsic* should not be equated with "bad." Then ask students if there are any items on that list that they wish came more from within.

Discuss the Photo

Many students will certainly question the ethics of separating a monkey from its mother. You may want to review the current ethics of experimentation at the end of Chapter 2.

▲ **Points to Stress** These will get your students focused on key chapter concepts by using familiar, but perhaps unconsidered, examples.

▲ **Discussion** - Here your class is provided extended opportunities to explore the issues under study. Discussions will often prompt students to discover new ways of understanding text material and how it relates to their lives.

▲ **Discuss the Photo** Photographs are wonderful anchors for students to attach ideas to. They're also useful for their ability to trigger responses. Discuss the Photo features take advantage of both of these properties, helping you further propel your students into the study of psychology.

---

classroom, and they will work for hours on it (because of intrinsic motivation). So what is the solution? The school structure is so big and so formalized that it won't work to take away grades (extrinsic). We need to find a way to add intrinsic motivation for students. If all of us were stuck on a desert island, it wouldn't be long before we were actually begging for a chance to learn something new.

Need for Stimulation All animals must have physical stimulation in order to develop properly. Monkeys that are not handled while they are growing up become cold, aloof, and unfriendly not only to others but also to their own offspring. Such monkeys can be partially "repaired" over a period of about six months if placed with other monkeys, but the fact that it takes so long shows the devastating effects of no stimulation (Suomi, 1983).

Psychologist **Harry Harlow** showed this need for **contact comfort** dramatically in a series of studies with monkey babies. Monkeys were placed in a cage with two fake mothers (see Figure 5.4). One of the "mothers" was made of wire and had a bottle attached to it where the monkeys could feed. The other mother was covered with terry cloth but provided no food. Once the animals had adjusted to having the two mothers, a fear test was performed.

While a mechanical, windup, teddy bear is fascinating to a child, it is very frightening to a monkey, so it formed the basis for the test. The mechanical teddy bear was put into the cage. The monkeys panicked. Here is the key point: even though the monkeys were fed by the wire mother, they consistently ran to the cloth mother for protection and comfort when faced with the teddy bear. This indicates the importance of contact comfort in development. While we would expect the monkeys to go to the mother that fed them, the pleasant physical contact of the cloth made them feel far more secure (Harlow, 1959).

There are parallel situations in humans. In one study during World War II, infants who were reared in an institution where there was almost no personal attention in the form of touching or holding were compared with infants who were reared in a prison nursery where they had contact with their mothers. The results were frightening: 37 percent of the institution children died within a year, despite being fed and kept clean (Spitz, 1946).

There is even physical evidence of these needs. At the base of the brain is a unit called the *cerebellum*, which registers and controls bodily movement and sensation. (For more detail, see Chapter 3.) The cerebellum has a number of connections to emotional systems. Without enough rocking and touching, the cerebellum does not develop properly, which is likely to create permanent emotional and physical scars (Prescott, 1979). We suspect that nature sees to this need, giving mothers the desire, almost automatically, to rock their infants.

Chapter 5 MOTIVATION AND EMOTION

contact comfort

The satisfaction obtained from pleasant, soft stimulation.

▲ *Figure 5.4 This monkey has the best of both worlds—contact comfort with the soft "mother" and food from the other one.*

139

139

Sample pages shown at reduced size.

▲ Additional WRAPAROUND EDITION features:

Lead-Off Activities /Introducing the Chapter /Pacing Charts /Demonstration, Experiment, and Cooperative Learning Activities /Chapter Projects (including interdisciplinary) /Critical Thinking /FYI, Teaching Hints, and Connections /Reading Assignments /Assessing Student Progress /Extra Credit /Additional Resources /School Involvement in Psychology /Speakers /Suggested Resources /Performance Tasks.

WEST PUBLISHING has put together an assortment of supplement materials that not only add variety and impact to any introductory psychology class, but also help you organize and simplify material presentation. You'll save time and find yourself better able to concentrate on the needs of your students.

PSYCHOLOGY AND YOU
Teacher Resource Materials

The following teacher resource materials are provided to you in one conveniently boxed package!

- **STUDENT WORKSHEETS (NEW!)** for each chapter including vocabulary, independent practice, enrichment, and reteaching have been prepared by Barbara Wiggins, a teacher from Montgomery, Alabama. Reproducible.

- **TEACHING MASTERS** - Tony Romano has prepared an extensive set of teaching masters to enhance presentations and ensure that students have a clear understanding of psychology concepts. Teaching suggestions for using the more than **100** reproducible blackline masters are provided in the Teacher's Wraparound Edition. Often incorporating cooperative learning techniques and performance-based assessments, these masters provide a variety of hands-on activities that appeal to different learning styles.

- **FULL-COLOR TRANSPARENCY ACETATES (NEW!)** - More than **50** transparencies of illustrations not found in the text are provided. These include sets of overlay transparencies, such as a depiction of the areas of the brain.

- **TEST BANK** - An outstanding Test Bank accompanies this edition of **PSYCHOLOGY AND YOU**. Available both on reproducible masters and in computerized form, the test bank contains two exams for every chapter. Preparer Joyce Waller, a high school teacher from Nashville, Tennessee, has identified all test questions by cognitive skill level as defined by Bloom's taxonomy. The text package also includes quizzes to test basic understanding.

- **ANNOTATED SOFTWARE RESOURCES LIST (NEW!)** Descriptions of applicable software for high school psychology classroom use have been prepared by Donna Hamilton, a high school teacher in Norman, Oklahoma. Compatible hardware, price information, and publisher addresses are included for each software package.

- **STUDENT WORKBOOK** - Includes a vocabulary review, projects, experiments, self-test questions, and key observations for each chapter. Prepared by Barbara Wiggins.

PSYCHOLOGY AND YOU

Videotapes

Unique videotapes offer a different and exciting approach to reinforcing and expanding on psychology concepts covered in **PSYCHOLOGY AND YOU**. The videotapes, from two widely acclaimed PBS series, cover a variety of issues, phenomena, and questions. *The Mind* consists of two complete episodes: *The Search for the Mind* and *Thinking*. These are two well-presented topics which correspond to topics in the text, and are inherently interesting to high school students.
The Brain videotapes are in a module format making them extremely powerful and flexible teaching tools. Each module is complete in itself, allowing you to choose individual topics at your discretion. *Your* lesson plans determine how the videotapes will be utilized!

Derived from current research in the psychology field, these video programs will enhance your class presentations, bringing a professional and dynamic visual dimension to your classroom. Detailed and clear graphics, computer-generated animation, and actual recorded footage (down to the microscopic level!) precisely show the workings of abstract or unfamiliar psychological and physiological concepts.

Correlations to related text material are provided.

Instructor's Manuals accompany the videotapes.

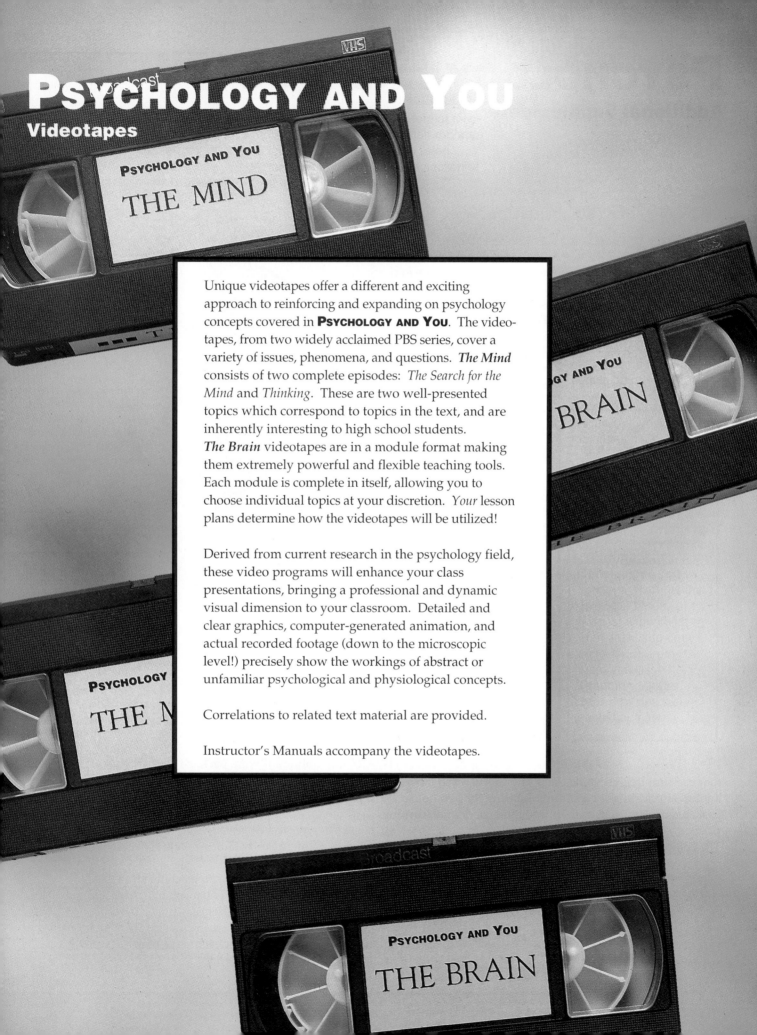

PSYCHOLOGY AND YOU
Additional Supplements

Videodiscs and Lecture Builder

New!

IMAGES OF PSYCHOLOGY: WEST'S VIDEODISC LIBRARY OF HUMAN BEHAVIOR - A two-videodisc set that provides nearly two hours of video footage to help you prepare exciting classroom presentations. Divided into thirteen units, each video segment has been carefully chosen to support major topics covered in **PSYCHOLOGY AND YOU**. Witnessing psychology concepts in action provides an instant spark that helps students understand human behavior.

Suggestions for using the videodiscs and related activities are provided.

INSTRUCTOR'S MANUAL - This accompanying guide references the videodiscs' footage, highlighting important concepts.

LECTURE BUILDER - This unique software program allows you to customize the videodiscs' presentation. With any MS-DOS or Macintosh computer using Windows operating system, you may program the order of the video segments from any part of a videodisc. An Instructor's Manual accompanies Lecture Builder.

PSYCHWARE and Mind Scope

PSYCHWARE - Available for Apple II computers, PSYCHWARE is a unique software package consisting of ten programs that use simulations, games, and tutorials to teach introductory psychology topics. PSYCHWARE emphasizes the most natural applications of computer learning for psychology. The programs reinforce understanding of classic experiments and basic psychological principles through experiential learning.

The complete package includes ten disks, an Instructor's Manual, and Student Study Guide in one convenient binder!

INSTRUCTOR'S MANUAL - Includes an overview of each program plus notes on teaching strategies and answers to the exercises in the Student Study Guide. The answers are also enhanced by teaching suggestions on topics designed to clarify and enrich the learning experience.

STUDENT STUDY GUIDE - Consists of a description of student objectives for each stage of a program and provides important background information the student may need to know. A series of worksheet exercises helps students apply what they learn.

PSYCHOLOGY AND YOU
Additional Supplements

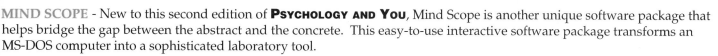

New!

MIND SCOPE - New to this second edition of **PSYCHOLOGY AND YOU**, Mind Scope is another unique software package that helps bridge the gap between the abstract and the concrete. This easy-to-use interactive software package transforms an MS-DOS computer into a sophisticated laboratory tool.

Designed for introductory level psychology courses, Mind Scope makes it possible for students to analyze aspects of their own psychology. Twenty exercises place the student into a subjective role where he or she performs psychological experiments that achieve real, not simulated, results. Exploring interesting phenomena such as reaction time, short-term memory, the stroop effect, and many others will help students become fascinated with the wonders of human response and behavior.

The complete Mind Scope package includes six disks, an Instructor's Manual, and a Student User's Guide grouped in one convenient binder!

WESTEST™ Computerized Testing

WESTEST™ is an easy-to-use computerized test bank. It allows you to create, edit, store, and print exams with the touch of a few keys! The system is menu-driven with a desktop format and offers the options of using keystrokes or a mouse, accelerator or function keys.

With WESTEST™ you may choose or edit existing questions and/or add new questions of your own. You may view summaries of the exam, prepare and preview their pages, and print the exam, answer sheet, answer key, or the entire test bank chapter. WESTEST™ also makes it possible to import graphics.

Available for Macintosh and MS-DOS computers.

PSYCHOLOGY AND YOU
SECOND EDITION

PSYCHOLOGY AND YOU
SECOND EDITION

Judith W. McMahon

Webster University
St. Louis, Missouri

Frank B. McMahon

Tony Romano

William Fremd High School
Palatine, Illinois

Wraparound Material
Written by

Tony Romano

West Publishing Company

Minneapolis/St. Paul   New York   Los Angeles   San Francisco

Copyedit: Nancy Palmer-Jones
Composition: Parkwood Composition
Cover image: Crowd #2 by Diane Ong; reprinted with permission of Superstock.

WEST'S COMMITMENT TO THE ENVIRONMENT

In 1906, West Publishing Company began recycling materials left over from the production of books. This began a tradition of efficient and responsible use of resources. Today, up to 95 percent of our legal books and 70 percent of our college texts are printed on recycled, acid-free stock. West also recycles nearly 22 million pounds of scrap paper annually—the equivalent of 181,717 trees. Since the 1960's, West has devised ways to capture and recycle waste inks, solvents, oils, and vapors created in the printing process. We also recycle plastics of all kinds, wood, glass, corrugated cardboard, and batteries, and have eliminated the use of styrofoam book packaging. We at West are proud of the longevity and the scope of our commitment to our environment.

Production, Prepress, Printing, and Binding by West Publishing Company.

02 01 00 99 98 97 96   8 7 6 5 4 3 2

TEACHER'S WRAPAROUND EDITION   ISBN # 0-314-02771-8
TEXAS WRAPAROUND EDITION   ISBN # 0-314-02968-0

Printed with Printwise
Environmentally Advanced Water Washable Ink

TEACHING AN INTRODUCTORY PSYCHOLOGY COURSE

Psychology can be one of the best courses a student takes in high school, and we hope that the suggestions in the teacher's wraparound edition will help to ensure this. The wraparound is not meant to create clones, with all of us teaching the same activities in the same way on the same day. Rather, we invite you to veer off, add, delete, and most of all, have fun with these suggestions. Regardless of how you use them, we trust that you will find that the ideas are original and lively and that they will inspire in students an authentic appreciation of psychology.

What follows are some general suggestions on teaching psychology and ideas on how to use the wraparound material in this edition. Not every wraparound category is addressed since many of the labels are self-explanatory.

Unit Opener Pages

Each unit opens with a two-page color photo. In the teacher's wraparound edition, these unit opener pages are equipped with

---

TEACHER'S BACKGROUND MATERIAL

Dealing With Stress

The text defines stress as the physical pressure and strain that results from the demands of the environment. It also states that conflict, anxiety, and frustration lead to stress. People have to cope with both the positive and negative changes in their lives, since both types cause stress.

Psychologists study how people respond to stress emotionally, physically, and behaviorally. When people react emotionally, they can become angry, anxious, irritable, and bitter. Physically, pulse rate increases, hands become sweaty, and eyes dilate. Behaviorally, people may appear restless as they bite their nails, tap their fingers, grind their teeth, or play with money in their pockets. Most disturbingly, they may start drinking more alcohol or displaying superstitious behaviors.

Three categories have been developed to describe stress-coping tendencies (Carver, 1989; Folkman and Lazarus, 1988). The first refers to individuals using **problem-focused** plans. These people attempt working out a way to either accept or change a situation so that it is no longer stressful. Proactive strategies such as strategic planning, problem-solving, restraint, and confrontation may be used. For example, if a person is accused of spreading rumors about one of the students in your class, what might you do? You could try talking to the person allegedly spreading the rumors. You may entertain a number of different ideas about how and why the rumors started before formulating a plan to put an end to the situation. You might try not to react to the rumors in front of your students. All of these instances revolve around the notion that addressing the situation, and changing it if possible, is the way to eradicate the stress it engenders.

Some people, however, employ **emotion-based** plans in the face of stress. In other words, they might try to change the emotional content of a situation in order to lessen its intensity. An example of this is relabeling your feeling of unrequited love for someone as dislike, in order to avoid the unpleasantness of low self-esteem. Other people may use repression or selective forgetting to deny that a problem even exists. Let's say you have an appointment with the dentist to have your wisdom teeth extracted. You have heard horror stories about this procedure from your friends, and are consequently fearful and anxious about it. Then you "forget" about the appointment and fail to show up at the dentist's office. Another tactic may be to tell yourself that the dentist is not qualified and made an incorrect diagnosis, or you may convince yourself that your teeth are fine and that the dentist is just trying to make a few extra dollars.

The third coping condition involves the **social support of others**. When people are under a great deal of stress they may seek the company and advice of others who have been in similar predicaments. Support groups can provide assis-

UNIT FIVE

PERSONALITY, ADJUSTMENT, AND CONFLICT

For people as in nature, from out of conflict and turmoil often come growth and greater understanding.

386

387

Discuss the Photo

Ask students to think of other parallels between nature and personality.

tance and emotional support, and some even offer legal help and psychological counseling for their members.

In a study of over 400 adults, researchers found that stable adjustment to stressful situations is enhanced when one uses problem-based strategies (Holahan and Moos, 1990). They also found that emotion-based plans, such as denial, lead to poorer adjustment and depression. Generally, the results showed that men tend to use more problem-solving plans than women, while women are more likely to use emotion-based plans and support groups. This is not surprising, as it reflects traditional, socially-enforced gender role traits, which are discussed at greater length in Chapter 13.

Other psychologists have identified still more stress-reducing strategies. One of these involves using physiological coping techniques such as progressive relaxation, exercise, and meditation. Another method is behavioral coping; for example, using a calender and schedule to utilize time more efficiently.

Cognitive restructuring (Meichennbaum, 1977) is another way to deal with stress, and requires rethinking and monitoring what you say to yourself. Most of us tend to believe that situations are worse than they actually are; Meichenbaum (1985) has outlined cognitive strategies that can enable people to avoid doing that. For example, a self-statement that can help when confronting a stressor is "Don't think about stress, just about what I have to do."

References

Full citations can be found in the Teacher Resources.

PERFORMANCE TASK

Overview: For this project, study groups will be assigned one of the four chapters of this unit. They will design a bulletin board using pictures, editorials, short articles, cartoons, tables, graphs, charts, and posters. Student-constructed materials are encouraged. These materials will be accompanied by a short paragraph explaining the material's relationship to the unit. Projects are to be displayed in the classroom, hallway, or in portfolios. Complete instructions for this activity and the supporting student worksheets can be found in the Teacher Resources.

background information relevant to the topic of each unit. This material is designed to supplement your lessons and enhance discussion. Referring to the theories and experiments presented here can help you further clarify and expand upon the concepts covered in the student text. These pages also provide descriptions of performance tasks; all tasks require students to organize, interpret, and present information relating to the subject of each unit.

Chapter Opener Pages

If you're looking for guidance while planning your lessons, look no further than the chapter opener pages of the wraparound. Here you'll find the **Psychology and You Resources** box which includes information about supplemental materials, such as the videos provided by West, software packages, relevant Teaching Masters, and Student Worksheets. A **Lead-Off Activity** and an **Introducing the Chapter** section suggest introductory activities and discussion topics, enabling you to get students immediately involved in the chapter material. There's also a **Pacing Chart**, which gives you a day - by - day breakdown of each chapter's highlights.

CHAPTER 4 PLANNER

DISCUSS THE PHOTO

Have students offer other possible perceptions of the photo (which is a difficult task once they read the caption).

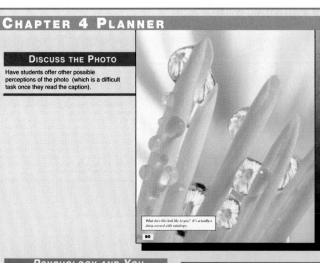

What does this look like to you? It's actually a daisy covered with raindrops.

90

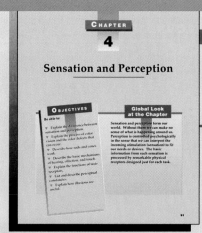

CHAPTER
4

Sensation and Perception

OBJECTIVES

Be able to:
▼ Explain the difference between sensation and perception.
▼ Explain the process of color vision and the color defects that can occur.
▼ Describe how rods and cones work.
▼ Describe the basic mechanisms of hearing, olfaction, and taste.
▼ Explain the functions of taste receptors.
▼ List and describe perceptual constancies.
▼ Explain how illusions are useful.

Global Look at the Chapter

Sensation and perception form our world. Without them we can make no sense of what is happening around us. Perception is controlled psychologically in the sense that we can interpret the incoming stimulation (sensation) to fit our needs or desires. The basic information from such sensation is processed by remarkable physical receptors designed just for each task.

91

INTRODUCING THE CHAPTER

Draw a grid on the chalkboard with 16 equal squares in it. Ask students how many squares they see. The immediate response will be, "16." A few seconds later, someone will say, "No, 20." You can find 30 with a little effort. Use this simple demonstration to make the distinction between sensation and perception. All of us *see* the same grid (sensation), but each of us may *interpret* it a bit differently (perception).

PSYCHOLOGY AND YOU RESOURCES

A variety of resources are available in the Psychology and You supplementary material. In addition, there are a number of additional resources listed to enhance your lesson plans.

Masters
▼ 4-1A Learning Goals
▼ 4-1B Answers to Learning Goals
▼ 4-2 Cutaneous Receptors
▼ 4-3 Perceptual Set
▼ 4-4 Identify the Perceptual Principle
▼ 4-5 The Dating Game
▼ 4-6 What Do You See? 1
▼ 4-7 What Do You See? 2

Worksheets
▼ Vocabulary Worksheet

▼ Independent Practice Worksheet
▼ Enrichment Worksheet
▼ Reteaching Worksheet

Test Bank
▼ Tests A and B

Multimedia
▼ The Mind Videotape The Brain #17
▼ The Mind Videotape Modules #11-14
▼ **Mindscope** Exercises 1, 2, 10, 19
▼ Psychology Videodisc

90

PACING CHART

Complete Coverage

Day 1: Assign the first two sections about sensation prior to class period. Choose an in-class demonstration from the wrap to illustrate the mechanisms of vision. In Focus: Color Vision will also be helpful.

Day 2: Build discussion around classroom demonstrations involving hearing, taste, smell, and/or the cutaneous senses. Have students read the "Perception" section for Day 3. Also, assign for homework an activity that involves conducting an experiment exploring sensation or perception, due on Day 5.

Day 3: Classroom demonstrations will best convey the concept of perception. Direct students to the In Focus box on size constancy. Use the question it presents to spark discussion about perception involving interpretation and expectation. Stress the concept of Gestalt and use In Focus: Moving Cubes to discuss illusions.

Day 4: Use Psychology in Your Life to discuss the evidence for and against the existence of extrasensory perception.

Day 5: Discuss and evaluate the results of students' completed activities assigned on Day 2. Give the Chapter Review quiz.

In Brief

Day 1: Use classroom demonstrations to highlight your lecture on sensation; the wrap provides several of these.

Day 2: Focus discussion on how perception is different from, yet connected to, sensation. Make sure students understand the concept of Gestalt.

Day 3: Discuss Psychology in Your Life, and conduct the demonstration it describes. Give the Chapter Review quiz.

LEAD-OFF ACTIVITY

Most students underestimate the abilities of our senses. To demonstrate our keen sense of touch, bring in ten lemons and ten blindfolds. With a marker, number each lemon. Have ten volunteers sit in a circle on the floor. After they are blindfolded, give each one a lemon and tell them their numbers. Allow them about a minute to "know" their lemons. Afterward, collect the lemons and randomly give a lemon back to each student. Still blindfolded, the students will pass lemons around the circle, attempting to find their assigned lemons. The rest of the class can observe how the group members communicate with each other without sight. Have fun varying this procedure by shortening the time limit, giving some students two lemons, and so on.

91

Activities

There's nothing like a hands-on activity to keep students alert, interested, and involved.

Demonstration, Discovery, and Experiment

In each chapter, several of these exercises can be found in the wraparound, and all of them promote understanding of key psychological concepts through active classroom participation; students learn by experiencing "psychology in action."

Cooperative Learning

If you are interested in cooperative learning, taking a class on the topic is an excellent way to experience the benefits of working together. Being a student in a cooperative-learning class also gives you valuable insight into your own students' reactions. The cooperative-learning ideas in the wraparound, however, are designed to work effectively even if you don't have this kind of training.

Here are some of the main principles and techniques of cooperative learning:

1. Small groups sit in a circle with desks touching. This helps the group members focus on each other and the task at hand. It also means that they don't have to shout to be heard by other group members, and consequently other groups will not be disturbed by loud voices.

2. Each group is given a specific task on which to work. The goals of the task are well defined.

3. Each member of the group is assigned or elects to perform a specific task, such as recorder, facilitator, artist, or timer.

4. If one member does not complete his or her task, it becomes difficult or impossible for the group to complete the group task. Knowing this creates a feeling of interdependency in the group.

If cooperative learning is new to you, you will probably want to gradually incorporate it into your lesson plans until you feel comfortable with it. Also, be prepared for a few objections from your students. Your better students may complain that group grades are unfair or that other students do not contribute their share. You can avoid this problem by making each student individually accountable in some way. If your "A" students are not satisfied with this,

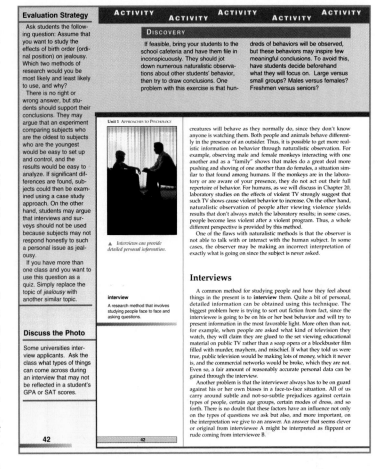

Evaluation Strategy

Ask students the following question: Assume that you want to study the effects of birth order (ordinal position) on jealousy. Which two methods of research would you be most likely and least likely to use, and why?

There is no right or wrong answer, but students should support their conclusions. They may argue that an experiment comparing subjects who are the oldest to subjects who are the youngest would be easy to set up and control, and the results would be easy to analyze. If significant differences are found, subjects could then be examined using a case study approach. On the other hand, students may argue that interviews and surveys should not be used because subjects may not respond honestly to such a personal issue as jealousy.

If you have more than one class and you want to use this question as a quiz. Simply replace the topic of *jealousy* with another similar topic.

Discuss the Photo

Some universities interview applicants. Ask the class what types of things can come across during an interview that may not be reflected in a student's GPA or SAT scores.

ACTIVITY

DISCOVERY

If feasible, bring your students to the school cafeteria and have them file in inconspicuously. They should jot down numerous naturalistic observations about other students' behavior, then try to draw conclusions. One problem with this exercise is that hundreds of behaviors will be observed, but these behaviors may inspire few meaningful conclusions. To avoid this, have students decide beforehand what they will focus on. Large versus small groups? Males versus females? Freshmen versus seniors?

Unit 1 APPROACHES TO PSYCHOLOGY

▲ *Interviews can provide detailed personal information.*

interview
A research method that involves studying people face to face and asking questions.

42

creatures will behave as they normally do, since they don't know anyone is watching them. Both people and animals behave differently in the presence of an outsider. Thus, it is possible to get more realistic information on behavior through naturalistic observation. For example, observing male and female monkeys interacting with one another and as a "family" shows that males do a great deal more pushing and shoving of one another than do females, a situation similar to that found among humans. If the monkeys are in the laboratory or are aware of your presence, they do not act out their full repertoire of behavior. For humans, as we will discuss in Chapter 20, laboratory studies on the effects of violent TV strongly suggest that such TV shows cause violent behavior to increase. On the other hand, naturalistic observation of people after viewing violence yields results that don't always match the laboratory results; in some cases, people become less violent after a violent program. Thus, a whole different perspective is provided by this method.

One of the flaws with naturalistic methods is that the observer is not able to talk with or interact with the human subject. In some cases, the observer may be making an incorrect interpretation of exactly what is going on since the subject is never asked.

Interviews

A common method for studying people and how they feel about things in the present is to **interview** them. Quite a bit of personal, detailed information can be obtained using this technique. The biggest problem here is trying to sort out fiction from fact, since the interviewee is going to be on his or her best behavior and will try to present information in the most favorable light. More often than not, for example, when people are asked what kind of television they watch, they will claim they are glued to the set viewing educational material on public TV rather than a soap opera or a blockbuster film filled with murder, mayhem, and mischief. If what they told us were true, public television would be making lots of money, which it never is, and the commercial networks would be broke, which they are not. Even so, a fair amount of reasonably accurate personal data can be gained through the interview.

Another problem is that the interviewer always has to be on guard against his or her own biases in a face-to-face situation. All of us carry around subtle and not-so-subtle prejudices against certain types of people, certain age groups, certain modes of dress, and so forth. There is no doubt that these factors have an influence not only on the types of questions we ask but also, and more important, on the interpretation we give to an answer. An answer that seems clever or original from interviewee A might be interpreted as flippant or rude coming from interviewee B.

42

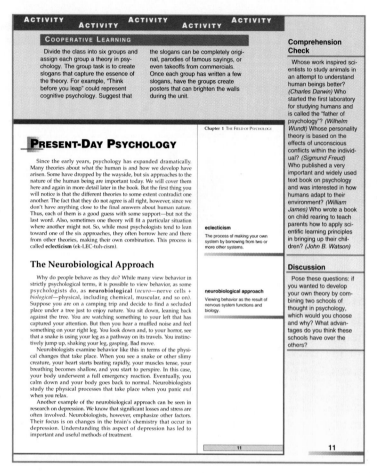

ACTIVITY ACTIVITY ACTIVITY ACTIVITY ACTIVITY

COOPERATIVE LEARNING

Divide the class into six groups and assign each group a theory in psychology. The group task is to create slogans that capture the essence of the theory. For example, "Think before you leap" could represent cognitive psychology. Suggest that the slogans can be completely original, parodies of famous sayings, or even takeoffs from commercials. Once each group has written a few slogans, have the groups create posters that can brighten the walls during the unit.

Comprehension Check

Whose work inspired scientists to study animals in an attempt to understand human beings better? *(Charles Darwin)* Who started the first laboratory for studying humans and is called the "father of psychology"? *(Wilhelm Wundt)* Whose personality theory is based on the effects of unconscious conflicts within the individual? *(Sigmund Freud)* Who published a very important and widely used text book on psychology and was interested in how humans adapt to their environment? *(William James)* Who wrote a book on child rearing to teach parents how to apply scientific learning principles in bringing up their children? *(John B. Watson)*

Discussion

Pose these questions: if you wanted to develop your own theory by combining two schools of thought in psychology, which would you choose and why? What advantages do you think these schools have over the others?

Chapter 1 THE FIELD OF PSYCHOLOGY

PRESENT-DAY PSYCHOLOGY

Since the early years, psychology has expanded dramatically. Many theories about what the human is and how we develop have arisen. Some have dropped by the wayside, but six approaches to the nature of the human being are important today. We will cover them here and again in more detail later in the book. But the first thing you will notice is that the different theories to some extent contradict one another. The fact that they do not agree is all right, however, since we don't have anything close to the final answers about human nature. Thus, each of them is a good guess with some support—but not the last word. Also, sometimes one theory will fit a particular situation where another might not. So, while most psychologists tend to lean toward one of the six approaches, they often borrow here and there from other theories, making their own combination. This process is called **eclecticism** (ek-LEC-tuh-cism).

eclecticism
The process of making your own system by borrowing from two or more other systems.

The Neurobiological Approach

Why do people behave as they do? While many view behavior in strictly psychological terms, it is possible to view behavior, as some psychologists do, as **neurobiological** (*neuro*—nerve cells + *biological*—physical, including chemical, muscular, and so on). Suppose you are on a camping trip and decide to find a secluded place under a tree just to enjoy nature. You sit down, leaning back against the tree. You are watching something to your left that has captured your attention. But then you hear a muffled noise and feel something on your right leg. You look down and, to your horror, see that a snake is using your leg as a pathway on its travels. You instinctively jump up, shaking your leg, gasping. Bad move.

Neurobiologists examine behavior like this in terms of the physical changes that take place. When you see a snake or other slimy creature, your heart starts beating rapidly, your muscles tense, your breathing becomes shallow, and you start to perspire. In this case, your body underwent a full emergency reaction. Eventually, you calm down and your body goes back to normal. Neurobiologists study the physical processes that take place when you panic *and* when you relax.

Another example of the neurobiological approach can be seen in research on depression. We know that significant losses and stress are often involved. Neurobiologists, however, emphasize other factors. Their focus is on changes in the brain's chemistry that occur in depression. Understanding this aspect of depression has led to important and useful methods of treatment.

neurobiological approach
Viewing behavior as the result of nervous system functions and biology.

11

11

give them a chance to hand in extra credit. Also, you might stress that sometimes the process of reaching consensus is as important or more important than the actual conclusion.

Once you become comfortable using cooperative learning and learn a few general strategies, you can apply these strategies in a variety of situations, regardless of content. For instance, Spencer Kagan (see Suggested Readings at the end of this introduction) recommends a method he calls *numbered heads together*. A useful reteaching strategy, the method works particularly well for review or as a comprehension check. Divide the class into groups of four, for example. Each group member picks a number from one to four. If one group has fewer members than everyone else, one member picks two numbers. The teacher asks a question and allows about 30 seconds for each student to write down an answer. Group members then put their heads together to formulate a single answer. At this point the teacher may want to rephrase the question. Rather than asking, "What is the definition of psychology?" the teacher says, "Make sure everyone in your group knows the definition of psychology." The teacher then calls on a number to answer the question. If the teacher calls "3," only 3s can answer. If only a few 3s raise their hands, the teacher might allow more time. This is an excellent strategy for keeping everyone involved in what could otherwise be a boring review.

You can create some friendly competition by using what Kagan calls *simultaneous numbered heads together*. In this case, all number 3s write down their answers on a group answer sheet. They then pass the answer sheet to the person whose number is called for the next question. You can use a spinner to make the number-calling seem more game-like. To motivate students, you might offer extra credit to the group with the most correct answers.

Projects

Each chapter includes a chapter project and at least one interdisciplinary project. Although these projects sometimes require extra planning and direction on your part, the results are usually worthwhile. The projects are practical; they lead to tangible results or products; and students get the opportunity to take charge, choose alternatives, and set goals.

Enrichment

In every chapter you will also find numerous enrichment ideas — tasks that send students searching for answers to intriguing questions. *Enrichment* may sound to you like a euphemism for plain *research*, but the process can be exciting if you find a way to sell it to your students. For example, you might require that each student complete at least one enrichment activity during the semester. As students complete them, they can report back to the class. If you stagger the due dates for each student (maybe you can pick them by lottery), you'll have reports throughout the entire semester! Or you might introduce the enrichment ideas from time to time for extra credit.

Journal Writing

Don't be afraid to make students write. They may complain from time to time, but they're just trying to condition you; condition them instead! The papers don't have to be lengthy, you don't need to take out your red pen, and you need not grade every page. In fact, much of the writing can be done in class, five or ten minutes here and there to allow students to *process* an activity or discussion. The very act of writing often helps us discover how we feel about a particular issue. If you're in the middle of a lively discussion and you don't want to cut it off to make time for writing, simply do it the next day. Many of the journal entries suggested in the wrap are designed just for this processing purpose.

If you decide that you want students to keep a journal in class, here are some general tips:

1. Limit journal-writing to about five to ten minutes.

2. Ask students to bring in a notebook that is exclusively for journal entries.

3. Encourage students to *free-write*—that is, they need not worry about spelling, grammar, or punctuation.

4. Use journals often. Once students realize that journals are part of the routine,

ACTIVITY   ACTIVITY   ACTIVITY   ACTIVITY   ACTIVITY

ENRICHMENT

Have students read a few case studies on the dismal conditions in some orphanages around the world, and they will acquire an appreciation for Harlow's studies. Harlow showed that infants need to be held and rocked, not simply "maintained."

Chapter 5 MOTIVATION AND EMOTION

classroom, and they will work for hours on it (because of intrinsic motivation). So what is the solution? The school structure is so big and so formalized that it won't work to take away grades (extrinsic). We need to find a way to add intrinsic motivation for students. If all of us were stuck on a desert island, it wouldn't be long before we were actually begging for a chance to learn something new.

Need for Stimulation All animals must have physical stimulation in order to develop properly. Monkeys that are not handled while they are growing up become cold, aloof, and unfriendly not only to others but also to their own offspring. Such monkeys can be partially "repaired" over a period of about six months if placed with other monkeys, but the fact that it takes so long shows the devastating effects of no stimulation (Suomi, 1983).

Psychologist **Harry Harlow** showed this need for **contact comfort** dramatically in a series of studies with monkey babies. Monkeys were placed in a cage with two fake mothers (see Figure 5.4). One of the "mothers" was made of wire and had a bottle attached to it where the monkeys could feed. The other mother was covered with terry cloth but provided no food. Once the animals had adjusted to having the two mothers, a fear test was performed.

While a mechanical, windup, teddy bear is fascinating to a child, it is very frightening to a monkey, so it formed the basis for the test. The mechanical teddy bear was put into the cage. The monkeys panicked. Here is the key point: even though the monkeys were fed by the wire mother, they consistently ran to the cloth mother for protection and comfort when faced with the teddy bear. This indicates the importance of contact comfort in development. While we would expect the monkeys to go to the mother that fed them, the pleasant physical contact of the cloth made them feel far more secure (Harlow, 1959).

There are parallel situations in humans. In one study during World War II, infants who were reared in an institution where there was almost no personal attention in the form of touching or holding were compared with infants who were reared in a prison nursery where they had contact with their mothers. The results were frightening: 37 percent of the institution children died within a year, despite being fed and kept clean (Spitz, 1946).

There is even physical evidence of these needs. At the base of the brain is a unit called the *cerebellum*, which registers and controls bodily movement and sensation. (For more detail, see Chapter 3.) The cerebellum has a number of connections to emotional systems. Without enough rocking and touching, the cerebellum does not develop properly, which is likely to create permanent emotional and physical scars (Prescott, 1979). We suspect that nature sees to this need, giving mothers the desire, almost automatically, to rock their infants.

contact comfort

The satisfaction obtained from pleasant, soft stimulation.

▲ *Figure 5.4 This monkey has the best of both worlds—contact comfort with the soft "mother" and food from the other one.*

Points to Stress

Some students may argue that they are intrinsically motivated at school. They enjoy learning; they work hard because they enjoy doing their best. But if these students were told that they would not be receiving diplomas after four years, no matter how hard they worked, would they still work hard or even attend classes? The point is that intrinsic and extrinsic motivation often go hand in hand.

Discussion

On one side of a sheet of paper, have students write down all the ways in which they are intrinsically motivated. The other side should include their extrinsic motivations. Do the lists balance? Remind students that *extrinsic* should not be equated with "bad." Then ask students if there are any items on that list that they wish came more from within.

Discuss the Photo

Many students will certainly question the ethics of separating a monkey from its mother. You may want to review the current ethics of experimentation at the end of Chapter 2.

139

ACTIVITY ACTIVITY **ACTIVITY** ACTIVITY **ACTIVITY** ACTIVITY **ACTIVITY**

DISCOVERY

Complete the preceding **Discovery**, but this time adopt a humanist point of view. Argue that *most* of the behaviors listed are motivated by free will. For instance, a humanist might say that it's preposterous to focus on a single behavior like hair-washing.

We wash our hair so we can concentrate on more important, self-fulfilling aspects of life. So in a sense, even hair-washing is based on free will. To encourage more involvement, you might have students pair up and have each partner adopt a humanist

or behaviorist stance. Their task will be to select any one item on their lists and to argue whether the behavior is motivated more by free will or by external reinforcements.

Journal Topic

"Describe a recent argument or disagreement you've had with a parent or friend." Then have students write or discuss how a proponent from each of the six approaches in psychology might view the argument. In other words, how would Freud, Skinner, and others view the argument? The Analyzing Your Neighbor section should be very helpful for this exercise. After students finish their journal writing, they may need to add some details so they have something to analyze.

Discuss the Photo

Rogers believed that many adult problems are the result of trying to live by other people's standards.

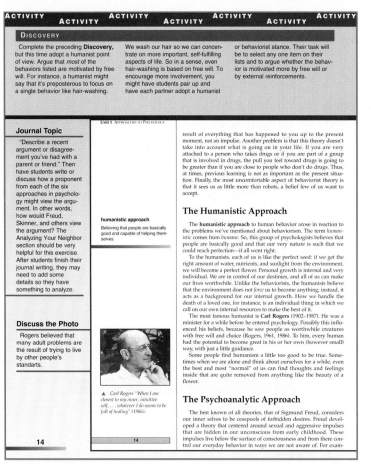

Unit 1 APPROACHES TO PSYCHOLOGY

humanistic approach

Believing that people are basically good and capable of helping themselves.

▲ *Carl Rogers "When I am closest to my inner, intuitive self, . . . whatever I do seems to be full of healing" (1986).*

14

result of everything that has happened to you up to the present moment, not an impulse. Another problem is that this theory doesn't take into account what is going on in your life. If you are very attached to a person who takes drugs or if you are part of a group that is involved in drugs, the pull you feel toward drugs is going to be greater than if you are close to people who don't do drugs. Thus, at times, previous learning is not as important as the present situation. Finally, the most uncomfortable aspect of behaviorist theory is that it sees us as little more than robots, a belief few of us want to accept.

The Humanistic Approach

The **humanistic approach** to human behavior arose in reaction to the problems we've mentioned about behaviorism. The term *humanistic* comes from *humane*. So, this group of psychologists believes that people are basically good and that our very nature is such that we could reach perfection—if all went right.

To the humanists, each of us is like the perfect seed: if we get the right amount of water, nutrients, and sunlight from the environment, we will become a perfect flower. Personal growth is internal and very individual. We are in control of our destinies, and all of us can make our lives worthwhile. Unlike the behaviorists, the humanists believe that the environment does not *force* us to become anything; instead, it acts as a background for our internal growth. How we handle the death of a loved one, for instance, is an individual thing in which we call on our own internal resources to make the best of it.

The most famous humanist is **Carl Rogers** (1902–1987). He was a minister for a while before he entered psychology. Possibly this influenced his beliefs, because he saw people as worthwhile creatures with free will and choice (Rogers, 1961, 1986). To him, every human had the potential to become great in his or her own (however small) way, with just a little guidance.

Some people find humanism a little too good to be true. Sometimes when we are alone and think about ourselves for a while, even the best and most "normal" of us can find thoughts and feelings inside that are quite removed from anything like the beauty of a flower.

The Psychoanalytic Approach

The best known of all theories, that of Sigmund Freud, considers our inner selves to be cesspools of forbidden desires. Freud developed a theory that centered around sexual and aggressive impulses that are hidden in our unconscious from early childhood. These impulses live below the surface of consciousness and from there control our everyday behavior in ways we are not aware of. For exam-

14

they'll soon comply. After a few weeks, many will realize the power of putting thoughts on paper.

5. Don't collect the journals until the end of the term. If students feel that you are checking up on them every week, they may not feel that they *own* their journals. You may, however, want to look around while students write to make sure that everyone is participating.

At the end of each term, students can process the journal as a whole. They can write an introduction to the journal in order to accomplish this. For example, have them write a page or two on this: "Pretend that you have lost your journal. Someone finds it and decides to write an introduction to the journal, summarizing what he or she thinks about the author of the journal. Write that introduction! Remember, you're writing from the point of view of the person who finds it. Don't spend too much time on *how* the journal was found. Get to the task at hand—the description of the journal and its author." See **Teaching Master 0-1—Journals** for a handout that lists this option, along with a few others.

At the end of the year, when students evaluate the class, you may be surprised at how many students genuinely appreciated the writing opportunities.

Critical Thinking

This feature provides tasks requiring students to apply learned information in various ways; students are encouraged to both deepen and broaden their knowledge.

FYI, Points to Stress, Teaching Hints, and Connections

FYI boxes contain relevant supplemental facts and background information, while the Points to Stress sections offers material to assist you in emphasizing important concepts. Teaching Hints suggest ways to facilitate students' understanding of some of the more complex ideas discussed in the text. The Connections feature highlights the relationships between ideas covered in a particular chapter and those found elsewhere in the text.

Reading Assignments

Students will groan about reading, too, of course. Many of them simply will not do it—or if they do, will not get much out of it—unless they are asked to respond to the reading. You will find plenty of ideas designed to elicit responses—in the wraparound, at the end of each chapter (the discussion questions in particular), in the Teacher Resources, and in the Student Worksheets.

At times, you may just want some assurance that students have read what they were supposed to read. The wraparound provides **Comprehension Checks** and **Evaluation Strategies** at regular intervals throughout each chapter. Also, Learning Goals for each chapter are listed in the Teacher Resources. Or you might simply have students take notes on the assigned chapter using a large note card. If they do a good job and do not merely copy the margin definitions, you might let them use the note card for the test. **Vocabulary Review** and **Reteaching Strategies** are other wraparound features you can utilize to reinforce students' learning.

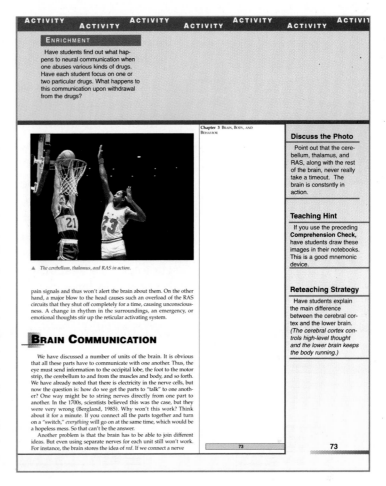

ACTIVITY ACTIVITY ACTIVITY ACTIVITY ACTIVITY ACTIVITY ACTIVIT

ENRICHMENT

Have students find out what happens to neural communication when one abuses various kinds of drugs. Have each student focus on one or two particular drugs. What happens to this communication upon withdrawal from the drugs?

Chapter 3 BRAIN, BODY, AND BEHAVIOR

▲ *The cerebellum, thalamus, and RAS in action.*

pain signals and thus won't alert the brain about them. On the other hand, a major blow to the head causes such an overload of the RAS circuits that they shut off completely for a time, causing unconsciousness. A change in rhythm in the surroundings, an emergency, or emotional thoughts stir up the reticular activating system.

BRAIN COMMUNICATION

We have discussed a number of units of the brain. It is obvious that all these parts have to communicate with one another. Thus, the eye must send information to the occipital lobe, the foot to the motor strip, the cerebellum to and from the muscles and body, and so forth. We have already noted that there is electricity in the nerve cells, but now the question is: how do we get the parts to "talk" to one another? One way might be to string nerves directly from one part to another. In the 1700s, scientists believed this was the case, but they were very wrong (Bergland, 1985). Why won't this work? Think about it for a minute. If you connect all the parts together and turn on a "switch," *everything* will go on at the same time, which would be a hopeless mess. So that can't be the answer.

Another problem is that the brain has to be able to join different ideas. But even using separate nerves for each unit still won't work. For instance, the brain stores the idea of *red.* If we connect a nerve

73

73

Discuss the Photo

Point out that the cerebellum, thalamus, and RAS, along with the rest of the brain, never really take a timeout. The brain is constsntly in action.

Teaching Hint

If you use the preceding **Comprehension Check,** have students draw these images in their notebooks. This is a good mnemonic device.

Reteaching Strategy

Have students explain the main difference between the cerebral cortex and the lower brain. *(The cerebral cortex controls high-level thought and the lower brain keeps the body running.)*

Assessing Student Progress

Most teachers probably rely on quizzes, tests, and assignments to assess students. Here are some additional ideas:

1. If you want students to invest more quality time studying for your tests, let them see any essay questions a day or two before the test. This encourages them to think about the questions for days, rather than for the 50 or 60 minutes of class time. You'll get better answers, which will make grading easier, and students most likely will retain more than they normally would. This technique is most effective when you use questions that focus on critical thinking skills.

2. Here's one way to motivate students to complete the numerous enrichment ideas listed throughout the wraparound. In order to receive a C for the quarter, students must complete at least one enrichment activity; for a B, two must be completed; for an A, three must be completed. All this would be in addition to any other requirements that you specify.

3. Consider having students develop portfolios of their work throughout the semester. You can still give tests and assignments,

but a major part of their overall assessment would include the portfolio that they hand in at the end of the semester. Here's one method for creating portfolios:

a. Students hand in assignments throughout the semester.

b. At the end of the semester, students select what they feel are the most significant works.

c. Students briefly analyze the strengths and weaknesses of this work, identifying problem areas and tracking their progress.

You will need to specify some minimum requirements for the portfolio. For example, the portfolio must include the following: a self-assessment, at least one write-up of an experiment, and at least one review of an outside source. Students should also write an introduction to the portfolio that includes their impressions of psychology. See **Teaching Master 0-2—Portfolio** for a student handout on portfolio formats.

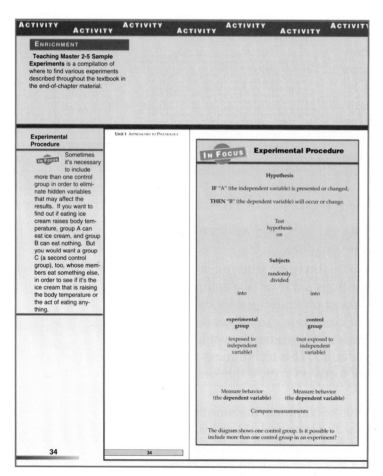

ACTIVITY ACTIVITY **ACTIVITY** ACTIVITY **ACTIVITY** ACTIVITY **ACTIVIT**

ENRICHMENT

Teaching Master 2-5 Sample Experiments is a compilation of where to find various experiments described throughout the textbook in the end-of-chapter material.

Experimental Procedure

IN FOCUS Sometimes it's necessary to include more than one control group in order to eliminate hidden variables that may affect the results. If you want to find out if eating ice cream raises body temperature, group A can eat ice cream, and group B can eat nothing. But you would want a group C (a second control group), too, whose members eat something else, in order to see if it's the ice cream that is raising the body temperature or the act of eating anything.

Unit 1 APPROACHES TO PSYCHOLOGY

IN FOCUS **Experimental Procedure**

Hypothesis

IF "A" (the independent variable) is presented or changed,

THEN "B" (the dependent variable) will occur or change.

Test
hypothesis
on

Subjects

randomly
divided

into   into

**experimental   control
group   group**

(exposed to   (not exposed to
independent   independent
variable)   variable)

Measure behavior   Measure behavior
(the **dependent variable**)   (the **dependent variable**)

Compare measurements

The diagram shows one control group. Is it possible to include more than one control group in an experiment?

34

34

Extra Credit

See **Teaching Master 0-3— What Can I Do For Extra Credit?** for a list of extra-credit possibilities that you can post in your classroom. Also, keep in mind that you may come across an idea in the wrap that sounds great, but you personally don't have the time to prepare it. In that case, let one of your students prepare and present it to the class for extra credit! For example, you may like the idea of conducting a taste test in class (see Chapter 4), but you don't want to bring in food. Have a student or a group of students organize this experiment for extra credit.

Additional Resources

At the end of each chapter, the wraparound provides lists of **Suggested Readings** and **Suggested Videos**.

Organizations to Join

You probably want to join your state's social studies council, but if you can join only one group, become a member of the American Psychological Association's High School Affiliate program. The cost is nominal, and the benefits are great: activity ideas, newsletters, journals, and automatic membership in APA's Teachers of Psychology in Secondary Schools (TOPSS).

Membership Office
American Psychological Association
750 First Street, NE
Washington, D.C. 20002-4242

School Involvement in Psychology

Psychology is such an exciting discipline that it's difficult sometimes to contain it within the walls of your classroom. If you think this is an exaggeration, try one of the following ideas:

1. Coordinate a psychology fair at your school in which your students prepare and present projects in the gym. The rest of the school learns about psychology through hands-on participation at each booth. See the Teacher Resources for details on the fair.

2. Start a psychology club. The focus can be on volunteering at mental health centers, preparing a newsletter that is distributed to the rest of the school, exploring issues discussed in class through the use of guest speakers—or all of the above and more.

Speakers

When students are asked to find speakers to visit class, they are initially reluctant, believing that no one will want to come. They're wrong. It's probably not accurate to generalize, but it does seem that most people who work in the field of psychology are eager to share their expertise, especially with young people. Some speakers are more compelling than others, of course, but there's nothing you can do about that at first. Save the business cards of the best speakers and call them back the next year.

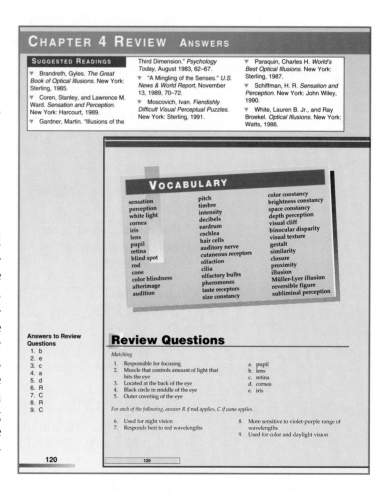

CHAPTER 4 REVIEW ANSWERS

SUGGESTED READINGS

▼ Brandreth, Gyles. *The Great Book of Optical Illusions.* New York: Sterling, 1985.
▼ Coren, Stanley, and Lawrence M. Ward. *Sensation and Perception.* New York: Harcourt, 1989.
▼ Gardner, Martin. "Illusions of the Third Dimension." *Psychology Today,* August 1983, 62–67.
▼ "A Mingling of the Senses." *U.S. News & World Report,* November 13, 1989, 70–72.
▼ Moscovich, Ivan. *Fiendishly Difficult Visual Perceptual Puzzles.* New York: Sterling, 1991.
▼ Paraquin, Charles H. *World's Best Optical Illusions.* New York: Sterling, 1987.
▼ Schiffman, H. R. *Sensation and Perception.* New York: John Wiley, 1990.
▼ White, Lauren B. Jr., and Ray Broekel. *Optical Illusions.* New York: Watts, 1986.

VOCABULARY

sensation
perception
white light
cornea
iris
lens
pupil
retina
blind spot
rod
cone
color blindness
afterimage
audition

pitch
timbre
intensity
decibels
eardrum
cochlea
hair cells
auditory nerve
cutaneous receptors
olfaction
cilia
olfactory bulbs
pheromones
taste receptors
size constancy

color constancy
brightness constancy
space constancy
depth perception
visual cliff
binocular disparity
visual texture
gestalt
similarity
closure
proximity
illusion
Müller-Lyer illusion
reversible figure
subliminal perception

Answers to Review Questions
1. b
2. e
3. c
4. a
5. d
6. R
7. C
8. R
9. C

Review Questions

Matching

1. Responsible for focusing
2. Muscle that controls amount of light that hits the eye
3. Located at the back of the eye
4. Black circle in middle of the eye
5. Outer covering of the eye

a. pupil
b. lens
c. retina
d. cornea
e. iris

For each of the following, answer R if rod applies, C if cone applies.

6. Used for night vision
7. Responds best to red wavelengths
8. More sensitive to violet-purple range of wavelengths
9. Used for color and daylight vision

120

120

Suggested Resources

Books and Magazines

Benjamin, Ludy T., and Kathleen D. Lowman, eds. *Activities Handbook for the Teaching of Psychology.* Washington, D.C.: American Psychological Association, 1981.

The Family Therapy Networker magazine. Contact: 8528 Bradford Road, Silver Spring, MD 20901-9955.

Fogarty, Robin, and James Bellanca. *Patterns for Thinking, Patterns for Transfer.* IRI Group, contact: 1-800-922-4474.

Hunt, Morton. *The Story of Psychology.* New York: Doubleday, 1993.

Johnson, David W., et al. *Cooperation in the Classroom*, Edina, Minn.: Interaction Book Company, 1988. Contact: 7208 Cornelia Drive, Edina, MN 55435, (612) 831-9500.

Johnson, Margo, and Michael Wertheimer, eds. *Psychology Teacher's Resource Book: First Course.* Washington, D.C.: American Psychological Association, 1979.

Kagan, Spencer. *Cooperative Learning.* Resources for Teachers, 1992. Contact: 1-800-WEE-COOP.

Makosky, Vivian Parker, Linda Whittemore, and Anne Rogers, eds. *Activities Handbook for the Teaching of Psychology.*, Vol. 2. Washington, D.C.: American Psychological Association, 1987.

Makosky, Vivian Parker, et al. , eds. *Activities Handbook for the Teaching of Psychology.* Vol. 3. Washington, D.C.: American Psychological Association, 1990.

Psychology Today magazine. Contact: P. O. Box 51844, Boulder, CO, 80321-1844.

Rainer, Tristine. *The New Diary.* New York: St. Martin's Press, 1978.

Rubinstein, Joseph, and Brent Slife, eds. *Taking Sides: Clashing Views of Controversial Psychological Issues.* 5th ed. Guilford, NY: Dushkin, 1988.

Video Series

The Brain. PBS Video, 1320 Braddock Place, Alexandria ,VA 22314-1698.

Discovering Psychology. Annenberg/CPB Project, c/o Intellimation, P. O. Box 1922, Santa Barbara, CA 93116-1922, 1-800-LEARNER.

The Mind. P. O. Box 68618, Indianapolis, IN 46268.

Seasons of Life. Intellimation, P. O. Box 1922, Santa Barbara, CA 93116-1922, 1-800-LEARNER.

Addresses for Books and Videos

American Psychological Association, 750 First Street, NE, Washington, D.C. 20002-4242.

Films for the Humanities and Sciences, Inc., P. O. Box 2053, Princeton, NJ 08543, 1-800-257-5126.

Insight Media, 121 West 8th Street, New York, NY 10024, (212) 721-6316.

Interact Publishers, Box 997, Lakeside, CA 92040.

J. Weston Walch, Portland, ME 04104-0658.

Social Issues Resource Series, Inc., P. O. Box 2348, Boca Raton, FL 33427-2348.

Social Studies School Service, 10200 Jefferson Boulevard, Room 3011, P. O. Box 802, Culver City, CA 90232-0802.

PSYCHOLOGY AND YOU
SECOND EDITION

PSYCHOLOGY AND YOU
SECOND EDITION

Judith W. McMahon

Webster University

St. Louis, Missouri

Frank B. McMahon

Tony Romano

William Fremd High School

Palatine, Illinois

West Publishing Company

Minneapolis/St. Paul   New York   Los Angeles   San Francisco

Copyeditor: Nancy Palmer-Jones
Dummy Artist: Diane Beasley
Proofreader: Julia Grondin
Indexer: Maggie Jarpey
Composition: Parkwood Composition
Interior Art: Barbara Barnett; Stan Maddock, Precision Graphics
In Focus Cartoons: Gary Carroll
Cover Art: *Crowd #2* by Diana Ong; reprinted with permission of Superstock.

WEST'S COMMITMENT TO THE ENVIRONMENT

In 1906, West Publishing Company began recycling materials left over from the production of books. This began a tradition of efficient and responsible use of resources. Today, up to 95 percent of our legal books and 70 percent of our college and school texts are printed on recycled, acid-free stock. West also recycles nearly 22 million pounds of scrap paper annually—the equivalent of 181,717 trees. Since the 1960s, West has devised ways to capture and recycle waste inks, solvents, oils, and vapors created in the printing process. We also recycle plastics of all kinds, wood, glass, corrugated cardboard, and batteries, and have eliminated the use of Styrofoam book packaging. We at West are proud of the longevity and the scope of our commitment to the environment.

Production, Prepress, Printing, and Binding by West Publishing Company.

Library of Congress Cataloging-in-Publication Data

McMahon, Judith W.
    Psychology and you / Judith W. McMahon, Frank B. McMahon, Tony Romano. — 2nd ed.
      p. cm
    Includes bibliographical references and index.
    ISBN 0-314-02772-6
    1. Psychology. I. McMahon, Judith W. II. Romano, Tony, 1957–.
III. Title
BF121.M2945 1994
150—dc20

93-41159
CIP

CONTENTS IN BRIEF

TABLE OF CONTENTS

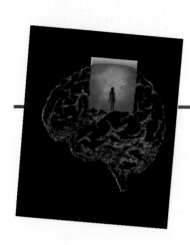

Chapter 2 Methods of Psychology   29

UNIT TWO **BRAIN, BODY,**
AND AWARENESS **57**

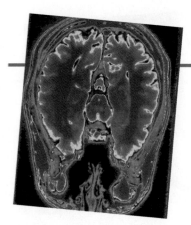

Chapter 3 Brain, Body, and Behavior 59

Chapter 4 Sensation and Perception 91

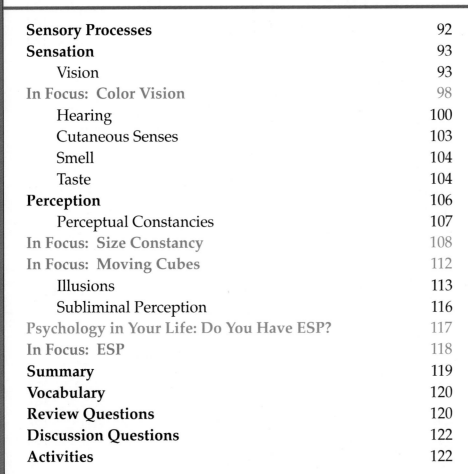

Chapter 5 Motivation and Emotion 125

Chapter 6 Consciousness   155

UNIT THREE   COGNITIVE PROCESSES   183

Chapter 7 Principles of Learning   185

Chapter 8 Acquiring, Processing, and Retaining Information 215

Chapter 9 Intelligence and Creativity

247

Chapter 11 Adolescence   309

Chapter 12 Adulthood and Aging   337

Chapter 13   Gender Differences   361

Unit Five PERSONALITY, ADJUSTMENT, AND CONFLICT   387

Chapter 14 Theories of Personality   389

Chapter 15 Measuring Personality and Personal Abilities 419

Chapter 16 Frustration, Conflict, Stress, and Drugs   443

Chapter 17 Toward a Healthy Personality

UNIT SIX **PSYCHOLOGICAL DISORDERS**   **501**

Chapter 18 Mental Disorders   503

Chapter 19   Treatment and Therapy   535

UNIT SEVEN SOCIOCULTURAL INFLUENCES AND SELF 563

Chapter 20 Sociocultural Influences and Relationships 565

Chapter 21 Sociocultural Influences: Attitudes and Beliefs   593

PREFACE

In the fall of 1990 the senior author of the first edition of this text, Professor Frank B. McMahon, died following a lengthy illness. He had devoted his professional life to the field of psychology and to his students. Teaching was his passion. Over a period of more than two decades, we collaborated on a number of projects, including college-level texts in the areas of introductory and abnormal psychology. The last such project was this high school text, *Psychology and You*. This revised edition embodies the philosophy and approach that we shared—to always keep the students' welfare and understanding in mind. It is an honor to be able to ensure that his contributions to his profession continue. With a sense of sadness and pride, this book is dedicated to his memory.

Psychology encompasses broad areas of research about human behavior, information that should be available to all high school students who want to understand themselves and others better. The goal of this text is to create active intellectual and emotional involvement by the student, not only in learning about the science of psychology, but in life as well. This edition retains all of the original features designed to stimulate students' interest and enhance their knowledge of the field. We believe that you will find it highly informational, up-to-date, and "user-friendly."

Learning abstractions and learning practicality do not have to be separate things. Almost every page of this book ties in scientific issues with corresponding applications to daily life. The special boxes—one for each chapter—called "Psychology in Your Life" apply some of the principles found in the chapter directly to everyday issues and concerns. In this edition, topics covered in these special boxes include substance abuse, problem solving, and abusive relationships. Additional

devices designed to keep interest high and improve retention are the inclusion of anecdotes, historical facts, unusual events, and humor, plus a writing style that talks to the students, taking them step by step through the subject matter.

With input from teachers who used the first edition of *Psychology and You*, each chapter was gone over carefully and updated and tightened or reworked in many places. For instance, the historical information in the first chapter is now more directly relevant to psychology. The chapter on functions of the brain and nervous system was reworked to make it more clear and inclusive, as was the chapter on abnormal behavior. A section on juvenile delinquency was added to the chapter on adolescence, and the chapter on adulthood and aging was almost completely restructured. Expansions of the text include additional information on: genes and chromosomes, characteristics associated with high intelligence, eating disorders, parenting styles, family issues, achievement in old age, gender differences in communication, the MMPI-2, defense mechanisms, and cultural influences on aggression.

This edition is extremely current. There are over 90 new references, the vast majority from 1990s sources. New references can be found in every chapter, and they cover all major areas in the field. For example, material in the chapter on abnormal behavior agrees with the diagnostic categories in the fourth edition of the DSM (1994). There is new material on self-concept and self-esteem as well as new coverage of the characteristics of the healthy personality. As the field of psychology has recently become more conscious of and sensitive to the impact of multicultural concerns on its findings and interpretations, so this volume reflects that increased awareness. This can be seen most clearly in a new section on cultural diversity and the two chapters on sociocultural influences, but multicultural issues also appear in various other places throughout the text.

Each chapter contains learning devices and exercises designed to enhance the students' understanding and retention of material. In creating these, Tony Romano, a high school teacher with a master's degree in psychology, has done his usual outstanding job. Especially noteworthy are his In Focus features, which condense and bring together subject matter that might be confusing or especially difficult. Mr. Romano has long been involved in setting up psychology science fairs for the counties in which he teaches, and his knowledge and skills are evident in the work he has done here.

Tony Romano also developed the wraparound teacher's edition and the teacher resource material.

Every effort has been made to be sure that you are getting the best possible psychology text for high school students. Several experienced high school teachers from across the country reviewed this edition and made many excellent suggestions for changes. They were especially thorough in their reviews of those sections that comprised substantive alterations to the original manuscript. Their help and encouragement are warmly appreciated and gratefully acknowledged.

David Boersma
Evergreen Park Community High School
Evergreen Park, Illinois

Sondra Gray
Chespeake High School
Pasadena, Maryland

Neil Lloyd
Carl Schurz High School
Chicago, Illinois

Ruth Martin
Memorial High School
Madison, Wisconsin

Jim Matiya
Carl Sandburg High School
Orland Park, Illinois

David Mejia
West High School
Denver, Colorado

Iris Roberts
Jefferson City High School
Jefferson City, Missouri

James Rostello
Olathe North High School
Olathe, Kansas

Dickee Six
Bath High School
Bath, Michigan

Marie T. Smith
Thomas S. Wootton High School
Rockville, Maryland

Swazette D. Young
Bowie High School
Bowie, Maryland

Without the patience, cooperation, and support of the Department of Behavioral and Social Sciences at Webster University, this project could never have been completed. Professor William HuddlestonBerry's help proved especially valuable.

West Educational Publishing Company has been very enthusiastic about the text and provided an enormous amount of assistance. In this regard, special thanks go to Clyde Perlee, Carole Grumney, Lynn Bruton, and Leslie King Deakin. We also want to thank Mario Rodriguez and Christine Henry for their production work, and Nancy Palmer-Jones for her diligent and extremely able copyediting.

Finally, to those of you who have used the book before, we hope that this revision pleases you. To first-time adopters, welcome. We are about to embark on an exciting educational journey, and we are delighted to have you all along.

Experimental Problems and Solutions

Experiments are designed to show a relationship between cause and effect. This relationship between variables can be obscured by problems within the experimental design. Two of the situations that can affect the relationship between variables in an experiment are known as the experimenter effect and the Hawthorne effect.

The term **experimenter effect** is used to describe the situation in which an experimenter unknowingly communicates to the subjects what is expected of them. For example, according to Fernald (1984), Hans was a very talented horse who reportedly could add numbers and subtract numbers and spell words. Clever Hans could "count" by stomping his hoof. For example, if Hans was asked to add 2+2, he would stomp his hoof four times on the ground. When the trainer stood in front of or off to the side of Hans, the horse would not miss a single problem. It was noticed that if the trainer stood behind Hans, the horse could not solve problems. Eventually, it was discovered that his trainer had unconsciously communicated to Hans when to start and when to stop counting numbers by giving visual cues such as nodding his head and blinking. Hans was not as clever as everyone thought.

Robert Rosenthal and Lenore Jacobsen (1968) also demonstrated the experimenter effect when they gave an I.Q. test to 370 students. Some children (selected at random) were labeled as being "spurters" or "bloomers." The teachers were told that these children would do very well academically in the current school year. Only the teachers were told which students were reported to be "spurters" or "bloomers" and they did not know that those students were selected at random. It was hypothesized that the teachers would somehow communicate these labels to the children. At the end of the school year, the children were given another I.Q. test. All the children showed improvement. The "bloomers," however, showed the greatest gains (an average of 12 points!) on the IQ test. Indeed, the teachers had communicated their belief regarding the children's potential by paying more attention to the "bloomer" children as well as through facial expressions and gestures. The expectations of the teacher influenced the behavior of the students in the same way that the experimenter can influence the subjects in an experiment. If the experimenter influences the subjects, the results of the experiment may not demonstrate the real cause and relationship it is designed to find.

Another problem occurs when the subjects try to please the experimenter. This is known as the **Hawthorne effect,** named after the classic experiment which took place at the

A pathway to understanding.

Discuss the Photo

This photo can be a metaphor for several things: the future of psychology as a science; an invitation to explore what's up ahead in one's life; and so on. Have students offer ideas.

Hawthorne factory in Chicago (Roesthlisberger, F. and Dickson, W. J., 1939). The company owning the factory produced telephones. Researchers wanted to test the effects of environmental conditions on the workers' productivity. They hypothesized that brighter light in the factory would positively affect productivity. The investigators found that no matter how bright the lighting was, the workers produced more telephones. This was confusing. It was concluded that simply because the subjects had been told they were subjects in an

APPROACHES TO PSYCHOLOGY

PERFORMANCE TASK

Overview

Class will select one topic to study. An example might be the effect of types of music on concentration while studying. Small study groups propose a research method such as experimental method, case study, etc., to explore the topic. Each group presents their method to the class, outlines step by step procedures, and concludes with what they see as limitations and advantages of their particular method as applied to the class topic. After a period of questions on appropriateness of the method, procedures, or ethical concerns, all students will write a short paper stating which method he or she would select to research this topic and why. Complete instructions for this activity and the supporting student worksheets can be found in the Teacher Resources.

experiment, they acted differently by working harder to produce more telephones.

The existence of the Hawthorne effect was further demonstrated when an experimenter asked subjects to complete 224 calculations (Orne, 1962). The subjects were given 2000 pieces of paper with 224 calculations on each one! For five hours the subjects calculated the results. The experimenter then asked the subjects to tear each answer sheet into little pieces before going on to the next set of problems. Without question or protest, subjects continued to calculate the questions and started ripping apart the answer sheets. Evidently, subjects wanted to please the experimenter!

It is for reasons like this that psychological experiments often use control groups and the double-blind format, discussed in Chapter 2.

References

Full citations can be found in the Teacher Resources.

DISCUSS THE PHOTO

The human mind is one of the world's most profound mysteries. Studying psychology can provide the tools needed to explore it.

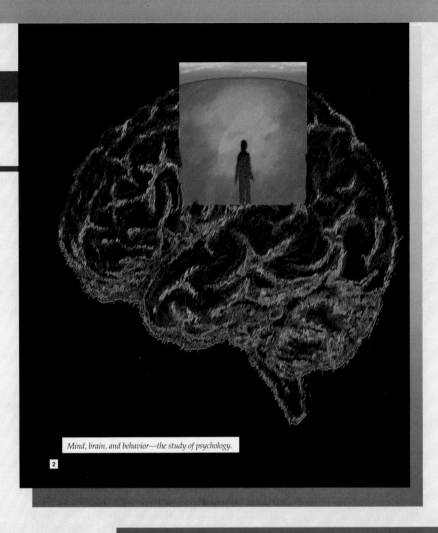

Mind, brain, and behavior—the study of psychology.

2

PSYCHOLOGY AND YOU RESOURCES

A variety of resources are available in the Psychology and You *supplementary material. In addition, there are a number of additional resources listed to enhance your lesson plans.*

Masters
▼ 0–1 Journals
▼ 0–2 Portfolio
▼ 0–3 What Can I Do for Extra Credit?
▼ 1-1A Learning Goals
▼ 1-1B Answers to Learning Goals
▼ 1-2 Vignettes
▼ 1-3 Six Approaches to Studying Behavior
▼ 1-4 Writing Your Own Magazine Article

Student Worksheets
▼ Vocabulary Worksheet
▼ Independent Practice Worksheet
▼ Enrichment Worksheet
▼ Reteaching Worksheet

Test Bank
▼ Tests A and B

Multimedia
▼ Psychology Videodisc

Student Workbook

PACING CHART

Complete Coverage

Day 1: Assign the first section of the chapter and Psychology in Your Life prior to class. Do activity #1 from the text as a group. Discussion question #2 can be used to illustrate the concept of theory as it applies to psychology. Have students define each of the occupations described in Psychology in Your Life as examples of either research or applied psychology. Assign "History of Psychology" for Day 2.

Day 2: Focus on the ramifications of introspection for psychological study. After evaluating the contributions of Darwin, Wundt, Freud, James, and Watson, direct students to the In Focus: A Few Who Have Shaped Psychology for review. Have students read "Present-Day Psychology" and "Analyzing Your Neighbor" in preparation for Day 3. Assign activity #5 in the text to be completed for Day 4.

The Field of Psychology

OBJECTIVES

Be able to:

▼ Define psychology and describe some of the work psychologists do.

▼ Explain the purpose of theory.

▼ Describe what Wundt was trying to accomplish with his laboratory work.

▼ Explain the approach of William James.

▼ Describe John B. Watson's areas of interest.

▼ Describe Freud's contribution to psychology.

▼ Give an example of and describe the six different approaches of present-day psychology to understanding human nature.

Global Look at the Chapter

Once science started to make progress in the 1800s, humans began to be viewed as creatures who could be studied and understood. Since then, the human body and mind have been explored in detail. In this chapter, we cover some of these explorations, trying to describe human nature as it was seen in the past and as it is understood now.

3

Before assigning any reading, have students pair up to answer two questions: (1) What is the definition of psychology?   (2) What do psychologists study? Most of their answers will be acceptable, but this exercise offers you an early opportunity to dispel misconceptions. In defining psychology, students will probably not include the term *scientific.* Stress how essential this term is to the definition. You can reinforce this point every time you conduct an experiment in class. Point out that in order to be scientific, psychology examines behavior, something that can be seen and measured and perhaps altered.

Day 3: Emphasize the way eclecticism works. Discussion question #3 can be used to facilitate understanding of the various approaches of eclecticism and situations in which such approaches can be combined.

Day 4: Have students share their conclusions after completing activity #5. This will provide an opportunity for a good discussion about the socio-cultural approach to psychology. Give the Chapter Review quiz.

In Brief

Day 1: Emphasize the concepts of theory and introspection. Assign in-class activities that involve constructing and evaluating theories.

Day 2: Focus on eclecticism. Facilitate a discussion requiring students to evaluate the application of the various psychological approaches. Give the Chapter Review quiz.

LEAD-OFF ACTIVITY

The purpose of this activity is to break the ice and to communicate to your students on the very first day that psychology will be different from any other course they've ever taken. Pass out index cards, and as you pass them out, shake each student's hand. Have students write the following on the cards: "This card proves beyond a shadow of a doubt that [student's name] is definitely cool." Walk around, initial each card, and announce that these are their official cool cards.

Explain that we all have a desire to appear cool at times, to be accepted by others, and that there's obviously nothing wrong with that. Because of this desire, however, we sometimes go out of our way to act cool, rather than being ourselves. Offer them some personal examples about times when *you* have tried to appear cool. (There may be cooler words to use than cool!) Since your students now have their official cool cards, they don't have to prove they're cool. It's acknowledged. In fact, the sooner they can be themselves in class, the more likely they are to enjoy the class and get something out of it.

DISCOVERY

Present a series of examples of pseudo-psychology and ask, "Is *this* psychology?" Possible examples: (1) Have students sign their names on index cards, collect them, and "analyze" their handwriting. (2) Ask a few students, "What's your favorite color?" Pretend to look up analyses in the teacher's manual. (3) Ask students to write down a number from one to ten. Predict that 90 percent wrote down the number seven (which may end up being right).

The reason none of these examples is real psychology is that they all lack scientific rigor. For example, even if handwriting analysis were widely accepted, a graphologist would need to collect more than just a simple signature. Ask students what procedures could be changed and made more scientific so that the tasks might be considered real psychology. This is a good time to explain that "lucky seven" is related to astrology, which has nothing whatsoever to do with psychology.

Discussion

Browse through the text with your class on the first or second day, perusing illustrations, photos, and so on. Discuss some of the issues raised in the captions. This should help generate interest in the wide scope of concerns in psychology.

TEACHING MASTER 1-1A

Learning Goals. A Learning Goals sheet for each chapter is provided in the Teacher Resources. These Learning Goals can be used as review sheets or worksheets. **Teaching Master 1-1B** consists of answers to these Learning Goals.

THE WORLD OF THE PSYCHOLOGIST

For most people, a psychologist is someone who sits across from you, listens to your problems, and tries to help. There are more than 100,000 psychologists in the United States, and roughly a third do in fact deal with personal problems. But that leaves two-thirds of the group doing something else. What are the rest of them doing? Well, some try to understand what the world is like for children or adolescents or older people—that is, what are their worries, hopes, needs, and so forth. Some help design spacecraft cabins so dials and switches are in the right place and so the captain in an emergency won't hit the "up" button instead of the "down" button. Still others study the effects of various drugs, while some counsel alcoholics or drug abusers. Another group works with delinquents, while others try to figure out what causes delinquency in the first place. Psychologists work in educational systems. They try to understand exactly what we measure with an IQ test (since we're still not completely sure); they try to keep the good students moving forward and help struggling ones get themselves together; they try to improve both teaching and learning. Some psychologists handle rape and suicide crises, while others try to figure out why such things happen and how best to prevent them.

As you have guessed by now, this list could go on and on. Figures 1.1 and 1.2 show the major areas of psychology. And at the end of the chapter, you'll find a fairly detailed outline of the tasks involved in some of the major fields of psychology.

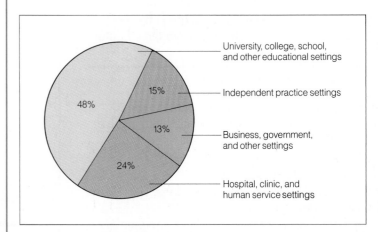

University, college, school, and other educational settings

Independent practice settings

Business, government, and other settings

Hospital, clinic, and human service settings

▲ *Figure 1.1* *Approximate proportions of job distribution among psychologists.*

INTERDISCIPLINARY PROJECT

Science. Most young people today understand that we need to clean up the environment, but even the concerned ones may be short on specifics. Have students study one part of the environment (landfills, ozone layer, and so on) from the point of view of natural sciences. Students should describe one specif-ic problem, explain the causes of the problem, and suggest possible solutions. At this point, they should address the following question: How can psychology help to clean up the environment? Point out that in answering this question, students are acting as applied psychologists.

If students become excited about this project, consider implementing some of their solutions. For example, they can try to increase recycling efforts at your school. They might discuss the advantages and disadvantages of placing a recycling bin at one location versus another. Or they can start an ad campaign. Explain *(continued on next page)*

Educational	Teaching
Military	Experimental
Adulthood and aging	Psychological testing
Engineering	Physiological
Rehabilitation	Developmental (children)
Community (problems	Personality and social
and needs)	behavior
Psychopharmacology	Clinical (abnormal)
Mental retardation	Industrial and
Consumer behavior	organizational
Psychology of women	Psychotherapy
	Environmental

▲ *Figure 1.2   Representative areas of specialization in psychology.*

Defining Psychology

At first, when we look at all the things that psychologists do, it doesn't seem possible to come up with a single definition for what psychology is. But there actually is one that fits them all: **psychology** is the scientific study of human and animal behavior.* The term *behavior* is not used here in its simple, everyday sense. It refers to almost *any* activity. Thus, the blink of an eye is behavior, and so is sweating, and so is thinking. Behavior includes attitudes, thoughts, and physical changes, as well as emotional changes. We are studying behavior when we want to decide if people take drugs for psycholog-ical or physical reasons. In other words, studying behavior means trying to figure out why it occurs.

The meaningful study of any subject requires some kind of struc-ture. In science, theory provides that structure. A **theory** is a general framework or idea about the nature of something. Because it covers so much, a theory is usually too complicated to be directly tested or researched. However, smaller aspects of it can be. When enough of these smaller parts prove true, the theory itself is supported. A theo-ry, then, is something like a tree, and its branches and leaves are testable ideas or assumptions.

In sciences such as chemistry and physics, theories are fairly straightforward. In psychology, though, things can get pretty confus-ing. After all, there may be many causes for a particular behavior. For example, people can be violent if they come from a family in which they have learned to deal with arguments by beating each other up. But there are also cases in which a person suddenly goes into a rage for no apparent reason. This might be a physical problem. As we will discuss in Chapter 3, there is a part of the brain that, when stimulated, causes a person to become extremely violent. In 1966, a man with a brain growth that was touching this area climbed

psychology

The scientific study of human and animal behavior.

theory

General framework for scientific study; smaller aspects can be tested.

Points to Stress

The definition of psychol-ogy in the text, though correct, may not seem adequate to some stu-dents. Emphasize that psychology can be viewed as a science, but it can also be viewed as a pro-fession. The two are intri-cately linked and comple-ment each other. For example, a clinical psy-chologist may help a depressed patient by using the findings of experimental research. The direction of new research, in turn, may be influenced by the results of therapy. Refer students to the **Psychology in Your Life** feature at the end of the chapter to show the broad concerns of psychology. Some psy-chologists focus on research, extending the knowledge base. Others treat people. And some do both.

---

*Words throughout the book that are in dark **boldface** are terms that are important; you should know the definition of them.

INTERDISCIPLINARY PROJECT

(continued from previous page) that applied psychologists use the information gathered by research psychologists; then encourage them to find some of that research. For instance, research on persuasion may teach them that ad campaigns shouldn't go too far in trying to make people feel guilty (in this case, making others feel guilty about throwing cans in the trash rather than in the recycle bin).

ENRICHMENT

You may want to have students debate the following issue: Should research psychologists have to prove that a particular study will be practical, at least someday, or will this block creativity? In other words, should research psychologists be funded and allowed to conduct research that may never be applicable?

FYI Good theories will summarize data that has been collected, help to direct future research, and allow us to predict behavior to some extent.

Teaching Hint

Draw two filing cabinets on the board. Explain that a study might find that reaction time slows down as one gets older and this information would belong in the "research" cabinet. Once this information becomes useful, it is moved to the "applied" cabinet. The main distinction between applied and research psychology is that the first is immediately practical and the second is not. Many researchers have to show that the results of their research will lead to practical benefits to get funding.

DISCUSS THE PHOTO

A psychologist may devote years studying a seemingly simple, isolated behavior, such as how a person's brain reacts when she is presented with a novel pattern after she has seen a series of similar patterns.

6

▲ *So much behavior to study and so little time.*

research psychologists

Those who study the origin, cause, or results of certain behaviors.

6

atop a tower at the University of Texas carrying rifles and ammunition and picked people off one by one. By the time the police got him, he had shot 44 people, killing 14 of them. So, psychologists study the physical as well as the psychological aspects of behavior (Valenstein, 1973).*

Research Versus Applied Psychology

Depending on how much attention you were paying to the first paragraph, you may or may not have noticed that there are two basic types of psychologists. One group studies the origins, causes, or results of certain behaviors. Another group uses such information to deal with people and problems directly. Psychologists in the first group are called **research psychologists.** Since the second group

*Psychology uses a special system for listing references. The last name of the author from whom certain information comes and the year he or she published that information appears in parentheses. These references are then listed in the back of the book under the author's name. (These are for reference only; do *not* try to memorize these names.)

Have volunteers study the government's most recent position on research versus applied science: Is the government willing to fund both? How have technology, the economy, politics, and changes in science itself influenced the government's position? What do critics say about the government's position? How might this position affect research in psychology?

makes direct use of ("applies") psychological studies, they are called **applied psychologists.** As we will discuss in Chapter 6, airlines have recently discovered a rather serious problem: pilots are falling asleep in the cockpit as you ride along at 30,000 feet. Research psychologists who study sleep patterns and basic body rhythms have determined why this happens; applied psychologists consult airlines and suggest ways to fix the pilots' schedules in order to avoid this problem.

HISTORY OF PSYCHOLOGY

For our purposes, psychology has the goal of understanding the human being, how and why we operate the way we do. To understand what psychology is today and how it got there, you need a brief history.

At the beginning of the 1800s, science as a whole was in its infancy. Psychology had not really begun to be a science in the formal sense. But in the 1800s, **Charles Darwin** went on a five-year sea journey around the world. He had two feet of walking space in his cabin and was seasick the whole time, but when he was on land, he noted that animals he knew well at home in England had developed differently in other places due to climate or food sources. Eventually he suggested that animals, including humans, had evolved and changed. His theory has been causing argument since 1859 when it

▲ *Charles Darwin as a young man.*

Chapter 1 THE FIELD OF PSYCHOLOGY

applied psychologists

Those who make direct use of the findings of research psychologists; deal directly with clients.

Announce this theory: *Personality is inherited.* Students will probably demand that you support your statement. The discussion that ensues will probably be very lively, since you've adopted such an extreme stance. It should also demonstrate the need for *objective* support. Finally, it should lead to a discussion about theories in general. What if you really wanted to test the theory? How could a psychologist study one aspect of the theory? For example, rather than focusing on something as broad as personality in general, a psychologist might study a single personality trait, like shyness.

Darwin's idea of adaptive functions for natural selection also applies to psychology. For example, he believed that human emotions evolved because they serve a useful purpose.

CHAPTER PROJECT/COOPERATIVE LEARNING

You can transform the critical-thinking exercise below into a group exercise by assigning each group a different behavioral goal to work on. Here's a handy list of goals (including those already mentioned) that your behavioral engineers can work on:

(1) increase alertness; (2) improve reaction time; (3) get people to wear seat belts; (4) get people to obey traffic laws; (5) make long-distance rides more comfortable; (6) eliminate drunk driving.

Remind students that the very design of the car should help accomplish these goals, and encourage them to be practical. For example, maybe the radio can fade out every time the speed limit is exceeded!

Critical Thinking

Give students a chance to think like applied psychologists by discussing automobile design. What kinds of changes would they make if they wanted to increase the alertness of the driver? Or they can modify parts of the car to meet other behavioral goals. For example, how would they improve reaction time? How can they get people to wear seat belts? Would there be any modifications that might persuade people to obey traffic laws? To begin the discussion, you can review any recent changes in automobile design that students have already noticed.

DISCUSS THE PHOTO

Psychology is still considered a "new" science. While being over 100 years old may not seem young to you, sciences like astronomy and physics have been studied for a much longer time.

▲ *Wilhelm Wundt "The work which I here present to the public is an attempt to mark out a new domain of science" (1873).*

was first published. He was so worried about the effect his book might have on religion that he hid his manuscript from his wife for 14 years in fear that it would upset her (Stone, 1980; Adams, 1969). The importance of Darwin's theory for our purposes lies in the fact that it inspired scientists to study animals in an attempt to understand the human better, something psychologists still do all the time. Indeed, animals have a great deal in common with us. Although the individual units in the brain differ in size and location, the overall structure of the human brain is quite similar to that of the rat, cat, or dog. Since other animals are less complex than human beings, scientists of Darwin's era assumed that if we understood how they worked, we could apply this information to ourselves.

By the mid 1800s, then, it looked as if science was going to be able to understand almost everything—including the human. Our species was going to be examined and understood in detail. At least that was the goal, but as you know, people are more than a little difficult to pin down.

Wilhelm Wundt

Wilhelm Wundt (pronounced VUNT) (1832–1920) is called the "father of psychology" because in 1879, he started the first laboratory for studying humans. Like many famous people, he got off to a rocky start. Darwin's father, for example, had called his son a bum and had told him he was too lazy and stupid to ever amount to anything. Albert Einstein, one of the world's greatest mathematicians, kept failing high school math as well as college-entrance exams. When he finally got through school, he claimed it had injured his mind. So, too, with Wundt: he spent most of his time in class daydreaming and failing, for which his teachers kept slapping him in the face (literally). Fortunately, a few teachers saw the promise of greater things in him and helped him to pull himself together. He eventually wrote so many books and articles that if you read 50 pages a day, it would take you three years to get through them all. Several well-known early American psychologists studied under Wundt or were strongly influenced by him (Benjamin, Durkin, Link, Vestal, and Acord, 1992; Fancher, 1979).

Because, in Wundt's time, sciences like chemistry were having success in breaking things down into parts, Wundt thought he might be able to break down the human mind in the same way. In other words, since chemists had found that water can be broken down into two parts of hydrogen and one part oxygen, maybe the same type of thing could be done with the human mind. If that was possible, psychology would understand the basics that go into making up our feelings and thoughts.

Wundt's idea was to train people to be very accurate in describing the sensations they got from objects they touched. For instance, if you

DISCOVERY

One way to show the limitations of introspection is to bring in various objects and have students jot down the sensations they experience. Write some of their reactions on the board, trying to find common threads. Is it possible for these common threads to represent every person's reaction? Before conducting this exercise, pick an object in the room and report some of your own sensations. This way, they'll have some idea about what to write down.

pick up something like a shoe, what sensations (sights, smells) does it cause? What images or memories? What emotions (love, hate, distaste, and so on) does it bring out? Or if you pick up a cat, what kinds of responses does it bring? Wundt hoped that, with responses to enough different objects, he would find certain things in common, and these would be the basic elements that humans use to build the thoughts they have.

There is no question that Wundt had an excellent idea here. Unfortunately, it didn't work. The number of descriptions he and his assistant got kept getting larger and larger. At one point, they had 44,000 different sensations that people had described, with only a small number in common.

What went wrong? Actually, nothing. Wundt was learning that the human is so complex that mechanical measurement alone won't work. The only way anyone can deal with things like emotions and sensations is to ask people what they feel. This process is called **introspection,** which means "looking into" yourself and telling what is there (Bringmann and Tweney, 1980). Once you do that, though, rigid science becomes less rigid. Even today we have to rely on introspection when trying to get information about complex feelings.

But Wundt's work was not all a waste of time. He and his followers showed that some things about the human can be measured in a scientific fashion and that if you are clever enough, you can get information in an objective fashion that is pretty reliable (Mueller, 1979).

Psychologists today will always try to be as objective as possible, even when they have to rely on introspection. But sometimes relying on introspection is not necessary. For instance, in Chapter 2, we will show you how an experiment is done. The issue we will deal with is an interesting one: are males *really* better at playing video games than females? The results might surprise you, but we don't want to give them away here. In any case, such a study does not require introspection even though, as you will discover, it deals with very complex social and personal issues.

Sigmund Freud

In the late 1800s and early 1900s, **Sigmund Freud** (FROID) (1856–1939), an Austrian physician, developed one of the first comprehensive theories of personality. His special areas of interest were how personality develops, what can go wrong, and how to fix it. His theory is based on the effects of unconscious conflicts within the individual. In other words, we are influenced by things we are not aware of. We are also influenced by our experiences in early childhood. In Freud's view, problems that appear in adolescence or adulthood can be traced to things that happened in the first five or six years of life.

Freud's theory had a huge impact on psychology through the 1950s. Its popularity then declined from the 1960s through the 1980s.

introspection

The process of looking into yourself and describing what is there.

▲ *Sigmund Freud "A man like me cannot live . . . without a dominating passion. . . . It is psychology" (1895).*

9

Teaching Hint

Ask students, "What's the first thing you think of when you think of psychology?" Many will mention Freud and some will say, "the black couch." This well-known image fostered by Freud, who really did use a black couch during therapy, shows the popularity his theory once had. Explain that the more likely scenario nowadays is to find the therapist and patient sitting up and facing each other.

DISCUSS THE PHOTO

Freud's theories have been applied to other disciplines besides psychology, such as literature, sociology, and political science.

Journal Topic

"You are a little boy (or girl) with your hand in your mother's purse. Your mother walks into the room. What are your thoughts?" Tell students to write as quickly as possible, not worrying about rules of punctuation, grammar, and capitalization. They should try to convey how they really think. Some call this stream-of-consciousness writing. Explain that William James would have probably viewed their journal entries as evidence of their individuality, while Wundt might have tried to find common elements in the entries in order to draw conclusions.

DISCUSS THE PHOTO

James also commented, "To the infant the world is just a big, booming, buzzing confusion." He was interested in how we organize and give meaning to these sensations.

DISCUSS THE PHOTO

Watson's belief that we are completely controlled by the environment is considered to be an overstatement by most psychologists today.

10

DEMONSTRATION

Here's a quick and simple activity to show the concept of *learning by association.* (Many more such activities are listed in the wraparound for Chapter 7.) Take a rubber band and extend it as if you're going to shoot it at your class. Students will cower and cringe because they have associated extended rubber bands with a stinging sensation. They have learned this. If they don't believe that they've learned this, ask them if a baby would cringe in the same situation. Obviously, no. Oh—and be careful.

Unit 1 APPROACHES TO PSYCHOLOGY

▲ *William James "Psychology is the science of mental life" (1890).*

▲ *John B. Watson "No one today knows enough to raise a child" (1928).*

Recently, though, psychology has renewed its interest in unconscious processes (Greenwald, 1992; Kihlstrom, Barnhardt & Tataryn, 1992). The current emphasis is somewhat different from Freud's. However, his work as a pioneer of this subject definitely set the stage.

William James

William James (1842–1910), a philosopher and Harvard professor, was one of the founders of American psychology. In 1890, he published a very important and widely used textbook on psychology. It took him 12 years to write, was 1,400 pages long, and filled two volumes. James himself apologized for the book's length. In fact, he even suggested parts the reader might skip to keep from getting bored (James, 1890).

James was interested in how humans function and adapt to their environment. Rather than breaking consciousness down into its elements, he preferred to look at human experiences as complete wholes. For example, he tried to understand thinking as a "stream" of ideas, not a series of separate thoughts. As far as James was concerned, each person perceives and reacts to the world slightly differently. While basic rules of behavior may apply in general, psychology must never lose sight of the individual (Leary, 1992).

John B. Watson

Working mostly in the 1920s, **John B. Watson** (1878–1958) was one of the first American psychologists to study the impact of learning on human emotion. Because of his emphasis on learning, he is associated with "behaviorism," an approach covered in more detail shortly. Watson believed that what we feel and do depends on connections and associations we have made. For instance, we are afraid of something because we have associated bad or unpleasant experiences with it. Most people would agree that learning plays a major role in our lives. According to Watson, though, nearly everything we are is caused by learning. Put another way, we are what we learn to be.

Watson believed that careful, structured parenting could prevent most psychological problems from ever happening. Frustrated by the haphazard methods most parents used, he wrote a book on child rearing. The goal of his book was to teach parents how to apply scientific learning principles in bringing up their children (Watson, 1928).

Learning theory was a major early force in psychology. It has been greatly expanded since Watson's time, and its popularity continues to this day. Several useful treatment approaches in mental health come from this school of thought.

COOPERATIVE LEARNING

Divide the class into six groups and assign each group a theory in psychology. The group task is to create slogans that capture the essence of the theory. For example, "Think before you leap" could represent cognitive psychology. Suggest that the slogans can be completely original, parodies of famous sayings, or even takeoffs from commercials. Once each group has written a few slogans, have the groups create posters that can brighten the walls during the study of this unit.

PRESENT-DAY PSYCHOLOGY

Since the early years, psychology has expanded dramatically. Many theories about what the human is and how we develop have arisen. Some have dropped by the wayside, but six approaches to the nature of the human being are important today. We will cover them here and again in more detail later in the book. But the first thing you will notice is that the different theories to some extent contradict one another. The fact that they do not agree is all right, however, since we don't have anything close to the final answers about human nature. Thus, each of them is a good guess with some support—but not the last word. Also, sometimes one theory will fit a particular situation where another might not. So, while most psychologists tend to lean toward one of the six approaches, they often borrow here and there from other theories, making their own combination. This process is called **eclecticism** (ek-LEC-tuh-cism).

eclecticism

The process of making your own system by borrowing from two or more other systems.

The Neurobiological Approach

Why do people behave as they do? While many view behavior in strictly psychological terms, it is possible to view behavior, as some psychologists do, as **neurobiological** (*neuro*—nerve cells + *biological*—physical, including chemical, muscular, and so on). Suppose you are on a camping trip and decide to find a secluded place under a tree just to enjoy nature. You sit down, leaning back against the tree. You are watching something to your left that has captured your attention. But then you hear a muffled noise and feel something on your right leg. You look down and, to your horror, see that a snake is using your leg as a pathway on its travels. You instinctively jump up, shaking your leg, gasping. Bad move.

Neurobiologists examine behavior like this in terms of the physical changes that take place. When you see a snake or other scary creature, your heart starts beating rapidly, your muscles tense, your breathing becomes shallow, and you start to perspire. In this case, your body underwent a full emergency reaction. Eventually, you calm down and your body goes back to normal. Neurobiologists study the physical processes that take place when you panic *and* when you relax.

Another example of the neurobiological approach can be seen in research on depression. We know that significant losses and stress are often involved. Neurobiologists, however, emphasize other factors. Their focus is on changes in the brain's chemistry that occur in depression. Understanding this aspect of depression has led to important and useful methods of treatment.

neurobiological approach

Viewing behavior as the result of nervous system functions and biology.

Comprehension Check

Whose work inspired scientists to study animals in an attempt to understand human beings better? *(Charles Darwin)* Who started the first laboratory for studying humans and is called the "father of psychology"? *(Wilhelm Wundt)* Whose personality theory is based on the effects of unconscious conflicts within the individual? *(Sigmund Freud)* Who published a very important and widely used textbook on psychology and was interested in how humans adapt to their environment? *(William James)* Who wrote a book on child rearing to teach parents how to apply scientific learning principles in bringing up their children? *(John B. Watson)*

Discussion

Pose these questions: If you wanted to develop your own theory by combining two schools of thought in psychology, which would you choose and why? What advantages do you think these schools have over the others?

ENRICHMENT

Volunteers can research how Skinner's early life and research influenced his theories about behavior. Or allow students to research any of the psychologists presented in the chapter.

Eclecticism.

IN FOCUS This question encourages students to personalize the different schools of thought, something they may not do without prompting. Have them list and then analyze a few specific behaviors.

Reteaching Strategy

Ask students the following question: Can psychology be as scientific as chemistry or physics? Answers will vary. Emphasize that the methods of research in psychology should be as scientifically rigorous as those in chemistry and physics. The conclusions psychology makes, however, may lack the precision of other sciences. For example, mix two chemicals together in a vial, and in most cases a chemist can accurately predict the outcome. But inject an identical chemical into two different people, and factors other than the chemicals will affect the outcome: motivation, experience, and so on. This should help to illustrate the complexity of psychology.

12

Unit 1 APPROACHES TO PSYCHOLOGY

behavioral approach

Viewing behavior as the product of learning and associations.

The Behavioral Approach

The **behavioral approach** states that we are the product of learning and associations. We are the end result of all the different events we have been exposed to throughout life and of the types of responses we have made to them. Whether or not you get involved with drugs has to do only with the types of punishments or rewards that have been part of your life up to the time you make the decision. If the praise and rewards for *not* doing forbidden things have been great enough, this will successfully counteract the desire to do something forbidden, such as take drugs. On the other hand, if you have

IN FOCUS

The eclectic is like a child in a candy store who knows that getting only one kind of candy will not be quite satisfying enough.

I'LL HAVE A LITTLE OF THIS AND SOME OF THAT...

COGNITIVE BEHAVIORAL SOCIOCULTURAL

NEUROBIOLOGICAL PSYCHOANALYTIC HUMANISTIC

"CANDY" COUNTER

Which jar would best explain your behavior during class?

DISCOVERY

Have students list about ten behaviors that they performed in the last 24 hours. Then have them check the behaviors that were performed out of free will. You'll never reach consensus as to which items to check, but try to challenge some of the checked items from a behaviorist viewpoint. For instance, a student may check, "I washed my hair." A behaviorist would contend that clean hair was probably reinforced in the past with praise; if dirty hair were reinforced, we wouldn't wash our hair. Some behaviors will be difficult to challenge. A few studies have found that creativity, for example, actually decreases when external reinforcements are introduced.

gotten attention over the years mostly for doing things that are not allowed, then the rewards for taking drugs can be greater than for not taking them.

John B. Watson was an early behaviorist, but one of the most famous recent behaviorists is **B. F. Skinner** (1904–1990). He disliked philosophy and focused only on what could be seen. He believed we are mechanically controlled by the environment in the sense that we become whatever the environment forces us to be—good or bad (Skinner, 1967). Shortly before his death, Skinner wrote a paper about his concerns over the direction psychology was taking. He saw psychology as moving away from the study of observable behavior. He felt that the focus on things we cannot see or study directly, such as cognition and unconscious processes, threatens to make psychology less scientific (Skinner, 1990).

In support of the behavioral theory, there certainly is evidence that we do a great number of things because we have been rewarded for them in the past. Such information is invaluable for those parents who are trying to figure out how to get started in making their offspring into reasonable human beings.

On the other hand, there are problems with this theory. For one thing, it takes away a person's "free will." In other words, if you decide "on the spur of the moment" to go get a pizza, the behaviorists say you really had no choice. Whether you went or not is the

Chapter 1 THE FIELD OF PSYCHOLOGY

▲ *B. F. Skinner "Whether behavior analysis will be called psychology is a matter for the future to decide" (1990).*

Discussion

Each school of thought in psychology helps us decipher one small piece of the human puzzle. Invite students to create another puzzle piece, another school of thought. What is yet another way to view behavior? Focus students by restricting your discussion to a particular area, such as aggression or love.

DISCUSS THE PHOTO

One of Skinner's more controversial ideas was that human "free will" is a myth. He called for a "designed culture" in which positive reinforcement encourages behavior patterns that will save the planet from overpopulation, pollution, and nuclear war.

▲ *Does school achievement come from learned motivation, natural personal growth, or social influences?*

DISCOVERY

Complete the preceding **Discovery,** but this time adopt a humanist point of view. Argue that *most* of the behaviors listed are motivated by free will. For instance, a humanist might say that it's preposterous to focus on a single behavior like hair-washing.

We wash our hair so we can concentrate on more important, self-fulfilling aspects of life. So in a sense, even hair-washing is based on free will. To encourage more involvement, you might have students pair up and have each partner adopt a humanist or behaviorist stance. Their task will be to select any one item on their lists and to argue whether the behavior is motivated more by free will or by external reinforcements.

Journal Topic

"Describe a recent argument or disagreement you've had with a parent or friend." Then have students write or discuss how a proponent from each of the six approaches in psychology might view the argument. In other words, how would Freud, Skinner, and others view the argument? The **Analyzing Your Neighbor** section should be very helpful for this exercise. After students finish their journal writing, they may need to add some details so they have something to analyze.

DISCUSS THE PHOTO

Rogers believed that many adult problems are a result of trying to live by other people's standards.

humanistic approach

Believing that people are basically good and capable of helping themselves.

▲ *Carl Rogers "When I am closest to my inner, intuitive self, . . . whatever I do seems to be full of healing" (1986).*

result of everything that has happened to you up to the present moment, not an impulse. Another problem is that this theory doesn't take into account what is going on in your life. If you are very attached to a person who takes drugs or if you are part of a group that is involved in drugs, the pull you feel toward drugs is going to be greater than if you are close to people who don't do drugs. Thus, at times, previous learning is not as important as the present situation. Finally, the most uncomfortable aspect of behaviorist theory is that it sees us as little more than robots, a belief few of us want to accept.

The Humanistic Approach

The **humanistic approach** to human behavior arose in reaction to the problems we've mentioned about behaviorism. The term *humanistic* comes from *humane*. So, this group of psychologists believes that people are basically good and that our very nature is such that we could reach perfection—if all went right.

To the humanists, each of us is like the perfect seed: if we get the right amount of water, nutrients, and sunlight from the environment, we will become a perfect flower. Personal growth is internal and very individual. We are in control of our destinies, and all of us can make our lives worthwhile. Unlike the behaviorists, the humanists believe that the environment does not *force* us to become anything; instead, it acts as a background for our internal growth. How we handle the death of a loved one, for instance, is an individual thing in which we call on our own internal resources to make the best of it.

The most famous humanist is **Carl Rogers** (1902–1987). He studied for the ministry before switching to psychology. Possibly this influenced his beliefs, because he saw people as worthwhile creatures with free will and choice (Rogers, 1961, 1986). To him, every human had the potential to become great in his or her own (however small) way, with just a little guidance.

Some people find humanism a little too good to be true. Sometimes when we are alone and think about ourselves for a while, even the best and most "normal" of us can find thoughts and feelings inside that are quite removed from anything like the beauty of a flower.

The Psychoanalytic Approach

The best known of all theories, that of Sigmund Freud, considers our inner selves to be cesspools of forbidden desires. Freud developed a theory that centered around sexual and aggressive impulses that are hidden in our unconscious from early childhood. These impulses live below the surface of consciousness and from there control our everyday behavior in ways we are not aware of. For exam-

14

DEMONSTRATION

Make this announcement: "We've been studying various types of psychologists, but we haven't mentioned child psychologists. Tomorrow, I want each of you to deliver a one-minute speech on one of your most memorable childhood experiences. What we'll try to do is view each experience through the eyes of a child psychologist." You will do no such thing, of course. Nor will they ever prepare or deliver the speech. You simply want to create a little anxiety. Once it's apparent that students are anxious, have them write down some of their thoughts: "I can't deliver speeches. People will laugh at me. The teacher is unfair." Do not explain yet that no speech is imminent. Afterward, have them report their thoughts to the class and analyze some of them. Are the thoughts rational and accurate? Explain that this is the kind of analysis that cognitive psychologists undertake.

---

ple, if you were very angry at your mother but knew better than to say anything, you might, when you call out to get her attention, say, "Oh, Bother!" The unconscious has replaced the "M" with a "B," showing your real feelings. Since these impulses are hidden, in order to understand them and have more choice about them, we have to *analyze* them with the help of a therapist. Thus, this approach to our behavior is called **psychoanalysis.**

In the last 15 years, many psychologists have considered Freud's theory to be too negative by itself, so they have combined it with other theories (eclecticism) that give the person more say-so in what fate has in store.

Currently, psychology's interest in unconscious processes does not focus on sex and aggression, as Freud did. Instead, psychologists try to understand what kinds of perception, thinking, and memory go on below our level of awareness and without our conscious control (Greenwald, 1992). Nevertheless, many of Freud's ideas are still around. His influence can still be felt today.

The Cognitive Approach

The fifth approach is one of the most popular in psychology today. It is called the **cognitive approach.** The word *cognition* refers to thinking or using mental processes. Once you understand that, the cognitive approach will be clear. For cognitive psychology, the most important human ability is that we can take information from the environment, analyze it, and come up with a solution to almost any problem. So, we are first and foremost thinking creatures able to compare the past with the present and make judgments. We humans are special because we can change our thought patterns after looking at different problems and deciding on the best approach.

To the cognitivist, our personalities are, to some extent, made up of the different kinds of sentences (thoughts) we have inside our heads. If you pay close attention, you will notice that there are many times during the day when you are carrying on a conversation with yourself inside your head. In fact, you are, in a sense, sitting there listening while this goes on, even though it's coming from you. These sentences can sometimes get us in trouble, as when we keep saying, "This math is completely impossible to understand." The cognitivists believe that if we replace such internal sentences with more useful ones like, "Joe Smaltz is stupid and *he* can do math; I am not an idiot, so I can, too," it will have an impact on how well we do (Hilgard, 1980; Haugeland, 1978).

A problem with the cognitive theory is that it badly downplays the effects of emotions. For most of us, hardly an hour goes by when we don't get involved in something at least partly emotional. Hence, even though the cognitivists say we can control these by thought, they don't give enough credit to the effect of emotions on what we do.

Chapter 1 THE FIELD OF PSYCHOLOGY

psychoanalysis

A system of viewing the individual as the product of unconscious forces.

cognitive approach

Emphasizing how humans use mental processes to handle problems or develop certain personality characteristics.

Comprehension Check

(1) Which approach in psychology emphasizes people's potential? *(humanism)* (2) Which analyzes internal sentences, thoughts? *(cognitive)* (3) Which focuses on learning? *(behaviorism)* (4) Which analyzes our chemical make-up? *(neurobiological)* (5) Which studies one's ethnic background? *(sociocultural)* (6) Which emphasizes sexual desires? *(psychoanalysis)*

DISCOVERY

Teaching Master 1-2 Vignettes offers students an opportunity to analyze situations using the six different approaches in psychology. It lists several vignettes that you can use in a variety of ways. (1) You can read the situations and discuss them as a form of review. How would Freud view the situation? And so on. (2) You can use the sheet for evaluation purposes. (3) You can have students role-play the situations and then have everyone write down how he or she views the problem. Next, have students match their personal interpretations with the school of thought in psychology that it most resembles. (4) You can break the class into six groups and assign each group an approach. Role-play the situations. Have each group interpret the role-play from its assigned point of view.

A Few Who Have Shaped Psychology.

 You might get some creative answers if you prompt students. You might want to use this as a journal entry.

Connections

If you like a challenge or if you do not like to "follow the book" chapter by chapter, here's a rough game plan. Have students read Chapter 1 so they get a general idea of the concerns of psychology. Then teach units on each of the main schools in psychology, telling students which pages to read from various chapters. Unit One could be psychoanalysis: Freud, Jung, Horney, Adler, Erikson. Unit Two could be behaviorism: Pavlov, Watson, Skinner. Unit Three could be neurobiology: brain, body, and awareness. And so on.

Unit 1 APPROACHES TO PSYCHOLOGY

sociocultural approach

Behavior viewed as strongly influenced by the rules and expectations of specific social groups or cultures.

The Sociocultural Approach

In recent years, psychology has begun to look more closely at how much we are influenced by our culture. Thus, the **sociocultural approach** studies the impact of specific social, ethnic, racial, and reli-

IN FOCUS   A Few Who Have Shaped Psychology

	What They Did	**Effect on Psychology**
Charles Darwin	Published his theory of evolution in 1859	Suggested that the study of animals could reveal something about humans
Wilhelm Wundt	Opened the first psychological laboratory in 1879	Inspired others to believe that humans could be studied scientifically
Sigmund Freud	Developed a personality theory and treated patients from the late 1800s to the early 1900s	Suggested that we are influenced by childhood experiences and unconscious forces
William James	Published a widely used psychology text in 1890	Suggested that humans be studied as complete wholes
John B. Watson	Studied learning during the 1920s	Created learning theories that are widely applied, even today
B. F. Skinner	Studied the effects of the environment from the mid 1950s to 1990	Emphasized that a scientific psychology should study observable behaviors rather than thoughts
Carl Rogers	Studied personal growth from the 1950s to the 1980s	Emphasized the positive side of human nature

Scientific psychology is just over 100 years old! How might this list change in the *next* 100 years?

DISCOVERY

Teaching Master 1-3 Six Approaches to Studying Behavior is the same as discussion question #5 from the end of the chapter. Students interpret a situation in light of the six approaches to psychology.

gious groups on behavior. For example, it's clear that a suburban white girl and a Native American boy on a tribal reservation live in very different worlds. They probably have different experiences and opportunities, activities and values, dreams and goals. They also follow different rules and have different expectations. Each child's culture influences how she or he spends time and plans for the future, what is learned, and so on. However, they are both affected by the overall American culture as well.

Which differences are the most important? What areas of life do these differences affect? How can we measure these effects? Do we need special ways of dealing with certain problems? These are some of the questions a person taking a sociocultural view of behavior might ask.

For a time, this approach looked mostly at such issues as racial prejudice and the fairness of IQ testing for different groups. Now, however, it has spread to nearly every area of psychology. One major concern is how to counsel people from cultures different from our own. Another has to do with education. Still others include such things as motivation and emotion, crime and criminal justice, family systems, and smaller social groups and their impact (Pedersen, 1991).

IN FOCUS — The Six Main Theories in Psychology

Neurobiology	Behavior viewed in terms of biological responses
Behaviorism	Behavior viewed as a product of learned responses
Humanism	Behavior viewed as a reflection of internal growth
Psychoanalysis	Behavior viewed as a reflection of unconscious aggressive and sexual impulses
Cognitive Psychology	Behavior viewed as a product of various internal sentences or thoughts
Sociocultural Psychology	Behavior viewed as strongly influenced by the rules and expectations of specific social groups or cultures

Can you place these theories in any chronological order?

Evaluation Strategy

Briefly describe a situation using events at your school and have students decide how each of the six approaches in psychology would view the situation. Or, photocopy a column from the school newspaper and have students analyze the events in the article.

The Six Main Theories in Psychology.

IN FOCUS Psychoanalysis, behaviorism, humanism, cognitive psychology, neurobiology, sociocultural psychology. (It could be argued that neurobiology should be listed at the beginning since many behavior disorders, such as schizophrenia, were thought to be biologically based in Freud's day.)

Unit 1 APPROACHES TO PSYCHOLOGY

ANALYZING YOUR NEIGHBOR

Strange things always go on next door or down the block. And everyone knows about them. So, we will look at the problem that John, who lives down the block, has, and we'll examine it, using each of the six approaches discussed. In this way, you'll get a better understanding of how each approach views the person.

John is 40 years old and lives alone with his mother. He has never been married but has a good job as an engineer. His life seemed to be going well—until one day a month ago his boss chewed him out for not doing something right. During the last month, John has been worried and depressed because he has started to forget things. He told his mother, who told Ethel who lives next door, and now everybody knows. Here are examples of what has been happening to him: he was supposed to turn in plans for a new project but forgot they were due. He had always remembered his mother's birthday, but it was a week ago and he completely forgot about it, hurting her, even though she pretended not to be upset. A month ago, a few days after the incident on the job, he met a woman he really liked and set up a date with her for later in the week. But he had forgotten that he was going to be out of town then, so he had to cancel the date.

Neurobiological Analysis

Psychologists know that memory is stored better if the learner is excited at the time of the event. Chemicals that aid in storage are much higher with excitement, anger, fear, or hope. But John's condition is such that just the opposite is going on: he is depressed. Depression lowers the level of brain chemicals that aid in memory. Therefore, John's memory problem is seen by neurobiologists as the result of a physical malfunction resulting from the trouble at work and other chaos in his life.

Behavioral Analysis

The behaviorists see the problem differently. When John was in grade school, he was comforted and hugged by his mother, not scolded, when he did things like forgetting to bring a book home to study for a test the next day. Not only that, but she let him stay home the next day because he "didn't feel well." So, over time, John has learned very bad habits from his early training. Something in John's present life is worrying him, just as an exam the next day used to. Now he is doing the same thing that worked well in the past: he is not forgetting textbooks, but he is forgetting other things to try to get love and attention from his mother.

▲ *Regardless of how we explain John's problem, only he can solve it.*

DISCOVERY

This is an activity to do at the end of the first week or at the end of the chapter. Have students pair up with classmates whom they don't know well. Allow them about ten minutes to interview each other. Then sit in a circle and have each student intro-duce the partner. Even the most with-drawn students handle this activity well.

Be prepared to allow an entire peri-od for this activity. Some of you may be reluctant to devote this much time to an activity that doesn't teach an academic concept, but if conducted properly so that students really listen to each other, this kind of activity will help promote the sharing and dis-cussing of ideas throughout the semester.

IN FOCUS

Questions That Psychologists Ask

Issue: Alcohol Abuse

Neurobiologists:	Is alcoholism a disease? What role does heredity play? How does alcohol affect the brain?
Behaviorists:	Is alcoholism learned? If so, can it be unlearned? Can new habits replace drinking habits?
Humanists:	Do people drink because they don't feel a sense of worth? Does alcohol give people a false sense of worth?
Psychoanalysts:	Is heavy drinking an indication of some deeper problem or conflict raging in the unconscious? Does drinking make people less inhibited, allowing their uncon-scious desires to surface?
Cognitive Psychologists:	What thoughts lead up to episodes of heavy drinking? If these thoughts are analyzed and changed, will the drinking be curbed?
Sociocultural Psychologists:	How does alcoholism differ from one culture to another? What are the unique pressures within a certain culture that might contribute to alcohol abuse?

Suppose a millionaire wanted to fund research to find answers to these questions. To which psychologists should the millionaire give money?

Humanistic Analysis

For the humanists, John will soon continue with his fine work as an engineer. But his inner world has suffered a number of setbacks. It was going so well, but now he is more and more distracted. Exactly what is it that is causing John so much worry? His individual self has been injured. His personal growth has been slowed because he made

---

Questions That Psychologists Ask.

IN FOCUS   Answers will vary, but you may want to discuss the pros and cons of support-ing or ignoring each school of thought. The millionaire's dilemma might prompt a good jour-nal entry or even inspire a good short essay ques-tion.

Reteaching Strategy

Have students write a paragraph comparing and contrasting any two approaches in psycholo-gy. Possible areas of focus: According to each approach, what charac-teristics are we born with (what is our nature)? What role does the envi-ronment play in forming personality?

ENRICHMENT

Have students complete the **Enrichment Worksheet** for this chapter located in the Teacher Resources.

Reteaching Strategy

Have students complete the **Reteaching Worksheet** for this chapter located in the Teacher Resources.

The **Vocabulary Worksheet** may be completed by the class as a pretest for chapter concepts or used as a reteaching worksheet for those students needing additional review.

Comprehension Check

Which psychologists would be associated with these statements? (1) We should study humans as wholes. *(James; Rogers is a good answer, too, although students won't know this yet)* (2) The unconscious affects everyday behavior. *(Freud)* (3) The environment is most crucial in forming personality. *(Skinner, Watson)* (4) Introspection can be studied scientifically. *(Wundt)*

20

mistakes and got upset about them and because he is starting to bring another woman into his personal life, which requires major adjustments. These distractions are causing the forgetting. But he still has the same basic internal strength and purpose. He will soon recover and get back on course if given patient understanding and a chance to regain his footing.

Psychoanalytic Analysis

The psychoanalysts focus on desires and needs such as sex and aggression. John is suffering from a conflict of wanting to stay with his mother but knowing that if he has a close relationship with the woman, which he also wants, he will someday have to leave home. Since the two desires cannot live side by side, he is getting more frustrated and aggressive toward others. This is shown by his forgetting his mother's birthday. But the more the conflict goes on, the more guilty he gets, so he tries to forget this "bad" side of himself. He forgets many things in his effort to hide from the ongoing basic conflict raging in his unconscious.

Cognitive Analysis

Cognitive psychologists focus on thinking skills rather than on previous learning or unconscious impulses. For them, John will have to sit down and take out a piece of paper and analyze (a cognitive process) exactly what his life is like. He has to focus on the kinds of things he is saying to himself that are causing him so much trouble. For example, he is convincing himself he is forgetful. He is talking himself into hopelessness because he made a mistake at work. He is telling himself he can never do anything right. If, however, he makes a formal, logical plan of action and decides what he is going to do about this "other woman" in his life, then his memory will improve all by itself.

Sociocultural Analysis

Sociocultural psychologists focus on cultural influences on our behavior. They would want to know what special social pressures exist in this man's particular world. In the case of John, we'll make it up. In John's subculture, being publicly chewed out is a serious disgrace and a threat to one's self-image. Also, when a father dies, his son, married or single, is expected to live with and care for his mother. So, John's depression makes sense after he has suffered public humiliation. His boss needs to know the importance of what happened so that John can get back some of his self-esteem. John's forgetting his mother's birthday and having to cancel his date were

COOPERATIVE LEARNING

Divide the class into eight groups and assign one of the occupational possibilities to each group. Pick a specific problem such as juvenile delinquency, and have each group suggest ways to reduce or eliminate the problem. For example, a clinical psychologist may suggest that the entire family of a delinquent be treated. Educational psychologists might suggest some alternative school structure that would discourage delinquency. Students may need to conduct some research on the occupational possibilities in order to do an adequate job.

---

caused by social conflict. The overall American culture is pressuring him to marry and set up his own family. His own culture is pressuring him to stay with his mother and take care of her, as a dutiful son is supposed to do. Part of the answer lies in everyone having a better understanding of the special conflicts John faces. Another part of the answer lies in John making some decisions about which social demands are the most important to him.

PSYCHOLOGY IN YOUR LIFE

Being a Psychologist—Occupational Possibilities

In case you become interested in psychology as an occupation (which we hope will happen), here is a brief synopsis of some major areas in the field. Most of these occupations will require an advanced degree, meaning a master's degree (two to three years beyond the regular four years of college) or a doctorate (four to five years beyond the four-year college curriculum).

Clinical/Counseling Psychologists

This group works with people who have marital, personal, or mental problems, using specialized techniques to increase their clients' self-confidence and to reduce behaviors that are causing them trouble. These psychologists give psychological tests and help people to understand themselves and others better. They can work in private practice, in a mental hospital or clinic, in industry, or in a school system.

School/Educational Psychologists

This group works in the school setting. The tasks are varied. Some help design and improve the learning systems and curricula involved in education. Some work directly with the students, helping them with personal or learning problems or with the choice of a career. Others try to improve the quality of the school system as a whole and act as educational advisers to the school administration.

▲ In psychology, one can find a job working with people of most any age group or type.

Environmental Psychologists

This group works in industry or for the government. Their task is to study the effects of *(continued on next page)*

PSYCHOLOGY IN YOUR LIFE

Enrichment
Explain that most of the psychologists listed in **Psychology in Your Life** are involved in applied psychology. Break the class into groups, assign one type of psychologist to each group, and have them research the subject.

Enrichment
Have students research how much education and training is required for each type of psychologist.

DISCUSS THE PHOTO

About 21 percent of those practicing psychology are school/educational psychologists.

ENRICHMENT

Ask interested students to make a few phone calls to invite various types of psychologists to your class. Before the visit have students work in groups to generate a list of questions to ask the speakers.

TEACHING MASTER 1-4

Writing Your Own Magazine Article. If you want students to read outside material, but you become bored with simple summaries and reactions, this handout might be helpful. Although the assigment calls for some summary, the emphasis is on originality and the writing process.

FYI You might want to warn students about the dangers of going too rapidly from research to application. One danger is that one research study might contradict another. (Chapter 20 discusses the conflicting research results on the possible influence of film on violence.) Another danger is that people may tend to generalize, or overapply, research findings. A mom may read that it's crucial to interact with small children and then spend every waking moment interacting with her children, which obviously wouldn't be healthy for either party.

Unit 1 APPROACHES TO PSYCHOLOGY

PSYCHOLOGY IN YOUR LIFE

Being a Psychologist—Occupational Possibilities

(continued from previous page) the environment on people. They look at the effects of disasters, overcrowding, and toxic materials on the health and welfare of the population as a whole or on individual families. They also study such things as how best to design an environment (such as a factory) in order to keep those working there reasonably comfortable.

Developmental/Child Psychologists
As you will find when you read the chapter on child psychology, children live in a world all their own and have sets of rules often beyond adult comprehension. Psychologists in this area study child development, but they also often work in a clinic or private practice to help disturbed children or to help parents who are trying to understand the problems they face in living with and rearing these "foreigners."

Industrial/Consumer Psychologists
Psychologists in this area "take sides," so to speak.

One group works with management to try to improve working conditions, to obtain greater efficiency from the work force, to increase sales, and to keep the corporation's image positive with the public. The other group works with the employees on any issues they might have, from difficult work conditions to problems at home.

Engineering Psychologists
Psychologists in this area work to design systems that help people become more efficient. These psychologists do everything from studying how to design the instruments on a machine or an automobile for greatest efficiency to figuring out the best physical design for a shopping mall so that people are able to get in and out efficiently and pleasantly.

Experimental Psychologists
These psychologists work in industry or universities. They perform research to understand better how the human operates physically

or psychologically. This work may include the study of drugs, of physical reactions, and of the effect of certain laboratory events on human beings or animals. The goal of all of these studies is to add to the literature—that is, the books and articles that are studied by other psychologists as well as made available to the public. For example, an experimental psychologist might try to answer the question, what leads to a heart attack?

Teaching
Teaching psychology can involve any of these fields. That is what the authors of this book do. It's the most exciting field in the world. We hope some of you will try it someday. The rewards of communicating with others and helping them to understand are beyond belief.

Before testing students on the contents of the chapter, you may want to review vocabulary terms that are especially important or confusing. Terms in this chapter that could require clarification are *eclecticism* and *theory*.

Wrapping It Up

An effective way to wrap up this first chapter is to return to the topic of applied psychology. There are several ways to do this: (1) Have each student find an article that would be considered an example of applied psychology. (2) The simplest and quickest option is to skim through back issues of *Psychology Today* and collect your own examples. You can easily spend an entire period discussing the articles. (See **Suggested Readings** at the end of this chapter's wraparound for a few sources.) (3) Present students with a series of questions that they can research. Here's a sampling that focuses on legal issues: (a) How might psychologists assist a lawyer in jury selection? (b) How do psychologists create profiles of criminals? (c) What kinds of testimony might psychologists offer in a courtroom? (d) Are lie detectors fool-proof? (e) How can a lawyer use psychology when examining witnesses?

Chapter 1 THE FIELD OF PSYCHOLOGY

SUMMARY

1. Psychologists work in just about every setting you can imagine. About a third help people with personal problems.
2. Psychology is the scientific study of human and animal behavior. Psychologists use theories (general ideas) about the nature of behavior as a framework for research. There are two basic types of psychologists—those who do research and those who apply the research.
3. Charles Darwin's theory in the mid 1800s suggested that animal studies might help us understand the human.
4. Wilhelm Wundt started the first human psychology laboratory in 1879. He tried to break the human mind down into basic parts, but both our complexity and the need for introspection kept him from reaching his goal.
5. William James wrote an important early psychology textbook. He tried to understand how we humans function and adapt to our environment.
6. Sigmund Freud developed a comprehensive theory of personality. His emphasis was on unconscious conflicts in early childhood.

7. John B. Watson studied the effect of learning on emotions. He wrote a book on child rearing based on his ideas.
8. Today there are six approaches to the understanding of human behavior:
   a. The neurobiologists see behavior as mostly influenced by bodily and chemical processes.
   b. The behaviorists, such as B. F. Skinner, see us as creatures who are formed and controlled by what we learn and the associations we make.
   c. The humanists, such as Carl Rogers, see people as basically good and able to achieve almost anything. For them, each of us is special and in control of his or her destiny.
   d. The psychoanalysts, on the other hand, find us controlled by unconscious impulses, especially sex and aggression.
   e. The cognitivists focus most on the thinking brain, which can talk itself into (and out of) almost any belief or behavior.
   f. Sociocultural psychologists emphasize the influence of specific cultures on attitudes and behavior.

SUGGESTED READINGS

▼ Loftus, Elizabeth, and Katherine Ketcham. *Witness for the Defense.* New York: St. Martin's Press, 1991.

▼ Kimble, G. A. and K. Schlesinger. *Topics in the History of Psychology.* New York: Erlbaum, 1985.

▼ Thompson, Dick. "Science's Big Shift." *Time,* November 23, 1992, 34–5.

▼ Sannito, Tom, and Peter J. McGovern. *Courtroom Psychology for Trial Lawyers.* New York: Wiley, 1985.

▼ Smith, Samuel. *Ideas of the Great Psychologists.* New York: Harper, 1983.

▼ Porter, Bruce. "Mind Hunters." *Psychology Today,* April 1983, 44–52.

VOCABULARY

psychology
theory
research
   psychologists
applied psychologists
Charles Darwin
Wilhelm Wundt
introspection

Sigmund Freud
William James
John B. Watson
eclecticism
neurobiological
   approach
behavioral approach
B. F. Skinner

humanistic approach
Carl Rogers
psychoanalysis
cognitive approach
sociocultural
   approach

Answers to Review Questions

1. theory
2. applied psychologists
3. research psychologists
4. psychology
5. Wilhelm Wundt
6. William James
7. False
8. False
9. True
10. False
11. True

12. a	18. e
13. d	19. c
14. e	20. d
15. b	21. b
16. a	22. c
17. f	

Review Questions

Fill in the blank; answer on a separate sheet of paper. (An answer may consist of more than one word.)

1. A general framework for doing more specific research is called a ___?___.
2. Psychologists who use research to solve practical problems are called ___?___.
3. Psychologists who study the causes of behavior are called ___?___.
4. The scientific study of behavior is called ___?___.
5. ___?___ is considered the father of psychology.
6. The psychologist who studied how people function and adapt to their environment was ___?___.

True/False

7. B. F. Skinner was an early behaviorist who wrote a book on child rearing.
8. Psychology is no longer interested in the study of unconscious processes.
9. The overall structure of the human brain is remarkably similar to that of a rat.
10. The process of introspection helped Wilhelm Wundt categorize sensations into five main areas.
11. Eclecticism refers to a combination of psychological theories.

Notes on Discussion Questions

1. A research psychologist might conduct surveys, compile statistics, and gather physiological data. An applied psychologist might take this information and use it to help treat a phobic. The physiological data might suggest the use of a biofeedback tool.

2. Some students have difficulty distinguishing fact from opinion. Write these two words on the board and have several students try to support their theories. List the facts they present on one side, opinions on the other. Are any of their opinions testable? (By the way, a woman invented windshield-wiper blades.)

3. Answers will vary. A neurobiological explanation focuses on the biological root of depression. The depressed person who prefers this approach is more likely to say, "I can't help being depressed. It's just the way my body reacts." A cognitive explanation might tend to encourage "ownership" of the

Matching (Answers can be used more than once.)

12. Rewards and punishments control behavior.
13. Physical changes are emphasized.
14. Humans are basically good.
15. The unconscious plays a great role in behavior.
16. The environment is all-important.
17. Ethnic and religious backgrounds influence behavior.
18. Humans control their own destinies.
19. A person's thoughts are emphasized.
20. Chemical changes in the brain influence behavior.
21. Sexual and aggressive impulses control behavior.
22. Internal sentences directly influence personality.

a. behavioral approach
b. psychoanalytic approach
c. cognitive approach
d. neurobiological approach
e. humanistic approach
f. sociocultural approach

DISCUSSION QUESTIONS

1. How could both a research and an applied psychologist possibly be involved in reducing someone's fear of heights? Explain. Offer examples of what each type of psychologist might do.

2. Each of us constructs "theories" about behavior based not on research but on our own experiences. Describe one of your "theories" and discuss what parts of the theory you might like to test if you were a psychologist. Sample: "When it begins to drizzle, male drivers tend to turn on their windshield wipers, turn them off, and turn them on again as needed. Females, on the other hand, turn the wipers on and leave them on." This is a silly theory, of course, but you could test its numerous assumptions: are females more safety-conscious than males? Are females lazier? Are males more fidgety? And so on.

3. If you were severely depressed for several weeks, would you rather have someone explain your depression to you using the neurobiological approach or the cognitive approach? Why? Explain.

4. Of the six main approaches to studying and understanding behavior (neurobiological, behavioral, and so on), with which do you tend to agree the most and why? With which do you agree the least? Explain.

5. Maria wants to ask for a raise but begins to sweat uncontrollably every time she even gets near her boss. Using the six approaches discussed in this chapter, briefly describe how each might explain this simple behavior.

depression: "I'm depressed because of my thoughts, and I can change my thoughts."

4. Answers will vary.

5. **Teaching Master 1-3 Six Approaches to Studying Behavior** includes a detailed answer to this question!

Notes on Activities

1. This is a good initial activity to force students to skim through the text. You might want to do this activity as a class, where each student, after skimming, writes down ten or 15 questions. Each student then reads aloud his or her best five questions. Have a poster-board ready to jot down some of the better questions overall. Throughout the semester, you can check off the questions that have been answered. Or if you like to assign independent projects, this list could provide possible topics.

2. Since this is the first research activity in the student text, you will prob-

ably want to specify your requirements, especially with regard to length. Length should not be the foremost concern, but your expectations must be clear in order to receive work that meets your standards. If you want more than a simple summary and reaction, see **Teaching Master 1-4 Writing Your Own Magazine Article** for an alter-

native magazine assignment.

3. If you decide not to assign this activity, keep it in mind for Chapter 10. Parenting is a lively topic, and students' reports are usually informative and varied.

4. To prepare students for this activity, analyze your classroom. The clock is usually placed in the back of the room so students aren't con-

ACTIVITIES

1. For this first activity, we want you simply to write down 40 questions that you want answered by this text or course. The questions can range from simple to personal to complex. Some examples: Why are my parents becoming grouchy lately—is it a midlife crisis? Do colors have any effect on a person's moods? Does ESP exist? Forty questions may seem like a lot at first, but you'll be surprised at how quickly you complete this activity, since psychology deals with so many interesting issues. Feel free to skim through the text for ideas. If your list of questions seems to end at about 25, leave it and come back to it in a day or two until you *can* complete it. It might be interesting to save this list or post it in the classroom, and at the end of the year check the questions that were answered.

2. Here's another simple activity to get you acquainted with the field of psychology. Find any three- or four-page article relating to psychology. Write a summary of the main points and a critique or reaction to the article. With which points do you agree or disagree? Is the material merely research, or can it be practical, or both? Does the material relate to your own life in any way? Be sure to make the description of your reaction as detailed as the summary of the article.

3. Often, the information that an applied psychologist borrows or uses from a research psychologist may seem practical at first, but then may not turn out that way. For example, Watson wrote a book to teach parents how to apply scientific learning principles in raising their children, but it is difficult to determine how successful this was.

   These kinds of books are still being written today. Your task is to find out how effective they seem to be by interviewing two or three parents with preschool children. Of course,

you will need to find parents who consult these books from time to time and who might have an opinion on the topic. A good area to focus on might be discipline.

   An alternative to interviewing could be to read various sections from a parenting book or two and write a report on *your* reactions.

4. In the next chapter, you will learn about how psychologists gather information about behavior and the environment through scientific experimentation, and you will eventually conduct your own experiments. For now, we want you to gather information about the environment through informal observations. Visit two of the following sites (or choose your own sites): grocery store, train station, fast-food restaurant, factory, doctor's office, office building. For each site, take detailed notes on as many of the following categories as possible: (a) colors used; (b) music played; (c) arrangements of products; (d) arrangement of furniture; (e) other appropriate details you may notice.

   Next, analyze your observations. *Why* does a store have red walls and low lighting? How will this influence your behavior? Does it make you want to hang around or leave quickly? Does it keep you awake or put you to sleep? Don't worry too much about the "correctness" of your analysis. The purpose of this activity is not to search for "right" answers but merely to make you more aware of how "psychology" is all around you. One final suggestion: some of the places you visit will be more thoughtfully designed than others, so use discretion when choosing your sites.

   These are the kinds of observations you might note if visiting a grocery store: (1) Milk, located at the back of the store, is a popular item. As you walk through the entire store to get to it, you might buy other

stantly watching it. The desks are too uncomfortable to sleep in; they're designed so that students face forward and sit up straight. The walls are painted in bright colors to help keep students awake, but they're not so bright that they distract. Once you exhaust your analysis, you can examine other sites from memory: courtrooms, stores, libraries, and

so on.

5. Stress that this is a creative-writing exercise. Here are some behaviors students might note: females walk wearing soft shoes, but when they get to work, they put on hard shoes. Conclusion: females want to be uncomfortable at work. Males also want to be uncomfortable at work. They wear long pieces of

cloth around their necks, and when they arrive at work, they tighten these cloths as if they were nooses. Chapter 2 discusses naturalistic observation. This activity may serve to point out the limitations of using only observations to collect data.

6. After reading this activity, students invariably ask, "Where will we find these people for interviews?" It's a good idea to post a list of mental health agencies in your area, not just for this assignment but for volunteer opportunities for students. You can usually get at least a few students to volunteer each semester. And there's certainly nothing wrong with offering extra credit as an incentive. The phone book is a good source as well, not only for interviews but also for guest speakers. You'll be surprised and pleased at how generous people are with their time.

items. (2) Children's cereals are stacked on the bottom shelf so children, at their eye level, can point out the boxes to their parents. (3) Snack items are located at the checkout counter. These items are inexpensive and promote impulse buying.

Divide your report into two parts. Part One should be an *analysis* of your sites, as described in the previous paragraphs. Part Two should be a *critique* of your sites. For example, do you agree that slow music should be played at a particular site? Why or why not? In your critique, be sure to include suggestions on how to improve the design of the site. If you visited a family restaurant, you might suggest that it hand out crayons and paper to kids to keep them busy (and, yes, quiet).

5. Pretend that all your knowledge of human behavior has been completely erased. You don't know, for instance, that traditionally, men in our society were trained to be dominant and women to be passive. Or you don't know that a clique tends to be exclusive and that its members are opposed to outsiders filtering in. You will observe all

the human behavior around you as if for the first time, and you will try to arrive at some new understanding of these behaviors. Write a creative report describing your fresh observations from this point of view, and then draw some new conclusions from these observations. What you will be doing, in a sense, is developing your own psychological theory for understanding behavior based on these simple observations.

6. The end of the chapter lists several types of psychologists. Contact a psychologist who fits into one of the categories listed and interview this person. Have a list of questions prepared beforehand. Possible questions: (1) What kind of education is necessary for your particular job? (2) Would you recommend one kind of graduate school over another? (3) Are there many jobs available today in your type of work? (4) What would a typical day at work be like for you—or is there no such thing as "typical"? (5) What motivated you to enter this line of work? Write a report of your interview and include your specific reactions.

DISCUSS THE PHOTO

A crucial part of the scientific method is careful observation.

Objectivity is a primary goal in psychological research.

28

PSYCHOLOGY AND YOU RESOURCES

A variety of resources are available in the Psychology and You *supplementary material. In addition, there are a number of additional resources listed to enhance your lesson plans.*

Masters
▼ 2-1A Learning Goals
▼ 2-1B Answers to Learning Goals
▼ 2-2 Reaction Time Experiment
▼ 2-3A Flawed Experiment
▼ 2-3B Answers to Flawed Experiment
▼ 2-4 Experiment Guideline
▼ 2-5 Sample Experiments
▼ 2-6A Drawing Conclusions
▼ 2-6B Answers to Drawing Conclusions

▼ 2-7 Interviews
Student Worksheets
▼ Vocabulary Worksheet
▼ Independent Practice Worksheet
▼ Enrichment Worksheet
▼ Reteaching Worksheet
Test Bank
▼ Tests A and B
Multimedia
▼ Psychology Videodisc
Student Workbook

PACING CHART

Complete Coverage

Day 1: Prior to class, assign the first three sections of the chapter. Focus on the components of a psychological experiment. Assign activities in which students must identify these components. In Focus Experimental Procedure and In Focus Independent vs. Dependent Variables can help clarify this topic. Assign Psychology in Your Life for Day 2.

Day 2: Discuss how stereotypes can bias psychological studies, how experiments can control for the influence of stereotypes, and finally how psychology studies can be used to test those stereotypes objectively, as in the Psychology and Your Life example. Assign the "Field Experiments" and "Other Methods of Studying Behavior" sections for Day 3.

Day 3: Conduct an activity or demonstration in which students can evaluate which method of studying behavior best applies to a given situation. Assign "Ethics of Experimentation" as homework.

Day 4: Discuss the ethics of experimentation. Do a group activity that will allow students to analyze

OBJECTIVES

Be able to:

▼ Explain the overall purpose of using scientific methods.

▼ Identify the independent and dependent variables, the experimental and control groups in an experiment.

▼ Describe the advantages and disadvantages of survey methods.

▼ Describe how naturalistic observation is done, and explain its usefulness.

▼ Indicate the pros and cons of the interview method.

▼ Explain what the case study method is used for.

▼ Explain the purpose of the longitudinal versus the cross-sectional methods.

▼ Discuss the pros and cons regarding the morality of experimenting with humans or animals.

Global Look at the Chapter

To avoid bias and false conclusions, psychology, as a science, tries to be as objective and factual as possible in its studies. This chapter covers some of the methods that are used to gain information about people and animals without allowing the personal bias of the researcher to distort the conclusions reached.

29

INTRODUCING THE CHAPTER

Spend a few minutes discussing the ways in which ninth graders and twelfth graders are different. Point out that their conclusions, though they may be accurate, are based on conjecture. Let them work in pairs to think of more scientific methods of finding differences between ninth and twelfth graders. Afterward, have them analyze the strengths and weaknesses of each method.

experiments according to the American Psychological Association's ethical guidelines.

Day 5: Allow students to analyze the arguments for and against animal experiments. Give the Chapter Review quiz.

In Brief

Day 1: Discuss the experiment in the text regarding men, women, and management, emphasizing the identification of its components. Assign for homework an activity that involves constructing an experiment.

Day 2: Focus on the concept that each method of studying behavior lends itself to certain situations better than others. Several activities in the wrap provide opportunities for the class to evaluate these methods as a group.

Day 3: Discuss the ethics of experimentation. Assign a short in-class activity in which students can evaluate the ethics of an experiment. Give the Chapter Review quiz.

LEAD-OFF ACTIVITY

See **Teaching Master 2-2 Reaction Time Experiment** for a simple reaction time experiment that you can perform in class. The purpose of the experiment, which is severely flawed, is (1) to teach students to detect those flaws; (2) to demonstrate the need for tight controls during experimentation; and (3) to warn students about experimenter bias when they conduct their own experiments or when they read about other studies.

DEMONSTRATION

To demonstrate the power of placebos, find a student in class who is not feeling well. Tell this person to place one hand palm up on his desk. With the other index finger he should press on the meaty part of the palm near the thumb for one minute. Explain that this pressure usually provides temporary relief of minor aches and pains. Tailor this explanation to the particular ailment of the student. Make sure you continue selling the cure for the entire minute, recounting how it relieved your headache one time, and so on. Even if the student does not report feeling better, this is an effective demonstration.

You might consider having the entire class participate, claiming that the procedure will make them feel more alert. This way you're more likely to get at least a few students reporting changes.

TEACHING MASTER 2-1A

Learning Goals. A Learning Goals sheet for each chapter is provided in the Teacher Resources. These Learning Goals can be used as review sheets or worksheets. **Teaching Master 2-1B** consists of answers to these Learning Goals.

Comprehension Check

How does a placebo work? *(Some people, when given "fake" medicine, feel better merely because they expect the medicine to bring relief.)*

placebo

A "medicine" that has no active ingredients and works by the power of suggestion.

double-blind study

A study during which neither participants nor researchers know to which group any subject belongs.

SCIENTIFIC METHODS

In a year we consume roughly one *billion* dollars' worth of pain relievers such as aspirin. The forms these tablets take include buffered, coated, capsule, with "added ingredients," so-called nonaspirin aspirin (acetaminophen), and crystals or tablets that dissolve in water. You can see immediately that this is a big business involving an enormous intake of drugs. As a result, advertisers fight vigorously for every cent they can wrench from us. Their techniques often involve TV commercials with questionable "studies," using distorted charts, diagrams, and claims. How well do these products really work? The only way to find out is to perform an actual, unbiased study of the product.

Psychologists do these kinds of studies because the question immediately arises, "How much, if any, pill-taking brings about a cure based on the power of suggestion?" In such a study, the goal of the researchers is to be completely objective. For instance, you would have to be careful about the age and sex of the subjects studied. Their overall health would have to be explored. If you happened to get a handful of people in the group you were studying who had a major illness or a disease that caused pain, the pain reliever would probably affect them differently than it would a person in good health but who has a headache. And you would have to determine whether it was actually the pain remedy that was responsible for the cure. As you can see, careful experimentation is very involved. Without it, we can draw no meaningful conclusions.

If we take an average of the studies in this area of pain relief, it turns out that roughly 50 percent of pain is "cured" by the power of suggestion (Frank, 1974). This is discovered when the experimenter uses one group that is given the real medicine and a similar group that is given a "medicine" with nothing in it that could cause a change. This second "fake medicine" is called a **placebo** (pla-SEE-boh). By comparing the cure rate between the two groups, we discover that 50 percent are getting better just because they get a pill they *believe* will bring relief.

The patients' expectations obviously play a major role here. Often, researchers' expectations have an impact as well. For instance, knowing that one group is only getting a placebo might change the experimenter's attitude. The patients' responses could be interpreted differently. Such a situation might well affect the accuracy of the results. It's better, then, if neither the patients nor their examiners know which group is which. When this is the case, it is called a **double-blind study.** This means that neither the participants nor the researchers know which group anyone belongs to until the study is finished.

Psychological studies provide broad scientific information about what we do, why we do it, and what changes go on during the

DISCOVERY

Teaching Master 2-3A Flawed Experiment includes a list of flawed experiments that students can correct and improve. Even before students can identify control groups, independent variables, and so on, they should be able to analyze these experiments using common sense and critical thinking. Results of these experiments appear in **Teaching Master 2-3B.**

process. Studies do not attempt to establish a "right" or "wrong" as much as to provide accurate information. For example, some people might decide that since 50 percent of the people get better without the painkiller, this group should not take pills for a headache. That, however, would be a highly questionable judgment, because other studies show that when people take a pill they *believe* will help them, their body chemistry actually changes to provide pain relief—even for those taking a pill that contains no pain reliever in it. Thus, fake pills can be necessary for triggering the body's own internal pain relievers.

One of our major goals in the first part of this chapter is to acquaint you with some of the terminology used in experimentation. This is best done by discussing a few different studies.

EXPERIMENTAL PROCEDURES: EFFECTS OF THE MOON

An area of interest that has been around since ancient times is the belief that the moon influences our behavior. In fact, the word *lunacy* (insanity) comes from the word *lunar,* which means "of the moon."

One study compared mental hospital admissions with the phases of the moon to see if there might be some relationship between a full moon and abnormal behavior. Researchers compared mental hospital

▲ *In this early drawing, these people are being driven mad by direct influence of the moon.*

Teaching Hint

Emphasize that hypotheses need to be clear and precise, and that the terms used in a hypothesis need to be defined objectively. Ask students if they think this is a good hypothesis: *Religious people tend to be more helpful than non-religious people.* Though this may be an interesting assertion, it is certainly not a good hypothesis—yet. Ask five students to define the word *religious,* and you'll probably get five different answers. Try to reach a consensus such as: *A religious person is one who attends church at least once a week.* Many will disagree on the definition you work out, but stress that you are merely defining the word for the purposes of one particular experiment. This way, the researcher can draw precise conclusions from data: *People who attend church at least once a week are more likely to . . .* Use the same process to define the word *helpful.*

DISCUSS THE PHOTO

In earlier times, people thought that madness could also be caused by devils and evil spirits.

COOPERATIVE LEARNING

Although **Teaching Master 2-5 Sample Experiments** lists numerous possible experiments that students can conduct, you may want them to think of their own topics. Have each group write 10 to 20 questions that they want answered through experimentation. As each group reports to the class, you can start to narrow the list of questions by pointing out which ones are impractical or unethical (see **Ethics of Experimentation** at the end of the chapter).

Points to Stress

Many of the so-called experiments that you and your students will perform throughout the semester are probably not experiments at all, mainly because your subjects will not be chosen randomly and you won't use enough of them. But this is OK. If you try to be too rigorous with your standards, the experiments will become tedious (which they really can become). It's probably enough simply to discuss what should be done in a real experiment. At the very least, you might want to recommend the following: (1) Do not use friends as subjects. (2) Treat all subjects the same. (3) Include the same number of subjects in the experimental and the control groups. (4) Treat subjects with respect.

hypothesis

A statement of the results that the experimenter expects.

subjects

People or animals on whom the experiment is conducted.

variables

Factors that change in an experiment.

admission rates for ten days before the full moon with the rates for ten days after the full moon (Blackman & Catalina, 1973). They did find what seemed to be a relationship between the full moon and "lunatic" behavior.

Hypothesis

We will use this experiment to help you become familiar with the terminology used in experimentation. The researchers started with a **hypothesis** (hy-POTH-ah-sis), which is a statement of the results they expect to get. In this case, the hypothesis was that there would be a relationship between the occurrence of the full moon and an increase in mental hospital admissions.

Choosing Subjects

Subjects are people (or animals) on whom an experiment is conducted. In this study, the subjects were people being admitted to a mental hospital.

Variables

Every experiment has **variables.** The term *variable* refers to things that can change (vary). In the present study, the variables were the phases of the moon and the rate of mental hospital admissions. Researchers want to examine how as one variable changes, the other changes. So, in this experiment, they asked, during different moon phases, does the admission rate vary?

Sometimes there are hidden or unexpected variables that you have to guard against. There was one in the moon study that was not discovered until after the study was over, and it invalidated the study. Hospital admissions drop over weekends. The time period right after the full moon happened to include a weekend. As a result, there was a sudden drop in admissions that was not connected with what was being studied—the moon's phases. Hence, the study cannot conclude that the moon has an effect on people's mental health. When the experiment was run again, eliminating a weekend, the moon's phases no longer showed up as having any influence on admissions. Researchers always have to watch out for this kind of problem (Campbell & Beets, 1980).

The finding of the second study is disappointing because most of us like to believe in the exotic. To date, studies of many kinds have found that no clear connection exists between the moon and mental problems or criminal behavior, except in horror movies (Rotton & Kelly, 1985).

One of the best ways to reinforce the terminology presented in the chapter is to have students conduct their own experiments. **Teaching Master 2-4 Experiment Guideline** provides students with a format they can follow when writing their reports. Ideas for experiments are listed throughout the book in the section at the end of each chapter.

Some studies have so many variables that it can be difficult to know what the truth is. This is the reason that there is so much confusion about what really causes heart disease. Some scientists claim cholesterol and salt cause heart problems; others say that this is not necessarily so. The conflicting studies occur because there are likely to be hundreds of things that must fall into place to cause heart disease (weight, age, life-style, family history, and so on), and only two of these factors might be cholesterol and salt intake. Since all these variables interact in knotty ways, sometimes salt or cholesterol shows up as a problem, sometimes not.

A STUDY OF STEREOTYPES

To acquaint you with some more terms, we want to examine an issue that relates to how we perceive other people. A stereotype is a set of fixed, generalized beliefs we hold about a given group. These beliefs are often inaccurate, but we nevertheless tend to assume that everyone from that group shares the same characteristics. For instance, if you believe that old people are crabby, you will probably expect that behavior from a friend's grandmother when you meet her for the first time.

Research: Men, Women, and Management

It has been shown repeatedly that stereotypes are strongest when people have little or no other information about a particular member of a group. For example, women traditionally have been perceived as unsuited for jobs in management. Imagine that you don't know anything about two people except that one of them is the president of a large company. Now imagine that one of these people is a man and the other a woman. Wouldn't you be likely to decide that the company president is the man rather than the woman? Most of us would be. One of the troubles with stereotypes is that they frequently result in discrimination. People may be treated unfairly simply because they belong to some group or other. In business, then, an individual woman may be denied the opportunity to prove herself because of a stereotype about women in general (Martinko & Gardner, 1983; Heilman, 1984).

One study of this issue had an equal number of men and women evaluate candidates for promotion to a managerial job. The subjects were given the job description and fictional summaries of several applicants' past professional experience. Half of the applicants were male, half female. The subjects were then asked to rank the applicants in order. All of the candidates had good work histories and

Chapter 2 METHODS OF PSYCHOLOGY

▲ *Getting an early start on heart disease?*

ENRICHMENT

Teaching Master 2-5 Sample Experiments is a compilation of where to find various experiments described throughout the textbook in the end-of-chapter material.

Experimental Procedure.

IN FOCUS Sometimes it's necessary to include more than one control group in order to eliminate hidden variables that may affect the results. If you want to find out if eating ice cream raises body temperature, group A can eat ice cream, and group B can eat nothing. But you would want a group C (a second control group), too, whose members eat something else, in order to see if it's the ice cream that is raising the body temperature or the act of eating anything.

Unit 1 APPROACHES TO PSYCHOLOGY

 **Experimental Procedure**

Hypothesis

IF "A" (the independent variable) is presented or changed,

THEN "B" (the dependent variable) will occur or change.

Test
hypothesis
on

Subjects

randomly
divided

into   into

**experimental
group**   **control
group**

(exposed to
independent
variable)   (not exposed to
independent
variable)

Measure behavior   Measure behavior
(the **dependent variable**)   (the **dependent variable**)

Compare measurements

The diagram shows one control group. Is it possible to include more than one control group in an experiment?

DEMONSTRATION

Propose a simple hypothesis: "In a game of catch, the way a ball is thrown will affect whether the ball will get caught." Lob a tennis ball around the room, making erratic throws, and note which throws are caught. Now that you've got their attention, explain about independent and dependent variables. The way you threw the ball was *independent* of any other factors: you could have thrown fast, slow, high, low. Whether the ball was caught was *dependent* on the type of throw (or the independent variable).

---

were described as successful in their previous jobs. The only difference, then, was gender, which the subjects could figure out by the applicants' names. We still aren't ready for the results, though. There is another twist to this story. The subjects differed from each other in one important way. Some of them had personal experience working under a female manager, the rest did not.

So, what were the results of this study? What questions would we like to have answered? Well, the first one might have to do with whether male or female candidates were ranked higher. Since stereotypes are strongest when there is little information about a person, and since in this study the subjects were given a lot of information about each candidate, it might not surprise you to learn that there was no evidence of a bias against the women applicants. (In fact, the women got slightly better ratings than the men did!) The more intriguing question to us, though, and the one we want to focus on, is whether having worked for a woman in the past made a difference. It did, and in a somewhat surprising way. The subjects who had never worked for a woman before ranked the men and women equally. The subjects who had personal work experience with female managers ranked the women applicants significantly higher than they ranked the men. In other words, these people showed a bias *in favor of* women as managers, something you might not expect to happen (Pazy, 1992).

It's always risky to draw broad conclusions from a single experiment. However, this study is backed up by many others who have made the same observation—namely, the more personal experience we have with members of a group, the less likely we are to apply stereotypes to them.

Variables: Independent and Dependent

This study shows the importance of two special kinds of variables that are part and parcel of scientific experiments. The first is called the **independent variable,** meaning that the researcher changes or varies this factor in a study. In the experiment just described, the independent variable is the experience a subject has working for female managers. The experimenter varied this by dividing the subjects into those with such experience and those without it and then looking at the responses of these two groups. The other special kind of variable is called the **dependent variable,** meaning that it will change as a result of what the other factor does. You might think of it as being dependent on the independent variable. Put another way, the results you get depend on what else has happened. In this study, the ranking of men and women changed as a result of the experience of the people doing the ranking. Thus, the dependent variable is the ranking of male and female candidates for promotion.

independent variable

The factor that the experimenter manipulates or changes in a study.

dependent variable

The factor in a study that changes or varies as a result of changes in the independent variable.

Comprehension Check

What are the independent (IV) and dependent variables (DV) in the following hypotheses? (1) Students score higher on SATs in the morning than in the afternoon. *(IV = time of day; DV = scores)* (2) People who wear uniforms will receive greater obedience than those who do not wear uniforms. *(IV = uniforms; DV = obedience)* (3) Strict parents raise children who rarely get in trouble. *(IV = discipline methods, strictness; DV = amount of trouble kids get into)*

FYI Here's a puzzle that is difficult to solve because of gender stereotypes: A father and his son are in a car accident. The father dies. The son is rushed to the hospital. The surgeon looks at the boy and says, "I can't operate on this boy; he's my son." How can this be? Answer: *The surgeon is the boy's mother.*

INTERDISCIPLINARY PROJECT

Math. As students conduct experiments, they should be expected, at the very least, to compute averages and percentages. You may want a few interested students to go a step further. Have them analyze their data with graphs, report correlations, and find the median and mode. Direct students to the Statistics Appendix. Another option is to invite a math class to analyze your data!

Independent versus Dependent Variables.

 IV = others watching; DV = jogging pace.

Teaching Hint

Have students note that the hypotheses listed in the preceding **Comprehension Check** are very general. Each key term used in the hypothesis would need to be defined more extensively and, of course, objectively. For instance, have students define obedience. All their answers may be right, but they may not be objective. Here's a possible definition: *Obedience, in this experiment, is defined as the number of times subjects obeyed the instructions of an experimenter who wore a uniform.* Have students define some of the other terms in these hypotheses. What constitutes a strict parent? What does it mean to "get in trouble"?

36

---

field experiments

Research that takes place outside the laboratory.

 **Independent Versus Dependent Variables**

How can you tell which is the independent variable and which is the dependent variable? Most hypotheses include the words *IF* and *THEN*. Here is a sample: If a request is made by a person in a uniform, then more people will reply to this request than to a request from someone without a uniform. The IF part of a hypothesis refers to the independent variable (what the experimenter controls). The THEN part refers to the dependent variable (what the experimenter measures). The independent variable in the above example is the uniform; the dependent variable is compliance.

Even when the words IF and THEN are not actually used, they are implied. For example, "people are more likely to obey instructions from someone who is near to them than from someone who is farther away." The IF part, the independent variable, is nearness. The THEN part, the dependent variable, is obedience.

Try to identify the independent and dependent variable in the following example: "People tend to jog at a faster pace than usual when others are around to watch."

FIELD EXPERIMENTS

Not all experiments are carried out in a laboratory. If they are not, they are called **field experiments,** meaning they happen away from the laboratory or "in the field."

Studying Jet Lag

As we will discuss in Chapter 6, a current and serious problem is the effect of the jet aircraft's speedy transportation on pilots and passengers. The disturbances created are called "jet lag" because the rhythm of the body lags behind (or runs ahead of) the time of day it would be at the person's place of departure. In other words, a person is still on the time at home while engaging in activities being done on a different schedule at a different place (eating lunch at 4 P.M., for example). The body is very sensitive to any kind of shift in the time of day when we eat, sleep, or work. The result of major shifts in time

Chapter 2 METHODS OF PSYCHOLOGY

Points to Stress

If students have problems identifying the independent and dependent variables, remind them that the independent variable is the *if* part of the hypothesis (if and independent both start with "i"!), and the dependent variable is the *then* part of the hypothesis.

Points to Stress

The experimenter varies the independent variable, but tries to keep other variables constant. For example, if you wanted to find out if older people are more tolerant than younger people (and, of course, you'll need to define all these terms for the experiment), you would not test some of your subjects at the beach and other subjects in an office. If setting is not part of the independent variable, it needs to remain constant.

DISCUSS THE PHOTO

Sometimes an inventor's early attempts seem primitive, but they may lead to sound results in the end.

are fatigue, stomach distress, dizziness, feeling "awful," and mental confusion.

Jet air travel causes a disruption in the normal cycle of behavior when we fly across the ocean. Flights across the ocean are usually made at night. The airlines claim that the passenger will arrive at his or her destination "ready for a day's work." That's not really true. Here's what actually happens. If you leave from New York and are flying east, you will cross five time zones and arrive in Europe five hours out of synchronization with your own body's time clock. Thus, arriving at 9:00 A.M. London time actually has you at 4:00 A.M. at home. Your body is operating on home time. And 4:00 A.M. is the low point in the day for almost everyone; it is the time when your body is least able to cope with any kind of stress. It will take you at least several days to get into synchronization with London time, yet you are expected to operate at full efficiency right away when you are weakest and least able to do so (Moore-Ede et al., 1982). So this shift in light and darkness, and the changes in habits that it causes, will create all the symptoms associated with jet lag. These effects have been demonstrated over and over and are the subject of considerable concern, even when they involve shorter time zone changes such as those that result from crossing the United States. But perhaps some

▲ *The man in the top photo avoided the pitfalls of jet lag by never getting off the ground.*

EXPERIMENT

The topic of field experiments provides a great excuse to leave the confines of your room! The cafeteria, the gym, or any other location where you won't look too conspicuous are good field sites. Divide students into groups to design an experiment and announce that the "best" one will be conducted. If you don't want to take the time for group work, here are a few possible experiments: (1) Students can walk around pretending to collect answers to a survey and, while doing so, invade people's personal space. (2) Have someone fall to see who helps or drop a wallet to see who returns it. (3) Get the cafeteria's permission to "steal" something in front of subjects to see if anyone reports this. Note: a certain

Discussion

You may want to mention to students that many of the psychological studies they will read about have primarily used white college students as subjects. Examine the possible flaws in this by asking the following questions: Are these white college students representative of the larger population? Were the subjects chosen randomly? (Selection was probably not entirely random if the sample was skewed by race.)

experimental group

The group on which the critical part of the experiment is performed.

control group

The group that does not participate in the critical part of the experiment.

people are still skeptical of these claims. How do we set up an experiment that will clearly show that the problem comes from rhythmic changes rather than just from the fatigue of flying itself?

To examine whether the effects arise from the disruption of body rhythms, the scientist uses the same experimental procedures that are followed inside the laboratory. To illustrate that the effects are not from fatigue, the experimenters can look at the different reactions of two groups of subjects. The first group will fly to Europe, crossing the time zones. This group is called the **experimental group,** since the critical part of the experiment is being performed on them. A second group is needed, however—one that does *not* cross time zones. In this way, we can note how the effects of the trip differ for the two groups. So, we have to *control* the critical part of the investigation, the flying across time zones. "Control," then, refers to removing, for one group, the factor being studied. (Note that this was done in the study on pain relievers: one group was given a "medicine" that did not contain any medically active ingredients so that it could be compared with the group that received the real painkilling medications.) Thus, we form what is called a **control group** that flies an equal time and distance but to South America. The shift in light and darkness and the alteration of sleep and eating times *do not* occur for this group because there is no time change.

What we discover is that the control group does not suffer the physical effects of jet lag, which show up dramatically in the experimental group. Hence, we have demonstrated that the problems come from time changes, not the length of the flight itself.

To go over it once more: the independent variable is the alteration of the usual light-dark cycle by using a time-changing flight path, and the dependent variable is the result of the alteration: fatigue, trouble making decisions, and disturbances of the body's rhythmic cycles. The control group, which does not undergo the specific factor we are studying, is then contrasted with the experimental group—which *does* undergo the critical variable.

Fighting Insomnia

So many technical terms can be difficult to grasp at first, so we will review them with an additional experiment. In this one, we want to determine if people who have trouble sleeping (insomnia) can be helped by taking a "sleeping pill" before going to bed.

The experimenter assembles two groups of insomniac subjects and administers sleeping pills to one group and placebos to the other group. Here are the experimental setup and the results:

Hypothesis X amount of sleeping pills helps the otherwise healthy person with insomnia to sleep better.

Subjects The subjects of the experiment are two groups of people

amount of planning is required for this type of activity to work well; you'll need to spend a few minutes ironing out details so that the experiment can be conducted in a scientific manner. At the very least, develop a hypothesis, define the independent and dependent variables, and identify the experimental and control groups. When students return, they can write about and then discuss their results.

in similar physical health, within the same age range, and with similar sleep problems.

Independent Variable   (This is the variable that the experimenter changes.) The experimenter regulates the "medicine," with one group receiving genuine sleeping pills while the other receives a placebo.

Dependent Variable   (This is what results from the experimenter's varying or changing the independent variable.) The results can *vary* among better sleep, worse sleep, or about the same amount of sleep.

Control   (This is the removal of factors that might cause the results, even though they are not the independent variable.) The experimenter will not use people who are sick, people with severe allergies, or people who are very old. Any one of these factors could alter the real effects of the medicine in the average person with insomnia.

Control Group   (This group consists of the subjects who are like the experimental group except the control group doesn't participate in the crucial part of the study.) The control group in this study consists of those subjects who receive a placebo, thinking it is a sleeping pill.

Experimental Group   (These are the people who participate in the crucial part of the study.) The experimental group consists of those subjects who get *X* amount of sleeping pills.

Results   The hypothesis turns out to be incorrect in a real-life study. Thus, we reject the hypothesis that those who receive the sleeping pill will sleep better. What is found is that subjects taking the sleeping pill over a period of days will still have insomnia, only worse. And the sleep they do get is worse (less restful) than the sleep the control group gets.

These results occur because most tranquilizers and sleeping pills interfere with dreams; they cause the person to feel worse because without dreams, sleep loses most of its "curative effect" (Hartmann, 1984). This subject is discussed in more detail in Chapter 6.

▲   *No sleep, no dreams, no rest.*

DISCUSS THE PHOTO

What are some ways that students deal with insomnia?

OTHER METHODS FOR STUDYING BEHAVIOR

In this section, we want to acquaint you with other methods that psychologists use to study behavior.

COOPERATIVE LEARNING

Divide the class into six groups and assign one of the six methods for studying behavior to each group. Each group's tasks: (1) Read the assigned section in the text. (2) Prepare a skit that shows psy-chologists using the assigned method. (3) Debrief the rest of the class. This should include a discussion of the advantages and disadvantages of using the particular method.

Methods of Research.

IN FOCUS Student answers will vary. This can be an excellent critical-thinking exercise if you ask students to explain their rankings.

IN FOCUS **Methods of Research**

	Advantages	Disadvantages
Laboratory Experiment	Researcher can be completely objective. Usually provides accurate information.	Somewhat artificial setting. May not reflect the "real world."
Field Experiment	Setting is more realistic than in a laboratory.	Often difficult to control all variables.
Survey Method	Can gather information on feelings, opinions, and behavior patterns. Can be amazingly accurate.	Survey's sample may not be representative of population as a whole. Questions used may not be phrased objectively. Interpretation of results may be distorted.
Naturalistic Observation	Behavior studied is completely natural.	Researcher cannot interact with subjects and may interpret subjects' responses incorrectly.
Interview	Researcher can obtain personal, detailed information.	Subjects' responses may not be completely honest. Researcher's biases can influence behavior.
Case Study Method	Provides background information that may shed light on present behavior.	Subjects' responses may not be completely honest. Researcher's biases can influence behavior.
Psychological Test	Provides accurate, objective information—little chance of distorting results.	Tests limited in the amount of information they can obtain.
Longitudinal Method	Necessary for certain kinds of research, such as studies on development.	Expensive and time consuming.
Cross-Sectional Method	Samples used are usually representative of population as a whole. Less expensive and less time consuming than longitudinal method.	Not appropriate for some types of research, such as studies on developmental changes over time.

If you were a psychologist and you wanted to study whether reading to children would affect their reading ability once they enter school, which of these methods would be most useful and which would be least useful? Answer this question by ranking the methods from 1 (most useful) to 9 (least useful).

DISCOVERY

Surveys seem to be easy to write, but when asked to create one, students usually have a difficult time. Their questions are often open ended, so the task of analyzing answers becomes arduous, if not impossible. When multiple choice answers are offered, the choices are sometimes too limiting; questions often include inherent biases, and so on.

To help students appreciate a well-devised survey, have them write their own. (This might be a good group activity.) Tell them to focus on a single topic, like dating, loneliness, or music. Afterward, analyze two or three of the surveys—on an overhead projector, if possible—comparing and contrasting them with surveys collected from magazines.

Survey Method

A **survey** involves asking questions of a carefully selected group of people. This allows you to gather information on feelings, opinions, or behavior patterns. Surveys can be done by mail (using questionnaires), in person, over the phone, or via television using a responding device set up in the home. Which method is used is not as important as the kind of people chosen to participate in the research. Suppose we wanted to find out if people think that there is too much crime and that the prison sentences given to criminals are too light. If, say, 30 percent of our sample is comprised of ex-convicts, we will get a distorted view of the general population's opinion on this subject—to say the least.

Since we can't interview everyone, a **sample** must be chosen that represents the general population. The sample should be composed of a correct proportion of people from various races, sexes, social classes, and age groups. If properly selected, a sample can produce results that are amazingly accurate. The Gallup Poll, for instance, is careful to include people from all the various groups. As a result, since 1950, the poll has missed the actual presidential election results only by a remarkably low 1.6 percent of the time (Myers, 1983).

The way a question is phrased can also be of major importance. Advertisers are infamous for phrasing questions in such a way that they get results favorable to their point of view. For instance, an advertiser might ask, "Which aspects of car X [the advertiser's car] do you like better than car Y?" This question forces a biased answer. After the survey, the advertiser places ads that ignore the original question and how it was phrased and, instead, say something like, "Ninety percent of people surveyed said they preferred car X over car Y!" Such advertisers would be afraid to ask the more meaningful question, "Do you prefer car X or car Y?"

Using a questionnaire sent through the mail can pose a big problem that may distort the results—namely, filling out the questionnaire takes time and trouble. Hence, many people will not bother to fill it out and mail it back. Usually only those with an ax to grind or a special devotion to the issue will go to the trouble of responding. Some surveys get as few as 20 to 30 percent of the questionnaires returned. It is hard to put much faith in such a low response rate. Too many opinions are missing.

Naturalistic Observation

In **naturalistic observation,** researchers secretly observe the subjects of the study—animal or human—in daily activity, carefully recording their behavior. The advantage to this method is that the

survey

A method of research using questions on feelings, opinions, or behavior patterns.

sample

A group that represents a larger group.

naturalistic observation

A research method that involves studying subjects without their being aware that they're being watched.

Journal Topic

This topic relates to the above **Discovery** activity. "Write about the process you went through when creating your survey. What difficulties did you encounter? How did you decide on a topic? What revisions did you make and why?" This won't be the most exciting journal topic for students, but it's the kind of task that promotes critical thinking.

DISCOVERY

If feasible, bring your students to the school cafeteria and have them file in inconspicuously. They should jot down numerous naturalistic observations about other students' behavior, then try to draw conclusions. One problem with this exercise is that hundreds of behaviors will be observed, but these behaviors may inspire few meaningful conclusions. To avoid this, have students decide beforehand what they will focus on. Large versus small groups? Males versus females? Freshmen versus seniors?

DISCUSS THE PHOTO

Some universities interview applicants. Ask the class what types of things can come across during an interview that may not be reflected in a student's GPA or SAT scores.

Evaluation Strategy

Ask students: If you wanted to study the effects of birth order (ordinal position) on jealousy, which two methods of research would you be most likely and least likely to use, and why?

There is no right or wrong answer, but students should support their conclusions. They may argue that an experiment comparing subjects who are the oldest to subjects who are the youngest would be easy to set up and control, and the results would be easy to analyze. If significant differences are found, subjects could then be examined using a case study approach. On the other hand, students may argue that interviews and surveys should not be used because subjects may not respond honestly to such a personal issue as jealousy.

42

▲ *Interviews can provide detailed personal information.*

interview

A research method that involves studying people face to face and asking questions.

creatures will behave as they normally do, since they don't know anyone is watching them. Both people and animals behave differently in the presence of an outsider. Thus, it is possible to get more realistic information on behavior through naturalistic observation. For example, observing male and female monkeys interacting with one another and as a "family" shows that males do a great deal more pushing and shoving of one another than do females, a situation similar to that found among humans. If the monkeys are in the laboratory or are aware of your presence, they do not act out their full repertoire of behavior. For humans, as we will discuss in Chapter 20, laboratory studies on the effects of violent TV strongly suggest that such TV shows cause violent behavior to increase. On the other hand, naturalistic observation of people after viewing violence yields results that don't always match the laboratory results; in some cases, people become less violent after a violent program. Thus, a whole different perspective is provided by this method.

One of the flaws with naturalistic methods is that the observer is not able to talk with or interact with the human subject. In some cases, the observer may be making an incorrect interpretation of exactly what is going on since the subject is never asked.

Interviews

A common method for studying people and how they feel about things in the present is to **interview** them. Quite a bit of personal, detailed information can be obtained using this technique. The biggest problem here is trying to sort out fiction from fact, since the interviewee is going to be on his or her best behavior and will try to present information in the most favorable light. More often than not, for example, when people are asked what kind of television they watch, they will claim they are glued to the set viewing educational material on public TV rather than a soap opera or a blockbuster film filled with murder, mayhem, and mischief. If what they told us were true, public television would be making lots of money, which it never is, and the commercial networks would be broke, which they are not. Even so, a fair amount of reasonably accurate personal data can be gained through the interview.

Another problem is that the interviewer always has to be on guard against his or her own biases in a face-to-face situation. All of us carry around subtle and not-so-subtle prejudices against certain types of people, certain age groups, certain modes of dress, and so forth. There is no doubt that these factors have an influence not only on the types of questions we ask but also, and more important, on the interpretation we give to an answer. An answer that seems clever or original from interviewee A might be interpreted as flippant or rude coming from interviewee B.

Case Study Method

The **case study method** involves developing information about a person's long-term background, often for purposes of psychological treatment. The goal is to find out as much as possible about how the personality has evolved from the early years in order to shed light on what might be the origin of present-day problems. Again, this method is subject to the same distortion as the interview, but it is still a useful way to get a rough idea of how a person views the world. People who are very pessimistic might not know they are giving away the fact that they see most things so bleakly, but if you talk to them for even a short period of time, you get clues that suggest the presence of this attitude. If you are lucky, you will also get some background information that suggests how they became such black-cloud creatures.

In real life, the psychological interview or case study method is most often used to get an overall sense of how a person approaches problems and of what his or her general feelings are; the psychologist generally doesn't rely too much on the specific content of what a person claims is the truth.

One word of warning about case studies—you cannot generalize from their findings. You *can* get a fair amount of detailed information about a particular person or situation, and that is the advantage of case studies. However, what is true for one case may or may not be true for others.

case study method

Research that collects lengthy, detailed information about a person's background, usually for psychological treatment.

Psychological Tests

One way to overcome bias in an interview is to use objective **psychological tests,** such as the IQ test. All of us have experienced the phenomenon of being deceived by people we meet for the first time. They seemed to be very stupid (or bright), but later we discover that we have misjudged them just because they looked the way they did or dressed in a certain fashion. Problems of this kind can be avoided by using the IQ test, since it has a fixed set of questions *and* answers for scoring. It leaves no room for personal bias to enter into the interpretation of the results. The test takers either answered the questions correctly or they didn't. In a way, then, the psychological test is a kind of fixed, rigid interview with minimal opportunity for personal distortion. As we will discuss in Chapter 9, the test is a much better method than the interview for finding out a person's intellectual potential.

Tests of personality or job aptitude are, again, more objective than the interview, but when we move into these rather vague areas, the tests are often not as useful as observation of a person on the job or in interaction with others. Too often people exaggerate the amount of

psychological tests

Observation and measurement of the subject using objective measures (as opposed to an interview).

Critical Thinking

Ask the class a very general question: What do you want to know about people? Write the answers on the board. If your question doesn't generate many answers, you can have them fill in the following blank: I wonder why people _____. Or, What puzzles me about people is _____. After you collect about 20 answers, discuss which method of research would yield the most accurate (or best) data for each question. Encourage students to think in practical terms. Matching a question to a particular method may be a challenging task for students, so consider allowing them a few minutes to write about it before you begin the discussion.

DISCOVERY

Have several students role-play a version of the **Journal Topic** scenario below. (Students can still do the role-play without completing the journal entry.) You might assume that researchers have placed a video camera in the kitchen that records constantly. The students role-play a family discussion on using the car, keeping curfew, or whatever else they choose. Remember, this is the first day of being watched, so some "family members" may put up a front for the camera.

Discussion

Ask students the following question: If you were a parent, would you allow your kids to be part of a longitudinal study? Remind students that these kinds of studies are time-consuming. (Answers will vary, but many students will argue that it depends on the type of study and whether they feel it is worthwhile.) This could be an interesting topic to pursue further; the potential worth of research *should* be examined. Ask students: What issues do they feel are worthy of pursuit, and which ones are not?

Journal Topic

"Pretend that your family has been selected to participate in a longitudinal study on parenting styles. Your family agrees to take part, but you do not want to participate. You're afraid of what the researchers will find out. You don't voice your objections, and today is the first day of the study. The researchers arrive and . . ."

44

cross-sectional method

A method of research that looks at different age groups at the same time in order to understand changes that occur during the life span.

longitudinal method

A method of research that studies the same group of people over an extended period of time.

information these tests provide. Such tests cannot predict behavior in the complex human with a high degree of accuracy, even though they can uncover important information that might be missed in an interview. The best of all worlds, then, is to combine and compare the results of both the interview and the psychological test.

Longitudinal and Cross-Sectional Studies

In addition to the fact that there are all these different methods for investigating behavior, you should be aware that there can also be different goals behind the investigation. For example, researchers might want to know what feelings large groups have regarding a problem that is current today, but they are not concerned with how the opinions developed or changed over time. Then there are other cases in which researchers want to examine a pattern over time in groups in order to observe the changes that might occur. For example, you may have heard that intelligence notably declines with age. This seemed to be true from early studies examining the issue. How were these studies done? Since the goal was to compare intelligence levels for people of different ages throughout our life span, the experimenters took subjects from different age groups, running from late childhood through old age, administered IQ tests to each age group, and then looked at how the results changed from one age group to another. This technique is called the **cross-sectional method** because a cross section (or representative sample) was taken from each major age group.

These findings on intelligence, however, turned out to be incorrect. There was a major flaw in the way the study was designed that no one saw at first. Using the cross-sectional method required that the researchers use different people from each age group. Therein lay the problem. The older people in the sample were from a generation that did not know as much as the generation following it. It seems that your generation will know more than we do, that we know more than our parents did, that our parents knew more than their parents, and so forth. (As long as we have to face up to this, we take some consolation in the fact that *your* children will know more than you do.) As a result, the cross-sectional method was measuring and comparing the older people, who had less knowledge to begin with, with younger people, who had more information. Thus, it *appeared* that as a person got older, intelligence declined.

How was the error discovered? To understand, you need to know that there is another system of conducting studies, called the **longitudinal** (lon-juh-TUE-di-nal) **method.** In the longitudinal method, the researchers follow the *same* group of people through the years, measuring them again from time to time. You can immediately see why this method is not used very often, given the length of time and the

EXPERIMENT

Obedience studies are presented in Chapter 21, but if you wait until the end of the course to try this activity, students may know you too well. Show up late to class one day, but leave the overhead projector turned on. Place a sheet of instructions on the overhead to see how obedient your students will be. Possible

instructions to the students include: sit in a circle; take off your shoes; pick a leader; read; and so on.

To make this more like an experiment, vary the instructions from class to class. One class's instructions could be expressed courteously; another's could be rude. Or you may want to arrange for a student or two

to lead the obedient behavior—or to disobey vehemently. Afterward, discuss the role of deception during experimentation. Is deception ever ethical? (There are no right answers to these questions, of course, but students should be encouraged to defend their positions.)

---

expense involved. But sometimes it is necessary, as in this example about intelligence or in child development research.

When the longitudinal studies were applied to the *same* group of people over the decades, researchers discovered that the cross-sectional studies were wrong. They found that in general, people maintain approximately the same level of intelligence as they age. Of course, there is a slowing of reaction time and a moderate amount of memory loss when a person is quite old, but overall there is little decline in a person's mental abilities over his or her life span. Similar studies show that old people who are cranky, selfish, forgetful, and rigid in old age were that way when they were 30 and often when they were 15 years old.

Most psychological studies are cross-sectional, but every now and then longitudinal research still appears today.

ETHICS OF EXPERIMENTATION

Throughout this book, you will read about studies that have required deception of subjects or the deliberate creation of frustration and anxiety in people to see how they react in certain situations. These studies have been justified on the grounds that we are seeking more information about the human being. The more knowledge we have of ourselves, the better off we will probably be, and the more likely it is that we can be helped or that we'll understand problems that arise.

But serious issues come up with this kind of research. How far can and should an experimenter go in trying to find answers? For example, in Chapter 21, we will discuss an experiment designed to determine the causes of deplorable conditions in prisons. The experiment in question was performed with college students, and for a time, it *literally* turned the college-student "guards" into vicious people and the college-student "prisoners" into helpless, miserable creatures. After the experiment, there was greater understanding of what causes today's prison conditions, but some of the subjects were psychologically scarred from finding out that they could act the way they did. Was it ethical and worth it? We don't know; the matter is still being argued back and forth.

Ethical Principles

The American Psychological Association has established ethical guidelines for experimenters. We want to cover the main points here so that you can make your own decisions about what is ethical (American Psychological Association, 1992).

1. *Subjects must always have the right to decline participation in an experiment or withdraw their participation at any time.* This ethical

Chapter 2 METHODS OF PSYCHOLOGY

Comprehension Check

Name a problem associated with each method of studying behavior: survey method *(results can be distorted by an unrepresentative sample; questions can be formulated to force biased answers);* naturalistic observation *(it is possible to make an incorrect interpretation of the subject's behavior);* interview *(interviewee may put up a false front; interviewer's personal prejudices can affect questions and interpretation of interviewee's answers);* case study *(cannot generalize from findings);* psychological tests *(cannot predict behavior with a high degree of accuracy);* cross-sectional studies *(differences in generations may distort results);* longitudinal *(expensive, time-consuming).*

CHAPTER PROJECT

This project will give students more experience designing an experiment. Point out that Ph.D. candidates who want to conduct experiments must go before a review board that determines if the experiment will add worthwhile knowledge to the field, and if the experimental procedure is ethical. Have students work in pairs designing an experiment. Their design can include the following sections: hypothesis, subjects, apparatus, procedure. (See **Teaching Master 2-4 Experiment Guidelines** for more details on these sections.) Then set up a hearing in which you act as the review board and students act as Ph.D. candidates who try to gain approval for their experiments. To make the hearing seem more authentic, you can sit behind a table, have a colleague join you as part of the board, and so on. This is an excellent activity, even if you don't want students actually to perform the experiments.

Connections

Discuss the ethics of Milgram's and Zimbardo's obedience studies found in Chapter 21. After reviewing the studies, have students decide if the four guidelines listed were violated. You may want to have several students formally debate the issue.

Comprehension Check

According to the guidelines established by the American Psychological Association, would it be unethical for a psychology teacher to give an "F" to a student who refused to participate in an experiment? Why or why not? *(Yes, it would be unethical. According to the American Psychological Association, subjects must always have the right to decline participation in an experiment or withdraw their participation at any time.)*

principle is rarely violated. No one should ever be forced to take part in an experiment. Still, there can be hidden pressure: "If I don't participate, what will the teacher think of me? Will my grade be affected?" In cases where participation in research is a course requirement, some other fair option must be made available to the students.

2. *Openness and honesty are essential to experimentation.* Here is a typical problem in this area: studies have been designed to examine under what circumstances a subject will cheat. The subjects are observed—unknown to them—in situations where cheating is possible. If the experimenter is honest with them, they will know they are being observed and will not cheat. How do we conduct this kind of study and still remain ethical? The general rule is that if researchers cannot disclose everything at the beginning of the study, they must do so as soon as possible afterward. They are obligated to clear up any misconceptions their subjects may have.

3. *Information obtained about a subject during the course of a study must remain confidential.* The major exception to this rule applies when an agreement to the contrary has been made beforehand. When it is likely that other people will have access to the information, the experimenter must inform the subject of this possibility. Sometimes, though, the experimenter can't foretell with certainty just who will have such access. How far should confidentiality procedures be taken, and with what kinds of information?

4. *The experimenter has the duty to assess carefully the possibility of any potential risks, physical or mental, to participants, inform them of existing risks, and correct or remove any undesirable consequences of participation.* This rule covers both immediate and long-term effects. If an experimenter does a study in which subjects are made to feel inferior (as would be the case with a deliberately difficult "IQ test"), then the subjects must be told the true nature of the test at the end of the study. Sometimes, however, as in the prisoner-guard experiment, the degree of potential risk could not have been anticipated. Even though the experiment was terminated early, the damage had already been done. In cases like this, there doesn't seem to be any way to help participants completely forget how they behaved during the experiment itself.

Experimentation with Animals

People all over the country are expressing concern about experimentation with animals. Since animals have many things in common with humans, they are frequently studied in order to find out more about us. At the same time, they are not merely objects or abstract creatures with no feelings. Some people believe that any physical or

Interested students can collect articles on the controversy over using animals for experimentation. Have students focus on psychology-related experiments. They can present their findings to the class and perhaps have a debate.

Chapter 2 METHODS OF PSYCHOLOGY

psychological suffering caused an animal must be aimed at removing a problem in the human that is equal to or greater than the unpleasantness caused the animal (Fox, 1983).

Some have pointed out that as the brighter creatures, humans have a moral obligation to protect animals rather than use them. Many people feel that since animals are part of the ecology of the whole planet, scientific researchers must show basic respect for them. Otherwise, scientists will not be taken seriously as individuals trying to foster the greater good of the world (Fox, 1980b).

Fortunately, the bulk of evidence obtained about the majority of experiments in psychology suggests that animal treatment is humane, but humans must always be on guard against abusing their power over a helpless creature (Coile & Miller, 1984).

We hope you can tell by reading this book that we love psychology but that we also love animals. We have tried to avoid mentioning experiments that seemed cruel because we don't want to give any more publicity to people who would do such things. In a few cases, however, we have not been in a position to decide for certain whether an experiment involved cruelty; in these cases, we have given the researcher the benefit of the doubt. We report only those studies that seem to be useful—and then we cross our fingers and continue to worry about it.

Reteaching Strategy

Tell students that they are budding psychologists who want to study communication. Which two methods of research would they use and why? Ask students to be specific. For example, if they want to conduct an experiment, have them briefly describe the procedure. If they want to use surveys and interviews, have them include a few questions.

EXPERIMENT

Bring in a video game (such as Tetris) that challenges spatial skills to test for potential gender differences. Randomly select several males and females as subjects. These students should have no previous experience playing the game. Compare male and female scores and discuss how to make the experiment more scientific.

PSYCHOLOGY IN YOUR LIFE

Critical Thinking
Ask students to respond (orally or in writing) to the following question: How might participation in sports influence spatial skills? Answers will vary, but might include the point that athletes in team sports need to know where their teammates are at any given moment. For example, good basketball players can make crisp passes without looking directly at teammates. They have a strong sense of where they stand in relation to their teammates, who occupy a different spot in space. (*Spatial* is a derivative of space.) Years of practicing would certainly have an effect on this spatial ability.

DISCUSS THE PHOTO

If you have students who spend time in a video arcade, have them keep track of how much time males versus females spend playing a particular game.

PSYCHOLOGY IN YOUR LIFE

Socialized Sex Differences?

▲ *Are females really inferior at playing video games?*

There is no hotter topic among the general population as well as in the scientific world than that of the differences between the sexes. (We will discuss this topic in some detail in Chapter 13.) Overall we find that there are far more similarities between the sexes than differences. One area of difference does stand out, however, and this is called *spatial ability*. Spatial ability is the ability to imagine how things look in space and to manipulate these objects mentally or physically. Thus, playing video games is a good measure of this characteristic. By and large, males take delight in the fact that females, as a group, don't compare well with males on this task. While we can't disagree with this fact, it clearly requires a more detailed examination. One of the major criticisms of the suggestion that innate differences are involved is the possibility that females either aren't interested in tasks involving spatial skills or, more likely, that society puts pressure on them to stay away from such activities.

We want to go through a real experiment on video games and male-female skills. The goal is to try to help you think through the basic problem and some of the issues that come up along the way in such a study. Then we'll give you the results of the study (Gagnon, 1986).

Fifty-eight students at Harvard University participated in the study, 34 males and 24 females. The purpose of the exploration was to determine if practice made any difference in video-game skills. If females don't play the games very often, could this be a factor in their relatively poor performance? In the study, one of the tasks to be performed was to play a video game called "Targ," which involves moving a spaceship through a maze while fighting off enemy ships.

As we proceed, asking each question, try to answer it for yourself before reading on.

What is the first step in the experiment?

First an hypothesis is formed and subjects are selected. In this case, subjects were categorized as "expert" or "novice" on video-game playing to form a back-

(continued on next page)

Chapter 2 METHODS OF PSYCHOLOGY

PSYCHOLOGY IN YOUR LIFE

Socialized Sex Differences?

(continued from previous page)
ground for analyzing their results later on.
Do you need a control group?
Yes. A control group was used and was given no time to practice after a pretest of their skills on the machine. Using a control group reduces the possibility of any other factors influencing the results. The control group, then, took the pretest on the machine to establish a starting point, did nothing in between, and then took a posttest on the machine. The experimental group took the pretest, got two and a half hours of practice on the machine over the period of a week, then took the posttest on the machine to detect whatever changes might have occurred.
Here is what the experiment looked like in diagram form:
Experimental group:
Pretest → 2 ½ hours of playing → Posttest

Control group: Pretest → wait during week → Posttest
Before starting, the experimenter would not have done the task properly if she hadn't obtained as much information on the subjects' school histories as possible.
What might she need to know, given that society might be influencing the results? That is, what school courses does society consider "masculine" and might be related to these skills?
The experimenter obtained from the subjects information regarding the math, science, or "engineering-type" courses they had taken, since these courses could be related to spatial skills.
What were the results of the study?
With practice, the improvement rate for females was such that there was no significant difference in learning between males and females. In other words, females clearly can learn

such skills rapidly. The second finding suggested that spatial skills are something that improve with practice and that cumulatively get better over time. Third finding: the number of math and science courses taken is related to improvement in video-game skills. Fourth: the control group did not improve in their skills (which was to be expected, but was a necessary part of the experiment).
This study has clear social significance. It strongly implies that we are dealing with a socially induced difference in spatial skills between males and females rather than with some kind of innate difference. In and of itself, the study is not conclusive, but it adds a bit of information to the broad study of male and female differences. It also helps call into question the assumption that females are less capable of dealing with so-called masculine pursuits of this type.

Reteaching Strategy

Have students complete the **Reteaching Worksheet** for this chapter located in the Teacher Resources.
The **Vocabulary Worksheet** may be completed by the class as a pretest for chapter concepts or used as a reteaching worksheet for those students needing additional review.

49

ENRICHMENT

Have students complete the **Enrichment Worksheet** for this chapter located in the Teacher Resources.

VOCABULARY REVIEW

Before testing students on the contents of the chapter, you may want to review vocabulary terms that are especially important or confusing. Terms in this chapter that could require clarification are *hypothesis*, *independent variable*, *dependent variable*, *experimental group*, and *control group*.

Wrapping It Up

Remind students that when we read or hear about experimental findings, we should view them critically. Too often we blindly accept reports without asking a single question. Who conducted the study? Are there any other variables that could have affected the outcome? Was the experiment fair to subjects (this includes animal subjects)? Is the information that the experiment provided worthwhile?

Unit 1 Approaches to Psychology

SUMMARY

1. In the scientific method of psychological experimentation, first the hypothesis is formed and the subjects are chosen; then the subjects are divided up into an experimental group and a control group.
2. A variable is any factor in an experiment that changes. The variable that is regulated by the experimenter is the independent variable. The second variable is the dependent variable, which is the change that occurs as a result of what the experimenter does with the independent variable.
3. Field experiments are conducted away from the laboratory, but they still adhere as much as possible to the rigid rules of experimentation.
4. A survey is used to ask questions of carefully selected people in order to understand opinions and feelings. The questionnaire is one such method, but it may not be too effective if administered by mail.
5. Naturalistic observation avoids interfering with the subject's behavior and focuses on hidden observation in order to record how the creature behaves when not aware that it is being watched.
6. The interview involves the face-to-face collection of people's ideas, actions, background, or behavior. The case study is somewhat similar in that it collects specific background information covering a greater period of years in order to help develop a picture of the person, usually to aid in psychological treatment.
7. Psychological tests are objective methods of gathering information about people. The questions are determined beforehand, and the range of answers is restricted.
8. The longitudinal method of research requires considerable time and expense. The same group of people is examined over and over during a lengthy period of time, often many decades. The cross-sectional method also studies the effects of time, but it uses people from different age groups and tests them all at the same time in order to provide the desired information.
9. Psychological research must conform to the ethical guidelines of the American Psychological Association. Subjects may decline or withdraw their participation. Researchers must be honest, maintain confidentiality, assess risks and correct any undesirable effects on their subjects.

SUGGESTED READINGS

▼ Bunker, Barbara Benedict, et al. *A Student's Guide to Conducting Social Science Research.* New York: Human Sciences, 1975.

▼ Edwards, A. L. *Experimental Design in Psychological Research.* 5th ed. New York: Harper, 1985.

▼ Keith-Spiegel, P., and G. P. Goocher. *Ethics in Psychology: Professional Standards and Cases.* New York: Random House, 1985.

▼ Stanovich, K. E. *How to Think Straight About Psychology.* New York: Scott Foresman, 1986.

SUGGESTED VIDEOS

▼ *Understanding Research.* Discovering Psychology series, part 2. 27 min. 1-800-LEARNER.

VOCABULARY

placebo
double-blind study
hypothesis
subjects
variables
independent variable
dependent variable

field experiments
experimental group
control group
survey
sample
naturalistic observation

interview
case study method
psychological tests
cross-sectional method
longitudinal method

Review Questions

Read the following sample experiment and fill in the blanks; answer on a separate sheet of paper.

Psychologists wanted to find out if people are less likely to help in an emergency if there is a full moon. An "emergency" situation (a flat tire) was staged for 20 males and 20 females, all in cars. One-half of the subjects (group A) was tested when there was a full moon. The other half (group B) was tested when the moon was not full. Helping was defined as "seeing the flat tire, stopping, and getting out of the car to assist in any way."

1. Hypothesis = ___?___
2. Subjects = ___?___
3. Dependent variable = ___?___
4. Independent variable = ___?___
5. Control group = ___?___
6. Experimental group = ___?___

True/False

7. Placebos have some medicinal ingredients but not enough for the brain to detect.
8. The experimental group is exposed to the independent variable.
9. The control group is exposed to the dependent variable.
10. In a double-blind study, the experimenter does not know who is in the control and experimental groups.

Answers to Review Questions

1. People are less likely to help when there is a full moon.
2. 20 males and 20 females
3. Stopping, getting out of car, assisting
4. Full moon
5. Group B
6. Group A
7. False
8. True
9. False
10. True

Notes on Discussion Questions

1. Other factors that might have influenced the results include: (1) Was the previous experience that the experimental subjects had with women a positive one? (2) Was the previous experience long or short term? (3) What were the ages of the subjects?

2. When confronted, people who did not help may lie or rationalize: "I didn't know it was an emergency." They may put up a front.

3. Answers will vary. Interviews and case studies will yield valuable information. To overcome the limitations of these methods, one might combine them with the longitudinal method. Ethical considerations pro-

hibit conducting laboratory experiments on alcoholism and the family.

4. Researchers would probably use field experiments. It would be simple to create mild stress on the job and then measure performance.

5. To discuss this, put a scale (numbered one to seven) on the board, one end representing those who want to end all experimentation on

11. d
12. a
13. b
14. f
15. e
16. g
17. f
18. d
19. c
20. b
21. g
22. c
23. e

Matching: match the answer that best fits the description. (Answers can be used more than once.)

11. Results can be easily distorted to mislead others.
12. Chance of personal bias distorting results is minimized.
13. Researcher has to be careful about own biases.
14. A representative sample from each age group is taken.
15. Subjects can act "normally."
16. Subject's past is studied in order to help with present problems.
17. This is not very useful for studies on long-term development.
18. Only a sample of the population can be studied.
19. This can be expensive.
20. As this is a face-to-face situation, subject may put up a false front.
21. Lengthy information about a subject's background is gathered.
22. Subjects are studied for a long period of time.
23. Researcher does *not* interact with subjects.

a. psychological test
b. interview
c. longitudinal method
d. survey method
e. naturalistic observation
f. cross-sectional method
g. case study method

DISCUSSION QUESTIONS

1. In your own words, explain the conclusions of the "men, women, and management" experiment. Make a list of other factors that might influence the results. Explain how these factors could make a difference. Decide how you might be able to control them.

2. Let's say that you started off conducting an experiment on why people do not help in emergencies. Immediately after the experiment is completed, you decide to interview those people who did not help. What potential problems might you have with these interviews? Explain.

3. The chapter describes several methods that psychologists use in their research. If you wanted to study the effects of alcoholism on the family, which of the methods described would you use to study this and why? Explain. Briefly describe how you might conduct this research. Why would you probably *not* conduct your research in the laboratory?

4. Which method of research would you probably use to study the effects of mild stress on job performance? Explain. Briefly describe how you might conduct this research.

animals, the other end representing those who feel these experiments should include no limitations. Take a poll to see where students fall on the scale, and then have them discuss their reasoning. If you have no students who adopt the extreme positions, assume one yourself or assign roles; this will keep the discussion lively.

Notes on Activities

1. Find an article yourself so you can show students what you expect. Then consider letting them work in groups; this is a good cooperative-learning activity.
2. The purpose of this activity is to get students to think critically about what they read by having them ask questions. They may find it helpful to remember this process when reading other articles.
3. This activity can be an eye-opener for students. Ask them if the results would probably be the same for other stereotypes.
4. Before students interview the adults, have them guess what the adults will say—which can lead to a discussion on yet another stereotype: the narrow-minded adult.
5. You can work on this experiment in class and then send students out into the hallway to collect data. In this way, you can collect a great deal of data in a short time.

5. Leo is an animal rights activist. He believes we should stop *all* experimentation on animals and find alternative means. He argues that if animals somehow could choose, they certainly would not choose to be part of the experiments. They suffer; they are part of the ecology; they should be given more extensive rights. Sam, on the other hand, believes we should experiment on animals as much as we like. He argues that only with this attitude will we ever find vaccines and cures that will improve the quality of life. He admits that animals will obviously not experience this quality of life at first, but in the long run, even they will benefit. Both of these views are extreme, but with whom do you tend to agree and why? Explain.

ACTIVITIES

1. Look up back issues of *Psychology Today* in your library. The magazine often includes reports on experiments that are fairly easy to read. Skim through some issues of the magazine and find information about three experiments. Briefly summarize each experiment, and then identify the following: the hypothesis, the subjects, the dependent variable, the independent variable, the control group, and the experimental group. Do the experiments seem to meet the ethical guidelines established by the American Psychological Association? Explain.
2. Regarding activity 1, consider any problems you may have had in figuring out what the studies mean, in a broader sense. What background information on the subject matter would help you understand these studies better? Where might be some good places to get this information? Come up with two specific questions that apply to each study but are not answered in the study itself. Write a summary of the general subject matter that is relevant to each of the studies you selected in activity 1.
3. Write down a numbered list regarding what you believe to be widely held stereotypes about high school students. Include all the characteristics you can think of. Using yourself and two other students you know as examples, go through your list and indicate which things apply to each person and which do not.
4. Using the list you compiled in activity 3, ask an adult you know (other than a teacher) how many of these characteristics he or she believes are generally true. The adult can be a relative but doesn't have to be. Ask that adult how much and what kind of experience he or she has with high school students. Now do the same thing with an experienced high school teacher and compare the results you get.
5. Here's a chance to conduct your own experiment. Reread the "men, women, and management" study discussed in this chapter. Instead of evaluating fictitious people for promotion, your subjects will decide for which fictitious person they would vote for class president, based on summaries of accomplishments that you have made up. It's important that your subjects not be students in this psychology class, so weed them out before you collect your data. Now make up two sets of honors, activities, and so on that you think make sense for a good candidate for class president. But they must be lists that can

apply to both males or females. If sports are on the list, for instance, tennis or swimming or running may be fine, but football and basketball are out, unless your school has coeducational teams. While you don't want both lists to be exactly the same, try to make them equivalent.

When writing paragraphs to describe each candidate, you may find it hard to avoid personal pronouns that would give away whether the candidate is male or female. Since you don't want "she" or "he" in your summaries, use the following format:

John (or Marcia) has been a student at _____ High School since 199____ and is running for president of the _____ class. As members of the election committee, we want to provide you with a brief personal history and a list of John's accomplishments. We ask you to give the candidates careful consideration before deciding on the one you will vote for.
—Born in Weleetka, Oklahoma, 1980
—Two brothers and one sister
—Plans to attend the University of Waxahatchie after graduation
—Honor student for three consecutive semesters
—Did volunteer work for Youth in Need
—Served as chair of the Labor Day Fund-Raising Committee

Of course, this is just an example. You put down what you think is the most important.

The next task you have is to alternate the names you use in the introductory paragraph. For one of your lists, use a clearly masculine name, such as "John," and place a small "2A" in the upper right-hand corner. For the other list, use a clearly feminine name, like "Marcia," and place a small "2B" in the upper right-hand corner. Make ten copies of each. Now, reverse the order,

putting Marcia's name with a small "3B" on what was John's list and John's name with a small "3A" on Marcia's list. Make ten copies of each of these as well. Since the two lists of accomplishments cannot be identical, you want to make sure that John *and* Marcia have a chance at both. Without realizing it, you may have put better things on one list than the other. What you want to count, though, is not the content of the lists but the gender of your candidates. By reversing the names, you have "controlled" your experiment.

Now you're almost ready to collect your data. First, though, you need to create standard instructions so that everyone you talk to gets the same information. Feel free to change the following example if it doesn't fit; just be careful not to give yourself away.

"I'm doing a project on what the average high school student thinks is important in a class president. I'd like you to read a couple of descriptions of candidates and tell me what you think. Would you be willing to take a few minutes to help me out?"

If some students say, "NO WAY!", thank them anyway and go on to the next subject. Remember, you can't force people to participate even if they're your friends.
After they have decided on a candidate, ask them what persuaded them, and take notes. Don't take down their names, though. Most subjects would rather remain anonymous.

Using the "John & Marcia #2" pair of lists, ask ten students to read them both and tell you which student they would vote for. Keep score. Do the same with ten more students for "Marcia & John #3."

You can compare your vote totals and answer the question of sex bias if you tally the results in the following way. For the lists labeled with a 2, add up the votes for A (John). Add up the votes for B (Marcia). Do the same thing for the number 3 lists. Look to see if there are differences between the number of votes each "student" got on the number 2 versus number 3 lists. If there are, make a note of it. This will tell you whether there was something in the lists themselves that made a difference. Now add both A's together. Do the same for both B's. If John got more votes, the A sum will be greater. And if John got a lot more votes, your subjects are probably biased in favor of having a male for class president.

One final thing. Since you asked your subjects why they voted the way they did, you may as well use the information you got. Their comments might clarify what was going on. Or they may give you an idea or two about other directions that future research could take.

6. As noted in this chapter, surveys gather information on feelings, opinions, or behavior patterns. Write your own ten-item survey to find out the feelings and opinions of at least 30 freshmen and 30 seniors at your school. The survey should deal with a single subject of your choice. For example, it might be interesting to find out how freshmen view dating and to contrast that with how seniors view it. Other possible subjects: parents; clothes; friendship; work; studying. Once you decide on a subject, write ten objective questions. Objective questions are those that have multiple-choice answers. Do *not* include open-ended questions that allow

participants to fill in the blanks. You might get 100 different answers in these blanks, and responses would then become difficult to analyze. Or consider using a scale similar to this one:

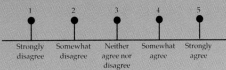

Then you would write ten statements below the scale and have participants place a corresponding number next to each statement. Sample statements: "The male should initiate and pay for the first date." "A movie theater is a good place to go for a first date."

Draw a simple chart summarizing all your responses and then analyze your results. Compare and contrast the freshmen responses with the senior responses. Any surprises? Were there any questions that could have been phrased more carefully? Explain.

7. One of the most controversial issues in psychological research involves animal experimentation. Find an article that presents more than one side of the issue and write a brief summary. Then write an argumentative paper either for or against animal experimentation. Include in your paper information from the article that you have summarized.

6. Have students show you their surveys before they administer them. A good survey may need to go through several drafts.
7. See if you can get two students who hold—or who will adopt—opposing viewpoints to debate.

Subliminal Perception

Subliminal perception refers to the senses receiving messages but registering them below consciousness. Studies have demonstrated that information actually can be processed subconsciously. In one study (Zajonc, 1980), subjects were shown shapes and faces at a pace where they could be seen clearly. The subjects were then exposed to shapes and faces that they had been shown previously along with many they had never been exposed to, but at such a high speed that they all appeared as flashes of light. Even though the speed of the presentation prevented the subjects from really "seeing" any of the shapes and faces, they reported a preference for those shapes and faces that had been presented to them initially.

A more recent study also reported that people are somewhat influenced by material presented subliminally (Krosnick, 1992). Subjects were shown slides of a person, and then their attitudes toward the person in the slides were measured. Some of the subjects saw unpleasant pictures, presented subliminally, before they saw the person in the slides. The other subjects saw pleasant pictures presented subliminally before they saw the person in the slides. Those who saw the unpleasant pictures reported more negative feelings toward the person in the slides, while those who saw the pleasant pictures reported more positive feelings toward the person in the slides.

These results are provocative, but other studies have concluded that while information can be processed subliminally, it has little effect on actual behavior (Dixon, 1981). Yet over $50 million has been spent on subliminal materials to alter weight, smoking, fears, self-confidence, and friendships (Natalie, 1988). Most of the audio tapes offer subliminal suggestions (for example, "Believe in yourself" or "You do not want that cigarette"). Several companies were even found to be producing "subliminal" tapes that did not include any embedded messages. Yet, people said the tapes helped them. The placebo effect, or just believing in the effectiveness of the self-help tapes, made the people evaluate the tapes as being helpful. If all of this were true, wouldn't it be great to make some tapes for your psychology students that would increase their self-confidence, test grades, and study habits!

Some psychologists have concluded that people can hear subliminal messages only after being prompted (Vokey and Read, 1985). In one study, researchers played the song "Another One Bites the Dust" by the rock group, Queen. If subjects were prompted, they easily heard the subliminal message (which advocates marijuana use). Subjects who were not prompted could not hear the embedded message. Recently, several different critics of rock music have said that

Images, sounds, feelings, sensation—ways we experience our world.

56

Discuss the Photo

For some people, this type of ride will *overload* the senses.

some recordings contain Satanic messages. Controversy rages over the possibility that such a recording affects the moral character of its listeners.

In another amazing study, subjects were told they would hear tapes that would enhance their self-confidence or memory (Greenwald et. al., 1991). The researchers recruited people who were interested in those two areas, and measured their levels of self-confidence or memory abilities. They were then given a tape to use every day for a month to increase their self-confidence or memory abilities. At the end of the month, the subjects were tested again to see if there

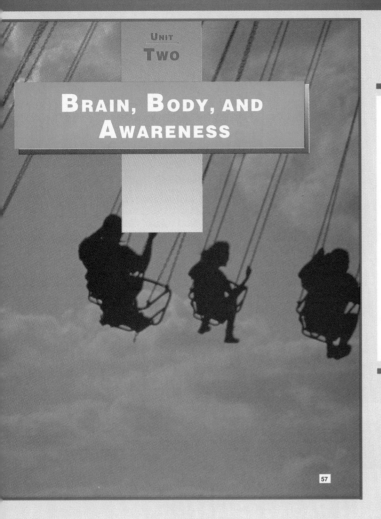

BRAIN, BODY, AND AWARENESS

57

PERFORMANCE TASK

Overview

Students demonstrate how the nervous system responds to incoming messages. Day one will be for planning, day two for construction, and day three for demonstration. Students decide on an incoming sensory message, what the response will be, and create a demonstration to illustrate the structure and function of various parts of the nervous system involved in the response. Small groups plan the nature of the illustration using models, charts, or enactments of the relevant portions of the brain and nervous system. Groups will collaborate with each other for the demonstration. Evaluation is based on clarity and effectiveness of visuals, as well as decision-making and problem-solving skills. Complete instructions for this activity and the supporting student worksheets can be found in the Teacher Resources.

had been any improvement. Some of the subjects who were interested in improving their self-confidence were given a tape marked "self-confidence." The tape, however, was actually designed for memory improvement. Other subjects who were interested in improving their memory abilities were given a tape marked "memory improvement." They actually received a tape about improving one's self-confidence. Would the subjects' self-confidence or memory abilities improve? What effect would hearing the incorrect tape have on the subjects' abilities?

Those subjects who wanted to improve their memory abilities but heard a tape on self-confidence improved their memory abilities. Those subjects who wanted to improve their self-confidence but were given a tape about memory abilities improved their levels of self-confidence. This evidence supports the notion that it is expectations (the placebo effect) that really influences behavior.

So why do people continue to buy products that have "subliminal" information when we know they are of questionable value? There are five ideas about why people continue to believe in subliminal persuasion (Patkanis, 1990). The first explanation is that subliminal persuasion is part of the appeal of what is called "pop psychology"; you can buy easy answers to complex problems. The second reason is that it easily fits in with the latest "conspiracy" story of the year. The third reason is that people believe that advertisers use subliminal material (although advertisers will not admit to it). The fourth reason is that the popular media does not report articles critical of subliminal persuasion. Magazines that did so would not sell as well as ones carrying articles about the effectiveness of subliminal seduction. The fifth reason is that subliminal persuasion helps people explain their behavior. People may feel relieved of responsibility if they believe that their alcoholism, lack of self-confidence, obesity, etc. are not owned by the self.

References

Full citations can be found in the Teacher Resources.

DISCUSS THE PHOTO

Through a variety of imaging techniques, doctors are now able to view how the brain processes information.

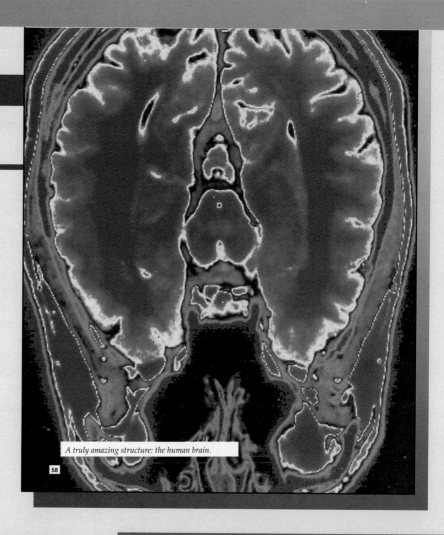

A truly amazing structure: the human brain.

58

PSYCHOLOGY AND YOU RESOURCES

A variety of resources are available in the Psychology and You *supplementary material. In addition, there are a number of additional resources listed to enhance your lesson plans.*

Masters
▼ 3-1A Learning Goals
▼ 3-1B Answers to Learning Goals
▼ 3-2A Puzzles
▼ 3-2B Answers to Puzzles
▼ 3-3 Motor Strip Dominance
▼ 3-4 Faces 1
▼ 3-5 Faces 2
▼ 3-6A Fill-in-the-Blanks
▼ 3-6B Answers to Fill-in-the-Blanks
▼ 3-7 Hemisphere Dominance Inventory
▼ 3-8 Brain Communication

Student Worksheets
▼ Vocabulary Worksheets

▼ Independent Practice Worksheet
▼ Enrichment Worksheet
▼ Reteaching Worksheet

Test Bank
▼ Tests A and B

Multimedia
▼ *The Mind* Videotape Modules #3–6
▼ *The Brain* Videotape Modules #1–6, 8, 10
▼ **Mindscope** Exercises 13 and 16
▼ Psychology Videodisc

Student Workbook

PACING CHART

Complete Coverage

Day 1: Have students read the first two sections of the chapter before class. Use the appropriate Teaching Masters noted in the wrap as a tool to have students identify the functions of the various areas of the brain.

Day 2: Concentrate on hemisphere specialization, using discussion question #1 in the text and "Wrapping It Up" in the wrap to enhance the lesson. Assign Psychology in Your Life for homework.

Day 3: After discussing the subject of "brain control" presented in Psychology in Your Life, focus on the functions of the lower brain. Have students create visuals of each part (the thalamus, cerebellum, hypothalamus, and RAS). Discussion question #2 in the text can serve to extend the evaluation. Assign "Brain Communication" for Day 4.

Day 4: Perform a chain exercise like the demonstration in the wrap to illustrate the mechanisms of neurons, synapses, neurotransmitters, and the spinal cord. Have students read "Looking at the

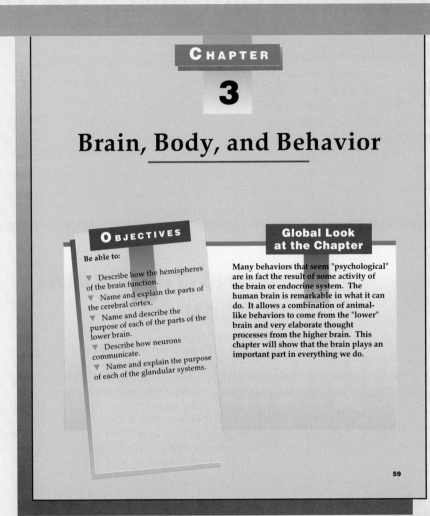

3

Brain, Body, and Behavior

OBJECTIVES

Be able to:

▼ Describe how the hemispheres of the brain function.

▼ Name and explain the parts of the cerebral cortex.

▼ Name and describe the purpose of each of the parts of the lower brain.

▼ Describe how neurons communicate.

▼ Name and explain the purpose of each of the glandular systems.

Global Look at the Chapter

Many behaviors that seem "psychological" are in fact the result of some activity of the brain or endocrine system. The human brain is remarkable in what it can do. It allows a combination of animal-like behaviors to come from the "lower" brain and very elaborate thought processes from the higher brain. This chapter will show that the brain plays an important part in everything we do.

59

INTRODUCING THE CHAPTER

Draw a 500-pound gorilla and a 150-pound human on the blackboard, side by side. Ask students what the gorilla's and the human's brains weigh. The gorilla's weighs about one pound; the human's weighs about three pounds. The absolute weight is important, but more essential is the brain-to-body ratio. Ask them to consider that difference: 1 to 500 versus 3 to 150. It's this amazing three-pound mass that separates us from all other animals. In fact, compare humans to other animals in any other area (strength, endurance, vision, hearing, and so on), and humans seem less than remarkable.

Glandular System" for homework.

Day 5: Use discussion question #5 in the text to review the functions of the endocrine system. Give the Chapter Review quiz.

In Brief

Day 1: Provide an activity requiring students to identify the functions of the different areas of the brain (the appropriate Teaching Masters noted in the wrap may be helpful).

Day 2: Focus on the task of hemispheres and the lower brain. Discussion question #2 in the text and In Focus Tasks of the Two Hemispheres can aid students' understanding.

Day 3: Use a demonstration like the relevant one in the wrap to illustrate the chain reaction characterizing the travels of neurotransmitters and the function of the spinal cord. After briefly reviewing the functions of the glandular system, give the Chapter Review quiz.

LEAD-OFF ACTIVITY

Teaching Master 3-2A Puzzles presents a variety of puzzles that you can photocopy for the students or show on an overhead projector. Directions to complete these puzzles are provided on the teaching master. Answers to the puzzles are given in **Teaching Master 3-2B.**

This activity should serve to create immediate interest in the material. It should also shed light on why some people excel at solving these and similar kinds of puzzles. This skill may have little to do with intelligence, although students often assume it does. Finally, it should clarify the commonly held assumption that the hemispheres operate independently from one another. On the contrary, they work together in nearly everything we do.

DEMONSTRATION

Have the entire class conduct the brief "experiment" described below in the student text. Not only should this generate a sense of wonder, but it should generate curiosity. How does the brain know that the arm and not the leg is moving? And how does the brain know it's the right arm and not the left? If you convey some of your own wonder, this is usually enough to spark a few questions. At this point you may also want to gauge what students already know about the brain and how it communicates with the body.

Journal Topic

"Imagine that you've been feeling down or blue for several weeks for no apparent reason. You decide to see a psychologist. Describe to the psychologist how you feel, and describe a typical recent day." This is a good opportunity to discuss or reinforce how physiology can affect behavior, emotions, and even personality. Ask a few students to share their entries and then ask about the probable cause of their lethargy. Most of them will cite personal difficulties, like not getting along with parents and so on. While this may certainly be true, a sluggish thyroid, a poor diet, or a lack of exercise may be compounding the problem—or may even be at the root of it.

Unit 2 BRAIN, BODY, AND AWARENESS

OBSERVING THE BRAIN IN ACTION

Let's start with an experiment. Put your right arm straight out, palm downward. Next, bring your hand in toward your head and put your finger gently into your right ear, saying, "I stretch my hand forth; I bring my hand back." Finally, take your finger out.

You have just done something that is almost beyond belief it is so remarkable. Here is what happened: Your brain analyzed the instructions. Next it sent a message to your arm. Then it called on the area that controls hand movements and put your finger into your ear. It didn't miss the ear and make you wind up with a finger in your eye or nose. While that was going on, the brain searched through the memory banks for the words you needed, put them together, and then used the speech areas of the brain to make those words.

The experiment is not over, though. Probably if you sense you were tricked into doing something weird, you now feel stupid, or irritated, or puzzled. These are emotions coming from yet another part of the brain. The brain decides whether you were treated fairly and triggers an emotional response that will vary, depending on how you interpreted the experiment.

There were a couple of reasons for our "experiment." First, in daily life, we all too often take for granted the wondrous thing that we are. In truth, it is worth considering how amazing it is that you are able to do what you just did. Second, as we move through the chapter, we wanted to be able to use a concrete example of something you have done, rather than talk in general terms about the workings of the brain.

EXAMINING THE BRAIN

Psychologists study the brain in detail because it is the part of us that controls every thought, action, and feeling. The brain, which looks like tightly compressed macaroni, is the most demanding organ of the body. If you spend a long time studying, it takes more energy and causes more aches and pains than jogging. The brain uses 20 percent of all our oxygen, eats up most of the sugar we take in, and operates on 20 watts of electrical power. Even though very elaborate, its workings are not hard to understand if you follow the description in this chapter step by step.

DEMONSTRATION

Have students rub their stomachs with one hand and pat their heads with the other. This activity illustrates the idea that we really do have two hemispheres that control opposite sides of the body. It also shows how well the two hemispheres work togeth-er. It's rare for your hands to get confused, as they do in this activity. It's also interesting to note that the brain will quickly adapt to dual tasks like this. Ask your drummers and piano players what their coordination was like when they first started playing.

Connections

Some students are surprised to see a chapter on the body and brain in a psychology text. "Is this biology?" they ask. Mention that many behavior disorders (Chapter 18) are biologically based, and in order to understand these disorders fully (or at least to the extent that we currently know about them), they will need to have a sound understanding of the material in this chapter. In fact, if you like to skip around, Chapters 3 and 18 may work well back to back.

The Hemispheres

Imagine that a friend of yours is sitting in a chair, and you are standing behind him or her. Looking down at the top of the head, *if only* you could see through hair, skin, and bone, you would notice an interesting characteristic of the brain. It is divided into two halves. In the middle, from front to back, is a depression, called a **fissure.** This fissure marks the division of one half of the brain from the other. Each half is called a **hemisphere.** "Hemi" means half, so we have two halves of a sphere. These are referred to as the right and left hemispheres. Each one controls the opposite side of the body—that is, the left hemisphere controls movements and sensations on the right side of the body, and the right half controls the left side.

If you were to pull these two halves apart, about midway down, you would see a bundle of fibers called the **corpus callosum** (KORE-pus kah-LO-sum). This unit contains several million nerve fibers that help each half of the brain communicate with the other, transmitting all kinds of information (Myers, 1984). We'll get back to this structure and talk more about the hemispheres shortly. First, however, it's important to understand the functions of different areas of the brain.

The Lobes

The brain is divided into four major sections, called **lobes.** To show you where they are, we need to look at the brain from the side. Figure 3.1 shows a side view of the left hemisphere, but the right hemisphere would show basically the same structure. If you think of this side view as resembling a boxing glove, you won't get confused about where the front and back parts are. (It even has a thumb!) About midway from the front to the back is another depression or fissure. It marks off the boundary between two lobes of the brain. The frontmost area is conveniently called the **frontal lobe;** the area behind it is the **parietal** (pah-RYE-eh-tul) **lobe.** Notice in Figure 3.1 that there is a shaded section on either side of the fissure. The section that is located in the frontal lobe is called the **motor strip.** Every part of the body that is capable of moving is represented on this strip. That is why it is called "motor"; the word *motor* means "relating to movement." During surgery, if the brain is exposed, the surgeon can stimulate different parts of this motor strip with an electrically active wire, and depending on the area touched, the arm, the leg, or the finger will move, the nose will twitch, and so forth.

The shaded section located in the parietal lobe is called the **sensory strip.** If this is stimulated in an exposed brain, the person feels a sensation in different areas—in the leg, ear, mouth, and so forth—depending on the specific area that the electricity hits. So, for the experiment you did at the beginning of this chapter, you used the

Chapter 3 BRAIN, BODY, AND BEHAVIOR

fissure

A lengthy depression marking off an area of the brain.

hemisphere

One-half of the two halves of the brain; controls the opposite side of the body.

corpus callosum

A large bundle of nerve fibers that transfers information from one half of the brain to the other.

lobe

Major division of the brain.

frontal lobe

Division of the brain that contains the motor strip and frontal association area.

parietal lobe

Area of the brain that contains the sensory strip.

motor strip

Band running down the side of the frontal lobe that controls all bodily movements (called motor functions).

sensory strip

Band running down the side of the parietal lobe that registers and provides all sensation.

DEMONSTRATION

Have students perform some of the tasks from **Teaching Master 3-3 Motor Strip Dominance** using both sides of their bodies! This test should demonstrate why athletes and musicians constantly drill: they're training not only their bodies but their minds as well. One task that works particularly well is cutting something with a pair of scissors. Hold a sheet of paper and have a student cut it with his or her non-dominant hand. (This will also demonstrate that scissors are designed for right-handers.)

Clapping works well, too. Have the entire class clap as they normally do; then tell them to clap with their non-dominant hands on top. You should hear a distinct difference.

Motor Strip Dominance. This handout is an inventory that measures which hemisphere's motor strip is more dominant. The more students answer *right,* the more it indicates that their left motor strip is dominant, and vice versa. There's not much more to the analysis than that, and students can certainly guess the conclusion, but it's a fun inventory to fill out in class.

Teaching Hint

Find out who likes to draw or paint and have these students discuss the process they go through as they work. Do they visualize the art before they begin? Does their mental image change as the process progresses? Point out that it is the occipital lobe that helps us visualize something, even before it exists.

occipital lobe

Area of the brain that interprets visual information.

Unit 2 Brain, Body, and Awareness

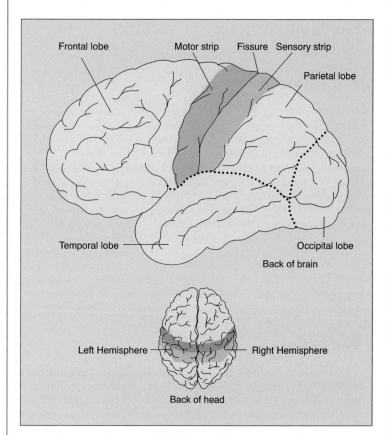

▲ *Figure 3.1   The sensory and motor strips.*

sensory strip to tell you when your finger actually hit your ear. The motor strip controlled the movement of your arm and finger.

The very back of the brain is devoted to making sense out of what we see. This area is called the **occipital** (ox-SIP-ih-tul) **lobe.** When you were reading the first part of this chapter images of the words you saw went through the lens of the eyes and landed on the back of the eyeball. What was received was coded and then sent through nerves to the occipital lobe.

The brain sits in a fluid that acts like a shock absorber, giving it some room to move back and forth and sideways. Sometimes that isn't enough, however. If you've ever been hit really hard in the front part of your head, you saw all kinds of images in front of you for a second (seeing "stars"). This is because the blow sent the brain sloshing backward, crashing the occipital lobe into the skull. The collision stirred up the electrical system of this visual area, and it made these strange images. If you've never been hit, you can still see this area in

DISCOVERY

Here's a simple and fun activity to demonstrate how the temporal lobe "hears" without actually hearing anything. Pick a song that every student knows, such as the "National Anthem." Have the entire class hum the song while you direct with your hand held high. Every once in a while, lower your hand to below your waist but continue conducting. When you lower your hand, students should stop humming aloud but continue to hum silently. As you raise your hand again, students resume humming aloud. Continue raising and lowering your hand to see if everyone can stay together. Afterward, mention that Beethoven continued composing music even after he became deaf!

Chapter 3 BRAIN, BODY, AND BEHAVIOR

 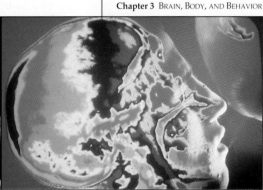

▲ *In the photo at right, the darker and red portions of the visual area at the back of the brain are showing electrical activity from colliding with the skull.*

DISCUSS THE PHOTO

You might convince a few students to find out the long-term effects of getting jabbed in the head.

operation. Lie on your bed in a dark room for about ten minutes. Then open your eyes and *VERY GENTLY*(!) touch the edges of your eyeballs. This will send electrical impulses to the occipital lobe that will create odd images "right before your very eyes."

The part of the brain in Figure 3.1 that looks like the thumb of a boxing glove is the **temporal** (TEM-pore-ul) **lobe.** The temporal lobe contains the major centers for hearing. This is also where some of the centers related to speech are located, although there is overlap into other lobes to handle all the different aspects of language. If you are actually speaking, for instance, a place in the frontal lobe's motor strip will also be involved; if you are reading a speech, the occipital or visual area will be activated. There is a circular spot whose sole job is to create sentences. It organizes words in the proper sequence so the meaning can be understood. If someone is unlucky enough to damage this area of the brain, he or she can still speak, but what is said is a jumble of words that make no sense. So, when you spoke the sentence about your hand at the beginning of the chapter, the speech was made up by this unit. It was spoken with the help of the motor strip, even if you didn't say it out loud. When we are "talking" silently to ourselves, as we all do, the same units are involved; the actual sounds that others hear come when you also activate the voice box in your throat.

For most people, these speech areas are only found in the left hemisphere. But about 25 percent of left-handers have them only in the right hemisphere. We'll talk about "lefties" shortly.

temporal lobe

Area of the brain responsible for hearing and some speech functions.

The Frontal Association Area

Once the words you received while reading the first part of this chapter were processed by the visual area, this information was sent all the way straight ahead to the frontal lobe. As you can see in

Discussion

Ask students the following question: How might creativity, shyness, general moodiness, or other traits be influenced by physiology? It might be a good idea to discuss this at the beginning of this unit, then again at the end. If you need to prompt discussion, ask how the following might influence behavior or personality: gender, hemisphere dominance, genetic makeup, hormones, brain chemicals.

ENRICHMENT

Interested students can research other cases of damage to the cerebral cortex. What have scientists learned about brain function through these case studies?

Comprehension Check

Name the part of the brain that is probably most active during each of the following activities: watching a movie *(occipital lobe);* running *(motor strip);* listening to music *(temporal lobe);* deciding whether or not to yell at someone who has knocked you over *(frontal association area).*

Unit 2 BRAIN, BODY, AND AWARENESS

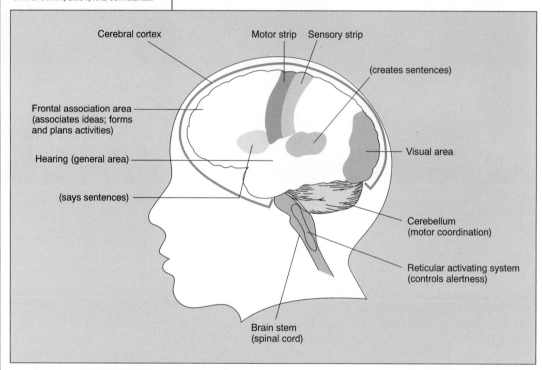

▲ *Figure 3.2*   *View of left hemisphere with skull removed.*

frontal association area

The forward portion of the brain that engages in elaborate associations or mental connections; it plays an important part in integrating personality and in forming complex thoughts.

Figure 3.2, this part is called the **frontal association area.** The frontal association area is very heavily packed with nerve cells because its task is very complex: to interpret what is going on and tell us what to do and what to feel. It decided how you reacted to our "experiment," for example. In many ways, the frontal association area seems to form the core of a person's personality, since so many decisions are made there.

In the 1840s, a railroad worker with the unlikely name of Phineas P. Gage was injured in a freakish accident, which gave us clues into the nature of the frontal association area. He was pushing some dynamite into a hole with a four-foot-long iron bar in the shape of a toothpick, about an inch in diameter. The dynamite went off, firing the bar upward through his jaw, through the frontal association area, and on out. Remarkably, he survived because none of the vital parts that control breathing, movement, or physical control had been damaged. Still, the injury to his frontal association area resulted in some *major* changes. While he had been friendly and normal, suddenly he became someone who swore all the time, undressed wherever he felt like it, went to the bathroom anywhere in public, and had temper

CHAPTER PROJECT/COOPERATIVE LEARNING

Assign each group three or four pages from the chapter. The task of each group is to create several original **In Focus** boxes based on these pages. Explain that the **In Focus** boxes are designed to simplify and clarify text material through illustrations and/or charts. Have the groups present their **In Focus** boxes to the rest of the class. The nice things about this project are that students can usually prepare their presentations in a class period or two; the presentations are short; and they can display their work.

tantrums. Thus, this complex area of the brain must play a large part in what we call social control as well as in our basic personalities.

The frontal association area also tries to make sense of the environment. Someone who has major damage in this part of the brain can know what is happening but not be able to bring together all the aspects of the situation. For example, a man with damage here can watch someone: (1) take a bullet; (2) put it in a gun; (3) cock the gun; and (4) aim the gun at him. He will not show any concern. He understands each act by itself but is not able to put them all together (Jouandet & Gazzaniga, 1979).

The size of this frontal association area likely reflects intelligence level from one species to another. Since we can't "talk to the animals," we will probably never know for sure, but it is interesting that the amount of the brain devoted to the frontal part depends on how advanced the animal is. Thus for the dog, it is 7 percent, 15 percent in the chimpanzee, and 30 percent in the human.

If you want, you can actually see the frontal association area in operation. Try this experiment, but pick a reasonably pleasant person to try it on. While the subject is standing in a line, go up to where he or she is and bump him or her from behind. Wait five seconds after the person turns around before you apologize. Note that the person will spend this time (a *long* time for the brain) looking at you, going back and forth mentally, while the frontal association area decides if what you did was on purpose or not and whether he or she should get mad.

Hemispheres and Handedness

Ten percent of the population is left-handed. Because they are different from others statistically, people wonder how "they got that way." Earlier we mentioned that the left hemisphere controls the right side of the body and vice versa. That *is* true, but we were referring only to major body movements. When dealing with small, fine movements, such as writing or putting your finger in your ear, one hemisphere has **dominance**. In other words, one hemisphere is always the preferred one to use. Most people are left-hemisphere dominant and right-handed. But if the right hemisphere is dominant, then the person will be left-handed for all fine movements.

Left-handedness does not seem to be inherited—at least not in the same sense as something like eye color, which follows a clear family pattern. Sometimes in identical twins, who come from the same egg and have exactly the same heredity, there will be one left-handed twin and one right-handed (Corballis & Morgan, 1978).

The genetic instructions that make the brain have got to be complex beyond imagination. We suspect that for some reason, accidental or otherwise, the part of the "program" that develops the brain gets slightly different signals for the left-hander and shifts the domi-

dominance

Either the right or left hemisphere is dominant in each individual; hence one of them is preferred and controls the majority of actions performed.

Points to Stress

Since the frontal lobe seems to form the core of one's personality, you may want to emphasize the effects of damage to this lobe. Effects will vary, depending on the extent of damage, but the following list includes likely consequences: inappropriate emotions; socially unacceptable behaviors, usually meaning fewer inhibitions (mention Phineas Gages's bathroom behavior—which is discussed in the **Frontal Association** section); inability to make long-range plans; easily distracted; difficulty in integrating facts. Possible scenario: *someone with frontal lobe damage walks into the bedroom to make the bed, becomes distracted by the wallpaper, which he decides needs to be changed, and rips it down!*

Unit 2 BRAIN, BODY, AND AWARENESS

▲ *A famous "leftie," Paul McCartney, who presumably is using his talented right hemisphere.*

nance to the other hemisphere. Or if the shift isn't complete, a very few become what is called "ambidextrous" (left- and right-handed). For these people, the instructions get "stuck" in the middle of the two hemispheres, so to speak.

The intelligence of right- versus left-handed people is about the same; that is, there seems to be about the same number of bright, average, and dull people in both groups. But statistically the left-hander will probably do better in art, music, and mathematics. And the odds increase that the speech areas will be in the right rather than the left hemisphere. They also tend to be better actors: try keeping track for a while of the number of leading men and women in movies and TV who are left-handed. We will explain why this is so in a few paragraphs.

Before going on, though, we should mention the myth that if a left-hander is forced by the parent to use the right hand in childhood, this may cause insanity. That's not true. But what a nuisance it can be, and so uncomfortable. People used to think that something was wrong with left-handers (there isn't anything wrong, any more than with right-handers) and tried to change their children. It's hard enough to grow up as it is without adding the burden of making children uncomfortable trying to do things in an "unnatural" way (Geschwind, 1983).

Tasks of the Hemispheres

Scientists have wondered for hundreds of years about why the brain has two halves. There must be some reason. Only recently have we begun to understand why this might be.

We have already mentioned that nerve fibers hold the two hemispheres together in a unit called the corpus callosum. The difference between the functions of the hemispheres was noted with patients who had to have the corpus callosum cut surgically to stop electrical disturbances in the brain. Experiments were set up in which information was fed through a part of the eyes that led to only one hemisphere or the other. This was possible because with a severed corpus callosum, most communication between the two halves is cut off. Hence, only one half of the brain would get the message.

In the first experiment (Figure 3.3), using a woman with a split brain, her right hemisphere was shown a photo of a nude woman (the left hemisphere "saw" nothing). The woman blushed and laughed nervously. When asked why she was blushing, she said she didn't know! In a second experiment, a picture of a spoon was shown to a man's left hemisphere. He was asked what he had seen and correctly said "Spoon." But, next, the picture of a spoon was shown to his *right* hemisphere. He was asked what he saw. He couldn't *say* what it was. But he could pick out a spoon from objects on the table to indicate what he saw (Gazzaniga, 1970). What do these findings mean?

DEMONSTRATION

Teaching Master 3-6A Fill-in-the-Blanks is a simple test to emphasize that the two hemispheres work together. Students are given a series of phrases in which they have to fill in the missing letters. The left hemisphere will be primarily responsible for reading and interpreting the letters. The right hemisphere will specialize in interpreting the spatial relationship between the letters and perhaps visualizing what the incomplete word would look like with various alphabet alternatives. Hypothesis: *A "balanced" brain should perform better than one in which one hemisphere tends to dominate.* Furthermore, females (and lefties) seem to have thicker corpus callosums than males and perhaps a more balanced brain. Therefore, females should do better on this test. (For extra credit, students can give the test to lefties and righties and compare results.) Answers to the fill-in-the-blanks are found in **Teaching Master 3-6B**.

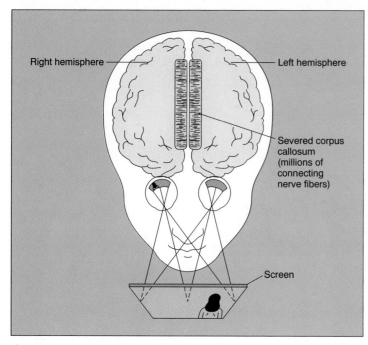

Chapter 3 BRAIN, BODY, AND BEHAVIOR

▲ *Figure 3.3   The hemispheres and the corpus callosum.*

Labels in figure: Right hemisphere — Left hemisphere — Severed corpus callosum (millions of connecting nerve fibers) — Screen

TEACHING MASTER 3-7

Hemisphere Dominance Inventory. This handout is a simple inventory that indicates hemisphere dominance. You can easily locate more extensive tests of this sort for interested students, but this short one is ideal for classroom purposes. This teaching master includes an analysis based on students' responses.

It seems that the left hemisphere (for right-handers and most left-handers) handles verbal or speech material (see Figure 3.4). So, when the man saw the spoon only with the right hemisphere, he couldn't *say* what it was (left hemisphere). The right hemisphere deals with objects in space, art, music, some mathematical reasoning, as well as emotional material. Hence, the woman had an emotional reaction because of what she saw in the right hemisphere, but couldn't say what it was (left hemisphere). For those who are left-handed, since the right hemisphere will dominate, the odds increase that they will be better at and deal more with their right hemispheres. This, in turn, increases the chances that they will do well in art, music, architecture, or the physical and emotional art of acting—all *non*verbal activities (Springer & Deutsch, 1985).

Before leaving this topic, we want to make a final comment. A lot has been written recently in the popular press about right-brain versus left-brain thinking and learning. Many people assume that the differences between the hemispheres are great and that each operates in a very specialized way. That is not really true. The hemispheric functions we have discussed are quite real and easy to demonstrate. However, it is important to keep in mind that the hemispheres work together in virtually everything we do (Hellige, 1990). Also, even though certain kinds of mathematical reasoning and nonverbal artis-

DEMONSTRATION

Call a student to the front center of the room, and have her sit facing the class. From the back center of the room, ask her a series of questions that tend to appeal to one hemisphere or the other. Hypothesis: *If the left hemisphere is working harder to answer the question, the subject's eyes should move to the right, and vice versa.* (Have all subjects wait outside while you explain the hypothesis to the rest of the class.) Explain that this is a demonstration and not an experiment. Though the point is to show that each hemisphere specializes in different functions, emphasize again that the hemispheres work together, even to solve the questions posed in the experiment.

Possible questions: (1) What is on the back of a dollar bill? *(right hemisphere)* (2) Spell *hypothesis. (right hemisphere)* (3) What is the sum of 77 and 83? *(left hemisphere)*

FYI According to David McNeil at the University of Chicago, the left hemisphere seems to specialize in linguistic encoding: syntax and grammar. The right hemisphere seems to specialize in imagery, which may be reflected through gestures. During discourse, it's common for split-brain patients to pause, then gesture, then resume speaking again. "He punched [pause] the man in the nose." During the pause, the speaker may gesture a punch, but since the right hemisphere initiates this, the left has to stop speaking momentarily to allow the right to "speak." Conclusion: Both hemispheres are involved in language. (See *Adler* in **Suggested Readings** at the end of this chapter.)

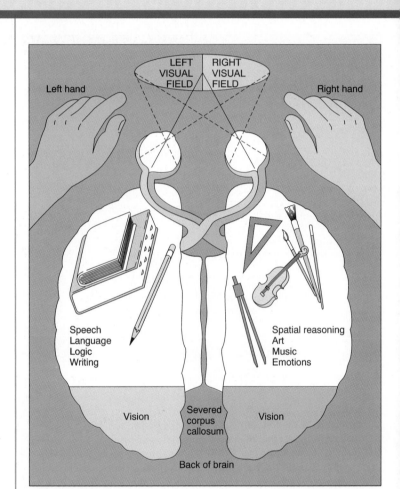

▲ *Figure 3.4*   *Assumed areas of "specialization" in the brain.*

tic abilities are primarily right-hemisphere functions, the majority of mathematicians and artists, like everyone else, are right-handed.

The Cerebral Cortex and the Lower Brain

While we haven't formally said so, all the parts discussed so far (hemispheres, lobes, frontal association area, and so forth) are part of the **cerebral cortex.** The cerebral cortex is the outermost layer of the brain, as indicated in Figure 3.2. This unit controls very high-level thought (*cerebral* means "relating to thought or intelligence"). In the human, the cerebral cortex takes up over two-thirds of the brain's

cerebral cortex

The unit that covers the lower brain and controls mental processes such as thought.

(4) Mentally walk through your house. How many clocks do you pass? *(right hemisphere)* (5) Picture a stop sign. How many sides does it have? *(right hemisphere)*

Students are fascinated by this demonstration—it's like glimpsing the brain at work—and sometimes the results seem eerily accurate, but make sure to discuss the many variables that make the demonstration unscientific: too many people watching; the subject may simply look to friends; being in front of the class may be an emotional strain.

 **Tasks of the Two Hemispheres**

Typical Right-Hemisphere Task

Which of the pieces, above right, would fit into space 4 on the left?

Typical Left-Hemisphere Task

Which of the following is correct?

a. I wish I was a rich man.
b. I wish I were a rich man.

The right hemisphere specializes in spatial functions such as piecing together a jigsaw puzzle. The left hemisphere specializes in the verbal skills needed to answer a "language" question.

Both hemispheres work together, of course. What would the left hemisphere contribute as you solve the puzzle problem above? What would the right hemisphere contribute in the language problem?

nerve cells. There are roughly 100 billion (100,000,000,000) of them, packed into macaronilike material. If the cortex were untwisted and spread out, it would be about the size of a large bath towel. We know of nothing in the universe that can equal it. These nerve cells can connect with one another in so many ways that if you emptied dump trucks full of computers night and day until you'd filled up a football stadium, this pile would not even come close to equaling our brain power. In fact, some people have estimated that the number of possible different connections the brain can make is greater than the number of particles in the universe (Sagan, 1977).

No matter how fantastic it is, though, the cortex will not keep the body running. For that, we need a "lower" brain. Deep inside the

Tasks of the Two Hemispheres.

IN FOCUS (1) The left hemisphere would help with reading the directions and understanding the task. (2) We take for granted the spaces between words (see the very beginning of Chapter 4), but if we remove the spaces, we understand how spatial skills help us to read. First answer: piece A; second answer: b.

Comprehension Check

Ask the students the following question: Split-brain Sam is blindfolded. With his left hand, he picks up a bell. He feels it, rings it, knows it is a bell. Would he be able to say it is a bell? *(You might fool some students with this one. Since both ears hear the bell, both hemispheres also "hear" it, and the talking left hemisphere would be able to say bell. If he does not ring the bell, then he probably would not be able to say the name of the object.)*

DISCOVERY

This can be a difficult chapter for students because of all the terms they need to remember. Sometimes a simple hands-on activity goes a long way toward overcoming this problem. Tell students to pair up and trace each other's heads. That's right: trace

heads. Students are usually creative, lying on the floor, using desks, tracing a shadow thrown from an overhead projector. Students then keep the trace of their own heads and use it as a template for a "mobile" they will create. When completed, the mobile will

show the parts of the cerebral cortex and the parts of the lower brain. Along with listing each part, students should include a visual that shows the function of the part. For example, the temporal lobe could include a picture of an ear. Most students will probably

Unit 2 BRAIN, BODY, AND AWARENESS

lower brain

Basic "animal" units common to animals and humans that regulate basic functions such as breathing.

The Cerebral Cortex and the Lower Brain.

 You could mention Phineas Gage as an example of someone who survived, but the loss of his "executive" impaired him greatly. You could also discuss patients who received lobotomies in the 1940s and 1950s, many of whom were reduced to what some call "vegetables."

skull lies the **lower brain,** with the cerebral cortex fitting over and around it. The word *cortex* means "bark," as on a tree; hence, the cerebral cortex covers the lower brain like a layer of bark. Use Figure 3.5 as we talk about the different parts of the lower brain. For most human responses (except automatic behaviors such as withdrawing a hand from a hot object), the cortex influences the animal-like lower units, and they, in turn, influence the cortex.

 **The Cerebral Cortex and the Lower Brain**

The brain could be compared to an office building in which executives at the top of the building (in the cerebral cortex penthouse) make the complex decisions about company goals and policies, while the custodians in the basement (the lower brain) regulate temperature, collect and deliver mail, and so on.

The executives (in the cerebral cortex) and the custodians (in the lower brain) obviously have a great deal of influence on the performance of the other. It should also be obvious that we couldn't live without the custodians. Could we live without the executives?

70

create two-dimensional mobiles, showing the cerebral cortex on one side of the trace, the lower brain on the other, but encourage them to consider other options, like making the mobile three-dimensional or adding hair to the heads. Hung from the ceiling, these head-mobiles make striking ornaments!

Connections

Chapter 7 discusses conditioning at length, but it focuses primarily on observable behavior. You can point out that unseen brain processes are also conditioned. For example, imagine someone from Florida visiting friends in Wisconsin in winter. This visitor will probably be more sensitive to the cold than his friends because his brain and body have not adapted; he shivers when cold—thanks to the hypothalamus—which generates heat, but he doesn't do it as productively as his friends, initially at least. Our brains and bodies can become conditioned to warm weather, too. The Florida man, because of conditioning, probably sweats more readily than his friends (thanks again, hypothalamus), which cools him, meaning he will be better able to tolerate high temperatures.

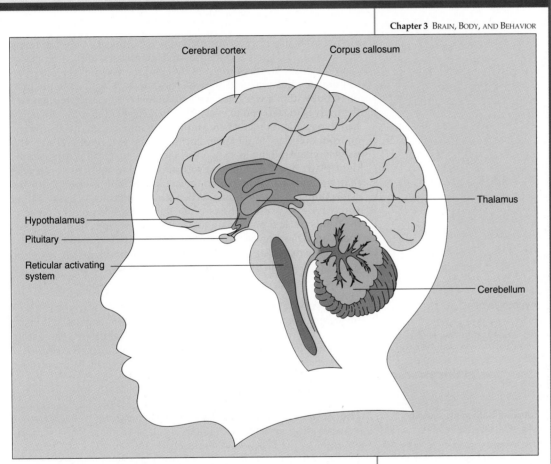

Chapter 3 BRAIN, BODY, AND BEHAVIOR

▲ *Figure 3.5* *The parts of the lower brain (left side of cortex removed).*

The Thalamus The term **thalamus** (THAL-ah-mus) comes from the Greek word for "couch." Note that it is shaped like one, an oval mass of nerve cells. It acts as a relay station to send incoming and outgoing messages to and from various parts of the brain. So, if you want to move your big toe, the brain sends a message to the thalamus, which then sends it to the correct place on the motor strip. Otherwise, you might wind up blinking your eye.

The Cerebellum The **cerebellum** (sarah-BELL-um) looks like a ball of yarn a little larger than a golf ball, and it hooks onto the base of the brain below the visual or occipital lobe. Its job is complex. Whenever you move, it makes sure you stay in balance, remain coordinated, and get where you want to go. It was responsible for you

thalamus

The portion of the lower brain that functions primarily as a central relay station for incoming and outgoing messages from the body to the brain and the brain to the body.

cerebellum

The portion of the lower brain that coordinates and organizes bodily movements for balance and accuracy.

71

DEMONSTRATION

You can easily demonstrate the functions of the lower brain through some simple actions. Thalamus: bring in junk mail from home and pass it out as if you were a postal worker separating and relaying correspondence. (Reminder—blot out your home address!) Hypothalamus: eat, shiver, fan yourself, become enraged. Cerebellum: extend your arm to shake someone's hand and miss, signifying damage to the cerebellum. RAS: lecture in a monotone and watch students fall asleep; suddenly become animated.

Teaching Hint

Ask students if they are hungry. If yes, their blood sugar and body temperature are probably low. The hypothalamus uses these cues, along with others, to tell us we're hungry. (See Chapter 5 for a discussion of external cues.) As we eat, our blood sugar level and body temperature rise, and our hypothalamus uses these new cues to tell us eventually that we're full. This explains why we sometimes sweat while we eat. It also explains why we tend to eat less when we're warm.

Comprehension Check

Have students match these images with the correct part of the lower brain: (1) thermostat (hypothalamus); (2) hamburger (hypothalamus, for hunger); (3) tightrope walker (cerebellum); (4) sleeping student (RAS); (5) post office (thalamus, for sorting); (6) angry teacher (hypothalamus).

Unit 2 BRAIN, BODY, AND AWARENESS

hypothalamus

The portion of the lower brain that regulates basic needs (hunger, thirst) and emotions such as pleasure, fear, rage, and sexuality.

reticular activating system/ reticular formation/RAS

The alertness control center of the brain that regulates the activity level of the body.

getting your finger into your ear in the experiment at the beginning of this chapter. Here's another example: think back to the first day of class this year. You had to go to different rooms from the ones you did the previous year, and all was chaos trying to remember the right ones. But within a week, the cerebellum and cortex had programmed themselves to take you to every class in sequence, and you no longer had to pay attention to where you were going. In fact, often you now go from one class to the other, turning right, left, right and so forth, while you are talking to someone—and you "magically" arrive at the right place. The cerebellum also contains thousands of nerve cells that are lined up in rows like the spokes of half a wheel, with the cerebellum core as the center. When someone throws a basketball to you, your eyes cause firing of cerebellum cells one after the other as the ball is tracked on its path toward you. The cerebellum calculates speed and direction as the cells fire, and it signals through the thalamus to the motor strip; then your hands will automatically go to the correct place to catch the ball (Llinas & Pellionisa, 1979).

The Hypothalamus   The **hypothalamus** (*hypo* means "below") sits below the thalamus. While only the size of a large pea, it helps control rage, pleasure, hunger, thirst, and sexual desire. Thus, if its rage center is electrically stimulated, it can cause a person to go wild and start smashing things. We will discuss the hypothalamus further in Chapter 5 when we talk about motivation and emotion.

The Reticular Activating System   The **reticular** (reh-TICK-you-ler) **activating system,** also called *reticular formation*, RAS for short, sits right at the base of the brain inside the spinal cord. Here is a good way to get a feel for what it is like: cut a two-inch square out of a woman's stocking and look at it. It looks just like a net. Insert it an inch or so into the end of a garden hose (the spinal column). Pretend that you insert the hose into the base of the brain, and you now have some idea of where the RAS is and a *very* rough idea of what it looks like. In fact, the word *reticular* actually means "net," since it *is* a kind of net that "catches" nerve impulses. The reason for its design, then, is that nerve impulses from the brain to the body and from the body to the brain pass through the RAS so that it can take a reading of the level of activity throughout the whole system.

The RAS regulates how alert or how sleepy we are. If a lot of things are going on, many impulses arrive from the body and brain, and alertness increases. If everything is quiet, this system heads us toward sleep. It is quite sensitive to steady sounds. Thus, if you go listen to a lecture somewhere and the speaker talks very slowly and dully, little change is noted by the RAS, so it starts to put you to sleep. If you are trying to get to sleep at night and count sheep passing by, that endless rhythm makes you drowsy. Drugs used for surgery dramatically slow down the RAS so it "doesn't care" about

ENRICHMENT

Have students find out what happens to neural communication when one abuses various kinds of drugs. Have each student focus on one or two particular drugs. What happens to this communication upon withdrawal from the drugs?

Chapter 3 BRAIN, BODY, AND BEHAVIOR

▲ *The cerebellum, thalamus, and RAS in action.*

pain signals and thus won't alert the brain about them. On the other hand, a major blow to the head causes such an overload of the RAS circuits that they shut off completely for a time, causing unconsciousness. A change in rhythm in the surroundings, an emergency, or emotional thoughts stir up the reticular activating system.

BRAIN COMMUNICATION

We have discussed a number of units of the brain. It is obvious that all these parts have to communicate with one another. Thus, the eye must send information to the occipital lobe, the foot to the motor strip, the cerebellum to and from the muscles and body, and so forth. We have already noted that there is electricity in the nerve cells, but now the question is: how do we get the parts to "talk" to one another? One way might be to string nerves directly from one part to another. In the 1700s, scientists believed this was the case, but they were very wrong (Bergland, 1985). Why won't this work? Think about it for a minute. If you connect all the parts together and turn on a "switch," *everything* will go on at the same time, which would be a hopeless mess. So that can't be the answer.

Another problem is that the brain has to be able to join different ideas. But even using separate nerves for each unit still won't work. For instance, the brain stores the idea of *red*. If we connect a nerve

DISCUSS THE PHOTO

Point out that the cerebellum, thalamus, and RAS, along with the rest of the brain, never really take a time out. The brain is constantly in action.

Teaching Hint

If you use the preceding **Comprehension Check,** have students draw these images in their notebooks. This is a good mnemonic device.

Reteaching Strategy

Have students explain the main difference between the cerebral cortex and the lower brain. (The cerebral cortex controls high-level thought and the lower brain keeps the body running.)

DEMONSTRATION

Have students simulate electrical activity inside the body by lining up single file. The line doesn't need to be straight; an open loop would be OK. Assign these roles to the first three students: dendrite, axon, neurotransmitter. Leave a space for the synapse and assign the same roles to the next three students, and so on. The front of the line could represent someone's foot, the back could be the head. Begin the chain reaction by tapping (or "firing") the first person in line. That person taps the axon, who taps the neurotransmitter, who jumps across and taps the dendrite, and so on. For mnemonic purposes, you can assign sound effects or gestures that you feel might fit each part. For example, neurotransmitters might "whoosh" across the synapse.

FYI Neurons can fire over and over again. How many times per second? On average, 300 to 400. Maximum is about 1,000 firings per second.

neuron

A nerve cell, which transmits electrical and chemical information (via neurotransmitters) throughout the body.

dendrite

The part of the nerve cell that receives information from the axons of other nerve cells.

axon

The part of the neuron that carries messages away from the nerve cell to the dendrites on another nerve cell.

from *red* to the idea of *rose*, that connection would work, but then how could we get the idea of *red* to the idea of *car* without triggering *rose* at the same time? Or how do we get the hypothalamus to signal rage without also sending out a signal for thirst, which would cause us to drink instead of yell? To solve these problems, we need many nerve cells that are separate but still able to alternate signals from one circuit to another. We certainly have more than enough of them, since each of our 100 billion nerve cells has thousands of connections to the others.

The Neuron

Each nerve cell, then, is separate, one from the other, and is called a **neuron** (NYOOR-ron or NOOR-on). As you can see in Figures 3.6 and 3.7, the body of the cell has a number of fibers sticking out from it. The shorter ones contain receptors (receivers) for neuronal messages. These short fibers are called **dendrites,** a word meaning "tree," since they look like branches. Dendrites receive information from other nerve cells and send it through the cell body to the **axon.** (The axon is the very long fiber shown in Figures 3.6 and 3.7.) The axon carries the message from the cell to other neurons. At the end of the

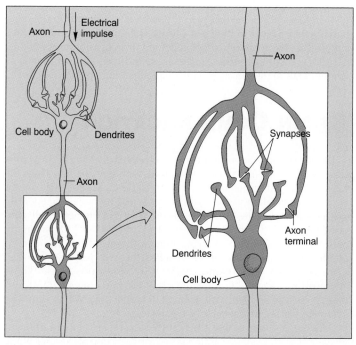

▲ *Figure 3.6   Artist's diagram of how parts of the nerve cells look and connect.*

Send students back to their seats and then apologize for misleading them. One neuron can actually communicate with hundreds, even thousands, of other neurons; the communication occurs instantaneously (which should be fairly obvious to students). There are over 40 known neurotransmitters that regulate which messages get through to the brain and which do not. Drugs, of course, can imitate or block neurotransmitters. For example, the drug curare (cue-RAH-ree) causes paralysis by blocking acetylcholine. Acupuncture, on the other hand, probably works by causing the release of endorphins, a neurotransmitter that inhibits pain.

Chapter 3 BRAIN, BODY, AND BEHAVIOR

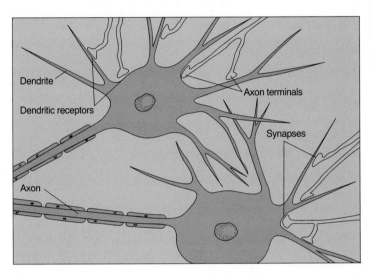

▲ *Figure 3.7* *Close-up drawing of parts of the nerve cell.*

axon are thousands of terminals, each sitting opposite a receptor for another neuron. So, the message comes to a receptor on a dendrite, goes through the cell, and then out the cell's axon to another neuron.

The Synapse

If you look carefully at Figures 3.6 and 3.7, you'll see that there is a space between the endings of the axon and the waiting dendrites. This space is called the **synapse** (SIN-apse), which means "junction point." Since the neurons work by electricity, we now have another problem: electricity will not go over a space, so it stops. And we have yet another problem: all electricity is the same. If you cut your finger and an electrical impulse goes up to the brain, how is the brain supposed to know it is a "pain message" and not a message to kick your foot?

Neurotransmitters

The solution to these problems lies in an amazing system of communication. Where the axon ends, just before the synapse, the area is filled with small containers that look like bubbles. They are called **vesicles.** Inside each of them sit thousands of chemical "messengers." Since chemical molecules can be any size or shape, they are not like electricity—you can identify them. So, if a circuit is for pain, the molecules inside that container will have a unique shape or makeup that means only "pain message" to the brain. If the circuit is for mov-

synapse

The junction point of two or more neurons; a connection is made by neurotransmitters.

vesicles

Bubblelike containers of neurotransmitters, located at the end of an axon.

75

Reteaching Strategy

Have students create their own illustrations to convey communication between neurons. Captions should be included.

INTERDISCIPLINARY PROJECT

Biology. Have several students who are interested in biology find out more details about neurotransmitters and neurons and then report back to the class. You could have them focus on how we perceive and block pain.

ENRICHMENT

There are numerous theories on why people feel phantom-limb pain. Have students research and report on these various theories. They might also find material on phantom hearing and phantom vision.

Discussion

Once students have an understanding of electrical and chemical activity in the body, they might be able to discuss phantom-limb pain. Ask students why someone who has lost a leg would still "feel" pain and other sensations in that leg. (Pain is registered and stored in the brain. For some reason, a neural chain reaction begins in the circuit for pain for that leg and causes the sensation of pain. Maybe a memory of the accident triggers the pain; maybe the cut nerves in what remains of the leg are still firing.)

DISCUSS THE PHOTO

Mention that we have 100 billion nerve cells and each has thousands of connections to the others!

neurotransmitters

Chemicals in the endings of nerve cells that send information across the synapse.

ing your arm, the container holds different-shaped molecules that will be used to signal only the movement circuit. These molecules are called **neurotransmitters** because they send (transmit) nerve (*neuro*) information from the end of the axon over the synapse to the dendrite receptor. Use Figures 3.8 and 3.9 to follow this discussion. Each circuit contains a different specific molecule for each activity that circuit controls: movement circuit, pain circuit, pleasure circuit, and so forth.

Here's what happens: You think, "Move my arm." The electrical impulse in the circuit for movement goes down the axon to a nerve ending (a terminal). The electrical impulse stops at the synapse, but when it arrives close to that area, the chemical containers (vesicles) holding molecules for "movement" are designed to float toward the synapse, where they lock onto a terminal and open up, flooding the open space with neurotransmitters for "movement." Once in the open space, the chemicals then float to the appropriate dendritic receptors for movement—in other words, each receptor is designed to accept only a specific type of chemical molecule (the "movement" molecules, in this case). Once accepted by a movement circuit, these molecules excite the dendrites there, which starts an electrical impulse through the new cell as the process repeats. The process continues until finally the impulse ends at muscle receptors, and your arm moves. Since these impulses go at about 120 yards a second, none of us is so tall that this presents a time problem. The response is almost instantaneous.

The same thing happens with the neurotransmitter for pain. Messages travel from a cut through a cell and down an axon to dendrites that will receive its pain molecules, through the cell to the next axon, and so forth until it reaches the brain where it is interpreted as

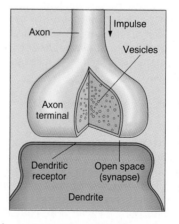

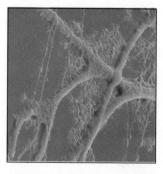

▲ *Figure 3.8 The startling complexity of a single nerve cell is shown under extremely high magnification.*

DEMONSTRATION

Now that students know a little more about neurotransmitters, you may want to try the **Demonstration** on page 74 once again. This time, one neuron will release one neurotransmitter, one that tries to excite the next neuron. Another neuron, located alongside the first, releases a neuro- transmitter that tries to stop the other excitatory neurotransmitter from send- ing its message. In practical terms, have two lines of students, represent- ing two neurons, stand side by side. Both will try to stimulate a third neu- ron (a third line of students) a few steps away. When the two neuro- transmitters try to bridge the synapse, they should struggle a bit (it could be just a verbal argument). One neuro- transmitter is trying to reach the next neuron; the other is trying to stop transmission.

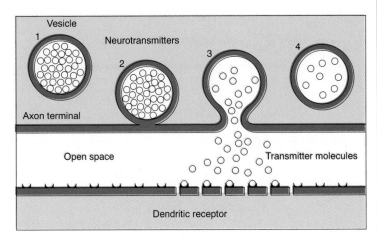

▲ **Figure 3.9** *A single container (vesicle) moving (1-4 is the same one) as the neurotransmitter is deposited into the receptor.*

pain. We now know of 60 different neurotransmitters, but we will probably eventually find hundreds of them (Snyder, 1984; 1986).

The most common and well-studied neurotransmitter is called **acetylcholine** (a-SEE-til-KOH-leen), or Ach (A-C-H) for short. One of its uses is to send information from one nerve cell to another when- ever we get ready to move some part of the body. Thus, if you are going to move your arm (as we've just described), the acetylcholine will *very* rapidly fire every nerve cell in sequence as your arm moves toward something. It will cause all the muscles in the arm to expand and contract, as necessary, so you can get the job done swiftly and accurately. Certain kinds of food poisoning, such as botulism, shut off the release of Ach. The result is paralysis.

Another neurotransmitter that is involved in motor functions or movement is called **dopamine.** A deficiency of dopamine seems to play a role in Parkinson's disease, which affects the body's ability to control movement. The same thing seems true, in part, for Alzheimer's disease, an illness involving increasing loss of neural function. Prescribing substances that produce dopamine often helps Parkinson's patients. A new technique holds some promise for Alzheimer's patients. In this technique, tissue from the adrenal glands that manufactures dopamine is implanted in the patient's brain. This is a controversial procedure, and the results are not yet all in. However, it at least points to neurotransmitters as central to the problem and possibly central to its solution as well (Kimble, 1990).

Neurotransmitters also exist that relieve pain and increase our sense of well-being. They are called **endorphins.** The term refers to the facts that they are made by the body itself (*endo*) and that they act as a natural form of morphine (*orphin*).

acetylcholine

Neurotransmitter that regulates basic bodily processes such as movement.

dopamine

A neurotransmitter involved in the control of bodily movements.

endorphins

Neurotransmitters that relieve pain and increase our sense of well- being.

Comprehension Check

Which two types of neurotransmitters are involved in motor func- tions? *(acetylcholine and dopamine)* Which type relieves pain? *(endorphins)*

77

DEMONSTRATION

Demonstrate the **Teaching Hint** below by standing behind a student and dropping tiny bits of paper on her head. Each time she feels a piece hitting her head, she should raise her hand: the neurons in the skin cover-ing her skull have fired. The pieces that were not felt did not supply enough stimulation for firing.

Explain again that the first neuron triggered the next one, which trig-gered the next, and so on. Also, it might be interesting to note that this chain reaction, once begun, is an all-or-nothing procedure. Some drugs, of course, can prevent the chain reac-tion from occurring in the first place.

Sizzling Neurons.

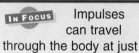 Impulses can travel through the body at just over 200 miles per hour.

Teaching Hint

The **In Focus** box uses the analogy of firecrackers as neu-rons. Students may ask, "Well, what stimu-lates, or fires, the first firecracker?" Explain that neurons will fire once stimulation reach-es a certain threshold. It's similar to striking a match; you have to supply a certain degree of friction for the match to light.

Unit 2 BRAIN, BODY, AND AWARENESS

 **Sizzling Neurons**

The A-B-Cs of Neurons!

Imagine that each tiny nerve cell, or neuron, is one complete firecracker. Imagine further that we have a bunch of these neu-rons, or firecrackers, throughout our bodies. When one of these neurons is stimulated, it begins a chain reaction.

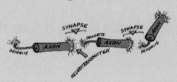

The wick (dendrite) receives the incoming message. The mes-sage is then carried along the length of the firecracker (axon). By the time the message gets to the end of the firecracker, it causes a chemical to leak (a neurotransmitter) from the vesicles. This chemical is responsible for bridging the tiny gap (synapse) between two firecrackers; it sends the message across the gap and lights the next wick.

The nice thing about all this is that you can use the wicks and firecrackers over and over again!

This diagram is simplified, of course. It appears that the den-drite is a single wick and that it can receive messages from only one other neuron. See the close-up drawings of neurons on ear-lier pages for more accurate illustrations.

The chain reaction above happens rapidly. Take a guess on the maximum speed: (a) 50 mph (b) 100 mph (c) 200 mph.

One final thing might have occurred to you. If you were breathing in and had no way to turn off the muscles that inhale, you wouldn't be able to exhale. Similarly, since the reticular activating system has to slow down in order for you to sleep, there must be a way to turn some of its cells off. There is. Some dendritic receptors are designed so that when a neurotransmitter arrives, the cell turns *off*. An exam-ple of this occurs when people drink too much. The alcohol molecule resembles a neurotransmitter that the body uses to turn cells off. So, when the alcohol gets into the system, cells begin to shut down. Cells turn off in the RAS, making the person sleepy; in the speech area, making him or her slur; in the cerebellum, causing him or her even-tually to fall over; and so forth.

The Spinal Cord

All the nerve impulses to the body from the brain and from the brain to the body must enter and leave the **spinal cord.** Figure 3.10 shows what is called a *cross section* of this unit. The drawing illustrates how the spinal cord would appear if you were cut in two and looked down on the bottom half. Sometimes, for our survival, the spinal cord must activate the muscles long before we are even aware of it, a behavior called a **reflex.** In the first stages of an emergency, the brain does not act but the spinal cord does. This happens in a close call when driving. You are about to hit another car, but "before you know it," you have swerved and missed it. The spinal neurons are short, direct, and very powerful in order to get us out of such messes. They have very few synapses to slow them down; just enough are available to send a message to the brain about what happened.

In theory, the spinal cord could operate by itself. For example, a frog has a very small cerebral cortex. If the frog's head is cut off, some of the parts of its body still work. If the foot is pinched, what is left of the frog will still draw its leg up—for an hour or so. But can the head still work? In a really gory experiment in France many years ago, scientists tried talking to the heads of men who had just had them cut off in an execution. The heads did not answer (Von Frisch, 1963).

Chapter 3 BRAIN, BODY, AND BEHAVIOR

spinal cord

The part of the body that functions as an automatic "brain" in its own right and is a relay station for impulses to and from the higher brain.

reflex

An automatic behavior of the body involving movement that is activated through the spinal cord without using the higher brain.

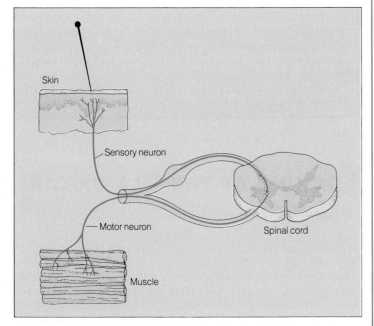

Skin

Sensory neuron

Motor neuron

Spinal cord

Muscle

▲ *Figure 3.10 The spinal cord.*

DISCOVERY

Have two students role-play a mother and father deciding whether to send their son to the doctor for growth-hormone treatments. The son has gone through puberty and is about four inches shorter than the average height for males his age. A third student could play the son in order to get his input and feedback.

Three Types of Neurons.

 Spinal cord interneurons would be stimulated in situations that require an immediate response, such as putting your hand on a hot stove. In this example, the impulse travels from the hand to the spinal cord. Rather than continuing to the brain, the impulse travels along the interneurons and then directly to the motor neuron which causes your hand to respond. A fraction of a second later, the brain receives a new impulse about the hot stove.

Points to Stress

Whereas the nervous system reacts instantaneously, it may take time for the endocrine system to affect the body. Hormones are released directly into the bloodstream, so it takes a bit longer for the body to respond to this.

80

Unit 2 BRAIN, BODY, AND AWARENESS

hormones

Chemical regulators that control bodily processes such as emotional responses, growth, and sexuality.

glands

Units of the body that contain the hormones.

endocrine system

The system of all the glands and their chemical messages taken together.

80

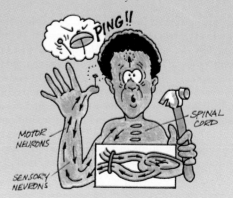

IN FOCUS   Three Types of Neurons

Neurons are like cars that can only travel down one-way streets.
1. Sensory neurons travel from the body to the brain.
2. Motor neurons travel from the brain to the body.
3. Interneurons connect sensory and motor neurons.

The illustration shows interneurons in the spinal cord, but there are also interneurons in the brain. The spinal cord interneurons are stimulated in the above example so that the person can respond more quickly—even before the brain knows that there is a need to respond.

Can you think of any other situations in which spinal cord interneurons would be stimulated?

LOOKING AT THE GLANDULAR SYSTEM

Communication by neurons is speedy and efficient, but it doesn't last very long. Some messages need to stay in the system longer. These messages come from chemicals called **hormones,** which are passed through the body using the bloodstream. *Hormone* comes from a word meaning "to activate," since that's what it does: hormones can turn on other parts of the body. These chemicals are held inside **glands.** All the glands and their chemical messages together make up what is called the **endocrine** (EN-doh-crin) **system.**

ENRICHMENT

Assign an emotion to each student. The task is to map out, in as much detail as possible, the internal activities that occur when we experience that emotion. Popular magazines like *Newsweek* and *Time* do an excellent job of depicting this sort of thing with diagrams, arrows, and illustrations. Find a sample that students can use as a model.

Hormones work like neurotransmitters in that they have a special molecular structure that must match the structure of a receptor. For example, there is a hormone-receptor pair designed only for a woman about to give birth. When the time comes, the hormone is sent through the blood to the proper area, where it locks onto its receptor and starts muscular contractions. If a woman never has a baby, this hormone is never used.

In the near-miss accident discussed in the previous section, once the message gets to the brain about what is happening, it declares an emergency that will require the body to be active for a period of time. The hypothalamus uses neurotransmitters to signal the pituitary gland (discussed next). The pituitary then sends out hormones through the endocrine system. They arrive at the adrenal glands (also discussed later), which stir the body up for the emergency. When you get enough of the adrenal hormone in your body, you start to shake all over and feel sick—this is the worst part of a near-miss.

In the sections that follow, we look at the major parts of the endocrine system. Be sure to note that the brain, our inner selves, the body, and the environment all work together; not one of them ever works all by itself.

The Pituitary Gland

The **pituitary** (pi-TUE-i-ter-ee) **gland** is called the master gland of the body. In Figure 3.11, you will see that it is a small bean-shaped unit that is attached to and controlled by the hypothalamus. Physicians many centuries ago thought that mucus running from your nose came from this gland. "Pituita" was a taboo slang word used for this substance, and everyone who heard the word was disgusted. They were wrong about what it does, but the term stuck. The pituitary has two jobs: (1) to send messages that will start other glands going and (2) to decide how tall or short we will be (Bergland, 1985).

The pituitary makes a **growth hormone,** but it does it in fits and starts. Sometimes its action is delayed, causing people in the growth phase to worry that they will never reach an average height. On occasion it seems to start too soon, creating youngsters who feel too tall and "not quite right."

Most of the time, these starts and stops in growth lead to an average height. But not always. When things are not working properly, there can be incredible growth: the tallest person in history was 8 feet 11.1 inches. He died at the age of 22, partly as a result of this growth. The shortest known person was 23.2 inches tall when she died at age 19. Today's medicine can handle most such situations if caught early enough, but these cases show what happens if the pituitary goes awry.

Like all body systems, the pituitary requires a normal environ-

Chapter 3 BRAIN, BODY, AND BEHAVIOR

▲ *The effects of the pituitary are clearly shown here. Entertainer David Frost stands between the world's smallest and largest men.*

pituitary gland

The master gland of the body that activates other glands and controls the growth hormone.

growth hormone

The hormone controlled by the pituitary that regulates the growth process.

Critical Thinking

Ask students the following question: What would happen if the pituitary, thyroid, and adrenal glands were overactive or underactive? (An overactive pituitary produces a giant—have students look up acromegaly; an underactive pituitary produces a short person. An overactive thyroid produces high metabolism, makes the person energetic; an underactive thyroid produces sluggishness and low resistance; a person's hair may fall out. An overactive adrenal gland produces high blood pressure and rapid heart rate; an underactive adrenal gland makes the person unable to deal well with stress: for instance, the liver, which normally releases sugar into the bloodstream for energy during emergencies, does not function efficiently.)

DISCUSS THE PHOTO

Have students write a journal entry from the point of view of one of these men.

DISCOVERY

Have four or five students assume the roles of different parts of the brain or body. Tell them they are all part of the same person and that they must communicate with one another. Give them this or another situation to act out: "You're sneaking into your house after curfew, and you hear your parents moving toward you." What would the hypothalamus say to the motor strip, or what would the frontal lobe say to the adrenal gland, and so on? If you want to convert this activity into group work, allow time for each group to prepare a simple skit.

Possible situations: (1) person wants to break off a relationship; (2) person wants to cheat on a test; (3) an older person wants to wear "young" clothes in order to feel younger; 4) the person is a baby getting his or her diaper changed.

FYI Regular injections of a synthetic growth hormone can increase a child's height by several inches. But side effects may also occur: leukemia, diabetes, and other problems.

Unit 2 BRAIN, BODY, AND AWARENESS

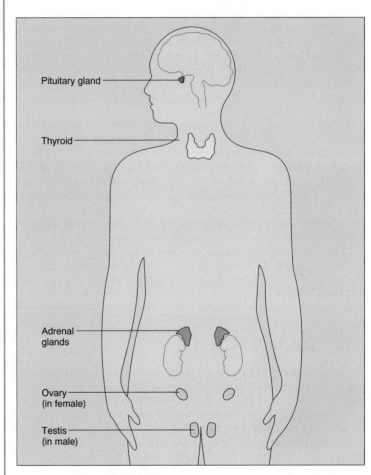

▲ *Figure 3.11* *The glandular system.*

ment. In one very sad case, a mother locked her growing child in a closet and allowed him out only to eat (from a dog-food bowl). As a result of the darkness and his poor treatment, he stopped growing. When freed by welfare workers, he began to grow again. Then, as a result of an error, he was sent back home. Locked in the closet once more, he stopped growing again. Fortunately, he was finally freed a second time and started growing again (Money, 1974).

Even diet can have a major effect on the pituitary. The Japanese as a group were very short compared to most Americans 30 years ago, but since their economy has picked up so greatly and food is more varied and accessible, today their average height is inches taller than

ENRICHMENT

The adrenal gland also plays a role in sexual development. Have students find out what happens to men and women when the adrenal gland is overactive. Possible effects: early puberty, baldness in women, breast enlargement in men.

it formerly was. Just the reverse is turning out to be true for Brazil. More than a third of its population lives with a severe lack of food, and each generation's average height is now becoming shorter and shorter (Simons, 1987).

The Thyroid Gland

The **thyroid gland** and the parts connected to it look like a bow tie sitting inside the neck (look again at Figure 3.11). The pituitary signals the thyroid, whose job is to control **metabolism.** Metabolism is the speed with which the body operates. People with a very active thyroid can be jumping around all over the place, not able to sit still. People with a slow thyroid, on the other hand, tend to be sluggish. A *very* slow gland from birth can lead to mental retardation.

We suspect that the thyroid gland may sometimes play a role in suicides. You will hear that suicides are highest around Christmastime, but that's not true. After all, that's the time of the year when people are usually pleasant and support you. Most suicides are in May. During April, everyone's thyroid gland begins to slow down because summer is approaching, and we don't need a fast-running motor during that season. If someone is having lots of troubles about this time and feels down and out, it may well be that the body slowing down will make him or her feel even more depressed and unable to cope, and this may tip the scale toward suicide (Zung & Green, 1974).

The Adrenal Glands

The **adrenal** (a-DREE-nal) **glands** are located on the right and left side of the body, slightly above the navel and to the back. When they operate at full force, they create an overexcited body, which none of us wants. But we don't go long without triggering them. In the near-accident example, the quick-acting spinal nerves make us swerve the car to avoid it. For a moment, we sigh with relief. But when all the activity gets to the reticular formation and then goes to the cerebral cortex, we begin to think about what *could* have happened. The cortex signals a major emergency to the hypothalamus, which tells the pituitary, which send hormones to the adrenal glands. The adrenal glands then dump **adrenaline** (a-DREN-a-lin) into the bloodstream. Adrenaline prepares us for an emergency: we begin to breathe rapidly, blood pressure goes up, muscles tense, sugar is dumped into the body for energy, and we are so excited that our armpits and feet sweat. This system is amazing: it even sends out a chemical that will help the blood clot faster just in case we get cut! These reactions are not designed by nature to deal with traffic problems, but the body

thyroid gland

The gland that controls and regulates the speed of bodily processes, called metabolism.

metabolism

The speed at which the body operates or the speed at which it uses up energy.

adrenal glands

The glands that cause excitement in order to prepare the body for an emergency or for some important activity.

adrenaline

The chemical that prepares the body for emergency activity by increasing blood pressure, breathing rate, and energy level.

Reteaching Strategy

Have students complete the **Reteaching Worksheet** for this chapter located in the Teacher Resources.

The **Vocabulary Worksheet** may be completed by the class as a pretest for chapter concepts or used as a reteaching worksheet for those students needing additional review.

ENRICHMENT

Have students complete the **Enrichment Worksheet** for this chapter located in the Teacher Resources.

Unit 2 Brain, Body, and Awareness

can't tell the difference between a real emergency (such as an accident we *don't* manage to avoid) and one we just think about. For instance, the whole emergency system is set into motion if we have to talk in front of a group or, for many of us, if we are about to take an examination. Hands tremble, armpits and feet perspire, we can hardly breathe, the heart is jumping, all saliva is gone so that we feel like we are choking, and we know for sure we are going to die right in the middle of the talk or the test.

The Gonads

The **gonads** are the sex glands; they make the sperm or eggs used for reproduction. The male sex hormone is called **androgen,** and the female one is called **estrogen.** *Both* males and females have *both* hormones in their bodies, but for the male, there will be more androgen, and for the female, more estrogen. These hormones make us look either male or female. For example, if a female is injected with extra androgen, she will grow body hair and a beard. Androgen also starts the sex drive for both males and females, but the sex drive doesn't really become very active until people are in their middle teens.

Earlier we mentioned that mind and body affect one another. Nowhere is this clearer than in the case of sex hormones. If you neuter a dog, it will lose its desire to reproduce. This is *not* the case with an adult human. Even after an accident that removes the source of the hormones, the sex drive can remain for years. So, even though our sex drive is at one time started by hormones, it is then taken over by the cerebral cortex, which makes it a social, symbolic behavior as well as a physical one. Many find this hard to believe, but because the cortex controls it, sex must actually be learned by humans. It is not like hunger or thirst. This fact is often a source of real confusion for adolescents because it takes a long time for anyone to understand what sex is all about. To add to the problem, sometimes their friends of the same age *pretend* they already know all about it. The presence of the cortex, however, does give humans the feelings of love, hope, warmth, respect, and care that can be attached to the sex act. On the other hand, the presence of the cortex also means that the opposite feelings—fear, anxiety, and psychological pain—can likewise occur.

gonads

The sex glands that make sperm or eggs for reproduction.

androgen

The male sex hormone.

estrogen

The female sex hormone.

Comprehension Check

Identify the gland that could be involved in each of the following situations: panicking at the sight of a snake *(adrenal)*; feeling tired all day *(thyroid)*; surpassing your parents in height *(pituitary)*; starting to look less like a child and more like a man or woman *(gonads).*

DISCOVERY

Discussion question #4 at the end of the chapter asks students to write about a brain transplant. Ask a male and female student to pretend that they have swapped brains, and have them role-play how they feel. This exercise is a fun way to end the chapter, and it might be a good preview for an upcoming chapter on gender.

PSYCHOLOGY IN YOUR LIFE

Brain Control

Endless television shows, movies, and science fiction books suggest that it might be possible to control people's brains. But what is the real, scientific evidence that we might be taken over and turned into robots?

It is startling to think about someone going berserk if a portion of the hypothalamus is electrically stimulated. We mentioned that event earlier because it shows what *can* happen. What we did not talk about, though, is the fact that the hypothalamus for each one of us is slightly different from that of another person. This is true of all parts of the brain and body. For example, each of us has a different-shaped stomach, and each person's stomach is located in a slightly different place. You can see the problem: it would take endless hours of work to locate the pleasure or rage center in the hypothalamus of one single person. You can imagine the impossible task of putting electrical control devices in enough people even to get a small mob going, much less control a larger group. To make it more difficult,

humans are so complex and variable that some of us respond with pleasure where the anger portion of the hypothalamus is supposed to be! So, you can rule out this method of controlling people.

But what about drugs? You have probably heard about a drug called a "truth serum." When it is administered (in the movies), the subject suddenly starts blurting out all his or her secrets. Surely that would be a good way to "get" things on someone and control him or her in that way. Well, no. Again the whole thing is exaggerated. The so-called truth serum only slows down the reticular activating system so that the victim is drowsy and fuzzy. This condition makes us all more suggestible in the sense that we don't worry as much about telling the truth. But such is not the case for those who have something to lose! Tests show that people lie all the time, if they need to, under this drug. Others make things up; for example, they confess to crimes they couldn't possibly have committed. So we have to rule that one out, too.

What about "confessions" given by prisoners of war or victims of the police? If enough psychological torture is used, sometimes prisoners will confess to things they didn't do. Historically, more often they will not do so. In any case, they have not really been "brainwashed" because as soon as they are free, they go right back to whatever they felt and believed before the torture. In fact, often the "confessions" from war camps are written in strange English to say the opposite of what the foreign captors think they are saying (Johnson, 1971).

We discussed the railroad worker who had an iron bar fired through his brain. That certainly changed his personality, didn't it? Not exactly. There's a big difference between *changing* a personality and damaging the brain so much that the person doesn't work right anymore. The iron bar had cut the connections between his frontal lobes and the lower "animal" brain. Hence, the frontal

(continued on next page)

(continued on next page)

PSYCHOLOGY IN YOUR LIFE

Teaching Master 3-8 Brain Communication. This handout can be used as a practice quiz. Students are asked to explain how a message is sent from the finger to the brain.

Connections

Chapter 5 reports on animals receiving stimulation to the pleasure center of the brain (located in the hypothalamus) if they pushed a lever; many stimulated themselves 20 times a minute. After 20 days, the number of pushes totaled 576,000!

Wrapping It Up

Most of the material on the cerebral hemispheres has been theoretical. Here are two practical applications.

(1) Often when students take notes, they condense what should be seven pages into a single page, and thus create few, if any, spatial relationships between one section and another. So when they take notes, study notes, and try to recall notes during tests they rely only on verbal skills, the strength of the left hemisphere. Encourage them to make better use of the right hemisphere by creating spatial relationships in their notes: skipping lines; indenting; using columns; boxing in material; underlining. Point out how common it is while taking a test to know where the material is located in one's notebook. These location cues are desirable as they often prompt more specific recall. (Some students use multicolored note cards to study: blue cards can include the parts of the cerebral cortex; red cards can be the lower brain!)

(2) Encourage students to draw pictures in their notebooks. When discussing the cerebellum, tell them to draw a person balancing on a tightrope. The best way to encourage them is to draw your own pictures on the chalkboard when discussing these brain parts. Explain that the pictures will also serve to create location cues and that both hemispheres will then be used more efficiently.

PSYCHOLOGY IN YOUR LIFE

Brain Control

(continued from previous page) lobes were no longer able to maintain control, and he acted like an animal. Strictly speaking, he was not turned into another, different person. Likewise, someone on drugs will behave strangely, possibly even violently, but when the drugs are removed, the basic person remains. We know of no method that will create major personality changes in an orderly, permanent fashion so that you can get a robot or make a different person.

Exotic as such ideas might seem, in most cases we are what we are and believe what we believe after years of a certain life-style. While we clearly can change bad habits and stop some of the awful things we do, there is no evidence at all that our brains can be taken over or altered to such an extent that we are not the same person we've always been.

SUMMARY

1. The upper outer covering of the brain is the cerebral cortex. The cerebral cortex is divided into two halves, called hemispheres. The halves are connected through the corpus callosum. The left half controls the right side of the body and vice versa.

2. The cortex is divided into sections or lobes. The frontal lobe contains the motor strip, which controls movement, and the frontal association area, which integrates the environment and carries on complex analyses. The sensory strip, which controls sensation, is in the parietal lobe. Hearing and speech are functions of the temporal lobe. The occipital lobe organizes visual information.

3. The lower brain controls basic bodily activity. The thalamus is a relay station to and from the cortex and the lower brain. The cerebellum guides coordination and balance. The hypothalamus is part of a system controlling rage, pleasure, hunger, thirst, and sexual desire. The reticular activating system keeps us alert or puts us to sleep.

4. Parts of the brain are connected to one another through neurons. The neurons have electricity running from the dendrite through the cell to the axon and out to the synapse. The brain is also connected to the body through neurons. Communication through the synapses is actually handled by neurotransmitters, chemicals that regulate different systems such as muscle movement or the recognition of pain.

5. The endocrine system uses hormones to provide a longer-lasting method of chemical communication than the neurons can provide. The pituitary is the master gland that guides growth, but it also signals the thyroid for metabolism, the adrenal glands for emergencies, and the gonads for sexual activity.

SUGGESTED READINGS

▼ Alder, Tina. "Gestures Offer Clues on Speech and Brain." *APA Monitor,* April 92, 41.

▼ Allman, William F. "How the Brain Really Works." *U.S. News & World Report,* June 27, 1988, 48–55.

▼ Coren, Stanley. *The Left-Hander Syndrome.* New York: Free Press, 1992.

▼ Gazzaniga, Michael S. *Nature's Mind.* New York: Basic Books, 1992.

▼ Llimàs, Rodolfo R. *The Workings of the Brain.* New York: W.H. Freeman, 1990.

▼ Maguire, Jack. *Care and Feeding of the Brain.* New York: Doubleday, 1990.

▼ Ornstein, Robert. *The Evolution of Consciousness.* New York: Prentice Hall, 1991.

▼ Restak, Richard. *The Brain.* New York: Bantam Books, 1984.

VOCABULARY

fissure
hemisphere
corpus callosum
lobe
frontal lobe
parietal lobe
motor strip
sensory strip
occipital lobe
temporal lobe
frontal association
    area
dominance
cerebral cortex
lower brain

thalamus
cerebellum
hypothalamus
reticular activating
    system
neuron
dendrite
axon
synapse
vesicles
neurotransmitters
acetylcholine
dopamine
endorphins
spinal cord

reflex
hormones
glands
endocrine system
pituitary gland
growth hormone
thyroid gland
metabolism
adrenal glands
adrenaline
gonads
androgen
estrogen

Answers to Review Questions

1. hemispheres
2. corpus callosum
3. sensory strip
4. motor strip
5. motor strip
6. parietal lobe
   or sensory strip
7. occipital lobe
8. temporal lobe

Review Questions

Fill in the blank; answer on a separate sheet of paper. (An answer may consist of more than one word.)

1. The cerebral cortex is divided into two halves called ___?___ .
2. The ___?___ connects the two halves of the cerebral cortex.
3. The ___?___ runs along a fissure and is located in the parietal lobe.
4. The ___?___ runs along a fissure and is located in the frontal lobe.
5. Most of our movements are controlled by the ___?___ .
6. The touch of a feather on your skin is registered by the ___?___ .
7. Visual information is organized and interpreted in the ___?___ .
8. Hearing and some speech functions are located in the ___?___ .

▼ Restak, Richard. *The Brain Has a Mind of its Own*. New York: Harmony, 1991.

▼ Restak, Richard. *The Mind*. New York: Bantam Books, 1988.

▼ *Scientific American*, September 92, entire issue.

▼ Springer, Sally P., and George Deutsch. *Left Brain, Right Brain*. New York: W. H. Freeman, 1985.

▼ Wonder, Jacquelyn, and Priscilla Donovan. *Whole Brain Thinking*. New York: William Morrow, 1984.

SUGGESTED VIDEOS

▼ *The Behaving Brain*. Discovering Psychology series, part 3. 27 min. 1-800-LEARNER.
▼ *Birth of a Brain*, 33 min. CRM/McGraw-Hill.
▼ *Nerves at Work*. 26 min. Films for the Humanities.

9. c	14. a	19. T
10. d	15. b	20. A
11. a	16. e	21. T
12. b	17. c	22. P
13. d	18. f	23. A
		24. P

Matching: match the function with the proper part of the lower brain.

9. Controls balance
10. Controls hunger and thirst
11. Sends messages to various parts of the brain
12. "Catches" nerve impulses in order to register activity level

a. thalamus
b. RAS
c. cerebellum
d. hypothalamus

13. Receive electrical messages from other nerve cells
14. The spaces between nerve cells
15. Carry electrical messages to the end of the nerve cell
16. Chemicals that send messages from neuron to neuron
17. Nerve cells
18. Containers for chemical messengers

a. synapses
b. axons
c. neurons
d. dendrites
e. neurotransmitters
f. vesicles

For each of the following, answer T for thyroid gland, A for adrenal gland, and P for pituitary gland. Each answer will be used twice.

19. Regulates metabolism
20. Activated especially during emergencies
21. May cause general sluggishness

22. The master gland
23. Helps regulate blood pressure
24. Helps determine height

Notes on Discussion Questions

1. A comb placed in the left hand of a blind person (whose corpus callosum has been cut) is registered in the right hemisphere. So the person would probably not be able to say "comb" but could probably draw a comb with the left hand (and only the left hand). If the comb were placed in the right hand, the information would go to the left hemisphere, which communicates well verbally, so the person could probably then say "comb."

2. The alcohol may disrupt coordination (cerebellum); it may cause fits of anger (hypothalamus); it may cause someone to be less alert (RAS); it may dull complex thinking processes (frontal association area); it may distort vision

DISCUSSION QUESTIONS

1. Suppose you met a blind person whose corpus callosum had been cut. If you were to put a comb in this person's left hand, would he or she be able to tell you what was in his or her hand? If yes, explain. If no, what other way could the person communicate "comb" to you? Explain. What if the comb were put in his or her right hand?

2. How do you suppose alcohol would affect each part of the lower brain (thalamus, hypothalamus, cerebellum, RAS) and each

part of the upper brain (frontal association area, occipital lobe, motor strip, sensory strip)? Explain.

3. Describe several situations where you might want your neurotransmitters to operate very efficiently and quickly. Describe several situations where you might wish your neurotransmitters to work inefficiently and slowly.

4. The "brain transplant" is a common science fiction theme. Just for fun, imagine that the

(occipital lobe); it would affect all movement (motor strip).

3. You may want neurotransmitters to work inefficiently before surgery. You may want efficiency when you're stealing a basketball pass.

4. Students' responses can lead to a discussion on values. How important is it to be happy or smart?

5. All glands will be affected by age. The adrenal gland would probably be least affected by age. The most noticeable might be the thyroid, however. As metabolism slows, weight usually increases. Ask them to look at pictures of their parents as teenagers and as they are today.

6. Have students bring in magazine ads or song lyrics and discuss their messages. Do these kinds of messages actually have any effect on people's choices? If not on students, do they have an effect on people from other age groups?

Notes on Activities

1. Mention that it is impossible for any ad to appeal to only one hemisphere. Each hemisphere may perform specialized functions, but it does not operate in isolation.

2. See number 1.

3. Some colleges have portable EEGs. See if you can borrow one for a day.

4. Suggest to your students that they obtain their research not only through nonfiction books, but also through movies (*One Flew Over the Cuckoo's Nest; Frances*) and novels that include scenes of lobotomies.

5. Again, students don't have to rely on books. They can interview a biology teacher, a university professor, or a zoo worker.

---

procedure has just become possible, and you have been chosen as the first candidate. Discuss the following:

a. Whose brain would you choose? Why?

b. If you had to choose between a smart, somber brain or a simple, happy brain, which would you choose? Why?

c. Regardless of your choices in (a) and (b), *who* would you be *after* the transplant? Would your identity be the same as it was before, because you would occupy the same body? Or would your identity be that of the new brain? Explain.

5. Which of the three glands discussed in the chapter would probably be most affected by the aging process? Explain your reasoning and provide supporting examples. Which of the three glands would be least affected by age? Explain.

6. The chapter explains that our sex drive has both physical and social aspects and that sex must be learned by humans. Other than actual experience and heart-to-heart talks, how *do* we learn about sex? Through TV? Through the media in general? Who or what teaches us? And what is the message being taught?

ACTIVITIES

1. Several advertisers explicitly use the theory of left- and right-hemisphere dominance to promote their products. For example, they openly claim that their products appeal to the left hemisphere and then supply statistics; at the same time, they claim that their products appeal to the right hemisphere and then supply vivid, emotional pictures.

   Other than these obvious examples, *do* advertisers direct their sales pitches to one hemisphere or another? To find out, collect ten magazine ads that appeal primarily to the left hemisphere, ten that appeal to the right hemisphere, and ten that appeal to both hemispheres. Neatly tape each ad onto a sheet of paper and provide captions explaining why you chose the ads.

2. An alternative to the activity in number 1 might be to videotape at random ten commercials and then analyze each one. Which ones appeal to the left hemisphere? To the right? To both? Explain your reasoning.

3. Contact a local hospital for information on the latest techniques for studying and examining the brain. Ask about MRIs, CAT scans, PET scans, and EEGs. Find out the advantages and disadvantages of each technique and under what conditions each would be used. Also find out the actual costs of each technique.

4. Conduct research on lobotomies, the surgical procedure for removing or disconnecting the frontal association area. Find out why lobotomies became popular and why they were eventually discontinued. Find out if any versions of lobotomies are still performed today. Compare your findings with any ideas about lobotomies that you may have had before you did this research.

5. Compare the size, development, and structure of the human brain to other animal brains. One of the more important areas you should compare is the ratio of brain size to body weight. Do any animals have a better brain-body ratio than humans? Another area you can compare is the cubic centimeter capacity, or the volume, of the brain.

DISCUSS THE PHOTO

Have students offer other possible perceptions of the photo (which is a difficult task once they read the caption).

What does this look like to you? It's actually a daisy covered with raindrops.

90

PSYCHOLOGY AND YOU RESOURCES

A variety of resources are available in the Psychology and You *supplementary material. In addition, there are a number of additional resources listed to enhance your lesson plans.*

Masters
▼ 4-1A Learning Goals
▼ 4-1B Answers to Learning Goals
▼ 4-2 Cutaneous Receptors
▼ 4-3 Perceptual Set
▼ 4-4 Identify the Perceptual Principle
▼ 4-5 The Dating Game
▼ 4-6 What Do You See? 1
▼ 4-7 What Do You See? 2
▼ 4-8 Color Experiment
▼ 4-9 Illusions

Student Worksheets
▼ Vocabulary Worksheet
▼ Independent Practice Worksheet
▼ Enrichment Worksheet
▼ Reteaching Worksheet

Test Bank
▼ Tests A and B

Multimedia
▼ *The Brain* Videotape Modules #28 and 29
▼ **Mindscope** Exercise 1, 2, 10, 19
▼ Psychology Videodisc

Student Workbook

PACING CHART

Complete Coverage

Day 1: Assign the first two sections about sensation prior to class. Choose an in-class demonstration from the wrap to illustrate the mechanisms of vision. In Focus Color Vision will also be helpful.

Day 2: Build discussion around classroom demonstrations involving hearing, taste, smell and/or the cutaneous senses. Have students read the "Perception" section for Day 3. Also, assign for homework an activity that involves conducting an experiment exploring sensation or perception, due on Day 5.

Day 3: Classroom demonstrations will best convey the concept of perception. Direct students to the In Focus box on size constancy. Use the question it presents to spark discussion about perception involving interpretation and expectation. Stress the concept of gestalt and use In Focus Moving Cubes to discuss illusions.

4

Sensation and Perception

OBJECTIVES

Be able to:

▼ Explain the difference between sensation and perception.

▼ Explain the process of color vision and the color defects that can occur.

▼ Describe how rods and cones work.

▼ Describe the basic mechanisms of hearing, olfaction, and touch.

▼ Explain the functions of taste receptors.

▼ List and describe perceptual constancies.

▼ Explain how illusions are useful.

Global Look at the Chapter

Sensation and perception form our world. Without them we can make no sense of what is happening around us. Perception is controlled psychologically in the sense that we can interpret the incoming stimulation (sensation) to fit our needs or desires. The basic information from such sensation is processed by remarkable physical receptors designed just for each task.

91

INTRODUCING THE CHAPTER

Draw a grid on the chalkboard with 16 equal squares in it. Ask students how many squares they see. The immediate response will be, "16." A few seconds later, someone will say, "No, 20." You can find 30 with a little effort. Use this simple demonstration to make the distinction between sensation and perception. All of us *see* the same grid (sensation), but each of us may *interpret* it a bit differently (perception).

LEAD-OFF ACTIVITY

Most students underestimate the abilities of our senses. To demonstrate our keen sense of touch, bring in ten lemons and ten blindfolds. With a marker, number each lemon. Have ten volunteers sit in a circle on the floor. After they are blindfolded, give each one a lemon and tell them their numbers. Allow them about a minute to "know" their lemons. Afterward, collect the lemons and randomly give a lemon back to each student. Still blindfolded, the students will pass lemons around the circle, attempting to find their assigned lemons. The rest of the class can observe how the group members communicate with each other without sight. Have fun varying this procedure by shortening the time limit, giving some students two lemons, and so on.

Day 4: Use Psychology in Your Life to discuss the evidence for and against the existence of extrasensory perception.

Day 5: Discuss and evaluate the results of students' completed activities assigned on Day 2. Give the Chapter Review quiz.

In Brief

Day 1: Use classroom demonstrations to highlight your lecture on sensation; the wrap provides several of these.

Day 2: Focus discussion on how perception is different from, yet connected to, sensation. Make sure students understand the concept of gestalt.

Day 3: Discuss Psychology in Your Life, and conduct the demonstration it describes. Give the Chapter Review quiz.

COOPERATIVE LEARNING

One of the things you will find, or have found, after teaching this chapter several times is that you never have time to do all the demonstrations that you'd like. To overcome this, break the class into small groups, maybe even pairs, and give each group an activity to perform and discuss. You can find numerous demonstrations in *Activities Handbook for the Teaching of Psychology* (3 vols.), from the American Psychological Association. See the introductory wraparound material for the address. These three volumes are highly recommended.

Unit 2 BRAIN, BODY, AND AWARENESS

SENSORY PROCESSES

We are so used to processing information from the senses that we take this ability for granted. Nonetheless, our ability to understand what is going on around us is truly remarkable. Our brains set up all kinds of methods for handling this complex information. If you receive information that is deliberately confusing—well, let's see what happens. We will give you a sentence, and you try to figure out what it says. We have put the "translation" of it somewhere in the next couple of paragraphs. Don't look for it until you have tried to figure the sentence out. Here it is:

ThEcOwgAvecOla

This is really a sentence, but you have trouble processing it because the normal shape and boundaries of the words and letters have been rearranged. Everyone must rely heavily on these shapes to be able to read as fast as we do. The eye skips and jumps from one part of the sentence to another; if a word is very common, like "and" or "the," we take only a glimpse at it as the eye looks at clumps of words all at one time. The normal method for reading is to focus on the beginning letters of a sentence and determine what basic *shape* the rest of the words in the sentence have. If everything looks familiar, we assume, after a very slight pause, that the words are known; if, as we read on, the sentence doesn't fit with what comes next, we stop and go back to find out what we missed. If you actually had to read every letter and word on this page, it would take you more than 20 minutes to read it and about eight hours to read this chapter—a fate no one deserves. So what is it we've done to make the example sentence so confusing? We've changed its physical structure. Here is the sentence written in something close to the normal structure; now you should have no trouble whatsoever with it: TheCowGaveCola (Dunn-Rankin, 1978).

All incoming sensation must be interpreted by the brain. As a result, quite often we see what we want to see and hear what we want to hear (or don't see or hear, according to what we really desire). So sensation is not merely a physical event—it can be very psychological. Here is a simple example of making something what it isn't. Read the following sentence from *right to left*, once, without stopping. *Don't* read it again yet.

".rat eht saw tac ehT"

Most people read one of two versions: "The cat saw the rat" or "The cat was the rat." Both of these are wrong. You made this mistake because if you had read the sentence backward the way it really is written, it wouldn't have made sense to you. Read it again, this time very carefully, and you will see what we mean (Dunn-Rankin, 1978).

One more example: we assign a symbolic "top," "bottom," and "side" to most objects we know, and we keep them that way, regardless of their position. Cut out a piece of paper with four equal sides,

Have students pair up, and give each pair one blindfold. Allow them about 20 minutes to walk around the school; each student will be blindfolded for ten minutes and will be a guide for ten minutes. Suggest some tasks to accomplish while blindfolded: (1) drink from a water fountain; (2) find a certain room; (3) make a phone call; (4) walk downstairs. (It might be a good idea to brainstorm possible tasks the day before the walk and photocopy a list that you want them to complete.) When students return, have them write a journal entry based on their reactions. Which tasks were harder or easier than they thought? Did their other senses become more alert? Even the most withdrawn students seem to enjoy this activity.

Chapter 4 SENSATION AND PERCEPTION

put it up on the wall, and call it a "square." Tilt your head and view it. It is still a square. Move your head around some more. It is still a square. Now, cut out the same basic square and call it a "diamond" before you put it up on the wall with one corner at the top. Tilt your head to the point where it actually looks like a "square." Is it? No, it remains a diamond in your mind.

In these examples, what started out as light energy coming into your eyes and going from there to the brain has been given a meaning not contained in the actual source of the light energy.

In this chapter, we will analyze some of our most incredible abilities: (1) **sensation**—the process of receiving information from the environment—and (2) **perception**—assembling and organizing sensory information to make it meaningful. These two processes actually go together and are intermixed. To make it easier to learn about them, however, we will divide the chapter into two sections, starting with sensation.

sensation

The process of receiving information from the environment.

perception

The process of assembling and organizing sensory information to make it meaningful.

SENSATION

In this section, we will look at the workings of each of the five human senses—vision, hearing, touch, smell, and taste.

Vision

Vision dominates the human senses. We always believe what we see first, and only secondarily do we accept information from taste, smell, hearing, or feeling. Thus, if you are brave enough to eat a green-colored steak, it will taste funny to you even if it has only been colored by a tasteless food dye. Despite the fact that your sense of smell says it is all right, that will make no difference in how it tastes.

Light   Light movement is based on the same principle as snapping a whip. In a whip snap, the energy starts at the wrist and is sent in the shape of a wave down to the end of the whip. Depending on how hard the whip is snapped, the waves can vary from long and slow to short and fast. Light starts out from the sun (or a light bulb) as **white light;** color is seen only after the waves of white light hit objects and bounce back to us at different speeds. There really is no such thing as "color": we simply give different light wavelengths certain names (see Figure 4.1). "Color" is seen because the eyes have different receptors for different wavelengths. Some speeds (such as that of ultraviolet light waves) are too slow for our eyes to be able to see the light, but these light waves can be used by other creatures: the bee seeks out flowers using ultraviolet light waves, for example. The

white light

Light as it originates from the sun or a bulb before it is broken into different frequencies.

FYI   Scientists are working on a system of artificial sight that might one day help the blind. Tiny electrodes placed in the occipital lobe pick up signals from miniature cameras attached to eyeglasses. The signals stimulate various parts of the occipital lobe so that a pattern is formed. If artificial devices are successful, it will be critical to offer them to blind newborns so that the occipital lobe develops properly. Experience changes the wiring of the brain, and these artificial devices will provide needed practice to the occipital lobe in processing images.

DEMONSTRATION

You can have fun distorting vision with a pair of goggles and two right-angle prisms. Simply cut a hole for each prism in the goggles and secure the prisms with duct tape. Blacken out the rest of the goggles so the volunteer can see only through the prisms. Depending on how you insert the prisms, the volunteer will either see everything upside down or with left and right reversed. Play catch with the volunteer, tell him to pick up a pen, and so on to show how quickly the brain adapts to the topsy-turvy messages it is receiving.

Teaching Hint

Make sure to return to this chart of the visible spectrum (Figure 4.1) during ensuing discussions on color vision. For example, the student text mentions that many fire trucks today are yellowish green—which is right in the middle of the spectrum and relatively easier to see. The eye cannot see the long waves at the far left or the short waves at the far right.

Unit 2 BRAIN, BODY, AND AWARENESS

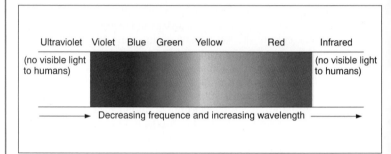

▲ *Figure 4.1   Energy waves arranged by frequency and wavelength.*

waves that are too fast for us to see (such as infrared light waves) are used by snakes to see at night.

The key to color, then, is white light waves hitting various objects in the environment and bouncing off at different wavelengths, which in turn hit receptors in our eyes. A good analogy is what happens if a shotgun is fired at the side of a hill: Some of the pellets hit dirt and are absorbed. Some hit leaves and are deflected. Some hit rock or other material and come back at us at different speeds. If these last pellets were light waves, they would be the ones we use for vision. Their speed of movement will vary depending on the texture and solidity of what they hit. For instance, snowflakes are built like crystals, so they have many flat surfaces. Sunlight, which is white, hits the slick flat surfaces of the flakes and bounces off without breaking up, so we see the snowflakes as white. In the same way, a polished wood surface gives out almost-white streaks where the bright light hits the glossy spots (directly reflected light), but if the end of a board is broken off, we can see a number of different colors. The light hitting the broken board breaks into different wavelengths, depending on which part of the board the light hits and how flat each part is. Water molecules are very strangely shaped and complex. Because of this, they absorb (remove from our vision) the energy at the red end of Figure 4.1, which would be the yellow and red light waves. This leaves two sets of rays that bounce back from water: green or blue. And this is why bodies of water look green or blue to us (Nassau, 1980).

Structure of the Eye   Figure 4.2 shows a top view of the eye if the eye were cut in half and the top taken off. The **cornea** (KOR-nee-ah) is a clear outer covering, behind which is a fluid. If you look at your eyes in a mirror, they seem shiny because you are seeing a reflection from the fluid behind the cornea. Next comes the portion of the eyes that lovers focus on. It is called the **iris** (EYE-ris) and is actually a colored circular muscle that opens and closes into larger or smaller circles in order to control the amount of light getting into the eye. To see it in operation, face a mirror, cover one eye, and turn on the light.

cornea

The clear outer covering of the eye, behind which is a fluid.

iris

A colored circular muscle that opens and closes, forming larger and smaller circles to control the amount of light getting into the eye.

DEMONSTRATION

Turn off the lights and ask students, "What's happening to the size of your pupils?" (The iris is trying to let in more light, and the pupil is getting wider.) Have students pair up before turning on the light again to view how the partner's pupils appear to get smaller as the room brightens. When the iris is open wide (or expands), the pupil appears about 15 times larger than when the iris contracts.

Chapter 4 SENSATION AND PERCEPTION

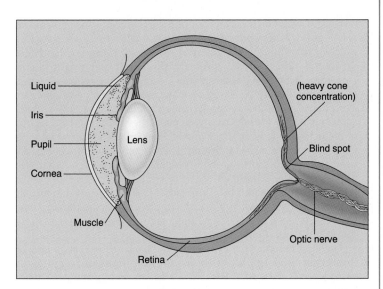

▲ *Figure 4.2* *Cross section of the eye as seen from the top.*

Stand so that the light will hit the covered eye when you remove your hand. Remove your hand, and watch how the iris, which had opened because it was dark behind your hand, quickly closes to a very small circle. When you leave a movie matinee, your irises are wide open to catch the limited light in the darkened theater; as you walk out into the sun, the light seems blinding at first because the irises aren't able to close fast enough; they let in too much light to too many receptors.

The **lens** of your eye is very much like a camera lens; it helps you to focus the objects you see onto the back of the eye where there are receptors. If the lens is not shaped correctly, the image coming in will either overshoot or fall short of the receptors at the back of the eye, and this causes images to blur. Eyeglasses are designed to change the angle at which the light hits the lens, causing the incoming light waves to land properly on the receptors. The lens automatically adjusts to whatever object we want to see. As the muscles controlling the lens make the adjustment, they give the brain information about how much they have moved, and this is one way we learn to judge how far away from us an object is.

What is the black circle in the middle of your eye? Nothing. The **pupil**, as you can see in Figure 4.2, is just an opening that changes size as the iris muscles move to cover and uncover the lens. Since it is dark inside your eye, the opening of the pupil looks black, but if you flash a light inside, the colors coming back through the pupil can vary across the whole range, depending on how the light is bent and what it hits in there.

lens

The part of the eye that focuses an object on the back of the eye.

pupil

The opening in the eye.

Critical Thinking

Ask students why they think we are much more likely to need glasses as we get older. Which part of the eye needs adjustment? As we age, the lens becomes more brittle and less flexible, and we cannot focus on near objects as well, a condition known as presbyopia (pres-be-O-pea-ah). You probably have several students who can describe their lens problems.

DEMONSTRATION

Have a volunteer stand in front of the room staring at a spot in the back. Stand a few feet to the side and a little behind the volunteer. Hold a colored sheet of paper at about eye level, at arm's length, and slowly inch toward the back of the room, gradually appearing in the volunteer's peripheral vision. When the volunteer notices the paper, she should say, "Stop." Still staring at the spot ahead of her, she should guess the color. The guesses are usually wrong because the image of the paper is falling on the sides of the eyeballs, and the cones aren't allowed much chance to participate. After a wrong guess, continue moving in the same direction until the cones can help. Try different colors to see if this makes a difference.

Teaching Hint

To facilitate student recall, you can compare the eye to a camera. Both use a lens to focus. The camera's aperture adjusts the diaphragm inside that determines how much light spills into the camera—which is similar to the function of the iris. The camera's film could be compared to the retina where images are processed.

Unit 2 BRAIN, BODY, AND AWARENESS

retina

The back of the eye, which contains millions of receptors for light.

blind spot

The portion of the retina through which the optic nerve exits and where there are no receptors for light waves.

Psychological factors can control the iris muscles and thus the size of the pupil. The pupils of our eyes get smaller if we see something unpleasant; they get larger if we see something we really like (Millodot, 1982). Those who learn this think they might be onto something. Since the pupils enlarge if someone likes you a lot, checking out pupils may be a way to make sure. In fact, years and years ago about the only way most women could survive was to marry someone. If they found a desirable male, they would put a few drops of medicine made from a poisonous plant called *belladonna* into their eyes, causing the pupils to widen. The women couldn't see very well until it wore off, but long before science, nature knew what wide pupils meant, and the men began to fall in love, not quite knowing why. *Belladonna* means "beautiful lady." Lest you go off thinking this is foolproof, best to tell you that the pupils open up all the way when someone is *afraid* also, because this makes it possible to explore the threat in the environment better.

The light entering the eye gets to the back of the eyeball and hits the **retina** (RET-in-ah). Millions upon millions of receptors are embedded in the retina. We will discuss them in a moment. Before leaving the overall structure of the eyeball, note in Figures 4.2 and 4.3 that there is a place where all the nerve cells leave the eye in what's called the optic nerve. Retinal receptors are to the right and left of this point, but there are none where this nerve bundle leaves. This is called the **blind spot.** We can't see anything when light waves hit that point. Still, the eyes dart back and forth so rapidly that we normally never notice it. If you want to find your blind spot, use Figure 4.4.

Receptors in the Retina Go outside as twilight approaches. Take a chair, a blue object, and a red object (or go where there are some blue and some red flowers). Sit in the chair, put the objects down,

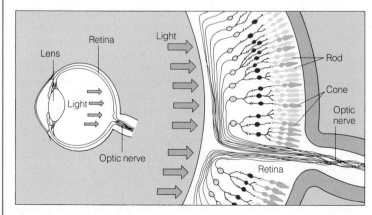

▲ *Figure 4.3* *Rods and cones transmitting impulses through the optic nerve.*

Change the procedure slightly to show how we can see slightly behind us. Once the volunteer says, "Stop," walk directly toward the volunteer and bring the paper to her head. If you walk straight, the paper will be slightly behind her eyeballs. Since the cornea is rounded, it serves as a

sort of lens that allows us to see things slightly behind us. If students don't believe you, have them hold the paper themselves at arm's length, stop when they see the paper, then have them bring the paper straight toward their heads.

▲ *Figure 4.4 Finding the blind spot. (a) With your right eye closed, stare at the upper right cross. Hold the book about one foot away from you and slowly move it back and forth. You should be able to find the position that causes the black spot to disappear. (b) Repeat this process, but stare instead at the lower cross. When the white space falls on the blind spot, the black line will appear to be continuous because your brain will fill in details for the place it can't find.*

and watch them as darkness approaches. The red objects will soon turn black and disappear, but the blue objects will not turn black until it is almost completely dark outside.

What you are experiencing is the fact that the retina is made up of two different kinds of receptors. The first type of receptor is called a **rod** because it is shaped like one (see photograph at right). The second is called a **cone** because that's the shape it has. Rods are very sensitive to the violet-purple range of wavelengths, but we will only "see" black and white with them because they have no color chemicals in them. There are about 100 million rods in the retina, and they are used for night vision because they respond very well to low levels of light. Since the rods are turning on as it darkens, they are keeping the blue objects visible. The cones are shutting off, so the red objects disappear. Thus, cones are used for color and daylight vision and respond best to wavelengths in the red range. They shut off at night. You can see color on a highway when you are driving through the city at night because the light level is almost as high as during the day. But if you watch carefully when you turn away from a populated area and drive down a dimly lit street, you will notice that the images you see are no longer sharp except where the headlights hit. This is because the cones, which provide sharpness of vision, have shut off, and rods by themselves only provide a rough outline of objects. Rods are very heavily packed into the sides of the retina. If you are trying to see something in a dark area, look *away* from where you think it is, and the rods on the sides of your retina will pick up its shape. Or have a friend sneak up on you in the dark and notice how you can spot him or her if you are approached from the side, but you have trouble if he or she moves toward the center of your line of sight, since the cones that have shut off are located mostly in the center of each retina. In daylight, on the other hand, the rods shut off, so when you enter a darkened movie theater, you can't see anything at first, since the cones can't handle darkness.

Chapter 4 SENSATION AND PERCEPTION

rod

A visual receptor most sensitive to the violet-purple wavelengths; very sensitive for night vision; "sees" only black and white.

cone

A visual receptor that responds during daylight; receives color.

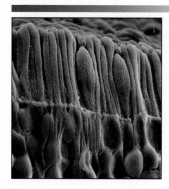

▲ *The visual receptors, rods and cones, are named for their shapes. The rods are the long, thin cells on the left; the cones are the roundish cells in between the rods.*

97

DISCUSS THE PHOTO

You can see here how these cells got their names.

Journal Topic

"Imagine that one of your senses is dramatically improved for a day. Describe some of the highlights of this day." These entries are fun to read aloud.

CHAPTER PROJECT

After showing students numerous illustrations of illusions and other perceptual principles and discussing them, have students create their own drawings. To generate interest, you may need to obtain a set of supplemental illusions or other illustrations from a science or social studies catalog. (See Teacher Resources for addresses.) You might want to discuss the project with an art teacher and invite him or her to talk to the class about illusions in art. (By the way, student photographers might be able to capture some perceptual principles on film!)

Unit 2 BRAIN, BODY, AND AWARENESS

Fire departments take rods and cones very seriously. Fire trucks used to be red. Today only a few are. Too many accidents occurred at twilight because automobile drivers couldn't see the red trucks very well. Most trucks today are a yellowish green, which is right in the middle of the color chart (Figure 4.1) between violet on one end and red on the other. This compromise coloring provides the best visibility for both day and night.

Color Vision   This is how *color vision* works: all the colors we see are red, blue, green, or a mixture of these three. You can understand the principle of mixture if you take red, blue, and green spotlights and shine them on a white wall. By mixing the lights, you will get every color possible. Throughout the center part of the retina are millions of cones connected together. Some receive red, some green, and

Color Vision.

 IN FOCUS   All the colors in the spectrum are absorbed by a black object.

Teaching Hint

Have the students look at someone in class who is wearing a black shirt or jacket. Is it *all* black? We're inclined to say yes because of color constancy (presented later in the chapter), but look closely. Because of the way light bounces off the material, you can actually see more than black—maybe even white.

IN FOCUS   **Color Vision**

A prism would show that white light is really made up of different colors. "Roy G. Biv" will help you remember the seven colors that comprise white light.

All the colors in the spectrum are absorbed by the apple, except for the red, which bounces off and hits receptors in the eyes.

Can you explain what happens when we see the color black?

DEMONSTRATION

Bring in a large flash unit from a camera. Tape a small shape cut from construction paper onto the flash, point it at four or five students at a time from a few feet away, and turn on the flash. If your volunteers close their eyes after the flash, they should see an afterimage of the shape—actually, since both eyes see the shape, two images may appear. If so, repeat the demonstration and have volunteers use only one eye.

DEMONSTRATION

There's nothing magical about the flag afterimage (see Figure 4.5 on page 100). You can design your own with colored construction paper. Paste various shapes or configurations onto whole sheets and follow the same instructions as in Figure 4.5. This could be a good extra credit project.

Chapter 4 SENSATION AND PERCEPTION

some blue wavelengths. Depending on the texture of the objects we are viewing, light from each part of the object will bounce back at different wavelengths, and the brain will mix these wavelengths, making the object appear a specific color (Normann et al., 1984).

Color Defects   A number of people have a defect called **color blindness,** the inability to see certain colors. The most common form of this problem is found in those who can see color only in the yellow-blue range and cannot see red or green color. The receptors *do* respond to the light wave energy, but they *don't* see it as "colored." About 8 percent of males have this inherited defect, only 0.5 percent of females. For these people, the red or green cone system does not work (in terms of seeing color). They still have a third color-receiving (cone) system that responds in the yellow-blue area (Mollon, 1982). In all other respects, their vision is completely normal.

Truly "color-blind" people are very rare. They respond to light waves only with rods. Even a moderately bright light can be very painful for them because all the rods are responding in unison to white light, something they are not designed to do.

People sometimes make things up out of nowhere and pass on the misinformation from one generation to another. You may hear that dogs and cats see everything in gray because they have no color vision. This is simply not true. Both animals have very elaborate rod and cone systems, just as we do (Muntz, 1981; McFarland, 1981). And you will hear that bulls go crazy when they see a red matador's cape. Bulls and cows have full color vision, but the idea of red inflaming them doesn't make sense. The bull is responding to movement, not color. If you don't believe us, try getting in a ring with one and waving a black or green or purple or whatever cape and see what happens!

Afterimages   All physical systems strive to stay in balance. If we are cold, we shiver to increase circulation; if hot, we sweat to cool down. The same principle applies to the cone network of the eyes. If you stare at a colored object for a minute or so, the chemicals in the cones for the colors you are seeing will be partially used up as changes in the chemicals cause electrical impulses (signals to the brain). The chemicals for all the colors you are *not* seeing are still intact. No message has been sent to the brain for them because you haven't seen these colors. As a result, the cone system is not in balance. If you look away from the object and stare at a white piece of paper, you will see the object in opposite colors. This **afterimage** results from the remaining "unused" cones firing so that all the cones can restore themselves to equal chemical levels at the same time. The same process will occur if you stare at a television for a while and then look at the wall.

You do not see these afterimages during normal viewing because you keep replacing one image with another, and each image fires a

color blindness

Inability to perceive certain colors, such as red and green.

afterimage

The firing of the cones not used after viewing something steadily in order to bring the visual system back in balance.

Journal Topic

"Imagine that you have lost the use of one of your senses. Describe a typical day for you, one year after this loss."

Comprehension Check

What would happen if the rods in your retina didn't work? *(You could not see well at night.)* If the cones didn't work? *(You could not see in color and your vision would not be sharp.)*

DEMONSTRATION

This activity will demonstrate how the eyes and ears help us maintain equilibrium or balance. Stack three or four books on the floor and balance a two-foot by six-foot board, about two feet in length, on the books. Have a volunteer step on the middle of the board and hand this person a blind-fold to put on. Surrounding the volunteer will be four people: you can stand behind as a spotter; two lifters will be at the sides; and one squatter will be in front. Tell the volunteer to place his or her hands on the shoulders of the person in front, who starts out standing. On your cue, the lifters will lift the board, raising the volunteer as high as they can. At least; that's what you'll say. Actually, the lifters will only raise the volunteer an inch or two. In the meantime, the person in front will slowly squat. When you say, "Down," the squatter will slowly stand and the lifters will bring the board

Points to Stress

When you stare at the U.S. flag in Fig. 4.5 and later see a red, white, and blue afterimage, your brain has little choice in the matter. It "sees" what it sees. Contrast this with how the brain processes this backward sentence: *.rat eht saw tac ehT.* In this case, the brain has a choice but usually does not accurately process what the eyes have seen. In the first case, the brain is fooled because of sensory changes. In the second case, the brain is fooled because of perceptual factors.

DISCUSS THE PHOTO

Have students look at these figures after discussing rods and cones.

FYI It seems that the temporal lobe operates like a keyboard in a way. As pitch increases, the temporal lobe responds in an orderly fashion, with higher-pitched notes processed at the bottom, lower-pitched notes at the top.

100

Unit 2 BRAIN, BODY, AND AWARENESS

▲   *Rod and cone behavior is illustrated by these two fire engines. Note that in daylight or bright artificial light, both engines are visible. Now move this picture to very dim light, and stare at the center of the red engine for about four minutes. Because the image is falling on the center portion of the retina, which is mostly cones, the red engine will disappear, while the blue engine (rods in dim light) can still be seen.*

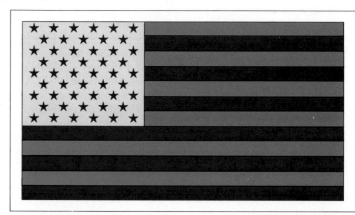

▶ *Figure 4.5   To prove the after-image for yourself, take a sheet of white typing paper, or other flat white surface, and put it aside. Focus your eyes on the last star of the flag (the one in the lower right-hand corner), and stare at it for one minute. Now quickly move your eyes to the white paper, and you should see the flag appear in red, white, and blue.*

audition

The sense of hearing.

100

different set of cones. Figure 4.5 gives you the chance to see the after-image principle in action.

Hearing

In hearing, or **audition** (aw-DISH-un), the energy form is sound waves, which have a much slower range of speeds but move in roughly the same fashion as do light waves. Many animals use sound more than humans do. The dolphin, for instance, sends out clicks, and the echoes that come back tell it the size and shape of what the sound waves have hit—whether the object is food, something dangerous, or a place of refuge (Fobes & Smock, 1981). Bats are

down. Let the volunteer step down and remove the blindfold. Ask the student "How high did you go?"

Get it? This is an effective illusion because the eyes are not allowed to help while the ears help too much. The fluid in the semicircular canals of the ears move hairlike filaments that

relay messages to the brain. In this case, since the subject has to bend forward to stay with the squatter, the message is that the body is tipping. The brain assembles these bits of information and tries to make sense of the situation.

---

amazing. They can find extremely small flying insects by bouncing sound waves off them. But nature has given their favorite food, the bat moth, a built-in detector for the high-frequency sounds emitted by the bats, so the moths can try to escape.

Characteristics of Sound   Sounds vary in terms of **pitch**, which means how high or low the sound is. Most men have a lower pitch to their voices than women do. Another characteristic of sound is something called **timbre** (TAM-ber), which refers to the complexity of a tone. The different sounds made by a piano, a flute, and a guitar are caused by variations in timbre.

Sounds also vary in **intensity**—how loud they are. Intensity is measured in **decibels** (DES-uh-bells). When sounds reach a decibel level beyond 130 (see Figure 4.6), they can become painful.

pitch

How high or low a sound is.

timbre

The complexity of a sound.

intensity

How loud a sound is.

decibels

A measure of how loud a sound is (its intensity).

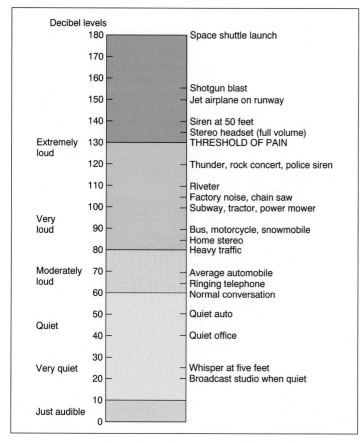

▲ *Figure 4.6 Decibel chart showing sound levels of various objects and events.*

Teaching Hint

To help students remember the characteristics of sound, try the following: Yell "intensity" loudly, and then say "intensity," softly. Vary the pitch of your voice and say "pitch; pitch." Have each student say "timbre," and notice the subtle differences in tone; you may have a few talented students who can create different complexities with their voices. Or you may need to bring in a couple of instruments to demonstrate timbre.

Comprehension Check

Your punsters may like these. Expect a few groans.

(1) What does a complex voice say when cutting down a tree? *(timbre)*

(2) What does a baseball catcher with a screechy voice say to the person on the mound? *(pitch)*

(3) A young worker asks his loud bosses where their ten kids live. Where? *(in ten cities—intensities)*

ENRICHMENT

If you can't get a speaker to visit class, have a few students research what it is like to be deaf or blind. Have the class brainstorm questions they would like to have answered by this research; this should provide your researchers with some focus. Remind them that research does not always mean reading books. Ask them to use the phone to gather information, too.

EXPERIMENT

This activity requires some preparation, but you might be able to get a student to help. Researchers have discovered that for most people, one ear is dominant. To show this, tape one word on the left track of a tape, another word on the right track. Subjects (wearing headphones)

Discussion

Ask students what they think it would be like to be deaf or blind. What tasks would be most difficult? What would they miss seeing or hearing the most? (Consider inviting a hearing- or visually impaired person to class.)

Unit 2 BRAIN, BODY, AND AWARENESS

eardrum

A piece of skin stretched over the entrance to the ear; vibrates to sound.

cochlea

A snail-shaped part of the ear, filled with fluid and small hairs that vibrate to incoming sound.

hair cells

Receptor cells for hearing and sense of smell; found in the cochlea and the nasal cavity; see *cilia*.

Continuous loud noises will actually impair hearing by killing receptor cells in the ear (Bohne, 1985). Sleep is disturbed by noise as high as that of a refrigerator (70) but is helped by a continuous sound of roughly 50 decibels (Gilbert, 1985).

Structure of the Ear   "My, what big ears you have, Grandma!" said Little Red Riding Hood.

"The better to hear you with, my dear."

Actually, the wolf was wrong. Ear size makes no difference, but the shape does have a purpose. The cupped design of the outer ear catches the sound waves and funnels them in toward the **eardrum** (see Figure 4.7), a piece of skin stretched tightly—just like a drum—over the entrance to the rest of the ear. When the sound waves hit the drum, it vibrates. This vibration causes a small bone to vibrate. This bone is attached to another bone and acts like a lever, causing it, in turn, to vibrate. A third bone is attached to a snail-shaped unit called the **cochlea** (KOKE-lee-ah). The cochlea is filled with fluid and small hairs, called *cilia*.

The key to hearing is the existence of these 20,000 **hair cells,** which we gradually lose as we age. They are lined up in the cochlea and "tuned" to receive different frequencies, just as the strings are tuned on a musical instrument. The hair cells will respond to movement of only a *trillionth* of an inch, about the space between two atoms. As this movement occurs, it causes a flow of electrical particles in the nerve cell connected to each hair (Loeb, 1985). The electrical impulse

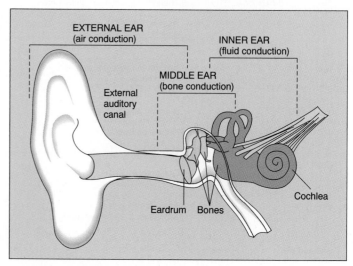

▲ *Figure 4.7*   *Structure of the ear ("conduction" means movement of sound by air, fluid, or bone vibration).*

should be presented with the words simultaneously to see which is comprehensible (which may have something to do with attention or the personality of the subject as well; you may want to compare students with teachers). Instead of words, you can also tape high and low tones on each track to see which ear hears which tone. Psychologist Diana Deutsch has found that ear dominance may be related to handedness. The results you find may vary, depending on the quality of the tape, but see if you and your students can draw any conclusions.

goes through the **auditory nerve** to the brain where the sound pattern is interpreted. How strong a sound is and when it arrives at one ear is contrasted by the brain with the strength and arrival time at the other ear, and the difference between them helps us locate where the sound is coming from.

Sound can have strong psychological implications. For instance, some cells specialize—that is, certain cells recognize specific important sound patterns. Thus, a bird mother makes sounds to her offspring inside the egg so she can be recognized later; the infant bird will then follow the mother's sounds as it moves about. Newborn human babies relax when hearing tapes of the mother's voice or heartbeat, so this must be a human phenomenon also.

Cutaneous Senses

Our skin contains three types of **cutaneous** (cue-TAIN-ee-us), or touch, **receptors.** Each sends a message to the brain where it is recorded. The first one records pressure. It can register a pinprick, a bruise, or even an ant crawling up the arm. The second kind responds only to changes in temperature. The third kind remains active continuously to record an injury or poison. These last receptors cause the painful feelings we all dread, because they fire for hours and hours after a burn or major cut. Figure 4.8 shows some of the cutaneous receptors.

Chapter 4 SENSATION AND PERCEPTION

auditory nerve

Bundle of nerves carrying sound to the brain.

cutaneous receptors

The nerve receptors in the skin that respond to pressure, temperature, or pain.

TEACHING MASTER 4-2

Three Kinds of Cutaneous Receptors. This handout offers students a visual of the three kinds of cutaneous receptors.

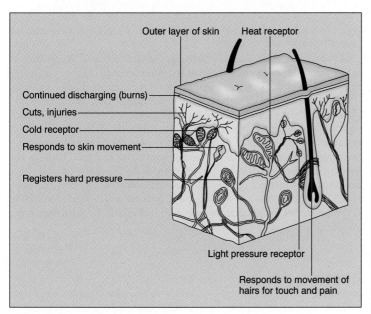

Outer layer of skin   Heat receptor

Continued discharging (burns)
Cuts, injuries
Cold receptor
Responds to skin movement

Registers hard pressure

Light pressure receptor

Responds to movement of hairs for touch and pain

▲ *Figure 4.8 The skin senses include pressure, pain, cold, and warmth. This drawing shows the different forms the skin receptors can take.*

ENRICHMENT

Psychologist Harry Harlow taught us about the power of touch by separating newborn monkeys from their mothers and depriving them of what he called "contact comfort." Have students find out the effects of this research and other research on touch. Also, have them discuss the potential practical applications of this research and the ethics of experimenting with animals in this way.

DEMONSTRATION

You can easily demonstrate how appearance affects taste by coloring various foods and liquids. Half of your subjects see before tasting; the other half is blindfolded. Then they rank how much they like the food.

Comprehension Check

Identify the sense associated with each of the following; auditory nerve *(hearing)*; cutaneous receptors *(touch)*; olfactory bulbs *(smell)*.

---

olfaction

The sense of smell.

cilia

Tiny hairs (that receive odor molecules). Some act as receptors in the nose.

olfactory bulbs

Units that receive odor molecules and communicate their nature to the brain.

pheromones

Odor chemicals that communicate a message.

taste receptors

Chemical receptors on the tongue that decode molecules of food or drink to identify them.

Smell

The sense of smell, or **olfaction** (ol-FAC-shun), depends on the ability to detect chemicals, and once again the human comes in a poor second to most animals. If you are upwind of a deer, it will take off before you ever see it because it is sensitive to your smell (no matter how often you bathe). A shark uses your odor molecules in the water to decide if you are worth eating.

Smell is the most animal-like of the human senses. Odors are very hard to define using words, but when an odor is associated with an emotional event, we never forget it. If we ever happen to smell that odor again, it will recreate a very strong emotional memory (Engen, 1987).

Mechanisms of Smell Inside the nasal cavity (Figure 4.9), embedded in a layer of mucus, are microscopic hairs, or **cilia.** They are similar in structure to the cilia found in the ear. However, they have a different function. These cilia collect molecules of odor. When the odor molecules attach themselves to the hairs, an electrical signal is sent to the **olfactory bulbs,** which generate a "code" that is sent to the brain for interpretation (Rivlin & Gravelle, 1984).

Smell Communication The most critical use for our sense of smell is information about food heading toward the mouth. In fact, smell is more important in eating than is taste. If you don't believe this, try holding your nose when you eat. The food will have almost no taste at all.

Animals use smell to communicate sexual interest. An animal's body sends out odor chemicals, called **pheromones** (FER-uh-moans), in order to reach a possible partner. Whether humans have such sexual communication is not clear. A few studies find some possible connection. Since almost all creatures communicate this way, it seems probable that the human would, too. This is difficult to study because human sexual interest is a complex mixture of things like clothing, perfumes, fads about body shape, and so forth. There is no evidence, however, that "musk" perfumes do anything to make the male more attractive. As a matter of fact, musk works best in cockroach courtship (true). Even so, there actually *was* a study in which the researchers found that people could tell males from females by smelling sweaty T-shirts (Russell et al., 1977).

Taste

Taste receptors operate by chemical communication. The major receivers are the little red spots (because of their rich blood supply) on the tongue. These are called "taste buds" because they resemble

DEMONSTRATION

To show that some parts of the body are more sensitive to touch than others, bring in toothpicks to conduct a simplified test of cutaneous two-point threshold. Tape two toothpicks together, but keep them slightly separated. Find a volunteer who is willing to be blindfolded and poked lightly by these toothpicks and by a single toothpick. The blindfolded volunteer reports whether you are applying one or two points. Try this on various parts of the body, and tally correct answers to assess sensitivity.

DEMONSTRATION

Obtain a variety of fluids that taste sweet, sour, salty, and bitter. With a dropper, place the various fluids on different parts of a volunteer's tongue. In this way, you can map out which part of the tongue is most sensitive to which taste.

Chapter 4 SENSATION AND PERCEPTION

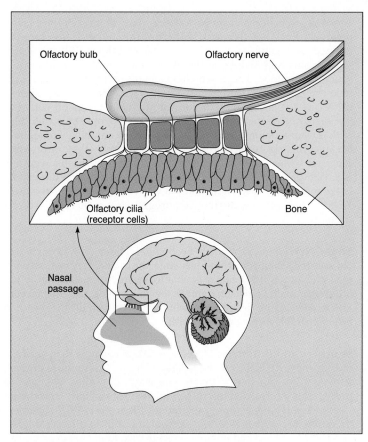

▲ *Figure 4.9* *Mechanisms of smell.*

flowers (see Figure 4.10). The mucus and saliva in the mouth cleanse the buds, but it takes a while to do so, as you may have learned on Thanksgiving if you have ever eaten some cranberries and followed them by a drink of milk—a horrible combination. There are four types of receptors—*salt, sweet, sour, bitter* (see Figure 4.11 on the next page). These combine sensations much as the cones in vision do to give us the subtle differences between, say, barbecued ribs and sweet-and-sour pork (Rivlin & Gravelle, 1984).

Salt Needs   Salt is necessary for survival. It operates nerve cells, helps keep body chemistry in balance, and is used for muscle contraction. A very low-salt diet can make you dizzy and sick. In healthy people, excess salt is quickly and efficiently removed from the body in the urine with no ill effects (Beauchamp, 1987). While some uses of salt may be learned (such as salting some cooked foods), the evi-

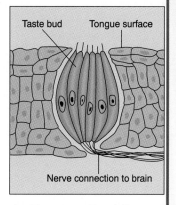

▲ *Figure 4.10* *Taste buds.*

105

DEMONSTRATION

Bring in a dropper and a variety of liquids—ammonia, perfume—and slowly expose students to the liquids. Release one drop onto a dish, wait about 30 seconds, release another, and so on. See how long it takes them to report the smell. This should demonstrate how well we smell. Ask them if they still smell anything after five minutes to show how quickly we adapt. If they say no, bring in someone from outside. Could this adaptation process have anything to do with how we usually don't know that we have bad breath?

You can also use water and simply suggest it's ammonia to demonstrate the power of placebos or suggestions. Or you can have confederates raise their hands, then discuss the power of the pressure to conform. *(Reminder: Handle ammonia with care. It is a strong chemical.)*

Unit 2 BRAIN, BODY, AND AWARENESS

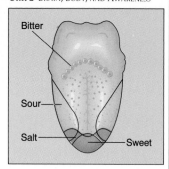

Bitter

Sour

Salt

Sweet

▲ *Figure 4.11* *Areas of the four types of taste receptors on the tongue.*

Discussion

Ask students if they would drink gray milk. Or would they actually eat green eggs and ham? Discuss how the appearance of food often affects our perception of taste. Grocers certainly know this.

dence suggests humans are born with a fixed sequence of need. The newborn does not like salt. But from the age of a few months onward, youngsters want salt. Until late childhood, this interest in salt remains high, while on the other hand, children dislike spicy, sour, or bitter food. This is why items on the children's menu at fast-food chains taste like cardboard with salt on it. That's all they want to eat (Cowart, 1981). The desire for salt gradually tapers off with age. But then, much later in life, it reappears. Old people love chili dogs with mustard, onions, pepper, salt, and almost anything else around, because their taste receptors are not as sharp as they once were. Pregnant women seek an extra supply of salt for the fetus; you will hear of a pregnant woman suddenly needing a pickle in the middle of the night. One scientist mentions a woman who ate approximately 1,500 salted herring during her pregnancy—probably a record (Denton, 1983).

Sugar Needs   Most animals need sugar. Human newborns a day old can tell when something has sugar in it, and they will actively seek it (Cowart, 1981). Sugar is vital for energy to run the body. Too little sugar makes a person tremble, feel faint, and causes mental confusion. Hence, the desire for something sweet is built in, even if it presents problems for those on a diet.

Sourness and Bitterness Detectors   We have more than one type of bitterness detector on the tongue. These detectors are critical. Almost all poisons are bitter in one way or another. We need to process this information instantly while we are still only considering swallowing what was put in the mouth (Bartoshuk, 1978). Sourness detection also serves a protective function, but to a lesser degree. Food that has gone bad often has a sour taste to it. However, we can usually smell this problem before we put the food in our mouths. Bitter poisonous substances, on the other hand, frequently have no distinctive odor.

PERCEPTION

The truly remarkable thing about the world "out there" is how stable and organized it seems. You go to the parking lot and put the key into the right car. You don't try to put it into a Honda if you own a Buick. At the supermarket, you buy three small grapefruit if that's what you need. You don't come back with three very large lemons. You go to another room to get a certain book. If the book is sideways, upside down, lying on the floor, whatever, you don't decide it is not the same book. But in every one of those positions, the book looks entirely different to the eye. What amazing creatures we are!

COOPERATIVE LEARNING

This is a five-minute activity for the beginning of class. Break the class into small groups and read these instructions: "Your group is an independent advertising agency with extremely poor judgment. In your last campaign, you thought it would be a good idea to push gray milk. Your job now is to think of equally rotten ideas for other foods." The point is to show how appearance has an effect on our perception of taste.

Through a combination of inborn abilities and experience, we gradually are able to handle billions of bits of information correctly. We make the world make sense. This is *perception*. Perception is the process of assembling sensory information so that we can understand what the incoming energy means. Perception is always a matter of *interpretation* and *expectation*. Benjamin Franklin used to entertain his friends by hooking himself up to an electrical laboratory apparatus; then they all held hands, supposedly getting a wonderful sensation. Everyone laughed and thought it was delightful, but it was only a matter of suggestion (Oster, 1970).

Perceptual Constancies

Our world is always in motion. So are we, in relation to the world. Things change from one split second to another. The word *constancy* means holding steady. And this is what we must do to the world in order to maintain order and control, to make sense out of our environment.

Size Constancy   In the 1500s, Spanish explorers arrived at the Grand Canyon, the likes of which they had never seen before. According to their records, they stood atop the south rim and looked across at the other rim, in some places more than ten miles across. They looked down at the river and estimated its width to be six feet across. The Native Americans in the area knew better because they had been down to the bottom and had discovered that the river was about two miles wide (Hawgood, 1967). Thus, when the Native Americans stood on the rim of the canyon, they perceived a two-mile-wide river that looked smaller "because it was far away"; they were using what is called **size constancy,** the ability to retain the size of an object no matter where it is located. This skill is so important that it appears in an infant only a couple of weeks old.

It is possible, though, to trick the brain, and this allows you to see size constancy in operation: the average cigarette pack is about three and three-eighths inches high. In a laboratory, a specially constructed cigarette pack only two inches high is put in front of people. They are asked to judge how far it is from them. They will claim the pack is much farther away than it is. Why? Because they know its usual size and it appears smaller. Hence, their brains tell them that it *must* be more distant—things get smaller only with more distance.

Color Constancy   As discussed, we have three different color receptors (for red, blue, and green) that blend varying energy waves together to give an object color. But notice that if you take an apple from a bright kitchen into a darkened room with just the TV on, the

▲ *The river winding below in the Grand Canyon is the one the Spanish thought was six feet wide.*

size constancy

The ability to retain the size of an object regardless of where it is located.

DISCUSS THE PHOTO

The Spanish *did* use size constancy: they estimated that a river that *appears* quite small is actually six feet wide. They just didn't use size constancy well—which should demonstrate that size constancy is influenced by experience.

INTERDISCIPLINARY PROJECT

Language arts/Sense poems.
Break the class into small groups. Have each group pick an emotion and describe what the emotion smells like, tastes like, and so on. For example: "Confusion smells like a cologne counter. Confusion tastes like a glass of orange juice after brushing your teeth." Encourage students to use concrete descriptions. Once they have listed several descriptions, have students arrange them into a poem. If you want to go a step further, groups can include illustrations and display the finished pieces around the room.

Size Constancy.

 We are born with the ability to use size constancy, but the environment certainly plays a role in developing this skill. (Psychologist Jean Piaget, though he didn't refer specifically to size constancy, demonstrated how size can easily fool children in the preoperational stage of development. See Chapter 10 for more on Piaget.)

Unit 2 BRAIN, BODY, AND AWARENESS

IN FOCUS   **Size Constancy**

If we stand on a railroad tie and look down the track, the railroad ties in the distance actually seem to get smaller. But because of size constancy, we're not fooled for a moment. The *eyes* record the railroad ties in the distance as tiny, but the *brain* STRETCHES them out to "normal" size.

Are we born with this size constancy ability? Does experience influence it?

DISCOVERY

Place two pieces of construction paper together and cut out eight squares. Sizes: two inches by two inches, three inches by three inches, and so on. Now you have two sets of eight squares. Number both sets from one to eight (smallest to biggest). Bring your class into the hallway, give one set of squares to a student, and send this student about 25 feet away. Randomly hold up a square but do not reveal the number. The lone student searches his squares for the identical one. The square in your hand certainly does not look the same size as the one in his hand, but the student should still do fairly well because of size constancy. Does practice help? Send both the student who has practiced and a new student 50 feet away. See who does better. (The no-practice subject should go first.) Later, ask the subjects if they used any cues to help them.

---

apple still seems exactly the same color. It hasn't turned darker. The light being reflected from the apple cannot be the same in the two locations. So how do we hold the color constant? The visual network works all by itself once we have decided what color something is. It has the ability to increase or decrease *mentally* the internal firing of visual receptors to equal what the brain tells it the color is (Mollon, 1982). This is called **color constancy,** but it only works—like the Grand Canyon example—when we already know what color something is.

Brightness Constancy   Possibly color constancy can be better understood after we look at **brightness constancy,** which follows roughly the same principles. Find a familiar black object. Look at it indoors, then take it outside on a very bright sunny day. The level of brightness reflected from the object is extremely high outside, yet it looks to be about the same color as it did inside, rather than "bright black." The brain causes the rods and cones to compensate for the brightness. If the object seems too bright to match our concept of "black," some of the visual nerve cells shut off.

To see this aspect of perception in action, look at Figure 4.12. We assume the light is hitting the object from the left side. This makes the right side darker, as it would be in real life. But if you cover the "shadow" at the lower right, the picture no longer makes sense in terms of a belief that light is coming from the left. It now looks like an open book, one side of which could be dark regardless of light direction. Further, since a book is printed, note that your visual system makes the "page" look much darker once you cover the shadow (Land, 1977; Beck, 1975).

color constancy

The ability to perceive an object as the same color regardless of the environment.

brightness constancy

By taking an average, the human visual network keeps brightness constant as an object is moved to various environments.

Critical Thinking

Ask students the following question: What kinds of factors will affect perception? (Students may mention motivation, attention, personal experiences, gender, genetic make-up, and so on. Have them offer examples.)

DISCUSS THE PHOTO

Students like brain teasers; see if any of them can draw one of their own, demonstrating any of the concepts discussed in this section of the chapter.

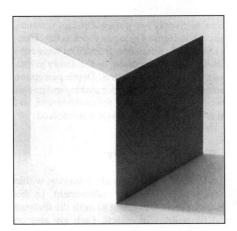

▲ *Figure 4.12*   *Depending on your assumptions regarding light direction, the brightness changes. See text.*

DEMONSTRATION

Each eye sees the world from slightly different angles, something called binocular disparity (see next page). Ask students if we can perceive depth with one eye. A few will blurt "no," but it's easy to convince them otherwise. Have them look at you with one eye when you're three feet away. Tell them to close both eyes. Move away from them another three feet. Have them open one eye again. They will have no difficulty judging that you are now farther away. Stress that we use several cues to perceive depth—binocular disparity being only one of them.

Teaching Hint

Another cue for depth perception is motion parallax, which means that close objects in motion seem to move a great distance, while far objects in motion seem to barely move. As a kid, you probably watched your finger jump by staring at it first with your left eye, then your right, then your left. Tell students to do this and then slowly move the finger away from them. As they do so, the finger will appear to move less and less—which is a cue for depth.

DISCUSS THE PHOTO

Refer students to Chapter 10 for other skills and reflexes that babies have from the beginning.

Unit 2 BRAIN, BODY, AND AWARENESS

space constancy

The ability to keep objects in the environment steady.

depth perception

The ability to see objects in space.

visual cliff

A large table with Plexiglas, used to demonstrate depth perception in small children.

Space Constancy The most common type of auto accident is the "rear-ender." Despite many warnings, people don't take "not following too closely" to heart—because they don't understand perception. We have to keep objects in the environment steady in order to survive. This is called **space constancy.** But we must allow some motion. There are two types of motion: *self-motion* and *object-motion*. We must choose between allowing ourselves to move in reference to the environment and allowing the environment to move in reference to us. If we allow both at one time, severe dizziness results. For example, we can focus on telephone poles as we move along in a car (object motion), or we can focus on ourselves and the inside of the car (self-motion), letting the poles blur. Usually when we drive, we are aware of our own movement. When that is the case, we must hold the cars in front of us steady in our minds. As a result, only a *major* change in the speed of the cars will be noticed. A small change, such as occurs during a normal stop, will not be perceived well (Probst et al., 1984). This is why auto manufacturers were forced to put a third brake-warning light at eye level starting with 1986 cars.

Depth Perception **Depth perception** is the ability to see objects "out there" in space. It is built into a baby from a very young age. This was shown by an experimenter who was on a picnic one day at the Grand Canyon. She wondered if her baby would crawl over the canyon rim or already "knew better." She sensibly decided not to try it at the canyon itself in case the baby failed to stop. So, in a laboratory, she constructed what is called the **visual cliff** experiment (Figure 4.13). This experiment uses a large table with retaining walls of wood

▲ *Figure 4.13* The "Visual Cliff." *The baby would like to crawl to the mother, but is not about to fall over a cliff to get to her.*

DEMONSTRATION

The pictures in Figure 4.14 will tend to look three-dimensional if you can get each eye to view each picture independently. One way is to cut out two holes in a piece of paper, one hole for each eye. Hold the paper close to your face and stare at the picture from about six inches away, or from wherever you can best focus. A better way to see three-dimensional is to order a set of stereopticons, model 707, from Taylor-Merchant Corp., 212 W. 35th St., New York, NY, 10001.

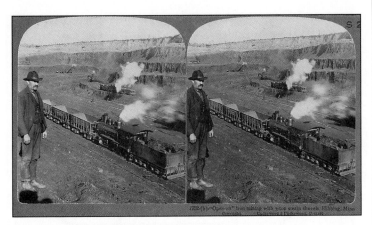

▲ *Figure 4.14* *Binocular stereoscopic pictures.*

on three sides. The fourth side is left open. A piece of heavy, clear Plexiglas covers the table and extends many feet beyond the open edge. To the baby's eyes, it looks as if anyone going beyond the end of the table will fall into space. Babies from six to 14 months old were placed on the table and enticed by rattles and goodies to leave the table and "fall" over the fake cliff. But the babies wouldn't go beyond the edge onto the Plexiglas (Gibson & Walk, 1960). This showed that humans have depth perception almost from the beginning.

Depth perception requires a number of brain skills. First, there is **binocular disparity** (di-SPAR-i-tee). There is a difference (disparity) between the images received by each of your eyes (binocular means "two eyes"). Hold your finger steady in front of your eyes; first close one eye, then the other, and notice how the finger shifts. This is the result of each eye seeing a different image. We have to bring these images together in our brains in order to see them correctly. In the process of doing so, we judge and "see" distance and depth (Poggio, 1984). See Figure 4.14.

Another cue to distance is called **visual texture.** "Texture" refers to how smooth or rough something appears to be—that is, how clear its details are. Note, in Figure 4.15 on the next page, that we gauge the distance of flowers in each row by how clearly we can see them. Since we can see the individual flowers at the bottom of the picture, we know they are close. As they become more distant, we see much less detail, and they appear "smooth," blending together, so we know these are "way out there." Others that we can't tell apart at all are "way, way out there."

Perceptual Organization   When given incomplete perceptual information, we tend to organize it so that it makes sense. We interpret things the way we think they *should* be, not in terms of how they

binocular disparity

The difference between the image provided by each eye. When the images are brought together in the brain, they provide a sense of depth.

visual texture

Depth perception based on how rough or smooth objects appear.

DISCUSS THE PHOTO

Ask students what problems a person may have if one eye is blind.

Comprehension Check

Name the property of perception utilized in each of the following examples: going back into a darkened movie theatre and spotting the purple jacket you left on your seat *(color constancy)*; knowing it is about three meters from your desk to the door *(depth perception)*; understanding an incomplete sentence *(closure)*; realizing that a plane up in the sky is really larger than any bird *(size constancy)*.

DEMONSTRATION

Teaching Master 4-3 Perceptual Set shows the classic old woman-young woman illustration, along with instructions for a simple student activity. Before handing this out, however, make a transparency and conduct the activity in class, following the instructions listed on the teaching master. Afterward, dis-cuss how expectations or *set* can influence perceptions. For example, when depressed, we tend to view the world from a distorted set: "No one likes me; life will never get better; I'm no good." Everything is viewed in absolutes and from a single perspective, and it's difficult to see the other side of the coin, just as it's difficult to see the young woman if we've been set up to see the old one. In other words, we become depressed or stay depressed in part because of our perceptions, our distorted thoughts. See Chapter 19 for a discussion on what cognitive therapists do to "fix" these thoughts.

Moving Cubes.

IN FOCUS   Texture; shadows; another cube in the distance—all these would add to the perception of depth.

DISCUSS THE PHOTO

Have students look at the floor near their feet to notice the texture. Have them gradually pan the floor with their eyes, shifting their gaze farther and farther. They should notice a distinct difference in texture.

112

Unit 2 BRAIN, BODY, AND AWARENESS

IN FOCUS   **Moving Cubes**

This illustration offers no cues for depth and causes the brain to view it in a variety of ways. Stare at the plus sign in the middle, and the front of the cubes will either appear to shoot out at you or to cave in away from you. You might even get one cube to shift toward you while the other shifts away.

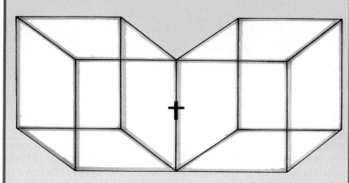

What types of cues could you add to help you perceive depth in this picture?

▲ *Figure 4.15*   *These rows of flowers allow for the principle of visual texture when gauging distance.*

actually are. For instance, part A of Figure 4.16 is actually two rows, each one made up of two black circles followed by two white circles followed by two more black circles. But that is not what we perceive. Instead, we see three rectangles, one made up of white circles and two of black circles. We have organized this information and constructed something more complete from it. In the language of perception, this is called a **gestalt** (gesh-TAHLT), meaning an organized whole, shape, or form.

Early researchers who studied how we go about making these interpretations were called Gestalt psychologists, and they found that we use certain perceptual cues to make sense of things. One such cue is **similarity,** in which we group like things together. We used this cue in part A of Figure 4.16 when we grouped circles of the same color together to form rectangles. It's almost impossible to see a square made up of both white and black circles, as is shown in part B of the figure.

Another process is called **closure,** by which we fill in (close) the details that aren't there to complete the picture. We used this principle, too, in our example when we filled in the dotted lines to form rectangles around the circles. Another example is shown in Figure 4.17. Here we see a complete word, although that is not a totally accurate perception.

Using the perceptual cue of **proximity,** we group things together that are near one another. Figure 4.18 shows how this works. We don't see a row of unequally spaced circles. Instead, we perceive the first two as belonging together, the third one standing alone, and the last three as belonging together.

Illusions

Illusions occur when we perceive something inaccurately. In a way, they are misperceptions. Nonetheless, they are important because they show how we construct the world. A striking illusion is the "Room of Mystery" often found at carnivals and amusement parks. When you go into one of these rooms, you seem to be walking at a very steep angle and feel like you might fall over if you don't hold onto something. Guides claim that there is a mysterious magnetic force involved. Actually, if you look at Figure 4.19, you will see the unique construction of such a room. It is built so that you can't tell it isn't a normal room; everything in the room is glued or nailed down. The room *is* on a slight angle, but since you expect to be able to walk and stand straight up, the unexpected information your brain is getting makes you feel as if you are going to fall. You are actually walking only at about the angle required to get to a higher level at a sports stadium. But because your eyes and your body are sending different clues to your brain, it decides you are in danger, which increases the effect. Try going through one of these or similar

Chapter 4 SENSATION AND PERCEPTION

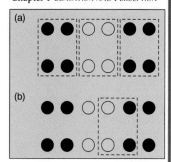

▲ *Figure 4.16* *Similarity.*

gestalt

Organized whole, shape, or form.

similarity

A perceptual cue in which we group like things together.

closure

The process of filling in the missing details of what is viewed.

proximity

A perceptual cue in which we group together things that are near one another.

illusion

An inaccurate perception.

Points to Stress

You may want to remind students that although William James would certainly not be considered a Gestalt psychologist, he did emphasize the need to view the human being as a whole.

Critical Thinking

Ask students to think of examples of closure and proximity in real life. (*Closure:* when we retell a story that we've heard but can't recall the details, we may tend to fill in the gaps to make the story seem whole. *Proximity:* photographs and newsprint make use of tiny dots that are close in proximity. Students may argue that these dots have gaps between them and we must use closure to perceive them correctly, but the gaps are so small that for all practical purposes, they're nonexistent.)

DISCOVERY

Here's a simple illusion for students that puts holes in their hands. Instruct them to roll up a sheet of paper like a telescope and, holding it with one hand, peer through it with one eye, focusing on a distant object.

Keep the other eye open. Bring the other hand next to the telescope. If they haven't changed focus, they should see a hole through their hand.

Reteaching Strategy

Ask students to respond either verbally or in writing to the following situation: Imagine that you have lost the ability to use one of the perceptual principles listed throughout the chapter. For example, you can no longer use size constancy. In a paragraph, describe your changed world.

Evaluation Strategy

See **Teaching Master 4-4 Identify the Perceptual Principle** for a set of illustrations that students need to match with the correct perceptual principle. Answers are listed at the bottom of the teaching master, so you may want to cover them when photocopying.

114

Unit 2 BRAIN, BODY, AND AWARENESS

▲ *Figure 4.17* *Closure.*

▲ *Figure 4.18* *Proximity.*

Müller-Lyer illusion

Two pictures in which one line seems longer than the other but really isn't.

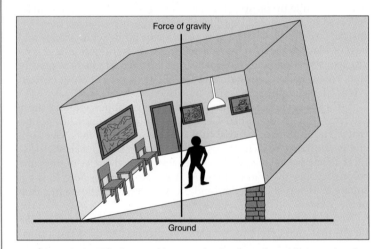

▲ *Figure 4.19* *Tilted room: objects are glued to the walls and floor causing the eye/brain mechanism to think the room is at a really severe angle.*

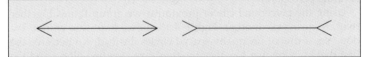

▲ *Figure 4.20* *Muller-Lyer illusion: both lines are the same size.*

distorted rooms with a friend (you trust) and keep your eyes closed. Now it's simple because you aren't getting mixed signals.

Most people think of illusions as "mistakes" that we make. That is not really the case. Instead, over the years, we learn to change what we perceive so that the world makes more sense. It is truly fascinating to see the eye-brain mechanism perform some of these changes. We will use what is called the **Müller-Lyer illusion** (MUE-ler-Liar) to illustrate the point. Look at Figure 4.20 and decide which of the two lines is longer. The "arrowhead" line looks much shorter. It is not; measure them. Some have thought the effect results from the arrowheads drawing the eyes in, but that is not the explanation. If the figures are flashed to the eyes faster than the eyes can move, the illusion remains. So, how do we explain it? The Müller-Lyer effect is an excellent vehicle for understanding what is going on.

Suppose you take two identical books and place them on a table, as shown in Figure 4.21. Stand them on their ends and align them side by side so that one book has the open pages facing you and the other has the cover facing you. Sit down in a chair directly in front of the books and look at them on the table from a distance of about six

INTERDISCIPLINARY PROJECT

Photography. Place the desks in your classroom on their sides, in rows. Have students squeeze into them, and have a student photographer take a snapshot. Try different poses: students reading their books, sleeping, and so on. Students should sit at their desks as though they were upright. You'll be pleased with the surreal illusion you've created, as if students are suspended in midair.

---

or seven feet. Next, ask yourself the length of each book's spine. Are they the same length? You will see them as being so, even though the images arriving on the back of the eye are *not* the same length. The images arriving at the eye can't be the same size since the spine of one book is seven or eight inches farther away from you than the other one. You are experiencing size constancy. Both spines appear the same length. This happens because we know both books are the same size.

Now, Figure 4.21 has been tampered with by an artist. Both lines representing the spines in that drawing are identical in length. Try measuring them. Follow this carefully and you will see how the eye-brain mechanism works: (1) Two identical lines for the spines arrive at the eye. (2) If the lines are the same length—which they are—then the spine of the book with the pages open and facing you is made "longer" by the brain since in real life, if the lines were equal, that book has to be bigger than the other one. Again, if the images of the spines are the same length, the books can't be the same size because the spine of one book has to be farther away than the other. Hence, the eye-brain mechanism makes the line in the book that is open toward you look longer than the other one—just as it would have to be if the books were real.

Finally, turn the page sideways and you will see that the books form a Müller-Lyer illusion. Now you know why the "arrowhead" part of that illusion looks shorter than the other part. The eye-brain system has so much experience in real life with seeing these kinds of angles and interpreting their lengths that just seeing part of a whole picture triggers a complete analysis of the length of the lines. We use this method to analyze the height or length not only of books but also of buildings, fences, windows, and so forth.

Many illusions come from the need for us to make sense of our surroundings. We make guesses in the context of what we think should be the case (Gregory, 1981). For instance, suppose you see a small dot far away on the opposite side of the highway coming toward you. You assume this is a regular-sized car. Next, suppose you are in a field with no roads anywhere and, across the field, you see a round object the same size as the one you saw before moving at the same speed, just at eye level, coming right toward you. Can you imagine your panic? Since it can't be a car, it must be—what? An enormous bee? A hawk? In any case, you form opinions about the nature of objects, and then they look that way to you—at least for a while. This is the case with what is called a **reversible figure.** Since the shape of the object shown in Figure 4.22 is such that it can be more than one thing, the eye-brain mechanism keeps "changing its mind." First you assume that it is a vase, but then all of a sudden the faces of two men nose to nose appear; then it looks like a vase again, and so forth. Obviously, something that appears to be an illusion is really the brain doing the best it can with an ambiguous figure, wanting to make certain it doesn't miss something important.

Chapter 4 SENSATION AND PERCEPTION

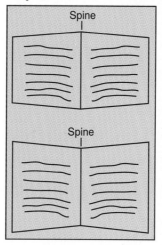

▲ *Figure 4.21* *Both book spines are the same size. Since the spine below seems farther away, our brain "stretches" it, as it usually does for distant objects.*

▲ *Figure 4.22* *This vase creates the face-goblet illusion.*

reversible figure

An illusion in which the same object is seen as two alternating figures—first one, then the other.

Although evidence suggests that subliminal messages have no effect on behavior, advertisers continue to insert these messages in magazine ads. If you're patient enough to study a few ads, especially those with pictures of ice cubes, you'll probably find a few hidden words or images. Just for fun, bring in a few ads to see if students can find subliminal messages. Even if they do not, this activity usually leads to a lively discussion. Is it ethical to include such messages without warnings? Is it ethical for department stores to urge people not to shoplift by piping subliminal messages through their sound systems? Are subliminal tapes worthwhile—you know, the ones that allegedly improve study habits, reduce weight, and build self-esteem?

TEACHING MASTERS 4-6 & 4-7

What Do You See?-1 and What Do You See?-2. The directions to the students are listed on these masters, but if you cover them up, you can conduct an experiment in class on the possible influences of subliminal messages.

TEACHING MASTER 4-8

Color Experiment. This reproducible handout is a test of colors and how our perceptions of colors may affect our thinking ability.

TEACHING MASTER 4-9

Illusions. This handout shows students how to create expectations that influence people's behavior.

subliminal perception
Stimulation presented below the level of consciousness.

Subliminal Perception

There are all kinds of audiotapes on the market today that claim to be able to reach your subconscious mind with wonderfully effective messages. Their advertisers say that just by playing the tapes, you can control your weight, stop smoking, increase your self-esteem, or become more popular, more successful, more whatever they can dream up. The part of the tape you can hear usually is comprised of easy-listening or classical music or some soothing sound like ocean waves or a gentle rainfall. Supposedly hidden at a much lower volume is a repeated message, such as "You are a winner." Other approaches have made use of videotapes in which a message, such as "Don't eat chocolate," is flashed on the screen over and over too fast to be clearly seen.

The idea behind all this is that while we cannot consciously hear or see the message, it will still be registered at the subconscious level. The principle involved is called **subliminal** (sub-LIM-uh-null) **perception**—perception that takes place below our level of conscious awareness. A lot of attention was given to this process in the 1950s when an advertiser very rapidly flashed "EAT POPCORN" on the movie screen at a theater. The advertiser claimed that popcorn sales increased 50 percent. Studies since then have not been able to duplicate these results. Some experimenters have flashed words on a screen and offered a lot of money to students who could say what the words were. However highly motivated these students were, none of them was able to do the task (Moore, 1984; McConnell et al., 1958).

Strangely enough, the lack of proof that these tapes do any of the things they claim hasn't made much difference in their popularity. Businesses sometimes use them to try to reduce shoplifting by customers and pilfering by employees. And, recently, there has been a great deal of public concern over the possible effects of subliminal messages in rock music. Regardless of all the furor, the best information we have is that subliminal perception or persuasion is simply not effective (McConnell, 1989; Pratkanis & Greenwald, 1988). The problem is a very basic one. The brain does not consider a faint message to be as important as one that is there for a while. So, it just doesn't pay much attention. (By the way, the word *subliminal* comes from the word *limen*, which means a line that marks off a boundary; hence, *sub*—beneath—the limen means below the level of everyday awareness.)

EXPERIMENT

Teaching Master 4-5 The Dating Game is a subliminal message game! Photocopy this handout four times and cut out the rectangles. Notice that there are several "3's" embedded on each card. With a bright marker, write a "Dating Game" type of question on each card. For example, "If you could be any animal in the world, which one would you be and why?" Using three students from your class as contestants and a student from outside the class as a subject, conduct a dating game simulation to see if the hidden "3" has any effect. The rules are simple. Assign each contestant a number. Place a barrier between the three contestants and the subject and you're ready to begin: the subject asks the questions; the contestants do their best to answer them; the subject picks one contestant.

The game is simply a fun device to discuss experimental design. Ask students: If we wanted to collect data scientifically, what changes would we *(continued on next page)*

PSYCHOLOGY IN YOUR LIFE

Do You Have ESP?

Most people you meet, possibly even you, will have had an experience similar to this one: You feel as if you have gotten a message that a friend is sick or lonely and needs you. You call and check—and it turns out to be the case. Was this mental telepathy? That is, did the two of you actually communicate in some special way?

Most psychologists don't believe in the phenomenon of *extrasensory perception,* or ESP (receiving information without the aid of our "normal" senses—vision, hearing and so on—hence, *extra* sensory or even beyond normal awareness) (Alcock, 1990). Nonetheless, there have been a few carefully done studies that suggest that this type of communication is possible.

Here is where the difficulty lies: many scientists say that the biggest problem with the existence of ESP is that there isn't any way to get the message from one person to another. For example, suppose you wanted to send a message to someone who is now in New York or California (that is, across the country, depending on where you live). How can it get to that person? Even if you got the message to the proper state, how do you guide it to the right street address? Since the brain is run by electricity, today's sensitive measuring devices can pick up electrical impulses about three or four inches from the skull, but beyond that they measure nothing. So electrical impulses don't seem to be the answer. Another problem is that the ESP ability seems to come and go; it is not consistent. Those who claim to have it on one day may not have it on another. That makes it difficult to study. Yet another problem is that most ESP demonstrations are fake. Stage shows in which someone "reads" another's mind are preplanned and use a confederate or stooge. Popular acts, such as bending a key with psychic forces, are magic tricks, not ESP.

Even though most scientists doubt that ESP exists, there are people who keep claiming they have these special powers. Maybe even you do. Never say "never." After

▲ *One would hesitate to disagree with anything Madam May says.*

all, most people believed the radio would never work. Next, people were certain television was impossible. Television certainly seems impossible. As you sit in a room reading this, all the shows on television are going through the air in the room (can't be!?). It is extremely important to remember that we (you, we authors, scientists, researchers, whoever) know

(continued on next page)

DISCUSS THE PHOTO

What are modern versions of circus fortune tellers? Maybe your area broadcasts the psychic network on cable TV.

PSYCHOLOGY IN YOUR LIFE

Demonstration

To demonstrate the need for tight controls when conducting ESP experiments, convince students that you know a colleague with ESP. Have the colleague wait outside the class while students pick an object in the room. Let's say they pick a clock. You will say five sentences to the colleague soon after she walks in. The first sentence will begin with **C**; *(continued on next page)*

EXPERIMENT

(continued from previous page)
need to make? The answers should be fairly obvious: (1) Include a control group–cards with no "3's." (2) More subjects should be tested. (3) Contestants' answers and voices should be essentially the same. (4) There shouldn't be an audience.

PSYCHOLOGY IN YOUR LIFE

(continued from previous page)
the next with **L**; then **O**; **C**; **K**. For example, you can say, "**C**ome in. **L**ook around. **O**kay, what do you think. **C**ome on, hurry. **K**eep thinking, class." To make the demonstration seem more realistic, the colleague can guess incorrectly the first time. When you debrief the class, emphasize that you're not trying to discredit the existence of ESP; you're trying to train them to think scientifically. You can also point out the power of labels. If you had labeled the colleague a magician, students' expectations would have been different.

ESP.

 Experimental procedure will vary, but emphasize the need for strict controls in the experimental design (see Chapter 2).

PSYCHOLOGY IN YOUR LIFE

Do You Have ESP?

(continued from previous page)
almost nothing in comparison to the vast intelligence of our universe. We can't even understand the smallest ant. If you take an ant apart, it's almost impossible to find a "brain" as we know it, yet ants can walk, communicate, build houses, carry, dig, breathe, avoid obstacles, see, and even interpret.

Here is something interesting to try: a few people are so sensitive that they can tell a difference in an object's color and pick the right one using only touch. Try it. You may be one of the *very* few who can do it. Have someone take three or four different-colored squares—all of exactly the same type of colored

paper—and put them under a thin piece of plastic so you can't tell differences by texture alone. Blindfold yourself and try to tell one color from another using just the tips of your fingers. It has been done—in one case, with 68 percent success in telling blue from white. Good luck!

IN FOCUS   **ESP**

Four Types of ESP Commonly Studied

1. **Telepathy:** (te-LEP-uh-thee) Reading someone's mind.
   Example: Your best friend is thousands of miles away. He hurts a foot, and at the same time your own foot starts to hurt. You have "read" the pain in his mind.
2. **Clairvoyance:** (klare-VOY-ence) Seeing or knowing something without being there.
   Example: Your best friend hurts her foot, and at the same time you "see" her do it. So you call her up, and she is amazed!
3. **Precognition:** (PRE-kog-NISH-un) Predicting the future.
   Example: You realize hours before he does it that your friend will hurt his foot.
4. **Psychokinesis:** (SIGH-koe-ki-KNEE-sis) Moving objects with your brain.
   Example: You concentrate and concentrate and you *cause* a log to move, over which your friend stumbles and hurts her foot. (Let's be thankful that there is no scientific evidence so far to support the existence of psychokinesis.)

How would you design an experiment to test the existence of ESP?

ENRICHMENT

Have students complete the **Enrichment Worksheet** for this chapter located in the Teacher Resources.

VOCABULARY REVIEW

Before testing students on the contents of this chapter, you may want to review vocabulary terms that are especially important or confusing. Terms in this chapter that could require clarification are *sensation*, *perception*, *gestalt*, and *illusion*.

Chapter 4 SENSATION AND PERCEPTION

SUMMARY

1. Sensation is the process of receiving information from the environment.
2. Vision is our most powerful sense. It uses light waves from the environment, which go through a lens in the eye and hit the retina. Information is then forwarded to the brain. The receptors in the retina are rods for night vision and cones for daylight color vision.
3. Audition uses sound waves to stimulate the eardrum. Sound varies in pitch, timbre, and intensity. The intensity is measured using decibels. Hair cells in the cochlea are tuned to receive the information and forward it to the brain.
4. Cutaneous senses respond to three basic types of stimulation: pressure, temperature, and pain.
5. In olfaction, the olfactory bulbs receive information from cilia in the nose and send this information to the brain.
6. Taste receptors respond to sweet, sour, bitter, and salt. Sugar and salty substances are necessary for human survival. Sourness and

bitterness receptors are used to detect bad food and poisons.
7. Perception is based on interpretation and expectation. To organize the world in order to understand it, our perception holds it steady by using size, color, brightness, and space constancies.
8. Depth perception arises from binocular disparity and visual texture. We also organize the world by using similarity, closure, and proximity.
9. Illusions are misperceptions, but they show how we organize the world. The Müller-Lyer illusion is an example of how we evaluate objects to determine their shape and size.
10. Subliminal perception does not work according to most studies. Still, people continue to believe in it.
11. ESP may be possible, but we cannot figure out any method by which it could be accomplished.

Wrapping It Up

The study of perception should teach us two things. On the one hand, we're all different. We all view the world from slightly different angles. This is only natural! Since this is true, let's respect the differences in others. On the other hand, there are ways in which we view the world similarly. This is natural, too, as the Gestalt psychologists tried to show us. So let's recognize that we're all in the same skin, regardless of race or ethnic background.

SUGGESTED READINGS

▼ Brandreth, Gyles. *The Great Book of Optical Illusions.* New York: Sterling, 1985.

▼ Coren, Stanley, and Lawrence M. Ward. *Sensation and Perception.* New York: Harcourt, 1989.

▼ Gardner, Martin. "Illusions of the Third Dimension." *Psychology Today,* August 1983, 62–67.

▼ "A Mingling of the Senses." *U.S. News & World Report,* November 13, 1989, 70–72.

▼ Moscovich, Ivan. *Fiendishly Difficult Visual Perceptual Puzzles.* New York: Sterling, 1991.

▼ Paraquin, Charles H. *World's Best Optical Illusions.* New York: Sterling, 1987.

▼ Schiffman, H. R. *Sensation and Perception.* New York: John Wiley, 1990.

▼ White, Lauren B. Jr., and Ray Broekel. *Optical Illusions.* New York: Watts, 1986.

VOCABULARY

sensation
perception
white light
cornea
iris
lens
pupil
retina
blind spot
rod
cone
color blindness
afterimage
audition

pitch
timbre
intensity
decibels
eardrum
cochlea
hair cells
auditory nerve
cutaneous receptors
olfaction
cilia
olfactory bulbs
pheromones
taste receptors
size constancy

color constancy
brightness constancy
space constancy
depth perception
visual cliff
binocular disparity
visual texture
gestalt
similarity
closure
proximity
illusion
Müller-Lyer illusion
reversible figure
subliminal perception

Answers to Review Questions

1. b
2. e
3. c
4. a
5. d
6. R
7. C
8. R
9. C

Review Questions

Matching

1. Responsible for focusing
2. Muscle that controls amount of light that hits the eye
3. Located at the back of the eye
4. Black circle in middle of the eye
5. Outer covering of the eye

   a. pupil
   b. lens
   c. retina
   d. cornea
   e. iris

For each of the following, answer R if rod applies, C if cone applies.

6. Used for night vision
7. Responds best to red wavelengths

8. More sensitive to violet-purple range of wavelengths
9. Used for color and daylight vision

Multiple Choice

10. If someone is said to be color blind, it usually means that
    a. he or she can see no color at all.
    b. part of his or her cone system is not working.
    c. his or her system of rods is not working.

11. For people who are truly color blind
    a. none of their cone systems is working.
    b. none of their rods is working.
    c. neither cones nor rods are working.

12. Cutaneous refers to the
    a. nose.
    b. ears.
    c. skin.
    d. eyes.

13. The hairs inside the nasal cavity are called
    a. pheromones.
    b. bulbs.
    c. cilia.
    d. bulb cells.

14. Smell chemicals are called
    a. pheromones.
    b. bulbs.
    c. cilia.
    d. nasalines.

Matching

15. Loudness
16. How high or low a sound is
17. Measurement of loudness
18. Hearing
19. Bone in ear
20. Complexity of sound

a. audition
b. decibels
c. intensity
d. pitch
e. timbre
f. cochlea

Fill in the blanks; answer on a separate sheet of paper. (More than one word can be used.)

21. Sally kisses John in a dark room. Although his face looks crimson, she knows it's really a bright red; this is an example of _____ _____.

22. Ballet dancers who spin a lot in circles don't get dizzy because of _____ _____.

23. Flying in an airplane, you look down at the "tiny" cars, but you don't perceive them as tiny because of _____ _____.

24. The fact that one of our eyes actually sees something different than the other is called _____.

25. We perceive objects that are outside in the same way whether it's cloudy or sunny because of _____ _____.

10. b
11. a
12. c
13. c
14. a
15. c
16. d
17. b
18. a
19. f
20. e
21. color constancy
22. space constancy
23. size constancy
24. binocular disparity
25. brightness constancy

Notes on Discussion Questions

1. Ultraviolet (UV) wavelengths are too slow for our eyes; infrared waves are too fast. If humans had receptors for UV, we might be able to see a deeper blue or a deeper purple. If we could see infrared wavelengths, we could probably function better in the dark. We might see heat in a different way; a pot of boiling water might glow.

2. Answers will vary. These are fun papers to read aloud in class.

3. People who meditate regularly often report a richer awareness of the world. Whether this improves the performance of their senses is arguable.

4. In comparing human sensory abilities with those of other animals, humans probably rate average or below average. Bees use ultraviolet light to find flowers; snakes use infrared light to see at night; dolphins and bats use sound waves in ways that

humans will probably never experience.

5. Experiments performed in the fifties revealed that two or three days of sensory deprivation cause mild hallucinations. It seems that when the brain is deprived of stimulation, it creates its own. If you've ever driven long distances, especially at night, you've probably experienced this

hallucinatory type of stimulation: shadowy creatures dart in front of the car; traffic signs become hitchhikers; viaducts become huge trucks.

6. Kinesthesia gives us feedback about our muscles, joints, and tendons. Circadian rhythm refers to the body's internal, natural clock (see Chapter 6). Equilibratory senses tell us where our body is in space.

DISCUSSION QUESTIONS

1. Briefly define *ultraviolet* and *infrared* wavelengths. Describe how the world might be different if humans had receptors for these wavelengths. Be specific.

2. Which of your senses is most important to you? Explain. If you had to give up one sense, which one would you give up? Why? What if you had to choose between giving up hearing and giving up seeing?

3. What if you could magically improve the performance of one of your senses? Which sense would you choose to improve? Why? Could you improve the performance of this one sense without magic? How? Be specific.

4. If we compare the performance of our senses as human beings to the senses of other animals, what conclusions can we draw? Do humans rate poorly, average, or above average? Why? Explain.

5. Each day our senses are bombarded with stimulation from the environment. What do you suppose would happen if we were

completely deprived of this stimulation for two or three days? List several possible side effects. *Hint:* try finding someone who has driven alone on the highway at night; how did the person feel once fatigue set in?

6. The chapter explains that ESP may be an extra sense. Do you think human beings have any *other* extra senses? To answer this question, you might research kinesthesia, circadian rhythms, and equilibratory senses.

7. Assume you are an experimental psychologist. Someone who claims to have ESP asks for an appointment with you in your laboratory. What kinds of questions would you ask? What types of experiments would you conduct?

8. Do you think that subliminal messages have *any* influence on people? Explain. Assume that these messages do influence people in some way; should the messages be regulated by law? Do you see any dangers in their use?

ACTIVITIES

1. Conduct a taste test on ten to 15 people (your "subjects") to demonstrate how smell contributes to taste. *Procedure:* Blindfold a subject and place four pieces of food in front of her or him. Don't tell the subject what foods you're using. The pieces can be taken from: (1) an apple, (2) a potato, (3) a pear, and (4) a carrot—or choose your own food groups. Guide the subject's hand to the first piece of food; tell the subject to hold her or his nose with the other hand while eating the food and to continue holding it until she or

he has guessed what the food is. Repeat this for each piece. Repeat the entire procedure for each subject.

Predict beforehand which kinds of foods the subjects will most often guess correctly. Which will they most often guess incorrectly?

After conducting the test, consider this: since your subjects could not use smell to guess what they were eating, they had to rely on other cues or hints. What were some of these cues? Explain.

Carnival rides tend to disrupt this equilibrium.

7. Have students refer to Chapter 2. The experiments should be conducted in an objective manner, with tight controls, so they can be replicated by other researchers. The study of ESP has been marred by sloppy experimental procedures. See "Psychic Abscam." *Discover*, March 1983, 10–11.

8. Answers will vary. See Natale, Jo Anna. "Are You Open to Suggestion?" *Psychology Today*, September 1988, 28–29.

Notes on Activities

1. This is a fun activity to conduct in class. If you don't want to do it yourself, you can always find a few students who will do this one for extra credit.

2. If you really want a speaker who is visually impaired to visit class, assign someone to call and arrange the visit.

3. Students who enjoy creative writing will like this one. If you like to combine classes, invite a creative-writing class to visit your class one day, and let them respond to the topic, too.

4. Definitely try this one in class. Offer them a hint: Forget logic and think of this as a spatial skills task. See if they remember which hemisphere specializes in spatial skills.

5. This kind of experiment works best in a setting outside school, somewhere like a grocery store, where people expect these kinds of tests. Make sure students obtain the approval of the store manager.

2. Look in a phone book to find a center for the vision-impaired. Find out if there are any speakers who would like to talk to a high school psychology class. If this is inconvenient, conduct your own interview with a blind person, and report what you learn to your class. Possible questions: Have your other senses become stronger? (This question wouldn't apply to someone blind from birth.) Do you dream in sounds, smells, or images? What's the most difficult part about being vision-impaired?

3. Describe an experience where a smell has had such an impact on you that you still remember it vividly and with emotion. Try to recreate the experience for your reader by providing vivid details.

4. Create your own illusion. Take a small sheet of paper. Make three cuts in it as shown in the diagram below. Hold the paper in your hand. With your left hand at the top of the left (shaded) side of the paper, turn this side over by pulling it toward you, so that your left hand ends up at the bottom, still on the left side of the paper. Put the paper down. The "FLAP" should now be sticking straight up. You can help to straighten it by folding it up and down. A top view of the finished illusion should look like the small drawing below. The illusion may not seem like an illusion to you since you have created it. But try it on your friends and family. They'll insist that you used glue or two pieces of paper. In other words,

what you have made *seems* impossible to make with a single sheet of paper.

Without offering your friends any instructions, give them a sheet of paper and let them try to create the illusion. What steps do they take? What problem-solving strategies do they use? Refer back to the chapter on brain hemispheres (Chapter 3). Which hemisphere *should* play a greater role in solving the illusion? Why? Which hemisphere do you think your friends primarily used? Why? Explain.

5. When you walk through a grocery store, do you avoid the generic sections? Do you perceive generic products as being inferior to brand name products?

Conduct a test to see if people, because of their perceptions of labels, prefer brand name products over generic products. *Procedure:* Buy a jar of peanuts (or another snack item). Empty half the peanuts into a brand name jar; empty the other half into a jar labeled "generic." Have people taste a peanut from both and decide which tastes better. Don't tell them you are conducting a psychology experiment or they will figure out that the peanuts are identical.

Analyze your results. Did people's perceptions affect their preferences? Discuss. To help with your discussion, you might look up some *Consumer Reports* issues on food products.

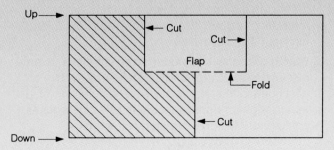

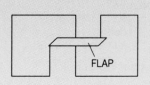

Ask students if they believe they would be this motivated if they were confined to a wheelchair.

Motivational forces in action.

124

PSYCHOLOGY AND YOU RESOURCES

A variety of resources are available in the Psychology and You *supplementary material. In addition, there are a number of additional resources listed to enhance your lesson plans.*

Masters
▼ 5-1A Learning Goals
▼ 5-1B Answers to Learning Goals
▼ 5-2 Which Needs Are Most Important?
▼ 5-3A Maslow's Hierarchy of Needs
▼ 5-3B Answers to Maslow's Hierarchy of Needs
▼ 5-4 Characteristics of Self-Actualizers
▼ 5-5 Setting Goals

Student Worksheets
▼ Vocabulary Worksheet
▼ Independent Practice Worksheet
▼ Enrichment Worksheet
▼ Reteaching Worksheet

Test Bank
▼ Tests A and B

Multimedia
▼ *The Brain* Videotape Module #29
▼ Psychology Videodisc

Student Workbook

PACING CHART

Complete Coverage

Day 1: Assign "Symbolism, Motivation, and Emotion" prior to class. Concentrate on the concept that humans attach emotional and symbolic importance to the satisfaction of hunger. The wrap provides several in-class activities and discussion topics to focus students. Assign "Motivation and Emotion: Physical Factors" and "Motivational Forces" for Day 2.

Day 2: After reviewing the physiological components of motivation, use the example of hunger in the text to differentiate physical and psychological motivating factors. Use Psychology in Your Life to highlight this discussion.

Day 3: Conduct classroom demonstrations (examples are in the wrap) to illustrate the motives described in the "Nonsurvival Needs" section of the text. Assign for homework an activity that requires analysis of Maslow's hierarchy of needs.

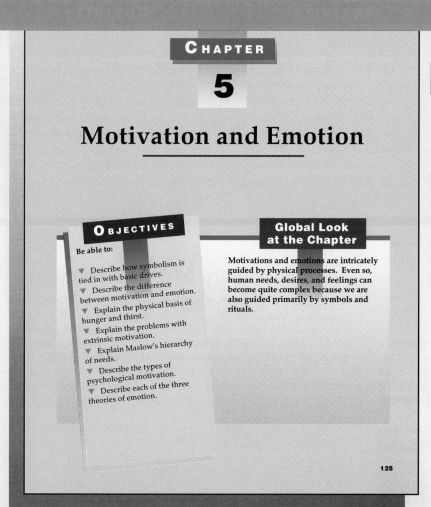

CHAPTER

5

Motivation and Emotion

OBJECTIVES

Be able to:

▼ Describe how symbolism is tied in with basic drives.

▼ Describe the difference between motivation and emotion.

▼ Explain the physical basis of hunger and thirst.

▼ Explain the problems with extrinsic motivation.

▼ Explain Maslow's hierarchy of needs.

▼ Describe the types of psychological motivation.

▼ Describe each of the three theories of emotion.

Global Look at the Chapter

Motivations and emotions are intricately guided by physical processes. Even so, human needs, desires, and feelings can become quite complex because we are also guided primarily by symbols and rituals.

INTRODUCING THE CHAPTER

Ask students: How does it feel when you do your best? This seems like an obvious question, but force students to elaborate and write their answers on the board. Next ask: If we know we're going to feel good when we do our best, why don't we do our best all the time, or at least more often? This is usually a great discussion starter! Explain that you will study several theories of motivation in this chapter.

LEAD-OFF ACTIVITY

Find a way to create a little fear in your class: scream, blare a horn, have someone charge in and crash cymbals. Then have students make note of any physical arousal they experienced. When did this happen? Immediately after being surprised? The moment they thought about it? If they can't agree, explain that psychologists can't agree either, but that you will study several theories about emotions in this chapter.

Day 4: Use In Focus: Unsatisfied Needs and discussion question #5 to aid a review of Maslow's theory. Assign "Emotions" for Day 5.

Day 5: Address and expand upon discussion question #8 as a group in order to understand the three theories of emotion. Give the Chapter Review quiz.

In Brief

Day 1: Focus on the example of hunger in the text to illustrate the interplay between physical and emotional motivational factors. Assign an activity for homework that involves analyzing the motivations behind eating, such as activity #1 in the text.

Day 2: Discuss Maslow's hierarchy of needs, using In Focus: Unsatisfied Needs as a visual aid. Discussion questions #5–7 in the text can be used as short essay homework assignments.

Day 3: Review the three theories of emotion. Give the Chapter Review Quiz.

DISCOVERY

Have a few students role-play a family dinner on Thanksgiving. The rest of the class should note how the rituals played out in class differ from their own dinners at home.

DISCUSS THE PHOTO

If you wanted to find other photo opportunities to express this caption, where would you go? Ever notice how many politicians nowadays punch the air to emphasize a point? But they use an odd fist—the thumb is on top. Maybe this serves to defuse the power of the punch, to make it seem less violent. Maybe they all attend the same speech classes!

Points to Stress

The symbolism and rituals we attach to satisfying hunger should add a dimension to your discussion of Maslow's hierarchy of needs later in the chapter. Although food satisfies level one, the rituals that surround it can be used to satisfy higher levels. For example, if a child violates table rules in front of visitors, this may threaten the parents' self-esteem. Or, a person who is self-actualizing may view family dinners as a sort of communion. Ask students how food rituals can satisfy any of Maslow's five levels.

Unit 2 BRAIN, BODY, AND AWARENESS

▲ *Using the hands is a necessity in conveying strongly felt emotions.*

SYMBOLISM, MOTIVATION, AND EMOTION

At first glance, both motivation and emotion seem reasonably straightforward, but nothing could be further from the truth. We will define and explore each of them shortly. But first, to illustrate how complex things can become, we will focus on hunger (a motivator) for a few moments. Satisfying hunger can be a mixture of social, psychological, and physical factors.

Visitors to the birthplace of William Shakespeare—Stratford-upon-Avon, England—are fascinated by some of the items on display. In an old tavern, there is a dining table from Shakespeare's era, the late 1500s and early 1600s. The table surface looks like it was worked on by a chain saw. Its appearance is the result of thousands of travelers in those days gouging and stabbing at food they placed directly on the table after they had removed it from community bowls. Some people carried with them their own wooden plates, but others just attacked bread and meat on the table. At upper social class functions, soup was served in individual bowls, but in places like this one, the same bowl was passed from person to person so that each could eat a spoonful as it continued its circular trip around the table. The fork was forbidden because it was considered an instrument of the devil; it did not come into general use until the mid 1700s. The French king, Louis XIV, prided himself on being the best in his kingdom in one respect: he was able to eat chicken stew with his fingers without spilling a drop. The famous French author of the time, Michel de Montaigne, complained that he often found himself eating so fast he was constantly biting his fingers. Two customs of that era survive today: (1) the napkin (a real necessity then) and (2) hand-washing between courses (this now takes place only at fancy restaurants) (Braudel, 1981).

Note how, as you read this discussion, you had emotional responses—mostly negative—to the different behaviors mentioned. Why? Because satisfying hunger is not just a basic motivation. We attach rules and regulations to the process. What appears to be a basic "animal" behavior—eating—is filled with all kinds of symbolism. Eating is a special ritual. If we have something to celebrate or if we desire companionship, we go to a special place and are served food in a formal way. For both the Jewish and Christian religions, eating and drinking wine have deep religious significance. (Next time you see a painting of the Last Supper, look carefully at the table—no forks.) Note also our rituals of drinking different substances from different-shaped glasses. There are beer steins, water glasses, martini glasses, wineglasses, and so forth. Further, different drinks have different meanings. For example, wine is often served at

DEMONSTRATION

You'll need three thermometers and a variety of snack foods for this activity. Procedure: Three subjects take their temperature, then eat one of the snack foods. A few minutes later, they take their temperature again. If their temperature rises, you can discuss how the hypothalamus reads this information and begins to send the message that the person is full. You may notice that foods that are richer in carbohydrates, such as doughnuts, will tend to raise the body temperature more than foods such as carrots. Subjects may need to eat quite a bit to raise their temperature. You should also notice that hot liquids like tea and coffee don't raise body temperature at all.

a formal Thanksgiving feast; many people think that serving beer or soda pop with the meal would seem very much out of place.

The human higher brain operates largely in terms of complex symbolism and ritual. We even have "uniforms" to wear while satisfying hunger. The higher brain thinks that such symbols are real, not imaginary. Here is a good experiment to demonstrate this point. Ask an adult why it isn't acceptable to wear a clean pair of jeans to a formal dinner party. The answer you get will probably resemble, "It just isn't done," or "It would be embarrassing." There is no real answer that makes sense. It is a rule based on symbolism. Ask some friends who aren't taking this class why—*really why*—it would be weird for someone to wear a dress or a suit when the group plans on getting pizza and spending the evening talking. They will come up with similar reasons, especially the circular one, "Well, it's just weird, that's all," which only proves our point and doesn't answer the question.

Finally, eating behavior in its most symbolic form consists of *not* eating. People with important causes go on hunger strikes to call attention to things they feel need correcting. Eating is so important that they are able to attract attention by not doing it.

MOTIVATION AND EMOTION: PHYSICAL FACTORS

Motivation is what drives us to seek a specific goal. Hence, we are motivated to drink, eat, make friends, and so forth. **Emotion** is a state of the body that causes feelings, which vary according to how we view a situation—with fear, hope, love, and so forth. Motivation and emotion involve both physiological and psychological factors. We will start with the parts of the body that are involved. Use Figure 5.1 so you get an image of what we are talking about. In that figure, the head has been sliced down the middle vertically so you can see the inner structure of the brain.

The Hypothalamus

Attaining pleasure and avoiding pain are often cited as primary motivators in human behavior. Scientists have located the centers for both pain and pleasure in a unit called the **hypothalamus** (high-po-THAL-ah-mus). Humans and animals alike have such centers. This unit also contains fear, rage, hunger, thirst, and sex centers.

Sending electrical stimulation through a small wire to the hypothalamus can produce any of these motivators or emotions, depending on which part is touched. Animals receiving stimulation to the

motivation

The drive to seek a goal, such as food, water, friends, and so on.

emotion

A state of the body causing feelings of hope, fear, love, and so on.

hypothalamus

A part of the inner brain that controls such basic needs and desires as pleasure, pain, fear, rage, hunger, thirst, and sex.

Discussion

Many Mediterranean families place a great emphasis on eating and often seem insulted if you visit their homes and don't eat (or don't eat enough!). See if any of your students have stories about this, and ask them if they can pick out any rituals or symbolism in the stories.

Points to Stress

Part of the hypothalamus, call it the "stop" signal, when stimulated, will cause us to feel full; another part, the "go" signal, will cause us to feel hungry. If you damage or remove the "stop" signal, the animal will simply never feel full.

DISCOVERY

Does motivation change as one gets older? To find out, ask students to make a list of several motivations they have for coming to school. At the same time, send several students around the school to ask teachers and administrators the same question. When both lists are completed, compare and contrast the two. Is one list more self-centered than the other? Is one more materialistic than the other?

Discussion

When students meet at a fast-food restaurant, what kinds of rules apply? Do they play with straws? Are napkins used as napkins, or do they serve other purposes? What kinds of "uniforms" are worn? Ask them to compare and contrast these rituals with rituals followed at other kinds of restaurants. Finally, ask if all these rules change as one grows older. In other words, in what ways, if any, do freshmen's rituals differ from those of juniors or seniors?

Points to Stress

The rat with the damaged hypothalamus weighs 1,080 grams. A normal rat weighs about 200 grams. Ask students to convert this into human terms by multiplying their own weights by five!

DISCUSS THE PHOTO

Discuss the ethics of damaging an animal's hypothalamus.

128

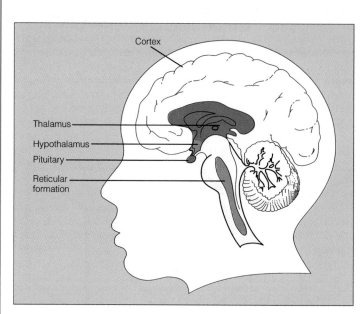

▲ *Figure 5.1 Major brain areas in motivation and emotion.*

▲ *Damage to the hypothalamus has resulted in this extraordinarily heavy rat, which lost the ability to stop eating.*

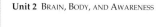

pleasure center if they push a lever have been known to stimulate themselves for up to 20 days at 20 responses per minute for a total of 576,000 pushes. Some of them preferred this to eating or drinking and died as a result (Valenstein, 1973; Olds, 1956).

Studies of the fear-rage portion of the hypothalamus have had their wilder moments. One experimenter connected a miniature radio receiver to the fear area of a bull's hypothalamus, and then he got into the ring with the bull. The experimenter was armed only with a radio transmitter. When the bull charged, he pushed a button sending an impulse to the bull's fear center. Fortunately, the bull came to a screeching halt (Delgado, 1969). The experimenter was taking quite a chance because right next to the fear area is an area for rage, which could well have been activated if the receiving wire had been off by a millimeter or so.

The Reticular Formation

Almost any emotional or motivational state involves taking some kind of action. Whether we run, fight, or seek something we need, we require an increase in activity level. Anyone who sits through a sporting event with no change in heart rate, blood pressure, or speech level has not been very involved in it. The **reticular** (re-TICKu-lar) **formation** shown in Figure 5.1 is at the base of the brain inside the neck. It controls not only sleep but also how high or low the level of activity in the body is.

The Pituitary Gland and the Adrenal Glands

Neither the reticular formation nor the hypothalamus can do its work all alone. Both frequently call upon the chemical system of the body to get us going. The controller of chemical responses is called the **pituitary** (pi-TUE-i-ter-ee) **gland,** a small structure located just below the hypothalamus. The bodily reaction when a person gets highly anxious, excited, or emotionally involved is controlled at least in part by the pituitary. When we see someone we love so intensely that he or she seems to be gradually killing us, the hypothalamus tells the pituitary, which uses chemicals to signal the **adrenal** (a-DREE-nal) **glands**—there are two of them, one on each side of and about even with the belly button (Figure 5.2). These glands secrete the chemical *adrenaline* (a-DREN-a-lin), which makes the heart beat faster, breathing increase, and perspiration break out when we see the object of our love—or when we are faced with an emergency.

Chapter 5 MOTIVATION AND EMOTION
reticular formation

The unit in the inner brain that registers and controls activity level, increases excitement, and helps generate sleep.

pituitary gland

The controller of other glands and hormones, as well as the producer of its own hormone that regulates growth.

adrenal glands

Glands that secrete adrenaline, which stirs up the body, changing the breathing, perspiration, heart rate, and so on.

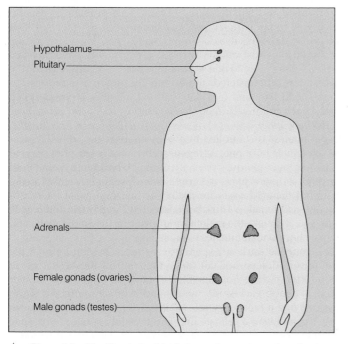

Hypothalamus
Pituitary

Adrenals

Female gonads (ovaries)

Male gonads (testes)

▲ *Figure 5.2* *Significant physiological areas in emotion and motivation.*

Critical Thinking

"Would you become obese if your hypothalamus were damaged and you never felt full?" This question goes back to the rituals and symbolism that humans apply to eating. Although we may never feel full, we still know that it is impolite to stuff our faces, so we probably wouldn't. The question also takes us forward in this chapter to **Factors Controlling Weight.** Some people eat because of external cues. If your hypothalamus were damaged and you knew this, you might avoid as many external cues as possible. Set points would probably change after damage to the hypothalamus also.

DISCUSS THE PHOTO

The root of the word *emotion* means "to move." It certainly does this, in more ways than one.

Connections

You may have already discussed the ethics of animal experimentation (Chapter 2) in a general sense, but there are several real examples in this hypothalamus section. Do these experiments go too far? Is the information learned worthwhile?

ENRICHMENT

Have students look for case studies on infants born with both male and female sexual organs, and have them report their findings to the class. Although this problem is rare, remind them that all of us have both male and female hormones (see Chapter 13).

DISCUSS THE PHOTO

Students can probably think of numerous examples when the adrenal gland is working hard. And point out that the event need not be life threatening.

Connections

Chapter 12 discusses the effects of aging on sex hormones. The level of androgen drops for males during middle age, and the level of estrogen drops for females during menopause.

Teaching Hint

Most students are familiar with the term *adrenaline* and its effects, but emphasize the speed at which adrenaline operates. You can do this by suddenly pulling someone to the front of the room. Tell the student that his or her task is to make the rest of the class laugh. After ten or twenty seconds, ask the person to report any physiological reactions: faster heart beat? Faster breath? Perspiration?

130

▶ *Adrenal glands are in full operation in an event such as a fire or other life threatening event.*

gonads

The sex glands.

testes

The male sex glands; make sperm.

ovaries

The female sex glands; make eggs.

androgens

Male hormones that control sexual interest in both males and females.

estrogen

The hormone that controls the female reproductive cycle.

The Gonads

The sex glands, called **gonads,** are of two types: the **testes** in the male and the **ovaries** in the female. They produce sperm and eggs, respectively, as well as sex hormones. The hypothalamus signals the pituitary, which in turn, causes the gonads to produce the sex hormones that will make a fetus into either a male or a female. Prior to birth, just a slight error by the hypothalamus can change the amount of sex hormone released, and the result, on occasion, is an infant who has both male and female sexual organs. This problem is usually handled well today with surgery and hormone supplements. When the physician discovers it, a decision is made regarding which sex the child should be. Most infants with this abnormality have physical parts that belong more to one sex than the other. So hormones for the desired sex are administered, and eventually surgery is performed to make the child look and feel like a natural member of the assigned sex. Most such children turn out well both physically and psychologically (Money, 1980).

Sexual interest is controlled by the male hormones, called **androgens.** The female hormone, **estrogen,** seems to have the primary goal of regulating the reproductive cycles of the body. There is some indication that estrogen plays a limited role in sexual interest for the woman, but the androgens are the key to starting sexual interest in both males and females. Thus, both sexes have both male and female hormones. Obviously, the male hormone dominates in the male, and the female hormone dominates in the female.

Once someone starts to experience sexual interest, usually at the beginning of adolescence, all the symbolism of the higher brain enters into the picture. For humans, sexuality, as opposed to hunger or thirst, is almost exclusively mental and symbolic, with the physical part playing a secondary role. This is why some individuals can give up sex and lead a celibate life. This certainly could not be done with hunger or thirst. The average person can go about three days without water and 60 to 70 days without food. You may have heard

ENRICHMENT

When discussing sex hormones, students may ask if an imbalance will cause homosexuality. Although hormones certainly play a role, most homosexuals and lesbians have normal hormone levels. Thus, an imbalance alone is probably not going to cause someone to become homosexual. What will? No one knows, but it's a complicated issue that might be worth exploring as a research project.

---

that if a person does not use the sex organs, the organs will gradually waste away. Or that each time they are used, people lose a little more of their "life energy." Neither of these rumors is true.

MOTIVATIONAL FORCES

Motivation is thought to result from **drives**—that is, forces that push the organism into action in order to reach a goal. For example, if you are thirsty, you have a need for water and are driven by the body to seek it.

The body's drives operate in cycles designed to maintain balance over the long run. A period of high activity, for instance, is followed by one of rest. This process of establishing physical equilibrium or balance is called **homeostasis,** literally translated as "standing (or staying) the same." Thus, we are driven by hunger to eat. Once satisfied, though, we stop eating and go on to other things. These "start-stop" or "on-off" mechanisms help keep the body on an even keel.

Homeostasis operates in all our basic drives. Now we will examine some of those basic drives in detail.

Hunger

In the middle 1800s, a man had part of his stomach left exposed after a shotgun accident. Experimenters talked him into becoming a guinea pig for their research on how the stomach works. A see-

Chapter 5 MOTIVATION AND EMOTION

drives

Forces that push an organism into action to reach a goal.

homeostasis

Bodily process of maintaining a balanced internal state.

▲ *Two male elephants trunk wrapping, the drive to establish dominance.*

Comprehension Check

Ask students the following question: How does an effective teacher affect the reticular formation of each student? *(walks around the room, asks questions, and tries to keep everyone involved)*

Critical Thinking

Assign students the following task: Compare and contrast homeostasis to Maslow's hierarchy of needs. Maslow believed that once a need is satisfied, it is no longer a motivator, at least for a while. This sounds very much like homeostasis. Maslow, however, added that after satisfying a need, we strive to satisfy higher-level needs. So while homeostasis is a state of balance (physical equilibrium), Maslow's hierarchy of needs suggests that the healthy individual goes beyond that and constantly strives.

DISCUSS THE PHOTO

What are some nonverbal behaviors that **humans** use (or try to use) to show dominance?

CHAPTER PROJECT/COOPERATIVE LEARNING

Divide the class into groups and assign one of the following to each group: athletes, artists, scientists, educators, legal experts, business leaders. Or let students pick their own job categories. Their task is to find people in the assigned field who are highly motivated. If you want them to work individually on this part, give them a minimum, such as two articles or two people. When they come together, their next task is to discuss what the motivated people have in common and to develop their own theory of motivation based on their research. Have each group briefly share their findings with the rest of the class.

Students often confuse motivation with some sort of success. The people they study were probably highly motivated before they became "successful." If they find this to be true, how does success affect motivation?

Points to Stress

Homeostasis works like a thermostat at home that automatically kicks the heat on when the temperature falls below a certain point and automatically turns it off when the home is warm enough.

Discussion

Before delving into the causes of hunger, ask students about their eating habits. You will probably find a wide range of hunger drives, from people who rarely eat lunch to those who feel they have to carry snacks around with them. What do they think accounts for these differences—their bodily requirements or habits they've learned?

Journal Topic

"Write an entry from the point-of-view of the man whose stomach was left exposed after a shotgun accident. Why did you hide out? Where did you go?" This point-of-view exercise can lead to a discussion on the ethics of experimentation.

132

Unit 2 BRAIN, BODY, AND AWARENESS

through covering was placed over the wound so the effects of various foods and other activities in the stomach could be viewed. After a while, the man got fed up with all this and fled to Canada, where he hid out. Later, when word came that he had died there, a doctor in the United States planned to try to get his body for a medical museum. The family heard about it and warned the doctor with a classic in telegrams. It read, "DON'T COME FOR AUTOPSY. YOU WILL BE KILLED" (Rosenzweig, 1962). Being extra cautious, the family kept the body exposed a long time so it decomposed and became useless to any museum. Because of the stench, it had to remain outside during the funeral.

During the time the man was studied, however, his stomach provided much information on how the digestive system functions. For example, when people feel depressed, the amount of acid in the stomach drops noticeably and salivation slows, both of which are needed for digestion. This may be one of the physical reasons why many depressed people don't want to eat. On the other hand, when we are angry, the opposite occurs: the stomach's mucous membranes become red and engorged with blood, acid production more than doubles, and the stomach begins violent contractions. You may have learned this from trying to eat during a family argument at the dinner table. Aside from the possibility of choking, the increased acid causes nausea. Either extreme—that is, too much or too little stomach acid—will affect our appetite.

What Causes Hunger? Researchers are still trying to understand fully how we know it is time to eat or why we feel satisfied after a meal. The earliest suggestion was that the stomach growled and contracted when it was empty. To see if this was the case, in the early 1900s experimenters had people swallow deflated balloons that were attached to a recording device. Then they were inflated to touch the stomach walls, so each stomach contraction was recorded (see Figure 5.3). The experimenters found that when a person is hungry, the stomach does indeed contract, *but* it also contracts at other times (Cannon, 1939). So contractions might be part of the answer, but certainly not the complete one.

A problem with the contraction theory arose when it was discovered that people who had operations in which the stomach was removed still experienced hunger. How were they getting signals of hunger? In the 1960s, it occurred to some researchers that the hypothalamus might be involved. Following up on this hypothesis, the researchers discovered that electrical stimulation of the side part of the hypothalamus would cause eating behavior even in animals that were full. Similarly, damage to a lower portion of the hypothalamus would cause the animal to stop eating (Margules & Olds, 1962).

Still, knowing that the hypothalamus is involved doesn't explain *how* it works. A clue appeared years ago but was not understood for a while: you may have noticed that if you skip a number of meals,

ENRICHMENT

Researchers are experimenting with different ways to stimulate the hypothalamus through external stimuli. For example, certain smells may stimulate the hypothalamus in such a way that we do not feel hungry. Ask students to find out about these experiments and whether they would be interested in using the products if they became available.

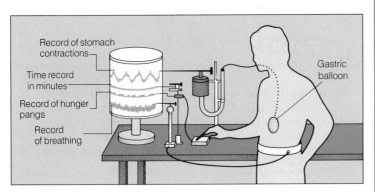

▲ *Figure 5.3*   *The subject pushes a key to indicate when stomach sensations are felt. This is then compared with actual stomach contractions.*

Chapter 5 MOTIVATION AND EMOTION

you begin to feel weak and sometimes dizzy. This is caused by a low **blood-sugar level,** a term referring to the amount of sugar (called **glucose**) in your blood. A low amount can be corrected for a short while by eating a candy bar or drinking a soft drink, because either will flood the body with straight sugar. But then your blood sugar zooms downward again. Eating something like meat, chicken, or pasta is a better solution because the body will convert part of it into a steady source of glucose. In any case, researchers found that the hypothalamus contains *glucose monitors* within it, which determine the level of blood sugar. If the level starts to fall too low, these monitors send out signals that make you feel hungry (Arkes & Garske, 1982). If you skip a meal, your hunger disappears after an hour or so because the body will dump some of its stored glucose into the system to tide you over until the next meal.

There are other factors involved. If you pay close attention the next time you eat, stop after five minutes or so and examine how you feel. Notice that you are already less hungry. But there hasn't been time for all you have eaten to get to your stomach, let alone to change your blood-sugar level. How can this be? The tongue, learning, and chemical responses all seem to play a role. From experience, we discover that food on the tongue means we will be satisfied. That is the learning part—previous association. When food hits the tongue, it communicates to the brain that you are eating. What if you stopped eating at that point? You would not be hungry for a while; in the intestines and stomach, however, there are other receptors that release a chemical to say when *they* are satisfied. As a result, since what you have eaten won't satisfy them, you will begin to feel hungry again (Whalen & Simon, 1984).

Taste is also a most important factor. It is critical to eating, a fact discovered in another unlucky event. A ten-year-old drank some boiling soup that fused his esophagus shut so he could not swallow. This was in the early 1940s when surgery was primitive. Nothing

blood-sugar level

The amount of sugar contained in the blood, which indicates the level of hunger.

glucose

Another name for sugar in the blood.

Points to Stress

The balloon-in-the-stomach experiment demonstrates the need for caution when formulating conclusions. It would have been easy to conclude that contractions cause hunger, and then stop there (which is what the researchers did at first). With such an attitude, however, any new evidence would have been discarded and further research would have been discouraged. This may explain why, nowadays, when breakthrough treatments for diseases are reported they are announced as preliminary findings.

Comprehension Check

Name some possible reasons why people eat when they are not hungry. *(They associate eating with the relaxation it can produce and so eat when anxious; they cannot accurately read the internal cues provided by the hypothalamus, blood sugar, and stomach, and so rely on external cues, such as availability.)*

COOPERATIVE LEARNING

Ask students to illustrate the **What Causes Hunger?** section using large butcher paper. Each group can focus on a particular aspect of hunger: (1) stomach contractions; (2) hypothalamus; (3) blood-sugar level; (4) the tongue: learning and chemicals, taste receptors; (5) external cues; (6) set points. Each group should complete one large illustration that includes captions. Emphasize that the finished product should be clear enough to stand on its own.

Feeling Hungry?

 Possible answers: time of day, seeing others eating, smelling food.

Discussion

Ask any long-term dieters in the class how it feels after the stomach has shrunk. Wrestlers who cut weight may have some good stories. What happens to appetite, to the amount of food needed to satisfy hunger? Many dieters report that appetite decreases and that relatively small amounts of food make them feel full.

Critical Thinking

This section includes some good questions that you might want to present to students *before* they read: (1) What causes hunger? (2) If we feel hungry when our blood-sugar level is low, why do we stop feeling hungry without having eaten? (3) Does learning play a role in satisfying hunger?

set point

The body-regulating mechanism that determines a person's typical weight.

Unit 2 BRAIN, BODY, AND AWARENESS

 **Feeling Hungry?**

Here are four possible reasons why:
1. Your stomach is contracting.
2. Your blood-sugar level is low.
3. Your taste receptors are "on."
4. You've lost weight, and shrunken cells are signaling you.

The reasons listed refer to physical factors. What are some "psychological" factors that might contribute to the feeling of hunger?

could be done for him except to insert a feeding tube through the area above the belly button into the stomach. The man lived a full life this way, but he found he didn't feel satisfied without taste. Hence, he would put a small amount of his (liquid) meals into his mouth first, spit that out, and then pour the rest into his feeding tube (Wolf & Wolff, 1947).

The importance of taste, however, is short-lived. As we continue to eat, the taste receptors begin to shut down so that we will stop eating. Notice toward the end of a meal how tasteless your food becomes.

Factors Controlling Weight Because obesity is so often a topic of concern, there has been quite a bit of research on the problem. One of the most prominent theories suggests that the very heavy person is not able to read accurately the internal cues provided by the hypothalamus, blood sugar, and stomach—cues that would help him or her decide when and how much to eat. Instead, such people operate on external cues. In other words, if an item *looks* interesting or tasty, some obese people pay little attention to whether they need food at the moment but are carried away by its availability. There is a reasonable amount of evidence that this is the case in *some* obesity problems (Schachter & Rodin, 1974).

We all know people who can eat enormous quantities of food and never gain an ounce, while others seem to enlarge after eating a single cookie. One explanation for this is that people differ in what is called their **set points.** A set point is the body's regulating mechanism that determines what an individual's weight should be (Bennett & Gurin, 1982). If you have a high set point, the body will keep moving upward in weight to that point, and vice versa if you have a low set point. Set points vary from one individual to another. You may have noticed that when you have tried to gain or lose weight, there is

ACTIVITY

DEMONSTRATION

Eat a doughnut in front of your students to show the power of external cues. Ask them what their eating habits would be like if they could only rely on external cues for hunger. (Dieting might be easier, as long as you're willing to live a reclusive life.)

Critical Thinking

Ask students the following question: How might a newborn's hunger differ from an adult's? Student answers might include: A newborn has to rely on internal cues—stomach contractions, low blood-sugar levels, and so on. An adult obviously uses these cues, too, but learning will have an effect on the internal processes. Even if we're not truly hungry, learning will prompt us to eat anyway: others are eating; it's "time" to eat; eating will make me feel better; if I don't eat, my parents will be angry.

a specific weight that is very difficult for you to get above or below. That is your set point. A set point *can* be changed but only with considerable work. A regular program of exercise will gradually change the set point to a limited degree in the case of those who are too heavy, or it will add muscle to those who are too thin (Thompson et al., 1982). Your set point is to some extent determined by your fat cells, which vary in both size and number from one person to another. Some people have trouble losing weight because as they start dieting, the size of the fat cells shrinks, which sends hunger signals to the body (Brownell, 1984).

It is risky to give an excuse to those people who want one for overeating, because overeating is almost always unhealthful. Still, the evidence is that a fair number of people are overweight based partly on their heredity and their metabolism, the speed at which the body uses up energy in the form of fat. Some people store fat more readily and have a slower body speed than is needed to use it up.

What we eat seems also to have some hereditary basis. Taste receptors can vary from one person to another as the result of inheritance. One inherited factor that can arise if both the mother and father have a dominant gene for it is a horrible, bitter taste when eating green, leafy vegetables (Rodin, 1984). This may help explain why some children have such an aversion to certain types of vegetables; many are just being "difficult," but a handful will actually experience a horrible taste from them.

Several researchers have reviewed more than a hundred studies on obesity and find that no single factor shows up consistently. Obese people seem to be quite variable in physical structure, psychological motivation, and eating behavior. Exceptions are those who are *very* obese—150 percent or more over their normal weight. These people probably have something wrong physically, as well as a tendency to respond to most food items, even a picture of a sandwich (Conger et al., 1980). In one extreme case, a girl was injured, damaging her hypothalamus. On her first day up and around in the hospital, her physician went with her to the cafeteria. On the way he asked her if she was hungry, and she said no. But when she got there, she ran behind the counter and started grabbing handfuls of food, pushing them into her mouth (Pribram, 1971).

Thirst

Humans are roughly 65 to 70 percent water. As mentioned earlier, we can't go long without water. Whereas we have storage units for excess fat in case of an emergency, there is no place to put water, and we always need a ready supply. The amount of water we need is determined by units that "count" the number of water molecules in certain body cells surrounding the hypothalamus. When the count gets low, the desire for water increases.

Chapter 5 MOTIVATION AND EMOTION

▲ *Something is very wrong with this man's set point. Obesity at this level is almost always physiologically caused.*

DISCUSS THE PHOTO

Contrast this photo with the one on anorexia (p. 314).

FYI Although set points are affected primarily by heredity, childhood eating habits certainly play a role. The person who develops more fat cells during childhood from overeating may find it difficult to control his or her weight during adulthood.

135

EXPERIMENT

Pass out something salty for students to munch on, perhaps using the premise that the snacks were left over from a party you had. Before class, arrange for two or three students to ask if they can get a drink of water after tasting these snacks.

When the students return, ask the rest of the class if hearing the request for water influenced their thirst. You can then discuss how the excess of salt created an imbalance of water in the body cells (the excess drew water out of the cells), and the

hypothalamus signaled thirst. Then discuss how learning—observational, in this case—can also play a role in thirst. You can conduct the activity without the salty food and focus solely on learning.

Reteaching Strategy

Hunger and thirst are such basic drives that students have a difficult time remembering that learning can affect how we satisfy these drives. Have them list the innate causes of hunger on one side of a sheet of paper and how learning may make us feel hungry on the other side. They can do the same for thirst.

Discussion

Discuss the following questions with the students to see if your school encourages or discourages curiosity: Are most of the desks in your school lined up in rows? Do the teachers do most of the talking? Are students allowed to work independently if they choose? Are students involved at any level in making decisions about school rules?

curiosity motive

A drive that moves a person to see new and different things.

While a dry tongue and the need to make it moist are important in thirst, there are also receptors in the intestine to make certain that this vital fluid actually gets into the body. Most animals have such receptors on the tongue, but we don't (Maddison et al., 1980). Instead, humans respond to temperature receptors on the tongue, which trigger a desire for cold drinks in summer and hot ones in winter (Kapatos & Gold, 1972). Thus, dryness of tongue, temperature of water, and balance of water in the body cells are all registered by the hypothalamus.

For most of us, water intake is controlled by learning rather than by a physical signal. Over time we learn the amount of water we need and the amount we tend to drink on a fairly regular basis. For example, studies show that right after playing tennis—before the bodily signals have been activated—the tennis player will gulp just the right amount of water to compensate for the loss that will be signaled shortly (Pribram, 1971).

A sometimes serious side effect of such learning is that we can come to associate eating food or drinking alcohol with the relaxation and grogginess it can produce. As a result, many times people get into the habit of eating and drinking at the first sign of any type of pressure or anxiety, trying to offset the upcoming upset. People with this problem must fight it by restricting drinking (of alcohol) and eating to only certain times of the day and for only a brief period (Bellack et al., 1973). We have also learned that children must never be given food as a reward for doing something good, or food will take on an abnormal interest that can, over time, become a dominant one for the child. This behavior can carry into adulthood. Best to give the child some other reward whose power as a motivator is not as likely to increase as the drive to eat is. On the other hand, infants are supposed to be chubby and should not be put on a diet except in the case of medical crisis or a disease.

Nonsurvival Needs

We humans do a good job of taking basic needs and making them symbolic. The brain never seems content with leaving things alone. For example, we have a psychological need for change. There is always something "new" that we want to do, such as rearranging our rooms, changing the decorations or the colors, and so forth. This constant need for cerebral (brain) changes is one of our stronger needs, even though it is not critical to survival.

Curiosity Motives   The strong psychological need to see new, odd, or different things is not confined to humans but is also found on a limited basis in "lower" animals. We have a German shepherd, for example, that drives us crazy with this **curiosity motive.** Naming it doesn't help. He has learned to open closet doors to find out what

DISCOVERY

To demonstrate the curiosity motive, simply perform an unusual behavior or task—without explanation—and mentally note students' curious reactions. Gaze at the ceiling. Or stare out into the hall. Or put a student's desk on top of your desk, leave it alone, and begin lecturing. If the students are not curious, continue lecturing for a short while, then perform another unusual behavior. Continue this procedure until their curiosity interferes with your lecture (if this doesn't happen, take their pulses), then discuss their curious reactions. How and when did they express their curiosity? What factors inhibited them from expressing their curiosity? Does school in general promote or stifle the curiosity motive?

---

is new in there. We might as well not even have doors on the closets because he opens them every time he is in the house. Discipline is not a solution because he would have to be beaten into submission to obey and we are too softhearted to do that. In humans, one of the most noticeable bits of evidence of this motive is the fact that in rush-hour traffic, people will slow down and jam things up hopelessly in order to view even the most minor accident.

Manipulation Motive   When we move up the scale from the dog or cat to the *primates* (such as monkeys, chimps, and humans), we find what are called **manipulation motives.** Manipulation is a drive to handle and use objects in the environment. Monkeys, for instance, love complicated mechanical puzzles of hooks, latches, and sliding bolts—just to have something to play with or examine. They will manipulate such things for hours with no other reward (such as encouragement or petting). Monkeys will work especially hard to be able to open a door and see a toy train going around in a circle, satisfying both curiosity and manipulation needs (Harlow et al., 1956). Monkeys and other higher primates also love new human inventions such as the video player. When a foot switch is rigged to turn on a video player, monkeys will hold it down 60 percent or more of every hour merely to be able to enjoy the show. This is especially true of males, who will watch tapes of female monkeys about 75 percent of every hour if they are given the chance (Swartz & Rosenblum, 1980).

Chapter 5 MOTIVATION AND EMOTION

manipulation motive

A drive that moves a person to handle and use objects in the environment.

DISCUSS THE PHOTO

Have students think of other animals whose curiosity motive is high.

▲ *The monkey's curiosity motive is very strong. It will work hard to get a chance to see this train in operation.*

EXPERIMENT

At the beginning of class one day, hand out an ice-cream bar stick to every student and go on with your regular lesson for the day. The lesson should be one in which students will remain in their seats. During the period, make mental notes on how students manipulate the sticks, and discuss this near the end of the class. If you have more than one class, try different objects to see if this makes a difference.

DISCUSS THE PHOTO

Contrast this portrait of curiosity and cooperation with the clinging desperation in Figure 5.4.

Points to Stress

The Harlow findings may seem painfully obvious to students nowadays, and students may not see the need for such research, but maybe the reason the findings are so obvious and full of common sense is *because* of experiments like Harlow's. Also, the practical implications of the research should point out how worthwhile the studies have been.

Critical Thinking

Ask students the following question: How could the very structure of school be changed to encourage more intrinsic motivation by students? Encourage students to offer concrete plans, something that could actually be presented to a principal or school board for consideration. This might be a good cooperative-learning activity.

Unit 2 BRAIN, BODY, AND AWARENESS

▲ *Hooks, latches, and sliding bolts are among monkeys' favorite things.*

intrinsic motivation

Seeking satisfaction that comes from within the individual for certain behavior.

extrinsic motivation

Seeking a reward from outside the organism for certain behavior.

The important factor in these findings seems to be that these animals feel a desire for some type of change. Animals that are in very elaborate cages, such as a psychedelically decorated one, eventually prefer a simple cage, and the reverse is true for those in simple cages. Apparently, change, in and of itself, helps meet some need of the brain and possibly of the body as well.

Intrinsic Versus Extrinsic Motivation   As mentioned, monkeys will play with latches and hooks endlessly if left on their own. But what happens if you start giving them a reward, such as a banana, for doing so? Something unexpected occurs: they will lose their incentive to play and start to focus on the reward instead. If it doesn't arrive, they quit playing. We explain this situation by what is called **intrinsic** versus **extrinsic motivation.** "Intrinsic" means coming from within the organism. "Extrinsic" means coming from outside.

You may remember how, as a child, you were curious about almost everything. Often, now, the reverse is true. This is one of the heavy prices we pay for organizing and structuring things into a formal school system. When we give people external rewards (such as grades and praise), we are using extrinsic motivation and to some extent removing intrinsic motivation. Thus, too many students begin to act like the monkeys, no longer able to get really deeply involved in what they're learning. But give these same students a problem outside the

ENRICHMENT

Have students read a few case studies on the dismal conditions in some orphanages around the world, and they will acquire an appreciation for Harlow's studies. Harlow showed that infants need to be held and rocked, not simply "maintained."

classroom, and they will work for hours on it (because of intrinsic motivation). So what is the solution? The school structure is so big and so formalized that it won't work to take away grades (extrinsic). We need to find a way to add intrinsic motivation for students. If all of us were stuck on a desert island, it wouldn't be long before we were actually begging for a chance to learn something new.

Need for Stimulation   All animals must have physical stimulation in order to develop properly. Monkeys that are not handled while they are growing up become cold, aloof, and unfriendly not only to others but also to their own offspring. Such monkeys can be partially "repaired" over a period of about six months if placed with other monkeys, but the fact that it takes so long shows the devastating effects of no stimulation (Suomi, 1983).

Psychologist **Harry Harlow** showed this need for **contact comfort** dramatically in a series of studies with monkey babies. Monkeys were placed in a cage with two fake mothers (see Figure 5.4). One of the "mothers" was made of wire and had a bottle attached to it where the monkeys could feed. The other mother was covered with terry cloth but provided no food. Once the animals had adjusted to having the two mothers, a fear test was performed.

While a mechanical windup teddy bear is fascinating to a child, it is very frightening to a monkey, so it formed the basis for the test. The mechanical teddy bear was put into the cage. The monkeys panicked. Here is the key point: even though the monkeys were fed by the wire mother, they consistently ran to the cloth mother for protection and comfort when faced with the teddy bear. This indicates the importance of contact comfort in development. While we would expect the monkeys to go to the mother that fed them, the pleasant physical contact of the cloth made them feel far more secure (Harlow, 1959).

There are parallel situations in humans. In one study during World War II, infants who were reared in an institution where there was almost no personal attention in the form of touching or holding were compared with infants who were reared in a prison nursery where they had contact with their mothers. The results were frightening: 37 percent of the institution children died within a year, despite being fed and kept clean (Spitz, 1946).

There is even physical evidence of these needs. At the base of the brain is a unit called the *cerebellum*, which registers and controls bodily movement and sensation. (For more detail, see Chapter 3.) The cerebellum has a number of connections to emotional systems. Without enough rocking and touching, the cerebellum does not develop properly, which is likely to create permanent emotional and physical scars (Prescott, 1979). We suspect that nature sees to this need, giving mothers the desire, almost automatically, to rock their infants.

contact comfort

The satisfaction obtained from pleasant, soft stimulation.

▲ *Figure 5.4   This monkey has the best of both worlds—contact comfort with the soft "mother" and food from the other one.*

Points to Stress

Some students may argue that they are intrinsically motivated at school. They enjoy learning; they work hard because they enjoy doing their best. But if these students were told that they would not be receiving diplomas after four years, no matter how hard they worked, would they still work hard or even attend classes? The point is that intrinsic and extrinsic motivation often go hand in hand.

Discussion

On one side of a sheet of paper, have students write down all the ways in which they are intrinsically motivated. The other side should include their extrinsic motivations. Do the lists balance? Remind students that *extrinsic* should not be equated with "bad." Then ask students if there are any items on that list that they wish came more from within.

DISCUSS THE PHOTO

Many students will certainly question the ethics of separating a monkey from its mother. You may want to review the current ethics of experimentation at the end of Chapter 2.

DEMONSTRATION

Before discussing Maslow's hierarchy of needs, pass out copies of **Teaching Master 5-3A Maslow's Hierarchy of Needs** and present this scenario: *You are shipwrecked alone on a desert island. Which of the five needs listed in the middle of the sheet would you need to satisfy first? After satisfying this need, which need would you satis-* *fy next? And so on?* Have students write the number 1 next to the first need they would satisfy, a 2 next to the second need, and so on. Once they've completed this arrangement, discuss their choices. Then briefly explain Maslow's order and have them insert each need into its respective level on the pyramid. (If their previous arrangement of the needs differs from Maslow's order, have them scratch this to avoid confusion.)

Finally, have them match the adjectives at the bottom of the sheet with Maslow's needs. (Answers are listed on **Teaching Master 5-3B.**) This activity should help clarify the logic in the order of the hierarchy.

TEACHING MASTER 5-2

Which Needs Are More Important? This handout asks students to rank which needs are more important to them. It should be used prior to discussing Maslow. Most students will probably not rank physiological and safety needs as most important. In that case, point out that since these needs are already met for them, these needs do little to motivate them.

TEACHING MASTER 5-4

Characteristics of Self-Actualizers. This handout is a list of qualities that Maslow believed self-actualizers possess. Ask students how often the descriptions apply to them.

DISCUSS THE PHOTO

Maslow called the tendencies for self-actualization "meta-needs". These include desire for justice, beauty, goodness, uniqueness, autonomy, and truth.

Unit 2 BRAIN, BODY, AND AWARENESS

▲ *Figure 5.5 Maslow's hierarchy of needs.*

hierarchy of needs

A system that ranks needs one above the other with the most basic needs for physical survival at the bottom of the pyramid.

physiological needs

The bottom of the hierarchy: hunger and thirst.

safety needs

Part of the Maslow's hierarchy: shelter, nest egg of money.

belongingness needs

Part of the hierarchy: friendship, closeness with another.

self-esteem needs

Part of the hierarchy: liking and respecting yourself, feeling important and useful.

The Theory of Needs

Psychologist **Abraham Maslow** developed a theory called the **hierarchy of needs.** A hierarchy (HI-er-arc-ee) is a system that ranks items one above the other in importance. Maslow's goal was to put human needs into such an arrangement. The most obvious needs are at the base of the pyramid shown in Figure 5.5—the physiological, or physical, needs. These **physiological needs,** such as hunger and thirst, must be met first. When people are starving or thirsty, this will almost always dominate their thoughts and behavior.

Once the physiological needs are satisfied, however, we move upward. On the next level are the **safety needs.** Once we have food and water, we begin to experience other less-critical but still basic needs, such as trying to provide a little shelter and possibly a small nest egg of money so that we are "safe" over the long run.

When we are reasonably safe, we seek contact and love with another. This is called the **belongingness need.** We cannot survive very well over time without friendship and closeness, so these needs appear after safety.

It is very hard for anyone to feel important in the scheme of things unless at least one other person cares about him or her. So, once we have satisfied the need to belong, we begin to feel acceptable. Now we need to develop that self-acceptance into a sense of being more than a cog in the machinery—a sense of being a real person. These are the **self-esteem needs,** with self-esteem meaning liking and respecting yourself (in the positive sense, not in the sense of being "stuck-up").

▲ *Psychologist Abraham Maslow.*

INTERDISCIPLINARY PROJECT

Language Arts/List Poems. Have each group write a list poem that relates to Maslow's hierarchy. A list poem is simply that: a list. What makes it a poem is the unique phrasing, the order of the items, repetition, rhyme, line breaks, and so on. The creative writers in your class will supply you with good models in no time. Here are some examples of what they can list: "How I Feel Safe"; "Why I Don't Do My Best"; "Ways to Improve My Life"; "How to Become Self-Actualized"; "How to Belong."

Students will probably think of better titles. Explain that at first, every line is a good line; they shouldn't be too critical. Once they have more lines than they will use, they can begin to eliminate some.

Chapter 5 MOTIVATION AND EMOTION

 IN FOCUS   ## Unsatisfied Needs

Let's compare Maslow's five hierarchy of needs with a set of five building blocks. Once we arrange the first block to our satisfaction, we add the second block, and so on. A problem arises, however, when we can't arrange a particular block just the way we want.

For example, in the diagram shown here, someone has arranged the first two blocks pretty well. The third block, however, keeps falling over. This represents the fact that the person feels that he or she can develop no close or intimate relationships.

What's the solution? One obvious solution is to continue working on "block 3." If a relationship doesn't work out as well as expected, try again. As we all know, this is not always easy, but it is usually worthwhile. At the very least, don't believe that one or two failed relationships are a sign that all future relationships will fail.

Another "solution" is just to keep fiddling with and focusing on the first two blocks, thinking that this will take care of the falling block. This behavior is typical of some anorexics who may feel that they're not loved, so they compensate by becoming obsessed with food (in other words, they keep rearranging the first block over and over again).

Still another "solution" is to forget the third block and put the fourth block on the stack. The person still has a difficult time developing close relationships, but the problem becomes less noticeable. This is typical of workaholics who try to attain self-esteem strictly through their jobs, at the expense of a meaningful private life.

To sum all this up: if a person cannot directly satisfy a need, he or she may compensate by becoming obsessed with some other more accessible need. To **compensate** means to substitute one need for another.

What if a student is obsessed with becoming popular at school? How might this student be compensating for some need that hasn't been filled?

Unsatisfied Needs.

IN FOCUS   Someone who wants to be popular may feel insecure (level two) and compensate by trying hard to fit in, to belong in many groups (level three). Or maybe this person has low self-esteem (level four) and compensates by looking for approval from many people (level three).

Discussion

To further clarify Maslow's hierarchy, ask students how they satisfy or have satisfied each of the five levels of needs. For example, one's safety needs might be satisfied by locking the doors at night and installing an alarm system. Note that these help provide for physical safety which may lead to a sense of psychological safety.

Have each group think of two or three famous people or organizations that seem to operate almost exclusively at one of Maslow's five levels. For example, for level one, students might include poor people who don't know when their next meal will come. These people are obsessed with satisfying level one. For level two, students might include the homeless, and so on. Students' choices are often original and creative. Have them provide brief reasons for their choices. Almost any choice is acceptable if the reasoning is in line with Maslow's theory.

Journal Topic

"Describe how you satisfy your physiological, safety, belongingness, self-esteem, and self-actualization needs. You can focus on one or more of these needs."

Critical Thinking

Show several commercials in class and have students jot down which of Maslow's hierarchy needs the product in the commercial satisfies and to which need the ad appeals (This is similar to activity # 3 at the end of the chapter). What patterns can students find?

Discussion

Ask students the following question: In your experience, has the need for affiliation and approval increased or decreased as you advance through high school?

self-actualization needs

The top of the hierarchy: establishing meaningful goals and a purpose in life.

need for affiliation

Psychological motivation for belonging to and identifying with groups.

need for approval

Psychological motivation for obtaining other people's good opinion of oneself.

need for achievement

Psychological motivation for personal accomplishment.

Having attained the needs of the bottom four levels of the hierarchy, we are in a position to go on to even greater things—the need to establish meaningful goals and a purpose in life, called **self-actualization needs.** This term refers to our ability to put into practice (actualize) whatever skills and talents we possess. If you have carpentry skills, then these are used to make a fine product, the best you can—not something shoddy that barely hangs together. If you have musical talent, then you develop it so that you can sing or play an instrument beautifully and meaningfully (Maslow, 1954).

Maslow's theory has had an effect on our understanding of people who have trouble in life. They may lack a sense of purpose because they have failed to satisfy their needs at one of the lower levels. For example, someone stuck at the belongingness level has a "hole which has to be filled, an emptiness into which love [needs to be] poured" (Maslow, 1968, p. 39).

Psychological Motivation

The discussion so far strongly suggests that physiological needs are only part of the motivational picture. Since most of us are fortunate enough to get basic needs like hunger and thirst met on a regular basis, we don't have to spend a great deal of time dealing with them. Instead, we direct our energies toward more psychologically satisfying activities. The specific goals we choose will depend largely on what we have learned to seek out.

From time to time, psychologists have tried to make complete lists of such psychological motives—that is, needs human beings seem to have that lack any clear survival value. The lists are many, and the number of possibilities is nearly endless. For example, there are people who are "joiners," who seem to need to belong to every club and organization that comes along. People like this are said to have a high **need for affiliation.**

Some people seem willing to do almost anything to get other people to like them. They are even concerned about the opinions of people they don't know. These people are high in the **need for approval.** Both of these groups have *learned* to value these goals and to associate them with good feelings or a sense of personal satisfaction.

Achievement Motivation One psychological motive stands out from the rest, probably because our culture values individual success so highly. The **need for achievement**—a strong desire for personal accomplishment and a high degree of competence—has long been a favorite subject for study. People who are high in achievement motivation tend to seek out challenges and to stick with tasks once they start. They also work harder and accomplish more than the average person.

Pass out several sections of newspapers and tell students they must find one example for each of Maslow's hierarchy needs. The article can relate to the need in any way, as long as support is offered. For example, a story about a starving person could show that this person has not satisfied level one and would therefore not care much about self-esteem or belongingness. On the other hand, if the starving person is actually staging a protest, then the story may be about someone who is self-actualizing, someone who is willing to sacrifice to convey a message.

Journal Topic

"I do my best when. . ." The concept of self-actualization can be elusive to students, and this entry might help to make it more concrete. If you don't like this opening, just tell them to write about times when they have done their best.

As is true of other psychological motivation, the need for achievement seems to be learned. The parents of high achievers encourage and reward this kind of behavior. So do the schools and society at large. There is also evidence that firstborn children are more often high achievers than later-born children (Falbo & Polit, 1986). One explanation of this finding is that parents are more involved with their firstborn because their attention is not so scattered.

While a high need for achievement is generally seen as a positive thing, it *can* be taken too far. People sometimes feel terrible pressure to constantly do more and more, better and better. When this is the case, they often have trouble relaxing and suffer more than most of us from the effects of stress. And since we are on the subject of motivation, another problem is worth mentioning: people who develop eating disorders (see the "Psychology in Your Life" section at the end of this chapter) often come from families that emphasize very high levels of achievement (Yates, 1989).

EMOTIONS

Emotions are part of our physical survival system. Without anger and fear, for instance, we could not protect ourselves. In this sense, we are very much like animals. Again, however, humans often express themselves in a social and symbolic context. Thus, rioters have been known to destroy police cars because the cars are a symbol of authority, not because the cars pose an immediate life-threatening danger to the rioters.

Scientists have been arguing for centuries about how many human emotions there are and how they differ. The issue still has not been settled. (Try sometime to come up with a clear distinction between anger and frustration, and you will see what the problem is.) However, people the world over seem to share certain basic emotions, such as joy, fear, anger, and sadness. Beyond this short list, though, we can't go very far. Significant cultural differences exist. For instance, what events produce which emotion? How and under what circumstances are emotions expressed? Each culture will have its own answers to these questions. It's usually a mistake, then, to assume that everyone everywhere responds and feels the same way (Mesquita & Frijda, 1992).

Cognition and Emotion

Cognition (symbolic thought processes) is intimately involved in the emotions we feel. Thus, in laboratory experiments, when one group of people is led to believe they will experience pain, that group becomes far more anxious than another group whose members are

Chapter 5 MOTIVATION AND EMOTION

▲ *These expressions of emotion are pretty easy to read.*

cognition
Symbolic thought processes.

FYI Although Maslow prided himself on being a scientist (in fact, he worked with Harry Harlow), he realized the limitations of science when it came to understanding human potential. He boldly ventured beyond science and explored self-actualization and other elusive concepts. For example, Maslow studied "peak experiences," fleeting moments when we feel completely fulfilled or happy. We can't manufacture these moments, but we all have them, and if we allow them to, they can change our lives.

DISCUSS THE PHOTO

After studying a large number of babies, one researcher found that we experience all the basic human emotions before age two.

Literature. Have students analyze characters in fiction in terms of motivation and emotion. You can use one short story for the whole class, or set them up in groups and assign a different story to each group. At what levels in Maslow's hierarchy are the characters operating? Emphasize that a character will probably operate at more than one level; tell them to look for this and use examples to support their conclusions. What theory of emotion best explains the character's feelings? Again, more than one answer may apply. Is there any other material in the chapter that helps to shed light on a character's motivation?

DISCUSS THE PHOTO

You might want to turn back to this photo when you discuss phobias.

Reteaching Strategy

Have students illustrate one of the concepts discussed in the chapter. For example, they might draw, with captions explaining the three theories of emotions, three people encountering a black cat.

Comprehension Check

Name the type of motivation in the following: you read your sister's diary *(curiosity)*; you read your favorite novel even though it is not assigned *(intrinsic)*; you rearrange your furniture *(manipulation)*; you do chores and receive an allowance *(extrinsic)*; you join a sorority or fraternity *(need for affiliation)*; you give into peer pressure *(need for approval)*; you work to become valedictorian *(need for achievement)*.

144

Unit 2 BRAIN, BODY, AND AWARENESS

▲ *Terror or exhilaration? You decide.*

told they will not be hurt. If the first group receives a minor shock, they overestimate how agonizing it is—just from the expectation of pain. Or take the sensation of starting to fall forward or backward. All of us immediately panic as we try to correct for it. But if we label the sensation as *fun*, then we don't react that way to the same sensations. Example? A roller coaster ride. Imagine how you would respond if all those sensations were present while you were sitting in class. So, how something feels becomes a matter of interpretation.

Often physical arousal cannot be identified as a specific emotion until we label it. For example, two people meet face to face, about to get into a fight. One is seven feet tall and weighs 275 pounds; the other is five feet tall and weighs 75 pounds. Both are fully aroused physically, and devices that measure bodily responses wouldn't show a difference between them. Even so, aren't they feeling different emotions?

Theories of Emotion

We will discuss three theories of emotion in the sections that follow. At present, our understanding of emotion is still incomplete, so all three theories can stand side by side as possible "answers," even though they are different. And one theory might fit a particular set of circumstances to which another one doesn't even apply.

James-Lange theory

For emotion, first the body responds, *then* one feels the emotion.

The James-Lange Theory   The **James-Lange** (Lang) **theory,** named after the two men who proposed it, is simple. But it can be confusing unless you pay close attention. The theory suggests that

ENRICHMENT

Have students find out what happens physically when we are emotional. The class might focus on four or five specific emotions that they would like to explore.

DISCOVERY

Ask the class to make a long list of emotions and transfer these emotions onto note cards. Divide the class in half and play a version of charades in which players act out the emotion. Don't allow students to communicate what the emotion sounds like or break the word up into syllables; they must act it out. Which emotions are more easily identifiable?

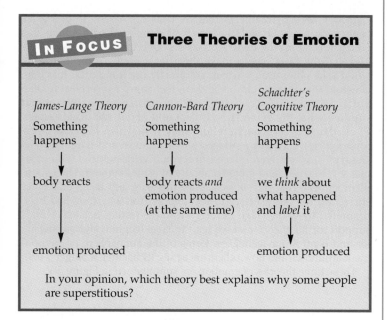

IN FOCUS **Three Theories of Emotion**

James-Lange Theory	Cannon-Bard Theory	Schachter's Cognitive Theory
Something happens	Something happens	Something happens
↓	↓	↓
body reacts	body reacts *and* emotion produced (at the same time)	we *think* about what happened and *label* it
↓		↓
emotion produced		emotion produced

In your opinion, which theory best explains why some people are superstitious?

emotions operate in reverse of the way most of us assume. In general, people think that we see a snake, feel an emotion, then run. These two men claimed that we see a snake, our bodies respond, we run, and *only then* do we feel an emotion because the body is so keyed up. They arrived at this theory because they believed that just thinking about or seeing a snake has no real effect until *after* the body has responded. So our physical feelings *are* the emotions.

The Cannon-Bard Theory   The **Cannon-Bard theory** of emotion is also named after two scientists. Their theory arose after the discovery of the thalamus as a physical unit of the brain that can instantly transmit messages (Chapter 3). They claim that when an emergency is perceived, both the bodily reaction and the emotional system respond at the same time. So, while James-Lange waited for the body to respond first, in this theory both occur together.

The Cannon-Bard theory might fit many cases, but for some the James-Lange would fit better. For instance, in a near accident, we respond physically first, by reflex, and then later we start feeling panic. In this situation, the brain takes roughly two seconds to respond, a *long* time in an emergency. Hence, what we are feeling over the near accident comes after the body is stirred up.

Schachter's Cognitive Theory   The psychologist **Stanley Schachter** (SHACK-ter) performed experiments to support his

Cannon-Bard theory

The bodily reaction and the emotional response to an event occur at the same time.

Theories of Emotions.

 James-Lange: we see a black cat; our heart races; fear. Cannon-Bard: we see a black cat; our heart races, and fear is produced at the same time. Schachter's: we see a black cat; "They are evil," we think; "I'm afraid," we think.

Discussion

Ask students their opinions on the following questions: Is one gender more emotional than another? Does one gender show more emotion? If so, does the showing or expressing lead to greater feelings? On the other hand, if we constantly hide or stifle our emotions, do we in fact become less emotional?

EXPERIMENT

Make a list of about ten words that may evoke emotion and mix these with ten neutral words. Ask a volunteer to report the first word that comes to mind when hearing each word. You should find that it takes the volunteer longer to process and respond to the emotional words. (You might have someone actually time the interval.) Some suggested emotion words: *rejected, fight, cry.* Some neutral words: *eraser, window, walk.*

ENRICHMENT

Have students complete the **Enrichment Worksheet** for this chapter located in the Teacher Resources.

Comprehension Check

Which of the three theories of emotion apply to the fact that usually when you cry at a wedding, you're happy; but when you cry at a funeral, you're sad? *(Schacter's cognitive theory)*

Reteaching Strategy

Have students complete the **Reteaching Worksheet** for this chapter located in the Teacher Resources.

The **Vocabulary Worksheet** may be completed by the class as a pretest for chapter concepts or used as a reteaching worksheet for those students needing additional review.

DISCUSS THE PHOTO

Do students have any anecdotal evidence of their own to support one of these theories?

Unit 2 BRAIN, BODY, AND AWARENESS

cognitive theory (Schachter)

We label a bodily response by giving it the name of an emotion we think we are feeling.

cognitive theory—the belief that we label our bodily responses as being certain emotions. His subjects were injected with adrenaline, which speeds up the body's processes. One group of subjects was told that the drug would make them feel "high" or on top of the world. The other group, which got exactly the same drug injection, was told the drug would make them feel angry. Subjects were then put in a room with stooges who were to act in a fashion that would support what the subjects had been told about the drug's effect. Thus, the subjects who were told they would feel high were surrounded by very happy stooges playing games and laughing. The "angry" subjects were placed in a room with stooges who complained, moaned, and groaned about almost everything. The experiment showed that the subjects, once the drug had taken effect and stirred up the body, began to feel and act the way they had been prompted to—either high or angry. In these results, Schachter finds support for his theory that we tend to label (cognitively) our behavior and control our feelings in terms of the atmosphere or environment around us and how others are acting (Schachter & Singer, 1962).

These three theories of emotion are summarized in Figure 5.6.

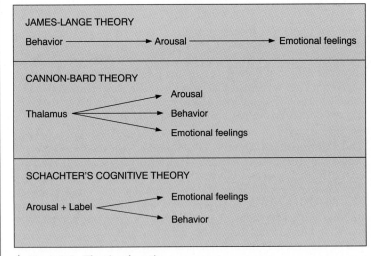

Theories of Emotion

JAMES-LANGE THEORY

Behavior ⟶ Arousal ⟶ Emotional feelings

CANNON-BARD THEORY

Thalamus ⟶ Arousal
Thalamus ⟶ Behavior
Thalamus ⟶ Emotional feelings

SCHACHTER'S COGNITIVE THEORY

Arousal + Label ⟶ Emotional feelings
Arousal + Label ⟶ Behavior

▲ *Figure 5.6   Theories of emotion.*

COOPERATIVE LEARNING

Break the class into three large groups and have each adopt as its own belief one of the three theories of emotions for a few minutes. Introduce the following situation and have each group interpret the situa- tion and argue that its own theory is correct: *Someone grabs you from behind by the shoulder and shoves you hard enough to throw you off balance. You don't fall, however, and you don't know who grabbed you.*

What emotion is evoked, if any? When is it evoked? The point is not to discard one of the theories or to imply that one is better than another but to clarify the fine points of each theory and to show that all are valid.

PSYCHOLOGY IN YOUR LIFE

Trying to Survive Body Size

▲ To the average Alaskan native male, the heavier Alaskan native woman is far more appealing than the skinny Anglo woman.

The average wolf weighs about 80 pounds. It is not unusual for it to eat up to 18 pounds of meat at one sitting (Lopez, 1978). Yet it would be rare to find an obese wolf, even in areas of plenty. Humans, on the other hand, have made the process of eating and not eating so complex that it often involves nothing but chaos, anxiety, and a great deal of injury to both psyche and body. If you have been trying to make sense out of all the conflicting claims in this area and have gotten lost, join the club. At best, things are murky. Some scientists say too much salt and cholesterol are bad; others say they are irrelevant. Some say too much fat is bad; others say it is not necessarily harmful. Alaskan natives used to put a premium on obesity in both male and female marriage partners, while every decade or so, people in the other states try to turn themselves into walking sticks with a cell or two hanging onto them. We want to outline here some of the things that seem to be pretty well established with the hope that at least a few partially reasonable facts will be available to you.

Most rats know better than to keep eating the same thing over and over and over. Some variety of foods seems necessary for humans, too. Certain types of food groups have been well established as providing vitamin and mineral needs. These are listed, with no preaching or discussion, in one of the half-dozen annual almanacs (such as *World Almanac* or *Information Please Almanac*) sold for a few dollars at drugstores and in supermarkets.

There is nothing inherently wrong with fat, salt, or sugar. They are all necessary for survival. And when the body doesn't have enough fat or sugar, it will make its own.

(continued on next page)

(continued on next page)

DISCUSS THE PHOTO

Not only does the ideal body size vary between cultures, but over time, it varies within cultures, too.

PSYCHOLOGY IN YOUR LIFE

Enrichment

Have students bring in commercials or other media material (propaganda?) that promote a certain body size. If they use print ads, they might trace the progression of the "ideal" body size from the 1950s to the present.

Discussion

Ask students at what age they believe people are most influenced by the "ideal" body size presented in the media. As we mature, do we become progressively immune to the messages?

DISCOVERY

Teaching Master 5-5 Setting Goals asks students to set four concrete goals for themselves. Emphasize the value of visualizing goals. You can probably offer a few personal examples. Or how about a musical example, such as Joe Jackson's "You Can't Get What You Want 'Til You Know What You Want"? Or maybe you can set a class goal. (Put together a psychology fair? See the Teacher Resources.)

Discussion

Ask students the following questions: How do cultural factors affect eating habits? (Answers will vary widely. Students may mention that it is acceptable to eat meat in America but not in some other countries. Not only that, but meat here is served quickly and inexpensively.)

Discussion

Do you eat more when you're upset—for example, after a bad day? If yes, does eating make you feel better, worse, or no different?

PSYCHOLOGY IN YOUR LIFE

Trying to Survive Body Size

(continued from previous page) On the other hand, we humans do not seem to have very good detectors for telling us when we are over-doing any of the three. We must have had these detectors at one time, but somehow over the centuries their effectiveness has been destroyed. The body still does show some wisdom in terms of a need for fruits and vegetables, since many people still get a craving for them. But we must remain skeptical of something like a "craving" for a hot dog.

Food can act in a fashion similar to a narcotic in that it can relieve tension by making a person groggy. This is especially true of chocolate, which has a chemical composition that makes us sleepy. Hence, many can fall prey to using food much as someone would use alcohol or drugs.

One of the toughest decisions many slightly heavy people have to make is what to do if the fashion of the moment is to be skinny. Set points are just plain higher for some people than for others. But there can be so much social pressure that it is hard to know how to handle it.

One of the most serious dangers is the possibility of developing an *eating disorder*. In eating disorders, the person's preoccupation with food and/or weight makes him or her unable to read accurately the body's signals about what food the body needs. Thus, the person eats or refuses to eat for the wrong reasons. (See Chapter 11 for a more complete discussion.)

In some kinds of eating disorders, people become so obsessed with dieting that they become dangerously underweight. Still, they refuse to eat. Over time, the body gradually adapts to lower and lower weights until eventually it is impossible to eat much of anything. Some people die of starvation because they simply can't hold down any food. In another kind of eating disorder, the person eats a great deal of food and then throws it up or takes heavy doses of laxatives in order to avoid gaining weight.

"Speed," or amphetamines, make people so jumpy and nervous that they don't want to eat. While weight loss is possible by taking these drugs, the odds are very great that the users will become addicted to them and wind up with much more serious problems than they had at the beginning.

If you want to make money, write a diet book, because there is always one on the best-seller list. These books often suggest dangerous paths to follow, though. Some fad diets can kill you by depriving you of absolutely necessary nutrients. Most people who go on one of these diets get off it within about six months anyway. A fad diet is not worth the risk. About the only consistent and safe way to lower weight is by exercising and eating less food (and, of course, not gorging on fat and sugars). If you are *actually* overweight, try eating at mealtimes only for a while and see what happens. Or try eating a little less on a consistent basis.

None of this may help, but maybe it will. A couple of final ideas to make life a little better for everybody: try to look at your body in a positive way; we *all* have our good points and bad points. And every one of us has such

(continued on next page)

VOCABULARY REVIEW

Before testing students on the contents of this chapter, you may want to review vocabulary terms that are especially important or confusing. Terms in this chapter that could require clarification are *motivation*, *emotion*, *drives*, and *cognition*.

PSYCHOLOGY IN YOUR LIFE

Trying to Survive Body Size

(continued from previous page)

oddities as hair follicles, funny-looking nostrils, and all the rest. If your weight is honestly out of control— either too thin or too heavy— you are not alone. But something needs to be done. One of the most comfortable ways to handle it is to join a group of other people who are working together on the same problem. You'll get plenty of support from the group as you work to improve your health.

SUMMARY

1. Motivation consists of drives that make us seek specific goals. Emotion involves various states of the body that cause feelings; these feelings vary in terms of how we view a situation.
2. The hypothalamus contains centers for pleasure, pain, rage, sex, hunger, thirst, and fear. It controls other units of the body as we seek satisfaction or respond to certain feelings.
3. The reticular formation controls the level of bodily activation. Given a need, it increases the body's activity noticeably.
4. The pituitary gland works under instructions from the hypothalamus and secretes chemicals that stir up the body.
5. The gonads control which sex the fetus will be and, later in life, they trigger sexual responses.
6. Hunger is signaled by the hypothalamus after taking into account stomach contractions, intestinal receptors, taste, and blood-sugar level.
7. A set point is the body's determination of what weight each individual should be.
8. Thirst is also controlled by the hypothalamus; here the dryness of the tongue and the amount of water in body cells are also registered to determine if water is necessary.
9. Curiosity and manipulation motives seem to be needs of the brain. The evidence is clear that physically we also need stimulation and contact comfort.
10. Abraham Maslow's hierarchy of needs ranks our needs in a pyramid of importance. Most basic are physiological and safety needs, followed by belongingness and self-esteem, and at the top is self-actualization.
11. Psychological motivation involves learned needs. These include a need for affiliation, a need for approval, and a need for achievement.
12. The James-Lange theory of emotion claims that the body is stirred up first and then the emotion is felt. The Cannon-Bard theory says that the thalamus causes both the body and the emotion to be stirred up at the same time. Schachter's cognitive theory suggests that we call a particular excited state of the body by a label or name, so emotion is actually a cognitive process.

Wrapping It Up

Maslow makes it easy to end on a positive note. Here are some practical applications of his ideas. As parents and teachers, we should recognize the potential in our children and allow them the freedom to reach that potential. As managers, we can motivate workers by allowing them to satisfy higher-level needs on the job, involving them in decision making rather than encouraging them to be obsessed with lower-level security needs. Companies hired Maslow to conduct how-to seminars on motivation. As doctors, we should view patients as human beings, not medical conditions. Maslow dropped out of medical school because he saw it as an inhumane environment. All in all, he believed we should view the human as a whole.

SUGGESTED READINGS

▼ Green, R., et al. *Human Motivation.* New York: Allyn & Bacon, 1984.

▼ Hoffman, Edward. *The Right to be Human.* New York: St. Martin's Press, 1988.

▼ Spence, J. T. ed. *Achievement and Achievement Motives.* New York: W. H. Freeman, 1983.

SUGGESTED VIDEOS

▼ *Motivation and Emotion.* Discovering Psychology series, part 12. 27 min. 1-800-LEARNER.

▼ *A New Look at Motivation.* 32 min. CRM/McGraw-Hill.

VOCABULARY

motivation
emotion
hypothalamus
reticular formation
pituitary gland
adrenal glands
gonads
testes
ovaries
androgens
estrogen
drives
homeostasis
blood-sugar level

glucose
set point
curiosity motive
manipulation motive
intrinsic motivation
extrinsic motivation
Harry Harlow
contact comfort
hierarchy of needs (Maslow)
Abraham Maslow
physiological needs
safety needs
belongingness needs

self-esteem needs
self-actualization needs
need for affiliation
need for approval
need for achievement
cognition
James-Lange theory
Cannon-Bard theory
Schachter's cognitive theory

Answers to Review Questions

1. A
2. R
3. P
4. P
5. A
6. R
7. estrogen
8. gonads
9. estrogen
10. androgens

Review Questions

For each of the following, answer R for reticular formation, P for pituitary gland, and A for adrenal glands.

1. Helps us react in an emergency
2. Regulates level of activity in the body
3. Signals other glands to release chemicals
4. Located just below hypothalamus
5. Releases chemicals that affect heart rate
6. Controls sleep

Fill in the blanks; answer on a separate sheet of paper. (An answer may consist of more than one word.)

7. The female hormone is called ___?___.
8. Sex glands are called ___?___.
9. ___?___ regulates the female reproductive cycle.
10. Male hormones are called ___?___.

For each of the following, answer yes *if it does cause hunger,* no *if it does not.*

11. Taste
12. Stomach contractions
13. Low blood-sugar level
14. High blood-sugar level
15. Cell size

True/False

16. We are born with certain set points, and they do not change with age.
17. A person's set point is partly determined by fat cells.
18. Inherited factors may lead to weight problems.
19. The hypothalamus regulates both hunger and thirst.

Matching

20. Bank accounts
21. Self-acceptance
22. Hunger
23. Doing your best
24. Friendship

a. belongingness needs
b. self-actualization needs
c. safety needs
d. physiological needs
e. self-esteem needs

Matching

25. Joining groups
26. Studying hard in order to make the honor roll
27. Being friendly to people you don't know

a. need for approval
b. need for affiliation
c. need for achievement

Matching

28. Body's reaction and emotion occur simultaneously.
29. Emotions are produced through labeling them.
30. Body reacts first, then emotion is produced.

a. James-Lange theory
b. Schachter's cognitive theory
c. Cannon-Bard theory

DISCUSSION QUESTIONS

1. The chapter mentions that eating is a special ritual. Analyze your own family's meals, taking into account both past and present gatherings. What "rituals" does your family seem to follow? What do these rituals say about your family? Have the rituals changed over the years? What does this say about your family?

2. Do you think that, in general, motivation changes as you get older? If so, in what ways

11. yes
12. yes
13. yes
14. no
15. yes
16. false
17. true
18. true
19. true
20. c
21. e
22. d
23. b
24. a
25. b
26. c
27. a
28. c
29. b
30. a

Notes on Discussion Questions

1. This is a fun issue to discuss in class, especially if your students represent a wide range of ethnic backgrounds.

2. If you discuss this question in class, break it down into categories. (1) How do developmental changes affect motivation? For example, as one becomes older, metabolism slows down. Does this motivate us to exercise more or less? (2) How do interpersonal changes affect motivation? For example, does marriage increase or decrease the need for safety? (3) How do career choices affect motivation?

3. You may find that some of your students *do* get cash for grades. Does it motivate them now? Did it motivate them when they were younger? Is there a prime age for using money in this way?

4. Most answers will fit somewhere on Maslow's hierarchy of needs. Relating students' answers to Maslow's theory should provide an effective summary.

5. Physiological and safety needs are extrinsically satisfied for the most part. Food, water, and housing are examples. Belongingness, self-esteem, and self-actualization needs are intrinsically satisfied for the most part. For example, if we enroll in a course, it's safe to assume that we belong in that course, yet for various reasons we may not

always feel as if we belong. We need to decide intrinsically that we belong; our enrollment registration card (an extrinsic symbol) may be insufficient. You can probably think of several exceptions to these examples. For instance, someone may extrinsically satisfy his or her safety needs by installing 17 dead-

bolt locks on the doors of his or her house, yet this person may still feel unsafe.

6. Answers will vary.

7. Many people do not strive to do their best because they haven't satisfied the lower levels in Maslow's hierarchy. Or perhaps some people don't do their best because then the

does it change? Be specific. If not, provide examples to show that motivation does not change.

3. Imagine that your parents gave you $100 for each A that you received on your report card. First, do you think that the money would motivate you? Why or why not? Second, assume that the money did motivate you. Would you actually learn more? Why or why not?

4. Besides money, what motivates your parent(s) to go to work every day? Explain. Which motivators are more important—money or the ones you've just listed? Explain.

5. Briefly define extrinsic and intrinsic motivation. Then analyze Maslow's theory and decide which of his hierarchy of needs are extrinsically satisfied, which are intrinsically satisfied, and which, if any, are satisfied in both ways. Explain.

6. Compare Maslow's hierarchy of needs to your own life. Which needs have you

adequately satisfied? Explain. (If you have indeed satisfied these needs, you don't spend much time thinking about them.) Which needs are you currently trying to satisfy? Explain. (These are needs that you *do* spend a great deal of time thinking about.)

7. According to Maslow, self-actualizers are people who strive to do their best, strive to reach their potential. If you look around, you'll probably agree that very few people consistently choose this path. Why not? Offer several reasons or explanations.

8. Think of a time when someone rejected you (for a job, a date, a favor, whatever). Which of the theories of emotions best describes how you felt after the rejection? Explain.

9. Write down five or six fairly basic emotions. Think about your friends, family, and teachers. Do they express these emotions differently? Describe the similarities and differences in emotional expression. What types of events or situations produce which emotions?

ACTIVITIES

1. The chapter explains that hunger is a product of both internal and external cues. Make a list of everything that you ate yesterday. Next to each food item, write *I* if the item was eaten primarily because of internal cues (for example, you were hungry), and write *E* if the item was eaten primarily because of external cues (it was time to eat, everyone else was eating, the food was there, and so on). For some items, both *I* and *E* may apply. In this case, pick the cue that seemed dominant, or stronger, at the time.

Analyze your list. Is there a pattern? Which cues seem to play a greater role in your eating habits? Explain.

If there is a pattern, this may have something to do with your family life. To find out, conduct a brief survey. Interview the person who does the grocery shopping and/or cooking for your household. Have this person make a list of everything he or she ate the day before. After the list is made, explain to this person about internal and external cues, and then have the person mark each item *I* or *E* just as you did for yourself. Urge the interviewee to be honest.

Did a pattern develop in your interviewee's answers? Compare these answers to your own answers. Can you draw any conclusions? Is there too much

best will be expected in the future. It's easier to be average. Students will think of numerous other valid answers.

8. Answers will vary.

9. This can be a good role-playing activity. How does a parent, a teacher, or a friend express anger (or another emotion)?

Notes on Activities

1. To prepare students for this activity, you might have each student find an article about dieting methods and follow this up with a class discussion. Do the diets try to curb the influence of external cues? What do the diets suggest people do about internal cues? Do diet plans work?

The few students who have tried different diets may not be willing to discuss their experiences, but they and others may be willing to discuss their parents' diets.

2. Contacting a fast-food restaurant is optional and requires extra effort by students. You may want to offer extra credit: no homework for one night?

3. Before assigning this activity, bring in several ads and analyze them according to the instructions in the activity. Some students may need this practice in order to complete the activity properly.

4. This is a good one to discuss in class after students have completed the assignment. Or you may want to conduct this activity in class yourself. Simply bring several ads and a radio into class.

5. See numbers 3 and 4.

---

food in your house? The wrong kinds of food? Explain.

2. Conduct an experiment to find out the influence of visual external cues on eating. Buy a package of cookies or some other snack that your family likes. One day, leave the snack on the table, the kitchen counter, or somewhere else very visible, and see how many cookies are eaten by the end of the day. Wait a few days, and buy the same snack. This time, make sure somehow that everyone knows about the snack, but stick it in a drawer or in the refrigerator or somewhere else that is *not* very visible. But don't hide it; everyone should know where it is. Again, count how many cookies are eaten by the end of the day. Compare your results. Discuss your conclusions.

   If you're ambitious, you can contact a local fast-food restaurant and have the owner conduct a similar experiment. In this case, the owner one day would put up pictures of, let's say, a hot dog, and the next day he or she would put up no pictures.

3. Some people feel that Maslow's theory has had an effect on the world of advertising. To understand how, collect 20 magazine ads, all for different products. Then take a sheet of paper, number it from 1 to 20, and divide it into three long columns. Label the columns as follows: *Product; Need That the Product Satisfies;* and *Needs* (notice plural) *That the Ad Appeals to.* For example, the first entry might look like this:

Product	Need That the Product Satisfies	Needs That the Ad Appeals to
1. Brand "X" soda	physiological need	belongingness needs self-esteem needs

In other words, soda satisfies a basic physiological need: thirst. Advertisers, however, in order to sell their products, appeal to our belongingness needs: they present images of friends having a good time. Also, they appeal to our self-esteem needs: they use slogans like "It'll make you feel better about yourself." Next, analyze your chart. Are the second and third columns identical or vastly different? Do any patterns develop in either column? If so, how do you account for this? Did your results turn out as expected, or were you surprised? Explain.

4. An alternative to the activity in number 3 might be to watch 20 television commercials or listen to 20 radio commercials, and then follow the same directions and answer the same questions. In this case, when you're analyzing the third column—*Needs the Commercial Appeals to*—you might take into account background music, narrator's voice, and dialogue.

5. This next idea will count as two activities (just in case your teacher is counting). Do *both* of the activities in numbers 3 and 4; that is, fill out a chart for magazine ads *and* a chart for television commercials. In this case, skip the questions listed, and focus instead on comparing the two charts. Do advertisers use different appeals in magazines than they do on television or radio? Explain. Point out numerous differences and similarities.

DISCUSS THE PHOTO

This photo could serve as a metaphor for the subconscious that lies just below the surface.

What seems to be reality is sometimes only its reflection.

154

PSYCHOLOGY AND YOU RESOURCES

A variety of resources are available in the Psychology and You *supplementary material. In addition, there are a number of additional resources listed to enhance your lesson plans.*

Masters
▼ 6-1A Learning Goals
▼ 6-1B Answers to Learning Goals
▼ 6-2 A Dream Assignment
▼ 6-3 Journal Topics
▼ 6-4 Dream Tasks

Student Worksheets
▼ Vocabulary Worksheet
▼ Independent Practice Worksheet
▼ Enrichment Worksheet
▼ Reteaching Worksheet

Test Bank
▼ Tests A and B

Multimedia
▼ *The Brain* Videotape Modules #15–17
▼ Psychology Videodisc
▼ **Mindscope** Exercises 1, 2, 10, 19
▼ Psychology Videodisc

Student Workbook

PACING CHART

Complete Coverage

Day 1: Have students read "Defining Consciousness" before class. Conduct an in-class activity or discussion focusing on understanding the term *construct*. End class with a discussion on the levels of consciousness, and assign "Chrono-biology and Unseen Forces" for Day 2.

Day 2: Focus on biological clocks and entrainment. The wrap contains examples of ways to encourage discussion and analysis of these topics. Assign "The Nature of Sleep and Dreams" and have students do the exercise in Psychology In Your Life for homework.

Day 3: Conduct an in-class activity requiring students to distinguish between REM and NREM sleep, as well as the brian-wave pattern changes during sleep. Have students read the "Psychology of Dreams" and "Practical Issues in Sleep" sections for Day 4.

Day 4: Have a few willing students share their dreams with the class to spark discussion about

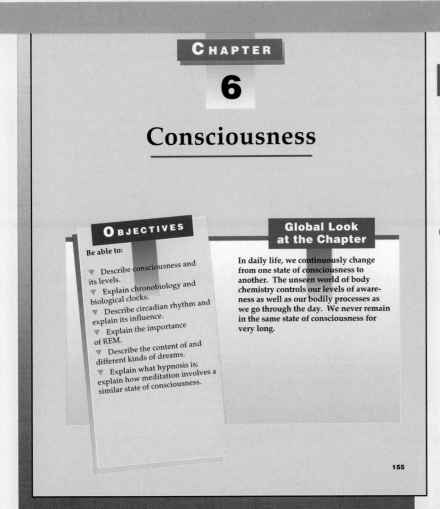

6

Consciousness

OBJECTIVES

Be able to:

▼ Describe consciousness and its levels.

▼ Explain chronobiology and biological clocks.

▼ Describe circadian rhythm and explain its influence.

▼ Explain the importance of REM.

▼ Describe the content of and different kinds of dreams.

▼ Explain what hypnosis is; explain how meditation involves a similar state of consciousness.

Global Look at the Chapter

In daily life, we continuously change from one state of consciousness to another. The unseen world of body chemistry controls our levels of awareness as well as our bodily processes as we go through the day. We never remain in the same state of consciousness for very long.

155

Ask students if they believe that love and hate exist. Can they prove it—that is, can they provide evidence that they exist? Explain that these terms are constructs and that the focus of the chapter will be another construct, namely consciousness. Can they provide evidence of consciousness?

LEAD-OFF ACTIVITY

Bring in a book on dreams, the kind that lists common dream images and what they allegedly mean. Most libraries stock such books. Ask students to think of objects or images they've dreamt about and consult your handy book for an interpretation. It shouldn't take long for students to realize that the interpretations are too pat, too general. Some of these books are better than others, and some may even be essentially sound, but emphasize that dream interpretation is hard work. Those who choose to pursue this work should note this: each of us is potentially the best interpreter of his or her own dreams.

dream content and the three major theories about why we dream (refer to the In Focus box). Provide an exercise that allows students to identify the various "practical issues in sleep" covered in the text. Assign "States of Consciousness" for Day 5.

Day 5: After reviewing the nature of hypnosis, encourage discussion about popular conceptions regarding its use. Contrast it with meditation. Give the Chapter Review quiz.

In Brief

Day 1: Use discussion question #1 to facilitate understanding of the term *construct,* and then use discussion question #2 or 3 in the text to make the connection between this term and *consciousness.* End with a review of chronobiology.

Day 2: Present an activity or discussion question regarding the psychology of dreams. Assign the exercise in Psychology in Your Life for homework.

Day 3: Discuss the etiology and uses of both hypnosis and meditation. Give the Chapter Review quiz.

DEMONSTRATION

Have students fill in the following blanks as they pertain to the last few hours: I tasted _____. I smelled _____. I saw _____. I touched_____. I heard _____. I remembered_____. I felt _____. I thought _____.

These sensations, feelings, and perceptions are processed and sometimes stored and accumulated to form our consciousness. Our consciousness is different each moment. Do the exercise again and students will probably fill in the blanks differently. Even if the answers are the same, it is with the added realization that they *are* the same!

Journal Topic

"Watch yourself from the outside. Pick a recent day in your life and describe it from the third-person point of view (using he or she). Don't be satisfied with merely reporting details; include opinions, evaluations, and so on. For example, 'She argued with her dad for 30 minutes and would not admit to herself that she was being stubborn.' Notice it's *she*, not I." This picture they paint with words, along with all the other pictures in their lives, makes up what we call consciousness.

TEACHING MASTER 6-1A

Learning Goals. A Learning Goals sheet for each chapter is provided in the Teacher Resources. These Learning Goals can be used as review sheets or as worksheets. **Teaching Master 6-1B** consists of answers to these Learning Goals.

156

Unit 2 BRAIN, BODY, AND AWARENESS

construct

A concept requiring a belief in something that cannot be seen or touched but that seems to exist.

consciousness

The awareness of, or the possibility of knowing, what is happening inside or outside the organism.

DEFINING CONSCIOUSNESS

Years ago a teacher told one of us that we couldn't prove that a rock rolling down a hill didn't know where it was going. The whole class sat there and looked at him. We didn't know what to say. In a way, though, he had a point. Exactly what is consciousness? It is a lot harder to define than you might think at first; we can't touch it, find it, or pick it up. It is a **construct.** A construct is a concept that requires a belief in something that cannot be seen or touched but that, according to evidence, actually is present.

The ancients (1500s) came up with an idea for measuring consciousness. They took people who were obviously dying and put them on large scales. Researchers were stationed in front of the scales at all times. The moment the person died, they watched the dial in order to measure any weight difference when the "soul" or "consciousness" left the body. As you might have guessed, no change occurred. Consciousness must not weigh anything—or at least it is so light we don't have any way of recording it. Yet it seems obvious that it is there.

We will do the best we can with a definition: **consciousness** is the awareness of, or the possibility of knowing, what is going on inside or outside the organism. This definition fits the fact that we can receive stimulation, analyze it, and then take some action.

Consciousness: Map of the Self in Relation to the World

Consciousness (for both humans and animals) is believed to come from our making a "map" of where we are in space and then more or less seeing ourselves on this map (Jaynes, 1976). Notice that when you think about something you did a while back, you actually seem to be watching yourself from the outside. Or if you want to, you can move inside the "you" that you are remembering and "look out" as you imagine doing what you did before. We think consciousness results from just such a series of stored and viewed images of ourselves. In other words, as we move about, different scenes, some from the environment, some from memory, flash before us, then fade and are instantly replaced by the next scene. Some of them are stored in memory for later use. This situation is a great deal like a motion picture at the theater. Movies are nothing more than a series of thousands of fixed images (in each "frame") flashed one after the other on the screen so it looks to us as if the people are alive and moving. Thus, all day long, we combine millions of brief memory images of ourselves with our current images of the world, and we call this consciousness.

ENRICHMENT

Ask students the following questions: Can the unconscious be studied scientifically? If so, what techniques could be used? (You could mention Freud and free association which they will learn about in Chapter 14.) Is free association a valid tool for studying the unconscious? Is free association scientific? The answer to these questions is *Probably not.* The responses that subjects provide are too open-ended. Several *scientific* studies, however, have focused on slips-of-the-tongue, which supposedly offer a glimpse into the unconscious. For example, subjects are presented with various stimuli to see if they will evoke slips. In one study, males were given a series of incomplete statements which they had to complete. An attractive female (the independent variable) presented the statements to half the subjects (the experimental group). These subjects' answers included more sexual connotations!

Levels of Consciousness

We are not necessarily conscious of everything we do. For example, experiments show that sometimes, when we are going to reach for something or get up and walk around, our brain circuits for these acts may fire *before* we consciously know we are going to do anything (Libet et al., 1983). Similarly, if a "forbidden" word is flashed on a screen in front of people very rapidly and then removed, the people's brains will respond electrically even if the people claim they didn't see the word. In such cases, it is likely that a kind of censoring has taken place, even though the people are not aware they are doing it (Loftus & Klinger, 1992; Posner et al., 1973). The level of awareness in these examples, then, is called the **subconscious,** meaning consciousness just below our present awareness.

An example of subconscious thought would be a very vague feeling that for some unknown reason, the people around you at a party are acting strangely toward you. You don't put the feeling into words, and for the most part, you ignore it; still, you feel vaguely uncomfortable or worried. You don't realize that you have *noticed* people's strange behavior toward you until you get home and you start to wonder why you didn't have a very good time at the party. Then you remember what your subconscious had picked up (and you wonder if maybe you had bad breath or something).

Many psychologists believe that we also have an even deeper level of awareness called the **unconscious.** The unconscious contains thoughts, information, or desires about which we have no true or direct knowledge (Greenwald, 1992). Unconscious thought is very easy to see in children: for example, a jealous brother keeps undoing the bolts on his brother's bicycle, but when caught, he really can't explain why he does it—even to himself. We will discuss the unconscious in greater detail in Unit 5, where we look at personality.

CHRONOBIOLOGY AND UNSEEN FORCES

Many of us spend money to be scared out of our wits by a horror movie. If you stop and think about it, what makes the horror movie so exciting is that there are things hidden in the background—the unseen. We have a similar show going on around us all the time—and it's not only free but far more fascinating than the best of horror films. This is because it is real: all creatures are controlled by forces that none of us can see or feel.

This area of study is called **chronobiology** (KRON-oh + biology). *Chronology* refers to time, so the focus of chronobiology is on forces that control the body biology at different times of the day or month

subconscious

Consciousness just below our present awareness.

unconscious

Thoughts or desires about which we can have no direct knowledge.

chronobiology

The study of forces that control the body at different times of the day, month, or year.

Connections

Find out if students recall (from Chapter 3) what probably happens internally when brain circuits fire before conscious awareness. One possible answer might involve reflexes, where the body reacts via nerves in the spinal cord, and the brain registers this a moment later. Sometimes the brain responds electrically (to a forbidden word), but there is never an awareness. Subliminal messages (Chapter 4) supposedly work in this way.

Teaching Hint

Ask students if they have ever walked or driven home and not remembered passing intersections, stopping at red lights, turning, and so on. This could be an example of subconscious thought.

EXPERIMENT

Have two or three volunteers take their temperatures once an hour for an entire day to monitor minor fluctuations. Ask them to pay close attention to mood and alertness to see if there is a correlation with body temperature. One may not necessarily cause the other, but they may be correlated.

ENRICHMENT

Have students do research to find out the effects of working night and midnight shifts. What if the shifts change every few months? What is the best rotational schedule?

DISCUSS THE PHOTO

Ask students to think of other animals that are nocturnal.

FYI Some people experience a winter slump because of briefer exposure to sunlight during the winter months. This condition is called seasonal affective disorder (SAD). Light therapy, in which the patient actually sits in front of a large panel of light, seems to be an effective treatment.

Comprehension Check

Ask students to name some examples of human chronobiology. *(Answers may include day/night cycle, female monthly cycle regarding reproduction, male monthly cycle, annual change in which people lose energy as summer approaches.)*

158

Unit 2 BRAIN, BODY, AND AWARENESS

▲ *The screech owl silently hunts for food at night.*

or year. The most obvious effects are those involving night and day cycles: the rat, hamster, and beloved cockroach awaken and wander around during the night, while the squirrel, sparrow, chicken, and human come out during the day.

There are monthly cycles that can cause changes in feelings and moods. The best known of these is the female monthly cycle designed for reproduction, but females are not alone. While most males deny it, studies show that males also have a monthly cycle in which they become listless, slightly depressed, and "different from usual" for three or four days (Luce, 1971; Moore-Ede et al., 1982).

Finally, there are annual cycles in which people slow down and lose energy as summer approaches. And there are annual changes in weight as well as in the chemical content of the body.

The most obvious annual rhythm in nature is bird migration. Birds don't fly south in order to be home for Thanksgiving; they are responding to a change in the light-dark cycle of the Earth as winter approaches. They perform this feat by using patterns of the stars as a guide during their flight. They are so accurate that some of them can go across country to the same 25-square-yard space they used the previous year. If the sky becomes overcast, built-in magnets in their brains, which contain small particles of the mineral *magnetite,* are used to orient them to the Earth's magnetic field so they can stay on course. To date, no similar system has been found in the human, although some studies show that many people are able to orient themselves to north, south, east, and west.

COOPERATIVE LEARNING

The content of this chapter is usually highly interesting to students, so it should be easy for them to write down some questions they would like to have answered. Assign one of the following topics to each group, and have each group write ten questions: biological clocks, sleep, dreams, sleep disorders, hypnosis, meditation. Students may need to skim through the chapter for ideas. If all the questions are not answered by the end of the chapter, they become good extra-credit opportunities!

Chapter 6 CONSCIOUSNESS

Biological Clocks

All creatures are under the control of **biological clocks.** Biological clocks are internal chemical units that control parts of the body all by themselves and are programmed and regulated by nature. Even fetuses inside the mother have working biological clocks (Schwartz, 1984). Our internal temperature is run by one of these clocks, keeping us, when healthy, at plus or minus two degrees of the same temperature no matter what the weather outside of us is (Mork, 1983). The kidneys also operate independently. Their clock has to ignore the outside world because they must get rid of poisonous materials at regular intervals in order to protect us. Those clocks that ignore the environment use what are called **free-running cycles** because they are under their own control.

Some clock systems can be changed, however. This is most obvious with sleep-wake cycles. Even here, though, some species are free-running. Dogs and cats, for instance, continue to free-run throughout the light-dark cycle. If you pay close attention to Fido and Kitty, you will find that they are quiet at night just to keep from getting into trouble with their owners. They do not follow the same pattern as humans; they fall asleep and wake up on and off throughout both day and night.

Even though the human is free-running at birth, we are able to change the sleep-wake cycle. Babies start off driving everyone crazy because they want to eat and sleep at odd times during the day and night. After about 20 exhausting weeks, parents have usually trained the babies to fit the adults' schedule. This process of altering the free-running cycle is called **entrainment** (as in "training"). The human body has a natural rhythm that free-runs on a cycle of 25 hours. If we lived in a cave (which some psychologists have done to prove the point), our body rhythms would go through a 25-hour cycle of sleep and wakefulness, of various chemical changes, and of the need for food or water. In other words, within 25 hours, each process would make a complete cycle of its own. Away from the cave, each of us has to entrain to the Earth, which has a light-dark cycle of only 24 hours. The body can adjust to this one-hour change with little trouble, but some of you may spend the weekend doing everything you can to destroy this learned rhythm, putting it off by many hours. The result of changing your rhythm even by an hour or two can be a genuinely awful feeling come Monday morning (Moore-Ede et al., 1982; Webb & Agnew, 1974).

You may have run across pamphlets, articles, and books that claim to be able to tell your personality and future based on "biorhythms." These have no scientific validity and are similar to fortune-telling.

Circadian Rhythms Every living thing on Earth is controlled by the unseen forces that we call biological clocks. For example, there are

biological clocks

Internal chemical units that control regular cycles in parts of the body.

free-running cycles

Cycles set up by biological clocks that are under their own control, ignoring the environment.

entrainment

The process of altering the free-running cycle to fit a different rhythm.

FYI If you are not a morning person, you are probably amazed (or annoyed) by people who are. Actually, this sort of disposition may have something to do with one's biological clock. Our body temperature fluctuates throughout the day, and people who wake early do so because their body temperature happens to be high at 6:00 A.M. or so. The rest of us need a few more hours for our temperatures to reach a high point.

ENRICHMENT

Here are some fun facts about biological rhythms from Richard Restak's, *The Brain:* (1) Blood pressure can fluctuate by 20 percent in a day. The lowest is in the morning, the highest in the afternoon. (2) Drugs that work on the white-cell count can have varying effects, depending on the time of day. When the doctor says, "Take two in the morning," there may be a reason. (3) Cancer drugs seem to work best when our body temperature is highest. (4) It is better to eat a heavy meal early in the day than late. The body is better able to "process" the meal early in the day. Ask students to find more "fun" facts about biological rhythms.

Natural Cycles and Entrainment.

 The question is mainly a rhetorical one, but see the following **FYI** for ideas for discussion.

FYI Point out that some cave dwellers have a 48 to 50-hour cycle, rather than the usual 24 to 25-hour cycle. They literally lose a day. Michael Siffre, one such cave dweller, compares his odyssey of isolation with brainwashing and says he would never do it again. He believes it took him five years to return to normal, after spending six months in the cave (Restak, 1984). After hearing this, students may have a new appreciation for sunlight, clocks, and even school bells.

Unit 2 BRAIN, BODY, AND AWARENESS

IN FOCUS **Natural Cycles and Entrainment**

The human body goes through a natural 25-hour sleep-wake cycle.

The earth, however, moves on a natural 24-hour light-dark cycle.

Through the process of entrainment, the human body adapts to this 24-hour cycle.

Which is more natural: entrainment or the body's 25-hour cycle?

circadian rhythm

Sequences of behavioral changes that occur every 24 hours.

plants that open up in the morning and close at night. Many think this happens so that the plants can get sunlight. Not so. If you take these plants into a lead-lined vault, they will open and close on schedule every 24 hours with no light at all. The plant is operating on what is called a **circadian rhythm.** *Circa* means "about" and *dian* means "a day," so the plant is changing its behavior twice in "about a day."

The human circadian rhythm is based on an entrained 24-hour cycle. Within that cycle, we have a high point and a low point. For most people, the lowest point (low temperature, low blood pressure, weakness, and so forth) is between 3:00 and 5:00 A.M. That is why, if you wake up at that time, even on a hot summer's night, you will

ENRICHMENT

Circadian rhythms are related not only to high and low body temperatures but also to other internal events: (1) Certain hormones are released on a daily schedule. (2) Brain neurotransmitters seem to follow a regular cycle. (3) The hypothalamus and pituitary operate in a rhythmic fashion. Have students find out more about these circadian rhythms.

feel cold and shiver. Although everyone does not have the same rhythm, most of us come close. What happens if it is ignored?

Fighting the Clock   A Boeing 707 approached Los Angeles Airport. The pilots had slept the previous day, but their home city—and basic rhythm—were set for a time that made it 3:00 A.M. for them when they arrived in the Los Angeles area. The people in the control tower watched in horror as the plane stayed at 32,000 feet instead of landing. It flew on out over the ocean. The staff in the control tower made noises through the radio to awaken the crew, all three of whom had fallen asleep while the plane was on automatic pilot. They awoke with just enough fuel to get back to the airport and land (Coleman, 1986).

A study of 30 pilots for Airline X found that the pilots started to fall asleep while flying on an average of 32 times a month. Fortunately, rarely do they all fall asleep at the same time. Some pilots keep a kitchen timer in the cockpit, and they set it in order to keep themselves awake (Moore-Ede, 1986; Winfrey, 1987). These pilots are competent, but the airlines are asking them to fight nature, and that's hard to do at 3:00 A.M. with the steady sound and rocking of the aircraft. Thus, the fact that you get some sleep is not always as important as *when* you get that sleep.

A person can change his or her basic rhythm so that the low point comes during the day, but this takes months to do, and airlines, hospitals, police departments, and factories rarely let it happen, since they keep changing the workers' hours.

Giving Up Sleep   What happens if we decide to give up sleep? It doesn't turn out too well, although most cases aren't as bad as the ones we describe here. A disc jockey set himself up in a phone booth on the street to do this. By the time he had been up for 200 hours, he saw things that were not there, and he thought people were trying to do him in. And in a laboratory study, one man, after 168 hours without sleep, suddenly went berserk, sobbing and falling to the floor because he thought a gorilla was trying to get him.

Both the disc jockey and the subject in the laboratory had all the time in the world to rest. So rest alone will not do it. There is something special about sleep. It is clearly necessary. As you will find out, nature has set it up so that we sleep in order to do the most important thing: have dreams. If people are awakened whenever they are about to have a dream, thus stopping it, they feel as bad as if they had had no sleep at all. The importance of dreams is also shown by the fact that *all* creatures—except for one species of bird—have what appear to be dream periods. Elephants, cows, rats, mice, cats, rabbits, and donkeys all have them. The donkey has to hurry up about it since it has only three hours of sleep per circadian cycle, while all the others sleep more than we do (Coleman, 1986).

Connections

Students may recall from Chapter 3 that a certain part of the lower brain serves numerous functions. It should come as no surprise that this part, the hypothalamus, also seems to play a role in regulating our biological clocks. Why? One possible reason is that the eyes send information about light and dark to the hypothalamus.

Discussion

You may have a few students who have experienced jet lag. Sunlight at your journey's destination may be sending the message that it is afternoon, but the body is not fooled; it is still running on the old light-dark cycle back home. Ask students how long it takes to adjust. Is motivation a factor? (Adjustment would probably depend on the length of the trip and the time difference. At best, motivation might reduce some of the effects of jet lag, but it won't eliminate the effects completely.)

CHAPTER PROJECT

Have students keep a dream journal during the course of the chapter. After a few days, some students will complain that they simply don't remember their dreams. You can help alleviate this problem in two ways: (1) Have an informal discussion on dreams at the very beginning of the unit. (2) Have students keep a "day journal" in class during the unit. Each day or every other day, assign a topic in class and allow them about ten minutes to respond freely to the topic. See **Teaching Master 6-3 Journal**

Topics for ideas. You'll note that many of the topics are similar to common dream themes. The idea is for students, during the day, to write down their conscious observations about these kinds of themes. In the morning, when they jot down their

---

FYI Record for the longest time awake: Randy Gardner, when he was 17, stayed up for over 264 hours (11 days). Then he slept for 14 hours.

Points to Stress

Circadian rhythms affect when we experience REM. For example, most people spend an increased amount of time in REM as sleep progresses. Patients with mood disorders, however, sometimes experience the opposite, with the longest REM period occurring early in sleep. In treating depression, doctors may consider altering the patient's sleep schedule.

Teaching Hint

When discussing REM sleep, have students look at a partner. Each partner should close his or her eyes and rapidly look left and right over and over again. Students won't forget what REM stands for.

162

---

twilight state
Relaxed state just before we fall asleep.

REM sleep
Rapid eye movement sleep when we dream.

THE NATURE OF SLEEP AND DREAMS

At first it seems that we simply get tired and go to sleep. But it's much more complicated than that. Sleep is far from just a time of peacefulness and relaxation. Only the first hour could be viewed this way, since it contains the deepest period of sleep, and during it, there is a dramatic fall in blood pressure, heart rate, and breathing. During the rest of the night, many unexpected events occur.

When we first lie down, electrical activity in the brain begins to slow. This is a period called the **twilight state,** with images and thoughts drifting in front of us, probably the one time during the day when we can totally relax and let the mind wander. Then, before you know it, you are heading for your deepest sleep.

There is no question that sleep helps restore the body. The making of new cells is at its maximum; chemicals the brain has used up during the day are restored. This is also the time when body hair grows most rapidly (Webb & Cartwright, 1978; Hartmann, 1973).

REM Sleep

The most important purpose of sleep—dreaming—is something of a surprise. Let's look at what happens to each of us every single night—four or five times. The brain begins to fire furiously; blood pressure zooms upward; our eyes move rapidly from side to side and up and down; breathing and heartbeat are very rapid—all within a paralyzed body (Dement, 1979). This is called REM sleep.

So sleep is not a single state of consciousness involving only a single behavior. Instead, it can be divided roughly into two major types: the first is **REM sleep** (pronounced as one word: "rem"), and the second is NREM sleep, which we'll discuss in just a bit. REM stands for *rapid eye movement*, and REM sleep is that period when our eyes are moving about in all directions within the eye sockets. You can watch this in action with a dog or cat. They have a REM period every 30 minutes or so after they first fall asleep. Or you can watch your friends or members of your family. You can actually see the eyeballs rotating in the sockets. They will have a REM period about every 90 minutes from the time they fall asleep until morning. If those you are watching are *really* in REM, you will not awaken them unless you call their name or make a *lot* of noise. In fact, as mentioned, they are paralyzed. Most likely you have had a number of dreams in which you were trying to get away from an attacker but were unable to move your legs to run. That's because you *couldn't* move your legs—literally. Sleepwalking, which we will discuss later, does not occur during REM.

dreams, they will write down their "unconscious" observations of these or other dream themes. The hope is that at some time, the two journals will intersect and provide students with some insights. The day journal may help students to remember their

dreams by sending a message to the brain that such themes are important. If this is too ambitious, the day journal at least serves as a reminder to write down their dreams. (See **Teaching Master 6-2 Dream Assignment** for student instructions on this project.)

Chapter 6 CONSCIOUSNESS

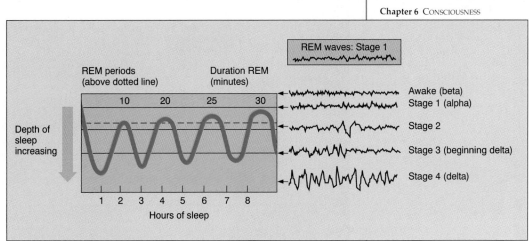

▲ *Figure 6.1 The sleep cycle.*

DISCUSS THE PHOTO

Dreams occuring early in the sleep cycle tend to reflect events of the preceding day. Later dreams are usually more surreal.

How long do REMs or dreams last? You may have heard that dreams are over in about a second. That's not true. The actual dream lasts as long as it *seems* to take—roughly 5 to 40 minutes. Throughout the night, REM periods occur roughly every 90 minutes with each REM lasting longer than the previous one. Figure 6.1 shows the typical pattern of a night's sleep. Note that REM periods come during times when we are *not* in deep sleep. Also notice that as the night progresses, sleep gets lighter. The chances are that the dreams you remember are those coming closest to the morning since they are the longest, have occurred most recently, and you are the closest to being awake when you have them.

We need to pause here and give you an overview of the whole cycle of sleep, dreams, and the changes that occur during this time period.

Brain Changes During Sleep

In addition to the waking state, there are five other brain-wave patterns and corresponding stages of consciousness (REM and stages 1 through 4). These are shown in Figure 6.1 on the right-hand side, with the typical brain-wave pattern shown next to each stage of sleep.

Using the figure as a guide, first look at the brain waves running from the top to the bottom of the right-hand chart, comparing awake (**beta waves**) with stage 1–relaxed, called **alpha waves,** and with the deepest sleep (stage 4, **delta waves**). Notice that the deeper the sleep is, the slower and "lazier" the brain-wave pattern is. In fact, the delta waves in stage 4 are very slow and regular.

Connections

See if students can think of a useful mnemonic device (Chapter 8) to remember beta, alpha, and delta waves.

beta waves

Rapid brain waves; appear when a person is awake.

alpha waves

Stage 1, fairly relaxed brain waves occurring just before going to sleep; relaxed.

delta waves

Slow, lazy, deep-sleep brain waves.

163

Remind students that the rest of the body is paralyzed during REM and that the eyes move involuntarily.

Comprehension Check

When does the shortest dream of the night occur, and about how long is it? *(before the end of the second hour of sleep; ten minutes)* When does the longest dream occur, and about how long does it last? *(towards morning; 30 minutes)*

Points to Stress

The stages of sleep are not always as orderly as described or illustrated here. For example, if we have been deprived of sleep for several nights, we may drift into a deep sleep immediately. Or if we have been deprived of REM for several nights, which can be caused by alcohol abuse, we may spend a lot of time in REM as soon as we fall asleep.

164

Unit 2 Brain, Body, and Awareness

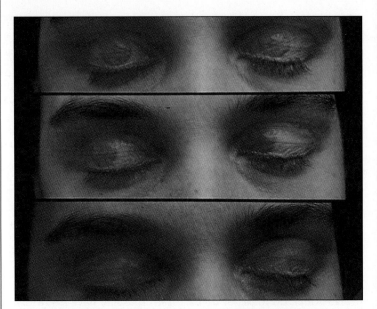

▲ *Time-lapse photography shows the movement of the eyes during REM sleep.*

The chart on the left of the figure shows the typical pattern of a night's sleep, starting at the top. Before bed we are awake (beta). We get into bed and relax (stage 1–alpha). As we begin to enter a twilight state, we are moving into stage 2, and the alpha waves disappear. Stage 3 is next as we drift into deeper sleep, and finally we reach the deepest, delta-wave sleep (stage 4). If you look to the left in Figure 6.1, you will note that by the time you reach stage 4, you are about one hour into sleep. At this point, you begin to go in reverse, heading from stage 4 back toward stage 1. Before the second hour, however, when you would be arriving back at the regular stage 1–relaxed alpha, something unusual happens: instead of going into the regular stage 1, you enter stage 1–REM; this is rapid eye movement, or dream, sleep. The first dream of the night occurs, lasting about ten minutes. (Note: you will not enter the stage 1–relaxed phase again until you awaken in the morning.) Thus, the rest of the night you will go from stage 1–REM to stage 4 and back again. Notice also that the length of dreams increases through the night, so that the last dream toward morning will be close to 30 minutes long.

Looking at the brain-wave patterns, you might assume that REMs are very close to the beta awake waves. The brain-wave pattern looks similar. But a person in stage 1–REM is almost impossible to awaken. Not only that but as mentioned, the person in this dream stage has periods of paralysis, and it is very difficult even to get a reflex from him or her. The similarity of brain waves between the two stages probably reflects the fact that during dreams, the brain is very active,

DISCOVERY

Dream Tasks. Photocopy **Teaching Master 6-4 Dream Tasks** and cut it into four parts. Hand out a separate part on four consecutive days. Students should not read the sheets until they are ready to go to sleep each night. Just before they turn off the lights, they should read the instructions on the sheet, which are dream tasks essentially, and sleep on it. By the way, most students will probably not dream about the tasks, mainly because they are only trying this for four days. Regardless of your results, this should lead to some good discussions on dream control.

---

just as it would be if we were awake and looking around (beta). In any case, we clearly are not part of the waking world during REM sleep (Webb & Cartwright, 1978).

NREM Sleep

The second type of sleep is called **NREM sleep,** which stands for *non–rapid eye movement sleep.* In Figure 6.1, all of the sleep below the dotted line is NREM sleep. During this "non-REM sleep," the brain is still active, providing partial thoughts, images, or stories. But these do not have the organization of the "stories" found during REM activity.

When you are not in REM, you are in NREM. NREM seems to be the time when the brain goes into "idle"; its operations are still going on, but they are neither at the level of wakefulness nor at that of REM dreaming. Some researchers feel that this is the time when the body rests. Remember, though, that you have to have REM sleep in order to feel halfway decent.

The Purpose of Dreaming

There are three major hypotheses about why we dream. Evidence supports all of them, so they can sit side by side at this stage of our knowledge.

NREM sleep

Non–rapid eye movement sleep; sleep involving partial thoughts, images, or stories, poor organization.

FYI During Stage 1 sleep, which usually lasts about ten minutes, we lose our perception of time. For example, if we were to awaken someone during Stage 1, the person might be fooled into thinking that she's been sleeping for hours. Ask the people who have fallen asleep in class for a minute about this. This distortion of how much time has elapsed may happen during other stages, but it seems most profound during Stage 1.

Comparing REM to NREM.

IN FOCUS Bed-wetting, sleepwalking, and talking or eating in one's sleep all occur during NREM—usually in Stage 4, delta sleep.

IN FOCUS
Comparing REM to NREM Periods of Sleep

REM	NREM
Rapid eye movement	Non–rapid eye movement
Increases in length as night's sleep progresses	Decreases in length as night's sleep progresses
Vivid dreams	Vague, partial images and stories
Nightmares	Incubus attacks (night terrors)
Paralyzed body	Sleepwalking and talking in sleep
Essential part of sleep	Less essential part of sleep

In your estimation, during which period would a child wet the bed?

Discussion

"Describe some memorable dreams that you've had. What do you think these dreams mean? What is the purpose of dreaming? Can you control your dreams?"

During discussion, students invariably ask: Is it true that if you die in a dream, you'll really die? If you have a sense of humor, you can foster this *myth* for a while, declaring that, oh, yes, you have absolute proof of this. There will usually be a student in class who can report having died in a dream but who is still breathing. On the other hand, it is rare to die in our dreams. Even then we tend to protect ourselves!

Three Theories About Why We Dream.

 To test the first and third theories, scientists would study the neurological and chemical activity that occurs during sleep. To study the unsolved problems theory, have subjects think about various problems before going to bed and wake them during REM to see if they are dreaming about the problems; wake other subjects during NREM.

DISCUSS THE PHOTO

Research has found that only eight percent of the population averages five hours of sleep or less per night. Also, many people who sleep longer than average per night tend to worry a lot during the day.

166

▲ *Rip Van Winkle trying to recover from a bout of 20 years' sleep.*

The first hypothesis is that dreams are used to get the brain re-organized after a day's work of thinking and dealing with problems. This makes sense because we know that brain chemicals are used up during the day. Notice how hard it is to study on nights when you have done a lot of mental work during the day. To restore the chemicals, we have to cut off the outside world in order to keep new problems—which would require more work—from getting in. The brain, however, cannot remain inactive. So dreams keep the brain busy with old material while it is being recharged, so to speak (Evans & Evans, 1983).

The second hypothesis is that dreams are designed to help work out unsolved problems left over from the day. You can find evidence for this in something that has happened to almost everyone. You go to bed with a problem of some sort that you haven't been able to solve—maybe in math or history, or maybe a personal problem. When you wake up the next morning, there's the solution, as obvious as can be (D. B. Cohen, 1980a; Webb & Cartwright, 1978). Further support comes from the fact that when we are under stress or depressed, we sleep longer, and the amount of time spent in REM increases. This fact strongly suggests that we are working on the things that are worrying us while we dream (Hartmann & Brewer, 1976).

 **Three Major Theories About Why We Dream**

To reorganize the brain:

Brain chemicals are used up during the day. While the brain replenishes these chemicals, dreams organize the past day or week or more.

To work out unsolved problems:

We go to bed with a problem. When we wake up, the problem is solved (or forgotten—which in itself may be a solution).

To make sense of random stimulation to the brain:

While we sleep, the brain flushes out the garbage we don't need. In the process, the brain is stimulated in a random or "crazy" way. So we dream to make sense of the random stimulation.

If you were an experimental psychologist, how might you test the validity of each theory?

DISCOVERY

Describe a dream and have students analyze it from the point of view of the three theories of why we dream described in the In Focus. If you discuss Freud in this chapter, they can add what he might say. Here's a sample answer. *Dream:* one's teeth have fallen out. *Reorganize brain theory:* the person may have a loose tooth or an impending dentist's visit. While he dreams he is organizing his thoughts of the day. *Solve problems theory:* during the day the person has been worrying about his appearance. Now that his teeth have fallen out (in his dream) the problem, in a metaphorical sense, is solved. There is no *need* to worry about appearance any longer; he can't do much about it. *Random stimulation theory:* the person's brain is randomly stimulated during REM sleep. The cerebral cortex tries to make sense of this stimulation by creating a story. This night it's a story about teeth; another night it will be a different story.

The third explanation comes from today's emphasis on the computer. It is possible that we get too much unnecessary material in our "files" from the day's tasks. Thus, dreams result from all the electrical realignments, revising, and updating going on in the brain. As various electrical circuits are being fired, different memory circuits are being triggered, and we have a dream (Crick, 1983; Evans & Evans, 1983). In other words, the brain is trying to make sense of the bits and pieces of information that are appearing while we are cleaning out the material, so it makes up a "story" to fit them. This would account for why we so often put odd things together in a dream.

There is one thing missing in our coverage to this point. What actually causes dreams, since there is no external stimulation? First, remember that all our memories, thoughts, and actions are controlled by electrical impulses within the brain. Add to this the fact that electrical bursts occur in cycles throughout the night. These bursts come from deep within the brain at regular intervals (90-minute cycles) and have special brain cells that turn them on and off. The electrical impulses move upward, hitting various portions of the upper brain, thus firing different memory circuits. The result is what we call dreams. These bursts also cause eye movements. We are not "watching" our dreams. Even people without sight from birth have rapid eye movements, but the content of their dreams centers on sound and touch (Coleman, 1986; Melnechuk, 1983).

PSYCHOLOGY OF DREAMS

Throughout history, dreams have been considered mystical and, in some cases, able to predict the future. There is no scientific evidence to support such claims. Since we know that dreams are made by electrical impulses causing the firing of our own memory circuits, it is obvious that the material is coming directly from us. If coming from us, then we should be able to tell the future just as much when we're awake as during a dream—if the future can be known. It also seems unlikely that dreams tell us much more about ourselves than we already know. A dream *can* trigger a memory that we have forgotten or deal with something that we hadn't paid much attention to, but this is far different from receiving a special secret message.

Dream Content

Most dreams, most of the time, are about very ordinary events. We dream about things from a normal day: family, friends, and school. Dreams also contain a lot of material about worries, fears, or feeling inferior because these are concerns we all have. And often dreams involve an argument. The good part about these kinds of dreams is

TEACHING MASTER 6-2

A Dream Assignment. This is an assignment sheet for the chapter project. Make it clear that you will not read any journal entries that are marked *Personal.* You may suggest that students rip out these pages, allow you to glance at them as proof of completion, and then not hand them in. If you find that some students just cannot remember their dreams, you might suggest that they write more day journal entries and then write a report based on this day journal, or complete some other alternative project.

INTERDISCIPLINARY PROJECT

Creative Writing. Ask students to create a fictional character and to describe this character in a paragraph or two. What are his or her goals, motives? What conflicts has he or she experienced lately? All of this is prewriting. Then have students imagine the kinds of dreams this person has, given the motives, conflicts, and so on. Finally, have them write down one of the dreams in vivid detail.

DISCUSS THE PHOTO

Scientists disagree over whether dreams have hidden meanings or not. What do students think?

FYI This is obviously not necessary, but it's a good idea to keep your own dream journal during the chapter. You'll better understand some of the frustration students may experience in remembering their dreams. You may also develop insights into how to remember dreams or how to interpret them (although there is no single, correct method).

TEACHING MASTER 6-3

Journal Topics.
This is a list of journal topics for the entire chapter. See the **Chapter Project** for more on this.

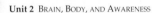

Unit 2 BRAIN, BODY, AND AWARENESS

▲ *The dreamer's world is not bound by time or space.*

that in them, we most always turn out to be right. That's not hard to understand since we're usually convinced we're right in the waking state. Still, it's nice to have our dreams agree with us (Webb & Cartwright, 1978).

While 70 percent of our dreams are about people we actually know, there are also other unexpected common images in dreams. For example, 40 percent of females dream about the sea or bodies of water, while only 27 percent of males do. Falling or being chased in a dream is very common and occurs about equally for males and females. Sex and romance are likewise typical. And the following themes occur with some frequency among completely normal males and females: violence, talking to dead friends or relatives, shoplifting, finding yourself naked in public, and discovering the "secret of the universe"—which unfortunately we forget by the time we wake up (Evans & Evans, 1983).

Bizarre dreams also occur. Usually the core of the dream is reasonable, but the story winds up happening in a strange place or with people you don't expect. Thus, ugly Uncle Harry is seen starring as the handsome leading man in a romantic movie. We suspect these strange combinations occur from the random nature of the electrical firing, putting things together we normally would not allow if we were awake and in control. Strange dreams do *not* mean something is wrong with you. The only time you should be concerned is if the same dream occurs over and over and really is bothersome. Then it's time to sit down with a friend and try to figure out what it means. It will probably then disappear, as long as you don't let it worry you.

The concept that dreams are symbolic or represent deep, hidden impulses, needs, or desires has been around forever. Even world leaders have been known to guide their movements by dreams. The story goes that Abraham Lincoln had dream warnings that it was dangerous for him to go to Ford's Theatre, where he was later assassinated. Most, but not all, researchers today believe that dream content of this sort is just a reflection of daytime, waking concerns that appear at night, rather than the result of some special message from another world or from our own unconscious world.

Finally, something we don't understand at all: about 50 percent of our dreams are in color, and 50 percent are in black and white. Despite numerous experiments, we can't figure out why this is so. No, we don't even have a guess. It's not related either to the scenes in the dream or to the amount of color we see when awake. Researchers have even put colored filters over people's eyes for a week to see if that makes a difference, but it doesn't change the proportion of color in their dreams.

After students complete the preceding interdisciplinary project, have them exchange papers (only the dreams, not the prewriting) to see if they can interpret their partners' papers! Can the partner get any insights into the dreamer's motives and conflicts by analyzing the dream?

Comprehension Check

Ask students to name some normal, common images that appear in dreams. *(Answers may include falling, being chased, sex and romance, violence, talking to dead friends or relatives, shoplifting, finding yourself naked in public.)*

Nightmares

There are two frightening experiences that can occur during sleep. The first happens during REM and is called the **nightmare.** Fortunately, nightmares are infrequent; only about 5 percent of the population has them as often as once a week. The odds that all of us will have a nightmare on occasion are very high since we all carry around bad memories that can be triggered. Nightmares are more likely when people have missed REM periods for a day or so from drinking too much alcohol or not getting enough sleep (Hartmann, 1984; Coleman, 1986). The reason nightmares appear then is that if REM is blocked, **REM rebound** occurs. REM rebound refers to the fact that the first time we go to sleep after being deprived of REM, both the length and the number of dreams increase (rebound) dramatically to make up for the loss. Hence, the chances of having unpleasant dreams increase. In general, however, we have no evidence that nightmares indicate something is wrong with the person. They seem to be just part of dreaming. And despite the fact that you will hear the rumor frequently, nightmares are not caused by eating something strange.

Incubus Attacks

The second frightening experience during sleep is another kind of dream that you may have been lucky enough to avoid. It is called an **incubus** (IN-cue-bus) **attack,** from the Latin meaning "to have a devil on your back." These are horrible dreams that are quite vivid and real.

What makes them so awful is that the incubus attack occurs during NREM, not REM. The body knows that a regular dream is coming every 90 minutes and prepares for it, but the body is caught completely unprepared by an unpleasant dream that gets triggered during NREM. The physical overload it causes sets off major bodily changes. Breathing rate zooms upward, the person feels choked, heart rate takes off to an unbelievable 170-plus beats a minute. These events create a feeling of panic and a fear of dying. The sleeper usually springs up in bed, sweating, nauseated, and afraid. Since to the body, which is unprepared, NREM is so much closer to reality than REM, we "know" it is "not" a dream, and it's too much to handle (Kahn et al., 1972).

The incubus attack, sometimes called a *night terror,* is fairly common in very young children. For some unknown reason, these

nightmare

Frightening dream during REM.

REM rebound

Increase in the number of dreams after being deprived of them.

incubus attack

Also called a night terror; a horrible dream occurring during NREM when the body is not prepared for it.

FYI Freud believed that dreams are the royal road to the unconscious. He looked at dreams as having two parts: the *manifest* part, the part we recall; and the *latent* part, the hidden meaning of the dream. This hidden meaning is usually associated with aggressive and sexual impulses. The reason these impulses need to remain hidden, even in dreams, is that we would wake otherwise. Therefore, we disguise the true nature of the dream with symbols. If we dream of a fortress, this may really represent a strong-willed father. If we are trying to knock down the fortress in our dreams, then maybe things are not going so well with Dad!

DISCOVERY

This activity works best if students have been completing a dream journal, but the journal is not essential. Tell students to recall a particularly vivid dream that they have had *recently*. Urge them to choose a dream that seems meaningful. Once they all have a dream in mind (in the next day or so), have them draw the dream in class with crayons. Afterward, have them sit in a circle, tape the pictures to the front of their desks, and briefly explain the details of the dream without providing any possible interpretations. After this brief explanation, the rest of the class will try to analyze the drawing. What colors does the person use? How intense are the lines? How

Points to Stress

Here's a good line by Carl Jung to display: *Never go beyond the meaning which has an effect upon the patient.* In other words, don't try to tell other people what their dreams mean. You can offer suggestions certainly, but don't get too excited by what you think the dreams mean.

 FYI When incubus attacks do not subside and treatment is called for, altering the patient's sleep schedule sometimes helps. For example, you might wake up the patient after an hour of sleep. This is sometimes enough to break the usual pattern and stop the attacks.

Comparing Nightmares to Night Terrors.

IN FOCUS Nightmares probably occur during the second half of the night because REM is longer. There's more opportunity for them to occur.

Unit 2 BRAIN, BODY, AND AWARENESS

 **Comparing Nightmares to Night Terrors**

Nightmares	Night Terrors (incubus attacks)
Occur during REM, usually during the second half of the night	Occur during NREM, usually during the first hour of sleep
Mild physiological changes	Drastic bodily changes: breathing and heart rate rise dramatically
Associated with vivid images	Associated with panic
Most likely to occur during REM rebound	Most likely to occur in children

Why do you think a person is more likely to have a nightmare during the second half of the night?

dreams seem to be connected with a maturing brain. Thus, in general, night terrors should *not* be treated by a professional, since all that would do is call attention to them and frighten the child even more (Dement, 1974; Coleman, 1986). The child will grow out of them. If incubus attacks occur with any frequency beyond middle adolescence, the chances are good that something physical is wrong, and this should not be ignored. A physical exam is clearly in order.

PRACTICAL ISSUES IN SLEEP

Patterns of sleep change as the years progress. Infants spend a good 75 percent of the time in REM sleep. The brain has so much building to do that chemicals are used up very quickly and need to be constantly restored. By adolescence, the brain is fully developed, but major physical and psychological changes are still going on. As a result, regular sleep is important—at least in theory. Adolescents usually have so many "social obligations" that their sleeping schedule is chaotic (Carskadon et al., 1980). Finally, toward old age, people require much less deep sleep, probably from changes in the brain cells that control sleep. In this section, we deal with issues that apply to the teenage years through age 25.

Social Entrainment

Problems can arise from too much *social entrainment* of sleep cycles. Sometimes, for social purposes, we alter our rhythms—

do these factors relate to the content? Explain that you're not searching for correct answers, just possible paths. If students treat this activity seriously (and they usually do and enjoy it), it can lead to a worthwhile discussion

on the purpose of dreams and dream content. If you're adept at analyzing literature, you should have fun deciphering their dream metaphors. You might invite an English teacher to visit and participate.

ENRICHMENT

Sleep research centers are becoming more and more common. Have a few students call to invite a speaker to class or to arrange an interview. If the speaker specializes in sleep disorders, ask about people who eat in their sleep. These people sometimes raid the refrigerator and prepare entire meals.

Chapter 6 CONSCIOUSNESS

because, for example, we are going to too many parties, visiting too much, or "hanging around" too much. Just getting eight hours of sleep is not enough. Sleep has to come at the right point in the circadian cycle. Otherwise the cycle gets off, which in turn makes the person feel terrible and also leads to errors on the job or to trouble solving problems. If there is not enough REM, the body craves more. The longer this goes on, the harder it becomes to get back to a reasonable rhythm (Weber et al., 1980).

Length of Sleep

People differ in the amount of sleep they need each night. For most of us, though, the body tends to seek about eight hours' worth (Weber et al., 1980). Some people need a little more and some a little less. You actually have to experiment to find out what the correct amount is. Almost no one can get by for any length of time with less than five hours of sleep a night. There *is* a case of a man who suffered damage to the brain cells that control sleep, so he never sleeps. But he feels so terrible that he can't hold down a job, and he lives a life of misery (Coleman, 1986).

Although, on occasion, a normal person can sleep up to 17 hours a night, too much sleep doesn't work either (Winfree, 1987). After 11 hours, the brain is "thick," and we do poorly on tasks requiring alertness. Long sleepers (ten hours plus) also tend to die earlier than short sleepers (six hours). But this is probably not related to sleep itself. For one thing, long sleepers are less active. Another factor centers on something we discussed earlier: those with problems need more REM, so they sleep more. If you worry a lot, your stress level is going to be much higher overall, and your body is more likely to give out earlier (Hartmann, 1984).

Walking and Talking in Your Sleep

A fair number of people sleepwalk or talk in their sleep. Neither indicates something is wrong with them. On the side of the brain, there are specific areas that control body movements and speech (Chapter 3). When random electrical impulses hit these areas, they cause walking or talking. Such behavior typically occurs during stage 4 sleep, a deep NREM sleep period, so the person is not really awake or making much sense. Trying to communicate is fruitless. You may have heard it is dangerous to awaken a sleepwalker. That's not true at all. Sleepwalkers are just asleep. Wake them up so they don't wander off and hurt themselves. Just be sure they're sitting or lying down first.

Discussion

Ask students about their weekday and weekend sleep schedules. Do they experience any problems because of social entrainment? Are we less able to alter our sleep schedules, to stay up late, as we get older? Most adults will answer *yes*. This may be related to the fact that as we get older we spend less time in Stage 4 sleep.

Critical Thinking

Several factors may affect our need for sleep. (1) *Age:* older people sleep fewer hours and the quality of their sleep is not what it used to be. Infants average about 16 hours of sleep a day. (2) *Situation:* stress may alter sleeping patterns. (3) *Body temperature:* daily fluctuations in temperature may affect when we get up and go to sleep.

ENRICHMENT

Since insomnia is so common, students may enjoy finding out how to prevent or deal with it. Although insomnia is caused mainly by drug use and getting out of the normal circadian rhythm, insomnia is also partially learned. For example, we often associate the bedroom with studying and phone calls and watching TV, instead of relaxation. The key for insomniacs (the rest of us usually can get by without such measures) is to use the bedroom only for sleeping purposes.

Parents with newborn babies are often told not to tiptoe around the house when the baby is napping. Let the baby learn to sleep through the everyday noises, like the ringing phone and the vacuum cleaner. If the house is too quiet, the baby may *need* quiet in order to sleep.

Comprehension Check

Ask students the following question: What is the difference between entrainment and social entrainment? *(Because of our 24-hour day, entrainment has become a natural process. It's no big deal to adjust a 25-hour rhythm to the 24-hour day. When we adjust the clock twice a year, it doesn't take long for our bodies to adjust. Social entrainment is a bit more "unnatural," mainly because our social schedules are usually so varied. The body never really adjusts because of the lack of routine; it does not know what it should adjust to.)*

FYI Far more males than females get apnea, something like 100 to 1. One in three men over 60 will get apnea. Just as with other sleep disorders, it is often misdiagnosed. The symptoms include snoring, hypertension, and lethargy.

172

---

insomnia

The inability to get enough sleep.

narcolepsy

Disorder in which a person falls instantly into sleep no matter what is going on in the environment.

sleep apnea

Breathing stops while someone is asleep.

hypnosis

A state of relaxation in which attention is focused on certain objects, acts, or feelings.

Sleep Disturbance

About 30 million Americans have trouble sleeping. Most such problems are self-created. Dogs and cats, for example, don't have **insomnia** (in-SOM-nee-ah), the inability to get enough sleep.

The two most common causes of insomnia are getting out of the normal circadian cycle and taking drugs or alcohol, especially before going to sleep (Webb, 1982; Blum, 1984). The irony is that these drugs (including "relaxers" or "sleeping pills") tend to block REM sleep. As a result, over a week or so, we are losing more and more REM and feeling worse and less able to sleep. By the end of a week, we are starting to feel depressed. The more depressed we are, the more we need REM, and so forth. Really heavy alcohol use for an extended period of time can cause such severe REM rebound that dreams appear while the person is still awake—in a form like the incubus attack. Bugs seem to be attacking, snakes are crawling under the bed, and so forth. These are the result of the continued heavy use of drugs or alcohol; on the other side, sometimes drugs can help bring on sleep for a very brief time after a trauma, such as a death in the family (Derryberry, 1983).

An infrequent problem that starts sometime between the teens and 20 years of age is **narcolepsy.** In this disorder, an individual can go into "instant" REM anywhere, anytime, even while driving a car or in the middle of talking to someone. Thus, although rare, it is extremely dangerous since the person immediately loses consciousness. Drugs are available that often help, so treatment is mandatory. We don't know the cause.

Another problem, usually with older people, is called **sleep apnea** (AP-nee-ah). The word *apnea* means to "stop breathing." Someone with this disorder literally stops breathing hundreds of times during sleep and keeps waking up. Normally the person doesn't know this is happening.

STATES OF CONSCIOUSNESS

So far, we have discussed cycles everyone goes through in the normal course of events. We are all subject to biological rhythms that include deep sleep, dreams, and wakefulness. However, some states of consciousness do not occur naturally. They require effort or training. For this reason, they deserve a section of their own.

Hypnosis

Hypnosis has a colorful history. It involves being in a relaxed state with a heightened ability to focus on specific things, while ignoring

DEMONSTRATION

This is a simple activity to demonstrate that hypnosis is not as mystical as it seems. Have students put out their hands straight in front of them, palms down. Tell them to look at their hands and then close their eyes. Then suggest, over and over, that their hands are sinking down, lower and lower, like a great weight is pushing them lower and lower, and that no matter how hard they try, their hands are sinking lower and lower and lower. Recite these instructions very slowly and rhythmically. After a minute or so, several hands will sink down. Have them open their eyes, and many of them will be amazed. This should demonstrate the power of a simple suggestion.

the usual distractions. Before we go on, it might help to give you a feel for why people think hypnosis is a strange and mysterious force. One of the words connected with "mystical" happenings that we still use is *mesmerize* (MEZ-mer-eyes), which means to put someone under your power. This term comes from Anton Mesmer, who worked in the late 1700s "curing" people of their ailments. Mesmer claimed that he had special magnetic powers and that people who needed help could have their body magnetism "realigned" if they came to him. He had an enormous bathtub filled with iron filings, water, and ground glass. Iron rods stuck out from the side of the tub, and the "sick" visitors were told to hold onto them. Mesmer then entered the room wearing colorful, flowing robes and touched the tub, claiming he was mixing his magnetism with theirs. Mesmer was clearly a quack, since for those who couldn't make it to his place, he sold bottles of his special magnetism for a "take-out" cure (Ellenberger, 1970).

The surprising thing is that many people were helped by this nonsense. We know today that such "cures" come from the power of suggestion. Suggestion is basic to hypnosis.

The Nature of Hypnosis The formal definition of hypnosis is that it is a state that helps a person focus attention on certain objects, acts, or feelings. The best way to understand hypnosis is to think back to a time in the past few days when you were both studying and listening to music. You could not do both of them equally well and at the same time. If you focused on the music, what you were reading faded, or if you focused on what you were reading, the music faded. So it is obvious that we have the power to control how

▲ *Fashionable people attending Mesmer's "bath" in the 1700s.*

Reteaching Strategy

Break the class into groups and assign a sleeping disorder to each group. The group then presents a role-play that shows someone suffering from the disorder.

FYI Here are the ingredients, or the variables, needed for successful hypnosis: (1) a good hypnotist; (2) a good subject, someone who is willing to "let go"; (3) a good relationship between the hypnotist and subject; and (4) a good atmosphere.

DISCUSS THE PHOTO

Approximately eight people out of ten can be hypnotized.

ENRICHMENT

Have someone invite a hypnotist to class. A good hypnotist can usually address a number of topics: goal setting, visualization, the unconscious, and meditation.

DISCOVERY

Most Americans have little or no experience with meditation. If you'd like to expand students' horizons a bit, obtain a copy of a meditation cassette tape, play it in class, and allow students to meditate for 15 to 20 minutes. A good tape will usually provide step-by-step instructions about body position and so on. To create a proper atmosphere, turn off the lights and have students spread out by themselves on the floor. If possible, eliminate any possible distractions or interruptions from outside the classroom: tape paper over any glass in the door so people can't look in, and so on.

DISCUSS THE PHOTO

Stage hypnotists informally screen subjects and choose only those subjects who are highly cooperative.

Unit 2 BRAIN, BODY, AND AWARENESS

▲ *While hypnosis is real enough, much of the stage variety is mostly entertainment and questionable.*

trance

Another word for the state of deep relaxation that can occur during hypnosis.

Journal Topic

"Write a dialogue between a hypnotist inducing a trance and her subject. Include the subject's thoughts (in parentheses maybe) throughout the induction." Reading some of these entries aloud should give you the opportunity to debunk several myths about hypnosis. And this may also help clarify that the subject does indeed maintain his or her thoughts and free will during hypnosis.

174

much attention we give to different things in the environment (Greenwald, 1992; Hebb & Donderi, 1987; Hilgard, 1986). And if we want, we can cut out some stimulation altogether. You have been doing that while reading this book. Here are some of the things you may have been blocking out: that you have shoes on your feet, that the room is light, that there is noise coming from an air conditioner or furnace, that your arms are connected to your body, and so forth. Once you are aware of these things, they come into focus, one by one, demonstrating our point. Memories are cut off also. You have "forgotten," for example, the sights, smells, sounds, and feelings of your first day in high school—until reading this sentence.

The brain is like a mammoth stereo system with billions of speakers, switches, and filters so that you can turn on one, then another, blend them, mix them, or make most of them turn off completely. Some people get so good at controlling incoming stimulation that they can stick a knitting needle right through the arm and not feel a thing.

Depending on the goal, hypnotists use the power of suggestion to aid in focusing or blocking whatever system is desired. Thus, a person can be aided in forgetting something, remembering something, reducing pain, and so forth. All of us can do anything without hypnosis that we can do under hypnosis. Some people just don't have enough confidence in themselves to believe that this is the case, so they rely on an outsider—a hypnotist—to aid them.

A Special State? Some people think hypnosis is a form of sleep. This belief may have arisen because subjects can get so relaxed they are like rag dolls and they act semiconscious. Or it may be because some hypnotists say, "You are getting sleepy." But the hypnotic state is really not related to that of sleep. Hypnosis is an intense form of relaxation with the person fully conscious.

Does the hypnotist really have control over the person? Only if the person wants to be under control, since he or she is still conscious (Spanos, 1986). If you tell someone in a deep **trance** to stay in the room and you'll be back in a couple of days, he or she may sit there for a while, relaxed, until what you've said fully registers. The person will then get up and leave. *Trance* is just another word for the state of relaxation that the person is in. The deeper the trance, the more likely the subject will be relaxed and will cooperate with the hypnotist's suggestions.

There is much arguing about whether someone can be made to do something "immoral" under hypnosis. This is very unlikely, unless the person really wants to do it and uses the hypnosis as an excuse. If, however, the subject is in a deep trance and is foggy, he or she may trust what the hypnotist says far more than normally, so that is a problem. In this sense, hypnosis *can* be dangerous, since the subject lets down defenses while putting faith in the hypnotist. Thus, hypno-

Afterward, discuss the difficulties students had in following the instructions on the tape. They surely will not experience many benefits after only 15 or 20 minutes, but perhaps they can guess what benefits they *would* experience if they meditated on a daily basis. Assuming that these ben-

efits will be experienced, ask why students do not meditate. (They may answer that the benefits aren't that valued; society doesn't promote it, and so on.)

Have students complete the **Enrichment Worksheet** for this chapter located in the Teacher Resources.

---

tized people could say or do things that would embarrass them later on. The actual physical dangers are few, but some subjects get a headache afterward or feel a little anxious or confused.

Uses of Hypnosis At one time or another, hypnosis has been claimed to cure almost everything. It *does* have some uses. It might help with reducing weight or with giving up smoking or drinking, but its effectiveness in these cases is only as great as the person's real *desire* to change (Wadden & Anderson, 1982). Hypnosis can help with minor pain, such as some dental work; it can help a woman through a *normal* childbirth; it can help reduce some headaches. Hypnosis cannot improve memory, but it can help you focus better on such things as study assignments, so it has been useful in education. While there is some disagreement about its use with major pain, most agree that in Western society, it is usually not too effective (Hilgard, 1986, 1974; Barber, 1969). Those who can stick knitting needles through the arm are different because they have spent a lifetime practicing self-control or self-hypnosis, which is essentially the same thing.

A great deal of "hype" is given to the so-called posthypnotic suggestion, with people claiming that it causes someone to do something that they can't control. This is quite an exaggeration. Since a person is suggestible under hypnosis but still quite conscious, he or she may later do what was suggested but doesn't *have* to do anything. The situation is roughly the same as the one in which you go to school and three people in a row say you don't look very well today. You don't have to believe them, but the repeated suggestion makes you wonder, and you actually start to feel not all that well, even if you were fine before they said anything. Or right now we can suggest that your right arm feels a little stiff. Aren't you moving it a little to check? No hypnosis involved, but you still check it because of the suggestion.

Meditation

Meditation is a form of self-control in which a person uses many of the "switches" and "filters" of the brain to cut off the outside world. He or she then focuses on some steady rhythm or sound, trying to put the brain more or less into "neutral" in order to feel peaceful and at ease. The steady sound can be a hum or a word or phrase that the person repeats, or even simply the ticking of a clock. Meditation can be very effective in lowering blood pressure or slowing heart rate. The techniques of meditation are actually tools to help us relax. Some people can do it without going through any ritual. And some people cannot relax, no matter what. When some try to relax, it makes them nervous (Holmes, 1984; Heide, 1985)!

▲ *Meditation is basically a form of intense relaxation.*

meditation

A form of self-control in which the outside world is cut off from consciousness.

With meditation, the suggestions come from within; with hypnosis, the suggestions come from the hypnotist. Otherwise, the two are highly similar.

Comprehension Check

How are hypnosis and meditation similar? *(Both can be used to make the brain block out the outside world in order to focus intently on something; one effect of this is relaxation.)* How are they different? *(For hypnosis, an outsider aids in the process described above, while meditation depends on self-control.)*

ENRICHMENT

Invite a speaker to discuss dream interpretation. Some psychologists who use dream journals as part of their therapy may be able to analyze a few students' dreams or at least explain the process they use to interpret them.

Points to Stress

The 2:00 P.M. low has nothing to do with lunch but is related more to the natural highs and lows we experience throughout the day.

FYI

Here's a story to show the priority Europeans place on their breaks (see also **Wrapping It Up**). I was on a train in Italy one summer day when the train came to a sudden stop between stations. When I learned that the conductors and other workers had gone on strike, I panicked and wondered how I'd get back to my grandfather's farm, 30 miles away. My cousins told me not to worry, that the conductors strike every day but that they return to work in a few hours. This was no strike. This was espresso time.

PSYCHOLOGY IN YOUR LIFE

Wandering in the World of Consciousness

Here are some practical and, we hope, interesting applications of the material discussed in this chapter:

Try using the dream state for problem solving. This might be a little difficult because you may want to go ahead and solve a problem, especially if the answer is due the next day. But if you can, look up a problem in a math book—a problem that you can solve but that will take some time. Look at it just before going to bed. You will probably have the solution by morning (or be very close) since your brain has been working on it.

Many people claim that the twilight state is the period when we are the most creative. Let your mind wander during this time and see if you don't come up with an unusual idea. If it sounds quite good, get up and write it down before you sink into deep sleep. Of course, it may not seem so hot in the morning—but who knows?

Try to *make* a dream. It can be done. Think about something very simple and not threatening, and tell yourself that you want it in the

dream. It will probably appear in some form during the night. If you're lucky, it may occur late, toward morning, and you will remember it. Sometimes, though, it will not appear until the following night.

If you see a horror movie that really scares you, it also might appear in a dream—something you *don't* want. The computer theory we discussed works pretty well in this case. Here's what you do: just before getting into bed, go over the part that scared you and reassure yourself that it didn't—and won't—really happen. If you do this, the odds are great that you will have "cleared" that problem from your memory system, and it will not appear in a dream.

Find something you want to memorize. For example, pick a few lines of a poem or a saying. Read them over about five times while you sit on the bed. Then forget them and go to sleep. By morning, you will have most of the material stored, and it will require only a little more work for you to retain it permanently.

Night dreams are not the only dreams we have. Every 90 minutes during the day we have daydreams, unless something is really distracting us. Now that you know this, think about a daydream *after* you've had one. (Don't try to "catch" it in midstream.) Notice how much more organized it is than a night dream. This is because you keep better control when you are awake.

Set your own internal alarm clock. You have one. Pick a time you want to wake up, but make it real; in other words, plan on doing something at that time. Your internal clock will time the number of 90-minute cycles and shorten the later dreams as you approach your wake-up time. The odds are that you will not hit the time exactly but that you will awaken just before or after the REM closest to the time you set.

Notice how much easier it is to get to sleep if you go to bed an hour later than you did the night before, rather than an hour earlier. This is because when you go to bed

(continued on next page)

PSYCHOLOGY IN YOUR LIFE

Wandering in the World of Consciousness

(continued from previous page)
an hour later, you are actually moving toward the body's free-running cycle of 25 hours. On the other hand, if you go to bed an hour earlier, you are just adding another hour *against* your natural rhythm, which makes sleep more difficult to attain.

If you have been up very late over the weekend and not slept late the next morning, note that the following night you will feel like you had more dreams than usual. This is true. REM rebound will occur, especially after two such nights in a row.

Most of us know if we are "night" or "day" people. To "prove" it, take your temper-ature every hour for 18 hours or so. It will start to increase and reach its high point for the day (roughly 99.5 degrees) either in the evening or late morning. This increase tells you that you are entering your best time of day. If you're really interested, and if you are a day person, get up sometime at 3:00 or 4:00 A.M. and notice how low your temperature is.

Don't ever *try* to get to sleep, no matter how important it is that you do. The brain will decide you are trying to do something critical and will signal an "emergency." This will change your body chemistry so that you will never get to sleep. Instead, count something like imaginary horses jumping a fence. Such rhythmic thoughts will distract the brain and lull you to sleep.

Some animals, such as cows, sleep with their eyes open. Observe your friends in a 2:00 P.M. class, and you will see behavior that resembles that of the cow. Chimpanzees, monkeys, and humans not only have a 3:00 A.M. dip in energy but also one at 2:00 P.M. This is a natural rhythm, not related to eating lunch. Recognizing this, many cultures allow for a nap in the early afternoon. Ours doesn't—hence, the condition of you and/or your classmates in that 2:00 class.

VOCABULARY REVIEW

Before testing students on the contents of this chapter, you may want to review vocabulary terms that are especially important or confusing. Terms in this chapter that could require clarification are *construct*, *chronobiology*, *REM sleep*, and *NREM sleep*.

Wrapping It Up

The chapter makes clear that we are all affected by internal rhythms. Society isn't always kind to these internal rhythms, however. Discuss possible changes we should make in our world to better accommodate our internal clocks.

For example, our body temperature is low at 2:00 P.M. Should we allow for this? In Europe, many businesses, stores, schools, and farms shut down in the afternoon for a few hours—for breaks, naps, social visits. When students stop cheering for this, tell them there's a catch: they can go home from about 1:00 to 3:00, but they would have to return to school until 5:00 or 6:00.

Reteaching Strategy

Have students complete the **Reteaching Worksheet** for this chapter located in the Teacher Resources.

The **Vocabulary Worksheet** may be completed by the class as a pretest for chapter concepts or used as a reteaching worksheet for those students needing additional review.

178

SUMMARY

1. Consciousness is our awareness of events inside and outside ourselves. Consciousness seems to result from a series of scenes put together into a whole as we move about. Levels of consciousness are the conscious, subconscious, and unconscious.

2. Chronobiology is the study of the effect of different rhythms on behavior. The rhythms are controlled by biological clocks that cause events to start or stop at certain times of the day, month, or year.

3. Sleeping and waking follow a 24-hour cycle called the circadian rhythm. Each of us follows this rhythm and has a high and low point every 24 hours.

4. Sleep is divided into REM and NREM periods. The REM period contains most of the dreams.

5. Dreams occur every 90 minutes throughout the night, with each dream longer than the previous one. The basic purpose of dreams seems to be to keep the brain active while the outside world is shut off. It is primarily during this time that the brain chemicals are restored.

6. Most dreams are about everyday events. Sometimes bizarre dreams can occur from random firing of the memory circuits. Likewise, sleepwalking and talking in one's sleep result if an electrical impulse hits the areas of the brain controlling these activities during NREM.

7. Hypnosis is the focusing of attention. People under hypnosis can control memories, bring them back, or make them disappear. Hypnosis is of some use in reducing pain and can help a person lose weight or stop smoking—but only if the person already really wants to.

8. Meditation is a form of self-control in which outside stimulation is greatly reduced to create a peaceful state.

SUGGESTED READINGS

▼ Begley, Sharon. "The Stuff That Dreams Are Made Of." *Newsweek,* August 14, 1989, 441–44.

▼ Dolnick, Edward. "What Dreams Are Really Made Of." *The Atlantic,* July 1990, 41–61.

▼ Faraday, Ann. *The Dream Game.* New York: Harper and Row, 1974.

▼ Hartmann, Ernest. "The Strangest Disorder." *Psychology Today,* April, 1981.

▼ Hobson, J. Allan. *Sleep.* New York: W. H. Freeman, 1989.

▼ Porter, Laurence M. *The Interpretation of Dreams: A Student's Companion to the Text.* Boston: Twayne, 1987.

▼ Restak, Richard. *The Brain.* New York: Bantam Books, 1984.

▼ Ullman, Montague, and Nan Zimmerman. *Working with Dreams.* New York: St. Martin's Press, 1979.

▼ Von Franz, Marie Louise. *Dreams.* Boston: Shambhala, 1991.

VOCABULARY

construct
consciousness
subconscious
unconscious
chronobiology
biological clocks
free-running cycles
entrainment

circadian rhythm
twilight state
REM sleep
beta waves
alpha waves
delta waves
NREM sleep
nightmare

REM rebound
incubus attack
insomnia
narcolepsy
sleep apnea
hypnosis
trance
meditation

Answers to Review Questions

1. unconscious
2. chronobiology
3. construct
4. 25
5. entrainment
6. 24
7. consciousness
8. A
9. B
10. A
11. D
12. NREM
13. REM
14. REM
15. NREM
16. REM
17. REM
18. d
19. c
20. a
21. b
22. false
23. false
24. true
25. false
26. true

Review Questions

Fill in the blanks; answer on a separate sheet of paper. (An answer may consist of more than one word.)

1. If someone is mad at his or her uncle but is completely unaware of this, the anger is probably hidden in his or her ___?___ .
2. ___?___ is the study of the body and the cycles that affect it.
3. A belief in something that can't be seen or touched is called a ___?___ .
4. The free-running daily cycle of most humans is ___?___ hours.
5. Most humans have altered their free-running cycle through ___?___ .
6. The human circadian rhythm is based on a ___?___-hour cycle.
7. Another name for knowing, or awareness, is ___?___ .

For each of the following states of consciousness, indicate A for alpha waves, B for beta waves, and D for delta waves.

8. Very relaxed
9. Awake
10. First ten minutes of sleep
11. Deep sleep

Notes on Discussion Questions

1. Any abstract concepts like love, hate, envy, and so on are acceptable answers. To help students think more critically, have them present their evidence in class, then discuss the validity of the evidence.

2. A greater level of awareness is probably more related to motivation, sensitivity, and open-mindedness than to intelligence. On the other hand, one's level of awareness could probably not be great without a certain degree of cognitive development. In other words, an adult would probably possess a greater level of awareness than a child.

3. This could lead to a discussion on values. Is it worthwhile to explore our innermost past and present feelings? Should learning about ourselves be a struggle (rather than an act of pushing a button)? Is there risk involved in exploring our inner selves?

4. For those who would give up sleep, what would they do instead? For those who want to sleep, why is it so important?

5. Answers will vary.

6. If you have a few talented actors, you might convince them to act this out in class. They can assume the roles of animals who reveal the content of their dreams by talking in their sleep.

7. Students may have

SUGGESTED VIDEOS

▼ *Chronobiology: The Time of Our Lives.* 58 min. Films for the Humanities.

▼ *Dream Voyage.* 26 min. 1985. Films for the Humanities and Sciences.

▼ *Dreams: Theater of the Night.* 28 min. Films for the Humanities.

▼ *The Mind Awake and Asleep.* Discovering Psychology series, part 13. 27 min. 1-800-LEARNER.

▼ *Secrets of Sleep.* 52 min. Time Life.

For each of the following, answer REM *or* NREM.

12. When the brain is idle
13. Associated with vivid dreams
14. Paralyzed body
15. When incubus attacks occur
16. Gets longer as night progresses
17. Associated with narcolepsy

Matching

18. Episode of panic and fear
19. Can be caused by drinking alcohol
20. Stop breathing
21. Falling suddenly into sleep

a. sleep apnea
b. narcolepsy
c. insomnia
d. incubus attack

True/False

22. Hypnosis has been proved to improve memory.
23. Hypnosis is regarded as a special sleep stage.
24. It is unlikely that a person will do something immoral under hypnosis.
25. Most doctors in the U.S. agree that hypnosis can help reduce major pain.
26. Meditation helps us shut out the outside world.

DISCUSSION QUESTIONS

1. Besides consciousness, can you think of another construct, or belief, that people have? (Remember, a construct can't be seen or touched.) What evidence would suggest that this construct actually exists?

2. Consciousness is an awareness of what is going on inside and outside the organism. Do you think that people who are highly intelligent experience this awareness at a greater level than people who are less intelligent? Explain.

3. The unconscious contains thoughts and desires about which we have no knowledge. If you could suddenly become aware of these "hidden" thoughts by simply pushing a button, would you do it? Why or why not?

4. If you could completely give up sleep without many physical side effects, would you do it? Why or why not? Remember, no sleep means no dreaming.

5. Do you consider yourself a long sleeper or a short sleeper? If you're a long sleeper, how do you feel when you can only sleep a short time? Explain. If you're a short sleeper, how do you feel when you've had too much sleep? Explain.

6. Since dogs and cats have REM, it's probably safe to assume that they "dream." What would you guess makes up the content of their "dreams"? Explain.

7. With which of the three major theories that explain why we dream do you most agree? Explain.

8. If you could automatically remember and control all your dreams, would you want this ability? Why or why not?

9. In general, do you believe that you could be hypnotized? Why or why not?

their own interpretations of dreams. Invite them to share these.

8. Mention that some people are better able to do this than others but that with practice most of us could control our dreams to some extent.

9. People who do not believe that they can be hypnotized probably never will be. A good hypnosis subject will believe, will be eager to follow the suggestions of the hypnotist, and will usually be highly imaginative. Perhaps you can compare students' attitudes about dreams to their answers to this question. Those same students who view dreaming as mystical and highly meaningful are probably the same students who believe that they can be hypnotized.

ACTIVITIES

1. Prepare a list of questions for an interview with your grandfather or grandmother or someone about the same age. Find out how sleep patterns generally change as a person gets older. Avoid too many questions that simply require a yes or no response. If you do receive a simple answer, ask the person to elaborate.

   Possible questions:

   a. How has the quality of sleep changed as you've grown older? Is it more satisfying now than 20 years ago, or less satisfying?

   b. Do you sleep more now than 20 years ago, or less? How does this affect your everyday routine?

   c. What kinds of events in your life forced you to alter your sleep-wake cycle?

   d. Are your dreams more vivid now than they were 20 years ago? Do you remember your dreams more today than you did then?

   Write a detailed report of your interview. Be sure to include your questions. Also, include your general reactions to what you found out.

2. This chapter mentions that there seem to be some differences between long sleepers and short sleepers. Find out if the differences also involve personality. Use 20 subjects and ask each of them the following questions:

   a. Do you consider yourself to be (1) highly imaginative, (2) somewhat imaginative, or (3) not very imaginative?

   b. Are you (1) usually introverted or (2) usually extroverted?

   c. When you are given an assignment, are you generally (1) a highly motivated worker, (2) a somewhat motivated worker, (3) a somewhat unmotivated worker, or (4) a highly unmotivated worker?

   d. In general, do you consider yourself (1) a leader or (2) a follower?

   e. How long do you usually sleep: (1) six hours or less; (2) seven hours; (3) eight hours; (4) nine hours; (5) ten hours or more?

   Analyze your results. Does there seem to be some correlation between personality and length of sleep?

3. Keep a dream journal for several nights. Write down each dream exactly as you remember it. After about a week of jotting down dreams, analyze them. Were there any common themes or common objects in many of them? Did you dream in color? Which colors? Did the dreams tend to be bizarre or somewhat orderly?

   What do the answers to all these questions say about your personality in general? Explain.

4. Write a report on Sigmund Freud's theory of dreams. Find out what Freud believed about the subconscious and the unconscious and what he said about how these concepts are revealed in our dreams.

Cognitive Processes

One of the most common requests we make of our students is to "Pay attention!" We often plead, beg, and even threaten students who do not pay attention at the appropriate times. The need to listen, to process the classroom material, to integrate the material into what is known, and reapply that information in new and novel situations is the basis of education. If more is known about the physiology of attention, there may be fewer children labeled in the school system as being disruptive and/or withdrawn.

In order for people to pay attention effectively they generally have to be able to (1) identify and focus on the important element of a situation; (2) maintain attention on that element while integrating important relevant information and ignoring unimportant and competing information; (3) retrieve memories related to what they are focusing on, and (4) redirect attention to new information when appropriate. Paying attention begins as a process in which we passively receive incoming information from the environment. Since we aren't able to process all of it, however, the brain limits sensory input within a narrow range. Stimuli that is sudden, dramatic, and novel is quickly processed, since our brains are designed to notice anything that may signal predatory danger. The sensory-input range also includes stimuli characterized by emotional intensity. One task of teachers today, however, is to help students attend to contemporary dangers that are subtle and gradual (such as pollution, global warming, the destruction of the rainforests, etc.); understanding the mechanisms of the human attentional system sheds light on just how challenging this task is.

From a teaching standpoint, it is valuable to know that attention often shifts from external events to highly subjective internal memories. This shift between what is being said in a conversation, for example, and the memories of past experiences triggered by that conversation is important in maintaining and updating long-term storage of memories, since it facilitates a connection between past experiences and the current situation. By recalling these memories, the neural networks that contain them are strengthened. Classroom activities that encourage this process can enhance learning.

Another fact about the attention process that is useful to understand is that the brain has a fast system to note *where* objects are located (the background) and a slower one to discern *what* the objects are (the foreground). Focusing on the foreground is especially problematic for children with dyslexia and Attention Deficit Hyperactivity Disorder (ADHD). The fast system is sluggish for those with dyslexia, so that words that have been read are not shifted to the background when new

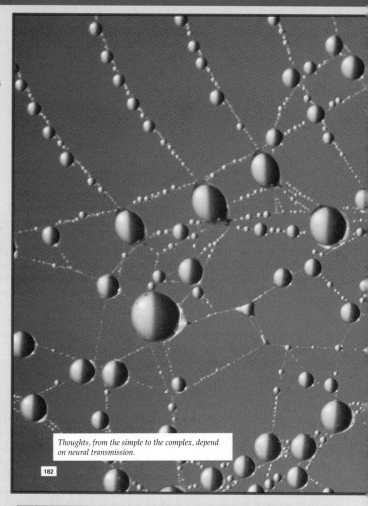

Thoughts, from the simple to the complex, depend on neural transmission.

Discuss the Photo

Neural transmission relies on chemical messengers called neurotransmitters. We know of 60 different neurotransmitters!

words are being read, causing them all to blur. ADHD seems to be the result of neurotransmittor deficiencies. Attention-focusing skills for all students can be strengthened by providing activities that require them to constantly make foreground and background decisions. If one is looking for a needle in a haystack, for example, the texture and quality of the hay must be of secondary importance to the appearance of the needle. (Have you ever tried to find "Waldo?") An interest-

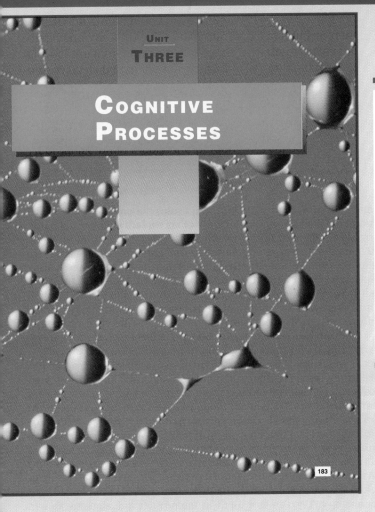

COGNITIVE PROCESSES

PERFORMANCE TASK

Overview

Students conduct a study of controversies regarding the development and testing of intelligence. Several topics, such as increasing intelligence through special programs, the relative influence of heredity and environment on intelligence, parental instructions of preschool children, or effects of daycare, can be used. On day one, students will research in teams and prepare a presentation for one side of an issue. On day two, one member of each group serves on a panel to present each team's argument to the class and answer questions. On the third day, other class members write statements stating which position they agree with, defending their choices with reasons. Complete instructions for this activity and the supporting student worksheets can be found in the Teacher Resources.

ing experiment called the Stroop test can illustrate this principle of selective attention. In the experiment, people are timed as they read aloud a list of words that denote different colors (i.e. the words "red," "blue," "green," etc.). People are then asked to read the words a second time. This time the letters of the words are printed in colors (i.e. the word "green" is printed in yellow ink, the word "blue" is printed in red ink, etc.). People often say the color of the letters instead of saying the word the letters spell. The point is that people have problems staying focused on the task because their attention is divided between the colors the words are printed in and the name of the color the word denotes. Speed and accuracy increase, however, with practice.

References

Full citations can be found in the Teacher Resources.

DISCUSS THE PHOTO

Some behaviorists may disagree, but as the caption implies, rewards can arrive from within. The bulk of the chapter, however, will describe *external* reinforcements.

A thing done well is often its own reward.

184

PSYCHOLOGY AND YOU RESOURCES

A variety of resources are available in the Psychology and You *supplementary material. In addition, there are a number of additional resources listed to enhance your lesson plans.*

Masters
▼ 7-1A Learning Goals
▼ 7-1B Answers to Learning Goals
▼ 7-2A Classical Conditioning
▼ 7-2B Answers to Classical Conditioning
▼ 7-3 Ways to Break Bad Habits
▼ 7-4A Classical and Operant Conditioning Practice Quiz
▼ 7-4B Answers to Quiz
▼ 7-5 Classical Conditioning Review Sheet
▼ 7-6 Operant Conditioning Review Sheet

Student Worksheets
▼ Vocabulary Worksheet
▼ Independent Practice Worksheet
▼ Enrichment Worksheet
▼ Reteaching Worksheet

Test Bank
▼ Tests A and B

Multimedia
▼ *The Brain* Videotape Module #21
▼ **Psychware** Exercises 2–5
▼ Psychology Videodisc

Student Workbook

PACING CHART

Complete Coverage

Day 1: Assign the first two sections of the chapter prior to class. Provide a means for students to identify the components of classical conditioning. Use discussion question #3 to initiate analysis of John Watson's theory. Have students read "Operant Conditioning" for Day 2.

Day 2: Compare and contrast classical and operant conditioning. Assign a short research project on B. F. Skinner for homework, such as activity #4 in the text.

Day 3: Focus on the importance of reinforcement for operant conditioning. Discuss the effects of the four schedules of reinforcement, using the question provided in In Focus: Schedules of Reinforcement to begin review of generalization, discrimination, and extinction. Assign "Social Learning" for Day 4.

Day 4: Review the concept of observational learning. Divide the class and set up a debate about the effects of television violence on children's behavior.

OBJECTIVES

Be able to:

▼ Explain the basic principles of classical and operant conditioning.

▼ Explain the different schedules of reinforcement and give an example of each.

▼ Describe social learning and explain how it differs from learning based on classical and operant conditioning.

▼ Describe some of the complexities of conditioning unknown to Pavlov or Watson.

▼ Explain the philosophy of the cognitive approach to learning and how this philosophy differs from other theories about how we learn.

Global Look at the Chapter

Most often when we think of learning, we think of the formal type that occurs in school. Learning, however, takes place continuously every day. In this chapter, we examine some of the mechanisms that aid in this process.

185

INTRODUCING THE CHAPTER

This can be a difficult chapter for some students because they tend to forget the "big picture" behind behaviorism. To help establish this big picture, discuss John Watson's assertion: *Give me a dozen healthy infants, allow me to control the environment, and I can make them into anything I want* (see discussion question #3 at the end of the chapter). You can discuss not only the feasibility of such a task but also the ethics involved. Watson's claims are limited mainly to behavioral results, but given his premise, could he mold less tangible qualities like generosity or pride?

Have students read "Cognitive Psychology in Learning" as homework.

Day 5: Use an activity from the text or wrap to clarify the term *cognitive map* before giving the Chapter Review quiz.

In Brief

Day 1: Stress the concept of association. Assign an in-class activity requiring students to identify the elements of classical conditioning.

Day 2: Outline B. F. Skinner's approach to learning. Focus on reinforcement as the basis for operant conditioning. Review the effects of the various schedules of reinforcement.

Day 3: Discuss Albert Bandura's belief in observational learning. Provide a demonstration illustrating the concept of what E. C. Tolman calls "cognitive maps." Give the Chapter Review quiz.

LEAD-OFF ACTIVITY

You're bound to have a student who has a small pet, like a hamster or mouse, who would be willing to bring the animal to class. Make sure the animal is hungry when it visits. Using some of the principles discussed in the chapter, particularly shaping, teach the animal some simple new behaviors. You can probably shape a few behaviors in a single class period. Throughout the chapter you can refer back to this training.

If you're unwilling or unable to have an animal in class, conduct activity #5 in the chapter-end material. Note that with both of these ideas, students are given the opportunity to observe *learning.* Be sure to emphasize this.

Teaching Hint

Consider having students read the **Psychology in Your Life** feature, and have them use some of the ideas presented there as they read the chapter, especially the suggestions on taking notes.

INTERDISCIPLINARY PROJECT

Literature. Many works of fiction deal with the theme of behaviorism gone wild: George Orwell's *1984* and *Animal Farm,* Aldous Huxley's *Brave New World,* Kurt Vonnegut, Jr.'s "Harrison Bergeron." Have students read one of these works, relate it to behaviorism, and speculate on whether such fictions could ever happen. "Harrison Bergeron" is a short enough story that you could read it aloud in class.

DISCUSS THE PHOTO

It is ironic that shock, which is usually regarded as inhumane, can produce such dramatic changes.

Critical Thinking

Even if you do not complete the interdisciplinary project above, you can still discuss the abuses of behaviorism in real life, either past or present. You might discuss how some cults condition members to discard their old value systems and adopt the cult's. You can also discuss how mainstream society conditions us to adopt its values. This process is less intensive than the one a cult might use, but students may be able to find some similarities. For example, most students do not swear during class. The rewards for swearing are few (a little attention, a few laughs maybe) and the punishments are usually severe.

186

Unit 3 COGNITIVE PROCESSES

conditioning

Making an association between two events by repeated exposure.

BASIC CONDITIONING

A nine-month-old baby lay in a hospital crib starving to death, his weight less than 12 pounds. The baby was so thin that his ribs stuck out and the skin hung from the bones of his arms. His eyes were wide and dull; he spent most of his time staring into space. Death seemed inevitable because each time he swallowed food, it would reach a certain point in its downward movement and then his muscles would contract in the opposite direction, causing him to throw up.

Some central part of the child's brain was sending a signal to "throw it into reverse" when the food reached a certain spot. All available forms of medical and surgical treatment had been tried, and now there seemed to be no hope. But then someone hit on the idea of using a basic psychological principle—conditioning. In **conditioning,** an association is made between two events by repeatedly having them occur close together in time.

The next step was to find the exact location in the digestive tract at which the reversal of the food movement took place. This point was located with little trouble. Then the process of conditioning began. A wire that could carry an electric shock was attached to the infant's leg. Each time the food arrived at the "reversal spot," a shock was sent to the leg at one-second intervals until the vomiting was over. At first there seemed to be no significant change, but the doctors kept on with it. Treatment lasted for two weeks. By that time the food revers-

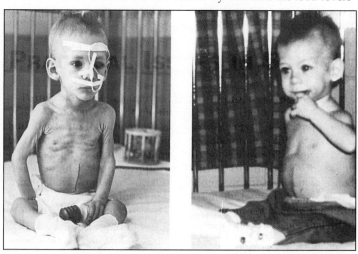

▲ *The power of conditioning is demonstrated in these two photos of the nine-month-old baby—before and after.* From "Case Report: Avoidance Conditioning Therapy of an Infant with Chronic Ruminative Vomiting" by P. J. Lang and B. G. Melamed, 1969, *Journal of Abnormal Psychology,* © by the American Psychological Association. Reprinted by permission.

DEMONSTRATION

Just before discussing Pavlov, bring a lemon into class. Cut the lemon in half and suck on it, allowing a few drops to drip to the floor. (Is your mouth watering already?) If a lemon is too sour for your tastes, use an orange. The important thing is to get several students to salivate. Once they admit that they are salivating, ask if their responses are learned. The initial reaction will probably be, "No, of course it's not learned. It's natural." There's no question that salivation is natural, but it's not natural to salivate after *seeing* a lemon. For example, flash a lemon in front of a baby's face, and surely no salivation will occur.

ing had been thoroughly associated with something very unpleasant for the infant. His brain decided to stop the reversal process in order to avoid the shock. Soon afterward, the infant began to gain significant weight, and he was discharged, well and happy (Lang & Melamed, 1969). Thus, it is possible to condition mental or physical behavior by a process of association.

Social Influence

This dramatic episode shows the value of conditioning, even at the most primitive level. However, conditioning can also be very subtle and complex. A good example is the concept of handsomeness, which is conditioned by each culture. Males in the Boloki tribe demonstrate their attractiveness and masculinity by chiseling their upper front teeth to V-shaped points (Frumkin, 1961). Apparently the women in the tribe like it, but it is hard to imagine this technique attracting many people in New York or San Francisco.

Changes in style occur in every society over time, and we adapt to each change by constant association. The best example of this is the sheer panic each generation of parents feels over the music that is currently popular with their offspring. And the offspring, having learned to hear a different sound as pleasing, cannot fathom how the parents can actually listen to the "old-fashioned" music they enjoy.

Four Types of Learning

In this chapter, we will discuss four types of learning. The first involves unavoidable physical association, such as the shock to the boy's leg. This is called *classical conditioning*. The second involves learning caused by the actions we perform. For instance, we learn that pressing one's finger very hard on the edge of a knife is not a good idea. This is called *operant conditioning*. The third type of learning is the learning that results from observing others. If someone dives into a black lagoon and does not resurface, you know not to do that. This is called *social learning* (because it results from viewing other people). The fourth type emphasizes thought processes in learning. It is called the *cognitive approach*.

CLASSICAL CONDITIONING

The most primitive learning is the kind we have just discussed in the example with the baby. It was first demonstrated by a physiologist and absentminded professor in the 1900s, **Ivan Pavlov** (PAV-lov).

Points to Stress

Conditioning (learning) occurs everyday. If we eat something and become nauseous, smelling that food later may make us queasy. Students are certainly conditioned by the school bell: their hearts race; they jump out of their seats. When an outsider visits class, you can really see this conditioning by noting the visitor's *lack* of response to the bell. Even before we are born, we learn. Crying newborns have been known to be soothed by music they heard while in the uterus. (Some parents take this too far and begin crooning the alphabet into the mother's belly button.)

DEMONSTRATION

Conditioning can be broken down into two basic parts: stimulus and response. To demonstrate this, turn the lights off, leave the classroom, and start to walk back in as though for the first time. Follow this sequence in slow motion, and report what is happening internally. *Stimulus:* dark-ness. *Response:* turn to look for a switch. *Stimulus:* switch. *Response:* flick switch. *Stimulus:* light. *Response:* step into room. We can break up most of our behaviors into stimulus-response patterns, which becomes very useful when we have problems like phobias or bad habits.

Comprehension Check

Ask students what specific associations they have about styles of clothing that are "in" right now. What associations come to mind regarding clothes that are out of style? *(Answers will vary.)*

Connections

In Chapter 5, students learned how hunger may be influenced by external cues. Conditioning would certainly play a role, too. Notice that if the school day is shortened (by shortening each period by twenty minutes), many people will still eat during the same lunch period, even if it's two hours earlier than usual.

DISCUSS THE PHOTO

The tube in the dog's mouth carried saliva to a lever, activating a recording device (far left).

He was a man with a very hot temper who blew up at assistants for the slightest mistake. He fined them for being late to work, even though they had to walk through an ongoing Russian Revolution to get there; when *he* was late, on the other hand, he did not dock his own pay (Miller, 1962; Windholz, 1987). Pavlov also became infuriated with the dogs used in his experiments because they were so bored with what was going on that they kept falling asleep. Despite these problems, his early discoveries led to major advances in understanding how people and animals learn.

Pavlov's original goal was to understand how the digestive system works. He wanted to discover how salivation and gastric juices aid in digestion. By today's standards, the experiments were both basic and simple, but such was not the case in the early 1900s. Pavlov surgically separated the stomach from the esophagus (food transporter) in dogs. This operation meant that: (1) food taken by mouth would never reach the stomach and (2) food could be put directly into the stomach without having to travel through the mouth.

Importance of Association

Pavlov was quick to note three strange things. First, food put directly into the stomach did not generate all by itself enough gastric juices for digestion. Thus, salivation at the time of eating is critical to proper digestion. Second, even though *no* food was placed in the dog's mouth, the animal would still salivate copiously just at the *sight* of the food. But Pavlov's third finding was the most surprising and important one: the sight of the *experimenter* who fed the animal would cause the dog to salivate even if that person was not carrying

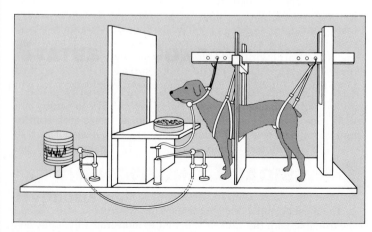

▲ *The type of apparatus used by Pavlov in conditioning his dogs.*

DEMONSTRATION

Raise one hand, make a loud noise with the other hand—by dropping a book or slapping your desk—then repeat this procedure several times throughout the class. Soon enough, your raised hand will evoke some of the same reactions as the loud noise. Ask students to identify the UCS (noise) and the UCR (anxiety), the CS (raised hand), and the CR (anxiety), and the neutral stimulus (raised hand).

any food. This meant that receiving food could be conditioned to (associated with) the mere presence of the (feeding) experimenter.

So far this is all clear and easy to understand, but from this point on, students almost always get confused. This is because classical conditioning involves a specific terminology, not because there is anything really complicated about the ideas.

Outline of Classical Conditioning

A Model T Ford is one of the first cars that Henry Ford produced. This makes it an item of first importance—a classic. Since Pavlov's experiments were the first in the learning area, they also are considered classical. This is how we get the term **classical conditioning.**

The following steps are involved in classical conditioning. You start with a reflexive or "natural" stimulus-response pair. The word **stimulus** refers to anything that causes some kind of reaction. That reaction is termed the **response.** Thus, since meat makes a dog salivate, meat is the stimulus (S) for the response (R) of salivation. The behavior involved is completely automatic; the animal salivates when food is put into its mouth. Here is a diagram of this activity:

Receives food (S) → Salivates (R)

So food is a stimulus (S) and salivation is a response (R) to that stimulus.

Note that no special *conditions* are needed for meat to cause salivation; it is natural and automatic. Hence, Pavlov called the food an **unconditioned stimulus** (UCS) and salivation an **unconditioned response** (UCR), because they occur without any special conditions needed. Replacing the diagram above with more accurate terminology, this is what we get:

Receives food (UCS) → Salivates (UCR) [*unconditioned stimulus and unconditioned response,* respectively]

Since seeing an experimenter will not elicit salivation all by itself, some specific conditions are necessary—namely, the animal must associate the experimenter with food. When that association takes place over time, then "seeing the experimenter" becomes a **conditioned stimulus** (CS). In other words, the special condition of associating the experimenter with food has been met. A diagram of this process of association would look like this:

Sight of experimenter (CS) → Receives food (UCS) → Salivation (UCR)

Eventually, the animal responds to the conditioned stimulus alone, by salivating, much as it did to the unconditioned stimulus of food. Salivation at the sight of the experimenter, since it is now triggered by a CS, with no food present, becomes the **conditioned response** (CR) (even though it's the same type of salivation). The last step is:

Sight of experimenter (CS) → Salivation (CR)

classical conditioning

Ivan Pavlov's method of conditioning in which associations are made between a natural stimulus and a learned, neutral stimulus.

stimulus

Anything that elicits a response.

response

A reaction to a stimulus.

unconditioned stimulus

A stimulus that automatically elicits a response, such as meat causing salivation.

unconditioned response

An automatic response to a particular natural stimulus, such as salivation to meat.

conditioned stimulus

A previously neutral stimulus that has been associated with a natural (or unconditioned) stimulus.

conditioned response

A response to a stimulus that is brought about by learning—for example, salivating at the word *pickle*.

Points to Stress

Classical conditioning deals with how we learn involuntary responses, while operant conditioning involves how we learn voluntary responses. See the **In Focus** box in Chapter 8—**Common Mnemonic Devices** for a mnemonic on this. Don't take for granted that students know the distinction between involuntary and voluntary. Involuntary means that we usually have no control over the behavior: blood pressure, salivation, heart rate, sweat, some fears. Voluntary denotes control: walking, talking, and so on.

Points to Stress

The unconditioned stimulus (UCS) automatically produces an unconditioned response (UCR). In other words, the UCS naturally produces the UCR. Remember, the UCR is an involuntary response. No learning is involved.

Evaluation Strategy

How could prejudice be learned through classical conditioning? Answers may follow this line of reasoning: If our parents constantly associated a certain ethnic group (N) with yelling (UCS), which naturally stirred up unpleasant feelings (UCR), the ethnic group (CS) would eventually evoke unpleasant feelings (CR). In supporting their answers, students should use the classical conditioning terms, as done here.

FYI Classical conditioning is usually fun to teach because once students learn about it, they usually have plenty of examples, especially pet stories. We don't endorse this, but pet owners with money to spare sometimes install a system that when activated, will shock a dog if it ventures beyond a certain boundary (something on the collar triggers the shock). The dog eventually associates the boundary (N) with the shock (UCS) and avoids the boundary (CS).

Evaluation Strategy

Have students respond (verbally or in writing) to the following question: How do advertisers use classical conditioning? Before we have heard of a product, it is neutral. If we associate the product (N) with pleasant images

(continued on next page)

Have groups think of five or six examples of classical conditioning in everyday life, and then have students identify the UCS, CS, and so on. Even before discussing extinction, ask them how they could reverse the conditioning in each of these examples.

Have students work in pairs to answer the following question: How could you use classical conditioning to help someone stop bedwetting? Sometimes the best way to extinguish a response is to create another response to take its place. Tell stu-

Here is a quick review to help set the terms in your brain. You hear someone mention that he or she desperately wants a juicy dill pickle. Note that just reading this is causing you to salivate. How is this possible? In the past:

Eating pickle (UCS) → Salivation (UCR)

Before you actually eat a pickle, you think or say to yourself, "Pickle."

Word *pickle* (CS) → Eating pickle (UCS) → Salivation (UCR)

Over time, the word *pickle*, which is only a sound and not a real object, becomes associated with a real pickle, which *does* cause salivation. So we now have:

Word *pickle* (CS) → Salivation (CR)

John Watson and Emotional Conditioning

Several years after Pavlov's early experiments, psychologist **John Watson** appeared on the scene. While he was working his way through school, one of his jobs was to take care of laboratory rats. Gradually the rats became Watson's pets and friends. One of his favorite pastimes was to teach them all kinds of tricks. The rats were able to find their way through elaborate mazes he built, to solve problems such as the need to dig through obstacles he had put in their path, to act as construction workers in tunnels he started for them, and so forth. Based on his observations, Watson eventually decided that what seemed to be the rats' complex behavior actually resulted from little more than a series of stimuli and responses, rather than from some exotic concept such as "intelligence." Watson went even further to suggest that at the human level, "deep emotions" are also just the result of association and learning. One of his most famous experiments involved trying to get a human to spread (or generalize) the emotion of fear from one object to another; this, he thought, would demonstrate that emotions can be mechanically induced (Cohen, 1979).

Watson's work in this area has concerned many people because of the ethics involved in how he dealt with a child. His research would never be allowed today, but since he did it, we might as well discuss it rather than let it go to waste. A woman who worked at the same clinic as Watson would bring her child with her while she was working. Unknown to the mother, Watson started a series of conditioning experiments with the child. This 11-month-old is now famous in psychology and is known as "Little Albert."

Before describing what happened to Little Albert, we need to give you some background information on fear. An unexpected loud noise makes anyone's heart race. We don't have to *learn* to be startled

dents about a device that attaches to a blanket and sounds an alarm when the blanket becomes wet. How does this make use of classical conditioning? Urge to wet bed = N. Alarm = UCS. Waking up = UCR. Then urge becomes the CS, and waking up

becomes the CR. In other words, the urge to wet the bed is so neutral, at first, that the child sleeps through it. You can get a brochure on the device by contacting Potty Pager, Ideas for Living, 1285 N. Cedarbrook, Boulder, CO 80304, (303)440-8517.

or afraid. It happens automatically. So, a sudden loud noise is an unconditioned stimulus for the unconditioned response of fear.

Watson put a white laboratory rat into the room with Albert. Albert loved the furry creature and played with it. While Albert played, Watson sneaked up behind him and smashed a steel bar with a hammer near the boy's ear, creating a horrible, startling noise. Albert fell forward, crying and burying his face in a mattress on the floor. The next time he reached for the rat, Watson repeated the crashing noises. Little Albert became terrified of the rat. Here is the situation:

Loud sound (UCS) → Fear (UCR)

followed by the association phase:

Rat (CS) → Loud sound (UCS) → Fear (UCR)

which then becomes:

Rat (CS) → Fear (CR)

Watson then went on to demonstrate what is called **stimulus generalization,** which means that a response can spread from one specific stimulus like the white rat to other stimuli resembling the original one in some way. To show this had occurred, Watson brought in a white rabbit, which also frightened Albert. Albert even showed some concern about a fur coat and a mild negative response to a Santa Claus mask, objects somewhat similar to the white rat.

Before the mother discovered these goings on and fled with Albert, Watson had shown two things: (1) conditioning of emotions to neutral objects is possible and (2) a conditioned emotion can gen-

stimulus generalization

A response spread from one specific stimulus to other stimuli that resemble the original.

(continued from previous page)

(UCS), which produce pleasant feelings (UCR), the product (CS) will later create pleasant feelings (CR). Companies are so convinced of this classical-conditioning process that they spend millions of dollars a year on advertising to strengthen the conditioning. However, students may argue that the pleasant images are not really unconditioned; they don't naturally evoke pleasant feelings. They may have a point, but you can mention that even babies will stare at a picture of a human face for a longer length of time than at a face with jumbled features. Note that in this example, advertisers are conditioning involuntary responses—namely, positive feelings toward a product. This may or may not lead to the operant response of buying the product.

DISCUSS THE PHOTO

It's amazing that more kids don't have this reaction. But children soon learn that Santa provides plenty of reinforcements.

▲ *Just like Little Albert this child is not too happy with Santa Claus.*

DEMONSTRATION

Record several sounds to which students are conditioned: school bell, telephone, alarm clock. At the beginning of class one day, inconspicuously start the tape, and go on with your lesson. Every ten minutes or so, the sounds on the tape will interrupt you. Seize the moment and ask students if the sound startled them or prompted them to move. Then discuss how they have become conditioned to respond to the sounds.

DEMONSTRATION

One day while checking comprehension or reviewing, respond to students' answers with more praise than you normally do. After a few minutes, ask if students were motivated at all by this reinforcement. Were any students *less* likely to answer because of the excessive praise? If you're try-

Teaching Hint

Students may ask, "How often does the neutral stimulus need to be paired with the UCS?" Sometimes conditioning will occur after one pairing, sometimes the pairing must occur numerous times. For example, someone may yell at us only once, but we immediately "learn" to raise our heart rate every time we see the person. Advertisers, on the other hand, constantly must bombard us with their products to evoke any reaction.

Critical Thinking

How would you extinguish the fear of a dog who has been beaten by hand? The dog is probably associating a raised hand with the beating. Every time you pet the dog, raise your hand, pause, then associate the raised hand with petting.

Connections

Chapter 19 discusses systematic desensitization, or gradual extinction, of fears: associate a feared stimulus with relaxation and progressively move the feared object closer and closer.

192

Unit 3 COGNITIVE PROCESSES

extinction

The gradual loss of an association over time.

operant conditioning

Conditioning that results from one's actions and the consequences they cause.

192

eralize to other objects that have similar characteristics. All of this is helpful to know, but there still is a problem: because no one ever located "Big" Albert after Watson's experiment and because no one since Watson has done a similar kind of experiment, we don't know how long such conditioned emotions last (Samelson, 1980). Most likely Albert's fear disappeared, since we do know from other studies (with adults) that if you stop pairing something like a frightening noise with an object, the original association will begin to disappear. This disappearance is called **extinction,** as in the verb "to extinguish." Thus, after a while, Pavlov's dogs would extinguish (stop) their salivation at the presence of the experimenter unless the experimenter continued to feed them occasionally.

Removal of Fears

One very important discovery was made as a result of Watson's experiments, and it came from a student who worked for Watson, **Mary Cover Jones.** Aware of the effect that Watson's experiments had had on Little Albert, she wondered if she could reverse the procedure and *cure* a child of a terrible fear. She found a three-year-old, "Peter," who panicked at the sight of a rabbit. In an experiment, she brought a rabbit into the room with Peter, close enough for him to see it. She then gave the child some food he liked. She moved the rabbit closer and gave more food, and she continued this process, associating the pleasure of food with the feared object. It worked: Peter lost his fear of rabbits. Jones had found the key to removing all manner of fears, called *phobias,* that can make people's lives miserable—fears of elevators, snakes, dogs, and the like. Associating something pleasant with a feared object is still used quite successfully today to reduce or stop such fears (Jones, 1924).

As a sort of footnote: Mary Jones was a close friend of Watson, so she never said anything negative about him. Even so, she does note that one day, when he was visiting her at home, she left him in a room with her child, who was about the age of Little Albert. From the other room she heard a very loud banging noise, but when she hurried back, everything seemed normal (Jones, 1974). Was Watson trying to set up another "experiment"?

OPERANT CONDITIONING

Despite the importance of the studies just described, most learning does not occur in a classical stimulus-response sequence. It usually is the result of some voluntary action taken by the learner. This type of learning is called **operant conditioning,** in which a behavior is learned or avoided as a result of its consequences.

ing to elicit simple behaviors or simple answers, reinforcement may be effective. When you're trying to stimulate critical thinking, however, reinforcement such as praise tends to limit possibilities. It sends the message to students that you're looking for *right* answers rather than possible answers. Why would a student continue to think about a question when another student's answer was highly commended? This assertion is arguable, of course, so test for yourself. Try this same exercise with another class but this time use critical thinking questions.

Classical Versus Operant Conditioning

In classical conditioning, learning takes place without any choice; in other words, meat on the tongue (or something that has been associated with meat) will automatically cause salivation without any choice by the organism. In operant conditioning, the organism plays some role in what happens. This theory claims that humans and animals learn as an end product of performing certain actions (or *operations*).

The distinction between classical and operant conditioning is often hard to grasp when encountered for the first time. But the brain has a way of remembering unusual things better than it remembers the commonplace (we will discuss this in Chapter 8), and we want to take advantage of this fact now by giving you an example that is truly absurd, so you won't ever forget it. Here we go:

Someone in your household decides to condition you classically to hate a certain vegetable. At random times this person, carrying a handful of the cold vegetable, sneaks up behind you and shoves it into your mouth while talking into your ear about something nauseating. After a few of these encounters, you will find the thought of that vegetable quite unpleasant. You have now been *classically* conditioned to dislike the vegetable, since you had no control whatsoever over what was happening. Second scene: You find three different varieties of canned vegetables in the cupboard. You have never eaten any of them. You reach in, take one out, cook it, and eat it. You do the same thing with the other two later on. The one you like best you will probably reach for and cook again. In this case, you have been *operantly* conditioned by your actions (operations) and their consequences to prefer one vegetable over another.

B. F. Skinner

Psychologist **B. F. Skinner** is best known for his work with the operant conditioning theory. He believed that how we turn out in life is the result of what we learn from all the operations we make over the years (Skinner, 1990). If our actions result in people getting angry and disliking us, we are being operantly conditioned to believe that the world is a dangerous and threatening place. If the environment rewards us when we perform certain acts, then we tend to repeat them. Thus, if you study hard, do a good job on a paper, and get a note of praise, you will tend to study hard and do a good job again; if you get a nasty note on your paper even though you've done well, you will lose your desire to repeat these actions.

The seeds of Skinner's work were planted when he was a boy. He set up a pulley system in his bedroom closet that kept a large sign, "Hang up your pajamas," visible until he opened the door and placed the pajamas on a hook, at which point the sign moved out of

Comprehension Check

If stimulus generalization occurred with someone who had learned to be afraid of the ocean, what other things could cause a fear response in that person? *(a lake, a river, a bath, etc.)*

Points to Stress

For classroom purposes, it may be valuable to learn that some behaviors are learned through classical conditioning while others are learned through operant conditioning, but the two types of conditioning are intertwined. Emphasize that nearly all behaviors have some elements of both classical and operant conditioning.

TEACHING MASTER 7-2A

Classical Conditioning. Students can practice identifying classical-conditioning terms with this handout. Answers are found in **Teaching Master 7-2B.**

193

COOPERATIVE LEARNING

Have groups discuss how to improve the performance of students at your school through conditioning. You can have each group focus on a different area of performance: attendance, grades, extracurricular activities, community involvement, recycling habits. Spend a few minutes discussing the kinds of performances they feel would be worthwhile to pursue at your school. Once each group has a topic, they can discuss the merits of using money, prizes, privileges, recognition, and so on, as reinforcement. And they can also discuss the merits of using punishment, as well—fines for skipping class, for example. If any of the plans are creative and practical, present them to administrators!

DISCUSS THE PHOTO

You may have students who can build a version of this Skinner box.

Points to Stress

In classical conditioning, the critical part of the conditioning occurs before the response: the stimulus actually *causes* the response. In operant conditioning, the critical part of conditioning occurs *after* the response: the reinforcement determines whether the response will occur again.

Discussion

According to operant conditioning, behaviors will cease if reinforcement does not follow the response. Ask students how behaviorists would explain charity. OK, OK, what if there were no tax write-off? *(Behaviorists would maintain that there has to be something that is reinforcing about giving away money.)*

▲ *Okay, I pushed the bar. Where's my food?*

reinforcement

Something that follows a response and strengthens the tendency to repeat that response.

primary reinforcement

Something necessary for psychological/physical survival that is used as a reward.

secondary reinforcement

Anything that comes to represent a primary reinforcer, such as money bringing food.

positive reinforcement

Strengthening the tendency to repeat a response by following it with the addition of something pleasant.

negative reinforcement

Strengthening a response by following it with taking away or avoiding something unpleasant.

view. He was operantly conditioning himself, and his action was probably reinforced by an absence of getting yelled at for being sloppy (Fancher, 1979).

Later Skinner was so concerned about how our surroundings affect us that he reared his daughter in what he called an "air crib." In this crib, the environment—such as the temperature, humidity, and light—was carefully controlled at all times. The child was also not confined by diapers. The "diaper" consisted of a continuous roll of sheetlike material that was fed in one side of the air crib and pulled out the other. Skinner wanted the perfect environment for his little girl. She turned out just fine, but we'll never know whether she was really helped by the special crib.

Operant Conditioning Processes

Reinforcement is an important ingredient in operant conditioning. It is something that follows a response and strengthens our tendency to repeat that response in the future. The word means the same thing in learning as it does in construction work: when something is reinforced, it is made stronger. For example, say that there is a bar inside an animal cage, and each time the animal presses the bar, food appears. The behavior of bar pressing is reinforced by the arrival of the food. After a while, when the animal is hungry, it will walk right over to the bar and push it.

One type of reinforcement is called **primary reinforcement.** The word *primary* means "of first and greatest importance." Thus, a primary reinforcer is something that is absolutely necessary for survival, such as food or water. The possibility of obtaining one of these when you perform an action is the strongest incentive to learn.

Not all of our behavior involves primary reinforcers, however. For example, we engage in a truly weird activity that we take for granted: we work, struggle, fight, and wish for rectangular pieces of gray and green paper. People even commit crimes, lie, and cheat just to get these pieces of paper. Where's the reinforcement? We're talking about money, of course. Since you can't eat or drink it, it can't be a primary reinforcer, but it certainly does reinforce. Money is a secondary reinforcer. **Secondary reinforcement** is anything that comes to *represent* a primary reinforcer. Because money can buy food and drink, it represents these primary reinforcers. All secondary reinforcers are related to some primary one. For example, you work for a high grade because it is a formal way of receiving praise, and this praise represents the physical love (primary reinforcement) in the form of hugs that you got from your parent(s) when you did a good job as a child.

We have been talking about **positive reinforcement** up to this point. Positive reinforcement occurs when something the organism wants (such as food) is added on (+, positive) after an action. Another type of reinforcement is called **negative reinforcement.**

DEMONSTRATION

Students may initially have difficulty distinguishing between what is an involuntary and voluntary response. Walk around the room and perform various behaviors and ask them to identify each one. Involuntary behaviors are much harder to show, so you may need to report them: my blood pressure is rising; I'm salivating! Then simply remind them that the conditioned involuntary responses are learned through classical conditioning; the voluntary responses are learned through operant conditioning.

Negative reinforcement occurs when something unpleasant (negative) is stopped or taken away (–, negative) if the organism does something. In both cases, the consequences of an action are something the organism wants. In one, something pleasant is added; in the other, something unpleasant is stopped or avoided. Try to remember that reinforcement always strengthens a response, rather than weakening it, and this will be easier to understand.

Chapter 7 PRINCIPLES OF LEARNING

 **Classical and Operant Conditioning**

Classical Conditioning:
How We Learn Involuntary Responses

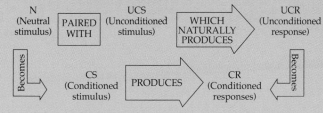

If we pair a neutral stimulus with an unconditioned stimulus, the neutral stimulus becomes a conditioned stimulus and then produces the same response as the unconditioned stimulus. An example:

Sight of Experimenter (N) + Food (UCS) ----▶ Salivation (UCR)

Sight of Experimenter (CS) ----▶ Salivation (CR)

Operant Conditioning:
How We Learn Voluntary Responses

Voluntary response | FOLLOWED BY | Reinforcement | THEREFORE ▶ Same voluntary response is likely to occur again.

If we receive a reinforcement for a voluntary behavior, we'll probably perform the voluntary behavior again in the future. An example:

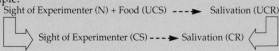
Study for test ----▶ High grade ----▶ Studying again for next test

If you want to teach your dog to bring you the newspaper every morning, how would you use both classical and operant conditioning?

Classical and Operant Conditioning.

 Operant: Reward the dog when he brings the paper. *Classical:* You probably couldn't teach a dog to fetch using only classical conditioning, but you could certainly create positive involuntary responses toward the newspaper by associating it with an unconditioned stimulus like food. As mentioned previously, emphasize that most behaviors have elements of both classical and operant conditioning.

Comprehension Check

What is the fundamental difference between classical and operant conditioning? *(In classical conditioning, learning takes place automatically, without any voluntary action on the part of the subject; in operant conditioning, the subject learns from the consequences of his or her voluntary actions.)*

Connections

Behaviorism begins to make less sense if you try to apply it to something like creativity (Chapter 9). Does conditioning ever play a part in the creative process? Can it motivate us to get started? To stay on schedule?

INTERDISCIPLINARY PROJECT

Government. Have students explore one of the following government-related issues to determine the role of conditioning in each: the patronage system, government lobbyists, senatorial courtesy, political parties. Students can then focus on two areas: (1) How has conditioning (mainly positive and negative rein- forcement) helped to create the current state of affairs? (2) How can new conditioning improve the current state of affairs? For example, if students see a problem with the patronage system, what incentives (reinforcements) would help to eliminate patronage?

If you don't want to use these examples, simply discuss how conditioning can help eliminate government waste. For example, students might propose a program in which citizens are rewarded for exposing waste. Or you can discuss how to encourage people to vote through reinforcement—make it mandatory? Offer voters a tax write-off?

Positive and Negative Reinforcement.

 Positive: parents let you use the car when grades are high. *Negative:* parents make you wash the car until you get good grades.

Discussion

What is the best (most effective) form of punishment for teens? Or would reinforcement be more effective? You might ask students to discuss the effectiveness of grounding or the removal of specific privileges.

Critical Thinking

Ask students this question: You want your child to mow the lawn every week. How do you use positive and negative reinforcement to achieve this? *Positive:* offer money, praise, privileges. *Negative:* yell and stop yelling when the work is done.

Unit 3 COGNITIVE PROCESSES

 **Positive and Negative Reinforcement**

Positive Reinforcement

Negative Reinforcement

Ann drives conscientiously, courteously, and carefully so she can receive a safe-driving certificate and reduce her insurance rates.

Terri drives conscientiously, courteously, and carefully to avoid getting any more traffic tickets.

What are some positive and negative reinforcements for earning good grades in school?

---

punishment

The process of weakening a response by following it with unpleasant consequences.

generalization

A behavior that spreads from one situation to a similar one.

If the floor of a cage gives an animal a shock and the animal learns to push a bar in order to stop the electricity, this is negative reinforcement; it strengthens a response (pushing the bar). Say that someone wants you to take out the trash, which you keep forgetting to do. So the nagging starts, and it keeps on and on. You are being negatively reinforced: all you want to do is find a way to stop the endless whining about what a mess you are. You take out the trash and therefore are performing an act in order to stop something unpleasant.

Punishment   Students often confuse negative reinforcement with punishment, but there is a very basic difference. **Punishment** is an attempt to *weaken* a response by following it with something unpleasant, not to strengthen it. There are two basic ways to go with punishment. First, something desired can be taken away, as when someone is fined for a traffic violation. Second, something unwanted can be added, as when students in the "olden days" had to write "I shall not talk in class" 100 times on the blackboard.

Generalization and Discrimination   As mentioned earlier, a classically conditioned response can spread or generalize to similar stimuli. **Generalization** can also occur in operantly conditioned behavior. For instance, a boy who pats a dog and gets a wagging tail is likely to approach the next dog he sees in the same fashion. If that dog also wags its tail, the boy's action will generalize to all dogs, for

COOPERATIVE LEARNING

See **Teaching Master 7-3 Ways to Break Bad Habits** for a list of methods to break habits. Assign one method to each group. The groups then think of an original habit and show, through a skit, how the habit would be broken using the method.

Chapter 7 PRINCIPLES OF LEARNING

the boy will assume they are all friendly. Suppose, however, that the third dog the boy pats bites him. In such a case, generalization has been instantly halted and replaced by **discrimination learning.** In other words, the child learns to tell the difference (discriminate) between dogs or between situations that are not all the same.

Babies often embarrass adults because of their generalizations. For instance, a baby girl hugs her father and says, "Dada." Daddy gets so excited about this that he praises her and runs to tell the mother that she has called him by name. The little girl generalizes the response, sensibly in her own mind, by calling every man she meets "Dada." When the other men don't give her the same positive reinforcement, she gradually discriminates between who is really "Dada" and who isn't—even though she doesn't actually know what that sound means.

discrimination learning

Learning to tell the difference between one event or object and another; the reverse of generalization.

Extinction   Often, when a response is no longer followed by reinforcement, a person will gradually stop making that response. This situation is called *extinction*, the same term used earlier with classical conditioning. In both classical and operant conditioning, then, extinction can occur. In both cases, an association has been weakened: in classical conditioning, because the unconditioned stimulus is no longer present; in operant conditioning, because reinforcement is no longer present.

Shaping and Chaining   So far we have been talking about fairly simple one-step behaviors. Is operant conditioning limited to them? The answer is "no." Two major techniques can be used to teach more complex or complicated responses.

The first such technique is called **shaping,** the "method of successive approximations." What does this mean? In shaping, increasingly closer versions (approximations) of the desired response are reinforced in turn (successively). We start out reinforcing a rough version of the response we're after. Once that rough version has been learned, the standard goes up. Now, a smoother or more accurate attempt is required before reinforcement will be given, and so on. Thus, a dog being trained to jump through a hoop will first be reinforced by praise or food for approaching the hoop that lies on the ground. Next it is reinforced for walking through the hoop as it is held vertically touching the ground. Then the dog is shaped to jump through the hoop held a few inches off the ground, and so forth. The same process is gone through when someone is learning how to play a tune on the piano or how to swim.

When we want a complete sequence done in order, we usually have to start by reinforcing each part of that sequence. Then, each part or link is connected to the others by reinforcement. This process is called **chaining,** as in "connecting together." In learning a new dance, for instance, people learn the different steps or parts of the dance first. Then they put the parts together like links in a chain.

shaping

The process of gradually refining a response by successively reinforcing closer approximations of it.

chaining

Reinforcing the connection between different parts of a sequence.

Connections

Behaviorists believe that depression (Chapter 18) is caused, in part, by a learned sense of helplessness. The essence of operant conditioning is that behavior is shaped by consequences. If we learn that no matter what we do, we cannot control the consequences, then we may become depressed.

Journal Topic

"Describe one or two of your worst habits. What keeps you doing this habit? Why don't you stop? How would it feel if you suddenly stopped?" If you can tie in extinction with students' own habits, you can spark a lively discussion.

EXPERIMENT

Here's a fun activity to demonstrate shaping. Have someone volunteer to be a "student mouse." Explain that clapping, not food, will be his or her reinforcer. Have the mouse leave the room. The rest of the class will choose a simple behavior it wants to shape: erasing the board, pulling down the projector screen, and so on. Invite the mouse back in. Every time he or she gets close to the desired behavior, the rest of the class will clap. Whenever the mouse moves away from the desired behavior, clapping should stop. Students enjoy this activity, and if you repeat the procedure two or three times on other mice, they become proficient at performing more and more complicated behaviors, such as doing somersaults, standing on your desk, and so on.

Generalization, Discrimination, and Extinction.

 The behaviors described are voluntary; therefore, they are examples of operant conditioning.

Connections

See the **Interdisciplinary Project** on recycling in Chapter 1. It fits in well with the material in this chapter.

Evaluation Strategy

See **Teaching Master 7-4A Classical and Operant Conditioning Practice Quiz** for a practice quiz. Answers are found in **Teaching Master 7-4B.**

Unit 3 COGNITIVE PROCESSES

 **Generalization, Discrimination, and Extinction**

Joe makes a wisecrack in his first-period biology class, and everyone laughs, even the teacher. The following types of learning may occur:

Generalization:

He makes wisecracks in other classes, in front of other teachers.

Discrimination:

He makes wisecracks in other classes, but when no one laughs or when the teacher glares at him, he stops. He decides to tell jokes only during first period.

Extinction:

He continues to make wisecracks during first period, but when others tire of his jokes and stop laughing, he stops.

Generalization, discrimination, and extinction occur during both classical and operant conditioning. Are the above situations examples of classical or operant conditioning?

Seeing Eye dogs for the blind are highly intelligent and remarkable examples of what shaping and chaining can produce. They can read stoplights and traffic patterns, find curbs and doors, discover dangerous holes that might trip their owner, or find things the owner drops. They even will resist dangerous commands from the sightless person. All these behaviors occur as a smooth, ongoing process that looks completely effortless—and is, after being done hundreds and hundreds of times. Since these animals are capable of forming close psychological bonds, only occasionally during training is a reinforcer such as food used. The dog wants to please the trainer to such a degree that a pat on the head or some other form of approval or praise is more than enough and is generally even preferred.

The Coast Guard Search and Rescue teams tested an unusual use for pigeons because a pigeon's vision is so much sharper than a human's. The pigeons were trained to search for an orange disk and, when it was located, to push a button with their beaks as a signal. After training, they went on helicopter rescue missions to watch for orange "disks"—life jackets attached to people in the water. Pilots have trouble seeing them, but the pigeons don't. Pigeons have a 90 percent success rate, whereas the pilots are stuck at 35 percent. The victims were thankful when the pigeon spotted the life jacket and pecked a signal to the rescuers (Fox, 1980).

ENRICHMENT

Invite someone who works with animals at a zoo to come to class and discuss techniques used to control the animals' behaviors. Nearly all animal shows are based on the principles of operant conditioning.

Reteaching Strategy

See **Teaching Masters 7-5 Classical Conditioning Review Sheet** and **7-6 Operant Conditioning Review Sheet.** These are review sheets to help students remember the principles of classical and operant conditioning: generalization, discrimination, extinction, and shaping.

Evaluation Strategy

Have students work in pairs to answer the following question: How could you use conditioning to get people to car pool to work? Have them devise a plan that is specific and practical, and have them identify whether the plan makes use of reinforcement (positive or negative) or punishment.

Schedules of Reinforcement

There are different methods of providing reinforcement during operant conditioning. So far we have focused on **continuous reinforcement**—that is, each time a desired behavior occurs, it is reinforced. In many cases, this is not a good method because the creature gets used to having something and will quit if it doesn't show up every time. This problem can be avoided by using different **schedules of reinforcement**, that is, different techniques. When the organism is not being continuously reinforced, it is on a **partial reinforcement schedule,** of which there are four. In partial reinforcement, the animal or person does not get a reward each time a desired act is performed.

Variable Ratio A pigeon quickly learns to peck at a button for food. But if you use continuous reinforcement, the pigeon will quit unless it is really hungry. On the other hand, if the pigeon gets food after five pecks, then after seven pecks, then three, or whatever variable numbers you want to use, once you stop the reinforcement, they will peck over 10,000 times before they finally give up (Skinner, 1957). This is the **variable ratio schedule;** "ratio" refers to numbers. Thus, with the pigeons, you vary the number of pecks required before reinforcement occurs. Humans can really get hooked on this type of schedule, which is how slot machines work. Since players don't know exactly when the money will fall through the chute, they work hard at it, just like the pigeons. Usually the machines are set to give a few coins as reinforcement every now and then but to give a jackpot only infrequently.

Fixed Ratio What would happen if you kept the ratio the same, so there is one reinforcement every time the creature performs a *certain number* of acts? For example, what if the pigeon is rewarded after

Chapter 7 PRINCIPLES OF LEARNING

continuous reinforcement

Each time a behavior occurs, reinforcement is given.

schedules of reinforcement

Different methods of reinforcing.

partial reinforcement schedule

Reinforcement is not given each time an act is performed.

variable ratio schedule

Reinforcement occurs after a desired behavior occurs, but a different number of the desired acts is required each time.

DISCUSS THE PHOTO

How would you use shaping to train a dog? Reinforce the small behaviors that lead to the big one.

▲ *Affection is often the only reinforcement Seeing Eye dogs need to learn incredibly complex behaviors.*

COOPERATIVE LEARNING

Break the class into four large groups (or eight smaller groups that double up on the topics). Each group is assigned one of the four schedules of reinforcement. Their task is to think of examples of behaviors that are reinforced according to their schedule. They should think of as many as they can in five minutes.

CHAPTER PROJECT

Print up several homemade bills with your name on them— "Smithdollars," for example. If students collect two (or three or four) of these bills, they can trade them in for one extra-credit point. Hand these bills out throughout the unit as reinforcement for various behaviors, such

as asking thoughtful questions, volunteering for an activity, and so on. (This is a token economy, which is discussed in Chapter 19.) At the end of the chapter, discuss the effectiveness of the bills. Did they improve education or did they interfere? Would it make a difference if the bills

Schedules of Reinforcement.

In Focus   The variable schedules are usually more difficult to extinguish. Gambling is a perfect example.

Reteaching Strategy

Have students make a list of ten behaviors that they have made in the last 24 hours. Next to each behavior, have them identify whether the behavior was learned through classical conditioning, operant conditioning, or both.

Points to Stress

The variable schedules are especially reinforcing because the person never knows when he or she is going to be reinforced. This is something that parents especially should keep in mind. If there is a behavior that they want to extinguish, they can't reward that behavior every once in a while and then expect it to disappear.

200

IN FOCUS   Schedules of Reinforcement

Variable Ratio

Reinforcement is given after a variable number of behaviors.

Fixed Ratio

Reinforcement is given after a fixed number of behaviors.

Variable Interval

Reinforcement is given after a variable amount of time.

Fixed Interval

Reinforcement is given after a fixed amount of time.

Which two schedules of reinforcement would produce behaviors that are difficult to extinguish?

fixed ratio schedule

Reinforcement occurs after the desired act is performed a specific number of times.

every five pecks? This is called a **fixed ratio schedule** since the relationship between the number of pecks and the number of reinforcements is always the same. With this method, the pigeons will peck as rapidly as possible because they know that the faster they go, the greater the number of reinforcements they will receive.

At first this seems like it might be a good way to squeeze every drop of work possible out of factory workers—but there are major pitfalls. Suppose that an auto company decides to put the workers on a fixed ratio schedule in which they are paid by the number of cars they produce. As workers are forced to speed up, they will put screws in halfway and leave out parts in order to save time and produce more cars. Even when this system looks like it might work—

were incorporated for a longer period of time? How could the system of awarding the bills be improved?

Variations: You can conduct the chapter project in several ways. One way is to announce which behaviors will be reinforced and consistently reinforce them. Another way, in another class perhaps, is to include numerous flaws in the procedure. For example, *don't* announce which behaviors will be rewarded; change the criteria for handing out the bills every 20 minutes or so. Including flaws should demonstrate the need for consistency with any kind of reward system. This can lead to a discussion about the reinforcement system at school and in students' homes. Are these systems consistent?

some workers may decide to try to outproduce the others—pressure from the group as a whole will force a quick end to this competition. On occasion it may work, as with individual farmhands who are paid by the bushel.

Variable Interval A third type of partial reinforcement is called **variable interval schedule.** Here the creature never knows (in terms of time, or "interval") when the reinforcement will arrive. It may come at the end of three minutes, then two minutes, then five minutes, and so forth. A real-life example can be found in that baffling activity called fishing, in which a person sits hour after hour holding a pole up in the air staring into space while apparently nothing happens. Actually, variable interval reinforcement is going on and keeps the person moving the boat or adjusting the line: the line is attached to a bobber that floats on the water and at unpredictable intervals (from the current or a small wave most often, but on occasion from a fish), the bobber will disappear below water level, causing considerable excitement and keeping hope alive (Kary, 1984). With variable interval reinforcement, animals will keep working at a steady, sluggish pace, just to be sure they are performing the right act when the prize comes. But they don't overdo it in terms of speed.

Fixed Interval A fourth type of schedule, called **fixed interval schedule,** gives a reward when a specific, fixed amount of time has passed. It has an interesting effect on the behavior of animals. Pigeons that learn they are going to be rewarded every five minutes no matter how fast they peck become very casual about it all. They walk over to the pecking button, hit it once, saunter away for a while, and then return, hitting it again. They mope about until just before the five-minute interval is over. Then they move to the button and peck rapidly.

If you look at Figure 7.1, you will see that Congress behaves just like the pigeons. There is no particular reason why the production of bills (laws) should not be more or less continuous throughout a congressional session, but with the reinforcement of upcoming vacation time, there is always a sudden flurry of activity. Note how steep the curve becomes (meaning a dramatic increase in output) as the summer months—and adjournment—approach (Weisberg & Waldrop, 1972).

SOCIAL LEARNING

In present-day psychology, most of the research has moved away from classical and operant conditioning. While both play a role in learning, they fall short of explaining complex learning processes.

variable interval schedule

Reinforcement occurs after varying amounts of time if a desired act occurs.

fixed interval schedule

A reinforcement is received after a fixed amount of time has passed if the desired act occurs.

Teaching Hint

Even after students learn about classical and operant conditioning, these processes may sound foreign to them, like mysterious algebraic formulas. Stress at the beginning and throughout these sections that *conditioning* is simply another term for *learning* or training. This little reminder may help eliminate confusion. (At the end of the chapter, you might clarify by adding that learning certainly encompasses more than conditioning, as the social and cognitive learning theorists have emphasized.)

EXPERIMENT

Recreate Bandura's doll experiment in class! The only catch is that you will have to invest in an inflatable punching doll. Arrange for one or two admired students to slug it as they walk into class. You might want to show up a few minutes late and have your sluggers record reactions. In another class, slug it yourself as students walk in; then make an excuse to leave. Be sure to plant an observer to collect data. Instruct the observer to slug the doll if no one else does it within two or three minutes. Were there any differences in the reactions to an adult versus a student model? If no one imitated the models, why not? Setting is probably a prime factor.

Comprehension Check

What does Albert Bandura think is the most important aspect of learning, which is not taken into account in classical or operant conditioning theories? *(the complex "inner person" who responds to stimulation after analyzing events and making decisions)*

Unit 3 COGNITIVE PROCESSES

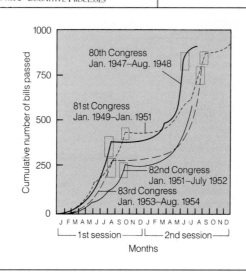
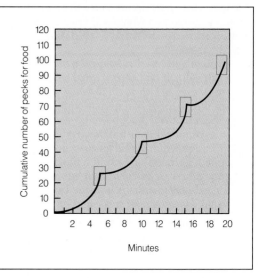

▲ *Figure 7.1   Cumulative number of bills passed during the Legislative Sessions of Congress from January 1947 to August 1954 (left) and cumulative number of responses of pigeons on the five-minute fixed interval reinforcement (right).*

Critical Thinking

Ask students the following questions: Why do we observe and imitate some models and not others? What kind of models are most likely to be imitated? Their answers should acknowledge that according to Bandura, models who are admired and models who have been rewarded are most likely to be copied. Once we copy a model's behavior, reinforcement may then play a part in whether we continue to copy the model.

social learning

All learning that occurs in a social situation.

observational learning

A form of social learning in which the organism observes and imitates the behavior of others.

One of the current theories about learning is called **social learning**, and its most prominent theorist is psychologist **Albert Bandura** (ban-DUR-ah). He claims that the most important aspect of learning was missed by Pavlov, Watson, and Skinner, for he feels that between the stimulus and the response is the complex "inner person" who is able to analyze events and make decisions before a response is given. (In case it slipped by you, the previous learning theorists we have discussed more or less ignored the individual and focused on robotlike patterns of stimulus and response or action and reinforcement.) Bandura feels that a more complex explanation for behavior is needed when analyzing group, or social, living. In order to survive, he says, we imitate directly the activities of those around us; "social learning" is the general term for this imitation.

Much of our behavior is acquired by **observational learning**, meaning that we learn patterns of behavior by watching others and deciding what to imitate. From the parent, a child learns speech patterns, personal habits, and how to react to other people. In other words, the child observes and then patterns behavior after that of the important people in his or her life (Bandura & Walters, 1963). Just in case you feel a little confused about the terminology: "Social learning" refers to *all* learning in a social situation; "observational learning" is *one* of the processes used for social learning in which we (and

Points to Stress

If you brought in a lemon to make students salivate during the lesson on Pavlov, apply that example to cognitive learning. If you had told them that the lemon you were going to show them was plastic (but it looked real), would any of them have salivated? Not if cognitive learning had taken place.

many animals) watch events, persons, and situations for cues on how to behave.

In a now-famous experiment, Bandura demonstrated that children who observe aggressive adult models become aggressive themselves as a result. The children watched adults slugging plastic stand-up dolls. When the children were left alone, they imitated this behavior.

We once had a neighbor who was so afraid of germs that she would disinfect her house every 48 hours. She would not enter any neighbor's house, preferring to stay outside where she thought the air would be fresher and more germ-free. We were very surprised, however, when her daughter began to wear gloves while riding her tricycle—surprised, that is, until we were invited over to the woman's house for the first time; during the whole time we were there, the woman wore thin, latex, surgical gloves (true story).

Don't miss the important point that Bandura is making: The child does not require a *specific* reinforcement such as food for learning to occur. Social learning can occur by exposure and imitation alone. Bandura felt that earlier explanations of learning were too simplified.

COGNITIVE PSYCHOLOGY AND LEARNING

Bandura's approach to learning is clearly more complex than earlier theories. Today psychologists are finding that even his version doesn't fully account for the elaborate task of learning. As a result, much of the present research looks at a means of learning called the **cognitive approach.** The word *cognitive* here means "knowledge-using," with "knowledge" meaning far more than just a stimulus and response or imitation. Using the cognitive approach, we are able to learn very abstract and subtle things that could not be learned simply through conditioning or social learning. For instance, some people have learned through the stories of others that it is very bad luck to walk under a ladder or to break a mirror: this kind of belief is very abstract and hence could not be learned by any method other than the cognitive one. When psychologists study cognition, then, they focus on how complex knowledge is obtained, processed, and organized.

Complexities of Conditioning

Cognitive psychologists support their position by pointing out that even classical conditioning is not as simple as it first appears. For example, the type of cage an experimenter keeps an animal in will

▲ *Albert Bandura.*

cognitive approach (to learning)

A way of learning based on abstract mental processes and previous knowledge.

DISCUSS THE PHOTO

Bandura believed that observational learning allows us to bypass trial-and-error learning.

Points to Stress

You might assume that only humans acquire superstitions. When Skinner trained animals in what we now call a Skinner box (in which a mouse, for example, presses a lever for a reward of food), he noticed that even a mouse can adopt seemingly superstitious behaviors. During conditioning, the mouse presses a lever for food, but this is preceded—coincidentally—by a twisting of the leg. He associates the twisting—along with his operant response of pressing the lever—with reinforcement, and continues to twist his leg every time!

COOPERATIVE LEARNING

Have students work in pairs to make a list of five operant behaviors. Next to each item have them list possible reinforcements for the behavior. Finally, have them interpret each behavior from the point of view of a cognitive psychologist. For example, cognitive psychologists would admit that studying is reinforced by high grades, but they would also point out other variables: the student's age, how the student views the studying or the teacher, and so on. This activity should demonstrate that learning is not always a simple matter of conditioning.

DISCUSS THE PHOTO

The relationship of the model to the learner would also have an effect on aggression.

Connections

This section on cognitive learning may remind students of the curiosity motive described in Chapter 5. Reinforcements may have little to do with satisfying curiosity.

Unit 3 COGNITIVE PROCESSES

▲ *These laboratory film clips show children imitating aggression after seeing it.*

affect the animal's learning ability, as will the amount of time the animal has previously spent in the cage. If an animal is in unfamiliar surroundings, it gets preoccupied with its new environment and doesn't pay attention to the experiment (Hall, 1980). And as in the case of Pavlov's dogs falling asleep, animals vary in the degree to which they are interested in the experiment itself. There are also strange individual preferences—for example, pigeons will tend to peck at lighted keys even without reinforcement, and they will peck differently if they are trying to get water as compared to food (Miller, 1983). Animals condition more easily to pictures of rats or spiders than they do to pictures of flowers and mushrooms (Marks, 1979). All of these findings make the animal far more complex than just a responder to stimuli. To see how complicated it can become at the human level, think about how the experimental results might have changed if Little Albert had been a bit older and had *known* that Watson was standing behind him banging the bar.

Under the cognitive theory, complexities Watson didn't know about take on a new light. For instance, at first it seems reasonable to assume that Watson's work with Little Albert can explain such human problems as phobias—in other words, that fears of closed spaces, heights, snakes, open places, or germs arise from straight

204

ACTIVITY   ACTIVITY   ACTIVITY   ACTIVITY   ACTIVITY   ACTIVITY   ACTIVITY

DEMONSTRATION

Call a student to the front of the class and have her give you directions to someone's house. Pick someone who is usually animated and uses a lot of gestures. Afterward, ask the other students if they believe a cognitive map was formed while the person gave the directions. As the person pointed and described various landmarks, could you almost "see" the person forming this map?

association. But this is not necessarily the case. Psychologists have discovered a strange quirk about phobias: while many of them may indeed come from association, there is clearly a cognitive (or knowledge-based) aspect to them, because phobias only develop in relation to some kind of *natural* danger. Thus, if you are in a closed space, you really may be trapped; if you are up high, you may fall; some snakes are indeed poisonous; if you are out in the open, you may be more vulnerable; germs can kill you. All of these are known phobias; in contrast, there are no phobias for neutral or "unnatural" things, such as umbrellas, trees, light switches, or automobile tires (Seligman, 1971). As you can see, the conditioning of fears seems to develop through a sophisticated cognitive process.

Cognitive Maps

In the 1930s, psychologist **E. C. Tolman** was already arguing that the mechanical stimulus-response view was too shallow an explanation for all learning. But only with the emergence of cognitive psychology has his early claim been taken seriously and studied extensively. Tolman claimed that even rats in a maze were able to form what he called a **cognitive map.** This term refers to the human and animal ability to form a mental image of where he or she is located in the environment. Thus, when a maze is changed, a rat is able to visualize the change after going through it once and then can run the maze to seek food using the new mental image (Tolman et al., 1946).

We now know that Tolman was right, that there is no such thing as a simple organism. Rats in mazes, for example, not only form some kind of cognitive map but they also use **strategies** (techniques for solving problems) of their own to explore carefully the alleyways of a maze without going over the same territory more than once. Chimpanzees in a maze are remarkable. An experimenter can carry a baby chimp through a complicated maze and deposit bananas in 18 different places in the alleyway while the chimp watches. When freed, the chimp can find an average of 12 of the 18 bananas quickly without duplicating any routes (Olton, 1979, 1978). Birds that store pine seeds in the ground for months at a time have the same excellent record; in fact, they even pass by storage places for other birds and pick up only their own seeds (Kamil & Roitblat, 1985).

One of the most amusing of these experiments involves bees who use a "scout" to find food (Gould, 1984, 1985). After finding the food, the scout flies back to the hive to tell the others where the food is. The location is indicated by an elaborate scout-bee "dance" that shows the direction and distance of the food location by the length of its up-down movement and the general pattern of its flying. One researcher took a scout bee out into the middle of a lake in a boat and exposed it to food. When it flew back to the hive, it dutifully reported direction and distance of the food to the others. Since the other bees also have cognitive maps, they presumably thought the scout was

Chapter 7 PRINCIPLES OF LEARNING

▲ *About as clear a case of observational learning as one would hope to find.*

cognitive map
A mental image of where one is located in space.

strategies
Methods for solving problems.

DISCUSS THE PHOTO

You might want to introduce the concept of identification, too. See Chapter 17. What other kinds of behaviors do children imitate?

Comprehension Check

What did E. C. Tolman believe? *(Tolman believed that animals and people form a mental image, or "cognitive map" of where they are located in an environment.)*

ENRICHMENT

Have students complete the **Enrichment Worksheet** for this chapter located in the Teacher Resources.

DISCUSS THE PHOTO

Walk-through mazes seem to have universal appeal. Maybe they satisfy our curiosity motive.

Reteaching Strategy

Have students complete the **Reteaching Worksheet** for this chapter located in the Teacher Resources.

The **Vocabulary Worksheet** may be completed by the class as a pretest for chapter concepts or used as a reteaching worksheet for those students needing additional review.

Four Types of Learning.

IN FOCUS *Classical:* the dog was associated with loud barks. *Operant:* a dog bit her one time when she went to pet it. *Social Learning:* she saw her sister scream when she got bit by a dog. *Cognitive Learning:* dogs look mean, so she has decided that they must be mean.

Unit 3 COGNITIVE PROCESSES

▲ *A walk-through maze that requires a cognitive map to "solve."*

mentally disturbed (Food in the middle of the lake? He's got to be kidding!) because not one bee moved. In the next step of the experiment, a scout bee was taken by boat to the shore at the other side of the lake, exposed to food, and let go. When it reported back to the same hive, all the bees came flying posthaste!

Here is an experiment for you to do; we will discuss the results below. Get a large piece of *unlined* paper. In the center, put where you live. Try to draw your map to scale, but don't use a ruler. Pick two places away from your home, one to the right and one to the left of it, approximately the same distance away. One should be a place you don't like for some reason, the other a place you have good feelings about. Draw a map of the streets from your home to each of these two places (Evans, 1980; Milgram, 1977).

The Map   Don't read this section if you haven't finished your cognitive map yet.

This experiment shows how psychological factors enter into a cognitive map. Note that you have made the distance to the unpleasant place greater than that to the pleasant place because you don't want to go to the unpleasant one. You have created a symbolic map that tries to move you closer to the pleasant place. In line with this symbolism, you have also straightened out the curves and bends in the road and generally altered the map to fit your own desires rather than strict reality. If the places are not actually equidistant from your home, you can still check with a ruler how much you "psychologically" changed the two distances.

IN FOCUS   **Four Types of Learning**

Classical Conditioning: Learning by association
Operant Conditioning: Learning through reinforcement
Social Learning: Learning by observing and imitating
Cognitive Learning: Learning through mental processing

Allison becomes extremely fearful around dogs. She could have learned this fear through *any* of these types of learning. Can you explain each possible way?

DISCOVERY

Consider conducting activity #6 at the end of the chapter, especially the part that asks teachers to poll their classes about study habits.

PSYCHOLOGY IN YOUR LIFE

Teaching Hint
These study tips are a good lead-in to Chapter 8. You can discuss interference and transfer as they relate to studying.

Points to Stress
While it is true that the brain stores new information we are working on and making connections to in a particular location, this does not mean that the brain is divided into sections or shelves with subject matter systematically coded and categorized. New information cannot simply be slotted into the appropriate shelf like *(continued on next page)*

PSYCHOLOGY IN YOUR LIFE

Trying to Learn How to Try to Learn

There are courses as well as many excellent books on how to study. How far you want to go into the subject is a matter of personal choice. Here, however, are a handful of firmly established facts about studying that have stood the tests of time and of many experiments. We hope you will take them all to heart; at least the more of them you use, the better off you will be. Some of them require no pain whatsoever.

First, two "don'ts": there are many courses in speed reading, but speed reading doesn't work for studying. As your speed increases, comprehension decreases. If you are a very slow reader (less than 70 words per minute on a novel or newspaper article), you might benefit from extra training just to get your speed up to 100 or so words per minute. But speed reading reduces learning when you read faster than 250 words per minute. Learning "in your sleep," by using a tape recorder or other such

device, also doesn't work. You learn only in proportion to how awake you are. All the machine will do is disturb your sleep (Evans & Evans, 1984).

The single most effective thing you can do to help you learn is to write a synopsis in your own words of every two or three paragraphs of the chapter you are studying. Stop when an idea seems to be completed and write it out in your own words. You should wind up with your own "minichapter" when you are done. Review your synopsis, note anything that isn't clear, and go back to the text to clarify that point, revising your notes. Keep your minichapters in a separate notebook so you can use them for review later.

Here is a technique you will like: the brain demands rest in order to bring together material properly. This might explain why, when you have tried to solve a problem and have finally given up and

▲ *A familiar method of learning.*

gone to bed, the solution will suddenly be there when you wake up. The brain has been working on the problem without all the clutter that normally distracts it during the day. While such a system won't work for regular studying, its principle can be applied. The maximum human attention span is about 30 minutes. So quit—eat or drink something, talk to someone, do anything different for about ten minutes.

(continued on next page)

DISCUSS THE PHOTO

Do students view this "familiar method" as useful or as busy work?

Connections

See **The Purpose of Dreaming** from Chapter 6 for more on how the brain organizes material during sleep.

(continued from previous page)
an addition to a library. It requires special attention to consolidation and is especially susceptible to interference. When attempting to establish neural pathways to this information, it is important not to "overload" the system by exhausting the neural networks involved. This is why taking a break from studying this material every 20 to 30 minutes is so helpful to remembering it. The break facilitates consolidation of the information. Switching to a very different subject lowers the risk of interference and negative transfer from similar associations that might otherwise occur.

Wrapping It Up

Have students make a list of ten things they have learned in the last few years. Next to each item, they should mark if they learned it through classical conditioning, operant conditioning, social learning, or cognitive learning. If their list is skewed, it probably means that they don't usually view many of their behaviors as being learned. If you want the list to be more balanced, tell them to think of a few examples for each type of learning.

VOCABULARY REVIEW

Before testing students on the contents of this chapter, you may want to review vocabulary terms that are especially important or confusing. Terms in this chapter that could require clarification are *conditioning, unconditioned stimulus, unconditioned response, conditioned stimulus, conditioned response, schedules of reinforcement,* and *cognitive map.*

PSYCHOLOGY IN YOUR LIFE

Trying to Learn How to Try to Learn

(continued from previous page) Then go back to studying for another 25 to 30 minutes.

The brain works on material on a specific subject in roughly the same location. History, for example, tends to be worked on in a particular area. This means that an area can get overloaded and fatigued for a short while.

Thus, you should change subject matters each study cycle (30-minute period), coming back later, if necessary, to the earlier ones. Keep away from similar material from one cycle to another. Put math between history and English, put English between math and chemistry, and so forth.

Finally, at the end of each subject studied, try to establish some principle that brings the material together. Ask yourself, "What exactly is the *issue* involved in what I've just studied?" Then review your summaries and leave them alone. If you have *really* studied, your brain will keep working on it.

SUMMARY

1. Classical conditioning results from an involuntary association of a neutral stimulus with a natural stimulus until each brings the same response.

2. Operant conditioning requires some action on the part of the organism. These actions can be positively or negatively reinforced, or they can be punished.

3. Schedules of reinforcement include fixed-interval, fixed-ratio, variable-interval, and variable-ratio.

4. Social learning centers on observation of other people. We learn appropriate behaviors by watching others and imitating them.

5. Cognitive learning is the focus of a currently popular area of psychology that studies the meaning and use of knowledge. The methods by which knowledge is used, manipulated, processed, and organized are the subjects of cognitive research.

Suggested Readings

▼ Bjork, Daniel W. *B. F. Skinner.* New York: HarperCollins, 1993.

▼ Hill, W. F. *Principles of Learning: A Handbook of Applications.* New York: Chandler, 1982.

▼ Kazkin, A. E. *Behavior Modification in Applied Settings.* New York: Dorsey Press, 1985.

▼ Skinner, B. F. *Beyond Freedom and Dignity.* New York: Knopf, 1979.

Suggested Videos

▼ *Learning.* Discovering Psychology series, part 8, 27 min. 1-800-LEARNER.

▼ *Pavlov: The Conditioned Reflex.* 25 min. b&w. Films for the Humanities.

▼ *Reward and Punishment.* 30 min. CRM/McGraw-Hill.

Vocabulary

conditioning
Ivan Pavlov
classical conditioning
stimulus
response
unconditioned stimulus
unconditioned response
conditioned stimulus
conditioned response
John Watson
Little Albert
stimulus generalization
extinction
Mary Cover Jones
operant conditioning
B. F. Skinner

reinforcement
primary reinforcement
secondary reinforcement
positive reinforcement
negative reinforcement
punishment
generalization
discrimination learning
shaping
chaining
continuous reinforcement
schedules of reinforcement

partial reinforcement schedule
variable ratio schedule
fixed ratio schedule
variable interval schedule
fixed interval schedule
Albert Bandura
social learning
observational learning
cognitive approach
E. C. Tolman
cognitive map
strategies

Answers to Review Questions

1. OP
2. SL
3. CC
4. SL

Review Questions

For each of the following, indicate whether the capitalized behavior is learned primarily through classical conditioning *(CC),* operant conditioning *(OP), or* social learning *(SL).*

1. Nino *EATS* at Lou's Pizza for the first time. Since he enjoys the food, he returns there every Saturday for dinner.
2. The main reason that Nino *EATS* at Lou's Pizza is because all his friends eat there.
3. Every time Nino drives into Lou's parking lot, his *MOUTH WATERS* because he knows he will eat soon.
4. Little Lauren *WEARS* her mom's clothes simply because she wants to imitate her mom.

Notes on Discussion Questions

1. Stimulus generalization means that Theodore would cry when hearing similar bell sounds. The fear might be extinguished by associating something pleasant with the bell sound.
2. If students can't think of an exam-

5. CC
6. OP
7. needle
8. fear
9. dentist
10. fear
11. dentist
12. secondary reinforcer
13. primary reinforcer
14. primary reinforcer
15. secondary reinforcer
16. positive reinforcement
17. negative reinforcement
18. negative reinforcement
19. positive reinforcement
20. b
21. c
22. a
23. b
24. d
25. a
26. c

5. Little Lauren's *HEART RACES* every time she wears her mom's clothes.

6. Little Lauren *WEARS* her mom's clothes often because she knows she will always get a laugh.

Read the following example of a behavior learned through classical conditioning: "The first time that Sarah went to the DENTIST, he stuck a long NEEDLE in her mouth, which naturally caused her to experience FEAR. After a few visits, she experienced FEAR not only when the needle was stuck in her mouth but also when the DENTIST appeared to call her into the office." Using this example, identify the following concepts (possible answers are capitalized above):

7. The unconditioned stimulus (UCS)?
8. The unconditioned response (UCR)?
9. The conditioned stimulus (CS)?

10. The conditioned response (CR)?
11. The stimulus that started out as neutral (N)?

Which of the following are primary reinforcers, and which are secondary reinforcers?

12. Money
13. Food

14. Love
15. A promotion

Which of the following are examples of positive reinforcement, and which are examples of negative reinforcement?

16. Tom hangs up his coat in order to get a dollar.
17. Tom hangs up his coat in order to stop his mom's yelling.

18. Mary stays at home every weekend so she won't run into her old boyfriend.
19. Mary stays at home every weekend because her new boyfriend always comes over.

Matching

20. Phil loves to talk, but when he discovers that no one really listens to him, he stops talking.
21. Phil learns that it's all right to talk during class discussions but not during tests.
22. Phil talks to a person in class wearing green shoes who actually listens to him. As a result, he tries talking to other people wearing green shoes in other classes.

a. generalization
b. extinction
c. discrimination

ple, encourage them to ask their parents about toddler fears that came and went. (See **Introducing the Chapter**.)

3. This is a good question to discuss in class at the beginning of the chapter. Perhaps you can relate their answers to the six approaches discussed in Chapter 1.

4. Removal of the reinforcement would probably work for other habits as well. If a person overeats, this person should not have large quantities of food in his or her house. If a person procrastinates, watching TV instead of doing homework, he or she should remove the TV from the room in which homework is done, or better yet, remove the TV from the house entirely (which may not be entirely realistic).

5. This is a tricky problem for students, but insist that after they read the chapter, they have the tools to solve it. Ignore the gorilla during undesirable behavior—like sitting in the doorway of his cage. Reward the gorilla for desirable behavior: you feed him when he moves and only when he moves.

6. Answers will vary. Perhaps you can discuss which methods their parents have used.

7. You might be able to get someone to research the techniques used by animal trainers. This is usually a lively topic to discuss in class.

8. One of the two variable schedules would be more likely to promote addiction than the fixed schedules. Point out the addictive nature of gambling (VR) and fishing (VI). A fixed-interval schedule would probably be least effective. A person could simply look at his or her watch and sit in front of the TV at the "right" times.

9. Answers will vary. Have students share their strategies in class.

Matching

23. Gamblers never know how many times they need to bet in order to win.
24. Factory workers get a break every three hours.
25. Whenever you kick a vending machine three times, candy bars fall out.
26. Every once in a while, candy bars fall out of the vending machine.

a. fixed ratio
b. variable ratio
c. variable interval
d. fixed interval

DISCUSSION QUESTIONS

1. One day little Theodore is extremely startled when he hears the doorbell, and he begins to cry uncontrollably. In the days that follow, stimulus generalization occurs. Describe what might happen during the following days. How would you extinguish his fear?

2. Describe a fear that you once had that is pretty much extinguished today. Why or how was the fear extinguished?

3. Psychologist John Watson once said, "Give me a dozen healthy infants and allow me to control the environment, and I'll make them into anything I want." In other words, he could make them become priests, doctors, or even criminals. Do you agree with him? Explain why or why not.

4. According to operant conditioning, people continue to perform certain behaviors mainly because of the reinforcement they receive. This applies even to bad habits. Name one of your bad habits. What are several possible reinforcements that you receive for performing the habit? How would you remove or change some of these reinforcements and possibly extinguish the bad habit? Here's an example: habit = biting nails; reinforcement = relieves tension; removing reinforcement = wear gloves.

5. Imagine a huge gorilla sitting stubbornly in the doorway of his cage, not allowing anyone to close the cage door. How would you use operant conditioning to get him to move? Explain.

6. Your grades have been slipping lately, and your parents have become concerned. They decide to use some of the principles of learning discussed in this chapter to motivate you. One month they try positive reinforcement, another month negative reinforcement, and finally punishment. Explain in practical terms what they might do each month, and explain what method would best motivate you.

7. Many animal trainers use the learning techniques outlined in this chapter to train their animals. If you have a pet, describe in your own words how you have trained the pet to perform certain behaviors. Do you see any similarities between your training techniques and the techniques described in the chapter? For example, did you use shaping and/or chaining? Explain.

8. If you wanted someone to become addicted to watching television, which schedule of

Notes on Activities

1. Consider conducting this activity in class.

2. To prepare students for this activity, you might want to use yourself as an example, pointing out the reinforcements you use to motivate students. Or invite a popular coach to class!

3. Try to get a few students to videotape their training sessions and show the tapes to the class. Or get permission to bring an animal to school and condition the animal in class.

4. Have the students who choose this activity present an oral report. Skinner's ideas can be good discussion starters.

5. You will probably need to conduct this activity in class if you want students to do it at home. Stress that you are looking for *behaviors.*

6. You might want to assign this as a class project and combine everyone's results.

reinforcement would be most effective? Explain. Which schedule would be least effective? Explain.

9. The end of the chapter discusses several techniques for studying. What strategies for studying have been effective for you? Explain.

ACTIVITIES

1. Reread the map experiment described at the end of the chapter and try the same experiment on five friends to see if the results are consistent. In addition to telling them to draw a map, give them the following instructions:
   a. "On another sheet of paper, draw yourself in the center. On one side of you, draw someone you like and on the other side of you, draw someone you do not like."
   b. "On the same sheet of paper, draw a food that you like on one side of you and a food you do not like on the other side of you."

   Analyze the drawings: the map, the people, and the food. Is there any consistency in them? Are all the unpleasant items drawn farther away from the center than the pleasant items? Explain. Are all the unpleasant items drawn on the same side of the paper? Are there any other patterns that you notice?

2. Analyze a typical school day OR a typical athletic practice OR a typical day at work. Point out how reinforcement (both positive and negative) is used by your teachers, coaches, or bosses. Discuss whether these uses of reinforcement are effective in motivating performance or behavior—not only your behavior but also your friends'. Finally, discuss whether these uses of reinforcement should be increased. If so, how? If not, why not?

3. The following activity is for the lover of household pets. Take a cat or a dog and train the animal to perform a simple behavior like rolling over or pushing open a door. The best way to produce this simple behavior is through shaping: every time the animal comes even close to performing the behavior you want, reinforce it with food. (Do the shaping when the animal is hungry.) Once the animal knows what it needs to do to get the food, put it on a fixed ratio schedule for a few days and then on a variable ratio schedule for a few days. (If it's at all possible, use two different animals and train each on a different schedule.)

   Which schedule seems to be most effective? Explain. Would it be more difficult to extinguish behavior learned through one schedule than through the other? Explain. Finally, jot down any general problems you have in training the animal(s).

4. B. F. Skinner has always been a controversial and fascinating psychologist. Write a brief report on his life. Focus particularly on how he applied the learning techniques he studied to his own life and to his family's life. Describe your reactions to his ideas.

5. Get a friend to participate in an experiment on shaping. Conduct the experiment where there will be few distractions. Sit across from the friend and read the following directions:
   "Imagine you're applying for a job and I'm the boss. I'm going to ask you a series of simple questions that will determine

212

whether I'll hire you. My decision to hire will be based not so much on the content of your answers, but on the behaviors that you happen to perform in the next few minutes. So just pay attention and try to produce as many positive responses from me as possible after each question. The more positive responses you receive, the better your chances will be of getting hired."

Have ready a list of 25 to 30 simple questions, such as name, address, and so on. Before you begin asking the questions, decide on a simple behavior you want to shape. For example, if you notice that your friend is slouching back in the chair, try to get him or her to lean forward and fold his or her hands.

Slowly read the list of questions. The answers, of course, are meaningless. But whenever the friend comes progressively closer to the behavior you want, nod and say, "OK." Your friend should interpret this as a positive response. If the friend continues to slouch, shake your head disapprovingly and say, "Uh-oh" (or something similar). Note: your first few responses will be negative since the friend has no idea what you're reinforcing. This whole process of shaping is similar to the "hot and cold" game that most of us played as kids. Whenever the person gets "hot," or close to doing what you want, you positively reinforce him or her; whenever he or she gets "cold," you offer no reinforcement.

Repeat this entire procedure with two other friends and compare results. Discuss whether the shaping was generally successful. On the average, how long did it take for your friends to figure out the behavior you wanted? (Note: even if your friends did not figure out the behavior but they still *did* the behavior by the end of your questioning, shaping can be considered successful.) Finally, what were some of the obstacles that interfered with the shaping process? Explain.

6. Find out who some of the top-ranked students in your school are. Interview two of them to find out about their study habits. Ask them this: "It's the night before an important test; what steps do you take to study? Be specific. How long do you study?"

Once you accumulate a list of specific studying behaviors, conduct an informal survey around the school, asking people whether they use any of the strategies on your list. Ask them to what extent they use the strategies: very often? once in a while? never? Finally, ask them their grade point averages.

Compare the grade point averages to the answers on your survey. Do you find that these are related in any way? Explain.

An alternative to a survey might be to convince two teachers to poll their classes about study habits. One class could be an advanced class, and the other could be a regular class.

DISCUSS THE PHOTO

Take a poll on which students prefer solitude and quiet and which prefer noise while studying.

Retention of learned material is easier when there are no distractions.

214

PSYCHOLOGY AND YOU RESOURCES

A variety of resources are available in the Psychology and You *supplementary material. In addition, there are a number of additional resources listed to enhance your lesson plans.*

Masters
▼ 8-1A Learning Goals
▼ 8-1B Answers to Learning Goals
▼ 8-2 Story Chain
▼ 8-3 Soft-Drink Memory Experiment
▼ 8-4 Organizing Memory
▼ 8-5 Touch Versus Touch-and-Taste Recall
▼ 8-6 Memory List 1
▼ 8-7 Memory List 2
▼ 8-8 The Assailant 1
▼ 8-9 The Assailant 2

Student Worksheets
▼ Vocabulary Worksheet
▼ Independent Practice Worksheet
▼ Enrichment Worksheet
▼ Reteaching Worksheet

Test Bank
▼ Tests A and B

Multimedia
▼ *The Brain* Videotape Module #21
▼ **Psychware** Exercises 2–5
▼ Psychology Videodisc

Student Workbook

PACING CHART

Complete Coverage

Day 1: Assign "Acquiring Information" prior to class. After reviewing the chemical and emotional influences on learning, use discussion question #3 to highlight the differences between positive and negative transfer. Have the class read "Information Processing" for Day 2.

Day 2: Assign an activity (activity #1 in the text, for example) that reinforces students' understanding of the concept *schema*. Use a demonstration and the In Focus boxes to illustrate the various special learning processes (elaboration, mnemonic devices, principle learning, and chunking). Have students read "Retaining Information" and assign the first two experiments in Psychology in Your Life for homework.

Day 3: Evaluate students' homework regarding the Psychology in Your Life experiments as you discuss the inference theory of forgetting. Review the function of short- and long-term memory and the sequence of memory loss.

CHAPTER 8

Acquiring, Processing, and Retaining Information

215

OBJECTIVES

Be able to:

▼ Compare learning curves when attention is high versus when it is normal.

▼ Explain transfer of training.

▼ Describe what a schema is.

▼ List and describe special learning processes.

▼ Explain how remembering differs when the task is recall versus when it is recognition.

▼ Explain what it means to store memories in "code."

▼ Explain the difference between short- and long-term memory.

Global Look at the Chapter

To acquire information, we must control what comes in and what is blocked out from the environment. Material that we retain is first sent through a short-term memory where it is processed and then moved to a permanent storage area where physical changes occur in the nerve cells.

INTRODUCING THE CHAPTER

Walk into class one day, get everyone's attention, make a few announcements, then have the students turn their desks around to the back of the room. Prepare a short oral quiz that tests students' recall of objects or signs in the front of the room. For example, "Where is the fire exit sign? What color is it? What does it say on the sign? Is there a flag in the room? Where is it? What color is my shirt?" Point out that poor performance on this quiz results from lack of attention to these objects.

LEAD-OFF ACTIVITY

Show the power of mnemonic devices by having everyone memorize each other's last names. Go around the room and associate each last name with a vivid image. The more bizarre and elaborate the image, the easier it will be to remember the names. For John Swanson, imagine John riding a swan and calling it son. For Judy Richards, imagine Judy with money stuffed in her pockets (rich) and playing "cards" (which is close to "ards," the last part of her name). You can mention that this memory game is an example of a mnemonic device which they will learn about in this chapter.

Day 4: After briefly discussing unusual types of memory, conduct an experiment (such as activity #4 or 5 in the text) to show the fallibility of eyewitness accounts. Have students complete the final experiment in Psychology in Your Life for homework.

Day 5: After discussing the results of students' homework, give the Chapter Review quiz.

In Brief

Day 1: Review chemical and emotional effects on learning. Assign an activity requiring students to identify examples of negative and positive transfer.

Day 2: Focus on the concept *schema.* Have students think up some mnemonic devices (use In Focus Common Mnemonic Devices for inspiration) while evaluating the various special learning processes. Assign the experiments in Psychology in Your Life for homework.

Day 3: Discuss forgetting, concentrating on the inference theory and incorporating the results of students' homework. Give the Chapter Review quiz.

EXPERIMENT

Read aloud the four passages presented at the beginning of the **Acquiring Information** section. Half of the class follows along in the text; the other half just listens. At the end of the class, see who has better recall. This shows that memory can be enhanced by multisensory input.

CHAPTER PROJECT

New theories about memory seem to appear every year, especially with the brain-imaging technology available today. To bring the class up to date on these theories, have students find the most recent articles on memory that they can find. You could refer back to **Teaching Master 1-4 Writing Your Own Magazine Article** for an assignment on magazine articles. Or simply have each student give a one-minute presentation on one article.

TEACHING MASTER 8-1A

Learning Goals. A Learning Goals sheet for each chapter is provided in the Teacher Resources. These Learning Goals can be used as review sheets or as worksheets. **Teaching Master 8-1B** consists of answers to these Learning Goals.

Discussion

How do teachers command attention? Students might enjoy some behind-the-scenes glimpses into your approach.

attention
Alert focusing on material.

ACQUIRING INFORMATION

All day long we talk, read, listen, discuss, fight, hope, believe, wish, despair, and analyze. All of these behaviors are taken for granted. But none of them is possible without learning and storing the information that we use in each case. We sit and mumble to ourselves, but we are mumbling *something,* and the something comes from things we have stored in memory. So, no issue is more critical than how we acquire and retain information.

To start off, we have listed here four passages for you to read. Read them only once, but in order for us to make the points we need to make, *please* don't reread these passages until we refer to them later.

1. In 1925, lawyer William Jennings Bryan prosecuted the teaching of evolution and won the case. In 1920, many states were won to the cause of the Eighteenth Amendment for prohibition of liquor. Fourteen years later, the Twenty-First Amendment repealed the Eighteenth.
2. Raoult's Law states that the depression of the freezing points and the elevation of the vapor pressures of liquids that are dissolved are in proportion to the number of molecules of substance dissolved.
3. If you are attacked by a dog, hit its nose hard and fast. Put your forearm in front of you and jam it into the dog's open mouth. Bring your other arm around behind the dog and press it against the dog's neck. Force the dog's head backward and over your arm, snapping the neck.
4. The following is a poem about outlaw John Wesley Hardin, who roamed the West in the late 1800s (McMahon, 1987). He had killed five people by the time he was 15. Later he became sheriff!

   John Wesley Hardin, meanest outlaw of the West,
   Killed over 40 men, and his reasons weren't the best.
   From a hotel room next to his, a snoring man disturbed his rest.
   So he simply fired through the wall and shot the man to death.

Learning Curves

Learning processes can be plotted out visually using graphs. For example, they can be used to study the influence of **attention** on learning. Attention refers to a person's alert focusing on the material to be retained.

Influence of Attention   When we attend to something, we become physically aroused, and this activates chemicals in the brain that aid our ability to learn (McGaugh, 1983). The item about John Wesley Hardin is a real attention grabber. Probably every one of you

DEMONSTRATION

We've probably all played the game in which the first person whispers a story to a second person, who whispers it to a third person, and so on. By the end of the chain, the story has significantly changed. In this case, have four or five students leave the room. Read a story to a volunteer in the room. Then have the students from outside return one by one. The volunteer who heard the story will recite it from memory to the first student; that student will recite it to the second, and so on. See **Teaching Master 8-2 Story Chain** for a story to use. After the activity, which only takes five to ten minutes, discuss how the story changed. What kinds of facts were deleted? Added? Was the doctor's name remembered? It was used four times! The game should demonstrate the unreliability of memory, which you can stress again when you discuss eyewitness memory.

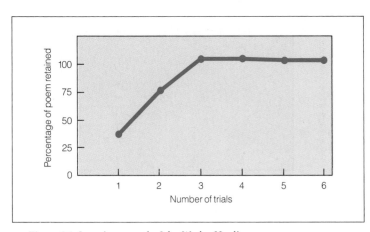

▲ *Figure 8.1 Learning curve for John Wesley Hardin poem.*

can repeat a good portion of its content without having to check back. A graphic view of learning the whole poem would look something like Figure 8.1. In other words, Figure 8.1 shows that on the first few trials, a person would probably make errors, but learning would take place rapidly until he or she reached 100 percent mastery. (A trial refers to each attempt to recite the material after a session of memorizing.)

Conventional Learning Compare the John Wesley Hardin poem with item number 2, Raoult's Law. Because the material is not an attention grabber for the average person, it involves a slower learning process. Motivation and attention are moderate, so learning is more of a struggle. Over a period of time and through a number of trials, the graph of learning this information will look like Figure 8.2. Note that here learning moves gradually upward with practice as the learning progresses, but the curve is nowhere close to the dramatic upward movement of learning the John Wesley Hardin poem. This curve (Figure 8.2) is the conventional (or usual) one that applies to most learning and is simply called the **learning curve**.

Chemical Influences on Learning

There are many chemicals that influence learning, and they fall into two broad categories: stimulants and depressants.

Stimulants, such as the caffeine in coffee, tea, and some soft drinks, can actually increase learning. They stir up the body's activity level, which in turn increases memory (Dunn, 1980). The soft drink must have sugar in it, too, not an artificial sweetener. Artificial sweeteners alter the normal firing pattern of brain cells, canceling the bene-

learning curve

A gradual upward slope representing increased retention of material as the result of learning.

Connections

Attention is certainly influenced by motivation (Chapter 5). If we are driving around and we are hungry, we'll pay attention to the restaurants that we pass. If we want friends, we'll pay attention to news about a party this weekend.

Critical Thinking

Are there any types of learning that do *not* follow a typical learning curve? For example, we can learn a fear after only one exposure to a stimulus. (See classical conditioning in Chapter 7.) Also, observational learning may defy the learning curve. We see something once, and we learn.

EXPERIMENT

This activity will enable you to create a conventional learning curve. Draw a graph on the board, labeling the horizontal axis, "Number of trials" and the vertical axis, "Number remembered." Number the horizontal axis from 1 to 10; the vertical axis from 1 to 15. Flash a 15-digit number on the overhead for about ten seconds, and have a volunteer try to recall the number exactly. Record on your graph how many digits the student remembers correctly, and repeat the procedure until the volunteer gets the entire number correct. Connect the dots, and you should have a conventional learning curve.

EXPERIMENT

You can label this activity an experiment, but it's far from scientific. Rather, it's a gimmick to help students remember that chemicals influence learning (or to convince students that gimmicks *do* enhance memory).

Unit 3 COGNITIVE PROCESSES

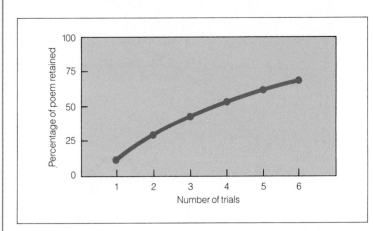

▲ *Figure 8.2* *Conventional learning curve for Raoult's Law.*

Points to Stress

State-dependent learning is similar to a victim returning to the scene of the crime and remembering details thought to be forgotten. This analogy, however, is flawed. When we return to a crime scene we rely primarily on *external* cues. State-dependent learning is enhanced by recreating the original *internal* state of the learner. If returning to a crime scene helps recreate the original internal state—through smells or temperature factors, for example—state-dependent learning may play a role in recall.

Comprehension Check

Ask students to name two things that enhance learning. *(stimulants, emotional involvement)*

fit of caffeine. (While there is as yet no conclusive evidence that these sweeteners do any direct damage, it would seem sensible to limit your intake of them or to avoid them altogether and take in a few extra calories from the sugar. This is especially true for very young children, since the cumulative effects of artificial sweeteners might not be desirable.) In any case, the stimulant is increasing the level of brain chemicals that allow for more rapid learning (Martinez et al., 1980). Strong stimulants, however, such as amphetamines (speed), overstimulate the brain and cause the reverse—loss of learning. Overall, the best of all worlds is to be naturally excited about what you are learning, because then your body will produce its own chemicals to assist in the task.

Anxiety about taking a test, at reasonable levels, acts just as caffeine does to stimulate the person, but some students "come apart" and drive the anxiety so high that it acts like the amphetamines, blocking learning.

Any depressant drug—such as a tranquilizer or alcohol—will block the firing of brain nerve cells and reduce learning. So will hot dogs or cold-cut meats. They contain a preservative that in low concentrations tends to depress learning ability (Martinez et al., 1979). But you have to eat three hot dogs or cold-cut sandwiches to get the effect, which is pretty hard to do without feeling horrible. Someone once said that "we are what we eat," which doesn't make much sense, but what we eat or drink *can* sometimes influence our behavior.

The fact is that taking in *any* chemical will alter a person's bodily condition or state. If someone learns something while in that altered state, the material learned will be easier to remember later on if the same state is reproduced. At the extreme, people who drink too much will not remember what happened once they are sober, but the odds are that the memory will return if they get in that condition

Put tinfoil around two cans of soft drinks. One should have caffeine and sugar, the other should not. Have two students drink the cans at the very beginning of class. Take attendance, discuss why they drank the soft drinks, discuss ways in which you could make the "experiment" more scientific, then pass out copies of **Teaching Master 8-3 Soft-Drink Memory Experiment** to your two drinkers. Send them to a quiet spot and give them two minutes to memorize the list on this master. Bring them back to class and have them write down everything they remember. You probably won't find much difference, but students will remember the hypothesis; emphasize that scientific studies have found that caffeine and sugar *do* affect learning.

Chapter 8 ACQUIRING, PROCESSING, AND RETAINING INFORMATION

state-dependent learning

The fact that material learned in one chemical state is best reproduced when the same state occurs again.

again. The same principles apply to studying when someone has drunk three cups of coffee. This is called **state-dependent learning,** meaning that the learning and reproduction of the material are reliant on (dependent on) the condition (state) of the body at the time of learning.

Emotional Factors in Learning

The most important learning is that centering on survival. Animals whose existence depends on remembering who or what is bad are in an excited state when a crisis arises, and this excited state increases the brain chemicals for learning; hence, the animals have increased memory potential (McGaugh, 1983). Similarly, a place that provides food is a good place to remember, and animals' brains seem to become primed for learning at the discovery of such a source.

For humans, the principle is the same but more complicated. Here are the results of an experiment called "Nancy's Visit to the Doctor": researchers gave subjects a long, tedious, and involved story about Nancy's visit. As you might have guessed, the subjects remembered little when they were tested later. In contrast, when the story was given to a different group and was altered to start off with the possibility of a major change or crisis in Nancy's life (an emotion generator), subjects remembered the details of the visit quite well (Owens et al., 1979).

So, emotional involvement increases learning. Another good example is the use of humor in the classroom. In moderation, it increases the level of brain activity. Too much humor, though, will wind up making humor itself the subject matter and will detract from learning. In some cases, the fact that a teacher is unpleasant can increase learning for a while because even though the emotion created is negative, it still *is* an emotion. After a while, however, the teacher's nastiness or ridicule becomes the major focus of attention and learning decreases (Klatzky, 1980).

Transfer of Training

One major learning process is called **transfer of training.** Its principle is relatively simple: learning task A will carry over (transfer) to learning task B if there are similarities between them.

Positive Transfer Police officers who shoot on a range at targets that dart, hide, and suddenly reappear will be better able to shoot at real-life targets because of the similarity of the task. Hence, the material in one situation *transfers* to that of a similar situation. This is called a **positive transfer** because the two tasks are similar. The same technique is used by airlines when they have pilots fly in simulators that recreate precisely the feel and movement of a genuine aircraft.

transfer of training

A learning process in which learning is moved from one task to another based on similarities between the tasks.

positive transfer

A transfer of learning that results from similarities between two tasks.

Discussion

Can the principle behind state-dependent learning apply to setting? If students are given gum every day while learning material, will they perform better on a test if they receive gum during the test? You might consider an experiment in which the class receives gum while learning the chapter and then only half chew gum during the test. You'll probably want to compare scores of several previous tests from other chapters before analyzing this data.

Points to Stress

The conclusion of the experiment titled "Nancy's Visit to the Doctor" (see **Emotional Factors in Learning** section) should be fairly obvious to students, yet many fail to apply the findings when they write. Point out that it might be to their advantage to hold their teacher's attention by expressing their emotions or appealing to ours.

EXPERIMENT

Bring in a tennis ball and have two or three subjects throw the ball into a waste basket 15 times from about five feet away. After 15 throws have them use their other hand to see if positive transfer occurred. (See the next **Experiment.**)

DISCUSS THE PHOTO

Someone who has been driving manual shift and then drives automatic may also experience negative transfer. The foot searches for a clutch that isn't there.

Teaching Hint

Explain to students that they may notice that musicians often play more than one instrument. The skills learned with one instrument often carry over to other instruments (positive transfer).

FYI Musicians may report positive transfer after taking an advanced reading class. The reading class actually helps them read music better. On the other hand, a saxophone player who tries to learn piano will probably report negative transfer. A D on one instrument is different from a D on the other because of different pitches.

220

Unit 3 COGNITIVE PROCESSES

negative transfer

An interference with learning due to differences between two otherwise similar tasks.

▲ *In the midst of this mess, all the person in the new manual-shift red sports car needs is to stall out from negative transfer.*

If you are interested in chemistry, you may have already been exposed to some of the elements found in Raoult's Law (item number 2 at the beginning of the chapter), and you probably remember at least part of what it said due to a transfer of training from your exposure to similar material. On the other hand, if you have never had any chemistry, chances are that Raoult's Law is already long gone from your memory storage area—or never even made it into your memory at all, as we'll discuss later.

So, positive transfer takes place when some useful similarity exists between what you have learned in the past and the new material. For example, a person who has taken courses in Latin will have an edge over others when taking Spanish, since many Spanish words are similar to Latin words.

Negative Transfer   There are occasions when transfer is not a useful thing, called **negative transfer.** If you learned to drive a car with an automatic transmission and then changed to a car that uses manual shifting, requiring a clutch, odds are that you stalled frequently, ground the gears a lot, and felt quite uncomfortable. If you learned how to drive with a manual transmission and then drove an automatic, you probably kept pushing an imaginary clutch to the floor and felt very foolish. The previously learned task is interfering with the present one.

Exercising the Mind?   Latin was picked merely as an example above. Still, for a while, educators believed that if you took very difficult and obscure courses like Latin, even if you didn't want or need

EXPERIMENT

Bring in two balls that are very different in weight. Have a student toss one ball into the wastebasket about twenty times. Then have her toss the other ball. She will probably do poorly at first because of negative transfer.

Chapter 8 ACQUIRING, PROCESSING, AND RETAINING INFORMATION

▲ *This is an example of either just plain sleep or consolidation of memory, depending on your point of view.*

to, somehow the pain and struggle involved in doing so "exercised" your mind so you would be smarter for most other courses. That has proved not to be the case. Some courses are considered a necessity for a proper education, and for many people they are not easy; such courses include chemistry, physics, and advanced mathematics. But although they are difficult, they don't "exercise the mind" in the sense of making it "stronger" for other courses. Chemistry and physics will transfer to one another because of some similarities, but there will be no transfer between, say, chemistry and history, physics and literature, or mathematics and Spanish.

INFORMATION PROCESSING

Learning and reproducing what we have learned is referred to as **information processing.** In other words, information processing is another term for the methods by which we take in, analyze, store, and bring back the various things we learn. Below we discuss studies of these various processes.

Using a Schema

Suppose we were to ask Little Red Riding Hood how to get to Grandma's house. She would not come out with the answer automatically but would have to go through a series of steps to figure it

information processing

The methods by which we take in, analyze, store, and retrieve material.

COOPERATIVE LEARNING

Have students work in pairs to draw a schema for answering this question: why did you come to school today? Have them refer to Figure 8.3 for ideas.

Connections

Jean Piaget used the term *scheme* to describe the way we organize knowledge (see Chapter 10). Scheme is synonymous, of course, with schema. Piaget believed that a three-year-old will form different schemas than a ten-year-old. The act of creating a schema is a developmental skill. You might ask how school helps to nurture this natural skill. Or does it?

Teaching Hint

When teaching about blocking out *incorrect* paths during a search for a memory, you may want to mention the concept of *constructive processing.* Instead of blocking out incorrect paths, we sometimes reconstruct the memory, adding new details in the process. If my mom tells me about the time my little sister hit me with a pot, I may not remember the actual pot in question, but I will assume it had a handle, that it was steel, and so on. These assumptions may become part of my own so-called memory of the event.

222

schema

An organized and systematic approach to answering questions or solving problems.

out. Various bits of stored mental information must be brought together in an ordered sequence before she can give an answer. Here are the steps: (1) Process words in the question asked. (2) Match the question to rough categories of information she knows in order to find the correct area where the information might be. (3) Within the area chosen, search to find a representation of Grandma in her house. (4) Hold that representation in her own consciousness while she locates the brain representation of where she herself is when the question is asked. (5) Find all the connections (streets and directions) between where she is now and where Grandma is located. (6) Answer the question step by step from where she is to Grandma's house, all the time blocking out incorrect connections that might appear (such as where Uncle Harry's house is) (Anderson, 1983). This process is diagrammed in Figure 8.3.

This organized and systematic approach to answering questions or solving problems is called "making a **schema**" (SKEE-ma). The word *schema* comes from the Greek, meaning an "outline or pattern." In other words, each of us has a plan for solving problems (Horton & Mills, 1984).

An organized search is required because of the complexity and amount of material stored in the brain. In fact, it truly leaves one in awe to think that any of us can *ever* come up with an answer to any question, much less do so in a matter of a few hundredths of a second. Figure 8.3 shows only a small part of the schema used to find Grandma's house (Craik, 1979; Klatzky, 1980). The original information given in the form of a question has to be processed through the correct sensory register (visual, auditory, smell, touch, taste)—in this case, auditory, since Little Red Riding Hood *heard* the question asked. Creating the answer requires, among other things, remembering how she got there (walking, running, riding), deciding whose house she is going to (aunt's, uncle's, grandmother's), and analyzing the types of houses possible (wood, brick, adobe, or gingerbread).

Importance of Organizing Information

The importance of organization is demonstrated in the following experiment: Pictures of rooms were given to subjects to see how many objects in a room they could recall when the picture was removed. If the picture contained an unnatural scene, such as having a kitchen knife on the coffee table, pots and pans on the dining table, and flowers on the stove burner, the picture was very hard to remember. This experiment suggests that in everyday activity, we form an organized, coherent, structured "map" of our world, and if what we see doesn't "match" our existing memory (that pans belong on the stove), we have to stop and overcome confusion (Mandler & Ritchey, 1977).

Many of our memory sequences have been thoroughly learned. If the brain fires the information memory of "capital" for "United

COOPERATIVE LEARNING

After students review the Little Red Riding Hood schema (see Figure 8.3), see if they can create their own. Split students into six groups and assign one of the following topics to each group: (1) You are late to a class and need to think of an excuse. (2) You are deciding if you should run for class president. (3) You are considering shoplifting. (4) You wonder if you should go to a party. (5) You wonder if you should get a summer job. (6) You wonder if you should break off a relationship. (See activity #1 at the end of the chapter for other suggestions.)

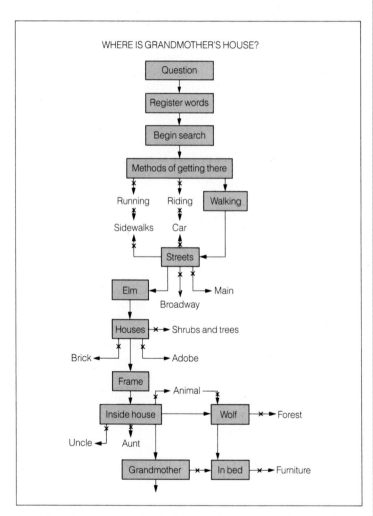

▲ *Figure 8.3* *Finding Grandmother's house. Make answer to where Grandma lives:* Wolf in bed in Grandmother's house on Elm reached by walking there. *Check answer:* match to question. *Redo answer to match question:* Grandmother's house is on Elm Street.

Connections

Students may recall from the end of Chapter 7 that cognitive-learning theorists believe we form cognitive maps. The material in *this* chapter shows that this map making is an organized and efficient process.

States," for example, the hookup is so well established that very quickly the answer will arrive: "Washington, D.C." (Anderson, 1983). Of course, there are always a few who will say, "Bowlegs, Oklahoma," but that's the way life is!

You should note that an important aspect of learning is the ability to eliminate or block out the *incorrect* areas we run across during the search for an answer. As you can see in Figure 8.3, and if you remem-

EXPERIMENT

This activity demonstrates how we store and/or retrieve information in an organized manner. Read the list on **Teaching Master 8-4 Organizing Memory** to one or two volunteers. Then have them count backward from 52 to zero—by fours (52, 48, 44); this

should prevent rehearsal. Now have the volunteers try to recall the items on the list. You will notice that the objects on the list can be clustered into several categories. When the volunteers try to recall the objects, they will probably recall them in clusters.

EXPERIMENT

Elaboration helps us store material by using a maximum number of associations. See if this applies to short-term memory as well. Have students pair up. Give one member of each pair a blindfold. Pass out **Teaching Master 8-5 Touch vs. Touch-and-Taste Recall,** face down, along with

---

Points to Stress

If we get stuck when recalling a memory during hypnosis, we're more likely than usual to fill in the blanks, even if what we fill in is a mistake. A hypnotized subject tends to be suggestible, so if the hypnotist asks, "How *fast* was the car moving?" the subject will probably assume that the car *was* going fast, even if it wasn't.

Also, a hypnotized subject may *believe* that hypnosis improves memory and will be more *willing* to make guesses—which will affect the schemas formed.

(See the section **Unusual Types of Memory** later in the chapter where eyewitness memory is discussed.)

---

ber the story, instead of meeting her Grandma, Little Red met a wolf with his snout sticking out over the bedcovers. So as she tries to answer the question, she runs into a chain of information connected to wolves—forests, other animals, snouts, nose size, and so forth—most of which must be blocked out in order to get the right answer to where Grandma's house is. The X's in the diagram show some of the areas that must be blocked.

Finally, when we learn something new, it must be stored in the correct area. If information about a car is stored where flowers and bushes are located, the chances of ever retrieving that information are remote. There is some suspicion today that a fair part of what we call "intelligence" may be the ability to store and block information properly.

Special Learning Processes

Using a flashlight in the dark, you can find an octopus easier in an aquarium than another kind of fish because it has so many tentacles sticking out. If you find one of the tentacles, it is easy to locate the octopus's body. The same is true when trying to locate something we have learned. The more elaborate we make it, the greater the chance that one of the side branches will be spotted by a brain search and that we can then get to the main memory.

So, now the question is, do you remember item number 1 at the beginning of the chapter, about William Jennings Bryan and about Prohibition? No? There is a reason for this. First, you didn't give it your full attention because it wasn't that interesting. Second, it was too factual, meaning it had few associations, or branches, and no emotional color to help you hook onto the basics. Go back and read it again, then read this version:

In 1925, lawyer William Jennings Bryan prosecuted a young high school teacher who wanted to give students information about evolution. The trial took on the atmosphere of a circus; it became a free-for-all with shouting by "liberated" (for that time) college students and young reporters who reflected the antireligious feeling that was then erupting all over the country. The teacher was found guilty, so Bryan won the case, but he was mocked so much during the trial that some people believe that this led to his death five days later.

In January 1920, a group of women, tired of having drunken, abusive husbands arrive home only after they had spent all of the family money at the local bars, organized the Anti-Saloon League to abolish alcohol. They rejoiced over the passage of the Eighteenth Amendment, which made the sale or possession of liquor illegal nationwide. Fourteen years later, it became clear that mobsters were reaping enormous profits from the sale of illegal alcohol and were using those profits in other crimes. Violations of the Eighteenth Amendment were rampant among

the items listed on the master, to the other member of the pair.

Half the blindfolded subjects will touch the items listed. The other blindfolded subjects will touch *and* taste the items. Randomly assign which half will follow which procedure. Explain that the items are common but that they have been assigned different names. The partners who are not blindfolded are simply your experimenters. Their directions are listed on the master. Be sure that the pairs are separated from each other during the collecting of data so subjects can't overhear one another. You may need to send some pairs just outside the room. The "taste-and-touch" subjects will theoretically use a greater number of associations to store the material than the "touch" group, so they should have greater recall. Tally and discuss your results.

---

all classes of people until Congress eventually gave in and passed the Twenty-First Amendment, which repealed the prohibition of alcohol.

The Elaboration Process   This revised passage should help you understand the process psychologists call **elaboration.** Elaboration is an effective method for storing learned material by using a maximum number of associations—as long as the associations make sense (Klatzky, 1984). Especially useful are colorful associations that grab your attention—such as the circus and the Anti-Saloon League women in the example just given—and help tie all the information together. The moral is that if you have to read something dull, try associating it with something important in your life. Parts that are especially difficult to remember can be treated with the device for learning isolated facts that we will talk about in the next paragraph, but here's an example of it: the Twenty-First Amendment is for those *21 or older* and not *for teens* (passed *fourteen* years after Prohibition started).

Mnemonic Devices   Elaboration is somewhat similar to a method called **mnemonic** (nee-MON-ick) **devices,** named after the Greek goddess of memory, Mnemosyne. She held an important position because memory was vital in those days before books or photocopy machines existed. Even when a type of paper was developed in 3000 B.C., everything was written on long scrolls that had no pages, and if they were unrolled a few times, the words on them would disappear. It is hard to imagine, but early English common law (part of the basis of our present legal system) was normally guided by memory, too, rather than by written record (Boorstin, 1983).

Mnemonic devices are unusual associations made to material in order to aid memory. They are not logical, but they can help you remember information. They can replace unthinking, rote memorization, which is the most difficult learning process because it lacks associations with material you already know. If you can already make sense of whatever you are trying to remember, don't use mnemonic devices. In this regard, it is interesting to take note of a special use for mnemonics. Students who are slightly mentally retarded usually have trouble organizing material, making elaborations and meaningful associations. When mnemonics are used more extensively in teaching them, they both learn better and remember better (Scruggs & Mastropieri, 1992).

Sometimes, mnemonics are helpful to all of us. For example, say you are at a party with mostly unfamiliar people. In the midst of them, you meet someone you like and want to remember, Harriet. Making a weird association with her name will keep you from forgetting it. If you are lucky, there will be something unusual about her hair (very long, bright green, shaved head, etc.). You keep saying to

Chapter 8 Acquiring, Processing, and Retaining Information

elaboration

The process of attaching a maximum number of associations to a basic concept or other material to be learned so that it can be retrieved more easily.

mnemonic devices

Unusual associations made to material to aid memory.

Points to Stress

Poets and fiction writers are masters at elaboration. When they create metaphors, in particular, they are making use of vivid, memorable associations.

Discussion

Discuss the value of mnemonics. To prompt discussion, have students make a list describing how they use mnemonic devices: to remember names of new faces; to remember information for tests; to remember routine tasks: blue key for this door, red key for that door.

DISCOVERY

Give students a chance to *elaborate*. Tell half the class to complete this sentence: "Last summer my family vacation was _____." The other half completes: "Going on a summer vacation with my family is like _____." The second statement usually elicits more vivid, metaphorical images; if it does not, encourage students to be creative. Then read everyone's name and answer. Distract the class for a minute, then have students write down everyone's name and how each person filled in the blank. The more vivid answers (usually from the second statement) are typically more memorable because of their rich associative qualities.

Elaboration.

 Give students a chance to work on this, and they should arrive at some creative answers. Clarify that any mnemonic device will be acceptable. For example, *Joe is from out of state. His memory improves when he goes back home. Conclusion: Material in one (chemical) state is best remembered in the same state.*

Comprehension Check

What are the limitations of mnemonic devices? *(If used excessively or if images are too bizarre, you won't remember the association; they won't work unless you use them from the beginning with whatever you are trying to remember; it becomes harder to use them the older you get.)*

Points to Stress

Students can probably think of some famous phrases learned through mnemonics, like ROY G. BIV (the colors of the spectrum).

226

 **Elaboration**

New material to be learned:	Associate this new material with "old" material:	The new material is effectively stored:
Rapid eye movement (REM) is associated with vivid dreaming.	New = REM Old = DREAM The new term, REM, is made up of nearly the same letters as DREAM, a word that's very familiar.	REM = DREAM
The cerebellum controls balance and coordination.	Associate the word CEREBELLUM with something else that represents balance or a lack of balance. Actually draw this in your notes:	An acrobat has excellent balance. An acrobat has a well-developed cerebellum.

How would you use elaboration to remember the definition of state-dependent learning (which can be found at the beginning of the chapter)?

yourself "Hairy-et"; you have formed a mnemonic device. Here's another great use of mnemonics. Most of us, at one time or another, are asked to give someone the license number of our car. Unless you have a special license plate, you probably have trouble remembering the number. Mnemonics solve this problem. For example, PWC-303 becomes "Put on a Warm Coat, or you'll FREEZE-OH-FREEZE." No,

EXPERIMENT

This is a simple activity to demonstrate the power of mnemonic devices. Send one student out of the room. Teach another student the mnemonic device described below. Then give both of them identical grocery lists to study for a minute or two. Distract them for 30 seconds. See who has better recall of the items.

One of the easiest mnemonic devices to learn is the method of loci (loci refers to location). This is a process in which the learner mentally places items to be remembered in a familiar location. For example, you can picture two items in each room of your house: milk and potatoes in the bedroom, catsup and oranges in the basement, and so on. The key is to *fill* the rooms: milk is drenching the carpet; potatoes are spilling out of the closet.

Chapter 8 ACQUIRING, PROCESSING, AND RETAINING INFORMATION

it doesn't make much sense, but it *is* hard to forget. (One of your authors still has several old, expired license-plate numbers rattling around in her head, taking up space.)

There are serious limitations to this system if used excessively or with images that are too bizarre, because then you won't remember the associations, much less the original information. Still, it is a useful technique for certain important things that you just keep forgetting. We hope you can see that mnemonics come down to little more than a type of elaboration in which you use the unusual to try to call attention to something later on during a mental search.

We should warn you about a couple of things before we leave this topic. First, mnemonics will *not* work unless you use them from the beginning with whatever you are trying to remember. Attempting to

Common Mnemonic Devices.

 Answers will vary. Do your "better" students make better use of mnemonics?

Evaluation Strategy

Have students write down how they plan to remember any five concepts in this chapter. They should explain what the concepts mean. Collect this paper. The next day, have them write down the meaning of the concepts they chose the previous day—all from memory. After all, this *is* a memory chapter.

IN FOCUS   Common Mnemonic Devices

Material to be learned:	Mnemonic device:	How information is stored:
Grocery list: milk, eggs, celery, and so on	**Method of Locations** Imagine a familiar location (like your house) and place the items to be remembered in various areas of that location. It's usually effective to enlarge the items in a bizarre way.	The sink is filled with milk that overflows onto the floor. Giant eggs roll along the table-top. On the chairs, sitting at attention, are giant celery stalks; they prevent the eggs from falling.
Voluntary = Operant conditioning Involuntary = Classical conditioning	**Acronym** Take the first letter of each item on a list and make a word.	**VOICE** V = voluntary O = operant I = involuntary C = classical "E" is thrown in to make a word.
A part of the brain: the cerebellum, which controls balance	**Narrative chaining** Tie together the material to be learned into a story.	He hit me in the cerebellum with a brick, and I was thrown off balance . . . .

As you can see, some of these methods overlap one another. With practice, we all develop our own personal mnemonic devices.

What mnemonic devices or "tricks" do you use while studying?

DISCOVERY

Have students bring in a notebook from another class. They should select from it a concept that they need to remember—something that will not be too easily recalled. Then have them study the concept in class using principle learning. Searching for the principle behind a concept may require more time than cramming, but the material to be learned is stored efficiently and recall is usually high—even weeks or months later. You might want to have students work in pairs so they can help each other.

Connections

Here's another example of principle learning. It's fairly common to remember a dream after sleeping late. It's not so common to remember a dream after a short nap early in the day. Principle: We don't dream as much early (in sleep) as we do late (in sleep). This may help us remember that we don't experience much REM *early* in sleep, but that we do *later* (Chapter 6).

Teaching Hint

One more example of principle learning: If you had to hand in blue attendance slips in the morning and pink in the afternoon, this might be hard to remember. But if you create a principle, it becomes elementary: Blue starts with b; pink starts with p. Alphabetically, b precedes p.

Principle Learning.

 Answers will vary. You might use this as a cooperative learning task.

principle learning

A method of learning in which an overall view (principle) of the material to be learned is developed so that the material is better organized.

attach them later won't help you remember. Second, you should start using them while you're still young. Old people aren't very good at this, even with practice. So, keep your imagination active (Baltes & Kliegl, 1992; Rust & Black, 1972).

Principle Learning   A very useful learning technique is called **principle learning**, which means you focus on the basic idea behind what is to be learned. See if you can't still recite the basic principle behind dog defense that you read about at the beginning of the chapter (item number 3). You should be able to; if not, one more reading and you won't forget it, because the method of defense is based on a principle of physics: pressure exerted at one point and at a counterpoint will snap something.

Another brief example: When learning a segment of history, tie it to a principle, and you can more easily make sense out of what the characters are doing. If you are studying the westward expansion of settlement in the United States, you can use a mental map as your principle. Then you will know that most of the pioneers wound up to the left of the map, most of the urban people were to the far right, the gold rush was to the left, and so forth. While this is a rather primitive example, it should demonstrate the basics of forming some kind of principle to guide learning.

 **Principle Learning**

New material to be learned:

Infants sleep 12–22 hours a day and spend 20 percent of that time in REM.

Children sleep 10–12 hours a day and spend 15 percent of that time in REM.

Young adults sleep 8–10 hours a day and spend 10–15 percent of that time in REM.

Old people sleep 6–8 hours a day and spend about 5 percent of that time in REM.

Tie the new material to the general principle:

The older you get, the less sleep you need and the less time you spend in REM.

Which mnemonic device will you use to remember what principle learning means? Explain.

228

DISCOVERY

Have the class make a list of common abbreviations that make use of chunking.

IN FOCUS **Chunking**

Without chunking	Number of items to be remembered	With chunking	Number of chunks to be remembered
Phone number:			
1234567	7	123-4567	2
Social security number:			
123456789	9	123-45-6789	3
Driver's license (in some states):			
A11001110111	12	A110-0111-0111	3
New zip codes:			
606060660	9	60606-0660	2

What are some other common examples of chunking?

Chunking   It is not a good idea to treat items separately if they can be united in some sensible fashion. We learn better if things are clustered together. **Chunking,** at its simplest, means putting things into "chunks," such as organizing information by "either/or" descriptions (good/bad; bright/dim; alive/dead). On a more complex level, chunking relies on putting, say, all trees together as trees, even though they don't always resemble one another that well. In other words, when we call both oaks and evergreens "trees," we are *chunking* on the basis of bark, leaves (counting a pine needle as a leaf), trunk, and so forth in order to form the concept of "tree."

How confused the world would be without chunking! Every single item would have to be learned separately. In one study, children who were blind until about 12 years of age and thus could not store information visually by chunking were extremely confused when finally able to see. For a while, their world was chaos. A rooster and a horse were confused because they both had tails. One boy who gained his sight at age 11 thought a fish was a camel because its fins looked like a hump (Delgado, 1969).

Both authors of textbooks and teachers have to have some basic organizational structure in their approach to their subject matter. This

chunking

Putting things into clusters or "chunks" so that items learned are in groups, rather than separate.

IN FOCUS   Phone numbers are sometimes chunked using letters: 1-800-TEACHES. Other examples: credit cards, account numbers, abbreviations (NOW, SCUBA, POW).

TEACHING MASTERS 8-6 & 8-7

Memory List 1 and Memory List 2. To demonstrate the value of chunking, hand out **Teaching Master 8-6 Memory List 1** to half the class; this is the "prechunked" list (no muss, no fuss). Pass out **Teaching Master 8-7 Memory List 2** to the other half; you will notice that this list is not ordered. Have each side memorize its lists. Students with the chunked list should have better recall.

DISCOVERY

You can demonstrate the concept of overlearning by making a list of popular advertising slogans or jingles. Recite these slogans to your class, but leave out a few key words, as in "____, it does a body good." (It's *milk.*) See if students can fill in the blanks. It seems that advertisers have mastered the concept of overlearning.

DISCUSS THE PHOTO

You probably have a few chess players in class who can discuss the strategies they use.

Teaching Hint

The old adage, "You don't know it until you teach it," relates well to overlearning. Describe to students the process of preparing a lesson plan and why overlearning occurs: because you're forced to think of the material in a variety of ways, because you have to think of examples for the material, because you have to make the material relevant to your audience, and so on. Part of the appeal of cooperative learning is that it often lets students become teachers for a while—which helps them overlearn the material.

230

Unit 3 COGNITIVE PROCESSES

▲ *Expert chess players chunk sets of moves to outwit their opponents.*

forgetting

An increase in errors when trying to bring material back from memory.

overlearning

The process of learning something beyond one perfect recitation so that the forgetting curve will have no effect; the development of perfect retention.

forgetting curve

Graphic representation of speed and amount of forgetting that occurs.

230

structure consists of units, or groupings within the whole subject. For example, in chemistry, first you learn basic principles about how molecules behave; later on, you learn basic principles about how water molecules interact with acid (not necessarily very well). In each subject, you can use the teacher's or author's units to form your own chunks of information that will tie together the separate facts you need to learn.

RETAINING INFORMATION

Learning material is not of much use unless we can hold onto it. In this section, we will discuss the methods and systems by which we remember and the factors that go into causing us to forget that which we have learned.

Principles of Forgetting

Forgetting does not necessarily mean losing what we have learned. Often it involves only an inability to bring back certain material. In other words, a memory may still be in the brain, but because other things interfere with it, it is hard to find. For example, if your home phone number that you have used for years is 555–2678, chances are you won't be able to retrieve easily a phone number of a recent acquaintance that is 555–2687 because the older learning will keep interfering. Viewed in this way, **forgetting** is an increase in errors while trying to bring material back (Isaacson & Pribram, 1975). But we are assuming here that there has been sufficient time to learn the material and that it has been stored. The next section shows what happens when there isn't time for enough practice.

The Forgetting Curve Forgetting occurs very rapidly. If you look at Figure 8.4, you will see what happens if we learn something only to the point of being able to recite it one time and then we don't practice it. By the end of one hour, roughly 50 percent of a poem is gone. Retention falls to 35 percent by the end of two hours, and so forth.

The only way that we can permanently store something of average interest (unlike the John Wesley Hardin poem or the phone number of a special friend) is by **overlearning.** This term sounds strange at first, but as you can see from the figure, if you just learn something to the point of one recitation, you aren't going to retain it. Hence, you have to *over*learn it, meaning that you rehearse it over and over beyond the one perfect recitation. After many rehearsals, the **forgetting curve** shown in Figure 8.4 will not apply. Such is the case with "I pledge allegiance to the ____ ____ ____" and so forth. Note that your brain keeps going on and on for a while, filling in blanks because the material has been learned so well, or overlearned.

Critical Thinking

Ask students the following question: If overlearning defies the learning curve, how can we overlearn material?" One way is to rehearse the material through drills, review sessions, tests. This approach, however, doesn't make the best use of elaboration or principle learning. A better approach would be to apply the knowledge—through papers, projects, and personal assessments.

Discussion

Discuss some of the advantages and disadvantages of taking recall (essay) and recognition (multiple-choice) tests. Recall tests allow students to explain their answers, but these tests require more preparation by students. Recognition tests are usually easier because they provide students with choices to aid memory, but they don't allow students to elaborate. What kind of tests do students prefer?

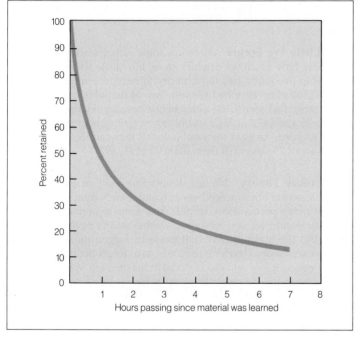

▲ *Figure 8.4 Forgetting curve. Amount retained after learning material once to the point of a perfect recitation.*

recall

The ability to bring back and integrate many specific learned details.

recognition

The ability to pick the correct object or event from a list of choices.

Recall and Recognition In tests of how much we have forgotten (or the reverse, how well we can remember), psychologists classify two types: **recall** and **recognition.** Both are tests of memory, but recognition is easier than recall. Recall requires bringing back and integrating many specific learned details—as in an essay test, for example. Recognition, on the other hand, is used in the familiar multiple-choice tests ("Which one is correct? A, B, C, or D?") in which you must *recognize* the right answer.

Here is an example of the difference between the two. You see someone a couple of times a week who wears a uniform (at a burger place, a worker at the school cafeteria, someone who pumps gas, or the like). You don't know this person as a friend, but you see him or her regularly. Then one day you are shopping, and you see this person out of uniform. You know that you remember his or her face from *somewhere,* but you can't quite get it. You are trying to *recall* who the person is, and you start a long search through all the possibilities, which can be innumerable. Eventually you might get it. If, however, you were given a *recognition* test, one of the items to choose from would be something like "Woman who works at the Taco Palace," and you would get it immediately. Why? Because a recognition test

EXPERIMENT

If you can obtain two identical, useless yearbooks (check your school library), try recreating a version of Bahrick's 1974 experiment. Have a volunteer scan about 50 photos. Then hand the volunteer a second set that includes not only the original 50 photos but 50 additional ones. Note that 90 percent of the faces were remembered in the original experiment, but the faces were of previous classmates. See activity #4 at the end of the chapter for another version of this exercise.

Evaluation Strategy

Have students prepare both a recall and a recognition quiz for a section of this chapter. You can make this a cooperative-learning activity and assign different sections to each group so that the entire chapter is covered. Discuss which quizzes are harder to prepare. Students can probably guess which are harder to grade. Consider having each group teach the material and then administer their quizzes at the end of the unit.

Points to Stress

Walk into your first class of 30 students on day one, and by the time you walk out, you can recall everyone's name. When you walk in the next day, you remember only five or six names. Why? Probably because you had three or four other classes where names interfered with your first class. Of course, the first class may interfere with later classes.

interference theory

The belief that we forget because new and old material conflict (interfere) with one another.

lists the memory storage areas for you to search; you need only to go to each storage area to see if there is a correct match.

How Little We Forget   Here are some rather startling findings that show how much we actually store, how little we really forget. Subjects in one study had the capacity to recognize roughly 90 percent of 2,560 slides they had viewed. Two of the subjects who scored in this range had seen 1,280 slides in just one day (Haber, 1970), and persons 35 years out of high school can *recognize* about 90 percent of their classmates' faces in the yearbook, but they can recall the names of only about 25 percent of them (Bahrick et al., 1974).

Interference Theory   No one doubts that many of the things we start to learn are not practiced enough and merely disappear forever without being permanently stored. And some material that we do store just decays for one reason or another and is never to be seen again. But the major theory that explains forgetting is called the **interference theory.** Interference causes us to forget because there is a conflict between new and old material in the memory system.

The theory goes this way: Bringing in new material can cause processing difficulties if we already have somewhat similar material stored. This would be the case if you are trying to learn a new telephone number. Or suppose you are trying to remember a sound, such as a musical note. You are in the process of storing tone A; the introduction of tone B shortly after A results in considerable interference, confusion, and difficulty in remembering A. The new tone, B, requires processing and will cause interference with remembering tone A, much more so than if there were a blank space of time after learning tone A (Massaro, 1970). The problem is that two memory systems for similar material operating at the same time cause confusion (Spear, 1978). Also, if new material is very much like old material, the brain has some trouble figuring out where it should go, since the two compete for the same space, so to speak, in the memory storage system. In either of these cases, the new material can fail to get stored properly or at all.

Mechanisms of Memory

People buy computers with a certain amount of storage capacity—for example, 3 million bytes of information. Since you are familiar with this, it should help you to understand how much we can store in our own memory banks. For starters, a single bacterium can store 200 *billion* bytes of information, using only thousands of nerve cells, which outdoes most computers (Benner, 1984). Compared to the very simple bacterium, humans have billions of nerve cells, each one with millions of connections, so our capacity is just about limitless. Suppose that you were to write out everything you have stored in

ENRICHMENT

Have students do research on the physical mechanisms of memory. They can focus on the brain (particularly the hippocampus), neuron traces, or chemical codes.

Most of the claims that we only use ten percent of our brains are made by people who want to sell self-improvement videos on late-night cable televi-

sion. Students should remember from Chapter 3 that the hemispheres work together. If one works harder than the other on certain tasks, it is probably for the sake of efficiency. So even if it's true that we use only 10 percent of our brains (which is nonsense), then there must be some advantage to using such a small percentage.

Some research with brain-imaging techniques, in fact, shows that the brains of highly intelligent people don't seem to work as hard as those with normal intelligence. Perhaps these intelligent people are simply more efficient.

---

your brain right this minute until the brain is empty. You would be writing a very long time, to put it mildly. If you are average, your present storage is the equivalent of 35 million pages the size of those in the book you are now reading! This is very hard to believe, but stop and think: you have stored so much that has happened to you—your first bed, your first room, the size and color of the seat on your first bicycle, the shape of the sidewalk in front of your home, and on and on (Sternberg, 1984). (You may have heard that people use only 10 percent of their "brain power." There is no evidence at all to support or disprove this claim. Someone just made it up decades ago, and it is still passed from one generation to another as a fact.)

When we remember something, it seems that we are "seeing" or "hearing" it. But that is not how the brain itself works. Memory is stored in some kind of physical chemical code, the nature of which we don't fully understand yet. We can grasp the principle but not the physical details. An analogy would be the computer code of strings of numbers such as 0-1-1-0 or 1-0-1-0, each standing for something different. Thus, a long string of 0-1-1-0-1-0 and so forth might stand for "horse." We believe today that nerve cells fire in certain sequences, just like the combinations of 0's and 1's, and in this way they reproduce any memory desired. As they fire in sequence, they produce what we call "thought" (Farley & Alkon, 1985).

The brain contains about 100 billion nerve cells that are separated one from the other but that can communicate by electrical and chemical information going from one nerve cell to the other. Each of these nerve cell junctions is called a *synapse* (SIN-naps) (also discussed in Chapter 3).

One basic theory of memory suggests that as we learn something, the physical structure of the synapses changes shape, a possibility introduced by microscopic studies of synapses after learning (Lynch & Baudry, 1984). These physical changes seem to alter which nerves will connect with which other nerves via synapses, how easily a set of synapses will fire, and what the sequence of firing will be. Thus, the memory becomes like a toy train with a series of switches turned on or off so that as you learn something, you increase the chances of the same sequence of nerve firings occurring for each memory. The more often you repeat the material, the more solid becomes the "track" over which the memory train will travel. Similar theories suggest that the chemicals used to make the connections across the synapses increase with each learning, making certain connections faster and easier (McGaugh, 1983; Squire, 1987).

A second theory centers on the idea that the synapses grow once a pattern is established. In other words, we make certain memories, and as they are stored, the synapses grow to hold them. Such growth is very obvious as a child develops. Learning, then, becomes a matter of using newly grown nerve cells in the synapses to form a map. If the memory is no longer useful, the growth slows down; later, a new

Chapter 8 ACQUIRING, PROCESSING, AND RETAINING INFORMATION

▲ *Some of the billions of nerve cells with synapses used to store information in the human brain.*

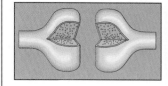

DISCUSS THE PHOTO

Flip to Chapter 3 for more close-ups of nerve cells.

Connections

You can use the term *repression* (Chapter 17) when referring to unwanted memories. Such a memory is probably stored, but you are *unwilling* to retrieve it. Compare and contrast this with depression (Chapter 18). As with repression, there is nothing wrong with your *ability* to remember when depressed; you simply don't concentrate or pay attention as well—which will affect not only memory but also the ability to learn new material.

DISCOVERY

Conduct a role-playing exercise in which one character has amnesia and the other is a therapist trying to bring the lost memories to the surface. After explaining the roles, whisper separate instructions to each volunteer. To the therapist: "The patient matches the description of a missing teen who ran away from home after a family argument. The family was trying to convince the teen to break off a relationship with someone whom they felt was a bad influence." To the teen: "You're a teenager. You feel restless, unhappy, but unsure why. You have little or no desire to find your identity. The therapist reminds you of someone close to you, possibly a parent, but you can't recall." This exercise should demonstrate that the retrieval of lost memories is like piecing together a jigsaw puzzle. Since the patient in this case does not really know his or her identity, the puzzle will never be solved. Instead, the *process* of rebuilding will be highlighted here.

Evaluation Strategy

To explain how memories may be stored, memory is compared to a toy train and to a map **(Mechanisms of Memory).** Have students draw an **In Focus** box to illustrate this, either using the above metaphors or other original images. The growth of synapses could be compared to the growth of plants. The visuals should include captions.

Connections

Mention that amnesia is categorized as a dissociative disorder (Chapter 18). When you *associate*, you join together; when you *dissociate*, you separate. In this case, you separate a memory from your *self*.

Points to Stress

The material on mechanisms of memory should clarify the complexity of memory. In other words, there is not a memory headquarters where all memories reside. Various parts of the brain contribute in different ways.

amnesia

The blocking of older memories and/or the loss of new ones.

growth starts for a new memory or for a modified memory (Rosenzweig, 1984). There is support for both this system and the one we just discussed. We don't know enough yet to bring it all together into a clear pattern.

While performing brain surgery, neurosurgeons have discovered that it is possible to touch parts of the brain with an electrically activated wire and the patient will relive, as if in a "movie" dream, a sequence from some earlier time in life, like a birthday party in childhood (Penfield, 1959). Such events certainly suggest that memories are stored in certain areas of the brain and that a whole sequence of nerve firings can occur from one stimulation.

Short- and Long-Term Memory

A common plot on television involves a man or woman who is struck on the head while witnessing a murder and forgets "everything." Fearful of exposure, the murderer follows this person around, waiting for a chance to do him or her in, not knowing that the memory of the murder is "gone."

Although this situation is exaggerated (as usual), a good solid blow to the head, a major trauma, or an electric shock can produce **amnesia,** the blocking of older memories and/or the loss of more recent ones. The term *blocked* is used because most of the material will return after a period, unless the person suffers a severe injury or the amnesia is from a disease (Graf et al., 1984). Strangely enough, the material that disappears is fairly selective. People rarely forget how to tie a shoe or brush their teeth. The most likely explanation for this is that these acts have been performed so often for so long that only massive brain damage would erase them, since they are so permanently fixed in memory. In some cases, however, once amnesia has started, people don't *want* to bring back certain memories, so they block them from returning even though physically they could be available.

Explaining Amnesia   There are two possible explanations for the phenomenon of amnesia: (1) Amnesia could result from a temporary reduction of blood supply from an injury. This will disrupt the proper nourishment of the cells and reduce their chemicals, which, in turn, will alter the firing of the nerve cells to produce a memory (Dunn, 1980; Parkin, 1987; McGaugh, 1983). (2) A blow to the head will cause major electrical changes that will disrupt the transmission across the synapses and temporarily dislodge older memory systems, meanwhile just about wiping out most newer memories that haven't been thoroughly stored (Kinsbourne & Wood, 1975).

You may hear that if a person has amnesia, another blow to the head will bring back the memories. As you can see, this is a ridiculous notion. The only possible results of another blow are further

You can show the limitation of short-term memory (STM) quickly by having someone memorize five, then seven, then nine, then 11 digits or items. Recall becomes increasingly difficult after seven items.

Journal Topic

"Write a diary entry from the point of view of someone with amnesia." Encourage students to forget every soap opera episode they have ever seen and to write from their new understanding of how amnesia really works.

Chapter 8 ACQUIRING, PROCESSING, AND RETAINING INFORMATION

DISCUSS THE PHOTO

Another amnesia victim recently appeared on a talk show and was later arrested. She didn't remember that she was wanted by the police for stealing money from her family.

▲ *This amnesia victim appeared on a talk show, hoping someone would recognize her.*

Comprehension Check

What are the two theories about mechanisms of memory? *(1) The physical structure of the synapses in the brain change when we learn something, and (2) synapses grow to hold memories.*

confusion and more disruption of the memory systems. It is truly hard to imagine how people can come up with such strange ideas.

Sequence of Memory Loss Most people with amnesia can recall events from the distant past but nothing recent. And when memory returns, it always starts with older memories and moves up to the present. This was our first clue to the fact that we have both a **short-term** and a **long-term memory** system. Thus, the memories immediately preceding an accident are gone forever because they never made it from the short-term storage system to permanent, long-term storage.

The two memory storage systems seem to be at least partially independent. In cases of injury to different parts of the brain, some people lose only short-term memory (STM), while others lose only large portions of long-term memory (LTM).

STM lasts from a few seconds to half of a minute. LTM can last from hours to days to a lifetime, depending on the amount of time a memory spends in the storage system where it becomes more and more solidified (Dunn, 1980). All incoming material goes first to the STM, where it is "processed"—that is, we make a decision about whether to keep it or not. Next, the material is either eliminated or moved to the LTM storage area where, over time, it is made permanent (Kellogg, 1980).

short-term memory

The memory system that retains information for a few seconds to a few minutes.

long-term memory

The memory system that retains information for hours, days, weeks months, decades.

ENRICHMENT

Have students find out more about "S" or about other extraordinary cases of memory ability or disability.

Connections

Subliminal messages (Chapter 4), if they are processed at all, are probably processed by the sensory memory system. The messages are flashed so faintly or so quickly that we don't make any kind of conscious decision about sending it along to STM.

Journal Topic

"Describe your earliest memory." Afterward, discuss how much of this memory *may* be based on a dream or a story heard from parents.

Journal Topic

"Describe a memory that has had a lasting effect on you."

236

Unit 3 Cognitive Processes

sensory memory system

Direct receivers of information from the environment—for example, iconic, acoustic.

iconic memory

A very brief visual memory that can be sent to the STM.

acoustic memory

A very brief sound memory that can be sent to the STM.

236

Under normal circumstances, the STM will hold only seven (on occasion up to nine) items before the material has to be moved on to the LTM (Miller, 1956). The only reason we can learn anything is because this memory system doesn't care how *long* each of the seven items is. This means we can group, or chunk, items together. Here are 13 items to learn: moon, cow, the, jumped, ate, over, the, hamburger, lunch, at, in, barn, the. The STM can't hold these 13 items. How do we do it? We chunk. The cow//jumped over moon//ate the hamburger at lunch//in the barn (Tulving & Partay, 1962). We now have only four items, which are easily put into STM.

In a very unusual case, a man called "S" had a defect of the STM system such that it *didn't* eliminate or block out any incoming material. His life became a private hell because he could not forget *any-thing* that arrived. When people talked, he could blank out nothing. Images came in, collided with one another, got mixed up, and triggered endless confusion. At times he felt that the word images were covered with smoke and fog. The more people talked, the less sense he could make of anything (Luria, 1968; Bruner, 1968).

We left out a slight technicality so you could understand the STM and LTM systems without any confusion. There *is* one additional system that comes just before STM, called the **sensory memory system,** which refers to direct receivers of information from the environment. The first set of receivers is called **iconic** (eye-KON-ick) **memory.** The word *icon* means "image"; so we see and hold an image in front of us. The iconic system is probably just an electrical trace left over from firing the visual network, because it lasts only a few seconds. During that time, we make a decision about whether to send the image to the STM or eliminate it (Cowan, 1984). A quite similar system is the **acoustic** (ah-KOO-stik; sound) **memory** in which we can hold words for a few seconds while again we decide if we want to move them to STM or forget them (see Figure 8.5).

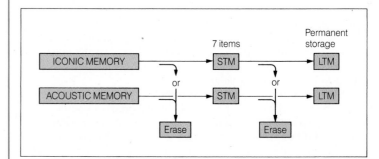

▲ *Figure 8.5 Diagram of the memory system.*

INTERDISCIPLINARY PROJECT

Law. Our court system gives great weight to eyewitness testimony in the determination of guilt or innocence. Have students find out about the reliability of eyewitness memory. Can the actual phrasing of a question alter one's memory? Do witnesses tend to "reconstruct" their memory, adding details based on assumptions rather than memory? Why aren't memories that are elicited through hypnosis admissible as testimony in most courts? If you want to focus on a single case of eyewitness memory, consider exploring the Kennedy assassination.

Unusual Types of Memory

You have no doubt heard stories of startling feats of memory. Usually these are tricks. When they are not, they may be caused by a defect in the memory system, such as occurred with the man called S.

Photographic Memory   One commonly claimed feat is photographic memory, called **eidetic** (eye-DET-ick) **imagery.** Supposedly people can look at a picture of something like a chain, and then when the picture is taken away, they can count the links in front of them even though the picture is gone. Some people *do* have longer iconic memories than others, possibly lasting a minute or so, and these are usually children (Furst, 1979). But in all of the psychological literature, only one or two people might have had eidetic imagery. So, for all practical purposes, it doesn't exist. Try it out for yourself on Figure 8.6.

Eyewitness Memory   Memory is vitally important in eyewitness testimony, but unfortunately it is often wrong. For example, descriptions frequently fit a stereotypical image of a "bad guy" rather than the actual criminal. Further, under extreme stress, perception can be

eidetic imagery

An iconic memory lasting a minute or so that keeps images "in front of the person" so objects can be counted or analyzed; also called "photographic memory."

FYI   Another unusual type of memory is sometimes called a flashbulb memory. When an event is extraordinary or devastating, the memory remains especially vivid, which may be somehow related to the adrenaline released during these events. For example, many people still remember exactly what they were doing when they heard about the assassination of John Fitzgerald Kennedy.

DISCUSS THE PHOTO

Try this same exercise with photographs from magazines.

▲ *Figure 8.6 Study this picture for 30 seconds, then look at a blank wall and try to reproduce it in as much detail as possible.*

If you really have the gift of eidetic imagery, you should even be able to tell how many trees there are.

EXPERIMENT

Find someone in your school whose face would not be readily recognized. Have this person charge into class, accusing you of hitting his or her car. To make the confrontation more realistic, have the "assailant" knock on your classroom door and call you outside. Argue for a while outside, out of view from students but not out of earshot. Then walk in, pretending to look for something in your desk. The assailant, after waiting outside for a while, can storm in and verbally attack you. Make sure the assailant doesn't stay in the room too long. See **Teaching Master 8-8 The** **Assailant 1** and **Teaching Master 8-9 The Assailant 2** for data sheets on this experiment.

This activity requires a good deal of effort on your part, but the results are worthwhile. As discussed in the chapter, people learn more efficiently when they are mildly aroused and

DISCUSS THE PHOTO

Most of us think what we see with our own eyes is the truth. Research has found, however, that a person's confidence in his or her eyewitness testimony is not positively correlated with its accuracy.

Comprehension Check

Which memory is at work for each of the following situations: A car speeds by and you glance at the license plate, but you do not process it. *(iconic)* You remember a license plate, but only for a minute. *(STM)* You remember a license plate you had several years ago. *(LTM)*

Reteaching Strategy

Have students complete the **Reteaching Worksheet** for this chapter located in the Teacher Resources.

The **Vocabulary Worksheet** may be completed by the class as a pretest for chapter concepts or used as a reteaching worksheet for those students needing additional review.

238

Unit 3 COGNITIVE PROCESSES

▲ *Eyewitness identification is usually quite inaccurate.*

faulty, and witnesses often either speculate or use their LTM banks to fill in details that never existed (Poole & White, 1991; Kassin, Ellsworth & Smith, 1989; Loftus, 1984).

Eyewitness testimony is so bad because our brains are never content to let incoming information stand on its own. We process it, reprocess it, and keep working on it so that it makes *complete* sense in terms of everything we know, even though the facts in real life—that is, what we saw—seldom fit together completely. Consequently, so-called eyewitness testimony often includes information obtained after the fact, rather than being limited to what the person actually saw and remembers (Kassin et al., 1989; Wells, 1984).

During class one day, a teacher staged a fake assault on himself. Later, during the "lineup," over 60 percent of the student eyewitnesses were wrong in their choice of who did it (Buckhout et al., 1972). In another (real) case, 17 eyewitnesses identified a man as the one who shot a police officer, but clear evidence later emerged that the man was not even near the scene at the time of the crime (McCloskey & Zaragoza, 1985).

Just to show you how easily memory can change, here is part of a laboratory study on eyewitness identification: in an accident case in which there was *no* broken headlight at all, two sets of witnesses were asked a slightly different question by the experimenter:

First group of witnesses: "Did you see *a* broken headlight?"
Second group of witnesses: "Did you see *the* broken headlight?"

ENRICHMENT

when they pay attention. This is a good opportunity to put these concepts into practice. Also, it will bring to life the material on eyewitness memory. If you *do* conduct this activity, warn students in your first class not to say anything about the activity to your other classes. And conduct this activity before students read

about eyewitness memory. Instead of having someone charge in, you may want to videotape a confrontation so you can use it again at any time.

Have students complete the **Enrichment Worksheet** for this chapter located in the Teacher Resources.

Chapter 8 ACQUIRING, PROCESSING, AND RETAINING INFORMATION

The experimenter found that the use of the word *a* leaves the issue of whether or not there was a broken headlight in doubt. Only 7 percent answered "yes." On the other hand, when the word *a* was changed to *the,* the witnesses assumed the presence of a broken headlight. The second group doubled the agreement based on just this one word change; 15 percent said they had seen one. Note how easily we are swayed by suggestion. So, the precise wording of questions is extremely important (Kassin et al., 1989).

Hypnosis doesn't make eyewitness accounts more accurate because under hypnosis, people are more suggestible than at almost any other time. Hence, the accuracy of identification can be even worse, depending on how the questions are formed (Laurence, 1983).

Identifying Faces and Seeing Through Disguises Much of what we have been talking about in this chapter, if applied to identifying faces seen during a crisis, suggests that people would be very inaccurate in doing so. And this turns out to be the case. For example, there is very little opportunity for elaboration (developing associations) during the brief time of watching a crime being committed. Without time to make associations, an eyewitness has little chance of picking the right person later. In addition, identification across racial lines is especially poor, particularly when white people are doing the identifying (Kassin et al., 1989).

Even after being warned in an experiment, subjects have problems remembering faces. One researcher gave subjects pictures of peoples' faces and told them that they were later going to identify one of these pictures as part of a second set. They were given a long time to analyze the first set. Later, one of the faces was put with a second set of pictures to see if it could be located. Most of the people failed the task, and there was none of the pressure in this experiment that would be involved in a real-life crisis (Harmon, 1973).

Our perception of others is quite faulty. This is clearly demonstrated by the effect of using disguises. If a person changes his or her hairstyle or, for men, adds a beard, accurate identification drops 25 percent. With both a new hairstyle and a beard, or with a change of hair color for a woman, it drops 52 percent; and if the person to be identified doesn't look straight at another but keeps a profile, accuracy of identification falls a full 61 percent (Patterson & Baddeley, 1977).

TEACHING MASTERS 8-8 & 8-9

The Assailant 1 and The Assailant 2. Use these masters in conjunction with the preceding experiment. Pass out **Teaching Master 8-8** to half the class and **Teaching Master 8-9** to the other half. Both sheets include leading questions. On **Teaching Master 8-8,** questions 3 and 8 are leading; on **Teaching Master 8-9,** questions 2 and 7 are leading. Point out that the use of the word *assailant* on both sheets may be leading.

ENRICHMENT

Have students find out about drugs that promote and block consolidation.

PSYCHOLOGY IN YOUR LIFE

Teaching Hint
Compare consolidation to gelatin. When information, such as a new phone number, is presented, the memory is unformed. It takes a while for it to "set."

Points to Stress
One of the reasons why sleep is a good consolidator is that sleep eliminates most chances for interference.

FYI Here are a few terms you may want to introduce that relate to interference. *Serial position effect:* we remember the first and last items on a list, but tend to forget the middle ones. *Retroactive interference:* new learning interferes with old learning. *Proactive interference:* old learning interferes with new learning.

PSYCHOLOGY IN YOUR LIFE

Testing Your Memory

An established principle of learning and memory is called *consolidation.* Consolidation is a process by which over time a memory will solidify until it becomes permanent. The term itself refers to the fact that the memory is brought together (consolidated) into a clear and organized whole. Here's a chance for you to test this out. You will need a partner to do so.

The first experiment involves short-term memory, which allows for no consolidation. Take the "Yellow Pages" and put it on a table about 25 feet from the telephone. Have your partner stand by the phone book. Find a number at random and circle it. Read it once. Now, try to get to the phone to dial it. All the time you are on your way, your partner is to shout random numbers out loud to you (5, 29, 3, 12, 8, whatever). You don't stand a chance of making it to the phone with the circled phone number intact in your brain, because each new number that your friend is calling out is fighting for a position among the magic quantity of

seven items that can be stored in the STM. One "old" number is knocked out as a new one comes in. You can even try talking or humming to yourself as you run to the phone, but even that won't work because now the STM is trying to store the words you are making or the humming sound (and you are still picking up some numbers from your shouting partner).

The second experiment centers on partial consolidation. This time put a pad and pencil next to the phone so, instead of dialing, you can write down what you would have dialed. That way you can see what we're talking about. First, remember that sleep is an excellent consolidator. All night the brain will be working on material you give it. The night before this experiment, pick a number from the phone book and write it down. As you sit on the side of the bed before going to sleep, rehearse it two or three times. Wait five minutes. Rehearse it again a few times. Then turn the piece of paper over so you can't see the number, and go to sleep. Next day: don't look

at that piece of paper next to your bed! When your partner arrives, do the same thing as before: Look at the piece of paper and review the number twice. Then head for the phone while your partner is shouting numbers. Write what you would have dialed on another pad. The odds are overwhelming that you will have most of the correct numbers, perhaps not yet in their exact sequence, but it will be obvious that they have been at least partially stored.

For the third part of the experiment, your partner—at random—picks a number you know very well and says it to you ("Amy's number"). You head for the phone as your partner keeps shouting numbers. This time you will be frustrated because you have to keep fighting STM storage as you bring back LTM (Amy's number), but you'll be able to do it because the number is permanently stored; it has been *consolidated.*

The final experiment involves being an "eyewit-

(continued on next page)

EXPERIMENT

Assign the eyewitness/photo experiment at the end of **Testing Your Memory** and discuss the results. It's a good experiment, but students won't do it, of course, unless it is as assigned.

VOCABULARY REVIEW

Before testing students on the contents of the chapter, you may want to review vocabulary terms that are especially important or confusing. Terms in this chapter that could require clarification are *information processing, schema, short-term memory, long-term memory*, and *sensory memory system*.

Connections

One of the theories of dreaming (Chapter 6) is that we dream to forget. REM may be a way of getting rid of redundant memories and consolidating others.

Wrapping It Up

Throughout the text and wraparound, references are made to study habits. This time let students offer the advice. What tricks or steps help them memorize material for tests? Answers are often creative, and when advice comes from classmates, it may sound less preachy than usual.

Another thought to leave students with is that improving memory is not magic. It's possible through work: pay attention, concentrate, and sleep. Since all of the brain contributes to memory, take good care of it. Alcohol use in particular can damage memory, especially over the long term.

PSYCHOLOGY IN YOUR LIFE

Testing Your Memory

(continued from previous page) ness." Somewhere in your home is a box of family photos. At least one photo you know very well, but you haven't seen it for a month or so. Tell your partner which one it is, and he or she can get it for you. Don't look at it. Next write out everything you think is going on in the photo—who is where, what they are wearing, and so forth. When you are done, compare what you have written down with the real photo, and note how many details you have added that are not in the actual photo— usually things that you wish were there or that you think would logically be there.

SUMMARY

1. Learning takes place most rapidly with a high level of emotion and attention.
2. In positive transfer, material already learned is moved to a new task that is similar. Negative transfer causes interference when you are learning two tasks that are similar but that have some significant differences.
3. A schema is an organized pattern for analyzing information in the memory storage areas.
4. Memory is greatly aided by elaboration.
5. When material to be remembered is not easily organized, mnemonic devices can aid in retention. If items can be put together under a general principle, retention is greatly increased.
6. Recognition is easier than recall because it involves matching memories rather than a detailed search for one. Recognition demonstrates just how much we actually are able to retain.
7. Memory is the result of learning that has altered the chemistry and/or structure of the nerve cell endings, called synapses. Memory is divided into three parts: the very brief sensory memory system, the slightly longer short-term memory, and finally the long-term memory.
8. Photographic memory seems to exist in only a few people, and it is probably the result of an ability to hold images iconically longer than normal.
9. Eyewitness memory is quite defective because it is based on what people think and want rather than on what they actually observe.

SUGGESTED READINGS

▼ Keyes, Daniel. *Flowers for Algernon.* New York: Bantam Books, 1968.

▼ Loftus, Elizabeth and Katherine Ketcham. *Witness for the Defense.* New York: St. Martin's Press, 1991.

▼ Neisser, U. *Memory Observed: Remembering in Natural Contexts.* New York: W. H. Freeman, 1982.

SUGGESTED VIDEOS

▼ *Memory.* 30 min. 1980. CRM/McGraw-Hill.

▼ *Memory: Fabric of the Mind.* 28 min. 1988. Films for the Humanities.

VOCABULARY

attention
learning curve
state-dependent
    learning
transfer of training
positive transfer
negative transfer
information
    processing
schema

elaboration
mnemonic devices
principle learning
chunking
forgetting
overlearning
forgetting curve
recall
recognition

interference theory
amnesia
short-term memory
long-term memory
sensory memory
    system
iconic memory
acoustic memory
eidetic imagery

Review Questions

Answers to Review Questions

1. positive
2. negative
3. state-dependent learning
4. schema
5. information processing
6. elaboration
7. principle learning

Fill in the blanks; answer on a separate sheet of paper. (An answer may consist of more than one word.)

1. Tracy knows Italian, so learning Spanish is easy for her. This is called __?__ transfer.
2. Stacy knows Italian, so learning Spanish is difficult because she confuses the two. This is called __?__ transfer.
3. A basketball player learns something at practice while sweating, forgets it at home, then remembers it again the next day at practice. This kind of learning is called __?__.
4. The mental outline we use to solve problems is called a __?__.
5. Taking in, storing, and bringing back the things we learn is called __?__.
6. __?__ is the process of associating new material in some way with something important in your life.
7. Focusing on the basic idea behind a concept is called __?__.

▼ *Remembering and Forgetting.*
Discovering Psychology series,
part 9. 27 min. 1-800-LEARNER.

True/False

8. Mnemonic devices often make use of weird images.
9. Chunking leads to negative transfer and should usually be avoided.
10. If we forget something from long-term memory, this usually means it is gone from the brain.

11. Overlearning will help to prevent forgetting.
12. The interference theory suggests that interference of ideas causes us to forget.

For each of the following, answer recall *or* recognition *or* both.

13. Essay tests
14. Matching tests

15. Fill-in-the-blank tests
16. True/false tests

Matching (Answers can be used more than once.)

17. Holds sounds for only a few seconds
18. Usually lasts for up to half of a minute
19. Visual sensory trace that lasts a few seconds
20. Photographic memory
21. Permanent memories stored here
22. Holds about seven to nine items

a. iconic memory
b. short-term memory
c. long-term memory
d. acoustic memory
e. eidetic imagery

DISCUSSION QUESTIONS

1. Describe the kind of anxiety you experience before a big test. For example, what kinds of physical reactions do you have? What thoughts race through your head? Does this anxiety generally block or help learning? Explain.
2. The chapter explains that emotional involvement will usually increase learning. Describe a teacher you have now or have had in the past who "creates emotion" in

class. What does the teacher do to "create" the emotion, and what is the effect? Explain.
3. In a few sentences, describe a time when you've experienced positive transfer and a time when you've experienced negative transfer.
4. Which schema would you guess would be more elaborate: (a) deciding to buy and actually buying a pair of shoes or (b) deciding to go to a party? Explain.

8. true
9. false
10. false
11. true
12. true
13. recall
14. recognition
15. recall
16. both
17. d
18. b
19. a
20. e
21. c
22. b

Notes on Discussion Questions

1. Answers will vary.
2. You might want to suggest that students not use any names.
3. Answers will vary. You might ask if certain subjects in school tend to promote one kind of transfer or another.

4. List on the board the possible steps involved in both situations. You'll probably find that deciding to go to a party will include more steps, since it involves an emotional element.

5. Consider discussing this one in class. Focus not so much on what kinds of tests students prefer but on what kinds of tests more accurately and thoroughly measure what they know. If students agree that recall tests more accurately measure knowledge, ask if a lengthy recognition test (100 to 200 questions) would compensate for the superiority of recall tests.

6. S would probably do well in occupations where incoming information needs to be processed and organized by the employee at a rapid rate: a worker at the stock exchange; a telephone operator; a secretary in the school's attendance office who must listen to 700 excuses every day. Even in these occupations, S would still have problems separating the

incoming information and deciding which bits of information are more important than others. If he could simply receive the incoming information and relay it to people who could discern the importance of the information, his skills might be valuable (although this is still unlikely considering the efficiency of computers).

7. This person may read a magazine, put it down, pick up the same magazine seconds later and start to read it without any recollection of having read it moments before.

8. You might want quick consolidation during important events that you want to remember later: your marriage vows, your child's first words, and so on. You may want to block consolidation during events that you

---

5. Teachers often use both recall and recognition in their tests. In your opinion, which method more accurately measures how much you actually know? (Be honest.) Explain.

6. The chapter explains that patient S's life became a private hell. This may be true, but S's ability might serve him well in certain occupations. Which ones? Explain. What problems would he have even in the occupations that you have listed? Explain.

7. Imagine someone having the opposite problem of S's—that is, he or she *does* eliminate *all* incoming information. Describe a typical experience this person might have.

8. Research has actually been done to find out which drugs will promote quick, solid consolidation and which drugs will tend to block consolidation. If these drugs were proved to be safe, what practical applications would each of these drugs have? In other words, when would you want quick consolidation, and when would you want to block consolidation? Explain.

ACTIVITIES

1. Take a close look at the chart of a schema in Figure 8.3. Using this chart as a model, design your own schema. First, pick a possible question or problem that needs to be solved. For example, "Should I quit my job?" or "Should I date ___?___ ?" Second, jot down a rough draft of your schema. Be creative. Perhaps brainstorm with a friend or two. Third, decide on a final version of the schema and transfer it onto a poster. Use arrows, different colors, and boxes to clarify and highlight the entire process. Also include a key that will explain what your arrows and other symbols mean.

2. The chapter explains that we form organized "maps" of the world; furthermore, objects that don't "fit" on this map are more difficult to remember. Test whether this is true. Take a photograph of your kitchen. Include in this photograph common kitchen objects. Take another photograph of your kitchen. This time include objects that don't belong in a kitchen. Be subtle: for example, put a

toothbrush on the table. Now repeat this procedure for your living room.

With these four photographs, test six subjects, repeating the following procedure for each subject: (1) Present photo number 1; allow the subject 30 seconds to memorize it. (2) Have the subject start at 50 and count down aloud to zero by fours (50, 46, 42, and so on). (3) Allow the subject as much time as necessary to write down as much information as he or she can remember from the photograph. (4) Repeat these three steps for the other photos.

Analyze your results. Which objects were best remembered? Least remembered? Which photo(s) elicited the most mistakes? Are there any other conclusions that you can draw? Explain.

3. Test the effectiveness of mnemonic devices on ten subjects. Write up a typical 20-item grocery list and *slowly* read each item aloud to each subject, explaining first that he or she will have to memorize the list. Once you

want to forget later: surgery, the breakup of a relationship, and so on. You can probably think of interesting dilemmas that would result from the availability of such consolidation drugs. For example, would a woman want efficient consolidation during the birth of her child? It may be a glorious event, but does she want to remember *everything*?

Notes on Activities

1. Stress that you're not looking for correct schemas. Schema diagrams should demonstrate thought and creativity. Perhaps you can brainstorm and draw a sample schema on the board.

2. Have students hand in their four photographs so you can better understand their reports.

3. This is a simple activity to conduct in class. The students who do not use the mnemonic device should wait outside while you explain the device to the "mnemonic subjects." A week later, surprise both groups of subjects by having them write down as many items on the list as they can remember.

4. The directions for this activity should be self-explanatory. Just insist that the yearbook be old in order to eliminate the chance of subjects recognizing the faces. Have students show their work by requiring them to hand in the photographs.

5. See activity #4. If you require students to conduct more than one activity, you should probably not allow them to do both numbers 4 and 5. Students might conduct only one of them and then try to get credit for both.

6. As with activity #2, collect the photographs used so you can decipher students' reports. Assure them that you will return the photographs without coffee stains on them.

finish, have each subject start at 50 and count down aloud to zero by fours (50, 46, 42, and so on). Then have each subject write down as many grocery items as possible without any time limit.

For half the subjects, teach them beforehand to use the following mnemonic device: Have them picture a room in their house. As each item is read, have the subject picture the item in some location in the room. In addition, have the person enlarge the item in a weird manner. For example, for "Milk," have the subject picture milk overflowing in the kitchen sink.

For the other half of the subjects, simply tell them to memorize the words.

Compare your results. Were the "mnemonic subjects" able to learn and use the mnemonic technique easily and effectively? (Ask them.) Why or why not? What conclusions can you draw in general? Explain. (An interesting side note: if the subjects using the mnemonic device did so effectively, they will often remember the list even a week or two later!)

4. The chapter points out that eyewitness testimony is not always reliable. See how well your friends do at picking out faces. Find an *old*, useless yearbook. Cut out 60 pictures (all males or all females) and put them into two equal piles. Have a friend study pile A for five minutes. Then, before giving him or her pile B, slip a picture from pile A into pile B. Tell your friend that he or she needs to identify the picture that you slipped in. Repeat this entire procedure on seven other friends.

How well did they do? If they did well, ask them what cues they used to help them. If they didn't do well, ask them what interfered with their remembering the face. Explain their answers and any conclusions you can draw from the experiment.

5. Read activity number 4 and follow the same instructions, but in this case, try the experiment on four male subjects and four female subjects.

Which group did better at remembering the faces? You were allowed to use all male photographs *or* all female photographs: do you think that this had any effect on your results? Explain. If you were to use 2,000 subjects instead of just eight, do you think you would get the same results? Why or why not?

6. Conduct the last experiment described in the "Psychology in Your Life" feature at the end of the chapter. In this case, *you* become the experimenter and use two or three family members as subjects. Find an *old* photograph and briefly describe the photo to your "subject" just so he or she knows which one it is. Have the subject write down everything he or she can remember about the photo. During this time, ask a few leading questions, like "What color is my sweater in the picture?" or "What time is it on the clock?" Be as subtle as possible. In actuality, there will be no sweater or clock in the photo. You're simply testing whether they will fill in details or reconstruct the scene according to what they think *should* be there. Repeat this entire procedure for five other old photos.

How influential were the leading questions? Explain. Did subjects fill in other details that weren't there even before you started asking the questions? Explain your results.

DISCUSS THE PHOTO

What types of factors stifle creativity?

Creativity is often apparent at an early age.

246

PACING CHART

Complete Coverage

Day 1: Assign "Understanding Intelligence" prior to class. Stress the differences between the Stanford-Binet and Wechsler Intelligence Tests, using the appropriate In Focus boxes as visual aids. Have students read Psychology In Your Life for Day 2.

Day 2: Concentrate on the uses and limitations of IQ test scores. In particular, emphasize the socio-cultural aspects involved. Balance the discussion by referring to the content of Psychology In Your Life. Assign "Superior Intelligence" and "Mental Retardation" for Day 3.

Day 3: After using a discussion question like number six in the text to discuss superior intelligence, assign an activity the class can do as a group to evaluate the practice of mainstreaming. Have the class read "Creativity" for homework.

PSYCHOLOGY AND YOU RESOURCES

A variety of resources are available in the Psychology and You *supplementary material. In addition, there are a number of additional resources listed to enhance your lesson plans.*

Masters
▼ 9-1A Learning Goals
▼ 9-1B Answers to Learning Goals
▼ 9-2 Binet's Task
▼ 9-3 Be Creative
▼ 9-4 Problem Solving
▼ 9-5 Creativity

Student Worksheets
▼ Vocabulary Worksheet
▼ Independent Practice Worksheet
▼ Enrichment Worksheet
▼ Reteaching Worksheet

Test Bank
▼ Tests A and B

Multimedia
▼ *The Brain* Videotape Module #22
▼ Psychology Videodisc

Student Workbook

9

Intelligence and Creativity

OBJECTIVES

Be able to:

▼ Explain Binet's four-part definition of intelligence.

▼ Describe the original formula for IQ.

▼ Explain why Wechsler developed a performance scale.

▼ Give evidence for both views regarding the source of intelligence: environment versus heredity.

▼ Describe the classifications of mental retardation.

▼ Describe psychology's concept of creativity as "breaking set."

Global Look at the Chapter

While most of us can recognize the end product of intelligence or creativity, scientists are not certain what each one is. A number of tests have been devised, however, to try to measure these characteristics. This chapter looks at the nature of these tests as well as the pros and cons of using them.

247

INTRODUCING THE CHAPTER

Write the word *intelligence* on the chalkboard and brainstorm a definition. What skills should it include? This should show how difficult it is to arrive at a single, concrete definition. Explain that intelligence, like consciousness, is a construct (Chapter 6). Intelligence cannot be seen or touched, but there's plenty of evidence that it exists. Then brainstorm examples of this evidence. Finally, you may want to spend a few minutes discussing how to measure intelligence.

LEAD-OFF ACTIVITY

Break the class into groups, and have each group fill in the following blanks with ten different answers: "Intelligence is _____. Smart people are _____ ." Encourage students to be creative. Afterward, help them analyze which answers are fact and which are opinion.

Day 4: Use a demonstration from the text or wrap to illustrate the concept *breaking set.* Review the differences between superior intelligence and creativity. Give the Chapter Review quiz.

In Brief

Day 1: Focus on the four elements Alfred Binet believed important for intelligence. Discuss why David Wechsler was dissatisfied with the Stanford-Binet Intelligence Test, and how his own test differs from it.

Day 2: Use one of the discussion questions in the text to evaluate the uses and limitations of IQ test scores. Briefly review the criteria for both superior intelligence and mental retardation.

Day 3: Assign an in-class activity to demonstrate *breaking set* and follow with a discussion about creativity. Give the Chapter Review quiz.

If you like the idea of students writing their own intelligence test (see **Chapter Project**), perhaps you can have students write a different sort of test this time, one that focuses on intelligence *at your school.* What skills and knowledge are necessary to adapt to *that* environment? The test could be administered to, let's say, sophomores, and with their scores you can establish a range of intelligence. The low end might indicate "likely to drop out or be kicked out." The high end could indicate "likely to be valedictorian." The questions don't have to be entirely serious, of course. For example, you can ask about detention schedules: "Which teacher monitors detention on Wednesdays?" Those who are *too* familiar with detentions are probably not adjusting

---

TEACHING MASTER 9-1A

Learning Goals. A Learning Goals sheet for each chapter is provided in the Teacher Resources. These Learning Goals can be used as review sheets or as work-sheets. **Teaching Master 9-1B** consists of answers to these Learning Goals.

Points to Stress

Note that it is the *ability* to understand and adapt to the environment that constitutes intelligence. A person who is unwilling (but able) to adapt may still be intelligent.

Discussion

If intelligence is the ability to understand and adapt to the environment, does the loss of this ability mean the loss of intelligence? (One of the reasons people are committed to mental institutions is that they cannot adapt to the environment; are all these people without intelligence?)

248

---

intelligence

The ability to understand and adapt to the environment by using a combination of inherited abilities and learning experiences.

Stanford-Binet Intelligence Test

The original intelligence test developed by Alfred Binet and refined at Stanford University.

248

Unit 3 COGNITIVE PROCESSES

UNDERSTANDING INTELLIGENCE

In this chapter, we tackle one of the oldest and most researched areas of psychology: intelligence. In a way, though, it seems that the more we study the topic, the more complex it becomes. So we will deal with considerable controversy and disagreement as we proceed.

Defining Intelligence

Of all the words used by professionals, none seems so clear when we hear it but on close examination becomes so vague as does "intelligence." A formal definition might help a little: **intelligence** is the ability to understand and adapt to the environment by using a combination of inherited abilities and learning experiences.

Psychologists first tried to measure intelligence in a mechanical way. In the late 1800s, researchers assumed that since mind and body are so difficult to separate, it might be possible to measure intelligence by a series of physical tests. Some of these measures seem outlandish today. For instance, there was one test item in which a pointed rubber plug was pressed against the subject's forehead with increasing pressure until it caused pain. The idea was to measure many supposedly "bright" and "dull" people, find out which group was better able to stand the pain, and then use these "test" results in order to measure other people with the plug and classify them as either dull or bright. As you might have guessed, this approach did not work very well for measuring intelligence.

The Stanford-Binet Intelligence Test

The first workable intelligence test was constructed in the early 1900s. In France, the minister of public instruction wanted to find some way of locating students who were not bright enough to be in the regular school system. His goal was to provide them with special instruction. He appointed a psychologist, **Alfred Binet** (be-NAY), to solve the problem. An updated version of Binet's test is still used today, 90 years later. It is called the **Stanford-Binet Intelligence Test** because it was refined at Stanford University in California.

Binet was not sure what an intelligence test should include. He, like everyone else, had trouble defining the term, but eventually he came up with four elements that he believed were important for intelligence: (1) *Direction* is the ability to set up a goal and work toward it. (2) *Adaptability* means that when faced with a problem, the person can make the adjustments needed to solve it.

COOPERATIVE LEARNING

well to school rules! The value of the activity is in the process: trying to establish validity, reliability, and standardization, deciding which questions are fair, and so on.

Ask students what can be done to make a test reliable and valid? Answers may include the following points. *Reliability:* (1) Subjects take the test more than once; compare these scores. (2) Compare the scores on the first half of the test with those on the second half. (3) Use two similar tests, and compare each subject's results. *Validity:* Compare scores with performance. If the SAT claims to predict success in college, see if it does.

Chapter 9 INTELLIGENCE AND CREATIVITY

Connections

Intelligence tests (Chapter 2) need to be reliable: if you take a test on Monday and take the same test on Friday, the scores should be similar. The tests should also be valid; they should measure what they are supposed to measure. Intelligence tests should be standardized: you have to find a norm so you have some basis of comparison; also, you should administer the test the same way every time.

▲ *We now know that intelligence and creativity come in many forms—not necessarily directly related to school activities.*

DISCUSS THE PHOTO

What other kinds of skills would reflect intelligence or creativity?

(3) *Comprehension* means having a basic understanding of exactly what the problem is. (4) Finally, the person working on the problem should have some idea of whether he or she has been able to solve it correctly. "Solving" the problem is worthless if the wrong solution is arrived at. Hence, Binet called the last item *self-evaluation.*

Binet's ideas seem obvious today, but that is because we're used to them. At the time, they were very innovative. He developed test items that measured each of these areas; then these items were put in order of increasing difficulty. As the items got progressively more difficult, they applied to higher age groups; in this way, he could test both older and younger students.

Test-Item Construction At the simplest level, typical Binet test items included naming major parts of the body (arms, legs, and so on) or selecting specific objects from a pile (pick up the toy train; pick up the ball) when asked to do so by the examiner. More difficult items appeared for older children: "Indicate which number is not in its correct position: 12, 9, 6, 3, 15." At a higher level of abstraction, we have this one: "Bill Jones's feet are so big that he has to pull his trousers on over his head. What is foolish about that?"

ENRICHMENT

Students might be interested to know that at one point, Binet tried to determine validity for his tests through head measurements! Ask students to find out more about Binet's early attempts to study intelligence.

COOPERATIVE LEARNING

Divide the class into four large groups. Each group writes five questions or statements that describe one of the following: direction, adaptability, comprehension, or self-evaluation. Direct students to the **In Focus** box, **Binet's Definition of Intelligence,** for ideas.

Binet's Definition of Intelligence.

IN FOCUS It may be easier for students to evaluate their own intelligence if given a focus—school, for instance. *Direction:* do they decide what grade they want early in the course? *Adaptability:* do they adjust this goal when scores are returned? And so on.

TEACHING MASTER 9-2

Binet's Task. This handout includes an excerpt from Elaine and Harry Mensh's *The IQ Mythology* (1991) that should generate some lively discussion.

Points to Stress

Students should note that mental age is merely a statistic. This makes an intelligent quotient merely a statistic, too. And as we've all heard, statistics sometimes lie.

250

---

mental age

The level of intellectual functioning in years, which is compared with chronological age.

> ### IN FOCUS   Binet's Definition of Intelligence
>
> Direction   — Set goal
> Adaptability   — Adjust goal
> Comprehension   — Understand problem
> Self-Evaluation — Assess solution
>
> Mighty Stacy walks up to the plate. Annette, on the pitcher's mound, decides she's going to strike her out, but she can't give her any easy pitches (*direction*). She throws three pitches inside, and the count is three balls and no strikes. She decides to give up speed for accuracy (*adaptability*) and throws the ball over the middle of the plate. Mighty Stacy swings and misses. Annette now understands the problem (*comprehension):* Mighty Stacy can't hit slow pitches. Annette throws another slow pitch over the middle. Mighty Stacy swings and misses. The count is three balls and two strikes. Annette winds up and lobs the ball over the plate. Mighty Stacy swings and launches the ball over the outfielders' heads. Annette sits on the mound and wonders whether slow pitches were the answer (*self-evaluation).*
>
> If you were to evaluate your own intelligence using Binet's four elements, what would be your conclusion? How well do you apply each element?

Before the test was finished, each item was administered to a large group of children of varying ages. The items were then put in order of increasing difficulty. For example, if all five-year-old children could solve a particular item, it was considered too easy for that group, so it would be tried with four-year-olds. Or if too hard for five-year-olds, it would be tried at the age-six level. The goal was to get items that most, but not all, of the children of a given age could answer. The final test was designed to measure mental ability from ages three to 15 years.

Mental Age   We expect the average five-year-old to pass most items at the five-year-old level, since that is how the test was designed. Thus, the child who is chronologically five years old (age based on birthdays), if average, should also have a **mental age** of roughly five years. But what if a certain five-year-old is brighter than the average five-year-old? This would mean that his or her mental age must be higher than that of the average five-year-old. Now, suppose this particular child answers all the items for five-year-olds as well as most of those at the six-year-old level. When the test is

DISCOVERY

Binet's four elements of intelligence, though not exactly a process, can be applied to writing tasks. Ask students to create an analogy or example applying Binet's elements to a writing assignment. *Direction:* I have to write a paper on WWII. *Adaptability:* There are too many sources, so I will have to focus on one aspect of WWII. *Comprehension:* I know what I will focus on. *Self-evaluation:* The assignment calls for five pages; I only have two. *Adaptability:* I need to do more research.

---

scored, the child's mental age has gone beyond age five into the six-year area. So, his or her mental age would be six and chronological age would be five, showing that the child is brighter than most other children of his or her physical age.

A term you hear all the time is "IQ." The IQ, or **intelligence quotient,** is a measure of brightness obtained by comparing mental age with physical age. A quotient is a number obtained by dividing one number by another. To make calculation easy, the number 100 was chosen as the center, or perfectly average, point of the test. An IQ of 100, then, is a perfectly average IQ.

Notice how we get this IQ of 100: take the mental age, divide it by the chronological age, and multiply by 100 (to get rid of any decimals). Thus, the following would occur for our perfectly average five-year-old:

$$5/5 \times 100 = 100 \text{ IQ}$$

The child we've described as having a mental age of six must have a higher IQ score. And that is the case:

$$6/5 \times 100 = 120 \text{ IQ}$$

We hope this formula helps you understand what an IQ means and where it comes from. However, you should be aware that the formula is no longer used today. For a number of reasons, it was replaced by statistical tables many years ago.

There is a wide range of possible IQs. Categories of IQs are shown in Table 9.1 along with the percentage of people falling into a given category as well as the label attached to each category. Note that most people do not have very high or very low intelligence quotients. The largest group (49 percent) falls within the average range.

The Wechsler Intelligence Test

The Binet test certainly served its purpose of locating children who would have trouble in school, since the Binet test deals almost exclusively with words, and they are the core of schoolwork. Almost

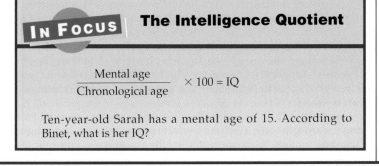

IN FOCUS   The Intelligence Quotient

$$\frac{\text{Mental age}}{\text{Chronological age}} \times 100 = \text{IQ}$$

Ten-year-old Sarah has a mental age of 15. According to Binet, what is her IQ?

Chapter 9 INTELLIGENCE AND CREATIVITY

intelligence quotient

A measure of intelligence originally obtained by comparing mental age with physical age.

Evaluation Strategy

Combine and scramble the questions and/or statements from the cooperative-learning activity above. Next to each question or statement, have students identify what it describes: direction, adaptability, comprehension, or self-evaluation. Use an overhead and you can complete this exercise in a few minutes. Students should refrain from answering their own questions, of course.

Comprehension Check

What are the four elements Alfred Binet believed were important for intelligence? *(direction, adaptability, comprehension, and self-evaluation)*

The Intelligence Quotient

 Her IQ is about 150.

DEMONSTRATION

Bring in several difficult questions from the game, Trivial Pursuit, or a paragraph from a dull journal. See if students can answer the questions or make sense of the paragraph. With your tongue in cheek, tell them that their responses are an indication of their intelligence. Actually, this exercise serves as a transition from Binet to Wechsler. The Trivial Pursuit questions were probably not relevant to students, just as Binet's questions were not relevant to many of the "low-intelligence" students Binet tested. Wechsler, of course, tried to compensate for this shortcoming by measuring a variety of skills.

Connections

Remind students about S's extraordinary ability (Chapter 8). He didn't forget anything, but he couldn't integrate material. Did he lack intelligence? Is the ability to integrate essential for intelligence? You might also mention Dustin Hoffman's character in *Rain Man*, who could compute faster than a pocket calculator but who thought a car cost $1.00.

Discussion

Ask students the following questions: Have you ever met someone who is not very street smart but does very well in school? Would you regard this person as intelligent? Students' answers, of course, will depend on a number of variables. Mention a few hypothetical variables throughout the discussion to see how their answers change. For example, what if this person *knows* he or she is not street smart? What if the person is so lacking in street smarts (that is, in the ability to adapt to the environment) that others take advantage of him or her?

verbal scale

IQ test items that rely heavily on word comprehension and usage.

performance scale

IQ test items that try to bypass verbal material and focus on problem solving without words.

Wechsler Adult Intelligence Scale-Revised (WAIS-R)

An intelligence test for adults that provides three IQs: verbal, performance, and a combined (total) IQ.

Wechsler Intelligence Scale for Children-Revised (WISC-R)

An intelligence test for children ages six to 16; similar in form to the WAIS-R.

▲ *Figure 9.1 Meaning of Intelligence Quotients*

IQ	Category	Percent of People
130 or above	Very superior	2
120–129	Superior	7
110–119	High average	17
90–109	Average	49
80–89	Low average	16
70–79	Borderline	6
69 or below	Mentally retarded	2

all the items require some kind of searching for a word answer, as in the question, "Brother is a boy; sister is a _____."

There were problems with the Binet test, though. One psychologist, **David Wechsler** (WEX-ler), worked at New York's Bellevue Hospital where he handled derelicts from skid row who were brought there by the police. Most of these people had had little formal education, and school-related material was not usually part of their life. Since Wechsler wanted to develop a program to help these people find jobs and get out of the mess they were in, he needed some measure of how bright they were in real-world intelligence rather than in schoolwork. The highly verbal Binet test just didn't do the job. Wechsler hit on the idea of a two-part intelligence test. The first part contained verbal items like the Binet **(verbal scale),** but a second part was a *non*verbal IQ test, called a **performance scale.**

Wechsler's performance scale relies minimally on the use of words, but it still requires the ability to reason. Here are a couple of the types of items he used when his test came out in the 1930s: In *picture completion,* the test taker was shown a series of pictures from which some important part had been removed. For example, at the simplest level, a picture of a pig with no tail was shown, and the taker was to indicate what was missing. In another type of item, the *object assembly,* a picture of a familiar figure or object (for instance, a picture of an elephant) was cut up like a jigsaw puzzle. The test taker first had to recognize what the parts made when they were fitted together; then the test taker was supposed to assemble them.

Wechsler eventually constructed different forms of his intelligence test for use with different age groups. They all provide three IQs. One is verbal, another is performance, and the third combines these two to give a total IQ. The **Wechsler Adult Intelligence Scale-Revised (WAIS-R)** is used with adults, people ages 16 and older. The **Wechsler Intelligence Scale for Children-Revised (WISC-R)** is for children ages six to 16. There is also a test for preschoolers, ages four to six years old.

Wechsler's idea worked well. Interestingly, studies over the years have shown that the Wechsler performance scale measures roughly the same abilities as are measured by the verbal scale. This probably

ENRICHMENT

Ask students to compare and contrast humans with animals, and arrive at a conclusion about intelligence. This task can help to refine the various definitions of intelligence that you may have discussed earlier.

▲ *The performance scale of the WISC-R.*

results from the fact that to solve the performance items, a person must call on symbolic skills ("This is an elephant; an elephant has a trunk over here"). Symbolic skills are very much involved with verbal problems, since words are symbols. So, all of our IQ tests are measuring the same general thing. This "same thing" may or may not be identical with a person's *real* intelligence, as you'll see in the next section.

What Is Intelligence?

Haven't we been spending all this time discussing intelligence? Actually, we have not, and this is very important: we have been discussing intelligence *testing,* which is quite a different matter.

Think about this for a few seconds: since we are not certain exactly what intelligence is, but we do depend on intelligence tests, what we *call* intelligence is, in fact, whatever the intelligence tests measure. That sounds absurd at first, but note the predicament we are in. We have these tests that can tell the difference between people's school abilities in a general sort of way. We use the tests all the time to try to estimate how bright a person is. Hence, we are constantly using the test results themselves as the equivalent of intelligence. There are some serious flaws in this system. For instance, all of us know people who score very high on these tests but who are blatantly stupid in most areas of life; we also know people who score low average but who are great problem solvers and really handle everyday life effectively (McClelland, 1973). Clearly the IQ test measures something important, but it certainly is not the final word on intelligence.

Discussion

What kinds of performance skills might reveal intelligence? Do students agree that picture completion and object assembly are valid criteria? If a basketball player excels at fooling the defense with his passing, is this a sign of intelligence? How about if a mediocre artist makes millions of dollars due to successful marketing techniques? (See the next **FYI.**)

DISCUSS THE PHOTO

This material is used by test-takers to do things like arrange a series of cartoon panels into a meaningful story and to copy designs with blocks.

Discussion

The fact that Wechsler worked with many derelicts who were bright raises a few questions. Is it possible to be highly intelligent and illiterate? If so, how would the intelligence be exhibited? Also, would learning to read increase the intelligence of an illiterate adult since reading encourages abstract thought? You might mention that up until 150 years ago, *most* people were illiterate.

CHAPTER PROJECT/COOPERATIVE LEARNING

Break the class into small groups, and have each group write several questions for an intelligence test. The questions should be designed so that someone in the students' own age group would probably be able to answer them. After each group has written five to ten questions, bring the class together again and discuss the questions. Do the questions seem reliable and valid? Can most students in the class answer the questions? Are the questions culturally biased? If someone from another planet looked at the questions, what conclusions would the alien draw about intelligence on earth? In other words, what kinds of abilities do the questions measure? Academic? Performance? Combine the questions, administer the test to several of

---

The Wechsler Test.

 The Binet test relies solely on verbal skills. The Wechsler test includes both a verbal and a performance score. Also, the Binet test yields one IQ score, while the Wechsler test includes multiple scores to show strengths and weaknesses in different areas.

Comprehension Check

What problems did David Wechsler find with Stanford-Binet Intelligence Test that prompted him to create his own test? *(The Stanford-Binet test was too verbal and did not measure how bright people were in "real-world" intelligence as contrasted to schoolwork.)*

Journal Topic

"Describe an incident that made you feel not so intelligent."

Unit 3 COGNITIVE PROCESSES

 **The Wechsler Tests**

Two frequently used intelligence tests are the Wechsler Intelligence Scale for Children-Revised, or WISC-R, and the Wechsler Adult Intelligence Scale-Revised, or WAIS-R (Wechsler, 1958). The Wechsler tests place more emphasis on performance tasks (such as doing puzzles) than does the Stanford-Binet. As a result, individuals who are not particularly skilled in the use of words will not be as likely to receive low IQ scores.

In addition to providing one overall score, the Wechsler tests yield percentile scores in several areas—vocabulary, information, arithmetic, picture arrangement, and so on. It is therefore possible to compute separate IQ scores for verbal and performance abilities. This type of scoring provides a more detailed picture of the individual's strengths and weaknesses than a single score does.

Below is a sample of questions from five of the verbal subtests of the Wechsler. (Test items courtesy of The Psychological Corporation, New York.)

General Information

1. How many wings does a bird have?
2. How many nickels make a dime?
3. What is steam made of?
4. Who wrote *Tom Sawyer?*
5. What is pepper?

General Comprehension

1. What should you do if you see someone forget his book when he leaves his seat in a restaurant?

Influence of Society on Definition of Intelligence Wechsler cautioned that definitions (and tests) always reflect the culture within which we live—in other words, they reflect whatever society at the moment views as worthwhile, meaningful, and valuable (Wechsler, 1975). In some times and places, for example, the skills needed to be an excellent farmer are far more important than the skills needed to be a lawyer.

One study compared the definition of intelligence used by the Australians with that used by the Malaysians and found that the latter group defines intelligence as the ability to get along well with other people and to do so in a socially efficient way. The Australians, on the other hand, are quite industrialized and emphasize academic skills, just as we do (Gill & Keats, 1980; Brislin, 1983).

your colleagues' classes to establish a norm, then to a test class to assess intelligence. Students who take this mock intelligence test should not write down their names. Even if you do not administer the test, this project puts students in the shoes of psy-chologists and gives them the awesome task of defining and measuring intelligence. They will probably realize that no single test can adequately measure intelligence.

2. What is the advantage of keeping money in a bank?
3. Why is copper often used in electrical wires?

Arithmetic

1. Sam had three pieces of candy and Joe gave him four more. How many pieces of candy did Sam have altogether?
2. Three men divided 18 golf balls equally among themselves. How many golf balls did each man receive?
3. If two apples cost 15 cents, what will be the cost of a dozen apples?

Similarities

1. In what way are a lion and a tiger alike?
2. In what way are a saw and a hammer alike?
3. In what way are an hour and a week alike?
4. In what way are a circle and a triangle alike?

Vocabulary

1. "What is a puzzle?"
2. "What does 'addition' mean?"

Simulated items of the Wechsler Intelligence Scales for Adults and Children. Copyright © 1974, 1981, 1955 by The Psychological Corporation. Reproduced by permission. All rights reserved.

What is the major difference between the Wechsler tests and the Binet test?

FYI Psychologist Howard Gardner (1983) has proposed a theory of multiple intelligences, arguing that there are several kinds of intelligence. They include not only language, logic, and spatial thinking but also athletic or dance skills, interpersonal skills, and the ability to know oneself.

Journal Topic

"Ways in which I am intelligent." You may want to mention Gardner's theory of multiple intelligences. (See the preceding **FYI**.)

While this situation makes the definition of intelligence that we use rather questionable in many cases, we can't throw the tests out just because they *do* reflect our culture. After all, we have to succeed somehow within the limits of our society. Also, some kind of test is better than none, and we don't know what to replace these tests with. Still, almost everyone knows that if you judge people's abilities just by the results of their IQ tests, you're going to miss some potentially very capable people who don't do all that well on the tests.

Is Intelligence Inherited? Most of the evidence indicates that heredity plays an important part in basic intellectual potential. The majority of investigators in this area have concluded that roughly 50 percent of what we call intelligence is the result of some kind of

DISCOVERY

Have students write a few questions in which the instructions are clear, but only to a limited audience. Perhaps *you* can be the audience, and you can challenge them to try to stump you. Topics might include dating, music, parties. Here's a sample question: What should you do if someone asks you to turn down the Def Leppard? (a) call a zookeeper, (b) lower the volume on the stereo. This activity may show that a test can be unfair because of the age of the test taker.

ENRICHMENT

Do graphologists believe that handwriting reveals intelligence? Have a few students contact one to find out. What evidence do the graphologists offer? Ask the graphologists to cite specifics: What type of handwriting indicates more intelligence than others? How do they know this?

FYI Notes from Michael Gazzaniga's *Nature's Mind* (1992): "Are their [monozygotic twins'] brains alike? Normally there is a great variation in the gross morphology of the brain. While all brains have a similar overall plan, they vary tremendously in details. Some brains, for example, have bigger frontal lobes than others. . . The fact that the overall cognitive skills of monozygotic twins are more alike than those of mere siblings would suggest their brains are physically similar to one another" (p. 102).

Points to Stress

It could be argued that the Scholastic Assessment Test (SAT) and the American College Test (ACT) are examples of group intelligence tests.

Points to Stress

Fraternal twins are as genetically alike as siblings. The IQ scores of fraternal twins may be more closely correlated than those of siblings, but it's because of environmental reasons.

256

Unit 3 COGNITIVE PROCESSES

individual intelligence tests

IQ tests administered on a one-to-one basis—one examiner to one test taker.

group intelligence tests

IQ tests administered to many people at one time; test is highly verbal and uses paper and pencil.

256

---

hereditary influence, while the other 50 percent comes from all kinds of things—education, social class, environment, nutrition, amount of stimulation, and the like (Mackenzie, 1984; Plomin et al., 1980).

These conclusions have been reached after examining studies of the IQs of twins. Some twins come from the same fertilized egg. These *identical twins*, therefore, have exactly the same heredity. If they have the same heredity, and IQs are to some extent inherited, their IQs should be very close to one another, even if they are reared apart. And indeed that turns out to be the case.

Other twins are called *fraternal*. These twins will have the same environment inside the mother and will share many of the same characteristics, but they come from two separate eggs; hence, the heredity is not identical. Their IQs should be close, but not as close as those of the identical twins. Again, this turns out to be the case.

Finally, to round out the analysis, a comparison is made between the IQs for nontwins within the same family—that is, brothers and sisters. They are as close in heredity as fraternal twins, but experience greater environmental differences because they are not the same age. Hence, their IQs should be closer to one another than to the IQs of other children down the block, but not as close as the twins'. That also turns out to be true (Munsinger, 1975; Kamin, 1978). Environment *is* important: a brother and sister who live together are much closer in IQ than those who are reared apart.

Issues in Intelligence Testing

We want to discuss here some of the issues surrounding IQ scores. You will find that this area of study is far from peaceful and quiet.

Individual Versus Group Testing Both the Binet and the Wechsler tests are administered individually. A psychologist sits at a table with a student, asking the test questions and demonstrating the problems contained in the test. These **individual intelligence tests** take an hour or so to administer, plus additional time for scoring. Such a lengthy process provides more opportunity for the test administrator to see the person in action and to understand some of his or her reasoning behind the answers. The biggest problem, though, is the cost. An individual test administration is expensive.

Other tests cost as little as 10 to 20 cents per person. These **group intelligence tests** are given to large numbers of people at the same time and scored by computer. Hence, they are done entirely on paper by marking the correct answer. Here are two group IQ test items:

1. A hat is to: (a) smell (b) look through (c) wear (d) smoke.
2. *Ear* is to *hear* as *eye* is to: (a) tear (b) see (c) spectacles (d) eyelash.

Considering the amount of money and time involved, you would expect the individual test to give a much better picture of a person's

DISCOVERY

Urge your school psychologist to visit your class to discuss a school's purpose in administering intelligence tests. If this person is willing to come in, have your class prepare a list of

"intelligent" questions for the visit. Also, ask the psychologist to bring in several sample test items, if possible, and to discuss the kinds of questions included on intelligence tests.

abilities. It does, when dealing with a person who has serious problems or when used to help make a specific important decision. Overall, however, group tests can be reasonably accurate in predicting school potential. They do, though, present the problem of being completely verbal with no opportunity for performance scales.

Uses and Limits of IQ Scores   In general, things like achievement in history, reading comprehension, and biology class are all related to how well one does on the IQ test.

But test results must be viewed cautiously, especially if school performance is better than IQ score. The test can be a poor predictor, most often failing to predict things like how well a person actually does a certain task in the real world (Lambert et al., 1976). And the IQ test *can* make errors, sometimes enormous ones, as great as 30 points. Errors are usually not that large, though, and on average vary about seven points from what the correct IQ is supposed to be. Still, people should never be content to let one low score stand as is. In such a case, it is very important to administer another IQ test to be certain the first one was not in error.

Court Cases   In recent years, federal and state courts have more and more been ruling that IQ test results alone cannot be used to make judgments about which classes or schools to place children in if the children haven't done well on the test (Matarazzo, 1990; Opton, 1979). There are good reasons for many of these decisions. IQ tests are constructed by and contain material from the white middle-class group. As a result, these tests label six times more nonwhites than whites as "mentally retarded" (see the last section of this chapter). This difference is so high that the test, rather than the basic abilities of the nonwhites, immediately becomes suspect. When a test unfairly measures the abilities of different cultural groups, it is said to suffer from **cultural bias.**

The problem is that certain concepts, words, thoughts, phrases, and ideas vary from one subgroup to another in our mixed society. Chinese Americans, Japanese Americans, Hispanics, African Americans, Irish Americans, and Italian Americans all come from cultures that are not identical to middle-class white America. The differences are a valuable and important part of the American way of life; nonetheless, these differences can influence test results in an often subtle but unfair fashion. What seems to be an identical question for all groups can turn out not to be. Thus, for some reason, African American children have trouble with the instruction, "Mark the apple that is whole." But they have no trouble with "Mark the apple that is still all there" (Wright & Isenstein, 1975). Since this is the same instruction, it becomes clear that how a question or instruction is worded—which is the result of the test maker's own race and social class—can alter test results.

Larger cultural issues are also involved. For instance, it has been argued that African Americans tend to value and emphasize differ-

Chapter 9 INTELLIGENCE AND CREATIVITY

▲ *Sometimes a judge must decide if an IQ score is being used fairly.*

cultural bias

The unfair measurement of cultural groups' abilities.

Comprehension Check

What major factors limit the validity of I.Q. tests? *(racial and sociocultural bias)*

Discussion

Can a person's handwriting reveal intelligence? Point out that graphology has not fared well under scientific scrutiny. Graphologists are not very accurate in assessing personality or predicting job performance.

DISCUSS THE PHOTO

One such case was the Larry P. vs. The California State Superintendent of Education. Larry P. was an African American child placed in a class for the educable mentally retarded due to an IQ test score. The prosecution demonstrated that twice as many African American and Latino children are found in these classes than should be expected based on the percentage of these ethnic groups in the general population. The judge agreed that this suggested a defect in the test, not the children, and ruled that IQ test scores alone can't be used to place children in these classes.

INTERDISCIPLINARY PROJECT

Multicultural Studies. Have students write a few intelligence test questions that they think are fair, focusing particularly on making them culturally fair. Then have them write a few questions that seem culturally unfair. Students may need to conduct some research to complete their project. See the following **Enrichment.**

Discussion

Is intelligence learned? If we are constantly told we are dumb, will our intelligence be affected? When children are placed in a low reading group in elementary school, does this label stick in their minds? When they come across a difficult passage, are they more likely to give up trying to understand it because they *believe* they are "slow"? And will this giving up lead to lower intelligence?

Critical Thinking

If a stimulating environment is beneficial and perhaps even crucial to intelligence, how can we make classrooms more stimulating? Would students' intelligence be increased if schools focused more on problem solving and decision making than on rote memorization? If so, how could schools shift their focus to more critical-thinking skills?

Students may detect a bias in the last question: that it is desirable to strive for increased intelligence. Do students agree?

258

258

ent types of thought processes (such as problem solving and classifying) and approaches to test taking from those of whites (Helms, 1992). Such differences could obviously have a negative effect on one's IQ score.

Here is another example: in Brazil and some other Latin American countries, most people pay little attention to time. One study shows that almost all the clocks in Brazil (even the official ones) and the watches are set incorrectly. If you arrive late for an appointment, nobody pays any attention (Levine et al., 1980). On the other hand, in the United States, people run around all the time clocking themselves to the vibrations of quartz watches, splitting the second down into little bits. A cultural difference of this sort can have a major impact on IQ test results when comparing someone from a Latin American culture with someone from a typical North American culture, since many items on an IQ test are carefully timed. If you run out of time, you lose IQ points!

The Effects of Mental Challenge

Inheritance clearly plays a role in what a person can become. But it only sets up certain limits. Within these limits, the environment plays its role (Turkheimer, 1991). For instance, a person inherits a basic body structure, a certain lung capacity, and a specific leg structure. What the person does with these inherited traits is the result of effort and environment if, say, he or she wants to become a runner. His or her parents may or may not have provided, through heredity, the equipment for this person to become an Olympic candidate. But what they have given are the physical limits for a maximum and minimum running ability; this is what their child has to work with.

In the intelligence area, intriguing studies show that brain changes can occur in animals depending on the type of environment in which they are raised. Rats who live in a stimulating, enriched environment with plenty of activity to perform *literally* grow a thicker, heavier brain than other rats. The brain's nerve cells actually branch out and weigh more if the rats have developed in a stimulating environment (Rosenzweig et al., 1972). Other studies show that if an animal's visual system is given very high levels of stimulation—rather than, say, its hearing or smell—the visual portion of the brain becomes much heavier than these other parts (Greenough, 1985).

Researchers believe that exactly the same types of changes take place in the human brain. Figure 9.2 is very interesting in this regard. It shows the brain cell development of the normal child from three to 24 months of age (Pribram, 1971). What these studies demonstrate is the importance of environment. They do not suggest that a child can progress faster than nature allows. As we discuss in Chapter 10 on child development, nature has built in a sequence of mental develop-

The idea that IQ tests are unfair to certain cultures or races is a hotly debated issue. Have students outline the main points being debated. They might look up sociologist, Adrian Dove, who devised the Dove Counterbalance Intelligence Test, a culturally biased test designed to highlight the problems of bias when measuring intelligence. (The test appears in Coon—see **Suggested Readings** for this chapter.)

Chapter 9 INTELLIGENCE AND CREATIVITY

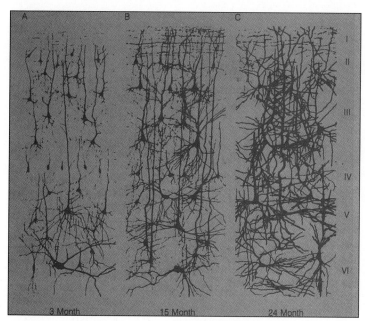

▲ *Figure 9.2* *Sections from the cerebral cortex of children ages three, 15, and 24 months. (Note increased branching and thickening of dendrites.) From the work of Conel (A) 1947; (B) 1955; (C) 1959. From* Language of the Brain *by K. Pribram, Prentice-Hall, Inc., 1971. Reprinted by permission.*

ment that the child follows with one stage leading into another. Training or stimulation *cannot* speed up the sequence of development. It is critical that the child be given a stimulating environment. As the brain develops, it can take in more and more from the environment, so the environment must contain stimulating objects and events.

SUPERIOR INTELLIGENCE

The heading of this section may seem offensive at first. However, if you reread Figure 9.1, you will see that the word *superior* is just one of the technical classifications at the upper end of the IQ range. The term *genius* is no longer used. Whichever term is applied, though, certain images are frequently associated with very high intelligence. Extremely bright people are often depicted as eccentric and strange, sickly and frail, and/or isolated from the rest of society. Is this an accurate picture? Stay tuned and you will find out.

DISCOVERY

Before students read about superior intelligence, draw a range of IQs on the board and have students list the characteristics they believe are associated with superior intelligence. Compare this list to the actual characteristics reported in the **Superior Intelligence** section. (If you complete the **Lead-off Activity** for this chapter, you can use some of those student responses for comparison.)

DISCUSS THE PHOTO

Creative thinking seems to have five stages: orientation, preparation, incubation, illumination, and verification.

Connections

A study that takes a number of years is called a longitudinal study (Chapter 2).

Critical Thinking

Once you dispel the myth that people with superior intelligence are nerds with pocket protectors who view life through thick glasses, ask students to speculate on which positive qualities *do* seem to emerge with superior intelligence.

Unit 3 COGNITIVE PROCESSES

▲ *Great inventions tend to occur to more than one person at the same time. This happened with the telephone: at the left the idea of Elise Gray; at right Alexander Graham Bell.*

Personal Characteristics

In the early 1920s, most people believed that high intelligence was linked to insanity and a number of other problems. But no one had ever carefully studied the issue. So, a man named Lewis Terman decided to find out what bright children were really like. He selected 1,528 children to participate in his study. The average IQ of this group was 150, a higher score than 99.9 percent of the whole population. He found them to be extremely successful in school, which was certainly no surprise. However, he also found that they were psychologically well adjusted, physically quite healthy, and they interacted well with other people.

These children were restudied several times over an extraordinarily long period of time—60 years, to be exact! In fact, the study went on so long that Terman died before it could be completed. The person who took over for him was one of the original subjects who, along the way, became a prominent psychologist. As adults and into old age, the subjects remained healthier and more successful than average. They also had lower rates of divorce, alcoholism, and suicide (Goleman, 1980).

Other studies have found that highly intelligent people tend to have greater self-esteem. They are also less gullible than most—that is, harder to hoodwink and influence or persuade of something they find difficult to believe (Rhodes & Wood, 1992). It would seem, then, that the popular image of extremely bright people is not very accurate.

Does intelligence alone account for these differences? Probably not, although it plays a major role. Most likely, several related factors have some input. For instance, early success in school may build confidence which has a positive effect on self-esteem. In addition, we

260

DISCOVERY

There are probably just as many stereotypes to describe the mentally retarded as there are for the highly intelligent. Refer to the range of IQs and have students write down the first thoughts that come to mind when they think of mental retardation.

(You may want students to go over the discussion of prejudice on page 600 to foster students' sensitivity while completing this activity.)

---

tend to like what we are good at, so those who do well are more likely to stay in school and get professional training. A good job means fewer worries, better access to medical care, less stress on a marriage, and so on. None of this guarantees that everyone with a high IQ will succeed in life. It does mean that as a group, these people have a somewhat better shot at making it. Please remember, though, that the reverse of all this does not doom someone to failure. We know too many people who have changed direction at various points in their lives to say that anything so complicated as one's happiness or success is set in concrete early on.

MENTAL RETARDATION

Mental retardation is usually present at birth, discovered at a young age, and affects quite a large number of people. There are about five million people with notable retardation in the United States. **Mental retardation** is defined as subaverage intellectual functioning in which an individual is unable to handle tasks appropriate to his or her physical age. Learning ability and social adjustment are impaired. The basic classifications for this problem follow, listing some of the things the people can and cannot do.

Basic Classifications

IQ 70–79: Borderline Mental Retardation Those labeled borderline score just below the "low average" group in IQ (see Table 9.1). They are slow learners, and most fail to complete high school. Generally, these people are employed in "nonintellectual" occupations and are not legally retarded in the sense that they would be entitled to disability benefits. (This is the classification of individuals about whom the courts are concerned when they restrict the use of the IQ test, as discussed earlier.)

IQ 52–69: Mild Mental Retardation Most people legally termed "retarded" fall into this category, and most attend special schools. The behavior of people in this group varies considerably depending on whether an individual's IQ is toward the higher or lower end of the range. Someone with a 69 IQ can function pretty well on his or her own, can usually marry, and can maintain a family. At the lower end of the range, some supervision is required, since these people have trouble with abstract reasoning and problem solving.

IQ 36–51: Moderate Mental Retardation People in this group have physical problems, often stemming from a serious disease. They are trained in how to take care of themselves and can live at home,

mental retardation

Subaverage intellectual functioning so that such a person is not able to perform at the level appropriate for his or her age.

Comprehension Check

What positive characteristics did Lewis Terman's study find regarding people with high IQs? *(success in school, generally physically healthy, psychologically well adjusted, interacted well with others, greater self-esteem than average, less gullible, lower rates of divorce, alcoholism, and suicide)*

Discussion

Students can probably cite several examples of people who do not seem intelligent yet are very successful.

Journal Topic

"Are you ever envious of people who seem to be smarter than you? Or do you ever wish you were smarter?"

ENRICHMENT

Students might want to explore some of the physical defects that cause mental retardation, such as Down Syndrome, cretinism, and phenylketonuria (PKU). Students might also want to study how poor nutrition and sensory deprivation may lead to retardation.

INTERDISCIPLINARY PROJECT

Literature. There are several classic works of literature that provide glimpses into what it means to be mentally retarded. Have students read a few passages from one of these works and report on any insights they glean about mental retardation. Students might read John Steinbeck's *Of Mice and Men,* Daniel Keyes's *Flowers for Algernon,* or William Faulkner's *The Sound and the Fury*. If you get a speaker to visit class, ask if these depictions of mental retardation are accurate.

DISCUSS THE PHOTO

Self-respect and a place in the community are as important to the mentally retarded as they are to everyone else.

Comprehension Check

Ask students to list several possible causes of retardation. *(heredity, poor nutrition, poor health, alcohol or drug abuse during pregnancy, lack of stimulation)*

Journal Topic

"Your IQ is 75 (borderline mental retardation). You know you are slower than most students at your school, which is why you have been in special classes your entire school life. Your parents have now decided to try mainstreaming you into regular classes. It's your first day." Set the proper tone for this entry and you'll get some moving narratives.

Unit 3 COGNITIVE PROCESSES

▲ *These real winners have just taken part in the Special Olympics.*

but with supervision. When fully grown, most have the skills of a four- to seven-year-old and can read, write, and speak at that age level.

IQ 20–35: Severe Mental Retardation   People in this group usually require constant supervision. About 75 percent have had a major disease or physical defect and cannot benefit from school (Cleland et al., 1980).

IQ 19 or Below: Profound Mental Retardation   The smallest group of people, about 1 percent of the mentally retarded population, fall into this category. Rarely do they mature mentally beyond age two, and even as adults, they can engage in only limited communication. They are unable to dress or care for themselves without considerable training (Robinson & Robinson, 1970).

Physical Defects

Only about 20 percent of those labeled retarded suffer from a known physical defect. Most of this 20 percent fall into the categories of severe or profound retardation, although a few are in the moderate group. The physical problems usually come from an injury or disease that has affected brain growth and development. The more common causes are lack of oxygen at birth, very poor nutrition, or exposure to toxic chemicals. Defects can also be inherited from the parents.

Most of the mentally retarded, then, do not have any obvious brain problem. You might expect, however, that if an autopsy was performed on the brains of a very bright person, an average person, and a mentally retarded person, there would be a clear difference among these brains. That is not the case. All three brains will look approximately the same. It is true that there are differences in the way the brains *work,* but with our present state of knowledge, we can't *see* whatever those differences might be.

Environmental Factors

Is it possible that some factors in the environment can lead to retardation? One thing we do know is that proper nutrition is absolutely critical to brain development. This is one of the reasons school lunch programs are so important. If the nutrients are absent during critical periods of brain growth, development is permanently slowed. Poor health and infection can have similar effects. Alcohol or drug abuse by pregnant women can also damage the unborn child. Finally, a lack of stimulation, as discussed earlier, won't actually damage the brain, but it can slow the growth of vital nerve cells. Any or all of these factors can be involved in mental retardation. Since the

ENRICHMENT

Invite a speaker from a local center that treats the mentally handicapped. Or you may have a special education teacher at your school who can discuss retardation.

COOPERATIVE LEARNING

Have each group prepare a 30-second public-service announcement on mental retardation. The message should be positive, focusing on what families can do to prevent problems later. Since students are focusing on positive action, ask them to avoid scare tactics, such as, "If you don't stimulate your baby, . . ." In fact, the announcement need not even mention retardation. Minimum requirement: Have them think of a slogan that will stick with the audience.

Potential Problems with Intelligence Tests

IN FOCUS

- Tests may unintentionally reflect a cultural bias.
- Tests may unintentionally reflect a middle-class bias.
- Individually administered tests are costly.
- Tests are sometimes a poor predictor of "success" in the real world—that is, outside school.
- Test scores might be inaccurate.
- Tests measure only a limited range of abilities.

Can you think of a question that would include a subtle cultural or middle-class bias?

Potential Problems with Intelligence Tests.

IN FOCUS Students can easily think of numerous examples (any reference to money, as in allowance, may be biased), but ask students to be subtle. Here's a sample of a not-so-subtle bias: "What should Paul do if his Rolls Royce breaks down?"

majority of people with this problem come from areas of poverty, we suspect that in many cases the environment is a major factor.

We have a lot to learn about mental retardation. There are puzzling cases in which the parents have done everything possible, the environment is reasonable, there is no *apparent* physical defect, yet the child is still retarded.

Methods of Treatment

For the mentally handicapped with physical defects, medicine is making great strides. For those suffering from environmental problems, many programs are available to provide intellectual stimulation. In the past, this generally meant sending virtually all such children to special education classes. In the case of some, this is the best alternative. In the case of others, though, these classes do not provide enough challenge, and the students feel isolated from other children.

Recently, efforts have been made to keep mentally retarded children in regular classes as much as possible. This approach is called **mainstreaming.** How well it works depends on many factors, but it can be remarkably successful. When both parents and teachers are truly committed to making it work and the child is not severely impaired, the results can be startling indeed. Many mainstreamed children learn much more than anyone thought they were capable of. And a number go on to become completely self-sufficient adults (Madden & Slavin, 1983).

For seriously mentally retarded children and adults, there are also programs that include training in motor coordination, practical social skills, and self-care. So, even though we don't completely understand the causes of retardation, large numbers of those who a few years ago would have been left in an institution are now able, at least partly, to take care of themselves.

mainstreaming

The practice of keeping mildly mentally retarded children in regular academic classrooms.

DISCOVERY

Ask students to agree that *we are all creative*. Then have them write down ways in which they are creative. You can prompt them with a few questions: (1) How can creativity be expressed when planning a party? (2) Can a basketball or a volleyball player be creative in the way he or she plays the sport? (3) Can the way one dresses express creativity?

DISCOVERY

Play some intriguing music in class. Classical music often works well. Some students draw what they see. Others write poems or narratives of what they hear.

FYI Many students who say they are not creative probably don't allow themselves *time* to be creative. This time for letting an idea form is often called "incubation." Students who complete an assignment at the last minute, without giving even a random thought to it beforehand, don't take advantage of incubation.

TEACHING MASTER 9-3

Be Creative. This handout includes ambiguous illustrations. Students are asked to write down what the illustrations look like. Often the students who claim they are not creative will think of the most original answers.

Comprehension Check

What do creativity tests measure? *(originality; ability to "break set")*

264

Unit 3 COGNITIVE PROCESSES

creativity
The mental processes that result in original, workable ideas.

set
A tendency to solve problems in the same old way over and over.

264

CREATIVITY

While intelligence tests have been the focus of much interest for generations, many psychologists have pointed out that these tests do not detect the "spark" that motivates a person to do an exceptional job in finding new and better ways of handling problems or in inventing something new—in other words, being creative. As a result, there is now a great deal of interest in trying to find a way to measure this dimension of the person. The IQ test doesn't tap whatever it takes to produce original, workable ideas—that is, it doesn't measure **creativity** (Helms, 1992; Getzels & Jackson, 1962).

Tests of Creativity

Suppose two people are shown a picture of a man sitting in an airplane and are asked to write a story about what he is doing:

1. Mr. Jones is flying home after a week away from the family. He will be happy to see his family again. The plane is only about an hour away from landing. He is hoping that soon he will have some good news about a promotion that he and his family have been waiting for. He decides to take a nap and dream about how well things have been going.

2. Mr. Jones is sitting in an aisle seat, looking toward the closed door leading to the cockpit at the far end of the plane. He wants to put on a leather flight jacket and goggles, burst into the cockpit, his scarf hanging from his neck and shimmering in the light as he takes over. He opens the windows and feels the cold air hit his face, invigorating him. He is going to show the pilots how a *real* aviator can do the job. He will take them all for a sightseeing trip over the North Pole.

Based on the same stimulus—a picture of a man in an airplane—these two stories show a striking difference. The first one is a standard, straightforward, dull account of a businessman flying home. The second is unexpected, novel, and humorous, showing a flair for the unusual—what some psychologists call "creativity," or at least an important aspect of it. They feel that a person must deviate from the expected in order to come up with creative products; invention is the result of unusual thinking. How many times have we all said, after seeing the solution to a problem, "Why didn't I think of that?" The answer was right before our eyes, but we didn't see it. Instead, we kept trying to solve problems in the old way. We were too conventional. We had what is called a **set,** a tendency to try to use the same old solution over and over again—even when it doesn't work.

Invention—and, we assume, creativity—is an ever-present necessity. Take the movie scene in a Wild West saloon where a man breaks

DISCOVERY

Tell students to find an object or two at home and *transform* it, which means that they will cut it or add to it or paint it or simply change it in some way until it has a different use. The use must be practical, at least in theory. The transformation must be original, not something they have ever seen before.

COOPERATIVE LEARNING

Ask students to consider what would happen if we changed to an eight-day week.

---

off the neck of a whiskey bottle and pours himself (and the barmaid) a drink. In real life, this procedure was often an actual necessity, rather than just a dramatic gesture, since sometimes a cork could be wedged so tightly into a bottle that 300 pounds of pressure would have been needed to remove it. The problem persisted until someone took a piece of metal, twisted it into a spiral, put a sharp point on it, added a handle to push down on the top—and there it was, the corkscrew.

Breaking Set

Creativity is in all of us. When we (your authors) were young, there was no such thing as a "pop-top" soft-drink can. A special pointed can opener was needed to open a can of soda. (Our generation was convinced, when the pop-top was first introduced, that it would not work and it wouldn't be around for long. This is standard practice for every generation when something new arrives.) In any case, if the opener was lost on a picnic, our ability to **break set**— think imaginatively with different objects—was remarkable. We used rocks, nails, fingernail clippers, hairpins (a failure), and tire irons to try to open the cans.

Psychologists, then, have come up with a definition of creativity as the ability to break set—to get out of the traditional mold and find a novel solution to a problem. But breaking set must be in the direction of something that works properly. An architect can break set and produce a bridge like no bridge anyone has ever seen before. But if it falls into the river, he or she wasn't demonstrating creativity. Truly creative people can move away from the expected but still keep enough of a hold on reality to make the solution workable (Barron & Harrington, 1981).

Tests of creativity, then, try to measure originality. One creativity test asks the test taker to give some uses for everyday objects such as a tin can or a brick. Creativity is measured by the kinds of responses given. If they deviate from the expected, then this counts toward a higher score. Answering "You can eat a brick" is original but not creative, since it is not tied to reality and shows no cleverness of thought. On the other hand, "Grind it up and put it in an enemy's red-pepper jar" has some merit in the creative sense. Tests of creativity, then, try to measure the unexpected but possible.

Creative Students

Evidence continues to mount that those who are creative are often different from the "very bright" as defined by the IQ test. Creative students are frequently unpredictable and disruptive. They may act a bit silly and have a tendency to contradict their teachers (Torrance, 1979). Often they have trouble fitting well into the standard educational system, which focuses on straight academic achievement

break set

To come up with unusual, unexpected ideas; to use something in a different way from how it is normally used.

TEACHING MASTER 9-4

Problem Solving. This is a simple problem-solving exercise. However, your instructions will make it seem impossible. Say, "The goal of this exercise is to connect A to A, B to B, and C to C. None of your lines can intersect each other or touch the outside boundary. You only get one chance to get it right. So don't let your pen touch the paper until you have figured it out." The lesson here is that we need to have the freedom to make mistakes in order to be creative. Once students connect A to A and B to B, the problem becomes simple. The solution is listed on the bottom of the master, so cover it before photocopying.

COOPERATIVE LEARNING

Bring several common, everyday objects to class: an eraser, a tape dispenser, an old shoe, and so on. (Be creative!) Each group picks two objects out of the bag, then thinks of ten original uses for each object. Let students demonstrate the uses to the class; this usually makes for a lively class period. Points to stress: most groups do not change or alter the object much. For example, they usually don't propose melting or cutting or *transforming* it. In fact, note how many of the uses for a particular object are similar, which indicates that students got stuck in a set. (Transformation requires one to break set.) You will also notice that few groups combine the objects; they work on one object at a time. Combining them requires *transform-*

TEACHING MASTER 9-5

Creativity. This is an adaptation of activity #3 from the end of the chapter. Photocopy enough copies of the master for half of your students and cut these sheets in half. Pass out the top to half of your class and the bottom to the other half. The top includes directions that are intended to create pressure; the bottom includes directions without pressure. After students complete the sheets, have them exchange papers to "grade" creativity by circling the items that break set. (See activity #3 for a description of how to do this.) Tally the number of items circled for each group, and compare the results.

DISCUSS THE PHOTO

Albert Einstein would probably be labeled as learning disabled today.

Unit 3 COGNITIVE PROCESSES

rather than on innovative approaches to problems (Helms, 1992; Merz and Rutherford, 1972).

Rarely could truly creative students be called "teacher's pets," but they actually do learn the material in the classroom. They seem to be on some side road to accomplishment that is parallel but not identical to that of the "bright" students. While they do very well on standard achievement tests, their grades may be a different story. Generally, their IQs are slightly above average but not necessarily extremely high. Beyond that, though, there seems to be no relationship between IQ and creativity. In other words, to be truly productively creative, you need an IQ of about 110 or so. However, having a higher IQ is no guarantee of being more inventive. So, the IQ test is measuring something different from creativity or innovation. If we look for creativity only among the top 20 percent of IQs, we miss 70 percent of the creative people (Barron & Harrington, 1981; Torrance, 1980). While a few students do get extremely high scores on both IQ and creativity tests, they are definitely the exception.

PSYCHOLOGY IN YOUR LIFE

What IQ Testing *Can* Do

We have covered some of the problems with IQ testing in this chapter, and they are important considerations. On the other hand, sometimes not enough attention is paid to the good that IQ testing can do. We feel that a large part of the controversy has come about because too often these tests are misused. When intelligence testing is done properly, the benefits usually outweigh the disadvantages.

The Wechsler scales measure several different abilities. The pattern of how well and how poorly someone does on the different parts or subtests can provide highly useful information. For example, some subtests are particularly sensitive to anxiety—that is, a person who tends to become very anxious under pressure will do poorly on

▲ *Albert Einstein*

(continued on next page)

ing the assumed rules of the task: you never told them that they had to work on the objects separately. Have each *person* describe the process the group went through: what promoted and what blocked creativity?

You may have noticed that many paper clips nowadays are slightly curved at one end to make fastening a bit easier and to avoid crimping. Pair students up and assign each

pair a common object like a spoon or pencil sharpener. Their task is to make an improvement on the object, just as someone has recently done with the paper clip.

Chapter 9 INTELLIGENCE AND CREATIVITY

PSYCHOLOGY IN YOUR LIFE

What IQ Testing *Can* Do

(continued from previous page) them. Others measure abstract reasoning without being affected much by the amount of schooling a person has had. Still others depend fairly heavily on one's formal education. And, of course, there is the overall division into verbal and performance tasks. If a tester is well-trained, she or he can analyze these subtests and come up with a great deal more than just an IQ score. This information can be extremely helpful when trying to determine in what type of program an individual should be placed. To support our point, we will discuss two real-life examples of the usefulness of IQ testing as a diagnostic tool.

In the first case, a young man was found wandering the streets. He was unable to tell the police or a social worker much about his situation. His speech was slow and halting, and he gave the impression of being mentally retarded. Later on, it was learned that the uncle with

whom he had been living had died recently, and now the young man had no relatives, no home, only an eighth-grade education, and no means of making a living.

An intelligence test was given to this young man. A careful analysis of the results showed that he was not mentally retarded. In fact, he was highly intelligent, as long as he didn't have to deal very much with words. He appeared to have a physical problem that interfered with his ability to understand and use language. Instead of being institutionalized, he was placed in a training program and learned to repair a variety of electrical appliances. Eventually he became completely self-supporting as an electronics technician.

The second case involves an adolescent girl who had recently transferred from a rural district to a new school in the suburbs. Her grades were a disaster, and school officials needed to know if she was capable of doing the work. Could she benefit from

remedial classes, or was special education the answer?

Test results showed that, indeed, she did have a low IQ—when only the overall score was used. Further analysis, however, found that her low score was due mostly to her nervousness about taking the test and a poor educational background. Her reasoning ability was actually slightly above average. So, she was placed in remedial reading classes and made excellent progress. Within a year, she had rejoined her classmates and was maintaining a C+ average in school.

Not every case turns out so well, of course. However, with all the criticism of IQ testing, it seems only fair to offer some balance on the issue. The important points to keep in mind in judging a test's usefulness are the type of test given, the purpose for giving it in the first place, and the qualifications of the person administering the test.

What abilities would a comprehensive IQ test reveal about you that an acquaintance, or a teacher, or even a close friend might not be aware of?

To dispel the stereotype that old people become "slow," some psychologists divide intelligence into two types: fluid and crystallized. Fluid intelligence refers to reaction time, rapid recall, and perceptual flexibility. Old people do show a decline in these abilities. Crystallized intelligence involves verbal skills and knowledge accumulated throughout a lifetime; this sort of intelligence steadily increases with age.

VOCABULARY REVIEW

Before testing students on the contents of the chapter, you may want to review vocabulary terms that are especially important or confusing. Terms in this chapter that could require clarification are *intelligence*, *intelligence quotient*, and *break set*.

Wrapping It Up

After reading about intelligence tests, students may wonder what the big fuss is all about. They're just tests. Some are better than others. This one measures verbal skills; that one measures performance. They have nothing to do with who we really are. Remind them that although the SAT and the ACT may not be intelligence tests in name, that's essentially what they are. With this in mind, students may suddenly appreciate the need for fair tests.

Unit 3 COGNITIVE PROCESSES

SUMMARY

1. The Stanford-Binet Intelligence Test was designed to locate students who were not very bright so they could receive special training. Direction, adaptability, comprehension, and self-evaluation were the aspects of intelligence for which Binet developed test items.
2. Originally, IQ scores came from comparing mental age with physical age and multiplying the result by 100 to remove decimals.
3. Since the Binet test is so verbal, the WAIS test was developed. It has a performance scale. Although an improvement, the performance scale is still measuring approximately the same thing as the verbal scales do (whatever that is). We do know, however, that different societies define intelligence in different ways.
4. Roughly 50 percent of intelligence is inherited; 50 percent is environmental. Heredity sets certain limits, and the environment fills in within these limits.
5. IQ scores can be as much as 30 points in error, but normally test error will stay within a range of seven points.

6. So many nonwhites score low on IQ tests compared to whites that the court system often forbids use of the test results in making decisions about nonwhites.
7. Mental stimulation can increase size and thickness of brain nerve cells.
8. Extremely bright people also tend to be well-adjusted, healthy, and successful. They have fewer divorces and suicides than average, and less alcoholism.
9. Most retarded people are not physically impaired. Those who are usually occupy the categories of the most severe retardation. Many environmental factors potentially influence retardation, especially poor nutrition and lack of stimulation.
10. Creativity is defined as the ability to break set. Those who do well on creativity tests need not have extremely high IQ scores, so we believe this ability is a dimension of the person not tapped by the IQ test.

SUGGESTED READINGS

▼ Carter, Philip and K. Russell. *Take the IQ Test.* London: Blandford, 1988.

▼ Coon, Dennis. *Introduction to Psychology: Exploration and Application, 6/e.* St. Paul, Minnesota: West Publishing, 1992.

▼ DeBono, Edward. *DeBono's Thinking Course.* New York: Facts on File, 1985.

▼ Gazzaniga, Michael S. *Nature's Mind.* New York: Basic Books, 1992.

▼ Goleman, Daniel et al. *The Creative Spirit.* New York: Dutton, 1992. (This accompanies the video series on creativity broadcast on PBS.)

▼ Mensh, Elaine, and Harry Mensh. *The I.Q. Mythology.* Carbondale: Southern Illinois University Press, 1991.

▼ Restak, Richard. *The Brain.* New York: Bantam Books, 1984.

▼ Von Oech, Roger. A *Whack on the Side of Your Head: How to Unlock Your Mind for Innovation.* New York: Warner, 1983.

VOCABULARY

intelligence
Alfred Binet
Stanford-Binet Intelligence Test
mental age
intelligence quotient
David Wechsler
verbal scale
performance scale
Wechsler Adult Intelligence Scale-Revised (WAIS-R)
Wechsler Intelligence Scale for Children-Revised (WISC-R)
individual intelligence tests
group intelligence tests
cultural bias
mental retardation
mainstreaming
creativity
set
break set

Review Questions

Matching (Answers can be used more than once.)

1. Deals mainly with verbal skills
2. Includes both verbal and performance scales
3. Uses picture completion
4. One of the first intelligence tests ever used

a. Wechsler Intelligence Scales
b. Stanford-Binet (or Binet)

Multiple Choice

5. The original purpose of the Binet Intelligence Test was to pinpoint
   a. above-average students.
   b. below-average students.
   c. students with brain damage.
   d. hyperactive students.

6. Which of the following best describes what Binet meant by "self-evaluation"?
   a. relating an IQ score to your personality
   b. feeling good about your IQ score
   c. knowing that a solution to an IQ problem is correct
   d. adding up your IQ score

Answers to Review Questions
1. b
2. a
3. a
4. b
5. b
6. c

7. a
8. c
9. d
10. true
11. false
12. true
13. false
14. true
15. true
16. false
17. false
18. d
19. b
20. c

7. Little Alfred is given a jigsaw puzzle, but he isn't able even to begin putting it together until he turns all the pieces over. This needed mental adjustment is what Binet called
   a. adaptability.
   b. comprehension.
   c. direction.
   d. self-evaluation.
8. Mental age refers to a person's
   a. chronological age.
   b. attitude toward problem solving.
   c. intellectual ability level.
   d. performance ability.

9. The Stanford-Binet intelligence quotient compares
   a. school grades with mental age.
   b. school grades with chronological age.
   c. performance with chronological age.
   d. mental age with chronological age.

True/False

10. Wechsler's performance scale measures basically the same thing as his verbal scale.
11. All countries define intelligence in basically the same way.
12. Heredity seems to play some role in intelligence.
13. The Binet and Wechsler tests are usually given to groups.

14. A stimulating environment may cause the brain actually to grow thicker and heavier.
15. An IQ score may be influenced by socio-cultural factors.
16. Highly intelligent people tend to have more psychological problems than the average person.
17. Mainstreaming mentally retarded children hardly ever works.

Multiple Choice

18. Which of the following is *not* a possible cause of mental retardation?
    a. lack of oxygen at birth
    b. heredity
    c. disease
    d. unaffectionate parents
19. Creativity is often increased through
    a. set.
    b. breaking set.
    c. heredity.

20. Set refers to
    a. brainstorming and putting similar ideas together.
    b. the first step in problem solving.
    c. looking at a problem in one way and only one way.
    d. flexibility in thinking.

Notes on Discussion Questions

1. Answers will vary. It might be interesting to contact a personnel director to see if intelligence is assessed in any way during the hiring process.

2. This might be an interesting question to debate in class.

3. This is another good question for debate.

4. This could lead to an interesting discussion on values. Also, notice that the word *safe* is in quotation marks. How many drugs have been deemed safe, yet have ended up having all kinds of side effects? Back in the fifties, many pregnant women took a synthetic hormone, DES, to avoid miscarriage, only to find that years later, their daughters would never be able to bear children.

5. This might be a good journal entry.

6. Intelligent people are more successful than average. They have greater self-esteem; they are less gullible. Factors other than intelligence that might account for these differences: parenting, experiences with other adults, and so on.

7. You can adapt this question for classroom use. Make a list of common objects, and write each object on a separate index card. Break the class into small groups. Each group picks a card and thinks of 20 original uses for the object. Then each group shares its list with the rest of the class.

8. Answers will vary. Discuss these policies one by one, and ask if each policy promotes or blocks creativity. You might get some interesting and surprising responses. For example, students may complain that the attendance and tardy policies are too strict, but these policies

DISCUSSION QUESTIONS

1. Your friend, Jorge, believes that studying intelligence is a waste of time. All it does is allow others to discriminate against people who have low "intelligence." Besides, you can never measure it accurately anyway. Your other friend, Maureen, disagrees. She believes that intelligence testing can single out people of low intelligence and help those people through special programs. With whom do you tend to agree? Why? Explain.

2. Imagine that IQ tests made virtually no errors whatsoever. Should grade levels in school then be determined by IQ or by the traditional chronological method? Explain.

3. Imagine you're the boss of a computer programming firm. You're aware of the potential problems with IQ tests (they can make errors), but the courts recently decided that using the tests for hiring is legal. Would you administer IQ tests to potential employees? Why or why not?

4. Fascinating research is currently being conducted on ways to increase the efficiency of the brain (despite its already remarkable efficiency). If you were a parent and you could increase the "intelligence" of your future children by taking certain "safe" drugs, would you do it? Why? (This may seem like an incredible possibility today, but it may not seem that incredible by the time you're a grandparent.)

5. One of the benefits of intelligence tests is that they may reveal strengths that remain otherwise hidden to observers. What hidden strengths might IQ tests reveal about you? See "In Focus: The Wechsler Tests" for ideas. Also, which of your strengths in intelligence would an IQ test probably *miss*?

6. Studies show that people with superior intelligence are different in many ways than people with so-called average intelligence. List some of the differences. Intelligence obviously plays a major role in creating the differences, but in your opinion, what are some other factors involved (other than the few mentioned in the chapter)?

7. See how creative you can be: write down "tin can" at the top of a sheet of paper and make a list of 20 original uses for the can. Since creativity is being highlighted here, don't feel restricted by the "tin can" suggestion. Choose a different everyday object if you like.

8. Do you think that school in general tends to promote or block creativity? List several examples to support your opinion.

9. In the book *Flowers for Algernon*, the main character, Charly, is retarded but seemingly happy, in spite of others' ridiculing him. He sees the ridicule as friendship. Later, he is the subject of an experiment that increases his intelligence dramatically. His happiness, however, is threatened because now he understands the ridicule. Which extreme would you find preferable: to know and to be usually miserable *or* to not know and to be happy? Explain.

may still promote creativity by forcing students to outwit the system in a creative way.

9. This is a great supplemental book if you have the time and money.

Notes on Activities

1. Instead of having students hand in written reports, you might have them summarize and organize their research on a poster and display it in class. If they find any sample intelligence test items, have them include these samples. If not, maybe they can devise their own sample questions.

2. Make sure students add some of their own interview questions.

3. Before students hand in this activity, you may want to write the name of an object on the chalkboard, have them list as many uses as possible for the object, and then analyze which uses are creative. This will provide students with practice in analyzing creativity.

4. Since the purpose of this activity is to test the creativity of your students, you should probably avoid

ACTIVITIES

1. It should be obvious that Binet and Wechsler are not the only ones ever to devise intelligence tests. Conduct research on other types of intelligence tests. Compare and contrast the criteria used for measuring intelligence on these tests to Binet's and Wechsler's criteria. Out of all of the tests, which one seems closest to your own personal definition of intelligence? Explain.

2. The chances are great that the person in your school who knows the most about intelligence testing is your school psychologist. Prepare a list of questions beforehand, and then interview this person. Possible questions: What kinds of intelligence tests do you use? How do these tests differ from one another? How have recent intelligence tests overcome the possibility of cultural bias? Do you ever encounter students who purposely do poorly on the tests so they won't be moved out of a special program?

    Write a report on the interview and your reactions to what you learned.

3. Many people argue that the creative process is intuitive, and if people are pressured into being creative, creativity will decrease. Find out if this is true. Take a sheet of paper and write down these four objects across the top of it: paper clip, can of hairspray, automobile tire, scissors. Find six friends to participate in your experiment. Tell three of them (one at a time) the following: "You have to help me with this experiment. You see these four objects? You need to think of as many uses as possible for these objects. And you only get five minutes. This is really important to me—I need to get a

good grade—so concentrate." You can use your own words, of course, but the idea is to create pressure. Tell the remaining three friends something like this: "Could you help me with an experiment? It's fun. You get five minutes to write down as many uses as possible for these four objects. Just do your best."

    Once you get all six lists, go through each use that is listed and circle the ones that you think break set. Breaking set will be your way of defining creativity. The more items you circle, the more creative the person will be (according to this limited definition). How will you know which ones to circle? A good guide to use is this: If someone writes that scissors can be used to poke a hole in paper, and in your lifetime you have actually seen someone doing this, then this is *not* an example of breaking set. On the other hand, if the person writes that scissors can be eaten, this also should not be circled since it is entirely unrealistic. If someone suggests that scissors can be used as a paperweight, this probably would be accepted as creative.

    Compare your results of the "pressured" group to the results of the "nonpressured" group. Who performed more creatively? Was pressure a factor? Were there any other factors that may have influenced your results?

4. Read activity number 3 and repeat the same experiment. This time, however, don't put pressure on any of the six subjects. This time, *you* are the one who will need to be creative. (Feel any pressure?) Once you get the six lists, it will be your job to develop a system that will measure creativity. In other

discussing a possible system for measuring creativity until after the activity has been completed.

5.   If possible, have the entire class read *Flowers For Algernon*. You can refer back to it again when you get to the unit on abnormal psychology. If obtaining a class set of the book is not feasible, consider showing the movie, *Charly*, which is based on the book.

6. Have students report their findings to the class. Ask students if they would send *their* kids to these elite organizations.

7. Don't forget to offer extra credit as an incentive for volunteering. Students should volunteer because they want to, but there's nothing wrong with prompting them.

words, you will need to decide on three or four criteria for measuring creativity. In the experiment in number 3, breaking set was one criterion. You may still use that one, but think of the three other original criteria. *Hint:* keep your eyes and ears open while your subjects fill out the lists; they may give you ideas for criteria.

According to your system, which friends were highly creative, moderately creative, uncreative? Explain.

5.   Find a copy of the book *Flowers for Algernon* and read (or reread) it. It's fast and fascinating reading. Write a report comparing and contrasting the main character's happiness level with his intelligence level. When does he seem happiest? Saddest? Why? Is Charly, the main character, the same at the end of the novel as he was at the beginning, or has he grown in any way? Explain.

6.   Contact a local college or university and ask about organizations that require special academic achievements or special "intelligence" to join. Once you find out, contact a member of the organization and interview the person. Possible questions: what criteria are used in choosing and rejecting members? Are there special privileges that members enjoy over other organizations? How would you define intelligence?

Another possibility is to contact a member of Mensa, an organization that claims outright that its members are highly intelligent. You can probably find the organization in the phone book, or try contacting the American Psychological Association (APA) for information. You should be able to find the APA or a local psychological association in the phone book.

Write a report on the interview and your reactions to what you learned.

7.   Visit or call a center in your area for the mentally handicapped and ask about the advantages and disadvantages of (a) special education classes and (b) mainstreaming. Maybe they can recount a few "success" stories. If the center treats people with physical impairments, ask about special training programs in motor skills, social skills, self-care, or any other special needs. Write a report on your visit and be sure to include your reactions.

Many of the centers welcome volunteers, so if this interests you, it could be a good opportunity to do homework and to help someone else at the same time.

Is Personality Inherited?

Have you ever heard people say, "You have your mother's personality?" or "You have the same disposition as your father!" These statements may not be entirely correct. We are probably not born with a personality. Rather, it can be argued that we are born with some attributes or traits that determine how we react to our environment and how others react to us, which shapes the development of what is commonly called a personality. These traits have been categorized and labeled by researchers as "temperaments." An individual's temperament refers to the nature of his or her response to stimulation, the intensity of reactions, and overall general mood. Temperament theorists believe that these attributes combine with environmental influences to form one's personality.

This theory was developed due to a longitudinal study of 133 children for over 30 years designed to examine genetic influences on personality (Thomas and Chess, 1977, 1980, 1986). The study has led the researchers involved to believe that there are inborn differences in children; that each child is born with a unique temperament. As an infant, each child was evaluated according to nine different factors.

1. **Activity level.** How active is the baby? Does he or she wriggle or not move when the diaper is changed?
2. **Rhythmicity.** Does the baby eat and sleep at regular times?
3. **Distractability.** Can the focus of attention be changed with different toys and activities?
4. **Approach/withdrawal.** How does the baby respond to a new toy or food?
5. **Adaptability.** What is the response to changes in routine?
6. **Attention span and persistence.** How much interest does the baby show with toys?
7. **Intensity of reaction.** How intense are the baby's reactions?
8. **Threshold of responsiveness.** What responses are elicited by changes in the environment?
9. **Quality of mood.** What is the overall mood of the baby? Content? Cranky? Indifferent?

From these evaluations, the researchers found three general patterns of behavior, or temperaments: they labelled children either "easy," "difficult," or "slow-to-warm-up." Easy children have regular sleeping and eating patterns, like new food, and often smile at their mothers. After napping, these children may play with crib toys quietly. It was found that

From seed to bud to flower, development is a natural process.

274

Discuss the Photo

Water and sun determine a flower's growth. What do humans need?

later in life children with an easy temperament generally find school enjoyable and eagerly meet new people. They are likely to have mostly positive interactions with parents. Difficult children are moody and require attention, soothing words of encouragement, and do not enjoy meeting new people. After napping, difficult children may cry and become quite restless in the crib. As they mature, these people seem to have a hard time with peers and parents, and their parents may feel discouraged. Slow-to-warm-up children are quiet,

HUMAN DEVELOPMENT

275

Overview

Students investigate moral development with an informal survey. They will compose questions to determine how their peers think about a particular moral issue of their choosing, conduct the research, compile results, and discuss findings with the class. As a group, the class then summarizes the findings, explains significance, and proposes ways to increase ethical/moral levels among peers. Complete instructions for this activity and the supporting student worksheets can be found in the Teacher Resources.

shy, and slow to react to people. Later, people with this temperament may have to repeat experiences and interact with people several times in order to develop some sort of trust and understanding. Their parents may react by being overprotective. Because of this, a slow-to-warm-up child may not be able to experience many new people and new situations. In all cases, the child's temperament plays a crucial role in the nature of parental interaction. Temperament, which seems to remain stable over a lifetime, predisposes the child to act and respond in certain ways, affecting the parents' response. When measuring the quality of this interaction, psychologists use the term "goodness of fit." The meshing of the child's temperament and the parents' ability to adapt to it is an important factor affecting personality development.

Most researchers agree that both biological factors such as temperament and environmental factors such as culture, family dynamics, and community influence the evolution of personality. However, some psychologists believe that temperament labels are meaningless because they are too broad, too general, or are too difficult to measure. Some question whether people go through these temperaments several times a day! Others, however, believe temperament to be the cornerstone of the personality that is further shaped by environmental forces. We may never fully understand where the influences of biological factors and the influences of the environment begin and end.

References

Full citations can be found in the Teacher Resources.

DISCUSS THE PHOTO

Did students play games when they were children that no one else would ever understand?

Exactly what are these kids doing? We don't know.

276

PSYCHOLOGY AND YOU RESOURCES

A variety of resources are available in the Psychology and You *supplementary material. In addition, there are a number of additional resources listed to enhance your lesson plans.*

Masters
- ▼ 10-1A Learning Goals
- ▼ 10-1B Answers to Learning Goals
- ▼ 10-2 What Would You Do?
- ▼ 10-3 Dr. Spock's Advice
- ▼ 10-4 The Mind of a Two-Year-Old
- ▼ 10-5 Kohlberg's Stages of Moral Development
- ▼ 10-6 Kohlberg Practice Quiz

Student Worksheets
- ▼ Vocabulary Worksheet
- ▼ Independent Practice Worksheet
- ▼ Enrichment Worksheet
- ▼ Reteaching Worksheet

Test Bank
- ▼ Tests A and B
- ▼ Midterm

Multimedia
- ▼ *The Mind* Videotape Modules #1, 9–12, 25–29
- ▼ **Psychware** Exercise 1
- ▼ Psychology Videodisc

Student Workbook

PACING CHART

Complete Coverage

Day 1: Assign the first two sections of the chapter prior to class. Use a discussion question in the text or an in-class activity to generate discussion about the effects of both heredity and environment on development. Have students read "Developmental Patterns" for homework.

Day 2: After discussing maturational processes, growth cycles, and critical periods, assign for homework an activity that gives students an opportunity to apply this knowledge. Have the class read "The Family and Child Development" for Day 3.

Day 3: Using discussion question #5, allow students to evaluate different parenting styles. Discuss what fosters children's healthy development. Assign "Sequences of Development" for Day 4.

Day 4: Provide an activity or project through which students can identify Piaget's stages of cognitive development.

Day 5: Use illustrative examples to help students evaluate Kohlberg's theory of moral development.

Infancy and Childhood

OBJECTIVES

Be able to:

▼ Explain the importance of heredity and environment in human development.

▼ Describe the way maturational processes work.

▼ Explain growth cycles, critical periods, and imprinting.

▼ Describe the role of the mother and the father in family life.

▼ Describe the three parenting styles and their effects on children.

▼ Explain the causes of child abuse.

▼ List and explain Jean Piaget's four stages of child development.

▼ List and explain Lawrence Kohlberg's three stages of moral development.

▼ Describe what is meant by children's rules of language.

Global Look at the Chapter

Throughout childhood, everything that happens to us arises from and is controlled by developmental processes that follow a fixed plan or sequence. Mental, moral, and physical growth must evolve at their own speed with the aid of a suitable environment.

277

INTRODUCING THE CHAPTER

Most students have probably never heard of Dr. Spock (no, not *Mr.* Spock), so explain that he was considered the foremost expert on child care for many years. In fact, his book, *Baby and Child Care,* which has been updated numerous times since it first appeared in the 40s, is still a popular resource for parents. **Teaching Master 10-2 What Would You Do?** asks students to assume the role of parents with small children. For example, what should you do if your child is throwing several temper tantrums a day? You can have students write down their answers, or break the class into groups and assign a few questions to each group. Compare students' answers with Dr. Spock's *updated* comments, which are listed on **Master 10-3 Dr. Spock's Advice.**

LEAD-OFF ACTIVITY

Have each group design one area of a children's museum. If students have never been to one, describe some of the ones you may have seen. For example, one corner has materials for projects: buttons, strings, glue. Another corner includes a long trough with water where kids can glide toy boats. Stress that each area should be educational, which can be defined very loosely (for example, the water area may teach kids about how water always seeks the lowest level), and each area should provide children with a hands-on opportunity.

Assign the final section for Day 6.

Day 6: Use discussion question #8 to enhance discussion about the development of language skills. Give the Chapter Review quiz.

In Brief

Day 1: Refer to Psychology In Your Life as you focus discussion on the impact heredity and environment have on development. Assign for homework an activity involving the study of identical twins.

Day 2: Use discussion question #8 in the text to review maturational processes, growth cycles, critical periods, and imprinting as they relate to the development of language.

Day 3: Use the relevant In Focus box to review Piaget's stages of cognitive development.

Day 4: Outline Kohlberg's theory of moral development, using the relevant In Focus box. Give the Chapter Review quiz.

ENRICHMENT

As a research project, have students compare Dr. Spock's advice found in **Teaching Masters 10-2 and 10-3** with another well-known child-care expert, Dr. T. Berry Brazelton.

FYI How many times does the average woman ovulate during her fertile years? 300 to 500. How many sperm cells are released on ejaculation? Over 300 million. How many sperm cells will reach the fallopian tubes? About 10,000 to 20,000. One of these may eventually reach and penetrate the egg. If so, a chemical reaction occurs that prevents other sperm from penetrating.

Teaching Hint

Compare heredity and environment to an automobile. Heredity gives us the chassis; the environment customizes it. The customizing during the early years is the most crucial. Without that, it is going to be difficult to fine-tune the engine or add pinstripes and details to the body.

heredity

Characteristics obtained directly from the genes.

environment

A person's surroundings, which have an influence on a person's characteristics and development.

nature/nurture

Contrasting views of how we gain certain characteristics: nature refers to heredity, nurture to environment

278

Unit 4 HUMAN DEVELOPMENT

THE WORLD OF THE CHILD

Here is a conversation between a researcher and a four-year-old boy (Phillips, 1969):

"Do you have a brother?"
"Yes."
"What's his name?"
"Jim."
"Does Jim have a brother?"
"No."

Is there something wrong with this child? No. As we start this chapter, we enter a foreign world—that of the developing child. While children partially resemble the rest of us, their thought processes can be quite foreign to our everyday thinking. The "problem" Jim's brother has is that he is not able to look at something from any point of view but his own—not yet. We will discuss a possible explanation for this a little later.

HEREDITY VERSUS ENVIRONMENT

For as long as scientists have studied animals and people, they have asked questions about what is caused by **heredity**—that is, what is actually contained in the genes themselves—and what is caused by the **environment**—which is what goes on in the world around us. The issue of which is responsible is called the **nature/ nurture** controversy. Things that do not depend primarily on learning are due to physical factors, or *nature;* things that are learned are due to the environment, or *nurture.* Before we can understand how children develop, we need to know which abilities and characteristics are mostly due to our physical nature. We already know that the environment, or nurture, plays a large part in the development of most skills, but almost all the time, the source of these skills is some combination of nature and nurture.

Until only recently, most people, including so-called experts, claimed that the world of the infant was chaos and confusion. How very wrong this view turned out to be! The interaction between environment and heredity can be seen clearly in some experiments that show just how alert and intelligent the seemingly mindless infant really is. To understand one study in this area, you have to know first of all that infants can vary their sucking patterns on nipples or pacifiers. Specifically constructed nipples that would register when the

DISCOVERY

To conduct a role-playing exercise, read the following directions to two volunteers: *You are the mother and father of a two-week-old infant. You learn that stimulation is essential for proper development.* Discuss the kinds of stimulation you want to pro-vide for your child. You might discuss mobiles, books, rattles, and so on.

Afterward, ask for two more volunteers to play out the same situation, but this time the child is two years old.

baby sucked were put in the infants' mouths, and earphones were put over their ears so they could hear voices. The infants had a choice of hearing their own mother's voice or that of a different mother. In order to hear their own mother's voice, the babies had to learn to slow down their sucking and to leave a fixed amount of time between suckings. If they speeded up, they got a different mother's voice.

Amazingly, these infants were able to vary their sucking so they could hear their mother's voice, and that became their favored pattern of sucking. This means that infants are able to learn from the environment, that they can make discriminations among different voices, that they have a memory system that can hold the voices, and that they can understand something as complex as an association between sucking and hearing a voice. This is a beautiful example of the importance of the environment and the use of already inherited skills on the environment (Stillings, et al., 1987; DeCasper & Fifer, 1980). Oh, yes, we forgot to tell you—all the infants were under 72 hours old!

Focus on Heredity

Genes are the basic units of heredity. They contain directions for many characteristics, such as eye color (and shape), hair color (and texture), adult height, general body build, and so on. Except for the effects that the prenatal environment can have (the pregnant woman's nutrition, injury to the fetus, and so on), everything babies are born with is determined by their genes.

Genes are carried on larger units, the **chromosomes.** Every kind of body cell contains 23 pairs of chromosomes, for a total of 46—every kind but one, that is. The reproductive cells, the egg and the sperm, each contain only 23 chromosomes, one half of each pair. When they unite at conception, the fertilized egg, or **zygote** (ZYE-goat), then has the necessary number, 46, for proper development.

While the environment is also critical to proper development, psychology in recent years has focused more and more on the influence that heredity has on many of our abilities and behaviors. The influence of heredity on intelligence is considerable, as we discussed in Chapter 9. And genes can clearly influence a child's activity level, how easily soothed an infant is, his or her emotional responsiveness, and such things as how a child reacts to new or novel things in the environment (Schwartz, 1979b). There are even indications that tolerance for alcohol may well have a genetic background. Note, though, that if something is inherited, this doesn't mean it can't be changed by the environment. A person may inherit the potential to be a great runner, but only with environmental training will he or she actually perfect this skill.

genes

Basic units of heredity.

chromosomes

Units of heredity containing genes; 23 in reproductive cells, 46 in all other cells.

zygote

Fertilized egg.

Connections

Students can apply what they have learned in Chapter 7 about *shaping.* An example is when babies learn to slow down their sucking to hear their mothers' voices.

Discussion

Describe the following scenario to your class: *You read about this experiment on sucking and the mother's voice. In practical terms, what effect does it have on you? Answer:* I realize that learning is going on every day, so I try to stimulate my baby in many ways.

Points to Stress

Infants are not the only ones to respond in a conditioned way to parents' voices, of course. Ask students, "Do you ever cringe at the sound of your mom's or dad's voice because you've heard that tone before and you know you're in trouble?" Infants may experience the same sort of learning process!

ENRICHMENT

Have students find out about early attempts to study genetics, such as Gregor Mendel's attempts to cross sweet peas to produce hybrids. They might also look up Thomas Scott Morgan.

ENRICHMENT

If any monozygotic (identical) twins attend your school, invite them to class for a question-and-answer session. If possible, invite a set of dizy- gotic (fraternal) twins on the same day, and compare and contrast answers. (You might ask students to submit questions ahead of time.)

Critical Thinking

Ask students which of the following aspects of personality are influenced by heredity: temperament, introversion/extroversion, intelligence, attitudes. Most of the evidence that students offer will be anecdotal, but this may prompt a few to search for other kinds of evidence.

DISCUSS THE PHOTO

If these triplets were raised apart from each other, would they still have similar interests? It's diffi- cult to say, but similarities are often striking in such cases.

Critical Thinking

Ask students why twins raised apart have such striking similarities at times. Because of their identical genetic struc- tures, perhaps twins are predisposed to react to the environment in similar ways or to pay more atten- tion to certain stimuli in the environment. But remind students that the environ- ment certainly influences heredity, which would account for the *differences* in twins raised apart.

280

Unit 4 HUMAN DEVELOPMENT

▲ *These triplets have identical heredity.*

dizygotic twins

Twins who develop from two differ- ent eggs fertilized by different sperm; have different heredity.

monozygotic twins

Twins who come from one fertilized egg; have the same heredity.

Twin Studies

There are two types of twins. One type develops from two differ- ent eggs fertilized by two different sperm. They are called **dizygotic** (dye-zye-GOT-ick) (or fraternal) **twins** because they come from two *(di)* fertilized eggs *(zygotes)*. Thus, their heredity, or genetic structures, are no more alike than are those of any other sibling pair.

The second type of twins develops from only one fertilized egg that for unknown reasons divides in two. These **monozygotic** (mah- no-zye-GOT-ick) (or identical) **twins** have the same (identical) genes or heredity. Psychologists study them thoroughly to see how they are alike—especially when they have not been reared together but have grown up in different homes. If they are reared apart and have simi- lar characteristics, the environment probably has had little influence on this fact, while heredity has played a major role.

A careful study of 15 pairs of grown monozygotic twins separated from birth has shown some startling similarities. For instance, these twins' basic temperaments, occupational interests, hobbies, prefer- ences for art and music, and athletic interests were quite similar, even though they had never actually met one another. At approximately the same age, the twins developed the same fears and nightmares, stuttering, bed-wetting, and bouts of depression. In one case, one twin was raised as a German Nazi while the other was raised as a Jew in the Caribbean. When they were first united in their late 40s, they both sported the same type of mustache, wore the same type of wire-rimmed glasses, liked the same foods, liked to scare people by sneezing loudly, stored rubber bands on their wrists, read magazines from back to front, and enjoyed eating alone in restaurants—some- thing few men like to do (Bouchard, 1983; Holden, 1980).

While not all monozygotic twins are this much alike, we now know that heredity plays a far more important role in development than we ever suspected. Most researchers today estimate that rough- ly 50 percent of our personality traits and intelligence are the result of genetic factors (Turkheimer, 1991; Bouchard, 1983).

DEVELOPMENTAL PATTERNS

An early study in psychology took a very unusual look at the process of development. A husband-and-wife team adopted a chim- panzee, a lovable seven-month-old female. They decided to rear this chimp along with their other new (human) child to see what hap- pened.

Both were treated identically, or as identically as possible, taking their physical differences into account. At first, this "experiment" looked like a disaster. In fact, the parents felt some panic for a while when the chimpanzee progressed faster than their son. For example,

COOPERATIVE LEARNING

Divide the class into groups and assign several pages of this chapter to each group so that the entire chapter is covered. Then, assign a particular age range (5-6, 7-8, 9-10, 11-12 years) to each group. Each group's task is to teach their material to their assigned age range. Fellow students will have to play the children! Students have great fun with this activity if both the "teachers" and "learners" remain in character throughout the lesson. Remind them that the lecture method does not work very well with kids; they should involve the audience as much as possible.

---

the chimp learned to feed herself, drink from a cup, and obey her "parents" much earlier and faster than the boy did. By the time both "children" reached the age of two, however, the boy had overtaken and passed the chimpanzee in every respect except physical strength and amount of body hair (Kellogg & Kellogg, 1933).

This dramatic study makes a point of major importance: development within a species (people, elephants, dogs, and so forth) is orderly and specific; it has its own timetable and pattern. The pattern is related to how complex the mature organism ultimately will be. At first, the boy living with the chimp developed slowly in comparison, but later he went beyond the chimp's abilities because human beings reach a higher level of intelligence and other skills. The human has the longest developmental period of all creatures. This state of weakness and helplessness that lasts for such an extended time is probably the reason we have an elaborate social structure of closely knit families who can protect and care for the helpless young ones.

Much of our development is a process of integrating our extraordinary brains with our bodies. Thus, the baby starts out with a series of reflexes or automatic reactions. These reflexes will occur with the proper stimulation, and the baby does not have any control over them—not at first. For instance, if you touch a baby's cheek, it will turn its head and start sucking. If you place your finger in the palm of an infant's hand, it will grasp it tightly—just as a chimp does, incidentally. And if a baby is startled, its arms and legs suddenly shoot out, away from its body. The sucking, grasping, and startle reflexes are some of the building blocks for later, more complicated behavior. With age, most of these reflexes disappear and can be regulated by the higher brain. In other words, they stop happening automatically and can be controlled; they become actions that we choose to do or not do. There are cases where adults have suffered certain kinds of damage to the brain, which result in the reappearance of these sucking and grasping reflexes. Such people find themselves automatically and unwillingly sucking when the cheek is touched and unable to let go of objects placed in their hands. For these people, the higher brain has, for want of a better term, been "disconnected" (Brown, 1976).

Maturational Processes

A child is preprogrammed for certain activities, such as walking, a natural skill that begins to develop sometime between nine and 15 months after birth. To the casual observer, this process seems to be "learned," but it is not. As uncoordinated as babies seem to be during the process of starting to walk, they will be able to walk on their own with no training at all. Some parents work and work with their children, thinking that somehow they are *teaching* them to walk. All this training does, at best, is to help the child walk about one month earlier than he or she normally would have, at roughly 15 months,

Chapter 10 INFANCY AND CHILDHOOD

▲ *Although bound, this infant will start to walk at the same age as children from other cultures.*

DISCUSS THE PHOTO

Point out that this infant will be rocked and stimulated and will develop normally.

Points to Stress

One of the original goals of the chimp experiment was to teach the animal to communicate. Although the experiment was not very successful, it inspired other experiments, years later, in which chimps learned to use sign language at the level of a human two-year-old. Critics argue that this is not really language but simply memorization of certain patterns. (See **Development of Language Skills** later in the chapter.)

DEMONSTRATION

Bring several educational toys to class, demonstrate how they work, and discuss what children can learn from the toys. If bringing in toys is not feasible, bring in a toy catalog and discuss the educational value of the toys in the catalog. If you need an update on new toys, talk to some teachers at your school who have recently had a baby. They'll tell you more than you'll want to know.

DISCUSS THE PHOTO

This toddler is about a year old. (Will she ever forgive her parents for allowing the use of this picture in a textbook?)

Points to Stress

Although learning to walk is influenced by the maturation process, there are two factors to consider. One, infants who are not allowed to practice crawling, sitting up, and other normal activities, because they are neglected in impoverished settings, will have very poor motor skills (Dennis, 1960). Two, it seems that infants who are strapped upright on the mother's back will tend to walk a month or two earlier than infants who spend most of their time on their backs or stomachs. But keep in mind that no infant will walk any sooner than its maturation will allow.

282

Unit 4 HUMAN DEVELOPMENT

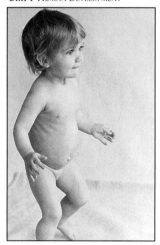

▲ *Baby's first steps.*

maturation

The automatic, orderly, sequential process of physical and mental development.

growth cycles

Patterns of development in which some areas develop more rapidly and some more slowly, but all in a way preplanned by nature.

282

which is an average. Walking at an earlier or later age (within the normal range) is *not* a sign of future intelligence or of being "slow" but is just a reflection of individual differences. Nature must take its course.

For some reason, many people have trouble believing that developing the ability to walk is automatic. But some Native American cultures, especially in the past, strapped an infant to its mother's back so she could go about her chores, thus preventing the baby from "practicing" walking. When these children were finally freed, they very quickly walked quite well on their own. This kind of skill, which develops automatically as the child becomes more mature, is part of the process called **maturation**—the automatic, orderly, and sequential process of physical (and mental) development.

The same rules apply to other skills, such as speech and reasoning, which we will discuss shortly. Sequencing and timing are clearly part of the development of general "intelligence." Many toys on the market claim to increase a child's intelligence more rapidly, but these claims should not be taken too seriously. There is no question that children need stimulation from their surroundings, and play is one of the best ways for that to occur. It is important for parents to spend time playing and "talking" with their babies, because this is a good way to stimulate the infants' brains. But it simply takes time for all the nerve cells to grow, develop, and branch out. No toy in the world can make that happen any earlier than it normally would. The child needs good nutrition, stimulation, and safety. A good environment is necessary for proper development, but it won't *speed up* the process. What we're saying here may require a moment's careful thought in order to be grasped: without a stimulating environment, the child's mental growth can be slowed; with a stimulating environment, it will proceed at its own internal pace, not exceed it. Many parents are too impatient; they can't accept what nature dictates (Rust, 1984; Kagan, 1975).

Patterns (sequences) of maturation are essentially the same for all children. The *timing* of development, however, will vary from one child to another. Only notable extremes are important. A child who develops very, very slowly and walks, for instance, at a much later age than the average child may have something wrong physically. The timing of a child's development would have to be quite a bit slower than the average, though, before parents should be concerned.

Growth Cycles

All of our parts do not develop at the same rate. There are **growth cycles** for different aspects of human development; in other words, some areas develop more rapidly, some more slowly, and some develop in spurts or increase dramatically all in a short time. For instance, at age eight, 95 percent of the basic structure of the brain

COOPERATIVE LEARNING

Group task: "Pick an age, any age, and think of a way to entertain, educate, and challenge children at that age." Each group focuses on a different way to achieve the task: (1) devise an original game that kids can play outside; (2) devise an original board game; (3) devise a new toy; (4) outline a new TV show; (5) plan an all-day field trip for kids; or (6) plan a birthday party with a theme.

has been completed, but the body has 55 percent left to go, and the reproductive system more than 90 percent.

There are also differences between the sexes in these cycles. Girls are more orderly and stable in their growth cycles. From infancy, they show a continuous movement forward in babbling, word making, and bone and muscle development. Boys grow in spurts and mature more slowly, although eventually they reach the same level.

Critical Periods

We can get insight into the human by studying animal behavior. Ducks and some other birds, for example, are programmed to accept a mother at a specific time in development. If there is no "real" mother around, some strange things can happen. One researcher found that shortly after ducks had hatched—somewhere around 16 hours—if the mother was not there, the ducklings would follow *him* around if he quacked and walked in a squatting position (Lorenz, 1952). They assumed that he was their mother.

As it turns out, ducklings are programmed to accept almost anything as a "mother" at this time. The term for this attachment is **imprinting**, which means that the animal's brain is ready to be engraved (or imprinted) with a mother image. The "mother figure" must move around for imprinting to occur. One of the most unusual studies of this sort involved imprinting ducklings on a tin can that was pulled around a pond in circles.

Imprinting occurs during a **critical period**. A critical period is a specific time period in an animal's maturation when a particular skill may be learned or an association made, but the learning or the associating can occur *only* during this period if it is to occur at all. Notice how in Figure 10.1, the duck's acceptance of the fake mother peaks at about 16 hours after birth. Imprinting seems to be the result of a chemical released by the body at a certain time. If an animal's chemistry is deliberately altered, the critical period can be extended or even eliminated (Colombo, 1982).

Critical periods must be part of all species because they show up in so many places. Dogs, for instance, form solid human attachments only up to 12 weeks of age. After that time, they can be unpredictable. Because of this, you want to get a dog that has been around humans quite a bit before that 12-week period is over, especially if the dog is a large and possibly dangerous one. Dogs from pet stores should always be bought before the end of 12 weeks because they are frequently isolated behind glass and have limited social experience.

Just as a dog automatically wags its tail, a baby will start to smile during its first month, even if no one is around. By the second month, smiling occurs in response to a pleasant sound or a caress. This happens with blind infants as well, so it can't be a matter of imitation. Smiling becomes associated with certain events through

imprinting

A process that occurs at a preset time in development, when the brain is ready to receive and respond to a specific stimulus.

critical period

A specific time of development that is the only time when a particular skill can begin to develop or an association can occur.

Critical Thinking

Ask students what factors other than maturation will affect growth. Answers may include genes, hormones, nutrition, major illness, and sensory deprivation.

Points to Stress

Parents whose young children have many ear infections know that their children's speech and language skills may suffer, since hearing well is *critical* during the first couple of years.

COOPERATIVE LEARNING

This is another version of the preceding cooperative-learning activity (you probably won't want to do both). This time, have the entire class focus on a birthday party. Each group thinks of a different theme and plans the party from beginning to end. For example, if the theme is clowns, children can come dressed as clowns, can draw clowns at the party, can play "Pin the nose on the clown," and so on. Decide if you want students to focus on one age group or on several different ones.

Points to Stress

Since language is affected by critical periods, this means that it is learned in an orderly, sequential fashion; in other words, it is part of the maturation process. And it begins early: children will coo, then babble, then make sounds that resemble words.

DISCUSS THE PHOTO

Imprinting also guides the selection of a mate of the same species. In other of Lorenz's experiments, a jackdaw who imprinted on Lorenz as an infant focused its mating ritual on him when it reached sexual maturity. Lorenz learned the hard way that part of this ritual involved stuffing worms into the mouth of the intended mate.

FYI Torsten Wiesel and David Hubel won a Nobel Prize for showing that there is a critical period for the development of sight. If the brain is not allowed to practice processing visual images during the first two years of life, a person will not be able to see.

284

Unit 4 HUMAN DEVELOPMENT

▲ *Walking and swimming together—Konrad Lorenz and his imprinted "children."*

learning at about four months. Both animals and humans need frequent touching, holding, and rubbing from birth onward, or the results are disastrous (the case of Genie, discussed later, provides more details about this). Finally, a most intriguing critical period occurs for humans: If you want to learn a foreign language with a correct and natural accent, you must start learning it before the age of

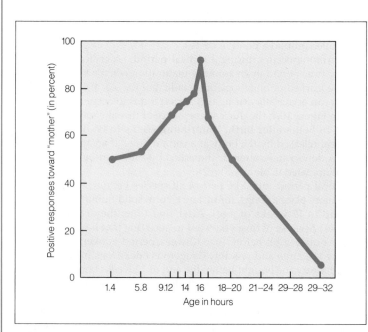

▲ **Figure 10.1** *Ducks' response to imprinting. Note the critical period peaks at 16 hours.*

ENRICHMENT

Harry Harlow (Chapter 5) thought that the first six months of a monkey's life were critical for social development. Although this is true, he later found that the effects of isolation during the first six months could be reversed. So, are the first six months critical or not? Have students answer this question by finding out what Harlow did to reverse the effects of isolation.

▲ *Chimpanzees prefer their own babies to ours.*

12 years. After that age, you can learn the language, but you will never have speech sounds that match those of the native speakers. There is one exception, though. A few people have a special ability to imitate sounds; these people are said to have an "ear" for languages. They will be able to get much closer to matching the correct accent, but the rule still applies for most of us.

You probably have heard tales about children who supposedly have been reared by animals. They are called **feral** (FER-al) **children**, the term *feral* meaning "wild, untamed." Such children supposedly walk on all fours and swing from trees. There has been one documented case of a boy who was discovered at age 11 or 12 after living in the woods by himself. The young man could not speak, and he did bite as any human child will, but he didn't growl, swing from trees, or act like an animal in other ways. The importance of critical periods and maturation within a social setting did show up. Since they were bypassed, he had almost no "human" skills. The boy eventually learned primitive speech and could print a few words, but he was never able to come close to what others his age could do in either area. He did learn the ways of society, in that he cleaned himself and ate the way we do and was able to accept and give affection as humans do, despite his childhood spent in isolation from other humans (Itard, 1932).

When you read about cases of children being brought up by animals, be careful not to accept them before asking yourself some questions. For instance, chimpanzees will almost automatically "adopt" an orphaned infant chimpanzee if its mother belonged to their group. They have even been known to take in an orphan whose mother was not a member of their group, but that is very, very rare. Chimpanzees

DISCUSS THE PHOTO

What if the parent was not around? The older sibling often assumes the role of caretaker when the parent is gone.

Comprehension Check

For most people, during what time in life is it probably easiest to learn more than one language? *(before age 12)* Why? *(Learning a language is a maturational process with a fixed critical period.)*

feral children

Children supposedly reared by animals.

285

DISCOVERY

Contact an elementary school teacher who might be willing to work with you on an extended project. Have your students write a children's story or poem and have the grade school teacher instruct his or her students to illustrate the story or poem. This pro-ject will force your students to focus on the reading abilities and interests of the grade school children. Once the project is completed, your students might, if feasible, read their story or poem to the children. Consider having the books displayed.

ENRICHMENT

Invite the owner of a local day-care center to class. Before the visit, have students prepare a list of questions; also, discuss what they believe con-stitutes a good day-care center.

Discussion

Students whose parents are divorced might be will-ing to discuss the hard-ships involved—from the inconveniences that divorce creates, to cus-tody battles, to the process of learning how to get along with step-parents.

Unit 4 HUMAN DEVELOPMENT

nuclear family

Parents and their children.

extended family

Nuclear family plus other relatives.

are more likely either to kill or ignore such an infant (Goodall, 1971). If they are this reluctant to take in a "foreign" baby of their own species, wouldn't they be much more reluctant to care for a human baby? Also, remember how long human infants are almost complete-ly helpless, unable to do much of anything for themselves, including eating. Unless an adult human is around to take care of them for at least the first year of life, and probably longer, they will die. Without that kind of care, abandoned infants could not survive long enough to be taken in by animals (Graber, 1988). As for stories about children reared by packs of wolves, human babies would probably be consid-ered food by the wolves, not welcome additions to their group.

THE FAMILY AND CHILD DEVELOPMENT

Many children in our society grow up in a **nuclear family,** made up only of parents and their children. An **extended family** includes other relatives, such as aunts, uncles, or grandparents. Most people think that the majority of Americans lived in extended families until very recent times. This is not actually true. On farms, grandparents and other relatives often lived on the family's land, but they usually had separate houses some distance apart. One estimate is that since our nation began, no more than one-fifth of the American people have ever lived in extended-family households (Degler, 1980).

The typical American family of today, however, is different in some important ways from the family of 20 or 30 years ago. For one thing, the divorce rate has steadily increased since the 1950s. By the 1980s, half of all marriages ended in divorce, and that rate shows no sign of slowing down. This means that before children reach the age of 18, 50 to 60 percent of them will spend at least one year in a single-parent family (Barber & Eccles, 1992). When a single parent gets mar-ried again, the children usually are not sure what the "new" parent means to their lives. Often, children resent stepparents and are afraid that they will try to take the place of the absent parent. When other children also come into the picture, confusion and jealousy are bound to occur. The best thing stepparents can do is go slowly. It takes time for everyone to get used to this new arrangement, and rushing things makes it worse. It is also important for the parent-couple to talk about these problems ahead of time and agree to back each other up. To do that, they must have similar ideas about what children should and should not be allowed to do. When the adults are prepared for confusion and are careful to treat everyone fairly, the new family has a much better chance of making it work.

286

DISCOVERY

Before students have read about discipline, ask the following question: Which methods of discipline are effective and which are not? Take five or six index cards, and write a misbehavior on each card: coloring a wall with crayons, throwing a ball in the house and breaking a lamp, swearing, and so on. One student chooses a card and role-plays the behavior, and another disciplines him or her. Afterward, discuss whether disciplinary methods should vary to fit the crime.

INTERDISCIPLINARY PROJECT

Film. Videotape several staged scenes in which children are misbehaving. Or, you may wish to tape portions of various TV sitcoms. Show the tape to your class, and have them decide how they, as parents, would handle each situation. Encourage them to be as specific as possible.

Chapter 10 INFANCY AND CHILDHOOD

Another recent change has to do with the roles family members play. Most families today need more than one income in order to have a decent standard of living, and nearly two-thirds of all mothers now have jobs outside the home. While it is true that household chores are shared more among parents and children, such changes are not as big as you think. Women still do almost all of the housework, especially the cooking and shopping (90 percent) and most of the childrearing, too (Phares, 1992; Burros, 1988).

Mothers Working Outside the Home

Mothers play an important part in their children's lives and are typically the first person babies become attached to. Many people today have asked what happens to children when their mothers work outside the home. Two important issues are (1) whether the amount of time children spend with their parents decreases and (2) whether the children's attachment to the mother is weaker.

Mothers who work outside the home obviously don't have as much time for their children as full-time homemakers do. In fact, full-time homemakers spend twice as much time with their children, playing with them, taking care of them, disciplining them, and so on. The issue is whether this difference in amount of time has a negative effect on the children of mothers who work outside the home. So far, the answer seems to be "not really." The most important thing is not the amount of time itself but whether the children feel loved and cared for. Apparently, this is possible, regardless of the amount of time spent, by giving children warm affection and by enforcing guidelines about which behaviors are acceptable and which are unacceptable (Barber & Eccles, 1992).

Children's attachment to the employed mother seems to be the same as to the homemaker mother, given a general sense from the mother of love and acceptance. Children who spend half their time in day-care centers develop just as strong an attachment to their mothers as the children of full-time homemakers (Belsky, 1990). Whether the mother is satisfied with what she is doing and whether she has her husband's support seem to be more important for everyone's welfare than whether she works outside the home or not (Levanthel-Belfer, Cowan & Cowan, 1992; Kagan, 1979).

The Father

While mothers generally do more of the childrearing, fathers are still important to a child's development. They spend less time with their children, but they do the same kinds of things as mothers do—playing with the children, taking care of them, disciplining and teaching them. Having a warm, affectionate father around provides a complete family unit and helps children become independent and better able to do things for themselves. Fathers also help children

▲ *While not critical, having a warm father around helps children develop self-esteem.*

Discussion

How has the role of the father changed in the last 20 or 30 years? Have students list ways in which fathers have remained the same and ways in which fathers have changed.

Comprehension Check

What seems to be the most important factor in whether a child forms a strong attachment to his or her mother? *(whether the child feels loved and cared for)*

DISCUSS THE PHOTO

Spending time with children is crucial. Ask students to pretend they have two children. They are offered a huge bonus if they will work out of state three weeks out of every month for a year. Would they accept this offer? Are males' and females' answers similar?

DISCOVERY

Have students interview their own parents about the parenting techniques they used from childhood to the present. Parents may focus on discipline, but students should also ask them about other issues as well: time spent together reading books or doing homework, religion, how one sibling was treated differently than the other, etc.

ENRICHMENT

Have students explore the issue of latchkey kids. What are the lasting effects of being left unsupervised for long periods of time?

Points to Stress

When children are surveyed about discipline, permissive parents are usually ranked as poor parents!

Points to Stress

The benefits of the authoritative style do not happen overnight. And no one is completely authoritative. In fact, it probably requires more discipline on the parents' part; these parents need to be open and consistent and patient, which is not always easy after a long day.

Connections

Ask students if they can think of ways in which the learning principles discussed in Chapter 7 could be applied by parents to motivate their children. For example, what if parents wanted their children to clean their rooms, to come in the house the *first* time they're called, to stop fighting with siblings?

Unit 4 HUMAN DEVELOPMENT

self-esteem

The feeling of being worthwhile and useful.

permissive parenting style

Style in which parents let children do as they wish; few rules made or enforced.

dictatorial (authoritarian) parenting style

Style in which parents rigidly set the rules and demand obedience.

authoritative parenting style

Style in which parents seek input from children; parents are consistent but flexible in enforcing rules.

develop **self-esteem,** which is a feeling that one is worthwhile and useful (Phares, 1992; Lamb, 1979).

When there is no father in the home, however, the effects are not always as bad as you might expect. Many problems found in homes where only the mother is present are caused by too little money and too much stress on the mother, rather than by the father's absence in itself. Boys from such homes are usually just as masculine as other boys, and neither girls nor boys necessarily get into more trouble at school. The important point is for children to feel loved and cared for. This is easier to do when two parents share the load, but it is not impossible with only one (Barber & Eccles, 1992).

Parenting Styles

There are three basic styles of parenting—permissive; authoritarian, or dictatorial; and authoritative. Generally, each one has fairly predictable effects on the children.

Permissive parents tend to let their children do whatever they want. These parents don't make many rules, and they fail to consistently enforce the few rules they do make. As a result, their children don't learn much about unacceptable behavior and its consequences. Children raised in this kind of atmosphere are usually impulsive and irresponsible. As you might expect, they don't have much self-discipline. They also tend to lack self-confidence and to have trouble making decisions and doing things for themselves. Because of these characteristics, they frequently don't get along very well with other children.

The authoritarian, or **dictatorial,** style of parenting is one in which the parents approach their children as tyrants approach their subjects. Dictatorial parents are rigid and inflexible. They set down the rules and demand compliance, often administering harsh punishment for disobedience. The children have very little, if any, input into how their lives are governed. Dictatorial parents don't trust their children to make decisions for themselves. Consequently, their children usually are not very good at making decisions. These children tend to be moody, have poor self-esteem, and often have trouble getting along with others.

The **authoritative** style puts parents in the role of authority figure but not dictator. Authoritative parents do make rules and enforce them. However, they are both caring and flexible, interested in their children's views. These parents try to help their children grow as individuals. They try to help them learn to make their own decisions and solve their own problems. Unlike permissive parents, they don't ignore or cover up an important issue. Unlike dictatorial parents, they don't simply hand down a solution that must be accepted by the child. Instead, authoritative parents listen and offer suggestions and support.

Have three students role-play the three types of discipline described here. Have the three students all respond to the same situation: *Your child is writing on the newly painted wall with crayons.* Mention that even permissive or dictatorial parents may explode at first, but they would probably resort to the styles they use most often. Here's another possible situation: *You look outside for your child who has been instructed to sit on the stoop, but the child is gone. You search and eventually find the child.* You might skip the permissive role-play this time and mention that these parents would probably not create nor enforce a rule of sitting in front. Would they look for the child? Probably.

Chapter 10 INFANCY AND CHILDHOOD

Children raised in this kind of atmosphere tend to be self-reliant, friendly, and self-confident. They take responsibility for themselves and their behavior and usually have stable relationships with others. They have a generally positive image of themselves and of other people as well. We should note that these characteristics are related to being well adjusted and psychologically healthy.

Other Influences

Before leaving this topic, a few points should be made. Parents are not all-powerful. They can and do have a lot of influence, but they are not completely responsible for everything a child does or fails to do. To make any sense of this complicated matter, you have to look at the importance of other children, brothers and sisters, school, teachers, and the rest of the outside world. Also, children are born individuals. A parenting approach that works well with one child may fail with another child.

Today you hear a lot about parents "teaching" foreign languages or an appreciation of classical music to their child before it is even born, while it is still in the womb! (No, it doesn't work.) And some parents are so worried about their child's success that they spend day after day trying to find the right preschool. Many psychologists are seriously concerned that the expectations placed on parents have gone too far. Psychologists are afraid that this pressure to be perfect parents may work against children, not for them. For example, when we put too much emphasis on parents' mistakes, we end up making the parents so insecure that they actually do a worse job, not a better one (Bell, 1983; 1979). Love, affection, guidelines, listening, encouragement—these are the most important things for a child's healthy development, and they are what most parents try hard to provide.

Child Abuse

We have mentioned discipline or guidelines as helping a child to grow psychologically. But the type of disciplining techniques or punishment that parents use is equally important. Physical punishment, like hitting, slapping, and so on, is not a good way to handle problems. It doesn't help the child learn very much about right and wrong, and it can also get out of control fairly easily. When physical punishment is too harsh, it becomes child abuse. Clearly, a child can be abused psychologically, too. But because that problem is much harder to define, most of the information we have focuses on physical abuse.

In this country, there are hundreds of thousands of cases of child abuse each year in which the authorities become involved. Such cases include broken bones, bruises all over the body, serious burns,

Discussion

Perhaps all parents are guilty at times of pressuring their kids to succeed. Maybe not. But students will probably have plenty of examples of times they have *felt* pressured. What lessons has this taught them? What will they do differently as parents?

Discussion

What are some practical ways in which parents can encourage independence in their young children? Ask students if they can remember any techniques their parents used.

Discussion

At what age is it OK to leave kids alone? For how long? Under what circumstances would leaving children alone be considered abuse?

CHAPTER PROJECT/COOPERATIVE LEARNING

The following project will require outside research and interviewing time for students to respond to the following scenario: *Allison and Roger have three kids. If one of them stays home with the kids, they know it will be difficult to make ends meet. What do they do?* Divide the class into groups, and assign each group one of the following tasks: (1) Show that day care is not harmful to children and may even be beneficial. (2) Show that day care can be harmful to children. (3) Explore the day-care possi- bilities in the community and assess which is the best. (4) What are the attitudes and feelings of parents who already send their kids to day care? Do they ever regret their decision? (5) What are the feelings and atti- tudes of parents who do *not* send

Connections

What would Erik Erikson (Chapter 14) say about separation anxiety? He would probably argue that the parents should avoid leaving the child with oth- ers if this causes anxiety because the child needs to develop a sense of trust early on.

DISCUSS THE PHOTO

Ask students how they would deal with such a crying baby.

TEACHING MASTER 10-4

The Mind of a Two- Year-Old. This is a brief conversation between a father and a daughter to illustrate the cognitive level of a two-and-a-half year old. If you are a par- ent, you can probably supply plenty of your own examples.

Unit 4 HUMAN DEVELOPMENT

▲ *Separation anxiety—it's time to panic.*

separation anxiety

The baby's fear of being away from the parent; the desire to avoid strangers.

and sometimes even death. But these figures are much lower than the actual occurrences of child abuse, since most cases are never reported. When a large number of parents were asked whether they had been violent enough with their children that they could have injured them, the number of people who said yes jumped to at least 1.5 million. But that figure is probably low, too, since it only includes parents who were willing to admit to such violent punishment (Phares & Compas, 1992; Starr, 1979).

Whether a parent will abuse a child depends on a lot of different things. We don't know them all, but we do know some conditions that make abuse more likely to happen. For example, most child abusers don't know much about children. They don't know how old a baby must be before it can be toilet trained or before it will sleep through the night and so on. Such parents are usually not very mature themselves and often are looking for love *from* a baby, rather than understanding how much work and responsibility are involved in being a parent. Often, these parents come from a violent back- ground themselves. While abused children run a higher risk of becoming child abusers themselves, the majority of child abusers don't fit this mold. Other factors that lead to child abuse are financial problems, unemployment, too much stress on the parents, alco- holism, psychological problems, and isolation or being far away from friends and family (Phares & Compas, 1992; Wolfe, 1985). For many of these reasons, teenaged parents are more likely to abuse their chil- dren than people who become parents at a later age.

SEQUENCES OF DEVELOPMENT

One of the most important advances in understanding children has been the discovery that we develop in the physical, moral, and intellectual areas in a sequential fashion. This finding is important to both parent and child. Nature requires that the brain and nervous system grow and mature before certain events occur. Thus, until about nine to 12 months after birth, most babies are happy to go from person to person and even to be left alone with a stranger. But from nine months on, the brain has developed enough that the child is very much aware of the mother or father and is just beginning to grasp the fact that parents can disappear and that in their place appears a "foreigner," the baby-sitter. So, from this time until about 18 months, the child completely panics when left with someone else; this is a normal phenomenon called **separation anxiety.** Separation anxiety can be seen in every culture and every normal baby. Obviously, then, it does not mean the parents are doing a bad job or that there is something wrong with the baby. All it does mean is that the brain has reached a certain level of development. Just as separa- tion anxiety seems to appear out of nowhere, it will eventually disap-

their kids to day care? Do they ever regret their decision? After the groups report back to class, have students process the information by writing about what *they* would do if they were Allison or Roger.

pear, and it has nothing to do with how the parents are rearing the child.

By about the child's fourth year, the brain is mature enough to grasp the concept of monsters and the possibility that they are sitting there in the dark next to the child. Comedian Bill Cosby used to do a routine in which a child smears Jell-O on the floor so the monster will slip on its way in. While this is clever and funny to us, it certainly isn't to the youngster. It is helpful to know that the child is not a "sissy," that a fear of the dark and of monsters is normal, and that the child shouldn't be punished because he or she is afraid. Often it helps to get children to say over and over, "I am brave—I can take care of myself," as they are exposed to longer periods of time in the dark. Some children simply can't adjust to the dark. All the commotion about whether to let them have a night-light is not sensible. What possible harm is it going to do? (None.) Fears and nightmares about creatures disappear by about age eight when the brain begins to deal with more complex concerns, such as bodily injury and physical danger.

Because understanding these patterns of development is so important, the next two sections will cover the core theories about how we develop mentally and morally.

Piaget's Theory of Cognitive Development

Jean Piaget (ZHAH Pea-ah-ZHAY) studied **cognitive development,** the ways in which a child's thinking and reasoning change and grow. Piaget divided this development into four basic stages. While not everyone agrees with every detail of his theory, it clearly has stood the test of time, and in its outline, it seems to apply to most children and to explain why they see the world the way they do. The stages and ages listed can overlap, and not all children follow the *exact* pattern, but in general, the system is valid (Beilin, 1992; Piaget, 1929).

Sensorimotor Stage (Birth to Two Years)   During the **sensorimotor stage,** the child spends time on two activities: sensation (sensory) and movement (motor responses; meaning arm, leg, and trunk movements). Thus, the baby sees, studies, and grasps a bottle, the milk providing a pleasurable sensation. So, learning requires the motor response and a connection with sensation. The two will later be tied together by symbols (the word *bottle*). The child also reaches for other objects that bring either pleasure or pain. A connection is made between these objects and the effects they create, and words are eventually attached to each.

These objects are not "permanent" during this learning process. From about three to five months of age, if an experiment is set up in

cognitive development

The ways in which thinking and reasoning grow and change.

sensorimotor stage

Piaget's first stage of child development in which knowledge is tied to movements and objects in the environment.

291

Critical Thinking

Ask students to put themselves in the role of researchers who want to find out if Piaget was correct in his assumptions about cognitive skills. What tests would they use to measure the cognitive skills that Piaget studied?

Points to Stress

Remind students that these stages are not as discrete as they seem. Although Piaget may have disagreed, skills within each stage develop gradually. The stages described here are the norms.

DEMONSTRATION

If you have pre-operational children of your own, you might videotape some of the tasks described in the preceding **Teaching Hint** and show the tape to your class. Or, some of your students may be willing to videotape their siblings.

Points to Stress

Piaget's method for studying object permanence involved hiding something, then observing the child's efforts to search for it. But if the child does not search for the object, does this necessarily mean the child believes it is gone? Is this type of test valid? (Probably not, according to many researchers today. A more valid test might simply track an infant's eye movements to see if he or she searches for an object when it disappears from view. For example, a child may watch a toy train disappearing into a tunnel and then look at the other end of the tunnel to see if the train exits.)

Connections

Piaget is an excellent example of an individual who applied naturalistic observations (Chapter 2). He began to study cognitive development by observing his own three children. He watched intently, interacted, and took notes.

292

Unit 4 HUMAN DEVELOPMENT

object permanence

Piaget's term for the awareness that specific objects are real and exist all by themselves.

preoperational stage

Piaget's second stage of child development in which logical thought is lacking; limited ability to see things from more than one perspective; acquire language and ability to use symbols.

reversibility

Piaget's term for the idea that a relationship that goes in one direction can go in the other direction also.

292

which the child is playing with a toy and the toy disappears through a trap door, the child doesn't show any concern—doesn't even look for the toy. How could this be? Apparently children this age are so self-centered that they view everything in the world from their own reference point. Thus, since the toy is no longer in their line of vision, it no longer exists. The concept of things moving somewhere else is not possible yet.

Children can see quite well. In the very beginning, their eyes focus most comfortably at a distance of somewhat less than a foot so they can focus on the breast for feeding. But their vision is sharp from the first few weeks. Even as adults, we are all programmed to respond to movement anywhere in our line of vision because it may signal danger. Since the child is still in training, so to speak, he or she will be most interested in the movement itself, not associating it yet with anything else (like danger). Thus, if you move a small white elephant toy along, pass it behind a screen, and bring out on the other side a red lion, a child younger than five months old will show no concern about the strange thing that has happened but will be fascinated by the movement alone.

In other words, the child has not as yet formed the concept of what is called **object permanence**—that is, specific objects do not exist all by themselves. They only exist as the child perceives them. The concept of permanent objects first appears at about ten months. Note that this is just about the time that separation anxiety appears; probably the presence and absence of the parent helps the child form this concept since when the parent leaves, an "object" of great importance is gone. Toward the end of the sensorimotor period, the child begins to name real things in a real world. Thus, there are endless requests for a bottle. The brain has replaced reaching for a bottle (motor) and getting it (sensation) with a symbol—that is, the word representing that object. The sensorimotor stage is over.

Preoperational Stage (Two to Seven Years) In the **preoperational stage,** children know that things can be permanent. The child is not yet able (pre) to operate effectively on and within the world. Children at this age are not logical creatures. They think that rocks have the same feelings they do, and they have long discussions with them. In fact, they have long discussions with just about everything and everyone. Language develops at an extremely fast rate during this stage and the child's vocabulary expands enormously. Many symbols, or words, are used to represent actions and objects. The child's point of reference, however, is still the child: the world only exists in terms of himself or herself. The conversation we quoted at the beginning of this chapter illustrated a child who could not imagine that his brother had a world different from his. During this stage, the child is unable to change places with someone else and see things from another point of view. The child cannot understand the principle of **reversibility**, which means that if a relationship goes in one

COOPERATIVE LEARNING

Divide the class into four large groups, and assign one of Piaget's stages to each group. Each group then divides up the following tasks among its members: (1) find more information on the stage; (2) prepare a skit that shows some of the main points of the stage; and (3) prepare a visual aid to illustrate the main concepts of the stage.

---

direction, it can be turned around and go the opposite direction, too. Thus, the little boy at the beginning of this chapter could only understand the relationship he had to his brother but not the reverse, the relationship his brother had to him.

Another interesting point is that children at this age cannot grasp something called **conservation,** the idea that you can change some of an object's characteristics while keeping others the same, or *conserving* them. For instance, the mass (amount) of an object stays the same (is conserved) no matter what you do to its shape. A ball of clay has the same mass if you stretch it out to look like a hot dog. A five-year-old will watch you take a glass of Kool-Aid and pour it into a taller, thinner glass (so the column of the drink is higher). If you ask the child which glass holds more Kool-Aid, he or she will insist that the taller one does, even though the pouring took place right there. By six years of age, a child will go back and forth and say that possibly the taller one has the same amount, but will not be certain.

The important point is that even though the child is so self-centered, he or she is beginning to notice differences between people and objects in the environment; these will finally become clear in the next stage.

Concrete Operations Stage (Seven to 11 Years)   The third stage of the Piaget system is called the **concrete operations stage.** The world has become fixed and real (that is, concrete), with separate objects being different and lying outside the child in the world. The idea of reversibility, or seeing things from someone else's viewpoint, is no longer a problem. Thus, the child's ability to reason in a logical way has gone up a rung on the ladder.

Children at this stage are still limited, however. While they can see objects as permanent and complete, they have some trouble seeing objects as having more than one dimension at the same time. So, a child at the beginning of this period will say about some pencils: "This pencil is long; this one is thin; this one is fat." By the end of the seventh year, they can compare pencils: "This pencil is longer and thinner than that one."

Conservation is much less of a problem, too. By age eight, children have no trouble at all insisting that the two glasses of different shapes hold the same amount of Kool-Aid. From ages eight through 11, the child seems to be bringing together all the principles we have just discussed. While doing this, however, he or she is forming rules and regulations that must be followed to the letter. It is hard for children at this stage to look at things in any other way than either black or white—gray areas are still a little too difficult to understand.

Formal Operations Stage (11 Years On)   Piaget's fourth stage of development, called the **formal operations stage,** appears sometime after 11 years of age and can become more elaborate and complex

---

▲ *Even though these beakers contain the same amount, this boy is convinced the taller one has more in it.*

conservation

Piaget's term for the idea that some of an object's characteristics can be changed while others remain the same; for example, changing shape does not change volume.

concrete operations stage

Piaget's third stage of child development in which the child understands that there is a real world with real objects, which exist apart from the child and which can be manipulated.

formal operations stage

Piaget's fourth stage of child development in which the ability to deal with the highly symbolic and abstract thoughts found in logic, math, philosophy, and ethics begins to appear.

293

Teaching Hint

Here are some common tests used to assess conservation. (1) Draw two rows of five coins on the board. In one row, the five coins should be nearly touching; in the other row, the five coins should be spread apart. Which row has more coins? The pre-operational child will claim that the longer row has more. (2) Draw two squares on the board to represent two grass fields. In one field draw six identical squares (representing houses) close together. In the other field, draw the same six identical squares, but spread these randomly around the field. Which field has more grass to cut? The pre-operational child will claim that the field with the houses close together has more grass to cut.

DISCUSS THE PHOTO

If you took two identical short beakers and filled them both with five ounces, the preoperational child will say they are equal. If you then poured the liquid from one of them into a tall beaker, the child will say that the taller one has more—even if you do the pouring in full view of the child.

ENRICHMENT

Just as intelligence tests (Chapter 9) can be unfair to test takers, Piaget may have been unfair to some of the children he tested. Often, the children had to rely on their limited verbal skills to answer questions. There's no doubt that two- to seven-year-olds

have more difficulty grasping reversibility and conservation than older children, but Piaget may have underestimated these abilities in younger children. Have students find out about Piaget's methods for collecting data.

ENRICHMENT

Have a few students interview a 1st- or 2nd-grade teacher. What attempts do the teachers make to match the lessons to the children's cognitive levels? Make sure the interviewers ask for concrete examples. For instance, students might ask

---

Piaget's Stages

 Parents can conduct the kinds of tests that Piaget conducted. (See Teaching Hints on previous page.)

FYI During the pre-operational stage, children are what Piaget called *egocentric.* Egocentrism is the tendency to look at the world from one's own point of view. Moreover, the egocentric child has difficulty seeing *any* other point of view. At age two or three, this difficulty is very literal. Little Joey sees a broken dish in the kitchen. He may say, "It's broke." Mom asks, "What's broke?" "*It's* broke." Since *he* sees the dish, he assumes she knows what he is talking about. The ability to view the world from many angles, not only literally but also in an abstract way, develops gradually.

294

IN FOCUS

Piaget's Stages of Cognitive Development

Approximate Age	Stages and Related Abilities
	Sensorimotor (birth to two years)
Birth	Raw sensation! Lights . . . sounds . . . smells . . . tastes
3 months	Significant movement! Reaches for objects
5–8 months	No object permanence yet—if object leaves vision, it no longer exists
9–12 months	Object permanence appears
	Separation anxiety!
2 years	Begins to move from world of all sensations and movements to world of thought
	Preoperational (two to seven years)
2 years	Object permanence well established
	No reversibility or conservation skills
	Self-involved—unable to view world from another's point of view
3–7 years	Growing awareness of reversibility and conservation
	Concrete operations (seven to 11 years)
7 years	Reversibility well established
8 years	Some conservation skills well established
9–11 years	Able to view world more and more from another's point of view
	Formal operations (11 and on)
11 and on	Growing ability to think abstractly and symbolically

If you were a parent and wanted to test informally some of these developmental abilities during the next several years as your child grows, how would you do so?

into young adulthood. The term *formal operations* refers to the ability to deal with highly symbolic thoughts, such as those found in mathematics, logic, and philosophy. While some people never make it to this stage no matter what, you can spot it developing in those who suddenly become concerned about issues such as truth and justice, fairness and personal rights. Such concerns are at their peak for most adolescents, but unfortunately too many people become calloused and begin to lose these concerns along the way into adulthood. According to Piaget, then, the formal operations stage is the highest level of cognitive development.

about reversibility and conversation. If a child does not possess these abilities, does the teacher avoid activities related to these skills? Or does the teacher try to encourage development of these skills?

Show students a videotape of an old TV situation comedy. As they watch, they should try to determine which stage of moral development seems to motivate each character. The old "Andy Griffith" episodes work well for this. Or if you want to spend

a little more time, *Twelve Angry Men* with Henry Fonda would be an excellent source. The great thing about this kind of activity is that in the course of debating possible answers, you can explain some of the finer points of the theory.

Chapter 10 INFANCY AND CHILDHOOD

Kohlberg's Theory of Moral Development

Moral development, the development of ideas about right and wrong, also seems to follow a maturational sequence, or series of stages. Like Piaget's system, there is not necessarily a fixed pattern of this development for every single person, and there can at times be a mixture of stages (Snarey, 1985). A major difference between this theory of moral reasoning and Piaget's cognitive system, though, is that a person may be at a high level of moral reasoning but still not be inclined to "be good." In other words, we have a choice regarding moral issues but not so with mental development. This moral system was developed by psychologist **Lawrence Kohlberg** and has many subcategories. For our purposes, however, the three main levels or stages should be enough to give you the general principle.

Preconventional Level (Younger Than Age Six)   At the early **preconventional level,** morality is determined by the sheer power of outside authority. Adults impose their own wills on the children. At these ages, it is impossible for the child to grasp the complexities of right and wrong; instead, the child focuses on whether he or she is being punished or rewarded. If punished, you are "bad." If you are not punished, or if you are praised, you must be doing "good."

Toward the end of this stage, children do begin to grasp that if people do something for you, you should do something for them. But the resulting behavior is not all that related to "morals": children are in it for what they can get at this time because they are still so self-centered.

Conventional Level (Seven to 11 Years)   The **conventional level** of moral reasoning focuses on the expectations of others as the major motivation for doing what is right or wrong. At first, children are seeking the approval of others. But gradually there emerges the idea of social order, or behaving in a certain way because society expects it. In time, the *intentions* of a person's actions become an important consideration in whether the child judges these actions to be right or wrong. In other words, whether or not someone meant to do something is taken into account, just as the legal system makes a distinction between involuntary manslaughter and deliberate murder.

The majority of older people, whether adolescents or adults, don't go much beyond this conventional level of moral reasoning. But some do make it to the final stage.

Postconventional Level (11 Years On)   A relatively small proportion of the population reaches what is called the **postconventional level** of moral reasoning. If this development occurs, it does so at

preconventional level

Kohlberg's early stage of moral development in which morality is determined by the sheer power of outside authority.

conventional level

Kohlberg's middle stage of moral development in which moral reasoning is based on the expectations of others regarding what is right or wrong.

postconventional level

Kohlberg's last stage of moral development in which personal ethics and human rights are dealt with.

TEACHING MASTER 10-5

Lawrence Kohlberg's Stages of Moral Development. This is a handout on Kohlberg's theory that outlines not only his three levels but his six stages as well.

Discussion

Conventional thinking would dictate that, in general, lying is wrong. To keep order in society, we must essentially be truthful with one another. But under what circumstances is it OK to lie? Monitor student responses to see if they are arguing *above*, *below*, or *at* the conventional level.

295

COOPERATIVE LEARNING

Have students work in pairs to answer the following questions: *You are a parent. What do you do to promote a high level of moral thinking in your children?* Answers might include the following: (1) Encourage children to view situations from more than one point of view. (2) When you do "good" things, like giving excess change back to a store clerk, explain why it would have been wrong to keep the money. (3) Treat children with respect. (4) When punishing children for inappropriate behavior, explain your reasoning.

Kohlberg's Dilemmas.

 Preconventional: self-interests. Conventional: social concerns. Postconventional: ethics.

Comprehension Check

Identify the level of moral development displayed in each of the following situations, according to Kohlberg's theory: Rebecca doesn't cheat because she's afraid of what her teacher would think *(conventional level)*; Jeff is nice to his younger sister because his parents will withhold his allowance if he isn't *(preconventional)*; Maria refuses to buy the products of a company that uses unfair hiring practices *(postconventional)*.

Reteaching Strategy

Teaching Master 10-6 Kohlberg Practice Quiz gives students a list of statements. Their task is to match the statements with the level of moral development. Answers are listed at the bottom of the master.

296

IN FOCUS Kohlberg's Dilemmas

Kohlberg compiled much of his information about morality through interviews with hundreds and hundreds of subjects. He would present these subjects with numerous moral dilemmas, similar to this one:

"Every day at the end of class, your teacher tells you to take down the attendance slip. One day a good friend runs into you before you reach the attendance office and begs you to take his name off the sheet. He says he can't tell you the reason why he cut class, but that it was important. Would *you* scratch off the name?"

For this example, Kohlberg would not be concerned so much with whether you would or would not remove the name from the attendance sheet. He was more concerned with the *reasoning* behind the decision. Kohlberg believed that this reasoning would reveal your level of moral development.

Typical Preconventional Reasoning

"It's all right to scratch the name off. There's no way I'll get caught."

"I'm *not* going to do it. I might get caught."

"I'm going to do it. Maybe someday I'll need a favor."

"No way. It's wrong. Besides, he wouldn't do it for me."

Typical Conventional Reasoning

"I better do it—what would my friend think of me if I didn't?"

"I'm *not* going to do it. What if the teacher found out? What would she think?"

"I'm not going to do it—you can't just break the rules whenever you want."

"I'm going to do it. One rule of friendship is that friends help each other out."

Typical Postconventional Reasoning

"I'm going to do it—the attendance system doesn't protect students' rights."

"I'm not going to do it. It's against my principles."

If you had to summarize each of these three types of reasoning in a word or two, which words would you use?

---

about age 11 or 12. Now that the brain and experience have primed the person for dealing with them, issues like personal ethics and human rights come to the foreground (Snarey, 1985; Kohlberg, 1963). Here is a comparison of answers given by people at the earlier preconventional level compared with those given by people at the postconventional level:

Problem: After a shipwreck, 11 men are in a lifeboat, one wealthy and powerful, ten poor. You can save either the one rich man or the ten poor men. Which would you save?

Preconventional answer: The rich man because he will give you a big reward.

Postconventional answer: The ten poor men because human life has value regardless of wealth or status.

You probably will take the second answer for granted, but that has required quite a bit of maturing. When you were very young, you probably would have given the first answer.

A complication with this system of moral development is that behavior differs depending on what kind of situation you are caught

DISCOVERY

Discuss the following dilemmas, making note of students' responses. Afterward, match some of their answers to Kohlberg's levels. And please be tactful. (1) You see someone shoplifting at a department store. Do you report this person? (2) A store clerk makes a mistake when totaling your bill and charges you $20 less for your merchandise. Do you point out the clerk's mistake? (3) You are a police officer on duty. You call home and find out that your home is flooding. There are several homes in your patrol area that are also flooding and *may* need your assistance. Do you go home or do you stay on duty and wait for a possible emergency call? (4) Use the attendance-slip dilemma from the **In Focus Kohlberg's Dilemmas.** You may be surprised at students' responses.

---

up in. Sometimes we let morality go out the window for our own convenience. With the intellectual development discussed by Piaget, we can't go backward, but with morality, sometimes we "know better" and we still don't care. Some psychologists believe that establishing right and wrong might actually arise from biological changes in the brain, despite the fact that the rules vary from one culture to another (Kagan, 1984).

THE DEVELOPMENT OF LANGUAGE SKILLS

Psychologists study communication in any form, even among and by animals. Some claims have been outlandish, though. In 1852, it was said that a captain captured a pirate ship and found a dog that could sing and dance. In 1600, supposedly there was a beautiful white horse who could dance and count and one day just climbed straight up the side of a church steeple to talk to the people (Thomas, 1983). Despite these claims, we do know that dogs, cats, birds, and most other animals can communicate by sound or action. So, before getting into the issue of human language, we want to set the stage with some other types of "language."

Chimpanzees can be taught to communicate symbolically using sign language somewhat similar to that used by the hearing impaired, and some chimps have learned as many as 1,000 different sign-language words. The ability to use sign language clearly shows that they can engage in a form of speech. They don't, however, have the necessary vocal apparatus actually to talk, nor do they show the same level of language skills found in the human. After all, how well would we do on tests of tree-swinging and mutual chimp maintenance (such as cleaning and grooming one another)—tasks they do with great expertise? The point is that we are asking them to perform unnatural acts, and they do themselves proud even though they are not destined to become as proficient in word language as we are (Premack & Woodruff, 1978; Schwartz, 1980).

Despite the chimpanzees' remarkable feats, it appears that only humans are destined to speak, to communicate through a verbal language. We are the only creatures with both the physical structures needed to make all the sounds and the brains to make rules of grammar and invent new words.

Processes of Language

Babbling is a natural activity for babies, even deaf ones who cannot hear their own or others' voices. Buried in all this noisemaking

Chapter 10 INFANCY AND CHILDHOOD

Journal Topic

Use the dilemmas mentioned in the **Discovery** above for journal entries.

Evaluation Strategy

You work at a stereo warehouse. Your boss has to leave early and tells you to lock up when you're done. You're tempted to steal equipment. Describe your reasoning as if you were at the preconventional level, the conventional level, and the postconventional level.

DISCOVERY

Most of us take language for granted. To remind students of the complexity of language and to make them more aware of the processes we undergo when learning a language, teach them some sign language throughout the unit. You can probably rent a video or locate a book to teach yourself; then introduce four or five signs each day!

DISCUSS THE PHOTO

Compare this picture with the photo of Konrad Lorenz that appears earlier in the chapter.

Points to Stress

There is a lot of debate on just how children learn the rules of language, but most people agree that listening alone would not do it. There needs to be a process of discovery. (See discussion question #8 at the end of the chapter.)

Unit 4 HUMAN DEVELOPMENT

▲ *You can imagine the kitten's initial reaction, but the new "mother" turned out to be patient, kind, and loving.*

are the sounds used in *any* human language. A basic blueprint of all speech sounds is programmed in the infant from birth. The environment, by providing examples to imitate, then guides the infant to the correct speech pattern for the society within which the infant lives. From this vast array of sounds, children pick and choose the ones that fit the language of those around them. This is why older foreigners have trouble learning new language. For instance, we use a *th* sound frequently, but it doesn't appear in German, so German children early on drop it from their supply of sounds unless they are also learning English.

Psychologists believe that language patterns develop because certain sounds are reinforced or rewarded whenever they occur. Thus, the sounds for "Da-da" and "Ma-ma" are among the first to be learned because they bring such joy to the parents.

Rules of Language

In the process of learning to speak, children follow rigid, fixed rules. For example, a child in an early Kohlberg stage will say that someone who breaks three cups accidentally is "badder" than someone who breaks one cup on purpose. Adding the "er" is a "rule" they learn and apply to almost any word to indicate a greater degree of something (Chomsky, 1980). Words like *doggie* are made plural by

ACTIVITY

ENRICHMENT

Have students find out what famous linguist Noam Chomsky believed about language acquisition. Chomsky argued that our capacity for language is innate, that children's first sentences formed certain patterns. Moreover, these patterns are universal.

Chapter 10 INFANCY AND CHILDHOOD

adding "s," so the rule is followed for all other words: "Those mans feeding corns to the sheeps." Correcting children does not affect their loyalty to these rules. They keep right on making the same mistakes, even though no one else speaks this way.

The most important thing at this stage is the location of the word. A child knows the difference between "Doggie eat" and "Eat doggie." Thus, grammar involving plurals and other rules are artificial and only learned from reinforcement at a later stage of development. Communication is the child's goal at the beginning.

Biology and Language

In 1970, authorities in Los Angeles found a 13-year-old, Genie, who had been strapped to a bed or chair for the previous 11 years. Her father never spoke, nor was there any television or radio. Hence, Genie heard a few sounds only when her blind(!) mother, separated from her father, visited her. Of real interest from this sad case is the fact that, after rescue, Genie learned to speak by following the exact principles all children use, moving from selected sounds through the rigid rules to making finer discriminations about grammar (Curtiss, 1977). Hence, there is a maturational process and fixed sequence involved when learning language. Sadly, though, Genie had missed so many critical periods in language learning that her speech level did not move much beyond that of a child aged four or five.

Since the sounds, words, word arrangements, and accents all vary from one culture to another and even from one section of a country

▲ *Although we might not find what these boys are saying all that funny, this type of interaction is critical to social development.*

Teaching Hint

Over a period of eight months, Genie learned about 200 words, which is amazing given her circumstances. Ask students to imagine learning 200 sign-language signs. How long would it take them?

DISCUSS THE PHOTO

Children learn to communicate with their parents well before they are able to speak. It appears that interaction with others is important for language development from birth onwards.

299

Ask students to name some of their heroes, real or fictional. Once you compile a list, analyze what kinds of morals these heroes seem to promote. Do these heroes have any effect on moral development? If family members are listed, the answer will certainly be affirmative, but what about the secondary models?

Comprehension Check

Why are humans the only creatures known to communicate through a verbal language? *(We have both the physical structures necessary to make sounds and a brain complex enough to make rules of grammar and to invent new words.)*

Unit 4 HUMAN DEVELOPMENT

to another, it is obvious that environment plays a critical role in speech development. There is a general feeling, however, that many basic ideas or concepts might be inherited rather than learned. This might explain why all known societies have a concept of something being "in here" or "out there" or of something being "big" or "little." The belief is that there is a biological program that is in us from the beginning but that needs an environment for fine-tuning (Bickerton, 1984; Chomsky, 1980). While controversy about inheriting "ideas" still exists, almost everyone now agrees that we do inherit the *potential* for speech sounds and that this is not environmental. It also seems obvious that sounds and words have to be stored over time, and this process in the normal child depends on brain development. By age two, the average child knows about 300 words, by age three roughly 1,000 words, and by age six can correctly use 5,000 words and understands almost twice that number. The average adult has a vocabulary of about 10,000 words but can grasp the meaning of at least 50,000 words, probably partly from context. There seems to be no doubt about it: humans are born to talk, and we will spend most of our lives in the world of words.

PSYCHOLOGY IN YOUR LIFE

How Much of You Is Still a Child?

In the early days, it was believed that a child was a miniature adult. As a result, there were few, if any, provisions made for the child's need to develop and mature. Assumptions were made that children could handle almost any problem and were fully accountable for their actions. Today we know that the world of the child is a unique one in which thoughts, actions, and beliefs do not necessarily match or even come close to those of adults for many years.

Some philosophers and psychologists went to the other extreme of claiming that children could be made into anything adults desired. In other words, children were like empty blackboards on which nearly anything could be written and it would last a lifetime. One psychologist, John Watson (discussed in Chapters 1 and 7), said that the best way to handle children was never to hug or kiss them(!) but, instead, shake hands with them just before they went to bed each night. He also maintained that he could take any healthy infant and turn him or her into any kind of person he desired.

Sigmund Freud, the founder of psychoanalysis (continued on next page)

COOPERATIVE LEARNING

Have each group find a short story that depicts a young person coming of age. They should analyze the character's cognitive and moral development. Also, how does the character fit in his or her family? How does the character break away?

PSYCHOLOGY IN YOUR LIFE

How Much of You Is Still a Child?

(continued from previous page) (Chapters 1 and 14), had tremendous influence on the whole course of beliefs about what makes people abnormal. He insisted that the first five years of life were the critical ones and that by the end of the fifth year, we had become what we were going to be—at least in terms of our abnormalities. It is hard, even today, to avoid hearing that someone who acts strangely probably does so as the result of something that happened in childhood. Few psychologists embrace this point of view any longer, but it continues nonetheless. Similarly, as we mentioned in this chapter, we still hear what a terrible disservice mothers who work outside the home are doing to their children—another belief that is not supported by the evidence.

While it is possible that what we write here today will not bear the scrutiny of time, at least today's views are far more balanced, have quite a bit of experimental support, and *seem* to make sense. A few very important discoveries have been that: (1) the child influences the parent by his or her behavior, rather than just the parent

controlling whatever happens to the child; (2) childhood friends have a striking influence on how we develop, often outstripping the influence of the parents; and (3) there are very strong genetic influences on what we are. Most of us tend to remain the same basic type of person from middle childhood on—at least in the most general sense. For instance, if we were very dependent on others as a child, the likelihood is great that we are still this way today—only we are now dependent on some person other than our parent. If we were very independent children, the same holds true today. This is different from the Freudian belief, because we are dealing with inherited characteristics on which we are free to build with all kinds of experiences throughout our whole life, not just during the first five years.

The evidence is very strong that we have within our power the ability to determine much of our fate. Very few children who were abused or who grew up under horrible circumstances become delinquent, criminal,

▲ *We rarely forget events that cause us to feel this way.*

horrible people. We only hear and read about a selected few.

You might want to try a little private research on yourself to see what you come up with. Sit down sometime and just think for a while about the course of your own development. For example, what childhood memories are the strongest? List a few. Did these events have or not have a major impact on what you are today? What interactions with your parents when you were a child do you remember? How much influ- *(continued on next page)*

(continued on next page)

PSYCHOLOGY IN YOUR LIFE

Journal Topic
"Answer the questions posed at the end of the **Psychology in Your Life** feature." There are plenty of good questions here for discussion and critical thinking, too.

VOCABULARY REVIEW

Before testing students on the contents of the chapter, you may want to review vocabulary terms that are especially important or confusing. Terms in this chapter that could require clarification are *nature/nurture*, *genes*, *chromosomes*, *critical period*, and *cognitive development*.

Wrapping It Up

We have probably all heard public-service announcements telling us to pay attention to children, to hug our children, and so on. Have students write some catchy slogans that could be used on such an announcement (or on a bumper sticker or a poster). For example, "All work and no play may pay the bills, but your kids will pay, too."

PSYCHOLOGY IN YOUR LIFE

How Much of You Is Still a Child?

(continued from previous page) ence did they have on what you are today? How much similarity is there in your basic personality (dependent, independent, adventuresome, shy, and so forth— don't lie to yourself) between what you were like as a child and what you are like today? What was the worst thing that ever happened to you, and did it really influence the course of your life up to the present? How similar or dissimilar are your real views on morality, the world, your friends, and so forth to those you think your parents had when you were growing up? And how much influence did your very good (or bad) childhood friends have on you? It is very hard to come to any final conclusion from such an exercise, but it will shed a great deal of light on your course of development, and a picture of yourself should emerge. There is no reason why your conclusions should be any less accurate than those of the "experts." In all probability, you will be *more* accurate, if you're being honest with yourself, since it has been your life, after all.

SUMMARY

1. The nature/nurture controversy assumes that both heredity and environment are important, but one side emphasizes the genes (nature) and the other side emphasizes the world (nurture) in which the child lives. Monozygotic twins play a major role in studies of heredity and its effects.

2. Developmental patterns show that each species has a fixed rate at which development proceeds. The speed with which it occurs seems to be related to the final potential and complexity of the particular species.

3. Maturation is an automatic, orderly, and sequential process of physical and mental development. Training has little effect on the speed or outcome of the process, although growth cycles are involved that vary the speed and timing of a child's development.

4. The nuclear family is the most common family unit in the United States and always has been. Evidence is that the mother's working outside the home does little damage as long as she and the child spend warm, affectionate time together and as long as

there is little family friction over her outside employment.

5. Different approaches to parenting have different effects on the child. The three major parenting styles are authoritarian (or dictatorial), permissive, and authoritative.

6. Child abuse results from two major factors: (1) pressure on a parent from unemployment, financial problems, and the like and (2) a lack of knowledge regarding development sequences, causing the parent to have unrealistic expectations of the child.

7. Separation anxiety occurs at about nine months of age and is a fear of being away from the parent.

8. Jean Piaget has a four-stage system of mental development that follows a sequence based on age and brain maturation. Lawrence Kohlberg has a similar three-stage system for the development of moral reasoning.

9. Language is a maturational process that starts off with a fixed set of rules for speech. Over time the child learns to conform more and more with society's grammatical system.

SUGGESTED VIDEOS

▼ *Development.* 33 min. CRM/McGraw-Hill.

▼ *The Developing Child.* Discovering Psychology series, part 5, 27 min. 1-800-LEARNER.

▼ *Development.* The Mind series. Part 2, 60 min., 1988.

▼ *The Discovery Year.* 52 min. Films for the Humanities.

▼ *Language Development.* Discovering Psychology series, part 6, 27 min. 1-800-LEARNER.

▼ *Rock-a-Bye-Baby.* 29 min. 1971. Time Life.

SUGGESTED READINGS

▼ Axline, Virginia M. *Dibs in Search of Self.* New York: Ballantine Books, 1964.

▼ Dennis, W. "Causes of Retardation Among Institutional Children: Iran." *Journal of Genetic Psychology* 96 (1960): 47–59.

VOCABULARY

heredity
environment
nature/nurture
genes
chromosomes
zygote
dizygotic twins
monozygotic twins
maturation
growth cycles
imprinting
critical period
feral children
nuclear family

extended family
self-esteem
permissive parenting
    style
dictatorial
    (authoritarian)
    parenting style
authoritative
    parenting style
separation anxiety
Jean Piaget
cognitive
    development
sensorimotor stage

object permanence
preoperational stage
reversibility
conservation
concrete operations
    stage
formal operations
    stage
Lawrence Kohlberg
preconventional level
conventional level
postconventional
    level

Answers to Review Questions
1. b
2. a
3. b
4. c
5. c

Review Questions

Multiple Choice

1. If we agree that violence is caused mainly by nurture, this means that violence
   a. is mainly inborn.
   b. is mainly learned.
   c. cannot be studied.
   d. is hereditary.
2. If violence is caused mainly by nature, this means that
   a. violence is mainly inborn.
   b. violence is mainly learned.
   c. violence is learned in nature.
   d. humans are as violent as other animals.
3. Once an ability is inherited, the environment
   a. cannot affect that ability.
   b. can affect that ability.
4. Which of the following statements about developmental patterns is *not* true?
   a. Development within a species is orderly.
   b. The human has a longer developmental period than animals.
   c. It's usually possible through training to speed up a species' developmental timetable by quite a bit.
   d. The development process integrates the brain and the body.
5. Dizygotic twins
   a. are also called identical twins.
   b. have the same heredity.
   c. develop from two different fertilized eggs.

▼ Dorris, Michael. *The Broken Cord: A Family's Ongoing Struggle with Fetal Alcohol Syndrome.* New York: HarperCollins, 1989.

▼ Elkind, David. *The Child and Society.* New York: Oxford University Press, 1979.

▼ Elkind, David. *Children and Adolescence: Interpretive Essays on Jean Piaget.* New York: Oxford University Press, 1970.

▼ Erikson, Erik. *Childhood and Society.* New York: W. W. Norton, 1963.

▼ Kagan, Jerome. *The Nature of the Child.* New York: Basic Books, 1984.

▼ Shurkin, Joel N. *Terman's Kids: How the Gifted Grows Up.* Boston: Little, Brown, 1992.

▼ Spock, Benjamin and Michael Rothenberg. *Dr. Spock's Baby and Child Care.* New York: Pocket Books, 1985.

6. d
7. c
8. b
9. d
10. c
11. a
12. b
13. b
14. true
15. true
16. false
17. false
18. false
19. true
20. true
21. false
22. b
23. c
24. a
25. d
26. a
27. b
28. c
29. b
30. d
31. b
32. b
33. c
34. a
35. c
36. a

6. Which of the following statements about growth cycles is *not* true?
   a. There are differences between the sexes.
   b. The brain develops sooner than the body.
   c. Girls develop in a more orderly and stable way than boys do.
   d. The reproductive system develops faster than the brain.
7. Children raised by permissive parents
   a. appreciate their freedom.
   b. mature faster than most children.
   c. are often indecisive.
   d. are less intelligent than most children.

8. Authoritarian parents
   a. supply reasons for their punishment.
   b. tend to be inflexible.
   c. are usually good listeners.
   d. were troublemakers themselves as children.
9. Authoritative parents
   a. are flexible.
   b. usually raise self-reliant children.
   c. encourage their children to make their own decisions.
   d. do all of the above.

Matching (Answers can be used more than once.)

10. Fertilized egg
11. Basic units of heredity
12. Most body cells contain 46 of them
13. Reproductive cells contain 23 of them

a. genes
b. chromosomes
c. zygote

True/False

14. Monozygotic twins have exactly the same, or identical, heredity.
15. Imprinting is affected by chemical changes in the body.
16. Critical periods apply to all animals but humans.
17. In time, a feral child will usually catch up to the ability level of others his or her age.
18. Extended families are more common today than in the past.

19. Studies show that mothers who work outside the home form just as strong an attachment to their children as mothers who don't work outside the home.
20. One cause of child abuse is the abuser's lack of knowledge about children.
21. Separation anxiety seems to have more to do with nurture than nature.

Matching (Answers can be used more than once.)

22. Conservation skills are not quite established.
23. The world becomes fixed.
24. Objects are not permanent.
25. This is the highest level of cognitive development.
26. Sensation and movement are particularly important.
27. Language develops at a rapid rate.
28. Conservation becomes easier.
29. Reversibility is difficult, if not impossible.
30. Logical and philosophical thinking take place.

a. sensorimotor stage
b. preoperational stage
c. concrete operations stage
d. formal operations stage

Matching (Answers can be used more than once.)

31. Others' approval helps us determine right and wrong.
32. Society's expectations help us determine right and wrong.
33. People's rights are given great consideration.
34. A person is extremely self-centered at this level.
35. This is the highest level of moral development.
36. Outside authority determines right and wrong for us.

a. preconventional
b. conventional
c. postconventional

DISCUSSION QUESTIONS

1. Some communities from time to time pass ordinances that ban the sale of toy guns, the implication being that violence is provoked in large part by what we learn in the environment. Do you agree or disagree with this type of ordinance? Why? Explain.
2. A similar controversy to that described in number 1 involves the portrayal of violence in television programs. In your opinion, do children learn to be violent themselves through these programs? Should the violence be censored in any way? Explain. *Note:* many cartoons include vivid violence.
3. Describe several aspects of your personality that are clearly influenced mainly by

heredity, and describe several aspects that are clearly influenced mainly by the environment.
4. Alisha is a mother who works outside the home. She argues that she spends at least two to three hours of quality time with her child every evening. Her friend, Tonya, is a mother who is not employed outside the house. She argues that these two to three hours may be quality time for Alisha but not necessarily for her child; maybe two to three hours of morning time (or afternoon time) would be the time when the *child* is most open to quality interaction. In other words, *maybe* the two to three hours in the evening

Notes on Discussion Questions

1. You might have students conduct research on communities that have banned toy guns. What reasons do these communities give for banning the toys?
2. Most students will probably insist that violence on TV does not affect children. Just make sure that students support their opinions. Don't allow them simply to state, "Well, violence doesn't affect *me*." In order to answer the question, they need to place themselves in the shoes of either young children or parents of young children. Ask, "If you were a parent, would there be any programs on TV that you wouldn't allow your children to watch?"
3. Answers will vary.

4. After students have explained their positions, discuss the general issue of mothers working outside the home. If a couple can afford it, should the mother stay at home with the children? If the mother has a higher-paying job than the father, should the father stay at home with the children? What factors other than money should be considered?

5. If you discuss this issue in class, present an additional situation: "You want to leave your child at a baby-sitter's house, and the child is clearly experiencing separation anxiety. Should you slip out without saying good-bye the moment the child becomes preoccupied with something? Or should you make it a point to wave good-bye and reassure the child that you'll be back?" Some students may argue that their answers will vary, depending on the age of the child. This is a valid point, so allow them to insert various ages into the situation.

6. Accept any answers that are properly supported. The following are possible answers: (1) If a judge is concerned with protecting people's *rights:* postconventional level. If a judge is interested in *bribery money:* preconventional level. (2) A teacher who strictly enforces *rules:* conventional level, because strict conformity in school is what society expects and wants. (3) If a

driver is concerned primarily with being *punished* by a traffic cop: preconventional level.

7. Someone at an advanced level of cognitive development will be able to think abstractly, which will help the person understand the long-term consequences of his or her actions. This understanding does not guarantee advanced moral development,

but without it, advanced moral development is not likely.

8. The child with little or no interaction will never be reinforced for any responses. Without some reinforcement, the child will remain a passive observer of life. Also, infants certainly need other kinds of stimulation, like touch and movement, to develop properly.

---

are a crabby time for the child, and the child benefits little from the interaction. With whom do you tend to agree? Explain.

5. The chapter mentions that all normal children will eventually experience separation anxiety. Not all parents, however, deal with the anxiety in the same way. For example, let's say that a stranger picks up the child, and the child begins to cry. Some parents will tend to take the baby away almost immediately to soothe the child; they let the child gradually decide when he or she is ready to approach the stranger. Other parents let the stranger hold the child, hoping that the child will get used to the stranger, despite the child's continuing anxiety. In your opinion, which approach would promote a stronger and longer-lasting sense of security for the child? Explain.

6. In your opinion, what level of moral development best describes each of the following situations? (a) A courtroom judge addressing a jury; (b) a teacher who rigidly enforces the rules of the school; (c) an automobile driver when a cop is around.

More than one answer may be possible for each of these situations, but defend your answer. For example, if one of the situations were "a politician addressing a crowd," you might answer *preconventional level,* arguing that politicians will grant us favors perhaps, but only if we vote for them.

7. If a person is at the postconventional level of *moral* development, this same person will probably also be at the formal operations level of *cognitive* development. Why? In other words, why would a person need to be advanced in his or her cognitive ability in order to be advanced in his or her moral development? Explain.

8. Imagine a very hypothetical situation where a child, for the first two years of his or her life, does little but watch educational programs like "Sesame Street" every hour, every day. Further, imagine that this child experiences almost no interaction with real people. Why would this child develop few, if any, language skills? Explain. (*Hint:* refer back to the principles of learning discussed in Chapter 7.)

ACTIVITIES

1. As suggested in the chapter, one of the best ways to learn about the effects of heredity and environment is to study identical twins. Try it. You can do it in one of two ways: (1) Find an article or two and write a report; emphasize the role of heredity and environment in the lives of the twins. (2) Prepare a list of questions and actually interview a set of monozygotic, or identical, twins. Ask around and you'll be surprised how easy it is to locate and contact a set of twins. Possible questions: What are some of

your common personality traits? Interests? Values? Which of these similarities do you think are influenced more by heredity and which are influenced more by the environment? Do other people sometimes have difficulty recognizing your individual uniqueness? In other words, do they look at you as *completely* identical?

Write a report on your interview and your reaction to what you learned.

2. This activity may help you discover how much your personality is influenced by your

Notes on Activities

1. Have students add their own interview questions.

2. When writing their lists, students will easily identify the physical characteristics that they share with their parents. The mental and behavioral characteristics, however, may be harder to identify, so you may want to spend a few minutes discussing these more elusive characteristics in class. Possible mental similarities: "My parents and I are both intelligent; we're highly competitive; we solve problems similarly; we're stubborn." Possible behavioral similarities: "My father and I both walk with our feet out; my mother's eyes twitch when she's worried, and so do mine; we both gesture wildly."

3. These kinds of papers are fun to grade and fun to share in class. Urge students to *show* rather than *tell* when describing their experiences. For example, rather than writing, "I was embarrassed," they can write, "My face turned crimson."

4. Once students note the similarities between "Sesame Street" and commercials, you might point out that advertisers appeal to the attention span of a child!

5. Try to get several children's drawings and analyze them in class. This should point out the need to brainstorm when analyzing the drawings. Also, it should help communicate to students that you're not looking for single, correct interpretations.

heredity and/or by your environment. Make a list of 20 characteristics that you have in common with your parents. The characteristics can be physical, mental, behavioral—just about any similarity that you can think of. After each item, write down whether the characteristic, in your opinion, is influenced mainly through heredity or mainly through the environment. The characteristics are most likely influenced by both, but choose the influence that you perceive to be slightly dominant.

Next, have one of your parents make the same list, following the same instructions—but don't let him or her see your list.

Compare the two lists. Were the characteristics listed pretty much the same? Were your conclusions about heredity and environment about the same? What general conclusions can you draw from this? For example, which kinds of characteristics (physical, mental, behavioral, and so forth) seemed to be most influenced by heredity? Least influenced by heredity? Explain.

3. We can all think of memorable childhood experiences that have helped to shape our personalities. Pick one of these memorable experiences and describe it in a couple of pages. Include all the rich and vivid detail that made the experience memorable for you. Write the description not as an essay but as if you were telling a story to a good friend.

4. Probably one of the most successful educational television programs for children is "Sesame Street." Watch about an hour of the program and take notes on the various teaching techniques used: length of skits, music, repetition, and any other techniques that you notice.

Next, watch about ten to 15 television commercials (don't rely on memory) and take notes on techniques that advertisers use to sell their products: length of commercials, music, repetition, and so on.

Notice any similarities? Write a detailed report comparing and contrasting "Sesame Street" to the television commercials. If possible, talk to parents whose children watch "Sesame Street" and ask them about the effectiveness of the techniques used.

5. Contact three teachers: one should be a first- or second-grade teacher (whose students will probably be preoperational); another should be a third- or fourth-grade teacher (whose students will probably be concrete operational); the third should be a fifth- or sixth-grade teacher (whose students will probably be formal operational). Ask the teachers if they would be willing to participate in a 15- to 20-minute experiment. All they'll have to do is allow their students to draw pictures, reading to their students beforehand the following instructions: "Draw a picture of a typical day at your home." Try to get all the teachers to use the same size paper and the same writing utensils—crayons, for example.

Analyze the three groups of drawings. You might look at some of the following aspects of the drawings: the size and proportions of objects drawn; the colors used; the number of people drawn versus the number of objects. (*Note:* artistic ability should probably not be given much weight in your analyses.) Try to relate these observations to Piaget's theory. Do the drawings reveal in any way the artists' stages of cognitive development? Explain.

Don't feel limited by these suggestions about your analyses. Although many therapists are trained in analyzing such pictures, most agree that there are no simple or set answers. They admit that their analyses depend on intuition and creativity to some extent. So be creative. Perhaps get a friend or two to help you brainstorm.

DISCUSS THE PHOTO

Do friends have a greater influence than parents during adolescence?

Friends have an enormous influence on most adolescents.

308

PSYCHOLOGY AND YOU RESOURCES

A variety of resources are available in the Psychology and You *supplementary material. In addition, there are a number of additional resources listed to enhance your lesson plans.*

Masters
▼ 11-1A Learning Goals
▼ 11-1B Answers to Learning Goals
▼ 11-2 Parents' Visit
▼ 11-3 Rating Scale

Student Worksheets
▼ Vocabulary Worksheet
▼ Independent Practice Worksheet
▼ Enrichment Worksheet
▼ Reteaching Worksheet

Test Bank
▼ Tests A and B

Multimedia
▼ *The Brain* Videotape Module #8
▼ Psychology Videodisc

Student Workbook

PACING CHART

Complete Coverage

Day 1: Have students read "Defining Adolescence" before class. Discuss the physical changes in adolescence, focusing on rates of maturation and self-esteem. Be sure to cover eating disorders. Assign "Psychological Issues" for Day 2.

Day 2: Use discussion question #4 in the text to facilitate analysis of conformity and group identity. Assign an activity for homework involving the evaluation of high school cliques.

Day 3: Concentrate on the concept of individual identity and Marcia's theory of identity states. (Use the corresponding In Focus box as a guide.) Have students read "Intellectual and Moral Changes" for Day 4.

Day 4: After reviewing Piaget's formal operation stage of cognitive development and Kohlberg's postconventional level of moral reasoning, discuss the family's influence on adolescence and how it

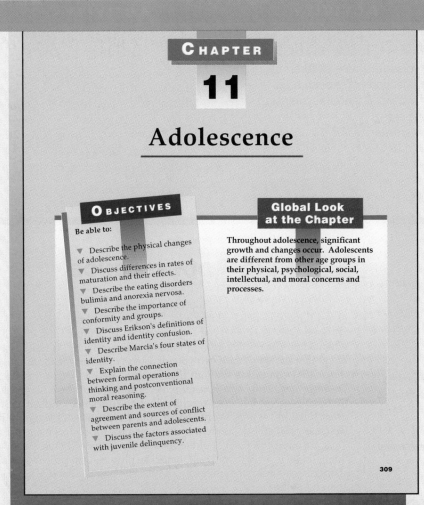

OBJECTIVES

Be able to:

▼ Describe the physical changes of adolescence.

▼ Discuss differences in rates of maturation and their effects.

▼ Describe the eating disorders bulimia and anorexia nervosa.

▼ Describe the importance of conformity and groups.

▼ Discuss Erikson's definitions of identity and identity confusion.

▼ Describe Marcia's four states of identity.

▼ Explain the connection between formal operations thinking and postconventional moral reasoning.

▼ Describe the extent of agreement and sources of conflict between parents and adolescents.

▼ Discuss the factors associated with juvenile delinquency.

Global Look at the Chapter

Throughout adolescence, significant growth and changes occur. Adolescents are different from other age groups in their physical, psychological, social, intellectual, and moral concerns and processes.

309

INTRODUCING THE CHAPTER

You will probably need to spend a few minutes discussing the meaning of the word *adolescence.* For many, the word denotes immaturity. Ask students to put aside any negative connotations and stress that if they would rather not label themselves as adolescents, that's OK.

affects juvenile delinquency. Assign Psychology in Your Life for homework.

Day 5: Discuss communication between parents and adolescents before giving the Chapter Review quiz.

In Brief

Day 1: Concentrate on the physical changes characteristic of adolescence. Discuss self-esteem and eating disorders in particular.

Day 2: Focus on Erikson's and Marcia's theories regarding individual identity. Assign for homework an activity analyzing conformity in adolescence.

Day 3: Discuss the family's influence on adolescence, including its relation to juvenile delinquency. Give the Chapter Review quiz.

LEAD-OFF ACTIVITY

Conduct in class activity #1 from the end of the chapter. Brainstorm ideas with the entire class for a few minutes, so that students understand the activity. Then break the class into small groups, and have each group create a rite of passage (which you will need to define). After ten minutes or so, have each group report its plan to the rest of the class. (See also discussion question #3 at the end of the chapter.)

ENRICHMENT

Have students find out the average growth of children whose pituitary does not produce enough growth hormone. Also, have them find out what it costs for these children to receive injections of growth hormones and what the effects of the injections are.

Points to Stress

If students want a more definite starting point for adolescence than age 11 or 12, you can agree that adolescence begins at puberty.

Discussion

When *does* adolescence end? Write students' answers on the board, and point out that all their responses are necessary. No single answer will suffice because our society sends mixed messages. Are there other significant ages besides 18 and 21 that mark the end? Would the end of adolescence be defined differently in different situations? For example, would a precocious 15-year-old who has a Ph.D. be considered an adolescent? How about a 22-year-old department-store clerk who still lives at home? What if the 22-year-old is in law school?

Unit 4 HUMAN DEVELOPMENT

early adolescence

The period from 11 to 14 years of age.

middle adolescence

14 to 16 years of age.

late adolescence

16 to 19 years of age.

puberty

The time of sexual maturation.

hormones

The body chemicals that control body growth, emotional responses, and physical changes.

pituitary gland

The gland that secretes growth hormones and increases the production in other glands of other hormones.

adrenal glands

The glands that produce adrenaline, the stimulating hormone; help sexual maturation, along with gonads.

gonads

The sex glands.

DEFINING ADOLESCENCE

The years between childhood and adulthood make up the period of development called adolescence. This period starts at age 11 or 12 and generally is considered over by 18 or 19. Pinpointing exactly when adolescence ends and adulthood begins, though, is not possible in our society. People can vote or join the military at 18. In most states, they can marry without their parents' permission at that age. On the other hand, a person must be 21 to have all the legal rights that adults enjoy. But even reaching that age does not automatically grant full adult status. Many people 21 and older are still single, still in school, and still dependent on their parents for financial support. They are adults in the eyes of the law but are not yet self-sufficient or living on their own. In any case, since the physical and psychological changes of adolescence are fairly complete by age 19, that is a reasonable end point.

The range of ages from 11 to 19 is further divided based on physical and psychological similarities within these smaller age groups. **Early adolescence** goes from 11 to 14. **Middle adolescence** runs from 14 to 16. **Late adolescence** ranges from 16 to 19. As we discuss these periods in greater detail, differences among the age groups will become clear.

PHYSICAL CHANGES

Throughout adolescence, the most startling developments are physical. Sudden changes take place in sexual maturation and physical growth. Changes in height and weight are dramatic and troublesome. The biggest problem, however, is that while these changes in physiology remove from adolescents the label *child*, they are not yet adults. They may feel for a while that they are "nowhere," neither adult nor child.

Sexual Development

Puberty, or the period of sexual maturation, is a notable feature of adolescence. **Hormones,** chemicals that control body growth, emotional responses, and physical changes, are responsible for sexual maturation. Several hormones are extremely active in adolescence. The **pituitary** (pi-TUE-i-ter-ee) **gland** secretes growth hormones and increases the production in other glands of other hormones. Two systems under the pituitary's control are the **adrenal** (ah-DREE-nal) **glands** and the **gonads** (GO-nads) or sex glands. Adrenaline from the adrenal glands and sex hormones from the gonads work with the pituitary to bring about sexual maturation.

DISCOVERY

One of the most worthwhile activities to conduct during this unit is to invite parents to class to discuss their own adolescence. Sell the idea of a parent visit to your students, and have several students promise to invite their parents. It helps to give them a form that parents can sign. The next day or so, find out how many parents will participate. If you can get at least five or six parents to visit, the discussion should be worthwhile. The main purpose of the visit is to compare and contrast adolescence today with adolescence 15 or 20 years ago. The parents who visit are not experts, but they can provide personal observations that are often more insightful than many written sources. See **Teaching Master 11-2 Parents' Visit** for a list of questions for the visit.

▲ *Growth does not occur at an even rate, or at the same time for everyone.*

During puberty breast development and the start of menstruation occur in females. Noticeable voice changes and the development of facial hair and thicker body hair occur in males. Both sexes begin the process of sex-organ maturation, which is accompanied by the growth of pubic hair (the word *pubic* means "downy" or "hairy"). Most people think sexual development is gradual from childhood through adolescence, but this is not so. Amazingly, 90 percent of sexual maturity occurs after puberty starts, which accounts for the concern and preoccupation with sexuality common for people in this period of their lives. Other effects of hormones include skin problems, like acne, and increased perspiration. While these are a natural outcome of the bodily changes taking place, they are also a source of embarrassment and concern for many adolescents.

It may surprise you to learn that the impact of hormones on an adolescent's emotional state is not clear-cut. It is true that adolescents generally are moodier than adults, but so are children, and children are not being bombarded with all these chemicals. The many intense changes taking place in adolescence probably have as much to do with emotional response as the hormones themselves. In any case, emotional ups and downs are more evident early on and largely disappear by late adolescence (Buchanan, Eccles & Becker, 1992).

Physical Growth

During adolescence, the body is moving upward and outward rapidly in what is called the **growth spurt.** When growth spurts

growth spurt

A rapid increase in growth during puberty.

Early maturation and identity foreclosure may be linked—when teenagers look like adults, they may be treated like adults, even though they may not be emotionally ready. The search for identity may be cut off to soon.

Discussion

If you are teaching juniors and seniors, it may be fun to discuss some of the physical changes students went through only a few years ago.

Connections

Remind students of the function of the hypothalamus—it instructs the pituitary to secrete growth hormones (Chapter 3).

DISCOVERY

Have two students role-play two early-maturing girls discussing their uneasiness about being taller than everyone else. Then have two males act as late maturers discussing the awkwardness of being shorter than everyone else. Make sure you pick students who are mature and who will not lapse into crude remarks about sexual development.

Journal Topic

"What emotional ups and downs did you experience during early adolescence?" Topics can include school life, family, friendships.

FYI As noted, growth spurts occur earlier for females than for males, and this includes muscle growth. This means that at a certain point, the average female will have more muscle than most males her age.

Discussion

Ask students to try to remember how classmates in junior high treated early and late maturers. If early and late maturers were treated differently, do you think this had an effect on their personalities? This is one time when you want to encourage generalities and insist on no names.

Unit 4 HUMAN DEVELOPMENT

early maturer

Someone who develops one and a half years or more ahead of average growth.

late maturer

Someone who develops one and a half years or more behind average growth.

occur, development is not orderly. Arms and hands may grow at a different rate from legs, for instance, while other parts of the body develop at yet another rate.

Although they may look gangly, teenagers have exceptionally good coordination. It is because growth is so rapid and uneven that adolescents may *feel* awkward and "not quite right." Most teenagers, however, handle puberty much better than people think. In fact, only a small number of adolescents, roughly 15 percent, have any real trouble adjusting to these dramatic changes (Petersen, 1987).

Growth spurts come earlier for girls than boys, but for both sexes, early adolescence is the time of maximum physical development. Between the ages of nine and 12, girls may grow as much as three inches taller in one year. For boys, this growth occurs between 11 and 15, when they may gain as much as four inches in height in a year. The exact time when this growth will occur for any individual, male or female, is unpredictable.

Rates of Maturation

Differences between boys and girls in the level of physical maturation are greatest and most obvious in early adolescence. By age 14, most girls have matured fairly completely, while most boys lag behind by two to three years. This difference between the sexes creates problems in relating to one another, especially where dating and dancing are involved. Most males are still shorter than females their own age, making the situation even more awkward. When girls start dating, many go out with older boys, largely because of these differences. By middle adolescence, the maturity gap between the sexes has narrowed considerably, and for most, by late adolescence it has disappeared altogether.

Besides overall gender differences in the rate and timing of physical maturation, individual differences exist as well. Small differences do not have much impact on the individual. When physical development occurs substantially earlier or later than average, however, there are psychological effects as well. The particular kinds of effects that occur depend on two factors: (1) whether the adolescent is an **early maturer** (one-and-a-half years or more ahead of the average) or a **late maturer** (one-and-a-half years or more behind the average) and (2) whether the individual is male or female.

Early maturation is more of an advantage for boys than girls. Boys who develop ahead of schedule have higher self-esteem and feel better about how they look. Early maturing girls feel awkward about being different from their friends. They are more self-conscious and dissatisfied with their weight and general appearance.

Development that starts later than average is worse for boys than girls. Boys who are late maturers, like early maturing girls, feel awkward about their bodies. They are more self-conscious, less self-

ENRICHMENT

Send students on a search to find the references cited here on early and late maturers: Peterson (1987) and Peskin (1973). Have them pick out five findings from the sources that surprised them. This search will also get students to pay more attention to the sources cited throughout the text. And it will send the message that if they want to know more about a certain topic, the citations are a rich source. If students can't find these sources, have them find *any* source from this chapter.

Discussion

Are high school girls more mature than high school boys? This should provoke interesting debates. Boys will probably argue that they are just as mature. You might then take a poll of how many girls only date older guys. If you get a high number, discuss why.

 **Maturation Timetables**

Early Maturers

Boys
High self-esteem

Satisfied with physical appearance

Girls
Generally low self-esteem

Dissatisfied with physical appearance

Highly self-conscious

Late Maturers

Boys
Generally low self-esteem

Dissatisfied with overall appearance

Highly self-conscious

Girls
High self-esteem

Satisfied with physical appearance

The feelings listed here are based on appearance. What other factors affect self-esteem during early adolescence?

Maturation Timetables.

 Students might mention success in school and in extracurricular activities, relationships with friends and family. You might mention Maslow's hierarchy (Chapter 5) and the kinds of needs that must be satisfied before a person can attend to self-actualization.

Points to Stress

The patterns that early and late adolescents exhibit are just that—patterns. There are plenty of adolescents who mature early or late who do not fit the pattern.

---

confident, and express greater dissatisfaction with their overall appearance than other adolescent males. Late maturing girls, however, do not seem to suffer many negative effects. Generally, they have high self-esteem and are satisfied with their physical appearance. They also have the advantage of being similar to boys their own age in height and overall maturation (Peterson, 1987; Peskin, 1973).

While pluses or minuses are created when maturation occurs later or earlier than average, their greatest impact is felt during adolescence itself. For most early or late maturers, neither the problems nor the advantages last into adult life.

Weight: Too Much or Too Little?

Along with rapid growth and sexual maturation come fluctuations in weight. Concern about weight is a common problem for adolescents. Being underweight or overweight can result from hormonal imbalances, physical changes, psychological difficulties, genetics, or

Comprehension Check

What aspect of physical development in adolescence can affect self-esteem? *(the rate or timing of maturation)*

DISCUSS THE PHOTO

Contrast this picture with the one that appears on p. 135.

FYI A girl who is 25 percent underweight will often stop menstruating.

Journal Topic

"Write about someone you know who has a weight problem. Does the person acknowledge the problem? If so, how does this person deal with the problem?" Assure students that this entry will remain confidential; even *you* will not read it if they so request.

FYI Potentially fatal health problems associated with bulimia: possible heart attacks, stomach ruptures, and hernias (from persistent vomiting).

314

Unit 4 HUMAN DEVELOPMENT

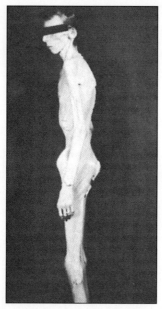

▲ *An extreme example of anorexia nervosa, a disorder in which people diet excessively.*

eating disorders

Conditions in which the person cannot read the body's nutritional needs and eats or refuses to eat for the wrong reasons.

bulimia nervosa

An eating disorder that involves binging on food and purging by vomiting or excessive use of laxatives.

anorexia nervosa

An eating disorder that involves severe loss of weight from excessive dieting.

some combination of these factors. For instance, some males try to compensate for a temporary "string-bean look" by eating too much. In addition, food can act as a sedative to relieve loneliness. Around issues of weight, patience is probably called for, as difficult as that may be. Physical changes *are* drastic during adolescence, but people in their early 20s are the leanest of all age groups.

Weight and body image are more often problems for females than for males. Society places more importance on physical appearance for women than for men. The "ideal beauty," that unrealistic picture of what the perfect woman should look like, has become thinner and thinner over the years. As two psychologists have noted, in the 1950s, a typical winner of the "Miss Sweden" title was five feet seven inches tall and weighed 151 pounds. Thirty-some years later, that title-winner was five feet nine inches tall (two inches taller) and weighed only 109 pounds (over 40 pounds less) (Wade & Tavris, 1993). A height-to-weight ratio like that borders on being seriously hazardous to one's health.

The damage done by social pressure to conform to such an impossible ideal is hard to overstate. At a minimum, it makes most women dissatisfied with their appearance. As many as three-fourths of American women think they are "fat" or at least should lose a few pounds. In reality, no more than one-fourth are even slightly overweight. At a more troublesome level, such social pressure can result in constant unhealthful dieting.

The evidence is absolutely clear that being somewhat overweight is nowhere near as risky as the attempt to become too thin. Also, excessive dieting can lead to **eating disorders,** conditions in which the person is unable to correctly read the body's signals about its nutritional needs and eats (or refuses to eat) for the wrong reasons. Whatever the specific disorder may be, the person is obsessed with food.

In the condition known as **bulimia nervosa** (bul-LEE-mee-uh ner-VOE-suh), people go on binges, eating large amounts of rich, calorie-laden foods. They then try to keep the food from causing any weight gain by either forcing themselves to vomit or taking excessive doses of laxatives. Thus, bulimia is sometimes called the binge-and-purge syndrome. As you might suspect, such people often develop problems in their digestive systems. Another side effect is severe irritation of the mouth and throat as well as erosion of tooth enamel from all that stomach acid. Most bulimics are adolescent or young-adult females. However, as many as 15 to 20 percent are young men. Males who become bulimic often are trying to maintain or qualify for a particular weight class in athletic competition. The motivation for females, though, is usually that same old sad story—they are trying to achieve an "ideal" weight that is unrealistic. Their self-esteem depends so much on how they look that they are sacrificing their health in the quest for unreachable perfection.

An even more serious eating disorder is **anorexia** (an-oh-REX-ee-uh) **nervosa.** In anorexia, the person basically has stopped eating and is at least 25 percent underweight. (Say that the normal weight for a particular woman's height and age is 130 pounds. If she is anorexic, she will weigh less than 98 pounds.) This condition is physically extremely harmful, even potentially fatal, because food intake decreases to the point of starvation. Nearly every system of the body can be damaged by the effects of anorexia. An additional problem is that as the body adjusts to an extremely low food intake, it becomes unable to handle nourishment except in very, very small amounts. Such people usually have to be fed intravenously to keep them alive. Their body images have become so distorted that even when they are little more than skeletons, they still see themselves as fat.

Anorexia is almost exclusively a problem for women. It has been estimated that 95 percent of anorectics are adolescent or young-adult females. Their motivation is similar to that of female bulimics. In addition, they often have gotten substantial praise in the past for dieting and losing weight. Over time they learn that not eating continues to bring praise. Eventually they become so thin that now they are getting attention for being sick. As is true for bulimics, their feelings of self-worth are excessively tied to their appearance.

PSYCHOLOGICAL ISSUES

Adolescence is often painted as a time of great difficulty and confusion. While the trials of this period vary from one culture to another, there is little indication that it is actually that bad for most adolescents. But many problems leave a number of teenagers in a type of limbo. One of the hardest issues to deal with is trying to find an identity. Until adolescence, there is no pressure to find out about yourself. Now it becomes necessary to try out different roles to see which ones fit. The problem is made worse in our society because the adolescent is normally not expected to take on adult responsibilities but, at the same time, *is* expected to show more maturity and a sense of commitment.

Other societies, especially primitive ones, handle the transition from childhood to adulthood more simply. This transition is made through some kind of initiation, or **rite of passage,** meaning that a change in status is recognized by a formal ritual. Adulthood rituals often involve cutting oneself, being decorated in some specific way, or drinking a foul-tasting potion as part of an elaborate ceremony. After the ceremony is over, the whole community is aware of the person's official adult status.

We have no such ceremonies, so adolescents by and large find themselves somewhat cut off from the mainstream of society, and they need to form their own subculture in order to avoid complete isolation. Subcultures invariably have all kinds of rules, regulations, and dress codes so that members can take pride in belonging and can

Chapter 11 ADOLESCENCE

rite of passage

A socially recognized and ritualized change in status, such as reaching adulthood.

Connections

How would Carl Rogers, B. F. Skinner, and Sigmund Freud (Chapter 14) diagnose weight problems? Rogers: "You need to work on your faulty perceptions and merge them with reality: 100 pounds is not fat." Rogers would not offer advice; he would allow the *client* to discover that 100 pounds is not fat. Skinner: "Someone probably paid great attention to your weight at one time. This reinforced behaviors related to your weight." Freud: "Giving up food is your attempt at remaining a child, so others will take care of you."

FYI Most bulimics are normal in weight or can even be a bit overweight.

COOPERATIVE LEARNING

The topic of cliques is usually a favorite one with high school students. Have students work in pairs to answer the following. What cliques exist at school? (Transfer students might offer more objective insights.) Any advantages to being in a clique? (They provide a sense of safety and belongingness.) What are the disadvantages? (You tend not to meet new people; you may conform to the clique's values.) Will cliques be less prevalent in college? (Do students consider fraternities and sororities cliques?)

DISCUSS THE PHOTO

Ask students if they think that such a ritual would make their lives easier. Do they have any ideas about what form this ritual could take?

Critical Thinking:

Ask students: Although it is true that our society provides no *rites of passage* into adulthood, can you think of any informal passages that people follow? (getting a driver's license, getting a part-time job, graduating)

Discussion

Beyond adolescence, is there less need to conform? Those who believe conformity needs remain the same may offer these kinds of examples: adults must conform to the workplace, dressing and behaving as expected; adults conform at home, by mowing their lawns and raking leaves. Other students may argue that adults conform less: adults have established identities; choose their own careers, are independent.

316

Unit 4 HUMAN DEVELOPMENT

▲ *Because our society as a whole does not have formal puberty—adulthood rituals as the Apaches do, the exact time of adulthood is not clear for most adolescents.*

be distinguished from "outsiders." Forming groups and achieving a sense of identity are two crucial psychological issues during adolescence. And they are related to each other in some interesting ways.

Conformity

Because adolescents are left to fend for themselves socially, they create small "exclusive" groups, which are used as a form of self-protection. In this way, they don't have to cope with the world all alone. When adolescents identify themselves as belonging to a particular group, they take on its dress code, use its slang, and engage in the group's "approved" activities. All these behaviors add to a sense of belonging. They also help separate adolescents from adults, sometimes by shocking the adults. Thus, adolescents may shave their heads, wear their hair long and shaggy, curl it into points atop the head, dye it green or purple, wear deliberately scuffed boots, or leave the laces untied on their tennis shoes—whatever happens to be in vogue at any given time. For example, when we were adolescents, anyone who wore green on Thursday was considered "weird" and was in for a very rough day, and this "rule" controlled adolescents from coast to coast for several years! Such conformity to the group is understandable: nobody wants to be alone.

Groups differ in terms of their size, how strictly defined they are, and how closely their rules must be followed. Fairly large groups, with loose rules and relatively changeable memberships are called

DISCOVERY

Have two volunteers role-play a situation in which one is complaining that the other has been spending too much time lately in a clique. In fact, the clique has changed this person. The clique person should be defensive at first; what happens after that is up to the volunteers. The discussion they have may be unrealistic, but it may bring up valid criticisms of cliques.

crowds. Crowds usually have shared interests, and the members dress similarly, but their structure is looser than more clearly differentiated groups. Both the **clique** (KLEEK or KLICK) and the **gang** are very tightly knit, have a limited membership, and strict rules for admission and proper behavior (Conger and Peterson, 1984). Major differences between the two are that cliques are usually based on common school-related interests, such as athletics or other types of activities. Gangs, on the other hand, have a rebellious or antisocial outlook and are based on out-of-school activities.

The need to conform to the group in dress and language is strongest in early adolescence, between ages 11 and 14. Toward the end of middle adolescence, around age 16, it has begun a sharp decline. This rapid decline continues through late adolescence so that rigid conformity has almost disappeared at age 18.

Group Identity

An expert in personality development, **Erik Erikson** (1902–1994), saw this support from social groups as necessary for exploring individual identity (Erikson, 1968). Others have expanded on his idea by referring to early adolescence as a time of **group identity versus alienation.** In other words, an adolescent who fails to get a sense of belonging by identifying with a group will feel like a foreigner, alienated from others of his or her age. This adolescent will also have more trouble forming a sense of individual identity toward the end of middle adolescence and through late adolescence (Newman & Newman, 1984).

Individual Identity and Erik Erikson

Personal background often plays a key role in determining what a person emphasizes in both personal and professional life. Such was the case with personality theorist Erik H. Erikson. He never met his Danish biological father, who deserted his mother before Erikson was born; he never even knew his name. His mother was Jewish and married a Jewish physician named Homburger when Erikson was a very small boy. For years, Erikson thought Dr. Homburger was his biological father, and until he was an adult, he used that last name. (His middle initial, "H," stands for Homburger.)

To protect young Erik from being confused and hurt, his mother and stepfather decided not to tell him about his father's abandonment. From a fairly young age, however, Erik felt that something wasn't right. For instance, his mother and stepfather were rather small, with dark hair and eyes, but he was tall, blond, and blue-eyed—obviously Scandinavian. He also felt out of place with his schoolmates. Those who were Jewish did not accept him because of

Chapter 11 ADOLESCENCE

crowds

Large groups with loose rules and changeable memberships.

clique

A very tightly knit group with limited membership and strict rules of behavior; normally tied in with school activities.

gang

A rebellious, antisocial group with strict rules but not connected with accepted school or social organizations.

group identity versus alienation

Erikson's idea that early adolescents either belong to a group or feel lost (alienated).

317

Discussion

What are the main differences between friendships in high school and friendships in junior high? Students will probably mention that friendships in high school are based more on trust and communication than on companionship. Stress that this greater openness, this process of self-disclosure among friends—discussing values and dreams—certainly has an effect on maturation.

Teaching Hint

Many students may initially balk at the idea that their friends have any influence on their individual identity. To illustrate the power of friends, mention Erikson's idea of a *negative* group identity, when young people turn to each other and join gangs or other destructive groups. Erikson warns, however, that when we as teachers, social workers, or administrators treat these young people as nothing more than hoodlums, then that is all they ever will be.

DISCOVERY

Role-play the following situations that highlight instances when parents and adolescents disagree. Afterward, discuss how realistic the role-plays were; then analyze *why* many parents and adolescents feel the way they do. (1) The parent wants the son to get a haircut or wear different clothes. (2) The parent objects to the type of music the adolescent listens to. (3) The daughter explains to her parent(s) that she is pregnant. (4) The parent and adolescent have just watched a TV show that implies that premarital sex is OK. The adolescent argues it *is* OK, as long as the two people love each other; the parent disagrees.

DISCUSS THE PHOTO

Analyze the groups at school—those with negative characteristics as well as positive—that might provide this sense of belonging.

FYI When Erikson finally did "settle down," he came to the United States and became involved in a variety of activities. He worked with World War II soldiers, Native Americans, and civil rights advocates in the South. These culturally varied experiences probably helped shape his theory that society has a great impact on personality. This contrasts with Freud's emphasis on biological forces or the power of the id.

Journal Topic

"What scares you about growing up?" Students may be willing to read these responses aloud.

Unit 4 HUMAN DEVELOPMENT

▲ *Group identity provides a sense of belonging.*

his physical appearance. Those who were Christian considered him Jewish because of his parents' religious beliefs.

From childhood on, he was confused about his own identity, unsure where he fit in the scheme of things. Eventually he learned the truth about his father, which added to his feelings of insecurity. When he graduated from high school, he had no idea what to do or be. For several years, he wandered around Europe as an artist, painting and sketching, but with no real goals. In fact, he was 25 years old before he decided what he wanted to do with his life. It was then that he met Anna Freud, Sigmund Freud's daughter, and began to study psychoanalysis and child development. As if to free himself completely from his crisis of identity, he took Erikson as his last name, reducing his stepfather's name to an initial.

Due to Erikson's circumstances at birth and to his experiences in childhood and adolescence through young adulthood, his sense of self was poorly defined. It took many years and a lot of trial and error before he understood who he was and knew which roads he wished to travel (Hall et al., 1985).

It should come as no surprise, then, that Erik Erikson emphasized the importance of forming an individual identity in his theory of personality development. According to his theory, from approximately age 12 until at least the end of the teenage years, accurately defining the "self" is our major psychological task. Belonging to a group is the

CHAPTER PROJECT/COOPERATIVE LEARNING

Tell students they have just been granted $100,000 to produce a public-service announcement for a teenage audience. Allow groups to choose their own issues: juvenile delinquency, teen pregnancy, AIDS, recycling, education, the future. The announcement will run on national television free of charge. Each group can pick an issue, write a script, then present it to the rest of the class, either live or on video. Set a time limit of one or two minutes. You may want to invite another class to view the announcements in order to have a real audience; this may provide added incentive for students to do a good job.

Chapter 11 ADOLESCENCE

first step. The next step is seeing how you are different from that group, how you are a unique person. Developing a sense of yourself as an individual means achieving **identity.** Never reaching this goal results in **identity confusion**—uncertainty about who you are and what direction you should take.

For Erikson, adolescence represents a crossroads, a time of upheaval, of selecting from many possibilities the ones that fit. This is not easy to do. As a result, adolescence is not an easy time. Too many decisions are forced on the adolescent too quickly. He or she must not only define the self and learn how to relate to the other sex but also make plans about occupations to pursue (Erikson, 1968). Because these decisions have long-range consequences, they create a lot of anxiety and insecurity.

It is natural for youth to flounder around, going back and forth before completing this task. Most adolescents experiment with a variety of roles, discarding one to try out another. In their search, some will identify with a public figure, perhaps an actor, actress, or rock star, taking on his or her mannerisms and style of dress, at least for a while.

Delaying the usual commitments of adulthood to find one's identity is called a **moratorium** (meaning a period of "time out"). In our society, this means that adolescents can engage in behaviors that are not allowed for adults. An obvious example is that teenagers are not expected to marry, start a family, or support themselves. On the other hand, think of how your community would react to a group of adults who dressed like teenagers and drove around the local hamburger

identity

A sense of oneself as a unique person.

identity confusion

Erikson's term for an uncertainty about who one is or where he or she is going.

moratorium

A term used by both Erikson and Marcia to describe the adolescent's delay in making the commitments normally expected of adults.

Discussion

It may be natural for adolescents to explore values, beliefs, and dreams, but what messages are they hearing from adults? Are they being urged to take their time or are they being pushed to hurry?

Teaching Hint

For the sake of argument, assert that society is becoming so complex and there are so many choices to be made that many young people are postponing adulthood. How do students feel about all the choices they have to make?

DISCUSS THE PHOTO

Have students write a journal entry from the point of view of this adolescent.

▲ *Quiet moments, deep thoughts—trying to sort it all out.*

DEMONSTRATION

Play several songs in which characters seem to belong in one or more of Marcia's identity states. After each song, break students into groups and discuss which identity state seems to fit which character. Groups should write down specific lines to support

their conclusions. This should serve both to summarize the main points of Marcia's theory and to clarify the particulars. For example, a singer may cry out about the pain and struggle that he is experiencing, which would signify a crisis, but if the singer turns

his back on the crisis and stops searching for values, beliefs, and so on, the "crisis" becomes pointless. If this same singer makes no commitment, he would be classified as identity diffused (and not in moratorium, as appearances might imply); if a

Discussion

Ask students if they have ever had a friend who "fell in love" and then completely neglected everyone else. Is this real love? (It may or may not be, but it's likely that the two people "in love" have become so dependent on each other that their individual identities have become anything but individual. They have been so obsessed with exploring the *other* that they may not know themselves.)

Teaching Hint

When discussing Marcia, emphasize two key words: (1) *commitment:* how deeply we believe in our values and beliefs and choices; and (2) *crisis:* the process of searching within ourselves for values, beliefs, and choices. Stress that although this crisis may be painful at times, it is a positive process and necessary for identity achievement. The word *crisis* usually denotes tragedy; in this case, it denotes opportunity for growth.

320

fidelity

Erikson's term for being faithful to one's ideals and values; loyalty.

foreclosure

Marcia's term for the state of accepting the identity and values an adolescent was given in childhood.

negative identity

Marcia's term for defining oneself as "bad" or as a "troublemaker."

diffusion

Marcia's term for the state of having no clear idea of one's identity nor attempting to find that identity.

place hanging out the car windows, shouting and waving at people they know. Moratorium is definitely reserved for adolescence.

Because achieving an identity takes so long, some youths try to make decisions about their identity too soon. By not giving themselves enough time to sort everything out, they decide on an identity that does not really fit. Such adolescents may end of up living a life that is not right for them. They may also marry the wrong person. During adolescence, falling in love is part of the identity process. Adolescents help confirm their own identity by gaining someone else's acceptance. As far as Erikson is concerned, real love between two people cannot exist until each knows who he or she is.

Gaining a sense of identity carries with it a number of specific characteristics. The first is developing a clear and unique definition of self, plus acceptance of that self-concept. Other characteristics are a commitment to goals and values, active planning for or working toward those goals, and confidence in the future, in the ability to achieve these goals.

When people have a sense of identity, they also have an understanding of **fidelity.** Fidelity is Erikson's term for being faithful to one's ideals and values as well as being loyal to others we care about, even if they don't always live up to our expectations.

Individual Identity and James Marcia

Researcher **James Marcia** (1980) expanded on Erikson's work and divided the identity crisis into four states. These are not stages but rather processes that adolescents go through. All adolescents will occupy one (or more) of these states, at least temporarily. Because these are not stages, however, people do not progress from one step to the next in a fixed sequence, nor must everyone go through each and every state.

Identity Foreclosure Adolescents who simply accept the identity and values they were given in childhood are in a state of **foreclosure** (not giving themselves a chance to explore alternatives). They have not experimented with other possibilities before deciding who they are. Instead, their self-concept has been defined by other people. For some adolescents, a **negative identity** results from foreclosure. These are the kids who were labeled *bad* or *troublemakers* in childhood and who have come to accept that label. Whether the identity is negative or not, foreclosure means blocking off certain possibilities for growth and individuality.

Identity Diffusion Adolescents who don't have a clear idea of their identity *and* who are not trying to find one are in a state of **diffusion.** These adolescents may have struggled with the issue of iden-

DISCOVERY

commitment is made, then the singer would be identity foreclosed (and not identity achieved, as appearances might imply). You can try the same activity with poems or even art.

Have students make a list of commitments they have made. Then have them rank each item on a scale of one to ten, one signifying "not very committed" and ten being "highly commit-

ted." This exercise may help students assess their own identity states. Follow this up with a journal entry based on discussion question #6.

Chapter 11 ADOLESCENCE

 **James Marcia's Identity States**

Foreclosure	Diffusion	Moratorium	Achievement
Individual makes *definite commitment* . . .	Individual makes *no commitment* . . .	Individual *delays commitment* . . .	Individual makes a *firm commitment* . . .
but commitment is *not* based on any internal "soul searching". . .	and does *no* "*soul searching*" . . .	and struggles a great deal with internal "*soul searching*" . . .	after experiencing meaningful "*soul searching*" . . .
thus, individual *conforms:*	thus, individual *wanders:*	thus, individual *searches:*	thus, individual *finds* identity:
"I think I'm going to be a plumber because my dad and his dad were plumbers."	"I think I'll do some traveling after graduation . . . or maybe I'll get a job . . . or . . ."	"I don't know what I want to do, but I don't want to rush into anything either. I want to find something that's right for me."	"It took me a while to find what I want out of life, but now I think I have a good idea."
In summary— Commitment: Yes Searching: No	In summary— Commitment: No Searching: No	In summary— Commitment: No Searching: Yes	In summary— Commitment: Yes Searching: Yes

Is it possible to be foreclosed or diffused and still be happy?

---

tity in the past, but they never resolved it, and they seem to have stopped trying. The outcome is a lack of self-identity and no real commitment to values or personal goals.

Moratorium   Adolescents who are trying to achieve an identity through experimentation and trial and error are in a state of *moratorium*, discussed earlier. Adolescents remaining in moratorium, or time out, may or may not achieve a sense of identity. Some give up the struggle and wind up in a state of diffusion.

Identity Achievement   Adolescents who have gone through the identity crisis and come out with a well-defined self-concept, who are committed to a set of personal values, beliefs, and goals, have reached the state of **identity achievement.** Their identities may well

identity achievement

Marcia's term for the state of having developed well-defined personal values and self-concepts.

James Marcia's Identity States.

IN FOCUS   If students argue that you *can* be happy, ask if the happiness is based on a solid foundation. Will it be long term? Students may end up more confused after a discussion of this, since happiness is such an elusive emotion.

Journal Topic

"Pretend that in the area of marriage, you are identity foreclosed. You chose your spouse for what you now realize were the wrong reasons. Write an honest letter to your spouse explaining your feelings."

INTERDISCIPLINARY PROJECT

Speech. If your school has a speech team, invite one or two of its members to join your class to read a brief short story or invite someone who is involved in school plays. After the reading, discuss the identity states of the characters in the story.

DISCOVERY

Choose a photo from this chapter and have students write a story about it. After they have written the story, explain that they may have projected their personalities (Chapter 15) into it. Did they project their identity states? For the sake of discussion, have them assume that they did, and have them explain which identity state.

Connections

What parts of Maslow's hierarchy of needs (Chapter 5) might match up with Marcia's identity states? Identity achievement and self-actualization: both involve striving and commitment. Identity foreclosure and safety: both emphasize security.

Critical Thinking

A convicted child abuser has to post a sign on his front lawn that announces his conviction and warns parents to beware. The American Civil Liberties Union (ACLU) has objected. What do students think? After the debate, point out the typical pre-formal operations stage response: "He did a bad thing and should be punished." A formal operations answer may argue the same point, but might also talk about deterrence, privacy, and so on. (By the way, this is a real case.)

DISCUSS THE PHOTO

A parent may be better able to help if he or she is aware of the child's intellectual and moral level of development.

322

Unit 4 HUMAN DEVELOPMENT

formal operations
Piaget's term for the ability to reason in abstract ways; complex thought processes.

▲ *When times are tough, often parents can help.*

322

be expanded and further defined in adulthood, but the basics are there, and such adolescents are well prepared to make meaningful lives for themselves.

INTELLECTUAL AND MORAL CHANGES

Since adolescents must deal with such a staggering number of issues, it is fortunate that their thought processes and moral reasoning have reached their highest level. Agreement that general reasoning abilities reach their peak in adolescence is easily demonstrated. The most popular individual intelligence test for adults starts at age 16 (Wechsler, 1981). Also, as discussed in detail in Chapter 10, Jean Piaget devised a theory of how thought processes progress as we mature. The last stage in Piaget's theory of cognitive development—formal operations—begins at age 11 or 12.

Jean Piaget's Formal Operations Stage of Cognitive Development

Formal operations in cognitive development include the ability to reason in abstract ways—to consider the possibilities instead of being struck with concrete realities. Adolescents are capable of logical thought, of testing hypotheses. When asked such questions as *"If such-and-such takes place, then* what will happen?," most adolescents think through the outcomes in systematic, logical ways that were not possible before. The ability to think abstractly helps the future become more real. Something that potentially exists is just as likely to be true as something that already does exist. Without formal operations, one is limited to the concrete, to the existing order of things. With formal operations, we can deal with what might be, what could be, *if* certain things took place.

Prior to this level of abstract thinking, the world was seen in concrete terms. Thus, if Mary got some extra money, so should Max—period. At the formal operations stage, however, the situation is seen differently. Suppose that Mary had been deprived while Max had had certain advantages earlier. The adolescent realizes that making up for past inequalities between the two is fair. Max does not need any money because justice demands that their situations be made more equal.

This high level of reasoning ability helps adolescents consider how the world could be a better place or why personal principles are sometimes more important than external rules and laws. Consequently, it is almost impossible to separate general cognitive abilities or thought processes from moral reasoning.

DISCOVERY

"What if people could run as fast as horses?" Have some fun with this; then explain that someone who thinks at the formal operations level will think of much more complex answers than someone below this level. For example, a ten-year-old might say, "That's stupid; people could never run as fast as horses." If you pursue an answer, the ten-year-old might talk about horses racing people and never get beyond that. On the other hand, a formal operations thinker may discuss how the world would change with this new ability. Maybe we would have fewer streets and more sidewalks; we would need to rethink our transit system, and what about special shoes? And so on.

Lawrence Kohlberg's Postconventional Level of Moral Reasoning

As explained in Chapter 10, Lawrence Kohlberg believed that moral development follows a maturational sequence. Individuals who have reached the **postconventional level** of moral reasoning make decisions about right and wrong according to basic principles. This holds true even if their actions must go beyond society's laws or authority's rules and regulations. Generally, this level of moral reasoning is not reached before middle or late adolescence.

Postconventional moral reasoning is subdivided into two stages. The first emphasizes **social contracts.** When people agree to something because they believe it is best for everyone involved, they are bound by this mutual agreement or social contract.

The second stage operates according to **universal ethical principles;** concepts like justice and honor are guidelines for right and wrong. This stage is the most complex and also the one least often reached by people (Lloyd, 1985).

Lawrence Kohlberg tested his theory by presenting moral dilemmas to people and asking them not only what they would do in the situation but why they would do it. It is the "why" that shows one's level of moral reasoning, not the "what." For instance, in the example in Chapter 10, a person could either save the one rich man in a lifeboat or the ten poor men, but not both. The postconventional answer given was to save the ten poor men because human life has value regardless of wealth. It would be possible, though, to give another answer from the postconventional viewpoint. Suppose a person said the one rich man should be saved because this one rich man could do more to improve the world through the proper use of his wealth than all ten poor men put together. Thus the final justification for this choice is that human life has value beyond the people in the lifeboat. This answer is also an example of postconventional moral reasoning. The same principle is involved in both answers—the value of human life. It is the interpretation of how to apply the principle that differs. But the fact that complex interpretation is going on is the key to this level of moral development.

The Family's Influence on Adolescence

We tend to take the existence of a serious "generation gap" for granted in this country. But does such a gap actually exist? And if so, is it as serious as we are led to believe? The topic of how parents and teenagers relate to one another raises a number of questions. As before, the answers are slightly different for early, middle, and late adolescence.

postconventional level

Kohlberg's term for the level of moral reasoning that uses basic principles.

social contracts

Kohlberg's term for agreements based on the concept of what's "best for everyone."

universal ethical principles

Kohlberg's term for concepts such as justice and honor.

Points to Stress

The few people who reach the universal ethical principles stage base their moral decisions on the effect those decisions will have on the human race. For example, when Martin Luther King broke the law to protest civil rights violations, he stated that he was actually showing great respect for the law; he wanted to make it better for everyone.

Points to Stress

The social contract stage emphasizes people's *rights.* In fact, the United States Constitution is based on this high level of moral thinking, providing us with the Bill of Rights.

COOPERATIVE LEARNING

Surveys such as the one below can always use updating. Have each group write ten survey questions that will be administered to teens and their parents to assess the level of agreement. The questions should actually be statements for which respondents can "strongly disagree," "strongly agree," and so on. See **Teaching Master 11-3 Rating Scale** for a scale that you can use; if you *do* use it, pass it out *before* students write their surveys. Each group can focus on one of the following issues: drugs; work; education; clothing styles; politics; sexual matters. Here are some sample issues: (1) It's OK for two adults to have premarital sex if they love each other. (2) A college degree is more important than a "business connection." (3) Marijuana should be

DISCUSS THE PHOTO

What are other perceptions that parents have of young people dating? Role-play a discussion on dating between a parent and an adolescent.

Discussion

"Why is it sometimes difficult for adults to understand adolescents?" Possible answers: adults may have forgotten what it is like to be 16 or 17; mention repression (Chapter 17). Though the term is overused, a *generation gap* can certainly cause difficulties. The world has changed, and adults will never know what it is like to be 17 when their kids are 17. Also, adults are dealing with their own life changes and this focus may interfere with their understanding.

Comprehension Check

Which topics do adolescents generally agree upon with their parents? *(education, work, drugs, and politics)* What topics cause the most disagreement? *(sexual matters and clothing styles)*

324

Unit 4 HUMAN DEVELOPMENT

▲ *Teenage couple on a date—as perceived by the girl's father. The Museum of Modern Art/Film Stills Archive*

Adolescents have been said to live in an "intense present." As a result, death seems quite foreign, and it is not a part of their thoughts very often. The distant future is also excluded from this daily living process. These feelings can be explained by the fact that the majority of adolescents are not tied to major lifelong responsibilities. Without these concerns, only the immediate past and present remain in focus most of the time, particularly in early and middle adolescence. By late adolescence, the future takes on greater importance as high school graduation nears.

Close scrutiny of the adolescent value system shows that what has been absorbed to this point is thoroughly locked in. Goals, such as trying to make life more moral, saner, and more humane—all improvements badly needed—reflect basically the same ideals that are held by most adults. More often than not, parents and teenagers are on the same wavelength. Most parents, at one point in their own past, were aiming for the same thing, and those ideals are still there. For many adults, though, actually working toward those goals has become a less urgent priority over time.

It is almost a tradition for the press to play up disagreements between children and parents. Despite this, teenagers and parents are in close agreement on almost every issue of importance. A survey of 986 people age 13 to 18 indicates that youth tend to agree with their parents on the importance of education and the necessity of work, and they have similar views about drugs and politics. The amount of agreement is high, ranging from 78 to 83 percent. Interestingly, these percentages reflect agreement with the mother. Across the board, teenagers and fathers don't see eye to eye as much, though the figures are still high: 69 to 76 percent. The lowest areas of agreement are about sexual matters (with the mother: 69 percent; with the father: 62 percent) and the clothing styles (mother: 65 percent; father: 53 percent) (White & John, 1984).

Most adolescents have a good and loving relationship with their parents. They share feelings of closeness and generally get along well together. As both parents and adolescents know, however, things do not always run smoothly at home. Research has shown that when children become teenagers, their parents, especially their mothers, experience greater stress, unhappiness, and dissatisfaction than at any other time.

Although the press has exaggerated the "generation gap," it is true that increased conflicts (arguing, nagging, and so forth) occur during a child's teenage years. This squabbling and bickering is at its worst in early adolescence—roughly between ages 11 and 14. During middle adolescence, it starts to decrease and usually is over for the most part by age 16. Late adolescence brings with it greater harmony with parents (Paikoff & Brooks-Gunn, 1991).

The distress is real even when teenagers and parents love each other and get along most of the time. Why, then, is there so much arguing and bickering between them? Some researchers see conflicts

should be legalized. (4) Ripped jeans should not be worn to school. Take the best five or six questions from each group and combine them into a comprehensive survey. Try to administer the survey to an equal number of parents and teens.

DISCOVERY

This activity appeals to students who are more artistic than verbal. Have students draw their families. Explain that the illustration and any necessary captions should clarify the role each person plays in the family. Who is the leader? The peace-keeper? And so on.

Chapter 11 ADOLESCENCE

▲ *Grandparents are often a ready source of comfort, and fun as well.*

between parents and their teenage children as both unavoidable and *necessary.*

Adolescence as a separate time given special emphasis is a fairly new idea. Many experts believe that it has only existed since the 1920s at the earliest. A century ago, children left home when they hit puberty, and they began to work as apprentices for adults other than their parents. This was particularly true for boys. Among girls, sexual maturity occurred several years later than it does today. For most girls, sexual maturity meant marriage. And marriage meant leaving home (Degler, 1980).

It is only in the recent past that adolescents have remained at home, financially dependent on their parents, for several years beyond puberty. Many agree this is an economic necessity. Others suggest this situation may be an unnatural or artificial arrangement. Those who take this position point to animal behavior for support: among many primates who live in groups, the offspring leave their group when they are old enough to start their own families. If they don't, they are forced out by the adults. A similar situation occurs even among solitary animals like the cougar. Cougars are "loners"; adult cougars stay together long enough to reproduce, and then they go their separate ways. The female rears her young alone. When they start to mature, she makes them go out on their own. A young cougar who doesn't want to leave home will be attacked by its own mother until it finally gives up and goes away.

Discussion

Years ago, adults seemed to command much more respect—or *obedience* might better describe it. Today, it seems that adults have to *earn* respect; it's not automatic. Do students view this as progress?

DISCUSS THE PHOTO

Ask students if they would want their grandparents living with them. What would be the advantages and disadvantages?

Discussion

"Do you feel that your parents are overprotective?" If you conduct the role-plays suggested earlier between a parent and an adolescent, this might offer a glimpse into the parent's point of view.

INTERDISCIPLINARY PROJECT

History. The period called adolescence has a relatively short history, beginning sometime around the early 1900s. Have students find out what life was like for children and teenagers before this time. You might ask them to focus on school and work. After they accumulate some material, ask them to write several diary entries from the point of view of a young teenager living back then. Remind students that since adolescence did not quite exist then, this teenager would have been considered an adult.

Teaching Hint

Many students will assume that adolescence evolved because of an increase in longevity. Stress that adolescence was a social creation, not a biological one. Three reforms helped to create it: juvenile delinquent laws, child labor laws, and compulsory education. Before then, children were looked on as *little adults*. With the introduction of these reforms, a greater distinction was made between adults and children, which began to create the gap that we now refer to as adolescence.

FYI Around 1900, two psychologists began to study childhood development: G. Stanley Hall in the United States and Sigmund Freud in Europe. These pioneers, the first to study children scientifically, helped to dispel the notion that children are merely little adults who need not be granted special rights.

Unit 4 HUMAN DEVELOPMENT

juvenile delinquency

Repeated violations of the law by those 17 and younger.

There is clearly a connection for various animals between sexual maturity, or puberty, and a "natural" desire to become independent of the family unit. Is there a similar connection for humans? Quite possibly there is. It has been noted, for instance, that tension between parents and teenagers is highest during puberty (Paikoff & Brooks-Gunn, 1991). It is to the advantage of the species for its youth to establish homes and families of their own. Consequently, it may be that puberty in some way triggers conflicts in order to make the separation easier for both sides (Steinberg, 1987).

To see how this might work, consider one more example from animals that live in groups, like wolves and chimpanzees. The increase in strength and size plus the additional adrenaline and sex hormones of puberty give both young male wolves and chimpanzees a push to challenge the older, more senior males. By winning such a fight, a younger male can improve his standing in the group. "Adolescent" female chimpanzees seem to provoke irritation in their mothers and are competitors for the males' attentions. In other words, the physical changes of puberty create different attitudes in young animals *and* differences in how they are perceived by their elders (Goodall, 1971).

Most cultures with rituals that mark one's entrance into adulthood (the rite of passage discussed earlier) are very clear about this issue. Once puberty starts, the children leave home. In some, even before puberty, older children no longer sleep in their family home. They see their family during the day, but at night they are with other adults or in "dormitories" constructed just for this age group. When they reach puberty, they marry and establish their own households. The separation from their original family is complete.

These studies suggest that making children and parents live together beyond the point of "natural" separation means that conflicts are bound to occur. In the words of one expert: "If teenagers didn't argue with their parents, they might never leave home at all" (Steinberg, 1987, p. 39).

JUVENILE DELINQUENCY

In 1990, 1.75 million people under the age of 18 were arrested. In fact, 30 percent of all the arrests made in that year involved offenders under 21 years of age (Zigler, Taussig & Black, 1992). **Juvenile delinquency,** the repeated violation of the law by those 17 and younger, is a serious problem in our society. In addition, juveniles who commit violent crimes or are substance abusers usually continue on this path well into their 20s (Buchanan, Eccles & Becker, 1992). The cost, in human suffering and dollars, is staggering, and each year it keeps getting worse. Obviously, society needs to address this issue. However, before looking for solutions, let us first consider what might influence such behavior.

DISCOVERY

Before students read this section, ask them to list the characteristics associated with juvenile delinquents. What is generally the income level of the family? What are some reasons for the delinquency? What is disci-pline like in the family? Afterward, compare their responses with the material in this section. How many responses were accurate? How many were simply stereotypes?

ENRICHMENT

Have students find out where money is being spent today on pro-grams to stop or prevent juvenile delinquency. Ask them to report back to the class. Then consider the cooperative-learning activity that follows.

Factors Associated with Delinquency

Over the past few years, psychologists have collected a great deal of information on juvenile delinquency. Before discussing their find-ings, though, we want to issue a word of warning. A number of char-acteristics are related to delinquency; these are factors that put ado-lescents at higher risk for getting into trouble. This does *not* mean that everyone with these characteristics is or will become a juvenile delinquent. Many, in fact, will overcome these obstacles and go on to lead productive lives. It is just more difficult for them from the out-set. Also, there are cases of loving families where the parents seem to be doing everything right, but their child has been difficult from the start and is always in trouble, nevertheless. Thus, there are no perfect predictions in this area.

Many people believe that adolescents from low-income families are more likely to break the law. However, research shows that this is sim-ply not the case. Income alone is not a factor (Hinshaw, 1992; Zigler et al., 1992). People also tend to believe that kids whose mothers work outside the home are more likely to get into trouble. Again, research shows this to be a myth (Silverstein, 1991). Interestingly, it appears that the father contributes more to his children's antisocial behavior than the mother does. A father who is aggressive, irresponsible, detached, and unaffectionate increases the risk of antisocial behavior in his children. When he has a history of criminal activity or substance abuse, the risk increases even more (Phares & Compas, 1992).

Delinquency, especially aggressive behavior, seems to grow best in an atmosphere of chaos, conflict, and discord far beyond the normal tensions that naturally occur in most families. Poor communication, abusive relationships in the family, and little affection or support from the parents make the situation worse. Also, when parents fail to provide and enforce reasonable rules and guidelines, when they are not involved in their children's lives, the risk is greater still. All these factors increase the likelihood that an adolescent will both do poorly in school *and* get into trouble with the law (Phares & Compas, 1992; Hinsaw, 1992; Phares, 1992; Zigler et al., 1992; Loeber, 1990). And like it or not, underachievement in school and delinquent behavior are related.

Preventive Programs

Many programs have been developed to deal with delinquency. Too many of them, though, are put into place after a delinquent behavior pattern has already been established. While some of these programs can still help adolescents turn themselves around, it is more difficult to produce change at such a late date. Oddly enough, the most successful programs were not even designed to deal with juvenile delinquency. They were set up to teach expectant mothers

Journal Topic

"Write a letter to your parents explaining to them that you want to leave home. Provide rea-sons and try to convince them that you are mature and responsible enough to be on your own." For a creative-writing exercise, have them write the likely parent response!

Evaluation Strategy

How might a juvenile delinquent fit into any one of the four identity states outlined by Marcia? If the person is searching for answers to his future: *moratorium.* If the person breaks the law just be-cause everyone else does: *foreclosed.* If the person breaks the law because it's fun and there's nothing else to do: *diffused.* If the person thinks that the laws are truly unjust and breaks them to send a message: *achieved?*

Comprehension Check

Name some factors associated with juvenile delinquency. (*abuse and/or poor communication in the family; lack of affection or support from parents; an aggressive, irresponsible, and detached father; parents who do not set and enforce rules*)

This activity sharpens problem-solving skills. *Directions:* "You have been given $1 million to help stop or prevent juvenile delinquency. You can only pour your money into a single project. It can be an existing project or a new idea. Describe the project you choose, and provide a list of reasons why it is most worthwhile." Students won't have much basis for comparison if they don't complete the preceding enrichment idea, but they may think of some creative, new ideas.

DISCUSS THE PHOTO

When considering the causes of juvenile delinquency, many researchers focus on children's attachment to their parents. Only a few have studied another important factor—the attachment of parents to their children.

Unit 4 HUMAN DEVELOPMENT

▲ *Harmony and interpersonal involvement within the family decreases the children's risk of getting into serious trouble.*

Recall Strategy

Which identity state would best fit these descriptions? (1) Jeremy ignored questions about what career to choose and went to work for his dad. *(foreclosed)* (2) Hazel dated the same man for six years, had some good times and some bad, then finally married him because she loved him. *(achieved)* (3) Josephine could not care less about a career and takes any job that comes along. *(diffused)* (4) Harold wants to make the right decision about college, but will not decide until he explores several possibilities. *(moratorium)*

how to be better parents or to help troubled preschool children do better in school. Many years later, researchers discovered that these programs had an impact on the probability of future juvenile delinquency.

The families in these original programs were at high risk for trouble. At the time, psychologists were not sure exactly what factors were involved in delinquency. However, looking back, we can see that these families had many of the problem characteristics we just talked about.

The successful programs did several things. They provided parenting classes and group meetings for the parents. They made in-home visits with the families and taught them how to solve problems. They helped find quality day-care services. They encouraged parents to participate in school activities and generally to become more involved in what their children were doing. Thus, nearly all the family issues associated with juvenile delinquency were dealt with, even though that was not the original goal.

Years later, when these children were in late adolescence or early adulthood, comparisons were made with a similar group who had not taken part in any preventive program. The results were clear and consistent. The children in the program were more likely to graduate from high school, go on to college, and have a stable job. Police records showed that there were far fewer arrests in this group, from one-fourth to one-half as many as for the comparison group. In addition, the arrests that did occur involved less serious offenses (Zigler et al., 1992).

DISCOVERY

If you have taken any assertiveness-training courses, these rules probably seem very familiar to you. Have students role-play various situations, first as they would normally handle them, then using some of the rules described here. If you can solicit real situations, it makes the role-plays and the discussion that follows much more vital. Have students try the following: express anger, make a request, refuse a request.

PSYCHOLOGY IN YOUR LIFE

Good Communication

The level of tension and conflict in any home comes from many different factors. One major source of trouble, though, is poor communication between teenagers and their parents. Most parents will never see this book, so we cannot deal directly with them. But since adolescents can change the way discussions take place, too, a few rules of good communication follow. Some of them may seem too obvious to bother with, yet very few people follow them, which causes no end of unnecessary problems.

1. Pick a convenient time and place to talk for *both* parties. An example of *not* following this rule is "Bob, get in here right now! I want to talk to you!" A different example: Bob tells his father he wants to talk to him; his father says, "Sure, I'll be finished with this in a couple of minutes"; Bob gets mad and shouts, "Oh, never mind! You're always too busy to talk to me anyway, so just forget it, okay?" A better approach is "When you have a few

minutes, there's something I want to talk about. How's right after dinner in the living room?" Be sure to set a specific time and place instead of leaving it open.

2. Be direct and clear when you speak, but also be polite rather than rude. If you're too subtle, your message won't get through; most people can't read minds. On the other hand, insults slam the door on communication. Amy tells her mother, "Your hair looks awful like that!" Laura says to her mother, "I saw a hairstyle the other day that would look great on you. Here, take a look at this picture I cut out of a magazine. Isn't that terrific? It's made for you, I can tell." Which one would you rather

▲ Genuine parent/child conflict increases notably with age. The complexities of modern society can require parents and children to live together too long.

listen to and maybe even cooperate with?

3. Take responsibility for your own feelings and accept what the other person feels. Saying, "*You* make me so mad when…" puts the responsibility for your anger on the other person. Saying, "*I* get so mad when…" puts the responsibility where it belongs. An example of acceptance is "My doing that really bothers you,

(continued on next page)

PSYCHOLOGY IN YOUR LIFE

What kinds of things block communication? *Examples:* We may enter a conversation with a certain bias that we cannot overcome. We process words faster than another person can talk, so we may listen carelessly. When the other person stops talking, we say, "But" or "Anyway," which can serve to discredit everything that was said.

DISCUSS THE PHOTO

Ask the students who get along well with their parents to share their tips on good communication.

Discussion

One pressure that you might want to discuss is moving from one neighborhood to another. Find out which students have moved the most and the effect the moving has had on the family. Is it easier to move in elementary or high school? Any advantages to moving?

Good Communication

(continued from previous page) huh?" Nonacceptance is shown by "Well, I don't see why you're upset! What's the matter with you, anyway?" or "It's dumb to get so mad when it's not that big a deal." Try to understand that not everyone responds the same way to the same situation.

4. Stick with the subject. This rule sounds so easy, but is broken all the time. For instance: "Oh, yeah? Well, what about the time you…?" or "I just knew that's what you'd say. You always say that. You've been saying that for so long, I'm sick and tired of hearing it" or "I don't see why I can't have my friends over when I want to. What about Aunt Esther? You let *her* stay here for three weeks, *in my bedroom!*" It's impossible to avoid emotional reactions to a sensitive subject completely. The goal is to be alert and get the

discussion back on track as soon as possible.
5. Don't play the "blame game." Trying to decide who's at fault is very tempting. But it usually doesn't solve anything. Eventually, it may be important to figure out how (not how much) each person contributes to the problem, so changes can be made. For the most part, though, it really doesn't matter who is more to blame. (Trust us!) The real point is that a problem needs to be solved. Looking at what needs changing rather than who is more responsible brings you closer to finding a workable solution.
6. Listen to what is being said. There are several parts to this rule. First, wait until the other person has finished speaking before you start thinking about your own reply. Second, never interrupt unless you honestly don't

understand; if you don't understand, ask direct questions. Third, try to rephrase in your own mind what the other person is saying. Fourth, open your mind to the possibility that you may not have "heard it all before."

It is important to remember that following these rules will not solve every problem. Sometimes, even with excellent communication, people still find themselves on opposite sides of the fence.

After you have a basic understanding of these rules, try them out with a couple of friends or classmates, in a group of three. Everyone takes a turn at playing each of three parts: the speaker, the listener, and the referee or "official" who decides when a rule has been broken. The subject you choose to talk about is up to you. However, the more strongly you feel about a topic, the more likely you are to break the rules of good communication.

SUMMARY

1. Physical growth in adolescence includes sexual development during puberty, which

is controlled by the pituitary gland and hormones from the adrenal glands and

VOCABULARY REVIEW

Before testing students on the contents of the chapter, you may want to review vocabulary terms that are especially important or confusing. Terms in this chapter that could require clarification are *rite of passage*, *identity*, *formal operations*, *postconventional level*, and *universal ethical principles*.

Chapter 11 ADOLESCENCE

gonads. Changes during puberty include maturation of the reproductive system, voice changes, breast development, and changes in facial and body hair.

2. Growth spurts happen earlier in girls, who may grow as much as three inches in one year; boys may later add four inches to their height in a year. In general, early maturation is an advantage for boys but not for girls, while late maturation is a problem for boys but not for girls.

3. Excessive concern about weight can lead to eating disorders, especially among female adolescents. In bulimia nervosa, the person binges on food and then purges the food from the system. In anorexia nervosa, the person stops eating and maintains a dangerously low weight.

4. Belonging to a group helps adolescents feel less alone and is a first step toward developing a sense of identity. Conformity to groups is highest in early adolescence, then falls rapidly from the end of middle adolescence on.

5. Crowds are fairly loose in structure and membership. Cliques are small, rigidly defined groups made up of adolescents with shared school-related interests. Gangs are small, rigidly defined groups with a rebellious or antisocial outlook, whose members share similar out-of-school interests. Those who do not have a group identity feel alienated from others.

6. Erik Erikson views adolescence as a time for developing a sense of identity. This means not only deciding who you are but also becoming committed to personal goals and values. During identity formation, a moratorium occurs, delaying adult commitments so that adolescents have the opportunity to experiment with different roles. Achieving an identity includes developing fidelity, or loyalty, to one's values and beliefs as well as to people one

cares about. Failure to achieve an identity results in identity confusion, or uncertainty.

7. James Marcia discusses four identity states. Foreclosure occurs when adolescents make identity decisions based on the identity and values given them in childhood by other people. Identity diffusion exists when adolescents have an unclear sense of self and have stopped trying to find themselves. Moratorium means trying out a number of possibilities. Identity achievement includes a clear definition of self and a commitment to the future.

8. During the formal operations stage, abstract thinking and logic are developed. Reasoning is systematic, and possibilities as well as realities can be carefully considered. Moral reasoning involves the application of social contracts or universal ethical principles to determine right and wrong.

9. Adolescents and their parents agree on most important issues, such as the value of education and work, their political views, and attitudes toward drugs. Mothers' opinions are somewhat closer to adolescents' than are fathers' viewpoints.

10. On the other hand, tension and conflict between parents and children are highest when the children are adolescents. Some researchers believe this is part of a natural separation process that occurs among animals and in more primitive cultures. The greatest conflict arises when the adolescent reaches puberty, regardless of the specific age at which puberty occurs.

11. Juvenile delinquency is a serious problem in our society. Among the factors contributing to juvenile delinquency are a chaotic and conflict-laden family life, poor communication, abuse, and lack of support, affection, and involvement from the parents. Preventive programs attempt to educate and encourage parents while the children are still small.

Wrapping It Up

Here's a challenge: write your own journal entry examining what fascinates you about the young people. Include the frustrations, too. If you're feeling bold, you may want to share your writing with your students to get their reactions.

CHAPTER 11 REVIEW ANSWERS

SUGGESTED READINGS

▼ Bell, Ruth. *Changing Bodies, Changing Lives.* New York: Vintage.

▼ Elkind, David. *All Grown Up and No Place to Go.* Reading, Mass.: Addison-Wesley, 1984.

▼ Elkind, David. *The Hurried Child.* Reading, Mass.: Addison-Wesley, 1988.

▼ Galbraith, Ronald E., and Thomas M. Jones. *Moral Reasoning.* San Diego: Greenhaven Press, 1976.

▼ Kaplan, Louise J. *Adolescence: The Farewell to Childhood.* New York: Simon & Schuster, 1984.

▼ Pogrebin, Letty Cottin. *Among Friends.* New York: McGraw-Hill, 1987.

▼ Satris, Stephen. *Taking Sides: Clashing Views on Controversial Moral Issues.* Guilford, New York: Dushkin, 1990.

Answers to Review Questions

1. L
2. E
3. E
4. M
5. M
6. L
7. false
8. true
9. false
10. true
11. true
12. false
13. rite of passage
14. alienation
15. identity confusion
16. fidelity
17. moratorium
18. c
19. a
20. d
21. c
22. b
23. d
24. b
25. a

VOCABULARY

- early adolescence
- middle adolescence
- late adolescence
- puberty
- hormones
- pituitary gland
- adrenal glands
- gonads
- growth spurt
- early maturer
- late maturer
- eating disorders
- bulimia nervosa
- anorexia nervosa
- rite of passage
- crowds
- clique
- gang
- Erik Erikson
- group identity versus alienation
- identity
- identity confusion
- moratorium
- fidelity
- James Marcia
- foreclosure
- negative identity
- diffusion
- identity achievement
- formal operations
- postconventional level
- social contracts
- universal ethical principles
- juvenile delinquency

Review Questions

For each of the following, answer E for early adolescence, M for middle adolescence, and L for late adolescence.

1. Don't care about what others wear
2. Highest level of arguing with parents
3. Females much more mature than males
4. A 15-year-old
5. Females slightly more mature than males
6. Less fighting, more harmony between adolescents and parents

True/False

7. Nearly 10 percent of our sexual maturity occurs during puberty.
8. Less than 20 percent of adolescents have a difficult time coping with biological changes such as growth spurts.
9. Early adolescence is a time of maximum physical growth for females but not for males.
10. An early-maturing boy generally has a higher self-concept than an early-maturing girl.
11. Both the clique and the gang have strict rules for how to behave.
12. Statistics show that adolescents from low-income families are more likely to break the law.

▼ Tannen, Deborah. *That's Not What I Meant! How Conversational Style Makes or Breaks Your Relations with Others.* New York: Ballantine Books, 1986.

▼ Tannen, Deborah. *You Just Don't Understand: Women and Men in Conversation.* New York: Ballantine Books, 1990.

SUGGESTED VIDEOS

▼ *Everybody Rides the Carousel.* 3 parts. 1975. Pyramid.

▼ *Kids in Crisis.* 52 min. HBO.

▼ *Moral Development.* 28 min. 1973. CRM/McGraw-Hill.

Notes on Discussion Questions

1. Students' answers may reflect their maturity or their perceptions of their maturity. Those who already consider themselves adults will probably not care how the end of adolescence is defined. Those who are confused or frustrated about their identities, which may be positive if they're actively searching for an identity, may welcome a clearly defined ending to adolescence.

2. Answers will vary, depending on students' definitions of "adult." Write *adult* on the chalkboard, and allow students a minute or two to write down their spontaneous reactions. Or brainstorm a definition of "adult." According to their reactions or definitions, do adults tend to be one-dimensional: responsible, bossy, and narrow-minded? Or can "certified adults" be irresponsible, rebellious, and playful, too?

3. A 15-year-old has probably been through puberty already, so physical changes would not be a major source of conflict or frustration. Also, the 15-year-old's cognitive development is probably relatively

Fill in the blanks; answer on a separate sheet of paper. (An answer may consist of more than one word.)

13. A ceremony or ritual marking the entry into adulthood is called a ___?___ .

14. According to some psychologists, the main conflict in early adolescence is group identity versus ___?___ .

15. Erik Erikson sees the main conflict in adolescence as identity versus ___?___ .

16. Sticking with your beliefs is called ___?___ .

17. Delaying commitments about beliefs and values is called ___?___ .

Matching (Answers can be used more than once.)

18. No identity and has stopped trying to find one
19. Makes decisions about identity too soon
20. Trial-and-error period
21. Tends to wander
22. Well-defined self-concept
23. Delays making a commitment, but still trying
24. Has made a commitment through searching within
25. Forms an identity based on others' expectations

a. foreclosure
b. identity achievement
c. diffusion
d. moratorium

DISCUSSION QUESTIONS

1. The chapter explains that in our society, it's difficult to determine when exactly adolescence ends. Do you think you'd rather have the end of adolescence more clearly defined, or do you prefer it loosely defined as it is now? Why?

2. If you could be considered, as of this moment, a full-fledged, 100 percent, certified adult, would you want that? Discuss.

3. Consider a 15-year-old from a primitive society who becomes an adult after an elaborate ceremony or ritual (rite of passage). Does this 15-year-old, since he is considered an adult and since he considers himself an adult, experience some of the same conflicts and frustrations that most adolescents in modern society experience? Explain.

4. Most of us at one time or another have been a part of a clique, whether we realized it or not. Why do people form cliques? Explain. Also, do cliques serve any positive or worthwhile functions? Explain.

5. Compare the ranges of adolescence (early, middle, late) to Marcia's theory of identity states. *When* would an adolescent most likely be foreclosed, diffused, in moratorium, and achieved? Explain. (In answering this question, you may be guilty of generalizing, but go ahead.)

advanced. The major source of conflict then would involve expectations. In our society, adolescents are expected to explore alternatives and to experience some confusion and frustration when forming identities. A primitive society would not expect these feelings. The question then is this: how important are society's expectations in influencing perceptions, attitudes, and maturity? Answers to this question will vary, and students may be able to offer several personal examples.

4. Many people probably join cliques to satisfy some kind of security or social need. If these people find it difficult to satisfy these needs in other ways, perhaps cliques serve a worthwhile function, at least for a while.

5. An adolescent may be diffused during early adolescence; at this time, the adolescent may not be ready for serious exploration of values or personal goals. During middle adolescence, an adolescent *may* be in a moratorium state; the adolescent is probably more capable now of struggling with difficult identity issues. During late adolescence, the adolescent could fit into any of the four identity states, the moratorium and foreclosure states being the most likely, the achievement state being the least likely. In other words, most adolescents are either strug-

gling over identity issues (in moratorium) or have given up and accepted the identity handed to them by others (foreclosed); furthermore, few adolescents have the maturity or experience needed to resolve the struggle adequately (achieved).

6. Answers will vary. You may want to use this as a journal topic.

7. If you invite parents to class dur-

ing this unit, ask them about the level of agreement between them and their children.

8. Most students will probably explain how they break away from parents, which is fine. But consider telling students to pick one vivid experience that served to help break them away from their parents and to describe that experience in detail.

6. Marcia acknowledges that part of an individual may be foreclosed, another achieved, and so on. For example, an individual may make a firm and personally meaningful commitment to career and be achieved in this area, but this same individual may wander and be diffused in matters of religion, for example. Pick three of the four identity states and explain how you might fit into each category at this stage in your life.

7. As mentioned in the chapter, surveys show that teenagers and adults agree on important issues: education, work, politics, drugs. If you and your parents were surveyed on these four areas, what would the results be? Would the agreement be high? Explain.

8. No matter how well we get along with our parents as adolescents, there comes a point

when we need to break away and begin to assert our own independence. There are several ways in which we do this, some of them deliberate and intentional and some of them not so intentional. For example, someone might join an activity at school for the enjoyment of it, which also causes this person to spend less time at home; as a result (but without really *trying* for this result), this person probably becomes more independent. Describe several ways, intentional or not intentional, that you use or have used to break away from your parents. Also, briefly describe your parents' past or present reactions to these ways.

9. Read through the rules of communication listed at the end of the chapter. Which one seems to be the hardest one for you to follow? Offer examples.

ACTIVITIES

1. Since our society has no rites of passage, it's unclear when adolescence ends and when adulthood begins. Here's your chance to eliminate any frustration or confusion that results from this. Think of an appropriate rite of passage into adulthood for our society today. Make the plan as specific as possible. How old would the person have to be? What exactly would the person have to do? And so on. Feel free to use humor if it helps you to get your point across.

   Once you have an appropriate rite of passage in mind, pretend that you're about to go through it yourself, and describe the experience and your feelings in detail. It may help to imagine that you're writing a journal or diary entry.

2. Often, cliques acquire stereotypical names: jocks, burnouts, brains, and so on. List the

names of ten cliques at your school and copy this list onto five other sheets of paper. Next, find five "strangers" or acquaintances at school (not close friends), and show each of them your list. After each clique, have them write down the following: (a) what a person needs to do in order to be admitted to the clique and (b) what is considered proper behavior within the clique. Without looking at their answers, follow the same procedure yourself.

   Finally, compare the lists. We don't want you to use friends for this activity since your friends will most likely have a similar perception of the cliques as yourself. We want to discover whether "strangers" have the same perception of certain cliques as you do. Do they? Explain.

   If you want to be bold, show your list to

These are good papers to read aloud.

9. You might ask students to volunteer a few examples and role-play them in class.

Notes on Activities

1. This activity seems simple enough, but students may need assistance. Spend a few minutes in class brainstorming ideas. For example, our society highly values the automobile. Therefore, you can propose that a young person needs to go through a rite of passage to attain a driver's license. In other words, only an adult should be able to drive a car. In this case, the rite of passage would dictate perhaps that the young person needs to prove that he or she can take apart a carburetor and put it back together again!

2. After students complete this activity, have a follow-up discussion. Students usually enjoy discussing the group structures at their school. You may notice that students find it easy to recognize clique behavior in others but rarely admit that they themselves belong to any cliques!

3. Students should have no difficulty finding information on these topics.

4. Parents enjoy this kind of involvement. You might encourage students to have parents help them compare the two lists; it might evoke more memories.

5. It might be fun to have some of your more creative students analyze the ideal male over the past ten or 20 years.

6. These papers are a pleasure to read, and they allow you to become better acquainted with your students. Assure students that the reports will remain confidential, that they will not be read aloud or discussed in class.

one of the clique members you described on your sheet. Does this person feel your perceptions are accurate?

3. Find an article or two on *one* of the following topics and write a report: teenage alcoholism, teenage suicide, teenage depression, teenage pregnancy.

    Part of your report will probably be a summary of the articles that you use. In addition to this, however, be sure to include your own reactions to your research: (a) compare and contrast your research findings with what actually occurs at your school; (b) discuss your agreement or disagreement with what the articles state as *causes* of these problems; and (c) propose a possible solution to these problems.

4. This activity will give your parents a chance to reminisce about their own adolescence. (If your parents are unavailable, find someone who would be about the same age as your parents.) Have your parents think back on their adolescent years, and have them make a list of things that an adolescent needed to do in order to be "cool" (or what it meant to be "uncool"). Ask them to include at least ten to 15 items. Without looking at their list, write your own list of things an adolescent needs to do today in order to be "cool." Again, try to think of at least ten to 15 items.

    Compare and contrast the two lists. What are some similarities and differences? Based on the lists, would you say that the period called adolescence has changed much in the past 20 or 30 years? Explain. Finally, show the two lists to your parents and discuss their reactions to the lists.

5. Along with beauty contests like "Miss America" and "Miss Sweden," the media certainly plays a part in helping to define the so-called ideal weight and appearance of a woman. Compile a series of commercials, magazine ads, songs, excerpts from TV shows, or other media material that seems to promote a particular ideal.

    Present these examples to the class, pointing out what the ideal is in each example. The primary focus of your analysis is appearance, but point out other characteristics that the media's ideal woman has. (Another option is to contrast recent media material with older material to see how the ideal has changed over the years.)

6. Marcia insists that an active searching for values, beliefs, and goals is essential to forming a meaningful identity. We want you to do some of your own searching. To do this, we want you to answer three main questions:

a. "Who am I?"
    What are some of your major beliefs and values today? What are some of your strengths and weaknesses?

b. "Where do I come from?"
    Describe several experiences from your past that have helped shape your personality. Describe the important people who have had an impact on your life.

c. "Where am I going?"
    What are some of your career goals? Personal growth goals? What are some of your fears about the future?

    The subquestions listed are merely suggestions; you need not address every one of them. This is one of those assignments, if taken seriously, that you can refer back to in years to come and really appreciate. (Trust us!)

DISCUSS THE PHOTO

Do students view the catcher's apparent vigor as atypical? (The catcher is in the middle.)

Growing older does not mean missing out on all the fun.

336

PSYCHOLOGY AND YOU RESOURCES

A variety of resources are available in the Psychology and You *supplementary material. In addition, there are a number of additional resources listed to enhance your lesson plans.*

Masters
▼ 12-1A Learning Goals
▼ 12-1B Answers to Learning Goals
▼ 12-2 Adulthood Questions
▼ 12-3 Will You Marry Me?
▼ 12-4 Poetry

Student Worksheets
▼ Vocabulary Worksheet
▼ Independent Practice Worksheet
▼ Enrichment Worksheet
▼ Reteaching Worksheet

Test Bank
▼ Tests A and B

Multimedia
▼ *The Brain* Videotape Module #7
▼ Psychology Videodisc

Student Workbook

PACING CHART

Complete Coverage

Day 1: Assign the first two sections of this Chapter prior to class. Note that the responsibilities of marriage, career, and children are usually assumed for the first time in young adulthood. Discuss the term *mutual respect* and the problematic distribution of child care and household duties. Have students read "Middle Adulthood: 40–59" for Day 2.

Day 2: Concentrate on the reassessment of one's life that often occurs in middle adulthood. Also point out the gender differences apparent during this process, and the conflict that this presents in marriage. Review the effects of the empty-nest period and menopause. Assign the next two sections for homework.

Day 3: Assign an in-class activity illustrating our culture's obsession with youth. Discuss the aging process, focusing on the factors affecting mental ability. Have the class read "Concerns in Old Age" for Day 4.

Day 4: Emphasize the three main fears present in

12

Adulthood and Aging

OBJECTIVES

Be able to:

▼ Describe the general characteristics of the period from 20 through 39.

▼ Explain what the midlife transition is.

▼ Explain what is meant by the "mellow 50s."

▼ Describe family relationships and crises (empty nest and menopause) during the middle adulthood period.

▼ Provide an overall view of the mental ability and health of the typical elderly person.

▼ Explain why "senility" can be a dangerous term.

▼ Explain the problems with our attitude toward death.

Global Look at the Chapter

The mental and social skills developed during childhood and adolescence have been more or less a training ground for what is to follow. Many problems have not been fully resolved, and in adulthood, the time comes to try to bring everything together into a whole.

337

INTRODUCING THE CHAPTER

Spend a few minutes discussing students' goals. Most of them will not project themselves too far into the future, so encourage them to go further. Also, some of them will not be realistic about their plans: "Well, I'm going to own three large companies by the time I'm 25." This may very well be true, but how is the person going to get there? That part of the answer is usually a bit more hazy. Ask students to clarify, but don't push too hard. There's nothing wrong with a little daydreaming.

LEAD-OFF ACTIVITY

Have students draw a time line on a sheet of paper. The beginning of the line represents their birth; the end represents their death. Have them place an X somewhere near the beginning of the line to mark the present. Above this X they should write their age; below the X they should write "The present." Have them fill in the rest of the time line in a similar way, marking significant ages and events of the past and making predictions about the future. How old will they be when they get married, have children, and so on? The purpose of the activity is to force students to think more realistically about their futures. The more often and effectively you can get them to think in this way, the more meaningful will be the material in this chapter.

old age. Concentrate particularly on society's attitude towards old age. Assign the last section for Day 5.

Day 5: Discuss our society's denial of death. Review the Kübler-Ross stages of dying before giving the Chapter Review quiz.

In Brief

Day 1: Focus on the responsibilities often assumed in early adulthood. Discuss the term of *mutual respect* and the negotiations made during this time between career and family.

Day 2: Use In Focus "Typical" Early and Middle Adulthood Tasks to begin discussion about issues in middle adulthood. Assign an activity for homework that addresses our culture's attitudes towards aging and death.

Day 3: Discuss the concerns of later adulthood, including mental capacity, retirement, isolation, bereavement, and institutionalization. Give the Chapter Review quiz.

Sociology. See **Teaching Master 12-3 Will You Marry Me?** for an activity that asks students to imagine living in a society in which marriages are arranged in a unique fashion: no courtships are allowed; a man and woman decide if they should marry each other after an extensive interview process. Teaching Master 12-3 provides more details, but here's a suggestion on how to conduct the activity. Allow students about 20 minutes to write out a list of questions for prospective spouses. The next day, send a male and female out of the room with their lists to "interview" each other. Select students who will complete the exercise seriously. Tell them that they are to assume they are attracted to each other. While they are out, you can discuss some of the questions written the day before. After five minutes, the male and female return to let you know if

---

TEACHING MASTER 12-1A

Learning Goals. A Learning Goals sheet for each chapter is provided in the Teacher Resources. These Learning Goals can be used as review sheets or worksheets. **Teaching Master 12-1B** consists of answers to these Learning Goals.

Points to Stress

The days of "Donna Reed" and "Father Knows Best" may have never been. Although the divorce rate was lower in the 50s than it is now, there were probably just as many problems in marriage then as now. The main difference was that television itself was newer then and did not take as many chances with controversial subjects.

DISCUSS THE PHOTO

Have students make a list of how their lives will change after graduation.

▲ *Look out world, here we come!*

DEFINING ADULTHOOD

In our society, once people over the age of 18 become self-sufficient and self-supporting, they are usually considered adults. However, adulthood is not just one time of life but many. For example, a 21-year-old and a 45-year-old have very different concerns, abilities, needs, and goals. Adulthood, then, can be divided into different periods. Officially, there is no real agreement regarding when these periods occur. For convenience, we will call the ages 20 to 39 early adulthood, 40 to 59 middle adulthood, and from age 60 on late adulthood.

As we discuss age ranges, remember that these are arbitrary. A person's actual age may well be less important than that person's experiences and outlook on life. The problems and activities that belong to one age group or another are only generalizations, and not everyone will fit into these neat categories. This is especially true in our present society, since people live longer and healthier lives. As time goes on, the categories of "middle age" or "old age" apply to later and later periods of life.

EARLY ADULTHOOD: 20–39

Although some start earlier and others later, sometime during their 20s and 30s, most people take on the adult responsibilities of marriage, career, and children. A sense of identity is gained through these duties, and this makes young adults more stable and less insecure than adolescents. They are more emotionally invested in the welfare of other people, particularly their spouses and children. They take responsibility seriously, and they can make personal decisions about their own lives—something they have wanted to do for years.

Marriage and Divorce

Despite the somewhat shaky image of the institution of marriage, nearly everyone does marry and expect the marriage to last. For about half of these couples, that expectation will be realized. No one really knows exactly what it is that makes any particular marriage work. Sometimes, the most unlikely combinations are wonderful successes. And in this brief space, there is little we can say on the subject. However, we do want to mention one critical ingredient—mutual respect, a term that encompasses a great deal. *Respect* means that you view others as important people, paying attention to them and seeing their ideas, abilities, needs, and wants as meaningful and worthwhile. *Mutual respect* means that two people both give *and*

they are getting married, and why or why not. This can lead to a lively discussion about students' values regarding marriage.

Follow-up discussion questions: (1) What if you could ask a prospective spouse only two questions? Which ones would you ask? (2) What would definitely make you decide, "No, I won't marry that person"? Would race or religion be a big factor? Would personal habits be a factor? (3) What qualities are most important in a marriage?

ENRICHMENT

You have probably heard of a few cases in which children try to and sometimes succeed in divorcing their parents. Have students report on the details of one or two cases, then discuss the merits of such a procedure.

---

receive these things. It means that you treat the other person with consideration, not demeaning or insulting him or her. This quality does not guarantee success. However, without mutual respect, a marriage simply cannot work.

The days of "The Donna Reed Show," "Leave it to Beaver," and "Father Knows Best" are definitely over. Less than 10 percent of the American population is comprised of married couples with children, with only the father employed. Among the majority of couples today, both work outside the home. For those who divorce, the odds are overwhelming that the mother will have custody of the children. Roughly 90 percent of single-parent families are made up of mothers and their children. Customarily, the fathers have visitation rights and the obligation of child support. Only about half the time, though, do the children actually receive all the support the courts have ordered. In too many cases, both the amount of support paid and the frequency of visitation start to decrease two or three years after the divorce (Levant, 1992). The effects on the children, both financially and psychologically, are not good. They often feel abandoned or rejected by their father if he is no longer involved in their lives. Perhaps these fathers do not realize how important they really are. In any event, divorcing parents can ease the heartache immensely by focusing on the children instead of each other and refusing to allow visitation, child support, or the children themselves to be used as weapons.

Family Life

While their careers may also be important, most young adult women, according to statistics, focus more on their families. Whatever changes may have occurred in our society, it is still true that most women are distressed by the prospect of reaching the age of 30 *un*married (Kaslow, 1992). In a marriage, women take care of more family obligations than men do, and they make more personal adjustments to the needs of their husbands than vice versa. Women do most of the child care as well (Denmark, 1992). Young women today face conflicts and stressors that simply did not exist a few decades ago. Because most married women work outside the home, they are often torn between their obligations to their jobs and their families (McWilliams, 1992).

So, where is the man all this time? Well, he is doing more than men formerly did. In early adulthood, men still tend to focus mostly on their careers, but they are also more involved in their family life than used to be the case. They spend more time with their children and are less likely to always let the job come first. For instance, a few years ago, it would have been almost unthinkable for a man to ask for special consideration at work in order to take care of a fairly routine family matter. Now such a request is not that unusual. Lest we get too carried away, though, the changes have not been great. In the

Discussion

If a marriage is failing, should a couple stay together for the sake of the kids? Most students will argue that in a failing marriage, the kind of interaction that goes on between the parents is not the best modeling experience for children.

Journal Topic

"Your parents are getting divorced and they have not been focusing on your needs. Write them a letter explaining how you feel." Explain that this is a fictional letter, even for students whose parents are divorced.

Comprehension Check

What responsibilities are usually assumed for the first time during early adulthood? *(marriage, career, and children)*

ENRICHMENT

Have students do some research on the "Donna Reed" days (family life as portrayed on TV) to find out if the 1950s were really as innocent as they were portrayed in the old TV shows.

DISCOVERY

Have students write brief poems in which the words *mother* and/or *father* (or *mom/dad*) appear in the title. Remind them that poems may be free verse and need not rhyme.

COOPERATIVE LEARNING

Give students about a week to interview one person from one of the following age brackets: 25 to 39; 40 to 59; over 60. The focus of the interviews should be on adult development. (See **Teaching Master 12-2 Adulthood Questions** for a list of questions.) When the interviews have been completed, group together all

DISCUSS THE PHOTO

Men may be more involved, but how many of them know their child's shirt size, pants size, or shoe size?

Points to Stress

In most cases, a husband does not do as much work around the house as the wife does, even if the wife works, but when the husband *does* perform some chore that the wife usually completes, he often expects adulation: "So, pretty good dinner, huh?" Also, the husband will often use the one chore as evidence of "how much he does around the house." This is a generalization, of course, but students may have examples to support it.

Discussion

Have students compare and contrast each of their parents' chores. Is the division of chores traditional (Mom takes care of the inside of the house; Dad takes care of the outside)? Do moms or dads from single-parent homes adopt both roles?

340

▲ *Although women generally do most of the child maintenance in the family, men are becoming more involved.*

1960s, men whose wives were employed did about 20 percent of the work around the house, including taking care of the children. By the late 1980s, that figure had moved up to around 25 percent—not exactly an astounding increase (Levant, 1992).

It seems that our society is somewhat hypocritical in its attitude toward parenting. On the one hand, it urges parents to devote themselves to their children. On the other hand, it provides few rewards for doing so and makes few allowances for the difficulties involved in raising a family. In many European countries, businesses routinely provide family leave and day care to their employees. Here, however, that is the exception rather than the rule.

MIDLIFE TRANSITION

Young adults eventually enter middle adulthood, but the progression is not always smooth. Serious questions about the real meaning of life arise. The ups and downs and stops and starts that can occur indicate that a person has entered the midlife transition.

In the United States, the age of 40 signals the true beginning of "middle age." At some point in their late 30s or early 40s, then, most people begin to reexamine their lives. They look closely at the direction their lives have taken and make decisions about where they want to be in the future. Of course, this happens at other ages as well. However, in midlife, there is often a sense of urgency involved. As

the students who focused on the same age bracket, and have them synthesize their findings. For example, are there any common feelings that 25-year-olds have? Do most 40-year-olds report a midlife crisis? If some groups are too large, divide them up into manageable sizes. Also, many students will avoid interviews with people over 60 because they feel that these "old" people will be offended, as if they don't know their own age and this interview might jolt them into awareness! Point out that the ones who are sensitive about the questions on old age are the young people.

people realize that they are no longer young, they begin to think in terms of how many years they have left. They start to focus on signs of physical decline and an awareness of aging. There is no question that things are not as they used to be. Their parents are becoming truly old. Their children are almost grown. A few friends have had heart attacks. The days of a wide-open future, with endless possibilities, are over. All of these facts contribute to feelings of vulnerability and uncertainty (McGrath, 1992; Kovacs, 1992).

As bad as this may sound to you, not everyone becomes miserable and depressed. For some people, this is a time for reassessing their life's goals and refocusing their energies on new interests and activities. For others, it is a time of terrible upheaval and loss of purpose, when they seriously question many of the values by which they have lived. Most people do experience some confusion, insecurity, and dissatisfaction during this transition, but a so-called midlife *crisis* is not inevitable.

MIDDLE ADULTHOOD: 40–59

Up to this point in time, most women have been primarily involved with their families and most men with their careers. During middle adulthood, however, priorities seem to shift, and both men and women reverse their focus. Perhaps because midlife is a time of reassessment and taking stock, they discover aspects of themselves that have been neglected, and they seek to give these aspects expression. This is potentially one of the best times of life.

In general, men begin to appreciate their more "feminine" characteristics and women their more "masculine" ones (McGrath, 1992; Levinson, 1978). Beginning sometime in their mid 40s, men become more emotionally expressive and warm, more giving of themselves than before. Relationships begin to be more important than career or money. At the same time, women are growing more independent and assertive, more determined to go out on their own and do what they want to do instead of making so many compromises for the family. For a while, this situation can create conflicts. As the husband turns to his family to develop his more tender side, the wife is out pursuing her own interests. The children, nearly grown, often have little need or desire for closer contact. Thus, the man may feel betrayed and unnecessary. The woman, on the other hand, may resent his demands coming at a time when she is finally free to accomplish what she wants on her own.

For most people in their 40s, marital satisfaction is at an all-time low. For some couples, these conflicts will be serious enough to end their marriage. It is true that most divorces take place when the couple is still young, usually in the first six or seven years of marriage. However, about one-sixth of the cases occur among those age 45 or

▲ *To most young people—to this man at the moment—life seems just about over at age 40. Studies show the opposite is really the case: he has taken the first step toward the "mellow" period of life.*

Comprehension Check

How is the re-examination of life that occurs during a person's midlife transition different than it is at any other time in life? *(There is a sense of urgency; when people realize they are no longer young, they focus on how many years they have left.)*

Discussion

Most of your students' parents are in midlife transition (chronologically). Ask students how their parents are reacting to this. Are they wearing "young" clothes or listening to "young" music? Do they seem to feel a sense of urgency?

Journal Topic

"You are going through a full-fledged midlife crisis. You are about to make some big decisions. Describe how you feel." Students might want to write about marriage, work, starting a business, religion, and so on.

DISCUSS THE PHOTO

Have students interview their parents on how they felt on their 40th birthday.

341

CHAPTER PROJECT

If you give students a week to find out as much as they can about adulthood, most will run to the library and ignore the "expert" resources in front of them: teachers, secretaries, custodians, administrators. Here's a *highly recommended* project that will involve the entire school. First, allow time in class to generate a variety of questions for these adults. Or see **Teaching Master 12-2 Adulthood Questions** for list of questions. Second, send students out of class with note cards on which the adults can jot their answers to these questions. Use one question and answer per card. (Some teachers may want to fill out several cards.) Third, have students pick what they feel are the most informative answers. Now comes the exciting part. Go back and photograph the adults whose answers were chosen, and use these pictures for a slide show! Pick a few students

Discussion

Many parents of students are probably approaching the age when the empty-nest period occurs. Ask students if they notice any changes in their parents.

DISCUSS THE PHOTO

This photo may remind students of themselves sitting at their desks. Have students think of parallels between taking stock during adolescence and taking stock during mid-life.

Points to Stress

It is probably not a coincidence that the effects of the empty-nest syndrome and menopause have been exaggerated. Both involve women and both reflect traditional gender stereotypes.

Journal Topic

"You never thought you'd be 'one of those,' but after 15 years of marriage, it has happened: you're divorced. It has been several months now since you signed the papers. Describe how you are doing, your reactions toward your ex, and your feelings about the future."

342

Unit 4 HUMAN DEVELOPMENT

▲ *Mid-life: taking stock.*

empty-nest period

The time of life when the children are grown and leave; for some people, this event leads to feelings of uselessness and depression.

menopause

The "change of life" period for women when menstruation and ovulation stop; some women experience major physical symptoms, such as dizziness and "hot flashes."

342

older (Wainrib, 1992a; McGill, 1980; Degler, 1980).

If people can be patient and tolerant, they will get a breather, so to speak. Marital conflicts don't have to last or cause real harm. The late 40s and 50s are a time when people become calmer and more accepting both of the changes in their lives and of each other. In fact, by their mid 50s (and beyond), men tend to see women as more powerful and dominant than men, a reversal of what was true in their youth (Belsky, 1992; Gutmann, 1987).

Some have called this decade the "mellow 50s," the prime of life (Levinson et al., 1975). Friends and earlier values become increasingly important; the dreams and goals of earlier years mellow into more realistic hopes. People generally are more satisfied with life. There is often a sense of relief that the struggle to achieve is less urgent. Marriages grow more settled, and people begin to sense a greater mastery over their personal world. Feelings of increased freedom and self-worth are common.

The Empty-Nest Period

At the beginning of this century, most women were widowed within two years of the marriage of their last child; thus, virtually all of their married life was spent rearing children. Now, most women who are finished with active motherhood still have 40 percent of their lives left to live, and most couples will be together another ten to 20 years (Wainrib, 1992a; Degler, 1980).

The **empty-nest period** is the time of life after the children leave home. It has been suggested that some parents, mothers especially, feel useless and depressed when the children leave and the "nest" is empty. While this period does bring major changes, the concept that such feelings are inevitable has been discarded. Most studies now show that the majority of women do not have these feelings. In fact, most marriages improve and most parents are happier once the children are gone.

Nonetheless, some women do suffer from the problem. Most often, they are people who have led rather restricted lives, who lack intimate contacts outside the home, and have few interests or activities of their own. In addition, their marriages tend to be not all that great, so they have little to fall back on (McGrath, 1992; McGill, 1980).

Menopause

At some time in their late 40s to early 50s, women go through a period commonly called the "change of life," or **menopause.** Menstruation and ovulation gradually stop as the result of a dramatic decline in the production of female hormones. Since both men and women have both male and female hormones, this means that as the

to write a script, mainly for the introductory and closing material. If you have a speech or drama team at school, the members might be willing to record the responses on tape, and the tape can be cued to the slide show.

Here are a few other suggestions:

(1) Add music behind the narration. (2) Borrow a dissolve unit for the slides. This allows one projection to fade into the next, and it adds a professional look to the show. Many colleges have such units that they will loan out. (3) Cap the show with "before" and "after" yearbook portraits of several teachers who have been at the school for a while. The *before* portrait would show the teacher in his or her first year at the school. The *after* would be the most current portrait. Watching people grow older before your eyes can be quite moving, especially with the right music.

IN FOCUS — "Typical" Early and Middle Adulthood Tasks

	"Typical" Male	"Typical" Female
EARLY ADULTHOOD (20–39)	Focuses on career but more with family than in years past	Takes care of more family obligations
	Still only does about 25 percent of housework	Does most of the child care
MIDLIFE	Feels a sense of urgency	Feels a sense of urgency
	Focuses on physical decline	Focuses on physical decline
MIDDLE ADULTHOOD (40–59)	Appreciates his feminine side	Appreciates her masculine side
	Becomes more emotionally expressive, warm, and giving	Becomes more assertive and independent
	During 40s, marital satisfaction at all-time low	During 40s, marital satisfaction at all-time low
	During 50s, mellowing occurs	During 50s, mellowing occurs

During middle adulthood, why do men tend to become more emotionally expressive and why do women tend to become more assertive?

"Typical" Early and Middle Adulthood Tasks.

IN FOCUS Men feel less need to prove themselves. They may not feel they are being tested as much. For many women, the kids have grown, and they welcome the freedom that this brings.

Connections

Men and women level out psychologically during middle adulthood, but their sex hormones level out, too. Females produce less estrogen, and males produce less androgen (Chapter 3).

female hormone diminishes, the male hormone becomes more dominant. Hence, there is a slight lowering of the voice, and facial hair becomes more prominent. Physical symptoms include "hot flashes," dizziness, insomnia, perspiring or "night sweats," and occasional heart palpitations. Some women experience menopausal acne. In addition, postmenopausal women are at higher risk of developing heart disease and/or brittle bones. Medically replacing the lost female hormone can alleviate these symptoms, but this procedure is still considered controversial by many. Some argue that all women as a matter of course should receive this hormonal therapy. Others believe that caution is called for because we do not yet have enough information about the therapy's long-term effects.

Much has been made of the psychological problems associated with menopause, but again they are exaggerated. Only a small number of women find it necessary to seek psychological help. Contrary to earlier beliefs, studies show that the likelihood of depression actually goes down, not up: the rate of depression among women in this age group is lower than that for younger women. It seems that more problems arise from society's ideas about what menopause is like than from the transition itself. Traditionally, women's value to society

DEMONSTRATION

Introduce the section on late adult-hood by writing the word *old* on the board. Go around the room and have each person name one thing that comes to mind when hearing the word *old*. You'll get responses like "frail, senile, lonely, wrinkled," and so on. Write all their responses on the board, and then review each one by placing an *M* next to each response that is *myth* and an *R* next to each response that is *reality*. (Have the class discuss and decide which responses are myth and which are reality.) You'll probably notice a pat-tern. Most of the reality responses will be associated with inevitable physical decline; most of the myth responses will be associated with intellectual decline or emotional defi-ciencies (lonely, withdrawn, and so on). This simple activity should make students more aware of their own myths surrounding old age, and it should prompt them to question those myths.

Comprehension Check

Name some problems that may occur during middle adulthood. *(marital dissatisfaction, depression due to the empty-nest period)*

Points to Stress

Can students think of other words with the *ger* root? (*Geras* comes from the Greek, meaning "old age.") Geriatric. Or remember Geritol?

Critical Thinking

Have students define "old" using several differ-ent criteria: chronology (age 65?); attitude (you're as old as you feel); biolo-gy (body starts to decline in your 30s!); performance (some old people can out-run young people!); cultur-al outlook (some cultures revere old people).

DISCUSS THE PHOTO

What do grandparents provide that a child's own parents may not? Time? Understanding? Cookies?

344

---

gerontology

The branch of psychology that studies the aging process and the problems of older people.

▲ *Growing older brings a very special reward.*

344

---

has declined when they are no longer able to bear children. Fortunately, however, there are clear signs that this attitude is chang-ing (Wainrib, 1992a; Belsky, 1992; Neugarten, 1980).

LATE ADULTHOOD: 60 AND OLDER

As we grow older, we become more philosophical. We attempt to bring the pieces of our lives together, to reflect on all that we have done, and to see ourselves as part of the cycle of life on Earth (Erikson, Erikson & Kivnick, 1986). Some of the major tasks we face include adjusting to an increased number of deaths among friends, accepting what we have not been able to do, and preparing for our own eventual death. Most older people take comfort in what they have accomplished and appreciate the fact that they will leave some-thing of themselves behind.

According to the 1990 census data, there are approximately 32 mil-lion people 65 and older in this country, and the percentage of the population in that age range is increasing steadily. In the mid-1980s, people over 60 outnumbered teenagers for the first time in our histo-ry. It is projected that by the year 2030, one in five people will be at least 65 years of age. Average life expectancy at birth is about 75 years, or nearly 30 years longer than it was in the early 1900s. However, women who have already made it into their 50s can expect to live another 30 years. Women live roughly six years longer than men, and the majority of women over 65 are widows. By age 80, there are three women for every man; 36 percent of the men this age are married, but only 6 percent of the women are (Wainrib, 1992a).

Along with the great increase in the number of older people has come a major expansion in a branch of psychology called **gerontol-ogy** (jer-un-TALL-uh-jee), which is the study of aging and older peo-ple. Gerontologists study the aging process and the psychological difficulties associated with it. The following sections describe some of the findings of their research.

THE AGING PROCESS

Aging in our country is a real challenge because as a culture we put a premium on youthfulness—to a ridiculous degree. We spend a lot of money on products designed to help us deny or hide the fact that we are getting older. While ours is not the first civilization to struggle with the facts of aging, we may deserve an award for being

INTERDISCIPLINARY PROJECT

Literature. Have students read Kurt Vonnegut's "Tomorrow and Tomorrow and Tomorrow." This is a farcical tale about a society that never ages because of an elixir that scientists have invented. Most of the story is dialogue, so you could probably read it together in class. The story should prompt a discussion on the ethics of extending life through technology. Another possible story, which has been made into a short film, is Nathaniel Hawthorne's "Dr. Heidegger's Experiment."

Chapter 12 ADULTHOOD AND AGING

the most blatant about it. People in other countries fight aging, but most recognize that older people may have grown wiser from their vast experience and should be valued and sought out for this wisdom, while Americans usually do not.

Cellular Time Clocks

The life span for different species is preprogrammed. Within a given species—horse, elephant, human, mosquito—each creature seems to have a fixed length of time on Earth (Jarvik, 1975). Today, individual people are not really living *longer* than people in the past did, but *more* people are living into old age. In other words, if you were able to avoid serious disease in the 1800s, your chances of living to about 70 were roughly the same as they are today. The big difference is that today fewer people are killed at young ages by disease or during childbirth. Unless we can figure out a method for controlling age by some manipulation of genes, humans will still die sometime around 110 years old, even if all diseases are eradicated (Rosenfeld, 1985).

As we age, our bodily functions slow down, problems with vision and hearing are likely to get worse, and we are more prone to disease and injury. Indications are that this occurs because body cells have internal "time clocks" that dictate how long each particular type of cell will continue to function and replace itself. Toward the end of the life span of a member of any species, the cells have notably deteriorated. In a fascinating study, researchers found that individual cells have a strict limit concerning the number of times they will divide through the course of a creature's life. In fact, if cells are allowed to divide a few times and then are frozen for a period, when they are thawed, they will continue the doubling process up to the same fixed number of times—no more, no less (Hayflick, 1979).

Mental Ability of the Aged

Just as bodily processes slow down with age, there seems also to be a slight slowing of certain mental processes. But we have to be careful about assuming that all older people automatically become forgetful and absent-minded. The bulk of evidence suggests that this is not the case. In animals and human beings, substantial memory deficits occur only in a minority (Jensen et al., 1980). The decline is most evident in tasks that are learned under pressure within a certain time limit and in things recently learned; long-term memory tends to remain intact. Further, the decline generally does not begin to appear until about age 70 (Hulicka, 1978).

Health and Mental Ability   Health is an important factor in mental ability. Old people in good health do about as well on learn-

Points to Stress

Is it healthy to get married? Maybe. On average, married people live longer.

Journal Topic

"If safe new wonder drugs were introduced that would stall the aging process, would you take them? Why or why not?" This could lead to a discussion on generativity (concern for the next generation). If you decide to take the drug, does that make you selfish for not "getting out of the way" to make room for the next generation?

Critical Thinking

"What would be the advantages and disadvantages of people living for 200 years?" Possible advantages: If wisdom increases with age, perhaps a 200-year-old could help the human race. Also, if we know that we are going to be around that long, perhaps we would take better care of the world. Disadvantages: Overpopulation! Also, if we begin to mess around with the life span, perhaps there would be unforeseen negative consequences.

ACTIVITY ACTIVITY ACTIVITY ACTIVITY ACTIVIT
ACTIVITY ACTIVITY

Connections

You may recall from the notes on Chapter 9 that some psychologists divide intelligence into two types: fluid and crystallized. Fluid intelligence refers to reaction time, rapid recall, and perceptual flexibility. Old people do show a decline in these abilities. Crystallized intelligence involves verbal skills and knowledge accumulated throughout a lifetime; this sort of intelligence steadily increases with age.

DISCUSS THE PHOTO

Share with your students how *you* will remain active after you retire.

Teaching Hint

Tell students: "You are probably going to be just as irritable and stubborn and rigid when you're 60 as you are now. You might as well do something about it now."

Discussion

Satchel Paige used to ask, "How old would you be if you didn't know how old you was?" In other words, take away all memory of birthdays, take away mirrors—how old? (Don't you have students who are already very old?)

346

DISCOVERY

Have students write a futuristic scenario about a society in which no one ever ages because of new wonder drugs. See the following **Enrichment** exercise.

ENRICHMENT

Have students watch the movie *Cocoon*, and ask them to examine how improved health affects the attitudes of the old characters in the movie.

Unit 4 HUMAN DEVELOPMENT

▲ *Like this man, the vast majority of older people are active and productive.*

346

ing tasks as younger people, as long as no time limit is imposed. Disease or accident, rather than aging itself, is responsible for most of the serious memory problems.

When older people *do* experience trouble with memory it is very distressing and frustrating for them, it has a strong negative effect on their self-concept, and it causes anxiety and depression (Hulicka, 1978). There are hints that in time we may be able to correct many memory problems of this sort. We know that the number of nerve cells in the brain decreases with age, but this may not be the real source of the trouble, since we have so many of them to begin with. In fact, for the typical elderly person, the brain has shrunk only about 8 percent of its original size by the age of 75. Instead, studies with aged animals and humans show the more important loss is of chemicals that are used to communicate from one cell to another (Smith, 1984). The first "brain transplants" performed involved taking tissue from the adrenal glands, which produce this nerve cell chemical, and placing it inside the brain. While this is probably not the final answer, a number of people gained improved memory from the process.

One often-neglected consideration is nutrition. Many older people get so fed up with fixing meals for three-quarters of a century or so that they don't eat as well as they should in their later years. In other chapters of the book, we have mentioned how disastrous poor nutrition is for the mental development of children and adolescents. The same is true for the elderly, only here we are not dealing with development as much as with preservation of the brain cells (Goodwin et al., 1984).

Intelligence and Aging Old age does not *automatically* indicate a decline in intellectual ability or achievement (Bromley, 1974). In many cases, when standard IQ tests are used, older people do not score as high as younger people do, but the reasons do not have to do with intelligence itself. For one thing, those who take such tests may be trying too hard to succeed and may be highly anxious. For another, the test items are usually too small for many of the elderly to see and to handle with comfort. The test is not supposed to be a measure of a person's vision. But most of all, the IQ test is designed to measure school potential, and that clearly is not relevant to older people.

Most experiments aimed specifically at the elderly show it is incorrect to assume that intelligence declines with age (Schaie, 1983). As we've already mentioned, an older person's memory is intact for the most part. Individuals who were bright and active in youth tend to be the same in old age. Most of the time, when you run into an older person who is irritable, stubborn, and rigid, you will find that he or she was also this way when young. Such behavior is usually not the result of aging itself (James, 1985).

ENRICHMENT

Most hospitals have several people on staff who deal with terminally ill patients. Invite one of these people to class. Without this sort of personal insight from a visitor, Alzheimer's will remain a disease "out there" that students simply have to remember for a test. Or some students may be willing to talk about family members who have Alzheimer's.

Senile Dementia   Many older people are labeled *senile,* a term that is not very flattering. But it doesn't mean what most people think it means. Senility simply refers to the state of being old. The proper diagnosis for diminished mental faculties resulting from aging is **senile dementia** (deh-MEN-sha). It is the word *dementia* that refers to the loss of *mental* capacity, not the word *senile.* Many believe that such dementia is inevitable with age. This is not the case. Only disease can result in changes sufficiently dramatic to have such an effect. *Genuine* senile dementia occurs in only 23 percent of the aged population. Of that 23 percent, only 3 percent are affected by age 70! To account for the remaining 20 percent, you must go all the way to 100 years of age (Reedy, 1983).

Substantial brain changes, however, can and do result from a blockage of the blood vessels going to the brain—a condition called **cerebral arteriosclerosis** (ar-teer-ee-oh-skluh-ROH-sis). The major cause of senile dementia, though, is **Alzheimer's** (ALTS-high-mers) **disease.** Alzheimer's results from a loss of the chemicals used to fire the brain cells; this, in turn, can cause debris to form in the brain. The disease most often seems to arise due to a genetic defect, and over time it leads to a disruption of speech, personality, memory, and body control (Wurtman, 1985).

There is a tendency in too many cases to label elderly people with senile dementia even when there is no evidence of brain damage. Brain damage is *very* hard to diagnose without evidence of disease or injury. The tragic aspect of all this is that a number of quite treatable ailments can produce the same symptoms. Somewhere between 15 and 30 percent of those diagnosed as having senile dementia in reality are suffering from other problems. Among them are depression, alcoholism, vitamin deficiencies, and the misuse of prescription medicines (Sloane, 1983; Jarvik & Cohen, 1973). Far too often, when the patient is old, no one bothers to make a thorough examination (Traxler, 1979). This neglect is probably a reflection of our youth-oriented culture, at least in part.

CONCERNS IN OLD AGE

Research shows that survival in old age is clearly related to having minimal physical and economic dependence on others. In other words, complete reliance on others is the worst thing that can happen to old people. When this occurs, they feel trapped because they can no longer make the changes they want; they no longer have *choice.* Most elderly people desire self-sufficiency, as well as some degree of freedom and activity. Their needs are clearly tied to the most basic fears they have: (1) poor health; (2) social isolation; and (3) a loss of feeling meaningful to society (Wainrib, 1992a, 1992b; Brody, 1974).

senile dementia

The loss of mental faculties as a result of aging.

cerebral arteriosclerosis

A blockage of blood vessels to the brain that results in the loss of mental faculties.

Alzheimer's disease

The loss of chemical nerve cell transmitters and other damage to nerve transmission that result in mental deterioration.

Connections

Do students recall the name of the chemicals that are used to communicate from one cell to another? Neurotransmitters (Chapter 3).

Comprehension Check

What factors can affect mental ability in old age? *(health, nutrition, level of chemicals used to communicate between cells, cerebral arteriosclerosis, Alzheimer's disease, depression, misuse of prescription medicine)*

Points to Stress

The ultimate effects of Alzheimer's are so devastating that victims may be unable to walk or sit up and may even "forget" to swallow. It may take years for someone to reach this stage, but the disease is terminal.

FYI   Though it is much less common in younger people, dementia can afflict people at any age.

ENRICHMENT

Have students contact a senior center to find out about the activities offered. This should dispel the myth that retired people sit in rocking chairs all day. You might even be able to get a few seniors to join you one day. If you do, ask them what they think of the euphemism *senior citizens.*

DISCOVERY

Have two students role-play this situation: *Two old people are talking about how they are dealing with the death of their spouses a year ago. They were both devastated by the loss but are coping well now.*

DISCOVERY

Have students complete this statement: You know you're getting old when _____. Some of the answers will be profound, some will be crude, but taken together, the answers should reveal some general attitudes about old age.

Discussion

Should people be forced to retire at a certain age? Students who argue for retirement may cite practical concerns, like making room for younger, cheaper workers. Others might counter that younger workers are cheaper for the company, but the overall cost for society will be greater. Also, older workers can probably add valuable insights into how the company for which they have worked for many years should be run.

Connections

Erikson (Chapter 14) asserts that the final stage of life, *integrity versus despair*, is the main concern in old age. If we look back on our lives with satisfaction, we will feel integrity. If we look back and feel that we have wasted our lives, we will feel despair. This focus on the *past* is in contrast to the *present* concerns described here: retirement, isolation, and so on.

Retirement

Most people look forward to retirement, and most retired people like their new lives. For a long time, it was believed that those who retired were a miserable lot. Some clearly are. For example, some men seem so lost that they follow their wives around the house, driving them crazy. They wind up doing such things as alphabetizing all the soup and canned goods in the cupboard. After that, they don't know what to do with themselves. These men, though, are the exception. We know less about women in retirement. Fewer women have been in the work force long enough, and most research in this area has looked only at men. From what we do know, however, it appears that the majority of men and women adapt well to this change in status and enjoy the freedom that retirement brings (Belsky, 1992).

You may think that the older someone is, the less active that person will be after retiring, but actually, age is not a very good predictor. Those people who have emphasized independence and personal involvement in life tend to stay active and to look forward to each new day, regardless of how old they are (Skinner, 1983; Birren, 1983).

Isolation and Bereavement

Social isolation is a fear that old people have, but it is a fear rather than a reality for most of them, according to the statistics. Those most vulnerable to isolation are in poor health or without a reasonable amount of money. Although overall our society leaves a great deal to be desired in terms of its approach to the aging, individual families do a pretty good job: the majority of old people are not isolated, withdrawn, or lonesome (Traxler, 1988).

There are exceptions to this generalization. The death of a close friend or spouse at any time changes one's life considerably, and this is far more likely to happen in late adulthood. We used to believe that the death of a spouse was always an extremely traumatic event for the elderly and that it was harder on men than on women. The upheaval in the survivor's life supposedly went on for years and years. Now it appears that these conclusions are only partly true.

There is no question that the death of a spouse involves a major loss and dramatic changes in a person's life. Research over the past ten years, however, reveals that most old people, women *and* men, do adapt. In fact, they usually have adjusted quite well within a year or so. In addition, there seem to be few differences between men and women concerning how well and how soon they recover (Belsky, 1992). Perhaps because loss is part and parcel of being old, people eventually develop ways to cope with it.

Women face greater burdens in this regard than men do. Since the average age of widowhood is 56, most married women will spend one-third of their lives without their spouse. And they will probably

DISCOVERY

Have students make a list of euphemisms or descriptive labels that our society has for old people. Here are a few examples: *old fogies, elderly, senior citizens, 70 years young, over the hill.* How many of these labels reflect ageism—that is, prejudice against old age? Note that even the positive labels may be prejudicial.

spend those years by themselves. Two-thirds of all widows live alone (Wainrib, 1992a).

As you might expect, older women are more likely to be put in the position of caring for a seriously ill spouse than older men are. However, you might be surprised to learn that this situation seems to be more stressful for women than for men. Since women have often spent most of their lives taking care of others, why would this be so? Some possible answers are that society provides less support and reinforcement for women in this position and that women are more reluctant to ask for help with this task. Women's traditional identity includes the role of care giver. Thus, the work they are doing is not seen as anything special. For men, though, it is. So, they generally get more praise and recognition for taking on this role. In addition, a woman may feel that her femininity is on the line, so asking for help may seem like admitting failure. Men do not experience the same constraint (Belsky, 1992).

Attitudes Toward Old Age

The negative attitude toward aging that exists in this country has a very sad side effect: many old people themselves have accepted it, and they wind up viewing themselves as a burden. This can lead to a sense of "giving up," which is very destructive. In fact, surveys show that old people themselves devalue old age *more* than younger ones do (Perry & Slemp, 1980). Even though most elderly are not in institutions (see the next subsection), those who are may be encouraged to remain dependent. Institutional staff frequently do too much for the elderly, keeping them in a subservient role. While their intentions are good, they are making these people feel even more helpless (Barton et al., 1980).

But positive changes are occurring. Young people are viewing aging in a better light, probably because older people today are so much more active for longer periods of time than used to be the case. If the shift in attitudes is real and continues in the same direction, we can predict that future generations of old people will have a more positive view of themselves. When that happens, we will have achieved a reasonable view of the life cycle as a whole.

Institutionalization

Everywhere we look, we get an image of the old person in an institution. But only about 5 percent of the elderly live in nursing homes. Most older people still have active ties with their family and friends, which is very good for them and for the family.

Even so, being in an institution is not *necessarily* a bad thing. Whether it is good or bad depends on whether institutionalization is

Chapter 12 ADULTHOOD AND AGING

▲ *Most old people are not lonely, but the possibility of loneliness is there and can be devastating.*

DISCUSS THE PHOTO

You may want to refer to Erik Erikson's eighth stage of development, integrity versus despair (Chapter 14).

Comprehension Check

What are some characteristics of a good nursing home? *(opportunity to visit with family and friends, field trips and other such meaningful activities)*

Evaluation Strategy

Have students interview their parents on the changes they have been through in the last few years. Students should peruse the chapter for ideas on questions, and then compare and contrast their parents' answers with those presented in the chapter.

DEMONSTRATION

Bring in a few general-interest magazines that you are ready to throw out. Flip through them in class, ripping out ads with people in them. Did you find a single person over 50? If so, what is the person marketing? Do you notice any other patterns?

ENRICHMENT

What kinds of institutions for the elderly are available in your community? You may have some students who work or volunteer at one of these institutions.

DISCOVERY

Have students role-play a situation in which a couple has to decide whether to institutionalize one of their parents. Instruct them to disagree at first but ultimately to reach a resolution.

Discussion

Students probably know a few achievement-in-old-age examples themselves. Allow them a few minutes to share these, then discuss what all these people have in common.

Journal Topic

Tell students to imagine that they are in middle or late adulthood. Have them write a paragraph describing how they feel about some of the changes they are going through. The paragraph should include some reference to material in the chapter.

Points to Stress

If you try the death-related theme activities suggested throughout these pages, remember to be aware of possible sensitivity on this subject. Some students, as you know, are extremely defensive about this topic, and you may notice increased levels of anxiety.

thanatology

The study of death and of methods for coping with it.

intended to "remove" a person from society and on the quality of life in the institution. If institutional life includes the opportunity to visit with family and friends and to take part in such activities as study groups, field trips, or even camping trips, then life can be quite pleasant. If the institution is not well run, however, its elderly residents risk experiencing isolation because they have no meaningful activities, no chance to be around children, and no opportunity to use any of their remaining skills. These circumstances can quickly lead to depression, giving up, serious physical illness, and even death (Bromley, 1974).

Achievement in Old Age

When discussing late adulthood, it is impossible to avoid such topics as poor health, senile dementia, widowhood, and so on. But we don't want you to leave this section discouraged or depressed. Aging is not simply an inevitable decline into disability; all is not gloom and despair. Many old people remain productive throughout their lives.

Providing a complete list of people who continued to make important contributions well into old age would fill a book all by itself. However, we can point out a few examples: Pablo Picasso, Michelangelo, Eleanor Roosevelt, Albert Einstein, Georgia O'Keeffe, George Burns, Katharine Hepburn, not to mention psychologists Erik Erikson, B. F. Skinner, and Jean Piaget.

THANATOLOGY

Thanatology (than-uh-TALL-uh-gee—*thanatos*, death, + *logy*, study of) is a relatively new area of study that came into its own in the 1970s. Until that time, the general attitude of psychology was that death was a "non-problem," a "nontopic"—something to be ignored. This has changed noticeably.

Hiding from Death

One of the most common complaints from thanatologists is that our society refuses to admit that death exists. We do everything in our power to hide from it and to shield others from its existence. The reality of death is denied by the sentimental or sensational deaths so often seen in the movies or on television. The portrayal of death as glorious and uplifting or at least sudden and dramatic ignores the reality of it all. We even hide the grossness and agony of killing in

Art. Bring construction paper and several boxes of crayons to class, and allow students about ten minutes to "draw death." They will probably have a variety of questions, but try not to give them any other suggestions. Afterward, have them briefly explain their drawings, then discuss their interpretations of death. Are they morbid, uplifting, depressing? Are their renditions of death influenced by Hollywood, books, fairy tales, or religion?

Have students find out how different cultures, such as various Native American tribes, bury their dead, both now and in the past.

Chapter 12 ADULTHOOD AND AGING

wartime by making it the action of patriots and heroes. While patriotism and heroism are not bad in themselves, in this case they are part of an attempt to escape from the basic fact of a person's death and the decomposition of the body.

Check out the sympathy cards sometime: there will actually be *no* reference to the fact that a life has ended. Mentioning death in such a card is taboo. Although flowers are the most popular picture on the cards, these flowers are not alive and growing, nor are they ever shown in some kind of container, like a vase (McGee, 1980). Apparently, the card manufacturers don't want to suggest anything resembling an urn.

Issues Regarding Death

One theme occurs continually in recent studies about those who are dying, and it is so basic that we usually don't pay any attention to it: death has never happened to any of us before. We may have read about it, come close to it, or seen someone else's death, but we ourselves have never experienced it. Thus, we face the ultimate unknown, and the fact that our society refuses to admit that it is a natural process gives the unknown an added dimension of terror (Kübler-Ross, 1975).

We must be careful about assuming that every normal person is afraid to die. In cases of terminal illness, a number of studies have shown that most old or dying people eventually come to accept death as a natural process, and they are more concerned about making preparations for the end than about the end itself. They may well have periods of being anxious and scared, but they benefit greatly from a chance to talk about their feelings.

▲ *Our society has real trouble accepting death as part of an ongoing process. This is a funeral for a 16-year-old whose heart was used for another person. In a way, from the death, life goes on.*

Discussion

Refer to the time line in the **Lead-off Activity,** and see if students can make any generalizations about different age brackets. One thing they may notice is that from ages six to about 18, life is pretty orderly; everyone does the same thing at about the same age: we graduate from elementary school, then from junior high, we get a driver's license, we graduate again, and so on. Beyond age 18, everyone's life becomes much more unpredictable. How do students feel about this?

DISCUSS THE PHOTO

While we see thousands of deaths on television, they are almost all violent, and most of us are unfamiliar with the slower process of dying from a disease.

INTERDISCIPLINARY PROJECT

Literature/Music. One of poetry's common themes is death. Have each student find a poem or song about death and present it to the class, explaining the poet's message. Students may be surprised to find that these messages are not necessarily morbid or depressing. In fact, good poetry, even when the topic is death, will usually be profound and uplifting in some way. Finding these poems should be relatively easy. Tell students to skim through the table of contents or index of a poetry anthology and look for a reference to death. Poet Raymond Carver, who knew his death was imminent when he wrote his last volume, *A New Path to the Waterfall*, would be a good choice.

Points to Stress

If you have ever dealt with insensitive hospital personnel, you can understand how valuable Kübler-Ross's theory is; it provides some insight into the dying patient's point of view. Also, it can help the family of the dying. For example, a patient, after several unsuccessful operations, may finally accept death. Meanwhile, the family may be bargaining for one more surgery, one last hope. After learning about these stages, perhaps the family will listen better to the patient and respect his or her final wishes.

Kübler-Ross's Stage of Dying.

 This knowledge might help because you would understand the other's point of view and allow the person to express these feelings. It might interfere if it creates expectations in you: "Oh, he's in denial; he'll be angry soon. Maybe I can make him less angry." The theory is a guideline, not a treatment manual.

What are terminally ill people most afraid of? They have three basic fears: (1) loss of mastery over oneself; (2) separation from loved ones; and (3) the gnawing fear of being replaced by another (Kavanaugh, 1974). Their major concern is about being left alone in an unpredictable situation where they are also faced with the frustration of not being able to do anything about it. A dying person, then, needs reduced conflict, time to assemble inner resources, and a continued relationship with a loved one up to the end.

Stages of Dying

A researcher on death, Elisabeth Kübler-Ross, proposed that people who are terminally ill go through a series of stages as they approach death. She suggested that first they *deny* that they are dying. This is then followed by *anger* or resentment that it is happening to them. Third, people try to *bargain* with God for a little more time. Fourth, they become *depressed*, and finally they adopt a more or less *peaceful acceptance* of or attitude toward the whole event, trying to tie up loose ends for themselves and their loved ones (Kübler-Ross, 1969).

IN FOCUS   **Kübler-Ross's Stages of Dying**

The Monologue of the Terminally Ill . . .

Denial "There must be some mistake with the test results. Are you sure you're looking at *my* results? This is nonsense. I'll just have to get another opinion—from a doctor who knows what he or she is talking about."

Anger "Why me? I exercise every day. I don't smoke. I do all those crazy things you're supposed to do to live longer. It's not fair."

Bargaining "Please, God, let me live another year and I promise I'll go to church every Sunday. It's just that there are a couple of things I want to accomplish. Just another year."

Depression "I become sad thinking about all the friends I'll miss. I grieve when I think of losing my family."

Peaceful Acceptance "I'm not afraid to die anymore. I know now that death is part of life. I still feel sad at times, but I've come to accept death, and I'm at peace about it."

If someone close to you had a terminal illness, how would knowing about these stages help you talk with this person? How might this knowledge interfere?

In many ways, Kübler-Ross created a double-edged sword with her suggestion. On the one hand, her system holds up in a general sort of way and helps explain many of the behaviors of people who are terminally ill. On the other hand, critics of her system feel that it takes away from the individuality and personal responses each of us may have if we face this crisis, so it may rob the dying person of respect for his or her personal feelings. Thus, if someone in this situation is angry about something, he or she may indeed have a legitimate cause other than the illness, but too many people will say, "Oh, he's going through the anger stage; that's all" (Kastenbaum & Costa, 1977). Today there is a movement toward acceptance of the fact that although emotions of the dying person may well follow a rough pattern, he or she should be recognized as an individual all the way up to the end.

Help for the Dying

Thanatologists point to the fact that dying away from home is a relatively new phenomenon and is primarily an outgrowth of our mechanized society. In many parts of the world, death is prepared for by the family unit, with everyone participating, including the person who is dying. One of the most frightening experiences is being alone when dying. If at home, the person feels considerably less alone. In fact, most present funeral rituals started out as something done within the home. Thus, washing and preparing the body were previously done by the family. The "wake"—in which family and friends stay with the body—was common before mortuaries existed.

The Amish (AH-mish) society has managed to hold onto its traditions separate from the hectic modern world and is a model for handling death. These people still make a living by farming, using horses instead of tractors, and in general have resisted so-called scientific advances. When someone dies, the immediate family is relieved of all work except for making a list of people to be notified. The family assumes responsibility for dressing the body in special funeral clothing. (Each person in the community has his or her own set of white garments to wear only when he or she dies.) Everyone is prepared for death, and the attitude is one of acceptance. Most Amish people die at home in the presence of their families. This is in stark contrast to the rest of our country in which most deaths take place in institutions.

One emerging trend is the use of **hospices** (HOS-pih-sez), places where terminally ill people can live out the remainder of their lives in relative comfort and away from the coldness of a hospital. Most hospices are "open" 24 hours a day for visits by family, friends, and pets. The goal is to provide a warm setting in which death is accepted. They are more like homes than hospitals, and they provide almost any activity desired as well as the opportunity to talk about feelings and concerns with others who are in the same situation (Melzack & Wall, 1982).

▲ *Hospices attempt to approach ensuing death with dignity and support, enriching the last days of many people.*

hospices

Places where terminally ill people can live out their lives in comfort and away from a hospital.

Points to Stress

Kübler-Ross devoted much of her adult life to studying the needs of the terminally ill. How? By simply listening to them.

Critical Thinking

Give students a few days to find out how other countries handle doctor-assisted suicide and how the United States is now handling it. Then debate the issue. Some may argue that doctor-assisted suicides allow terminally ill patients to die with dignity. Furthermore, throughout history doctors *have* assisted; it's just that nowadays, the doctor-patient relationship is not as strong as it used to be, and technology interferes. Those who are against doctor-assisted suicides may argue that no one has the right to end another's life. And what if a mistake is made, and the patient did not really want to die?

DISCUSS THE PHOTO

A hundred years ago, most people died at home. In the United States today, only 30 percent do.

ENRICHMENT

Invite a marriage counselor to class. Ask if there are any common problems that seem to break up marriages. And ask if there are any steps one can take before getting married that might prevent some of these problems. Students can write an extensive list of questions before the visit.

COOPERATIVE LEARNING

Ask students to break into groups and spend a few minutes discussing how they would explain death to a six- or seven-year-old child. What are some things *not* to do? For example, why wouldn't you say that the dead person is simply sleeping or on vacation? What are some things that you would do? Consider reading *Freddie the Leaf,* by Leo Buscaglia, in class beforehand. Ask if the book would be appropriate for explaining death. Can students think of any other stories that appropriately explain death?

PSYCHOLOGY IN YOUR LIFE

Cooperative Learning

If you like the idea of panel presentations (where four or five students present reports to the class), this chapter lends itself well to this method. Possible topics include mercy killing, life-support machines, near-death experiences, living wills, abortion, suicide, funeral homes, hospices, Alzheimer's disease, and institutionalization.

Tell students that they should focus on discussion questions that *involve* the class. You may even demand that each panel write 10 or 20 discussion questions, explaining that a major portion of their grades will be based on the thoughtfulness of these questions. If you're worried that students will not conduct enough research with this emphasis on discussion, simply require them to hand in a written report before the presentations.

PSYCHOLOGY IN YOUR LIFE

Trying to Look to the Future

Of all the chapters in this book, this one probably seems the most unrelated to you at this point in your life. This might be a good place, therefore, to try to bring together some of the overall issues discussed and to offer a little speculation that may give some order to the subject matter.

First of all, you may have noticed that many of the descriptions concerning the different age groups had a somewhat negative tone to them. This is not because from your age onward, everything is a disaster or something close to a disaster. Instead, it merely reflects the fact that if all is going well, there's hardly anything to say about it—in other words, there's not much research to report. Psychologists rarely are involved when life is moving along wonderfully; we just wish the people well and hope for their continued success.

There is one problem, however: parents and other people tend to wrap a cocoon around their children, but when the children are older, as you are, the adults never draw the line and say "*Now* let's tell the truth in its entirety." One of the best examples of this is the information you get about marriage. Despite all the research, the truth of the matter is that we don't know how to predict a good marriage. While it is obvious that if two people can't get along before marriage, they are not going to get along after marriage, the rest is vague. Love is one of the most powerful emotions in the world, and the old question "Is this *true* love?" is a rather silly one. All love is true love—for as long as it lasts. The real question is how long and enduring it will be and how compatible two people are. Nobody knows the answers to these questions—no psychologist, no test can accurately predict them. The truth is that you find out if your marriage is a good one only if and when it continues to make you and your partner happy and allows you to grow, while all the time you are putting a lot of hard work into the relationship. The point is that the tinge of negativity in some places in this chapter is just to keep you from feeling too abnormal later if things start to go wrong with your marriage, job, or family. People still tell their children that marriage is the most wonderful thing in the world. That is too sweeping a statement. With luck and work, it will be wonderful. You won't know beforehand—the 50 percent divorce rate shows that.

Most older people you are around will act as if they know a big secret that you are not privy to yet. This "secret" is almost always hinted at in the phrase "Wait until you…" All this means is that you have not yet experienced the trouble or difficulties that the older people have had. There is no real secret, but it makes the adults feel a little more important to have survived the crises you still face.

For example, the period of middle age has extreme ups and downs, just as you have at times. True stability is hard to hold onto at any age. All the parent's love for you is still basically there, but friction is inevitable until you, *(continued on next page)*

354
354

DISCOVERY

In Chapter 11 we suggested that you invite parents to class to discuss adolescence. Try the same thing here—the topic this time being adulthood. See **Teaching Master 12-2 Adulthood Questions** for an extensive list of questions.

VOCABULARY REVIEW

Before testing students on the contents of this chapter, you may want to review vocabulary terms that are especially important or confusing. Terms in this chapter that could require clarification are *gerontology*, *senile dementia*, *thanatology*, and *hospices*.

Connections

During early adulthood we begin the crisis that Erikson calls generativity versus stagnation (Chapter 14). You may want to introduce some of that material here. Generativity means a concern for future generations, a need to contribute something important to the world. This may be one psychological reason why people start families during this period. Stagnation, or deterioration, results from the feeling that one has not contributed to the world. Although this crisis is highlighted during adulthood, high school students may experience some of these feelings.

Wrapping It Up

You are the resident expert on adulthood in your classroom, so share some of the changes that you have gone through, comparing and contrasting yourself with the typical characteristics described in the chapter. As a result, students will retain the material better, and they will understand that each person develops in his or her own way, at times typical and at other times defying the norm.

PSYCHOLOGY IN YOUR LIFE

Trying to Look to the Future

(continued from previous page) too, have gone through the trials of adult life—bills, health problems, job threats, threats to family integrity, feeling inadequate, and so forth. It is sort of an initiation, so everybody gets back together again after you have spent some years with your share of unpleasantness. This may seem weird, but it is very common. In many

ways, the whole thing is like a tribal rite.

To state the obvious, death is something we all try to avoid. But that does not mean that we should also avoid old people. The majority of them are not sitting around waiting for and fearing death. There are so many stories about old people being "senile" and long-winded that many young people do avoid them. This is

a sad situation, since most old people have cast off their prejudices and are quite interested in younger people, in what they think and do. Those who are boring were boring when they were in high school and on through adulthood. A friendly relationship with an interesting older person can bring incredible rewards to both of you.

SUMMARY

1. During late adolescence and early adulthood, most people start their families and careers. In very general terms, the male devotes most of his time to career and the female to family, even if the woman works outside the home.
2. At some point around the age of 40, most people go through a midlife transition. This is a time for reexamining one's life.
3. In middle adulthood, people's priorities shift with men becoming more giving and emotionally expressive while women become more independent and assertive. The 50s are usually a time of mellowing.
4. Two major changes occur in middle adulthood, the empty-nest period and menopause.
5. Late adulthood begins in one's 60s, and more people are living longer than ever before.

6. Aging results from a slowing down of cellular growth. Mental ability for most people is quite good, although a little slower than before. Senile dementia occurs in a minority of the elderly. The symptoms of Alzheimer's disease result from nerve cell chemicals being depleted.
7. While isolation or institutionalization are feared, neither is the common lot of the elderly person.
8. Thanatology is the study of death; it emphasizes making death a natural part of the life cycle. Dying people should be an active part of the family as much as possible. There is much criticism of how we handle death in this country.

SUGGESTED READINGS

▼ Bender, David L., ed. *Problems of Death: Opposing Viewpoints.* Saint Paul, Minn.: Greenhaven Press, 1981.

▼ "How Medicine Mistreats the Elderly." *U.S. News and World Report.* January 18, 1993, 72–81.

▼ Kotre, John and Elizabeth Hall. *Seasons of Life.* Boston: Little Brown, 1990.

▼ Kübler-Ross, Elisabeth. *On Death and Dying.* New York: MacMillan, 1969.

▼ Sheehy, Gail. *Passages.* New York: Dutton, 1976.

VOCABULARY

empty-nest period
menopause
gerontology

senile dementia
cerebral
   arteriosclerosis

Alzheimer's disease
thanatology
hospice

Answers to Review Questions

1. false
2. true
3. false
4. true
5. true
6. false
7. false
8. thanatology
9. gerontology
10. six
11. cerebral arteriosclerosis
12. senile dementia
13. d
14. a
15. b
16. b

Review Questions

True/False

1. The midlife transition, though not as tragic as everyone used to think, is inevitable.
2. Marital satisfaction is typically at a low point during the midlife period.
3. The majority of divorces takes place during midlife.
4. Men and women tend to reverse their focus—or adopt the others' characteristics—during middle adulthood.

5. Studies show that the majority of women never experience feelings of uselessness and depression during the empty-nest period.
6. The onset of menopause tends to create significant psychological problems for the majority of women.
7. Studies show that the majority of old people are isolated, withdrawn, and lonesome.

Fill in the blanks; answer on a separate sheet of paper. (An answer may consist of more than one word.)

8. The study of death is called ___?___ .
9. The study of older people is called ___?___ .
10. Women live roughly ___?___ years longer than men.

11. The blockage of blood vessels going to the brain is called ___?___ .
12. The loss of mental capacity in older people is called ___?___ .

Notes on Discussion Questions

1. Answers will vary—and so will the honesty of the answers.

2. Consider having two or more students debate the issue in class for a few minutes and follow this up with a general discussion.

3. Students may have difficulty viewing the situation from the point of view of someone other than a young person who will soon need a job. Remind them that one day *they* may be the ones forced to retire.

4. Again, students may have difficulty putting themselves in the shoes of an old person. Emphasize the need to answer the question from an older person's point of view.

5. Here are some other examples of how we ignore death. The words *death* and *dying* often become "passed away," "deceased," "put to sleep" (as with animals), "no longer with us," "united with God." Dead people are often referred to as the "beloved." These examples may be trivial, but they're representative of a more general evasion of the existence of

Multiple Choice

13. Alzheimer's disease disrupts
    a. speech.
    b. body control.
    c. personality.
    d. all of the above.
    e. a & b only.

14. Which of the following is *not* a myth about senility but is true?
    a. Senility is caused by disease.
    b. Senility occurs in a majority of older people by the age of 70.
    c. The brain cells lost during aging lead to mental impairment.
    d. Senility is inevitable with age.

15. Those people who were highly active in youth usually
    a. slow down in old age.
    b. remain active in old age.
    c. live very long lives.
    d. experience fewer worries about old age.

16. If a person living in the 1800s avoided disease, the chances of that person living to 70 were
    a. still worse than today.
    b. about the same as today.
    c. better than today.

DISCUSSION QUESTIONS

1. If you're a male, would it bother you if your wife's career was more "significant" than yours and if she made much more money than you? Why or why not? Be honest. If you're a female, would it bother you if you made more money than your husband? Why or why not?

2. When you hear about research on manipulation of genes to prolong the life span, do you tend to become excited about the prospect, or do you think the life span is something that really shouldn't be toyed with and manipulated by science? Argue for one of these points of view.

3. The number of people over 65 has increased dramatically and will probably continue to increase. Let's assume that many of these people choose *not* to retire; consequently, the unemployment rate among young people rises sharply. Should the older people be forced to retire? Why or why not? Explain.

4. If you were about 75 years old and were unable to live independently, do you think you'd prefer to live in a well-run nursing home so you could associate with others your age, *or* do you think you'd rather live with your own children (assuming they welcome you!)? Explain.

5. The chapter describes several ways in which our society tends to ignore the reality of death. For example, even sympathy cards avoid mentioning words like *death* and *dying.* What are some other ways in which we ignore it? Explain. Consider language, hospital procedures, and funeral rituals.

6. If you found out that you had only a year to live, would you be likely to continue to live life as usual, or would you drastically alter your life style? Explain. If you *were* to change your life drastically, what would you do differently? Be specific.

death. Point out, however, that often this evasion serves a worthwhile function. For example, when a person dies, the wake, the funeral, and the burial, though they may seem to encourage an evasion of death at times, allow the family and friends of the dead person time to grieve and time to accept the reality of the death.

6. You may want to use this one as a journal topic.

Notes on Activities

1. This activity should be highly interesting to students since it offers insights into their near futures. Have students who complete this activity share these insights with the rest of the class.

2. Consider conducting this activity in class over the course of a week, allowing about ten minutes per journal entry. Afterward, try to get volunteers

to read aloud one of their favorite entries.

3. Students clearly have fun conducting this experiment. Remind them, however, that they need to remain objective and scientific when collecting data. For example, they need to drop the contents of the bag in an identical manner for every subject. You may even want to bring a

shopping bag to class and have a student or two demonstrate how they will drop the contents in the bag. Tell students to consider videotaping the experiment and showing the video in class.

4. Students will do a great job with this one! Encourage them to be creative and humorous.

5. Pick one or two of the better dia-

ACTIVITIES

1. Graduating from high school and breaking off with friends can often be a shock to young people. In fact, college students seem to be one of the groups hardest hit by depression. Contact someone who graduated from high school within the past year or two and interview the person. Possible questions: (1) Do you still see many friends from high school? Why or why not? (2) What's the biggest adjustment you had to make after high school? (3) What kinds of things get you down? (4) What worries you most about the future?

2. For this activity, we want you to consider your future—not only what you'll be doing but also how you'll feel about yourself. Imagine yourself at the ages of 30, 40, 50, and 60. Then write your journal entries (one for each age) in which you assume the point of view of one of your future selves each time. *Note:* the ages are approximate. If it makes more sense to you, for example, to use the age 33 instead of 30 go ahead. You might save this journal for the future to see how accurate your predictions turn out to be.

3. If we summarize some of the findings discussed in the chapter, we might say that adults in early adulthood (20–35) tend to be stressed and anxious, while adults in middle adulthood (45–60) tend to become more compassionate and mellow. This is obviously a generalization and not true for everyone, but we want you to use this as a basis for this next activity. Conduct an experiment to determine whether "middle" adults, being more relaxed, will be more likely than "early" adults to help a stranger.

General procedure: Walk through a mall with a shopping bag that has a ripped bottom. Stuff the bag with pre-purchased merchandise and some papers. As you approach someone in the mall, allow the contents of the bag to slip through the bottom of the bag and then record if the person helps. Repeat this procedure 20 times, half the time on "early" adults, half the time on "middle" adults. (You'll have to use your own judgment here as to ages.)

Specific points: (1) The reason you want to include papers in the bag is that papers will tend to cause a mess and will create a *need* for help. If you simply dropped an item or two, others may not feel that you need any help from them. (2) You probably want to conduct this experiment with a friend. One person can drop; the other can record. (3) Record not only if the person bent down to help you but also what the person said or didn't say, and so on. In other words, record as much information as possible about each subject. (4) If possible, test only subjects who are alone. If they're with others, this may be a factor that influences their helping behavior, and this is not what you're testing in this case. (5) If possible, divide your subjects equally between men and women. If this is not possible, try to use all men or all women. Again gender is not a factor that you're studying either, and this will be one way of partially eliminating this factor.

Discuss your results. Can you draw any conclusions? Was our hypothesis about the characteristics of the two age groups supported by your findings? Explain. Be sure

logues, and have students play them out in class.

6. Consider having students present their information to the class. High school students probably don't know a great deal about this topic and oral presentations provide a good opportunity for them to ask questions.

7. Have students write down the name and number of their contact at the site they visited. Maybe you can invite the person to class.

to include the specific reactions of each subject.

4. As mentioned in the chapter, our society is obsessed with youth, and many products on the market today reflect this obsession. In fact, many products seem to be designed to stall or deny the aging process. Collect several advertisements that promote these kinds of products and organize them in a creative way for a collage. *Note:* some products may not be specifically designed to stall or deny the aging process, but perhaps you can somehow display these products to show how they reinforce the obsession with youth.

5. Write a dialogue between a husband and wife arguing about whether they should invite one of their parents to live with them. The parent in question is not always able to move around easily. One person in the dialogue should support housing the parent; the other should be against it. End the dialogue with some kind of resolution. The dialogue will certainly be influenced by several factors: if the husband and wife have children living at home; if the husband and wife both work; and so on. You can fill in these details in any way you like.

You don't need to use quotation marks, but make it clear when a new speaker is talking—maybe by using different colored pens or skipping lines or introducing each speaker with *H:* and *W:* (for "husband" and "wife") or giving names to your characters.

6. Conduct research on Alzheimer's disease and organize your information into a report. Be sure to include your own reactions to the material—not reactions like "Oh, it's horrible," since no one would disagree with

that, but more along the lines of what should be done to help these people or to increase public awareness, and so forth. Also answer some of the following questions: (1) What are the stages of the disease that an Alzheimer's patient experiences? (2) What are the possible causes? (3) What research is being conducted on "cures"? (4) Is there anything one can do to reduce the risks of getting Alzheimer's disease?

7. Visit one of the following three sites and write a report from the point of view of whether you would ever want to be a "customer" at the place—assuming you *needed* the services. Explain in detail why you would or would not want to be a customer.

a. Nursing home: talk to someone in charge who can inform you of the services and activities that the facility provides. Also, find out the costs of the care. If possible, visit with a few of the residents to get their feedback on the facility.

b. Funeral home: this may sound a bit morbid, but visiting such a place when you don't really *need* to can be fascinating. Again, find out about services and costs. Ask the director about the main functions of funeral homes in our society.

c. Hospice: more and more hospitals are developing hospice programs as an option for terminally ill patients. The chances are good that you can find a hospice in your area. Find out about the services provided, how a hospice is different from a normal hospital setting, and the functions that hospices serve.

DISCUSS THE PHOTO

This picture probably doesn't raise many eyebrows. What if these two kids were playing with dolls?

Gender similarities at work.

360

PSYCHOLOGY AND YOU RESOURCES

A variety of resources are available in the Psychology and You *supplementary material. In addition, there are a number of additional resources listed to enhance your lesson plans.*

Masters
▼ 13-1A Learning Goals
▼ 13-1B Answers to Learning Goals
▼ 13-2 Gender Survey
▼ 13-3 Battle of the Sexes: Spatial Skills
▼ 13-4 Battle of the Sexes: Verbal Skills
▼ 13-5 Complete the Story
▼ 13-6 Sex Roles

Student Worksheets
▼ Vocabulary Worksheet
▼ Independent Practice

Worksheet
▼ Enrichment Worksheet
▼ Reteaching Worksheet

Test Bank
▼ Tests A and B

Multimedia
▼ *The Brain* Videotape Modules #8, 9, 23
▼ **Mindscope** Exercise 4
▼ Psychology Videodisc

Student Workbook

PACING CHART

Complete Coverage

Day 1: Have students read the first three sections of the chapter before class. Discuss the role hormones play in gender differences. Assign "Intelligence" and Psychology In Your Life for Day 2.

Day 2: Focus on the reasons why evidence about the causes of gender differences regarding certain abilities is inconclusive. Assign an activity for homework requiring evaluation of environmental influences on the development of skills for both sexes. Have students read "Social Skills" for Day 3.

Day 3: Discuss the social factors involved in gender differences regarding self-confidence and drive for success. Provide a group activity or demonstration aimed at analyzing gender differences in communication. Review male and female characteristics in mate selection. Assign the last two sections for homework.

Day 4: After briefly reviewing the effects of hormonal cycles, concentrate on the factors affecting

13

Gender Differences

OBJECTIVES

Be able to:

▼ Explain the role of hormones in gender development.

▼ List and describe the areas of mental ability in which males and females show differences.

▼ Explain why in each of these areas we cannot come to a firm conclusion about the results.

▼ Discuss gender differences in communication.

▼ Describe how mate selection differs for males and females.

▼ Explain whether or not the evidence is clear that women have strong maternal drives.

▼ Explain the process of identification.

▼ Describe androgyny and the positive and negative aspects of pursuing it.

Global Look at the Chapter

There are all kinds of myths about differences between the sexes. In this chapter, we explore what science has learned about the differences between males and females. In general, the two sexes are quite similar. A few differences have been found, but most of them have social rather than biological sources.

361

INTRODUCING THE CHAPTER

The topic of gender differences is a favorite one for students, so you may want to give them a chance to air some general impressions they have of the opposite sex. Ask this question: What are some nonsexual behaviors that the opposite gender gets away with that you would never be able even to attempt? Males may complain that females can talk their way out of a traffic ticket by crying or pleading. Females may complain about the rude comments that males can make. (See **Teaching Master 13-2 Gender Survey** for a list of gender-related statements that you can discuss.)

gender role identification. Conduct activity #3 in the text to evaluate society's rules and expectations regarding gender role behavior.

Day 5: Discuss the concept of androgyny before giving the Chapter Review quiz.

In Brief

Day 1: Discuss the effects hormones can have on male and female behavior. Focus on the factors that make evidence about differences in abilities between the sexes inconclusive. Assign an activity for homework that addresses cultural bias regarding characteristics of each gender.

Day 2: Focus on the sociocultural influence on males and females in the areas of self-confidence and drive for success. Use the relevant In Focus box to review gender differences in communication.

Day 3: Discuss the factors in gender role identification, and review the concept of androgyny. Give the Chapter Review quiz.

LEAD-OFF ACTIVITY

Have students take the **In Focus** gender quiz. All the statements are false, except for the first one. Number 2 is a 100-year-old claim, so we hope no one gets that one wrong. Number 3: males may do better on SAT scores, but females do better in math courses and on math advanced placement tests. There's no evidence for either gender having a natural ability for math. Number 4: this is simply a myth that society has fostered. Number 5: new mothers with no experience with babies will be just as lost as new fathers. Number 6: males also have a monthly hormonal change (one milder than females) that is related to moodiness. Number 7: men look more at physical attractiveness; women look more at character and status. Number 8: androgynous people tend to be more psychologically healthy than people with very strong gender identities.

CHAPTER PROJECT/COOPERATIVE LEARNING

Have each group write 25 questions about gender differences or sexuality. Have each group member take four or five of the questions and find the answers. You might want to spend a class period in the library, but remind students that other teach-ers are good sources, too. For exam-ple, a social studies teacher could address questions about gender dif-ferences across cultures; a biology teacher might shed light on the role of hormones in sexual development.

TEACHING MASTER 13-1A

Learning Goals. A Learning Goals sheet for each chapter is provided in the Teacher Resources. These Learning Goals can be used as review sheets or worksheets. **Teaching Master 13-1B** consists of answers to these Learning Goals.

Connections

Remember, it is the Y chromosome, which can only be supplied by the male, that makes a male (Chapter 10). Without this, the embryo will have two X chromosomes and will be female.

Gender Quiz.

 See the **Lead-Off Activity.**

Unit 4 HUMAN DEVELOPMENT

MALE AND FEMALE—A BRIEF HISTORY OF MYTHS

The word **gender** refers to the sex of an individual, either male or female. Studying the similarities and differences between the sexes, as you might imagine, has had a rather colorful history. In the old days, the males' desire for domination led to some bizarre "scientif-ic" attempts to show that the male is smarter than the female. We might look at a few of them.

One of the claims by males 100 years or so ago concerned brain size. Since women have smaller heads than men, their brains must be smaller, so the male scientists said that females were not as bright. This idea was finally given up when it was discovered that physical brain size is not related to intelligence. Then the scientists decided that the front part of the brain was better developed in the male. So that must be the area showing that men were smarter! But they found this, too, to be false since it was eventually shown that the female was as developed in this part of the brain as the male was. These disputes became stranger when it was claimed that the male hormones kept men's minds cool and "dry," leading them to have a

---

IN FOCUS **Gender Quiz**

Complete this true/false quiz before reading the chapter. (See activity number 5 at the end of the chapter for answers to the quiz.)

1. Females have fewer genetic defects and have greater endurance than men.
2. The front part of the brain is more developed in males than in females.
3. Males have a natural ability to handle mathematics better than females.
4. Males are more oriented toward achievement than females.
5. Women seem to have a special, natural ability to take care of children—some might call it a "maternal instinct."
6. Only females experience monthly hormonal changes.
7. When it comes to choosing a mate, men and women look for the same characteristics.
8. People with very strong gender identities are generally more psychologically healthy than people who engage in both masculine and feminine activities.

ACTIVITY ACTIVITY ACTIVITY ACTIVITY ACTIVITY

ENRICHMENT

When an infant's gender is unclear, this is called hermaphroditism (her-MAF-roe-dite-ism). Ask students to find out what parents and doctors do about this.

Connections

During puberty the adrenal glands release hormones that contribute to the development of sexual characteristics, like breasts in females and voice changes and facial hair in males (Chapter 12).

Chapter 13 GENDER DIFFERENCES

clever, "dry" wit. Then it was said that females should not be educated because this drained vital fluids from their bodies. And so forth. The point is that male/female relationships have been dominated even in science by mudslinging rather than by research. Today, the studies are much more scientific and accurate, and we hope we can shed some light on what differences, if any, really exist between the two sexes.

THE ROLE OF HORMONES

Each of us, male or female, has both male and female hormones, regardless of gender. **Hormones** are chemical agents that cause physical changes in the body. There are two types of sex hormones, **androgen** and **estrogen.** Males have more androgen, and females more estrogen. Whether a person becomes male or female results from which hormone is present in the fetus in greater quantities. Until the second month of development, male and female fetuses are exactly the same. Basically, it is a matter of one hormone being dominant in each individual. Thus, which sex we become depends on genetics, which causes certain mechanisms to increase the amount of one hormone over the other.

Hormones have some interesting effects on male/female behavior. For instance, injection of androgen into a pregnant monkey can produce an offspring that by nature should be female but that also has some physical male characteristics. Androgen injected into a human adult female can increase her aggressiveness. And male monkeys with too little androgen will show many patterns of behavior normally found in female monkeys.

Levels of sex hormones can be off slightly without producing serious abnormalities, yet they can result in slight changes in behavior. For example, some years ago a number of pregnant women were given medication that had the side effect of making their bodies produce more androgen than normal. Their female offspring tended to be somewhat "tomboyish." On the other hand, males who before birth had their androgen production reduced were a bit less rough and aggressive. In both cases, though, it is important to remember that the children were not abnormal; they were behaving within the normal range for their sex (Ehrhardt, 1979). When the levels of hormones are genuinely defective, children with characteristics of both sexes can be born. For instance, some can have the internal equipment of males but the external parts of females, or vice versa.

Despite these findings, hormones play a lesser role in humans than they do in other animals. For the most part, we are able to limit their effect on our behavior and on how masculine or feminine we feel.

▲ *A distinctly unfeminine lady, old West outlaw Belle Starr and her husband "Blue Duck." Note handcuffs.*

gender

The sex of an individual, male or female.

hormones

Chemical agents that cause changes in the body.

androgen

The male hormone.

estrogen

The female hormone.

DISCUSS THE PHOTO

Because the "masculine" traits are highly valued in our society, most parents would be less troubled if their daughter was a "tomboy" than if their son displayed "feminine" behavior.

Comprehension Check

How can the hormone androgen affect the behavior of both males and females? *(It increases aggression.)*

FYI Boys suffering from stuttering outnumber girls four to one. Girls usually develop language skills sooner than boys.

363

363

ENRICHMENT

Ask students to find out the definition of sociobiology. (Sociobiology is a branch of social psychology that studies how evolution has shaped not only physical changes but also social behaviors and characteristics, such as assertiveness and sensitivity.) Have students find out what conclusions sociobiologists have made with regard to gender differences. You might mention that sociobiology is a controversial field.

Teaching Hint

Have students list evidence that males are aggressive—an easy task. But it does not follow that females are not aggressive or even that they are less aggressive. This is a good example of how partial evidence can bias our perceptions and conclusions. Also, it's always easier to look generally at a behavior like aggression and suggest a theory about why it occurs than to measure such behavior objectively and *predict* it.

Points to Stress

Psychologists often make the distinction between sex and gender. Sex refers to being biologically and sexually male or female; gender refers to the attributes and disposition that cultures attribute to each sex. Also, gender roles refer to rights and obligations expected of each gender. Definitions of gender and gender roles vary between cultures and even within cultures when class and race are taken into consideration.

364

Unit 4 HUMAN DEVELOPMENT

364

MALE/FEMALE DIFFERENCES

Males are bulkier and stronger as a group compared to females, but females have fewer genetic defects, live longer, and have greater physical endurance. The other obvious, major male/female difference is that the female bears the offspring and provides the nourishment for the infant, which creates a very strong bond between the two.

The only activities, then, that clearly and absolutely belong to one sex are those involved in reproduction. All other differences are simply a matter of degree or frequency of occurrence. In other words, there are certain trends for one gender versus the other, but no rule holds hard and fast.

Aggression and Activity Level

We usually see aggression as primarily a masculine characteristic, and males do indeed generally show more aggression than females (Cohn, 1991; Deaux, 1985). Does this mean, then, that females are not aggressive? Absolutely not. Given the right circumstances, females may not only equal males in aggressive behavior but may also exceed them (De Bold, 1983). What it does mean is that more males than females are more likely to behave this way in more situations. For instance, when packed together in a big crowd, men tend to get aggressive, but women tend to get nervous (Schettino & Borden, 1976).

This is important: researchers note that attention is rarely given to gender similarities. And yet the sexes are far more alike than they are different. In other words, gender differences are the exception; gender similarities are commonplace (Money, 1980). We can discuss what differences do appear, but we are always faced with the additional problem of sorting out which differences are biological and which are learned—a formidable task.

Gender differences in *activity level* appear in infants as early as 45 hours after birth, with males more active. When asleep, male children twitch and jump, use their muscles more; females smile more. Male children engage in more physical activity than females. This difference also shows up in monkeys, suggesting a biological origin. From infancy, male monkeys are wrestling, pushing, and shoving one another, while females are relatively quiet (Caplan, 1984). Such findings have, in the past, been interpreted to mean that the female wants to be dominated. *Very* few people now agree with that suggestion. In fact, when a male monkey gets a little too heavy-handed, the female will clobber him one; this has been known to happen among humans, too. The best-documented difference between males and females, then, is in the area of rough physical play, probably the result of different hormone levels.

EXPERIMENT

Here's a simple test to assess whether females have stronger verbal skills than males. Give students three minutes to think of as many synonyms as they can for these words: hot, weak, tired, win. Tally and average the results, and you'll probably find that females have the edge.

Hormones.

IN FOCUS Males tend to produce fewer androgens than usual, and females tend to produce less estrogen than usual.

FYI The SAT scores of males and females are beginning to level out.

IN FOCUS Hormones

Material to be learned	Mnemonic device	How memory is stored
Androgen = male hormone	Associate new material with old material (elaboration).	Andy—androgen
Estrogen = female hormone	Associate androgen with a familiar male name.	Esther—estrogen
	Associate estrogen with a familiar female name.	If you simply remember the names ANDy and ESTher, the first three letters of each name will give you a cue; once you have the proper cue, remembering the rest is easy.

Each of us has both male and female hormones. What happens to the level or balance of androgen and estrogen as we age?

INTELLIGENCE

In infancy, the basic intellectual processes of the male and female seem the same. Over time, however, each sex develops more elaborate skills in a given area than the other sex does. Despite this, scientists suspect that males and females are very close in overall intellectual abilities (Feingold, 1988).

Spatial Skills

At about 11 years of age, boys begin to score better on tasks involving mathematics and spatial skills. **Spatial skills** refer to the ability to imagine how something would look in space—for example, getting a three-dimensional image of the parking lot if the cars were parked at right angles to the curb and then mentally rotating them so that they are parked parallel to the curb. Video games involve con-

spatial skills

The ability to imagine how an object would look if it was moved about in space.

EXPERIMENT

Pass out **Teaching Masters 13-3 and 13-4 Battle of the Sexes: Spatial Skills; Verbal Skills** to create some friendly competition between the males and females in your class. Propose the hypothesis that males have better spatial skills than females and that females have better verbal skills. Use these masters to test this hypothesis. Set a time limit for both tests. Tally the results, and try to draw several conclusions. (Answers are listed on the masters.)

Comprehension Check

Do males have a greater natural ability for math than females? Why is this question still unanswered? *(Test results are inconsistent; evidence is tainted by the fact that society expects boys to be better at math and tells girls they must act "dumb" to attract males.)*

DISCUSS THE PHOTO

You might point out that the SAT scores of males and females are beginning to level out.

▲ *Academic skills being put to good use.*

siderable spatial skills. In general, boys are better at these games than girls, but there is a "trick" here in that girls don't get involved with these machines very often. When they do, they learn the skills quite well. (See Chapter 2, where we discuss a study comparing males and females on video games.) There also are unexplained research findings such as this one: a study of 3,000 junior and senior high school students found that 13-year-old girls scored better on spatial skills than boys the same age (Meece et al., 1982). Whatever differences exist are best explained at the moment as resulting from differences in social role, social class, ethnic background, and the type of test given, rather than from differences between the sexes.

Some people have suggested that there might be physical differences in the brains of males versus those of females. Indeed, the brains do differ: certain areas in the brains of one sex will have more cells than the same areas in the brains of the other sex and vice versa, but to date we have not been able to relate these facts to any differences in mental abilities (Swaab & Fliers, 1984). In fact, such findings can lead to the same type of claims cited at the beginning of the chapter with men trying to show that women are not as bright. This would be hard to prove because school-age girls take an early lead in verbal skills (word problems, reading, and the like), for example, and continue to hold a slight edge in this area through the years.

Mathematical Ability

A study of 40,000 seventh-grade students showed that by age 13 males did better than females on the part of the Scholastic Assessment Test (SAT) that measures mathematical reasoning. There were 13 boys to every one girl scoring over 700 (95 percent) on the math portion of the test. Boys *seem* to have a wide lead in the area of mathematics (Benbow & Stanley, 1983). This difference is real, but explaining it is a whole other issue.

A few have argued that because girls can have the same formal training as boys in mathematics if they want to, these tests must indicate some innate, basic difference between the sexes (Benbow & Stanley, 1985). But evidence for this claim is at best quite mixed.

Problems that contradict a theory of male superiority in math show up in other studies using the same group that took the Scholastic Assessment Tests. These show that girls did better than boys in math courses and in advanced placement math tests. It seems unlikely that the SAT would measure math skills while the math courses wouldn't (Beckwith & Woodruff, 1984). Other studies show no difference at all between girls and boys on tests of high-level reasoning, such as geometry proofs (Senk & Usiskin, 1984). Possibly the answer lies in the fact that without even knowing it, many people have a bias against girls being involved in math, which has traditionally been part of the male domain. For example, some studies show

INTERDISCIPLINARY PROJECT

Politics. Have students explore whether the media uses a double standard in its coverage of male and female candidates during major elections or confirmation hearings. For example, will the husband of a female candidate undergo more scrutiny about his background than the wife of a male candidate? Students' analyses need not be restricted to the media. Does the substance of a government background check or a Congressional committee inquiry differ simply because of gender?

If you feel that such a project is too time consuming, have students look at the male/female voter breakdown for the last few major elections, and discuss possible reasons for any differences. Why was a candidate successful in attracting a particular gender's vote?

that a number of teachers give more attention to boys than girls in math classes (Sadker & Sadker, 1985).

So, at present we can only come to this conclusion: taken as a whole, the studies do not show that there is some basic difference between the sexes in the ability to handle mathematics. A great number of things would have to be cleared away first before we could conclude that there *is* a difference. Here are some: (1) The test results would have to be more consistent from one study to another. (2) We would have to compensate for the fact that teachers and parents expect males to do better than females in this area. (3) We would have to look at the fact that more boys than girls claim they "enjoy" math. If it's really true that boys tend to like math more, then we have a serious problem comparing the sexes in math abilities (Meece et al., 1982). (4) In general, a lot of people don't want to struggle with math. It may well be that females take advantage of the social forces claiming they are not that skilled in this area in order merely to bypass it and avoid the hassle.

Much of the difficulty in drawing conclusions about male/female abilities can be demonstrated by the fact that statistically speaking, most girls do not know how to insert a battery properly into a flashlight. This has got to be the result of environmental pressure on girls "not to know," since it is such a simple task that certainly anyone can learn it (Jacobson & Doran, 1985).

The fact that no conclusion can be reached is in itself very important, since this leaves the question wide open, and this is certainly a critical area that should not be closed without very hard evidence.

Environmental Influences

There is no way to remove environmental influences from the development of all kinds of skills. We have already noted that teachers call on boys more often in math classes. Actually, teachers call on boys more often, period. They give boys more of their attention and time and are more likely to ask boys than girls to expand on their answers and think things through (Hyde, 1990).

With spatial or mathematical abilities, environmental influences reach far beyond the classroom. For example, research has shown that more mathematical toys are given to boys. Also, boys play with toys such as footballs, which require spatial orientation in order to catch and throw them (Mossip, 1977).

The real clincher has both its humorous and sad sides: right at junior high school age, females as a group take a sudden and dramatic drop in grades and in intelligence test scores. Does female intelligence suddenly plummet like a rock at this age so that they know hardly anything anymore? Naturally that is ridiculous. Many females have been convinced by the "system" that they are supposed to be dumb to be appealing to males. Interestingly, females who refuse to go

Points to Stress

The flashlight experiment is *one* study. Bring in a flashlight, and try it with your students! You might also take a poll on who knows how to change a flat tire.

Journal Topic

"Would you vote for a female presidential candidate? Why or why not?" Afterward, you might ask the males if they would feel comfortable dating someone with such high ambitions.

DISCOVERY

Teaching Master 13-2 Gender Survey includes a list of gender-related statements, such as "Males are not as emotional as females." Students are asked to mark their level of agreement or disagreement.

Even if you don't bother to tally and compare male and female answers, the statements are an excellent source of discussion topics. (See **Introducing the Chapter.**)

DISCUSS THE PHOTO

Ask females who have had a job usually dominated by males if they experienced any discrimination.

Discussion

Ask the females if they ever play dumb in front of males. If they won't admit to it themselves, maybe because they really *don't* play dumb, perhaps they know females who do. Why do *they* do it? Do they achieve their goal?

Unit 4 HUMAN DEVELOPMENT

▲ *Women in jobs like these, once a rare sight, are becoming almost commonplace.*

along with all this and assert themselves show no decline in intellectual ability (Maccoby & Jacklin, 1974). Also, when females are past that "dumb" period, they really soar, especially in college where their grades are almost always better than those of males. Finally, we must not forget that there are many women who can leave men in a cloud of mental confusion just from watching their mathematical and spatial skills in operation. In fact, nearly 40 percent of mathematics professors are female.

At this point, then, there do seem to be a few differences between the male and female, but except for size, weight, endurance, genetically caused diseases, and the ability to give birth, the differences *do not* mean we are dealing with innate, biological factors. Environment plays a major role. Thus, we would probably find differences in knowledge about how an elevator works if we compared the explanations given by a group of people from Chicago with those given by a group from an island out in the Pacific Ocean. Such differences would not be biological.

SOCIAL SKILLS

Social factors play an important part in how we view the sexes. As a result, much of what you hear about sex differences is a myth.

EXPERIMENT

If you are a man, propose that males are more athletic than females; if you are a woman, propose the opposite. *More athletic* will be defined as the ability to throw a ball into a wastebasket from increasing distances. Mark a starting line on the floor, and mark six spots where you will place the basket; the first spot should be one foot away from the starting line and be worth one point; the second spot, worth two points, should be two feet away, and so on. Use as many subjects as you like. See the discussion that follows.

Discussion

The real purpose of the above experiment is to observe how males and females compete against one another. Is the *drive for success* similar? Who treats the game more seriously? Who is more vocal? Who jokes around more? *Why?* Does one gender use jokes to cover up real feelings about the game?

You probably don't want to go too far with any conclusions that you draw—after all, it *is* only a game—but ask students to be honest with their responses to these questions, and you should be able to arrive at some interesting insights. Since *you* are the only one aware of the true purpose of the game, pay close attention while it is going on; you might even want to sit in the back of the room, pretending to keep score, but actually noting behaviors and comments.

Self-Confidence

Females are not more influenced by others' suggestions than males; in fact, surprisingly, studies show males are more likely than females are to go along with the group (Eagly, 1978). Females consistently rate themselves as high on self-confidence as males do, at least through childhood and adolescence. Both have about an equal tendency to explore novel environments, engage in unusual activities, and refuse to be stepped on by others. Also, girls feel as important as boys—at least until the middle of high school.

In some studies, girls *claim* that in their daily lives, they are more anxious and fearful than boys. But we can't put scientific faith in this finding either, because girls may be feigning weakness as part of a social role. When faced with something frightening, boys sweat and swallow a lot and girls screech, but privately they admit to being equally terrified. So, what conclusion can be reached about self-confidence? No notable difference exists.

Drive for Success

Achievement is often described as a masculine goal. But research indicates that females are, in fact, just as oriented toward achievement as males. Large numbers of studies find no overall sex differences in this regard (Zuckerman & Wheeler, 1975). Why, then, do people have this image of men being more driven to achieve? The evidence points to societal beliefs that suggest that there is something wrong with a woman who seeks success. Girls are told not to be "too important" or they won't appeal to boys. Stop and think for a minute: isn't there at least a hint of this belief even in your own group?

The causes are all around us. Watch the TV ads carefully sometime, and note how the women are almost always connected somehow with ads for soap or for food products that need cooking. The men tend to be the focus in any ad involving something mechanical, such as a product that would be used with a car or lawnmower. In this way, then, both sexes are subtly indoctrinated. Females who are presently in college have been exposed to even more of this propaganda. When they get higher grades than males—which is the norm—they still anticipate doing poorly in the future; the males, including those who have not done well in school, expect future success (Dweck et al., 1980). Females who are presently in high school by and large are aware that they don't have to restrict themselves any longer to "female" occupations but can become involved in the wide spectrum of occupations available to all (Rubenstein, 1992; Zuckerman et al., 1980).

DISCOVERY

Find a short story that includes a good deal of dialogue between a male and a female character (or divide the class into groups and have each group find a story). Analyze the communication style that each character uses. Do your conclusions match the material presented in the student text?

DISCUSS THE PHOTO

For extra credit, students can walk around the school shooting their own photos of males and females conversing.

Discussion

One reason why women may be empathetic is that women seem to be better at interpreting subtle cues about how another person is feeling. Or is it the other way around? Are women better at interpreting subtle cues *because* they are empathetic? You may not arrive at definite conclusions, but the discussion may inspire some good questions. Is empathy innate to some degree?

Points to Stress

If we empathize with another, we *understand* what the other is going through and share in their feelings, almost as if it were happening to us. If we sympathize, we feel compassion or pity for the other, but we feel it from a distance; we don't internalize the other's feelings so much.

370

Unit 4 HUMAN DEVELOPMENT

▲ *Male and female conversational styles. Which one are you more comfortable with?*

Communication

Do men or women talk more? Are men or women more likely to touch someone they're talking to? In both cases, the answer is women, right? Wrong! Men not only talk more than women, they also interrupt other people's conversations more often. And it is men who tend to touch people while they are talking, but women more often are the ones being touched (Hyde, 1990). Let's try another one. Do men or women reveal more about themselves in a conversation? In this case, the answer *is* women. Many studies show that women engage in more self-disclosure than men, especially when they are talking with special friends or family members. This situation has been of some concern to psychologists because it can sometimes create problems for men in a lot of areas. For instance, self-disclosure is necessary in counseling and in close relationships. It is hard to express your feelings, find emotional support, or get your needs met if you cannot talk about what is going on inside. The magnitude of this problem, though, seems to have been exaggerated. Fortunately, the most recent evidence shows that sex differences in the amount of self-disclosure engaged in are actually quite small, only about 10 percent (Dindia & Allen, 1992).

Still, when it comes to understanding each other and being understood, it almost seems as if men and women come from separate planets. We don't exactly speak different languages, but we do place very different interpretations on what is said to us. A book by

DISCOVERY

Have two girls role-play this situation: *You think your boyfriend is interested in someone else. Tell a friend.* You can vary the situation in several ways: have the girl talk to her boyfriend. Or reverse the roles and have a suspicious male report his feelings to both a male and a female. It's probably a good idea to try this activity before students have read the material on communication so you get more natural responses—or at least as natural as role-playing allows.

Deborah Tannen (1990) sheds a great deal of light on this subject. Deborah Tannen is a specialist in the use of language, and the following material is derived from her work.

Before going any further, we need to explain that men and women seem to operate from very different overall views of the world. Men tend to see the world in terms of a hierarchy, where keeping or improving your status and independence is critical. Women, on the other hand, tend to see it as a cooperative network, where being more closely connected to others is what matters most. These basic

Chapter 13 GENDER DIFFERENCES

Points to Stress

The Tannen material refers primarily to general conversation and self-disclosure. These characteristics may not apply in other situations. For example, during a job interview, a male interviewer will certainly maintain eye contact.

Male and Female Communication

IN FOCUS   The males are not looking at each other. The male listener tries to minimize, then solve the problem. The females are looking at each other. The female listener empathizes with the friend.

IN FOCUS   Male and Female Communication

MY PARENTS ARE REALLY BUGGING ME ABOUT QUITTING MY JOB.

AH, JUST IGNORE THEM. IF THEY KEEP BUGGING YOU, TELL THEM THAT YOU'll PAY FOR PART OF THE PHONE BILL OR SOMETHING WITH THE MONEY YOU MAKE.

MY PARENTS ARE REALLY BUGGING ME ABOUT QUITTING MY JOB. THEY TREAT ME LIKE A TEN YEAR OLD.

I KNOW HOW YOU FEEL. WHEN I GOT MY JOB, MY PARENT WANTED ME TO QUIT EVEN BEFORE I STARTED...

What differences do you notice in these conversations?

371

ACTIVITY
ACTIVITY
ACTIVITY
ACTIVITY
ACTIVITY
ACTIVITY
ACTIV

DISCOVERY

Have students rank the following criteria for selecting a mate: personality, sense of humor, physical attractiveness, intelligence, character (honesty and integrity). A ranking of 1 means this characteristic is the least important; 5 means it is the most important. Tally the answers, and compare male and female responses.

Discussion

One way to show sympathy is to cry. Discuss how often students have seen a male cry, other than at a funeral. Why do males hold back? Are they afraid that others will think less of them? *Do others think less of them when they cry?* Does the holding back of emotions cause harm? Does it lead to a lessening of emotions?

Comprehension Check

One person is telling a male listener about a failing test grade. What might the listener say? *(The listener probably makes suggestions on how to study [or how to guess]. Or the listener might remark that it's only one test; there will be more.)* What might a female listener say? *(The female will tend to show empathy and may try to elicit more discussion from the speaker. For example, she may recount a time when she failed and explain that she felt the same way.)*

372

Unit 4 HUMAN DEVELOPMENT

differences in approach can account for the vast majority of problems the sexes have in understanding each other. For instance, when a woman checks with her husband before making plans, this supports her feeling of connectedness. On the other hand, a husband's checking with his wife may threaten his image of control and self-reliance, especially if other people are around.

Even in childhood, males and females communicate differently. Boys tend to sit beside each other to talk. To boys, this is less confrontational than sitting face-to-face, or head-to-head, as it were. Girls sit facing each other to talk. This allows for more direct interaction and clearer observation of facial expressions or gestures.

There is not enough space here to delve fully into this subject matter. But there is room for one example. Someone says to a friend, "I'm having a terrible time getting along with my boss," and then briefly describes the situation. How does the friend respond? Women are likely to empathize or tell about a similar problem they have. Men are likely to offer a solution or minimize the magnitude of the problem. In both cases, the friend is showing interest and concern. By minimizing how bad the problem is, the man is offering reassurance. By offering a solution, he is trying to help. After all, it doesn't do your status any good to have a big problem with someone more powerful than you. Negating the problem will improve your standing; solving it will let you avoid a confrontation and add to the friend's status as well. When another man gets these responses, he will probably react positively. A woman, though, is likely to feel insulted or ignored by either one of them. Why? When she expresses her feelings and those feelings are accepted by another person, she feels closer. But when a solution is given instead, the woman feels cut off. To her, negating or minimizing her problems implies a lack of concern. She is seeking connectedness, which she will get from discussing it further or hearing that someone else has had the same experience. A man, however, is likely to feel challenged or insulted by these responses. To him, saying that you've had a similar problem may mean you are trying to upstage him, and telling him you know how he feels may be interpreted as condescension. Is it any wonder that men and women so often seem to be at cross-purposes?

Selecting a Mate

Psychologists have been studying the characteristics that people want and value in a potential mate for decades. Gender differences are clear-cut and consistent. They hold true across generations and across cultures. They have resulted in women complaining that men are superficial and interested only in a woman's looks. They have resulted in men complaining that women are materialistic and interested only in a man's income. So, who is right? It appears that both are, to some extent.

DISCOVERY

Send all the males or all the females out of the room and give each group a chance to discuss the following: (1) Describe the ideal date. (The word *date,* or even the concept of dating, may be *outdated* to students; they can insert their own term.) (2) If a great deal of money is spent on a date, let's say for the prom, do most males expect something in return? (3) When a girl says no, does this always mean no? (Afterward, clarify, if no one else did, that even if a girl *seems* not to mean it, "no" must be taken at face value and respected.)

You may want to break students into smaller groups to facilitate discussion. And you may want groups to report back to the class in an anonymous fashion so that you get honest but discreet answers.

Chapter 13 GENDER DIFFERENCES

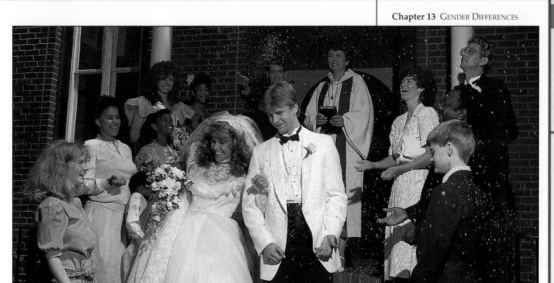

▲ *While this is generally a happy time for a marriage, stress increases until the children are grown, at which time the happiness surpasses that of the first year.*

A massive analysis of research done in this area over the last 25 years or so provides some interesting insights. The characteristics most often studied are social and economic status (middle class, working class, and so on), physical attractiveness, personality, intelligence, ambition, character (honesty and sincerity), and sense of humor. Women give more weight to socioeconomic status, ambition, character, and intelligence in mate selection. Both sexes value physical attractiveness in a mate, but men give this characteristic more weight than women do. The sexes are equal in the importance they attach to personality and sense of humor.

As to why these differences are so far-reaching, the answer probably has less to do with ego than with concern for the next generation. In other words, the situation is probably best explained in terms of the welfare of the (potential) children. For instance, general physical appearance to some extent reflects a person's genetic makeup. This will be passed on to the offspring. Thus, people look for physical characteristics that will benefit their children. In our society, children's survival depends on having access to good housing, medical care, education, nutrition, and so on. Look at the characteristics that women emphasize. They are all related to the ability to survive with some degree of comfort (Feingold, 1992).

The reasons we have just given for these sex differences may be arguable, although some psychologists believe this explanation fits the facts quite well. The differences themselves, though, are not in dispute. The differences are real.

DISCUSS THE PHOTO

It's probably easier to get married than it is to get a driver's license. Should couples have to take a course on marriage before tying the knot?

Discussion

Have students write a response to discussion question #3 at the end of the chapter, about males taking the initiative in selecting a mate, and talk about their responses in class. For enrichment, students can research whether male initiative is common in animals.

373

COOPERATIVE LEARNING

If you like the idea of separating the males and females for a few minutes (see the preceding **Discovery**), but you want to try something lighter, have each gender try to think of questions to which the other gender will not know the answers. You could make a game of it: the gender that stumps the other the most wins. (Hint: You may want to walk around and put your stamp of approval on the questions.)

Discussion

Students might enjoy talking about the breaking up of a relationship at this point. Get their response to this theory, which is based solely on conjecture: Males will tend not to break off a relationship. Instead, they will begin to act so rudely that the female will take the initiative of breaking up. In other words, males are essentially cowards in this area.

DISCUSS THE PHOTO

Before students read the section on maternal instincts, have them debate the question posed in the caption.

Discussion

Should companies provide males with time off to take care of the kids? Men who have been given time off often complain that the boss then perceives the man as unreliable and unwilling to sacrifice for the company. Also keep in mind that this attitude of employers has disadvantaged women in the workplace more often and for a much longer time.

374

Unit 4 HUMAN DEVELOPMENT

▲ *Maternal care—instinct or learned behavior?*

374

In our society, the man's status is also important for part of his family's identity. When a woman marries, she usually takes her husband's name. Children are usually given their father's last name. We tend to trace our ancestry more through our father's family line than our mother's. It is tempting to believe that because our culture does things a certain way, everybody else does it that way, too. Usually, though, this is not the case. It is not the case here, either. Among the Sioux, for instance, this tradition was reversed. Wives kept their own names, and the children belonged to the mother's clan, not the father's. Family property was held by the mother, and a child's lineage was traced through the mother's ancestry (Kelton, 1993).

Maternal Instincts

Do women *really* have a special empathy with, concern for, and ability to take care of children? Besides the ability to conceive and bear children, is there really something that makes women different in regard to kids? The answer seems to be a qualified "no" (Cosse, 1992; Eisenberg & Lennon, 1983). Women generally show more empathy for and intimate involvement with others of all ages. But the cause remains unclear (Cohn, 1991). One way to determine whether females have an inborn "maternal instinct" that males do not have is to search the animal world, where creatures are not guided by social forces to the same extent we are. There are exceptions to the rule we're about to describe, and the male lion is one of them. He is a genuine slob (there just doesn't seem to be a word that will fit better). He demands that the female go get food for him. He won't take care of his offspring; in fact, he will eat them when they are very small unless the mother lion keeps constant vigil. He doesn't even bother with personal hygiene as much as he should. So, we can give up on him. But in the animal world as a whole, the story is different if the male is forced to take care of the infants. For instance, male rhesus monkeys typically respond to their babies with either hostility or indifference. The close bond is between mother and infant. Yet in a series of studies, researchers have taken away the mother, forcing the male in the family to be left alone with the infant. At first the father complains and objects violently, but within a short time, he begins to groom, care for, and show strong attachment toward his infant. And there are male rats who also act awful about being left alone with their offspring. But, within a day or so, they "suddenly" manage to find their own version of the maternal instinct and begin to care for the infants in the same way the mother did.

The human mother with her first baby usually does not have the faintest idea what to do with this creature she suddenly faces. For one thing, the baby's head looks like it is going to twirl and wobble off at any moment. The task of caretaking seems absolutely hopeless.

ENRICHMENT

The effects of hormones on behavior can be fascinating. New discoveries are made nearly every day. Have students conduct research on the role of hormones on behavior, particularly male and female hormones. Encourage students to use updated material.

Teaching Hint

Take a poll on how many of your students baby-sit. Females usually outnumber males overwhelmingly. When these female baby-sitters have their own children, their "baby skills" will probably be evident, and others will look at them and declare, "Ah, she knows just what to do—it's instinct." A few students may turn this example around and argue that it's instinct that makes the female want to baby-sit in the first place. Explain that baby-sitting has more to do with societal expectations than instinct.

Points to Stress

Ask the baby-sitters in class if they have noticed male infants being treated differently than female infants.

Mothers must, of necessity, call on other women with experience or frantically read baby-care books to find out "what to do." So, taking care of the new baby is hardly "instinctive."

The evidence, then, is that "maternal" behavior is a matter of convenience for nature. Since the female animal gives birth to the infant, she must be programmed to take care of it, which *is* what happens. This "instinct," however, must also exist in the male animal. There is no evidence that any difference in ability or knowledge exists. Apparently, nature has made the female animal (in most species) more involved while allowing the male to hide from the task as ingeniously as he can—behavior we can sometimes see reflected among humans (Suomi, 1983; Berman, 1980; Degler, 1980).

HORMONAL CYCLES

With large numbers of women now employed in very responsible positions, some discussion has focused on what effect **menstrual cycles** have on their behavior. Menstruation occurs approximately once a month when the lining of the woman's uterus, which could have been used to hold a fertilized egg, is eliminated because it is not needed. The lining comes out as a harmless bloody fluid. It will build anew the following month to complete the cycle. Because there are so many hormonal changes that go along with this process, many females have physical discomfort and moderate changes in mood. From these facts arises the common belief that females will act strangely once a month. This belief has sparked comments concerning whether a woman, in light of these hormonal changes, would be able to handle the office of president of the United States.

Much of this is nonsense. In the 1870s, advertising headlines screamed "A FEARFUL TRAGEDY" over the story of a clergyman murdered by his wife, who "had become insane from 16 years of suffering with female complaints." Supposedly she would have been all right if she had taken Lydia E. Pinkham's Vegetable Compound, a liquid mixture of exotic ingredients, including a notable amount of alcohol, that was popular at the time (Jackson, 1984). In the 1950s, women were expected to come apart during "that time of the month"; they literally would not swim, play games, or go to work, and it was considered dangerous to take a bath. In the 1980s, female defendants have claimed they were under the influence of menstrual symptoms when they murdered their husbands. This defense has been used fairly successfully in England.

As usual, we must try to get a little perspective on the issue. Just as there are some diseases that are made much worse by something like alcohol, in extreme cases the menstrual cycle can have severe physical and psychological effects on a handful of women. But this

menstrual cycles

Monthly cycles that revolve around the elimination of the lining of the uterus because the woman's egg has not been fertilized.

ENRICHMENT

Have students compare and contrast gender differences in our culture with gender differences in one or two other cultures. Is men's work more valued than women's work in the United States (as suggested in Chapter 12)? In other cultures? Are women more involved with the children? Are men more dominant?

Evaluation Strategy

Ask students to explain to a child five ways in which males and females are different and five ways in which they are the same. They should assume that the child knows about the basic anatomical differences and similarities. (Similarities: we both have male and female hormones; we both experience monthly cycles; we both can be aggressive; we have similar drives to achieve; neither seems to possess a natural instinct for caring for an infant. Differences: the level of sex hormones differs; females have fewer genetic defects; females live longer; females seem to be less active; males *score* higher on tests that measure spatial skills; females *score* higher on tests that measure verbal skills.)

Comprehension Check

To what extent does the menstrual cycle affect most women's behavior? (*a negligible amount—if at all*)

376

Unit 4 HUMAN DEVELOPMENT

premenstrual syndrome (PMS)

Anxiety, irritability, and mental confusion resulting from monthly female hormonal changes.

gender role behavior

Acts that reflect society's view of what is appropriate for males versus what is appropriate for females.

identification

The process of modeling behavior patterns after (usually) a member of the same sex.

376

happens so very rarely that it is not something for the average female to worry about.

On the other hand, there is a condition called **premenstrual syndrome (PMS),** which is extremely uncomfortable for about 10 percent of women (Helas, 1984). PMS usually occurs three to seven days prior to menstruation itself and causes anxiety, irritability, and mental confusion (Turkington, 1984). Most women do not have severe symptoms, but when they do occur, they are very unpleasant (although rarely leading to murder!). Medical treatment to reduce the severity of the symptoms is available (Muse, 1985).

As we discussed in Chapter 6, all of us are controlled by unseen forces, especially bodily rhythms. The female's monthly cycle is one of these. And as we mentioned earlier, males also follow a monthly cycle. Males have a monthly hormonal change that is not as major as the female one, but it does cause mild depression, lethargy, and moodiness about once every 28 to 30 days (Luce, 1971). When a husband and wife live together for a long time, their cycles tend to become synchronized—that is, they happen at the same time, which is not necessarily a blessing (Nicholson, 1984).

GENDER ROLE BEHAVIOR

Many of our ideas about sex role behavior come from society, and we start picking up these ideas at a very young age. For instance, the color blue is used for baby boys; this comes from an old superstition that evil spirits threatened boys in the nursery and that blue, borrowed from the "heavenly blue" of the sky, would ward off these spirits. Later, legend suggested that baby boys were often found under cabbages (which are often blue in Europe). Girls were supposedly born inside pink roses, so that is their color (Brasch, 1967).

Identification and Gender Role

Gender role behavior involves acts that reflect society's view of what is appropriate for males versus what is appropriate for females. A simple example is society's idea of who should play with dolls versus who should play with soldiers. Gender role behavior is thought to arise from **identification.** Identification is the process of modeling one's behavior after the behavior patterns of another person, usually of the same sex. Even though the mother tends to have more influence than the father on children of both sexes, a child will most often actually *imitate* the parent (or another adult) of the same sex (Green, 1974). But it is a little more complicated than that. Fathers who are very warm and affectionate toward their daughters tend to produce a *mild* tomboyishness in them (Sears et al., 1966). On the other hand, extreme

EXPERIMENT

Hand the top portion of **Teaching Master 13-5 Complete the Story** to half of your students and the bottom portion to the other half. Note that the top portion includes the name Jim, while the bottom portion uses the name Jane. Do *not* make students aware of this. Have students complete the directions on the master.

The purpose of the experiment is to see if students will write more positive endings to the *Jim* story than to the *Jane* one. See the **Discussion** that follows. (You may want to complete this experiment early in the chapter so students do not guess the hypothesis.)

Discussion

Collect students' responses to **Teaching Master 13-5 Complete the Story** and read them aloud in class. After each one, decide if the ending is basically positive, negative, or neutral, and keep a tally on the chalkboard. If the Jim stories are much more positive than the Jane stories, you might conclude that traditional gender-role expectations still influence many of your students. If so, discuss why. Do their parents still promote this? Does society? What if the situation were altered a bit, and Jim and Jane were just graduating from college with degrees in art or education? Would students' responses be different? If there are not any significant differences between the two stories, discuss why. Do students' parents or society promote *this?* In what ways?

Chapter 13 GENDER DIFFERENCES

▲ *Noisy gender role identification in action.*

DISCUSS THE PHOTO

Ask students, "Which gender role behaviors do you think you learned from your parents?"

strictness, severe control of the child, or unusual physical punishment tend to dispirit both male and female children. These children become docile, at least externally, and they submit to others (Block, 1973). This submissiveness can be deceptive, though, because a time may come when such a child will "explode."

Boys whose fathers were not present during preschool years—that is, up to the age of five—tend to be less aggressive and not quite as active in sports (Biller, 1970). This finding, even though it is only a statistic and does not apply to all males, deserves a little elaboration. The assumption that males should be football players and females powder puffs in order to be "normal" turns out to be just the opposite of what is actually the case. The most normal people in terms of mental health are those who lean slightly away from excessive masculinity or femininity. This is an important finding because many single mothers panic unnecessarily, afraid that something is going to go wrong with their fatherless children (Lebovitz, 1972). Most boys in such a position tend to find a role model outside the home very quickly and imitate some older male, perhaps a teacher or an uncle.

Critical Thinking

If gender role behaviors reflect society's views of what is appropriate for males versus for females, what messages do music videos send? Are these videos more powerful than commercials, since they are so graphic, slick, and emotional? Do they have any effect on gender roles?

Discussion

Part of our sexuality includes our knowledge and attitudes about sex. How do most people learn about sex and what it should mean? Do parents discuss it with their children? Should they? If so, at what age?

Discussion

Have students think of ways in which gender roles have loosened up a bit in the past 20 or 30 years. For example, high school boys rarely wore earrings in the past, but it's fairly common now. High school girls in the early 1960s usually didn't wear pants to school. After you list a few of these simple behaviors, you might ask how far we should go in loosening up the roles. Should a female be allowed to join a high school wrestling team? (You might be interested to know that males who have to wrestle a female will often forfeit the match, believing that it's a no-win situation for them.)

DEMONSTRATION

Try to get a current grade school reading book, and read several of the stories to your class. Do these readers promote traditional gender role behavior? If possible, also obtain a grade school reader used ten or 20 years ago, and compare and contrast this one with the current reader. If you can't obtain any readers, try comparing and contrasting *any* old and new children's books.

Unit 4 HUMAN DEVELOPMENT

Identification can be complicated. In families where either the mother or the father is unusually dominant, the children tend to identify with that dominant parent, even across sex lines. If there is no striking dominance, some daughters identify with the father, some sons with the mothers, and some identify with both. In addition, children can identify with brothers and sisters. Boys who have only brothers and girls who have only sisters tend to adopt more traditional gender roles than those in families with a mixture. And girls who grow up without an older brother are more competitive than those who have one (Stewart & Winter, 1974). (Remember in all this discussion that we are not trying to say that one kind of behavior is "better" than another; instead, we're just trying to demonstrate how complicated identification can be.)

Psychologically Generated Gender Roles

As far as we can tell, animals of all kinds are very aware of gender. Monkey mothers carefully examine their newborn babies' genitals and treat babies differently depending on the offspring's gender. For instance, they do not allow as much fighting and bickering among females (Money, 1980). Among humans, parents strongly encourage activities that are socially defined as appropriate for the child's gender, especially when the children are quite young. Fathers, though, are somewhat more determined about this than mothers are (Lytton & Romney, 1991). As mentioned, playthings for boys contrast noticeably with those for girls. There is no reason at all why boys would not want to play with doll furniture, since they usually spend considerable time with miniature soldiers and tanks. In fact, when families send their children to nontraditional nursery schools where fixed gender roles are not taught, the children do not show the usual tools-only-for-boys and teacups-only-for-girls interest (Secler & Hilton, 1972). So, we know that much of gender role behavior is the result of social training.

Research shows that adults will treat a baby differently depending on whether they think they are dealing with a boy or a girl. Even with a baby only a few months old, if adults are told it is a boy, they will have some kind of male toy ready and vice versa for a girl. In one study, subjects were introduced to a baby (who was actually a boy) and later asked to describe the infant's characteristics. Those who were told that the baby was a girl described him in "female" terms as being soft and smiling (Sidorowicz & Lunney, 1980).

Mixing Gender Roles   By strictly defining gender roles and emphasizing differences when they don't exist, we tend to restrict the full range of possibilities for both men and women. "Masculine"

DISCOVERY

If your class enjoys role-playing, assign female roles to males and vice versa. Print the following situations on index cards, and have students pick one as they volunteer: (1) A boy asks a girl for a first date. (2) Two girls talk about another girl whom they do not like. (3) Two boys talk about another boy whom they do not like. (4) A girl breaks off a relationship with a boy (and vice versa). (5) A girl calls home, pleading with her mom to let her stay out later. (6) A boy pleads with his dad to use the car. (Remember, the mom and dad are played by the opposite gender, too.)

Some of this role-playing may become exaggerated and downright silly, but it can lead to an interesting discussion of each gender's perception of the other. After each situation is played out, list on the board the perceptions portrayed by the role-players. Discuss why these perceptions exist and whether they're accurate.

---

men, for instance, have difficulty enjoying and showing affection toward babies, playing with small animals, or even listening to someone's personal problems. "Feminine" females often can't assert themselves or make independent judgments. Thus, it would seem that a mixture of so-called feminine and masculine behaviors makes for the richest life, and we restrict this potential when we stress gender differences (Bem, 1975).

It is difficult to describe what is strictly masculine or strictly feminine. In our culture, masculinity tends to be associated with dominance, assertiveness, achievement, and leadership, while femininity is associated with compassion, sociability, and tenderness.

The problem is that people who fall into the more extreme gender roles are more rigid and have fewer options open to them in different situations. Nothing says that people can't be in between. For this reason, psychologist Sandra Bem (1975) developed a concept she called **androgyny** (an-DRAH-ja-nee), a term that means that a person is relatively high in both masculine (*andro*) and feminine (*gyn*) characteristics. The ideal androgynous person would be both an achiever and a social creature, capable of expressing emotion *and* of taking action.

Bem found that androgynous people are in better psychological health than those with very strong gender identities. This makes sense when you think about it, because the broader the base of one's activities, the more varied and exciting life can be. There are serious pitfalls, though. A woman who adopts what society considers to be too many masculine characteristics is not going to fit in very well. Worse in society's view, however, is the man who adopts too many feminine traits—he's in for even more trouble. To complicate Bem's proposal, society values masculine traits more highly than feminine ones. According to society, then, both men and women are better off with masculine characteristics (Bernard, 1980).

Despite these problems, Bem's work is important because it focuses on the extremes that too many people adopt. Her basic idea about androgyny is useful because it leads the way to more flexibility and a greater willingness to share the characteristics of members of the opposite sex. Even changing one's view moderately and realizing that every boy doesn't have to play ball nor every girl play with dolls can make life more rewarding for both groups (Taylor & Hall, 1982).

Chapter 13 GENDER DIFFERENCES

▲ *A nursery school version of androgyny.*

androgyny

The quality of having both masculine and feminine characteristics.

DISCUSS THE PHOTO

In what ways is androgyny encouraged at this age? In what ways is it not encouraged?

Discussion

Is androgyny more difficult to achieve for males? Imagine a man adopting traditionally feminine traits and a woman adopting masculine traits. Who will encounter more difficulties?

Comprehension Check

What are some possible advantages of androgyny? (*Androgynous people are healthier psychologically than those with strong gender identities; they do not restrict their activities according to gender role expectations, making life more interesting and exciting.*)

ENRICHMENT

Teaching Master 13-6 Sex Roles asks students to interview women who were 16 between 1955 and 1965, a volatile time for gender roles.

DISCOVERY

Have students write their own "Psychology in Your Life" section. After all, each of them is an expert, in a sense. Maybe the focus could be "What the opposite sex doesn't know about us." Or maybe you should let students choose their own focus. Have a few volunteers read their selections to the rest of the class.

Teaching Hint
You can appreciate society's impact on gender roles by studying language. One can think of numerous labels for females who are promiscuous, but very few for males. Students may mention the male "player," but even that contains a reference to *play*—an innocent term that in this case is far from innocent. Many years ago, *lecher* was used, and it's still a good word. But the list does not go much further.

Critical Thinking
Have students speculate on why males are ruder and why females flock to the rest room together. Is there any way to test whether the conclusions are accurate?

Journal Topic
Have students address the questions listed here and then discuss their responses.

PSYCHOLOGY IN YOUR LIFE

Searching for Gender Differences

We want to look here at some differences in the behaviors of the sexes. As far as we know, there have been no formal psychological studies of any of them, but there do seem to be real differences—at least in the sense that society apparently encourages them. Observe them for yourself, and see if we aren't correct. You might want to try to figure out why they occur. We have our own ideas for each, but they're just guesses, so try your own.

Note the difference in how males and females talk to members of their own sex when they are close friends. Males are very rude and aggressive to those they like best ("Hi there, ugly!"). Apparently the ruder the men are to one another, the closer the relationship. Females don't usually express affection in this fashion.

Note that females will hug one another, put an arm around the other's shoulders, and touch one another's hands. Males, on the other hand, will hit the other in the shoulder with a fist, shove the other person, or, in

sports, pat one another on the posterior.

When a group goes out to a restaurant, note how females tend to get up and go to the restroom together. Men go the the restroom separately, usually not getting up en masse to exit as the females do.

The male readers may have balked at an earlier statement about females doing better in school than males do. Try this out: ask ten males and ten females their grade point averages. Take the numbers, add them up for each sex, divide by the number of people you asked, and you have the average. Note that the female grade point average is higher than the male one.

In the next paragraphs, we have constructed a "quiz" of sorts, which might be fun to try out the next time a group is together. You'll be surprised at the major differences in responses between the sexes, and we hope it helps you gain some insight into the opposite one. If you actually reach the point where you can explain the opposite sex, you will have

done something nobody has done before.

1. (a) Think about the pluses and minuses of being a male in America today; of being a female. In your opinion, do males or females have it better? Why?

(b) Imagine that you are a member of the opposite sex. How would you be better off? What would the problems be?

2. (a) If you were married, would you want your mate's income to be above, below, or equal to yours? (Think about it, and answer truthfully!) How important is this to you, and why? Ask yourself the same questions about intelligence and looks.

(b) Suppose you had to choose between your mate's having a job with more prestige and status than yours and your mate's having a job that pays more than yours. (It must be one or the other; it can't be both or neither one.) Which would you choose and why? Compare your answers with those of the opposite sex.

3. If you could decide your

(continued on next page)

VOCABULARY REVIEW

Before testing students on the contents of the chapter, you may want to review vocabulary terms that are especially important or confusing. Terms in this chapter that could require clarification are *gender role behavior, identification,* and *androgyny.*

Reteaching Strategy

Have students write a paragraph arguing for or against androgyny as a model for psychological health.

Wrapping It Up

As mentioned near the beginning of the chapter, the similarities between the sexes are greater than the differences. Just so students do not forget this, have them make a list of similarities: we experience the same emotions, needs, and motivations. Also, we develop in much the same way (Chapter 10). There are differences, of course, but whether those differences are due to biology or society is not as important as the respect we afford those differences. There's nothing wrong with being different; differences should not affect equality.

PSYCHOLOGY IN YOUR LIFE

Searching for Gender Differences

(continued from previous page) baby's sex, would you? If so, would you prefer a boy or a girl? Would your answer change if you already had a child of that sex? If you could decide what your baby would become as an adult, including talents, personality, and occupation, would you? If not, why not? If so, what would your decision be? Is there a difference between the kinds of answers given by males versus females to these questions?

4. (a) A millionaire will give you, absolutely free, a brand-new car of your choosing if you agree not to speak to any of your friends for a month. During that time, if you tell anyone why you are doing this, the deal is off. Would you accept the offer?

(b) The same millionaire will give you $25,000 if you agree not to take a bath or shower, not to change your clothes, and not to wash your hair or comb it for two

months, while keeping the reason secret. Would you accept this offer? (Do more males or females answer "yes" to either offer?)
5. If you had all the money you wanted to spend on entertainment, what would you plan for one 24-hour period for yourself and no more than three friends of the same sex? (No dates allowed, please.) How do males versus females differ in their answers?

SUMMARY

1. Hormones control the basics of physical gender development. Both sexes have both male and female hormones but, in each sex, one kind of hormone dominates over the other.
2. The major difference between males and females is the fact that females bear children. Another difference that shows up in humans and animals is that the male tends to be more aggressive more often and to have a higher activity level.
3. When taken together, studies show no clear-cut differences between the sexes in: intelligence, self-confidence, drive for success, or "maternal instincts." When such differences exist, they can be explained as coming from social training.
4. Males and females do communicate differently. They also differ somewhat in the characteristics they seek in a mate.
5. Menstrual cycles can cause emotional upset and physical distress, but normally these changes are at a reasonable level, not exaggerated as they have been by the press.
6. Identification can be quite complex, and a person can identify with a brother or sister as well as with either parent or another adult. But, in general, males identify with older males and females with older females—usually the parents, if they are available.
7. Androgyny seems to be a goal worth working for, but there is a risk of social disapproval if a person goes too far in mixing gender role behavior.

SUGGESTED READINGS

▼ Francoeur, Robert T. *Taking Sides: Clashing Views on Controversial Issues in Human Sexuality.* Guilford, NY: Dushkin, 1991.

▼ Tannen, Deborah. *That's Not What I Meant! How Conversational Style Makes or Breaks Your Relations with Others.* New York: Ballantine Books, 1986.

▼ Tannen, Deborah. *You Just Don't Understand: Women and Men in Conversation.* New York: Ballantine Books, 1990.

▼ Zunin, Leonard and Natalie Zunin. *Contact: The First Four Minutes.* New York: Ballantine Books, 1986.

VOCABULARY

gender
hormones
androgen
estrogen

spatial skills
menstrual cycles
premenstrual
  syndrome (PMS)

gender role behavior
identification
androgyny

Answers to Review Questions

1. d
2. a
3. d
4. a
5. a
6. true
7. false
8. false
9. true
10. false
11. false
12. false
13. true
14. true
15. b
16. d
17. M
18. F
19. M
20. M
21. F

Review Questions

Multiple Choice

1. Injecting an animal with androgen would probably increase
   a. breast size.   c. moodiness.
   b. brain size.   d. aggressiveness.
2. The female hormone is called
   a. estrogen. b. androgen. c. androgyny.
3. Which of the following characteristics apply to females?
   a. greater endurance
   b. live longer than men
   c. fewer genetic defects
   d. all of the above
4. Evidence indicates that males are naturally
   a. more physical than females.
   b. less physical than females.
   c. equally as physical as females.
5. Which gender *performs* better on tests of spatial skills?
   a. males b. females c. neither

True/False

6. The brains of males are different from the brains of females.

7. Evidence indicates that males are naturally better than females at math.

8. Surveys consistently show that males have higher self-confidence than females.
9. Females are as oriented toward achievement as males are.
10. Studying animal behavior helps us realize that the maternal "instinct" is present only in females.
11. Premenstrual syndrome afflicts a majority of women.

Multiple Choice

15. Androgynous people on the average are
    a. less healthy than people with strong gender identities.
    b. more healthy than people with strong gender identities.
    c. just as healthy as people with strong gender identities.

12. Males experience their own hormonal cycles that start and end every three months.
13. Overly strict parents will tend to dispirit their children.
14. Children tend to identify with the dominant parent.

16. Which of the following reasons might discourage a person from becoming androgynous?
    a. Society values masculine traits over feminine traits—so why be feminine?
    b. Women who are masculine may not be accepted by society.
    c. Men who are feminine may not be accepted by society.
    d. all of the above

For each of the following, answer M for males and F for females, as it applies to communication skills.

17. Interrupt conversations more often
18. Self-disclose more often
19. Concerned about improving status

20. Sit beside each other rather than face-to-face
21. More likely to empathize than to try to solve another's problem

DISCUSSION QUESTIONS

1. If you were a parent, would you ever consider buying your daughter a toy truck or football? Why or why not?
2. If you were a parent, would you ever consider buying your son a doll or a toy kitchen set? Why or why not?
3. If you took a survey, you'd probably find that despite a leveling of gender role differences today, males still are primarily responsible for asking females out for a first date. In your opinion, why do a majority of females usually refrain from initiating dates? Explain.
4. Many people advocate passage of an Equal Rights Amendment (ERA) that would ban sex discrimination. Others argue that laws already exist to stop this discrimination. Furthermore, passage of the ERA would mean that women could be drafted in the event of a war. Do you think that the ERA should still be passed? Why or why not?

Notes on Discussion Questions

1 and 2. Consider reading students' responses aloud in class. Are there any patterns that develop? Is one sex more flexible or more open-minded than the other? If so, in what way does society promote this flexibility or inflexibility?

3. After students answer this question, ask the males in class why *they* often refrain from asking girls for dates. Compare and contrast these responses to the responses to the discussion question. You'll probably find some striking similarities. For example, both males and females will certainly admit their fears of rejection. The main difference then will be society's expectations of what each sex should do.

4. In the event of a war, it's clear that women will see combat. How do students feel about this?

5. Students may understand this question a little better after a few role-plays in class.

6. Mention that there's nothing wrong with a little sarcasm here to make a point.

7. Compare and contrast male responses to female responses. Is one sex more willing to admit its androgyny?

8. These responses can be hilarious. Consider requiring students to write at least a page on this question, and then read the papers aloud in class.

Notes on Activities

1 and 2. Students should have fun with these activities. The chances are slim, but if you have a student named Roanoke in your school, make up a different name.

3. Since students won't be able to rip out the ads from old magazines found in the library (and warn them

not to), have them briefly describe the ads that they use. If you think it's necessary, you may even have them include a rough sketch of some of the more important ads that they use.

4. Some students do an excellent job with this activity. Again, warn them not to rip out the ads from the magazines found in the library.

---

5. Which of the characteristics of male and female communication styles apply to you? For example, if you are a male and a friend tells you about a problem, do you attempt to solve the problem? If you are a female, do you tend to empathize? Provide examples to support your answer.

6. If it's true that females and males communicate differently, maybe we can all use some advice from the opposite sex. What

advice about communication would you offer to the opposite sex?

7. All of us are androgynous to some extent. Describe several of your own characteristics that reveal your androgyny. In other words, describe some of your "masculine" traits and some of your "feminine" traits.

8. This part of the question is for the males: describe the advantages of being a female. This part is for the females: describe the advantages of being a male.

ACTIVITIES

1. Neatly print the following information onto two index cards:

    "The reason I want to be an engineer is because I've always done well in math and I enjoy it. For example, in third grade, I won first place in a math test in the area, and ever since, I've always been excited about math classes. I know that my other grades are just average, but I've always gotten an A or B in math."

    At the top of one of the cards, print "Georgia Roanoke"; at the top of the other, print "George Roanoke." Take another index card and print the following information onto it:

    How would you rate the chances of this person succeeding in a career in engineering?

0	1	2	3	4	5	6	7	8
DIS-MAL	VERY POOR	POOR	BELOW AVER-AGE	AVER-AGE	ABOVE AVER-AGE	HIGH	VERY HIGH	OUT-STAND-ING

    Are you beginning to get the idea? Find 32 high-school subjects, 16 males and 16 females. Eight of the males and eight of the females will see the "Georgia" card; the other eight males and eight females will see the

"George" card. Record their ratings onto some kind of data sheet.

In order to get accurate and honest ratings, you must make sure that your subjects don't find out the purpose of the experiment—which is to see if the male, with his supposedly "superior" math skills, will be rated higher, despite *identical* qualifications. To make sure your subjects don't know your purpose, you might say something like this: "In English class, we're learning about how to write résumés and how to fill out job applications. We all had to write a paragraph, exchange the paragraph with someone in class, and then that person goes around and collects ratings. We thought the ratings would be more accurate if we exchanged paragraphs rather than collecting our own ratings. So be completely honest."

Analyze your results. What was the overall average rating for Georgia? For George? What was the female average rating for both cards? What was the male average rating for both cards?

Draw a simple chart and list all these ratings. Discuss your results. Did our

5. To prepare students for this activity, discuss the questions listed in **Psychology in Your Life** at the end of the chapter. The nature of the questions should provoke lively responses. As you listen to these responses, run to the chalkboard every once in a while to write down several of them. Afterward, analyze the responses on the board: are they sexist and traditional? If you have time, you might also want to brainstorm in order to come up with the interview questions needed for the activity.

hypothesis seem to be supported by your findings: is there a sex bias against females involved in math? Were you surprised by your results? Why or why not?

2. This next activity is a variation on the previous one. Follow the same procedure, except this time you'll use middle-aged adults as your subjects to see if people with more traditional backgrounds will, in fact, be "traditional" with their ratings. Discuss your results in detail. (Try to choose subjects whom you consider to have "traditional" backgrounds.)

If you're conducting this experiment *and* the previous one, compare and contrast the results—*or* maybe you can conduct one activity while a friend conducts the other, and then you can compare and contrast each other's results.

3. Most libraries save back issues of the most popular magazines for years and years. Sift through them to find several magazine ads from 1955, 1965, 1975, 1985, and the present. As you look through these ads, jot down information about the ones that seem to promote traditional gender role behavior and the ones that seem to defy traditional gender role behavior.

Organize your notes into a report. Which products and brand names are most commonly linked to gender roles? How has the nature of the ads changed from 1955 to the present? Do you notice any patterns? Be specific. Finally, are ads today still sexist? Explain.

4. Follow the same directions as in activity number 3, but instead of doing a written report, hand in a visual report. For example, you might take several poster boards and create charts to *show* how ads have changed. Include headings and captions. You might want to put together a magazine of ads, including some from the past up to the present. You can include your own explanatory captions for the ads. Or if you're ambitious, you might even put together a slide show (or videotape) with appropriate music and narration.

5. Take another look at the "Gender Quiz" at the beginning of the chapter (see In Focus). As you found out while reading the chapter, all but question number 1 are gender myths. Show the quiz to eight males and eight females and record their answers. Then go back to the person who got the highest score and the one who got the lowest score, and interview these two people. If there is a tie for highest or lowest, randomly pick one of the people who tied. For your interview, you can use the questions listed in "Psychology in Your Life" at the end of the chapter, or you can write your own—as long as both people are asked identical questions.

This will be your hypothesis: the person who scored lowest on the quiz probably has less knowledge about gender differences and similarities than the person who scored highest. The person who scored lowest then would also tend to exhibit more traditional attitudes about sex roles—simply because this person doesn't know any better. In other words, you're testing whether ignorance breeds sexist attitudes.

Analyze and compare the two interviews in detail to determine if this hypothesis seems to be true. The most difficult part of this analysis is trying to decide objectively whether the answers are, in fact, traditional and sexist—or not so traditional. You'll have to use your judgment. Just make sure you can support your judgment in some way. Also, try to be fair. The answers to questions numbers 1, 2, and 3 in the "Psychology in Your Life" quiz will probably be the most revealing.

Dealing with Stress

The text defines stress as the physical pressure and strain that results from the demands of the environment. It also states that conflict, anxiety, and frustration lead to stress. People have to cope with both the positive and negative changes in their lives, since both types cause stress. Psychologists study how people respond to stress emotionally, physically, and behaviorally. When people react emotionally, they can become angry, anxious, irritable, and bitter. Physically, pulse rate increases, hands become sweaty, and eyes dilate. Behaviorally, people may appear restless as they bite their nails, tap their fingers, grind their teeth, or play with money in their pockets. Most disturbingly, they may start drinking more alcohol or displaying superstitious behaviors.

Three categories have been developed to describe stress-coping tendencies (Carver, 1989; Folkman and Lazarus, 1988). The first refers to individuals using **problem-focused** plans. These people attempt working out a way to either accept or change a situation so that it is no longer stressful. Proactive strategies such as strategic planning, problem-solving, restraint, and confrontation may be used. For example, if a person is accused of spreading rumors about one of the students in your class, what might you do? You could try talking to the person allegedly spreading the rumors. You may entertain a number of different ideas about how and why the rumors started before formulating a plan to put an end to the situation. You might try not to react to the rumors in front of your students. All of these instances revolve around the notion that addressing the situation, and changing it if possible, is the way to eradicate the stress it engenders.

Some people, however, employ **emotion-based** plans in the face of stress. In other words, they might try to change the emotional content of a situation in order to lessen its intensity. An example of this is relabeling your feeling of unrequited love for someone as dislike, in order to avoid the unpleasantness of low self-esteem. Other people may use repression or selective forgetting to deny that a problem even exists. Let's say you have an appointment with the dentist to have your wisdom teeth extracted. You have heard horror stories about this procedure from your friends, and are consequently fearful and anxious about it. Then you "forget" about the appointment and fail to show up at the dentist's office. Another tactic may be to tell yourself that the dentist is not qualified and made an incorrect diagnosis, or you may convince yourself that your teeth are fine and that the dentist is just trying to make a few extra dollars.

The third coping condition involves the **social support of others.** When people are under a great deal of stress they

For people as in nature, from conflict and turmoil often come growth and greater understanding.

386

Discuss the Photo

Ask students to think of other parallels between nature and personality.

may seek the company and advice of others who have been in similar predicaments. Support groups can provide assistance and emotional support, and some even offer legal help and psychological counseling for their members.

In a study of over 400 adults, researchers found that stable adjustment to stressful situations is enhanced when one uses problem-based strategies (Holahan and Moos, 1990). They also found that emotion-based plans, such as denial, lead to poorer adjustment and

PERSONALITY, ADJUSTMENT, AND CONFLICT

387

Overview
For this project, study groups will be assigned one of the four chapters of this unit. They will design a bulletin board using pictures, editorials, short articles, cartoons, tables, graphs, charts, and posters. Student-constructed materials are encouraged. These materials will be accompanied by a short paragraph explaining the material's relationship to the unit. Projects are to be displayed in the classroom, hallway, or in portfolios. Complete instructions for this activity and the supporting student worksheets can be found in the Teacher Resources.

depression. Generally, the results showed that men tend to use more problem-solving plans than women, while women are more likely to use emotion-based plans and support groups. This is not surprising, as it reflects traditional, socially-enforced gender-role traits, which are discussed at greater length in Chapter 13.

Other psychologists have identified still more stress-reducing strategies. One of these involves using physiological coping techniques such as progressive relaxation, exercise, and meditation. Another method is behavioral coping; for example, using a calender and schedule to utilize time more efficiently.

Cognitive restructuring (Meichenbaum, 1977) is another way to deal with stress, and requires rethinking and monitoring what you say to yourself. Most of us tend to believe that situations are worse than they actually are; Meichenbaum (1985) has outlined cogni-

tive strategies that can enable people to avoid doing that. For example, a self-statement than can help when confronting a stressor is "Don't think about stress, just about what I have to do."

References
Full citations can be found in the Teacher Resources.

DISCUSS THE PHOTO

Ask students if they believe that their personalities are consistent from one situation to the next.

People are seldom exactly what they appear to be.

388

PSYCHOLOGY AND YOU RESOURCES

A variety of resources are available in the Psychology and You *supplementary material. In addition, there are a number of additional resources listed to enhance your lesson plans.*

Masters
▼ 14-1A Learning Goals
▼ 14-1B Answers to Learning Goals
▼ 14-2 Personality Survey
▼ 14-3 Biography

Student Worksheets
▼ Vocabulary Worksheet
▼ Independent Practice Worksheet
▼ Enrichment Worksheet
▼ Reteaching Worksheet

Test Bank
▼ Tests A and B

Multimedia
▼ Psychology Videodisc

Student Workbook

PACING CHART

Complete Coverage

Day 1: Assign the first two sections of the chapter before class. Define personality. Focus discussion on psychoanalysis, covering its major components. Discuss the idea of becoming fixated at one of Freud's five various stages of personality development. Assign for homework an activity exploring the concept of the unconscious.

Day 2: Focus on archetypes and the collective unconscious. Use the results of students' homework to assess the ideas of Freud and Jung. Assign "Social Psychoanalytic Theories" for Day 3.

Day 3: Review how the neo-Freudians' emphasis on social factors changes psychoanalytic theory. Provide an activity requiring students to identify Erikson's eight stages of personality development. Have students read "Behaviorism" for homework.

Day 4: After outlining the importance of reinforcement in the behaviorist approach to personality theory, concentrate on Bandura's emphasis of observation and modeling. Assign the last two sections for Day 5.

14

Theories of Personality

OBJECTIVES

Be able to:

▼ Explain psychoanalytic theory and the unconscious.

▼ Describe how introducing social factors changed the basic psychoanalytic theory.

▼ Describe the two approaches to behaviorism discussed.

▼ Explain the humanistic philosophy.

▼ Describe the role of heredity and environment in personality traits.

Global Look at the Chapter

Personality is a term referring to long-lasting patterns of behavior. This chapter discusses different theories, each one of which views human beings as motivated by different forces. Some suggest we are the product of unconscious forces, some that we are what we learn, and some that we inherit our personalities.

389

INTRODUCING THE CHAPTER

Make the distinction between mood and personality. Moods come and go. Personality is more enduring and consistent. When we say someone has a good personality, what we really mean is that the person is likable. Some of the person's enduring personality traits may contribute to this "good personality," but the two uses of the word *personality* are not the same.

LEAD-OFF ACTIVITY

Hand out **Teaching Master 14-2 Personality Survey** which asks students to mark their level of agreement regarding statements about personality. (The second page of this master explains which psychologist would strongly agree with each statement.) Throughout the unit, as you discuss each psychologist, students can refer back to this activity and say, "Oh, yeah, I agreed with that. . . ." In other words, this activity will serve to *personalize* the theories of personality.

Day 5: Discuss the evidence for both hereditary and environmental influences on personality traits before giving the Chapter Review quiz.

In Brief

Day 1: Review the definition of personality. Focus on Freud's theory of psychoanalysis, emphasizing the key terms. Outline Freud's five stages of personality development.

Day 2: Discuss archetypes and the collective unconscious. Move on to outline the theories of the neo-Freudians, focusing on Erikson's eight stages of personality development.

Day 3: Concentrate on the behaviorist approach to personality. Focus on Bandura's theory about observation and modeling.

Day 4: After reviewing humanist personality theories, discuss the role of heredity and environment on personality traits. Give the Chapter Review quiz.

INTERDISCIPLINARY PROJECT

Art. Have students sketch some of the great thinkers in psychology presented in this chapter, and post the sketches around the room. They could write concise summaries of the approach used by each thinker to be posted under each sketch.

ENRICHMENT

The mistakes we make when speaking are often called *Freudian slips*. We say one thing, but we really mean something else, which slips out. For example, a student wrote this note to a teacher: "Here's the artwork you wanted. Try to *contract* me." He meant to write "contact," but he apparently wanted to know if the teacher was going to pay him. Have students find out if current research supports Freud's claims that slips reveal the unconscious.

TEACHING MASTER 14-1A

Learning Goals. A Learning Goals sheet for each chapter is provided in the Teacher Resources. These Learning Goals can be used as review sheets or worksheets. **Teaching Master 14-1B** consists of answers to these Learning Goals.

Points to Stress

Some theories are useful because they inspire other theories. For example, Horney and Adler (described at the end of the chapter) place great importance on love and feeling worthwhile. Maslow's hierarchy of needs includes both these concepts.

Connections

Psychologists view personality as a construct (Chapter 6). We know it exists, but it can't be seen or touched.

Unit 5 PERSONALITY, ADJUSTMENT, AND CONFLICT

DIFFICULTIES IN UNDERSTANDING PERSONALITY

In this chapter we try to get a handle on personality. And what a difficult task that is. People aren't always what they seem. For instance, many professional comedians are very quiet at home, and some of the better ones suffer from serious bouts of depression. Classmates and teachers often misunderstand what you are really like and what you really feel. They may think you are aggressive when you are really shy; they may think you are outgoing when in fact you look forward to being alone. They may see you as a loner when you actually need company. And as if this isn't complicated enough, we all assume different personalities at different times. When we are eating alone at home, our manners may be disgusting; when we are out for dinner, no one would suspect how sloppy we can be.

You can see, then, that trying to pin down personality is a rough task. And we won't succeed completely. Still, it is worthwhile going over some of the theories about how our personalities develop. These theories attempt to bring together in an organized, coherent way a set of beliefs about how we become who we are.

The Usefulness of Theories

What is the purpose of having theories? There are a couple of answers to this. First, part of a theory may turn out to be correct. Thus, eventually we might be able to explain how we got the way we are by combining the most workable parts of a number of theories. Second, theories give us a framework in which to study people; then we can either accept or reject the claims of the theory based on what studies show to be the case. For instance, at one point it was said that those who abuse and beat their children had parents who beat *them* when they were children. As it turns out, in reality this may or may not be the case. But the hypothesis was useful because it gave us something to study, to either accept or reject. While abusive parents may themselves have been abused, this is not the only or even the major cause, so we have to look elsewhere to explain it.

Defining Personality

Some people are cheats and liars on one day and super-religious on the next. But most of us most of the time respond roughly the

DEMONSTRATION

Bring in two or three library books that include photographs of Freud and his family and show them to your students. If the books include synopses of his case studies, you may want to recount briefly several of these. Another way to bring Freud to life is more dramatic. Get a pair of costume glasses and a cigar and *become* Freud for 20 or 25 minutes. Announce one day that you have invited a guest speaker to class, leave, then return as Freud: "My name is Sigmund Freud. I was born in 1856, and unfortunately, I died in 1939. . ." This role-playing requires a good deal of preparation, but most students appreciate the extra effort. After your presentation, encourage students to ask questions. Stay in character, of course.

---

same way in many situations. In fact, this is the definition of "personality." **Personality** consists of broad and long-lasting patterns of behavior. These patterns are fairly consistent from one day to the next. Thus, the odds are that a person who is afraid of canoe trips, hiking, swimming, and heights will also be afraid of a roller coaster. On the other hand, those who constantly take chances, drive like fools, and will bet on anything will ride a roller coaster that has all the support bolts loosened. Once we assume that some aspects of personality are fairly stable, we can look at theories that try to explain their origin.

PSYCHOANALYSIS

Psychoanalysis is a personality theory based on the assumption that how we develop and behave is the result of impulses or needs that are unknown to us. In other words, what we are comes from hidden forces. The theory arose from a belief that people with psychological problems were unable to see the origin of their difficulties. To view these forces requires a trained professional who will *analyze* one's thoughts, feelings, and history to reveal what is going on beneath the surface. That's how we got the term psycho*analysis*.

Sigmund Freud

The most famous psychoanalyst was **Sigmund Freud** (FROID) (1856–1939). His theory of how we develop and what controls us dominated psychology from the early 1900s through the late 1940s. Freud believed that the core of one's personality appeared within the first five or six years of life and was more or less fixed by that age. For him, individual development had its source in the family and the conflicts that every family has. Our feelings about ourselves come from jealousies, anxieties, and guilt regarding how we relate to other family members and how they view us.

This emphasis is not hard to understand since Freud's own family life was chaotic. His father was 20 years older than his mother, had a couple of children by a previous marriage, and he had a mistress as well. Freud's mother then had eight children. At one point, there were the eight children, a half-brother the age of Freud's mother, the father, and a nephew all living in the same cramped 30-foot-by-30-foot room (Clark, 1980). It makes sense that the family friction and unwanted intimacy this brought about would lead to many of Freud's beliefs.

Freud studied to become a physician and for a while actually practiced medicine in the traditional sense. But two things changed the course of his life: (1) as he listened to patients, he became more and

---

Chapter 14 THEORIES OF PERSONALITY

personality

A person's broad, long-lasting patterns of behavior.

psychoanalysis

A theory that personality is based on impulses and needs in the unconscious.

▲ *Sigmund Freud, the founder of psychoanalysis.*

Comprehension Check

Why is understanding personality difficult? *(People act differently in various situations; people's true feelings can be misunderstood by others.)*

Points to Stress

The word *psyche* (SIGH-key), refers to our thoughts and feelings. Psycho*analysis is* the process of analyzing the psyche.

DISCUSS THE PHOTO

Some of the observations Freud used to develop his theory of psychoanalysis came from his personal experience. He conducted an extensive self-analysis based on his own dreams.

EXPERIMENT

To demonstrate the possible existence of the unconscious, break the class up into groups of three, and have each group choose one theme—for example, "The time I was in the hospital," or "My most embarrassing moment," and so on. Two members from each group will recount real experiences on the group's theme; the third member will tell a lie, from beginning to end. Each story should last about a minute. Allow students very little time to prepare (four to five minutes). Then have each group come to the front to present its stories. The point is that the liar cannot successfully lie; the unconscious will slip out. Test how true this is by having the class vote on who's the liar after each group presentation. Here's a variation on the experi-

Points to Stress

When students learn about Freud's theory, they sometimes dismiss it as ancient and thus never attempt to understand it. To help students appreciate Freud's ideas, you might want to provide them with a vivid picture of Freud's background; if students can view Freud as a person and not just as the owner of a theory, they may become more interested in his ideas.

FYI Freud didn't publish his first book, *The Interpretation of Dreams* (1900), until he was in his mid-40s!

Connections

Are people who suffer from hysteria faking it? Absolutely not. People show actual physical symptoms, yet there's nothing wrong with them. The term used today to describe hysteria is *somatoform disorder* (Chapter 18).

392

unconscious

According to psychoanalytic belief, the psychological part of us that contains childhood conflicts we are unaware of but that continue to control our behavior.

free association

Freudian process in which the person says everything that appears in the mind, even if the ideas or images seem unconnected.

392

more convinced that the problems they were having were coming from psychological forces rather than physical ones, and (2) he couldn't stand the sight of blood. At one point, Freud tried to treat his patients by giving them cocaine. Eventually he became addicted himself and just about ruined a very meaningful career before overcoming the problem (Reisman, 1966).

One of Freud's early patients was a woman who couldn't drink water but who stayed alive by eating only fruit such as melons. This clearly wasn't a "normal" sickness, and Freud couldn't make sense of it at first. A physician friend of Freud's told him that he had been successful in using hypnosis with patients with strange symptoms in order to find out what was going on. So, Freud thought he would try it. Under hypnosis, the woman recalled that when she was a child, she one day found a hated servant's dog drinking out of a water glass in the kitchen. Thus, it seemed that hypnosis helped Freud get to parts of the patient's mind that were unknown to her normally (Freud, 1938). Another colleague of Freud's had a truly bizarre case: he was treating a female patient for dizziness, fainting, and coughing spells. Before long, the woman had what is called an "hysterical pregnancy." The word *hysteria* refers to physical symptoms that come from a psychological problem. In hysterical pregnancy, the patient has all the symptoms, pains, and even a major swelling of the abdomen (from body water) that goes on for nine months, so you expect a baby when it is all over. But there is no baby in there (Schultz, 1969). A few such cases still occur every year, even on occasion to males.

You can see how Freud began to believe that we are guided by impulses and needs that don't show up on the surface. From this belief arose his famous concept, the unconscious.

The Unconscious

Freud believed that childhood conflicts within the family are removed from conscious memory but are still "in us." These events are held in the **unconscious,** the part of us we are not aware of. Our true feelings sometimes appear in dreams or in mistakes we make when speaking. Freud claimed that if he talked to a patient long enough, he found some of the material that was causing the trouble buried below the surface. So, he gave up hypnosis as not needed and used his "talking cure." Freud reached the unconscious by using **free association,** a process in which the patient says *everything* that appears in the mind, even if seemingly not connected. In other words, no "censoring" is allowed. The basis for this method of treatment was Freud's assumption that the unconscious always seeks expression in one way or another. If the patient talked long enough, more and more of the unconscious would appear in what was being

ment. Rather than simply voting on who's the liar, ask students to think of a more systematic way to pick the liar. For example, you can count the number of pauses or the number of fillers, like "you know"; you can note eye movements, abrupt gestures,

and so on. Send the "best" three liars out of the room to think of new stories while the class devises its system, and then test the system on the liars. (As before, only one student lies.)

Another way in which the unconscious theoretically reveals itself is through body language and handwriting. Though many regard these topics as pop psychology, students are highly interested in them. Have a few interested students research these topics.

said. The analyst could then put it all together into a coherent picture and thus explain problem-causing behavior. For example, if you have a deep-seated anger toward a friend, the more you talk about this person the more likely it is that some unconscious material about what caused the anger will appear.

Freud was quite taken by the theory and writings of Charles Darwin. Darwin's work suggested that the human was basically an animal, even though we have higher mental abilities as well as the ability to make moral decisions. As a result, Freud focused on our behavior as mostly animal-like. In other words, he focused on our very strong drives to satisfy bodily needs—food, comfort, sex, self-preservation. Since all human societies in one way or another try to block expression of too much animal-like behavior, we can't always satisfy these needs—or even admit we have them. Since they won't go away, we try to hide from them by putting them into our unconscious. If everything we wanted to do was good, there would be no problem. But all of us have desires that we would just as soon no one else know about, so we make them "disappear." This disappearance is called **repression**. According to Freud's theory, from childhood on, needs and desires that are forbidden cause guilt. As a result, they are pushed out of consciousness (repressed) into the unconscious where they live. They do not remain quiet, however, but reappear as conflicts and anxieties that interfere with daily life and normal functioning.

The Libido

Freud's theory emphasizes an interaction between conscious and unconscious forces. Because Freud developed his theory during a time of great scientific discovery in the fields of chemistry and physics about electricity, magnetism, and energy forces, he absorbed some of these ideas and assumed that the human had *real* (biological, not symbolic) energy inside, which controlled behavior. This energy he called **libido** (luh-BEE-doe). The libidinal energy constantly seeks some kind of discharge, just as lightning does when it finds a high tree and discharges into the ground. In the process of seeking discharge, this energy creates tension. If this tension is not released in real life, the desires appear as dreams or fantasies. An attempt at release can also appear as psychological disturbance.

Freud's Map of the Mind

Freud divided the individual's inner world into three parts. One is responsible for survival needs, another for society's rules of behavior. The third part deals with the real world and tries to keep the demands of the other two in balance.

repression

The process of pushing the needs and desires that cause guilt into the unconscious.

libido

Freudian term for internal energy forces that continuously seek discharge.

Points to Stress

Freud certainly did not discover the unconscious, but he was the first to attempt to study it scientifically. As a result of his extensive efforts, we now take for granted the idea of the unconscious.

Connections

If we use repression well enough, we may even forget our identity. In that case, we will be suffering from amnesia. Or we may develop new personalities to block out dangerous memories (Chapter 18).

DISCOVERY

Ask three students to role-play the id, ego, and superego. Have them play out a situation that involves conflict: "I want to eat that chocolate cake, but I'd better not; I want to ask him out, but I'd better not; I want to yell at her, but I'd better not." Remind them that the three-part dialogue theoretically occurs in one's mind. Afterward, point out the accuracy or inaccuracy of some of the lines used during the role-playing.

DISCOVERY

Pass out crayons and have students draw their versions of the id, ego, and superego. This will only take five or ten minutes, and students may think of fitting images.

Points to Stress

The ego's job is to follow what Freud called the reality principle. This means that the ego tries to satisfy id impulses, but is realistic about it. The ego may delay satisfying the id, or may find alternative behaviors. If the id says, "I want to eat—I want to eat NOW," the ego says, "Well, it *is* the middle of class; you will probably get in trouble. Let's wait." The superego, on the other hand, tries to *stop* the id, primarily through guilt: "How could you even *think* about eating at a time like this? What would your mother and father say?"

Points to Stress

Freud believed that once our repressed conflicts surface and we face them, whatever physical or psychological symptoms we have will eventually disappear. The movie, *Ordinary People*, illustrates this quite well, as does the last episode of "M.A.S.H."

DISCUSS THE PHOTO

In what ways do the ego and superego keep this behavior in check?

394

Unit 5 PERSONALITY, ADJUSTMENT, AND CONFLICT

id
Freudian psychological unit containing our basic needs and drives.

superego
Freudian psychological unit roughly synonymous with the conscience.

ego
The "self" that allows controlled id expression within the boundaries of the superego.

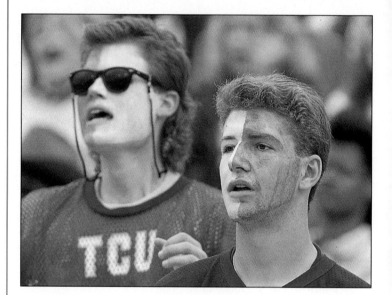

▲ *Freud might say this somewhat primitive masquerade is merely an expression of the id.*

Id All of our basic needs and drives make up the **id.** Therefore, it contains our major energy force (libido), which is constantly seeking expression. We cannot know, directly, what goes on in the id because it is unconscious. It is also completely unconcerned about any reality except its own desires. Because of its emphasis on sexual and aggressive impulses, the id can cause many psychological problems. Without it, however, we would not eat when hungry or defend ourselves if attacked. Without it, we could not survive.

Superego Although the id is necessary, if we acted out any impulse we had at any time, society would fall apart. To hold the id in check, we each have, according to Freud, a **superego,** a term that is an approximate synonym for conscience. The superego causes guilt for being bad and pride for doing the right things. It develops out of the punishments and rewards we get from our parents, the first representatives of society's laws and customs. We need a superego, but like the id, it exists only for what it wants. If allowed to operate unchecked, it would block all our drives and instincts, letting us die rather than break a rule.

Ego The third portion of the individual is called the **ego.** The ego is roughly the same as the *self*. The job of the ego is really to allow the id to express itself in some safety. In other words, the ego pays attention to reality and monitors what is going on in the environment as

DEMONSTRATION

Go around the room and find students with a pencil, gum, or a finger in their mouth, and jokingly point out that these are examples of *oral fixation*. Fixation refers to being *stuck* in one of the psychosexual stages. For example, Freud smoked cigars, despite developing cancer of the mouth, and claimed that he was orally fixated. Someone whose parents were overzealous during toilet-training will probably become fixated at the anal stage. This person may later become obsessed with neatness. Someone who fears authority is probably fixated at the phallic stage because he or she never identified with the same-sex parent and continues to fear that parent.

well as listening to what the superego has to say. If the id wants to steal wallets at a police station, the ego will listen to the superego and examine reality, saying, "That's not a very clever idea." So the ego acts as a controller attempting to balance our desires with the demands of reality.

Our personalities show how good a balancing act we have developed. For instance, if the id takes over because the superego is not strong enough, we will develop personalities that are more and more demanding of animal needs. If the ego loses its ability to strike a balance, we become pouty, whining individuals who are never satisfied. On the other hand, if the superego dominates as the result of endless control of our every desire, we become guilt-ridden, shy, fearful, and withdrawn.

Stages of Development

Freud's five stages of personality development go from birth through adolescence. As mentioned earlier, Freud believed that personality is basically formed by age five or six. Consequently, all the major conflicts and psychological tasks we must deal with take place in the first three of his stages. The two later stages are necessary for completeness, but neither one presents any important new crises or demands.

According to Freud, adults' psychological problems have their roots in early childhood and can be traced to unresolved conflicts during that time. When a conflict is not adequately resolved, some libidinal energy gets stuck, or *fixated*, at that stage. Such energy fixations create psychological trouble eventually. In fact, many behaviors that indicate trouble in one of Freud's first three stages appear later on in life, not in childhood. Examples of this include such problems as alcoholism, eating disorders, and severe depression. We give more examples of these behaviors in each of the following paragraphs.

Oral Stage: Birth to Age One-and-a-Half   In the **oral stage** of development, feeding is the main source of infants' pleasure, and weaning is the task to be dealt with. When a child is weaned too early or too late, personality problems develop. Examples of oral-stage behaviors are too much dependency on other people, rejection of others or being very sarcastic, and either overeating or self-starvation.

Anal Stage: Ages One-and-a-Half to Two-and-a-Half   The psychological task during the **anal stage is** toilet training. Toilet training that is either too lenient or too harsh will cause psychological problems. Anal-stage behaviors include such things as being excessively stingy or overly generous as well as sticking very rigidly to rules and regulations or being irresponsible and rebellious.

oral stage

Freudian stage of development during which feeding and weaning are the child's main issues.

anal stage

Freudian stage of development during which toilet training is the child's major concern.

395

Critical Thinking

Ask students to hypothesize what would happen to a person who has a very weak or very strong superego. Students might reply that with a weak superego there's no force stopping the id, so the person will tend to be very self-centered, always trying to satisfy his or her own needs. With a strong superego the person will be driven by guilt. Just thinking "bad" thoughts will create guilt, even though the person rarely follows through on the thoughts.

Discussion

The id and superego are both irrational, to the point that a person can become self-destructive if the id and superego are not controlled by the rational ego. Ask students to think of examples: We overeat because the id *wants* and because the superego says we don't deserve to be skinny. We stay up late, drive too fast, and so on.

DEMONSTRATION

The two main drives of the id are sex and aggression. (Remember, Freud wanted his theory to encompass all of human nature. We are sexual so we can ensure the existence of future generations. We are aggressive so we can fight off other aggressors and ensure our present existence.) Challenge students to think of behaviors that are *not* motivated by these two drives. To address their responses, you will need to refer to sublimation in Chapter 17. When we hit a baseball, we have channeled our aggression into the swing. We channel our sexual energy into activities that we enjoy, like reading a book or painting a picture. Here's another way to say that we are motivated by sex and aggression: the two most important things in people's lives are *love* and *work*. Students may be more willing to accept the idea when it's put this way.

Critical Thinking

Ask students to think of examples of the Oedipal complex. They might suggest one of the *Star Wars* movies, in which Luke tries to kill Darth Vader, who in turn tries to convince him that he is his father. (This is only partially depicted since the mother/son relationship is not present.) Read the newspaper, and you'll find several examples.

Teaching Hint

Another reason why Jung split with Freud is that Jung did not believe that humans were doomed to be neurotic (anxious and rigid). He thought we could *transcend* this. Ask students if they have studied any authors in English who wrote about transcendentalism. Students will probably mention Ralph Waldo Emerson and Henry David Thoreau.

DISCUSS THE PHOTO

According to Jung, you should be having an emotional reaction to this symbol; it represents the most ancient archetype of all.

396

Unit 5 PERSONALITY, ADJUSTMENT, AND CONFLICT

phallic stage

Freudian stage of development during which the child experiences romantic interest in the opposite-sex parent and hostility toward the same-sex parent.

latency stage

Freudian stage of development during which the child's earlier conflicts are hidden or go below the surface.

genital stage

Freudian stage of development during which the individual seeks an appropriate marital partner and earlier conflicts reappear.

▲ *A mandala, Jung's symbol for the collective nature or oneness of human experience.*

Phallic Stage: Ages Two-and-a-Half to Five or Six   During the **phallic stage,** children experience the "Oedipus complex" (conflict), named for a character in a Greek play who killed his father and married his mother—without knowing it at the time. The Oedipus conflict, then, involves a desire to marry the opposite-sex parent along with jealous and hostile feelings for the same-sex parent. Because parents are bigger and more powerful than children, there is also a fear of punishment involved. In turn, the possibility of being punished causes guilt because, in the child's mind, one is only punished for being bad. A complicated set of emotions must be dealt with during this stage.

The only way to cope with all of these romantic, jealous, aggressive, anxious, and guilty feelings is to "identify" with the parent of the same sex, which means taking on as many of his or her characteristics as possible. Failure to resolve this conflict through identification can result in a wide range of psychological disorders. Freud believed that unreasonable anxiety, extreme guilt, phobias, and depression, for example, originate in the phallic stage of development.

Latency Stage: Ages Six to Preadolescence   When something is latent, it is below the surface, hidden, not obvious. In the **latency stage,** conflicts and problems from the earlier stages remain subdued or latent. No new ones arrive on the scene during this period.

Genital Stage: Adolescence Onward   As people seek an appropriate marriage partner and prepare for adult life, the conflicts of early childhood reappear. No new conflicts arise during this **genital stage,** but all of the old ones resurface. Although the ways in which they are expressed may have changed, their content is left over from the first five years of life.

Carl Jung

Carl Jung (YOONG) (1875–1961) was a friend and follower of Freud. The two men became quite close, so that when their relationship later got rocky, strange things happened. For example, Jung one day told Freud that he (Jung) had had a dream about corpses in coffins. Freud thought this meant that Jung wanted him dead, and as a result he fell over in a faint. Then they started calling one another names fitting to their profession, such as "crazy" or "neurotic," (Brome, 1967). In any case, Jung began to doubt the Freudian theory's emphasis on animal functions and eventually went off on his own, emphasizing what he really believed: the unconscious is a well of mystical and religious beliefs that controls our behavior.

Pursuing his belief, Jung studied very old paintings, statues, relics, and books about myths and religion. The more he read, the more it

DEMONSTRATION

Have a volunteer role-play this situation: *You are excited because you finally have a date with someone with whom you have been infatuated for a long time.* The volunteer should convey this excitement to several differ-ent people: a friend, a teacher, a par-ent, a co-worker. Four other students can play these roles. This should show how we take on different per-sonas, depending on the situation and the audience.

Points to Stress

Our society may be a bit obsessed with personas. Actors frequently tell sto-ries of running into people who can't separate who the actors really are from the personas they usually portray.

---

became clear to him: no matter what civilization he studied—ancient, old, or new—he kept finding stories about and pictures of great heroes and concepts of "mothers" as strong and supportive, especial-ly "Mother Earth" as something that provides us with food and care. And the concept of God in one form or another kept repeating itself (Jung, 1933, 1958). He called these basic inherited ideas **archetypes.** An archetype is a universal human concept. It is like the master recording that is then used to manufacture large numbers of CDs or tapes. If such concepts appear everywhere throughout history in sep-arate civilizations that have had no contact with one another, Jung figured that they must be part of all humans from the very beginning of each life.

Instead of being guided by an unconscious that seeks bodily plea-sure, then, all humans must be controlled by certain beliefs we inher-it. All these archetypes together make up the **collective unconscious.** It is called collective (meaning "everyone together") because the ideas are shared by the entire human race. Jung felt that it was "unconscious" since we are not fully aware we are part of these forces.

So, each generation inherits beliefs in certain ideas or roles that are connected with certain behaviors—for instance, all civilizations have beliefs about mother, hero, wise old man, and so forth. Without even knowing it, we imitate the fixed images about these concepts and develop personalties to fit them. Thus, despite the fact that a new mother may be unsure about what her baby needs, she nonetheless *pretends* to know all and be all for the child. A skinny, weak, and hopelessly shy male will actually feel guilty if he doesn't stand up to another male who is six-foot-four and weights 240 pounds. The man feels he should be a "hero." While both the man and woman are being unrealistic, it would seem they are trying to fit into the myths of this collective unconscious.

At least one part of Jung's theory certainly is true of all of us. He claimed that in the process of trying to become like these mythical people, we hide our real feelings and our real personalities. The fake personality that we then develop is called a **persona** (per-SONE-ah), which comes from Latin and refers to the frowning or smiling masks that were worn by players in Greek and Roman stage plays. We use psychological masks to fit what we think we are supposed to be, rather than let ourselves be what we actually are. How many times, for instance, have you smiled and been pleasant around someone who is irritating you?

archetypes

Jung's term for inherited universal human concepts.

collective unconscious

Jung's term for the portion of a per-son that contains ideas (such as hero, mother, and so on) shared by the whole human race.

persona

Jung's term for a "mask" people wear to hide what they really are or feel.

FYI Two common archetypes: anima, our feminine side; animus, our mas-culine side. Jung believed that we need to acknowledge both.

Points to Stress

Critics call Jung's ideas unscientific and too spiri-tual for psychology. They're right about the unscientific part, but spiri-tuality is an area that interests many psycholo-gists today.

Points to Stress

Freud was often criti-cized for being sexist. Horney, for one, was cer-tainly critical of Freud for not understanding female psychology.

Assessment of Freud and Jung

Since both Freud's and Jung's theories emphasize the importance of unconscious forces, criticism of this emphasis applies to both. As much as we hear about and use the term *unconscious,* the truth of the

DEMONSTRATION

Play a simple body-language game. Have five subjects leave the room. Assign various roles to five other students who remain in the room: (1) You are a family doctor, shaking the hand of a long-time patient. (2) You are a politician, shaking the hand of a stranger who may vote for you. (3) You are a nurse returning from the operating room who must tell someone in the waiting room very bad news. (4) You are a father, shaking the hand of your child who has just graduated. (5) You are a teacher, shaking the hand of someone you must fail.

The subjects should return one at a time and shake the hands of each role-player. After each handshake, ask the subjects some questions: what is the role-player's age? Is this

---

FYI Here's a Freud quote you may want to post: "No mortal can keep a secret. If the lips are silent, he chatters with his fingertips. Betrayal oozes out at every pore." Freud also said, "The eyes are the windows to the soul."

Comprehension Check

According to Freud's psychoanalytic theory, which part of the mind is at work during the following situations? You feel an urge to hit someone who is making fun of you. *(id)* You think about the fact that fighting at school will get you suspended. *(superego)* You respond to the person with a cutting remark instead of your fist. *(ego)*

Points to Stress

One of the main criticisms of Freud's theory is that he derived his ideas from his clinical experience. Since he dealt with people who were sick, maybe his theory only applies to people with *deficiencies,* to use Maslow's term.

398

Unit 5 PERSONALITY, ADJUSTMENT, AND CONFLICT

matter is that we have no *direct* evidence it exists (Balay and Shevrin, 1988). We all know about things we want to do that we shouldn't, but the mere fact that we *do* know about them makes them conscious, rather than unconscious. We certainly have things stored in us that we can't remember for the time being. Often we do things we shouldn't that are obvious to others but that we deny. But none of this proves an active unconscious that controls us against our will.

Sigmund Freud's organized theory of human development, the conscious, and the unconscious revolutionized how the human was viewed. His beliefs and ideas have filtered down into everyday language and have influenced how people with problems are viewed—all the way up to the present. But by and large, today's psychology deemphasizes the influence of an unconscious and focuses far more on a person's ability to control current, ongoing behavior, rather than dwelling on childhood influences and unconscious impulses.

As for the three-part system of the person, there is little evidence it exists. Freud had hoped that someday it would be found, showing the ego, superego, and id as having a biological basis. This has not happened.

As you will find out shortly, many have objected to the idea that we are little more than animals. But in fact, this may have been Freud's greatest contribution—not that we are animals but that sometimes we do indeed lose control and behave in a fashion that is completely unacceptable. In other words, his theory focuses on the fact that humans are not completely rational and in control, something we often lose sight of.

Jung's personality theory is not discussed in psychology very much anymore. Still, it was worth considering here because it adds quite a dimension to the possibilities of how we might get at least part of our personalities. There is no proof for it. On the other hand, we know animals of all kinds inherit certain broad rules of behavior. Try building a bird's nest sometime, and you'll realize just how incredibly complicated it is. Somehow this behavior is programmed in the bird. So, very complex and elaborate things can be passed on. Why not some of Jung's concepts, many of which do indeed seem to be universal?

SOCIAL PSYCHOANALYTIC THEORIES

Both Freud and Jung dealt with an unconscious that was thought to be biological. In other words, they thought that inborn needs or mythological beliefs control people, with little influence from what happens in the environment. A number of psychoanalysts agreed

ACTIVITY
ACTIVITY
ACTIVITY
ACTIVITY
ACTIVITY
ACTIVITY

person related to you? *Why* is this person shaking your hand? It's rare for someone to guess the precise role being played, but students often make some close guesses. The point you hope the students pick up on is that the unconscious is often revealed through nonverbal means.

DISCOVERY

Have students think of metaphors to illustrate or symbolize the unconscious. A vat full of sludge represents a reservoir of all the unacceptable impulses we have ever had. If we sift through the sludge, we'll find what we're looking for, but it will be messy and a lot of work.

with the concept of an unconscious but objected to the fact that the early theories ignored the impact of social forces. These psychoanalysts believed that the unconscious also holds all the worries and concerns about how well we get along with others. Think about how sweaty and anxious you got the last time you met someone of the opposite sex you wanted very much to like you. While the desire to associate with that person might start off biologically, it quickly becomes a social issue. Given this different focus, this splinter group of psychoanalysts came to be known as social psychoanalysts, or **neo-Freudians,** the latter term meaning "new" (revised) Freudians.

neo-Freudians

Those psychoanalysts who broke away from Freud to emphasize social forces in the unconscious.

Karen Horney

Psychoanalyst **Karen Horney** (HORN-eye) (1885–1952) was outspoken about breaking with the Freudian tradition. She strongly disagreed with Freud's focus on biological drives (Murphy & Kovach, 1972). Horney felt that dealing with impulses from an id was less important for personality than coping with the stress of social needs. Hence, she was a neo-Freudian. She claimed that the human feels most helpless, anxious, and lost in life around the issues of getting enough love. All of us need love badly, so we are constantly afraid that important people (like our parents when we are very young) will not like us. This is so threatening that we build our personalities around fighting rejection. As a result, we go along with people when we don't want to. A person who does not receive love is one who is always anxious and afraid (Horney, 1950). For this person, anxiety gradually builds up in the unconscious because of confused or inadequate social relationships. The person's behavior will then be dominated by social concerns because of the constant pressure from the unconscious.

Alfred Adler

Alfred Adler (1870–1937) was a follower of Freud who also had trouble with the heavy emphasis on biological needs. He believed, like Horney, that social interaction was the key to proper development. He said that one of the biggest problems people face is trying to feel important and worthwhile around others. Those who are insecure struggle to make themselves look better. They spend their lives trying to dominate and control others in order to avoid their own inner feelings of inferiority. School bullies are perfect examples of this type of behavior. When one gets beneath the surface to the unconscious, one finds that these people doubt themselves, are afraid and weak; hence, they take off after those who are physically weaker in order to try to make themselves feel important and strong.

Points to Stress

Freud believed that the healthy individual balances the forces of id, ego, and superego. Horney stresses a different dynamic. Part of us wants to *socialize;* part of us at times wants to *withdraw;* and there's a part of us that *competes* with others. We must learn to balance these three urges. As a teacher, you see these sorts of dynamics every day. How do you deal with them? You may wish to share this with the class.

Journal Topic

"What makes *you* feel important and worthwhile?" To prepare students for this entry, have them make a list of major choices they have made in the last year: getting a job; quitting a job; choosing a college; and so on. How many of these choices would apply to the question?

COOPERATIVE LEARNING

The material on Horney provides an opportunity to discuss loneliness. Have students work in pairs to answer the following questions. Why do people become lonely? What is the difference between loneliness and being alone? Loneliness can stem from being alone, and this kind of loneliness is relatively easy to fix, provided that the person has some social skills. The other type of loneliness, when we feel that no one understands us, when we feel lonely even in a crowd, is much more devastating and harder to overcome. Ask students what they do to overcome both types of loneliness.

CHAPTER PROJECT/

Several theories of personality are presented in this chapter, each offering a different viewpoint. Some emphasize early childhood development, some look at present behavior, and some try to focus on the individ-

Points to Stress

Note that Erikson's fourth stage, *industry versus inferiority* is similar to Adler's main focus. We all struggle with feelings of inferiority at times, especially in childhood. Adler also agreed with Freud, who believed that much of our personality is formed during the first five years.

DISCUSS THE PHOTO

Erikson's theory is highly regarded and valued, although it is difficult to prove scientifically.

Points to Stress

Although trust or mistrust is established early, this is a conflict that reoccurs throughout our lives. We are constantly reassessing whether to trust people or not.

Unit 5 PERSONALITY, ADJUSTMENT, AND CONFLICT

▲ *Erik Erikson, a socially oriented psychologist.*

Erik Erikson

As mentioned, Freud felt that personality is pretty well set in the early years. Very few psychologists believe this anymore. As we'll talk about later, some aspects of personality tend to remain the same, but there are many things about us that change throughout life.

One theorist who supported the idea of change is **Erik Erikson** (1902–1994). His theory divides life up into eight stages. Like Horney and Adler, Erikson believed that social forces are most important, so it is the type of relationships a person has during each of the stages that forms his or her personality. Erikson's theory is appealing because it implies that we can "rescue" ourselves from problems almost anytime in life, all the way up to old age.

Stage one is in infancy. Erikson stressed the importance of warm relationships with the mother during feeding. Depending on how the mother and child get along, the child either relaxes and feels trusting or is tense and mistrusting of others. Erikson, therefore, called this stage *trust versus mistrust.*

Stage two comes at year two of the child's life. During this time, the child tries to become an individual—of sorts. Clearly he or she is pretty helpless but nonetheless is seeking a feeling of being a separate person. If the parents don't allow this, the ego is injured and the child feels shame. If the parents allow some freedom, a feeling of independence occurs, called autonomy (aw-TON-oh-mee). Erikson called stage two *autonomy versus shame.*

Even in *stage three*, from ages three through five, children are still very dependent on the parents. But this is the time when children try to take control of their environment—within limits. Thus, making a pile of rocks of their own design is important. Pretending to be a teacher or police officer or parent begins, and children make up their own rules about how these tasks are performed. They are taking the initiative in developing the behavior and rules of their pretend work. If not allowed this chance, the child begins to feel bad and guilty for having failed. This stage is called *initiative versus guilt.*

In *stage four* (ages six to 12 years), children begin to develop all kinds of skills and to get rewards for what they do. These can range from stars pasted on the forehead (for the younger ones, we hope) to extra TV privileges. The children are being molded to do more and better things (that is, to be "industrious"). If the skills or rewards are not forthcoming, they feel inadequate. This stage, then, is called *industry versus inferiority.*

Erikson saw *stage five*, adolescence (also discussed in Chapter 11), as very important. One tries to get a hold on the inner self by seeking an answer to the question, "Who am I?" Finding self-identity requires the safety of a group. For this reason, adolescents form tightly knit groups to keep the self free from adult or "outsider" influence. The groups even have uniforms of sorts, which adults can't seem to handle without coming unglued. Certain types of shoes, clothing,

COOPERATIVE LEARNING

ual as a whole. Since none of these theories provides a complete picture, have groups devise their own theories of personality. They can address the following questions: (1) Are we born with certain characteristics?

(2) What is the role of the environment in shaping personality?
(3) Which personality traits seem to remain the same throughout a lifetime? (4) How do you define a healthy individual?

Points to Stress

During the second stage, autonomy versus shame, children strive for a *physical* separateness. The focus during the third stage is on an *intellectual* separateness. This "why?" stage can drive parents crazy. Parents may try to participate in the child's games, but the parents have no idea what to do because the rules keep changing. Parents, of course, should be tolerant and allow children to experiment. Problems arise when siblings are not quite so tolerant.

▲ *Erikson's industry stage: can you still do it if you don't stick out your tongue?*

DISCUSS THE PHOTO

How can a teacher encourage industry? Maybe by allowing students to leave their seats and gain hands-on experience.

special language, hairdos, and the like all help to keep the group together for this important process and exclude both older and younger people. This is also the time for falling in love so the person can find out the answer to "Will someone love who I am?" (Muuss, 1975). (Fortunately, for almost all of us, there usually is *someone* somewhere who will see us as a little more than merely adequate.) Finally, this is the time when young people start a search for solutions to religious, vocational, and personal issues (finding a "role" in life) (Erikson, 1968). Stage five is called *identity versus identity confusion*. In other words, failure to develop a strong sense of self results in uncertainty about what one is supposed to be and do.

Stage six occurs during adulthood, starting in the late teens and running until about age 30. This is a time of forming permanent relationships and sharing on an intimate level, usually with a member of the opposite sex. This intimacy provides a true feeling of satisfaction because you are important to at least one special person. There is a sharing of a special closeness with another, a true process of give and take. Without it, there is loneliness. Hence, this stage is called *intimacy versus isolation*.

Middle adulthood is *stage seven*, from age 30 to 65. During this time, a person must either expand and give (generate) something important to the world in the way of a family or job, or he or she psychologically stands still and produces nothing (stagnates). This stage is called *generativity versus stagnation*.

Points to Stress

The emphasis during the fourth stage is on building and taking things apart, learning how things work. (The curiosity motive discussed in Chapter 5 is very evident at this stage.)

401

DISCOVERY

Have students find pictures that correspond to each of Erikson's eight stages. They should provide two pictures for each stage, one picture showing someone successfully dealing with the stage, the other showing an unsuccessful response. Have them provide captions for each picture. You might even have them bring in pictures of themselves at various stages!

Erikson's Eight Stages.

IN FOCUS Trust: rock the child; provide warmth. Autonomy: encourage child to dress herself, feed herself, and so on. Initiative: when the child asks, "Why?" be patient; allow her to make up her own rules for games. Industry: don't yell when the child takes apart the television.

Discussion

This topic concerns the sixth stage, *intimacy versus isolation.* Ask students who have had a long, romantic relationship to name the kinds of things that encourage intimacy. Students may mention honesty and trust and all that, but add that allowing room to breathe helps, too. No one wants to feel like he or she is tied down.

Connections

The seventh stage is the longest stage, but not much space is devoted to it here since Chapter 12 discusses adulthood in great depth. You may want students to flip to those pages to peruse that material.

402

Unit 5 PERSONALITY, ADJUSTMENT, AND CONFLICT

IN FOCUS — Erikson's Eight Stages

Trust Infant is totally dependent on others—learns to trust these others	versus	**Mistrust (Birth to two years)** or learns to distrust them.
Autonomy Child tries to become a separate individual	versus	**Shame (Ages two to three years)** or if not allowed, feels shame.
Initiative Child tries to take control of environment	versus	**Guilt (Ages three to five years)** or if not allowed, child feels guilty for having failed.
Industry Child wants to do more and better things—to be industrious	versus	**Inferiority (Ages six to 12 years)** or if child does *not* do better, child feels inferior.
Identity Adolescent searches for role or identity in life	versus	**Identity Confusion (Ages 13 to 18 years)** and feels confusion if no role is found.
Intimacy Young adult shares special or intimate feelings with one special person	versus	**Isolation (Ages 18 to 30 years)** or without the sharing, loneliness and isolation prevail.
Generativity Adult feels need to generate or contribute something important to the world	versus	**Stagnation (Middle adulthood)** or if nothing important is contributed, the adult deteriorates or stagnates.
Ego Integrity Person looks to past and feels a sense of accomplishment or integrity	versus	**Ego Despair (Late adulthood)** or person looks back and feels no sense of accomplishment and feels empty and despairing.

As a parent, what kinds of things will you do with your child to promote trust, autonomy, initiative, and industry?

In late adulthood, *stage eight,* from age 65 on, that which has gone before should, with a little luck, make some sense. One should be able to accept that the end is coming and find that life has been a worthwhile event, that something good was accomplished from living (Erikson et al., 1986). The self (ego) should feel reasonably complete when viewing what has happened, despite all the problems along the way. If a person doesn't feel this, he or she despairs, feeling life has been meaningless. Thus, this stage is called *ego integrity versus ego despair.* (*Integrity,* in this context, means a feeling of wholeness or completion.)

Assessment of the Neo-Freudians

The neo-Freudians brought an important new dimension to psychoanalysis: the influence of social forces. Clearly they provided more to work with in analysis than simply biological drives. Erikson's theory was especially helpful in allowing the possibility that we all have a chance to "repair" ourselves as we go along in life and are not stuck with something from childhood. Despite these alterations, however, the problem of whether we have an unconscious or not still exists.

BEHAVIORISM

Not all personality theories deal with the unconscious. In fact, in **behaviorism**, the unconscious is ignored altogether. Early theories in this area focused on our acts or behaviors as if we were robots. According to these theories, our personalities evolve from a series of rewards or punishments without concern about any deep motives. For example, those who drop out of school to work will, in the long run, lose a great deal of money. But for the short term, each week or so they get a lot more money than their friends who are still in school. Thus, they are getting a continued series of rewards that are more important than the pleas of their parents to stay in school. Note that the psychoanalysts would claim that these people have a deep-seated fear of failing in school or that they feel unimportant. As a result, they use the fact that they are making more money than their peers to feel superior. The Freudians, then, approach personality with much greater depth and complexity than the behaviorists.

John B. Watson

John B. Watson (1878–1958) was an early behaviorist. He believed that if he had complete control of a person's environment from infancy, he could make that person become absolutely anything at all—doctor, lawyer, beggar, or thief. His best known research was on learned fears (see the "Little Albert" study in Chapter 7). According to Watson, we are afraid of objects or situations because of frightening associations we have made to them in the past.

B. F. Skinner

Perhaps the best known behaviorist is **B. F. Skinner** (1904–1990). Skinner had a very strict religious upbringing. His grandmother used to hold his face over a stove of hot coals to show him "what hell was like." Later, when he was in school, he chose to withdraw from social

behaviorism

A personality theory that focuses on overt acts or behaviors rather than on consciousness or unconsciousness.

Comprehension Check

How do the neo-Freudians' views differ from Freud's? *(They believe that social factors, not just biological drives, influence behavior and personality.)*

Critical Thinking

Ask students how a behaviorist would view personality traits like confidence, friendliness, and rebellion. They should note that if these traits are reinforced, they will continue to occur.

DISCOVERY

Ask students to make a list of ways that freshmen model themselves after seniors. Students may have difficulty at first recalling specific behaviors that they copied as freshmen, but a little prompting may jar their memories: "Imagine freshman year. What kinds of things did seniors do that were cool? Did they hold their books or walk in a particular way? Did they hang out in certain places or sit in a particular area of the cafeteria? Did they wear cool clothes? Was there anything about their lockers that was cool? What about the way they talked?" If you can get students to describe ten or 15 concrete examples of modeling, your point that modeling is a complex process should hit home. If this process is complex at school, imagine how complex it is at home!

FYI Although Skinner's ideas are presented in this chapter on personality, Skinner would not call his theory a personality theory. He would call it a theory about behavior, some of which is enduring because of reinforcements and some which is not.

DISCUSS THE PHOTO

Have students make a list of the traits they ascribe to these people.

404

Unit 5 PERSONALITY, ADJUSTMENT, AND CONFLICT

activities, and he spent his time reading science books instead of going to movies, hanging around, or dating much (Skinner, 1967). If we were using the psychoanalytic method, we might come up with the idea that these early events in his life were part of what led him to see people in mechanical terms: the negative associations he had with religion and social activities may have developed his later picture of people as mechanical rather than as thinking, reasoning creatures. (Of some interest, as he entered Erikson's stage eight he mellowed quite a bit and viewed the human in less mechanical terms.)

In any case, for the early Skinner, everything we do is the result of a mechanical association of events with their consequences. For example, if you plan to go over to a friend's house tonight but then later in the day you decide to find a different friend with whom to go

▲ *After looking at these three pictures for a short period, note how many personality characteristics and traits you give the people just on the basis of appearance.*

DISCOVERY

Ask students to make a list of fears they have. Have them *check* each fear that has been created through modeling; have them *star* each fear that has been reduced through modeling. You might prompt some examples by asking them to think about experiences with siblings.

---

get something to eat, this was *not* a voluntary decision on your part, according to Skinner. Instead, you added up the number of pleasant experiences you have had with friend number one and those you have had with friend number two, and you chose the second friend because you had more positive associations with that person. While you *think* you had a choice, you really didn't. In the months to come, the number of positive experiences with different people might change so that you will choose friend number three. Thus, all our behaviors are the result of a series of **reinforcements** (see Chapter 7). Those who make clothing know that there are certain parts of the shirt that take more of a beating than others. If you haven't bought something really cheap, the manufacturer will have used extra stitches or material to *reinforce* these parts—make them stronger. A similar thing happens to humans, according to Skinner's system. Each time you laugh or share with friend A versus friend B, you reinforce the odds that you'll want to see friend A again. The same thing applies throughout all personality development: if studying is reinforced by good grades, you will study more often; if skipping school offers more reinforcement than it creates guilt, you will continue to skip school.

reinforcement

Events that strengthen a behavior by bringing the desired results.

Albert Bandura

Note again the last sentence. A person might base behavior on feelings of guilt. Guilt obviously is a broad, internal concept that doesn't fit that well with Skinner's mechanical view of behaviorism. Skinner's system is flawed because it doesn't give a person enough credit for being a thinking creature.

This was the complaint of **Albert Bandura** (b. 1925), a behaviorist who has elaborated on Skinner's system. He does not deny that we learn a great number of things just by straight association. If you're bitten by a dog, a cat, a raccoon, and a snake when you are growing up, there's no question that your personality will include a clear-cut fear of animals. On the other hand, we learn many things by using our ability to think, analyze, and interpret. Bandura feels that much of our personality comes from observing others and **modeling** ourselves after them. This process can be very complex, rather than just mechanical: if you observe an alcoholic uncle in the family who is very friendly and outgoing and an aunt who is a teetotaler but nasty and aggressive, your feelings for or against alcohol are going to be very complex—something Skinner's system doesn't allow for. Bandura still is behavioristic, though, because he believes learning is a process of association, but the organism interprets and chooses between associations rather than just "counting" them and responding automatically to the one that for the moment has the most positive reinforcements. In other words, the organism performs an internal analysis.

modeling

Bandura's term for learning by imitating others.

Connections

See the wraparound material for Chapter 7 for a variety of activities and discussion questions on behaviorism.

Discussion

Ask which kind of therapist students would choose to see: a psychoanalyst, a behaviorist, or a humanist. Most will pick a humanist. What if the reason to see a therapist is to break a habit or decrease a fear? The better choice would be a behaviorist.

Literature. Select a short story that the entire class can read. Then break the class into groups and assign each group one of the following viewpoints: *psychoanalysis, social psychoanalytic theories, behaviorism* (this group can refer back to Chapter 7), *humanistic theories* (this group can refer back to Chapter 5). Each group should analyze the story from its assigned viewpoint. For example, if the story is about a fight between siblings, the psychoanalyst group might see the fighting as a symbol of unconscious forces; the behaviorist group would stress the reinforcement the siblings receive for fighting, and so on.

Unit 5 PERSONALITY, ADJUSTMENT, AND CONFLICT

Points to Stress

In a way, humanism is a balance between psychoanalysis and behaviorism. Humanists acknowledge that the environment is important, but they insist that inner forces are important, too. In their view, the inner forces, if given a chance to be expressed, will push us to be our best.

Evaluation Strategy

Have students pair up to interview each other. They can ask questions about each other's past, family, and goals. Each student then analyzes his or her partner's answers from three angles: as a psychoanalyst, as a behaviorist, and as a humanist.

Points to Stress

How does one become fully functioning? We all need someone with whom we can be completely open. This person provides what Rogers called unconditional positive regard, which means that this person will accept us no matter what we do (under any *conditions*).

humanism

A personality theory that places emphasis on the positive potential of the person.

ideal self

Rogers's term for the goal of each person's development; perfection.

Bandura's studies on modeling have been very important. They have shown that if children observe someone beating up a plastic doll, these children will become aggressive themselves (see Chapter 7). More important, perhaps, Bandura showed that if someone is really, seriously afraid of snakes, for instance, he or she can lose that fear over time by seeing another person handling snakes comfortably. The person with the fear of snakes can model his or her behavior on that of others who handle snakes with little fear and with nothing happening to them. The important point is that we can relearn or retrain ourselves by deliberately developing a new set of associations (snakes are harmless) to replace the old.

Assessment of Behaviorism

We have mentioned most of the problems with behaviorism as we've gone along. The biggest one, especially for Skinner, is that it shortchanges the human's ability to think. On the positive side, though, the theory does show that we learn many behaviors just because they have been reinforced by positive associations.

HUMANISTIC THEORIES

As you might have guessed, some people soon objected to what they saw as a rather depressing picture of us either as a bubbling id trying to express itself or as a robot. These people considered Freud's unconscious filled with id impulses unacceptable and the behaviorists' failure to acknowledge the importance of personal experience unworkable. In reaction to these theories, some psychologists developed **humanism,** which emphasizes the whole person with his or her positive potential and which accepts the person as an individual human with all kinds of good qualities. So the focus is on *human* qualities, which explains how the name of this theory came about.

Carl Rogers

The leading humanist, **Carl Rogers** (1902–1987), was a minister for a while, but he had trouble with the idea that people are sinful and bad. Instead, he believed that we are basically good. The biggest problem we have, he said, is living up to what he called the **ideal self.** The ideal self is as close to perfection as one can get. We come into the world ready to become this ideal self, but at times we fall by the wayside while trying to get there. We are like a flower in our potential. If the environment is halfway decent, we will grow into a

ACTIVITY
ACTIVITY
ACTIVITY
ACTIVITY
ACTIVITY
ACTIVITY

COOPERATIVE LEARNING

Ask students to work in pairs to find any possible connections between one personality theory and another. Maslow's hierarchy of needs, for example, takes into account both Horney's emphasis on love (Maslow's third level) and Adler's emphasis on feeling worthwhile (Maslow's fourth level). For Maslow, both concerns are essential, but one need must be satisfied before the other. See Chapter 5 for more on Maslow.

FYI Unlike Maslow, who started out studying animal behavior in the laboratory and later studied self-actualizers, Rogers conducted therapy and was very successful at it. In fact, his methods inspired other therapists. See Chapter 19 for details of his therapy.

Chapter 14 THEORIES OF PERSONALITY

IN FOCUS Rogers's Fully Functioning Individual

Both individuals have the power to be fully functioning, but only the second individual realizes this, through the help of that individual's environment.

If the person on the left went to three psychologists—a psychoanalyst, a behaviorist, and a humanist—how might each psychologist describe the person's problem?

human who can be proud and internally beautiful. This can be accomplished by almost anyone who has the acceptance and warmth of love from parents in the early stages, from friends in the next stage, and from an intimate, personal relationship with someone as an adult. When we have united what we *should* be with what we *are,* we have become what he called a **fully functioning individual** (Rogers, 1951).

Abraham Maslow

Psychologist **Abraham Maslow** (1908–1970) followed in Rogers's footsteps. He saw the human as having deep needs for beauty, goodness, justice, and a feeling of completeness—all the hopeful and positive things about human beings. Each of us has inherited something unique, and *if* the environment will cooperate a little, we have the opportunity to become great (Maslow, 1970). Maslow does not mean "great" in the sense of "famous" but in terms of *actualizing* (bringing to life) our personal skills. Thus, the fulfilled person is **self-actualized.** We can accomplish this despite personal problems. For instance, he saw Abraham Lincoln as self-actualized, even though

fully functioning individual

Rogers's term for someone who has become what he or she should be.

self-actualized

Maslow's term for the state of having brought to life the full potential of our skills.

Rogers's Fully Functioning Individual.

IN FOCUS Psychoanalyst: "Talk about your past. Let the old conflicts resurface. Only in this way can we get to the root of the problem." Behaviorist: "Let's analyze the behaviors that upset you. And let's work on a program of reinforcement that will help eliminate those problems." Humanist: "I'm here to listen and support you. I think you know yourself well enough, and you know why you're upset. . . . So you say you can't do anything right? What do you mean by that?"

407

DISCOVERY

Ask students to interview their parents to see if there are any traits that the parents identified in the student early on. For example, parents may say, "Oh, yeah, you were shy from the beginning and you never changed." Or "You were colicky as a baby, and you haven't quieted down since."

Points to Stress

Carl Jung (presented earlier) used the term *self-actualization,* too, before Maslow. Both used the term to describe inner peace and wholeness. While Maslow felt that we become self-actualized by striving to reach our potential, Jung felt that we achieve self-actualization by balancing the dual natures within us—the masculine and feminine sides, for example.

Comprehension Check

Match the following descriptions to psychoanalysis, behaviorism, or humanism: (1) unconscious ignored *(behaviorism);* (2) unconscious very important *(psychoanalysis);* (3) being healthy means reaching one's potential *(humanism);* (4) being healthy means balancing inner forces *(psychoanalysis);* (5) being unhealthy means one has many bad habits *(behaviorism);* (6) being unhealthy means one is not striving to be his or her best *(humanism).*

408

Unit 5 PERSONALITY, ADJUSTMENT, AND CONFLICT

personality traits

The more or less permanent personality characteristics that an individual has.

the man suffered endless bouts of deep depression (Maslow, 1968). A truly self-actualized person would be a student who comes from a terrible environment but who propels himself or herself to a level of outstanding achievement. (Maslow is discussed more thoroughly in Chapter 5.)

Assessment of Humanism

Humanism is very upbeat; it makes us feel good. It also positively encourages a person to take charge of his or her own fate in a reasonable fashion. Unlike other theories, it emphasizes what goes right rather than what goes wrong in personality development—a welcome change. Critics argue that it goes too far in a positive direction. However, a fair amount of research backs up the basic ideas that humanism supports. The major problem, perhaps, is that this theory is too simple and vague to account very well for the great variety we see in the human personality.

EXAMINING PERSONALITY TRAITS

The more or less permanent characteristics each of us has are sometimes called **personality traits.** In this section, we cover recent studies on traits, discussing what is known about them and where they might come from. A great deal has been learned from major research being conducted at the University of Minnesota, where 350 pairs of twins are being studied. Since identical, or monozygotic, twins have exactly the same heredity (they come from the same fertilized egg in the mother), they can be compared with fraternal, or dizygotic, twins (who do not have as much heredity in common since they are from different fertilized eggs) or with just brothers and sisters (least amount of common heredity). If the same trait shows up in the identical twins but not in the other pairs, then the odds are very good that it is an inherited trait.

Major Permanent Traits

The most recent evidence from these twin studies suggests that there are three traits that seem to be inherited or at least that appear from an early age (Lykken et al., 1987). The first one is how well people get along in social situations. The second is how traditional the person is—that is, will he or she follow the rules most of the time or be rebellious? The third is how comfortable a person feels. In other

DISCOVERY

Draw a scale from 1 to 10 on the board. Next to 1 write "not at all like me," next to 10 write "very much like me." Read the following statement: "You are at a wedding reception and you know only one or two people. During the course of the night, you take the intiative and meet several new people." Students then pick a number from 1 to 10 that best applies to them. Change the setting—to a party, a sporting event at school, the first day at a new school—and have students supply new answers for each setting. If the answers are consistent for each setting, the trait (introversion or extroversion) is probably a central trait—one that is enduring. You can try the same exercise by reading statements regarding how traditional the person is and how comfortable a person feels.

Chapter 14 THEORIES OF PERSONALITY

▲ *Is this behavior the result of inherited characteristics or the environment? Do people who engage in activities like this have certain personality traits in common?*

DISCUSS THE PHOTO

Students might be able to provide plenty of anecdotal evidence to answer the question posed in the caption.

Critical Thinking

Ask students to consider the following question: How would a behaviorist view traits? They would balk at the very concept of a trait, since it implies permanence. Behaviorists would argue that if we were to change the person's environment and reinforce behaviors inconsistent with the trait, the trait would eventually be extinguished.

words, is the person relaxed and confident, or does he or she feel alone and not quite with it?

A different type of study followed 10,000 people—ages 25 to 74—for nine years to see how they changed over this period. Again, three characteristics tended to remain the same regardless of age. These three are very close to the ones just mentioned: (1) degree of friendliness; (2) how eager people are to do different or novel things; and (3) how anxious or comfortable they feel (Lykken et al., 1985; Costa & McCrae, 1986; Costa et al., 1987). (Since you have to remember this material, just learn the second list; it is the clearest, and it is close enough to the first one that you'll be safe.)

People *do* change throughout life in terms of how satisfied they feel, how high their morale is, and how active they are. To this point in time, only the three traits mentioned in the last paragraph seem pretty well set, maybe in "plaster," by the early 20s. Remember, though, that these three traits appear from birth and only later are they reinforced or not as other people respond to them. Thus, learning does have an influence, but only after certain tendencies have already been inherited. We all know of families in which two children were very different from birth; one was aggressive and cried a lot while the other was quiet and smiled. Parents and others respond in a certain way to these differences, and thus they continue to add to whatever inherited tendencies are already there.

ENRICHMENT

Have students find out more about trait theories by studying Gordon Allport and Raymond Cattell. Students should be able to find numerous similarities and differences between these two theorists.

The Big Picture: Major Personality Theories.

IN FOCUS Any answer is acceptable, as long as it is supported. You might mention that psychoanalysis is not a great force in psychology any longer. And humanism, as important as it is, is not always practical.

Comprehension Check

Which three personality traits appear to be fairly constant throughout life? *(degree of friendliness, eagerness to do new things, and level of anxiety).*

Unit 5 PERSONALITY, ADJUSTMENT, AND CONFLICT

IN FOCUS | **The Big Picture: Major Personality Theories**

	Early Psychoanalysis	Social Psychoanalysis	Behaviorism	Humanism
Major Theorists	Freud Jung	Horney Adler Erikson	Skinner Bandura	Rogers Maslow
Main Beliefs	Personality and behavior determined by hidden, or unconscious, forces	Personality influenced by the unconscious, but this unconscious is not all biological—social factors help shape the unconscious	Personality shaped by rewards and punishments and by modeling—forget the unconscious	Personality influenced by the unique potential within each of us
Role of the Environment	Plays big role during first five years of life—but after this, inner forces are more important	Plays big role in supplying love and making person feel important	Is all-important—it makes us who we are	Decent environment needed to nurture inner potential
Definition of Healthy Personality	One that adequately balances conflicts between conscious and unconscious forces	One that recognizes the social forces of the unconscious and that tries to repair itself by resolving conflicts	One that receives effective rewards and punishments—the individual has little choice in this	One that is fully functioning and self-actualized

Which personality theory seems most applicable or accurate in today's world?

Effects of the Environment

Most scientists who study personality today feel that roughly 50 percent of the total personality is controlled by heredity. Obviously, the environment will have an effect, but we seem to lean toward certain types of behavior from birth, as we've just discussed.

An environment, however, is not simply "good" or "bad." One of the more interesting recent findings is that even what seems to be exactly the same environment for the children in the family is, in fact, different for each child since each has a different personality from the

COOPERATIVE LEARNING

Birth order is a favorite topic for students, so you might want to spend some time on this. Group all the first-borns, middle children, last borns, and only children. Give them about ten minutes to discuss any common experiences they have. For example, last borns may complain about their slim photo albums. Firstborns may complain that they had to "break in" their parents. Only children may complain that there was no one else around to blame when something happened. No one pays attention to the poor middle children, so ignore this group for a while to make them feel at home.

beginning. So, they react differently to the same thing. If two children in a family are taken to a movie together, for example, it will have a different effect on each child. Such findings suggest that parents cannot control how children will respond; parents can only provide the best possible environment for their kids.

You will sometimes hear that birth order (whether one is the first, second, or third child, for example) is very important in how a child turns out. But after thousands of studies in this area, there seems to be very little support for any lasting effect. Parents in normal families tend to treat the children as equally as possible, and for the most part, they succeed. But each child sees what is going on from a different point of view. Finally, current studies are showing that interaction with a brother or sister or with playmates or school groups carries far heavier weight over time than do the parents. Of course, this assumes that the parents are not causing the children to live in a house of horrors but are providing an acceptable environment (Plomin and Daniels, 1987; Daniels, 1986).

Reteaching Strategy

Have students complete the **Reteaching Worksheet** for this chapter located in the Teacher Resources.

The **Vocabulary Worksheet** may be completed by the class as a pretest for chapter concepts or used as a reteaching worksheet for those students needing additional review.

PSYCHOLOGY IN YOUR LIFE

Finding Yourself in Personality Theories

As we mentioned at the beginning of this chapter, we don't have enough information yet on how accurate different personality theories are. Still, it might be interesting for you to explore some things about yourself, and see if you can find support for the theories discussed. Don't take it all too seriously; we're just doing an "experiment," so to speak.

Start with the Freudian theory. Go back in your mind to the last time you had a secret desire to do something you didn't think proper or moral. Note that you didn't merely go out and do it without caring. Instead, what probably happened was that you felt a very strong internal "push" to go ahead and do it. Next you began to feel concerned and guilty, and you had a sinking feeling in your stomach that you might actually do it. Then you weighed the pros and cons, the rights and wrongs of the situation. Finally, you did or didn't do it. Note how very close this comes to your ego (your*self*) trying to let the id have its way, but also balancing the reality and morality of the situation by listening to the superego. It certainly seems like Freud might have been partly right, doesn't it?

Now the behavioral theory. Pick a habit you have that you're not necessarily *(continued on next page)*

DISCOVERY

Try the activity described near the end of the **Psychology in Your Life** section.

ENRICHMENT

Have students complete the **Enrichment Worksheet** for this chapter located in the Teacher Resources.

PSYCHOLOGY IN YOUR LIFE

Enrichment

This chapter includes some colorful people who have had a great impact on psychology. Have students read a biography of one of these psychologists, or of any other psychologist, and then complete the biography assignment outlined on **Teaching Master 14-3 Biography.** The assignment asks students to write a list of interview questions, the likely answers to those questions, and an obituary. If you don't want to assign the reading of an entire biography, have students read a chapter or two.

PSYCHOLOGY IN YOUR LIFE

Finding Yourself in Personality Theories

(continued from previous page) happy with: biting your fingernails, humming, doing funny things with your fingers, tugging at your socks, or who knows what. Go back in your mind to the last couple of times you did this behavior. You didn't want to do it, but it came automatically. Such habits are very hard to trace in some cases, but here is how they probably get started: sometime in the past you felt a lot of stress and strain. The way the body is constructed, when stress occurs, we prepare to take some kind of action, like running away. That's natural. But we can't actually run away—society won't allow it. So, rather than run, you started doing something—anything—with your body to relieve the tension. Having done *something*, your body relaxed a little; this made you feel better, which reinforced the behav-

ior (even though what you did wasn't *really* helpful). Thus, you tend to repeat this something—humming, nail biting, and so on—year after year; each time, the reinforcement adds up so that the drive to do it gets stronger and stronger. The behavior becomes part of you. As you can see, this is the behavioral explanation for how we gradually develop patterns of activities that come to represent our personalities.

For the third example, the humanistic theories, you have to use your "Freudian superego" and not cheat. At a certain point, we will tell you not to read any further. Please don't, or you'll spoil the experiment. Don't even peek a line ahead. Here we go: in private write down the three things that you most admire about yourself. Beneath that, write the three things about yourself that

you find obnoxious, gross, or unpleasant. Be *very* honest. Don't read any further until you have finished writing.

Now you need to examine your inner feelings very carefully. Notice how much stress and strain you felt, how physically uncomfortable you were, when you wrote the bad part. Note how you avoided and wanted to get away from it. Why? Could it be that you are basically a good person seeking self-actualization and fulfillment and that you are destined to be good? That these negative things just don't seem to belong to you and should go away? That's what the humanists would say. (Don't forget to destroy what you wrote! And remember that defects are part of all of us, and you're not alone at all in feeling bad about certain aspects of yourself.)

412

VOCABULARY REVIEW

Before testing students on the contents of the chapter, you may want to review vocabulary terms that are especially important or confusing. Terms in this chapter that could require clarification are *psychoanalysis*, *unconscious*, *collective unconscious*, *neo-Freudians*, and *personality traits*.

Chapter 14 THEORIES OF PERSONALITY

SUMMARY

1. Freud's system focuses on unconscious impulses that are constantly seeking expression. The id contains our animal needs and tries to do what it wants. It is controlled by the ego or self, which balances the desires of the id with the restraints and judgments of the superego, or conscience.

2. Carl Jung felt we were guided by a collective unconscious, which holds all the myths about personality types (such as "mother" or "hero") and passes them on from one generation to another. He believed we also make up "fake" personalities or masks, called personas.

3. Karen Horney thought that social influences were most important in personality development. We live from birth with a dread that we will not be accepted by others, and this concern colors our personalities. Alfred Adler agreed about the importance of social factors and stressed that we feel inadequate and spend our energies trying to be important to offset such feelings.

4. Erik Erikson developed an elaborate theory in which life is divided up into a series of eight stages. In each of these stages, we have to deal with others; how we turn out depends on how good these relationships are during each stage.

5. Behaviorism sees personality as arising from learning and association. B. F. Skinner claimed that we act strictly in terms of the kinds of reinforcements we get, rather than in terms of conscious choices. Bandura focused on learning also, but claimed that we are more than just robots, that we can accept or reject certain kinds of behavior that we have learned by a process called modeling.

6. Humanistic theories stress that we are basically good and are aiming to fulfill our potential if the environment cooperates even a little bit. Carl Rogers saw us as destined to become fully functioning individuals. Abraham Maslow called people who found a place in life and did their jobs with excellence "self-actualized."

7. The three personality traits that seem to be inherited (or, at least, that are with us from a very early age) are degree of friendliness, novel behavior, and how anxious or comfortable we feel.

8. Aside from our parents, the most important influences from the environment on our personalities seem to come from brothers, sisters, playmates, and school groups.

Wrapping It Up

Were people the same hundreds of years ago as they are now? Did they experience fear and joy and shame as we do? Most people would concede that we have not changed much, if at all. And after over 100 years of studying people, psychology still has only *theories* about human personality. Those students who hate to be pigeon-holed into types should be encouraged by this idea. It implies that we are so complex that we have to rely on theories, as opposed to laws, to explain what we are.

SUGGESTED READINGS

▼ Axline, Virginia. *Dibs in Search of Self.* New York: Ballantine Books, 1964.

▼ Bettelheim, Bruno. *Freud's Vienna and Other Essays.* New York: Vintage, 1989.

▼ Bloom, Harold, ed. *Sigmund Freud.* New York: Chelsea, 1985.

▼ Bjork, Daniel W. *B. F. Skinner.* New York: Basic Books, 1993.

▼ Erikson, Erik. *Identity and the Life Cycle.* New York: W. W. Norton, 1980.

▼ Freud, Sigmund. *Basic Writings of Sigmund Freud.* New York: Random House, 1938.

▼ Gay, Peter. *Freud: A Life For Our Time.* New York: W. W. Norton, 1988.

▼ Hall, Calvin. *A Primer of Freudian Psychology.* New York: Signet, 1954.

▼ Stafford-Clark, David. *What*

VOCABULARY

personality
psychoanalysis
Sigmund Freud
unconscious
free association
repression
libido
id
superego
ego
oral stage
anal stage

phallic stage
latency stage
genital stage
Carl Jung
archetypes
collective unconscious
persona
neo-Freudians
Karen Horney
Alfred Adler
Erik Erikson
behaviorism

B. F. Skinner
reinforcements
Albert Bandura
modeling
humanism
Carl Rogers
ideal self
fully functioning
    individual
Abraham Maslow
self-actualized
personality traits

Answers to Review Questions

1. c
2. d
3. b
4. c
5. b
6. c
7. a
8. b
9. a
10. d
11. a
12. d
13. superego
14. free association
15. persona
16. neo-Freudians
17. Horney
18. intimacy
19. self-actualized
20. true
21. false
22. true

Review Questions

Matching (Answers can be used more than once.)

1. The unconscious is biological and remains basically unaffected by the environment.
2. Anxiety and fear stem from a lack of love.
3. Free will does not really exist.
4. Sigmund Freud
5. Observing others helps shape our personalities.
6. Critics argue that it reduces humans to little more than animals.
7. Carl Rogers
8. B. F. Skinner
9. The whole person is emphasized.
10. Conflicts exist throughout life that need to be resolved in order to feel worthwhile.
11. Humans have a powerful potential for good.
12. The unconscious is concerned about how we get along with others.

a. humanism
b. behaviorism
c. early psychoanalysis
d. social psychoanalysis (neo-Freudians)

Freud Really Said. New York: Shocken, 1966.

▼ Torrey, E. Fuller. *Freudian Fraud: The Malignant Effects of Freud's Theory on American Thought and Culture.* New York: Harper-Collins, 1992.

SUGGESTED VIDEOS

▼ *Dr. Carl Rogers.* 50 min., 1969, Penn State.

▼ *Discussion with Carl Jung.* 36 min., 1968, Penn State.

▼ *Maslow and Self-Actualization.* 2 parts, 30 min. each, 1969, Psychological Films.

▼ *Reactions to Psychoanalytical Concepts.* 30 min., 1982, Karol Media.

Notes on Discussion Questions

1. Psychoanalysis became popular, in part, because of its initial emphasis on sex. Since sex was not openly discussed in Freud's time, people welcomed the introduction of an appropriate way to discuss it: psychoanalysis.

Answers to the second part of the question will vary. Mention that students' analyses need not be conducted by a Freudian, who would emphasize sexual motivation, but might be made by a neo-Freudian, who would emphasize social forces.

2. Horney would probably argue that Sharon is not receiving enough love. Adler would insist that Sharon does not feel important or worthwhile.

3. This might be a good journal topic.

Fill in the blanks; answer on a separate sheet of paper. (An answer may consist of more than one word.)

13. According to Freud, the part of the personality that makes us feel guilty is called the ___?___.
14. Freud's method for studying the unconscious is called ___?___.
15. One's psychological mask, or ___?___, hides one's real personality.
16. Those psychologists who broke away from Freud to emphasize social forces are sometimes referred to as ___?___.

17. ___?___ argued that love is an essential ingredient for a healthy personality.
18. Erikson's term for sharing a special closeness with another is called ___?___.
19. According to Maslow, a person who strives to fulfill his or her potential is becoming ___?___.

True/False

20. Evidence suggests that friendliness does not change much with age.
21. Studies consistently show that birth order has a significant effect on personality.
22. Evidence suggests that a tendency to feel anxious does not change much with age.

DISCUSSION QUESTIONS

1. There was a time when it was very fashionable to be psychoanalyzed. Why do you suppose it was popular? Also, do you think you would ever want to be psychoanalyzed? Why or why not?
2. Sharon suffers from a severe bout of depression. How would Horney's explanation of her depression differ from Adler's?
3. Freud was probably correct to some extent in saying that much of our personality remains the same as we grow. Erikson was also probably correct to some extent in saying that much or our personality *does* change. Think back on your junior high school years. Describe aspects of your personality that have changed and aspects that have remained essentially the same.

4. If you were suffering from depression over the breakup of a relationship and you decided you wanted to see a therapist, would you prefer to talk with a behaviorist or with a humanist? Why?
5. Implementing humanism in the classroom in the 1960s turned out to be a disaster. Despite this, some people might argue that there's nothing wrong with applying humanistic ideas in the classroom, as long as certain guidelines are set. Propose a humanistic change you'd like to see adopted at your school. Make the proposal practical and somewhat detailed. (A "humanistic" change would be one that would encourage students to handle their own fates.)

4. Students will better understand this question after they read Chapter 19. For now, be sure they support their answers with material from the chapter. A behaviorist would analyze depression in terms of behavior: is the person sleeping less, eating less, crying more? The behaviorist would then try to pinpoint the specific conditions that cause or are associated with these behaviors. A humanist, on the other hand, would view the depression in a more holistic manner: how is the person feeling about life, about the depression? Ultimately, according to the humanist, the person has the inner strength to heal himself or herself; the humanist would simply help the person realize this strength.

5. Students enjoy criticizing school policies but rarely offer practical alternatives. This is their chance to do the latter. Here are some possible humanistic changes that students may mention: (a) Students should be given more long-range due dates for assignments. It will be up to students to budget their time. In college, most assignments are handled in this way. Can high school students handle this? Probably not. Even a behaviorist would admit that changing one small aspect of the environment may not be enough to alter behavior. (b) Students should be

allowed to roam the halls whenever they like. The ones who disturb classes can be put in study halls. (c) Students should be able to choose their own classes, teachers, and schedules.

6. You should get some interesting responses to this question. Categorize some of their answers as psychoanalytical, behavioral, or

humanistic. The purpose of this categorization is not to pigeonhole their responses or personalities but to elucidate the three theories.

7. Make sure that students offer specific examples.

8. The most likely responses will be that Freud's theory best explains mental disorders—Freud treated hysterical patients—and that humanism

---

6. If you could magically change one aspect of your personality—right now—would you choose to change something? If so, what would you change and why? If not, why not? Also, what is one aspect of your personality that you would never change? Explain.

7. The chapter explains that three personality traits seem not to change with age:

friendliness, trying new things, and anxiety. Does this conclusion accurately describe your own life? Why or why not?

8. Out of all the theories presented in the chapter, which one seems best suited to understanding someone with a severe mental disorder, and which one is best suited to understanding someone who is relatively healthy? Explain.

ACTIVITIES

1. When we think of modeling, we usually think of the long-term effects that our parents as models have had on us. It might be fun to examine if modeling is a factor at all between strangers. You'll need to go to a mall (or a similar setting) with a friend to conduct this experiment. The hypothesis will be this: people are more likely to be influenced by a model who resembles them than by a model who is vastly different.

   General Procedure: Either you or your friend should dress in a "traditional" manner. *You* decide what might be considered traditional for your area. The other person should dress in a more "radical" manner. Again, you decide what radical means. Your task will be to find 20 people who fit your "traditional" definition.

   Specific Procedure: The traditionally dressed person, or the *model* in this case, will sit next to a subject. After about a minute of so, the radically dressed person will approach the model and say, "I'm doing a report for school on shoppers in malls. Would you mind filling out a survey?" Repeat this procedure ten times. Half the time, the model will say, "Yes, I love filling out surveys"; the other half of the time, the model will say something like this: "Nothing personal—but it seems that every time I come here I fill out ten surveys. I'd rather not right now." After

each "yes" or "no" from the model, the survey person will then ask the subject, who has been overhearing all this, the same question. Record whether the subjects agree to take the survey and if the subjects' responses match the model's. Finally, repeat this entire procedure, using the "radical" person as the model this time.

   The survey mentioned is mainly camouflage, but if the subject agrees to take the survey, you need to have something ready. So just write a quick survey with questions like, "How often do you shop?" and "Do you usually shop with friends or by yourself?"—and make 20 copies of the survey. If you want, you can include one or two "meaningful" questions that you *will* analyze, which might relate to your modeling hypothesis. For example, "Should male store clerks be required to wear ties? Should female store clerks be required to wear dresses?"

   Analyze your results. It might be helpful to draw a simple chart summarizing your results for each model. *Did* the traditional model have a greater effect on responses than the radical model? Make several guesses as to why or why not. What other conclusions can you draw from your results? Discuss. Finally, describe some of the memorable reactions you received from your subjects.

best explains healthy behavior, since it emphasizes self-actualization.

Notes on Activities

1. Since the directions for this activity are so lengthy, you might want to spend a few minutes in class fielding questions. Also, have students make a list of clothes (and hairstyles) that a traditional and a radical model would wear. If you can pare down this list and convince all traditional models and all radical models to dress almost identically, perhaps you can tally everyone's results and draw overall conclusions with some degree of validity. Even if you do not plan on combining everyone's results, it's probably a good idea to devise a consistent and somewhat objective definition of traditional and radical for your area; this will communicate to students the need to be consistent when collecting data.

2. See activity #1. In this case, all you'll need to determine is what constitutes *young* and *old*.

3. Again, since the directions are so lengthy, spend a few minutes in class fielding questions. Encourage students to be sincere in their descriptions; the more sincere they are, the more meaningful the activity will be. Consider allowing students to choose their own five categories for the activity; this freedom of choice may make the activity more appealing. Finally, assure students that their descriptions will not be read aloud in class, which may promote more openness on their part.

4. Discuss the results of this activity in class. It can lead to an interesting discussion on dating.

2. This next activity is a variation on the previous one. Follow the same procedure, but this time both experimenters should dress "traditionally" (since dress will not be a factor examined this time). This time you will examine what *kinds* of subjects are most likely to be affected by modeling. To find out, use *one* of the following three categories for your subjects: (a) ten "young" versus ten "old" subjects; (b) ten females versus ten males; (c) ten people alone versus ten people in a group. Analyze your results, draw a chart, discuss your conclusions, and describe memorable reactions, just as in the previous activity.

3. As explained in the chapter, we all have some notion of our ideal selves, how we would ideally like to be. Pretend that you have, at this moment, become this ideal self. Don't make this ideal so perfect that you could never possibly achieve it. Simply envision how you would like to be in the near future. With this notion of your ideal self in mind, consider the following categories and describe your attitudes toward these categories from the point of view of your ideal self:

a. school   b. money   c. gender roles
d. family   e. friends.

Remember, you should describe your ideal attitudes—not your material ambitions. For example, for the money category, you wouldn't describe how much money you'll make as your ideal self, but your attitude toward money in general. Here's a sample (remember, the ideal self is writing): "I used to think that I wanted to be rich, but it's not that important to me now." You might write something like this, for example, if you presently seem too preoccupied with money. Write approximately a paragraph for each category. (If writing from the ideal point of view is awkward, write it in any way you like, as long as you still describe your ideal attitudes.) Write your descriptions before reading further.

Write all five categories listed above on each of four separate sheets of paper. Hand two of the sheets to two friends and the other two sheets to two family members. Instruct them to write about what they perceive to be your *real* attitude today toward these categories. Have them write about a paragraph on each category. In other words, these four people will describe your *real* self, as they see you. Tell them to be as specific as possible.

Compare you *ideal* descriptions with others' *real* descriptions in detail. Are they very similar or dissimilar? Explain. According to your comparison, would you say that you're a "fully functioning individual"? Explain.

4. Not only do we have notions about our own ideal selves but we also have notions about ideal relationships. Survey five males and five females at random, and have them describe, in order, the top three *ideal* personality traits of someone they'd like to date.

Next, survey five males and five females (not the same people as before) who have been dating the same person for over a month. Ask them to describe, in order, the top three (*real*) personality traits of their dating partners.

Compare the *ideal* traits with the *real* traits in detail. Are they very similar or dissimilar? Explain. What conclusions can you draw about dating from all this? Explain. Finally, answer this discussion question:

According to Rogers, if a person feels a big discrepancy between his or her real and ideal self, that person can work to bridge the "gap." What if a person's conception of an ideal dating partner doesn't match the real traits of his or her partner? Can the person who feels this discrepancy do anything to bridge *that* gap (besides breaking up or trying to *change* the other person)? Explain.

DISCUSS THE PHOTO

Perhaps the very process of measuring special abilities interferes with the performance of those special abilities.

Special abilities may be difficult to measure precisely.

418

PSYCHOLOGY AND YOU RESOURCES

A variety of resources are available in the Psychology and You *supplementary material. In addition, there are a number of additional resources listed to enhance your lesson plans.*

Masters
▼ 15-1A Learning Goals
▼ 15-1B Answers to Learning Goals
▼ 15-2 Inkblot Analysis
▼ 15-3 Résumé 1
▼ 15-4 Résumé 2

Student Worksheets
▼ Vocabulary Worksheet
▼ Independent Practice Worksheet
▼ Enrichment Worksheet
▼ Reteaching Worksheet

Test Bank
▼ Tests A and B

Multimedia
▼ Psychology Videodisc

Student Workbook

PACING CHART

Complete Coverage

Day 1: Have students read the first four sections of the chapter before class. Assign an in-class project addressing the factors involved in designing a personality test (standardization, establishing norms, validity, and reliability). Discuss the problems inherent in personality inventories and projective tests. Assign "Aptitude and Achievement Tests" for homework.

Day 2: Using the SAT as an example, discuss the differences between tests measuring aptitude and those measuring achievement. Review the design and purpose of vocational interest tests. Have students read the next two sections for Day 3.

Day 3: When discussing alternatives to testing, utilize an activity to illustrate the halo effect. Point out the difference between testing and situational assessment. Assign the last section for Day 4.

OBJECTIVES

Be able to:

▼ Explain the purpose of using psychological tests.

▼ Discuss the importance of validity, reliability, and norms.

▼ Compare projective tests with personality inventories.

▼ Describe the differences between aptitude and achievement tests.

▼ Explain the construction of the Strong-Campbell Interest Inventory.

▼ Discuss alternate methods to testing.

Global Look at the Chapter

Psychological tests are designed to measure facts about the individual objectively. The goals are to avoid bias of the type found in an interview and to compare individuals as factually as possible. The major tests are for personality, aptitude, achievement, and vocational interest. So far, such tests are the most accurate method we have to evaluate people in these areas.

419

INTRODUCING THE CHAPTER

See the **Lead-Off Activity.** At this point in the course, your savvy students may see through your inkblot charade, which is OK. Have them point out what they perceive to be the problems with your inkblot analyses. Regardless of their answers, this discussion should provide a lead-in to the material on norms, validity, reliability, and projective tests. Explain what these concepts mean, and relate them to the inkblot test. Ask if there are any ways to make the inkblot test more reliable and valid. For example, what if the test included multiple choices (which would make it less projective)? What if the test were used along with other tests? What if the test were administered to the same person over a period of months—would this make it more reliable? Is it possible to establish norms for projective tests?

LEAD-OFF ACTIVITY

Create three or four ink blots similar to those shown in the chapter. An art teacher at your school may be willing to help. Display the ink blots in class, and announce that you are going to analyze some of the students' personalities. Ask for a volunteer to come to the front of the room to examine each ink blot closely. The volunteer should report what he or she sees in each ink blot. Make a note of the responses; you might even want to pretend that you are timing how long it takes the student to respond. Repeat this entire procedure with three or four other students.

Afterward, refer to **Teaching Master 15-2 Inkblot Analysis** and pretend that you are carefully comparing their responses to a list or a key of possible responses that will, in turn, provide a professional analysis of personality. Insist that it has taken years of research to arrive at these professional analyses. Randomly apply some of the nonsense analyses on the master to each student. Some may actually seem to apply, so use your judgment as to what analysis to use each time. See **Introducing the Chapter** above.

Day 4: Outline the ethical standards of testing and give the Chapter Review quiz.

In Brief

Day 1: Review the following terms: standardization, norms, validity, and reliability. Use discussion question #3 in the text to illustrate the purposes and shortcomings of personality inventories and projective tests.

Day 2: Discuss the differences between aptitude and achievement tests. Review the purpose of vocational interest tests.

Day 3: Point out the problems characteristic of alternatives to testing, such as the halo effect. Review the ethical standards applied to testing. Give the Chapter Review quiz.

CHAPTER PROJECT/COOPERATIVE LEARNING

Have students create their own personality inventory. Each group can focus on a particular aspect of personality: friendliness, introversion, shyness, risk taking, assertiveness, anxiety, or any other trait they want to explore. Suggest that they look at the Locus-of-Control Scale in Chapter 17 for a sample. You may not want to take the time to establish a norm, but you can discuss the process, along with those of establishing validity and reliability.

TEACHING MASTER 15-1A

Learning Goals. A Learning Goals sheet for each chapter is provided in the Teacher Resources. These Learning Goals can be used as review sheets or worksheets. **Teaching Master 15-1B** consists of answers to these Learning Goals.

Discussion

You have probably seen surveys that ask, "What do you look for in a friend or a mate?" Personality is usually ranked high in importance. How do we assess personality in everyday life? How long does it take to really get to know someone? What if you were going to get a roommate for the next year—what would you want to know?

Unit 5 PERSONALITY, ADJUSTMENT, AND CONFLICT

psychological tests

Objective measures of what people know, how they act, think, and feel, and what their goals are.

WHY PSYCHOLOGICAL TESTS ARE USED

The first thing we want to do is find out how many criminals and dangerous characters there are in your class. We can do this by using a book from 1911. According to its author, the really evil ones have the following four characteristics: (1) very low forehead; (2) strangely shaped head and jaw; (3) eyebrows growing together over the bridge of the nose; and (4) very protruding ears (like Mickey Mouse?) (Lombroso-Ferrero, 1911). You may find it hard to believe—or maybe not—but after the book came out, police frequently held people who looked this way on suspicion.

Next, let's divide up your classmates by body type. The very heavy ones are smiling, happy people, really good-natured. Those with muscular bodies love adventure and athletics and have muscles in the brain. Those who are skinny are extra sensitive to pain and read books all the time (Sheldon, 1936).

What do you think? The first theory you probably don't believe because it never became part of our culture. The second one, however, is a little harder to fight since so many people accept it, even though studies over the years have shown it to be false. While there are happy heavy people and brainy thin people, overall the body does not reflect a specific type of personality. For example, Sherlock Holmes, the brilliant fictional detective, fit the stereotype of thinness. However, his older *and even smarter* brother, Mycroft, was a very large man, quite overweight.

To try to find out what a person is really like and to avoid such wild speculation, psychologists use **psychological tests.** A psychological test is an objective measure of what people know; how they act, think, or feel; or what their goals are or should be. A psychological test can measure personality, intelligence, occupational needs, or job skills. These tests try to be as factual and unbiased as possible and provide a picture of personality or personal skills.

MAKING A PERSONALITY TEST

Suppose you wanted to make a test to find out what Sally X is really like. One of the first things you might do is pick test items that could reflect personality. Here are some. Did you have nightmares about monsters as a child? Do you sometimes hate school more than anything else in the world? Did you ever wet your bed? Do you ever have trouble getting to sleep?

These sound like they might give us some useful information for exploring Sally's inner workings. But if you take these items and ask

DEMONSTRATION

Bring in a photo from a magazine and have students write down their impressions of one of the people in the photo. Afterward, explain that they have assessed personality.

What's wrong with their assessments? Are they valid? Reliable? Did they arrive at them through standardized procedures? Were students guilty of using the halo effect?

Connections

Students may recall from Chapter 14 that there are three traits that seem to be present from childhood: how well a person gets along with others, how traditional a person is, and how much anxiety a person feels.

Chapter 15 MEASURING PERSONALITY AND PERSONAL ABILITIES

Sally to reply and she says "yes" to all of them, does she have a personality problem? The answer is *no*. All of us will answer "yes" to all these questions, if we are being truthful. So, we have a problem: if everyone answers "yes," we have no way of focusing on an individual personality.

Standardization

How can we make up a test that will work? Before going any further, we must have clear directions for taking the test, scoring it, and interpreting it. These procedures make up what is called **standardization.** When a test is standardized, it is given and "graded" exactly the same way for every person who takes it.

Establishing Norms

For the next step, you have to come up with many items covering many areas. Once you do that, you must give the items to a large number of different people—older, younger, male, female, and so forth. You do this to find out how most people in each group answer the questions. The answers will vary, depending on the group. You want to know what are the *normal,* expected, responses for most people in a specific group. By doing this, you are finding what are called **norms.** Norms show you the pattern of answers for different types of people. Since, in a personality test, we are trying to find something *individual* about the person, we will focus on the answers that are *not* common to those of her group to get a clue about Sally. If she answers questions like "I feel very happy most of the time" or "I never lie down when I'm studying" differently from her norm group, we believe we are picking up something special about her. In this way, we try to form a personality picture of her as compared to others. (Note that for purposes of testing, we assume that if most people feel a certain thing, it must be "normal." While this is not necessarily a good idea, it's the only way we can do it.)

Establishing Validity

The test has been given to enough different types of people to establish some norms. Can we now give the test to Sally X? Suppose her answers differ from the norm group in that she finds things upsetting that others do not, she has trouble getting along with teachers, and she can't seem to accept the standards of society. Can we tell her she has a personality problem and needs help? If we do, based on these findings, we are making the same error as the developer of the "criminal test" mentioned in the first paragraph. Just because something sounds good and we *think* it is the case, this

standardization

Clear directions for taking, scoring, and interpreting a test.

norms

Patterns of test answers from different types of people.

Points to Stress

Most students have taken tests under standardized procedures: "Open your test booklet . . . do not turn the page. . . ." In fact, recite these directions and students will probably have a Pavlovian response.

Teaching Hint

Draw a bell-shaped or normal curve (see the Statistics Appendix) and explain the normal frequency distribution. Most people, the norm, fall into the middle of the curve; the people least similar to the norm fall at either end of the curve.

ENRICHMENT

The Federal Bureau of Investigation (FBI) and other law enforcement agencies sometimes create a profile of a criminal at large based on the norms that other criminals have created. For example, criminals who know their victims often strike the face; if a criminal at large has done this to a victim, the profile may suggest an intense investigation of family, friends, and coworkers. Critics warn that these profiles often mislead the police, however. You can probably get a few students to find out about psychological profiles.

A Good Personality Test.

 IN FOCUS Seniors' answers would provide a norm.

Comprehension Check

You own a school that trains pilots. You have 200 students in your introductory class, but you can only accept 100. You are convinced that good pilots have certain personality characteristics and you want to be able to find out quickly who has them, using a personality inventory. How would you test the reliability and validity of this test? *(Reliability: give pilots similar tests at varying times to see if the scores remain the same. Validity: give the test to all 200 students, and track the progress of these 200 students. Do the top scorers also perform better on simulation exercises? Do the top scorers become better pilots—fewer accidents, mistakes, or however you want to define "better")? See the Chapter 9 wraparound material for more on validity and reliability.*

422

Unit 5 PERSONALITY, ADJUSTMENT, AND CONFLICT

IN FOCUS   A Good Personality Test

A thousand seniors sit in a classroom taking a personality test. Their answers will form the **NORM** for other seniors.

Suppose that 96 percent of the seniors say they study for at least one hour every school night. (Hard to imagine, but just suppose. . . .) What would this information begin to tell us?

Hint: it's one of the boldfaced words above.

doesn't make it so. As a matter of fact, if these are Sally's "problems," they match the answers of a group of highly creative students who deviate from the norm about as much as those who have serious personal difficulties.

DEMONSTRATION

Bring in several intriguing photos from magazines and have students write a paragraph about one or two of them, similar to what a subject taking a TAT test would do. Tell students to write only a code name on the papers. Collect and mix them up, then randomly hand the paragraphs back to students for analysis. The analysis is just for fun, but it should give them insight into problems with validity and reliability.

Chapter 15 MEASURING PERSONALITY AND PERSONAL ABILITIES

▲ *Although certainly not perfect, aptitude or achievement tests are still the best measure of what has been learned.*

So, how do we ever make certain a test is measuring what it is supposed to? For example, apart from personality, if we want to develop a test that will predict how good an accountant you would be, what do we do? Once the items are chosen, the test can be given to a group of students about to enter an accounting class. We would score this test, wait until they finished the class, and compare the scores they made with how well they did in the course. If the high scorers did well in the course and the low scorers did poorly, we know the test works. This is called test **validity.** If a test is valid, it measures what it is supposed to measure. Thus, before we can give the test to Sally, we first have to establish the validity of the test items we are using. This could be done by giving the personality items to large numbers of students and then finding out if those who answer certain items deviating from the norms drop out of school, are sent to the principal, get into fights, and so forth. If these people have all kinds of trouble, we have established validity; if not, the test is not valid—it doesn't measure what it is supposed to be measuring.

Establishing Reliability

One final thing must be done before we can have confidence in the test Sally will get. Test items can always be affected by what is going on around us. Most personality tests contain items such as "I feel

validity

Whether a test measures what it is supposed to measure.

Points to Stress

Late-night cable stations often try to sell videos that include personal assessment tests and improvement programs. Warn students that these tests probably have poor validity.

DISCUSS THE PHOTO

Find out if any of your students experience test anxiety during these types of tests and ask them how they overcome this anxiety.

ENRICHMENT

Students may want to find out about the selection process for astronauts. What personality characteristics does NASA look for? How high is personality ranked compared to skills and training?

Unit 5 PERSONALITY, ADJUSTMENT, AND CONFLICT

FYI On the Minnesota Multiphasic Personality Inventory 2 (MMPI-2), recipients answer "true," "false," or "cannot say" to a variety of statements, such as "I enjoy taking walks," or "A friend should never disagree" (these are not actual test items). Individual answers will not reveal much, but if answers form a pattern, psychologists can assess a variety of disorders, like depression or schizophrenia, by comparing subjects' profiles to the norms. With this information, students will probably start to recognize how valuable computers have become in scoring personality assessments.

reliability

Whether test results are consistent over time.

personality inventory

A list of items about a person's beliefs, habits, hopes, needs, and desires.

MMPI-2

Latest version of the Minnesota Multiphasic Personality Inventory, the most widely used personality inventory.

depressed" or "I feel left out and don't have many friends" and so forth. Suppose that Sally goes to a movie the night before the test. To her it is a very sad, depressing movie that makes everything seem hopeless. But her companion doesn't agree and hence cannot share Sally's emotions regarding the film. If Sally takes the test the next day, the odds that she will say she feels depressed and left out by her friends are very high—even though this may not be her typical state. So, answers to test questions should not be too influenced by temporary changes. In other words, the test must have **reliability.**

Reliability means that the answers must be reasonably consistent over time. A friend who shows up one time for a date 20 minutes early, one time three minutes late, one time 50 minutes late, and so forth is clearly unreliable. So, too, with the test. It is unreliable if it is inconsistent. One way to measure reliability is to give a test to group A on a given day. Then you give the same test to the same group, A, two weeks later. If their answers are mostly the same, then the test is reliable. If many answers have changed, the test is unreliable. You can see what would happen with the accounting test if one week you got 98 percent and the next you got 34 percent on the same test. Obviously, the test would not be measuring with any accuracy and couldn't be used to measure a person's accounting abilities or anything else.

In summary: A test must have a large number of items. It must be standardized, so everyone takes it the same way. It must be normed so that we know how different groups of people tend to answer the questions. It must be valid and measure what it claims to measure. And, finally, it must measure reliably.

PERSONALITY INVENTORIES

A **personality inventory** is a list of items about beliefs, habits, hopes, needs, and desires. The test is given using a test booklet and answer sheet. Its format is objective—that is, it consists of multiple-choice or true/false questions. The questions are very similar to the ones we've been talking about: "I believe people like me." "When I get bored, I stir things up." "I have a happy home." And so forth.

Probably the best known and most widely used personality inventory today is the *MMPI,* or Minnesota Multiphasic Personality Inventory. The MMPI has been in use since the 1940s and underwent major updating and revision in 1989. The new version is called the **MMPI-2.** A number of other personality inventories are based in part on this test. The MMPI-2 contains over 500 true/false items. These items are divided into scales, with cutoff points for the normal range of scores within each one. For example, there are scales for social shyness, depression, suspiciousness, anxiety, and so on. In addition, there are scales that try to determine how well the person under-

ENRICHMENT

For some reason, students enjoy analyzing projective tests and/or having their own answers analyzed—it seems to have the appeal of magic. As long as students don't take the tests too seriously, there's nothing wrong with their fascination. In fact, you can probably convince several students to study projective tests and become "experts." These experts can then analyze the stories, answers, or drawings of other students. You might suggest to your experts to find out about the house-tree-person test. See the **Suggested Readings** for this chapter. Or if you have a school psychologist, this person may be willing to help.

---

stood the questions and how much he or she lied or tried to put on a good act. Three more such scales were added to the revised edition.

The test used most often in schools is the **California Psychological Inventory.** It has 480 items, which are scored in terms of categories like feelings of self-acceptance, self-control, desire to achieve, how you get along with others, and the like (Gough, 1960). The test is one of the best of this type, but even given that, it is only *fairly* valid and reliable. Thus, it can be faulty for any given person, even though overall it is useful for locating quickly some people with difficulties. The trouble with these tests is that too often they also pick out people who *don't* have problems.

Another major problem with personality inventories is the meaning people attach to the items. For instance, answering "true" to the statement "People talk about me" might indicate a touch of paranoia. However, it could also indicate a source of pride. That is, it could be interpreted as proof that you are important enough that people are interested in discussing you. Similarly, believing that you are an agent of God *could* be an indication of some kind of distortion in your thought processes. On the other hand, it could simply be a statement of faith that all people are, in some way, agents of a higher spiritual power.

Still another problem is that the test score itself gives no clue about how well the person is handling life. Saying "I certainly feel useless" appears on the surface to express a personal problem. However, it tells us nothing about whether the person sees that as a serious difficulty with no solution in sight. He or she may feel that it is just an occasional fact of life to be endured until it passes and is of no particular significance. Even if it is seen as a problem, the person may also have a plan for resolving it.

Personality inventories are useful for general screening in order to locate those who might need help. Caution is always called for, though. A score that indicates the existence of a problem must always be followed up by a face-to-face discussion with a counselor or psychologist to avoid serious error (Anastasi, 1988).

PROJECTIVE TESTS

It is not too hard to "fool" a personality inventory by merely checking items to reflect the way you *wish* to be or the way you see yourself (which might not be that accurate). The inventories do have built-in lie scales to catch those who are not telling the truth. For example, one of them has a question, "I read every editorial in the newspaper every day." Nobody does that, so it trips up those who are faking. Also, personality inventories seem to deal pretty much with the surface, rather than getting down to the nitty-gritty of our deeper personalities.

California Psychological Inventory

Personality inventory most often used in schools.

Points to Stress

Personality inventories are fairly successful at picking out liars. For example, the same question might be asked three times in the same test, perhaps phrased a bit differently each time. During a lengthy test, it's difficult to remember how you answered the question the previous time. So it's best to be honest from the start.

Teaching Hint

This may be an obvious point, but ask students why projective tests don't use more definite stimuli, like a *real* cactus. In that case, there would be nothing to project. Ink blots, on the other hand, force subjects to process and create from within, not simply label something.

DISCOVERY

Projective tests. Have students bring in a picture that represents their personalities. For example, if a student is highly motivated and ambitious, this person might bring in a picture of a locomotive. The pictures should represent their personalities, not their interests. Someone who enjoys hockey should not bring in a picture of a hockey player. Students should not show anyone their pictures. In fact, have them (at home) tape their pictures onto a piece of loose-leaf paper to make everyone's pictures more uniform. Collect the pictures facedown, mix them up, and tape them onto the chalkboard. These pictures will be the "projections" of their personalities. (The pictures may not be projections in the strict sense of the term, but for the

---

Points to Stress

When using ink blots, although content is important, psychologists pay more attention to the process the subject uses. Does the subject use the entire picture each time? Parts of it?

Points to Stress

Subjects taking the TAT are often asked to expand on their stories or to create a new one for the same picture to see if there are any thematic similarities. As a teacher, you have probably noticed that you don't really get to know a student until the third or fourth paper. A psychologist analyzing the responses to a Rorschach test might pay attention not only to content but to the length of the answers, how much or how little of the picture the subject uses, and so on. With the TAT, only content is analyzed.

426

Unit 5 PERSONALITY, ADJUSTMENT, AND CONFLICT

projective tests

Tests measuring inner feelings elicited by a vague stimulus, such as an ink blot or unclear picture.

▲ *Figure 15.1*   *Example of a projective test.*

Rorschach test

Ink blot projective test developed by Hermann Rorschach.

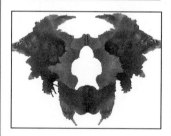

▲ *Figure 15.2*   *Ink blot test similar to the Rorschach.*

TAT

Thematic Apperception Test, a projective test using unclear pictures about which people make up stories.

To try to offset these problems, **projective tests** were designed. (You have to pay close attention here to get the logic of how these operate.) *Projection* here means the same thing that it does for a singer. A singer must project (throw) the voice outward until it lands on the audience. The same is true of the projective test. The test taker projects his or her innermost self onto the stimulus provided. For example, look at Figure 15.1. What is it? Some will say a cactus, some a fork, some a flower, and so forth. The answer will vary, depending on the person's experiences in life. Such an example is simple, but it shows the principle of the projective test. If the stimulus is more complex and the test taker is told to list a number of things it looks like, psychologists assume that some of the answers are coming from deeper in the personality.

The Ink Blot Test

The most famous projective test is the "ink blot," called the **Rorschach** (ROAR-shock) **test** after the designer, a Swiss psychiatrist named Hermann Rorschach. (Incredible as it seems, his nickname in school, "Klex," means "ink blot.") Rorschach spent much time in his basement splashing ink onto the middle of pieces of paper and then folding them together to get designs similar to that shown in Figure 15.2. After going through hundreds, he finally settled on ten of them, some in color, which were printed on cards. He believed that those who look at the card and see something moving in the blot (projection) have a lot of emotion and a good fantasy life. Those seeing color are explosive people. Those seeing lots of white space are negative people. What Rorschach based his conclusions on has never been clear, and the validity of the Rorschach is terrible. So is its reliability, because the second time around most people see entirely different things.

The TAT

The Thematic Apperception Test, or **TAT** for short, is another projective test. In the TAT, test takers are shown pictures that are vague and can be interpreted in many ways. They are asked to make up stories about what is happening in the pictures. The themes of their stories (hence, the word *thematic* in the name of the test) are then interpreted by the psychologist.

If you look at Figure 15.3, you will see a picture of two women. One person might say that the woman in front is listening to the evil part of herself, telling her to do something. Such an answer might indicate a conflict in the test taker. Or it might just be a theme from a television show or novel. But if the test taker sees enough cards and tells enough similar stories about personal problems of the same

sake of this activity, assume that students' choices reflect their innermost self.) For each picture, have the class try to develop a brief profile of the person who brought it in. Is the person male or female? Extroverted or introverted? Cautious or easygo-

ing? Under each picture, write down some of the class's responses. Afterward, go back to each picture, and have the owner of each remark on how accurate, the profile was. If the profiles are accurate, point out that the profiles were made by

friends and acquaintances. Would an objective outsider have developed the same profiles? If the profiles are not that accurate, this should demonstrate how difficult it is to measure personality through an open-ended test such as this one.

---

type, the tester can get a rough idea of some of the core problems that might exist. Again, validity and reliability are low, but they are better with the TAT than the Rorschach.

The Principle of Projection

According to the principle of projection, you see a vague stimulus, and you are asked to give responses. The more responses given, the more likely you are to dig into your deeper self. Even if this works, though, it is still hard to know what the responses given really mean.

Are projective tests of any use? Probably some, but not as much as you might think. They do offer the counselor or psychologist a chance to talk to the test taker, and they give some idea of how the test taker approaches problems. If the test taker is very disturbed, he or she might see bizarre, strange objects and events in the pictures (Anastasi, 1988). Some psychologists ignore the poor validity and claim the tests help them understand the person. While they are entitled to their views, in general high validity is much preferred.

APTITUDE AND ACHIEVEMENT TESTS

The major goal of any kind of testing is to sort out individual skills or characteristics when dealing with large numbers of people. An attempt is made not only to understand people but also to aim them in the right direction. For instance, a person whose eyes widen and who secretly begins to feel terrified and wants to scratch the floor on an airplane in an attempt to escape should avoid working toward being a flight attendant or pilot. On the other hand, people who love small detail and are precise should check out their skills in bookkeeping or accounting to see if these might be the fields for them to pursue.

We will discuss some of the tests available in these areas, but first we have to sort out some confusing terminology. *Intelligence*, which was discussed at length in Chapter 9, is supposed to be a measure of our overall ability to handle general mental problems. The word *general* is used because intelligence is not thought to be specific. The two types of tests we will cover here *are* specific; they deal with specific, not general, abilities.

Aptitude Tests

The word **aptitude** is part of our everyday vocabulary. We say so-and-so has an aptitude for medicine, or for law, or carpentry, or

---

Chapter 15 MEASURING PERSONALITY AND PERSONAL ABILITIES

▲ *Figure 15.3   Card from the Thematic Apperception Test.*

aptitude

One's special skills.

FYI Students may have heard of serial killer Jeffrey Dahmer. He had been given projective tests several times while incarcerated for minor violations, and he managed to fool nearly everyone with his innocuous responses.

DISCUSS THE PHOTO

Students may enjoy making up their own stories about this card.

Teaching Hint

The movie, *Miracle on 34th Street*, includes a hilarious scene in which the store psychologist gives Santa Claus an inkblot test. Santa ends up hitting the psychologist on the head with his umbrella. The psychologist, in this case, deserved it; he took the test too seriously.

INTERDISCIPLINARY PROJECT

Physical Education. Ask students to create an aptitude test for a particular sport. For example, for tennis, the test could measure one's knowledge of basic physics, which may influence whether one will understand about the rotation of the ball, the motion of the swing, and so on.

Points to Stress

Another value of projective tests: if subjects freeze up on other, more objective tests because of the nature of the questions, projective tests may reveal how they really feel.

DISCUSS THE PHOTO

The answer is: to the left.

Comprehension Check

Ask students to offer examples of an objective and a subjective personality test. *(Objective tests provide choices: personality inventories. For subjective tests, subjects must provide their own answers: projective tests.)*

Discussion

What do students think about the weight that the SATs carry in the college admissions process? Should grades count more? Is there any problem with using grades as the *sole* criteria for admission into a college?

428

---

aptitude tests

Tests that measure one's special skills (in carpentry, medicine, and so forth).

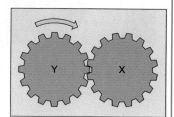

▲ *Figure 15.4   A mechanical aptitude test item: if the gear on the left turns in the direction of the arrow, what direction does the gear on the right turn?*

---

engineering. We mean that this person seems to have special skills in that area.

Aptitudes are hard to measure with tests. But there are some **aptitude tests** available. These tests are usually grouped together, in the sense that the person takes all of them to see in which categories he or she scores highest. Here are some examples:

Mechanical Comprehension   This test attempts to predict success in fields involving repair of autos, refrigerators, air-conditioning equipment, and the like. A typical item is shown in Figure 15.4. If gear X is moving in the direction of the arrow, will gear Y move: (a) clockwise or (b) counterclockwise? This item and many *very* complex ones are used to measure a person's understanding of mechanical devices. The scores are compared with the scores of people who are already in these fields to see how well the test taker does. (Remember norm groups and validity?)

Verbal Skills   This test measures a person's interest in and knowledge about words. We assume that someone who scores poorly in this area will not do well in occupations requiring a great deal of reading or writing. An example of a simple test item in this area is: which word is spelled incorrectly? (a) horse (b) house (c) humit (d) hanger.

Clerical Speed and Accuracy   Attempts to measure some of the skills necessary in clerical and office jobs fall into this category. This particular test is a timed, speed test because even though you might be able to get the answers, if it takes you forever to do so, you won't be much use on the job. A typical item is: as quickly as you can, find the underlined test items and mark them on your answer sheet.

Test Item	Answer Sheet
MS MQ <u>MP</u> MF	A. MF MQ MP MX
A7 B2 AB <u>C3</u>	B. C3 B3 B2 A7

This sampling should give you an idea of the kinds of aptitude tests available. None is accurate enough to predict success in a field. But they can give clues to areas in which you might do well or that you should avoid. Their validities and reliabilities are good, but they measure only a small part of what would be involved in any given occupation (Cronbach, 1990).

Achievement Tests

Another kind of test is given in elementary school and high school to measure student progress. These tests are often used to determine

ENRICHMENT

Invite a reading teacher to class to administer a sample SAT test. The person can probably offer students valuable tips on taking the actual test.

how well a school system or class is doing, but they can also be useful when counseling an individual student. They resemble the exams given in history, English, or math courses, but they are usually normed for the whole country or for certain segments of it. Sometimes they are used to give advanced placement in a certain subject to a student. Such tests are called **achievement tests** because they contain specific content that was (or should have been) learned in the classroom. Those who do best in class achieve the most in a certain area. The tests are not designed to predict future performance or skills, as is the case with an aptitude test—even though we assume that if you do well now in a particular area on the test, you will do so in the future.

Most students who plan to go to college run head-on into one of life's dreaded experiences: taking the **Scholastic Assessment Test,** or SAT for short. It used to be called the Scholastic *Aptitude* Test, which created a lot of controversy. The name change may help, but problems remain nonetheless. The issue is whether the SAT measures potential for learning, one's aptitude, or instead taps what one has already learned, one's achievement.

The SAT is made up of advanced verbal and mathematical problems. You have to be able to define the meaning of words as they fit into certain sentences, solve word puzzles, and deal with fairly complex logic and mathematics problems.

But there are some difficulties. The SAT is supposed to be a *predictor* of college work, not an achievement test. Is that even possible? Doesn't the test require that you have learned specific math techniques in order to answer the questions? Or that you have had a course in social science in order to deal with verbal social science problems? That certainly seems to be the case. For example, let's take this:

Columbus discovered America in: (a) 1492 (b) 1700 (c) 1859 (d) 1950.

This item is a good *achievement* test item for a history test in fourth grade. We would expect this information to be part of a course in basic American history. It is assumed that by high school, everyone has already learned the answer and remembers it. We certainly hope you do (it's not 1950). So, this same item can become part of an *aptitude* test for high school students. How is this possible? Aptitude tests use such items based on the assumption that as one goes through school life, those who absorb and retain the most material are also going to be the best in that area in the future because by then they will know even more. You see how complicated this is? There seems to be no way to write an aptitude test item without getting involved in how well you've done in school and how much you remember from school. Thus, the SAT does measure achievement, in large part, especially the verbal section. The mathematics part relies more on reasoning than remembering formulas (Cronbach, 1990).

achievement tests

Tests that measure the amount of specific material remembered from the classroom.

Scholastic Assessment Test

SAT, test designed to measure ability to do college work.

Evaluation Strategy

Ask students to respond to the following situation: You meet someone to whom you are attracted, but before you convey this, you would like to know more about this person. You get to administer two personality tests to this person, one with high validity and one with low validity. Which two do you use? (High validity: personality inventory or interest test. Low validity: probably a projective test.)

Comprehension Check

What is the difference between achievement and aptitude? *(Achievement refers to what we know. Aptitude refers to our potential for certain skills.)*

ENRICHMENT

Ask students to visit their school counselors to take a vocational interest test. Have them look at the three occupations in which they scored highest, and then have them interview someone who is currently employed in that occupation.

Students can use questions adapted from the vocational interest test for the interview. Afterward, have them assess how accurate the interest test seemed to be. If students complain that they do not know anyone in the three occupations in which they

scored highest, have them consult the yellow pages. They might even conduct an interview over the phone.

Journal Topic

"Some people are more aware or sure of their vocational interests than others, but just for fun, envision yourself in an occupation, even if it seems unrealistic. What would you enjoy about the job? Describe what you think would be a typical day on the job." You might get a student or two who "can't" think of an occupation. Assign them a job they are familiar with.

Unit 5 PERSONALITY, ADJUSTMENT, AND CONFLICT

vocational interest test

A test that attempts to predict a good occupational area for an individual.

The biggest problem with the SAT is that environments differ so much from one person to another. We knew a psychologist who had never before been out of New York City and had never seen a live horse, cow, or pig. He was giving a talk to some grade-schoolers in a rural part of West Virginia. The children couldn't believe it when he asked them if any of them had the task of milking the cows that were in a pen next to the school. The problem was that the "cows" were pigs.

It is, then, impossible to measure aptitude without at the same time measuring achievement, which makes the SAT somewhat questionable (Green, 1978; Owen, 1983). Since schools vary as much as does the overall environment, the test leans toward those from well-to-do schools. There are other problems: a low score can damage a person's self-esteem, and the test *can* err as much as 30 points in either direction just by chance. Expensive coaching for the test beforehand can help some students, again giving an advantage to those with money. But on the average, coaching doesn't help to an extent that matches the cost. Some people claim that the test is biased against minorities, and there is support for this (Morgan, 1984).

On the positive side, the test has good validity and reliability for enough students to make it worthwhile. And it does a much better job of predicting college success than an interview or letters of recommendation (Kaplan, 1982). While high school grade averages are better predictors of college success than the SAT, the test can add a little bit to predicting a person's chances for success (Weiss & Davidsom, 1981). (Note, though, that college success is only about 50 percent predictable, no matter how many or what measures are used.)

VOCATIONAL INTEREST TESTS

Probably one of the most important long-term goals any of us ever strives for is the one involving occupation. If things turn out well, most of us stay in the same general field throughout life, even though we may change where we work a number of times.

Areas of interest keep changing for most students until their junior or senior year in high school. Then they begin to become focused—at least in a general sort of way.

One of the most useful tests a student can take is the **vocational interest test.** Fortunately, the major tests in this area have some of the highest validities in psychological testing. Hence, their ability to predict is exceptional compared to the other tests we have discussed. Over 50 percent of people in some studies have been checked up on for more than 20 years after taking the test and are still reasonably happy in the selected occupation (Walsh & Betz, 1985).

ENRICHMENT

Consider inviting a counselor or your school psychologist to class to discuss how he or she uses tests, how students can prepare for achievement tests, and how reliable and valid personality, aptitude, and vocational interest tests are. If this person can't visit, maybe he or she can give you some sample tests to administer to your students.

▲ *Which job are you best suited for?*

Chapter 15 MEASURING PERSONALITY AND PERSONAL ABILITIES

DISCUSS THE PHOTO

Have someone assume the role of a teacher or a construction worker or an underwater performer, and allow the rest of the class to interview this person.

The Strong-Campbell Interest Inventory

The most used interest test is called the **Strong-Campbell Interest Inventory.** It is named after the two developers of the test. The test taker is provided with a test booklet answer sheet. The test contains hundreds of statements and choices to which the test taker responds with "like" or "dislike," "agree" or "disagree." Or the person is asked to choose among such things as being an actor, being an artist, or being a botanist. This is simple enough, but the test is actually more clever than it seems at first. Most people starting out, when faced with a choice of occupations, aren't sure at all what they want to be. Hence, it might do no good to ask these questions; if you already knew the answers, you wouldn't need the test. So the test's authors took thousands of people reasonably successful in all kinds of occupations and gave these occupational questions to them. Also included in the test were all kinds of questions not related directly to occupation, such as "Would you rather drive along the side of a mountain, discuss the purpose of life, or go fishing?" and so forth.

Next, all the test answers (occupational and otherwise) for all these people were divided up according to what occupation they were in, *not* according to how they answered the questions. When new test takers answer questions, a computer compares their answers with those of the people in each of hundreds of occupations and points out the occupational groups with which the test taker has the most in common. The content of the item is *not* important, which might well be the key to the success of the test. For example, if you agree that you would like to be an "auctioneer," this carries a *negative* weight for a score high on engineering since real-life engineers don't want to be auctioneers. We don't know why—they just don't. It turns out that as a group, real-life lawyers might prefer to be skydivers—at least on paper—and so, if you check the same answer they do on that item, you are given a plus toward a career in law. Hence, the test is showing you how similar you are in hobbies, activities, interests, and the like to people already in different occupations. If you

Strong-Campbell Interest Inventory

The most widely used interest test; based on answers of people successful in certain fields.

Comprehension Check

What *don't* vocational interest tests measure? *(Your aptitude for an occupation in which you score high)*

DISCOVERY

Have your own career day in class by inviting people from various careers to visit. Why did they choose their careers? Do the careers match their other interests? What advice can they offer on matching interests with careers? The easiest way to conduct this activity is to invite the parents of your students.

Discussion

If you don't obtain a vocational interest test, discuss the following choices. Perhaps students can rank them: which would they most and least like to do? (1) Would you like to work with your hands, building or fixing things (for example, as a carpenter)? (2) Would you like to work in a lab doing research? (3) Would you like to work with a pen or brush or camera, creating? (4) Would you like to help people (for example, as a counselor or a police officer)? (5) Would you like to work as a businessperson (for example, as an investment consultant or salesperson)? (6) Would you like to work at a desk?

have that much in common with them, you will probably like that occupation (Cronbach, 1990).

The results from the test are reported on a computer printout showing many occupations that fall into such categories as working outdoors, working in science, engaging in artistic tasks, helping people directly, working in sales or politics, and doing business or clerical work. How high you score in these areas is shown as you are compared with others in the various fields.

One of the biggest problems faced in using these tests is a misunderstanding about how they work. Students might score high on an occupation like "funeral director" and come away from the test saying, "Oh, ick, I don't want to deal with dead bodies." But none of the occupations is to be taken at face value in that way. A funeral director is interested in running a small business, dealing with the public, helping people who are in need, and the like. If used in the right spirit, the test can be enormously helpful. Finally, the test is very good at helping you to eliminate certain occupations. If you score low in most occupations within a certain area, the chances that you will like any of those occupations are quite remote (Walsh & Betz, 1985).

Cautions About Interest Tests

It is critical to understand that the interest test does not show that you have the aptitude or ability for an occupation in which you score high. So, try not to set your sights on jobs that deep in your heart, you know you are not qualified for. But we all can adapt goals to a different type of work in a field we like. For example, in real life, the pilots think they are the most important part of an airline, the mechanics feel *they're* the most important, the flight attendants feel the airline would fail without their aid and public relations work, and the executives think they are really keeping it all together. The point is that a person with clear-cut aviation interests will fit into one (or more) of these subcategories better than the others and can still be in his or her desired field.

A SECOND LOOK AT TEST VALIDITY

Tests of all kinds have a way of seeming more powerful and accurate than they really are. This is a lot like the idea that if you read something in print, it *must* be true. Stop and think about any obnoxious or goofy people you know. Someday some of them will be writing things that find their way into print. Would you believe something you read if you knew they had written it? The same principle applies to tests.

DISCOVERY

Administer a personality inventory to your students. Here are some addresses of organizations that may be able to supply you with tests: (1) Consulting Psychologists Press, Inc., 577 College Avenue, Palo Alto, CA 94306; (2) Institute for Personality and Ability Testing, PO Box 1188, Champaign, IL 61824-0188; (3) Psychological Corporation, 757 3rd Avenue, New York, NY 10017.

Chapter 15 MEASURING PERSONALITY AND PERSONAL ABILITIES

IN FOCUS   Tests and More Tests

	Personality Inventory	Aptitude Test	Achievement Test	Vocational Interest Test
General Purpose	Reveals beliefs, habits, hopes, needs, desires	Reveals or measures one's special skills	Measures amount of material remembered from classroom—*not* designed to predict future performance	Predicts suitable occupation Does *not* show aptitude for an occupation or ability
Positive Aspects	Locates those who might need help	Locates areas in which one might do well and areas one should avoid	Can be used to evaluate a school system or an individual—can help with advanced placement	Usually high validity—helps one eliminate certain occupations
Problems	Sometimes singles out those who don't really have problems	Not accurate enough to predict success in a field	Sometimes *used* as a predictor of future performance	Individuals may misinterpret their scores
Examples	California Psychological Inventory MMPI	Mechanical comprehension Verbal skills	SAT	Strong-Campbell Interest Inventory

Imagine that you are an expert at interpreting the results of these tests. Subject "A" completes all of the above tests. Assuming you avoid the problems listed above, what information about "A" would the tests still not reveal?

Tests and More Tests.

IN FOCUS   The tests may not reveal a person's determination, which may be a better predictor of success than any test. Any answers are acceptable, but insist that students provide support for their answers.

This is a good place to look again and a little more closely at *validity*. We will use completely imaginary numbers just to help you grasp the point. Suppose you had a tub filled with 100 red marbles and 100 white marbles, mixed. We will blindfold you and have you pull out 100 marbles. White means no error; red, an error. We will call perfect validity 100 white marbles. You pull out 53 white and 47 red ones. That means you made an "error" 47 times. Such is the case with validity—which is never perfect. In fact, in real life, tests that produce results like this would be considered to have good validity. Why? Because, as you'll see in the next section, many methods, such as interviewing, will only produce perhaps 20 white marbles. Hence, tests work better than interviewing. In any case, always check with a counselor about any test results, and then,

ACTIVITY
ACTIVITY
ACTIVITY
ACTIVITY
ACTIVITY
ACTIVITY
ACTIVI

EXPERIMENT

See **Teaching Masters 15-3 Résumé 1** and **15-4 Résumé 2.**

These handouts allow you to conduct an experiment on the halo and reverse halo effect. Pass out copies of one of these masters to half of your students and copies of the other master to the other half. Students simply follow the directions and fill in the blanks. The masters are nearly identical except for the grade point averages of the applicants. See if you find a difference in students' ratings. Consider having students collect data in the hallways using the two masters. In that case, subjects should write their answers on a separate sheet of paper.

Points to Stress

Despite problems, interviews remain a highly valuable tool. For example, many hospitals now hire psychologists to work the emergency rooms to screen some patients before releasing them. This is part of the new awareness in this country that we must heal the mind and not just the body—otherwise, many patients will just keep returning. These psychologists conduct brief interviews that include questions like "Are you thinking about suicide?" In this case, there's no substitute for such directness. An interview also gives the psychologist a chance to observe nonverbal cues as well, which might range from the tone of voice to whether the person's clothes are on backward.

Points to Stress

Another limitation of interviews: the interviewer may allow his or her personality to interfere with the interview.

halo effect

The situation where a person who has one positive characteristic is assumed to have other positive traits.

reverse halo

The situation where a person with one negative characteristic is assumed to have other negative traits.

standoutishness

Doing or wearing something that is so startling it detracts from one's real abilities.

---

assuming you are being truly honest and reasonable with yourself, go with your instincts about whether the results are right or not.

ALTERNATIVES TO TESTING

Despite the problems we have mentioned, a test remains the most valid and reliable method for getting information. All of us like to think we are as objective as the tests if we are called on to be so, but that apparently isn't the case.

Interviews

One of the worst problems in interviewing is the **halo effect.** The halo effect applies when a person with one positive characteristic is assumed to have other positive traits as well. No one checks to see if this is actually the case; it is simply assumed to be correct. We all know students who play up to the teacher so much that they seem to have a "halo" glowing above their heads. Often these students get special treatment and recommendations when everyone in the class knows they are unpleasant and devious people. In almost any kind of interview, they will come off well, making the interviewer think they are bright, helpful, useful—all of which may be false.

There is also the **reverse halo,** where a negative characteristic leads to the assumption of other negative aspects. The student who does dumb things, like throwing things in class, may have great potential, but it is hidden by this behavior. So, in this case also the teacher or interviewer tends not to see the real person; they are taken in by the reverse halo.

Since the interview takes place in person, there is another pitfall, called **standoutishness** (Hollingsworth, 1922). In a job interview, for example, a male wearing a red-and-yellow-checked jacket and a tie that lights up or a female wearing four-inch-long birdcage earrings complete with miniature chirping birds will completely distract the interviewer from noticing whatever qualities he or she possesses that are appropriate to the job. This description is deliberately exaggerated to get across a point. While such things shouldn't have any effect on how your intelligence or skills are viewed, they clearly do, and there's no way to get around it. A test measures the relevant qualities better because it doesn't know what you look like or how you act.

Should the interview be skipped? No, it can add important information if well done, but it must always be viewed with caution (Kaplan, 1982).

Situational Assessments

Another alternative to testing is secret observation of people in action. Especially for research purposes, people are watched to see how they act

DISCOVERY

Have students respond to the following scenario: *You open a restaurant, and you need to hire workers. Do you give them tests that measure how honest they are? Why or why not?* Remind students that no test is foolproof. Would any students use such a test as the sole basis for hiring? Would using such tests threaten morale from the outset?

when they think they are alone. For example, researchers wanted to understand what might lead people to help others in trouble. One study used stooges who faked a "flat tire" at the side of the road. Few people stopped to help. *But* if, a few blocks before this, another scene was set up in which stooges were obviously helping someone who had a flat tire, then when the people being observed arrived on the scene of the second "flat tire," they tended to stop and help. Clearly, this results from a form of imitation, but it also shows that the specific situation alters behavior (Bryan & Test, 1969). The researchers in this study were engaging in what is called **situational assessment.**

The biggest difference between testing and the situational approach is that with the latter, the researcher is observing and can't interfere or ask questions. Hence, we can never know what is going on in the minds of those whose behavior is changing. The moment we start to ask questions, we are testing, not observing.

ETHICS OF TESTING

When you take a test in math, history, English, psychology, or what have you, the worst outcome is that it will show that you haven't studied or that you have trouble with that subject. It is not a personal threat to you. Such is not the case with the personality tests we have been discussing. They almost always require answers to things that many of us prefer not to talk about. Hence, they can be extremely threatening. As a result, certain ethical standards exist to protect the test taker. Here are some of the core ones:

1. Depending on your age and state or federal law, someone—either you or your parent(s)—must give permission for you to take personality tests. And the reason for giving such a test should be spelled out.
2. Your privacy must be respected. Remember, however, that somehow law enforcement people can always find a way to see just about anything. So, be careful when you take a personality test. You might be merely joking when you agree to answers that are strange, but they could become part of your permanent record. If you are truly deeply worried about personality problems, which can happen to almost anyone at some point, it is worth taking the test if you have a counselor in whom other students have faith. Often these counselors can help a great deal.
3. When personality tests are being given for research, you always have the right to refuse to take them. That's standard practice.

And here are some general tips on testing that might be of use:

1. Whether or not you have to take an intelligence test is controlled by many state and federal laws. Court battles are going on in this area all the time. Your counselor can inform you of your rights.

situational assessment

The process of looking at how the circumstances surrounding an event influence people responding to that event.

Comprehension Check

Which interviewing problem is present in each of the following situations? A man with scuffed shoes and a stain on his shirt is assumed to be lazy and not very intelligent. *(reverse halo effect)* A woman with a degree from a prestigious university is thought to be honest, well-mannered, and cheerful. *(halo effect)* An interviewer can recall little about an interviewee except that person's overwhelmingly loud, cackling laugh. *(standoutishness)*

FYI Rating scales are often used during situational assessments to make sure that a variety of behaviors are observed. When your administrator evaluates you, he or she probably uses some sort of scale. See activity #3 for an example of a rating scale.

FYI Companies that use tests for hiring and promotion must be careful. Some states limit the use of tests for these purposes. For example, an owner of a retail store might want to find out if a prospective employee would steal. This employer may not be allowed to use a test that allegedly assesses honesty. Why? Tests sometimes make mistakes.

Comprehension Check

List the three main ethical rules that apply to personality testing.
(Permission must be given for someone to take the test; privacy must be respected, and [in the context of research] you always have the right to refuse to take a personality test.)

2. If you *do* take an intelligence test for some reason, a record will be made of the score. If you have any reason to doubt its accuracy, you should request a reexamination before you leave high school. This is important because these tests can make major errors at times, and you might carry along on your permanent record a lifetime score that does not reflect your real ability.

3. It is to your benefit to take a vocational interest test. We know of none that is a disguised personality test. Not taking the SAT or a similar test will likewise hurt you. Many colleges require one for admission. You can always take it again or go to some school that doesn't require it if you don't like your scores. Most colleges *do* look at your high school records, so if the SAT scores are below average and your grades have been good, the grades tend to carry more weight with most admission committees. Remember that the SAT, at its best, *only* measures school potential and has nothing to do with the possibility of great success in thousands of occupations.

4. As mentioned, anyone who takes a personality test may feel exposed and vulnerable. The worst part about this is that you might begin to feel that there *really* is something wrong with you just from the types of questions on the test. The chances that you are sane and about as normal or abnormal as most of the rest of us are overwhelming. The test has not made you the victim of some all-seeing, all-knowing psychologist. To illustrate this last point, we have developed the "Learned Pig Personality Test." Maybe it will help you rest more easily.

DISCOVERY

The primary method for making this unit exciting is to administer a variety of tests. See **Suggested Readings** for this chapter and try to get a copy of *The Mind Test*. It includes inventories on stress, anxiety, interpersonal relationships, and assertiveness. You may want to be careful about administering some of the tests. For example, if you give the test on depression and a student finds that he or she is depressed, then what? You haven't offered any tools for dealing with this information. Most of the tests are good; quite a few are taken from journal articles. They are all somewhat brief, and an analysis follows each test.

PSYCHOLOGY IN YOUR LIFE

The Learned Pig Personality Test

Please answer each of the following eight questions either true or false as it applies to you. At the end, we will tell you how to score your answers, and we will discuss the test.

1. I worry more often than I wish I did about the future. While sometimes the future seems reasonably clear, at other times it's too unknown.
    True   False
2. I have had a recent upsetting experience that is hard for me to forget. Sometimes it will pop into my mind at the strangest times.
    True   False
3. I worry about my body. It doesn't seem to be all that it should be, especially when I compare it with some other people's.
    True   False
4. I worry that I don't have enough really close friends. Many of my relationships seem too superficial.
    True   False
5. I'm not all the way sure who I *really* am. Sometimes I feel like my personality is pretty good, but it doesn't feel all the way right at other times.
    True   False
6. I'm uncomfortable about sexual matters. Lots of other people seem to know what's going on, but sometimes it makes me uncomfortable, and most of all it doesn't always make a lot of sense. Also, it seems to be out of proportion— but I'd never tell anyone that because they'd think there was something wrong with me.
    True   False
7. Being in love feels so good, and it's supposed to be a natural state. But I worry because sometimes things are so messed up about it that I wish it would go away.
    True   False
8. People always say that adolescence is the time when you don't really have any worries or burdens. There must be something wrong with me because that sure doesn't seem to be what my life is like.
    True   False

Scoring Key: Count the number of "true" responses you made. If you checked seven to eight "true," you are normal. If five or six, you're either awfully lucky or fooling yourself. If you checked four or fewer, you're either lying or not human.

There are a number of goals behind this little experiment. First, it should make you feel a little more at ease about your personality. We are all worried more often than we wish we were, and things don't go smoothly no matter what area of life we're dealing with. Second, you can see that a test can be made up in such a way that persons can be made to *appear* abnormal when in fact, they are not. And third, it should show you that many of the things that seem to be deep, all-knowing questions from psychologists are often just statements of the obvious made to look like there is special knowledge behind them.

(continued on next page)

(continued on next page)

PSYCHOLOGY IN YOUR LIFE

Connections
Many self-proclaimed psychics rely on this Barnum effect to convince others that they have ESP (Chapter 4).
Enrichment
Have students find out if any employers in your area use tests for hiring and promotion.

VOCABULARY REVIEW

Before testing students on the contents of the chapter, you may want to review vocabulary terms that are especially important or confusing. Terms in this chapter that could require clarification are *standardization, norms, reliability, validity,* and *aptitude.*

Reteaching Strategy

Have students complete the **Reteaching Worksheet** for this chapter located in the Teacher Resources.

The **Vocabulary Worksheet** may be completed by the class as a pretest for chapter concepts or used as a reteaching worksheet for those students needing additional review.

Wrapping It Up

All of the tests described in this chapter have some limitations, and for this reason, more than one test is usually administered to a person. And we're talking about the *valid* tests! Warn students (again perhaps) about people trying to make money by hawking so-called personality tests. For example, students should stay away from books that try to match the contours of the face to various personality traits. Most of these traits, of course, are described in such general terms that they can apply to anyone.

PSYCHOLOGY IN YOUR LIFE

The Learned Pig Personality Test

(continued from previous page)
Around the turn of the century, a famous circus called "Barnum and Bailey's" thrived. P. T. Barnum, one of the founders, said there was a "sucker born every minute." He was referring to the fact that you can fool people with great ease. Such foolery is still done today through palm reading and horoscopes, and the few remaining circuses usually have a "fortune-teller." All these people merely state the obvious or the common in such a way that it seems they know the deep, inner recesses of our minds. This is called

the *Barnum effect,* and it is a serious problem because so many of the things these people say seem to be mysteriously probing us when they aren't (Meehl, 1956).

We called our test the "Learned Pig" test because for about 100 years, starting in the late 1700s, pigs became the "in" thing in touring acts and stage performances. The pigs were supposed to have incredible abilities: they supposedly could sing, dance, spell, tell time, tell your age, and speak in many languages. In those days, people sometimes believed that women were very frail and

would "swoon" (fall into a faint) if they weren't dealt with very carefully. As a result, the promoters had to promise that ladies who attended the performance would not have their personalities revealed by the Learned Pig—thus, no one would know the ladies' secrets (Jay, 1987). The point is that the personality test we made up is similar to the one used by the pigs (on men only). The pigs would stick their snouts toward certain items on a big card that listed personality characteristics— in that way, they "told the future."

SUMMARY

1. Tests must be standardized and norms must be established by using different groups. Tests also must have good validity and reliability to work.
2. Personality tests are of two general types. The first is objective and uses factual questions to which the person responds. An attempt is made to build a picture of the person's personality using these statements.
3. Because personality inventories don't seem to reach "deep" enough and are subject to problems like faking, a second type of test, projective tests, like the ink blot are sometimes used. These tests are designed to get material from the test taker that is more hidden, since the stimulus he or she is responding to is so vague.
4. An achievement test is designed to measure

what has already been learned. An aptitude test is intended to predict how well a person will do in the future, but these tests still have to use the person's current knowledge.
5. Vocational interest tests are used to predict a person's satisfaction in certain job areas. These tests measure interest only, not aptitude.
6. Interviews provide information, but it is usually less accurate and more subjective than test results.
7. Situational assessments are used primarily for research purposes. They involve observation of how people behave when they think they are alone. They do cast light on behavior, but they don't provide an opportunity to find out why the people are doing what they are doing.

SUGGESTED READINGS

▼ Aero, R., and E. Weiner. *The Mind Test.* New York: Morrow, 1981.

▼ Buck, John. *House-Tree-Person Projective Drawing Technique: Manual and Interpretive Guide.* Los Angeles: Western Psychological Services, 1992.

▼ Cattell, R. B. *The Scientific Analysis of Personality.* New York: Penguin, 1965.

▼ Cronbach, L. J. *Essentials of Psychological Testing.* 3rd ed. New York: Harper, 1970.

SUGGESTED VIDEOS

▼ *Dr. Henry Murray.* 50 min., 1966, Penn State.

▼ *Personality.* 30 min., 1971, CRM/McGraw-Hill.

VOCABULARY

psychological tests
standardization
norms
validity
reliability
personality inventory
MMPI-2
California Psychological Inventory

projective tests
Rorschach test
TAT
aptitude
aptitude tests
Scholastic Assessment Test
achievement tests

vocational interest test
Strong-Campbell Interest Inventory
halo effect
reverse halo
standoutishness
situational assessment

Answers to Review Questions

1. b
2. a
3. c
4. d
5. b
6. a
7. c
8. c
9. d
10. b
11. a
12. d

Review Questions

Matching (Answers can be used more than once.)

1. Some are projective in nature
2. Can include clerical speed tests
3. Measures how much one has learned in the past
4. Helps one to eliminate certain career choices
5. Helpful in singling out people who need help
6. Designed to predict future performance, but sometimes not accurate enough
7. Not specifically designed to predict future academic performance—but often misused in this way
8. Useful for placing advanced students
9. Strong and Campbell developed a widely used one
10. At times, identifies abnormalities that don't exist
11. Reveals special abilities
12. Its ability to predict is very high

a. aptitude test
b. personality test or inventory
c. achievement test
d. vocational interest test

techniques that professionals use to catch liars. For example, a professional may ask essentially the same question in five or six different parts of the test, varying the wording, then noting whether the test taker is consistent in his or her answers each time. Could someone overcome these traps? Maybe. Shyness is probably more elusive than lying and

harder to measure and identify. Someone may be shy in one situation but may become bold when taking tests, for example.

4. This is one of those questions where students will point out how other students attempt to achieve a halo effect but will deny that they ever attempt the same. After discussing which kinds of students are

13. reliable
14. halo effect
15. norm
16. validity
17. situational assessment
18. false
19. false
20. true
21. true
22. false

Notes on Discussion Questions

1. The scores, if made readily available, may be misinterpreted by nonprofessionals. Even if the scores are interpreted correctly, the nonprofessional may exaggerate the importance of the test, perhaps not realizing that no test is perfect.

2. Reasoning may vary slightly, but most students will probably agree that the scores should *not* be made easily available. Two possible reasons are listed in number 1. Another problem might involve students comparing scores and ridiculing those with low scores.

3. Accept any answers that are logically supported. The chapter mentions

Fill in the blanks; answer on a separate sheet of paper. (An answer may consist of more than one word.)

13. If we take a test in April and score high and take the same test in May and score low, the test may not be highly___?___ .
14. Teachers' pets often benefit from the___?___.
15. If 98 percent of the population answers a question in a similar way, they are establishing a pattern, or a___?___ .

16. Test "A" is supposed to measure intelligence, and it *does*! The test, therefore, has a high degree of ___?___ .
17. Gathering information by observing people in different settings and situations is called ___?___.

True/False

18. A personality test can usually be administered to someone without permission.
19. A personality test need not be taken too seriously since the score will probably not be recorded on your permanent record.

20. You have the right to refuse to take a personality test used for research.
21. Certain laws exist that control whether you have to take an intelligence test.
22. Vocational interest tests are usually disguised personality tests.

DISCUSSION QUESTIONS

1. You may have filled out a personality inventory or two in your lifetime, but you were probably never made aware of your score. Why do you suppose scores are not made more readily available? Explain.
2. Should personality information be made more easily available? For example, should personality inventory scores be routinely sent out in the mail? Why or why not? Explain.
3. A reliable personality inventory should paint a somewhat accurate picture of various personality traits. What trait would a personality inventory have an easier time identifying: honesty or shyness? In other words, Joe fills out a personality inventory; if you (as an expert) were to analyze his answers, would it be easier to draw conclusions about whether he is honest or whether he is shy? Explain.

4. In your opinion, do students attempt to achieve a halo effect more often during junior high school or high school? Why? Does it have anything to do with peers?
5. Describe several experimental situations where researchers would want to use situational assessment rather than interviews. Remember that the problem with interviewing or asking questions is that the answers may not be truthful or accurate; also, once someone knows that he or she is being tested, that person's behavior automatically tends to become less natural.

more guilty of trying to achieve a halo effect (junior high or high school?) and after discussing how this halo effect is achieved, ask them about this tendency to see in others what we will not see in ourselves.

5. Possible situations where situational assessment might be preferred include the following: (a) You want to find out how children play with each other and how this affects development. (b) You want to find out when or why people will help in an emergency, so you stage an emergency and observe. (c) You want to find out the effects of mild stress on job performance. In all of these situations, if the subjects know they are being observed or tested, their behavior may become less than natural.

Notes on Activities

1. Keep in mind that many counselors are former teachers who might welcome the opportunity to visit a class to talk about these testing issues!

2. If students have difficulty finding information on personality and achievement tests, mention that their counselors and school psychologist probably have a great deal of information about these topics.

3. If students conduct all the activities for this chapter, their counselors will be kept busy! After completing the interest test, some students may complain that they do not know anyone in the three occupations in which they scored highest. Suggest that they consult the yellow pages and conduct an interview over the phone.

4. Consider reading students' responses aloud in class.

ACTIVITIES

1. Your school counselor probably has a great deal of knowledge about the purposes and uses of various aptitude, achievement, and vocational interest tests. Prepare a list of questions and interview your counselor. Include questions about: (a) the differences and similarities among the three types of tests; (b) the general strengths and weaknesses of each type of test; (c) the main kinds of tests your counselor uses and why—and whether these tests are "valid" and/or "reliable"; (d) students' rights in regard to testing—especially intelligence testing.

   Write a report of the interview and include your reactions.

2. As you may have gathered from reading the chapter, many of the personality and achievement tests commonly used often inspire controversy. Collect several articles that clarify and explain these controversies. Then design a detailed chart that presents the pros and cons of using these tests. Finally, in about a page, argue either for or against using these tests.

3. Visit your school counselor and tell him or her that you'd like to take a vocational interest test. Fill out the test and take a look at the three occupations in which you scored highest. Pick any one of these occupations and interview someone who is currently employed in that occupation.

   The main purpose of the interview will be to discover the similarities and differences between you and the interviewee. You might want to make a list of activities that you enjoy and have the interviewee rate each activity—perhaps like this:

   Activity = Fishing
   Rating: (a) enjoy very much (b) enjoy (c) do not enjoy at all

   Briefly summarize your similarities and differences. Would you say that the vocational interest test that you took is highly valid, valid, or not valid? Why?

4. Find one article on test anxiety and summarize it. Then imagine you are an advice columnist and you have just received this letter: "Dear _____, I'm a high school senior who suffers from test anxiety. I need to take the SAT next month and I'm afraid I'll flop. Can you help? Signed: Testaphobic." What advice would you give Testaphobic? Try to incorporate some of the material from the article and the chapter in your advice.

DISCUSS THE PHOTO

Have students think of other good slogans for signs.

Using drugs to relieve stress only makes things worse in the long run.

442

PSYCHOLOGY AND YOU RESOURCES

A variety of resources are available in the Psychology and You *supplementary material. In addition, there are a number of additional resources listed to enhance your lesson plans.*

Masters
▼ 16-1A Learning Goals
▼ 16-1B Answers to Learning Goals
▼ 16-2 Frustration

Student Worksheets
▼ Vocabulary Worksheet
▼ Independent Practice Worksheet
▼ Enrichment Worksheet
▼ Reteaching Worksheet

Test Bank
▼ Tests A and B

Multimedia
▼ *The Brain* Videotape Module #29
▼ Psychology Videodisc

Student Workbook

PACING CHART

Complete Coverage

Day 1: Have students read the first four sections of the chapter. Review the four types of conflict and two types of stress. Discuss the physical changes that accompany stress. Focus on the fight or flight response and the effects of adrenaline.

Day 2: Discuss stress and personality. Provide examples to analyze the general adaptation syndrome. Assign "Substance Abuse" and Psychology In Your Life for Day 3.

Day 3: Review the principle of how drugs affect the body. Discuss the factors involved in substance abuse, and the general course taken to overcome it. Assign for homework an activity requiring students to evaluate society's attitudes toward substance abuse.

Day 4: Focus on the causes and effects of alcoholism, noting especially the synergistic effect. Review the indicators of alcoholism and the problems associated with referring to alcoholism as a

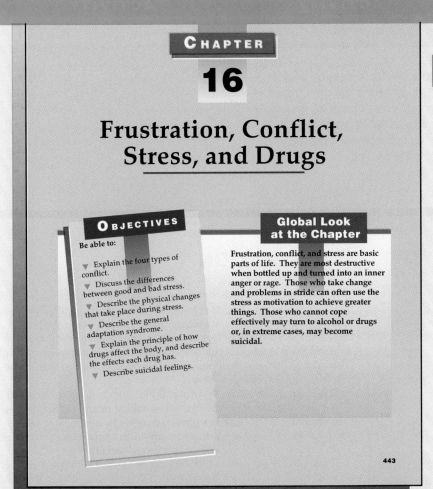

OBJECTIVES

Be able to:

▼ Explain the four types of conflict.

▼ Discuss the differences between good and bad stress.

▼ Describe the physical changes that take place during stress.

▼ Describe the general adaptation syndrome.

▼ Explain the principle of how drugs affect the body, and describe the effects each drug has.

▼ Describe suicidal feelings.

Global Look at the Chapter

Frustration, conflict, and stress are basic parts of life. They are most destructive when bottled up and turned into an inner anger or rage. Those who take change and problems in stride can often use the stress as motivation to achieve greater things. Those who cannot cope effectively may turn to alcohol or drugs or, in extreme cases, may become suicidal.

443

INTRODUCING THE CHAPTER

Ask students to define stress; tell them to describe how their body reacts to stress and how they deal with stress. You may find that many students do not believe that stress has to occur: if they have a problem, they simply deal with it and move on. If these people ever have children, they may change their minds.

"disease." Assign the last section for Day 5.

Day 5: Discuss the common stressors that contribute to suicide, and address the issue of the media's treatment of this subject. Give the Chapter Review quiz.

In Brief

Day 1: Review the four types of conflict and the two types of stress. Discuss the physiological responses to stress.

Day 2: Focus on stress and personality. Outline the three stages of the general adaptation syndrome.

Day 3: Use discussion questions in the text to analyze society's attitude toward drug and alcohol abuse.

Day 4: Discuss the media's treatment of teenage suicide before giving the Chapter Review quiz.

LEAD-OFF ACTIVITY

Teaching Master 16-2 Frustration provides a fun activity to demonstrate a particular aspect of frustration. Your hypothesis will be this: if people know ahead of time that they will be frustrated and if they understand the nature of this frustration, they will feel less frustrated than people without this knowledge or understanding. In other words, people who wait in line to buy tickets and who know that the wait will be 30 minutes will experience less frustration than people who wait in the same line without this information. **Teaching Master 16-2** provides directions for a game you can play to test this hypothesis.

COOPERATIVE LEARNING

Break the class into small groups and have each group think of a creative example for each of the four types of conflict described. After five to ten minutes, have each group report their examples to the rest of the class. Consider offering a prize for the most creative group: a candy bar, extra credit, the option of not having to complete the next minor assignment. This last prize is usually highly valued. Warn them that the examples must be not only creative but accurate as well.

TEACHING MASTER 16-1A

Learning Goals. A Learning Goals sheet for each chapter is provided in the Teacher Resources. These Learning Goals can be used as review sheets or worksheets. **Teaching Master 16-1B** consists of answers to these Learning Goals.

Journal Topic

"Describe some of the frustrating experiences you have had in the past few weeks. For example, you got caught in a traffic jam; you went to the store and it was closed; and so on." Afterward, ask students if they lost their sense of perspective during these times. In other words, did they blow the situation out of proportion? Was their response atypical for them?

444

frustration

The blocking or hindering of goals we are seeking.

conflict

A problem that demands a choice between alternatives in order to be resolved.

approach-approach conflict

A choice between two attractive alternatives.

approach-avoidance conflict

One part of the situation is attractive, but the other part is not; the choice is whether to do or not do something.

FRUSTRATION

If you plan on wearing something that matches your blue sweater, this item is bound to be either lost or all rolled up in a ball. If you are really in a hurry to get somewhere, the traffic will be unbelievable, and all the stoplights will turn red just as you reach them. If there is a sale and there is one CD you want badly, there are two possibilities: (1) you don't have enough money, or (2) you have the money, get the CD, but your player breaks down.

These are the frustrations of daily life, which do take their toll. While these problems may not be earthshaking in and of themselves, they gradually wear us down since each of them causes us to tighten our muscles, clench our teeth, and want to run screaming down the street. Such frustrations can't be good for us—and they aren't.

Frustration is defined as the blocking or hindering of goals we are seeking. Most frustrations are relatively minor, if we can keep them in perspective. The problem is that since there are so many of them, we can get buried and lose that sense of perspective. Some minor frustrations are still hard to handle for almost anyone—try those irritating busy signals seven calls in a row. And frustrations can be serious, as when someone doesn't have the skills to play a particular sport or lacks some other talent in an activity that is special to him or her.

CONFLICT

Conflicts are particularly difficult to deal with because they demand a decision. A **conflict,** then, is a situation in which we must decide between two or more alternatives (to do one thing or another, or to do or not to do something). Conflicts will not go away by themselves. There are four types of conflict.

Approach-Approach Conflict

The **approach-approach conflict** is not all that bad. It involves two attractive alternatives. We have to choose between two things we want to do (approach). There are two movies you want to see for example, but you have money for only one. You have to choose.

Approach-Avoidance Conflict

The **approach-avoidance conflict** can be distressing. One part of the situation makes it attractive, but the other part makes you want to run away. You want to go out with someone, say, but are afraid

COOPERATIVE LEARNING

Have students work in pairs to answer the following question. "Tom tries to decide what to wear to the prom. How might each of the four types of conflict be involved in his decision?" The stereotype is that females worry about this sort of thing more than males. Students may have fun reversing the roles.

you won't really be liked. The process of trying to decide what to do can leave you drained and feeling hopeless for the moment.

Avoidance-Avoidance Conflict

You can't win with the **avoidance-avoidance conflict,** the worst of the three because it involves two unattractive alternatives. If you don't go to the dentist, your teeth will rot (bad), but if you do go, he or she will bring out the whirling monster that sends bits of teeth and water flying all over the room while you squirm in agony (also bad).

avoidance-avoidance conflict

A choice between two unattractive alternatives.

Double Approach-Avoidance Conflict

The **double approach-avoidance conflict** is the one we face most often. It is called "double" because there are both good and bad parts no matter which way we go. For example, if you have a vote on whether your family moves to another city, the school might be better, but you aren't used to it; special new friends could be there, but you have to leave behind those you already know and care about.

All of these types of conflict are normal. They can't be avoided. Still, a steady diet of painful conflicts, especially when one feels alone and not supported, can result in feelings of hopelessness. After a while, a person in this situation will begin to make incorrect decisions or will be unable to make any decision, and eventually he or she can develop psychological and physical symptoms from the steady drain on the body and psyche.

double approach-avoidance conflict

A choice between alternatives, both of which have good and bad parts.

ANXIETY

Conflict and frustration lead to **anxiety,** a feeling of dread that something is seriously wrong and that disaster sits right around the corner. Anxiety results when we cannot resolve a conflict or when frustration builds too high. Any feeling of helplessness when we are trying to solve problems can lead to anxiety, and this, in turn, can become a general feeling that we can't cope. If such anxiety goes on for a long time, it can eventually do a person in. Severe attacks of anxiety can cause a rapid heartbeat, fatigue, breathlessness, chest pains, dizziness, fainting, feelings of doom, and headaches.

anxiety

The feeling that something is wrong and disaster is imminent.

stress

The physical strain that results from demands or changes in the environment.

STRESS

Stress is defined as the *physical* pressure and strain that result from demands or changes in the environment (Mandler, 1984). Stress

Comprehension Check

Students should answer *true* or *false* to the following statements: Mario faces an approach-avoidance conflict when he has to choose between going to see his favorite band play or watching his favorite basketball team play. *(false)* An example of approach-avoidance conflict is wanting to go to a certain out-of-state college, but not wanting to be far from home. *(true)* Tanya realizes that taking an after-school job has both pros and cons and that *not* taking it also has positive and negative consequences. She's facing a double approach-avoidance conflict. *(true)* You want to buy an item of clothing that costs all the money you have, but you also don't want to be broke. This is an avoidance-avoidance conflict. *(false)*

Connections

Anxiety disorders (Chapter 18) include phobias, panic attacks, and obsessive-compulsive disorder (OCD).

DEMONSTRATION

Play a game in which you create the conflicts described here. Draw a starting line on the floor and place two baskets about two feet from the line. The goal is to throw balls into the baskets. Divide the class into teams. Both baskets are worth points (approach-approach). Next, move one basket farther from the line. Close shots, worth only one point, will be easier than far ones, but far ones are worth five points (double approach-avoidance). After a while, you can change the rules: every bas-ket missed results in points being subtracted (avoidance-avoidance, because students may not want to try *any* baskets). You will probably think of other rule changes as you go along. You may want to sit in the back and observe how students react

Conflicts.

 Approach-approach: two colleges accept Colleen; she likes them both. *Approach-avoidance:* Colleen likes what one out-of-state college offers, but she can't afford to move that far away. *Avoidance-avoidance:* she does not want to go to college, but she does not want to be without a college diploma. *Double-approach-avoidance:* college A is close to home, which is good, but it does not offer many of the courses she wants; college B is far away, which is bad, but it is prestigious.

Reteaching Strategy

Ask students to make a list of conflicts they have experienced lately. Afterward, have them identify the conflicts by type and explain their reasoning.

Unit 5 PERSONALITY, ADJUSTMENT, AND CONFLICT

 **Conflicts**

Approach-Approach

Two attractive alternatives, but you can only choose one:
"Should I eat a hamburger or pizza? I only have enough money for one."

Avoidance-Avoidance

Two unattractive alternatives; avoiding one brings you closer to the other:
"I hate liver, but if I don't finish it, Mom will never let me hear the end of it."

Approach-Avoidance

One goal or choice that is both attractive and unattractive; the person reaches for the positive feature of the goal, but the goal includes both positive and negative features:
"I want to have a candy bar, but I don't want to get any more cavities."

Double Approach-Avoidance

Both alternatives include attractive and unattractive features:
"Should I eat liver, which is not very tasty but is nutritious, or should I have the dessert, which is rich in calories but makes my mouth water just thinking about it?"

Colleen has to decide which college to attend in the fall. How could each of these types of conflict be involved in her decision?

Critical Thinking

Write *stress* on the board and ask for the first thoughts that come to mind. Do students include any positives? Then write *events.* Ask them what events cause stress. Again, you will probably not get answers like marriage, moving, a new job. Have students refer to the social readjustment rating scale that appears later in the chapter and explain that stress can be caused by positive events, too.

to the different types of conflict. Does it take students longer to decide what they will try when the conflicts are more complicated?

Chapter 16 FRUSTRATION, CONFLICT, STRESS, AND DRUGS

arises whenever we have to readjust. Conflict, frustration, and anxiety can all lead to stress. But *any* kind of change, even a positive one, causes stress, because we must adapt to a new environment. We'll talk more about this shortly.

Good Stress

Stress is not necessarily a bad thing in and of itself. Its impact is relative to the individual: what is terribly difficult for one person can make another person feel interested and alive. For example, meeting new people can be a very stressful situation. Most of us are uncomfortable if the person we are meeting is someone we want to like us or someone who might be important to us. But since never making any new friends or getting a job or leaving home is much worse than stress, we have to go ahead and do these things. In fact, in these cases, stress turns out to be a good thing because it keeps the body going, and this, in turn, keeps us moving toward a new goal. Similarly, at least in theory, stress from doing homework is good in the long run because one learns. When stress is "good," leading to something desirable, it is called **eustress.**

Bad Stress

On the other side of the coin, the negative effects of stress are great. These include confusion, inability to make decisions, avoidance of people, as well as, eventually, physical or psychological illness (S. Cohen, 1980). When stress is "bad," or overwhelms our ability to cope, it is called **distress** (Cohen & Williamson, 1991).

How we view a particular problem has a lot to do with whether stress is bad or good. Moving to another city, for instance, can be seen as a chance to make a new and better life for ourselves, or it can be seen as a hassle and a loss (Pittner & Houston, 1980). Making up your mind to make the best of a situation—even though this is often easier said than done—can work wonders in terms of how stress affects you.

Physical Changes with Stress

The effects of stress come from the physical responses that occur whenever we are facing change, conflict, or frustration. To understand this, we need to look for a moment at the animal world where things are a little simpler to grasp.

Fight or Flight   In the wild, animals are designed to deal first of all with physical safety. The key to safety for them is an environment that remains the same. For example, an animal will sleep as long as

eustress

The stress that motivates us to do something worthwhile.

distress

The stress that is nonproductive and that causes physical problems.

FYI You may have heard that exercise helps one deal with stress. It seems that aerobic-type exercise will help us if we do it *before* the stress—our bodies will be better prepared to deal with stress—but will not be so helpful *after* the stress. Apparently, it takes time for the benefits of exercise to appear, at least as they relate to stress (see Holmes in **Suggested Readings** for this chapter).

447

DEMONSTRATION

This activity will take about five seconds, but it should guarantee that students will recall the meaning of a fight or flight reaction. Hide a horn inside your desk, and in the middle of the period, nonchalantly sound it. You can see students coming to alert status. (Ask a coach to lend you a horn; horns are used during games to stop the action.)

Comprehension Check

How can pregnancy be an example of both eustress and distress? *(It would depend upon the parents' feelings about parenthood and their emotional and financial readiness to support a child.)*

DISCUSS THE PHOTO

Ask students for examples of situations in which they experienced the fight or flight reaction.

Points to Stress

After you sound a loud horn (see preceding **Demonstration**) to create a fight or flight reaction, explain that if you had *announced* a pop quiz, the physical response would have been the same, though the intensity may have been different.

fight or flight reaction

The body's reaction to a crisis; these are the only two possibilities for action.

Unit 5 PERSONALITY, ADJUSTMENT, AND CONFLICT

▲ *When stress is prolonged and severe, as in the recent San Francisco Earthquake, some physical comforting is almost a necessity.*

everything around it is calm. Any change in the environment, such as an unusual sound followed by some type of movement immediately signals the possibility of danger. Some life-threatening event could be about to happen, and the sound and movement are warning signs: there might be a predator creeping up. As a result, the vision and hearing systems of all animals (including humans) are physically designed to detect immediately *any* change in the surroundings. (How about when you are at home alone some night, especially after seeing a horror movie? You are sitting there and it is completely quiet, when all of a sudden you hear scratching, creaking sounds, and you see some kind of movement outside the window. Your body goes into full alert.) Thus, any kind of change triggers a physical alarm. That is nature's design.

Assume that the animal is correct about coming to alert status: there is a creature on its way to attack. The animal's body is fully mobilized to do one of two things—fight or flee. There is no third choice. Thus begins what is called the **fight or flight reaction.** In nature, the animal either wins, loses, or escapes. If the battle is won or the animal runs away, special chemicals are then sent through the body to cancel out the ones that were triggered in order to handle the emergency.

The Human Response The major parts of the human that respond to emotional stress are the higher brain, the part we do our

ENRICHMENT

Students might enjoy reading a chapter or two from a book on positive mental attitude. Although many of these books are not scientifically based, they offer practical strategies for viewing life positively and reducing stress. Warn them that these books should not be worshiped but simply used as possible sources of inspiration. Before they read anything, check their choices to see if you approve: is the reading level appropriate? Is the material specific and practical?

Chapter 16 FRUSTRATION, CONFLICT, STRESS, AND DRUGS

thinking with; the lower brain, the animal part that controls all the basic bodily functions; and the **adrenal** (ah-DREE-nal) **glands** that sit to the right and left and above the kidneys and that stir up the body's activity level. Here are three examples of the kinds of things that can trigger an emotional response: anticipating having an operation; going out on a first date with a new person; having to accept the fact that a loved one has died. Notice that all three of these human problems involve a *psychological* change because they deal with *mental* issues. This does not reduce their potential for distressing us; instead, it makes them harder to handle than real life-and-death physical struggles.

In each case, the higher brain assumes that threat and danger exist. It signals the lower brain about the emergency. The lower brain secretes a special chemical called the **stress hormone,** which signals the adrenal glands to send to the body *adrenaline* (ah-DREN-ah-lin). This causes the muscles to tense, the heart to beat faster, and the liver to send out more sugar to be used by the muscles when we either fight or flee (Axelrod & Reisine, 1984). Thus, the body can't tell the difference between a physiological and a psychological threat and will respond in the same way to either kind of "danger."

If we were able to solve these problems immediately, the human body would go back to normal quickly, as it does with animals. But because our concerns are often more abstract than physical, it is tough to find an end to them. Hence, the stress lasts a long time, and eventually it can cause physical problems because we are running (on the inside) at full alert too much of the time (G. E. Schwartz, 1979).

Examining Stress

Some stress results from change, whether the change is good or bad. In this regard, Table 16.1 might be of some interest. Two stress researchers estimated the amount of change involved in certain life events and called their estimates *life change units* (Holmes & Rahe, 1967). This table is interesting because it shows how upsetting certain events can be. For example, serving a jail term and getting married are not that far apart as stressors. But one would hope that the changes involved in getting married would quickly pass from those of a stressful event to those associated with a warm, happy relationship. Hence, one cannot add up these scores and predict how much damage will occur. Those who are subjected to major stressors, however—such as the death of a spouse, loss of a family member, getting fired, and the like—are more likely to develop disease or sickness later on, especially if a couple of these stressors happen at about the same time (Krantz & Manuck, 1985).

Stress research also focuses on things that do not cause an actual change in one's life. For example, a continued beating from all of life's little annoyances, such as we discussed at the beginning of the

adrenal glands

The glands that secrete chemicals that activate or energize the body.

stress hormone

A special chemical that signals the adrenal glands to activate the body.

Discussion

Ask students to think of a time when an event caused them distress but later turned out to have positive consequences. Students may not be able to think of a situation on the spot, so you may want to give them a few minutes to write about the topic. Point out that their *attitude* probably determined that the event was distress. Would a change in attitude have made it "good" stress?

COOPERATIVE LEARNING

In class conduct activity #1 at the end of the chapter, where students make their own social readjustment rating scale. Be sure to discuss point values before administering the test.

FYI According to Holmes, a score of 300 or more is highly stressful and is likely to cause an illness. A score below 150 means "little stress."

Points to Stress

In the last chapter, we stressed that students should not take the results of rating scales too seriously. This is a good case in point. For example, divorce is ranked second, but remember, one's attitude may reduce the effects of stress. Divorce may be a welcome event for some people, as hard as that may be to believe.

Connections

Stress actually slows down the immune system, and we become less able to fight off infection (Chapter 17).

Unit 5 PERSONALITY, ADJUSTMENT, AND CONFLICT

▲ *Table 16.1 Social Readjustment Rating Scale*

Rank	Life Event	Mean Value	Rank	Life Event	Mean Value
1	Death of spouse	100	23	Son or daughter leaving home	29
2	Divorce	73	24	Trouble with in-laws	29
3	Marital separation	65	25	Outstanding personal achievement	28
4	Jail term	63	26	Wife begin or stop work	26
5	Death of close family member	63	27	Begin or end school	26
6	Personal injury or illness	53	28	Change in living conditions	25
7	Marriage	50	29	Revision of personal habits	24
8	Fired at work	47	30	Trouble with boss	23
9	Marital reconciliation	45	31	Change in work hours or conditions	20
10	Retirement	45	32	Change in residence	20
11	Change in health of family member	44	33	Change in schools	20
12	Pregnancy	40	34	Change in recreation	19
13	Sex difficulties	39	35	Change in church activities	19
14	Gain of new family member	39	36	Change in social activities	18
15	Business readjustment	39	37	Mortgage or loans less than $10,000	17
16	Change in financial state	38	38	Change in sleeping habits	16
17	Death of close friend	37	39	Change in number of family get-togethers	15
18	Change to different line of work	36	40	Change in eating habits	15
19	Change in number of arguments with spouse	35	41	Vacation	13
20	Mortgage over $10,000	31	42	Christmas	12
21	Foreclosure of mortgage or loan	30	43	Minor violations of the law	11
22	Change in responsibilities at work	29			

Reprinted with permission from T. H. Holmes and R. H. Rahe, "The Social Readjustment Rating Scale," *Journal of Psychosomatic Research*, 1967, Table 3, p. 216. © 1967, Pergamon Press Ltd.

ENRICHMENT

Have students find out the effects of overcrowding on a person's health. They might look at statistics on inner-city projects, some of which have been poorly planned.

Chapter 16 FRUSTRATION, CONFLICT, STRESS, AND DRUGS

chapter, if added to an environment of poverty, overcrowding, poor health, or the like, weakens a person's defenses to illness. In fact, some researchers feel that the accumulation of many moderately stressful problems might well be the real cause of early sickness or death (Lazarus & Folkman, 1984).

Pushing Too Hard   Excessive, continued, and unnecessary stress leads to trouble (Kobasa et al., 1980). One study that supports this belief examined 32 sets of male identical twins. In each pair, only one had heart problems. When the researchers looked into the history of each set of twins, they found that the ones whose hearts weren't working well had much more trouble with their marriages, took little time off, drove themselves too hard at work, and overall were less satisfied with their lives (Liljefors & Rahe, 1970). The last item seems more important than the others: we can overcome or avoid all kinds of problems if we can find some satisfaction within ourselves and some meaning in our lives.

Personal Attitude   In fact, personal meaning or attitude is a key factor in how well we survive. While it can be extremely hard to do, it is probably worth it to convince ourselves that if so-and-so doesn't like us or if so-and-so is better at something than we are, who cares—that's just the way it is. If we can find alternatives to what we think we want or need or if we can even take a break from life's responsibilities for a *short* while, we will dramatically reduce the effects of stress (Grant et al., 1981).

Stress and Personality

The higher brain, as mentioned, makes our problems abstract. How many animals do you know who fret and worry about a history exam? Our concerns are certainly real enough, but we make life so complicated. People in groups—that is, society—do the same thing. For instance, there are rules against punching a rude salesperson. We couldn't survive as a group without such restrictions. On the other hand, these restraints *do* cost us something. The more angry we get without being able to do something about it, the more the walls of the stomach engorge (fill up) with blood, putting pressure on that organ; the more our muscles tighten up; the higher our blood pressure gets—until we make ourselves sick (Krantz & Manuck, 1985).

Unrelieved Tension   In one study, researchers deliberately frustrated the subjects. Then the researchers allowed half of the group a chance to get back at them verbally (no injuries allowed). The other half wasn't allowed to do that. The blood pressure and heart rate of those who were able to pay the researchers back dropped noticeably,

Points to Stress

Note that the top three stressors on the social readjustment rating scale apply to adults. In fact, the majority of items ranked 1 to 24 apply mainly to adults. Do we experience more stress as we get older? You can provide students with an answer to this. Or is the test simply not valid for younger people? Both guesses probably include some truth.

Discussion

A pattern of pushing too hard may begin at an early age. Ask students if they take time off. What kinds of things add meaning to their lives? You might have them write about this for two minutes so they can get their thoughts together before beginning the discussion.

DISCOVERY

Have students respond in writing to the following scenarios: *Decide if you tend to be a type A or type B person. Then assume the opposite point of view, and describe your reactions to the following situations: (1) Your teacher has just announced that a major term paper is due in a month; (2) You can get tickets to a concert for tomorrow, but you have to work; (3) You have just received a rejection letter from the college of your choice.* There are certainly times when the two types do not understand each other or when they frustrate each other; this exercise of walking in another's shoes might provide some needed insight. After they write, have them role-play their responses.

FYI There used to be a delicatessen in Chicago whose workers would intentionally yell at customers. It was a gimmick, but these workers probably looked forward to work so they could relieve any bottled-up tension!

Connections

What part of the personality, according to Freud, restrains us from punching a rude salesperson? Superego (Chapter 14). Yet even Freud agreed that too much superego is unhealthy!

FYI Friedman and Rosenman, cited here for identifying type A and B personalities, are cardiologists who studied the differences in the two types for several years.

type A personality

People who are always operating at full speed, are impatient, and are filled with distress.

type B personality

People who are open to change, are flexible, enjoy life, and have low levels of stress.

general adaptation syndrome

The sequence of behavior that occurs in reaction to prolonged stress. It is divided into stages: **alarm reaction,** preparation for an attack; **stage of resistance,** trying to restore balance; and **exhaustion,** giving up the battle.

while those of the other subjects did not. So, bottling up your feelings *too much* isn't good for you (Case, 1985). There's a limit to this, however. No one wants to be around people who have no control over themselves. The point seems to be that a person needs to learn to pass off most things and to take a stand only on things that really matter. In actuality, there aren't that many things that matter deeply, if we are truthful.

Personality Types Much research has focused on what is called the **type A personality.** Type A's are always running full speed ahead. They can make people uncomfortable because even if you get them to sit down, they don't really seem to be with you in a conversation. They are impatient, thinking of other things, and can't be corralled long enough to share what they're thinking or feeling (Friedman & Rosenman, 1974; Yarnold & Grimm, 1982). They keep comparing how they are doing with how others do. But all type A's don't seem to suffer major problems. The ones who do are those who distrust others and are angry most of the time (Case, 1985). The type A's who see others as a threat, who misinterpret events, and who refuse to accept that they act the way they do are the ones most prone to physical disorders such as heart problems (Miller, Turner, Tindale, Posavac & Dugoni, 1991; Friedman, 1984).

The **type B personality** is the opposite of type A. These are people who are open to change and are flexible, who enjoy life because they don't put competition first, and who like a variety of activities (Weinberger et al., 1979).

One study compared over 150 male executives from the same company. Roughly half the group had become physically ill following some stressful life events, and the other half had not. Both groups had experienced roughly the same kinds of stress with the same severity, so they didn't differ in that respect. Analysis of the men showed that those who didn't get sick were type B's—those more open to change and who viewed problems more as a challenge than as a threat. They felt that they were in control and could do something to improve themselves and their environment (Kobasa et al., 1981). These studies suggest how critical it is to be a little more flexible and to try out a few new things, while accepting upsets without letting them eat up your insides. Doing this should not require a complete personality change, just a little loosening up and giving things a chance. The hardest part is figuring out what is important and what isn't, and then forgetting those things that aren't.

The General Adaptation Syndrome Any creature put under major stress for long periods of time will eventually collapse. The events that occur under such stress have been outlined in what is called the **general adaptation syndrome.** Translated, this term refers to "the overall (general) process by which the creature adjusts

COOPERATIVE LEARNING

Ask students to work in pairs to think of ways in which our society promotes type A behavior. (We stress the need to get to the top. We tell young people to set goals, to stay on schedule. We pursue material goods fervently. You may want to read portions of *The Great Gatsby*, which is an eloquent indictment of materialism.)

DISCOVERY

Role-play a type A person conversing with his or her type B spouse. Possible issues: buying a house, getting a pet, planning a party, deciding to have a baby, deciding where to go on vacation. What would be the best and worst combinations of types in a marriage? Any combination would work as long as each partner respected the other's type. Time permitting, you might want to role-play other combinations.

Chapter 16 FRUSTRATION, CONFLICT, STRESS, AND DRUGS

 Personality Types

Type A Personality

Someone with a type A personality is like a SPRINTER who needs to reach the finish line before everyone else.

Type B Personality

Someone with a type B personality is like a JOGGER who is willing to try different routes every day.

In the long "run," which person is more likely to become sick?

(adapts) to various levels of stress." The word *syndrome* means a set of symptoms or signs. This syndrome assumes that the same pattern is followed each time stress is heavy. As with all things, we can't make a rule that fits every case, but the following three-part sequence of the general adaptation syndrome seems to occur frequently (Selye, 1956).

The first stage is called an **alarm reaction.** The body sends out emergency signals that stir it up in preparation for an attack—either psychological or physical.

Next, the **stage of resistance** occurs. This means that the organism tries to fight back against the attack. The organism wants to restore psychological and physical balance. If the threat is removed at this point, the body and psyche begin to restore themselves to their normal chemical and emotional balance.

If the stress doesn't let up, continuous fighting becomes impossible. This third stage, **exhaustion,** means the battle is over, and we have lost or, at least, have quit.

Personality Types.

IN FOCUS A study of 150 executives showed that type A personalities were much more likely to become sick after a stressful event. Some type A personalities are also more prone to suffer heart problems.

Critical Thinking

Ask students the following question: Although there are potential dangers involved in running full speed ahead, what are the advantages of being a type A personality? (Work gets done; there's a sense of urgency to the work; type A personalities don't let obstacles get in their way. The type A people in your class are probably saying, "So, what's wrong with that?" Possibly nothing, but these people should be aware of the dangers.)

DEMONSTRATION

Before students read about the general adaptation syndrome, ask them to describe final exams week or some other equally stressful period. Listen for examples of alarm, resistance, and exhaustion, and identify them as such afterward on the chalkboard. You might ask, "What did you do *before* finals to prepare? *During* finals? And *after* finals?" Ask for specific answers.

The General Adaptation Syndrome.

IN FOCUS Students should have no difficulty thinking of examples, but have them describe the specific stages they experience (as shown in the illustration).

Critical Thinking

Ask students to discuss what a type A person diagnosed with high blood pressure might do to change. (Our society does not promote meditation, but meditation might be valuable and even necessary in this situation. See Chapter 6.) At the very least, the person should learn how to relax. Or maybe the person can emulate the characteristics of self-actualizers (see **Teaching Master 5-4 Characteristics of Self-Actualizers**). Finally, it may not be possible to learn how to laugh, but it is possible to take the time to laugh.

Unit 5 PERSONALITY, ADJUSTMENT, AND CONFLICT

IN FOCUS The General Adaptation Syndrome

Can you think of any other situations that you encounter at school that might produce this kind of reaction to stress?

The three-stage sequence is easiest to see in an accident, such as breaking your leg. When the limb is broken, the first response is one of panic or alarm, and the body starts the heart beating rapidly, increases the breathing rate, and so forth. Next comes an attempt to see if the leg will move despite the pain, trying to offset it somehow, to make it all go away (resistance). Finally, when the pain is too much and the break is obvious, you give in and lie there helplessly. Note that this would be the case if the break happens around others. But if it occurs when you are alone, then the stage of resistance is seen very clearly because you struggle, fight, and drag yourself toward help before you collapse.

One thing might be bothering you: stress, frustration, conflict, and anxiety have been defined. They are each slightly different, but they

454

Chapter 16 FRUSTRATION, CONFLICT, STRESS, AND DRUGS

all interact. Stress can cause anxiety; anxiety can cause stress; conflict can cause frustration; frustration can cause stress. So, just learn the differences among them in a formal sense, and don't be too concerned about the fact that they seem to get mixed together when we talk about them.

There are many ways of handling stress, conflict, and frustration—some reasonable, some disastrous. In the next two sections, we will cover the two worst methods for handling problems: substance abuse and suicide. The reasonable ways are discussed in the next chapter.

SUBSTANCE ABUSE

Misuse of drugs is formally called either **substance abuse** or **chemical dependence.** Using drugs to alter consciousness is not just a human activity. Reindeer, cattle, and rabbits eat intoxicating mushrooms; tobacco plants are preferred by baboons; elephants in the wild seek out fermented grain such as would be found in beer. There is some indication that stress is a factor in these behaviors because when elephants are restricted in the amount of space they have, they dramatically increase their consumption of the grain (Siegel, 1983). For humans, most scientists agree that stress, conflict, and frustration are major factors in drug use. The user is trying to alter the world enough to make it more tolerable. Also important is peer pressure: some who get started on drugs do so because others are doing it and they don't want to feel left out of the group.

One of the biggest problems we face in writing this section on drug abuse is that people have been lied to so often and in such exaggerated terms that it is hard to get anyone to listen to what the scientific findings are. For instance, a poster (Figure 16.1) put out by the government in the 1930s about marijuana warned that the drug caused murder, insanity, and death. It does none of these things.

On the other hand, there *are* problems with telling the truth about drugs. Many people have the ability to read what they want into whatever is actually said. For example, bypassing the fact that some believe that drinking alcohol in any form or quantity is wrong, we can report that the scientific evidence does not support the claim that alcohol is dangerous in and of itself. It is illegal to drink alcohol unless you are 21 years of age or older, but for adults, a glass of wine or a beer with dinner can be enjoyable and relaxing. But some will read this as saying that if one glass of wine is safe every now and then, so are three or four—or more. That is not true. The chances of becoming an alcoholic are very high as one increases the amount and frequency of drinking.

Another point is that over the years roughly half the population has used alcohol in one way or another on a fairly regular basis. To avoid the stigma attached to "drug" use, people often discuss alcohol

substance abuse

The use of drugs to excess in order to alter consciousness.

chemical dependence

The same as substance abuse.

Points to Stress

As noted earlier, the adrenal gland plays a key role during alarm reactions. What are the key symptoms during alarm? Racing heart; tense muscles; upset stomach; shortness of breath.

Points to Stress

The stage of resistance can last weeks. Imagine someone awaiting her own court trial. She worries, can think of nothing else, becomes surly at work, angry at home. This behavior may be very much unlike her, but the resistance is wearing her down and her ability to handle new stresses, even if they are minor, diminishes. This is when people are most susceptible to illness.

INTERDISCIPLINARY PROJECT

Government. Have students trace the government's attempts to legislate drug habits over the years. They can focus on the prohibition of alcohol in the past, and the prohibition of marijuana and other drugs now. What seems to be the effect, if any, of prohibiting the use of drugs? If the government insists on legalizing *some* "recreational" drugs, is the current division of legal and illegal drugs acceptable, or should a new system replace it? For example, should marijuana be made legal and alcohol be made illegal? This is highly unlikely, but an argument could be made that alcohol is more harmful. Students might also look at the system of providing methadone to heroin addicts. Why is this legal? Methadone may be less harmful in some ways, but it is just as addicting.

Critical Thinking

Introduce the section on substance abuse by writing this on the board: *How does society promote drug use?* Have students think of numerous ways in which our society promotes this message. You can either do this together as a class or allow students to work in small groups. Possible ways that our society promotes drug use: (1) alcohol commercials and ads (have students think of numerous slogans); (2) commercials and ads for aspirin and other pain relievers; (3) events sponsored by alcohol manufacturers: football games, concerts, and so on; (4) TV shows—past and present (have them think of specific references to drugs); (5) movies; (6) radio station disc jockeys; (7) parents (do their parties *always* include alcohol?); (8) friends.

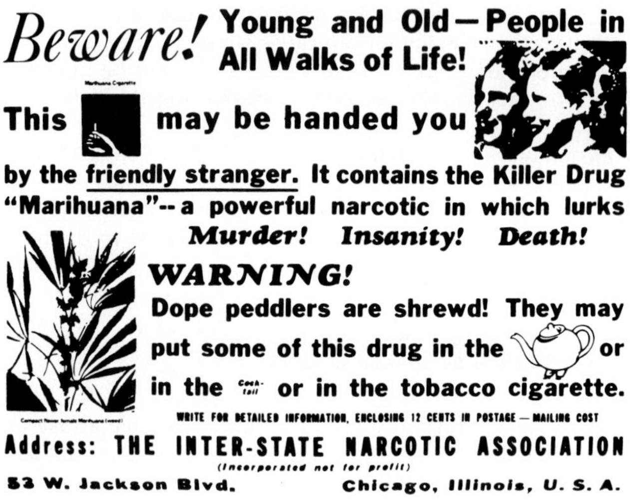

456

▲ **Figure 16.1** *1930s poster warning against using marijuana. (Courtesy of Lester Grinspoon.)*

as if it were not a drug. This is false. Alcohol works exactly the same way other drugs do, as we will describe in a moment. In fact, its general method of action is about the same as the popular tranquilizer, Valium.

The final point that should be made is that once a drug habit really gets started, it takes heroism to get rid of it. This does not mean that having taken a drug a few times, a person can never stop or is already damaged. On the other hand, no matter what "they" say, no one can have a steady intake of a drug and not eventually wind up in a very messy and painful situation. This is just common sense. The user becomes too attached to the sensations the drug produces to give it up. Such users keep saying, "I'll give it up tomorrow," but it doesn't work that way. If tomorrow ever *really* comes, a terrible battle must take place before the person can win.

How Drugs Work

It is hard to grasp some of the issues about drugs without at least a rough idea of how they work. So that's what we want to do now. Drugs all operate on the same general principle. If you look at Figure 16.2, you will see a nerve junction. The brain has billions of nerve cells, connected one to the other using these junctions. The space between the junctions helps keep different thoughts and feelings separate from one another. If certain nerve cells have to connect in order

ENRICHMENT

Contact a drug and alcohol rehabilitation center in your area for a speaker. These centers typically have several staff members who are eager to visit high school classes; in some cases, speaking to groups is the main responsibility for particular staff members.

Chapter 16 FRUSTRATION, CONFLICT, STRESS, AND DRUGS

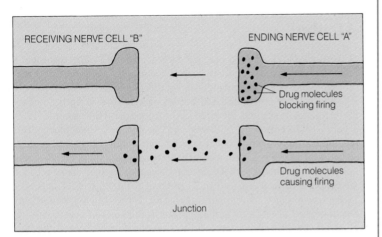

▲ *Figure 16.2*   *Nerve junction.*

to complete a feeling or thought, chemical messages are sent across the junction to the next nerve and then, if needed, on to the next nerve and so forth until the whole thought or feeling is complete. So, at the end of each nerve cell, there are chemicals that either send a message across or block one from crossing the junction.

Drugs have a molecular structure that physically resembles the different chemicals already in the nerve cells. Hence, when we take in a drug, it lodges in the endings of specific nerve cells designed to receive certain types of chemical molecules. The body will do what these drug molecules say because it thinks they are coming from inside, not outside. For instance, alcohol and tranquilizers have a structure similar to the chemicals that tell the nerve cells *not* to fire. When these drugs arrive in the brain, they hook onto certain nerve cells endings and give a message to stop firing. As more and more cells are stopped, the person becomes slower or "thicker," more dazed, and eventually can lose consciousness. Drugs that speed up the body are molecularly similar to the nerve cell chemicals that make the cells fire. Hence, as a person takes in greater quantities of these drugs, more and more cells begin to fire, and the person becomes more and more agitated. A third kind of drug causes its effect because normally the nerve cells are designed to keep different parts of the brain separate—hearing, seeing, smelling, and so on. Drugs like LSD lodge in different systems of the brain and cause the circuits in more than one of these areas to start firing together (Jacobs, 1987). As a result, people who take such drugs feel like they are "hearing colors" and "seeing sounds" and often wind up in a world so strange that it is terrifying.

Comprehension Check

What are some causal factors in substance abuse? *(stress, conflict, and frustration)*

Points to Stress

In general, there are four types of drugs: those that *speed* up the body, those that *slow* it down, those that relieve *pain,* and those that cause *hallucinations* and/or distort perceptions.

Discussion

Do students agree that peer pressure prompts some young people to use alcohol and other drugs? Many students refute this because they define peer pressure as someone with beady eyes coming up to them and pushing marijuana or a can of beer in their faces. Explain that peer pressure is usually much more subtle. Does this subtle pressure influence substance use or abuse?

DISCOVERY

Pass out index cards and take an anonymous poll to assess how often students have used alcohol: 1 = never; 2 = once or twice; 3 = occasionally; 4 = regularly; 5 = often; 6 = every day. Whatever you need to do to maintain confidentiality, do it. You may want to leave the room for a few minutes. Tally the numbers. Do students feel the results are representative of the school as a whole, of teens in general? If a poll showed quite a few 4s and above, do students consider this a problem?

Discussion

Years ago, *party* was used primarily as a noun. Now, it's common to say, "Let's party." This usage shift seems to be an indication of how important "partying" is to many people. Why is it so important? Is alcohol an integral part of a party? What if it were not available? Would people still show up?

Teaching Hint

Before students read the material on alcohol, have them make a list of the positive and negative uses and/or effects of alcohol. Which list is longer? Then have them peruse the material in the text and add more items to the list as they go along.

Unit 5 PERSONALITY, ADJUSTMENT, AND CONFLICT

Alcohol

Certain drugs tend to become fads for a while. For instance, in colonial America, alcoholism was twice as prevalent as it is today. Not unusual was the party given by the governor of New York for 120 guests: they consumed 120 bottles of Madeira, 36 bottles of port, 60 bottles of beer, and 30 bowls of rum punch (Rorabaugh, 1979). Twenty-five years ago, LSD was very popular. Its popularity then declined greatly until about five years ago when it began to increase again. Marijuana was very popular about 20 years ago, but the number of current users among 12- to 17-year-olds has dropped from 40–50 percent to a little over 20 percent (*Statistical Abstracts . . .*, 1986). Cocaine use by this same age group is roughly 10 percent, having increased about a percentage point in the last ten years. Through all the years and all the fads, though, alcohol has remained the most used drug. Roughly 70 percent of all teenagers have used alcohol, but not all of them necessarily to excess.

Obviously, not everyone who uses alcohol is an alcoholic, but there are more than 11 million known alcoholics across all age groups, and many more we don't know about (Blum, 1984).

Chemical Effects   Because many people who seem halfway reasonable when sober do wild things when they drink too much, some believe that alcohol is a stimulant. What actually happens is that the first few drinks remove a person's inhibitions about making a fool of himself or herself. This creates an impression of freedom. Alcohol is really a *depressant,* which is why country and western songs have so many drinkers crying in their beer. As the amount of alcohol in the body increases, more and more cells are shut off. Eventually this leads to unconsciousness.

Alcohol is absorbed by the body in two to six hours, depending on how much is taken in, how much the person weighs, and, to a large extent, how much has been eaten. Eating prior to or during drinking helps reduce the effects notably, if we're talking about a reasonable amount of alcohol (Blum, 1984).

Physical Effects   Repeated heavy drinking causes serious damage, but it takes a while to show up. About 10 percent of alcoholics develop permanent liver damage, and about the same percentage develop irreversible brain damage. Alcohol over time can directly destroy the liver. On the other hand, you will hear that every time people take a drink, they destroy large numbers of brain cells. There is no real support for this claim (Blum, 1988). Hundreds of brain cells do die every day all by themselves. We have so many of them (100 billion) that most people can get to over 100 years of age and still function quite well. The real trouble comes from the fact that alcohol is basically a food product: it fills you up and is high in calories but

EXPERIMENT

Have students use discussion question #6 at the end of the chapter to conduct an informal survey. They need to find five people who drink and five people who do not drink to answer the question. Collect everyone's data and see if you can draw any conclusions. A possible hypothe-sis is this: nondrinkers may argue that the ads *do* affect drinking habits (but *they* are strong enough to resist this influence); drinkers may argue that the ads have little or no effect on drinking habits (*they* drink because they choose to drink).

Chapter 16 FRUSTRATION, CONFLICT, STRESS, AND DRUGS

very low in nutrients. Hence, as people continue drinking over time, they gradually reduce their regular food intake, causing a vitamin loss. Vitamin loss is one of the few things that directly and perma-nently damages the brain cells.

Severe cases of alcoholism can lead to nightmarish experiences. When alcoholics can't get to a drink, they may experience what are called the "horrors," or an **alcohol withdrawal delirium.** The first symptoms are weakness, anxiety, and severe stomach cramps. These are followed by gross and terrifying **hallucinations**—that is, seeing or hearing things that are not really there. Typically, the person is being attacked and eaten up by bugs, snakes, and other crawling things. The progression of the delirium is from confusion to disorien-tation, to stupor, and often to death. Ironically, one translation of the word *alcohol* is "the water of life" (Blum, 1984).

The Synergistic Effect   The liver gets rid of foreign substances in the body. But it cannot handle two chemicals of slightly different structure at the same time. In fact, when two drugs are present in the liver, each of them *increases* in its potency. This is called a **synergistic** (sin-er-JIS-tic) **effect** (Gold, 1985). Hence, people run a notable risk when they take both barbiturates, or tranquilizers, and alcohol in the same period of time, since the effect of each will increase and can be fatal.

Causes of Alcoholism   You will hear that body chemistry, aller-gies, brain waves, and who knows what have been discovered as the cause of alcoholism. We obviously assume that the alcoholic is or has been under some kind of stress, but are there other factors that lead to alcoholism? We don't know for certain. While many studies find some common problem in one group of alcoholics, the problem doesn't show up in the next group that is studied. Thus, there is no known "cause."

Heredity is sometimes cited as the origin. We don't know that, either. We do know that if one's parents and other relatives are alco-holic, then the chances are good that the offspring will be also. But this type of finding does not separate out the influence of environ-ment. Someone living in an alcoholic family is clearly exposed to an alcoholic environment. To show you how difficult studies of heredity are—even with rats—here is a typical finding: some types of rats pre-fer alcohol as a drink while other kinds of rats don't. This certainly would suggest that some rats have an inherited desire or need for alcohol. But other studies of rats show that some groups of them like to drink alcohol in one type of laboratory setting but not in another kind. Hence, it could be environmental as well. Other studies of humans show a possible link to genetic defects—that is, certain abnormalities appear in alcoholic parents and in their offspring who also become alcoholic—but again this finding does not appear con-

alcohol withdrawal delirium

The "horrors" that can result from severe alcoholism; includes weakness, anxiety, cramps, hallucinations.

hallucinations

Seeing or hearing things that are not physically present.

synergistic effect

The result of taking two drugs in combination, which makes each more potent than either one by itself.

▲ *Alcohol is a drug, a depressant.*

459

Connections

Richard Restak, in *The Mind,* cites studies in which animals learn to associate music with drug injections. Eventually, the music alone evokes psy-chological symptoms of withdrawal (see the sec-tion on conditioning in Chapter 7). The same process happens to addicts who after getting "clean," return to their old neighborhoods, which elicit conditioned symp-toms of withdrawal. If pos-sible, addicts should move to new locations after coming clean. Another possibility is similar to sys-tematic desensitization (Chapter 19): the abuser prepares the drug but is not allowed to take it. This way, the drug eventually becomes associated with *not* taking it. This is a remarkable example of how societal cues can influence addiction.

DISCUSS THE PHOTO

Since alcohol is so readi-ly available on most col-lege campuses, should the drinking age in the United States be lowered? Have students debate the issue.

ENRICHMENT

Have students find out what it means to be legally drunk and how many drinks it takes for a 150-pound person to get there. While they're at it, they can check other weights, too.

Connections

Alcohol reduces REM. Withdrawal from alcohol tends to produce REM rebound, a sharp increase in REM (Chapter 6).

FYI Scientists are investigating whether alcoholics are deficient in the brain chemical, dopamine. If so, the theory asserts, this deficiency causes the blues, so alcoholics may drink to compensate for this. The alcohol does *not* compensate, but drinkers may believe it does.

Journal Topic

"Write a letter to someone whom you believe has an alcohol problem. Use a different name for confidentiality. If you do not know someone, write an 'open letter' to anyone with an alcohol problem."

sistently. For the moment, we are stuck with the possibility of a genetic (inherited) factor but not enough evidence to prove it (Waller et al., 1984; Tabakoff et al., 1984; Vaillant & Milofsky, 1982; Schuckit, 1980).

An indication of the importance of social factors in drinking is the consistent finding that Orthodox Jewish people have almost a zero rate of alcoholism. This is probably because alcohol is used as a basic part of their religious tradition and is frequently part of family celebrations at home during religious holidays. Since it is, excessive drinking is not considered clever or funny, which is certainly at least one factor that influences many people to start drinking. From their early years, Jewish children drink small amounts of wine and other beverages; as a result, alcohol becomes just another "thing" in their environment, not something to be sought after because it is forbidden—which is another reason people start drinking (Blum, 1984).

Indicators of Alcoholism A person clearly has a serious problem with alcohol if any of the following signs show up: (1) frequent drinking sprees—"frequent" is a little vague, but drunkenness once a week suggests real trouble; (2) a steady increase over time in the amount of alcohol drunk at one sitting; (3) morning drinking—to almost everyone, alcohol in the morning is nauseating, so if the day starts off with a drink, then alcohol has become a crutch the person needs to get started; (4) going to school or work drunk—this shows that the alcohol has taken over life to the point that *it* has become the major goal rather than anything else; (5) blackouts—rather than periods of unconsciousness, this term refers to memory loss of events that occurred while the person was drinking; (6) drinking whenever faced with a crisis—most people drink on occasion to "relax," but when drinking goes along with facing most problems, it has become a serious problem itself.

Concerns About Alcoholism as a "Disease" Of late, many scientists have expressed concern about calling alcoholism a "disease." Over time, alcohol can certainly devastate the body, but that alone does not qualify it as a disease. Being beaten up repeatedly can have similar effects, but no one would put that in the same category as something like cancer. Excessive use of alcohol seems to be an individual behavior that people engage in for almost as many reasons as there are people who drink. Normally, what we're saying here would seem to be little more than an argument about which words to use, but as you will see, the issue is far more important than that. In most cases, a disease is something that continues on its own course with very little chance for the victim to control it. If medicine can't help, people are at the mercy of the disease, and that can make them just give up trying to fight it.

ENRICHMENT

Have a student invite a speaker from Alcoholics Anonymous to talk about the organization's philosophy.

DISCOVERY

Several years ago, tobacco commercials on TV were banned. Given the harmful effects of alcohol, do students think alcohol commercials should be banned as well? Have several students debate the issue.

Chapter 16 FRUSTRATION, CONFLICT, STRESS, AND DRUGS

By assuming that alcoholism is this kind of disease, we become its victims, unable to do anything about it. The evidence to date, however, is pretty strong that anyone can stop the heavy use of alcohol. The keys to ending the problem are (1) really wanting to stop and (2) stabilizing one's psychological well-being enough to do so. The major problem with calling alcoholism a "disease," then, is that it tends to make the alcoholic feel hopeless. Another problem is that younger people overall feel quite good (at least compared to the rest of us), and the suggestion that they are suffering from a disease is usually seen as ridiculous, so it is ignored.

Since there is almost no evidence that alcoholism is indeed a disease in the formal sense, a leading researcher in the field of alcohol use and abuse has suggested merely calling the problem "heavy drinking" (Fingarette, 1988). At first, this seems to be a simpleminded distinction. But not so. A heavy drinker is headed for trouble—physically, legally, financially, and what have you. Too many people who are heavy drinkers talk themselves into thinking that they are not "alcoholics" and thus they do not have a problem. But if society sees "heavy drinking" itself as the problem, then these people will have to look at what they are doing. For example, if certain people get drunk at most parties, it may mean any number of things, but most clearly it means that they are unable or unwilling to be themselves. They can't trust who they are when they're sober; they can't relate well to others unless they are in a fog. They are afraid. By avoiding the label *alcoholic,* they can also avoid the obvious fact that they need to stop depending on alcohol and gain the strength simply to be whoever they really are. Since there is no question that they are drinking to excess, it would be much harder for them to avoid the label *heavy drinker,* which would let them know they need to get help.

One final point should be mentioned. Alcoholics Anonymous has had considerable success with a number of heavy drinkers and considers alcoholism a disease. None of the current researchers desires to take anything away from this organization's fine work. On the other hand, membership in AA does not include anywhere close to all the heavy drinkers around, and researchers feel that the term *heavy drinker* is more appropriate than *disease* for general use, experimentation, and understanding.

Marijuana

The use of marijuana has steadily declined since the 1960s and 1970s (Sarason & Sarason, 1993; *Statistical Abstracts…,* 1986). There are no obvious personality defects among those who use the drug on occasion (Loftus, 1980). But the heavier smokers—those who use the drug once or more a day—seem to have more than their share of personal problems. The effects of the drug are also influenced by social

Critical Thinking

"Are there any advantages in considering alcohol a disease, as Alcoholics Anonymous does?" AA's philosophy emphasizes that relapses are common and that alcoholics need to go without a drink *one day at a time.*

Discussion

What should you do if you know that someone has a problem with alcohol? Talk to that person? Report him or her? Will these direct methods backfire? A speaker from a rehabilitation center once suggested, "Do nothing." One of the ways in which alcoholics get away with drinking is by getting others to cover up for them—calling in for them, doing their work, and so on. This is what he meant by "Do nothing."

461

Discussion

Would you vote for a president who admits to having been an alcoholic? What if the candidate had smoked marijuana? What if the candidate still smokes marijuana? Why or why not?

Break the class into groups to tackle the following drug-related issue. What should we do as a society about drug abuse? Tougher enforcement? No restrictions at all?

Mandatory education? More public-service announcements? Have each group devise a plan. Groups should explain the advantages and disadvantages of their plans.

Points to Stress

Unlike opiates, which cause a physical dependence, marijuana does not seem to be addictive. But like cocaine, psychological dependence may develop.

DISCUSS THE PHOTO

Are photos like this effective at all in deterring young people from using drugs?

FYI Even people who smoke marijuana a few times a month will still have traces of it in their bodies at any given time.

Connections

Stimulants are sometimes used to treat narcolepsy (Chapter 6).

Unit 5 PERSONALITY, ADJUSTMENT, AND CONFLICT

psychedelic

A drug that distorts or confuses the user's perception of the world.

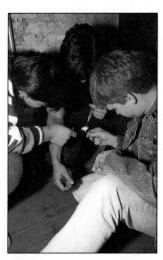

▲ *No matter what the drug, if it is being injected, the person is in very serious trouble.*

tolerance

The need to take larger and larger dosages of a drug while still only getting the same effect as from the original dose.

paranoia

The belief that others are out to get you.

surroundings. Thus, those taking it alone tend to be quiet and subdued; those using it in groups are more talkative and outgoing (Blum, 1984).

Marijuana is a **psychedelic** (sigh-kuh-DEL-ik) drug, which means it distorts or confuses the user's perception of the world. Especially notable effects are that time seems to stretch out longer than usual; the person becomes sleepy and has a floating feeling. While alcohol causes more problems with coordination and makes people more aggressive than marijuana, it still is not safe to perform any task involving coordination when taking this drug. When experienced pilots took marijuana and then were studied in flight simulators, the pilots made all kinds of serious errors (Blum, 1984; Zeichner & Pihl, 1979).

Many studies suggest that marijuana reduces the level of the male sex hormone in the user. The major concern here would be the danger involved in a pregnant woman using marijuana. During the first four months of pregnancy, the male fetus's sex characteristics are developed by this hormone. Hence, if a pregnant woman uses marijuana, damage to the developing male fetus is possible.

The most serious clear-cut effect of marijuana is on the memory system. People have short- and long-term memories, as we discussed in Chapter 8. Everything we learn must first go into the short-term system and then be transferred to the long-term, permanent storage. While the drug does not affect long-term memory, it does wipe out the short-term storage for a few hours after being taken, so newly learned material is never transferred and hence not retained. The result is that frequent use of marijuana typically leads to very poor school achievement (Lipton & Marel, 1980; Miller & Berman, 1983).

Amphetamines

Stimulants called amphetamines are very dangerous. They do create a feeling of excitement, freedom, and energy, but they also create a heavy **tolerance** in the user. Tolerance refers to the fact that if at first the person takes, say, one tablet, then two tablets will soon be needed to produce the same effect, then three, and so on. Hence, tolerance means that the body adapts to each dosage. In a short time, the user is taking a dosage hundreds of times greater than the original one in order to get the same effect. Heavy dosages, in turn, result in bizarre mental images, trembling, convulsions, and notable **paranoia** (pair-uh-NOI-ya), the belief that others are out to get you (Kokkinidis & Anisman, 1980).

Such drugs should never be used for weight loss; they do a poor job, and tolerance will build up quickly. Continued use to stay awake for studying will backfire, too, not only because of the buildup of tolerance but also because of the temporary memory loss that begins to occur.

ACTIVITY
   ACTIVITY
   ACTIVITY
   ACTIVITY
   ACTIVITY

ENRICHMENT

Ask students to find out the latest estimate on how many people in America have used cocaine. How has this estimate changed in the last ten or 20 years?

Chapter 16 FRUSTRATION, CONFLICT, STRESS, AND DRUGS

Cocaine

Cocaine, which comes from coca leaves, is also a stimulant producing many of the same sensations as amphetamines. The first soda fountains in the 1800s in the United States served soda pop that contained cocaine. Among the brand names were Koca Nola, Nerve Ola, Wise Ola, and, believe it or not, Dope. The best known, of course, is Coca-Cola, which originally contained alcohol as well (Musto, 1989). These drinks were quite a success, as you might have guessed, until some of the dangers of cocaine were noted, and the drug was made illegal. Today's Coca-Cola uses caffeine to provide stimulation (Blum, 1984).

Sniffing (snorting) is the most popular way to take this drug. It creates a warm "rush," which radiates through the body for about ten minutes. Cocaine in any form leads to severe hallucinations, mental confusion, and paranoia after a time (Siegel, 1985). *Crack* is very dangerous because it is a highly purified form of cocaine with great potency. It is cocaine in paste form, normally smoked, which means

▲ The effects of cocaine are spelled out in this old ad, but the damage and long-term problems cocaine can cause were unknown in the early "Coke" days.

Critical Thinking

"What if marijuana were legal and alcohol were not?" Students might consider health hazards, long- and short-term effects, the addictive quality of the drugs, and social changes that would occur. See the **Interdisciplinary Project: Government.**

Points to Stress

Amphetamines don't *add* anything; they simply cause the body to work faster, which will eventually cause wear and tear on the body. This stress may result in ulcers, high blood pressure, infections, and other problems.

DISCUSS THE PHOTO

Considering the known dangers of alcohol, you might wonder why it hasn't been made illegal too.

FYI Amphetamines last a few hours. Cocaine lasts about 20 minutes. After withdrawal from cocaine, a person may still be psychologically dependent on it for years.

DISCOVERY

Have several students debate whether there should be mandatory drug testing of athletes at your school. Prepare for the debate by having students interview program participants, if your school has a testing program.

Points to Stress

Many of your students may have seen the commercial in which monkeys, when given cocaine "on demand" in laboratory studies, preferred cocaine to sex and even food. Many of the monkeys, of course, died. As enrichment, have students read "Cocaine and the Chemical Brain," by S. Hammer and L. Hazleton (see **Suggested Readings** for this chapter).

Connections

Endorphins are the brain's natural opiates (Chapter 3). What do endorphins do? Inhibit pain.

Comprehension Check

What type of drug is each of the following?
(1) alcohol *(depressant)*
(2) marijuana *(psychedelic)*
(3) cocaine *(stimulant)*
(4) heroin, morphine, and opium *(opiates, or sedatives)* (5) LSD *(psychedelic)* (6) steroids *(artificial male sex hormones)*

464

psychological dependence

A craving by the psyche for a drug, although the body doesn't demand it.

opiates

Sedatives; drugs that reduce body functioning.

physical dependence

A craving by the body itself for a drug.

hallucinogen

A drug that produces major hallucinations.

steroids

Artificially produced male sex hormones.

464

that within a very brief time it is absorbed by the lungs and quickly enters the brain through the blood, causing an intense "high."

Cocaine produces a very strong **psychological dependence,** which means that although the body doesn't demand it, the user wants it so much that life becomes empty and intolerable without it. Most people who use cocaine do not die from it. Nonetheless, it can cause an instant heart attack and death in young and apparently healthy people who are using only an average dose. The exact cause of the heart spasms is not clear, and there is no way to know beforehand who or when it will kill (Isner, 1987).

Opiates

Heroin, morphine, and opium are all **opiates**—that is, sedatives—that dramatically depress nerve operation in the brain. At first, they make people feel very good and on top of the world, but suddenly the person comes crashing down into a deep depression. Opiates not only cause psychological dependence and create a drug tolerance but they also cause **physical dependence,** which means that the body itself, not just the psyche, begins to crave the drug. Most people are killed by these drugs from the additives put into them and from unsterile equipment (Ruttenber & Luke, 1984). These drugs can make those addicted to them so desperate that some have been known to cut open a vein in order to pour the drug in if they can't find a syringe (Stephens & Cottrell, 1972).

LSD

LSD is a very potent psychedelic drug called an **hallucinogen** (ha-LOOSE-en-uh-jen) because it produces major hallucinations. Doses as small as 1/250,000th of an ounce can cause marked changes in behavior. It makes the brain cells from different areas fire at random and mixes the senses, as we discussed earlier. Most of the danger from this drug comes from panic by users who can't cope with the sensations, often running around or mutilating themselves.

Steroids

Steroids are artificially made male sex hormones that are used by many athletes, mostly male but also a few females. Since the (normal) male sex hormone helps build muscles, these people are hoping to increase their body size and strength with the drug. While this works, many users experience severe problems. They lose control of their emotions, often going way up and then way down. They begin to feel an unrealistic sense of power. For example, some have thought they could jump out of a window three or four stories high without

ENRICHMENT

How do other cultures regard suicide? More specifically, how do religion, tradition, and the legal system affect attitudes toward suicide?

Points to Stress

This may be an obvious point, but the majority of people who are suicidal suffer from depression (see Chapter 18). It is the *depression* that most likely causes conflicts with family and school, work and social life.

Chapter 16 FRUSTRATION, CONFLICT, STRESS, AND DRUGS

hurting themselves (they couldn't). One deliberately drove a car into a tree at 40 miles an hour while his friend made a videotape of the scene. The symptoms usually end when intake of the drug is stopped, but while on it, the individual is quite unpredictable (Pope & Katz, 1987).

SUICIDE

For the population as a whole, roughly 13 people per 100,000 kill themselves every year. Approximately double that number *try* to commit suicide. Among those age 25 to 64 years, roughly 16 per 100,000 kill themselves; for ages 65 to 74, about 20 per 100,000 commit suicide; for those 75 to 84, the figure jumps to 25 per 100,000 (Wainrib, 1992b; *Statistical Abstracts...*, 1986). More males than females *actually* kill themselves, while females attempt it more often. The reason for this difference seems to be that males don't consider it "manly" to use methods such as taking drugs or inhaling carbon monoxide from the car exhaust. Hence, they have less of a chance of being rescued. Males most often use a gun; females most often take drugs.

Common Stresses

Some of the most common stressors leading up to suicide are the loss of important friends, substance abuse, serious conflicts within

FYI The number one cause of death among teenagers is accidents. Homicide is number two and suicide is number three.

Points to Stress

It is difficult to measure the suicide rate, of course. For example, when we hear the tragic story of someone getting hit by a train, it may officially be listed as an accident, but the truth may be otherwise.

DISCUSS THE PHOTO

Many hot line operators are trained to listen using nondirective techniques. See the material on Carl Rogers in Chapter 19.

▲ *Suicide hot lines have become a point of contact for thousands throughout the country.*

465

DISCOVERY

Have several students role-play the steps someone experiences when trying to overcome substance abuse. Afterward, discuss how realistic the role-play was.

Overcoming Substance Abuse.

 Yes, relapses are common. But abusers can learn from their mistakes.

Critical Thinking

Ask students to discuss some of the warning signs that someone has decided to commit suicide. First of all, clarify that sometimes there simply aren't any signs, at least not in the classical sense, like the giving away of prized possessions. Prolonged depression may certainly be a sign. But the number one sign is that the person tells you he or she is considering suicide. This may seem painfully obvious, but it's easy to dismiss such a statement as trivial: "Oh, he (she) doesn't really mean it." It's important that we take this direct sign seriously.

Unit 5 PERSONALITY, ADJUSTMENT, AND CONFLICT

IN FOCUS **Overcoming Substance Abuse**

Are relapses common? What can the abuser gain from them?

the family, and severe trouble at school or work. Usually added to these specific problems is a feeling that everything is meaningless and boring and that there is no point in trying to make things better (McMahon & McMahon, 1983).

Teenage Suicide

The suicide rate for people ages 15 to 19 is about 12 per 100,000. This rate stays roughly the same year after year, varying only a frac-

Have students complete the **Enrichment Worksheet** for this chapter located in the Teacher Resources.

Chapter 16 FRUSTRATION, CONFLICT, STRESS, AND DRUGS

tion of a percentage point. So, the number of suicides for this age group is not very high, but each one of these suicides causes pain and anguish. The media's claim that adolescent suicide is taking over like the plague is clearly false. The press also distorts the facts by using percentages: a small group of communities will have, say, one adolescent suicide during a year. If, for whatever reason, this happens to change to three people the following year, what we read is that suicide among teenagers in that area is up 200 percent!

Here is an example of the point we are making: about a month before we wrote this section, there were a couple of "shoot-outs" between motorists on California highways. The press kept playing this up in article after article. With each article, another couple of shootings would occur, illustrating the effects of stress and press exaggeration.

In all such cases, suggestible people are involved. The same thing results from the media's focus on the occasional teen suicide. There is an increase in suicides by a few cases every time these events are reported. The facts are that adolescents are not on a suicide rampage. The leading cause of teenage death is accidents—about 10,000 per year.

Comprehension Check

Name some common stressors that can lead to suicide. *(loss of friends, serious family conflict, severe school or work trouble, feeling that everything is meaningless and boring)*

Connections

See the wraparound material for Chapter 12 for discussion questions on doctor-assisted suicides.

PSYCHOLOGY IN YOUR LIFE

Preventing and Overcoming Substance Abuse

Substance abuse is a serious problem in our society. Of all the categories of psychological problems, it affects the largest number of people (Neal & Turner, 1991). It is associated with unemployment, dropping out of school, violent crime, and child abuse and neglect. The financial cost to society is tremendous, in terms of general health care, mental health care, incarceration, and drug and alcohol treatment programs. The emotional costs are staggering. Substance abuse destroys individuals and tears their families apart. While adequate treatment is an important goal, prevention is a much better alternative. When you can avoid the problem beforehand, you are way ahead of the game.

Probably no one is completely immune to the temptations of chemical substances. However, some people are at higher risk than others. If prevention programs are to be effective, these risk factors must be identified. The adolescent *(continued on next page)*

PSYCHOLOGY IN YOUR LIFE

Points to Stress
As noted earlier, the anticipatory feelings that a substance abuser goes through are conditioned.

Journal Topic
"You are in the first stage of substance abuse, when others see a problem, but you do not. Your friends are trying to convince you that you have a problem. What do you think of these friends?"

Connections
A relapse can particularly frustrate people who "awfulize" everything (Chapter 19). Everything is seen in black and white; one relapse means there is absolutely no hope—ever.

PSYCHOLOGY IN YOUR LIFE

Preventing and Overcoming Substance Abuse

(continued from previous page) years, for example, are a particularly vulnerable time.

We tend to assume that social class and drug use are automatically related, but that's not true. Only *extreme* poverty is a factor, and even its effects are limited. Children with behavior problems who also live in extreme poverty are at higher risk for substance abuse in adolescence or young adulthood. The risk increases dramatically when the neighborhood in which they live is unstable. An unstable neighborhood is one where there are many vacant buildings, the people do not identify much with their community and move frequently, and there is general chaos and disorder. In areas where drugs are readily available, there is also a higher rate of drug use.

In addition to these societal or cultural factors, personal factors contribute to risk. Children with certain characteristics are more likely to become adolescent substance abusers. For instance, very impulsive children who are big risk takers or thrill seekers are more vulnerable than others. We used to think that coming from a broken home increased one's risk of substance abuse. Now, however, we know more about this issue. The problem is not divorce but the absence of any real bond between children and their parents, along with a great deal of family conflict.

Obviously, if adults in the family use drugs or have permissive attitudes about the children using drugs, the child is at risk. This finding holds regardless of ethnic or racial background. It is true for whites, Hispanics, African Americans, Native Americans, and Asian Americans. Other family factors include a lack of parental involvement in children's activities and a lack of firm, consistent, and humane discipline.

Associating with drug-using friends is an especially powerful factor for adolescents. Where substance abuse is involved, peers have a stronger influence than parents do. And again, this is true whether you are white, African American, Hispanic, Native American, or Asian American (Hawkins, Catalano, & Miller, 1992).

In this chapter, we listed several signs of alcoholism. There is, however, a simpler test for substance abuse, if people can be truly honest with themselves. Feeling a strong need for the substance or looking forward with real anticipation to its use indicates a problem, regardless of how often a person uses it. Also, if someone's life is being damaged by substance use, that person should take a very close look at his or her behavior. Finally, if a person's family and friends repeatedly say that person has a problem, it is most likely true.

Treatment programs are many and varied. We are not in any position to evaluate the ones in your area. However, the process one goes through in overcoming substance abuse seems to take the same general course. Stopping for a short while is not that difficult. Staying off the substance, though, is very difficult indeed. People often become discouraged and think it can't be done. However, relapsing and trying again are part and parcel of eventually winning out over an addiction.

There are several stages to becoming substance-free. In the first stage, others see a problem, but the substance *(continued on next page)*

VOCABULARY REVIEW

Before testing students on the contents of the chapter, you may want to review vocabulary terms that are especially important or confusing. Terms in this chapter that could require clarification are *distress*, *eustress*, *fight or flight reaction*, *general adaptation syndrome*, and *synergistic effect*.

Reteaching Strategy

Have students complete the **Reteaching Worksheet** for this chapter located in the Teacher Resources.

The **Vocabulary Worksheet** may be completed by the class as a pretest for chapter concepts or used as a reteaching worksheet for those students needing additional review.

PSYCHOLOGY IN YOUR LIFE

Preventing and Overcoming Substance Abuse

(continued from previous page) abusers do not. They may even quit using for a while because of the pressure from other people. However, they will quickly take it up again. Next comes the time when the person is aware that a problem exists but has no commitment to doing anything about it. Among smokers, this stage has been known to last for years. In the next phase, the person is preparing or intending to solve the problem or has

done a little something toward the goal of abstinence. For example, he or she may have cut down the number of cigarettes smoked or switched to a low-tar brand. This also can go on for quite a long time. The next-to-last step is changing behavior and actually abstaining from the substance. Why isn't this the last step? Because achieving abstinence is only part of the solution. Maintaining it is the real answer and the last

step. Keep in mind that relapse is the rule, not the exception. Most people are embarrassed when a relapse happens, and they feel like failures. With each relapse, though, you gain a little bit over the last time and learn from your mistakes. The next time through, you are more likely to succeed. The key is to keep at it and refuse to give up (Prochaska, DiClemente & Norcross, 1992).

SUMMARY

1. Frustration results from the blocking of goals. Conflict occurs when a choice must be made between alternatives. Stress and anxiety are brought about by frustration, conflict, and change.
2. With stress, the human body prepares for an emergency just as animals do. But, for humans, social restrictions make it more difficult to discharge the stress through either fighting or fleeing. Our higher brains tend to see abstract crises that are much harder to handle.
3. Any kind of change can trigger a stress response. Being under stress for too long can lead to physical problems such as heart disease. The type A personality—the opposite of type B—drives too hard for too long and is in serious trouble if the person is

also angry most of the time. Fighting off stress involves a three-part sequence called the general adaptation syndrome.
4. Drugs affect the brain in a number of ways: blocking the firing of nerve cells, increasing their firing, or by disturbing one's normal ability to keep hearing, seeing, or smelling apart as different sensations. Depending on which drug is used, drug tolerance, physical dependence, and/or psychological dependence make them very hard to stop taking.
5. Suicide results from feelings of loneliness and loss. The frequency of teenage suicide is grossly exaggerated, but a few of those who are suggestible are influenced by press reports of other suicides to attempt it.

Wrapping It Up

When you discuss substance abuse, it may be that students who already use are probably tired of hearing of the dangers and tend to believe the dangers don't apply to them—no way. Those who don't use may be bored, thinking, "This stuff doesn't have anything to do with me." They may forget that the material may very well apply to someone dear to them. And they may not realize that none of us is immune to the dangers of substance abuse. Something could happen tomorrow to trigger the beginning of such behavior. So the moral for the students to understand is that everyone needs to hear about substance abuse, even at the risk of being bored.

SUGGESTED READINGS

▼ Cherey, L. "The Man Who First Named Stress." *Psychology Today,* March 1978: 64.

▼ Davis, Martha, and Elizabeth Eshelman. *The Relaxation and Stress Reduction Workbook.* Oakland, CA: New Harbinger, 1988.

▼ Hammer S., and L. Hazleton. "Cocaine and the Chemical Brain." *Science Digest.* [1984]: 58–61 and 100-103.

▼ Holmes, David S. "Psychological Effect of Aerobic Exercise and Fitness." *The Psychology Teacher Network,* American Psychological Association [March/April 1992]: 2–4.

▼ Mandler, G. *Mind and Body: Psychology of Emotion and Stress.* New York: W. W. Norton, 1984.

▼ Restak, Richard. *The Mind.* New York: Bantam Books, 1988.

Answers to Review Questions

1. c
2. b
3. a
4. d
5. b
6. a
7. d
8. c
9. b
10. d
11. a
12. c
13. true
14. true
15. false
16. true
17. false
18. true
19. true
20. true
21. false

VOCABULARY

frustration
conflict
approach-approach conflict
approach-avoidance conflict
avoidance-avoidance conflict
double approach- avoidance conflict
anxiety
stress
eustress

distress
fight or flight reaction
adrenal glands
stress hormone
type A personality
type B personality
general adaptation syndrome
alarm reaction
stage of resistance
exhaustion
substance abuse
chemical dependence

alcohol withdrawal
delirium
hallucinations
synergistic effect
psychedelic
tolerance
paranoia
psychological dependence
opiates
physical dependence
hallucinogen
steroids

Review Questions

Matching (Answers can be used more than once.)

1. "Should I go to Europe or Florida for vacation?"
2. "Should I quit my job? If I do, I can spend time with my friends, but I won't have much money. If I don't quit, I can buy a new stereo, but I won't have much time to listen to it with my friends."
3. "I don't want to do my homework, but I don't want to fail."
4. "I want to stay home from school, but I know my dad will find out and punish me."

a. avoidance-avoidance conflict
b. double approach-avoidance conflict
c. approach-approach conflict
d. approach-avoidance conflict

5. "Should I go out with Gail, who has a good sense of humor, but can never be serious or with Terri, who is a good friend and a good listener but doesn't laugh much?"
6. "Should I crash into the oncoming car, or should I swerve and perhaps injure a pedestrian?"
7. "Should I watch TV? If I do, I won't have time to finish my homework."
8. "Should I treat myself to dessert or have a snack later? I know I can't have both."

a. avoidance-avoidance conflict
b. double approach-avoidance conflict
c. approach-approach conflict
d. approach-avoidance conflict

Multiple Choice

9. Eustress is "good" because it
   a. helps us to live longer.
   b. helps push us toward new goals.
   c. blocks out "bad" stress.
   d. causes us less pain than "bad" stress.
10. Stress can be good or bad depending primarily on
    a. the body's initial reaction to a problem.
    b. the number of problems a person encounters.
    c. the type of problem.
    d. how a person views a problem.

11. If an animal experiences a fight or flight reaction and then no longer needs to fight
    a. chemicals will be released to balance or calm the body.
    b. chemicals will be released to further intensify the body's reaction.
    c. the animal will then run away.
    d. the animal will probably fight the next animal to come along.
12. The purpose of the Social Readjustment Rating Scale is to show that changes in life
    a. will cause sickness.
    b. can cause an early death.
    c. can result in stress.
    d. should be avoided.

True/False

13. Evidence indicates that extreme type A personalities often develop heart problems.
14. According to the general adaptation syndrome, we respond to stress in an established sequence.
15. There is clear evidence that heredity is the sole cause of alcoholism in an individual.
16. Drug users often become dazed because drugs may stop nerve cells from firing.
17. Alcohol acts as a stimulant to the body.

18. Marijuana use seems to have an effect on short-term memory.
19. Studies suggest that marijuana use reduces the level of male sex hormones.
20. Steroids operate as male sex hormones.
21. Relapses are rare among people who ultimately stop abusing drugs.

Notes on Discussion Questions

1. You might point out that divorce is ranked second and new residence is ranked 32nd on Holmes's scale.

2 and 3. Consider using these topics as journal entries.

4. If students agree that the illegality of alcohol promotes drinking, why doesn't this hold true for other illegal behaviors? Burglary, for example, is illegal, yet this illegality does not make burglary an attractive possibility for most people. This logic is simple and perhaps the analogy is not quite fair, but it should lead to the idea that there are numerous reasons why young people drink. Discuss these reasons.

5. It might be interesting to compare students' answers to the behavioral and humanistic approaches discussed in earlier chapters. A behaviorist would probably argue that the association of alcohol with positive images certainly would condition us to respond positively to alcohol. A humanist might argue that we are not so easily swayed by 60-second spots on TV; our decision to drink or not to drink will be based more on internal motivations.

6. We pop pills, have parties where alcohol is readily available, and so on.

7. Those who want restrictions on the press may argue that widespread coverage tends to glorify suicide. Some restrictions may include the following: (1) The dead person's face should not be flashed on the nightly news or printed in the newspaper. (2) The method of suicide should not be explained. (3) The dead person's friends should not be hounded with questions by reporters.

Notes on Activities

1. If you want to create *one* good chart that all your students can use to collect data outside of class, have everyone make a chart, and then combine the best from all of them. Or brainstorm ideas in class, and create a chart together. Warn students that their analyses should be

DISCUSSION QUESTIONS

1. If you had to create a chart similar to the Social Readjustment Rating Scale, which would you rank as more stressful: moving to a new school or breaking up with someone whom you have been dating for two months? Explain.

2. If someone had followed you around with a video camera from the beginning of this school year to the present—and only filmed you at school—what conclusions would a person viewing the video draw about your personality? Would your behavior indicate a type A or a type B personality? Explain. *Note:* conclusions should be based only on your behavior, not on your thoughts. What if you were filmed only at home?

3. Answer the question in number 2, but this time, imagine someone is reading only your thoughts and not seeing any behavior. What conclusions would be drawn in this case? Explain.

4. You are probably familiar with the theory that one of the reasons young people drink alcohol is that it is illegal or forbidden. Do you think this reason applies to the young drinkers in your area? Why or why not? Explain.

5. It should be fairly obvious to you how advertisers glorify alcohol use. Some people claim that this type of glorification has little effect on nondrinkers, that it will not significantly alter drinking habits. Furthermore, the purpose of the ads is to promote or highlight a particular brand name, not drinking in general. Others argue that the constant barrage of alcohol ads certainly does affect drinking habits. The ads send the message that it is perfectly acceptable to drink. With which argument do you tend to agree and why? Explain.

6. As stated in the previous question, advertisers explicitly condone alcohol consumption. Some would argue that not only do advertisers promote this drug use but also our society as a whole condones the use of alcohol and other kinds of drugs. What are some of the subtle ways in which our society says it is all right to use drugs? Explain.

7. As noted in the chapter, the press often plays up suicide. Should there be restrictions on what the press can report when a suicide occurs? Why or why not? Explain.

ACTIVITIES

1. The chapter includes a chart that awards a stress ranking for various kinds of life changes (Table 16.1). We want you to adapt this chart to your school by making a list, not of *life* change units, but of "school change units" that may cause stress. The following are possibilities: an upcoming test, being called down to the principal's office, getting caught cheating, being expelled, being asked to deliver a speech because of your high grades. *Note:* include both positive and negative changes. You can probably come up

as specific as possible. As the chapter suggests, one cannot simply add the scores and predict illness. Students should compare not only overall scores with illness but also major stressors with illness.

2. If you do not assign this activity, consider conducting it on your students, comparing one class with another.

3. Students usually do a good job with this activity. If you do not assign this one, perhaps you can have each student bring in two pictures, one that glorifies drugs and one that shows the reality of drugs. With these pictures you can decorate the entire room—or just a bulletin board or two.

4. Have students add their own questions to the ones already listed in the text.

---

with at least 20 or 30 of these changes that potentially cause stress.

Next, assign a ranking to each of these changes—a ranking of 100 would be most stressful; a ranking of five or ten would be least stressful. This ranking process will, of course, be subjective, but try to be fair. Before deciding on a final ranking you might consult with friends and teachers to get their input.

Once you've decided on your final rankings, place the items in order and include the numerical rank next to each item (just like in Table 16.1).

Next, either photocopy the chart so that each person in your psychology class can have a copy, or transfer the chart onto a poster so that everyone in class can see it. Ask your understanding psychology teacher for about five minutes of class time. Have everyone in class check the changes that they have experienced in the past month. Then have them add up the rankings for these changes. Finally, have them write down all the "illnesses" they have had in the past month—including sore throats, minor pains, and so on.

Collect their scores and their descriptions of their illnesses, and compare the two. Is there any relationship? Explain. Draw several possible conclusions from your results.

2. When we think of stress, we usually regard it as negative, as "distress." Conduct a simple experiment to see if a moderate amount of stress will actually improve performance. *Procedure:* Write out ten multiplication problems, all involving three-digit numbers multiplied by two-digit numbers; 336 × 75, for example. Find 20 subjects to solve the problems. Put ten of the subjects under moderate stress and the remaining subjects under no stress. The stressed subjects should be told that they have only a minute to complete as many problems as they can as accurately as they can. The remaining

subjects should simply be told to do their best, that it is just an assignment *you* need to complete. Don't tell them they are being timed. In other words, all 20 subjects will be allowed just one minute to solve the problems, but only half of them will know that they will be stopped at the end of a minute.

Compare the results of your two groups. Which group solved more problems? Which group answered more problems correctly? Based on your results, would you say that moderate stress increases performance?

3. Sift through several magazines and cut out ads that clearly glorify alcohol or any other kind of drug use. Next, find several pictures that show the possibly ugly realities of alcohol and other drug use. For example, you might use a picture of a vagrant sleeping on a bench with a pint of whiskey at his or her feet. Arrange both sets of pictures into a creative collage in which the message is clear that alcohol and drug use are often *not* glamorous activities. Your collage doesn't have to preach against anything; it should simply present two sides of an issue. It may be helpful to give a title to your collage or to include captions.

4. One of the most successful groups to deal with alcohol and drug abuse is Alcoholics Anonymous (AA). Contact an AA center in your area and interview someone there. Possible questions: (1) What are some indicators that might reveal whether a person has an alcohol or drug problem? (2) How common is it for a person to deny these indicators, to deny that a problem exists? (3) In what ways does this denial often express itself? (4) What steps need to be taken in order for a person to recover? (5) Is there such a thing as a cure for alcoholism?

Write a report on your interview and include your reactions.

DISCUSS THE PHOTO

What ingredients (other than those listed in the caption) are important for psychological health?

Thinking well of yourself, caring for others, and enjoying life are important ingredients for psychological health.

474

PSYCHOLOGY AND YOU RESOURCES

A variety of resources are available in the Psychology and You *supplementary material. In addition, there are a number of additional resources listed to enhance your lesson plans.*

Masters
▼ 17-1A Learning Goals
▼ 17-1B Answers to Learning Goals
▼ 17-2 Power of Suggestion
▼ 17-3 Possible Reactions to Stress
▼ 17-4 Defense Mechanisms
▼ 17-5 Self-Concept
▼ 17-6 Healthy Characteristics

Student Worksheets
▼ Vocabulary Worksheet

▼ Independent Practice Worksheet
▼ Enrichment Worksheet
▼ Reteaching Worksheet

Test Bank
▼ Tests A and B

Multimedia
▼ *The Brain* Videotape Modules #28 and 29
▼ Psychology Videodisc

Student Workbook

PACING CHART

Complete Coverage

Day 1: Assign the first two sections of the chapter and have students rate themselves on the Locus of Control Scale prior to class. Discuss the mind's power over the body, paying particular attention to the issue of control. Evaluate the way stress affects the immune system. Assign "Controlling Thoughts" and "Coping with Psychological Stress" for Day 2.

Day 2: After reviewing the concept of cognitive strategies (with pain control as a primary example), provide an activity designed to clarify each of the psychological defense mechanisms. Assign for homework an activity requiring the in-depth analysis of at least one of these psychological defense systems.

Day 3: Discuss self-concept and self-esteem. Assign the last section and Psychology In Your Life for homework.

17

Toward a Healthy Personality

OBJECTIVES

Be able to:

▼ Give examples of how the body and mind interact.

▼ Explain how stress affects the immune system.

▼ Define the psychological defense mechanisms and give an example of each.

▼ Describe the psychologically healthy personality.

Global Look at the Chapter

The healthy personality is one that is able to reduce or cope with stress, frustration, or pain. As you will discover, the evidence is overwhelming that we are able to gain control of all of these by the use of mental powers.

475

INTRODUCING THE CHAPTER

Ask students to work in pairs to make a list of things in their lives that they can't control. For example, students who receive low grades sometimes complain that it's the teacher's fault. (Why aren't *high* grades ever our fault?) As they report back, ask them to support their answers. For example, someone may say, "I can't control my mother. She's always telling me what to do." You might ask about the kinds of requests the mother makes, the student's reaction, the mother's response to the reaction, and so on. Can *any* part of this chain be controlled? Granted, the student cannot control the mother, but he can certainly control his reaction. See how many items on their lists might come under their control, at least to some extent, with a bit of cognitive readjustment.

LEAD-OFF ACTIVITY

Have students turn to the **In Focus Locus of Control Scale** that appears later in the chapter, and have them answer the questions on a piece of paper. Afterward, ask students if they feel the test is a valid one; they're not going to do any follow-up studies to determine this, of course, but do their scores *seem* to describe them correctly?

Day 4: Focus on problem-solving when evaluating the characteristics of psychological health. Give the Chapter Review quiz.

In Brief

Day 1: Focus on the connection between cognition and the body, emphasizing the importance of feeling in control (refer to In Focus Locus of Control Scale). Review the effects of stress on the immune system, as well as the two cognitive strategies for reducing pain.

Day 2: Conduct an activity involving the evaluation of psychological defense mechanisms. Review the terms self-concept and self-esteem.

Day 3: Discuss the characteristics of psychological health before giving the Chapter Review quiz.

EXPERIMENT

Teaching Master 17-2 Power of Suggestion includes directions for an experiment that students may want to conduct outside of class. You can probably run a version of the experiment in class.

TEACHING MASTER 17-1A

Learning Goals. A Learning Goals sheet for each chapter is provided in the Teacher Resources. These Learning Goals can be used as review sheets or worksheets. **Teaching Master 17-1B** consists of answers to these Learning Goals.

Discussion

We have all heard stories in which one spouse dies and the other dies soon after. Ask students if they believe this is a coincidence, or can we will our deaths—not suddenly as described here, but over a period of weeks or months? (See discussion question #2 at the end of the chapter.)

476

Unit 5 PERSONALITY, ADJUSTMENT, AND CONFLICT

BODY-MIND INTERACTIONS

In one East African tribe, during the wife's first month of pregnancy, the husband suffers along with her, supposedly "feels the growth of the embryo in his own body and develops great thirst." And in a study at a Boston maternity ward, 41 percent of the husbands showed physical health problems—nausea, faintness, leg cramps— that were not present before the woman's pregnancy (Munroe & Munroe, 1971). No matter how one views these situations, two facts are clear: (1) the man is not pregnant, and (2) the man's symptoms have to be connected with the woman's symptoms by the power of suggestion.

In similar fashion, study after study shows that there is a strong connection between mind and body. For example, if we are told about a butcher slicing off a finger, we can actually feel a real discomfort, possibly nausea, just from hearing about it. And we all know people who have used a headache or stomachache as an excuse so often that by now the pain has become real and the person doesn't even know how it got started.

And the reverse is true: giving the brain important information can reduce physical problems. For instance, "rehearsing" people who are scheduled for medical treatment—either by letting them observe someone getting the same treatment or by putting them through a dry run—reduces the pain they feel during the actual treatment compared to those who have not been rehearsed (Neufeld & Davidson, 1971). Patients told before an operation exactly what kind and how much pain they will feel after it is over have much less trouble coping with the pain, and they actually get out of the hospital earlier than those not briefed because their fear of the unknown has been reduced. So, the connection between the cognitive (thought processes) and the physical is very strong.

If you want literally to feel the power of suggestion in operation— actual nerve impulses "moving," so to speak—think right now about your right foot, especially the big toe and the second toe that is touching it. Maybe you should wiggle the big toe a little. Doesn't it feel a little large? Doesn't that make you want to wiggle your second toe? Now, are they both going or at least trying to? Note that you weren't even thinking about them before we gave you a mental suggestion.

An Extreme Case: Voodoo

Dramatic cases of death illustrate the effects of cognitive control over the body. There is a form of "religious magic" called *voodoo* in which believers might wind up with a hex put on them. A *hex* is a "spell" in which victims may be told the day and time they will die.

Have students research the topic of learned helplessness. According to the theory, if we learn to be helpless, as the rats did in the passage below, we will be more likely to become depressed. Students can look at ways in which humans learn to be helpless and how to overcome this feeling of hopelessness.

Chapter 17 TOWARD A HEALTHY PERSONALITY

Some scientists followed up these cases to see if such voodoo "works." Indeed it does. Most believers will die right on schedule. The scientists even paid off a few corrupt "witch doctors" to remove the hex, and the victims survived *as long as they knew the hex had been removed*. In a few cases, the word didn't get to them in time, and they died (Cannon, 1942). Autopsies show that what is going on in this **sudden death phenomenon** is that as the "time of death" arrives, people panic so badly that they send major electrical impulses through the critical nerve controlling the heart, causing it to get out of rhythm and stop (Lachman, 1983).

Issue of Control

It is obvious from the previous discussion that we can affect our health by the way we view life. Those who see themselves as worthless and who are anxious, depressed, angry, or hostile increase stress dramatically and set themselves up for heart problems and a generally weakened body.

One of the more important factors leading to a damaged body and psyche seems to be the degree to which we feel we have lost control of our lives. In an experiment using a pair of rats, each of them was placed in a separate cage with a wire attached to the rats' tails. Both were then subjected to a series of shocks. One of the rats was an "executive." It was able to stop the shock by turning a wheel with its paws. This ended the shock for the other rat also—but the other rat had no control over what was happening. Hence, both rats got the same amount of shock, but only one of them was "in charge," so to speak, because it could turn the wheel. The health of the rat controlling the wheel remained good, while the other one suffered ulcers and sickness—despite exactly the same level of shock (Weiss, 1972). The key here seems to be the ability to *feel* in control of a stressful situation, even though the stress must still be faced. Also important, in cases where control isn't really possible, is whether or not there is a sense of *complete* helplessness. If an event can be predicted or at least partially controlled, the negative effects are reduced dramatically (Burger & Arkin, 1980). Many studies on many different types of creatures, including the human, support these claims.

Such studies are important because they show that we are able to handle our fate in far more instances than might first be suspected. You may believe that there are too many cases where we can't do anything about it, but that is not completely true. Suppose, for instance, that you have a teacher or boss who makes life miserable. Since you can't quit school or work, what is going on seems impossible to deal with. It isn't, though. Control often comes from *inside* us. Thus, you take a good, objective look at this person causing you all the trouble. Is he or she really a nice person compared to you? Is the person more important than you? Again, probably not. He or she merely claims to be. And usually people who are like that haven't

sudden death phenomenon

A death resulting from panic and overload of the major nerve going to the heart.

Points to Stress

You might point out that some people who claim to have extraordinary mind-body powers are really charlatans. For example, *anyone* can sit on a bed of nails or walk across a bed of hot coals. If you know what you're doing, you can even stick your hand into a pot of boiling lead. Your school physics teacher might be able to explain how these feats are possible and to describe some other not-so-remarkable feats.

DEMONSTRATION

You might want to try a game presented in the wraparound material from the last chapter that deals with the issue of control. See **Teaching Master 16-2 Frustration.**

Points to Stress

If students complete the **In Focus Locus of Control Scale,** you may want to warn them not to take their scores too seriously. Assure them that their scores will be confidential.

FYI The American Dental Association published an article that quoted *American Health Magazine* which, in turn, quoted *The Journal of the Canadian Dental Association,* citing one study that showed that putting ice cubes on the web of the hand between the thumb and first finger will greatly reduce or eliminate pain from a toothache. We have no way of knowing if it works, but given the history of acupuncture, there is always the possibility that it might.

Unit 5 PERSONALITY, ADJUSTMENT, AND CONFLICT

IN FOCUS   **Locus of Control Scale**

Instructions

Answer the following questions the way you feel. (Do not write in your textbooks; use a separate sheet of paper.) There are no right or wrong answers. Don't take too much time answering any one question, but do try to answer them all. One of your concerns during the test may be, "What should I do if I can answer both yes and no to a question?" It's not unusual for that to happen. If it does, think about whether your answer is just a little more one way than the other. For example, if you'd assign a weighting of 51 percent to "yes" and assign 49 percent to "no," mark the answer "yes." Try to pick a response for all the questions.

The Scale

_____ 1. Do you believe that most problems will solve themselves if you just don't fool with them?

_____ 2. Do you believe that you can stop yourself from catching a cold?

_____ 3. Are some people just born lucky?

_____ 4. Most of the time do you feel that getting good grades means a great deal to you?

_____ 5. Are you often blamed for things that just aren't your fault?

_____ 6. Do you believe that if somebody studies hard enough he or she can pass any subject?'

_____ 7. Do you feel that most of the time it doesn't pay to try hard because things never turn out right anyway?

_____ 8. Do you feel that if things start out well in the morning, it's going to be a good day no matter what you do?

_____ 9. Do you feel that most of the time

parents listen to what their children have to say?

_____ 10. Do you believe that wishing can make good things happen?

_____ 11. When you get punished, does it usually seem it's for no good reason at all?

_____ 12. Most of the time, do you find it hard to change a friend's mind (opinion)?

_____ 13. Do you think that cheering more than luck helps a team to win?

_____ 14. Do you feel that it is nearly impossible to change your parent's mind about anything?

_____ 15. Do you believe that parents should allow children to make most of their own decisions?

_____ 16. Do you feel that when you do something wrong there's very little you can do to make it right?

_____ 17. Do you believe that most people are just born good at sports?

_____ 18. Are most of the other people your age stronger than you are?

_____ 19. Do you feel that one of the best ways to handle most problems is just not to think about them?

_____ 20. Do you feel that you have a lot of choice in deciding who your friends are?

_____ 21. If you find a four-leaf clover, do you believe that it might bring you good luck?

_____ 22. Do you often feel that whether or not you did your homework has much to do with what kind of grades you get?

_____ 23. Do you feel that when a person your age is angry at you, there's little you can do to stop him or her?

(continued)

COOPERATIVE LEARNING

Have students work in pairs to think of characters from books or movies who are primarily external or internal thinkers. For example, many of Shakespeare's characters, like Romeo and Juliet, are externally motivated.

IN FOCUS   Locus of Control Scale

(continued)

_____ 24. Have you ever had a good-luck charm?

_____ 25. Do you believe that whether or not people like you depends on how you act?

_____ 26. Do your parents usually help you if you ask them to?

_____ 27. Have you felt that when people were angry with you, it was usually for no reason at all?

_____ 28. Most of the time, do you feel that you can change what might happen tomorrow by what you do today?

_____ 29. Do you believe that when bad things are going to happen, they just are going to happen no matter what you try to do to stop them?

_____ 30. Do you think that people can get their own way if they just keep trying?

_____ 31. Most of the time, do you find it useless to try to get your own way at home?

_____ 32. Do you feel that when good things happen, they happen because of hard work?

_____ 33. Do you feel that when somebody your age wants to be your enemy, there's little you can do to change matters?

_____ 34. Do you feel that it's easy to get friends to do what you want them to do?

_____ 35. Do you usually feel that you have little to say about what you get to eat at home?

_____ 36. Do you feel that when someone doesn't like you, there's little you can do about it?

_____ 37. Do you usually feel that it is almost useless to try in school because most other students are just plain smarter than you are?

_____ 38. Are you the kind of person who believes that planning ahead makes things turn out better?

_____ 39. Most of the time do you feel that you have little to say about what your family decides to do?

_____ 40. Do you think it's better to be smart than to be lucky?

Scoring the Scale

The scoring key is reproduced below. You should circle your yes or no response on your answer sheet each time it corresponds to the keyed response below. Add up the number of responses you circle, and this total is your score on the Locus of Control Scale. Record your score at the top of your answer sheet.

1.	Yes	14.	Yes	27.	Yes
2.	No	15.	No	28.	No
3.	Yes	16.	Yes	29.	Yes
4.	No	17.	Yes	30.	No
5.	Yes	18.	Yes	31.	Yes
6.	No	19.	Yes	32.	No
7.	Yes	20.	No	33.	Yes
8.	Yes	21.	Yes	34.	No
9.	No	22.	No	35.	Yes
10.	Yes	23.	Yes	36.	Yes
11.	Yes	24.	Yes	37.	Yes
12.	Yes	25.	No	38.	No
13.	No	26.	No	39.	Yes
				40.	No

Reprinted by permission of Stephen Nowicki. From the Instructor's Manual prepared by Wayne Weitan for *Psychology Applied to Modern Life*, Second Edition, by Nowicki and Duke, published in 1986 by Brooks/Cole Publishing Company.

(continued)

Critical Thinking

Ask students to examine the advantages of having an external locus of control and the advantages of having an internal locus of control. (External thinkers may be nice people to be around; they are likely to be humble, since they feel they have had little to do with their successes. Internal thinkers are likely to take responsibility. So when these people feel down, they are likely to believe that *they* can bring themselves up again through determination. And as noted on the scale, their stress tolerance tends to be high.)

COOPERATIVE LEARNING

Have each group propose a new policy at school that would give students more control. For instance, students might want greater control when choosing a schedule. They might want to teach class for a day.

Or they may want to write a menu for the cafeteria. Afterward, have each group assess whether their plan would improve the attitude and even the mental health of students.

Connections

Chapter 16 discusses the importance of attitude when dealing with stress. A flexible, open-minded attitude may actually reduce the effects of stress. Remember, internal thinkers tend to have a high tolerance for stress; they feel *they* are in control and not the stress.

Unit 5 PERSONALITY, ADJUSTMENT, AND CONFLICT

 **Locus of Control Scale**

(continued)

What the Scale Measures

Locus of control is a personality dimension originally described by Julian Rotter (1966). According to Rotter, people vary in regard to how responsible they feel for their own fate. Individuals with an *internal* locus of control tend to believe that we are responsible for our own successes and failures. Conversely, people with a relatively *external* locus of control tend to attribute successes and failures to luck, chance, or fate. The scale you just responded to was developed by Stephen Nowicki and Marshall Duke (1974) in order to remedy some technical problems that were characteristic of the original Rotter (1966) scale. Like the original, it measures one's belief about whether events are controlled internally or externally.

Interpreting Your Score

Norms

External Score:	16–40
Intermediate Score:	7–15
Internal Score:	0–6

External Scorers: A score above 15 suggests that you have a fairly strong belief that events are beyond your control. In other words, you do not feel that there is much of a connection between your behavior and your outcomes. This means that you are relatively less likely than others to take credit for your successes or to take the blame for your failures. Instead, you tend to believe that success and failure are primarily a matter of luck and chance.

Intermediate Scorers: A score in this range means that you have inconsistent views about the degree to which you control your own fate. You probably believe that you do control your own fate in some areas of your life, while believing that you have little control in other areas.

Internal Scorers: A score below seven indicates that you have a firm belief in your ability to influence your outcomes. Your relatively internal score means that you generally do not attribute your successes and failures to good and bad luck or chance factors. Instead, you feel that you can influence the course of what happens to you. An internal locus of control is often associated with relatively great stress tolerance.

done much that is very meaningful with their lives, and that isn't the way you want to be. So, you have got the situation under control: you see it for what it is, and you have things in perspective. You do have to put up with the nastiness, but if you accept it within reason for what it is (the *other* person's problem), you can come out actually reducing your stress and anger greatly. You triumph despite some unpleasant moments.

It should also be noted that some people and cultures find strength through strong spiritual or religious beliefs that do not emphasize the individual's power. In such cases, they believe that the control starts from outside them, but they still benefit because they believe (inside) that there *is* some control somewhere on their behalf over what is happening.

ENRICHMENT

Ask students to find out if heredity seems to contribute to the likelihood of getting an ulcer. In other words, are some people predisposed to an excess of acid in the stomach, and will these people be more likely to develop an ulcer during stress than others?

Chapter 17 TOWARD A HEALTHY PERSONALITY

Comprehension Check

How does stress affect the immune system? *(It slows it down and decreases antibody secretions.)*

COPING WITH BODILY STRESS

If you get a splinter in your finger and leave it, some intriguing changes take place. The area surrounding it will first become reddened, but after a while a yellowish circular mound will form around the splinter. What has happened is that the body's defensive system has gone into action. It has dispatched special cells to that area to surround the foreign object, swallow it up, and kill any bacteria that have gotten into the wound. The result of the battle is the yellowish fluid of dead invader cells that comes out if you squeeze the splinter area.

This reaction is part of what is called the **immune system.** The immune system is our body's method of fighting off injury, disease, or illness, ranging from the splinter all the way through pneumonia. There are a number of types of these fighting cells, called **antibodies,** that are sent to various locations to ward off the invaders.

The chemicals that are triggered by stress actually slow down the immune system. While this doesn't "make sense," we didn't design the body—that's just the way it is. When people are depressed or anxious, the immune system is operating on a very low level, and these people are easily infected. The antibody secretions of students during exam time are decreased because of the stress, leading to an increase in the number of sick students. Evidence is pretty clear that a psychological catastrophe, such as a death in the family, can cause the immune system to be weakened to a point that some of the survivors are in life-threatening danger (Ornstein & Sobel, 1987; Schleifer, 1985; Jemmott, 1984). And the reverse is true to a more limited degree; optimism can increase the number of immune cells (Rugg, 1985). Thus, we play an active mental role in our health. You will read that even diseases like cancer can result from a "poor" attitude. That is quite exaggerated, but it has a *grain* of truth. What it refers to is that people who are beaten down by life have a weakened immune system, which can allow any incoming disease microorganisms to take over with greater ease. It doesn't mean that we can completely fight off cancer by having a healthy outlook.

The same principles apply to the illnesses discussed next. The evidence is again present that physical problems such as ulcers, asthma, and headaches can get worse as the result of psychological factors, but certainly psychological factors are not the "cause" of these difficulties (Friedman & Booth-Kewley, 1987).

Ulcers

Many medical people have tried to relate stomach **ulcers** to psychological stress. An ulcer is a severe irritation of the stomach lining that can become an open wound inside. Some ulcers probably result from an excess of acid in the stomach. When people are under stress,

immune system

The body's method for fighting disease or injury.

antibodies

Cells that fight off invading foreign bodies that might prove injurious; part of the immune system.

ulcer

Wound in the intestine or stomach resulting from severe irritation.

FYI Antibodies are produced by white blood cells. This is one of the reasons that doctors are concerned when our white blood cell count is low: we are more susceptible to infection.

TEACHING MASTER 17-3

Possible Reactions to Stress. This handout illustrates the various ways that we react to stress. You might want to post it in class.

481

INTERDISCIPLINARY PROJECT

Health. Have students examine the benefits of exercise on mental health. They can look at various kinds of exercise programs, then analyze which ones are more beneficial than others and in what way. Studies are showing that even a little exercise is better than none.

Discussion

You may have a few students in class who experience frequent headaches. Ask them their techniques for dealing with the headaches. If any of them have been to doctors, ask them to describe the procedures used to figure out what is causing the headaches. If any of these sufferers have an artistic bent, you might have them draw what the headaches feel like.

FYI Do you ever overhear people in restaurants request, "No MSG"? Monosodium glutamate (MSG) affects blood flow to the brain, which in turn may trigger migraine headaches.

Points to Stress

Migraine sufferers who are not helped by drugs may turn to biofeedback, discussed next, to develop control over the blood supply to the brain.

482

Unit 5 PERSONALITY, ADJUSTMENT, AND CONFLICT

asthma

Muscle spasms and tissue swelling in the air tubes of the lungs.

muscle contraction headache

Headaches from holding oneself in a fixed position, causing the muscles to spasm and putting pressure on the nerves.

migraine headache

A headache resulting from an insufficient supply of the brain chemical serotonin.

the amount of acid increases dramatically. We in the United States spend about $8 million a year on antacids, so our stomachs must not be in very good shape. The easiest way to get an ulcer is to drink alcohol and take aspirin. The chemical combination of the two breaks down the protective lining of the stomach (Davenport, 1982). Overall, the origin of most ulcers is not well understood. Nonetheless, the studies on control that we've already discussed do support the likelihood that people who feel helpless and who feel they lack control over their environments will get ulcers more often than people who feel a sense of control and who are relaxed and easy-going.

Asthma

In bronchial (BRON-kee-al) **asthma,** the muscles spasm and the tissues swell in the bronchial (air) tubes entering the lungs. This makes it very difficult to breathe. Physicians often claim that this is a psychological disorder, but it more likely is related to allergies or defects in the immune system (Friedman & Booth-Kewley, 1987). One would expect a person having trouble breathing to panic at times, so there also is a psychological component. Stress can make asthma worse, but it is probably not the origin of the problem.

Headaches

It may be hard to believe, but the brain itself has no pain receptors at all. Hence, it cannot hurt. Because of the thick, sturdy skull, nature considered pain receptors inside unnecessary. Your brain can be touched, squeezed, and pinched, and you will feel nothing. Even so, we spend about $1.8 *billion* a year on headache remedies, so there is a problem somewhere. Actually, the "head" ache is coming from the muscles and blood vessels pushing against nerve endings that surround the neck and head.

There are two types of headaches. The first type is called a **muscle contraction headache.** It comes from stress or from spending long periods of time holding oneself in a certain position. These headaches can develop from driving long distances without getting out of the car and moving about or from those (rare) cases when one studies too long. Muscular headaches also appear because when we are under stress, we tighten our muscles and hold ourselves in rigid positions for extended periods.

The second type of headache is called a **migraine headache.** People with migraine headaches have trouble with sleep and digestion, have disturbances of mood and emotional responses, and have improper operation of the blood vessels in the head. These factors, as well as pain responses, are controlled in part by a brain chemical called *serotonin.* People who have migraine headaches seem to have a

DISCOVERY

See **Teaching Masters 19-2** and
19-3 (from Chapter 19) for two activities on cognitive strategies.

Comprehension Check

Which of the following are examples of *distraction* and which are *redefinition?* (1) You feel a sharp pain shoot up your leg, and you imagine it to be a river. *(redefinition)* (2) Your back hurts, but you forget about it as you listen to music. *(distraction)* (3) Just as you are stuck with a needle, you think of a pleasing childhood memory. *(distraction)* (4) You focus and focus on your broken arm until it feels like it's floating. *(redefinition)*

defect of the serotonin system so that not enough of the chemical is available. This results in unpleasant changes in all these areas of behavior as well as the triggering of headaches of staggering proportions. While professionals used to believe that such headaches were caused by stress or psychological problems, these do not seem to be the origin of the difficulty—although they can add to the effects. We are dealing here with a biological malfunction; drugs that restore serotonin to proper levels are showing great promise in treating migraines (Brody, 1988). Some people who are not helped by the drugs have been able to develop sufficient control over their bodies to reduce the pain, but this takes a considerable amount of training.

Chapter 17 TOWARD A HEALTHY PERSONALITY

▲ *Maybe distraction would help this woman's headache.*

CONTROLLING THOUGHTS

The key to handling pain, anxiety, or worry is to learn to control one's thoughts. While this may sound simpleminded, it actually works.

Cognitive Strategies

A **cognitive strategy** is a mental technique in which we try to convince our brains to feel something different from what the incoming impulses say is going on. In the area of pain relief, there are two cognitive strategies: (1) **distraction,** in which we think of something else during pain and (2) **redefinition,** in which we talk ourselves into believing that the incoming stimulation is something other than pain (that is, we define the sensations over again).

Distraction works best with minor pain. You think of something like a beautiful sunset or some pleasant experience while being stuck with a needle. Redefinition works best with chronic (unending) pain. In the latter case, the task is to accept the incoming impulses, rather than distract them, but to reinterpret what they mean. Thus, you tell yourself that the impulse coming from an injured ankle is a warm, soothing one that will make you feel good. Or if you are out camping and starting to get cold, you imagine how warm the air is getting. If the dentist is getting ready to drill, you concentrate on something pleasant happening. Developing these opposite cognitive messages actually does a reasonable job of reducing pain, and it requires little practice (McCaul & Malott, 1984; Brown & Chaves, 1980).

Cognitive strategies work for two basic reasons: (1) they reduce the stress and anxiety aspects of pain, which are really a large part of it, and (2) they put into operation the brain's ability to alter incoming messages from "pain" to "no pain." If you approach a situation with the attitude of catastrophe, the stress and pain will be much greater. Those about to be operated on who think about the horrors that have

cognitive strategy

An organized mental task designed to deceive the brain about incoming information.

distraction

The cognitive strategy that consists of thinking of something else during pain.

redefinition

The cognitive strategy that consists of talking ourselves into believing that incoming stimulation is different from what it is.

Discuss the Photo

If the woman thinks of pleasing images, she is using distraction. If she imagines the pain as a great weight that she needs to lift, she is using redefinition.

Teaching Hint

Tell students that when Mom used to tell them to rub their heads when they bumped them, she may have been right. She may have been trying to distract them. Also, when they rub it, the brain has to decide whether to process the pain or the rubbing.

483

Someone from a hospital may be willing to speak on biofeedback and bring in equipment. You can probably find cheap biofeedback equipment at an electronics store, but the key word here is *cheap.* Don't waste your money if you're looking for accuracy.

FYI Since one benefit of biofeedback is relax- ation, it is sometimes recommended for peo- ple who can't sleep.

Teaching Hint

Ask if someone is willing to leave the room and return in 30 minutes with a lower temperature in her hands. She can only sit; she can't pour water on her hands or fan them or anything. Don't actually send her out, but ask how confident she is of her ability to do it. Most peo- ple would not be very assured because they would not know what to do to lower the tempera- ture. Biofeedback supplies the "what" part by provid- ing subjects with constant feedback: "Ah, I relaxed my fingers, and I noticed that the temperature went down."

DISCUSS THE PHOTO

This is an example of biofeedback.

484

Unit 5 PERSONALITY, ADJUSTMENT, AND CONFLICT

biofeedback

A method of mental control in which a machine attached to the body records events going on (for example, high blood pressure) so that the individual can change them.

▲ *As this person views different scenes, changes in brain wave pat- terns are being reported. He will then try to duplicate them on his own.*

484

occurred in their lives make the experience much worse than those who concentrate on some very warm, happy memories.

Preparing the brain beforehand also works. Providing detailed information about and methods for coping with childbirth consis- tently reduces the pain for those who take such courses. Whether or not this suggests that one should use "natural childbirth" (no anes- thesia) is another question entirely. While there may be less pain using psychological methods, women still rate the pain as severe and usually request medical assistance in reducing the pain during the late stages of labor (Melzack, 1987). This brings up the important point that mental control really won't work well for a major opera- tion or for stopping major pain, even though it may reduce it somewhat.

A practical hint: if some medical or dental procedure is being done to you, *don't* close your eyes. By doing so, you cut off all distracting stimulation from the environment and cause the body to focus only on the cut, stick, or drill.

Biofeedback

A popular method for developing control is called **biofeedback.** In biofeedback, a machine is attached to some part of the body and records its condition. The machine doesn't change anything—it merely gives information. Thus, it is useful for measuring stress (as recorded by muscle tension), anxiety (as recorded by the amount of sweat), and high blood pressure (Miller, 1985). Information about the body's condition is given to the conscious mind by the machine. We take this information into account and try to achieve conscious con- trol over the body. For example, if anxiety is too high, we try to relax until the machine says we are successful.

We don't know exactly how people are able to control themselves using biofeedback, but there are a few clues. First of all, using this technique causes us to *expect* benefits. Expectation is a large part of almost any "cure." Second, merely going through the procedure of biofeedback gives us *something* to do rather than remain helpless. Third, when we focus on any object—in this case, a machine—our attention gets locked in, and we typically go into a state of relaxation. Overall, relaxation is the most important aspect of the training.

Hypnosis, which we discussed at length in Chapter 6, is similar to biofeedback, since hypnosis also involves expectations and distrac- tion. As mentioned, hypnosis is just the focusing of attention on some idea or object. So, hypnosis, like all other methods we have dis- cussed, will only work if you really want it to. There is no way to reduce weight, stop smoking or drinking, be relaxed, and the like unless you genuinely want to make a change. Some people don't want to give up certain styles of life; nothing is going to change them, other than themselves. This can apply to biofeedback, too.

COOPERATIVE LEARNING

Have students work in pairs to illustrate a defense mechanism. Ask them to include captions.

ENRICHMENT

Sometimes repressed memories are so sensational that TV movies are made from them. The victim of abuse may suddenly remember a traumatic experience, which is triggered usually by some cue from the past. If you have any students who enjoy fiction, recommend Jane Smiley's *A Thousand Acres*, a novel whose main character slowly remembers her past. Some critics have called it a modern version of Shakespeare's *King Lear*. Or have students bring in other fiction or poetry that highlights one of the defense mechanisms.

Chapter 17 TOWARD A HEALTHY PERSONALITY

COPING WITH PSYCHOLOGICAL STRESS

Real problems in the real world have a definite impact on our well-being. However, a lot of the frustration and anxiety we feel has little to do with reality. To a large extent, the amount of stress we experience will depend on how much threat we perceive, how much we dwell on problems, and what we do about them.

Psychological Defense Mechanisms

When threatened, we all do our best to keep some kind of balance. We protect our inner selves from too much attack by using **defense mechanisms,** psychological distortions, or "tricks," designed to keep us stable. If someone says you are a slimy, rotten worm of a person, your defenses go into action instantly, and you either think how terrible that person is or you try to make yourself look better to offset the comment. Thus, we use defense mechanisms to reduce threats to ourselves and to feel like a decent person. Defenses are normal in and of themselves, but they can be used too often. When that happens, we are refusing to face reality, and this is not adaptive. In the next subsections, we cover several different defense mechanisms. Usually these are not fully conscious because we use them to protect ourselves. If we fully admit that we are using a defense mechanism, it loses its effectiveness; we have to believe at least partially in what we are saying to and about ourselves while we are saying it. As you might have guessed by now, the idea of defense mechanisms comes from psychoanalytic, or Freudian, theory.

Repression With **repression,** we do not allow ourselves to remain aware of painful material; we push it out of consciousness. If we hate someone and want to do him or her in, we force these feelings and impulses out of our awareness (repress them).

Repression operates to some extent in all defense mechanisms. After all, if we are going to distort something, we cannot afford to remember it clearly. Repression is usually unhealthy. For example, those who repress the feeling that someone important, like a parent, doesn't love them are asking for trouble. Pushing this feeling away can interfere with the ability to give and receive love. Better to find out where this belief comes from and resolve it. People who come from very abusive backgrounds often repress many of the terrible events of their childhood. This repression is helpful in the short run because it lets them survive the trauma. But the original problems continue to have an effect. For instance, these people may have a lot

defense mechanisms

Psychological distortions used to remain psychologically stable, or in balance.

repression

The process of pushing a painful event or thought out of consciousness.

Points to Stress

Biofeedback machines often provide visual or auditory feedback that corresponds with internal changes. For example, a decreasing pitch might be associated with a lowering of body temperature. Or every time the temperature decreases, a light goes on.

Connections

Freud believed that the ego, trying to balance the pressures from the id, superego, and external forces, uses defense mechanisms (Chapter 14).

Evaluation Strategy

Teaching Master 17-4 Defense Mechanisms asks students to match a variety of examples to the appropriate defense mechanism.

485

ENRICHMENT

You might have students read the following short story for a comic look at denial: "The Whole Truth," by Stephen McCauley. It appeared in the July 1992 issue of *Harper's* magazine.

Points to Stress

If you have had children recently, you and your spouse probably had to view films on labor. In the films, the moms, before delivery, are clearly in some agony; a few weeks later, during a quiet moment under the soft glow of a lamp, they describe labor as a beautiful experience. The camera may have influenced the moms' responses, but the point is still valid: it doesn't take long to repress painful memories.

Connections

Denial, according to Kübler-Ross, is a typical first response to news of a terminal illness. The person is not ready for the news, and denial proves valuable (Chapter 12).

Journal Topic

"Write a letter to someone close to you whose constant use of a particular defense mechanism drives you crazy. Tell the person how you feel." You might want students to use a fictitious name "to protect the innocent."

486

Unit 5 PERSONALITY, ADJUSTMENT, AND CONFLICT

denial
The process of refusing to admit that there is a problem.

displacement
The process of venting our feelings on something or someone other than the true or original target.

reaction formation
The process of expressing the opposite of what we feel.

486

of trouble relating to or trusting others, but because of the repression, they may not know why. Only by facing their terrors, however painful the memories are, can these people understand themselves and get on with their lives.

Denial   In some ways, **denial** is similar to repression. With denial, we *refuse* to admit that anything bad has even happened. When given some terrible news, the first thing people usually say is something like, "Oh, no! That can't be true." Denial, then, is a common *first* response to tragedy. Most of us, however, go on to accept reality. People who routinely deny having done or said things whenever they cause a problem are in for trouble. They may avoid facing the music for a short while, but eventually they lose out. Because they are less than truthful and do not take responsibility for their actions, others cannot trust them. Also, you simply cannot get anywhere in solving a problem if you cannot admit that one exists in the first place.

Some authors make a distinction between denial and repression, but it's a very fine one. With repression, we are at least partly aware of the problem, and then we push it out of consciousness. With denial, we don't let the problem into consciousness in the first place. The point is that either of these defenses puts distance between ourselves and what we should be facing.

Displacement   Sometimes we have trouble directly expressing what we feel because of the threat (real or imagined) of something terrible happening as a result. So, we vent our feelings elsewhere or on someone else, engaging in **displacement.** This behavior is so commonplace that even animals do it. If a male bird is threatened by a more dominant male, he may, instead of responding directly, turn away and furiously peck at a leaf. In the human arena, if we dare not talk back to our boss, for instance, we might yell at a friend instead. Most of us have had this experience when we are in a bad mood because of something that happened earlier in the day. Again, a little of this type of behavior is to be expected. However, too much displacement causes trouble because it allows us to avoid facing a problem that may only get worse rather than going away. Another problem is that when we displace anger onto innocent bystanders, we unnecessarily hurt people we care about.

Reaction Formation   In **reaction formation,** what we express is the opposite of what we really feel. Say that a man feels extremely hostile toward his mother and even thinks about physically harming her. This same man feels very guilty about his hostility because he believes that people should love their parents. He is horrified and terrified by his wish to harm his mother. In order to keep these feelings both secret and under control, he displays a high degree of protectiveness and concern for her. He calls her often to ask about her

DISCOVERY

Quietly assign a defense mechanism to each of two students, and then have them leave the room. While they are out, the class should pick a situation: a husband and a wife are walking to a train station; a boss is questioning an employee about absences; and so on. The two students outside should then return and act out the situation, one or both of them using their assigned defense mechanism. For example, the employee in the second situation could use denial to explain an unexcused absence from work. The rest of the class should try to guess which defense mechanism is being used.

Chapter 17 TOWARD A HEALTHY PERSONALITY

IN FOCUS — Defense Mechanisms

Repression (to forget) • **Rationalization** (to make excuses) • **Projection** (to point finger) • **Regression** (to go backward) • **Denial** (to not admit)

Reaction Formation (to express opposite feelings to your own) • **Displacement** (to redirect anger) • **Identification with Aggressor** (to adopt another's characteristics) • **Intellectualization** (to stifle emotions) • **Sublimation** (to channel impulses)

Should we try to avoid using defense mechanisms entirely?

Defense Mechanisms.

IN FOCUS Trying to avoid using defense mechanisms altogether is unrealistic. In fact, defense mechanisms protect us. When we use them too often, however, they become maladaptive.

Points to Stress

People who use reaction formation are often vociferous in their support or disapproval of an issue. Note that these defense mechanisms are not just lies or excuses. We use them to fool ourselves. So it makes sense that people who use reaction formation may *vehemently* support something that they are really against. On the other hand, it would be silly and dangerous to suggest that all who are vehement about something are using reaction formation.

DISCOVERY

Have students write down the word *Excuses* and let them free-write. Later, have them relate some of their excuses to the defense mechanisms described here.

COOPERATIVE LEARNING

Have students work in pairs to answer the following questions: "How do you feel *while* you are using defense mechanisms? Afterward? Do you usually accomplish what you mean to accomplish when you use defense mechanisms?" You might need to give students a few minutes to write down their answers to these questions so they can collect their thoughts before pairing up.

Points to Stress

A doctor may intellectualize his or her emotions when performing surgery, when breaking bad news to a family, and so on.

Connections

When a child experiences conflict with a parent, he or she may use the defense called identification and try to become more and more like this parent (Chapter 14).

Comprehension Check

Which defense mechanisms might be involved in the following situation? John throws a temper tantrum *(regression)* after he wrecks his new bike. He goes home and yells at his little brother *(displacement)*. A week later he completely forgets that he yelled at him *(repression)* and suggests that maybe it was his brother who was yelling at *him* *(projection)*.

Unit 5 PERSONALITY, ADJUSTMENT, AND CONFLICT

intellectualization

The process of removing our feelings about an event and discussing it in a coolly rational and unemotional way.

identification with the aggressor

The process of taking on characteristics of someone who has mistreated us in order to psychologically avoid the abuse.

health and well-being. He runs errands for her. He never misses a birthday or Mother's Day, and so on. The danger here is fairly obvious. The man's resentment will grow. The problem will get worse. Eventually, he will probably explode in a furious outburst.

Reaction formation is sometimes a little hard to see in operation, since we can't read people's minds. Grade school, though, offers a perfect and harmless example. How does a little girl know that a little boy likes her? Because he studiously and deliberately ignores her in the hallway and makes faces at her on the playground.

Intellectualization   When the emotions we feel are too overwhelming, we may try to eliminate them altogether. Talking coolly and "rationally" about a tragedy as if it were simply an event that we observed is called **intellectualization.** We have taken all the feelings out of our description. Intellectualization can be somewhat healthy, at least for a short while. People who have been widowed or seriously assaulted, for instance, may appear very calm at first. They may concentrate on seemingly unimportant tasks and talk about what happened to them as if they were objective observers, uninvolved and untouched. It is only when this approach goes on too long that it becomes troublesome. The problem is that the emotions have not really disappeared. Refusing to express them, face them, and deal with them on an emotional level gives them more power, not less.

Identification with the Aggressor   When we are mistreated for a long time by someone much more powerful than we are, we may take on some of that person's characteristics, or **identify** with him or her, to try to curry favor. By being like that person, perhaps we can avoid the abuse, perhaps that person will like us better, or perhaps we can also become powerful, at least in our own minds. This defense mechanism can help explain some puzzling events. For instance, some people who are held for long periods of time as prisoners of war become like their guards. Instead of treating the guards as the enemy, they treat them as friends—despite the fact that they have been beaten or tortured by these same people. When the war is over, the psychological conflicts begin. These former prisoners usually have great difficulty explaining their behavior to themselves and often come to feel like traitors. Although the behavior has stopped, the confusion and guilt they feel have not.

Similarly, a child may take on the characteristics of an abusive parent. Thus, he or she may end up engaging in the very actions that were so hated and feared in childhood. Such people often find themselves doing things to their own children that they swore they would never do. As was true in our other example, guilt is often one result. However, in this case, the abusive behavior has no clear-cut built-in stopping point, so the cycle may continue to repeat itself.

DISCOVERY

Students usually enjoy learning about defense mechanisms because they can easily identify with them. The *value* of learning about these defenses is that it tends to make us more aware that we are using them, and with this knowledge, maybe we can curb their use. Remember, defense mechanisms are valuable, so we don't want to stop using them altogether. But if we are yelling at someone, like our own kids, and we *know* we're yelling because we've had a bad day, having a label for what we do may make us stop and think. In this case, we *would* want to stop using displacement altogether. Have students make a list of instances when the use of particular defense mechanisms would be valuable and beneficial and times when their use would be harmful.

Regression With **regression,** we defend ourselves by "moving backward" and behaving like children. This defense is a reaction to the extreme frustration of having to be an adult and take responsibility. We regress (move backward) to a time when we were helpless children and someone had to take care of us. What we want when we are on the firing line is to be home in bed with someone bringing us chicken noodle soup. Regression is sometimes seen in sports events when the player lies down on the ground and has a temper tantrum, just as a child would. It is also seen in general behaviors such as pouting, sulking, and name-calling. If we can find someone willing on occasion to take care of us, regression might offer some comfort, but usually it tends to make others reject us, since anyone acting this way appears ridiculous. It is not a very useful defense in the long run.

Rationalization With **rationalization,** we explain what we do in such a way that we avoid any responsibility for a bad outcome. Say we take some money that we need for something important and spend it on something frivolous. We could rationalize this behavior by saying that we are all entitled to *some* enjoyment in life. However, we still need whatever it was, but now we don't have the money to pay for it.

On the other hand, rationalization can be used to our benefit to get rid of something we can't do anything about anyway. If someone we have loved very much tells us to shove off, we could rationalize by thinking of some defect that he or she has (terrible breath? strange smile? who knows what?). So we are "tricking" ourselves into believing we didn't want the other person anyway.

Projection **Projection** refers to the process of mentally giving to someone else our own thoughts or feelings. For example, if a person is fired from a job for genuinely poor performance, he or she might claim that it is the supervisor who is incompetent. In this way, the responsibility is shifted onto someone else. All of us, at times, have a few bad days in a row. We decide that those around us are acting strangely and making life difficult for us on purpose. For a while, this is all right, but a continued pattern of projection is self-destructive, since it doesn't help us face up to how *we* might be causing the problems.

Sublimation **Sublimation** occurs when we channel our emotional energy into a constructive or creative activity. It is the only defense mechanism that is truly healthy and adaptive. Instead of giving in to unacceptable aggressive impulses, we become gymnasts or play football. Sublimation allows us to express the lingering sadness we feel over losing someone close to us through painting or writing poetry. Or rather than just getting angry about social injustice, we may become active in an organization designed to change an unfair law.

Chapter 17 TOWARD A HEALTHY PERSONALITY

▲ *Tantrums—the adult and child versions.*

regression

The process of going backward in behavior and thought to a period when we were taken care of as a child; childish behavior.

projection

The process of attributing our thoughts to someone else.

sublimation

The process of channeling emotional energy into constructive or creative activities.

rationalization

The process of explaining away a problem so that we don't have to accept the blame.

489

DISCUSS THE PHOTO

How long should a parent allow a child this age to scream before intervening. Or should the parent intervene at all?

Connections

Regression is influenced by conditioning (Chapter 7). The childhood behavior worked in the past; the person thinks it will work now. The behavior was never completely extinguished.

Points to Stress

Rationalization, at first glance, seems harmless, but it can be dangerous. For example, a husband who batters his wife may claim that the wife asked for it. Nobody wants to be labeled an abuser, and for the husband, rationalization takes care of that quite well.

DISCOVERY

Have students fill in the following blank with 20 different answers: "I am _____." The first few answers will be obvious, like "I am male" or "I am tall," but that's OK. Explain that the sum of these blanks makes up our self-concept. As a follow-up, you might ask students to have their parents or close friends fill in this blank 20 times: "*You* are _____." The "you" refers to your students. Students can then compare how they see themselves with how parents or friends see them.

Connections

You may want to introduce the concept of the ideal self (Chapter 14). A fully functioning person, according to Carl Rogers, is one who establishes congruency between the ideal self, the self-concept, and the real self. Consider having students complete activity #3 from Chapter 14. Or see **Teaching Master 17-5 Self-Concept** for a similar activity.

Journal Topic

"None of us is perfect, and some of these qualities listed in **Healthy Characteristics** will apply to us more than others. Pick one characteristic that you wish applied to you better than it does and explain why. For example, you might write on how you wish you were more open to new ideas."

490

Unit 5 PERSONALITY, ADJUSTMENT, AND CONFLICT

self-concept

The image we have of ourselves.

self-esteem

The degree to which we think we are worthwhile.

Self-Concept

What we define as troublesome and our reactions to it are related to how we perceive ourselves. For example, if we feel confident in a social situation with new people, we won't see the situation as much of a problem, and we will probably enjoy ourselves. If not, we may well become anxious and withdraw instead of striking up a conversation. These different views and reactions come from different **self-concepts.** A person's self-concept is the image that person has of herself or himself. It is a mixture of characteristics that we see as belonging to us, which make up who we believe we are. It may or may not be in line with the way others see us.

All of us can think of people whose self-concept is not very accurate—a boring person who thinks she's hilariously funny, a drop-dead gorgeous guy who thinks he's ordinary-looking. When a *large* gap exists between our self-image and others' image of us, we may be failing to see a problem that can get worse if we keep ignoring it. However, most of us see ourselves in a somewhat more positive light than we really deserve. Is that a dangerous thing to do? Probably not, as long as it is within reason. In fact, it may help us maintain a sense of well-being. It is interesting to note that depressed people are usually both more negative and more accurate about their self-concepts than nondepressed people are (Haaga, Dyck & Ernst, 1991).

There is another way in which a gap between our self-image and others' image of us can cause problems. Childhood versions of self-concept come from what other people tell us about ourselves. As we grow older, we add our own information and experience. But when important other people, such as our family, hold up an unrealistic idea of who we should be, we usually end up feeling inadequate. As a consequence, our **self-esteem** suffers. Self-esteem refers to how worthwhile we think we are. Self-esteem is different from self-concept, but the two are related. For instance, a self-described nasty, ugly, mean, lazy slob can have high or low self-esteem, depending on the value those characteristics have for that individual. Similarly, people you think are kind, attractive, intelligent, athletic, and socially adept can still have low self-esteem. They may see themselves as not really having those characteristics or not having enough of them. When we are expected to meet impossible standards, we often stop trying altogether and just give up (Heatherton & Baumeister, 1991). The key is to develop our own positive idea of who we are, one that is not so dependent on other people's opinions.

HEALTHY CHARACTERISTICS

Psychology often tends to emphasize what goes wrong rather than what goes right. We know much more about various mental disor-

DISCOVERY

Teaching Master 17-5 Self-Concept asks students to pick the top several adjectives that apply to them, rank these adjectives, and then have a friend or parent do the same.

Complete directions are listed on the master. The purpose is to clarify whether students' self-concepts are consistent with others' perceptions.

Chapter 17 TOWARD A HEALTHY PERSONALITY

▲ *One of the tastier benefits of family life. Looks good, doesn't it?*

Connections

You may want to compare these healthy characteristics with Maslow's characteristics of self-actualizers. See **Teaching Master 5-4 Characteristics of Self-Actualizers.**

DISCUSS THE PHOTO

Simple chores can often bring a family together.

Connections

Compare some of these healthy characteristics to type A and type B personalities (Chapter 16). For example, taking responsibility would tend to be type A; type A personalities, however, may go too far, taking on more responsibility than they can handle. Type B personalities would be more "open to new ideas."

ders than we do about healthy behavior. However, certain personal characteristics are common to people who are resistant to stress and cope well with life's problems.

At the top of the list is accepting yourself, along with accepting and being interested in others. Being able to perceive reality fairly accurately is another important characteristic. This means not distorting things to suit your own purposes or denying that problems exist. Psychologically healthy people feel basically in control of their lives, at least in Western cultures. They have a few close personal relationships and are able to make commitments. They are tolerant of and try to understand different points of view. They have a sense of purpose in their lives and are problem-centered. People who are problem-centered set specific goals and then go about reaching those goals. They do not just sit for hours stewing and worrying about things. They take steps to make constructive changes. Related to all these characteristics is a sense of responsibility. This means both taking credit for successes *and* taking the blame for failures. Some people do only one or the other, and leaving either one out is a bad idea. For example, some people take complete responsibility for nearly everything that goes wrong in their lives. This not only makes these people feel terrible most of the time but it also allows other people to behave irresponsibly (Folkman & Lazarus, 1988).

CHAPTER PROJECT

Most students probably know someone who possesses many of the healthy characteristics described here. Have students interview this person to get some insight into how this person "acquired" these characteristics. Here are some starting questions, but students will need to add more: (1) Imagine that you have been working for a company for several years, and because of restructuring, the company does not need you any longer. How would you react to this news, immediately and in the long run? (2) Describe one of the toughest ordeals that you have had to face. How did you get through it? Did you learn from it? (3) Do you think it is important to set goals?

Comprehension Check

Complete this sentence with the five different endings below and ask students to identify each statement as *true* or *false*. Psychologically healthy people (1) dislike being alone *(false)*; (2) are able to make commitments *(true)*; (3) do not take themselves too seriously *(true)*; (4) are rigid in their beliefs and activities *(false)*; (5) are tolerant of different points of view *(true)*.

Connections

Students may recall that self-esteem is placed near the top of Maslow's hierarchy of needs (Chapter 5). In other words, a good foundation must be in place for self-esteem to flourish, according to Maslow.

Unit 5 PERSONALITY, ADJUSTMENT, AND CONFLICT

A certain amount of independence is also part of this recipe. Healthy people have respect for social order, but they are not overly conforming. They also like their privacy and like to have some time alone. This means that they not only enjoy their own company but also are not too dependent on other people. They are not rigidly locked into a specific philosophy or way of doing things but are open to new ideas, concepts, and activities.

"Take time to stop and smell the roses." Psychologically healthy people are experts here. They have a fresh appreciation of life, even things they have experienced many times before. They continue to marvel at a tree blossoming or the beauty of a snowfall or the changing shapes of the clouds or the miracle of being alive, regardless of how old they are. Finally, healthy people do not take themselves too seriously. They are able to laugh at the absurdities of life. Having a sense of humor smoothes the roughest and most difficult of times. A good laugh not only releases tension, but it can help you see things in their proper perspective (Miller et al., 1991; Kobasa et al., 1979, 1980; Maslow, 1968).

PSYCHOLOGY IN YOUR LIFE

Solving Problems

We have mentioned problem-solving skills at several points in this chapter, so it seems like a good idea to provide some specific steps here. They are important both in dealing with everyday foul-ups and in maintaining a general sense of having some control over what happens to you. They can also be an enormous help in trying to make changes in your life.

Since so many problems we experience involve other people, we want to remind you of something before we go any further. Please keep in mind that *the only person you can change is yourself.* You simply cannot change someone else, however much you may want to. You cannot make someone else love you. You cannot make someone else act the way you think he or she should behave. You can change the way you react to other people, though, and that is usually enough to make a very real difference.

As you go through these steps, take your time. If you get stuck, leave it for a while and do something else. Our brains have a way of working on things even when we're not aware of it. Yours may give you valuable insights if you give it the chance. These insights often come out of the blue, once

(continued on next page)

492

492

PSYCHOLOGY IN YOUR LIFE

Solving Problems

(continued from previous page) we relax and stop trying to force the issue.

1. The first step is to define the problem. Not only is this the first step but it is also the most important step. How you define a problem will determine the direction you take in trying to solve it. Defining the problem may sound simple, but doing it properly will require you to look at things a little differently. Your definition needs to be workable, objective, specific, and goal-oriented. The statement "I want Elmo/Zasu to love me," is not a workable definition. Why? *The only person you can change is yourself.* The statement, "I am not very happy," may be true, but it's still not a good definition of the problem. Saying "I want to be happier" makes it more goal-oriented, but it is still too vague to be of much use. So, pare it down further. What's the real issue? Is it money? Is it your social life? Is it making friends? Is it grades? If the problem involves more than one

area, go through these steps for each one in turn. If you try to tackle everything all at once, you'll get discouraged before you have a chance to succeed. The goal you choose needs to be as narrow as you can make it, at least for starters. Virtually all big problems can be broken down into smaller, more manageable ones. The more you do that, the less overwhelmed you will feel. Once you have a particular subject in mind, you can set about changing things. Once you have selected the subject and defined the problem, *write it down.* We know this sounds trite, but it really does work.

2. Now that you have your problem defined, think about different ways it can be approached. Let's say you want to improve your grades. There are several ways to go about this. One is to spend more time studying. Another is to pay more attention in class. Another is to find better ways of learning. Still another is to get outside

help. Think carefully about what you, as a unique individual, need. Maybe your biggest problem is in writing papers. Or it may be that you are trying to do too many things at once. Or perhaps you only have trouble in one subject. Whichever area you decide is the most important one for you, write down all the approaches you have come up with. Again, be as specific as possible.

3. Now, assess or evaluate how workable you think each approach is. You can make up a scale from 1 to 5, for instance, and label each approach. Just be sure that the labeling is yours and yours alone. What sounds good to other people may not be right for you. You know what will work for you, so trust your own judgment.

4. From all the approaches you have evaluated, select the best one, and come up with as many specifics for implementing it as you can think of. For

(continued on next page)

PSYCHOLOGY IN YOUR LIFE

Discovery
The steps described here for solving problems are specific enough to assign as is. Problems can include finding a job, raising a grade, choosing a college, or any other concrete problem. Check students' plans and have them hand in a follow-up report a couple of weeks later in which they evaluate their progress. See activity #7 at the end of the chapter.

ENRICHMENT

Have students complete the **Enrichment Worksheet** for this chapter located in the Teacher Resources.

Reteaching Strategy

Have students complete the **Reteaching Worksheet** for this chapter located in the Teacher Resources.

The **Vocabulary Worksheet** may be completed by the class as a pretest for chapter concepts or used as a reteaching worksheet for those students needing additional review.

PSYCHOLOGY IN YOUR LIFE

Solving Problems

(continued from previous page) instance, say you have decided that your study skills are good, but you need to spend more time studying. List all the possibilities for finding more study time, but be realistic. Maybe you have an hour free after school every day, but you're not at all in the mood to study then, or you honestly need to give your brain a break. So, pick another time.

Gathering information is an important part of this step. It applies even in the rather straight-forward example we are using. For instance, you might find that the best time for you to study is a time when you are obligated to do some chore around the house. By talking with your family, you might discover that you can make a switch and free that hour.

5. Put your implementations into action for a specific time period. This is probably the hardest part of problem solving. One thing that can help is to make the changes a habit. For example, if

you decided to study for an hour after supper, do it every evening, whether you have any assignments or not. Read ahead in one of your textbooks, or outline a chapter, or do extra-credit work, just *do something*. The point here is to be consistent so that you do it almost without thinking.

You may have noticed that this step has a time limit to it. The goal is to give yourself enough time to succeed but not keep you stuck doing something that isn't going to work. If you set a one-month time limit, for instance, you will continue working at your solution for that period. During this time, if you find yourself backsliding, you can make a renewed effort to try again. It is very important here not to second–guess yourself, though. Don't waste your energy wondering if your choice is the right one. Put all your efforts toward making that choice work.

6. Once the time period is over, evaluate your

success, being as honest with yourself as you possibly can be. For instance, did you really spend that time studying? Or did you spend it doodling in the margins and staring into space, daydreaming? Did you actually succeed quite well, but you are disappointed because in the back of your mind, you somehow imagined that you could go from all C's to all A's if you really applied yourself? Depending on the evaluation you make, you might want to continue with this plan, make a few changes, or try a different approach altogether.

These problem-solving steps sometimes seem artificial, but they can be applied to both short-term and long-term goals. They can help you clarify what is really going on, give you something tangible to deal with, and help you think up workable solutions. By using them, you can take vague dissatisfactions and transform them into constructive change.

Before testing students on the contents of the chapter, you may want to review vocabulary terms that are especially important or confusing. Terms in this chapter that could require clarification are *cognitive strategy, biofeedback, defense mechanisms, self-concept,* and *self-esteem.*

Chapter 17 TOWARD A HEALTHY PERSONALITY

SUMMARY

1. There is a very strong connection between mind and body. Everyone can fall prey to the power of suggestion. Voodoo is an extreme example of this.

2. The key to handling many of life's problems seems to be either actual control of various situations or at least the belief that one is in control. Helplessness can be the most destructive of attitudes or feelings.

3. The immune system is critical to survival. It is active or inactive as a function of our state of mind as well as of our physical health. Stress reduces the effect of this protecting system.

4. Cognitive strategies are methods of using thoughts to reduce pain. The same principles probably apply to stress or frustration.

5. Psychological defense mechanisms are used to keep the psyche in balance. By using them in moderation, we are able to protect our sense of well-being enough to recover from personality defects, mistakes, or problems. But using them often is not a healthy system for surviving.

6. Self-concept is the image one has of oneself. Self-esteem refers to how worthwhile we think we are. Either one or both may agree or disagree with others' views of us.

7. Personal characteristics associated with a psychologically healthy personality include accepting yourself and others, being realistic, flexible, problem-centered, responsible, and having a good sense of humor.

Wrapping It Up

When discussing the mind-body connection and the healthy personality, most people in our culture readily accept that psychological factors can make us sick, but we have a harder time believing that we can make ourselves well. There's nothing wrong with a little skepticism, but in this case, the doubt may be self-defeating. Optimism, tempered with a pinch of realism, may go a long way toward making or keeping us healthy.

Suggested Readings

▼ Alberti, Robert E., and Michael L. Emmons. *Your Perfect Right: A Guide to Assertive Living.* San Luis Obispo, CA: Impact, 1984.

▼ Buscaglia, Leo. *Personhood: The Art of Being Fully Human.* New York: Fawcett, 1986.

▼ Houston, Jean. *The Possible Human.* New York: St. Martin's Press, 1982.

▼ James, Muriel, and Dorothy Jongeward. *Born to Win.* Reading, Mass.: Addison-Wesley, 1973.

▼ Morgan, William P., and Stephen E. Goldston. *Exercise and Mental Health.* New York: Hemisphere, 1987.

▼ Peck, M. Scott. *The Road Less Traveled.* New York: Simon & Schuster, 1978.

Vocabulary

sudden death phenomenon
immune system
antibodies
ulcers
asthma
muscle contraction headache
migraine headache

cognitive strategy
distraction
redefinition
biofeedback
defense mechanisms
repression
denial
displacement
reaction formation

intellectualization
identification
regression
rationalization
projection
sublimation
self-concept
self-esteem

Answers to Review Questions

1. immune
2. antibodies
3. sudden death phenomenon
4. muscle contraction headaches
5. migraine headaches
6. c
7. b
8. d
9. d
10. a
11. c
12. b
13. g
14. f
15. e
16. h

Review Questions

Fill in the blanks; answer on a separate sheet of paper. (An answer may consist of more than one word.)

1. The ___?___ system helps the body fight off disease.
2. The actual cells that fight disease are called ___?___ .
3. The nerve that controls the beating of the heart can sometimes trigger ___?___ .
4. Sitting in the same position for a long time can cause ___?___ .
5. Defects of the brain chemical system controlling serotonin may cause ___?___ .

Multiple Choice

6. Cognitive strategies work because
   a. they completely block out pain messages.
   b. they increase stress, which helps the body deal with pain.
   c. they tend to reduce anxiety.
   d. of all of the above.

7. Biofeedback works because
   a. it fools the body just as drugs fool the body.
   b. it gives the user information about the body.
   c. it puts the user in a hypnotic trance.
   d. of all of the above.

▼ Powell, John. *Why Am I Afraid to Tell You Who I Am?* Niles, IL: Argus, 1969.

▼ Seligman, Martin. *Learned Optimism.* New York: Knopf, 1990.

SUGGESTED VIDEOS

▼ *A New Look at Motivation.* 32 min. CRM/McGraw-Hill.

▼ *The Self.* Discovering Psychology series, part 15, 27 min. 1-800-LEARNER.

Notes on Discussion Questions

1. Opinions will vary. Most students will probably agree that the brain, in theory, is powerful enough to block the virus. Asked if *they* could block the virus, most students will be less confident. The implicit lesson here is that mental strategies can be learned and developed. Students could argue that distraction and redefinition may help. Or they might suggest some sort of visualization where the person could imagine fighting off the virus with imaginary shields. How much all this will help is questionable.

2. Students may be able to provide examples of people who have "willed" themselves to die. For example, if a woman dies, her husband may become so distraught that he dies the following month.

3. Be sure that students offer examples. Are there any steps they can take to increase the feeling of control?

4. Those who feel a lack of control over their environments would probably not change their life-styles; these people probably feel that they cannot do anything to change it!

8. Defense mechanisms are usually used
   a. unconsciously.
   b. to reduce threatening thoughts.
   c. to protect ourselves.
   d. for all of the above.

Matching

9. Will is unable to remember an accident he witnessed 24 hours ago because the accident was too traumatic.
10. Jill claims she flunked her math course because the teacher didn't like her.
11. Bill hates his teacher, but he won't admit it. Instead, he claims that the teacher hates him.
12. Phil runs to his dad for advice whenever problems become too intense.
13. Stan dislikes football but says he loves it.
14. Ann channels her anger by petitioning for social change.
15. Jan yells at her little brother when she's having a bad day.
16. Dan expresses his feelings unemotionally.

a. rationalization
b. regression
c. projection
d. repression
e. displacement
f. sublimation
g. reaction formation
h. intellectualization

DISCUSSION QUESTIONS

1. Imagine you are locked for an hour in a room in which a virus has been released into the atmosphere. Do you believe that there are any mental strategies you could use to prevent the virus from entering your body? If so, what kinds of strategies would you use? If not, why not? Explain.
2. The chapter explains that sudden death phenomenon occurs because of a person's cognitive outlook: the person *believes* he or she will die. Do you think that a person can literally kill himself or herself, not only because of beliefs but also because of a *desire* to die? In other words, can a person wish to die and, simply through wishing, actually die? Explain.
3. We all experience times when we feel that we have little control over circumstances. Do you tend to feel this way more often at school or at home? Explain.
4. If you found out today that: (1) many people who get ulcers feel helpless and lack control over their environment and (2) that you have an ulcer, would you change anything about your life-style? If so, what specifically would you change? If not, why not? Explain.
5. If you suffered from migraine headaches and you could eliminate these headaches either

5. Students' answers will relate to their locus of control. Those who feel that they have little control over their lives will probably opt to take medicine, not believing that they can do anything about their headaches.

6. This is a good question to discuss in class. Some students may not want to know, out of fear that the headaches will then return. These people probably feel that they have little internal control over their lives. The ones who would want to know probably feel that they *do* have great internal control over their lives; knowing about the placebos then would reaffirm these ideas.

7. Students need to be creative with this question. They can describe their reactions to painful visits with the doctor and the dentist, and compare these visits to how their parents react to pain.

8. You might want to stress that their answers will remain confidential.

Notes on Activities

1. If you feel that it's worthwhile, you might have students read an entire book rather than just 20

by taking medication for the rest of your life or by undergoing an *intensive* five-days-a-week, training program in three-month biofeedback, which would you choose and why?

6. Let's say that five years ago you suffered from severe headaches. Your doctor, however, prescribed pills that virtually eliminated these headaches. If the pills that the doctor prescribed were, in fact, placebos—nothing but sugar pills—would you now want to know this? Why or why not? Explain.

7. If it is true that responses to some pain must be learned, what have you learned about pain and from whom have you learned it? Discuss.

8. Describe a time when there was a gap between your self-image and other people's image of you. Be specific. If you can't think of an example, ask a friend or parent to help!

ACTIVITIES

1. There are numerous "self-help" books on the market today that are indeed helpful and very interesting. Books alone are obviously not going to make someone's personality healthy, but they often supply needed inspiration. Have your psychology teacher recommend several of these worthwhile self-help books, or simply go to a bookstore or library and choose your own (you will be surprised at the wide selection); then read any 20 pages out of one of them. Write a review of the pages and include the following information: (a) a summary of the pages; (b) your personal reactions to the pages; (c) whether the information seems practical and helpful; (d) whether you would recommend the book to a friend and why or why not.

2. When we hear of programs that train people to integrate the powers of the mind and body, we often dismiss these programs as impractical and too mystical. We want you to unveil a bit of that mysticism by visiting a center in your area that emphasizes, in one way or another, the integration of mind and body. Before you dismiss this activity as impractical, please read on. Some

organizations will outwardly claim that their goal is to integrate mind and body. Examples include yoga centers, meditation programs, and acupuncture centers. These kinds of places are probably the places you would visit. If none of these is available in your area, then you need to be a bit more creative. For example, some organizations may not outwardly claim to integrate mind and body, but this, in fact, is their goal. For example, pregnant women often take Lamaze classes to learn how to "relax" (as much as that is possible under the circumstances) and to minimize pain during labor and delivery. Or people with high blood pressure often become involved in biofeedback programs. Where do you find these kinds of programs? Your best bet is to contact a local hospital and ask about the special programs that the hospital provides.

Once you contact one of these centers, interview one of the directors or trainers there. Find out: (a) the goals and philosophies of the training program; (b) specifically *how* the program achieves its goals; (c) what a typical training session is like; (d) how long it usually takes before a

pages. This might be especially appropriate if your school offers Psychology 2 or an advanced-placement course in psychology.

2. Consider inviting to your class one or two of the people that your students find.

3 and 4. Allow students a few minutes to show their work to the rest of the class.

5. These papers are usually a pleasure to read. Insist that students use specific examples.

6. Weeks after they complete this activity, you might want to have students write a brief follow-up!

person realizes any benefits from the program; (e) costs, if any.

Finally, include your specific reactions to the program. If you had a desire to enroll in such a program, would you enroll in this particular one? Why or why not?

3. Pick any four of the defense mechanisms described in the chapter and find four songs that seem to correspond well to each. For example, if a singer sings about not admitting his or her feelings for another, you might use this as an example of *denial*. Then write out the lyrics of each song and underline key words and phrases that reveal the defense mechanisms at work in the song. Finally, write about a paragraph on each song, explaining why the song appropriately illustrates the defense mechanism.

4. Take a look at the cartoons used in the In Focus on defense mechanisms. Pick any four of the ten defense mechanisms described and create your own visual for each. Feel free to deviate from the kinds of visuals used in the In Focus. Be creative. For example, instead of using a single cartoon, you might want to use a comic strip. Make the visuals large enough so that they can be displayed in class.

5. Write a three- to four-page paper describing the defense mechanisms that you typically use. How do others respond to your use of defense mechanisms? Do they use their own defenses? Include a paragraph or two assessing how the defense mechanisms you use are both beneficial and harmful.

6. Pick a personal problem that you would like to "solve" and write a detailed report on that problem using the steps outlined at the end of the chapter. Remember to narrow your problem and to be as specific as possible. Follow your plan of action for about a week and describe your progress. Did you encounter any obstacles that you hadn't predicted? What was the value of writing down the plan?

Abnormal Behaviors

Several well-publicized stories about people with mental disorders have grabbed the national headlines and news programs. Attention has been focused on Kenneth Bianci, Dan White, and John Hinkley. Bianci pleaded insanity, yet he was found guilty of a series of Los Angeles rapes and murders. After being dismissed from his job as a city supervisor, White killed the mayor of San Francisco and another city supervisor. He was found innocent because of his "diminished capacity." Hinkley shot President Reagan in order to gain the attention of an actress. He was found to be innocent by reason of insanity. Because of all of the publicity these cases have generated, many people believe that criminals commit crimes and then plead innocent by reason of "insanity" in order to avoid punishment. Actually, this controversial defense has been successfully used in less than 1 percent of all felony cases (APA, 1983).

Insanity is a legal term, not a medical or psychological diagnosis. It indicates that a person cannot be held responsible for his or her actions because of mental illness. For centuries, Western law has stated that a person who is mentally incompetent should not be punished if he or she violates the law. We do not punish children for breaking a law because the law states that people must be able to appreciate the significance of their actions. The term "insanity" is based on a nineteenth century case involving a Scotsman named M'Naghten who suffered from paranoid delusions. He believed the prime minister of England was after him. He mistakenly killed the prime minister's secretary. He was acquitted of the crime at the trial and sent to a mental hospital, since it was decided that his mental condition prevented him from understanding what he was doing at the time of the murder (M'Naghten Case, 1843).

An adjunct to the M'Naghten ruling came a few years later and is called the doctrine of "irresistible impulse." In this case, the reasoning is that if a person knows his or her criminal act is wrong but was unable to control his or her behavior due to mental illness, he or she is not held responsible.

In 1954, the Durham Rule was established. This broadened the insanity defense even more. Under the M'Naghten Rule, only psychotic disorders were the basis for the defense. The Durham ruling allowed other diagnostic labels (obsessive-compulsive, phobic, etc.) as a basis for insanity as well. The rule states that a person is not criminally responsible if his or her act was the product of mental illness. Several states have revised the law to include a "guilty but mentally ill" defense. This version of the insanity defense is used when a person is found to have a disorder of thought or

Neurotransmitters, such as serotonin, are involved in many types of mental disorders.

500

Discuss the Photo

Remind students that neurotransmitters are chemical messengers that help bridge the gap between nerve cells.

mood that affected him or her at the time of the crime, impairing judgement or behavior, and it allows the defendant to receive therapy for the disorder. After the therapy, the person is sent to prison for the duration of the sentence.

The insanity defense continues to be a very controversial topic for people in the field of psychology. Many people believe that a civilized society needs to allow for people who are mentally disturbed, and that these disturbed people should be treated differently

PERFORMANCE TASK

Overview

Students research the career of a professional in the treatment of mental disorders to prepare for a discussion in panel format. Students then present their findings to the class with a moderator prepared to ask them questions about the particular career they have researched. Training, degrees, job prospects, typical assignments, salary, as well as advantages and disadvantages of a particular career might be included. On the next day, students will complete individual charts comparing the careers as possibilities for themselves and conclude with a short paper stating their reasons for preferring a particular career. Complete instructions for this activity and the supporting student worksheets can be found in the Teacher Resources.

than others. Yet, some criminals do try to take advantage of this. In one case, for example, a girl killed a young boy because she wanted his coat. In court she unsuccessfully pleaded innocent by reason of insanity, claiming that she had an "urban psychosis" that drove her to kill the boy for his coat.

One of the most famous cases to illuminate this controversy involved John Hinkley's attempt to murder President Ronald Reagan in 1981. He was found to be legally insane and was acquitted of the crime. People were very upset with the court ruling, and this prompted the Insanity Defense Reform Act (1984), which was designed to make it more difficult for an alleged criminal to use the insanity defense. It has changed some of the language and shifts more responsibility to the defense from the prosecution.

Psychiatrist Thomas Szasz calls all of this "legal fiction." He believes that people are being told they don't have to be responsible for their behaviors, while others are placed inappropriately in mental hospitals. He estimates that 90 percent of all patients in mental hospitals are there involuntarily, and believes that committing the mentally "ill" to institutions is a civil rights issue (Szasz, 1987). His views raise important questions about how our society should handle those who behave "abnormally."

References

Full citations can be found in the Teacher Resources.

DISCUSS THE PHOTO

You probably have a few talented photographers in class who can make photographs that would be appropriate for this caption.

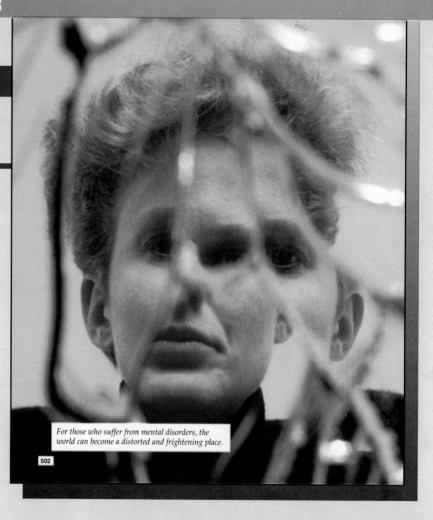

For those who suffer from mental disorders, the world can become a distorted and frightening place.

502

PSYCHOLOGY AND YOU RESOURCES

A variety of resources are available in the Psychology and You *supplementary material. In addition, there are a number of additional resources listed to enhance your lesson plans.*

Masters
▼ 18-1A Learning Goals
▼ 18-1B Answers to Learning Goals
▼ 18-2 Obsessive-Compulsive Behaviors
▼ 18-3 Obsessive-Compulsive Scale
▼ 18-4 Presidential Poll 1
▼ 18-5 Presidential Poll 2
▼ 18-6 Behavior Disorders
▼ 18-7 Case Study

Student Worksheets
▼ Vocabulary Worksheet

▼ Independent Practice Worksheet
▼ Enrichment Worksheet
▼ Reteaching Worksheet

Test Bank
▼ Tests A and B

Multimedia
▼ *The Brain* Videotape Modules #24 and 26
▼ Psychology Videodisc

Student Workbook

PACING CHART

Complete Coverage

Day 1: Assign the first two sections of the chapter and Psychology in Your Life prior to class. When evaluating the definitions of abnormal behavior and the purpose of the DSM-IV, use discussion question #1 in the text and refer to Psychology in Your Life. Have students read the next three sections and complete an activity involving characterizing abnormal behavior for homework.

Day 2: Review the differences between panic disorder, phobias, and obsessive-compulsive disorder. Distinguish between conversion disorder, hypochondrias as well as amnesia and fugue. When discussing dissociative identity disorder, emphasize that it is unrelated to schizophrenia. Have students read "Mood Disorders" for Day 3.

Day 3: Require students to differentiate dysthymic disorder from major depression. Focus discussion on bipolar disorder and the suspected causes of mood disorders in general. Assign the next two

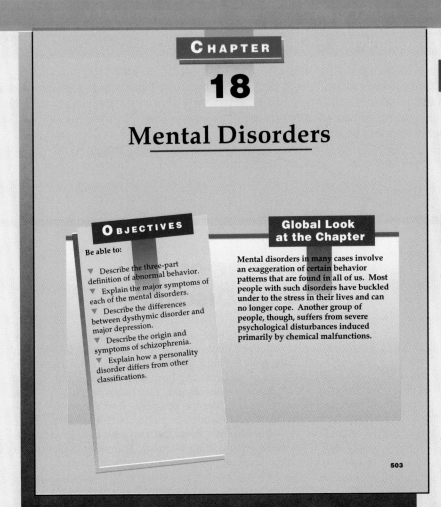

503

CHAPTER

18

Mental Disorders

OBJECTIVES

Be able to:

▼ Describe the three-part definition of abnormal behavior.

▼ Explain the major symptoms of each of the mental disorders.

▼ Describe the differences between dysthymic disorder and major depression.

▼ Describe the origin and symptoms of schizophrenia.

▼ Explain how a personality disorder differs from other classifications.

Global Look at the Chapter

Mental disorders in many cases involve an exaggeration of certain behavior patterns that are found in all of us. Most people with such disorders have buckled under to the stress in their lives and can no longer cope. Another group of people, though, suffers from severe psychological disturbances induced primarily by chemical malfunctions.

INTRODUCING THE CHAPTER

Warn students that as they progress through the unit, some of them will be tempted to personalize the disorders: "That's me... and that's me, too." The same thing happens when we flip through a medical book and begin to believe we suffer from some of the ailments. Explain that this is a *normal* temptation, but that's probably all it is. Any one of us will have *some* of the symptoms described in the chapter.

LEAD-OFF ACTIVITY

Students often have many misconceptions about behavior disorders, the foremost being that there is a clear-cut distinction between "abnormal" and "normal." While the distinction may be clear-cut between two particular individuals at a certain point in time, the distinction often becomes hazy and ambiguous at another time or for two other individuals. To demonstrate this ambiguity, simply act "crazy" while discussing the definitions of behavior disorders. Knock over desks, talk to the pencil sharpener, put your left shoe on your right foot. Meanwhile, ask questions: What is normal? What is abnormal? If someone puts his left shoe on his right foot, is this normal? You may get plenty of laughs, but you'll also get students to think. For example, normal depends on the situation, on the culture in which the behavior occurs, on the year (1960 versus 1999). Point out the three criteria for abnormal listed in the text: (1) the person suffers discomfort; (2) the person behaves in a bizarre way; (3) the person is highly inefficient. Afterward, explain that your craziness was not a mockery, that you were not trying to make light of people with serious disorders. You were just trying to illustrate a point.

sections of the chapter for homework.

Day 4: Review the four major symptoms used to identify psychosis. Concentrate next on the types, characteristics, and possible causal factors of schizophrenia. Assign "Personality Disorders" for Day 5.

Day 5: Discuss both antisocial personality disorder and borderline personality disorder. Give the Chapter Review quiz.

In Brief

Day 1: Review the definition of abnormal behavior, as well as the purpose of the DSM-IV. Ensure that students can identify the characteristics of the major anxiety, somatoform, dissociative, and mood disorders.

Day 2: Discuss the nature of psychosis and then focus on the types and causal factors of schizophrenia.

Day 3: Evaluate the differences between antisocial and borderline personality disorders before giving the Chapter Review quiz.

Points to Stress

If mental health is all a matter of degree, this implies that we're all a little crazy—or at least we all have the *potential* to be crazy. Writers like Edgar Allan Poe, Rod Serling, and Stephen King know all about this continuum. They describe people who are walking a tightrope between madness and normalcy and who can fall at any time. If their stories were about people who were just severely disturbed, they wouldn't be as compelling. A good example is the movie, *Silence of the Lambs.* The main character is certainly disturbed, but he commands our attention because there's a part of him that *seems* normal: he reads poetry, listens to classical music, is highly intelligent. If the entire movie had focused on the other disturbed character (the kidnapper), the one without any normal qualities, it would have been a typical slasher movie without any real suspense. (This is not a movie recommended for classroom use, but many students may be familiar with the reference.)

Mental Health: It's All a Matter of Degree.

 A severe disorder may refer to psychosis, when the person is out of touch with reality. Mild disorders would refer to nonpsychotic disorders.

504

As a follow-up to the **Lead-off Activity,** have students work in pairs to define abnormal. When should these abnormalities warrant commitment? The first task will probably be more difficult than the second because there are numerous ways to view abnormal; one view is usually inadequate.

Unit 6 PSYCHOLOGICAL DISORDERS

THE NATURE OF MENTAL DISORDERS

There are about 1.5 million people presently hospitalized in the United States for mental disturbances. An additional 4 to 5 million people annually seek psychological help of one sort or another. Despite these facts, it is surprising how incredibly difficult it is to define a mental disorder. It is obvious that those people who think they are someone famous like the president (but are not) or those who carry on loud conversations in public with themselves have something very amiss in their lives. But very few people with psychological problems are anything like that. Television depictions of those with severe problems are almost always inaccurate. The ax murderer who goes from house to house on Halloween chopping people up because of some early childhood experience shows little grasp of reality—on the part of the person who wrote the script. While a handful of the disturbed are dangerous, the average mental patient is confused and withdrawn, bothering no one. Statistically, mental patients are less violent than those making up the "normal" general public.

If you pick an emotionally disturbed person at random, the odds are that he or she will not be that much different from you or your friends in most areas, except for an exaggeration of certain behaviors. In other words, the person distorts or exaggerates characteristics that are shared by all of us. It comes down to a matter of degree.

 **Mental Health— It's All a Matter of Degree**

ABNORMAL	SEVERE DISORDER	MILD DISORDER	RELATIVELY HEALTHY	NORMAL	SUPER-NORMAL OR SELF-ACTUALIZING

All of us fall somewhere on this scale. Furthermore, we all fluctuate from week to week or month to month from one point to another. The further left we fluctuate, the more likely it is that we will need outside help. The two end points are theoretical, of course—no one is either completely "abnormal" or "super-normal."

In your opinion, how would someone with a severe disorder differ from someone with a mild disorder?

ENRICHMENT

Have students talk to lawyers to get their opinions on the insanity plea. When and how often is it used? How does a lawyer "prove" insanity? Have there been any changes in the insan-ity plea in the last few years? Students might ask about the plea "Guilty, but insane." Should the insanity plea be revised further?

Definitions of Abnormal Behavior

It's important to note that there is something "abnormal" in all "normal" people. Have you ever done anything "strange" that you don't want others to know about? We have. By itself this is not significant. One very workable definition of those who *do* need help has three parts to it: (1) The person suffers from *discomfort* more or less continuously. The discomfort shows up as extreme anxiety, endless worry, or long periods of depression. In addition, the person feels that something is wrong with his or her life far more than the average person does. (2) Another possibility is that the person is behaving in a *bizarre* fashion. He or she constantly misinterprets what is going on and what others are doing or saying. For instance, this person could be afraid to go to work or school. He or she frequently comes completely apart over minor things or sinks into a depression about them. (3) Finally, people who need help can be very *inefficient*. This means that they are unable to perform their life roles properly. Examples would be an alcoholic who refuses to accept that there is a problem; a person who does nothing while his or her family life is falling apart; a parent at home with the children who cannot even cope with the dirty dishes; a student who reads no assignments, doesn't attend class, and has nothing but trouble with most of the teachers.

Any one of these symptoms or a combination can indicate trouble. In addition, just as the degree of disturbance will vary, so will the degree of the symptoms. For example, the student just mentioned is in far worse shape if we add that he or she has no friends, locks himself or herself in a room most nights, and doesn't talk to family members (Buss, 1966).

Many people in need of help have trouble getting along with others and are typically *inflexible*. This means they can't go with the flow of life but instead plow ahead with a fixed set of responses to almost everything. Thus, a shy, withdrawn male goes to a party, and a few people are nice to him. This should help his self-image, but instead he misinterprets, just as he always does, and thinks they are only "feeling sorry" for him. Or a person who cannot tolerate elevators never accepts the fact that they are reasonably safe, even after hundreds of forced trips. So, feelings, thoughts, and actions won't vary much. These people establish self-defeating boundaries around themselves that won't budge (Bower, 1981).

Another characteristic is that these people constantly see a *threatening environment*. A number of studies suggest that their world is colored a gloomy gray because the worst is always expected or seen. Their thoughts and feelings are hardly ever warm and outgoing but instead are tinged with fear. They see danger, rejection, and failure around every corner (Hearn & Seeman, 1971).

A woman we knew a number of years ago provides a good example of disordered behavior. She was a secretary whose job was typing

▲ *At least on the surface, one would suspect marital problems, but sometimes it is difficult to tell if a person is just eccentric or is seriously disturbed.*

TEACHING MASTER 18-1A

Learning Goals. A Learning Goals sheet for each chapter is provided in the Teacher Resources. These Learning Goals can be used as review sheets or worksheets. **Teaching Master 18-1B** consists of answers to these Learning Goals.

DISCUSS THE PHOTO

What could be one revelation about this person that would convince students that this person is disturbed?

Journal Topic

"What do you know about mental illness? What would you like to know?" If you are courageous and don't mind sacrificing a little organization, you can structure the entire unit around students' questions!

Have groups think of famous people or fictional characters who suffer from the various disorders presented in the chapter. For each person or character, the groups must list evidence that the person is mentally ill, diagnose the disorder, and decide if the person should be committed. If the person in question were to break any laws, would the courts probably find the person sane or insane? See the preceding **Enrichment.**

Comprehension Check

What are some signs of abnormal behavior? *(continuous discomfort, acting in a bizarre fashion, inefficiency, inflexibility, constantly perceiving a threatening environment)*

Points to Stress

How does the court system view mental illness? A defendant can be deemed either insane or sane. An insane person is one who does not know the wrongfulness of his or her actions, or cannot control those actions. In this case, according to the insanity defense, the person should not be held responsible for those actions.

Comprehension Check

What do the initials DSM—IV stand for? *(the fourth edition of the Diagnostic and Statistical Manual of Mental Disorders)*

506

Unit 6 PSYCHOLOGICAL DISORDERS

Diagnostic and Statistical Manual of Mental Disorders IV

A book that classifies the symptoms of mental problems into formal categories.

anxiety disorder

Disorder whose major symptom is anxiety.

letters for the manager. This was during the days before word processors. She was determined to be the best secretary ever hired and began to put more and more pressure on herself to succeed. She tried to turn out a *perfect* letter each time with no corrections. Not only was this impossible to do, but she spent so much time on every single letter that her boss became impatient with her. She, in turn, was upset that he didn't appreciate her work, became irritable with other people, and finally grew quite depressed.

CLASSIFYING DISORDERS— THE DSM-IV

In the next sections, we discuss several classifications of mental disorders. These are part of a system in the mental health field that categorizes people according to the types of symptoms they have. There are hundreds of different sets of symptoms, each of which fits each into a certain classification. These are contained in a book called the *Diagnostic and Statistical Manual of Mental Disorders IV* (1994) (DSM-IV), which is used by mental health workers to determine what classification a particular person belongs in. The first DSM was published in 1952. Over the years, it has been revised several times to incorporate new information.

The classifications we will use are accurate, but we have taken some liberties with them just for the sake of clarity, since you are being exposed to them for the first time. In any case, remember that even though these categories have names and symptoms, no person really fits into any one category perfectly, and symptoms overlap with one another. The DSM system is used only to provide some degree of order when trying to decide the kind of problem the patient has. To keep you from getting lost, please refer to the In Focus titled "Mental Disorders" as the chapter progresses. It contains the basic information you will need and will keep you from losing your way in all the details.

ANXIETY DISORDERS

The three categories of problems we are about to cover—panic, phobia, and obsessive-compulsive disorder—have in common one thing: the person suffering from them also suffers from severe anxiety. Hence these are called **anxiety disorders.** Except for substance abuse, anxiety disorders are the most common type of mental disorder (Neal & Turner, 1991).

DEMONSTRATION

Students enjoy reading or hearing about real cases of behavior disorders. The text includes several case studies but you can easily find more in a casebook. (See the **Suggested Readings.**) You can either present these real examples as you go along, or you can use them at the end of the chapter for review. If you do the latter, present the examples, but describe only the symptoms, and students can try to identify the disorders described. You might also want to get a copy of the latest revision of the *Diagnostic and Statistical Manual of Mental Disorders (DSM).*

Mental Disorders.

 Anxiety and mood disorders are most common. Somatoform and dissociative disorders are least common.

Chapter 18 MENTAL DISORDERS

IN FOCUS **Mental Disorders**

DISORDER	MAIN SYMPTOMS
ANXIETY DISORDERS	anxiety, fear
Panic disorder	
Phobic disorders	
Specific phobia	
Agoraphobia	
Obsessive-compulsive disorder	
SOMATOFORM DISORDERS	physical impairments
Conversion disorders	(but no physical cause)
Hypochondriasis	
DISSOCIATIVE DISORDERS	memory loss,
Amnesia	disconnection from
Fugue	personal identity
Dissociative identity disorder	
MOOD DISORDERS	depression
Dysthymic disorder	
Major depression	
Mania	exaggerated elation (feeling "up")
Bipolar disorders (manic-depression)	mood swings (highs and lows)
SCHIZOPHRENIA (a psychosis)	thought disorders,
Catatonic schizophrenia	hallucinations, delusions,
Paranoid schizophrenia	inappropriate emotions
Undifferentiated schizophrenia	
PERSONALITY DISORDERS	
Antisocial personality	criminal behavior, lack of guilt
Borderline personality	dependency, possessiveness

Which two disorders do you think are most common? Which two do you think are least common?

Discussion

One of the problems of labeling someone mentally ill is the stigma attached to the label. There's nothing wrong with labels; we use them all the time. But when the labels limit us, because of our own shame or because of the attitudes of others, then the labels become destructive. Warn students that mental illness is a heavy load in itself, and each of us needs to avoid attaching any extra burdens with our own stereotypes and irrational fears. Ask students to share their experiences with mentally ill friends or relatives and discuss ways of being supportive of these individuals.

DEMONSTRATION

Associate an object with something unpleasant, like a loud noise or the slap of a ruler on a desk. For example, if your desks move, you can hold up an eraser, then tip over a desk (provided that the noise is jarring). It

won't take long to get students to cringe when seeing the eraser. This demonstrates the role of conditioning in acquiring phobias. (Remember Little Albert from Chapter 7?)

FYI Valium is sometimes prescribed to treat the anxiety that precedes an attack. Therapy, which may include biofeedback, is also used.

Points to Stress

It's very likely that a person with panic disorder will develop phobias. For example, if the person has an anxiety attack near a dog, she may associate the dog with the attack and later feel uneasy around dogs. Chapter 7 describes this sort of conditioning in detail.

FYI Anxiety attacks can last up to one or two minutes. This seems short, but remember, the attacks can be overwhelming.

anxiety

A generalized feeling of apprehension and pending disaster.

panic disorder

A type of anxiety disorder in which one cannot relax and is plagued by frequent and overwhelming attacks of anxiety.

phobic disorder

A type of anxiety disorder in which a person becomes disabled and overwhelmed by fear in the presence of certain objects or events. Examples include specific phobia and agoraphobia.

specific phobia

A major anxiety that arises when faced with a specific object or situation, such as a snake, dog, elevator, heights, and so on.

Anxiety is a generalized feeling of apprehension and dread that includes many bodily upsets. The palms sweat, the throat closes up, breathing is erratic, the heart pounds, hands tremble, and the armpits become a perspiration disaster. The feeling is a great deal like the one you get in a public speaking course when your turn comes to talk. All of us experience anxiety, but people with anxiety disorders may have anxiety attacks a few times a day, and in between they are restless, sleep poorly, don't eat well, and are not capable of calming down.

Panic Disorder

The person with a **panic disorder** is afflicted by frequent and overwhelming attacks of anxiety. Sometimes a panic disorder originates in the person's psyche, probably developing from years of feeling insecure and helpless. But often such a disorder starts because something is physically or chemically wrong with the person. Once they have occurred, these panic attacks tend to repeat themselves whenever the person is under stress. In other words, the anxiety at first is not really connected to anything specific; it is just a physical occurrence. Soon, however, the panic begins to spread, as the fear of dying or making a fool of oneself is associated with more and more objects, events, or people. Eventually, the person may reach a point where activities are severely limited because of these fears. When that happens, the problem is no longer simply physical but is psychological as well. Still, many who suffer can be treated with drugs that will reduce the symptoms (Fishman & Sheehan, 1985). Psychotherapy is also very effective and is discussed in the next chapter.

Phobic Disorders

In a **phobic disorder,** the person becomes disabled and overwhelmed by fear in the presence of certain objects or events. Anxiety is still extraordinarily high but usually only in the presence of the problem. The word *phobia* means "fear of," and there are two basic types of phobic disorders.

A **specific phobia** centers on particular objects or situations: dogs, enclosed spaces, snakes, heights, elevators, water, even knives. Faced with the object of fear, the person becomes extremely anxious. (Note the difference here: a panic attack is not attached to something *specific*, as the phobia is.)

The most common explanation for phobias today is that they result from association or learning. If a little boy cut himself and the parent began screaming, crying, and running around shouting, "You're bleeding! You're bleeding!" the child, with repeated such incidents, could easily develop hematophobia, a fear of blood *(hema).*

All of us have mild phobias. Many people fear that they will jump

DISCOVERY

Have students create a list poem of fears. "Fear of becoming your parents, fear of the ambulance in front of your house. . ." See Raymond Carver's poem, "Fear," for ideas. You can find it in his collection, *Where Water Comes Together with Other Water* (New York: Vintage, 1984).

Chapter 18 MENTAL DISORDERS

 **Phobias**

Achlophobia: Fear of crowds
Acrophobia: Fear of heights
Aerophobia: Fear of high objects
Agoraphobia: Fear of open spaces
Ailurophobia: Fear of cats
Algophobia: Fear of pain
Androphobia: Fear of men
Anthrophobia: Fear of people
Apiphobia: Fear of bees
Aquaphobia: Fear of water
Arachnephobia: Fear of spiders
Astraphobia: Fear of storms
Aviophobia: Fear of flying
Baccilophobia: Fear of microbes
Bacteriophobia: Fear of germs
Ballistophobia: Fear of bullets
Bathophobia: Fear of depth
Belonephobia: Fear of pins and needles
Brontophobia: Fear of thunder
Claustrophobia: Fear of enclosed places
Cynophobia: Fear of dogs
Decidophobia: Fear of making decisions
Demonophobia: Fear of demons
Domatophobia: Fear of being confined in a house
Entomophobia: Fear of insects
Equinophobia: Fear of horses
Ergophobia: Fear of work
Gephydrophobia: Fear of crossing bridges
Gynephobia: Fear of women

Hematophobia: Fear of blood
Herpetophobia: Fear of reptiles
Hydrophobia: Fear of water
Iatrophobia: Fear of doctors
Monophobia: Fear of being alone
Mysophobia: Fear of dirt
Necrophobia: Fear of dead bodies
Nucleomitiphobia: Fear of nuclear bombs
Nyctophobia: Fear of night
Ombrophobia: Fear of rain
Ophidiophobia: Fear of snakes
Optophobia: Fear of opening your eyes
Pathophobia: Fear of disease
Peccatophobia: Fear of sinning
Pediphobia: Fear of children or dolls
Phobophobia: Fear or your own fears
Psychrophobia: Fear of cold
Pyrophobia: Fear of fire
Sitophobia: Fear of food
Sophophobia: Fear of learning
Syphilophobia: Fear of syphilis
Taphephobia: Fear of being buried alive
Technophobia: Fear of technology
Thalassophobia: Fear of the ocean
Thanatophobia: Fear of death
Topophobia: Fear of performing on stage
Triskaidekaphobia: Fear of the number 13
Tropophobia: Fear of moving
Xenophobia: Fear of strangers
Zoophobia: Fear of animals

As you can see, people can develop phobias for many things. What are some phobias that might be added to the list because of technology?

Phobias.

 Laser-phobia? Virtuophobia (fear of virtual reality)?

Discussion

Pose this question to students: If you had a fear of water, would you rather learn to swim by being thrown in or by sticking your big toe in, then your leg, and so on? The first method can be dangerous. The second is called systematic desensitization (Chapter 19).

Points to Stress

It's ironic that people who fear heights, when in a high place, will tend to *imagine* jumping down! Or if they fear needles, they will imagine the needle piercing their skin.

EXPERIMENT

See **Teaching Master 18-4 Presidential Poll 1** and **Teaching Master 18-5 Presidential Poll 2.** Use these handouts to conduct an experiment on the effects of labeling someone as mentally ill. Pass out

one of the masters to half the class and the other master to the other half. Note that electroconvulsive therapy has been changed to electroshock therapy, a more familiar term to students. This should avoid

questions about the term during class, questions that will confuse the divorce control group and that will ruin the experiment. While handing out the masters, you may even want to insist that no questions be asked.

Points to Stress

If you have ever lived in an air-conditioned house for several weeks, you know that you can start to feel trapped, almost claustrophobic.

Discussion

You will probably find that many students are compulsive, although not to the point that they need help; they should be able to provide numerous examples. Give them a chance to list these examples, and add any of your own. This shows that we're all a little anxious.

Points to Stress

An OCD example: you kill a spider in the bathroom, clean your hands, look at your hands, look again. You comb your hair, but you can't help thinking that you missed the spider, and it's going to get in your hair. So you wash your hands again and look. . . .

Unit 6 PSYCHOLOGICAL DISORDERS

agoraphobia

The fear of leaving a familiar environment, especially home.

off high buildings; others are hesitant to use public rest rooms for fear of getting germs. But for true phobics, the danger is so real that they live in mortal fear of being anywhere near the object. Caution: trying to get real phobics to overcome their fears by deliberately forcing them into the feared situation can be very dangerous. Phobics have been known to die from an overload on the system. The problem usually can be treated both efficiently and safely by a professional in a matter of a month or so.

A second type of phobia is called **agoraphobia** (ah-GORE-uh-pho-bee-a), meaning the fear of leaving a familiar environment. Agoraphobics are so fearful of the world outside that they become virtual prisoners in their own homes. The following case (McMahon & McMahon, 1983) is interesting because it shows how an accidental event, such as an ear infection, can trigger a mammoth psychological event—the agoraphobia—that will go on and on.

A 42-year-old married salesman had been in traveling sales work for ten years. One night when on the road at a motel, he developed an infection which spread to the inner ear making him feel very dizzy. He decided to go to the bar and get a drink to "pick himself up." While sitting at the bar, things began to whirl around and the next thing he knew, he was lying on the floor, looking up at strangers all peering down at him as in a nightmare. He was certain he was dying because his heart was racing and people were saying things about a heart attack. He felt desperately alone, frightened, and embarrassed. The infection cleared up and everything seemed to be all right. But a week or so later, when driving down the highway, he started to feel "funny," weak, dizzy. He pulled off to the side of the road and waited the attack out. Instead of going on, he turned around and went back home where he felt safe. Within a matter of a month, he began to have anxiety attacks every time he left the house, and called in sick more and more often so he wouldn't have to leave home.

The word *agoraphobia* literally means a fear of open places. *Agora* is from the Greek for "marketplace" (an ancient shopping mall). We label the poor salesperson as agoraphobic because his basic fear is one of being away from the closed, secure atmosphere of his home and out in public. Some believe such trouble starts in childhood when a child is accidentally lost in a place such as a department store. But many agoraphobics are women, especially homemakers without an outside job. In these cases we suspect that the frequent isolation of this occupation makes them feel threatened about relating to other people in the "outside" world, and the fear grows and grows over time.

One oddity of agoraphobics might be of interest. Most of them have a specific boundary beyond which they cannot go. It varies from person to person. Thus, some people can go up to three blocks,

Chapter 18 MENTAL DISORDERS

▲ *If you have acrophobia (fear of heights), this picture should be enough to get you started.*

some ten, some another number, from home. If they go even a few feet beyond, they come apart, but if they stay within the boundary, they are all right.

Obsessive-Compulsive Disorder

An **obsession** refers to an endless preoccupation with some type of urge or thought. All of us have experienced this to a limited degree when we can't get a popular tune out of our minds. Eventually it disappears, but magnify this many hundredfold and you have the concerns of the person suffering from this disorder. The thoughts simply will not leave such a person alone.

A **compulsion** is a symbolic, ritualized behavior that a person must repeatedly act out. Each time the person does so, whatever anxiety he or she feels is decreased, so the behavior becomes self-rewarding and is repeated. Most people have minor compulsions, such as a desire to step on a crack in the sidewalk. Genuine compulsions are different because the people *must* carry out the act or they get more and more anxious. Some, for instance, wind up checking dozens of times to be certain the front door is locked before going to bed each night. That's not normal.

The two words, **obsessive-compulsive,** are generally used together. Most compulsive people are obsessed with their compulsion; for instance, the compulsive hand washer is obsessed with the thought that he or she is "dirty." And being obsessed with cleanliness leads to compulsive washing.

The stranglehold that this disorder can exert is remarkable.

obsession

An endless preoccupation with an urge or thought.

compulsion

A symbolic, ritualized behavior that a person must keep acting out in order to avoid anxiety.

obsessive-compulsive disorder

Having continued thoughts (obsession) about performing a certain act over and over (compulsion).

Connections

Freud's term for OCD was anal retentiveness or anal fixation (Chapter 14).

511

FYI OCD patients seem to have an imbalance of serotonin (discussed later in the chapter under manic depression). Antidepressants have been found to be an effective treatment.

CHAPTER PROJECT/COOPERATIVE LEARNING

Assign each group a behavior disorder, and ask them to prepare an installment for Mental Health Theater. They will present a five- to ten-minute episode, with props, that dramatizes the nature of their assigned disorder. They might have scenes at a psychologist's office, at home, at work.

They can include flashbacks to illustrate the onset of the illness. This is optional, but you may want to have each student conduct research on the assigned disorder and incorporate this research into the show. It is especially useful if students find a few case studies on their disorders.

DISCUSS THE PHOTO

Put a movie star next to the aluminum foil ball and suddenly the behavior is perceived as creative.

Points to Stress

People with OCD are usually good workers. They will try to do a perfect job and also tend to like routine.

Comprehension Check

Name the disorder described in the following situations: chewing food exactly twenty-five times before swallowing *(obsessive-compulsive);* being suddenly overcome by a racing heart, difficulty breathing, and a feeling of impending doom for no apparent reason *(panic disorder);* intense fear of leaving home *(phobia, particularly agoraphobia).*

Unit 6 PSYCHOLOGICAL DISORDERS

▲ *Believe it or not, this is an enormous ball of tinfoil. Hobby or obsessive-compulsive behavior?*

somatoform disorder

Condition in which psychological issues are expressed in bodily symptoms in the absence of any real physical problem.

Compulsive gamblers are examples. (These people are actually listed in the DSM slightly differently, but they serve our purposes well here.) They are constantly obsessed with the desire to keep on gambling no matter what. Thousands every year wipe out all the family finances, certain that the next hand of cards will change their luck. The strength of the problem is illustrated by a patient who entered a program in which he wanted to learn *not* to play a slot machine by having the act associated with something unpleasant, a shock. A slot machine was put in his hospital room, and he was wired up to receive a 70-volt shock to the forearm each time he pulled the lever. Over a period of time, he received 672 shocks. Only then did he decide to stop gambling. But his "cure" lasted only 18 months, at which point he started again and had to go back to the hospital for a series of "booster shocks" (Barker & Miller, 1969).

Obsessive-compulsive behavior seems to result from faulty attempts to resolve guilt, anxiety, or insecurity. For instance, insecurity and anxiety can result in someone *having to* get up and check the front door dozens of times before finally going to sleep.

Some behavior in this classification is quite symbolic. For example, many children are told that something they did was "dirty." This makes them associate cleanliness with goodness. Over time, whenever they feel "dirty" (guilty), they will wash their hands—up to hundreds of times a day. Just the act of doing *something* (even though it doesn't work) reduces their anxiety and guilt (Turner et al., 1985). Hence, they come to repeat it, rather than seeking a more sensible solution. On the other hand, recent research has found that there is a defect in the amount of some brain chemicals for many people with this problem. The result is the triggering of circuits in the brain over and over to repeat endlessly things that are reasonably normal for most of us. There are new drugs that help people begin to get it under control, at which point most can handle the problem effectively and understand themselves better (Rapoport, 1989).

SOMATOFORM DISORDERS

In **somatoform** (so-MAT-ah-form) **disorders,** psychological issues are expressed in bodily symptoms, but there is no actual physical problem. Most of us feel worse physically when life is not going too well. Somatoform disorders, though, present a far more dramatic picture.

Conversion Disorder

You may have heard of "hysterical blindness" or "hysterical paralysis." The technical term for both of these situations is **conversion**

512

ENRICHMENT

Have students compare and contrast two movies about dissociative identity disorder: *Three Faces of Eve* and *Sybil*. Which character was more believable? Did they note any behaviors that were not usually associated with this disorder?

ENRICHMENT

Some husbands experience sympathy pains when their wives are pregnant. You wouldn't call this a disorder, but if it went further and the husbands' bellies actually began to enlarge, conversion disorder would be a fitting description.

Points to Stress

You may have seen evangelists on TV who allegedly heal the crippled and the blind. These evangelists *may* actually be curing some people. But there's a catch. There's probably some sort of screening process before the show to find out *when* people were crippled. If they were crippled from birth, they go to the back of the line. If they were mysteriously crippled as an adult and doctors can't explain it, they may be suffering from a somatoform disorder, and these are the people who will be put on stage!

Connections

Conversion disorder was called hysteria in Freud's day (Chapter 14).

Points to Stress

With the spread of AIDS in recent years, hypochondriacs have more fuel for getting attention and worrying themselves.

Chapter 18 MENTAL DISORDERS

conversion disorder

Disorder in which a serious psychological trauma is changed into a symbolic physical dysfunction.

disorder. In a conversion disorder, a serious psychological trauma is unconsciously changed (converted) into a symbolic physical dysfunction. For example, a person who has witnessed terrible human torture and slaughter may be overwhelmed by the horror, so the mind shuts the visual system down. The person can no longer see. Or someone else was in an awful automobile accident and managed to get free of the car. He or she could hear other people screaming but, frozen by fear, was unable to move, to go get help. That person might develop some type of paralysis in response. These people are not faking it. Say that someone has, psychologically, lost feeling in the right leg. If you sneak up behind the person and stick a pin in that leg, he or she will not feel it. The dysfunction is real. There simply is no physical basis for it. Interestingly, however, such people show very little concern about their physical condition. As you might imagine, conversion disorders are quite rare.

Hypochondriasis

hypochondriasis

Disorder characterized by feeling excessive concern about one's health and exaggerating the seriousness of minor physical complaints.

A less unusual somatoform disorder is **hypochondriasis** (high-po-con-DRY-ah-sis). Hypochondriacs are overly concerned about their health. They see disastrous illness in the most minor physical complaint. Thus, a slight headache is interpreted as a symptom of brain cancer; a case of the sniffles is really pneumonia; and so on. Often, such people, as children, were given affection or support from other people only when they were sick. They never learned better ways of getting attention. Also, now that they have spent years focusing on their health, they have trouble breaking the cycle. Needless to say, these people spend a great deal of time in doctors' offices.

DISSOCIATIVE DISORDERS

dissociative disorders

Disorders in which a part of one's life becomes disconnected from other parts; amnesia, fugue, and dissociative identity disorder are examples.

Dissociative (dis-SO-see-ah-tiv) **disorders** are best known from soap operas on television. The major character develops amnesia and forgets she is married to a prominent attorney. She falls in love with a wealthy physician at the local hospital where she is treated for the flu. The physician is married to the head nurse, who has dissociative identity disorder and who got the woman-of-the-year award but steals drugs, which she sells on the street. Meanwhile . . .

If one paid any attention to television, it would seem that this sort of thing goes on all the time. Actually, dissociative disorders—amnesia, fugue, and dissociative identity disorder—are extremely rare. The word *dissociative* refers to the fact that people with these disorders can disconnect or "disassociate" certain events or behaviors from one another. There is a bit of this ability in all of us. We have things we want to forget, and we can do a good job of getting rid of them. It is a

513

DISCOVERY

Have each student attach a brief biography to their school ID (if your school uses them) and collect the two together. Randomly hand the IDs and bios back, and have students assume the identity of the person they get for the rest of the period.

Make sure students don't get back their own IDs. (You may want to warn students against being derisive.) Give the class tasks to perform so that everyone has a chance to interact for a few minutes. For example, "Find someone who likes to

draw." Let's say John approaches Sarah, and her assumed bio says "likes to draw"; she will have to pretend she likes to draw and talk about it. Afterward, ask students to imagine what it would be like if they changed personalities like this nearly every-

---

Points to Stress

When you *associate*, you join together; when you *dissociate*, you separate. In this case, you separate a memory from your *self*.

Teaching Hint

How would one distinguish between psychogenic amnesia and an organic type of amnesia? Organic: usually, only recent memories are hazy. The person may have difficulty paying attention, and he or she will seem disoriented. Psychogenic: past memories are lost, too. Attention may be seemingly unimpaired. The memory loss is preceded by an argument, a firing, and so on.

Points to Stress

During hypnosis, you are asked to "leave yourself" for a while. As mentioned in Chapter 6, you are still fully in control; you are simply focused. In the case of dissociative disorders, your ability to control this "disconnection" is impaired.

514

---

amnesia

A dissociative disorder in which traumatic events "disappear" from memory.

selective forgetting

"Forgetting" only things that are very traumatic.

fugue

The condition of having amnesia for one's current life and starting a new one somewhere else.

---

rare individual who doesn't "absentmindedly" miss a doctor's appointment, for example. We have a bit of dissociative identity disorder also, which we carry out all the time—without getting confused as to which part we are playing. For instance, no one uses the same language or discusses the same (sometimes crude) thoughts at a family dinner as he or she does when alone with close friends. So, dissociative disorders are very elaborate behaviors that have seeds in our everyday activities (Bower, 1981). Most of us can change our behavior in different circumstances and rebound to whatever our "core" personality might be. People with dissociative identity disorder, however, are different because they have an aspect of themselves that causes such guilt (for example, a repeated tendency to violate the law) that they cannot face this aspect and thus block it off. Since this part won't disappear, for these people it grows and grows until eventually they form a separate personality that can do these acts and not be responsible and guilty for them when they return to their "good" personality.

Amnesia

In psychogenic **amnesia,** a dissociative disorder, memories related to a terrible trauma "disappear." They are still "in" the person, but they are cut off from consciousness. While some amnesias can be caused by a high fever or a blow to the head, the term *psychogenic* means the problem is psychologically *(psycho)* caused *(genic)*. In fact, people with this problem often show little concern that parts of their past seem to be gone. Hence, there must be a psychological benefit involved, or they would indeed be alarmed at losing some of their memories.

A common and easily understood type of psychogenic amnesia is a soldier's loss of memory for nightmarish events that happened in battle. In such cases of amnesia, **selective forgetting** is involved, which means that only the traumatic portion of the memories disappear. For example, a soldier may completely blot out the part of his identity connected with his fighting battalion and everything in the more recent past leading back to a horrible war experience. The terror and guilt these memories produce therefore disappear, occasionally reappearing in nightmares (Neal & Turner, 1991; Hartmann, 1984). But only certain events are gone: the soldier doesn't forget how to tie a shoe, childhood friends, old memories, and so forth. In fact, amnesia in all these cases is selective.

Fugue

The **fugue** (FYOOG) state is an extensive, complicated type of amnesia. The person disconnects all of his or her current life from

day, and it was more or less out of their control! Discuss the obvious differences between this exercise and true dissociative identity disorder. With true dissociative identity disorder, the person is not faking it; other personalities do exist. And after a

while, the other personalities develop vivid histories of their own. With dissociative identity disorder, the purpose of switching personalities is to repress some painful memory.

FYI Sometimes the various personalities are called *alter egos.* These *alters* can be different genders, possess varying degrees of talent, and some can even be animals.

awareness, moves somewhere else, and starts all over. More men than women exhibit this problem. It seems to be caused by serious and unresolved conflicts, often with a spouse. Fortunately, this condition usually does not last very long. When the person "comes out of it," he or she cannot remember what happened during the fugue state.

Dissociative Identity Disorder

Dissociative identity disorder, formerly called multiple personality, in the basic form is also similar to amnesia. Instead of forgetting specific events, though, such individuals "forget" a portion of themselves, and that portion begins to live a life of its own. Although multiple personalities are all over television and are usually called schizophrenics, which they AREN'T(!), they are actually extremely rare (Kluft, 1991).

Again, all of us have secret fantasy lives that we don't want others to know about. In a fashion similar to the true dissociative identity disorder, we make a division that is usually based on a "good" person and a "bad" person. But for the true dissociative identity disorder, the dissociative behaviors are exaggerated to the point of becoming at least partly independent of each other.

Dissociative identity disorder is probably so rare because a number of conditions must align themselves in just the right way in order to produce it. Such conditions typically include a haunted, confused personality, a history of very upsetting traumatic experiences or childhood abuse, and a long-term habit of escaping from almost any problem. Usually these people have very strong, conflicting desires and needs in their life-styles. For example, a withdrawn and righteous man (call him A) who desperately wants to give vent to animal impulses develops mammoth guilt over these desires. To distance himself from this pain, another personality gradually creeps into the picture containing these unacceptable desires. This is evil personality "B." He can then go about doing whatever he wants as long as he is B. When A returns, he becomes very self-righteous, even prim, prissy, and obnoxiously good. Complete amnesia can be involved, with A not knowing about B and vice versa. Sometimes, however, the dominant or stronger personality knows about the weaker; the weaker rarely knows about the stronger one (Gruenewald, 1971).

The dissociative identity disorder is not schizophrenia. In dissociative identity disorder, there is really only one person involved with two or more sides that tend to live independently. But the basic core personality is the same, and this core is well aware of general reality as we know it, does not have trouble thinking or communicating, and does not believe things that don't exist. These facts are the opposite of what happens in schizophrenia, discussed in detail later.

dissociative identity disorder

Condition in which a person divides himself or herself into two (possibly more) separate personalities that can act independently.

Points to Stress

It seems that different personalities of a sufferer of dissociative identity disorder may serve different functions. For example, one may be the "work personality," and the other personalities will allow this one to be dominant during the work week for obvious reasons. Or personality A may start a fight, become apprehensive, then fade into the background to let personality B fight the battle.

FYI With selective forgetting, sufferers of amnesia will retain talents, abilities, and general knowledge about the world, unless one of these causes trauma for some reason.

DISCOVERY

Have students *draw* their perception of depression. For example, one student might draw people having a great time at the top of the hill, but at the bottom is someone alone; this might convey how we feel left out when we are depressed. Point out that artistic ability is irrelevant. While they are drawing, you may want to play lugubrious music in the background. Afterward, have students explain their interpretations.

COOPERATIVE LEARNING

The preceding **Discovery** calls for each person to draw depression. You may want to assign a *different* disorder to each group and have them draw what it might feel like to have the disorder.

Comprehension Check

Selective forgetting of events is involved in which kind of dissociative disorder? *(amnesia)*

Discussion

Since depression is so common, spend some time allowing students to explain why they get depressed and how they overcome it. Consider putting them in a circle to promote a certain degree of openness and intimacy. This is not meant as a therapy session, but the discussion may help some of them realize the universal nature of depression.

FYI Some psychologists view depression as the flip side of anxiety. Rather than feel anxious, which can be quite disturbing, we become depressed. In fact, antidepressant drugs are often used to treat anxiety disorders—even when no depression is exhibited.

516

mood disorders

A category of mental disorder characterized by one's emotional state; includes depression and mania.

dysthymic disorder

A moderate depression.

major depression

An extremely low emotional state, severe depression; involves loss of appetite, lack of energy, hopelessness, and suicidal thoughts.

516

MOOD DISORDERS

The *mood* of an individual is his or her emotional state—elated, depressed, angry, neutral, and so forth. Thus, mental disturbances characterized by a depressed mood, an exaggerated "up" mood, or an alternation between up and down are called **mood disorders.**

Dysthymic Disorder

The term **dysthymic** (dis-THIGH-mik) **disorder** comes from the Greek for "low spirits." Hence, it is a moderate depression. In any given year, between four and 12 percent of the population will be affected by it. Thus, it is a fairly common problem and of all the mental disorders in this chapter, dysthymic disorder is the most likely to clear up eventually without treatment. For both of these reasons, it is referred to as the common cold of mental health (Weissman, 1985). Typical symptoms are lack of energy, unhappiness, loss of interest in activities and people, loss of sense of humor, sadness, and rock-bottom feelings of self-worth (Beck, 1967). All of these feelings can occur in the normal person who, for instance, loses a loved one.

The best way to know whether depression of this sort is normal is to see if it has served its "function" or instead has taken on a life of its own that just keeps on going. Loss of a friend, for instance, would trigger these problems in any normal person, but if they go on and on with the same degree of severity, something else is probably wrong. Or if they appear "out of nowhere" or arise following an insignificant event, again one's emotional makeup may include a tendency to become depressed.

In the sections coming up, we discuss severe or major depression and bipolar disorders. Since the causes are similar in all mood disorders, we will save further discussion of these causes for the end of those sections.

Major Depression

Typical symptoms of severe or **major depression** are very slow speech, deep ongoing depression, disturbances in appetite and sleep patterns, lack of energy, a sense of hopelessness, extreme feelings of worthlessness, and frequent thoughts of death or suicide. Most patients in this category have trouble carrying out simple daily tasks. Some may even lie motionless in a rolled-up fetal position for hours at a time. It is as if all the joy has gone out of their lives. Underneath it all, though, there is frequently a great deal of anger, sometimes directed at the self, sometimes broad and unfocused. The depression may last from a couple of weeks to a matter of months.

ENRICHMENT

Have students find recent surveys on who gets depressed most and at what ages. For example, do people in certain professions report depression more often than those in other professions? Are certain age groups associated with higher rates of depression?

ENRICHMENT

Novelist William Styron has written an account of his ordeal with major depression that is powerful and insightful. The book is short enough to finish in a night or two. See the **Suggested Readings.**

Critical Thinking

Ask students why they think more women than men report being depressed. (It's possible that many women are still affected by old gender stereotypes: being reactive rather than proactive, acting out emotions, and so on.)

Chapter 18 MENTAL DISORDERS

DISCUSS THE PHOTO

The man who is squatting is probably suffering major depression. The other man probably has a dysthymic disorder.

Connections

How do behaviorists explain depression (Chapter 19)? Learned helplessness: we realize that our behaviors have little to do with consequences, so we become depressed. How do cognitive psychologists explain depression? Irrational thinking: when we are depressed, our thoughts are distorted.

Points to Stress

People who suffer major depression can become psychotic.

▲ *Different degrees of depression.*

Mania

The word *mood* refers to any kind of emotion. Some people go in the opposite direction from depression and have extreme *up* moods. This might sound at first like something that wouldn't be all that bad, but unfortunately that is not the case. This behavior, called **mania** (MAIN-ee-ah) from the Greek for "mad excitement," involves agitation, restlessness, inability to concentrate, and extremely rapid speech. The speech problem is the most notable part of the behavior. The patients' thoughts are moving so quickly through their minds that they literally collide with one another into a mass of confused speech, making comprehension almost impossible. This problem is called a **flight of ideas,** meaning that thoughts are running so fast they are flying in all directions. Here is a brief example: "I went to the store where I kept the containers of milk which all babies should have in order to survive which not everybody can do because of the threat of nuclear war between countries which are divisions of various parts of the land which is filled normally with rock and dirt." These patients often get so excited that they begin to have delusions that they have special powers or great influence, so they make plans for controlling the world or some such project (Depue et al., 1981).

Bipolar Disorders

On occasion, people experience swings between the ups of mania and the downs of a major depression. The official term for this prob-

mania

A mood disorder involving extreme agitation, restlessness, rapid speech, and trouble concentrating.

flight of ideas

A confused state in which thoughts and speech go in all directions with no unifying concept.

517

ENRICHMENT

Prozac has gotten a lot of press, both positive (as the wonder drug for depression) and negative (side effects allegedly have driven patients to violence, but this involved such a small number that the danger has been more or less dismissed). Have students find out how Prozac works and why it became popular in a relatively short time. See Kramer in **Suggested Readings.**

ENRICHMENT

Have students explore postpartum depression. What percentage of women report this? How long does it usually last? What seems to cause it?

Points to Stress

Just as depression may be one way to deal with anxiety, as noted earlier, mania may be one way of overcoming, albeit briefly, the feelings of worthlessness typical of depression.

Observable Mastery

Teaching Master 18-6 Behavior Disorders includes a list of fictional case studies and a list of disorders. Cut them out and hand either a case study or a disorder to each student. Students then walk around trying to find their match. If you want to make this more challenging, have students write their own case studies.

Bipolar Disorder.

IN FOCUS Mania is characterized by rapid speech, restlessness, and agitation.

Unit 6 PSYCHOLOGICAL DISORDERS

bipolar disorder

A disorder with up and down swings of moods from "high" to "low."

lem—which you may have heard of as "manic depression"—might confuse you at first, but it is logical. First, remember that the Earth has two poles, north and south. The word *pole,* in this sense, means "one of the two most extreme possibilities"—one pole is at the top, the other at the bottom. They couldn't get farther from one another. Next you need to understand the word *bi. Bi* means "two" of something. So, people who have these wild swings from up to down and back are categorized as having a **bipolar disorder.** Here is a case history of such a disorder (McMahon & McMahon, 1983):

The patient, a 25-year-old woman, was admitted to the hospital for observation after the fire department was called by a neighbor who saw smoke. The patient was dressed in a grass skirt she had purchased in Hawaii during her honeymoon. She had built a "bonfire" in the middle of the living room floor and was dancing around the fire, leaping, jumping, and singing what seemed to be college football cheers.

At the hospital she was not only dancing, but trying to throw touchdown passes at the same time, mixing obscenities and

IN FOCUS **Bipolar Disorder— The Manic Depressive**

Unlike a playground swing, the highs and lows of this illness can last several days to several months.
What is one characteristic of mania?

quarterback play calls in a continuous outpouring. She seemed only partially aware of her surroundings.

The same patient was readmitted to the hospital 17 years later at the age of 42 with a diagnosis of bipolar disorder. Her husband brought her to the hospital because she had refused to eat for three days, slept only two or three hours a night, and spent long hours staring off into space. She would speak to others, but only after more or less continuous coaxing. In very slow, monotonous speech, she commented that she was talking to her dead sister who was wearing a white gown, but her face was eaten up by worms and part of her eye socket was missing. This hallucination was intermixed with a conversation with God, a combination of pleading with Him to do something about her sister and blaming Him for her hospitalization.

In the years between her first hospitalization and her present admission, she had been treated on several occasions in the outpatient clinic for depressive episodes, but there had been one additional manic episode.

Note that in this case, the person suffered from hallucinations. Whenever hallucinations are present, the patient is considered to be *psychotic,* a term that is explained shortly. While most people with major depression are not psychotic, such elements are sometimes present. A similar situation exists with bipolar disorders, but psychotic elements are more frequent here. In fact, one type of bipolar disorder used to be classified as "manic-depressive psychosis."

Causes of Mood Disorders

We don't understand the origin of mood disorders too well. In fact, strangely enough, they disappear all by themselves (at least 80 to 90 percent of them) within about six months, although they tend to recur in many people (Rennie, 1972). Just as the dysthymic disorder may be caused by the loss of a loved one, major depression, we suspect, may come from a lifetime of many separations, losses, and unpleasant setbacks (Benjaminsen, 1981; Strauss, 1979). Again, like the dysthymic but at a more severe level, these people have a very poor self-image. They see themselves as responsible for many bad events and don't even struggle to put up a defense against such an unrealistic burden (Lewinsohn et al., 1980; Beck, 1972).

The problems associated with mood disorders can be so bizarre and severe and they can appear (and disappear) so rapidly that we suspect some chemical imbalance is involved. Probably psychological components then help send the person over the edge, so to speak. Studies show a pretty clear pattern of a chemical defect in the brain. One brain chemical that helps keep the brain active in normal people, called **serotonin** (ser-uh-TONE-in), is very high—much higher than normal—in many manics; the same chemical is very low in depressives (Snyder, 1984).

serotonin

The brain chemical that in excess leads to mania; in too low concentrations, it leads to depression.

INTERDISCIPLINARY PROJECT

Music. Have students create a medley of music, parts of which will match each disorder. For example, depression might be conveyed by a sonorous oboe, anxiety by a busy fiddle, schizophrenia by dissonance, and so on. This is not something you can do every year, but if you happen to have a few talented musicians in class, or even in the school, they are usually excited by this kind of project.

Points to Stress

Here's a simple way to distinguish psychosis from other types of disorders: when people are psychotic, they are out of touch with reality. As noted in the next few pages, schizophrenics are not out of touch with reality all the time.

FYI In general, the chances of becoming schizophrenic are about 1 percent. If your brother or sister is schizophrenic, your chance is about 10 percent. If your identical twin is schizophrenic, your chance is roughly 50 percent.

psychosis

Severe mental disorder involving major problems with emotional responses, disorganized thought processes, and distorted perceptions of the world.

thought disorder

A serious distortion of the ability to think or speak in a lucid and coherent way.

hallucinating

Seeing or hearing something that is not present.

delusion

A belief in something (for example, that you are a king or queen) that is not true.

schizophrenia

The most serious mental disturbance, involving loss of contact with reality, thought disorders, hallucinations, and delusions.

Could this defect be inherited? It is possible, but we can't be certain. Here is the problem: there is typically a family history of depression when you interview the patient. *But* depression is psychologically "contagious," so it may be that being around depressed family members is the cause rather than a specific gene (Kidd, 1985). We'll have to wait for the results of further research, but for the moment a combination of psychological factors with a physical or chemical defect seems a good bet as the source of mood disorders.

CHARACTERISTICS OF PSYCHOTIC DISORDERS

A **psychosis** or **psychotic disorder** involves a major disorganization of thought processes, confused and extreme emotional responses, and distorted perceptions of the world. There is a loss of contact with and difficulty in recognizing reality. Thus, it is a very serious mental disturbance. Most researchers do not think that it is an extension or outgrowth of less severe disorders but that it is a separate problem that arises all by itself.

There are four major symptoms that can appear in psychosis. All four may not be present in one individual, but typically at least two are. (1) The first symptom is a serious distortion of mental processes. Often it is hard to understand exactly what psychotic people are trying to say or to grasp what they are thinking. This behavior comes and goes so that they are lucid for a while, then very confused. This symptom is called **thought disorder.** (2) The second symptom involves seeing or hearing things that are not there. Again, this comes and goes. It is not unusual for psychotics to hear voices or see objects that are not present. This behavior is called **hallucinating.** (3) Next, many psychotics hold grossly inaccurate beliefs, such as thinking of themselves as avenging angels or as victims of persecution by some secret organization. Such a belief is called a **delusion.** (4) Finally, psychotics have a great deal of trouble with emotional responses. The emotions shown are quite inappropriate; they might show no response at all when something interesting happens, for example, or they might laugh at a tragic event. We seriously doubt that they really think it is funny; instead, we think that they are quite confused and dominated by a malfunctioning brain.

SCHIZOPHRENIC DISORDERS

Schizophrenia (skitz-oh-FREN-ee-ah), a psychosis, is the most serious of all mental disturbances. It affects about one percent of the

DISCOVERY

Here's an alternative to the preceding **Interdisciplinary Project**. If you have students who are interested in making short films, they can create a video montage that conveys the essence of each disorder. For example, anxiety might be conveyed by quick cuts, depression by darkness, schizophrenia by unusual camera angles. In fact, you may want to combine this project and the interdisciplinary one!

---

population. Obvious symptoms of this problem are disorganized thoughts and garbled speech, as well as hallucinations and delusions. Researchers doubt that schizophrenia is a single disorder but instead feel that there are different causes and degrees of severity. For example, about a third of such patients have one episode and get better, never to have it happen again; a third have very severe symptoms and do not respond to very much treatment at all; the final third are in and out of institutions most of their lives (Restak, 1984). We suspect that schizophrenia results mostly from some physical or chemical problem because it appears in late adolescence or early adulthood, almost never earlier. This fact would tend to rule out the suggestion that it is mostly psychological, because psychological causes should result in the problem appearing at almost any age.

In some cases, schizophrenics will speak what is called **word salad.** Like the ingredients of a tossed salad, the words are all mixed

word salad

Speech in which words are mixed together incoherently.

Points to Stress

The fact that some schizophrenics get worse, some get better, and some go both ways is sometimes called the *rule of thirds.* This is a label that may help students remember this material. Also, schizophrenia is *not* the same as dissociative identity disorder.

Schizophrenic Word Salad.

IN FOCUS   Schizophrenics may intend to say one thing but never quite get there. Here's another example: "Sometimes it tastes bitter like pound cake, 150 pounds on my hands and legs and I need a hammer."

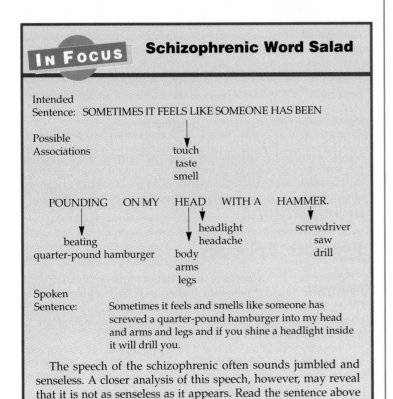

IN FOCUS — Schizophrenic Word Salad

Intended
Sentence: SOMETIMES IT FEELS LIKE SOMEONE HAS BEEN

Possible
Associations   touch
                      taste
                      smell

POUNDING   ON MY   HEAD   WITH A   HAMMER.

beating   headlight   screwdriver
quarter-pound hamburger headache   saw
                       body   drill
                       arms
                       legs

Spoken
Sentence: Sometimes it feels and smells like someone has
            screwed a quarter-pound hamburger into my head
            and arms and legs and if you shine a headlight inside
            it will drill you.

The speech of the schizophrenic often sounds jumbled and senseless. A closer analysis of this speech, however, may reveal that it is not as senseless as it appears. Read the sentence above and note the possible associations that the schizophrenic may make while mentally constructing the sentence below.

What is another spoken sentence that could be derived from the possible associations?

Points to Stress

Although clang associations are amusing, they are relatively uncommon. If you have students write journal entries from the point of view of patients with disorders, students will enjoy writing their own clang associations: "Hey, tan man. Too much fun sun?"

FYI Catatonic schizophrenia is relatively rare. Paranoid schizophrenia is the most common.

Points to Stress

Catatonics are so rigid at times that you can actually raise their hand or arm, and it will stay where you put it. And since catatonics sometimes remain in one particular posture, circulation problems may develop. At the other extreme, every once in a while, they will leave their stupor and become quite animated.

Unit 6 PSYCHOLOGICAL DISORDERS

clang associations

Psychotic speech in which words are rhymed.

catatonic schizophrenia

Type of schizophrenia characterized by disturbances of movement.

paranoid schizophrenia

Schizophrenia marked by strong feelings of suspiciousness and persecution.

undifferentiated schizophrenia

Schizophrenia that lacks any distinguishing symptoms.

psychotic episodes

Periods of psychotic behavior that can alternate with periods of relative coherence and calm.

---

together: "The house burnt the cow horrendously always" (Vetter, 1969). Or there are what we call **clang associations,** which refer to the fact that the speech has a rhythm like a bell: "You wear clothes and how much does this watch cost? Have you a sister? I have three and they are all fine girls, curls, furls, isn't that funny?" (Sherman, 1938). The clang comes with "girls, curls, furls."

Types of Schizophrenia

All schizophrenia has certain symptoms in common, especially thought disorders. However, there are several subtypes, three of which are described here.

Catatonic   The hallmark of **catatonic schizophrenia** is a disturbance of movement. Catatonics usually do not speak, or they say very little. They appear to be in a stupor much of the time. They may rigidly hold a peculiar posture or simply stand or sit, unmoving, for hours.

Paranoid   **Paranoid schizophrenia** is marked by strong feelings of persecution and suspiciousness. It often includes grandiose beliefs as well. For instance, a paranoid schizophrenic might believe that he or she has some kind of special or superhuman power.

Undifferentiated   **Undifferentiated schizophrenia** is just what the term implies. That is, there is nothing special to differentiate or distinguish it. Many professionals consider this a catchall category. In other words, this category is used when a schizophrenic does not fit into any other subtype.

Psychotic Episodes

Schizophrenics are not necessarily out of touch with reality all the time. Their unusual behavior (called **psychotic episodes)** often comes in cycles, and in between the person is reasonably lucid. But often even those who seem unaware of their surroundings are not really as completely lost as they may appear.

One story about this involves a loud and obnoxious student nurse who frequently made unflattering remarks about the patients. One day she leaned over to make a bed next to the one on which a catatonic schizophrenic patient had been sitting immobile for many hours. She commented on how stupid she thought his behavior was and suddenly received a good solid kick in the rear. By the time she had whirled around, the patient had "resumed his 'poker face' expression and former posture" (O'Kelly & Muckler, 1955).

DISCOVERY

Students may have heard of post-traumatic stress disorder (PTSD). It's used most often to describe the trauma soldiers experience after a war: nightmares, insomnia, reliving in their minds the horrors of war. The disorder can also afflict victims of disasters and violent crimes. Now that PTSD is listed in the *DSM*, attorneys are beginning to use it to defend clients who live in what they might call "inner-city combat zones." Those who agree cite statistics showing that there's a better chance of getting shot in some of these inner cities than in real combat zones. Others argue that such a defense will encourage more violence, since it diminishes individual responsibility. Ask students to discuss and/or debate the issue.

Environmental Factors in Schizophrenia

We know that the odds of a person becoming schizophrenic are moderately high if that person's close family members have this problem. The studies of direct inheritance, though, are confusing. When we look at identical twins, if one has the disorder, the odds are fairly good that the other will, too. For the population as a whole, however, the suggestion is strong that heredity is not the key factor. For 90 percent of schizophrenics, there are no other schizophrenics in the immediate family. In addition, when children from schizophrenic families are adopted at a young age into other families, the children's risk of becoming schizophrenic is lowered somewhat. It is still fairly high but not as high as it would be if they had remained with their original families (Dohrenwend et al., 1979; Mosher et al., 1973). Environment, then, may play a small part in this disorder. Consider the following case study of a schizophrenic named Michael (McMahon & McMahon, 1983):

Michael W., a 29-year-old married male, was brought to the hospital emergency room after refusing to eat or speak and staring out the window for four days. An interview with family members revealed that Mr. W. had had such episodes before, but they had never lasted this long. In addition, he had periods in which he was suspicious of everyone in his family and claimed they were trying to poison him. During these periods, he accused his wife of infidelity and became extremely agitated and hostile towards her. He had never been physically abusive, but his behavior was so irrational and out of control that she was quite fearful of him at those times.

Following high school graduation and vocational training, Mr. W. had been regularly employed in television repair until two years ago when economic conditions forced his employer to lay him off. Since that time, he worked occasionally at different jobs, the last one delivering for a local pizza parlor. He was fired from that job six months ago. Apparently, he would leave the parlor to make his deliveries, but would then become confused, park his truck, and sit for hours before returning with no deliveries made. Lately he had stopped seeking employment.

According to the older brother, he and Mr. W. had been reared by an unmarried aunt who was in her 50s when they came to live with her as small children. Their mother was killed in an automobile accident shortly after Mr. W.'s birth, and their father afterwards developed a drinking problem, eventually becoming totally unable to care for them. The brother described his aunt as an emotionally cold woman who resented caring for her nephews, but he stated they were well-fed and clothed and their physical needs generally were attended to. Visits from their father were rare, and usually resulted in bitter arguments with

Points to Stress

It makes sense that paranoid schizophrenics would develop grandiose beliefs. Maybe this helps them deal with their delusions of persecution.

FYI Another type is called disorganized schizophrenia, which is marked by extreme thought disorders. These people are usually part of the third of schizophrenics who never get better, who spend most of their lives in institutions.

Comprehension Check

Which type of schizophrenics have grandiose beliefs? *(paranoid).* Which display a disturbance of movement? *(catatonic).* Which have thought disorders? *(all types).*

DISCOVERY

The *DSM* has gone through several revisions. For example, homosexuality was listed as a disorder until 1974. People with borderline personalities may have been listed as schizophrenic in past versions. Post-traumatic stress disorder is one of the newer listings. A new label that has been under consideration is "self-defeating personality disorder." Have students debate whether this should be included as a disorder. Self-defeating personalities dig holes for themselves; they date people who are not good for them, not just once or twice but always; and they reject offers from people who try to help them. Students probably know someone who acts like this at times. But what if someone establishes a pattern of self-defeating behavior?

DISCUSS THE PHOTO

Approximately half of all patients admitted to mental hospitals are diagnosed as schizophrenic.

Points to Stress

One family factor that researchers have studied is called double-bind communication. This is when a parent expresses love and a sort of hostility at the same time. For example, a parent may say, "Why don't you ever tell me you love me? And when you do, you don't mean it. What's wrong with you?" These kinds of messages probably don't make us schizophrenic, but they certainly wear on us. (From a distance, however, this type of communication can be hilarious. A lot of sitcoms depict parents talking this way. Watch Jerry Seinfeld's show on TV.)

Unit 6 PSYCHOLOGICAL DISORDERS

▲ *This series of paintings by Louis Wain reflects a troubled personality. Wain was a British illustrator who became schizophrenic in middle age. As Wain's psychosis progressed, his cat paintings became highly abstract and fragmented. In many ways, Wain's paintings resemble the perceptual changes caused by psychedelic drugs such as mescaline and LSD. Recent research suggests that psychosis may, in fact, be the result of mind-altering changes in brain chemistry. (Derik Byes/Courtesy Guttman-Maclay Life Picture Service.)*

their aunt, after which the boys were denied supper and confined to their room for the remainder of the day. Neither had seen nor heard from their father for over 10 years, and the aunt died six years ago.

During the interview, Mr. W. answered no questions, but merely stared at the opposite wall. Every now and then he would jerk his head sideways and inhale sharply. He sat in a very peculiar posture, his right hand and arm held rigidly at a 45° angle, the left stiffly at his side. When he walked, his knees bent only slightly with each step, giving him a robotlike appearance. He was admitted to the hospital and given antipsychotic drugs.

After several days of observation and drug treatment, Mr. W. began to respond to direct questions, but did so in a monotone. He revealed that he believed himself to be controlled by magnetic fields beamed at him by the communists, and that he thought his wife and brother were working with them. Because of his severe motor problems, the diagnosis given was schizophrenia, catatonic type, with paranoid elements.

As you can see from the case study of Michael W., the home life of the schizophrenic can be very disturbed. We suspect that a bizarre family may be enough to tip the balance for people who are already potentially schizophrenic. But in far more cases the family is quite normal, things are very pleasant, other children seem to be fine, yet still one of them will develop the psychosis. From the available evidence, then, it seems clear that environmental factors are not a major cause of this disorder. They may contribute to its development, but only if a predisposition already exists.

ENRICHMENT

Ask students to find out if the brains of schizophrenics are structurally different than the brains of nonschizophrenics. There is some evidence that they *are* different.

ENRICHMENT

Have students find out the latest theories on the connection between dopamine and schizophrenia.

Chapter 18 MENTAL DISORDERS

Chemical Factors in Schizophrenia

Think back to the last time you were at a party with some good friends and everyone was sitting in a circle. When the discussion really got going, people were talking rapidly and were agitated; thoughts were moving *very fast*. When that was happening, the level of one of the chemicals that fires nerve cells in the brain was quite high, causing a speed of speech and thought that eventually would exhaust most people. This chemical is called **dopamine** (DOUGH-pa-mean) (Wong, 1985).

A major discovery about many schizophrenics is that they have abnormally high levels of dopamine in the brain (Bower, 1985; Snyder, 1980). This certainly can explain many of their thought problems. If thoughts are running through their heads at maximum speed hour after hour, day after day, this would cause confusion and eventually stupor from fatigue—which is just the way many schizophrenics act. Studies with animals show that drugs that increase the levels of dopamine far beyond normal produce bizarre behavior in the form of strange posturing and robotlike movements—again symptoms often seen with schizophrenics (Kokkinidis & Anisman, 1980). Finally, some schizophrenics get much better when they are given drugs that reduce dopamine levels. The only problem is that these same drugs can cause all kinds of side effects in some patients, including uncontrollable tremors (Breggin, 1983). Of importance here, though, is that scientists are on the right track. But they have not been able to refine the medication enough so that it works safely for most patients. We should add that some researchers feel that psychological problems can also cause the body to manufacture too much dopamine, so we are not limited only to a physical problem that can be cured by merely chemical means. Still, we are on our way toward solving one of life's most destructive disturbances.

Two additional points: (1) The rapidity of thought with the schizophrenic does not ever resemble that of the manic discussed earlier. Schizophrenics speak and act as if they are exhausted from too much thought. (2) The chemical defect in mood disorders does not involve dopamine. That chemical, as mentioned, is serotonin. There is some very subtle difference in these chemicals that we don't completely understand yet.

dopamine

The brain chemical present in excess in schizophrenics, which causes nerve cells to fire too rapidly and leads to thought and speech confusion.

Points to Stress

The dopamine theory is not as simple as it might seem. Increasing the level of dopamine may cause schizophrenic symptoms, but it doesn't necessarily follow that schizophrenics have high levels of dopamine. It is possible that schizophrenics have a *normal* dopamine level, but too many dopamine *receptors* in the brain.

FYI Amphetamines seem to raise one's dopamine level.

PERSONALITY DISORDERS

To avoid hopeless confusion, we have limited the previous discussion to disorders involving anxiety, guilt, conflicts, depression, and the like. Just for completeness, you should be aware of one additional category of people with problems, a group that has nothing in com-

ENRICHMENT

Here are some other types of personality disorders that you may want to have groups research: narcissistic, paranoid, schizoid, histrionic, avoidant, passive-aggressive.

Critical Thinking

"If you wanted to find genetic links to antisocial personality disorder, what direction might your research take?" Students might compare identical and fraternal twins; compare criminal records of adoptees and their biological relatives; compare the rate of alcoholism in adoptees and their biological relatives. Some studies have even looked at the effects of injected adrenaline in people who have antisocial personality disorder. The guess is that these people are born with less *ability* to be aroused and thus never learn guilt or shame. Even if this turns out to be the case, environment certainly plays its part (see Schachter and Latanè in **Suggested Readings**).

Points to Stress

It is possible, of course, to have more than one disorder. For example, many people with borderline personality disorder also tend to be diagnosed with major depression.

526

personality disorder

A disorder in which the person has formed a peculiar or unpleasant personality.

antisocial personality disorder

A personality disorder in which the person is in constant conflict with the law and seems to have no conscience.

sociopath

Same as antisocial personality disorder.

borderline personality disorder

Personality disorder marked by unstable emotions and relationships, dependency, and manipulative self-destructive behavior.

mon with the others discussed so far. These individuals do not fit into the categories we have mentioned. They are not out of touch with reality, so they are not psychotic, and they do not show the guilt or anxiety so common in other disorders. Instead, they seem to have formed peculiar and unpleasant personality patterns. For example, some are very secretive, some very self-centered and selfish, some suspicious all the time. Hence, we use the term **personality disorder** because their personalities are "off center."

Antisocial Personality Disorder

There are many personality disorders, but one in particular causes serious problems for society: the **antisocial personality disorder.** Originally, people with an antisocial personality were called *psychopaths*, a term you will still sometimes hear used. The label was given to those who committed crimes ranging from beating up little old ladies to committing ax murders.

A lack of conscience is central to this disorder. It is for this reason that the term **sociopath** is sometimes used, meaning that the behavior of these people toward society is clearly abnormal (*path* from "pathology," abnormal).

These people repeatedly come into conflict with the law and show little or no concern, guilt, or anxiety. Nothing in the way of drug or psychological treatment works to help them. They are very smooth and agreeable on the outside and will go along with almost any treatment that is suggested. They will cooperate, tell you they are getting better, thank you, and seem to be well. But as soon as they are released, they go right back to whatever their favorite crime happened to be.

In truth, we don't understand how these people got the way they are or what to do with them. For many, there is a family history of neglect and rough treatment. The parents are often alcoholic and abusive, but there must be millions of people over the years who have had such a background and didn't act this way. Sociopaths don't even abide by the rules usually followed by criminals. Most criminals have at least some standards. Measures of body chemistry and studies of genetic patterns have yielded nothing of any real significance regarding the origin of the sociopath's behavior.

Borderline Personality Disorder

The diagnosis of **borderline personality disorder** has only been around since 1980. Intense and unstable relationships with other people are a major characteristic. Borderline personalities are very dependent people, but they cannot admit this to themselves. So, they constantly test other people's concern and often sabotage their own relationships. They appear to be "clingy" and emotionally needy. However, as soon as the slightest thing fails to go their way, they become extremely angry with the other person, often insulting and belittling him or her. In addition, they frequently use self-destructive behavior to manipulate others. Thus, they may make suicide threats and attempts, or deliberately cut themselves, or purposely have accidents. It is as if they are so afraid of being abandoned that they are almost daring other people to do just that. Their emotions are also unstable, and they have trouble controlling their impulses. In some cases, perceptions and thoughts are quite distorted (Millon, 1981).

The causes of borderline personality are not yet clear. It does tend to run in families. However, because of the nature of this problem, it is hard to tell whether biology or learning is most involved. For instance, children who grow up with a borderline-personality parent will know very little about how to develop and maintain healthy relationships. Angry outbursts or threats of suicide when things don't go their way could come from imitating a parent who behaved that way. In other words, their early home life is so chaotic and emotionally charged that it is almost impossible to separate hereditary and environmental factors.

Borderline personalities are difficult to deal with in psychotherapy. Because they are so suspicious and manipulative, they have trouble developing a positive working relationship with a therapist. Consequently, they tend to switch from one therapist to another over and over again, rarely sticking with it long enough to be successful.

Points to Stress

When discussing borderline personalities, warn students (again!) not to assume that they suffer from this disorder. Some of the characteristics of borderline personalities seem very common, but the intensity of the emotions and the long history of self-destructive behavior are certainly not common. Borderline personalities are clingy and so on the *majority* of the time, not occasionally.

Comprehension Check

What type of disorder does a sociopath have? (*antisocial personality disorder*)

PSYCHOLOGY IN YOUR LIFE

Do You Need Help?

This question, as it stands, is simple enough to answer. Of course you do. So does everybody. The standards of perfection set up for all of us are something to work toward, but they cannot be attained. The closer the better, but you're still not perfectly normal. The important point, though, is that after reading a chapter like this, most people begin to worry that something might really be wrong with them. Since we don't know you personally, only you can get some kind of fix on how reasonable your problems are. What we *can* do, however, after years and years of experience, is go through some of the thoughts and feelings of adolescents that are so common that you should be able to relax a little about most of them.

For example, your body has by no means stabilized. All kinds of changes are going on, which may seem

(*continued on next page*)

DISCOVERY

If you have any kind of mental health center near your school, try to take a field trip there. No matter how much book knowledge students absorb, they may never overcome their misconceptions about mental illness without such a visit. Besides, it's fascinating. One misconception that students may have about the visit is that you will be able to walk through the wards and gawk at the patients. Not likely. However, state hospitals regularly conduct open commitment hearings to decide which patients can and cannot be released, and these cases are riveting. Perhaps you can arrange to attend one of these hearings. If you do attend, students will realize how essential the *DSM* is. Testimony regarding the diagnosis of mental illness must be linked to the *DSM*.

PSYCHOLOGY IN YOUR LIFE

Enrichment

Have students read a case study (an entire book) on a behavior disorder. These books are usually written by a therapist, a family member, or even the patient himself or herself. And students usually enjoy them. See **Teaching Master 18-7 Case Study** for an assignment sheet on this.

Reteaching Strategy

Have students complete in class activity #8 at the end of the chapter.

Reteaching Strategy

Have students complete the **Reteaching Worksheet** for this chapter located in the Teacher Resources.

The **Vocabulary Worksheet** may be completed by the class as a pretest for chapter concepts or used as a reteaching worksheet for those students needing additional review.

PSYCHOLOGY IN YOUR LIFE

Do You Need Help?

(continued from previous page) simple at first but which actually are major. Growth, for instance, involves a major hormonal upheaval. As a result, you will not feel quite right physically. Even if you are in good shape, follow all the rules, and have good coordination, your body doesn't seem to "fit" completely. This feeling is something like having a key that works in a lock but doesn't do so smoothly. You probably are not able to look in the mirror and see what you really want.

It is extremely hard for anyone to get social relationships and friendships to work out perfectly and smoothly. Add to this the fact that emotional chemistry and physical changes are running rampant during your age period, and you start to understand how friendships can appear and disappear in a matter of minutes no matter how intense or perfect they seemed to be. If you have one or two good friends for a reasonable amount of time, you're doing well.

The chances of feeling lonely, lost, or depressed for brief periods of time are very high. On the other hand, if you are subject to bouts of depression for two or three days at a time fairly often and can't even relate to a few friends, then you do have a problem and need someone to help. But when you try to analyze whether you have a serious problem, don't exaggerate. If you do have one, it can be handled, but the odds are that you don't. There is no way you can completely get away from feeling some loneliness and feeling not quite in step.

Most likely, adults are not going to feel totally comfortable around you. Many adults are not able to get their lives together either, and they may resent the lost years that you still have ahead of you. But the worries or concerns you have about relating to adults will simply disappear with physical age. And you belong to a different (not better) generation from your parents. Toleration in both directions is necessary; friction is at times inevitable.

Sexuality means trouble for every single person you will ever meet of any age beyond 12 or 13. There is a heavy toll carried by the pleasure it gives. For everyone—no matter whom—it also provides anxiety, confusion, awkwardness, guilt, feelings of emptiness, short depressions, and loneliness. If this is bothering you, trust us: it bothers everybody. It's part of the human condition.

Finally, in terms of being lost about where you are heading, try to compare yourself and your goals objectively with those of others. Don't just focus on the handful of students who seem to have their act together. Look around. More than half the students you see don't know where they are or where they are going for the time being.

If after reading this, you are still convinced that something is seriously wrong, you may be right. But it's not the end of the world. In fact, it is good to know it so early. We will discuss treatment and therapies in the next chapter.

VOCABULARY REVIEW

Before testing students on the contents of the chapter, you may want to review vocabulary terms that are especially important or confusing. Terms in this chapter that could require clarification are *anxiety disorder*, *dissociative disorders*, *mood disorders*, *psychosis*, and *personality disorder*.

Chapter 18 MENTAL DISORDERS

SUMMARY

1. Most people with mental disorders exhibit an exaggerated version of characteristics we all have. Symptoms include discomfort, inefficiency, and bizarreness. Such people often are inflexible and tend to find the environment threatening.

2. Anxiety disorders are characterized by apprehension and fear. With panic disorder, one has severe anxiety attacks unconnected to anything specific. In specific phobias, the fear is attached to a specific object or situation. With agoraphobia, fear is triggered by anything outside one's familiar home environment. An obsession is thinking constantly about a certain object, urge, or event. A compulsion is repeated ritualized behavior usually related to an obsession.

3. Somatoform disorders are characterized by bodily symptoms without any actual physical problem. Types include conversion disorder, in which the symptom symbolizes a psychological issue, and hypochondriasis or exaggerated concern with one's health.

4. In dissociative disorders, part of the person's memory system is separated from the remainder. In amnesia, the person forgets certain upsetting things. In fugue, the person forgets his or her current life and starts over elsewhere. With dissociative identity disorder, the person acts out conflicting desires, usually to be good and

bad, independently of one another.

5. Mood disorders involve disturbance in one's emotional state. Dysthymia is a moderate depression. Major depression is a severe, disabling depression. In mania, the person's mood is extremely elevated. Bipolar disorders involve both mania and depression. We suspect that both physical and psychological problems exist in mood disorders.

6. Psychotic disorders involve major disorganization of thought processes, hallucinations, that is, hearing or seeing things that are not there, and/or delusions, false beliefs. Schizophrenia, a psychotic disorder, is divided into three types: catatonic, paranoid, and undifferentiated.

7. Schizophrenia involves severely disabled thought processes and bizarre speech patterns. It usually appears in late adolescence or early adulthood. We suspect that it has a chemical or physical basis rather than psychological causes.

8. In personality disorders, people have formed peculiar and unpleasant personality patterns. The antisocial personality has no conscience and uses other people. Borderline personalities are dependent, unstable, and emotionally intense. They are demanding, suspicious, and manipulative in their relationships with others.

Wrapping It Up

The treatment of mental illness, discussed in the next chapter, has had a colorful history. In the old days superstitions prevailed. Atrocities were committed. Although we are now more "enlightened," many people with behavior disorders are still regarded as freaks. As teachers, we can hope that education will breed understanding and tolerance. In your own way, make a plea for this tolerance. This does not mean that we must be somber when discussing mental illness. Some of the case studies we hear about *are* funny, and we laugh and call the behaviors crazy—there's nothing wrong with that. If we agree that we're all a little crazy, maybe we're actually just laughing at ourselves.

SUGGESTED READINGS

▼ American Psychiatric Association. *DSM-IIIR Casebook.* Washington, D.C.: American Psychiatric Press, 1989.

▼ Barron, Judy and Sean Barron. *There's a Boy in Here.* New York: Simon & Schuster, 1992.

▼ Berger, Diane and Lisa. *We Heard the Angels of Madness.* New York: William Morrow, 1991.

▼ Bloom, Amy. *Come to Me: Short Stories.* New York: HarperCollins, 1993.

▼ Friedland, Bruce. *Personality Disorders.* New York: Chelsea, 1991.

▼ Keyes, Daniel. *Flowers for Algernon.* New York: Bantam Books, 1968.

▼ Kesey, Ken. *One Flew Over the Cuckoo's Nest.* New York: Viking, 1962.

▼ Kramer, Peter D. *Listening to Prozac: A Psychiatrist Explores Antidepressant Drugs and the*

Answers to Review Questions

1. e
2. d
3. a
4. b
5. c
6. false
7. false
8. true
9. false
10. true
11. delusions
12. word salad
13. clang associations
14. mania
15. bipolar
16. a
17. b
18. b
19. c
20. d
21. c
22. d

VOCABULARY

Diagnostic and Statistical Manual of Mental Disorders IV
anxiety disorder
anxiety
panic disorder
phobic disorder
specific phobia
agoraphobia
obsession
compulsion
obsessive-compulsive disorder
somatoform disorder
conversion disorder
hypochondriasis
dissociative disorders

amnesia
selective forgetting
fugue
dissociative identity disorder
mood disorders
dysthymic disorder
major depression
mania
flight of ideas
bipolar disorder
serotonin
psychosis
thought disorder
hallucinating
delusion
schizophrenia
word salad

clang associations
catatonic schizophrenia
paranoid schizophrenia
undifferentiated schizophrenia
psychotic episodes
dopamine
personality disorder
antisocial personality disorder
sociopath
borderline personality disorder

Review Questions

Match the symptoms below with the appropriate anxiety disorder on the right.

1. An anxiety attack—but not directed at a specific object
2. Extreme anxiety when a dog is seen
3. Thoughts that won't go away
4. Unable to leave a familiar environment
5. Repeated actions

a. obsession
b. agoraphobia
c. compulsion
d. specific phobia
e. panic disorder

Remaking of the Self. New York: Viking, 1993.

▼ Podvoll, Edward M. *The Seduction of Madness.* New York: HarperCollins, 1990.

▼ Schachter S. and Latanè L. "Crime, cognition, and the autonomic nervous system." In D. Levine ed. *Nebraska Symposium on*

Motivation. Lincoln: University of Nebraska Press, 1964.

▼ Styron, William. *Darkness Visible: A Memoir of Madness.* New York: Random House, 1990.

▼ Torrey, E. Fuller. *Nowhere to Go: The Tragic Odyssey of the Homeless Mentally Ill.* New York: HarperCollins, 1989.

True/False

6. A dissociative disorder can be referred to as the common cold of mental illness.
7. Psychogenic amnesia refers to a biological inability to remember.
8. Someone suffering from selective forgetting still retains abilities and skills learned before the onset of the amnesia.
9. A person who suffers from dissociative identity disorder can also be labeled schizophrenic.
10. In a dissociative identity case, it is possible for one personality to be aware of another.

Fill in the blanks; answer on a separate sheet of paper. (An answer may consist of more than one word.)

11. Someone who thinks he is Napoleon is having ___?___ .
12. Schizophrenics often mix words together, which is called ___?___ .
13. Schizophrenics also seem to chant in a rhythmic pattern; these patterns often include ___?___ .
14. The "up" part of an extreme mood swing would be called ___?___ .
15. A person suffering from major up and down mood swings would be suffering from a ___?___ disorder.

Multiple Choice

16. A high level of serotonin might cause a person to become
    a. manic.   c. withdrawn.
    b. depressive.   d. dissociative.
17. The fact that the onset of schizophrenia usually occurs during late adolescence suggests that the cause of schizophrenia may be
    a. psychological. c. learned.
    b. biological.   d. easily prevented.
18. High levels of dopamine may trigger
    a. a mood disorder. d. all of the above.
    b. schizophrenia.   e. a and b only.
    c. a bipolar disorder.
19. A sociopath would most likely have
    a. a high level of serotonin.
    b. a high level of dopamine.
    c. abusive parents.
    d. all of the above.
20. Someone with a personality disorder would probably exhibit high levels of
    a. depression.   c. anxiety.
    b. guilt.   d. none of the above.
21. People who become blind because of a conversion disorder
    a. can suddenly see again when taught to relax.
    b. are usually faking their impairment.
    c. actually cannot see.
    d. have retinal damage.
22. Borderline personalities
    a. are easily angered.
    b. tend to be too dependent.
    c. are often self-destructive.
    d. are all of the above.

Notes on Discussion Questions

1. Listed here are possible abnormal behaviors, followed by situations where the behaviors might be considered normal:

a. Talking to yourself—while praying

b. Walking around nearly nude—at the beach

c. Gambling every day—if you always win

d. Standing in the middle of the street waving your arms wildly—and you are a traffic cop.

2. You may be surprised at students' answers. Some may argue that yes, the person should seek help since the alcohol is clearly in control. Others may argue that no, the person only uses alcohol on weekends, it doesn't disrupt the person's life. The best answer would take into account the fact that drinking alcohol is illegal for people under 21 years of age. Other things to consider are: How does the person react to the alcohol? Does the person become violent toward himself or herself or others? If so, the person should definitely seek help. If not, perhaps the person does not need professional help. The person may still need to quit drinking for other obvious reasons—damage to the liver and so on—but profesional help *may* not be necesary.

3. This is an interesting question to discuss in class. The crux of the issue seems to be this: can psychiatrists accurately determine the state of a person's mental health? They may be able to determine mental health

532

Discussion Questions

1. Other than violent behaviors, list five behaviors that our society would consider abnormal. Then, for each of the five behaviors, describe a situation where the abnormal behavior *might* be considered normal. For example, eating another human is certainly regarded as abnormal, but if this happened three weeks after a plane crash in which the person had died and the survivors were stranded, the behavior *could* be construed by many as normal.

2. If a high school student has been drinking alcohol for a year and has gotten drunk *every* weekend—but only on weekends—should this person get help from a professional? Yes? No? Depends? Explain.

3. Courts today still sometimes use the verdict of "not guilty by reason of insanity." The logic here is that the person was unaware of his or her actions and should not be held responsible. Most likely, the person who is awarded this verdict will be committed to a mental institution until psychiatrists determine that the person is "sane"—at which time the person will be released. Do you agree that this type of verdict should be allowed, or should "insane" criminals be treated just like any other criminals? Explain.

4. Why would it be unlikely that a person suffering from a personality disorder would be found "not guilty by reason of insanity"? Explain.

5. Describe a specific phobia that you have. As noted in the chapter, this specific phobia is probably the result of learning. You may not have ever thought about it, but make several guesses as to how you learned this specific phobia.

6. If a person supposedly suffering from dissociative identity disorder committed a felony and his or her lawyer pleaded not guilty by reason of insanity, what are several ways that you might be able to determine whether the alleged criminal is truly suffering from the disorder or faking it? Explain.

Activities

1. Back in the 1960s, legislators decided that they wanted to shift the emphasis from large state-run mental institutions to local mental health centers. As a result, thousands of hospitalized mentally ill patients were eventually let out into the community. One of the problems of this deinstitutionalization process was that communities were not prepared to handle all these patients. Do some research on: (a) the original intentions of this deinstitutionalization; (b) the problems that arose as a result; and (c) what solutions are being proposed today. After you organize this information into a report, discuss which solution you support and why.

2. One of the most controversial verdicts of "not guilty by reason of insanity" involved John Hinckley after he shot President Reagan on national television. Research the case. Find out: (a) the nature of Hinckley's mental illness; (b) the insanity defense used by his lawyers; (c) the changes that have occurred

on a short-term basis, but can they predict future mental health? Even on a short-term basis, can psychiatrists avoid being duped by patients who fake mental illness?

4. People with personality disorders are in touch with reality. They understand the consequences of their actions. They simply have no conscience to guide their actions.

5. Students need not be too descriptive about their phobias. Descriptions alone may get their palms sweating.

6. You might measure the person's brain waves with an electroencephalograph (EEG). There seems to be evidence that each personality of a dissociative identity disorder evokes unique EEG patterns. You might also try other methods of measuring brain activity—like positron emission tomography (PET) scans or computerized tomography (CT) scans.

Notes on Activities

1. Students should have no difficulty finding information on this topic. Tell them to consider contacting a mental institution for information.

2. Again, students should have no difficulty finding information on this topic.

3. Students may want to add other phobias to the ones already listed in the activity. They can refer to the **In Focus** box on phobias for ideas. Also, they may want to add an "other" category.

4. Since this section includes three activities that require research, consider spending a class period in the library so that students can gather information.

5. This could make a good cooperative-learning exercise.

6. Warn students not to go too far with their mental illness. Otherwise, the entries become so bizarre and unintelligible that they lack conflict and are uninteresting.

since then in the types of verdicts allowed—for example, the verdict of "guilty but insane." Also, include your reactions. Should Hinckley ever be allowed freedom, given his verdict? Do you agree with the changes in verdicts that have occurred? Explain.

3. Ask three of your teachers if you can use five minutes of class time to survey the classes about phobias. Copy the following onto a sheet of paper and photocopy enough copies for the three classes:

Phobias Survey

Use the scale below to rate how anxious you usually become around the following items.

1	2	3	4	5
NOT ANXIOUS	NOT VERY ANXIOUS	SOMEWHAT ANXIOUS	VERY ANXIOUS	EXTREMELY ANXIOUS

Place a number from the scale next to each item below.

___ 1. Spiders	___ 6. Snakes	___ 11. Giving speeches
___ 2. Heights	___ 7. Dogs	___ 12. Open spaces
___ 3. Elevators	___ 8. Tall buildings	___ 13. Tests
___ 4. Water	___ 9. Closed spaces	___ 14. Cats
___ 5. Knives	___ 10. Needles	___ 15. Crossing bridges

(Notice that we didn't list just 13 items—fuel for another phobia.) Tally your results and create a table.

Place the phobia that received the highest average rating at the top, and work your way down to the phobia that received the lowest average rating. Transfer your table onto a poster and include appropriate captions—then put the poster up in class.

If you're ambitious, create another chart that shows the differences between males' and females' phobias. In this case, you would have each person mark "male" or "female" at the top of his or her rating sheet.

4. Another category of disorders not mentioned in the chapter is called "childhood disorders." Do some research on one of the following childhood disorders and write a report: hyperactivity *or* infantile autism. Focus on: (a) common characteristics; (b) how commonly the disorder occurs; (c) symptoms; (d) possible causes; (e) effective treatments. Some of the treatments used, especially for autism, are controversial. Discuss your reactions toward these treatments.

5. Pick three characters from movies, TV, or books who seem to suffer from mental disorders. Assume that you are a psychologist who has been hired to render a diagnosis of each character. What are your three diagnoses? Provide ample evidence, citing specific scenes or behaviors that the characters exhibit.

6. Write an extended journal entry (about three or four pages) from the point of view of someone suffering from a mental disorder. Decide beforehand whether this "character" knows or suspects that he or she has a mental disorder. Other related options: (a) write several short journal entries; (b) write a letter instead; (c) write a monologue—what someone might say to a therapist, for example; (d) write an extended dialogue in which one of the characters suffers from a mental disorder.

DISCUSS THE PHOTO

Ask students, "If you had a phobia, would you prefer attending a group session like the one pictured or a private session?"

In group therapy problems are aired with others. In return the group and therapist offer support and suggestions.

534

PSYCHOLOGY AND YOU RESOURCES

A variety of resources are available in the Psychology and You *supplementary material. In addition, there are a number of additional resources listed to enhance your lesson plans.*

Masters
▼ 19-1A Learning Goals
▼ 19-1B Answers to Learning Goals
▼ 19-2 Cognitive Distortions
▼ 19-3 Cognitive Diary

Student Worksheets
▼ Vocabulary Worksheet
▼ Independent Practice Worksheet
▼ Enrichment Worksheet
▼ Reteaching Worksheet

Test Bank
▼ Tests A and B

Multimedia
▼ *The Brain* Videotape Module #27
▼ **Mindscope** Exercise 20
▼ Psychology Videodisc

Student Workbooks

PACING CHART

Complete Coverage

Day 1: Assign the first three sections of the chapter before class. Evaluate the differences between the various types of mental health workers. Focus discussion on the methods of psychoanalysis. Assign "Humanistic Therapy" and "Behavioral Therapy" for Day 2.

Day 2: When discussing humanistic theory, focus on the terms client-centered, non-directive, and unconditional positive regard. Concentrate on systematic desensitization, aversive conditioning, and the token economy when reviewing behavioral therapy. Have students read the next two sections for homework.

Day 3: Focus discussion on the concepts of irrational ideas and internalized sentences. Then review the two purposes of group therapy, pointing out the pitfalls of encounter groups. Assign for homework an activity from the text or wrap requiring students to apply one or more of the therapies they have learned about to a particular situation. Have

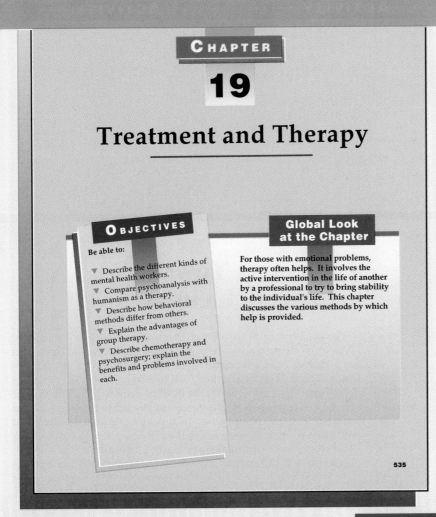

CHAPTER

19

Treatend and Therapy

OBJECTIVES

Be able to:

▼ Describe the different kinds of mental health workers.

▼ Compare psychoanalysis with humanism as a therapy.

▼ Describe how behavioral methods differ from others.

▼ Explain the advantages of group therapy.

▼ Describe chemotherapy and psychosurgery; explain the benefits and problems involved in each.

Global Look at the Chapter

For those with emotional problems, therapy often helps. It involves the active intervention in the life of another by a professional to try to bring stability to the individual's life. This chapter discusses the various methods by which help is provided.

535

INTRODUCING THE CHAPTER

One of the goals you want to accomplish early in this chapter is to communicate that there's nothing wrong with seeing a therapist. One way to achieve this is to solicit students' preconceptions about *therapy:* "What is the first thing you think of when you hear the word therapy? What kinds of problems do therapists treat? Do people see therapists only when there's a problem? (A couple may simply want to *improve* communication skills in their marriage, for example.) What is a typical session like?" Clear up any misconceptions—for example, clients most likely do not lie on a black couch—and stress that there is nothing wrong with seeing a therapist.

LEAD-OFF ACTIVITY

The chapter includes several exchanges between therapists (or analysts) and clients (or patients). Have students come to the front of the room to role-play the situations. All they have to do is read the parts. Afterward, have students work in groups to discuss the similarities and differences that they can identify about each approach. The labels alone, therapist versus analyst and patient versus client, should provide key insights. Based on these exchanges, which approach do students prefer?

students read the rest of the chapter for Day 4.

Day 4: Discuss the students' homework in relation to the commonalities and effectiveness of therapy. Review the uses of chemotherapy, ECT, and psychosurgery.

Day 5: Discuss the controversy over the term "mental illness" before giving the Chapter Review quiz.

In Brief

Day 1: Differentiate between the different types of mental health workers. Discuss the components of psychoanalytic therapy.

Day 2: Review the main characteristics of humanistic, behavioral, cognitive behavioral, and group therapies.

Day 3: Discuss chemotherapy and the ethical considerations regarding ECT and psychosurgery. Give the Chapter Review quiz.

Unit 6 PSYCHOLOGICAL DISORDERS

ATTITUDES TOWARD MENTAL ILLNESS

People typically are afraid of anything odd or unknown. Historically, reactions have been most violent, however, to those with some kind of emotional disturbance because the origin of the problem is often unclear. Before the 1700s, mental problems were thought to be the result of influence by the devil or demons. Behavior such as hearing voices or speaking strangely usually led to gross torture and hanging. In some communities, such people were boiled alive, and their parts were hung on posts in the public square (Deutsch, 1946). When there were outbreaks of disease, such as the Black Death plague in the 1300s, mental patients were blamed and "extremities were jerked from the . . . sockets, feet were torn from limbs, thumbs were squashed, and skin was torn with red-hot pincers" (Anderson, 1970).

With the arrival of the age of science, a search began for some method of treating those with serious mental problems. This new atmosphere was triggered by the work of a French physician, **Philippe Pinel** (Phil-LEAP Pea-NELL), who was put in charge of a hospital for the insane during the early 1700s. With great fanfare he entered the hospital, which was really a dungeon, and freed the "patients" who were chained to the wall. Given their freedom, they did not go on a rampage and pillage the town but showed signs of improvement. This was the beginning of humane treatment.

People in the town were very suspicious of Pinel as a result. When a cholera epidemic broke out later, they blamed him for poisoning the water supply, and an angry mob tried to kill him. The story has a romantic, but true, ending. Pinel was rescued from the mob by some of those he had freed (Reisman, 1966).

Even today, mental problems are still one of the most feared maladies for people to be around, but attitudes have changed a fair amount regarding therapy or treatment. Therapy for those with such problems as phobias, moderate depression, and the like is so common that a person having treatment is no longer considered all that unusual (Garfield, 1981).

TYPES OF MENTAL HEALTH WORKERS

Many people use the terms *psychologist* and *psychiatrist* without being aware that these are different occupations. Before discussing therapies, we should make the differences clear.

DISCOVERY

If you have a school psychologist, invite this person to class to talk about the types of classes and training involved in graduate school. This person can also describe his or her primary duties as a school psychologist.

Chapter 19 TREATMENT AND THERAPY

Psychologists

Psychologists who work directly with people, seeking to assist them with their problems, are called either *counseling* or *clinical psychologists*. **Counseling psychologists** deal mostly with people who do not have formal classifications of mental disturbance. Typically, they work with people who have marital or family problems or general problems with living. **Clinical psychologists** perform all the tasks of the counseling psychologists, but some of them also work in mental hospitals and clinics with "classified" patients.

Although many counseling psychologists have a doctor of education (Ed. D.) degree, the typical clinical psychologist has a doctor of philosophy (Ph. D.) degree. After graduating from college, members of both groups continue in graduate school for an additional four to five years, studying psychology. Clinical psychologists must also have a year's internship in a mental health facility. Most states require an additional one to three years of supervised training, so the total winds up being six to nine years before it is all over.

Psychiatrists

Psychiatrists are medical doctors who spend four years as graduate students learning about physical medical problems rather than mental ones. After this general medical training, they can specialize in the mental health field. Training in their specialization can include one to three years of hospital residency—which resembles an apprenticeship. The most striking difference between psychiatrists and psychologists is that the former can prescribe medicine. As a result, most psychologists downplay the role of medicine for the average person in treatment, and most psychiatrists do just the opposite. There probably is something to say for both sides. Your authors are psychologists, so, if you pick up any bias in how we cover the material, it is not intended—but we are probably right!

Other Mental Health Personnel

Other mental health personnel include **psychiatric social workers**, who usually hold advanced degrees in social work. They help patients find jobs or housing and assist families, among others, in dealing with problems. **Psychiatric nurses** are registered nurses with special education in psychiatric medicine.

In the early years, mental health workers were mostly physicians (medical doctors) or ministers. Ministers today are still active in the field, but we can't specify their education or training because it varies so much from one individual to another.

counseling psychologists

Psychologists who deal mostly with problems not fitting into the formal classifications of mental disturbance.

clinical psychologists

Psychologists who deal with emotional disturbances of any kind; may work with classified mental patients.

psychiatrists

Medical doctors with special training in mental disorders.

psychiatric social workers

Mental health workers with a degree in social work; help patients and families deal with problems.

psychiatric nurses

Registered nurses with special education in psychiatric medicine.

Comprehension Check

Ask students to answer *true* or *false* to the following statements. (1) Psychologists can only prescribe antidepressant drugs. *(false)* (2) Psychiatric nurses can prescribe medicine. *(false)* (3) One can become a psychologist after four years of college. *(false)* (4) Psychiatrists are medical doctors. *(true)* (5) Clinical psychologists must serve as interns for a year. *(true)*

Points to Stress

As noted, psychoanalysis is costly, especially if free association is employed. Today, many analysts will be more directive in order to save time and money.

Points to Stress

Just as patients transfer their feelings onto the therapist, therapists sometimes experience countertransference, which means that they develop feelings toward the patient. For example, the patient may remind the therapist of an old friend. The therapist, then, needs to separate those feelings during treatment.

Comprehension Check

What emerges from free association? *(desires in the unconscious)*

538

---

psychotherapies

Broad term for any method used to try to help people with emotional and psychological problems.

psychoanalysis

Therapy practiced by followers of Freud, who analyze the psyche via the unconscious.

▲ *The world's most famous couch—it was here that Sigmund Freud had his patients recline as they explored the unconscious.*

538

Psychotherapists—The Blanket Term

In the next sections, we discuss the major methods used to try to help people with their problems. All these techniques are called **psychotherapies,** a term meaning that there is an attempt to relieve (therapy) problems of the *psyche* or mind. *Psychotherapist* is a broad term for any professional who tries to help others psychologically. Thus, a psychotherapist can be a psychologist, a psychiatrist, a social worker, a minister, or a psychiatric nurse. In each of the different methods (psychotherapies) used, the goal is for the therapist actively to help the person change his or her views that are causing trouble, to help reduce tension, to remove certain behavior patterns or habits that are causing trouble, or just to provide a source of support in a time of trouble.

PSYCHOANALYTIC TREATMENT

Psychoanalysis (analysis of the psyche or mind) is a very symbolic and complicated treatment. It usually involves from three to five hours of treatment per week over a period of years. Thus, it is reserved for those who have quite a bit of money. Its method is based on the theory of the psychiatrist Sigmund Freud.

The Freudian system focuses on *anxiety* as the main problem people face. According to this theory, as you may remember from Chapter 14, anxiety arises from deep-seated animal impulses that we all have. Thus, we have strong sexual and aggressive impulses that we want to act out, but since such expression is taboo, we live in constant anxiety that our impulses will break loose. And we suffer guilt whenever we partially act out the desires. This guilt in turn produces more anxiety.

These desires operate at the unconscious level, causing endless battles within the self. The self is caught between the animal desires, which go all the way back to childhood, and the conscience, which has, over the years, developed to try to prevent these behaviors.

The animal desires are viewed as a physical force within the person. This physical force is trying to be heard, and its voice can get louder and more demanding as it seeks expression. But since it is operating at the unconscious level, we are not aware of it. The psychoanalytic theory claims that some of the unconscious energy is released and can appear as symbolic dreams. On occasion, it is freed enough actually to express itself in the acts we perform. But most of the time it stays bottled up, building greater force, which increases anxiety. It is the task of the psychoanalyst to help the patient free some of this energy in a safe form.

DISCOVERY

See the wraparound material for Chapter 14 for a variety of activities on psychoanalysis and the unconscious.

Free Association

Free association is a major technique of psychoanalysis. The process involves the patient saying *whatever* comes to mind, no matter how disconnected or unimportant the material might seem. The theory behind this is that since desires in the unconscious are seeking escape, they will often hook themselves onto what at first might seem innocent sentences. For instance, the male patient might claim that he wants to *tell* his parent something. Instead, he says, "I want to *kill* my parent." This "slip of the tongue" is the unconscious impulse escaping. Freudians believe that the longer the patient talks, the greater will be the amount of information coming from the unconscious. The therapist then points out to the patient the kinds of things that are being said, asks what they might mean, offers interpretations, and in this way puts the patient more in control of those impulses. In other words, the psychoanalysts believe they are allowing inner conflicts to come out, be explored in safety, and be resolved.

Transference

Another important aspect of psychoanalytic treatment is called **transference,** meaning that the patients transfer their emotional conflicts of earlier years onto the therapist. Since the therapist is emotionally neutral and is not personally part of any of the patients' conflicts, the therapist has no ax to grind one way or the other; he or she is emotionally objective. So, here lies the crux of the treatment: since the therapist is neutral, whatever the patient claims about the therapist is made up by the patient's unconscious trying to find expression. If patients can recognize this behavior for what it is, they will see that the therapist is being blamed for something he or she had no part in. As a result, the patient's inner conflicts become visible. Once they are visible, this provides an opportunity to deal with them "out in the open," so to speak, rather than hidden where they can cause us grief without our understanding the source. The following is a condensed excerpt that illustrates the basic principle of transference:

Patient: I don't feel well today. I had a headache and I was going to stay in bed.

Analyst: You really didn't want to come in.

Patient: Yes, you might say that. I had a bad night, and I dreamed that I was falling and falling—off a building, you know—and I couldn't find anything to grab hold of.

Analyst: You feel like you might be losing control of the situation?

Patient: Well, of course. That's true. But I don't need a dream to tell me that. So I had a dream, so what?

Chapter 19 TREATMENT AND THERAPY

free association

The process of saying whatever comes to mind; uncovers the unconscious in psychoanalysis.

transference

The process in which the patient transfers emotional conflicts of earlier years onto the therapist.

Journal Topic

Have students free-write for a few minutes about their reaction to some key terms. This process is similar to free association; they should not worry about grammar, punctuation, or spelling. You may want to break their writing into two to three minute segments, supplying a new question or word each time. Students hear the word or question and just write whatever comes to mind. Possible starters: (1) tell me about your parents; (2) sixth grade; (3) secrets. You don't need to supply any words at all, of course, but they might be helpful. Afterward, discuss the process. Did the writing take students in directions that surprised them? Did any "hidden" material come to the surface? (You need not probe the content of this.)

Before discussing Rogers's nondirective therapy, conduct a role-playing activity. One person should be given a hypothetical problem to talk about. For example, her parents always fight, or a relationship is breaking up, and so on. Be sure that the problem is not a real one for the students involved. The other person should respond like he normally would in such a situation. This will probably involve advice, questions, rebuttals, and so on. Then discuss the things that a listener should and should not do in such a situation. Is it OK to offer advice? Should the listener recount his or her own story about a similar problem? Finally, discuss Rogers's method of listening and contrast this with the methods discussed in class. Once students understand Rogers's ideas,

Discussion

"Do you consider yourself to be a good listener?" Ask students to provide evidence, and then discuss Rogers's approach to listening.

DISCUSS THE PHOTO

Contrast this picture with Freud's couch presented earlier.

Critical Thinking

"As you might guess, a client-centered therapist rarely, if ever, offers advice. What's wrong with advice?" Advice can be poor, which does no one any good. And advice can be good, which makes the client dependent on others for solutions, rather than using his or her own resources. Note that these ideas represent one philosophy about therapy—and not everyone agrees with it, of course.

540

Unit 6 PSYCHOLOGICAL DISORDERS

▲ *Traditional therapy involves support and reassurance as a key ingredient in the healing process.*

humanistic therapy

Therapy that emphasizes the individual's own ability to heal himself or herself with some assistance.

client-centered therapy

Rogers's humanistic approach; reflects belief that the client and therapist are partners in therapy.

540

Analyst: [*silence*].

Patient: No comment about that? You should say something, you know. [*silence*]. Well, why shouldn't you say something? You know I come here endlessly—for what? I feel anxious right now and you say nothing. I feel like I'm losing control, just like in the dream, and when I come in here it just gets worse. So, why should I come? You don't know what it's like.

Analyst: You seem rather angry with me.

Patient: [*silence*]. Well, shouldn't I be? Angry, I mean? I keep trying to get myself straightened out and you just sit there—like a lump. So know-it-all and pompous.

Analyst: Do your feelings seem familiar? Do I remind you of someone?

Patient: Now let's not start that crap.

Analyst: [*silence*].

Patient: Well, OK. Sure. Who cares? Yes—yes, you remind me of my father. Isn't that beautiful? But you really have a lot in common. Every time I started to do something, there he was, like some kind of god, ready to jump all over me.

HUMANISTIC THERAPY

You may have felt when you read the previous section that the psychoanalyst lives in a pretty gloomy world regarding the human condition. We can't say that this view of the human is incorrect. Still, there are other theories that take the opposite approach. These other therapies are based on the principle that people have within themselves the potential to know where they are heading. Eventually they will be able to reach this potential and blossom like a flower. Thus, there is no unconscious filled with baser desires. It is the therapist's function to bring out the best in people, a "best" that is already in us from the beginning but that needs to be freed. These therapies are called **humanistic** because they emphasize the power within the individual human to control his or her own fate and movement toward fulfillment. In the sections that follow, we will cover the major therapeutic methods in this area.

Client-Centered Therapy

The term **client-centered therapy** gives a clue to the orientation of this approach. To begin with, note the word *client*. This term means something very different from the term *patient*. Humanists have no

role-play the same situation with the listener this time using Rogers's technique. The situation may seem less natural this time, since everyone is aware of what is supposed to happen. In fact, even in a real situation, the listener may initially feel that simply mirroring responses is artificial, that it is a game. Point out, however, that if the listener sincerely cares about the other person, this artificiality will soon fade. Remember, the main purpose of mirroring responses is to show the other person that you're listening and to provide a nonjudgmental atmosphere.

---

patients, only clients, because to them the word *client* conveys a working relationship in which the two (therapist and client) are partners or coworkers working toward a common goal. *Patient* always has a one-above, one-below feeling to it. The client-centered approach, which is most closely associated with psychologist Carl Rogers, has also been called Rogerian therapy, or **nondirective therapy.** The word *nondirective* is designed to convey the idea that these therapists do not prod or push (direct) the clients, but instead let them decide for themselves what is important to be talking about and in which direction the therapy should be going.

nondirective therapy

Same as client-centered therapy

Points to Stress

Nondirective listening seems natural, but it's not. It requires discipline and hard work. Conduct the above **Demonstration** to convey this point.

Client-Centered Therapy.

IN FOCUS   A therapist may show he or she is listening by nodding, asking for clarification, and paraphrasing the client's words.

IN FOCUS   **Client-Centered Therapy**

The therapist's primary role in client-centered therapy, according to Carl Rogers, is to listen actively to the client in a nonjudgmental way. Also, the therapist should provide unconditional positive regard. Together, these factors provide a safe environment for the client, and in time, the client will shed the layers of defenses that he or she has created.

I SHOULDN'T TALK SO MUCH. PEOPLE TELL ME I TALK TO MUCH...

MY FATHER USED TO TELL ME TO SPEAK UP. SO I TALK A LOT...

I'M AFRAID PEOPLE DON'T LISTEN TO ME BECAUSE THEY DON'T LIKE ME —

I'M ALWAYS SAYING THE WRONG THING.

I GUESS I SHOULDN'T WORRY SO MUCH ABOUT WHAT PEOPLE THINK. I'M A GOOD PERSON. I HAVE IMPORTANT THINGS TO SAY...

What are some ways in which a therapist can show that he or she is listening actively?

DEMONSTRATION

Some students will be skeptical of the power of paraphrasing. They may perceive it as a game. Point out that without unconditional positive regard, it *will* be a game. The therapist needs genuinely to accept the client in order for this type of therapy to be effective. You can sometimes convince skeptics that paraphrasing works by using it in class during a discussion. What is the result of this paraphrasing? It creates an open atmosphere in which people feel free to participate.

Points to Stress

Rewording the client's feelings is key in client-centered therapy. This is sometimes called paraphrasing, and as a teacher, you are probably an expert at it. The beauty of paraphrasing is that you avoid being judgmental, at least verbally, and you show in very practical terms that you are listening. In turn, the client should open up.

Comprehension Check

What is the most crucial thing a humanistic therapist must provide for patients? *(unconditional positive regard)*

unconditional positive regard

A principle of humanistic therapy in which the client's feelings and thoughts are accepted for whatever they are; Carl Rogers's term.

The technique of client-centered therapy rests on the assumption that each of us aims toward living a meaningful life. To reach that state, we must accept ourselves for what we are, not for what others may think we should be. Since we are basically good, the humanists feel this is safe to do. Disturbed behavior, then, arises from worrying too much about the mismatch between what our inner selves are telling us and what others claim things should be like. Therefore, the therapist helps clients to clarify and accept inner forces and directions.

What if the direction one is going in is wrong? This supposedly results from a distorted environment blocking the inner forces for good. So, according to the humanistic theory, distressed people will be able, over time in therapy, to see for themselves that they are on the wrong track.

In the actual therapy, the therapist acts as a mirror that is held up to the client, a mirror that tries to reflect what the client is saying, *not* trying to put interpretations on the statements. Atmosphere is crucial: the therapist must provide a safe, nonjudgmental environment so the client can freely explore problems. So, the therapist reflects on and rephrases the client's own feelings and thoughts. You can see this in the small excerpt of dialogue that follows:

Client: I don't feel well today. I had a headache and I was going to stay in bed.

Therapist: You just didn't feel like coming today?

Client: Yes, you might say that. I had a bad night and I dreamed that I was falling and falling—off a building, you know—and I couldn't find anything to grab hold of.

Therapist: It sounds like that dream really bothered you and you feel insecure or afraid.

Unconditional Positive Regard

One final point about this treatment method: the critical thing that the therapist is to provide is called **unconditional positive regard.** This term means that the client's thoughts, feelings, hopes, and desires are to be accepted for what they are—a part of the growing person. The people themselves are not to be judged. Obviously, a client who wants to kill someone is not holding an acceptable goal, but the Rogerians maintain that the *feeling* can be accepted as part of the person, even though the idea itself must be rejected. So, there are no conditions on acceptance, and clients are free to talk, to listen to themselves, and to grow (Meador & Rogers, 1973).

This method of treatment may still seem a little vague to you. Basically, the therapist sits and listens, then rewords and reflects what the client is saying. The client "hears" himself or herself

DISCOVERY

The skills inherent in nondirective listening are so practical that you can have students try to use it with friends. Warn them, however, that this type of listening is not easy. It requires uninterrupted, concentrated attention. It's exhausting. For prac- tice, ask students to write (double-spaced) a short fictional dialogue. Collect the papers and pass them back to students other than the writers. Students should fill in appropriate paraphrased comments.

---

through the therapist's words. Over time, then, the client is talking to his or her inner self through the therapist. And since the client is basically good, eventually the right road will be discovered.

BEHAVIORAL THERAPY

Behavioral therapy involves techniques designed to bring about changes in people's behavior by using principles of learning. While the goals are the same as those of other therapies, its philosophy is different. Behavioral therapists believe that most mental disorders are not complex problems but instead are the result of unacceptable behaviors learned over a period of years. Both "normality" and "abnormality" are learned. Thus, whatever symptom the person has is not from some deep-seated problem but is simply the result of learning poor habits or responses to problems. Behavioral therapists say basically that if someone is afraid of elevators, it doesn't make any difference where the problem came from; instead, let's just get rid of the fear and ignore its origin, whatever that might be. We will bring about a relearning to reduce the fear.

This type of treatment is rapid (usually a matter of a few months) and highly effective for dealing with problems that center on some kind of specific fear or bad habit. It is not as useful with issues that are quite complex, such as friction between members of a family. In

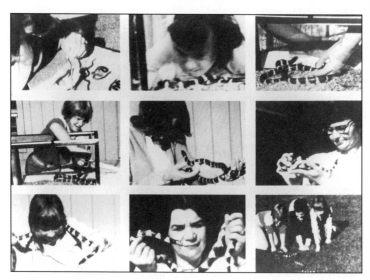

▲ These photographs show models interacting with snakes. In an attempt to over-come their fears, people with snake phobias watch the models handling the snakes.

Chapter 19 TREATMENT AND THERAPY

behavioral therapy

Therapy that uses principles of learning to alter the person's actions or behavior.

Journal Topic

"When I have a problem, I _____." Students usu-ally don't like to read their journal entries aloud, but you can probably get them to discuss this issue in general terms. Are their methods for solving prob-lems similar to the thera-pists' approaches present-ed in the chapter? Do they turn *in* (becoming quiet, wandering off alone) or *out* (talking to people) when they have problems?

DISCUSS THE PHOTO

See Chapter 18 for a list of other phobias. How would you use systematic desensitization to over-come some of these fears?

DISCOVERY

Ask students to make a list of fears that they would like to overcome. Have them make a hierarchy for attacking any *one* of those fears. What would be a safe first step? Step two would be a bit less safe, and so on. The activity is meant only to clarify the theory of desensitization. In actual therapy, relaxation would be taught at each step.

ENRICHMENT

Students usually enjoy researching uses of aversive conditioning. Some of it is quite controversial. For example, not only might alcoholics be given medication that nauseates them but they may be subjected to electric shocks.

Connections

As noted in the wraparound material for Chapter 16, the psychological craving for drugs after withdrawal can be reduced through systematic desensitization.

Points to Stress

The opposite of systematic desensitization is implosion therapy, where the person is flooded with the object or situation he or she fears. Needless to say, this can often be dangerous.

Points to Stress

Systematic desensitization may work simply by watching others face what we fear.

Unit 6 PSYCHOLOGICAL DISORDERS

systematic desensitization

A behavioral technique in which the therapist step by step increases the patient's anxiety and counters it with relaxation in a graduated sequence.

aversive conditioning

A behavioral technique in which unpleasantness is associated with acts that are to be avoided.

such a case, the behaviors involved are an interplay of so many factors that it is hard to focus on exactly what behavior one is trying to remove by using learning principles.

Systematic Desensitization

The goal of behaviorists is to weaken a habit that the person has and replace it with something else that is newly learned. The most elaborate method in this area is called **systematic desensitization.** The term refers to a process in which the therapist step by step (systematically) increases the anxiety the patient feels, but each time it is increased, that level of anxiety is replaced by relaxation. In this way, the person becomes much less sensitive (desensitized) to the problem.

Here is a real case: a college student had a phobia (unreasonable fear) about dissection to the point that she could not even enter a room where it took place. This meant that she was going to fail biology. First, the student was taught how to relax. The therapist then made up a list of items in order of increasing anxiety. The first item was presented to the student. Perhaps it was something like being on campus near the biology building. She was told to relax while thinking of this item. The next step was thinking about approaching the biology building. As anxiety built up at this thought, she was to relax once again. Then thoughts about the odors and atmosphere of the biology lab were introduced, creating greater anxiety. She again relaxed. Over time, she began to relax at the actual thought of cutting up a frog and hence was able actually to participate in such an activity—if she found it acceptable (McGlynn & O'Brien, 1972).

This procedure sounds almost simpleminded. But surprisingly, it works quite well with thousands of people every year. Its only drawback is that it is not very effective with long-term, complex, symbolic issues, such as not being able to get along with other people. It does work well with any kind of specific phobia, and it is the fastest, most efficient, cheapest method of treatment in such cases.

Aversive Conditioning

In **aversive conditioning,** the goal is to make certain acts unpleasant so that they will be avoided. For example, alcoholics can be given a medication that will make them nauseated when they take alcohol. The relearning process involved is to try to associate the aversive (negative) feeling with taking the alcohol and hence reduce its use. The rate of improvement for this method is about 50 percent, with the "cure" lasting about six months. Thus, it is not a solution as much as a good beginning for a number of alcoholics (Ullmann & Krasner, 1969; 1975).

544

COOPERATIVE LEARNING

You may have heard stories in which parents who catch their child smoking make the child smoke an entire pack in an hour or two—or until the child gets sick. Parents, in this case, are practicing aversion therapy. As noted previously, aver- sion therapy is often controversial, and in this case may even constitute abuse. Ask students to work in groups to see if they can think of other situations in which aversion therapy could be more detrimental than beneficial. Are there any instances in which it is justifiably the best method of treatment? The groups should elect one member to report their conclusions to the class.

Chapter 19 TREATMENT AND THERAPY

IN FOCUS | **Systematic Desensitization**

Systematic desensitization works well in reducing the fear of animals. For what other kinds of fears could this method be used? How might it be applied to more complex situations?

Systematic Desensitization.

 This method would work for most fears: water, heights, flying, even ago- raphobia (by gradually stretching the established boundaries).

Points to Stress

Aversive conditioning has sometimes been used with autistic children. Autism is a severe devel- opmental disorder that causes language prob- lems and sometimes self- mutilation. Aversive condi- tioning might call for a slap or a pinch or some other unpleasant conse- quence every time the child tries to hurt himself or herself.

DISCOVERY

"Should" statements make up a good portion of our irrational beliefs. "The house should be clean. . . . I shouldn't have called her. . . . He shouldn't talk to me that way." These should statements foster guilt and resentment, and they don't get us any nearer to where we want to be. Ask students to write down all the "should" statements they have used in the last two weeks. Are there some that show up often? Do the students feel guilt?

ENRICHMENT

Albert Ellis is a compelling character who is outspoken and independent. Students would probably enjoy learning more about him.

Points to Stress

One of the reasons why token economies are often successful is that they supply immediate reinforcement for behaviors. The reinforcements are secondary—patients (or clients) will cash in tokens for something else—but it is still immediate. Some systems make you pay tokens if you do not perform desired behaviors. For example, if parents use such a system at home, they might charge a dollar if the child's room is not cleaned up.

Connections

See the **Chapter Project** for Chapter 7 for ideas on incorporating a token economy system in your classroom. The project is designed to expose students to a token economy system on a short-term basis. It probably would not work well over the long term. As a teacher, you are probably more concerned with stimulating thinking, rather than shaping behavior, which is the goal of a token economy.

546

Unit 6 PSYCHOLOGICAL DISORDERS

token economy

A behavioral technique in which rewards for desired acts are accumulated through tokens, which represent a form of money.

cognitive behavioral therapy

Therapy in which thoughts are used to control emotions and behaviors.

546

The Token Economy

The **token economy,** a buying system (an economy) in which patients use tokens to purchase things, sounds again like something a little too simple. But it works quite well with certain types of mental patients in hospital wards. The tokens—paper slips, poker chips, or the like—are given for good behavior, such as making the bed, brushing one's teeth, or taking a shower. In day-to-day living in close quarters, doing these things vastly improves the comfort of the living conditions and reduces episodes of frustration and increased abnormality. The tokens give the patients something to do and a tangible reward. It is always a problem to figure out what the patients should be doing with their days, so here is a solution that solves this problem and gives a reward at the same time.

Major changes take place on wards using this method. Patients work for tokens with which they can buy extra walks on the grounds, more television time, candy, and the like. As a result, they become less withdrawn, have fewer confused thoughts, and improve their social relationships (Gripp & Magaro, 1971).

We need to add a word here about the term *behavioral*. Students almost always have trouble with the word, but you need to understand it for the material that follows, so here we go: there are three processes possible in therapy. These are mental (cognitive), verbal (talking), and behavioral (performing actions). In the techniques just discussed, taking action (behavioral) was the most important aspect—going into the biology lab, not taking a drink, making a bed. The therapies did not involve the verbal (talking) aspects that the Rogerians or Freudians use. The treatment also downplayed the mental (cognitive). Now you should have some idea how the word is used and be prepared for the next section.

COGNITIVE BEHAVIORAL THERAPY

We mentioned the limitations of straight behavioral therapy in terms of its inability to handle complex problems arising from mental, symbolic issues. Because of this failing, it wasn't long before a psychologist, **Albert Ellis,** (b. 1913) came up with the idea of uniting behaviors with cognitions (thoughts) as a method for helping people. This therapy becomes one of actively working on the client's thought processes (cognitions) and having him or her change actions and emotional responses to be more appropriate (behavioral) (Goldfried, 1980). Thus, this is called **cognitive behavioral therapy.**

Ellis's approach to problems is based on a belief that we humans are made up of two components: the rational (mental) and the emo-

COOPERATIVE LEARNING

Teaching Master 19-2 Cognitive Distortions provides a list of several common cognitive distortions. Assign one distortion to each group, and have students perform a skit in which one or more of the characters uses the distortion. Directions are listed on the teaching master.

ENRICHMENT

Have students read portions of Aaron Beck's *Love is Never Enough* (New York: HarperCollins, 1989). It's a guide to communication for couples. You can role-play some of the situations presented in the book.

---

tional (emotive). Treatment focuses on getting emotions under control by using reason; thus, this technique is called **rational emotive therapy** (Ellis, 1980). Most emotional upset occurs because we hold **irrational ideas,** ideas that don't hold up when challenged by careful logic. Put another way, we are disturbed "not by things but by the view we take of them." External events can't do us in half as fast as how we think about them. For instance: (1) A woman loses a job. She becomes depressed. (2) A woman loses a job and looks forward to greater opportunities at a *new* job. Two entirely different responses to exactly the same set of circumstances. This is the key to Ellis's system. Each woman's beliefs are based on what Ellis called **internalized sentences.** To understand what he means, stop and listen to yourself for a few minutes. Notice how you talk "inside" all day every day. How well you do in life depends on what kinds of sentences you are giving yourself. If they are "I'm doomed," "I'm hopeless," or the like, you've got trouble.

Someone who is important to us rejects us. We can **awfulize** (Ellis's term) the whole thing and say to ourselves, "This is just terrible. I'm no good, no good at all, and no one will ever like me again. I'm not worth anything. Doom. Doom." But we can change (behavioral) such internal sentences (cognitions) to read: "That's upsetting and disappointing. Maybe I'll have better luck next time." Sometimes this is very hard to do, but Ellis's ideas are well worth considering and trying to put into action for better mental health.

In therapy itself, Ellis and his followers assume people are straight thinkers and can be reached by reason to redo their internal sentences. Sometimes the therapy can get pretty rough, as the excerpt that follows shows, but the patient knows the therapist cares, which offsets the roughness.

Client: I don't feel well today. I had a headache and was going to stay in bed.

Therapist: Well, why didn't you?

Client: Well, I . . . uh . . . well, I thought maybe I should come in because I was supposed to.

Therapist: That's not much of a motivation. Why are you coming here at all? Out of some obligation to me?

Client: No . . . I'm coming . . . well, you know, because . . .

Therapist: You tell me.

Client: Because . . . well, because I need some support. I need someone to talk to. I have some friends, but my parents . . . especially my father, don't *really* care about me. You know.

Therapist: So your father doesn't really care about you? So what? If you think that's the end of the world, then that's just stupid. Do you really believe that all fathers care about their

---

Chapter 19 TREATMENT AND THERAPY

rational emotive therapy

Treatment centering on getting emotions under control by using reason; Ellis's term.

irrational ideas

Ideas that do not hold up when challenged by careful logic.

internalized sentences

The opinions we form of ourselves by listening to our own inner voice; Ellis's term.

awfulize

To see things in the worst possible light; Ellis's term.

Critical Thinking

"How could you incorporate a token economy system at school?" Here are some examples: Students can be paid (or given a token) for attendance or grades. This payment can be in the form of real money or in the form of coupons that can be exchanged for privileges. For example, people who make the B honor roll could be given free lunches for a week from the school cafeteria. (Students may groan that this is not a reward.)

Points to Stress

Contrast this exchange with the client-centered exchange earlier. This therapist is direct, confrontational, and offers advice.

CHAPTER PROJECT

Once students are familiar with some cognitive distortions (See **Master 19-2 Cognitive Distortions**), have them keep a diary of their thinking for several days, similar to what a cognitive behavioral therapist might recommend. Once they accumulate several examples of cognitive distortions that they use, work on how to correct these distortions. See **Master 19-3 Cognitive Diary** for an assignment sheet on this project.

INTERDISCIPLINARY PROJECT

Language arts. This activity requires absolutely no preparation. Bring in a radio and flip through the stations. Whenever you come across what sounds like a love song, stop and listen. Pick out several irrational

---

Main Types of Therapy.

 Cognitive behavioral therapy is most effective for depression. Behavioral therapy works best for phobias.

Discussion

As mentioned, cognitive behavioral therapy can get rough, which is in sharp contrast to client-centered therapy. If students had to see a therapist, which type would they prefer? Those who choose client-centered therapy may feel empowered to help themselves most of the time. See the **Locus of Control Scale** from Chapter 17. Or maybe cognitive therapy seems too much like homework! Those who choose cognitive behavioral therapy may be less internally motivated and might appreciate guidance. Maybe this therapy just seems a bit more concrete to these students. Note that cognitive behavioral therapy does not need to be rough. Not everybody conducts therapy like Ellis does.

548

Unit 6 PSYCHOLOGICAL DISORDERS

IN FOCUS — Main Types of Therapy

	Main Goal	How Goal Is Achieved	Main Technique(s)	Characteristic(s) of Therapist
Psychoanalysis	To reduce anxiety and guilt over unconscious impulses	Verbal processes	Free association Transference	Emotionally neutral
Humanistic Therapy	To help one see and fulfill one's potential	Verbal processes	Nondirective therapy	Nonjudgmental mirror—but demonstrates unconditional positive regard
Behavioral Therapy	To change one's unwanted or "abnormal behaviors"	Behavioral training	Systematic desensitization Aversive conditioning Token economy	Probably objective
Cognitive Behavioral Therapy	To unite behaviors and thoughts	Mental training	Rational emotive therapy Analysis of internalized sentences	Analytical—perhaps rough, but caring

Which method would probably be most effective in treating depression? In eliminating phobias?

---

group therapy

Therapy in which more than one person at a time is treated.

---

children? I mean, just because it's written someplace that you should love your child doesn't mean everyone does. Don't you have friends? Didn't you just say that?

Client: Yes, but . . .

Therapist: No buts. If you've got friends, you should stop saying to yourself, "I'm not cared for, I'm not loved." That's just not true, is it? No! It's not true. If your father doesn't like you, he doesn't like you.

GROUP THERAPY

Group therapy has two purposes: (1) It is an attempt to treat more than one person at a time; this makes it cheaper for the client and

ideas in the songs. You can make it a sort of challenge by seeing how many you can find in ten minutes. For example, "I can't live without you," "Without you, I'm nothing," and so on.

Break students into groups and ask them to discuss if they have ever gone on a retreat with their church or some other organization. They should list the most positive experi-

ences and analyze what promoted or prevented openness and intimacy. Would students ever consider encounter therapy?

Chapter 19 TREATMENT AND THERAPY

more efficient for both therapist and clients. (2) People can share their feelings and problems with one another and learn that they are not alone in their difficulties, a very important aspect of this method. Its usefulness is most noticeable when dealing with people suffering from grief or an addiction, not only because it offers companionship but also because if one or two can overcome the problem, it encourages the rest to follow suit.

The Group Method

In group therapy, people sit in a circle and talk to one another about problems under the guidance of a mental health worker. This type of therapy provides a more realistic world than individual therapy in which there are only two people and very little of the give-and-take of interaction found outside the therapy. The group can provide support, go deeply into certain problems, or deal with social skills. As long as the therapist is skilled and knows how to handle the group, there is little danger to the clients. One of the things that makes many people what they are is an extreme sensitivity to the feelings of others in most cases. The odds of their being understanding and sympathetic are very high.

Group therapists don't really follow a particular system such as Freudian, behavioral, cognitive, what have you. The therapy usually involves a mixture of a little bit of all of them. On occasion, a given therapist sometimes prefers one approach to another.

Encounter Therapy

You may have heard about **encounter groups.** In such a group, "normal" people are brought together to share their sensitivities and problems. The label *encounter* is used because people are forced to reveal inner conflicts and to share secret emotions and feelings. The purpose behind this is supposedly to expose people's psyches in order to make them more aware and stronger.

Give this therapy wide berth. In regular group therapy with a professional, there are either implied or stated rules that prevent anyone from taking more psychological abuse than he or she can handle. In encounter groups, the goal is to expose oneself in order to get in touch with the "inner self." While some people survive and possibly even become better for the experience, the process is too dangerous for most to handle. Many wind up revealing inner feelings to others that they come to regret later. They feel exposed, betrayed, helpless, and too open to the world after it is all over and everyone has gone home (Yalom & Lieberman, 1971; Kuehn & Crinella, 1969).

encounter groups

Type of group therapy in which people are forced to share their inner conflicts and emotions.

Comprehension Check

According to Albert Ellis, what are the two components that make up humans? *(the rational and the emotional)*

FYI Role-playing is a common technique used during group therapy. Many of the role-playing activities listed throughout the wraparound are similar to those that might occur during group therapy. The differences, of course, lie in the intensity and the goals: a classroom should never be used for therapy. Classroom role-playing will more likely lead to discussion than personal enlightenment, which would be the primary goal of group therapy.

ENRICHMENT

Have students find out about the various support groups available at your school and in your community. If you are willing to travel, you can find a support group for just about any conceivable disturbance.

DISCUSS THE PHOTO

Are students surprised by the informal setting here?

Comprehension Check

Identify each statement as being descriptive of *group therapy* or *encounter groups:*
(1) People are sometimes forced to share inner conflicts and secret feelings *(encounter group).*
(2) Patients talk to each other under the guidance of a skilled mental health worker *(group therapy).* Rules exist to prevent anyone taking too much psychological abuse *(group therapy).* Many participants feel exposed and betrayed afterward *(encounter group).*

550

Unit 6 PSYCHOLOGICAL DISORDERS

▲ *For many people, group therapy is an inexpensive and effective alternative.*

COMMONALITIES OF THERAPY

All therapies have certain factors in common that are important to note: (1) They are all designed to help the person resolve conflicts and problems, especially "Who am I, what do I want in life, and how do I get it?" (Orlinsky et al., 1970). (2) There is some direct relationship with a therapist for the purpose of trying to answer these questions. (3) There is the anticipation of some kind of positive change (Frank, 1971).

People benefit from therapy in a number of ways, usually: (1) they start some kind of program to find better methods for handling problems; (2) they learn new rules for understanding and correcting their behavior; (3) they feel better for having developed a relationship with someone who wants to help; and (4) they overcome present problems and are therefore better equipped to handle new ones that will arise later on (Harper, 1968).

EFFECTIVENESS OF THERAPY

You will sometimes hear that people with problems often get better all by themselves. While that is possible, it is unlikely. Certain fac-

ENRICHMENT

Psychotherapist Irvin Yalom's *Love's Executioner* (see **Suggested Readings**) presents several of his cases. Have students read one or two of these and then have them write ten conclusions about therapy and/or therapists. Students will probably conclude that therapy is more intuitive than they had imagined. Clarify that this "intuition" is based on years of experience.

Chapter 19 TREATMENT AND THERAPY

tors work behind the scenes to help those who don't enter formal therapy. For example, those with a higher education will tend to do better in the long run because this usually reduces financial and environmental stresses. Those who are married tend to get better because they have a spouse who can care for and support them emotionally. And those who have a job get better more quickly because they have something that provides income and meaning to life. It doesn't seem to be the passage of time itself that cures people but rather this "informal therapy" (Eisler & Williams, 1972; Jansen & Nickles, 1973).

In terms of formal treatment by a therapist, the evidence suggests that therapy is both helpful and useful (Nicholson & Berman, 1983). Millions claim they feel better and lead more useful lives after therapy.

Which therapy is best? The answer partly rests on the type of problem (Matarazzo, 1985). Behavioral therapy works very well with phobias, smoking, or overeating. With depression, a combination of drug therapy and cognitive behavior therapy seems to provide the best and longest-lasting improvement (Simons, 1984). The client-centered humanistic approach works very well with anxiety problems. Behavioral relaxation programs also help with anxiety (Phillips & Bierman, 1981). There is further evidence that it doesn't make much difference which type of therapy one is getting because feeling comfortable with and trusting the therapist carry such heavy weight in how effective the therapy is. In other words, if a person has a good therapist of any type whom he or she trusts, the chances of getting better notably increase.

Certain principles of psychoanalysis have proved useful in other therapies. For example, other therapists often explore childhood in *brief* fashion, or they assume that all is not as it appears on the surface. Even so, strict psychoanalysis is the most questionable of the therapies. There is no doubt about the fact that Freud laid the foundation for much of the treatment present today nor about the fact that he was a brilliant thinker. Even so, there are serious difficulties presented by his treatment method. For example, one study that followed up over 100 patients who had undergone an average of *600*(!) psychoanalytic sessions found that 60 percent showed substantial improvement (Brody, 1962). This is a fairly typical showing for any therapy, but at today's rates, that would have cost between $80,000 and $100,000. And in another study, 14 percent of the patients were worse off after therapy than before, and 26 percent showed no change at all (Kernberg et al., 1972; Garfield, 1981). One suspects that the problem with psychoanalysis is that it often involves continuous dwelling on problems dating all the way back to childhood, only partly dealing with the present. This may well increase the patient's feelings of being overwhelmed by the idea of a lifetime of problems. Given the speed and relatively inexpensive nature of other available treatments, we find it hard to recommend this one.

Comprehension Check

Which type of therapy works best with the following problems? (1) Anxiety *(client-centered and behavioral programs)* (2) Phobias *(behavioral therapy)* (3) Depression *(drugs and cognitive behavioral therapy)*

DISCOVERY

You may have a few film buffs who can rattle off movie scenes that depict therapy sessions. Have them either list several scenes or edit some together on video. Then have them identify which approach the sessions most resemble. Students might look at *Prince of Tides* and *Ordinary People* for starters.

FYI Since psychologists can't prescribe drugs, they often work closely with a psychiatrist who can.

Discussion

If one learned about therapy only through the movies, what conclusions would one make? (See the **Discovery** above.) All the conclusions discussed don't have to be entirely serious.

Unit 6 PSYCHOLOGICAL DISORDERS

chemotherapy

The use of drugs to relieve psychological disturbance.

CHEMOTHERAPY

Chemotherapy (KEE-mo-therapy) involves the use of drugs to relieve symptoms, so this treatment is handled only by a psychiatrist. The main drugs used are tranquilizers, antidepressants, and antipsychotics. The drugs alter the rate and pattern of firing of the brain nerve cells (Tosteson, 1981). Thus, if one is dealing with a depressed patient, the drug of choice would be one that *increases* the level of brain firing and thereby increases alertness. With someone very nervous and anxious whose nerve cells already are firing rapidly, a tranquilizer would be more appropriate. The reaction of a particular patient to a particular drug is unpredictable, however; so-called tranquilizers can act as energizers *or* tranquilizers, depending on the person and the dosage.

Given in moderation and with careful supervision, these drugs can be quite useful in lessening anxiety or depression and reducing psychotic symptoms. Many patients are able to function in life after taking the drugs when that was not the case before. Thus, there is no question about their usefulness. Still, as you will note in the next paragraph, the drugs don't work all that well with many patients and are used too often just to keep the patients quiet. While this benefits the staff trying to control them, it leaves many patients with serious problems unresolved. The general public and, to some extent, many professionals may think the problems of these patients are under control when they aren't. Finally, in too many cases, the patients are helped enough to be able to leave the hospital but not enough that they are able to function on their own, so the streets of every major city are filled with homeless and lost schizophrenics who don't know where to go or how to get help.

Most of us are accustomed to the idea that certain drugs treat certain diseases. This is not the case in the mental health area. The majority of the drugs currently used only make the patient more manageable and reduce symptoms somewhat. There is no drug that makes the person "well." So, a problem exists. Some workers in the field are concerned that the patient is only being "helped" by being made semiconscious. In some hospitals, for instance, the daily dosage of a tranquilizer for psychotics is the same one used by veterinarians to subdue a 400-pound lion. It is no wonder that these patients complain of their lives being filled with "empty feelings" (Breggin, 1983). And continued use of some antipsychotic medication can cause permanent disability in the form of involuntary arm, leg, and mouth movements (Bower, 1985).

ENRICHMENT

No one knows how ECT works, but one theory is that the brain of a depressed patient is too active, and ECT somehow reduces that activity.

Students interested in biological aspects of psychopathology can research theories about the method and effects of ECT.

ELECTROCONVULSIVE SHOCK THERAPY

In **electroconvulsive therapy (ECT),** a shock is deliberately sent through the patient's brain to produce convulsions. The procedure is not painful, but it certainly is quite terrifying to many patients. The treatment is very controversial. A major objection to it is that no one knows what it does, why it works when it does, and whether the risks involved are worth it (Weiner, 1984; Scovern & Kilmann, 1980). The actual physical changes that occur after ECT are best summed up as confusion and loss of memory, which disappear after a few hours. With continued shock treatments, however, the memory loss persists for longer and longer periods, and eventually ECT can result in brain damage (Freeman, 1985; Squire, 1985; Breggin, 1984).

What also makes the treatment worrisome is the fact that it is so primitive. It resembles a treatment used in the very early days of mental hospitals around Pinel's era, called the "snake pit." Patients who were depressed or behaving strangely were thrown in a pit that contained dozens of nonpoisonous snakes. Patients were left there until they "quit acting strangely." But from the previous chapter, you may remember that all psychotic patients have periods when the symptoms disappear. The hospital personnel were convinced that these patients were getting better as a result of the "treatment."

There are two final things to say about ECT that are important. First of all, it will lift some people out of a deep, suicidal depression, so *maybe* there is some justification for using it in such cases. Second, it doesn't work with any category of mental disturbance other than depression and should not be administered to people who fall into those other categories. For example, it makes schizophrenics worse, probably convincing some of them that their previously false belief

electroconvulsive therapy (ECT)

Therapy in which an electrical shock is sent through the brain to try to reduce symptoms of mental disturbance.

Points to Stress

Shock therapy was popular when it was first introduced, lost some of that popularity with the introduction of new drugs to treat depression, and now has gained back some of that popularity in treating severe depression that does not respond to other treatment. Why? It seems to work for many patients.

 FYI ECT was first used in 1938.

Points to Stress

It's true that ECT seems primitive, but the administration of ECT has become much more humane. Recipients are sedated, and the convulsions are very much reduced. The voltage lasts about two seconds and the seizures last about 30 to 60 seconds.

DISCUSS THE PHOTO

Most experts agree that ECT should be regarded as a last resort if antidepressant medication has failed.

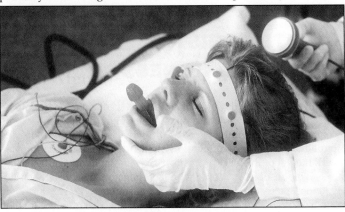

▲ *Patient is prepared for electroshock therapy.*

ENRICHMENT

Have students find out the effects of lobotomy on language, reasoning, and perception.

COOPERATIVE LEARNING

Szasz suggests that no one is mentally ill until *others* say so! Ask students to debate in groups this remarkable statement. Each group should elect two members to present to the class the main points on each side, pro and con, of this argument.

Points to Stress

Destroying or disconnecting the frontal lobe is called lobotomy. The technique was introduced in the 1930s and was performed for over 15 years! The introduction of drugs, particularly tranquilizers, made lobotomies obsolete.

FYI Estimates suggest that over 50,000 lobotomies were performed between the mid-1930s and early 1950s.

Reteaching Strategy

Have students go back to Chapter 18 to find a list of behavior disorders **(In Focus Mental Disorders).** For each disorder, students should explain which method of therapy would be most effective. Answers will vary; just be sure that students support their answers.

554

Unit 6 PSYCHOLOGICAL DISORDERS

psychosurgery

Surgery that destroys part of the brain to make the patient calmer, freer of symptoms.

554

that someone is trying to hurt them is true (Weiner, 1984; Scovern & Kilmann, 1980).

In a way, it may seem that we are being too harsh on this treatment. On the other hand, there is a real stigma attached to any person getting electroshock treatment. People think something really horrible is wrong with them. And most patients fear it. Since it *is* useful with some cases of *severe* depression, one could hardly fault its use in many of those cases. Nonetheless, the evidence is pretty clear that it does little good and sometimes harm with cases other than severe depression, yet it is still used for people with other disturbances. Some claim that this is the case because there is money to be made. We won't be cynical, but using something that is of little value and has so many negative aspects deserves to be questioned.

PSYCHOSURGERY

Any technique that involves entering the brain to alter one's psychological state is called **psychosurgery.** The most common operation involves destruction of part of the front portion of the patient's brain, just behind the forehead. This part, the *frontal lobe*, contains most of the nerve connections that control what we call "personality," especially our complex emotional responses. Usually a laser or probe is aimed at this portion, and enough tissue is damaged to try to slow down the patient. Unfortunately, brain tissue never restores itself, so the effects are permanent. Another problem: if the wrong area is hit, the patient can get much *more* violent and unmanageable. This is a treatment that is very hard to justify. Fortunately, it is almost never done today. When it is, the grounds are that the patient is uncontrollable otherwise. This justification is hard to believe, given our arsenal of tranquilizing drugs.

CONTROVERSY: MENTAL ILLNESS

As discussed in the previous chapter, the evidence mounts that psychotics have a physical or chemical problem. They probably could, in the broad sense, be said to have an "illness," a term that implies a physical defect. But psychotics are a minority among those with mental problems.

For the rest of the people who have serious problems, the issue is whether they should be listed as having a mental *illness*. Once a person has an illness, they are either supposed to be "cured" or removed from society—a distressing idea (Woolfolk, 1985). It has recently been

ENRICHMENT

It's ironic that patients are roaming the streets because now more than ever, patients' rights are given high priority during mental health court proceedings (at least in procedure). If the court deems that the hospital is not the "least restrictive environ-ment," the patient will be released to a less restrictive facility or into the community. Ask students to research some of the problems resulting from early release of patients from care facilities.

---

suggested that even the term *mental disorder* should be applied with care (Wakefield, 1992). In any case, if you say someone has a "dis-ease," you are labeling him or her forever. Is that justified? What about the Uncle Harrys and Aunt Marthas who spend a lot of their time in the attic chatting with imaginary friends? Are they really hurting anyone? Should they be removed from society just because they are a little quirky?

One psychiatrist has suggested that rather than "disease" or "ill-ness," we should say a person has "problems in living" (Szasz, 1961). Look what a difference just a change in wording would make, and decide for yourself: a man you slightly know is behaving strangely and seems distracted, so you ask a mutual friend what's wrong with him. Answer: "He has some problems at work. His marriage is in trouble. It's all getting to him." Now, here's the second scenario: "Charlie has a mental illness and had to be hospitalized."

Both describe the same person. Is there any difference in how you would respond to Charlie the next time you saw him, depending on which version you got?

PSYCHOLOGY IN YOUR LIFE

Seeking Professional Help

There are so many television shows and movies that dis-tort the reality of what those with problems are really like and what happens to them in therapy that we have our work cut out for us here. Having read the box at the end of the last chapter, you may have decided you have a serious problem. You could be right. But you do *not* have a serious mental disturbance or illness. There is an enor-mous difference! A serious mental disturbance involves seeing things that are not there, believing things that never have happened, and having extremely confused thought processes. If these applied to you, chances are close to zero that you would even be reading this.

As mentioned several times, everybody has prob-lems. Quite a number of people cross the line from having day-to-day problems to being involved with one that is so disruptive that it makes it hard to function. This still does not mean that you have a serious mental disturbance. It means that someone will have to help you get back on track. The odds of your doing it on your own are remote because the problem gets distorted when it fills up so much of your time and thinking. You need someone objective.

Only a handful of coun-*(continued on next page)*

Comprehension Check

Name the treatment described by the following characteristics: (1) in-volves destruction of the frontal lobe *(psycho-surgery)* (2) can jar peo-ple out of deep, suicidal depression *(ECT)* (3) drugs used to relieve symptoms *(chemothera-py)* (4) produces convul-sions *(ECT)* (5) rarely used and difficult to justify *(psychosurgery)* (6) treat-ment can only be adminis-tered by a psychiatrist *(chemotherapy)*.

Evaluation Strategy

Have students list four problems that might cause someone to seek mental health therapy. For each problem, students should describe possible treat-ment, based on one of the approaches discussed in the chapter. Each problem must be matched with a different approach.

ENRICHMENT

Students can look at some unique techniques that various therapists use: art therapy, music therapy, dream analysis, play therapy.

ENRICHMENT

Have students interview a therapist in your area. (See activity #2 at the end of the chapter.)

ENRICHMENT

Have students complete the **Enrichment Worksheet** for this chapter located in the Teacher Resources.

PSYCHOLOGY IN YOUR LIFE

Enrichment
Find the nonemergency number of a mental health hot line in your area, and assign one person to interview someone at the hot line. What kinds of techniques do these people use to keep the person talking? What kinds of questions do they ask? What kinds of things do they absolutely avoid? Have each student report his or her findings to the class. Compare and contrast these findings to the therapies presented in the chapter.

PSYCHOLOGY IN YOUR LIFE

Seeking Professional Help

(continued from previous page) selors or psychologists today are very interested in trying to uncover deep dark secrets. Most of them are interested in rapid, clear results. They want to work with you to get to the heart of the problem and get it over with for you, not delve into every nook and cranny of your personal life. Most therapies today are measured in months, not years, to completion.

One of the most important ingredients in getting yourself repaired, so to speak, is some degree of confidence in the therapist. School counselors are like people in every other profession. There are good ones and bad ones. You can get a feel for what one is like by discussing other areas, such as occupational choice, with him or her to see if you think he or she might be the kind of person who can help you deal with more personal issues. Go to your school counselor if you feel good about doing so, but don't base your decision on bizarre rumors that crop up among students. Sort out

what seems to be real from fiction.

From the outset, you can count on the fact that for a counselor or a psychologist, the problem you have is not something new and startling. Lots of other people have had it—whatever it is. If you decide to go to the counselor, be certain to ask him or her what the rules are about confidentiality. Counselors will be happy to tell you. The rules vary, and you don't want to get yourself into a position in which your problems become part of a school record.

If you decide to go to an outside psychologist, you will need your parents' cooperation and help in most states—but not always. It is likely that your parents will be somewhat upset if you approach them about it. But that is not because you are so weird. It's because they endlessly worry that somehow they haven't done right by you. It's almost inevitable that they have done the best they can and that they have little to do with what is both-

ering you. When you talk to them about the problem, be direct, but don't exhaust them with details so they think you are worse off than you are. With or without parents, one of the best sources for finding help is to contact a hot line, such as suicide prevention or runaway or anything like that. You don't have to have that particular problem to call them. All these organizations have endless sources of help available in almost any problem area.

Two things to trust us about: (1) You will find that therapy, when conducted properly, is very close to just sitting down and talking with a friend. Nothing strange or really different goes on. (2) *Don't* stick with a therapist you are not comfortable with. If you do, you will wind up fighting two battles—first, your problem, and second, your negative feelings about the therapist. Change therapists. But if you keep wanting to change, your expectations are probably too high.

VOCABULARY REVIEW

Before testing students on the contents of the chapter, you may want to review vocabulary terms that are especially important or confusing. Terms in this chapter that could require clarification are *free association, unconditional positive regard, systematic desensitization, token economy, internalized sentences, chemotherapy,* and *psychosurgery.*

SUMMARY

1. A psychologist has an advanced degree in psychological principles and methods. A psychiatrist is a medical doctor who has added a number of years to his or her training during which mental abnormality is studied. Psychotherapist is a broad term applied to almost any professional working with psychological problems.

2. Psychoanalysis is based on a theory that assumes unconscious animal impulses are seeking expression. Treatment focuses on free association and transference to reveal the inner forces and to reduce their strength and the anxiety they cause.

3. Humanistic therapy centers on the belief that the person is basically good. The therapist mirrors the thoughts of the client to bring out the potential that lies inside.

4. Behavioral therapy tries to change people's behavior or actions. Three methods used are systematic desensitization, aversive conditioning, and the token economy.

5. Cognitive behavioral therapy, using the rational emotive technique, tries to reorient internal sentences so the individual has better control over his or her emotions.

6. Group therapy benefits the patient because it is closer to real-life relationships than therapy involving just therapist and client. This treatment is also cheaper because more than one person is handled at a time.

7. There doesn't seem to be a "best" therapy. People benefit most from working with a therapist they can trust. Therapy in general is effective, but your return for the money with psychoanalysis is highly questionable.

8. Chemotherapy is drug treatment. Drugs in reasonable doses seem beneficial to many, but there are dangers. Electroconvulsive therapy is controversial. It does seem to help those who are severely depressed. Psychosurgery is a highly questionable method involving brain destruction in an attempt to make the patient more manageable.

Wrapping It Up

One of the best ways to convey that there is nothing wrong with seeing a therapist is to bring in several therapists during the chapter. Students will see that therapists are normal people with normal jobs, and they may even learn something about therapy, too.

Reteaching Strategy

Have students complete the **Reteaching Worksheet** for this chapter located in the Teacher Resources. The **Vocabulary Worksheet** may be completed by the class as a pretest for chapter concepts or used as a reteaching worksheet for those students needing additional review.

Suggested Readings

▼ Burns, David. *Feeling Good: The New Mood Therapy.* New York: Signet, 1980.

▼ Burns, David. *The Feeling Good Handbook.* New York: Plume, 1989.

▼ Ellis, A., and R. Harper. *A New Guide to Rational Living.* Englewood Cliffs, NJ: Prentice-Hall, 1975.

▼ Engler, Jack, and Daniel Goleman. *Consumer's Guide to Psychotherapy.* New York: Fireside, 1992.

▼ Yalom, Irvin D. *Love's Executioner: And Other Tales of Psychotherapy.* New York: Basic Books, 1989.

Vocabulary

Philippe Pinel
counseling psychologists
clinical psychologists
psychiatrists
psychiatric social workers
psychiatric nurses
psychotherapies
psychoanalysis
free association
transference
humanistic therapy

client-centered therapy
nondirective therapy
unconditional positive regard
behavioral therapy
systematic desensitization
aversive conditioning
token economy
Albert Ellis
cognitive behavioral therapy

rational emotive therapy
irrational ideas
internalized sentences
awfulize
group therapy
encounter groups
chemotherapy
electroconvulsive therapy (ECT)
psychosurgery

Answers to Review Questions

1. c
2. b
3. a
4. c
5. d
6. b
7. d
8. c
9. d
10. a
11. b
12. a
13. false
14. false
15. true
16. false
17. false
18. true
19. true

Review Questions

Matching (Answers can be used more than once.)

1. Treatment often lasts years.
2. Client essentially heals himself or herself.
3. Treatment often works relatively quickly.
4. Therapy is based on Sigmund Freud's theory.
5. Client's thought processes are analyzed.
6. The therapist reflects what the client is saying.
7. Therapy is based on Albert Ellis's theory.
8. Patient transfers emotional conflicts onto therapist.
9. Goal is to unite the mental, or rational, with the emotional.
10. The origin of the problem is essentially ignored.
11. The therapist remains completely nonjudgmental.
12. Disorders are the result of learned responses.

a. behavioral therapy
b. humanistic therapy
c. psychoanalysis
d. cognitive behavioral therapy

Notes on Discussion Questions

1. Psychoanalysis may be a better treatment for deep-seated, complex problems stemming perhaps from child abuse, neglect, or some other severe trauma. Theoretically, this abuse will cause resentment and guilt that will eventually be repressed. Psychoanalysis supposedly helps bring this resentment and guilt to the surface so they can be resolved. Behavioral therapy may be a better treatment for eliminating or reducing specific behaviors that interfere with day-to-day living. These behaviors can range from simple bad habits, like smoking or mildly overeating, to more severe problems, like never eating or washing one's hands 500 times a day.

2. You might want to ask students for specific examples. *How* did these people show unconditional positive regard?

3. The principal would first have to decide which behaviors will be rewarded—which raises ques-

True/False

13. In group therapy, "normal" people get together to share feelings without the guidance of a mental health worker.
14. The goal of most encounter groups is to train group members to become therapists themselves.
15. Psychoanalysis often tends to become a very expensive method of treatment.
16. A common treatment used by psychologists is chemotherapy.

17. One or two treatments of electroconvulsive therapy will tend to cause long-lasting memory loss.
18. One reason why electroconvulsive therapy is still used today is that it seems to work well on deeply depressed individuals.
19. Psychosurgery is sometimes used on patients who are difficult to control.

DISCUSSION QUESTIONS

1. What kinds of problems would be better dealt with using psychoanalysis, and which problems would be better dealt with using behavioral therapy? Explain.
2. Describe a person, in your past or present, who consistently has demonstrated unconditional positive regard toward you. What effect, if any, did (or does) this have on you? Explain.
3. If your principal wanted to incorporate a token economy system at your school, what are several ways in which to do this? Be specific. Do you think adopting your suggestions would realistically have any effect on students' behaviors? Explain.
4. Despite the many problems associated with chemotherapy, why would it be virtually impossible and even undesirable for a

mental institution to eliminate chemotherapy completely? What kinds of problems would result? Explain.
5. Imagine that one of your parents has been severely depressed for several months, that he or she has been completely listless and uncommunicative. All kinds of treatments have been ineffective. The last resort seems to be ECT; however, the hospital needs your approval to administer it. Do you give your approval? Why or why not? Explain.
6. Do you think it would ever be justified to use psychosurgery as punishment for criminals in prison? Why or why not? Explain.
7. Of all the therapies and treatments discussed in the chapter, which one would you tend to prefer if you had a problem? Explain.

ACTIVITIES

1. Take out a sheet of paper and write down the first ten things that come to mind when you think of a mental hospital. Your list needs to be somewhat detailed—not just a list of

single words and phrases. Then contact a mental health hospital and interview someone there, focusing particularly on the accuracy or inaccuracy of the ten items on

tions about the ethics of behaviorism. Why should the principal get to decide? If not the principal, then who? In other words, who determines what is "desired" behavior? Consider discussing these ethical issues in class.

4. As mentioned in the text, drugs given in moderation and under careful supervision can be quite useful. Without these drugs, many patients would simply not be able to function.

5. This would work well as a journal entry.

6. If you decide to discuss this question in class, use discretion. Students who believe that psychosurgery should be used as punishment may unintentionally appear cruel or sadistic. To avoid this, do not debate the question. Simply ask for the advantages and the disadvantages of using psychosurgery as punishment.

7. See discussion question #1.

your list. Also, prepare beforehand a list of other questions to ask about the hospital. Write a report on the interview. Be sure to include a comparison between your original list and what you learned. Was your list accurate?

2. Contact someone who conducts therapy on a more or less daily basis and interview this person. Possible questions: (a) What are the most common kinds of problems that you treat? (b) Would your answer to question (a) have been the same five or ten years ago? (c) What are the typical kinds of treatments and therapies that you use? (d) What is the average length of treatment time for your clients? (e) What are your feelings about chemotherapy? (f) Do you ever get tired of listening to other people's problems? Write a report on your interview and include your specific reactions.

3. You will need to do this next activity with a classmate. Instead of being evaluated on any written work, you will be evaluated this time on three role-playing situations that you will present to the class. First, choose a hypothetical problem on which you want to focus: depression over the breakup of a relationship, anxiety over a weight problem, frustration with parents, and so on. Second, select three of the four main types of therapists presented in the chapter and brainstorm how each would deal with the problem. You might refer back to Chapter 14 on personality theories for more insight into this. Next, write a dialogue between a patient (or client) and one type of therapist. Write two or more dialogues for the other two types of therapists. Try to make each dialogue about two or three minutes long. Finally, rehearse your dialogues: one of you will be the therapist, the other will be the client. Then arrange with your teacher a time when you can present the dialogues in class.

Note: your dialogues do not have to be entirely serious—have some fun with them—but they should be informative and accurate. Also, as we mentioned, be sure the problem you choose is *hypothetical* (for instance, do not use a person with a weight problem to play the role of someone who has a weight problem); a classroom is not the ideal setting in which to discuss your own personal problems.

4. This next activity is similar to the previous one in that you and a classmate will present a skit to the class. You are probably familiar with therapists who conduct therapy on television or on the radio. As with anything, some of these therapists seem qualified and helpful while others should seek therapy themselves. Regardless of the therapists' qualifications, this kind of "fast-food" therapy is a natural target for parody. We want you and a classmate to prepare a five- to six-minute skit in which one of you will be a new TV or radio therapist and the other a client. Again, arrange a time when you can present the skit in class. Definitely have fun with this one!

5. In the next couple of days, pay special attention to the problems of two of your close friends. "Friend" can be broadly defined: family member, boyfriend or girlfriend, and so on. What you will be looking for is a time when your friends seem to feel a need to talk about a problem. The problems can range anywhere from frustration over studying for a test to irritation over serious family problems. If in the next couple of days your friends don't seem to have any problems in mind, perhaps you can prompt them with a simple question about a past problem. If, on the other hand, you encounter five or six friends with problems, pick the two with the most serious ones.

Notes on Activities

1. If you do not have a mental health facility in your area, you and your class may want to compose a questionnaire or a letter that you can send to a state mental hospital.

2. Mention to students that if the therapists who are interviewed seem particularly excited about sharing their expertise, perhaps they can invite the therapists into class to speak.

3 and 4. These activities can be highly entertaining. However, be sure to follow up each role-playing situation or skit with a brief analysis. Was the dialogue essentially accurate? Was each therapist depicted accurately? Also, make it clear that despite the humor in some of the skits, intended or otherwise, real therapy is not something to laugh about. Moreover, we shouldn't ridicule or look down upon those who decide to consult a therapist. All of us, at one time or another, may need the help of a professional, and it requires courage to admit this.

5. This activity can be a rewarding one for students. However, before assigning it, review Rogers's nondirective technique. Otherwise, students may regard the exercise as a game and manipulate their friends into talking about their problems. The real purpose of the exercise is not to manipulate but to support and demonstrate concern, which, in turn, will encourage the "troubled" person to open up.

6. This activity can easily be adapted and used for in-class journal writing. Simply have students keep track of their day-to-day negative internalized sentences for about a week, and have them analyze these sentences.

As your two friends (one at a time) begin to discuss their problems, we want you to try to act as a mirror and simply rephrase your friends' own feelings and thoughts. In other words, you will be using Rogers's nondirective technique. Reread the sample dialogue from the chapter to get an idea of how to do this. Some pointers to keep in mind: (1) Don't give *any* advice. (2) Simply put their words into your words. (3) Be completely nonjudgmental—show unconditional positive regard. This entire experience may seem like a game at first, like you are simply repeating or mimicking what your friends say. But if you are sincerely concerned with your friends' problems, you will probably find that the experience is worthwhile.

Once you've tried this on two friends, write a report describing your reactions. Include how you felt at the time, whether you thought the experience was worthwhile and effective, whether you would use the technique again—for real—not just for an assignment. Be specific about your reactions, but do NOT disclose the content of your conversation—which should remain confidential.

6. We want you to practice identifying negative internalized sentences and supplying the more rational response after each sentence. Situation A: you have to give a speech tomorrow in front of your entire psychology class. Situation B: you decide you are going to ask someone out for a date. Write down these situations on two separate sheets of paper. For each one, write down ten possible negative internalized sentences—leave plenty of room after each one. For example: "No one will like my speech; everyone will think I'm stupid." After each sentence, write down the more rational response. For example, after the sentence above, you might write: "It's probably an exaggeration to say that *no one* will like my speech. Even if the speech as a whole is not that good, there will be parts of it that will be OK—and there will be *some* people who will recognize this. And not *everyone* will think I'm stupid; people in class know how difficult it is to give a speech." Notice how the rational response is not just a single sentence: you will need to explain yourself. So, you will be writing a total of 20 sentences with rational responses after each. This is typical of the approach cognitive behavior therapists might use. (Sounds like homework, doesn't it?)

As mentioned, this whole exercise is just practice. If you'd rather use two real situations from your own life, go ahead. It will probably make the activity much more meaningful. Your answers will not be read aloud in class.

Once you complete your two lists and the rational responses, write down your reactions to the exercise. How did you feel as you filled out the sentences and responses? Was it difficult? If you were to choose real situations and if you had more practice at this, do you think this kind of exercise would be helpful? Why or why not? Explain.

Cognitive Dissonance

Imagine that you are a student in a class taking a test. You happen to notice that another student's answer sheet is lying out on the teacher's desk. You decide to look at the answer sheet. Not only do you look at the sheet but you also change some of your answers to match those on the other student's sheet. Most teachers would say that you cheated on the test because you copied someone else's answers. You believe that cheating is dishonest, and that only lazy students need to cheat in order to pass. If you are like most students, this is an upsetting situation. You want to believe that you are an honest person and a good student, but given the opportunity, you willingly copied someone else's answers. Your beliefs are in direct conflict with your behavior. This stressful condition is known as cognitive dissonance. **Cognitive dissonance theory** contends that you can reduce this psychological tension by either changing your belief system or changing your behavior.

So, what do you do? Should you confess to the teacher? Doing so would reinforce the notion that you are honest. Alternatively, you may change your belief system by telling yourself cheating is not immoral.

Another way to eliminate the discomfort of cognitive dissonance is to try to reduce or modify the number of thoughts that support one of the conflicting ideas. In other words, you might try to rationalize that it was the teacher's fault for leaving the test answers out to be seen. You could say that by doing that, the teacher showed a lack of concern over whether students cheated or not. Yet another tactic is reducing the importance of the cognitive elements. You may think, for example, "I was just trying to test myself to see if I'm gutsy enough to break a rule. It was just an experiment so it doesn't really count." By doing any of these things, the distressing notion that "I am a dishonest person" is negated and the uncomfortable dissonance is reduced. It should be noted that cognitive dissonance is fairly common in everyday life. The text describes an experiment by Stanley Milgram that illustrates the idea of conflict between beliefs and behavior. Many of the subjects in his experiment had a difficult time believing that they were capable of harming another person.

Social psychologist Daryl Bem (1972) disagrees with the cognitive dissonance theory. Instead, he thinks that people infer their own attitudes from their behavior and the situational context in which it occurs. His **self-perception theory** is based on the idea that different situations make people alter their perceptions of themselves. In other words, attitudes and beliefs are dictated by one's behavior. If you pass up an opportunity to cheat during a math test, you conclude that

With others or by ourselves, we are never completely alone, for humans are social creatures.

562

Discuss the Photo

The individual has an influence on the group, and the group has an influence on the individual. These influences are what interests the social psychologist.

you must be an honest person. However, if you find yourself cheating in your English class, you then decide that in fact you are capable of dishonesty, in certain situations.

It is also thought that people seek consistency between their own beliefs and those of people they like. Like cognitive dissonance theory, Fritz Heider's **balance theory** (1958) focuses on the notion that people strive for cognitive harmony. He contends that rather than allowing our beliefs to conflict with those of

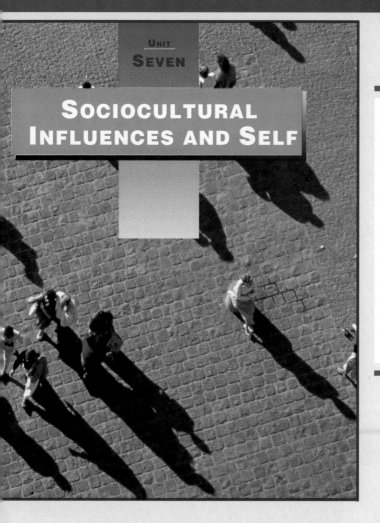

SOCIOCULTURAL INFLUENCES AND SELF

PERFORMANCE TASK

Overview

Students research the prevalence of prejudice in society and the processes used to try to reduce it. Areas to investigate may include attitudes and societal treatment of the aged, women, the impoverished, or ethnic groups. Students design interviews or questionnaires and use them to reveal peer attitudes and relevant behaviors. Students may ask interviewees how they think a particular prejudice originated, and may also ask for suggestions about how to attempt to resolve it. Their findings and conclusions are then reported to the class. The class will want to discuss ways to reduce the negative impact on the groups affected. Complete instructions for this activity and the supporting student worksheets can be found in the Teacher Resources.

someone we like, we tend to either compromise our beliefs or else withdraw from the relationship.

Another variance of the cognitive dissonance theory is called **reactance theory** (Brehm, 1966). Parents of teenagers are familiar with this one; if you tell your teenage daughter she is forbidden to see a certain boy, he suddenly becomes the only boy she's interested in and she defiantly continues to see him on the sly. Beliefs are influenced by the perception that one's freedom to choose has been limited. What is not available becomes more desirable.

Experiments which seem to show that people do indeed change their attitudes to match their behavior have been challenged. Why? If seems that subjects tend to report a change in attitude in order to *appear* consistent to others, even if their *real* attitude has not changed.

References

Full citations can be found in the Teacher Resources.

DISCUSS THE PHOTO

What types of attitudes and beliefs are influenced by culture?

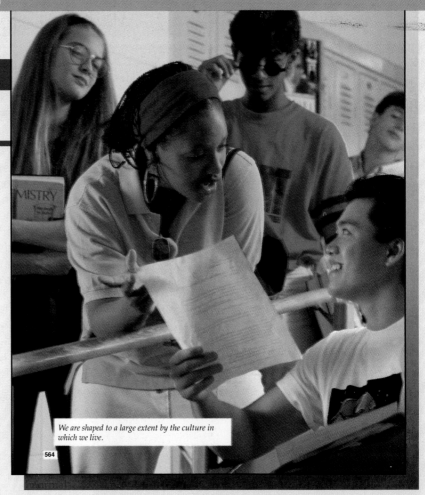

We are shaped to a large extent by the culture in which we live.

564

PSYCHOLOGY AND YOU RESOURCES

A variety of resources are available in the Psychology and You *supplementary material. In addition, there are a number of additional resources listed to enhance your lesson plans.*

Masters
▼ 20-1A Learning Goals
▼ 20-1B Answers to Learning Goals
▼ 20-2 First Impressions
▼ 20-3 Changing Careers 1
▼ 20-4 Changing Careers 2

Student Worksheets
▼ Vocabulary Worksheet
▼ Independent Practice Worksheet
▼ Enrichment Worksheet
▼ Reteaching Worksheet

Test Bank
▼ Tests A and B

Multimedia
▼ *The Brain* Videotape Module #30
▼ Psychology Videodisc

Student Workbook

PACING CHART

Complete Coverage

Day 1: Assign "Hidden Influences Behavior" prior to class. Concentrate on the three parts of the attribution theory. Assign activity #1 in the text addressing the role of antecedents in people's judgments. Have the class read "Interpersonal Attraction" for Day 2.

Day 2: Discuss the roles that associations, physical attraction, and familiarity play in "falling in love." Assign Psychology in Your Life and the "Aggression and Violence" section for homework.

Day 3: Begin with a discussion about abusive relationships. Review the biological and social factors in aggressive behavior, focusing on the concept of deindividuation. Set up a debate regarding the influence of the mass media on violence. Assign "Helping Behavior" for Day 4.

Day 4: Discuss the conclusion psychologists have drawn regarding helping behavior, focusing on the term "evaluation apprehension." Have students

Sociocultural Influences and Relationships

565

OBJECTIVES

Be able to:

▼ Describe attribution theory and how we use it.

▼ Describe the role of physical attractiveness in falling in love.

▼ Describe how it is possible for physical factors to start aggression.

▼ Explain the evidence that social factors can cause aggression.

▼ Give the evidence for both sides regarding whether TV causes violence.

▼ Describe the key factors in whether people will help one another.

▼ Describe territoriality and distinguish it from the protection of one's personal space.

▼ Explain the difference between density and crowding.

Global Look at the Chapter

This chapter focuses on the social and cultural factors that guide our feelings and actions toward one another. We will look at the external influences that interact with an individual's personality to create beliefs about and actions toward other people.

INTRODUCING THE CHAPTER

This chapter and the next deal with issues studied by social psychologists. Students may ask what the difference is between sociology and social psychology. Sociologists study groups and societies. Social psychologists also study groups, but the focus is on how groups affect the individual and how individuals affect groups.

LEAD-OFF ACTIVITY

Walk into class and drop a pile of papers all over the floor. Act frustrated and slowly bend down to retrieve them. Afterward, ask students why they did or did not help. Maybe they did not think you needed help. Maybe status is a factor. If you have more than one class, you can vary the procedure each time. One time, drop the papers close to someone and look the person in the eye. Another time, drop the papers in the middle of the class period, a time when most students are glued to their seats. It's difficult to include many controls when you can only drop papers a few times, but the activity should lead to some interesting observations.

read the last section of the chapter for homework.

Day 5: Give the Chapter Review quiz after reviewing environmental influences on behavior.

In Brief

Day 1: Focus on attribution theory and use discussion question #1 or 2 to evaluate the factors involved in interpersonal attraction.

Day 2: Discuss the biological and social factors in aggressive behavior. Note particularly the controversy over the effects of mass media and imitation learning. Assign for homework an activity analyzing helping behavior.

Day 3: Review the concept of personal space to discuss environmental influences on behavior. Give the Chapter Review quiz.

EXPERIMENT

See **Teaching Master 20-2 First Impressions.** Send one person out of the room. Read the top portion of this handout to a student in class, and follow the directions on the master. Invite the other student back in,

read the bottom portion, and again follow the directions. The top and the bottom of the masters are slightly different, but essentially the same. The purpose is to see if the slight differences cause different attributions.

Learning Goals. A Learning Goals sheet for each chapter is provided in the Teacher Resources. These Learning Goals can be used as review sheets or worksheets. **Teaching Master 20-1B** consists of answers to these Learning Goals.

Points to Stress

The prefix *ante-* means "to come before." Card players will be familiar with the ante put in the pot before the cards are dealt.

Discussion

Students usually attribute a variety of characteristics to cliques, but when asked, "What clique do *you* belong to?" most will claim that they do not belong to any. If this happens, ask why people do not like to admit to belonging to, or do not regard themselves as belonging to, a clique.

566

---

attribution theory

A theory about the process by which we form opinions about another.

antecedents

Information and beliefs we have beforehand about another.

attribution

The causes we use to explain another's behavior.

consequences

Our emotional responses, behavior, and expectations regarding another.

HIDDEN INFLUENCES IN BEHAVIOR

We all do things that at times can surprise even us. The surprise is not necessarily pleasant, especially when we discover things about ourselves that we don't like. For example, say that you are walking down the sidewalk on a busy street. A person falls down in front of you moaning, rolling up into a ball. Would you stop and help? You claim you would. But is that true? Since we don't know you personally, we can't say you won't, but statistically, in real life, the odds are staggering that you will walk on by. Later we will discuss why this happens so often. But first let's look at some of the details about how people think in their relationships with others and how they view the actions of others.

Attribution Theory

Much social interaction is colored by our own psychological makeup. A major factor in how we interpret the behavior of others is covered by **attribution** (at-trih-BYOO-shun) **theory,** which concerns the process by which we form opinions about another. Attribution theory can be divided into three parts, each of which interacts with the others. (1) The first consists of **antecedents,** a word that means "things that come before"—that is, we rely on information, beliefs, and motivations we already have in forming our opinions. (2) The next part is the actual **attribution,** which refers to the causes that we come up with to explain why people do what they do. In other words, we "attribute" (give) reasons to them for their actions. (3) The final part involves **consequences,** such as our behavior (what we do about the situation), our emotional responses, and our expectations (what we think will happen in the future) (Weiner, 1985).

Here is an example of what we are talking about: you have an acquaintance named Maria, a classmate you know casually; the two of you speak when you meet at school. You are going home at 4:00 on a Tuesday afternoon, and you see Maria coming down the sidewalk. As usual, you say, "Hi." *Not* as usual, however, she replies, "Go away!" and stalks off. Maria is usually a friendly, pleasant person, has always seemed to like you, and you in turn value knowing her. Those beliefs are part of the *antecedents* (what existed before you were rejected). You had already formed a concept of what Maria was like, and now you must try to explain her behavior within this framework. There are two possibilities. Either something about the situation caused her to act this way, or there is something personal involved. Perhaps something happens on Tuesday afternoons, causing Maria to behave that way. Because you want to find out what is

DISCOVERY

See **Teaching Master 20-3 Changing Careers 1 and Teaching Master 20-4 Careers 2.** Use these handouts to conduct in class textbook activity #1 at the end of the chapter. Pass out one master to half the class and the other master to the other half.

Chapter 20 SOCIOCULTURAL INFLUENCES AND RELATIONSHIPS

IN FOCUS   **Attribution Theory**

Situation: Ann sees her boyfriend talking with her best friend.

Assume that you know Ann is a jealous person. With this antecedent in mind, what is *your* attribution for her thoughts above?

Attribution Theory.

 One possible attribution is that Ann is jumping to conclusions.

Points to Stress

An actor steps from the black-and-white screen into the theater audience in Woody Allen's fantasy film, *Purple Rose of Cairo.* When he finds out that the girl he "loves" (remember, he's not a real person) is battered by her husband, he wants to fight him: "It's written into my character to do it, so I do it." This might be a good way to describe how antecedents influence attributions. Certain antecedents, after a while, are written into our character.

going on, you keep trying. So, the following day you say "Hi" to her again, and this time she says "Hi" back. The same thing happens the next day, and the next, and so on. The following Tuesday, however, at 4:00, when you say "Hi," she says "Go away!" and stalks off.

Now you have additional information, characteristics that can be noted and that are consistent. Only on Tuesday does she act this way. On further investigation, you find that Maria has a standing appointment at the dentist at 4:30 on that day, is having painful procedures done, and hates going there. Now you can make an *attribution;* that is, you make up a cause for her weird behavior. You perceive it as rooted in the fact that she has to go to the dentist.

Once an attribution is made, it leads to *consequences:* you can now explain Maria's behavior and not take it personally. Had the antecedents been different—if you had viewed her as an unpredictable, explosive person, for instance—you might have attributed

DISCOVERY

Spend a few minutes discussing popular definitions or descriptions of love: love is for the birds; love is a many-splendored thing; and so on. You can generate plenty of ideas by having students think of popular songs. Then tell students to write "Love is ____" at the top of a sheet of paper. Allow them about five min-utes to fill in the blank with as many "definitions" of love as possible. (You may want to break them into groups.) Encourage them to be creative and even humorous. You should receive some wacky answers. Collect all the papers and without revealing names, read the definitions. As you do this, look beyond the wackiness of some of the answers and perhaps find wis-dom in them. For example, if some-one writes, "Love stinks," ask, "In what way does love stink? Do you mean it causes pain? Is the pain worth it?" Of course, you don't want to overanalyze each answer, but you may get more out of some definitions than you expect.

Critical Thinking

Read the following sce-nario to students: *A teacher sees a student sleeping in class. To what might the teacher attribute this? (What reasons might the teacher use to explain this?)* (1) Oh, that's just the way he is. (2) He must have had a bad night. (3) I am a boring teacher. (4) It's 7:30 a.m.! The actual attribution will depend on how often this student sleeps in class, how many other students sleep, and other factors.

Discussion

When a team is on a winning streak, what attri-butions do we make? (The other teams in the conference are weak; the team is lucky; the team is working hard.) What if the team loses? (They were playing above their level before; they had a let-down; it was the coach's fault.) The attributions we ultimately make depend on what we focus on. And antecedents, along with other factors, influence this.

Unit 7 SOCIOCULTURAL INFLUENCES AND SELF

her actions to instability, not bothered to investigate, and avoided her in the future.

Thus, we are always seeking an explanation for why something happens, even if we unknowingly come to a false conclusion. Using such a system can lead us to accept or reject others. For instance, if a Republican publicly praises another Republican, most people pay no attention to what is said since both politicians belong to the same political party and since politicians are not very high on people's lists of most trusted people. But if we hear a Democrat praising a Republican, we are much more likely to attribute honesty to that per-son and tend to believe in him or her, even though that might not be sensible (Quattrone, 1985).

Now that you grasp attribution, note that its principles are used all the time. We use it to explain the behavior of our friends, parents, and people we work with. For groups we don't like, we attribute all kinds of strange things to them—they don't bathe, the family has strange rituals it performs—and then look for clues that might sup-port our beliefs. With groups we like, such as the ones we belong to, we see the members as having all kinds of positive characteristics, some of which don't really exist.

Attributions can be quite distorted. When it was discovered that the Earth was round, many famous people of the time believed that there was a whole race of oddly acting creatures who got that way from living "upside down" at the bottom of the Earth. They were called *Antipodes. Anti* means "opposite," and *podes* is another word for "feet." These Antipode people had their feet going the opposite direction, or upside-down. They lived at the bottom of the Earth where trees grew upside-down and rain fell upward. They were not creatures at all like the rest of us. Some people did object to this strange idea, but they tried to fight it by claiming that the Earth was a *cube* (Boorstin, 1983). That wasn't much of a solution because using the logic of the day, you would then have some people who grew sideways as well as some who grew upside-down!

Attributions are a subtle part of any relationship. In the very early stages, however, the critical factor in people getting together is how they view one another emotionally. Hence, in the next section we will review the factors involved in what seems to attract one person to another.

INTERPERSONAL ATTRACTION

One of the more difficult subjects to handle scientifically is "love." Equally hard is trying to tell the exact differences between "like" and "love." We know what we feel, but we cannot define it very well. So, we will report here the valiant attempts by scientists to understand these feelings.

ENRICHMENT

Ask some students to explore whether love is viewed in similar ways around the world. How do courtships and marriages differ in various countries?

ENRICHMENT

Have students research what kinds of physiological changes occur when we become infatuated with someone.

Discussion

Compare and contrast romantic love with other kinds of love—family bonds, platonic love, and so on. Ask students if it is important to *tell* family and friends that we love them. Or is *showing* love enough?

Chapter 20 SOCIOCULTURAL INFLUENCES AND RELATIONSHIPS

We can start with that overwhelming feeling we all have had at one time or another, "falling madly in love." There is no feeling quite like it since it can consume us one minute, make us feel wonderful the next, and miserable and lost the minute after that. The most obvious characteristics of this state are the physical responses: rapid heartbeat, stomach contractions, and general body chaos. Ironically, these "symptoms" are identical to those of fear and anxiety. The major difference is that the behaviors have become associated with someone we find physically attractive. When this association occurs, we know it isn't "fear" but "love" (Sherrod, 1982). So, we start off with a physical base, add emotional responses, and then top it all off by getting involved psychologically with the person.

Importance of Associations

We also know that there is a considerable amount of high-level emotional association going on in this state, which is what makes it so special. For example, most people in love have a special song that "belongs" to them. It was heard during a special moment together. Now the song is associated with them and the emotions they felt the first time they heard it. Thus, each time they hear it again, the emotions recur. There are also special places they have gone; again, these places and the things connected with them get associated with this high level of emotional arousal. As a result, we build more and more associations to the core response we had at the beginning. The more connections we have, the more associations and the stronger the feeling gets. What starts off as a physical feeling takes on broad emotional and mental associations.

Ingredients in Liking and Loving

Creatures don't fall in love with just anyone. There is something special that occurs. Many species of birds pick a specific mate for life. The wolf is quite selective in choosing a mate, and the couple tends to stay together as a unit with the "family." A male peacock will spread out its beautiful plumage to attract a female. Some females will like what a particular male shows; others won't and will prefer a different male. Finally, as is also true for humans, the female peacock is far more selective than the male.

Physical attractiveness is a large factor in interpersonal attraction when people first meet and get to know one another (Edinger & Paterson, 1983). At that point, there is little else on which to judge someone. The pitfall here is that we tend to see more attractive people in a generally more positive light, to see them as competent, confident, and so forth. In fact, just from appearance we attribute all kinds of good things to those who are more in line with society's

▲ *Studies suggest that love starts out as physical attraction, but whether it lasts depends on personality factors.*

DISCUSS THE PHOTO

What kinds of personality factors does lasting love depend on?

Points to Stress

Just as density may contribute to violence (see the end of the chapter), proximity, which refers to nearness, contributes to liking. This seems like a painfully obvious point, but we choose many of our friends because we happen to live next door to them, or sit next to them in school, or work with them.

Comprehension Check

List three components of "falling in love." *(physical attractiveness, familiarity, and emotional associations)*

569

COOPERATIVE LEARNING

You will probably have several students who have had relatively long dating relationships. Ask these people to share their ideas on why or how liking turns to love. Students may feel uncomfortable using the word love in this context, but they probably will answer more general questions such as "In what way did your relationship change as time went by? Do you worry sometimes about becoming too close to the other person? Does it require work to keep the relationship going? Does the relationship ever get boring?"

Points to Stress

Another tip from a marriage counselor: marriages have a better chance of succeeding when spouses allow each other to be themselves. Compromises are certainly going to be made, but that's what they are: *mutual* compromises, which are very different from one person trying to change the other. In a word, marriage requires tolerance.

expectations of attractiveness. Again, females are far more discriminating; they are more likely to view the whole person rather than just the body or hairstyle.

Less attractive people, by society's standards, are at a disadvantage—but only in the beginning. There is a saying that "beauty is in the eye of the beholder." Scientifically, this saying seems to be true because studies show that people tend to match up more or less with people who are roughly the same level of attractiveness (Reis et al., 1980; Cash & Janda, 1984; White, 1980). In any case, over time, personalities become more important to others than the physique. While physical looks can often get a first date, whether or not there will be a second one will usually rely heavily on personality. So, there is at least some hope for most of us.

Both liking and loving are based on *familiarity*. In other words, the more we see specific people, the more we like them (if there is something to them), since we tend to find that the familiar is less threatening. This principle holds true as long as the interactions are spaced over time. There is a lesson here: in beginning relationships as well as in long-standing ones, we can overdo ourselves and exhaust the other person no matter how wonderful we are. Too much closeness too fast often reduces attractiveness. It is better to maintain *some* distance at first so that there is still psychological territory for the other person to explore and be fascinated by (Myers, 1983).

Revealing oneself to the other person has its place, time, and limits. While love seems to grow with mutual understanding and sharing of intimate feelings, endless exposure of the self turns the other person off, especially if it comes early in the relationship and involves ongoing baring of the soul. Believe it or not, our problems, shared in excess, are rather boring to others. Limited sharing, though, can deepen a relationship. At the very least, the partner needs a chance to talk about *some* of his or her problems (Franzio, 1985).

You will hear that those with opposite interests are best suited for a long-lasting relationship, but there is no evidence to support this claim. Hundreds of studies have explored this area, and most conclude that those who stay together the longest are more alike than they are different (Nias, 1979). Variation is interesting, but major differences are threatening.

While it is probably not applicable to your life at present, this is a good place to mention a few tips from seasoned marriage counselors. These ideas are too important to ignore: (1) Marrying someone with the intention of helping him or her get over a drug or alcohol problem almost never works. Things inevitably get worse. (2) A little jealousy goes a long way. Most experts agree that someone who is very, very jealous will make daily life miserable, and the odds against getting rid of this problem are staggeringly high. (3) Any kind of violence in a relationship is there to stay. The odds of the victim being able to avoid it are so low that the time to end the relationship seems to be immediately, before it gets a foothold. (4) Love in the best of circumstances is a *very* fragile mixture of self-esteem and self-importance, of both giving and taking, and trying to keep a decent balance between them (Davis, 1985).

AGGRESSION AND VIOLENCE

War and violence are as old as human records. Fossil remains from the Neanderthals (100,000 years ago) show wooden weapons and spear tips embedded in human bone. As the result of such findings, many people claim that aggression appears among animals of any kind and that we are merely an advanced animal. However, virtually all animal species can and do control their aggressive impulses. Such control is absolutely necessary for survival.

At the human level, there are societies in which daily activities center on chances to cheat and be as cutthroat as possible toward one another. Other societies exist in which violence is absent or very rare, and people live in basic harmony.

Most of the evidence suggests that humans began as hunter-gatherers—that is, we wandered the forests where food was usually available. In such groups, violence would be at a minimum. Similar groups still exist in remote forest lands and show little aggression (Montagu, 1974). This finding leads some to think that aggression may have arisen from some natural disaster that stripped the forest bare and left people fighting for food. Whether we are supposed to be carnivores (meat eaters) or not is still argued. The evidence is ambiguous. Our intestinal systems are long, winding mazes, the kind that are normally found in creatures that require a lengthy digestion process for vegetation, as opposed to the relatively short and direct intestine of a meat eater such as a dog.

Be all that as it may, though, violence does indeed erupt all around us, and since most of us have more than enough to eat, we have to assume that at least part of such behavior is the result of imitation or social learning.

Influence of the Brain

Given our elaborate brains, we produce all kinds of variations on situations; we can be either peaceful or violent depending on how we *interpret* situations (Lazarus, 1974). For instance, people leaving a movie that had aggressive content who are "accidentally" pushed (by experimenters) are more likely to get aggressive than those who just saw a peaceful movie. The people are stirred up, but they don't know that it is from the movie; hence, they attribute (remember attribution?) the cause of their arousal to the person who jostled them (Rule & Nesdale, 1976). Thus the current hypothesis for aggression focuses on mental activity rather than on the fulfillment of basic

Chapter 20 SOCIOCULTURAL INFLUENCES AND RELATIONSHIPS

▲ *Victims of aggression in Somalia.*

Connections

Alcohol may inhibit our ability to control our aggressive impulses (Chapter 16). Alcohol also leads to *deindividuation* (presented later in the chapter).

DISCUSS THE PHOTO

You might point out that the American soldiers are not the aggressors. They were sent to Somalia to try to *restore* order.

Connections

Male hormones may contribute to greater aggression (Chapters 3 and 13).

571

COOPERATIVE LEARNING

Ask students to debate in small groups the following question: *Would you be willing to sacrifice individual rights for greater security and less violence?* If so, ask students for specific rights they would surrender. Would they agree to a curfew? Fewer violent TV programs? Restrictions on aggressive sports, like boxing? This is not meant to suggest that staying out late, TV, and boxing cause violence but to show that there are many freedoms we take for granted.

ENRICHMENT

Have students explore possible factors that contribute to the relatively low rate of violence in Japan. Could we successfully apply any of these factors in the United States? Is the occurrence of violence in Japan on the increase? For what reasons?

Comprehension Check

Describe the various influences on aggression.
(1) Cultural *(emphasis on individualism and competition)*
(2) Social *(focusing male upbringing on masculine activities; anonymous nature of society, or deindividuation; risky shift phenomenon; possibly the media)*
(3) Biological *(allergies or drugs affecting the hypothalamus)*

Unit 7 SOCIOCULTURAL INFLUENCES AND SELF

needs (such as getting food). At least once a week, we read about someone stabbing or shooting a family member to death because they lost the *TV Guide* or some equally absurd thing. A moment's reflection and it becomes obvious that this aggression is the end product of some kind of symbolic issue, rather than of deprivation, starvation, or a specific basic need that has not been met.

Culture and Aggression

Human aggression also develops from environment and culture. The United States has always been a very violent country, and we are getting worse, not better. All types of violent crime increased throughout the 1980s. You are between seven and ten times more likely to be murdered in America than in most European countries. In fact, homicide is the second highest cause of death among our youth, killing more people between the ages of 15 and 24 than anything else except accidents (Lore & Schultz, 1993). Japan, on the other hand, is relatively free of violence despite notable overcrowding. Although violence is on the rise in Great Britain, the rule is still that police officers do not carry firearms, even when they are capturing thieves, burglars, or petty criminals.

Many experts believe that the high value Americans place on individual rights and freedoms plus our emphasis on competition have contributed to this problem. In other words, when the individual is overemphasized, getting along with others becomes less important. When one person is strongly encouraged to win over another, hostility and aggression are likely to result. Other cultures place greater value on the welfare of the group, which in turn encourages people to cooperate and find ways to get along with other people.

To get another perspective on how humans vary in their aggressive behavior, we might consider the frontier West, which is often thought to have had very high crime rates. This was not the case. Murder was very rare among ordinary citizens. In Bodie, California, from 1878 to 1882, bodies did pile up at a rate three times that of today's most murderous urban areas. But these were the bodies of young men who wanted to go around "shooting it out," not of everyday citizens. During this four-year period, only one woman was robbed, and there were no reported rapes. Juvenile crimes were nonexistent (McGrath, 1985). In fact, even among the worst of criminals, it was strictly taboo *ever* to bother a woman in any way. That was the code of the West.

Humans also seem to set up special places for aggression, such as football games, boxing matches, and bars. One psychological study focused on all the bars in one city—185 of them. Only a few accounted for the majority of the aggression that took place in bars. The psychologists found that those who entered these few bars *expected* either to attack or to be attacked before the evening was over. Such

History. In many ways, war seems to be the ultimate act of aggression. Have students select a war and find examples of deindividuation. What fostered an atmosphere of deindividuation, and how did this lead to aggression? For example, in the Persian Gulf war, there was not as much face-to-face combat as in most other wars. It was essentially fought from the air, which would certainly contribute to deindividuation.

bars had certain characteristics in common: unclean and cheap surroundings, ill-kempt patrons, patrons drinking rapidly, people talking loudly to themselves, unfriendly bartenders, downtown location, and poor ventilation (Graham et al., 1980).

Social Factors in Aggression

There is much more violence among men than women. While one could make a case for hormones causing this, social learning—that is, the childhood training received by males versus females—seems more important.

More often than not, aggressive behavior starts early in life and continues on through adolescence. Most of it seems to result from family upbringing focusing on "masculine" activities that are typically aggressive—such as fighting back and standing up to someone "like a man." This kind of training has to be tempered very early, many feel, or it is too late to do anything about it. Aggressive patterns apparently are somewhat set by middle childhood (Eron, 1980).

In addition to family influence, psychologists point to the anonymous nature of our society as a cause of aggressive behavior. When people are ignored as individuals, this can lead to antisocial behavior. The term used for this is **deindividuation** (DE-in-di-vi-ju-AYE-shun), meaning a loss of one's sense of individuality (Diener, 1976). A study performed on Halloween supports this hypothesis. When children were given an opportunity to steal change from a money bowl about two feet from the candy bowl, they stole about 8 percent of the time if they were alone and if the person answering the door knew who they were, but they stole about 20 percent of the time under the same conditions if they were *with a group* and known—probably the result of group "bravado." The figure jumped to 57 percent, though, when the group was *not* known to the person answering the door. In one case, an experimenter answering the door told the children that she was going to leave the room, pointed to the smallest child, and said if she found any money missing when she came back, she was going to hold that child responsible. The stealing soared to 80 percent since the group then had someone to blame (Diener et al., 1976).

As you can see, individuals reduce the sense of their own responsibility when they are with other people. In other words, in a group, each person apparently feels less responsible for what happens. Also, the individual feels more powerful and less vulnerable when with other people. This situation has been called the **risky shift phenomenon**, meaning that when in a group, the risk or danger for each individual is shifted (divided up) among all the group members (Wallach et al., 1962). Hence, group behavior fosters much more risk taking than individual members would engage in by themselves. The risky shift may help explain horrible events like lynch mobs, gang beatings, and mass riots.

deindividuation

A loss of one's sense of individuality and responsibility when in a group.

risky shift phenomenon

The situation where the danger of an act is split among the members of a group; hence, it is smaller for each person.

573

Points to Stress

Offer examples of the risky shift phenomenon that occurred during the 1992 riots in Los Angeles after the not guilty verdict was announced for the police officers who allegedly beat Rodney King. At least one innocent driver was pulled from his vehicle and beaten. The attackers did not think they would be held responsible. Ironically, videotape captured their actions.

DEMONSTRATION

Sometimes newspapers and news magazines will print picture after picture of children killed in the last year by gunshots. The apparent goal is to discourage deindividuation and perhaps reduce violence. If you can find this kind of photo spread, show it to the class and ask for their reactions.

ENRICHMENT

Have students explore other unusual acts of aggression by people who were otherwise usually calm. Restak's *The Mind* would be a good source; see the **Suggested Readings.**

FYI Psychologist Irving Janis (1982) uses the term *groupthink* to describe a process similar to the risky shift phenomenon. If a group is unanimous, it creates an illusion of power and security, and individual members are not likely to oppose the group. Before the space shuttle Challenger crashed, individuals had reservations about going ahead with the launch, but many did not voice their opinions, nor did the majority give much credence to the few people who did express doubts.

Biological Factors in Aggression

There is evidence that some aggressive behavior can have physical causes. We discussed in Chapter 3 the fact that in the inner core of the brain, roughly midway between the nose and the back of the head sits a unit called the *hypothalamus,* which controls rage, anger, pleasure, and other behaviors. We believe that the rage portion of the hypothalamus might well be responsible for uncontrolled outbursts of violence.

Here are a few examples: allergies to certain substances can cause dramatic changes in a person's behavior. There was a case of a child who was perfectly normal until he ate bananas. After doing so, he would try to tear up the room and destroy his toys. This only occurred after eating that fruit. Another child would bang his head against the wall whenever he ate wheat. And we personally knew about a very sweet, normally calm mother who every now and then at breakfast would throw dishes against the wall and stomp on the silverware. This behavior was restricted to breakfast time and lasted only about 20 minutes. Of course, very few people can witness small children in action at breakfast without feeling a little crazy, but this was truly out of the ordinary. After careful exploration, it was discovered that just before these episodes, she would sample pancakes she was cooking. She normally didn't eat them. It turned out that she was allergic to the yellow dye some manufacturers use to make the pancakes look more "eggy." Normally, when people are allergic, they break out in hives, but in these cases, they were "breaking out" inside their heads, causing the brain tissue to swell and put pressure on the rage center in the hypothalamus (Moyer, 1975). Thus erupted the woman's uncontrollable morning episodes.

Amphetamines ("speed"), used over time, can cause brain cells to start firing at random and can make the world so confusing that the person feels threatened and begins striking out at others to protect himself or herself from being harmed—even though no one is really even paying attention to that person. The effects of alcohol are very much involved with changes in the psychology of the person. Alcohol reduces inhibitions and leads to violence in people who are insecure or obnoxious to begin with and who, when they drink, can no longer hold these traits in check.

Recent attention has focused on other factors as contributors to aggression, especially in television and movies. We will take a look at that next.

Effects of Mass Media

It may seem hard to believe, but for 50 years in colonial America, newspapers and books were considered a danger to the general public. Printing presses were carefully controlled, and what few things

574

Ask students to describe possible ways groups could avoid groupthink (see the preceding **FYI**). (They might suggest procedures that could be built into a group's decision-making process that would welcome contrary opinions. You have probably con-ducted several exercises in class that encourage students to view situations from various points of view through role-playing and journal writing; perhaps these kinds of exercises could be implemented when major decisions are being made.)

Have several students debate whether people who commit acts of violence that are prompted by drugs, allergies, or other physical abnormalities should be held responsible for their acts.

Chapter 20 SOCIOCULTURAL INFLUENCES AND RELATIONSHIPS

▲ *At-home example of the effects of viewing violence.*

Ask students, "If these were your kids, would this behavior disturb you? Would you turn off the TV?"

Discussion

Video games sometimes include a great deal of violence. Some might argue that video games are worse than TV because young people *participate* in the violence, in a sense. Some of your students have probably spent many hours with these games. Do they believe the games have any short- or long-term effects on aggression? Will they let their children play video games? If so, are there *any* restrictions that parents should establish?

were published had to have government approval. The fear was that somehow freedom of publication might damage the morals of the general public. In the 1600s, a highly spiritual book (today considered a Christian classic), the *Imitation of Christ*, was banned because it might lead to differing views about religion. In Nathaniel Hawthorne's classic novel, *The Scarlet Letter*, a woman had to wear a large red letter "A" (for adulteress) on her clothing because she had a child outside of marriage. The book was banned in the 1850s. Later, in 1925, censors would not allow the movie based on the book to be shown unless the main character was married—which destroyed the whole point of the story (Tebbel, 1974).

Today, movies and television programs are at the center of attention in the same general way, with much concern expressed about violence and sex as part of their content. While there may well be important issues involved here, we have to move cautiously to keep from winding up with the same restrictions and censorship that existed in earlier centuries. There have been a few studies on the issue of sex in movies and television, but roughly 100 or so on violence, so we will focus on the latter to try to get some perspective.

Basic Film Studies An early core study on the influence of film violence involved showing part of a movie called *The Champion*, starring actor Kirk Douglas. In the part shown to subjects, Mr. Douglas received a grotesque beating. After seeing the movie, subjects were told to judge the merit of a drawing made by a young man whose outline could be seen behind a screen. If they didn't like his work, they were to administer shocks to him. The shocks were not real, but

INTERDISCIPLINARY PROJECT

Speech. Students should choose to support the affirmative or opposition for the following statement: The content of children's television should be more regulated than it is today. The sides should choose members to sit on a panel that will debate this question. All members should research the issue and help formulate supporting arguments.

Discussion

Whatever effect TV has on aggression, it is important that parents watch TV with their kids at times to clarify and monitor any misconceptions that may arise. Ask students if they watched TV with their parents when they were children. Did they discuss the content and values of various shows?

imitation learning

The process of learning behaviors by viewing others and then doing the same things they did.

the subjects thought they were because the person would groan. Again unknown to the subjects, all the drawings used for different groups were identical.

In one variation of the experiment, the "artist" was introduced as "Kirk" to some subjects and by another name to other subjects. The intensity of shock administered to "Kirk" was much greater than that to the person with another name. These findings suggest that we can identify with violent behavior and carry the activity seen on the screen into real life (Berkowitz & Geen, 1967).

In a second version that used the same arrangement, some subjects were told before viewing the scene from the movie that a bad guy was receiving the beating. Another group was told that a good guy was getting the blows. In other words, for the first subjects, the beating was justified; for the second, it was unjustified. This study showed that *justified violence* bred greater violence (shocks) against the stooges than unjustified violence.

Some principles emerged from these studies. First, violence can breed violence. Second, justified violence is likely to breed greater violence than unjustified violence does. Thus, violence in the name of right, honor, and good in movies and television actually leads to more violence, at least in laboratory settings (Diener & Woody, 1981). In a way, society has condoned violence if it is "right." This is important because few of us ever feel that we are *not* justified in "paying someone back" (Collins & Zimmerman, 1975).

These studies are based on the principle that people imitate all kinds of behavior, including violence. What, then, are the effects on children of viewing television? First of all, in the laboratory, if children see a movie with violence, they tend to become violent themselves by a process called **imitation learning** (Bandura et al., 1963). Logic, then, suggests that TV can contribute to imitation and aggression (Roberts & Bachen, 1981). But the evidence is not all one-sided. "Good" (nonviolent) television leads to imitation for a short while, but children seem to lose interest in it. Instead, they actively seek out the novelty in strange and wild programs such as the "Three Stooges" series (Comstock et al., 1978). Some suspect the key to appropriate TV programming, for children at least, is plenty of non-violent novelty.

There is only one clear finding. The short-term effect of violent TV and movies is a very high level of *physical* arousal, which could lead to aggression if the person is then provoked in some way. This arousal lasts only about 20 minutes, however (Doob & Climie, 1972). No one disputes this finding on the short-term effects, but some question the long-term effects.

Trying for Perspective It is hard to get perspective on an issue once it "goes public" and becomes controversial. This is especially true in an area that involves something like TV, when the average child two to 11 years old watches 27.3 hours a week (Nielsen, 1985).

DEMONSTRATION

To test whether your students will imitate aggressive behavior, bring in a large, inflatable toy. Arrange beforehand for a few students to punch the toy around while the class is waiting for you to show up to class. Arrive a few minutes late. Ask your models to carefully observe the reactions of the rest of the class then discuss these reactions.

For example, one psychologist brought together all the research on TV and aggression and concluded that there was no clear-cut and strong relationship (Freedman, 1984). More recently, other psychologists looked at nearly 30 studies done in this area and reached very different conclusions. According to these researchers, media violence is directly linked to aggressive behavior, not only in children but among people of all ages (Wood, Wong & Chachere, 1991).

Here are some basic findings: government reports and newspaper accounts say that there are 2,500 or more studies on TV and aggression, but this number is misleading. The same studies are being reported over and over, only each time a little information is added to one of them. Actually, there are about 100 studies directly relating to the subject, most of them from the laboratory. Most such studies show a relationship between TV and aggression. But the fact that filmed or videotaped aggression leads to aggressive behavior in a laboratory may or may not reflect what happens in real life, so let's turn our focus to the nonlaboratory studies.

In *field studies*, behavior is directly observed in a natural, nonlaboratory setting; in this case, subjects are watched after they view violent and nonviolent TV. Taken as a whole, these studies give only weak support to the belief that TV aggression causes real-life aggression. In fact, some aggressive people are *less* aggressive after seeing violence, and some nonaggressive people are *more* aggressive. Why this happens is not clear. In any case, there is insufficient evidence in field studies to conclude that TV viewing leads to aggression. Some unclear, but important, difference exists between laboratory studies and the behavior of people outside the laboratory.

Examination of the overall behavior of children (not just their television viewing) does show something important. Children who are already aggressive and view a lot of TV get progressively worse. In addition, already aggressive children actively seek out aggressive television (Eron, 1983).

The final item is clearly ironic. The most popular programs on television over time are those that contain emotional conflicts and have little or no violence (Diener & Woody, 1981). Apparently, program makers are adding an ingredient (violence) that people don't care all that much about, and then everyone is getting upset about it.

Conclusions? (1) Studies to date show mixed results concerning the relationship between TV and later violence *in the average person.* (2) Aggressive people seek out aggressive television and then become even more aggressive (Eron & Huesman, 1985).

Catharsis   Before ending the discussion, we should make one more comment. You will hear that seeing violence might help us get rid of our aggressive impulses—that is, that it can "discharge" the energy connected with those impulses. The psychological term for this is **catharsis** (ca-THAR-sis), which comes from the Greek mean-

catharsis
The supposed ability to get rid of aggressive energy by viewing others acting aggressively.

Discussion

Solicit anecdotal evidence for increased aggression during and after sporting events. Are certain sports more likely than others to incite aggression in fans? If so, this could be an example of imitation learning. Sometimes, however, fights after a game seem to be more related to the outcome of the contest than to modeling. One explanation might be too much identification with the teams.

Points to Stress

Novelty shops often sell items that you punch, and this punching allegedly reduces stress. Catharsis? Probably only a gimmick.

COOPERATIVE LEARNING

Before students read about the reasons why people do not help in emergencies, tell them about the Kitty Genovese attack. Explain that since the incident, psychologists have been fascinated with finding reasons for people's *apparent* apathy during emergencies. Then divide students into small groups, and have each group think of two possible hypotheses about why people do *not* help in emergencies and how to test each hypothesis. You will probably need to review some terms from Chapter 2. This activity should demonstrate how difficult it is sometimes to think of hypotheses and to devise a plan to test them. If students do not get a chance to devise these plans, they may perceive the altruism experiments presented in the text as

---

Points to Stress

As neighbors watched Kitty Genovese being killed, minute by minute, they established a norm of not helping. Chapter 21 explores the power of conforming to expectations.

Points to Stress

Another word for helping behavior, which might prove *helpful* to you, is *altruism*.

DISCUSS THE PHOTO

One of the rules of helping is that the bystander needs to define the situation as an emergency. This may be a good example of evaluation apprehension.

Critical Thinking

Is there a difference between males and females in helping behavior? Ask students to assume that there *is* and to think of reasons why one gender might help more than the other. If they want to test their theories, see the next **Experiment.**

578

▲ *Apparently very strict "rules" guide whether or not someone in need gets assistance.*

ing "to cleanse or purify." The idea is that by fantasy, we can purify ourselves of this need in real life. As much as one might like this theory to be true, the evidence over a number of years shows that it doesn't work. Instead, people merely get more agitated (Geen, 1977).

Violence obviously leads to victims who need help. As a result, social psychologists also study the other side: under what circumstances will people come to the aid of someone in an emergency? The answer is surprising.

HELPING BEHAVIOR

At 3:00 A.M. in New York City, a young woman by the name of Kitty Genovese was attacked on the street in front of her apartment house by a man bent on killing her. She let out endless bloodcurdling screams and broke away from him, only to be caught again and attacked once more. It took the man over half an hour to murder her, during which time 38 of her neighbors stood at their windows and watched. One of the neighbors was seen opening his door, going to the top of a stairwell, watching the attack going on down below him, and then returning to his apartment. Fifteen minutes later that man was the first person to call the police (Seedman & Hallman, 1974).

These events and others like them have been the topic of almost endless discussion in the news media. Have people lost all sense of right and wrong? Don't they care anymore?

Two experimenters examined these issues using a series of elaborate psychological observations. They wanted to learn why people sometimes will not help others in obvious distress (Latané & Darley, 1970). The experimenters set up situations in which people were sitting in a room when one of the following events occurred: smoke began to creep through one of the air vents, or a man was having an epileptic seizure (fake) in the other room, or a woman fell down in an adjacent room and was apparently seriously injured, indicated by all kinds of noise, moans, and groans coming from her. Each of these events was staged in such a way that the behavior of those who were "bystanders" to the event could be observed. (1) In the smoke experiment, different arrangements were tried: a student was placed alone in a room taking a test when it happened, then two students were in the room, three students, and so forth, all observed through a two-way mirror. (2) In the epileptic experiment, subjects were isolated from one another but "found out" that one of the subjects was epileptic. The subjects were to carry on a discussion with one another via earphones and microphones, so they could hear but not see one another. They were told that this was to allow them more freedom of speech. When the "seizure" came, they could hear it going on and had access to help if they wanted it just by getting up and looking for the laboratory assistant. (3) The same basic setup as in number 1 was

simple and uninspiring, and the conclusions may seem like common
sense. If they get the chance to
devise their own experiments, they'll
probably realize how insightful the
actual experiments are.

used for the "injured" woman, but the door to the testing room,
where differing numbers of people were, was left open so they could
hear the woman.

After all these experiments, the subjects were interviewed. The
findings are quite consistent and strong. First of all, though, no particular personality type responded to the need for help more than
others. Second, all the subjects were quite concerned about the plight
of the person in need, so there was no lack of feeling. Some came to
the rescue; large numbers did not. What was the difference? The
answer is so simple that it is startling and at first unbelievable, but
this type of study has been done so often over the years that there is
no question about it.

The factor that controlled whether or not someone helped others
was how many people the subject was with at the time the emergency arose. That makes sense, doesn't it? But there's a twist to it,
because the *more* people present at the emergency, the *less* likely any
one person was to give aid to the victim, and this held true for all the
experiments. The results, part of which are shown in Table 20.1, are
striking. In this table, the subject is the person being observed to see
if he or she will respond to the cry of the epileptic; the victim is the
epileptic; "others" are just added people put into the situation by the
experimenter.

How do the experimenters explain why this happens? Here are
some of the conclusions that have been clearly demonstrated over time:

1. When others are present, we are inhibited from acting for fear
   we will make fools of ourselves in public.
2. If others are also observing the emergency, we use them as a
   guide for how to act, just as when we go to a party with people
   we don't know, we use others at the party as a guide for how to
   behave. If they don't help, we don't; if they do, we do.
3. Subjects who think or know that others are present are less likely
   to take personal responsibility because they feel that it is
   someone else's job. This is called **diffusion of responsibility,**
   meaning that the more people there are, the less responsibility
   each of us has to take (because responsibility is diffused, or
   spread out, among the members of the group).
4. But why don't people at least phone for help? Calling the police,
   in and of itself, admits that there is an emergency. If we admit
   that, then we get ourselves into a bind (Milgram, 1977): if it is
   indeed an emergency, we should do something more about the
   problem than just hang up the phone and wait for help to arrive!
5. We won't help in a strange environment where we don't know
   the rules. Here is a study that shows that: a well-dressed man on
   crutches fell down. Would someone help? He was a stooge for an
   experimenter and was not really injured. The first series of
   experiments was done in a subway, and 83 percent of passersby
   came to his aid. In a second set, he fell down at an airport. Only
   41 percent tried to help. Is this some kind of social class

Chapter 20 SOCIOCULTURAL
INFLUENCES AND RELATIONSHIPS

▲ **Table 20.1 Effects of Group
Size on Likelihood and Speed
of Response to Epileptic
Emergency (Letané & Darley,
1970)**

Group Size	Percent Responding by End of Seizure	Percent Ever Responding
2 (subject and victim)	85	100
3 (subject, victim, and one other)	62	85
6 (subject, victim, and 4 others)	31	62

diffusion of responsibility

For an individual member of a
group, responsibility for others is
spread out among all group
members.

Discussion

Children are taught to
stay away from strangers,
yet they are also told they
should be polite and helpful. How do we teach children to decide which
behavior is appropriate?
(When children are very
young, parents may sug-
gest that they only help
when the parents are
around. As children
become older and they
are better able to discriminate, parents may give
children specific warning
signs. Believe it or not,
some parents may even
role-play a variety of scenarios with their children.)

Points to Stress

Although it is mentioned
here that subjects were
interviewed after the altruism experiments, point out
that the *interviews* did not
yield the results. The interviews were merely follow-
up. The results consisted
of subjects' *responses* to
the situation.

EXPERIMENT

You can probably conduct your own mini-experiment on helping behavior just outside your classroom. Assign four students to be experimenters. Tell them that they can be a few minutes late to class for the next several days. Instead of rushing to class, they should drop their books several times on the way and notice who helps. (These experimenters may need partners to record the data.) Have the class decide on a hypothesis they want to test. Perhaps two experimenters could drop books in a more secluded hallway; the other two could drop books in a crowded one. Or two experimenters could complain after dropping the books, and the other two could remain silent. Whatever hypothesis and variables are chosen, make sure that *all* exper-

Journal Topic

"Imagine that you are living in a war-torn country. A husband and wife knock on your door, and ask you to hide them for a number of days. If you do not, they will most likely be captured and killed—not for any crimes but for their ethnicity. If you do hide them, your own safety will be threatened. They leave you alone for a few minutes to collect your thoughts. You decide to write down your thoughts. Go ahead." Mention that these situations actually occurred during World War II.

Comprehension Check

What is the difference between deindividuation and evaluation apprehension? *(With deindividuation, the focus is off the individual and on the group. With evaluation apprehension, the individual focuses too much on himself or herself.)*

evaluation apprehension

The concern about how others will judge us; we make our behavior conform to what we think they will approve of.

territoriality

An attachment to a fixed area designated as ours alone and the tendency to defend it against intruders.

difference? No. The people were interviewed, and here is the finding: those familiar with the airport were more likely to respond to the need for help; those familiar with the subway were likewise more likely to help. The difference comes from the fact that an airport is familiar to far fewer people; this was the deciding factor in whether or not help was forthcoming (Pearce, 1980).

The issue of familiarity is critical to behavior. We are always concerned about the proper behavior and what others will think about us. This feeling is called **evaluation apprehension,** which means that without our even knowing it, we are apprehensive or concerned about how others will judge our performance. If we see someone helping someone, we tend to join in because that is expected; if not, we stand back (Schwartz & Gottlieb, 1980).

Finally, you may have thought that these studies might somehow seem "fake" to the subjects, but that was not the case. To prove the point, experimenters used experienced stuntmen to enact an apparently genuine violent situation with people fighting in public, beating each other up over an allegedly stolen item. The results were identical to the previous studies. So, we are without doubt influenced by those around us—especially by the number of them. But none of the subjects later interviewed ever was aware of this influence (Shotland, 1985).

ENVIRONMENTAL INFLUENCES ON BEHAVIOR

How we feel and how we interact with others can be strongly influenced by the physical environment. For example, a noisy environment can be distracting and nerve-racking. Students from schools with a great deal of noise are edgy, uncomfortable, and tend to have higher blood pressure than students from other schools (Russell & Ward, 1984).

All animals have a sense of **territoriality,** an attachment to a fixed area set aside for their use, and they will attack anything that comes within this space. While humans may not immediately attack any and all intruders, we are also territorial. We acknowledge this when we knock on someone's door instead of simply entering unannounced. The invasion of our territory is highly likely to be seen as a direct threat. In fact, this connection is so strong that the law usually allows an aggressive defense of one's home.

Human territoriality can also be "carried around" with us. Think for a moment about how uncomfortable you feel when someone moves too close to you. This "invisible bubble" we carry around with

imenters drop their books in the same manner each time. Practice in class! (Note: If you're not testing for gender differences, the experimenters should probably all be the same sex.)

IN FOCUS **Helping Others**

Diffusion of Responsibility

No Opportunity for Diffusion of Responsibility

How could evaluation apprehension play a role in the situation on the left?

Helping Others.

IN FOCUS Perhaps the people watching don't help because they are afraid that others will laugh.

Connections

Chapter 21 explains that if just one person disobeys orders, this makes it much more likely that others will disobey, too. The same applies for helping behavior. If just one person lends a hand, others will follow suit. This is a practical point that may hit home with students. Ask them if after learning about why people do not help, they will be more likely to offer help in the future.

EXPERIMENT

Have students conduct a "bench experiment" at a park or in a school hallway. One third of the time, an experimenter could sit at the end of a long bench, which would hypothetically encourage the greatest number of subjects to sit on the same bench.

Another third of the time, an experimenter could sit in the middle, which would encourage the fewest number of subjects to sit on the same bench. During the final trials, an experimenter could sit between the middle and the end of the bench, which

would encourage a moderate or average amount of subjects to sit on the same bench. You may have some version of a bench right at your school.

Teaching Hint

During the course of the semester, note where students sit. Even if you don't keep a seating chart, students will rarely move around from one day to the next. Ask them if they sat in the same area of the cafeteria their entire first year of high school. Ask if they can think of other common examples of territoriality.

Comprehension Check

How does a person often feel when a stranger invades his or her personal space? *(uncomfortable and threatened)*

DISCUSS THE PHOTO

Students may want to shoot their own photographs of high density at school.

582

Unit 7 SOCIOCULTURAL INFLUENCES AND SELF

personal space

The "invisible bubble," or portable area, around us that we try to keep from being invaded.

density

The actual number of people per square foot in a given space.

crowding

A psychological feeling of too little space.

582

us is our **personal space.** An invasion of personal space will not cause quite the same kind of reaction as an invasion of territory, but it will usually be seen as threatening. On the average, for strangers, our personal space is roughly two feet; if a stranger comes any nearer, we feel uncomfortable. The psychological closeness you have with another person determines the exact distance you place yourself from him or her. For someone you truly love, personal space can approach zero most of the time. Males generally have a larger personal space than females. And cultures differ in this regard as well. In many Middle Eastern countries, for example, people stand very close together in conversation. An American caught in this situation will probably start backing away and be seen as very rude in the process.

Overcrowding is another problem. When animals are in crowded conditions, their behavior patterns become abnormal, some of them kill one another, they fail to breed, they develop brain defects, and many die from the stress of this situation (Calhoun, 1962; Fox, 1968).

Human reactions to space are highly psychological. Thus, ten people living in a 500-square-foot room for a couple of days will be overwhelmed by the feeling of closeness; the same number of people on a train for a day or so with approximately the same total square feet can feel lonely (Russell & Ward, 1984). Psychologists therefore divide lack of space into **density** and **crowding.** Density is the actual number of people per square foot, while crowding is the *feeling* of being

▲ *When density is this high, feeling crowded is almost inevitable.*

EXPERIMENT

Bring your class to the cafeteria, and have students pretend they are taking a survey. Have them write down some questions on school policy. As they conduct their survey, they should gradually move closer to subjects and invade their personal space. Students enjoy this activity and usually return to class with some amusing data. Since this activity is more experiential than scientific, there's no need to analyze the data.

Simply discuss their reactions. Did your students feel uncomfortable themselves? You might want them to write their reactions in their journals.

Chapter 20 SOCIOCULTURAL INFLUENCES AND RELATIONSHIPS

too close. Density at a rock concert can be high but crowding low; sitting at a restaurant counter with someone on your right and your left can feel very crowded, but density compared to the rock concert is low (Stokols, 1978).

Much work has been done with prison density, since high density can create such serious problems as riots. One very workable system that is far cheaper than dealing with trouble in a prison is to give each prisoner an individual cell. Interestingly, it makes no difference how small the cell is (as long as the person can move!) or how cheap it looks (Cox et al., 1984).

PSYCHOLOGY IN YOUR LIFE

Abusive Relationships

This chapter covers interpersonal attraction. It also covers aggression and violence. When the two come together, a physically abusive relationship exists. However, it is extremely important to keep in mind that abuse can occur without any actual physical violence. This is what is referred to as emotional or psychological abuse. In an abusive relationship, one person dominates the other through physical harm or threats or by belittling, degrading, and demeaning the other person. By definition, such a relationship lacks any sense of equality. One person has far more power and freedom than the other. Mutual respect and love, in the real sense of these words, simply cannot exist in this type of situation. In the overwhelming majority of cases, the male is the abuser.

It may be hard for you to understand how such a relationship can happen, and most women think it could never happen to them. However, abusive men as a rule do not start off being violent or abusive. In the beginning, they are often quite charming. Abusive behavior is a problem that usually starts small and then escalates, following a fairly predictable pattern. In addition, when people fall in love, they tend to overlook or explain away things that would otherwise make them wary. Another contributing factor is that in our society, women are expected to give and forgive more in a relationship than men are. In order to keep things going smoothly and keep the man happy, women usually make more compromises.

The pattern of abuse is cyclical. First, there is a buildup of tension, with increasingly frequent arguing. Then comes the violent outburst. It may or may not include physically hurting the other person. Next come profuse apologies, pledges of *(continued on next page)*

(continued on next page)

Evaluation Strategy

Ask students to list three conclusions about aggression and three conclusions about helping behavior that they want to remember. They should be specific and describe how to apply these conclusions in real life.

Reteaching Strategy

Have students write a letter to the editor of your school newspaper proposing a plan that, if implemented at school, might increase helping behavior or decrease aggression. The plan should be specific, practical, and simple to implement. See activity #1 at the end of Chapter 21.

ENRICHMENT

Invite to class a therapist who treats women who have been abused. Or maybe an organization that helps women who have been raped or battered can send a speaker. These organizations are usually eager to educate young people.

ENRICHMENT

Have students complete the **Enrichment Worksheet** for this chapter located in the Teacher Resources.

PSYCHOLOGY IN YOUR LIFE

Journal Topic
"Imagine that you are dating someone who is extremely jealous. Write a letter telling this person how you feel."

PSYCHOLOGY IN YOUR LIFE

Abusive Relationships

(continued from previous page) love, and promises that it will never happen again. These are followed by a "honeymoon" period, when everything seems to be even better than ever. Eventually, however, the cycle repeats itself. Each time it does, the interval between cycles gets shorter, the violence increases, and the "honeymoon" period is shorter and less intense.

Recently, there has been an alarming increase in domestic violence among married couples. However, there are also signs of an increase in abusive dating relationships, and that is what we want to focus on. In the following paragraphs, we will discuss several warning signs, behaviors that are associated with actual or potential abuse. Most of them involve a desire for control and/or a failure to take responsibility for one's actions, blaming the other person instead. It is not necessary for all of these behaviors to be present. Even two or three should be enough to send up a large red flag.

1. Does the man try to control the woman by telling her what she can and cannot do, where she can and cannot go, whom she can and cannot see? This is sometimes interpreted as having an interest in her welfare, but it also shows a lack of respect for her decisions, interests, and needs. When there are *major* and *frequent* disagreements in this area, it is probably not the girlfriend he is concerned about but himself.

2. Is he extremely jealous? A certain amount of jealousy in a close relationship is probably to be expected, and most people find it flattering. However, too much jealousy can quickly become a serious problem. This is especially true if he blames her for encouraging the attention of other men.

3. Does he try to isolate her from her friends and family? By cutting off or damaging her relationships with other people, he increases his own control. If she has no one to turn to, to discuss her problems with, to seek help from, she is more likely to stay with him.

4. Does he frequently belittle or insult her? Is he quick to point out her flaws or faults? None of us is perfect, and all of us have faults. But love should make us feel better about ourselves, not worse. Humiliation is just another weapon for gaining control.

5. Do they as a couple always do what he wants to do and rarely or never what she wants to do? Again, this shows a lack of respect for her and increases his control in the relationship.

6. Does he blame her for his own mistakes, problems, or shortcomings? When he mistreats her, does he use his love for her to excuse his behavior? This is simply another indication of his failure to accept responsibility for his own actions. Also, she is more likely to forgive his abuse if he can make her believe that either she or his love for her is somehow responsible. Neither is true, period. No one can
(continued on next page)

CHAPTER PROJECT/COOPERATIVE LEARNING

Divide the class into two large groups. One group will focus on ways to reduce aggression in society or in some designated area they choose. The other group will focus on how to increase helping behavior. Break each group into two or three sub-groups, assigning a different task to each. Possible tasks: (1) increasing public awareness about aggression or altruism through posters, commercials, or magazine ads; (2) creating an incentive program within the school for being less aggressive or more helpful; (3) writing a how-to manual for parents who want their children to be less aggressive or more helpful.

PSYCHOLOGY IN YOUR LIFE

Abusive Relationships

(continued from previous page)

make someone else do something. That is his decision.

7. Does he have a short fuse? Someone who is very quick to anger is likely to act without thinking first. This behavior by itself does not necessarily mean the person is abusive, but in combination with one or more other warning signals, it usually means trouble.

8. Does he become angry and difficult when he drinks? Does he use being drunk as an excuse? The problem here is that it is his choice to drink in the first place. And once he knows how he acts when he is drunk, his behavior is solely his responsibility. Alcohol is frequently involved in cases of domestic violence.

9. Do her friends repeatedly ask her why she puts up with him and with the way he treats her? Do they frequently suggest that she leave him? When those who know us really well become this concerned, it is usually a sign that we should take a very close look at what is going on. People outside of an emotional situation sometimes have a more objective and clearer perspective.

10. Has he ever forced her to do something sexually that she truly did not want to do? If so, his behavior is not only abusive but he has broken the law. This is true even if an actual rape was not committed. The goal of both sexual assault and rape is to demean and dominate the victim. These things simply have no place in an intimate relationship.

Finally, just about the only way an aggressive or violent person learns to control that aggression is when the negative consequences of such behavior are swift and sure (Lore & Schultz, 1993). It is usually best to leave the relationship after the very first instance of physical abuse. Failing that, you should never give anyone more than one second chance. Failing that, it is never too late to get out. Having invested a lot of time and energy in a relationship is not a good reason to stay when it has gone this bad. No relationship is worth it when one of the parties is being abused. No one deserves to live that way— no one.

Reteaching Strategy

Have students complete the **Reteaching Worksheet** for this chapter located in the Teacher Resources. The **Vocabulary Worksheet** may be completed by the class as a pretest for chapter concepts or used as a reteaching worksheet for those students needing additional review.

VOCABULARY REVIEW

Before testing students on the contents of the chapter, you may want to review vocabulary terms that are especially important or confusing. Terms in this chapter that could require clarification are *attribution*, *deindividuation*, and *territoriality*.

Wrapping It Up

Most of the psychological findings on aggression and altruism are interesting, but do they do any good? Are students any more likely to help in an emergency after studying altruism? Are they now less likely to imitate aggressive behavior? Most of them will probably tell you what they think you want to hear, but explain that none of us can predict what we will do in any one particular situation. If studying altruism and aggression causes students at least to pause and consider someday, then the studying will have been time well spent.

Unit 7 SOCIOCULTURAL INFLUENCES AND SELF

SUMMARY

1. In attribution theory, we rely on what we already know, try to interpret and explain the present event, and then guide our beliefs and behavior by combining the two.
2. The emotions of love and like seem to start from a physical base. This base is typically related to how attractive the person seems to us. After that, closeness develops by a process of association of many events and actions with the other person, and the person is viewed in more ways than just the physical.
3. Aggression and violence may be natural to animals and humans when in dire physical need. But the evidence leans toward psychological and sociocultural causes for human violence in most cases. Some instances of violence develop from physical defects or allergies.
4. Research on the connection between viewing televised violence and behaving aggressively provides mixed results. Most laboratory studies show a connection, but field studies are less conclusive. Those who are already aggressive seem to be negatively influenced by the aggression they see on television.
5. Whether or not we help other people in an emergency seems primarily related to the size of the group we are part of when the emergency arises.
6. Humans and animals have a sense of territoriality. Humans also have what is called personal space, which indicates the distance away from us that we desire people to stay when interacting with us.
7. Density and crowding can have a notable influence on behavior. Crowding is the more important psychological factor, since it represents how "closed in" we feel. Density is more a measure of the actual physical space the person has to work or live in.

Suggested Readings

▼ Aronson, Elliot. *The Social Animal.* 6th ed. New York: W. H. Freeman, 1991.

▼ Buscaglia, Leo. *Love.* New York: Fawcett, 1972.

▼ Eysenck, H. M. *Mindwatching: Why People Behave the Way They Do.* New York: Anchor, 1983.

▼ Fromm, Erich. *The Art of Loving.* New York: Harper & Row, 1956.

▼ Janis, I. (1982). *Groupthink.* 2nd ed. Boston: Houghton Mifflin, 1982.

▼ Myers, David G. *Social Psychology* 4th ed. New York: McGraw-Hill, 1992.

▼ Restak, Richard. *The Mind.* N.Y.: Bantam Books, 1988.

Vocabulary

attribution theory
antecedents
attribution
consequences
deindividuation
risky shift
   phenomenon

imitation learning
catharsis
diffusion of
   responsibility
evaluation
   apprehension

territoriality
personal space
density
crowding

Answers to Review Questions
1. d
2. a
3. b
4. e

Review Questions

Multiple Choice

1. According to the attribution theory, our opinions about others are influenced by
   a. our own motivations.
   b. our emotional responses.
   c. our beliefs.
   d. all of the above.
2. An antecedent refers to the information we
   a. have before an event happens.
   b. receive while an event happens.
   c. conclude after an event happens.
   d. block out during all of the above.
3. Studies show that couples who stay together a long time are
   a. more different than alike.
   b. more alike than different.
   c. exactly the same.
   d. none of the above.
4. The risky shift phenomenon suggests
   a. that we will take fewer risks when in a group.
   b. that we will take more risks when in a group.
   c. that risk in a group is shifted to other group members.
   d. none of the above.
   e. both b and c.

SUGGESTED VIDEOS

▼ *Judgment and Decision Making.* Discovering Psychology series, part 11, 27 min. 1-800-LEARNER.

▼ *Understanding Aggression.* 29 min. Prentice-Hall.

▼ *When Will People Help: Bystander Intervention.* 25 min. 1976. Harcourt Brace.

5. true
6. true
7. true
8. false
9. true
10. false
11. false
12. c
13. d
14. a
15. crowding
16. density
17. evaluation apprehension
18. personal space
19. territoriality

True/False

5. Studies show that we tend to form relationships with others who are at about the same level of attractiveness as we are.
6. Revealing personal information about ourselves is best done in small doses, especially at the beginning of a relationship.
7. Men tend to be more violent than women.
8. Deindividuation will lead to a stronger sense of personal identity.
9. People are more likely to be violent when they justify that their violence is right.
10. Most people agree that exposure to violence on TV will have long-term effects on children.
11. Field studies clearly show that violence on TV causes real-life violence.

Multiple Choice

12. Which of the following is *not* a valid conclusion about TV and violence?
    a. The average person acquires no long-lasting violent tendencies after being exposed to violence on TV.
    b. Already aggressive people are most affected by violence on TV.
    c. Watching violence on TV will actually reduce the need to be violent in real life.
    d. None of the above—they are all valid conclusions.
    e. Both a and c are not valid.
13. Experiments on helping behavior tend to show

    a. that people do not help because they do not care.
    b. that people are more likely to help when there are a greater number of people around.
    c. that some types of personalities are more likely to help than others.
    d. none of the above.
14. The diffusion of responsibility theory suggests that during an emergency, we
    a. assume less responsibility.
    b. assume more responsibility.
    c. assume others will be responsible.
    d. do both a and c.

Fill in the blanks; answer on a separate sheet of paper. (An answer may consist of more than one word.)

15. The feeling of being closed in is called ___?___ .
16. If there are three fans at a football game, we can assume that the ___?___ is low.
17. Worrying about what others expect during an emergency is called ___?___ .
18. If we stand so close to someone that we can count his or her cavities, we would probably be violating that person's ___?___ .
19. Animals who have a strong sense of ___?___ will attack others who attempt to take their "space."

DISCUSSION QUESTIONS

1. A nonhuman but intelligent being captures you and explains that the only way it will set you free is if you adequately define the concept of *love*. Define it.

2. Some people argue that love is a subject that should not be scrutinized under a microscope by psychologists. Do you tend to agree or disagree with this? Explain.

3. If it's true that an emphasis on individual rights may contribute to a high rate of violence, would you be willing to sacrifice some of those individual rights in order to create a more peaceful society? If so, what exactly would you sacrifice that might help reduce violence? Be specific. If not, why not?

4. Imagine a high school where there is a real possibility for violence on a daily basis. You can probably assume that a certain amount of deindividuation exists at the school. Give several possible reasons for this deindividuation. For example, you might say, "The school is probably very large." Then describe several ways in which you might decrease this deindividuation.

5. As made clear in the chapter, psychologists have accumulated a great deal of information about why people help or do not help others. What should we do now with this information in order to increase helping behavior in our society? Explain. Or do you believe that nothing *can* be done to increase helping behavior? Explain.

6. How might diffusion of responsibility occur within a typical family situation? Describe several examples.

7. The chapter explains that evaluation apprehension during an emergency decreases the likelihood of someone helping. In what ways could evaluation apprehension help to *create* emergencies? Also, offer several real examples of emergencies perhaps caused by evaluation apprehension. For example, one could argue that those who saw problems with the **Challenger** space shuttle before it exploded did not voice their opinions loudly enough because of evaluation apprehension.

8. Describe a personal experience where density was low but crowding was high, and describe an experience where density was high but crowding low. Be specific.

ACTIVITIES

1. Conduct an experiment to determine the role of antecedents in people's judgments. What you will do is supply the antecedents and then measure "attributions" and "consequences." Write all of the following on an index card:

    Read the description below and answer the two questions beneath it.

    Melissa Weeber is 28 years old. She has been a high school counselor for six years. She enjoys the job but feels that her role has been reduced simply to scheduling students for classes. She now wants to become a marriage counselor. When asked to describe her, students commonly use the following

8. Students might refer to parties or concerts.

Notes on Activities

1. Before assigning this activity, be sure that students have a good grasp of attribution theory.

2. Mention to students that their photographs need to be somewhat uniform. For example, they should *all* be black and white or *all* color; none of the people in the photos should be wearing eyeglasses—or they should all be wearing them; all the photos should be portraits rather than candids; and so on.

3. By now, you may be tired of grading dry research papers. This activity should provide a welcome variation—for both you and your students. Consider using a similar format for other research activities listed throughout the text.

4 and 5. These are two more activities that force students to present their research in a creative fashion. Consider assigning half the class activity #4 and the other half activity #5. Then conduct an informal debate in class.

6. At this point in the course, students should be quite proficient at conducting experiments and analyzing data. However, they may still need to be reminded that they must fall in an identical way each time, that their appearance must remain constant for each trial, and so on. What varies and what remains constant, of course, will depend on the chosen hypothesis. As suggested in the activity, be sure to approve the hypotheses; students can formulate some bizarre ideas.

7. Before students begin this experiment, have them show you their data sheets to make sure they are prepared.

8. You might want to take the time to find a sample that students can read before they write this.

---

adjectives: caring, dependable, and hardworking.

How would you rate this person's chances of becoming an effective marriage counselor?

1	2	3	4	5	6	7	8	9
EXTREMELY LOW	VERY LOW	LOW	BELOW AVERAGE	AVERAGE	ABOVE AVERAGE	HIGH	VERY HIGH	EXCELLENT

If you were responsible for hiring this person as a marriage counselor, what would be the likelihood that you would hire her?

1	2	3	4	5
VERY LOW	LOW	AVERAGE	HIGH	VERY HIGH

Write down the same information on another index card, but this time replace the adjective "caring" with "efficient." Show the first card to 20 people; show the second card to 20 other people. Record their ratings.

Analyze your results. The first question measures attribution; the second measures consequences. Were the subjects' answers to the first question similar to their answers to the second question? What were the average ratings for both questions on the first card? On the second card? Discuss why you think you got the results that you did.

2. As mentioned in the chapter, attractive people are initially perceived as more competent than others. Conduct a simple experiment to test this assertion. *Procedure:* (1) Find a paragraph or poem that you had to write for one of your classes, or use a poem or paragraph from a book. Neatly copy the material onto an index card. (2) Sift through an *old* yearbook and photocopy four pictures: an "attractive" male, an "attractive" female, an "unattractive" male, an "unattractive" female. Your choice of photos will be subjective, so maybe a few classmates can help you with your final decision. Also, remember that the pictures should be *old* so that your subjects will not recognize the

people. (3) Write the following information on another index card:
How would you rate this person's writing skills?

1	2	3	4	5	6	7
AWFUL	POOR	BELOW AVERAGE	AVERAGE	ABOVE AVERAGE	GOOD	EXCELLENT

(4) Show the paragraph (or poem), *one* of the pictures, and the rating scale to 20 males and 20 females. Here's how: (a) five males and five females will see the attractive male; (b) five males and five females will see the unattractive male; (c) five males and five females will see the attractive female; and (d) five males and five females will see the unattractive female.

Record your subjects' ratings on a separate data sheet and analyze your results. Were the attractive pictures rated higher? Were female subjects less influenced by attractiveness, as suggested in the chapter? Half the time, subjects saw pictures of the opposite sex; were these ratings higher than the others? Discuss why you think you got the results that you did. Also, make a chart summarizing all your results.

3. Collect several articles on jealousy and write a report. This time, write your report using the format of an advice columnist for a newspaper. For example, you can list several questions written by a jealous husband or wife, and then you can assume the role of an advice columnist and answer the questions. The answers should be informative, and they should be primarily based on the articles you collected, but you can also include several "creative" responses. Be sure to make up a name for your column.

4. The chapter mentions that about 100 studies have been done on the effects of filmed violence on real-life violence. Find an article that describes in detail the findings of one or

two of these studies and present a brief summary of these findings. Then, write a paper from the point of view of a parent who wants to persuade other parents to act or *not* act on these findings. Notice that you are trying to convince other parents to *act*, not just agree. So make your suggestions practical and specific. For example, you might propose that young children should not be allowed to watch television after 6:00 P.M. or that young children and parents should watch TV together. Again, be specific and support your proposals with information found in the article that you summarized.

5. In order to do this activity, you will need to do the previous one as well. This time, you will write a complete rebuttal to your proposal in number 4. This is a good exercise in persuasion, and it may force you to think about a side of the issue you hadn't considered.

6. Conduct an experiment on helping behavior. The procedure will be simple: fall down, stay on the ground for about 15 seconds, holding your ankle the whole time. Do this in exactly the same way 20 times.

   This time *you* will supply the hypothesis. For example, half the time you can fall in an environment familiar to your subjects; the other half the time, the environment will be unfamiliar. Look back through the chapter for other ideas, or think of an original hypothesis. Be sure to have your teacher approve your hypothesis.

   Also, you should probably get a friend to help record responses. A few remarks about responses: devise a data sheet that will outline the degree of help that your subjects offer. The following is one example: Level 1 = "completely ignored"; Level 2 = "stopped, but did not help"; Level 3 = "offered help"; Level 4 = "helped

immediately." In addition to recording these levels, write down as much information as possible about each subject. This information will give you something on which to base your conclusions.

   As always, analyze your results in detail and draw conclusions. You might consider videotaping this experiment and showing it to the class—perhaps your teacher will give you extra credit for this.

   One final option: if you do not think you are bold enough to fall in front of strangers, consider testing helping behavior in another way—maybe through dropping money or a wallet— and see who helps. Be creative.

7. Stand close to someone you do not know in the hallway and gradually move closer. Or go to a mall and sit close to customers who are resting on benches. Bring something to read and move progressively closer. Do this to about ten different people and record their reactions. (a) Did they ignore you completely? (b) Did they look at you, then look away? (c) Did they move slightly or turn away? (d) Did they get up? (e) Did they swear at you? Notice that these questions are measuring the degree of your influence. Your data sheet should reflect these degrees. Write a report analyzing your results and describing your reactions in detail.

8. Domestic violence is often the subject matter of novels and movies. Write an original scene that might appear in such a novel or movie that conveys some of the warning signs associated with abuse. It serves no purpose, for this activity, to describe graphically the actual abuse; instead, describe a time leading up to the abuse or a time soon after the abuse. The scene can include the two principal characters, or the abused and a friend, or any other situation that you think might be interesting. Some dialogue would probably work well.

DISCUSS THE PHOTO

Based on what they have learned so far, ask students how they think the field of psychology can pay more attention to multiculturalism.

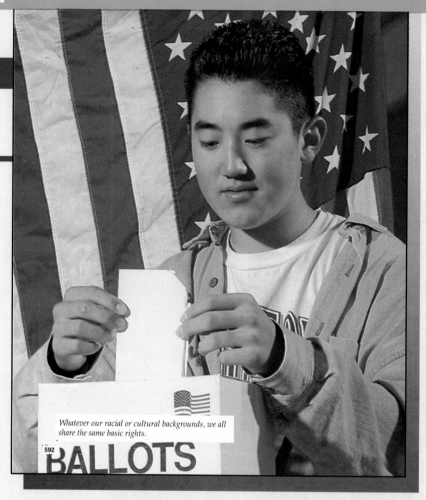

Whatever our racial or cultural backgrounds, we all share the same basic rights.

592

BALLOTS

PSYCHOLOGY AND YOU RESOURCES

A variety of resources are available in the Psychology and You *supplementary material. In addition, there are a number of additional resources listed to enhance your lesson plans.*

Masters
▼ 21-1A Learning Goals
▼ 21-1B Answers to Learning Goals
▼ 21-2 Occupational Survey
▼ 21-3 Reference Groups
▼ 21-4 Groups
▼ 21-5 Memory Test
▼ 21-6 Illusory Correlations Data Sheet
▼ 21-7 Analyzing Commercials

Student Worksheets
▼ Vocabulary Worksheet

▼ Independent Practice Worksheet
▼ Enrichment Worksheet
▼ Reteaching Worksheet

Test Bank
▼ Tests A and B
▼ Final

Multimedia
▼ **Mindscope** Exercise 17
▼ **Psychware** Exercises 9 and 10
▼ Psychology Videodisc

Student Workbook

PACING CHART

Complete Coverage

Day 1: Assign the first section of the chapter before class. Differentiate between culture, race, and ethnic groups before discussing how multiculturalism is affecting the field of psychology. Have students read the next two sections for Day 2.

Day 2: Discuss the concept of internalizing beliefs while evaluating group influences on behaviors and attitudes. Use discussion question #1 in the text and refer to Zimbardo's study when discussing reference-group influence.

Day 3: Focus on stereotypes, scapegoats, and the factors involved in prejudice and discrimination. Conduct an activity in class illustrating illusory correlations. End by talking about how prejudice can be overcome.

Day 4: Discuss the ways attitudes can be changed, concentrating on cognitive dissonance. Then focus discussion on Milgram's experiment.

21

Sociocultural Influences: Attitudes and Beliefs

OBJECTIVES

Be able to:

▼ Describe the cultural makeup of the United States.

▼ Describe cultural biases in the field of psychology.

▼ Explain how a reference group influences attitudes.

▼ Describe the usefulness of stereotypes.

▼ Explain how prejudice can be reduced.

▼ Explain how cognitive dissonance changes attitudes.

▼ Explain the techniques of "brainwashing."

Global Look at the Chapter

Although it may seem that we arrive at attitudes and beliefs on our own, closer examination shows that we form many of them based on the behavior and actions of others. This chapter looks at the cultural and group origins of many of the thoughts and feelings that people have.

593

INTRODUCING THE CHAPTER

Have students complete two lists. List 1: what are some stereotypes that you tend to believe in? List 2: in what ways are you prejudiced? Just give them a minute or two for each list; they may feel a bit uncomfortable spending too much time on this. Assure them that their answers will remain confidential. Explain that it's nearly impossible to avoid using stereotypes and being prejudiced at times. Warn students not to distort your point: just because we prejudge at times and generalize, this does not give us the right to discriminate—which we certainly *can* avoid.

LEAD-OFF ACTIVITY

Pass out **Teaching Master 21-2 Occupational Survey** and ask students to rank the various occupations listed from most credible to least credible. Complete directions are found on the master.

Day 5: Review methods of verbal and social persuasion, as well as ways to resist them. Give the Chapter Review quiz.

In Brief

Day 1: Review the definitions of culture, race, and ethnic groups as well as the effects of multiculturalism on the field of psychology.

Day 2: Refer to Zimbardo's experiment when discussing group influences on behavior and beliefs, then concentrate on stereotypes and the factors involved in prejudice. Assign an activity for homework involving illusory correlations.

Day 3: Focus on how attitudes are changed, especially in relation to compliance with authority.

Day 4: Review defense against verbal and social persuasion before giving the Chapter Review quiz.

This is a great end-of-semester activity to celebrate cultural diversity. Have an "ethnic day" when students bring in food that is unique to their cultural backgrounds. If you encourage it, some students will bring in old photos, family heirlooms, even unique apparel.

Critical Thinking

Ask students to assume that there is such a thing as a universal norm—informal rules that nearly all humans follow. What are some of these norms? Possible answers include: taboos against incest; people of lower status show respect to people of higher status; and men are the dominant gender. (Remind students that they need *not* agree or disagree with their answers.)

Have students think of situations where this mosaic can be easily seen. Sports is one such situation in which team members overlook differences and work toward a common goal.

594

Unit 7 SOCIOCULTURAL INFLUENCES AND SELF

culture

A set of beliefs, attitudes, and values held in common by a large number of people and passed down from one generation to the next.

race

A set of hereditary physical characteristics that distinguishes major groups of people.

ethnic group

People with the same country of origin, as well as racial and cultural features.

▲ *An American mosaic.*

594

CULTURAL DIVERSITY

The United States is often called a "melting pot" of a wide variety of cultures, races, and ethnic groups. These terms are similar, but not identical. A **culture** consists of a set of beliefs, attitudes, and values that are held in common by a fairly large number of people and passed down from one generation to the next. **Race** refers to a set of hereditary physical characteristics that distinguishes one major group of people from another. An **ethnic group** includes people who share both racial and cultural features and usually also encompasses one's, or one's family's, country of origin.

Historically, the United States is largely a country of immigrants, and religious freedom is one of our basic constitutional rights. Primarily for these reasons, we enjoy a great deal of cultural and religious diversity. You should be aware that other countries operate very differently. China, for instance, just recently opened its borders to foreigners. Only a decade or two ago, it was extremely difficult to visit there.

Much has been said about racial problems and disharmony in the United States. These are serious issues, and a lot of this chapter is aimed at addressing them. To get some perspective, though, we should note that these concerns are as old as the human race itself. Furthermore, almost no other country has our level of cultural diversity *and* the expectation that we will all learn to live together in peace. One of the few countries that included several races, cultures, and ethnic groups is the former Soviet Union. Without the control of a strong central government, it quickly broke up into warring factions. These factions were often based on ethnic and cultural differences. When almost the entire population shares the same culture, race, religion, and history, as is true in many places, the risk of intergroup conflict is much lower. Our point is *not* that multicultural harmony is impossible. Our point is to acknowledge that it is difficult. Because of that difficulty, we must never become complacent or let up in our efforts to achieve a tolerant and peaceable society. After all, war is also as old as the human race, but peace is still a better alternative.

Multicultural America

The multicultural composition of the United States is changing. Since the early days of our history, whites have made up the majority of the citizenry. Today white people account for about 75 percent of the population. However, this margin is smaller than ever before, and it continues to shrink. Within that majority are numerous subcultures, immigrants, and ancestors from many different countries, each with its own customs and values.

African Americans are the next largest group, roughly 12 percent

INTERDISCIPLINARY PROJECT

Multicultural Studies. Have students think of ways to promote harmony among different cultures using principles of psychology. The ideas should be practical and detailed, and the psychological principles they intend to use should be spelled out.

Consider conducting this activity as a cooperative-learning exercise. To motivate groups, announce that the best idea will be submitted to the student council for possible implementation. Or maybe there's a better way to implement the idea at your school.

You might refer students to Chapter 7 for ways to reinforce behaviors, or send them to the end of this chapter for material on persuasion.

Chapter 21 SOCIOCULTURAL INFLUENCES: ATTITUDES AND BELIEFS

of the total. They are the only major group that did not choose to come to this country. Because their ancestors were sold into slavery, they were forced to leave much of their cultural heritage behind. That heritage originated in a variety of places, especially the coastal countries of the African continent. Most African countries are, in turn, comprised of various tribes. Each tribe has its own culture and often its own language as well.

The largest recent increases have been among the Asian American and Hispanic populations. Approximately 9 percent of our population is Hispanic, a growing minority. Their numbers increased nearly one-third in the 1980s. However, within this group, Puerto Rican Americans are not exactly the same as Mexican Americans, who are also different from Spanish Americans or Argentinean Americans, and so on. The biggest increase has been in the number of Asian Americans. During the 1980s, their numbers swelled by 70 percent. About 2 percent of the total population in the United States is Asian American. This group is also diverse. Korean or Vietnamese Americans may have little in common with Japanese Americans or Chinese Americans. Their countries of origin don't even share the same language.

Native Americans make up the last and smallest major group. There has been no notable increase here, and they comprise less than 1 percent of the total population. We tend to think of this group as a single entity, but that is far from the truth. In fact, there are hundreds of separate tribes, each with its own beliefs and traditions (Yetman, 1991).

In the face of this head-spinning diversity, we may sometimes feel overwhelmed. Actually, though, we in this country are very fortunate. Most people have to travel far and wide to experience "exotic" cultures. All we have to do is look around us.

Multicultural Psychology

All of us are shaped by the culture in which we live. It influences how we dress and speak, our daily activities, goals and dreams, and how and what we think. It even has an impact on simple physical reactions. Take, for instance, an impending sneeze. Does the person try to hold it back or loudly let it go? Do others look away or say something? What do they say? The correct answers will depend on the culture (Segall, Dasen, Berry & Poortinga, 1990). What does this have to do with psychology? These things are behaviors and as such are part of the field.

Psychology has primarily been studied in the United States, Europe, and Canada. Consequently, it has a North American and European bias. The truth is that we do not know whether much of our information can be generalized to other places. Within the United States, our focus and research subjects are most often white and mid-

Comprehension Check

Which of the following refers to *race, culture,* or *ethnic group?* (1) Inherited characteristics *(race)* (2) Learned characteristics *(culture)* (3) Includes both inherited and learned characteristics *(ethnic group)*

ENRICHMENT

Have students choose a single behavior, like hugging or making eye contact, and research how different cultures view that behavior. For example, males in America shake hands while Europeans often hug.

ENRICHMENT

Have students make a list of roles that family members play in our culture. For example, in two-parent families, the father more often works to support the family and the mother takes care of the kids more than the father does. Have students look at the roles of family members in one or two other ethnic groups. This should demonstrate the power of cultural influences.

Discussion

Give students a few minutes to think about the following question: If reference groups provide us with a particular way of viewing the world and if friends are one of your reference groups, how have they influenced your view of the world?

Have them look around the room at the clothes they're all wearing. Any similarities in language? In attitudes toward school, or the future? See **Teaching Master 21-3 Reference Groups** for more ideas.

Points to Stress

Students often view conformity as an evil (how's that for a stereotype?), and material that appears later in the chapter will add fuel to this attitude. Point out, however, that conformity to society's norms is often beneficial. For instance, we nod to mean yes; we are generally polite to one another; we use utensils when we eat; and we generally look out for other's feelings.

596

Unit 7 SOCIOCULTURAL INFLUENCES AND SELF

internalize

To make as part of ourselves the attitudes or beliefs of others.

reference group

A group with which one identifies and that provides standards of behavior.

dle class (Graham, 1992). American psychology has not ignored minority groups. But it has failed to give them enough attention. Also, when psychology does study minorities, too often it simply makes a direct comparison with the dominant white culture. The frequent implication is that one culture is better or worse than the other. But sometimes different is just that: different. Such comparisons are not necessarily called for. We know, for instance, that psychological tests designed by and for white middle-class people may not be appropriate for other groups. We also know that family roles and the relative influence of peers and family are determined partly by one's ethnic group. Consequently, at least some of the information we have gathered from white subjects is probably not applicable to subjects with other backgrounds. Too often, we simply assume that what is true for whites is true for other groups as well.

Regrettably, psychology does not have a very enviable record in its dealings with diversity. Throughout the 1800s, for instance, racial inferiority of some groups was accepted as fact. As late as 1920, the notion of mental or intellectual differences based on racial group was also accepted as fact. It was not until around 1940 that psychology began in earnest to study prejudice as an unjustified or irrational attitude (Duckitt, 1992). We have made substantial progress since then, but we still have a long, long way to go. With the current heightened interest in multicultural issues, our perspective should broaden. In the meantime, we must be alert to our biases and proceed with caution.

GROUP INFLUENCES

The groups people belong to clearly influence how they think, feel, and behave. For example, normally the school principal is set apart from other teachers, the teachers form their own group, and the students are a third group. The principal and possibly a vice-principal are often symbolically alone and they behave and dress as they believe all principals do. Teachers normally do not dress as formally as the principal. Students follow their own dress code, which is designed to resemble that of the other two groups as little as possible. Dress, eating habits, patterns of speech, hobbies, entertainment—these are all partly the result of the group we belong to. The more important a particular group is to us and the longer we have associated with it, the stronger its hold on us will be. In other words, the more we identify with a group, the more we **internalize** (take as part of ourselves) the attitudes, beliefs, and uniform of that group.

Reference Groups

A **reference group** is a group with which a person identifies and that provides standards of behavior. A person can have more than

DEMONSTRATION

See **Teaching Master 21-3 Reference Groups.** To demonstrate how reference groups affect attitudes, pass out copies of this master and have students describe their attitudes toward the categories listed.

For *Republican,* they might write, *Concerned with America's future, conservative, I'd prefer to vote for a Republican,* and so on. Have students ask their parents and a friend to respond to the same categories

and compare and contrast the two lists in class. This should demonstrate which reference group is most important for each attitude.

Chapter 21 SOCIOCULTURAL INFLUENCES: ATTITUDES AND BELIEFS

▲ *One of these graduates clearly seems to be taken over by her own reference group.*

one reference group—for example, family, church, workplace, and school groups. Reference groups often provide for us a particular way of seeing things in the world, and in fact, they can sometimes actually control *what* we see.

Here is an example of this in terms of cultural reference groups. An experimenter used what is called a *stereoscope,* which can show two separate pictures to a subject, a different one to each eye. Quickly flashed to one eye was a picture of a baseball player and to the other, at the same time, a bullfighter. Mexican subjects almost always saw only the bullfighter, while United States subjects saw only the baseball player, if the viewing time was kept short (Bagby, 1968). In another study without the stereoscope, experimenters showed subjects obviously satirical cartoons making fun of prejudice. Prejudiced subjects saw the cartoons as *supporting* their distorted and biased ideas (Cooper & Tahoda, 1964).

Fitting Attitudes to the Group

As we've said, people with whom we associate help form our attitudes. Many of our beliefs begin very early in the family and tend to remain firmly implanted. But when new reference groups come along, they can change the earlier values. A study of college students demonstrated this power. A group of conservative students entered a liberal college where they formed new reference groups. By the time

DISCUSS THE PHOTO

Will there ever be another moment in this graduate's life when she will feel *this* uninhibited in public? Or put another way, do we become less playful as we get older?

TEACHING MASTER 21-4

Groups. On this handout, students are asked to list the groups to which they belong, and then they are asked some questions about those groups. Afterward, you can discuss how we conform at home, at school, at work. Students may not view their behavior as conformity, but this activity may demonstrate that conformity isn't always bad.

COOPERATIVE LEARNING

You can say that society acts as a reference group by establishing norms for behavior: when waiting in line, we don't cut in front; we speak quietly in the library; we face the front of elevators; we shake hands (while in Europe, people embrace). Have students work in pairs to make a list of norms in our society. Discuss how different ethnic groups would respond to these norms.

Discussion

Discussion question #2 at the end of the chapter asks students to list several stereotypes of teachers. To illustrate the concept of stereotypes in class, ask the same question, but use additional labels: kindergarten teacher, nerd, old person, pizza delivery person, and so on. At times, there may be more than one label to describe a single group. For example, "cop" and "police officer" both refer to the same occupation, but one label might evoke different stereotypes than the other. You may want to try using different labels: one class can describe "cop"; another can describe "police officer." Afterward, discuss whether most of the stereotypes listed for the labels were primarily positive or negative.

DISCUSS THE PHOTO

Could Zimbardo's experiment be conducted today? See the experimental guidelines established by the American Psychological Association (Chapter 2).

598

the students graduated, they were quite liberal in their outlook, except for the ones who did not form strong ties to a new group but stayed close to their families. Twenty-five years later, these two groups (both those who had changed and those who hadn't) had held onto their college attitudes, showing the staying power of group influences (Newcomb, 1963).

The Prisoner-Guard Experiment   One of the most dramatic—and frightening—examples of reference-group influence occurred in an experiment that took place in the basement of a building at Stanford University in the 1970s. A psychologist set up a mock prison, complete with cells, "security" doors, and drab surroundings. He then hired 24 male students for a "live-in" experiment. Twelve of them were *randomly* assigned to the role of guards, and 12 were assigned to be prisoners. Each group was then given the proper attire—guard uniforms or prisoner garb, thus increasing identification with their new reference groups through these symbols.

At that point, the experimenter left the two groups living on their own. He acted as "warden" but did not intervene in the situation. The result was a nightmare no one expected. By the end of six days, the "guards" had become genuinely brutal and vicious toward the "prisoners," who in turn had become docile and bitter. The experiment had to be stopped because it literally was getting out of control.

Most of the young men never lost the memory of how they had acted, whether they were guards or prisoners, and a number temporarily suffered emotional upset that had not been evident prior to the experiment. When there was an investigation, two consultants—a 16-year inmate of a real prison and a prison chaplain—commented on how closely the behavior of the students had come to resemble that of real prisoners and guards (Zimbardo, 1972).

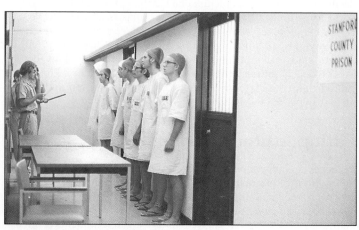

▲ *Photo from the actual "prison experiment" that turned so vicious.*

DISCOVERY

Ask students to break a norm: walk down the wrong side of the stairs; face the back of the elevator; slurp your soft drink. It's when we break norms that we feel their power. (If you're concerned about your stu-dents' choices, you may want to approve their ideas first.) Afterward, have them write a journal entry on their reactions to violating a norm. Was it liberating? Or did it make them tense?

HOW WE VIEW OTHERS

We assume we judge others objectively, relying on their individual characteristics. But that generally is not the case.

Stereotypes

Stereotypes are printing plates used to reproduce printed material. When the word **stereotype** is used in the realm of human relations, it refers to one group's ability to turn out *identical* information about every member of another group. For instance, a group may believe that all members of group A sleep on the floor at night or that all people in group B have a bad character trait such as laziness. Stereotypes can become so broad and familiar that dozens of meanings are summarized by just one derogatory name; when using the name, all within hearing range are supposed to know the bad characteristics of the group being stereotyped.

The origin of stereotypes can be seen in studies in which subjects were given descriptions of a certain group of foreigners whom they never actually met. Most of the subjects preferred those people who were said to have characteristics similar to their own (Katz & Braley, 1958).

What purpose do stereotypes serve? They solidify the "in-group," thereby increasing the group's self-esteem by making the stereotyped group seem "worse" or inferior. Stereotypes also tend to ward off the possibility that different cultural ways will "take over" one's own group. In other words, the in-group wants things to stay the way they are; ridiculing the other group reduces that group's importance and influence.

Stereotypes can be very subtle. For example, group members do not pay as close attention to their own people as they do to outsiders. Thus, when evaluating job applicants, if the evaluator is female, far more attention is given to the small details (dress, speech, and so on) of a male applicant than of a female one; if the evaluator is white, then far more attention is given to the details of a black applicant. Such is not always negative, even though it may be unfair. For example, studies show that a white evaluator of black and white applicants with exactly the same credentials will rate the black applicant higher. A female, rating two applicants, male and female, with the same credentials will rate the male higher. This probably results from the fact that because of the careful scrutiny, the rater becomes more familiar with the "outsider" applicant and therefore more conscious of the fact that he or she fits the job qualifications (Linville & Jones, 1980).

"Doctor" and "Reverend" also generate stereotypes associated with those titles. Society reserves such titles for properly trained indi-

stereotype

A fixed set of beliefs about a group that may or may not be accurate.

Comprehensive Check

What did the behavior of Zimbardo's subjects chiefly demonstrate? *(internalization of attitudes in accordance with their reference group, either prisoner or guard)*

COOPERATIVE LEARNING

Have each group make a list of the various cliques at your school, and have them list the characteristics of each clique. Afterward, compare the lists. Which characteristics seem accurate? Which are stereotypes (probably all of them)? Of the stereotypes, which are based on material considerations, like how much money one has? Which are based on behaviors, or on clothes, or on hair?

DISCUSS THE PHOTO

How many of students' stereotypes are influenced by the man's age?

Journal Topic

"You find out that the company for which you have worked for the past five years is discriminatory in its hiring policies. Would this bother you? Would you talk to someone at the company? Would you report the company to authorities?" Have students examine their answers afterward. It might give them insight into how they approach problems in general. Are they direct about it? Do they try to sidestep the problem?

Connections

Ask students to recall John Watson's statement from Chapter 7: "Give me a dozen healthy infants and allow me to control the environment, and I'll make them into anything I want." This statement becomes haunting when applied to prejudice.

600

Unit 7 SOCIOCULTURAL INFLUENCES AND SELF

prejudice

A judgment of people based on the group they belong to rather than their individual characteristics.

discrimination

Mistreating or denying rights to people because they belong to a particular group.

▲ *What stereotypes do you form of this man?*

viduals to ensure the well-being of its members and to reassure them that they are in good hands.

Prejudice and Discrimination

Stereotypes are not, in and of themselves, bad. In fact, most evidence suggests that they cannot be avoided, since it is impossible for us to evaluate everything we see or hear on a case-by-case basis. If we think of a foreigner of a specific race, for instance, even though every single person looks different, we "take an average" so to speak and come up with a stereotype of what "those foreigners" look like. We do the same thing regarding what a teacher will look like, a mechanic, or a nurse. The nurse will be female and will always appear in white, even though many hospitals use different colored uniforms today, and many nurses are male.

We need a basis, then, for categorizing and analyzing our environment, and the stereotype helps us do this. The problem arises when stereotypes cause **prejudice,** a judgment of other people based on the group they belong to rather than on their own individual characteristics. Given human nature and the world we live in, most of us find it very difficult to erase all of our prejudices completely. However, we can become aware of them. And we can avoid **discrimination,** mistreating or denying certain rights to people because they are members of a particular group.

EXPERIMENT

See **Masters 21-5 Memory Test** and **Teaching Master 21-6 Illusory Correlations Data Sheet.** These handouts are a variation of activity #3 at the end of the chapter. The masters include complete directions for in-class use.

Illusory Correlations A stereotype will fight off incoming information that contradicts it. This is because we tend to form **illusory** (il-LOOSE-uh-ree) **correlations.** That is, we see relationships that match our previously set beliefs, and we ignore others. Because these relationships match (correlate), we think we have seen the two together far more often than is really the case (illusion), thus making the stereotype even stronger. A simple experiment illustrates the principle: subjects are shown several pairs of words an equal number of times; one of the pairs of words is *bacon-eggs,* a connection we already have. The number of times *bacon-eggs* appears is identical to that of other pairs that appear, but subjects think it has been seen far more frequently than it has. In the same way, if we have a stereotype that the fictitious "Slobian" race is lazy, all we have to do to start the "bacon-egg" process is to see a couple of "Slobians" on different occasions lying down under a tree instead of working. We will then be convinced they "all" act that way (Hamilton, 1979; Hamilton & Rose, 1980). Another example is that most males of a certain generation are convinced that females are bad drivers—at least compared to the males' incredible expertise! What happens to feed this illusory correlation is that the males store in their memories every incident in which they see a female doing something stupid in a car, all the while ignoring males who do the same thing or females who perform an excellent avoidance maneuver. Or if these males do store positive events that involve female drivers, they put them into the "chance happening" category.

Perception is clearly changed by these correlations. For instance, if you flash on a screen a picture of a well-dressed man holding a spoon while he stands on a subway train, adult viewers are puzzled because they see a spoon. But if you show them a teenage male holding a spoon in the same situation, they more often than not see it as a knife.

Overcoming Prejudice On the positive side, when students from a mixed-race class rate one another *individually* on personal characteristics, stereotypes do not show up, not even across social class or race (Sagar & Schofield, 1980). This suggests that stereotypes can exist for a group even though an individual member is viewed differently. Again on the positive side, the longer one lives around a different culture, the more the original negative beliefs toward that culture begin to fade (Smith et al., 1980).

In the same vein, the odds that someone will help another across races are affected by whether the helping behavior is face to face or "remote"; that is, in the latter case, the potential helper and helpee are not physically within one another's view. In face-to-face studies, experimenters set up a situation in which a black or a white man dropped a grocery bag at a market. There was no difference in helping regardless of the race of the helper or the individual helped. The result was the same if a black or white man with a cane fell down in a

illusory correlations

Seeing relationships between things that match already held beliefs and ignoring what does not match these beliefs.

Connections

One's belief in ESP (Chapter 4) may be influenced by illusory correlations. The phone rings and we know who it is before we even pick it up! Amazing! We tell stories about the call. The call carries great weight in our memory. What about all the other calls when we *didn't* know who it was?

Journal Topic

"You find out that a good friend of yours is extremely racist. Describe your feelings. Would you talk to the friend? Would it affect the friendship?"

DEMONSTRATION

One of the reasons we become prejudiced is that we lack knowledge about another. Atticus, in Harper Lee's *To Kill a Mockingbird,* urges his children to live in someone's shoes for a while before they judge anyone. As a teacher, you can certainly provide opportunities for students to get to know each other, to walk in each other's shoes. Cooperative learning is one excellent way to break barriers (see the Aaronson citation at the end of the **Overcoming Prejudice** section), but there are smaller gestures that can help, too. For example, if you have a deaf student in class, ask the person to present a "sign of the day"; by the end of a semester, the entire class could be fairly proficient with the alphabet and numerous signs. Look for students who might

---

FYI The blue eyes-brown eyes experiment sounds like an innovative and worthwhile activity, doesn't it? A teacher in Illinois who recreated the experiment got fired for it. Someone apparently missed the point of the exercise: to *raise* sensitivity.

Points to Stress

When we blame others for our ills, we often gain something in the process. For example, in the 1950s, communists were convenient scapegoats, and Senator Joe McCarthy used this for political gain. When the Soviet Union collapsed, some columnists worried that America would lose a competitive edge without its long-standing scapegoat.

Unit 7 SOCIOCULTURAL INFLUENCES AND SELF

subway car. But a difference does show up in the "remote" setup because illusory correlations are in control with no "real person" present—just a stereotype. In one study, different college applications *with pictures* were left in a phone booth at an airport, with a stamped, addressed envelope and a note to "Dad" to please mail (hence, "Dad" must have dropped it on the way to his plane). As compared with the face-to-face arrangement, the response was different. Those applications with an opposite-race picture were mailed less often (Lerner & Frank, 1974). So, even though prejudice is still around, the face-to-face type is decreasing noticeably (Ransford & Palisi, 1992; Crosby et al., 1980).

Perhaps you have heard of the "Blue Eyes–Brown Eyes" experiment. It was designed to increase students' awareness of the negative effects of prejudice and discrimination. In this study, a teacher divided her class according to eye color. She then announced that people with brown eyes are smarter, better students, and generally superior to those with blue eyes. For the next two days, the "Brown Eyes" got special privileges and extra praise. The "Blue Eyes" were treated like second-class citizens. Then the teacher made a second announcement: it is not people with brown eyes who are superior, after all, but those with blue eyes. The students' roles were reversed. For the next two days, the "Blue Eyes" were treated specially and the "Brown Eyes" viewed as inferior. As you undoubtedly know, eye color actually has no bearing on one's intelligence or other abilities. When the study was over, both groups had learned a great deal. They were all much more sensitive to the issue of prejudice (Peters, 1971). In daily life, it might be a good idea for us to stop now and then and try to put ourselves in someone else's situation.

Prejudice can be reduced. For example, groups "at war" with one another, as in a sports competition, feel strongly toward their own group and "hate" the other group. In one experiment, when a truck taking two opposing teams back to town from a game broke down (courtesy of the experimenter), the two groups had to cooperate and thus became one group working toward a common goal. The rivalry disappeared (Sherif, 1982). If students in racially tense classes are given projects requiring every group member's help to complete them, racial barriers also go down (Aaronson, 1972).

On a personal level, we can speak up. When someone makes a racial or ethnic slur, we can let that person know how we feel. Often, even when we are uncomfortable hearing such a remark, we don't say anything, just to avoid creating a touchy situation. The trouble is that our silence may be interpreted as agreement or approval.

Scapegoats

If things go wrong at school or at home, most of us tend to blame someone else. Even if we are fairly open-minded, we are likely to say,

DISCOVERY

be victims of any type of prejudice to take a leadership role in the class. Ask these students to discuss *their* own prejudices, as well.

DISCOVERY

The text describes how Nazis used Jews as scapegoats. Do certain groups today still use scapegoats? To find out, have students scan the newspapers and weekly magazines for several days and pick out possible examples.

ENRICHMENT

The book, *Flowers for Algernon*, depicts the boycotting of deviates quite well. The main character's developing intelligence threatens his coworkers, and they get him fired. See the **Suggested Readings** for Chapter 18.

"Yes, it was partly my fault, but *he* (or *she*) was mostly responsible— at least, *he* (or *she*) started it," or some variation on this theme. Psychologically, we retain balance—keep ourselves safe—by not taking the full blame.

The same mechanism works with groups; others are blamed for whatever goes wrong. Prejudice is built on this process, called **scapegoating,** in which group A blames group B for its ills. The word *scapegoat* comes from the biblical reference to a sacrificial goat on which sins were symbolically laid before it was killed as an offering. A blatant example of scapegoating was the Nazi movement of the 1930s, which managed to incite people to the point of mass murder. Germany had been plunged into despair; in 1933, millions of Germans were unemployed. Adolf Hitler, a scrawny man who had been rejected by the army, came up with just the right formula: "We are the result of the stress *for which others [the Jews] are responsible,*" he shouted (Bullock, 1953). Things got so far out of control that eventually a group of 80,000 "technicians" (experts at efficient murder) exterminated approximately 6 million Jews. Assembly lines were set up in the camps, and each worker was assigned a gruesome specific task. One removed the clothing; another formed victims into lines; some took out gold fillings to get money for the Nazi cause; others worked on methods of increasing the heat to burn the bodies that were piling up. All of this resulted from Germany identifying a scapegoat to blame for its ills.

Removing Deviates

In less dramatic but still serious cases, group members will try to "drive out the demons" by ejecting those whom they feel threaten the group's integrity. In other words, they try to remove anyone who might make the group look different from the desired image. A group may also be threatened by the prospect of including people who compromise its goals or ideals. In group workshops, for example, where people explore ways to improve their lives, their business conditions, and so forth, the group will on occasion turn against "masculine" women who express anger or against "feminine" men who express supposedly nonmasculine emotions (Kahn, 1980). This behavior becomes quite cruel at school or in the workplace when someone is "boycotted" or kept out of a group because of certain characteristics that the group doesn't like, such as manner of speech, body size, appearance, or a physical defect.

CHANGING ATTITUDES

We join groups that believe the same things we do, and thus we strengthen our ideas by associating with those who agree with us.

Chapter 21 SOCIOCULTURAL INFLUENCES: ATTITUDES AND BELIEFS

scapegoating

Blaming someone else for one's own problem.

▲ *The human race never seems to completely get rid of the temptation to find a scapegoat for its problems.*

603

Comprehension Check

Ask students to respond with *true* or *false* to the following statements. (1) Prejudice cannot be reduced once it exists in a person *(false)*. (2) Someone who believes a stereotype tends to ignore evidence that contradicts that stereotype *(true)*. (3) Blaming a group for your own group's problems is called making illusory correlations *(false)*. (4) Since stereotyping is a way we all categorize and analyze our environment, discrimination cannot be avoided *(false)*.

DISCUSS THE PHOTO

Students can probably give examples of scapegoating that occurs at school. Make sure no names are mentioned.

DISCOVERY

Have students make posters designed to change a person's attitude about a particular issue. For instance, someone might create a poster on drinking and driving or on the dangers of using drugs or alco-

hol. Warn students that they should not go too far with scare tactics because they may backfire. If you scare people too much, they may simply turn away.

DEMONSTRATION

This will require some thought and preparation on your part, but the results can be insightful and entertaining. Record some instructions on a cassette tape, place it inside a cassette player with headphones, and hand it to someone in class. Press

Points to Stress

Students like to claim that they don't give in to peer pressure. Asch's experiment may challenge this idea. The confederates in the experiment were strangers to the subjects. The subjects had nothing material to gain or lose, yet they went along. Imagine the impact that *friends* have.

Teaching Hint

The makeup of the group is important where conformity is concerned. For example, ask students what they think would happen if college students in Asch's experiment were put in a room with high school confederates.

Points to Stress

When subjects in Asch's experiment were shown the first set of lines, the confederates perceived correctly. This helped to set up the second trial in which the confederates answered incorrectly.

604

Unit 7 SOCIOCULTURAL INFLUENCES AND SELF

cognitive dissonance

A contradiction between actions or events and beliefs, which must be reconciled or justified.

604

The more we think and talk about things that everybody around us agrees with, the more extreme our beliefs can become. Thus, people with strong opinions on, say, gun control typically join an official group and become even more involved in their positions. The more frequent the contact with the group, the greater the emotional investment, and the harder it is to alter one's opinion (Tesser, 1978).

How, then, do attitudes change? We have already seen the influence of new reference groups. The subjects in the prison experiment discussed earlier had no idea that they would adopt the attitudes they eventually did. So, playing a role, such as a guard, can be a powerful agent in attitude change. There is more than a grain of truth in the old saying that you will understand people better after you have walked a mile in their shoes. None of us can be certain how we will respond to certain circumstances until they occur.

Cognitive Dissonance

If we find that our beliefs (cognitions) are contradictory (dissonant), it makes us uncomfortable and puts us in a state called **cognitive dissonance** (DIS-o-nance) (Festinger, 1957). Suppose you fall madly in love with someone who later tells you that you are stupid and a bore. Since you can't reconcile the love with the insults, you are in a state of cognitive dissonance. (Cognitive dissonance, then, creates an imbalance of beliefs.) You must do something to relieve the discomfort this causes; you must find some way to justify what happened since it is not in harmony with what you feel about yourself or about the other person. Since you cannot change what happened, you change your beliefs, thus providing a justification and saving face. After the initial hurt, you will probably decide that your "loved one" wasn't that great a bargain after all.

Many experiments demonstrate cognitive dissonance in operation. For instance, psychologists have measured people's attitudes on a particular topic and then had them take the *opposite* position by giving speeches and writing essays to get others to believe that point of view. Just completing the exercise has some effect. But if the subjects were then led to believe that their arguments were successful and had changed other people's minds on the subject, the subjects became very uncomfortable indeed, especially if they knew the people they had affected. As a result, their own attitudes shifted in the direction of what they had been preaching (Cialdini et al., 1981).

Yielding to Others

Group pressure toward conformity can be very hard to fight. In a classic experiment, subjects were asked to judge the length of differ-

Play. The first student might hear, "I want you to help me in an experiment on listening. When I tell you to press Stop, do it, and hand the cassette player to the tallest person in the room. Then come back to your seat and take your left shoe off. Press Stop now." Each request on the tape should be a bit more

involved, but don't go too far. Afterward, discuss why people obeyed. For example, listening through headphones during class is probably a novel activity, so students were curious and went along; you are a legitimate authority; and so on. See some of the activities that follow for similar ideas.

ent lines drawn on a piece of cardboard. Subjects were formed into groups, but only one member of each group was not "in" on the experiment. All the other members worked for the experimenter and had the task of exaggerating the length of the line shown to the group. The goal was to put pressure on the one subject to see whether or not he or she would yield and go along with a ridiculous claim that the line was much longer than it really was. So, it was a study on how much people will conform to pressure from those around them. Roughly 25 percent of the subjects consistently buckled under and agreed that the line was much longer than it really was. About the same portion held on to their beliefs that the line was shorter than the group claimed, despite the pressure from the others to agree. The remaining subjects went back and forth in their judgments. This study showed just how strong is the need that most people have to "go along with the crowd."

Using basically the same experimental setup, researchers had just one of the stooges go over to the subject's side and agree that the line was shorter than everybody else said. With only one stooge on the person's side, what had been unanimous group pressure disappeared, and the subject's agreement with the exaggerated length of the line declined dramatically (Asch, 1952).

Compliance with Authority

Unquestioning obedience can be very dangerous. In a now-famous laboratory experiment, the subjects, young adults, were told that they were to be a part of a "learning experiment." The task was simple. On the other side of a screen from the subject sat a person who was a "learner." Each time this person (a confederate of the experimenter, but the subject didn't know this) made an error, the subject's task was to increase progressively a shock going to the learner by turning a dial marked off in voltages. The dial was labeled from "mild shock" through "danger" all the way to a setting of 450 volts. The final point was marked in red, suggesting that it might trigger a fatal charge of electricity. Even when the stooges cried out "in pain" (they were not really receiving shocks), many subjects obediently continued to give the erring "trainees" seemingly agonizing shocks.

In fact, a full 65 percent of the subjects obeyed instructions to give severe shocks as a penalty for failure to answer questions properly. Interviews after the experiment indicated that the subjects were genuinely concerned that they might be injuring the people (Milgram, 1971). Incidentally, there was no difference between male versus female behavior in this experiment.

Sometimes people are skeptical, thinking that the subjects had somehow caught on to the experiment and would not do this in "real

▲ *Photographs taken during Asch's experiment on conformity. In the top photograph, Subject 6 (sixth person from left) listens to the others express identical (but wrong) answers that differ from his own. He has to make a choice: does he express the judgment he knows to be correct and risk being different from the group, or does he conform to the group's judgment? In the next two photos, Subject 6 shows the strain of being in repeated disagreement with the group, but he did stand by his own opinion, saying that "he has to call them as he sees them."*

Teaching Hint

You might note one minor flaw in Asch's experiment. The subjects were in the same room as the confederates, who had to act in an identical way each time. Is this possible? Future experiments of this type attempted to eliminate this variable: subjects responded to a tape recording.

DISCUSS THE PHOTO

Have students make a list of the practical implications of Asch's study.

FYI In one version of his experiment, Milgram had the experimenter called out of the room, and a substitute experimenter was brought in. As you might expect, compliance dropped dramatically. You've probably seen the same response at school with substitute teachers.

Points to Stress

For realism, "teachers" in Milgram's study were given an initial minor shock.

ENRICHMENT

Asch's experiment is classic but dated. Would subjects react the same way today? Have students find out if follow-up studies on Asch's experiment have yielded similar results. See the following **Demonstration.**

DEMONSTRATION

Pick someone who won't be embarrassed, and use this person as a subject in a re-creation of Asch's experiment. The preparation is simple: draw a few sets of lines and recruit some confederates.

DEMONSTRATION

As noted, most people blindly obey authority because they are not given full responsibility for their own actions. This can easily be demonstrated in class. Without explanation, order a student to bring a notebook to your desk. Order another student

---

Conformity to Group Pressure.

IN FOCUS Five friends say that they liked the movie, and we go along, even though we hated it. Or everyone else is wearing the newest sandals, so we have to have a pair.

Discussion

Ask a shop teacher to rig up a panel of authentic-looking voltage meters so you can recreate Milgram's experiment in class. Are you *shocked*? You should be. Although Milgram's subjects were not harmed, they were put under a fair amount of stress. Thus, this is **not** an experiment to recreate in class. Pretend, however, that you intend to conduct the experiment at school. Many students will get excited and begin offering ideas on how to make it work. Encourage this for a while to see if anyone objects. If no one does, halt the discussion, and as if it suddenly dawned on you, discuss the ethics of conducting such an experiment. Explain that such an experiment would likely not be approved today— even at a university.

606

IN FOCUS **Conformity to Group Pressure**

Which of the three lines on the right is most like the one on the left?

A
A
A

A B C

WHAT A BUNCH OF STOOGES...BUT WHAT IF I'M WRONG?

UH...A

Twenty-five percent of subjects agreed with group.
Twenty-five percent of subjects disagreed with group.
Fifty percent of subjects wavered between agreement and disagreement.
Describe a real-life situation where this kind of *subtle* group pressure exists.

---

life." But in an identical experiment, with puppies right in view, subjects were willing to shock them at the command of the researcher as a "training" device. The shocks did cause the puppies to yelp and squirm uncomfortably, but the shocks were not great (again unknown to the subjects). As in the other experiment, the subjects had a dial in front of them that indicated increasing voltages (Sheridan & King, 1972).

to bring something from his or her pocket. Order another to take off his or her shoes. And so on. The orders should become progressively more outlandish—but don't go too far! Most students will readily comply since they probably believe that what hap-

pens in your class, under your orders, is *your* responsibility. Even after explaining your point about blind obedience and responsibility, some students will continue to comply if you demand something.

Chapter 21 SOCIOCULTURAL INFLUENCES: ATTITUDES AND BELIEFS

▲ *The machine and procedure used in the studies of obedience. Note in the photo at right that the man at the controls is forcefully holding down the arm of the "learner" who is screaming in agony. (Copyright © 1965 by Stanley Milgram. From the film OBEDIENCE, distributed by the New York University Film Division and the Pennsylvania State University, PCR.)*

Psychologist **Stanley Milgram** (1977), who pioneered these studies, was very distressed at how things turned out. He decided to try the experiment using physical contact with the victim, figuring *that* would make a difference. But the victim crying out, pleading heart trouble—nothing seemed to stem the blind obedience of most subjects to go ahead with the punishment and torture on command. Naturally, at that point, Milgram began to worry about the "kind of character produced in American democratic society that can't be counted on to insulate its citizens from brutality." He said this after he found that subjects ordered to force the victim's hand onto a shock plate supposedly containing 150 volts were willing to drag the person over to it and place the hand on the plate. In one case, the subjects were dealing with a screaming 50-year-old man.

We are faced here with a frightening amount of obedience to authority. In fact, one experiment shows that it is possible to get these kinds of results using a telephone, so the "authority" is not even present in the room. This study was set up at a real hospital, and 22 nurses were *telephoned* by a "physician" unknown to them. They were told to administer a drug to a patient while the physician was en route to the hospital, so the drug would have started taking effect by the time he got there. The experimenters used the name of a fictitious drug and had already placed the bottle, clearly labeled with a maximum dosage in the nursing station drug locker. On the phone, the "physician" prescribed an administration of *double* the safe dosage. Twenty-one of the 22 nurses had to be stopped as they left the nurses' station, medicine in hand to give it to the patient as ordered (Hofling et al., 1966).

Is there any saving grace in this mess? A little, at least in terms of learning a lesson. As two social psychologists have summarized, the key to a lot of this destructive obedience may lie in the fact that people are often not given full responsibility for their own actions. When

FYI Some results of Milgram's experiment: if the learner was not seen or heard—almost 100 percent compliance; if the learner was not seen but was heard—60 percent compliance; if the learner was seen and heard—40 percent compliance; forcing hand on plate—30 percent compliance. (Compliance refers to those who gave the full 450 volts.)

DISCUSS THE PHOTO

Contrast the subject in this photo with Asch's subject presented earlier. Milgram's subject appears amazingly calm.

Points to Stress

One technique that will almost always guarantee obedience in the above **Demonstration** is your use of distance. If you ask someone from across the room to take off a shoe, the person may not do it. Stand face-to-face with the same person, and the rate of obedience soars. Try it, and then discuss whether it seems to work.

607

EXPERIMENT

If possible, send students out in the hall to make small requests from people in the cafeteria: "Call this number for me; lend me a quarter; can I sit in that chair? It's *my* chair." Before you send them out, decide what you want to test for: making a request from near versus far; making a request with a question versus with a demand; effects of offering a compliment before a request; gender differences; effects of how the experimenter is dressed; number of people in the hall.

DISCOVERY

See **Teaching Master 21-7 Analyzing Commercials.** This handout asks students to analyze a variety of commercials for credibility, sincerity, and so on. If you want to use it in class, tape several commercials and present them.

Comprehensive Check

What does the evidence of Stanley Milgram's studies suggest? *(People tend to comply with authority, even if it means torturing innocent others. One possible explanation is that in obeying authority, people do not feel responsible for their actions.)*

Teaching Hint

Students find it hard to believe that subjects would administer full shocks, especially after they heard screaming. Point out that we're used to obeying. If a doctor says to take off your clothes, you do. A doctor is a legitimate authority. In Milgram's experiment, subjects saw the experimenter as a legitimate authority, too. Ask students to think of other authority figures people might obey without question (police, military officers—anyone in a uniform?). (Note how some criminals use this tendency to obey by dressing up as authority figures to help solicit unquestioning cooperation.)

608

---

immunization

An attempt to train a person beforehand to resist persuasion or propaganda.

608

---

subjects are told that they are in charge and must account for what happens, obedience to these outlandish commands drops dramatically (Worchel & Cooper, 1983).

VERBAL PERSUASION

Verbal persuasion is all around us. It runs the gamut from a radio commercial to a defense attorney's plea to a jury. Persuasion by itself is neither good nor bad; each of us tries to convince others of our point of view. While none of us is totally immune to the effects of persuasion, how resistant we are to an appeal depends on a number of factors.

Defenses Against Persuasion

Psychologists have studied techniques for fighting off persuasion, called **immunization.** Can a subject be immunized against propaganda as if it were the measles? Results are inconsistent, but a few points do stand out. For one thing, a two-sided argument in which opposing viewpoints are stated and compared seems to be a more effective immunizer than merely giving the person a one-sided lecture. This technique helps prepare the listener before he or she hears the opposite point of view from the actual "persuader," so the propaganda loses some of its punch (McGuire, 1964). In the same way, lawyers gain an advantage by presenting some of the opponent's views in watered-down form or in a way that makes those views seem insignificant. Doing this unconsciously impresses judges and juries since the lawyer seems more "open" about the issues, less biased. As a result, when the opposing attorney gets up, everyone has "already heard that argument"—only they got it from the first attorney who probably slipped in his or her own slant (Cialdini et al., 1981).

A second point is that passively reading arguments is not as effective as having to work out one's own case against something. Actively working on arguments about things like nuclear disarmament or capital punishment results in our becoming more certain of the side we are taking, since we begin to think that this was our view all along (Eagly & Himmelfarb, 1978). Of some interest, if we hear a counterargument before this new argument is settled in the brain, we tend to return to our original beliefs (Rogers & Thistlethwaite, 1969). As you can see, people *gradually* change beliefs so that their beliefs match what they are saying, but it requires work on their part.

Thus, immunization works to some extent. Complete resistance to new points of view is impossible and a fiction. Nonetheless, long-standing beliefs can be very resistant to change.

DEMONSTRATION

Advertisers know all about keeping the audience involved and active: scratch and sniff; flaps in magazines that must be unfolded; slogans that stick with us for years: "Is it live, or is it _____ ? I can't believe it's not _____." As a teacher, you know about the importance of involving the class. You're usually not trying to persuade students about any particular message, but you are certainly trying to persuade them to think. (As an activity, you can write a list of incomplete commercial slogans to see how well students do. Explain that advertisers _count_ on them to do well, to remain _involved_ even years later!)

DEMONSTRATION

Have students bring in and "sell" a product to the class using the tips presented in the **In Focus How to Persuade.** After each of these commercials, have the class briefly analyze the persuasive techniques used.

IN FOCUS — How to Persuade

Present _both_ sides. You'll seem more open-minded!

Actively involve your audience!

Have experts sell your message!

How you say something is often more important that _what_ you say.

Suppose you wanted to convince your audience not to abuse alcohol and other drugs. How could you use each of these suggestions?

How to Persuade.

IN FOCUS You admit that alcohol is widely accepted, but you show the dangers (two sides). You ask the audience questions and maybe have them role-play (which involves them). You might get a former substance abuser (an expert of sorts) to speak to the audience. You might try to get a charismatic speaker (who knows how to keep an audience awake).

Reteaching Strategy

Have students bring in several magazine ads that they can analyze in class with a partner. Direct them to the **In Focus How to Persuade.** Do the ads follow the tips presented there?

DISCOVERY

Here's one exception to the advantages of offering two sides. If you know that the audience already tends to agree with you, it is usually more effective to present only one side. Why confuse people who have already made up their minds and who agree with you? On the other hand, maybe presenting dissenting opinions will prevent blind submission, and blind submission could come back later to haunt you.

Have students make a list of commercials or ads that mention competitors. In other words, the ads present two sides, not equally perhaps but still two sides. Are these commercials effective? *Should* Coke mention Pepsi, for instance?

Critical Thinking

"You are given $100,000 to produce a commercial for foot-odor spray. You decide you want to use a personal appeal, someone talking directly to the audience. What qualities do you want your speaker to have?" Someone who is attractive and sincere. An expert. Someone who is well known can accomplish much of this immediately without saying a word. Which is one reason why celebrities can make huge amounts of money endorsing products.

Points to Stress

Lately, advertisers seem to be mocking credibility. For example, they might get a (fictional) politician, a role not high on many people's list for credibility, to sell a car. And since the commercials ridicule credibility, they probably receive high marks for sincerity.

Points to Stress

Sometimes even pseudo-experts are used to sell products: Remember this one: "I'm not a doctor, but I play one on TV"?

610

Effect of Having an Expert

As a general rule, we are more likely to listen to a genuine expert on a subject (or one who seems to be!) than to an appealing but relatively unknowledgeable person. Advertisers should pay more attention to this fact given their tendency to use movie or television personalities in ad campaigns. If a tennis star is advertising sports equipment, it works reasonably well, but having the same person push a laundry detergent is a different matter, since the viewer knows full well that stars rarely do their own laundry.

In many cases, it doesn't make as much difference *what* the person is saying in a commercial or a persuasive argument as *how* it is said. If you make up lots of "impressive" statistics and claims, the true facts of the situation may be hidden and might not play a role in the opinion the listener forms.

Consciously or unconsciously, realistically or not, we are always evaluating the source of our information before we act on it. If we feel it is reliable, we tend to agree; if not, we don't. Consider the following experiment: trying to determine the influence of source credibility on saving energy, experimenters sent out two batches of identical "Consumer Energy-Saving Tips." One was sent from the electric company and the other from a "public service group." Those who received the utility's letter did not cut their energy use, while those who thought it was from the service group reduced their use by 7 percent (Stern, 1984).

SOCIAL PERSUASION: BRAINWASHING

In war and terrorist activity, it is not unusual for a captive to "confess" to something that is untrue or even to defect to the enemy. This is commonly called brainwashing. Why this happens is very complex, but we do have clues that might help explain it.

Friendliness

Having a common enemy usually unites a group of prisoners around the prisoners' own ideals and goals. In World War II, torture was common in prison camps, thus bringing the prisoners closer together. In such situations, they did a good job of resisting exposing secrets or confessing. But in the Korean and Vietnam wars, prisoners dealt with a new situation: captors who at times were unusually friendly. This approach was unexpected and, as a result, caused the

ENRICHMENT

Have students find out why people join extremist cults, why they stay, and how they get out. A good source might be the local police station, where you can probably find a speaker, too.

ENRICHMENT

Salespeople know all about persuasion. Have a few students interview salespeople to find out what methods they use. Or invite one in. Clarify what you mean by salespeople: the ones who do it as a career, not the part-time assistant manager/stockpersons who work in the mall.

Points to Stress

It's easy to convince new parents that they need to buy thousands of dollars of safe equipment for their child. The moral of the story: if you want to persuade someone to buy something, know your audience.

Points to Stress

As noted, sensory-deprived subjects began to see and hear things that weren't really there. (This is a prime time to introduce the concept *propaganda*. Sensory deprived subjects are a bit spooked; they are more willing to believe.) If you have ever driven long distances at night, you may have experienced some of the effects of sensory deprivation.

DISCUSS THE PHOTO

If any of your students have ever used isolation chamber "therapy," ask them to describe how it affected them.

Comprehension Check

List three methods of brainwashing. *(friendliness towards victim, sensory deprivation, and a reward system)*

Chapter 21 SOCIOCULTURAL INFLUENCES: ATTITUDES AND BELIEFS

prisoners confusion about resisting the enemy (Lifton, 1961). It was a calculated technique that weakened the prisoners' resolve to resist.

Sensory Deprivation

Other prisoner-of-war incidents have called attention to a phenomenon called **sensory deprivation,** a severe type of punishment that involves no physical torture, as such, but that deprives the person of the use of his or her senses. Sensory deprivation is accomplished by using gloves, earmuffs, and a blindfold, in some cases suspending the person in water set at body temperature. Because our bodies require stimulation, this treatment becomes intolerable very quickly.

Many a cocky college student has been taken down a peg or two by this procedure. In one study, students were asked to volunteer for a sensory-deprivation experiment in which they had to do absolutely nothing but wear some of the equipment mentioned above. They were paid the equivalent of $100 a day. Despite this, only the stoutest students could last a full three days. Deprivation induces a fear rather like that of being lost in a vast wasteland without a sight or sound around. Because there is no stimulation, the brain begins to call on its own inner resources to make things up. For instance, visual hallucinations—seeing things that are not there—are common (Heinemann, 1970). Confusion, worry, disorientation, regret, and panic are common symptoms (Zubek, et al., 1971).

One has to assume that the students' symptoms were moderate, since they knew they could quit at any time. Prisoners are left in a state of deprivation until they agree to whatever the captors want. As far as we know, everyone gives in to this psychological pressure.

You will hear about a "therapy" using isolation chambers. People lie in an enclosed tank of water and meditate. This has helped some get more in touch with themselves, but it is completely voluntary, relatively brief, and not externally controlled. Hence, there is no comparison with psychological torture (Kamrnerman, 1977).

Reward System

Difficult to fight is a reward system in which prisoners are given, say, extra food for providing basically useless information about others. This technique is clever because once a person has given in a little, each similar behavior is a bit easier to obtain. Along the same line, minor (but useful) confessions may be elicited for a reward (Schein et al., 1961). Larger confessions soon follow. Probably the most destructive aspect of this method is that it undermines the prisoners' group structure. Every person walking around with extra food is immediately suspected by the other prisoners, and they don't know exactly who is giving significant information to the enemy and

sensory deprivation

Removing all external sensations and stimulation.

▲ *Blindfolded students who were wearing gloves and earmuffs and whose arms were wrapped and feet covered, were placed in an isolation chamber. This kind of sensory deprivation becomes intolerable for anyone after roughly three days maximum. Human beings cannot remain oriented without some sort of stimulation, and without it we will begin to see and hear things that are not really present.*

611

DEMONSTRATION

See the wraparound material for Chapter 2 for a few social psychology experiments and activities. Here's an example from Ch. 2 (if you didn't use it then) that would work well here: Show up late to class one day, but leave the overhead projector turned

on. Place a sheet of instructions on the overhead to see how obedient your students will be. Possible instructions: sit in a circle; take off your shoes; pick a leader; read; and so on. To make this more like an experiment, vary the instructions from

class to class. One class's instructions could be courteous; another's could be rude. Or you may want to arrange for a student or two to lead the obedience or to disobey vehemently. Afterward, discuss which factors influenced obedience.

Teaching Hint

If you've ever bought a new car, you're familiar with the salesperson's masterful techniques, where small requests are followed by a reward and then by larger requests: "If you did buy a car from us, what color would you like? Sharp color. Would you get just a radio or a CD player as well?" And so on. (Milgram's experiment worked on the same principle: start with a small shock, and it becomes easier to administer a bigger shock.)

Discussion

One way that commercials try to achieve sincerity is by using cameras that seem to be hand-held. The image shakes and tilts. Or we, the audience, witness a real taste test with the help of a hidden camera. Or we may overhear two people talking about the laundry soap they use. We're in on their secret. These commercials are intended to seem natural, since they are not "slick." Ask students if they can think of any other similar advertising techniques. Are they really fooled by any of this?

612

to what extent. The same basic approach is often used by the police, and it rarely fails. They bring in two suspects who were working on a "job" together. They question each one separately. Neither knows what the other said, but the police officers make one of them think that the game is up by being very friendly, suggesting that a confession has already been obtained from the other suspect (Nizer, 1966).

Brainwashing and the Consumer

Brainwashing and other forms of control are often based on the principle of compliance with a small request, followed by a reward, followed by a larger request. This same system is used by advertisers who enter you in a contest if you simply write down the name of their product or send in a box top. Having gotten you to do one small act, they assume that you will probably engage in the larger behavior of buying their product.

Studies have been fairly consistent in showing that such small requests are a good method for getting people to comply with larger ones. In one study of such techniques, women were called on the phone and asked a few questions about some household product such as soap. A few days later, the same women were called and asked if the experimenter could bring *five men* and take a two-hour inventory of the products in the home. Having given in to the small request, 52 percent of the women agreed to the larger request. To see if the first request had made a difference, another group was given only the larger request. Only 22 percent of them agreed to allow the inventory (Freedman & Fraser, 1966). While there is a difference between giving in on soap and other products versus a major issue, the principle is fairly sound.

Finally, despite the commotion we hear on occasion about thought control and such, rarely does a person change deep-seated opinions. While we may be willing to "change" our beliefs for a short while, when the pressure is over, lifelong philosophies reappear.

CHAPTER PROJECT/COOPERATIVE LEARNING

The media are constantly taking polls on one attitude or another. Have each student group choose a topic and then write a ten-question attitude survey on that topic. Explain that the survey will be given to other high school students. Groups can focus on attitudes toward dating, school, money, part-time jobs, parents, the future, and so on. (They may need to review the material in Chapter 2 on surveys. Or, you may want to bring in some sample surveys from magazines. Warn them that open-ended questions are very difficult to analyze. Encourage them to use scales and quantify the responses.)

PSYCHOLOGY IN YOUR LIFE

Winning Over Attitudes and Beliefs

Getting a job involves a direct confrontation of the values, attitudes, and beliefs held by two different generations. The interviewer, unfortunately, is probably prejudiced and may have a stereotype of you—sight unseen. It is a form of psychological war in which, more often than not, you have to "lose" for the moment in order to gain over a longer period of time. There are some tried-and-true psychological principles and details that deserve consideration. It may well sound like we are dictating what you must do. That's not our purpose. Sometimes to win you have to swallow your pride. None of the suggestions presented here should compromise your integrity; they are only nuisances that will eventually put you on top. Follow these ideas for a job interview, and you will increase your odds of success dramatically.

1. There are important rules about eye contact. Try not to look down at the floor. In "body language," this indicates submission, guilt, and weakness. When someone is talking to you, look directly at them. If you are talking for a long time, look away for a brief period, but return your eyes again. When you are talking to the other person, look at them only for brief periods because the other person will be watching you. The goal here is to avoid the threat of continuous eye contact, which can be distressing, so most people automatically follow these rules.

2. Try to avoid using slang whenever possible. It's also a good idea not to say "like" and "you know" too often, as in "He, like, told her about it, you know, and like, I thought that was, you know, like not right." While these sound acceptable when with friends, to others they sound terrible and may, in and of themselves, be enough for you to lose the job. Don't kowtow or be too subservient, but saying "Mr. ____" or "Ms. ____" on occasion sounds awfully nice.

3. Rules for clothing, males: Find the most boring thing you own and have it cleaned and pressed. Use solid colors—not too bright. Wear only regular shoes or boots, not sandals. A tie is an inexpensive and helpful touch. Check your fingernails for cleanliness just before going in for the interview. Females: Wear a skirt or dress. The more you accentuate your "good looks," the *smaller* will be your chances of getting the job. Watch out for too much makeup or eye shadow. Both male and female interviewers are usually highly prejudiced against a "flashy" woman. So look reasonably conservative and well-groomed.

4. Look up something about the company with the help of your librarian, and ask a few sensible questions

(continued on next page)

(continued on next page)

PSYCHOLOGY IN YOUR LIFE

Discovery
Have students write a brief résumé that highlights their potential job skills. Have students read point number 6 in this section. It might help if students have a specific audience, a particular employer in mind, when writing the résumé.

ENRICHMENT

Have students complete the **Enrichment Worksheet** for this chapter located in the Teacher Resources.

VOCABULARY REVIEW

Before testing students on the contents of the chapter, you may want to review vocabulary terms that are especially important or confusing. Terms in this chapter that could require clarification are *culture, internalize, prejudice,* and *cognitive dissonance.*

Reteaching Strategy

Have students complete the **Reteaching Worksheet** for this chapter located in the Teacher Resources. The **Vocabulary Worksheet** may be completed by the class as a pretest for chapter concepts or used as a reteaching worksheet for those students needing additional review.

Wrapping It Up

Here's a role-playing exercise in which *you* should probably participate. Make up a clever name for a company—your company—and interview several students for an important job opening. Afterward, have students point out the positive and negative aspects about each student's responses. Next, discuss the job interview techniques outlined at the end of the chapter. Finally, interview several more students, and this time students should try to incorporate some of these techniques during the interview.

PSYCHOLOGY IN YOUR LIFE

Winning Over Attitudes and Beliefs

(continued from previous page) during the interview so you appear interested in the company. Try also to ask a question or two about something that the interviewer tells you about the company— again to show interest.

5. Be sure to nod occasionally so you seem interested. But watch out for the "nodding-dog-on-a-spring" effect.

6. Write down beforehand the skills you have developed, no matter how trivial they might seem. Try to cover everything you have done. Then, if the issue of a certain skill comes up and you have done something using a similar skill sometime in the past, be prepared to say, "I had some related experience when I…"

7. Regarding apprehension and anxiety, both of which are natural: there is a useful, workable "trick" that psychologists suggest for clients who panic when they have to face other people. It sounds silly, but it really will help.

Visualize the interviewer in underwear or some other awkward situation. This will make him or her seem more like a plain old human rather than some great authority figure, and it will help you feel more equal and less threatened by that person.

8. You must rehearse these things for a few days beforehand with a friend or parent. They are not natural and must be learned.

SUMMARY

1. The United States is comprised of many different cultures, races, and ethnic groups. Whites make up the majority. African Americans are the largest minority group, followed by Hispanics, Asian Americans, and Native Americans.

2. The field of psychology has a North American and European bias. Some of our research information may not apply to minority groups.

3. We identify with a reference group that helps form and continues to support a set of beliefs that we have internalized.

4. People form stereotypes because they bring organization to our world. They are not bad in and of themselves but can lead to prejudice and discrimination. Once prejudice

starts, it is kept going via illusory correlations. Scapegoats are people who are not responsible for but are blamed for our own problems.

5. Many of our attitudes are changed because cognitive dissonance causes us to feel uncomfortable, so we realign our beliefs. We also will often yield to pressure from others without even knowing it. Obedience studies show that any of us might yield too much to the pressure of authority.

6. Brainwashing is not a technique that normally has lasting effects. To change opinions for a limited time, friendliness and sensory deprivation are the most effective methods.

SUGGESTED READINGS

▼ Allport, G. *The Nature of Prejudice.* New York: Doubleday, 1958.

▼ Milgram, S. *Obedience to Authority.* New York: Harper & Row, 1974.

▼ Miller, A. G. *The Obedience Experiments: A Case Study of Controversy in Social Science.* New York: Praeger, 1986.

▼ Zimbardo, Philip, and E. B. Ebbesen. *Influencing Attitudes and Changing Behavior.* Reading, Mass.: Addison-Wesley, 1977.

VOCABULARY

culture
race
ethnic group
internalize
reference group

stereotype
prejudice
discrimination
illusory correlations
scapegoating

cognitive dissonance
Stanley Milgram
immunization
sensory deprivation

Answers to Review Questions

1. stereotype
2. prejudice
3. internalize
4. reference groups
5. scapegoats
6. illusory correlations
7. immunization
8. cognitive dissonance
9. true
10. false
11. true
12. true
13. false
14. true
15. true

Review Questions

Fill in the blanks; answer on a separate sheet of paper. (An answer may consist of more than one word.)

1. The statement, "All Slobians are lazy," is an example of a __?__.
2. Treating all members of an ethnic group the same way is a sign of __?__.
3. When we __?__ a group's beliefs, we adopt them as our own.
4. We often perceive the world differently because of the various __?__ with which we identify.

5. If we blame tall people for indirectly raising clothing prices, tall people then are __?__.
6. When we use __?__, we only see in others what we want to see and ignore other information.
7. Two-sided arguments often lead to __?__.
8. Contradictory beliefs lead to __?__.

True/False

9. Stereotypes often lead to prejudice.
10. Illusory correlations tend to weaken stereotypes.

11. Recent studies indicate that face-to-face prejudice seems to be decreasing.
12. When faced with cognitive dissonance, most people will change their beliefs.

Notes on Discussion Questions

1. Students may want to examine family, friends, and coworkers.

2. This question may give you some insight into how your students view *you!*

3. You might want to follow this up with a discussion on intercultural and interracial dating.

4. This question would work well as a journal topic.

5. To discuss this question in class, write two columns on the board. "List A" should include what Milgram learned through his studies. "List B" should include how Milgram performed his studies and any drawbacks to this method. Have students work in pairs to complete the lists. Then have them share their answers with the class.

6. Advertisers establish credibility by showing doctors (or actors playing doctors) promoting aspirin, physically fit people eating healthy foods, attractive people using beauty products, and so on.

7. The following workers may be affected by sensory deprivation: truck drivers, air traffic controllers, factory workers on an assembly line, security guards, English teachers who must listen to 93 speeches in a row.

8. This is a good end-of-the-year activity!

Suggested Videos

▼ *Constructing Social Reality.* Discovering Psychology series, part 20, 27 min. 1-800-LEARNER.

▼ *Eye of the Storm.* 25 min., 1970, ABC.

▼ *Obedience.* 44 min., 1969, Penn State.

▼ *The Power of the Situation.* Discovering Psychology series, part 19, 27 min. 1-800-LEARNER.

13. Milgram's subjects delivered "high" voltages of shock because they suspected that no one was actually getting hurt.

14. Someone who will be held responsible for his or her actions is less likely to obey an authority.

15. Without external stimulation, the brain creates its own stimulation.

Discussion Questions

1. Describe two of your most important reference groups. Discuss several similarities and differences between these two groups. Overall, are there more similarities or differences? Explain.

2. List several stereotypes of teachers and discuss (without using names) whether your teachers this year fit these stereotypes.

3. If you were dating someone for several months and then found out that this person was extremely prejudiced against a certain ethnic group, do you think you might eventually stop dating this person for this reason? Yes? No? Depends? Explain.

4. Compare some of the attitudes you have today with those you had when you were in junior high school. Have they remained basically the same? If yes, do you *express* them differently? Explain. If your attitudes have changed, in what ways? Explain.

5. While Milgram's obedience studies are fascinating, they also put the subjects involved under a great deal of stress at times. Experimenters always need to strike a balance between *how* they get their results and *what* they find out. Some might argue that Milgram's studies do not achieve this balance, that it is not ethical to put subjects under this great stress, regardless of what is learned. Do you agree? Why or why not? Explain.

6. How do advertisers establish credibility for their products? Describe several real advertising examples to support your answer.

7. As noted in the chapter, sensory deprivation may cause hallucinations. What kinds of occupations would be most affected by this problem? Explain. Keep in mind that not all the senses need to be deprived at one time to cause problems.

8. One of the suggestions listed at the end of the chapter was to write a list of job skills that you have developed. You may not have an interview soon, but this will be good practice. So, go ahead and write down your skills now.

Activities

1. Write a "Letter to the Editor" to your school newspaper on the issue of multicultural harmony. If your school has achieved what you perceive to be true harmony, the letter could be written in a congratulatory tone and might include reasons why people are getting along. Or you can discuss how other schools can adopt your school's policies and attitudes. If your school needs improvement in multicultural harmony, state the problems,

Notes on Activities

1. Make sure that you read these letters before allowing students to submit them anywhere; check to see if the tone is appropriate.

2. You may want to give students the option of *not* allowing you to read their letters. Maybe they can simply show them to you to prove that they wrote them.

3. See **Teaching Masters 21-5 Memory Test** and **21-6 Illusory Correlations Data Sheet** for a variation of this activity.

4. Students should have no difficulty finding information on this topic.

Consider inviting a police officer to class to speak about cults.

5. Tell the class exactly what your grading criteria will be before you assign this one.

---

then offer numerous concrete, practical solutions to the problems. Ask your teacher about the length of the letter and about the possibility of actually submitting the letter to the newspaper.

2. Pick two people who have helped to shape your attitudes and beliefs, and write a letter of appreciation to each of them. Be specific as to the kinds of things that the person did or said and what effect these things have had on your past and present values and beliefs.

   Something unexpected usually happens after writing these kinds of letters: you not only feel better about the people to whom you are writing but you also tend to feel better about yourself! No one will force you to do this, but once you receive credit for the letters from your teacher, why don't you mail them and spread some of the positive feelings you experience to others?

3. Conduct the illusory correlation (or "bacon-eggs") experiment described near the beginning of the chapter. Think of five familiar word pairs: bacon-eggs, lion-roar, and so on. Think of five unfamiliar word pairs; night-fork, gamble-bed, and so on. Write *each* of these ten word pairs, both familiar and unfamiliar, onto five separate index cards. In other words, five cards will say "bacon-eggs," five will say "lion-roar," and so on. You will have a total of 50 index cards.

   Procedure: Mix up the cards and hand them to your first subject. (*Note:* do *not* mix them blindly as you would with playing cards; make sure the same word pair does not appear two times in a row.) The subject will look at the first card for three seconds (yes, time it), and then you will announce, "Next." The subject will then put the card face down onto the table or desk and look at the next card. Then have a separate sheet of paper with all the word pairs listed and ask the subject how many times the word pair appeared on the cards. This list should mix the familiar and unfamiliar word pairs evenly: Word pair number 1 would be familiar, number 2 would be unfamiliar, and so on. Record the subject's answers. Repeat this entire procedure on 20 subjects. Of course, analyze your results in detail. By this point in the text, you should be an expert at this!

4. Do some research on extreme kinds of reference groups: cults. Find out: (a) the broad definition of a cult; (b) *how* new cult members internalize the beliefs and attitudes of the cult; (c) what the established members of the cult do to promote this internalization process; (d) why people join cults; (e) how and why people leave cults. Organize this information into a report and include your reactions.

   You will probably acquire your information from books or magazines, but at least consider another source: a police station. Often there will be someone there who, through necessity, has become a sort of expert on the topic.

5. This chapter mentions that advertisers often use celebrities to promote products about which they probably know little. In other words, these ads do not seem highly credible. Flip through several magazines and find a bunch of ads that *do* strike you as credible for one reason or another, and also find ads that do not strike you as credible. Organize these ads into a creative collage. Be sure that the collage somehow presents the message about credibility versus incredibility. Perhaps you can do this by including appropriate captions. For example: "Would this man do his own laundry?" Once the collage is completed, display it in class.

STATISTICAL MEASURES: REPORTING EXPERIMENTAL FINDINGS

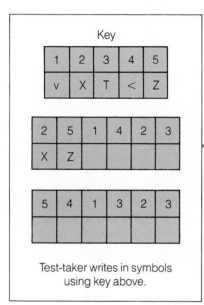

Test-taker writes in symbols using key above.

▲ *Figure A.1* *Digit-symbol task.*

Statistics are nothing more than a kind of shorthand, a way to collapse large groups of numbers into one or two, so comparisons can be made easily. **Statistics,** then, include any numerical process used to group, assemble, organize, or analyze information.

GRAPHICAL ANALYSIS

In some studies, the experimenter has varied the instructions on a particular task in order to vary the amount of pressure put on the individual who has been asked to solve a problem. As pressure to solve the problem increases, anxiety increases, and, with high anxiety, efficiency decreases drastically.

One study shows the effect of anxiety on test performance. Discussing the results will show how graphs work and how they help to clarify the findings of a psychological study.

One experimenter administered a questionnaire to a large group of students (Sarason et al., 1952). From the information he obtained through the questionnaire about their feelings and responses to test situations, he was able to pick out two smaller groups. One group was what might be called "high-anxious"—or, in everyday terminology, high-strung, prone to nervousness, or quite jumpy in a tight situation. The other group was low on the anxiety rating, meaning these people were calm, not nervous or jumpy under pressure. The two groups were given a test in which each subject worked individually on the task of matching various symbols with numbers. The experimenter used a key that showed the subject a series of figures that were already numbered (see Figure A.1). The test was too long to be completed in the time allotted, yet the subjects were given the instructions that they were "expected to finish."

The subjects were given five chances to succeed at the task. In other words, they took the test five times in succession. In psychological terminology, these five chances are called five **trials.**

Here is a report of the results: The scores varied from 27 through 43 for the five trials for each of the groups. The low-anxious group scored consistently higher (better) for each of the five trials, and in every case did better on the task than the high-anxious group. Even on the fifth trial, the low-anxious group continued to score better than the high-anxious group.

Although this verbal report is accurate, the results of the experiment are difficult to visualize, no matter how well the report is organized or written. This problem comes up frequently in the reporting of psychological experiments. **Graphs** are used to clarify and organize facts visually. A graph of this experiment is shown in Figure A.2.

The horizontal line at the base of Figure A.2 is marked off to indicate the number of trials (1, 2, 3, 4, 5). The vertical line at the left indicates the scores obtained by the subjects. A legend, similar to one found on a road map, shows the reader which lines within the graph represent which group in the study. The lines themselves connect a series of dots. Each dot represents a point on the horizontal axis (trial line) and a point on the vertical axis (score line).

The two arrows you see in Figure A.2 do not appear in real graphs, but have been added here to explain how the position of the

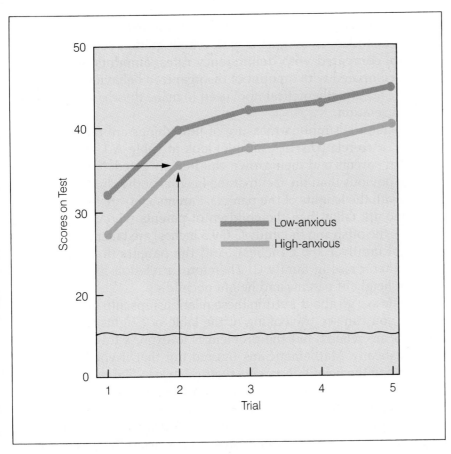

▲ *Figure A.2* *Test performance of high- and low-anxious subjects.*

dots is determined. Assume that the experimental results show that, on trial 2, the average score of all the subjects in the high-anxious group was 35. An arrow moves from 35 on the score axis (vertical) over to the right until it meets an arrow coming up from trial 2 on the trial axis (horizontal). The point at which they meet is the point where the dot is placed. Put another way, the dot represents trial 2, for which the average score of high-anxious subjects equaled 35.

With that out of the way, notice how easy it is to see the results of the experiment just by looking at the graph. The dotted line (high-anxious) is consistently below the straight line (low-anxious); high anxiety, then, appears to keep the level of performance low through all five trials. If this explanation is not completely clear, go back to the paragraph in which the results of the experiment were described, and compare the verbal description with the graph in Figure A.2.

You will see hundreds of graphs in scientific reports. They all follow the *same* principle as the one we've just shown you.

CORRELATION

Almost all psychological studies involve comparisons. The intelligence of a student is compared with school grades; problems in the home are compared with delinquency rates; amounts of narcotics taken is compared with amount of disorganized behavior; and so on. One statistical (mathematical) tool used to make these comparisons is called **correlation.**

Correlation is simply a measure of how things are related to one another, or co-related. For example, look at Table A.1 in which the heights of parents and their grown children are listed. Nothing could be more obvious than the fact that the heights of the children are correlated with the heights of the parents. Parents who are tall have children who are taller than the children of parents who are short. For example, the offspring in family C (69.5 inches) are taller than the offspring of family E (68.2 inches). And the parents in family E are shorter than those in family C. Therefore, a relationship must exist between height of parents and height of children.

How do we go about putting these relationships into numbers?

Well, you can see by looking at the table of heights that the two variables are related, but the problem is to express this relationship mathematically. Mathematicians figured out that if you plot points representing the height of parents (vertical axis in Figure A.3) and the height of children (horizontal axis) and then draw a diagonal that comes as close as possible to all the points and still is a straight line, then the amount of distance *between the dots and the line* will indicate how close a relationship there is between the two different characteristics (height of parents and height of offspring).

▼ *Table A.1*
Average of Heights of Parents and Offspring (in inches)

Family	Parents	Offspring
A	72.5	72.2
B	71.5	69.9
C	70.5	69.5
D	69.5	68.9
E	68.5	68.2
F	67.5	67.6
G	66.5	67.2
H	65.5	66.7
I	64.5	65.8

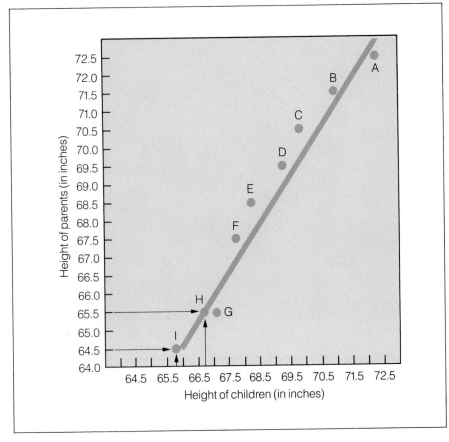

▲ *Figure A.3* *Correlation of average heights of parents and children.*

For example, Figure A.4 (hypothetical) shows a perfect relationship; there is no difference between the points and the straight line. Figure A.5 (hypothetical) shows a weak relationship; there is a great difference between the points and the line of best fit. It is possible, with highly accurate graph paper, actually to measure the distances between points and the diagonal line and to place them in a formula to determine the degree of relationship. Rather than do all this measuring, however, we can obtain the same results by dealing with the numbers *directly* by means of a mathematical formula. The reason for using graphs here for correlations is to provide a visual image of what we are talking about.

Reading, Interpreting, and Reporting Correlations

Correlation, then, is a measure of the apparent relationship between two different things. The numbers for correlation are called **correlation coefficients** and vary from 0 to 1. Zero means no relationship exists, while 1 means a perfect relationship exists.

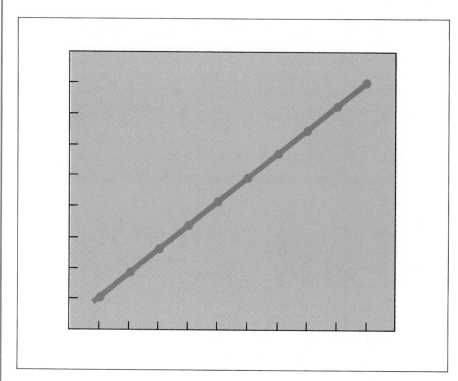

▲ *Figure A.4*   *Perfect correlation.*

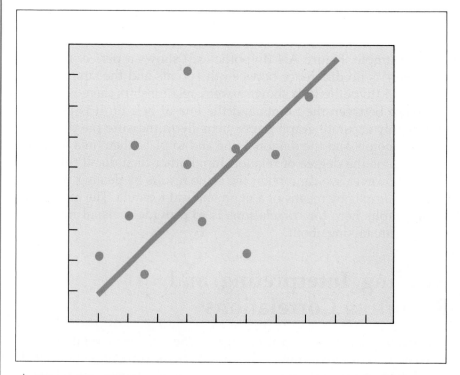

▲ *Figure A.5*   *Weak correlation.*

Words of caution: It is a rare student who does not confuse correlation with percentages at the beginning. A correlation is not in any sense the same as a percentage. Correlation numbers *look like* percentages. They are *not*. Nonetheless, at least one similarity does exist—the higher the number, the more the two items seem to be related.

So, the size of the correlation indicates the strength of the relationship; the higher the number, the stronger the relationship:

Typical correlations:

.00   .15   .38   .59   .70   .89   .90   1.00

Relationship getting stronger   →   →   →

The number .00 means no correlation exists; 1.00 means perfect correlation exists. A correlation coefficient can be *any* number between 0 and 1.

Now, suppose we examine the relationship between bottle feeding and age. As age increases, bottle feeding will decrease. At age five, there are a few hangers-on, and maybe one by age seven. Look at Figure A.6, where this correlation is plotted. Something is different. For one thing, the line is running in a direction opposite from the ones seen previously. For another, even though the line fits pretty

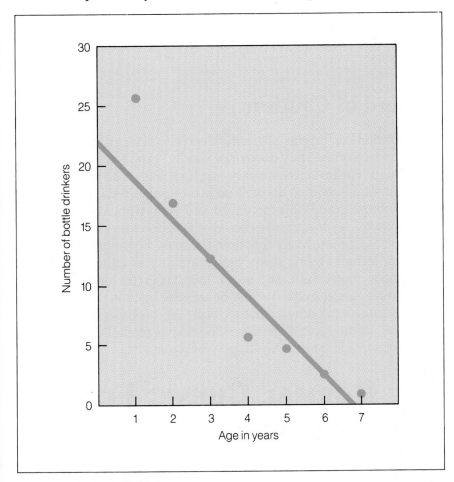

▲ *Figure A.6*   *Correlation of bottle feeding with age.*

squarely between dots, if you report something like this—
"Correlation between age (through age 7) and bottle feeding is .90"—
you are saying that, as age *increases*, bottle feeding *increases*, which
obviously is wrong. Yet we know there is a strong relationship
between age and bottle feeding. To allow for this kind of situation,
scientists use the correlation coefficients in the negative (minus)
direction as well as the positive (plus) direction; both mean the *same
thing* in terms of *degree* of relationship. A negative .90 correlation
(–.90) is just as strong as a positive .90 correlation (.90). The negative
correlation means that, as one variable (age) goes one way (increases), the other variable (bottle feeding) goes the other way (decreases).
The positive correlation means that, as one variable goes one way, the
other variable goes the same way (as height of parents goes up, that
of the children goes up).

The following *rough* guides can be used to interpret correlation
coefficients:

- From .00 to + or –.20 means an indifferent or negligible
  relationship exists.
- From + or –.20 to + or –.40 means a low correlation exists; a
  relationship is present but slight.
- From + or –.40 to + or –.70 means a substantial or marked
  correlation exists.
- From + or –.70 to + or –1.00 means a strong to perfect relationship
  exists.

A Word of Caution

Correlation coefficients show the degree to which two things are
related to each other. They do *not* necessarily show a cause-and-effect
relationship. For instance, suppose we find that students with good
grades in school tend to do well on achievement tests. Given these
two numbers, grade point average and achievement-test performance, can we say that grades cause the test scores or vice versa? No.
Instead, it is far more likely that both are caused by other things, like
basic intellectual ability, study habits, quality of education, home
atmosphere, motivation, and so on. Similarly, the length of one's
arms and legs are correlated with one another, but it is not very likely
that one causes the other. Instead, both are probably caused by a
"program" in the genes that directs the body's overall development,
with nutrition and general health playing a role.

THE NORMAL CURVE: FITTING PEOPLE INTO GROUPS

All sciences must bring order to a large number of facts. This
holds true for psychology, also; somehow people and their character-

istics have to be brought together in an orderly fashion. Otherwise, people can't be studied in a way that permits comparison.

The scientist putting things and people into categories often uses diagrams to represent these categories. Take the case of the investigator who, by the use of numbers, must show the difference in wealth among various groups in the United States. For example, how many families in the United States make under $10,000 a year? How many make between $20,000 and $40,000, and how many make more than $100,000? Grossly approximating for purposes of illustration, we could say that 3 million families fall into the first category, 15 million into the second, and about 3 million into the third.

Suppose that you draw a line to equal, in length, the number of families in each category:

		3 million	
Under $10,000		___ ↓	15 million
$20,000–$40,000		_____	↓
Over $100,000		___	

You have created a visual representation of income and families divided by categories. If you wanted to include more data, you could draw a line for each of a large number of income categories, making wealth appear to be a little more equally distributed than it actually is; you would obtain something approximating this diagram:

Number of Families

1	Under $10,000	___
2	xxxxxx	_____
3	xxxxxx	_____
4	xxxxxx	_____
5	$20,000–$40,000	_____
6	xxxxxx	_____
7	xxxxxx	_____
8	xxxxxx	_____
9	Over $100,000	___

(The larger the number of families, the longer the line.)

Now you can turn the diagram on its side, connect the highest points, and remove the lines, as shown in Figure A.7. The curve that results is called a bell-shaped or **normal curve.** This same curve represents the distribution (in a rough fashion) of such a large number of

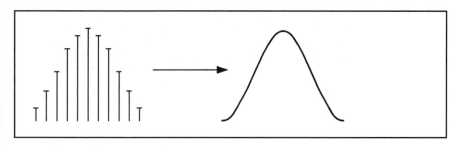

▲ *Figure A.7* *A bell-shaped curve.*

things in the world that psychologists use it frequently to illustrate characteristics of people as a whole or to categorize people along a certain dimension. It is used to represent visually how large numbers of people are distributed.

You can see how it works if you take a hypothetical curve of cleanliness. Most people (the norm, or normal—that is, what is to be expected) are going to be in the middle in the more-or-less clean group (see the rectangle in Figure A.8). Some groups of people are going to deviate from this norm, or normal position. At the far right of the curve in Figure A.8 might be the superclean, the bathtub dwellers. As we move along the curve toward the superclean, the number of individuals becomes smaller and smaller. Sliding to the left, we move away from the norm toward the superdirty, represented at the far left (and fortunately they also are in the minority). The technical name for this figure (A.8) is a *normal frequency distribution*. This means that, after having counted (determined frequency), we have a distribution (arrangement) that fits the normal (quite frequently found) arrangement of things: few superdirty, few superclean, most in the middle (Figure A.9).

Height of individuals is a characteristic that also fits this curve. Another is intelligence-test results, which would include the very bright and the very dull, one at each end of the curve, and the average in the middle.

Figure A.10 shows the percentage of subjects (persons, things, events, and so on) that would fall within a certain area of the curve if the curve were perfect. It is never perfect, but sometimes it comes close. The largest group of people fall into the middle (68 percent); 95 percent of the subjects are included within the second set of lines; and at 99 percent, the third set of lines, nearly everyone is accounted for. For example, 68 percent of a typical group is average clean. (In other words, if we have studied and categorized 100 individuals along the curve, 68 of them would fall between the two lines indicated.) All people vary somewhat, but they can be classified according

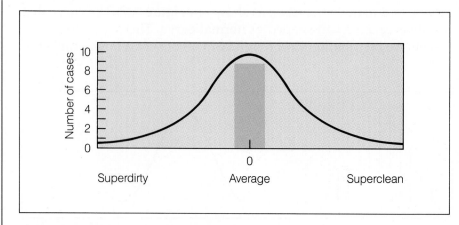

▲ *Figure A.8* *Normal frequency distribution.*

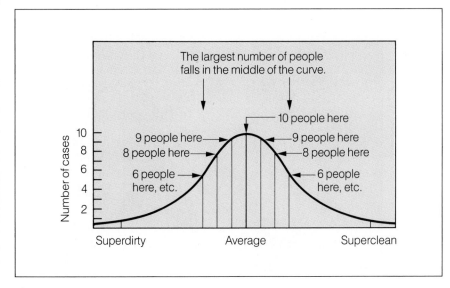

▲ *Figure A.9* *Normal frequency distribution.*

to these individual differences. Some are cleaner than others, some brighter than others.

The student new to psychology usually finds the concepts of statistics somewhat difficult to grasp at first. The purpose of this discussion has been to acquaint you in a general way with a distribution curve. The normal curve is a representation of the way in which people are distributed throughout a given population according to certain characteristics, such as intelligence or height. The normal curve does not fit all situations, however. The normal curve is an idealized one, so, of course, the psychologist will run into other ones, some of

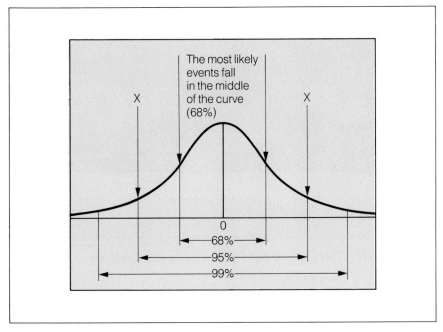

▲ *Figure A.10* *Breakdown of normal curve.*

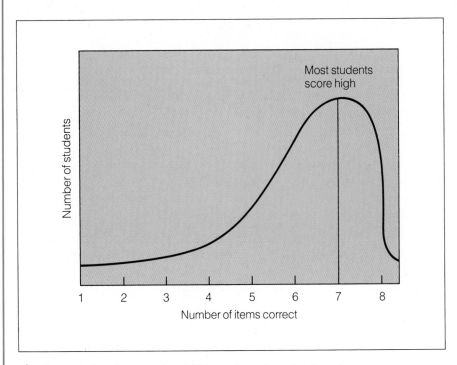

▲ *Figure A.11*   *Test results of fifth-graders given third-grade test.*

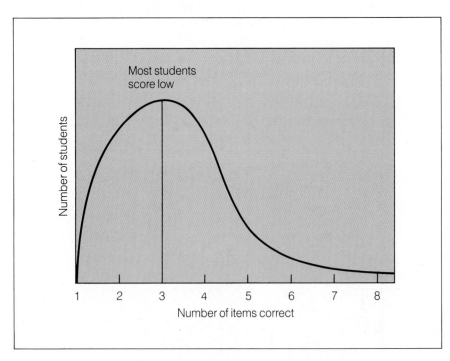

▲ *Figure A.12*   *Test results of third-graders given fifth-grade test.*

them very oddly shaped. For example, if fifth-grade children were given a third-grade test, they would get most items right, and the curve would look something like Figure A.11.

Reverse the procedure and give the fifth-grade test to the third-graders, and the curve will look something like Figure A.12.

Since Figures A.11 and A.12 deviate so much from the normal curve, they serve the useful function of showing immediately that we are dealing with an unusually distributed behavior or occurrence. So, the last two curves are not normal curves, and the percentages discussed earlier do not apply to them. These curves do, however, give a visual representation of many numbers pertaining to grouped individuals, and they can quickly supply a general idea of performance, removing the need for tedious research into the specific numbers obtained for each subject. Since all these kinds of curves are used so frequently, it is important that you grasp the general idea of what these curves are, how they are constructed, and how you read them.

MEAN, MEDIAN, AND MODE: REPRESENTATIVE NUMBERS

Three other mathematical measures are used in psychology to condense information into accessible form. If we had five scores of 25, 26, 24, 24, and 21, for example, we could get a number that would closely represent all these numbers by adding them together and dividing by the number of entries (5). The result, 24, is very close to representing all these numbers, and this number is called the arithmetic **mean**—in everyday language, it is called the average.

These numbers present no problem; but, if we took the scores 3, 5, 6, 7, and 30 and figured the mean, we'd obtain 10.2, which would not be very representative of the many small scores we have (four out of five are below 10). The major problem with the mean, therefore, is that it can be inflated by a few extremely high or low numbers. This problem is sometimes an advantage, since the mean is sensitive to extreme scores and includes them in its calculation. As you will see, neither the median nor the mode takes extreme numbers into consideration. In the case of the numbers we have just listed, we can get the best possible representative number by using what is called the **median,** or halfway mark—the mid-point of a list of ordered numbers. Since we have an odd number of digits (5), the midpoint or median will be the middle number, 6; this number is much more representative of the scores than 10.2. If your list of numbers is even, merely take the middle two numbers in the list, add them together, divide by 2, and you have the median. (For example: 3, 5, 5, 6, 7, 30. Add: 5 + 6 = 11; divided by 2. Median = 5.5.)

The third representative numerical measure is the **mode.** It is very simply calculated: It is the most frequently appearing number. The mode is adequate if you have a set of scores such as 3, 7, 9, 9, 12, and 14 because the mode 9 occurs close to the middle of the series. On the other hand, the most frequent number might appear at a strange place in the list: 3, 3, 3, 9, 9, 12, 14, and 17. Here the mode is 3 and certainly does not represent the group of numbers.

Of the three kinds of representative numbers we have discussed, the mean is the most frequently used. It is typically used with other statistics, but it can be used by itself.

Probability, Chance, and Odds

We consider next the topics of probability, chance, and odds, since almost all the studies mentioned in this book are based on mathematical measures (statistics) that relate to probability and chance.

For example, consider that the basic issue in extrasensory perception is whether individuals even have such power. To show how statistics might help determine whether this power exists, suppose that we were to predict that the next flip of a coin would be heads, and indeed it was. Would you then agree that we had special powers of prediction? Hardly—but why not? Simply because our prediction could have come true just by chance. In other words, a single prediction had a 50-50 chance of being right. We could have predicted tails and been correct; that is, we could have been correct just by chance.

No one knows what chance is; we do, however, assume that certain fixed laws operate in the universe and influence, for example, the roll of dice. In addition to these laws, there is chance itself: the unknown factors influencing the roll, which might be the tilt of the floor, the particles in the air, the angle of the hand, and so on. Even though the mechanical laws operate, unknown or chance factors constantly enter into any occurrence. So, at any given time, almost anything could occur just by chance maybe once, maybe even twice, or possibly a few more times. But suppose we could correctly predict the roll of dice 99 percent of the time for 1,000 throws. We assume you would then give us the credit we deserve for our special abilities. Why? Because something other than chance must be operating.

The same considerations apply to studying extrasensory perception or even the problem of finding that a person is a delinquent and comes from a broken home. We might be able to guess a card someone is holding just by chance alone. Or the delinquent may come from a broken home just by chance, and there might be no relationship between the home and the child's later behavior. We need a statistic that will determine just how far-fetched it is to assume that chance is operating. If, for example, we were to apply a statistic to our 99-percent-correct predictions of dice rolls, we would find that the idea that chance alone is working *this often* is quite remote. In fact, we can be almost certain that something other than chance is operating, even if it is nothing more than our having loaded the dice.

How far the results of a given study are removed from the effects of chance are reported numerically in the same fashion as other statistics are. We will get to this in a moment, but first it might be worthwhile to start the discussion all over again with another example to clarify these concepts.

One universal fact about human beings is that not everyone behaves in the same way. How, then, is it possible to make *any* statements about human behavior? We have already discussed correlation, but other statistical methods also give information about experimental findings. Suppose, for example, that we were to take the weights of a group of men found loitering on the corner somewhere and noted them to be 150, 165, 140, 160, and 325. Immediately we are struck by the highly deviant weight of 325, something expected very rarely. Also, we begin to speculate on how this man became so heavy. Maybe a glandular problem, maybe overeating. No one, however, tries to speculate on how a man comes to weigh 140 or 160 pounds. There's nothing unusual about it.

Reverse the situation. A group of experimenters think they have found a drug that induces weight increase. They administer it to a group of four males and then examine them ten years later, finding that their weights are 140, 150, 180, and 175. Assuming that their physiques correspond roughly to these weights, we can conclude that this is a very ineffective drug for increasing weight. Using another drug, the experimenters find ten years later that the subjects weigh 325, 298, 310, and 170. These heavier weights are extremely rare. Because of this rarity, the researchers can entertain the hypothesis that the drug induces weight gain. Chance might have given them one unusual weight, but it is highly unlikely that they would obtain three out of four strikingly deviant weights just by chance. In other words, the likelihood of this event occurring just by chance is remote. The scientist is always trying to demonstrate that the results obtained would be highly improbable if chance was the only factor operating.

Psychological experiments, including social studies, ESP experiments, intelligence testing, predictions of group behavior, and so on, never produce 100 percent rare events, just as the last study did not: 170 is not an unusual weight. On the other hand, the psychologist is looking for results that approach statistical rarity. The best way to understand this is to return to coin tossing.

In coin tossing, using a fairly new and untampered-with coin, the **probability,** or odds, that you will get either heads or tails is, in lay terminology, 50-50 (in statistical language, $p = .50$, where p stands for "probability"). In other words, *in theory*, every 100 tosses of a coin should yield 50 heads and 50 tails. In actuality, for any given set of 100 coin tossings, you might get 40 heads, 60 tails; 55 heads, 45 tails; and so on. Chance (unknown or accidental) factors are operating to give slight variations in the number of heads or tails. The nature of these chance factors is unspecified, but they are assumed *not* to operate in a consistent fashion; in other words, they temporarily influence the appearance of heads a few more times, or tails a few more times, eventually canceling one another out to result in overall figures close to 50-50.

If you have any money riding on the flips and they come up 20 tails and 80 heads, you should investigate the coin immediately on the grounds that something other than chance is operating—for example, a weighted coin. The discrepancy is too far removed from what normally occurs just by chance.

This is exactly what experimenters do: They look for results that are very remote from chance, just as it is very remote that 20 tails and 80 heads would occur merely from chance. (Note that it *is* physically possible for this to happen, but so rare as to be considered improbable.) It is more logical to search for a reason—a loaded coin—than to assume chance is the cause.

It is interesting to see what happens if you toss 10 different coins, 1,024 times. First of all, even with so many coins, the law of probability will still work. We could expect 5 heads and 5 tails from the 10 coins more often than any other combination; next most probable would be 4 heads and 6 tails or 6 heads and 4 tails. Something to be expected *very* rarely would be 10 tails or 10 heads. Figure A.13 shows a curve that quite closely represents the results obtained from throwing a group of 10 coins 1,024 times. You will note that a toss of 10 heads or 10 tails comes up only once in 1,024 tosses. The odds are 1,024 to 1 of getting either 10 heads or 10 tails.

Figure A.13 is the normal curve again, and we can mark off the percentage of occurrences on the curve (Figure A.14). Take the combination of 10 heads. The point on the curve where it falls (indicated by the arrow that points off the page) is beyond the 99 percent level of the curve, actually a little beyond the 99.9 percent point, meaning

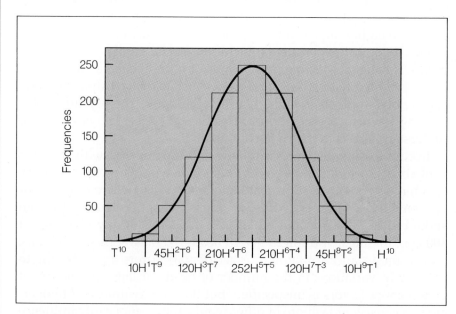

▲ *Figure A.13*   *Normal frequency distribution in coin tossing.*

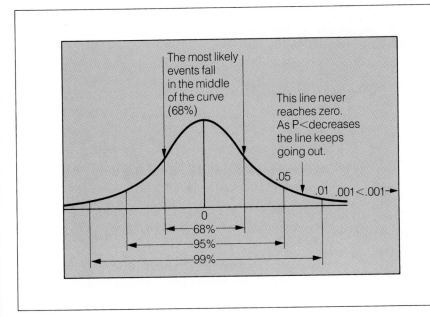

The most likely events fall in the middle of the curve (68%)

This line never reaches zero. As P<decreases the line keeps going out.

.05

.01 .001 <.001

0

68%

95%

99%

▲ *Figure A.14*   *Breakdown of normal curve.*

that over 99.9 percent of all other combinations fall below this point on the curve. Looked at another way, 10 heads leaves only .1 percent (one-tenth of 1 percent) of the curve.

The whole curve, 100 percent, is going to equal 1.00 when the percentage is changed to a decimal (1.00). To find out how much of the curve representing 10 heads is left, we change 99.9 percent to .999 and subtract it from 1.00(0); .001 is the remainder. This figure as a fraction is $1/1,000$ and means that one time in 1,000 (actually, in our case, $1/1,024$) could this occur by chance alone. Thus, it is *extremely* rare.

In the sciences, even though we know that events *could* conceivably occur with a *p* (probability) of .001 and still be chance, such an event is so rare that scientists assume that the result is more likely caused by the variable studied than by chance. Thus, if scientists find that statistics demonstrate that what they found in a study could occur only once in 1,000 times just by chance alone, they assume that chance is not the important factor. Another way of saying this is that the results reached the .001 level of **significance,** meaning that only 1 out of 1,000 times would such a finding occur by chance.

The .001, .01, and .05 levels are typically agreed on by scientists as indicating significant (important) findings, and are reported in scientific studies as $p = .001$, $p = .01$; $p = .05$, respectively. The experimenter decides before the experiment what significance will be acceptable. For most studies, a significance level of .05 is considered good enough, but if the results turn out to be even more significant, say .01 or .001, so much the better.

GLOSSARY

A

Acetylcholine Neurotransmitter that regulates basic bodily processes such as movement.

Achievement tests Tests that measure the amount of specific material remembered from the classroom.

Acoustic memory A very brief sound memory that can be sent to the short-term memory (STM).

Acupuncture A system of pain relief that involves inserting needles into the skin.

Adrenal glands The glands that produce adrenaline, the stimulating hormone that activates the body; help sexual maturation, along with gonads.

Adrenaline The chemical that prepares the body for emergency activity by increasing blood pressure, breathing rate, and energy level.

Afterimage The firing of the cones not used while viewing something steadily in order to bring the visual system back in balance.

Agoraphobia The fear of leaving a familiar environment, especially home.

Alcoholic withdrawal delirium The "horrors" that can result from severe alcoholism; includes weakness, anxiety, cramps, hallucinations.

Alpha waves Stage 1, fairly relaxed brain waves occurring just before going to sleep; relaxed.

Alzheimer's disease The loss of chemical nerve cell transmitters and other damage to nerve transmission that result in mental deterioration.

Amnesia The blocking of older memories and/or the loss of new ones. Also a dissociative disorder in which traumatic events "disappear" from memory.

Anal stage Freudian stage of development during which toilet training is the child's major concern.

Androgen The male hormone.

Androgyny The quality of having both masculine and feminine characteristics.

Anorexia nervosa An eating disorder that involves severe loss of weight from excessive dieting.

Antecedents Information and beliefs we have beforehand about another.

Antibodies Cells that fight off invading foreign bodies that might prove injurious; part of the immune system.

Antisocial personality disorder A personality disorder in which the person is in constant conflict with the law and seems to have no conscience.

Anxiety The feeling that something is wrong and disaster is imminent.

Anxiety disorder Disorder whose major symptom is anxiety.

Applied psychologists Those who make direct use of the findings of research psychologists; deal directly with clients.

Approach-approach conflict A choice between two attractive alternatives.

Approach-avoidance conflict One part of the situation is attractive, but the other part is not; the choice is whether to do or not do something.

Aptitude One's special skills.

Aptitude tests Tests that measure one's special skills (in carpentry, medicine, and so forth).

Archetypes Jung's term for inherited universal human concepts.

Asthma Muscle spasms and tissue swelling in the air tubes of the lungs.

Attention Alert focusing on material.

Attribution The causes we use to explain another's behavior.

Attribution theory A theory about the process by which we form opinions about another.

Audition The sense of hearing.

Auditory nerve   Bundle of nerves carrying sound to the brain.

Authoritive parenting style   Style in which parents seek input from children; parents are consistent but flexible in enforcing rules.

Aversive conditioning   A behavioral technique in which unpleasantness is associated with acts that are to be avoided.

Avoidance-avoidance conflict   A choice between two unattractive alternatives.

Awfulize   To see things in the worst possible light; Ellis's term.

Axon   The part of the neuron that carries messages away from the nerve cell to the dendrites on another nerve cell.

B

Behavioral approach   Viewing behavior as the product of learning and associations.

Behavioral therapy   Therapy that uses principles of learning to alter the person's actions or behavior.

Behaviorism   A personality theory that focuses on overt acts or behaviors rather than on consciousness or unconsciousness; Skinner and Bandura are examples of behavioral psychologists.

Behaviorists   Those who believe we are the product of associations.

Belongingness needs   Part of Maslow's hierarchy of needs; friendship, closeness with another.

Beta waves   Rapid brain waves; appear when a person is awake.

Binocular disparity   The difference between the visual image provided by each eye. When the images are brought together in the brain, they provide a sense of depth.

Biofeedback   A method of mental control in which a machine attached to the body records events going on (for example, high blood pressure) so that the individual can change them.

Biological clocks   Internal chemical units that control regular cycles in parts of the body.

Bipolar disorder   A disorder with up and down swings of moods from "high" to "low."

Blind spot   The portion of the retina through which the optic nerve exits and where there are no receptors for light waves.

Blood-sugar level   The amount of sugar contained in the blood, which indicates the level of hunger.

Borderline personality disorder   Personality disorder marked by unstable emotions and relationships, dependency, and manipulative self-destructive behavior.

Break set   To come up with unusual, unexpected ideas; to use something in a different way from how it is normally used.

Brightness constancy   By taking an average, the human visual network keeps brightness the same as an object changes environment.

Bulimia nervosa   An eating disorder that involves binging on food and purging by vomiting or excessive use of laxatives.

C

California Psychological Inventory   Personality inventory most often used in schools.

Cannon-Bard theory   Theory of emotion stating that the bodily reaction and the emotional response to an event occur at the same time.

Case study method   Research that collects information about a person's background, usually for psychological treatment.

Catatonic schizophrenia   Type of schizophrenia characterized by disturbances of movement.

Catharsis   The supposed ability to get rid of aggressive energy by viewing others acting aggressively.

Cerebellum   The portion of the lower brain that coordinates and organizes bodily movements for balance and accuracy.

Cerebral arteriosclerosis   A blockage of blood vessels to the brain that results in the loss of mental faculties.

Cerebral cortex   The 100-billion-nerve-cell unit that covers the lower brain and controls very high-level thought.

Chaining   Reinforcing the connection between different parts of a sequence.

Chemical dependence   The same as substance abuse;

the use of drugs in excess in order to alter consciousness.

Chemotherapy   The use of drugs to relieve psychological disturbance.

Chromosomes   Units of heredity containing genes; 23 in reproductive cells, 46 in all other cells.

Chronobiology   The study of forces that control the body at different times of the day, month, or year.

Chunking   Putting things into clusters or "chunks" so that items learned are in groups rather than separate.

Cilia   Tiny hairs that receive sound waves in the ears or odor molecules in the nose.

Circadian rhythm   Sequences of behavioral changes that occur every 24 hours.

Clang associations   Psychotic speech in which words are rhymed.

Classical conditioning   Ivan Pavlov's method of conditioning in which associations are made between a natural stimulus and a learned, neutral stimulus.

Client-centered therapy   Roger's humanistic approach; reflects belief that the client and therapist are partners in therapy.

Clinical psychologists   Those who deal with emotional disturbances of any kind; may work with classified mental patients.

Clique   A very tightly knit group with limited membership and strict rules of behavior; normally tied in with school activities.

Closure   The process of filling in the missing details of what is viewed.

Cochlea   A snail-shaped part of the ear, filled with fluid and small hairs that vibrate to incoming sound.

Cognition   Symbolic thought processes.

Cognitive   Concerning mental processes or thoughts.

Cognitive approach   Emphasizing how humans use mental processes to handle problems or develop certain personality characteristics.

Cognitive approach (to learning)   A way of learning based on abstract mental processes and previous knowledge.

Cognitive behavior therapy   Therapy in which thoughts are used to control emotions and behaviors.

Cognitive development   The ways in which thinking and reasoning grow and change.

Cognitive dissonance   A contradiction between actions or events and beliefs, which must be reconciled or justified.

Cognitive map   A mental image of where one is located in space.

Cognitive strategy   An organized mental task designed to deceive the brain about incoming information.

Cognitive theory (Schachter)   A theory of emotions stating that we label a bodily response by giving it the name of an emotion we think we are feeling.

Collective unconscious   Jung's term for the portion of a person that contains ideas (such as hero, mother, and so on) shared by the whole human race.

Color blindness   Inability to perceive certain colors, such as red and green.

Color constancy   The ability to perceive an object as the same color regardless of the environment.

Compulsion   A symbolic, ritualized behavior that a person must keep acting out in order to avoid anxiety.

Concrete operations stage   Piaget's third stage of child development in which the child understands that there is a real world with real objects, which exist apart from the child and which can be manipulated.

Conditioned response   A response to a stimulus that is brought about by learning—for example, salivating at the word *pickle.*

Conditioned stimulus   A previously neutral stimulus that has been associated with a natural (or unconditioned) stimulus.

Conditioning   Making an association between two events by repeated exposure.

Cone   A visual receptor in the eye that responds during daylight; receives color.

Conflict   A problem that demands a choice between alternatives in order to be resolved.

Consciousness   The awareness of, or the possibility of knowing, what is happening inside or outside the organism.

Consequences   Our emotional responses, behaviors, and expectations regarding another.

Conservation   Piaget's term for the idea that some of an object's characteristics can be changed while others remain the same; for example, changing shape does not change volume.

Consolidation   The process of strengthening a memory and its parts over time until they are very solid.

Construct   A concept requiring a belief in something that cannot be seen or touched but that seems to exist.

Contact comfort   The satisfaction obtained from pleasant, soft stimulation.

Continuous reinforcement   Each time a behavior occurs, reinforcement is given.

Control group   The group that does not participate in the critical part of the experiment.

Conventional level   Kohlberg's middle stage of moral development in which moral reasoning is based on the expectations of others regarding what is right or wrong.

Conversion disorder   Disorder in which a serious psychological trauma is changed into a symbolic physical dysfunction.

Cornea   The clear outer covering of the eye behind which is fluid.

Corpus callosum   The large bundle of nerve fibers that transfers information from one half of the brain to the other.

Counseling psychologists   Those who deal mostly with problems not fitting into the formal classifications of mental disturbance.

Creativity   The mental processes that result in original, workable ideas.

Critical period   A specific time of development that is the only time when a particular skill can begin to develop or an association can occur.

Cross-sectional method   A method of research that looks at different age groups at the same time in order to understand changes that occur during the life span.

Crowding   A psychological feeling of too little space.

Crowds   Large groups with loose rules and changeable memberships.

Cultural bias   The unfair measurement of cultural groups' abilities.

Culture   A set of beliefs, attitudes, and values held in common by a large number of people and passed down from one generation to the next.

Curiosity motive   A drive that moves a person to see new and different things.

Cutaneous receptors   The nerve receptors in the skin that respond to pressure, temperature, or pain.

D

Decibels   A measure of how loud a sound is (its intensity).

Defense mechanisms   Psychological distortions used to remain psychologically stable, or in balance.

Deindividuation   A loss of one's sense of individuality and responsibility when in a group.

Delta waves   Slow, lazy, deep-sleep brain waves.

Delusion   A belief in something (for example, that you are a king or queen) that is not true.

Dendrite   The part of the nerve cell that receives information from the axons of other nerve cells.

Denial   The process of refusing to admit that there is a problem.

Density   The actual number of people per square foot in a given space.

Dependent variable   The factor in a study that changes or varies as a result of changes in the independent variable.

Depth perception   The ability to see objects in space.

Diagnostic and Statistical Manual of Mental Disorders IV   A book that classifies the symptoms of mental problems into formal categories.

Dictatorial (authoritarian) parenting style   Style in which parents rigidly set the rules and demand obedience.

Diffusion   Marcia's term for the state of having no clear idea of one's identity nor attempting to find that identity.

Diffusion of responsibility   For an individual member of a group, the idea that responsibility for others is spread out among all group members.

Discrimination   Mistreating or denying rights to

people because they belong to a particular group.

Discrimination learning   Learning to tell the difference between one event or object and another; the reverse of generalization.

Displacement   The process of venting our feelings on something or someone other than the true or original target.

Dissociative disorders   Disorders in which a part of one's life becomes disconnected from other parts; amnesia, fugue, and dissociative identity disorder are examples.

Dissociative identity disorder   Condition in which a person divides himself or herself into two (possibly more) separate personalities that can act independently.

Distraction   The cognitive strategy that consists of thinking of something else during pain.

Distress   The stress that is nonproductive and that causes physical problems.

Dizygotic twins   Twins who develop from two different eggs fertilized by different sperm; have different heredity.

Dominance   Either the right or left hemisphere is dominant in each individual; hence one of them is preferred and controls the majority of actions performed.

Dopamine   The brain chemical present in excess in schizophrenics, which causes nerve cells to fire too rapidly and leads to thought and speech confusion.

Double approach-avoidance conflict   A choice between alternatives, both of which have good and bad parts.

Double-blind study   A study during which neither participants nor researchers know to which group any subject belongs.

Drive   Forces that push an organism into action.

Dysthymic disorder   A moderate depression.

E

Eardrum   A piece of skin stretched over the entrance to the ear; vibrates to sound.

Early adolescence   The period from 11 to 14 years of age.

Early maturer   Someone who develops one and a half years or more ahead of average growth.

Eating disorder   Condition in which the person cannot read the body's nutritional needs and eats or refuses to eat for the wrong reasons.

Eclecticism   The process of making your own system by borrowing from two or more other systems.

Ego   Freud's term for the "self" that allows controlled id expression within the boundaries of the superego.

Eidetic imagery   An iconic memory lasting a minute or so that keeps images "in front of the person" so objects can be counted or analyzed; also called photographic memory.

Elaboration   The process of attaching a maximum number of associations to a basic concept or other material to be learned so that it can be retrieved more easily.

Electroconvulsive therapy (ECT)   Therapy in which an electrical shock is sent through the brain to try to reduce symptoms of mental disturbance.

Emotion   A state of the body causing feelings of hope, fear, love, and so on.

Empty-nest period   The time of life when the children are grown and leave; for some people this event leads to feelings of uselessness and depression.

Encounter groups   Therapy in which people are forced to share their inner conflicts and emotions.

Endocrine system   The system of all the glands and their chemical messages taken together.

Endorphins   Morphine-like substances produced naturally within the body.

Entrainment   The process of altering the free-running cycle to fit a different rhythm.

Environment   A person's surroundings, which have an influence on a person's characteristics and development.

Estrogen   The female hormone.

Ethnic group   People with the same country of origin, as well as racial, and cultural features.

Eustress   The stress that motivates us to do something worthwhile.

Evaluation apprehension   The concern about how others will judge us; we make our behavior conform to what we think they will approve of.

Experimental group   The group on which the critical part of the experiment is performed.

Extended family   Nuclear family plus other relatives.

Extinction   The gradual loss of an association over time.

Extrasensory perception   The receipt of information without the aid of the "normal" senses such as hearing, seeing, feeling, and so on.

Extrinsic motivation   A reward from outside the organism for a certain behavior.

F

Feral children   Children supposedly reared by animals.

Fidelity   Erikson's term for being faithful to one's ideals and values; loyalty.

Field experiments   Research that takes place outside the laboratory.

Fight or flight reaction   The body's reaction to a crisis; these are the only two possibilities for action.

Fissure   A lengthy depression marking off an area of the brain.

Fixed interval schedule   Reinforcement occurs after a fixed amount of time has passed if the desired act occurs.

Fixed ratio schedule   Reinforcement occurs after the desired act is performed a specific number of times.

Flight of ideas   A confused state in which thoughts and speech go in all directions with no unifying concepts.

Foreclosure   Marcia's term for the state of accepting the identity and values an adolescent was given in childhood.

Forgetting   An increase in errors when trying to bring material back from memory.

Forgetting curve   Graphic representation of speed and amount of forgetting that occurs.

Formal operations   Piaget's term for the ability to reason in abstract ways; complex thought processes.

Formal operations stage   Piaget's fourth stage of child development in which the ability to deal with the highly symbolic and abstract thoughts found in logic, math, philosophy, and ethics begins to appear.

Free association   Freudian process in which the person says everything that appears in the mind, even if the ideas or images seem unconnected; technique used in psychoanalysis to uncover the unconscious.

Free-running cycles   Cycles set up by biological clocks that are under their own control, ignoring the environment.

Frontal association area   The forward portion of the brain that engages in elaborate associations or mental connections; it plays an important part in integrating personality and in forming complex thoughts.

Frontal lobe   Division of the brain that contains the motor strip and frontal association area.

Frustration   The blocking or hindering of goals we are seeking.

Fugue   The condition of having amnesia for one's current life and starting a new one somewhere else.

Fully functioning individual   Rogers's term for someone who has become what he or she should be.

G

Gang   A rebellious, antisocial group with strict rules but not connected with accepted school or social organizations.

Gender   The sex of an individual, male or female.

Gender role behavior   Acts that reflect society's view of what is appropriate for males versus what is appropriate for females.

General adaptation syndrome   The sequence of behavior that occurs in reaction to prolonged stress. It is divided into stages: alarm reaction, preparation for an attack; stage of resistance, trying to restore balance; and exhaustion, giving up the battle.

Generalization   A behavior that spreads from one situation to a similar one.

Genes   Basic units of heredity.

Gerontology   The branch of psychology that studies the aging process and the problems of older people.

partner and earlier conflicts reappear.

Glands   Units of the body that contain the hormones.

Glucose   Another name for sugar in the blood.

Gonads   The sex glands.

Group identity versus alienation   Erickson's idea that early adolescents either belong to a group or feel lost (alienated).

Group intelligence tests   IQ tests administered to many people at one time; test is highly verbal and uses paper and pencil.

Group therapy   Therapy in which more than one person at a time is treated.

Growth cycles   Patterns of development in which some areas develop more rapidly and some more slowly, but all in a way preplanned by nature.

Growth hormone   The hormone controlled by the pituitary that regulates the growth process.

Growth spurt   A rapid increase in growth during puberty.

H

Hair cells   Receptor cells for hearing and sense of smell; found in the cochlea and the nasal cavity; see *cilia*.

Hallucinations   Seeing or hearing things that are not physically present.

Hallucinogen   A drug that produces major hallucinations.

Halo effect   The situation where a person who has one positive characteristic is assumed to have other positive traits.

Hemisphere   One-half of the two halves of the brain; controls the opposite side of the body.

Heredity   Characteristics obtained directly from the genes.

Hierarchy of needs   A system that ranks needs one above the other with the most basic needs for physical survival at the bottom of the pyramid.

Hormones   The body chemicals that control body growth, emotional responses, and physical changes.

Hospices   Places where terminally ill people can live out their lives in comfort and away from a hospital.

Humanism   A personality theory that places emphasis on the positive potential of the person; Rogers and Maslow are examples of humanistic psychologists.

Humanistic approach   Believing that people are basically good and capable of helping themselves.

Humanistic therapy   Therapy that emphasizes the individual's own ability to heal himself or herself with some assistance.

Hypochondriasis   Disorder characterized by feeling excessive concern about one's health and exaggerating the seriousness of minor physical complaints.

Hypnosis   A state of relaxation in which attention is focused on certain objects, acts, or feelings.

Hypothalamus   A part of the brain that regulates basic needs such as hunger and thirst, as well as emotions such as pleasure, fear, rage, and sexual desire.

Hypothesis   A statement of the results that the experimenter expects; an educated guess as to what the results will be.

I

Iconic memory   A very brief visual memory that can be sent to the short-term memory (STM).

Id   Freudian psychological unit containing our basic needs and drives.

Ideal self   Rogers' term for the goal of each person's development; perfection.

Identical twins   Same as monozygotic twins.

Identification   The process of modeling behavior patterns, usually after a member of the same sex.

Identification with the aggressor   The process of taking on characteristics of someone who has mistreated us in order to psychologically avoid the abuse.

Identity   A sense of oneself as a unique person.

Identity achievement   Marcia's term for the state of having developed well-defined personal values and self-concepts.

Identity confusion   Erikson's term for an uncertainty about who one is or where he or she is going.

Illusion   An inaccurate perception.

Illusory correlations   Seeing relationships between things that match already held beliefs and ignoring what does not match these beliefs.

Imitation learning   The process of learning behaviors by viewing others and then doing the same things they did.

Immune system   The body's method for fighting disease or injury.

Immunization   An attempt to train a person beforehand to resist persuasion or propaganda.

Imprinting   A process that occurs at a preset time in development, when the brain is ready to receive and respond to a specific stimulus.

Incubus attack   Also called a night terror, a horrible dream occurring during NREM sleep when the body is not prepared for it.

Independent variable   The factor that the experimenter manipulates or changes in a study.

Individual intelligence tests   IQ tests administered on a one-to-one basis—one examiner to one test taker.

Information processing   The methods by which we take in, analyze, store, and retrieve material in memory.

Insomnia   The inability to get enough sleep.

Intellectualization   The process of removing our feelings about an event and discussing it in a coolly rational and unemotional way.

Intelligence   The ability to understand and adapt to the environment by using a combination of inherited abilities and learning experiences.

Intelligence quotient   A measure of intelligence originally obtained by comparing mental age with physical age.

Intensity   How loud a sound is.

Interference theory   The belief that we forget because new and old material conflict (interfere) with one another.

Internalize   To make as part of ourselves the attitudes or beliefs of others.

Internalized sentences   The opinions we form of ourselves by listening to our own inner voice; Ellis's term.

Interview   A research method that involves studying people face to face and asking questions.

Intrinsic motivation   Satisfaction that comes from within the individual for certain behavior.

Introspection   The process of looking into yourself and describing what is there.

Iris   A colored circular muscle that opens and closes, forming larger and smaller circles to control the amount of light getting into the eye.

Irrational ideas   Ideas that do not hold up when challenged by careful logic.

J

James-Lange theory   For emotion, first the body responds, *then* one feels the emotion.

Juvenile delinquency   Repeated violations of the law by those 17 and younger.

L

Late adolescence   The period from 16 to 19 years of age.

Late maturer   Someone who develops one and a half years or more behind average growth.

Latency stage   Freudian stage of development during which the child's earlier conflicts are hidden or go below the surface.

Learning curve   A gradual upward slope representing increased retention of material as the result of learning.

Lens   The part of the eye that focuses an object on the back of the eye.

Libido   Freudian term for internal energy forces that continuously seek discharge.

Lobe   Major division of the brain.

Longitudinal method   A method of research that studies the same group of people over an extended period of time.

Long-term memory   The memory system that retains information for hours, days, weeks, months, decades.

Lower brain   Basic "animal" units common to animals and humans that regulate basic functions such as breathing.

M

Mainstreaming The practice of keeping mildly mentally retarded children in regular academic classrooms.

Major depression An extremely low emotional state, severe depression; involves loss of appetite, lack of energy, hopelessness, suicidal thoughts.

Mania A mood disorder involving extreme agitation, rapid speech, and trouble concentrating.

Manipulation motive The drive that moves a person to handle and use objects in the environment.

Maturation The automatic, orderly, sequential process of physical and mental development.

Mediation A form of self-control in which the outside world is cut off from consciousness.

Menopause The "change of life" period for women when menstruation and ovulation stop; some women experience major physical symptoms, such as dizziness and "hot flashes."

Menstrual cycles Monthly cycles that revolve around elimination of the lining of the uterus because the woman's egg has not been fertilized.

Mental age The level of intellectual functioning in years, which is compared with chronological age.

Mental retardation Subaverage intellectual functioning so that such a person is not able to perform at the level appropriate for his or her age.

Metabolism The speed with which the body operates or the speed with which it uses up energy.

Middle adolescence The period from 14 to 16 years of age.

Migraine headache A headache resulting from an insufficient supply of the brain chemical serotonin.

MMPI-2 Latest version of the Minnesota Multiphasic Personality Inventory, the most widely used personality inventory.

Mnemonic devices Unusual associations made to material to aid memory.

Modeling Bandura's term for learning by imitating others.

Monozygotic twins Twins who come from one fertilized egg; have the same heredity.

Mood disorders A category of mental disorder characterized by one's emotional state; includes depression and mania.

Moratorium A term used by Erickson and Marcia to describe the adolescent's delay in making the commitments normally expected of adults.

Motivation The need to seek a goal, such as food, water, friends, and so on.

Motor strip Band running down the side of the frontal lobe that controls all bodily movements (called motor functions).

Müller-Lyer illusion Two pictures in which one line seems longer than the other but really isn't.

Muscle contraction headaches Headaches from holding oneself in a fixed position, causing the muscles to spasm and putting pressure on the nerves.

N

Narcolepsy Disorder in which a person falls instantly into sleep no matter what is going on in the environment.

Naturalistic observation A research method that involves studying subjects without their being aware of being watched.

Nature/nurture Contrasting views of how we gain certain characteristics; the nature refers to heredity, nurture to environment.

Negative identity Marcia's term for defining oneself as "bad" or as a "troublemaker."

Negative reinforcement Strengthening a response by following it with taking away or avoiding something unpleasant.

Negative transfer An interference with learning due to dissimilarities between two otherwise similar tasks.

Neo-Freudians Those psychoanalysts who broke away from Freud to emphasize social forces in the unconscious.

Neurobiological approach Viewing behavior as the result of biology plus nerve cells.

Neuron   A nerve cell that transmits electrical and chemical information (via neurotransmitters) throughout the body.

Neurotransmitters   Chemicals in the endings of nerve cells that send information across the synapse.

Nightmare   Frightening dream during REM sleep.

Nondirective therapy   Rogers' system of reflecting and bringing together whatever the client exposes.

Norms   Patterns of test answers from different types of people.

NREM sleep   Non-rapid eye movement sleep; sleep involving partial thoughts, images, or stories, poor organization.

Nuclear family   Parents and their children.

O

Object permanence   Piaget's term for the awareness that specific objects are real and exist all by themselves.

Observational learning   A form of social learning in which the organism observes and imitates the behavior of others.

Obsession   An endless preoccupation with an urge or thought.

Obsessive-compulsive disorder   Having continued thoughts (obsession) about performing a certain act over and over (compulsion).

Occipital lobe   Area of the brain that interprets visual information.

Olfaction   The sense of smell.

Olfactory bulbs   Units that receive odor molecules and communicate their nature to the brain.

Operant conditioning   Conditioning that results from one's actions and the consequences they cause.

Opiates   Sedatives; drugs that reduce body functioning.

Oral stage   Freudian stage of development during which feeding and weaning are the child's main issues.

Ovaries   The female sex glands; make eggs.

Overlearning   The process of learning something beyond one perfect recitation so that the forgetting curve will have no effect; the development of perfect retention.

P

Panic disorder   A type of anxiety disorder in which one cannot relax and is plagued by frequent and overwhelming attacks of anxiety.

Paranoia   The belief that others are out to get you.

Paranoid schizophrenia   Schizophrenia marked by strong feelings of suspiciousness and persecution.

Parietal lobe   Area of the brain that contains the sensory strip.

Partial reinforcement schedule   Reinforcement is not given each time an act is performed.

Perception   The process of assembling and organizing sensory information to make it meaningful.

Performance scale   IQ test items that try to bypass verbal material and focus on problem solving without words.

Permissive parenting style   Style in which parents let children do as they wish; few rules made or enforced.

Persona   Jung's term for a "mask" people wear to hide what they really are or feel.

Personal space   The "invisible bubble," or portable area, around us that we try to keep from being invaded.

Personality   A person's broad, long-lasting patterns of behavior.

Personality disorder   A disorder in which the person has formed a peculiar or unpleasant personality.

Personality inventory   A list of items about a person's beliefs, habits, hopes, needs, and desires.

Personality traits   The more or less permanent personality characteristics that an individual has.

Phallic stage   Freudian stage of development during which the child experiences romantic interest in the opposite-sex parent and hostility toward the same-sex parent.

Phantom-limb pain   Severe pain that feels as if it is coming from a missing limb.

Pheromones   Odor chemicals that communicate a message.

Phobic disorder A type of anxiety disorder in which a person becomes disabled and overwhelmed by fear in the presence of certain objects or events.

Physical dependence A craving by the body itself for a drug.

Physiological needs The bottom level of Maslow's hierarchy of needs; hunger and thirst.

Pitch How high or low a sound is.

Pituitary gland The gland that secretes growth hormones and increases the production in other glands of other hormones.

Placebo A "medicine" that has no active ingredients and works by the power of suggestion.

Placebo effect Physical reaction to the power of suggestion.

Polygraph A lie detector; machine used to measure physiological changes in a person.

Positive reinforcement Strengthening a response by following it with something pleasant.

Positive transfer A transfer of learning that results from similarities between two tasks.

Postconventional level Kohlberg's last stage of moral development in which personal ethics and human rights are dealt with.

Preconventional level Kohlberg's early stage of moral development in which morality is determined by the sheer power of outside authority.

Prejudice A judgment of people based on the group they belong to rather than their individual characteristics.

Premenstrual syndrome (PMS) Anxiety, irritability, and mental confusion resulting from monthly female hormonal changes.

Preoperational stage Piaget's second stage of child development in which logical thought is lacking; limited ability to see things from more than one perspective; acquire language and ability to use symbols.

Primary reinforcement Something necessary for psychological/physical survival that is used as a reward.

Principle learning A method of learning in which an overall view (principle) of the material to be learned is developed so that the material is better organized.

Projection The process of attributing our thoughts to someone else.

Projective tests Tests measuring inner feelings elicited by a vague stimulus, such as an ink blot or unclear picture.

Proximity A perceptual cue in which we group together things that are near one another.

Psychedelic A drug that distorts or confuses the user's perception of the world.

Psychiatric nurses Registered nurses with special education in psychiatric medicine.

Psychiatric social workers Mental health workers with a degree in social work; help patients and families deal with problems.

Psychiatrists Medical doctors with special training in mental disorders.

Psychoanalysis A theory that personality is based on impulses and needs in the unconscious; also a system of therapy practiced by followers of Freud, who analyze the psyche via the unconscious.

Psychological dependence A craving by the psyche for a drug, although the body doesn't demand it.

Psychological tests Observation and measurement of the subject using objective measures (as opposed to an interview).

Psychology The scientific study of human and animal behavior.

Psychosis/psychotic disorder Severe mental disorder involving major problems with emotional responses, disorganized thought processes, and distorted perceptions of the world.

Psychosurgery Surgery that destroys part of the brain to make the patient calmer, freer of symptoms.

Psychotherapies Broad term for any method used to try to help people with emotional and psychological problems.

Psychotic episodes Periods of psychotic behavior that can alternate with periods of relative coherence and calm.

Puberty The time of sexual maturation.

Punishment   The process of weakening a response by following it with unpleasant consequences.

Pupil   The opening in the eye.

R

Race   A set of hereditary physical characteristics that distinguishes major groups of people.

Rational emotive therapy   Treatment centering on getting emotions under control by using reason; Ellis's term.

Rationalization   The process of explaining away a problem so that we don't have to accept the blame.

Reaction formation   The process of expressing the opposite of what we feel.

Recall   The ability to bring back and integrate many specific learned details.

Recognition   The ability to pick the correct object or event from a list of choices.

Redefinition   The cognitive strategy that consists of talking ourselves into believing that incoming stimulation is different from what it is.

Reinforcement   Something that follows a response and strengthens the tendency to repeat that response.

Reference group   A group with which one identifies and that provides standards of behavior.

Reflex   An automatic behavior of the body involving movement that is activated through the spinal cord without using the higher brain.

Regression   The process of going backward in behavior and thought to a period when we were taken care of as a child; childish behavior.

Reliability   Whether test results are consistent over time.

REM rebound   Increase in the number of dreams after being deprived of them.

REM sleep   Rapid-eye-movement sleep when we dream.

Repression   The process of pushing memories, needs, and desires that cause guilt or pain into the unconscious.

Research psychologists   Those who study the origin, cause, or results of certain behaviors.

Response   A reaction to a stimulus.

Reticular activating system/reticular formation   The alertness control center of the brain that regulates the activity level of the body.

Retina   The back of the eye, which contains millions of receptors for light.

Reverse halo   The situation where a person with one negative characteristic is assumed to have other negative traits.

Reversibility   Piaget's term for the idea that a relationship that goes in one direction can go in the other direction also.

Reversible figure   An illusion in which the same object is seen as two alternating figures—first one, then the other.

Risky shift phenomenon   The situation where the danger of an act is split among the members of a group; hence, it is smaller for each person.

Rite of passage   A socially recognized and ritualized change in status, such as reaching adulthood.

Rod   A visual receptor most sensitive to the violet-purple wavelengths; very sensitive for night vision; "sees" only black and white.

Rorschach test   Ink blot projective test developed by Hermann Rorschach.

S

Safety needs   Part of Maslow's hierarchy of needs; shelter, nest egg of money.

Sample   A group that represents a larger group.

Scapegoating   Blaming someone else for one's own problem.

Schedules of reinforcement   Different methods of reinforcing.

Schema   An organized and systematic approach to answering questions or solving problems.

Schizophrenia   The most serious mental disturbance, involving loss of contact with reality, thought disorders, hallucinations, and delusions.

Scholastic Assessment Test (SAT) Test designed to measure ability to do college work.

Secondary Reinforcement Anything that comes to represent a primary reinforcer, such as money bringing food.

Selective forgetting "Forgetting" only things that are very traumatic.

Self-actualization The top of Maslow's hierarchy of needs; establishing meaningful goals and a purpose in life; bringing one's life to its fullest potential.

Self-concept The image we have of ourselves.

Self-esteem The feeling of being worthwhile and useful.

Self-esteem needs Part of Maslow's hierarchy of needs; liking and respecting yourself, feeling important and useful.

Senile Dementia The loss of mental faculties as a result of aging.

Sensation The process of receiving information from the environment.

Sensorimotor stage Piaget's first stage of child development in which knowledge, movements, and objects in the environment are tied together.

Sensory deprivation Removing all external sensations and stimulation.

Sensory memory system Direct receivers of information from the environment—for example iconic, acoustic.

Sensory strip Band running down the side of the parietal lobe that registers and provides all sensation.

Separation anxiety The baby's fear of being away from the parent; the desire to avoid strangers.

Serotonin The brain chemical that in excess leads to mania; in too low concentrations it leads to depression.

Set A tendency to solve problems in the same old way over and over.

Set point The body-regulating mechanism that determines a person's ideal weight.

Shaping The process of gradually refining a response by successively reinforcing closer approximations of it.

Short-term memory (STM) The memory system that retains information for a few seconds to a few hours.

Similarity A perceptual cue in which we group like things together.

Situational assessment The process of looking at how the circumstances surrounding an event influence people responding to that event.

Size constancy The ability to retain the size of an object regardless of where it is located.

Sleep apnea Breathing stops while one is asleep.

Social contracts Kohlberg's term for agreements based on the concept of what's "best for everyone."

Social entrainment (of the sleep cycle) Fitting sleep and dreams to your social schedule.

Social learning A form of learning in which the organism observes and imitates the behavior of others.

Sociocultural approach Behavior viewed as strongly influenced by the rules and expectations of specific social groups or cultures.

Sociopath Same as an antisocial personality disorder.

Somatoform disorder Condition in which psychological issues are expressed in bodily symptoms in the absence of any real physical problem.

Space constancy The ability to keep objects in the environment steady.

Spatial skills The ability to imagine how an object would look if it was moved about in space.

Specific phobia A major anxiety that arises when one is faced with a specific object, such as a snake, dog, elevator, heights, and so on.

Spinal cord The part of the body that functions as an automatic "brain" in its own right and is a relay station for impulses to and from the higher brain.

Standardization Clear directions for taking, scoring, and interpreting a test.

Standoutishness Doing or wearing something that is so startling that it detracts from one's real abilities.

Stanford-Binet Intelligence Test The original intelligence test developed by Alfred Binet and refined at Stanford University.

State-dependent learning The fact that material learned in one chemical state is best reproduced when the same state occurs again.

Stereotype A fixed set of beliefs about a group that may or may not be accurate.

Steroids Artificially produced male sex hormones.

Stimulus Anything that elicits a response.

Stimulus generalization A response spread from one specific stimulus to other stimuli that resemble the original.

Strategies Methods for solving problems.

Stress The physical strain that results from demands or changes in the environment.

Stress hormone A special chemical that signals the adrenal glands to activate the body.

Strong-Campbell Interest Inventory The most widely used interest test; based on answers of people successful in certain fields.

Subconscious Consciousness just below our present awareness.

Subjects People or animals on whom the experiment is conducted.

Sublimation The process of channeling emotional energy into constructive or creative activities.

Subliminal perception Stimulation presented below the level of consciousness.

Substance abuse The use of drugs to excess in order to alter consciousness.

Sudden death phenomenon Death resulting from panic and overload of the major nerve going to the heart.

Superego Freudian psychological unit roughly synonymous with the conscience.

Survey A method of research using questions on feelings, opinions, or behavior patterns asked of a large group of people.

Synapse The junction point of two or more neurons; the connection is made by neurotransmitters.

Synergistic effect The result of taking two drugs in combination, which makes each more potent than either one by itself.

Systematic desensitization A behavioral technique in which the therapist step-by-step increases the patient's anxiety and counters it by association with relaxation in a graduated sequence.

T

Taste receptors Chemical receptors on the tongue that decode molecules of food or drink to identify them.

Temporal lobe Area of the brain responsible for hearing and some speech functions.

Territoriality An attachment to a fixed area designated as ours alone and the tendency to defend it against intruders.

Testes The male sex glands; make sperm.

Thalamus The portion of the lower brain that functions primarily as a central relay station for incoming and outgoing messages from the body to the brain and the brain to the body.

Thanatology The study of death and of methods for coping with it.

Thematic Apperception Test (TAT) A projective test using unclear pictures about which people make up stories.

Theory General framework for scientific study; smaller aspects can be tested.

Theory of multiple intelligences The assumption that, besides an "IQ," each of us has special skills—music, carpentry, design, and so forth—at which we are proficient.

Thought disorder A serious distortion of the ability to think or speak in a lucid and coherent way.

Thyroid gland The gland that controls and regulates the speed of bodily processes, called metabolism.

Timbre The complexity of a sound.

Token economy A behavioral technique in which rewards for desired acts are accumulated through tokens, which represent a form of money.

Tolerance The need to take larger and larger dosages of a drug while still only getting the same effect as from the original dose.

Trance Another word for the state of deep relaxation that can occur during hypnosis.

Transfer of training A learning process in which learning is moved from one task to another based on similarities between the tasks.

Transference The process in which the patient transfers emotional conflicts of earlier years onto the therapist.

Type A personality People who are always operating at full speed, are impatient, and are filled with distress.

Type B personality People who are open to change, are flexible, enjoy life, and have low levels of stress.

Twilight state Relaxed state just before we fall into deep sleep.

U

Ulcer Wound in the intestine or stomach resulting from severe irritation.

Unconditional positive regard A principle of humanistic therapy in which the client's feelings and thoughts are accepted for whatever they are; Rogers's term.

Unconditioned response An automatic response to a particular natural stimulus, such as salivation to meat.

Unconditioned stimulus A stimulus that automatically elicits a response, such as meat causing salivation.

Unconscious According to psychoanalytic belief, the psychological part of us that contains childhood conflicts we are unaware of but that continue to control our behavior.

Undifferentiated schizophrenia Schizophrenia that lacks any distinguishing symptoms.

Universal ethical principles Kohlberg's term for concepts such as justice and honor.

V

Validity Whether a test measures what it is supposed to measure.

Variable interval schedule Reinforcement occurs after varying amounts of time if a desired act occurs.

Variable ratio schedule Reinforcement occurs after a desired behavior occurs, but a different number of the desired acts is required each time.

Variables Factors that change in an experiment.

Verbal scale IQ test items that rely heavily on word comprehension and usage.

Visual area The area at the back of the brain that interprets everything we see.

Visual cliff A large table with Plexiglas, used to demonstrate depth perception in small children.

Visual texture Depth perception based on how rough or smooth objects appear.

Vocational interest test A test that attempts to predict a good occupational area for an individual.

W

Wechsler Adult Intelligence Scale-Revised (WAIS-R) An intelligence test for adults that provides three IQs: verbal, performance, and a combined (total) IQ.

Wechsler Intelligence Scale for Children-Revised (WISC-R) An intelligence test for children ages six to 16; similar in form to the WAIS-R.

White light Light as it originates from the sun or a bulb before it is broken into different frequencies.

Word salad Speech in which words are mixed together incoherently.

Z

Zygote Fertilized egg.

SPANISH EQUIVALENTS FOR IMPORTANT PSYCHOLOGICAL TERMS IN ENGLISH

A

Acetylcholine   Acetilcolina

Achievement tests   Pruebas de ejecución

Acoustic memory   Memoria acústica

Acupuncture   Acupuntura

Adrenal glands   Glándulas suprarrenales

Adrenaline   Adrenalina

Afterimage   Imagen consecutiva; Imagen accidental

Agoraphobia   Agorafobia

Alcoholic withdrawal delirium
Delirio por síntomas sufridos por el adicto al suspender alcohol

Alpha waves   Ondas alfa

Alzheimer's disease
Enfermedad de Alzheimer

Amnesia   Amnesia

Anal stage   Etapa Anal

Androgen   Andrógeno

Androgyny   Androginia

Anorexia nervosa   Anorexia nerviosa

Antecedents   Antecedentes

Antibodies   Anticuerpos

Antisocial personality disorder
Trastorno de la personalidad antisocial

Anxiety   Ansiedad; desesperación

Anxiety disorder   Trastorno de ansiedad

Applied psychologists
Psicólogo aplicado

Approach-approach conflict
Conflicto de atracción y atracción

Approach-avoidance conflict
Conflicto de atracción y evitación

Aptitude   Aptitud

Aptitude tests   Pruebas de aptitud

Archetypes   Arquetipos

Asthma   Asma

Attention   Atención

Attribution   Atribución

Attribution theory   Teoría de atribución

Audition   Audición

Auditory nerve   Nervio auditivo

Authoritive parenting style
Estilo autoritario de criar niños

Aversive conditioning
Acondicionamiento por aversión

Avoidance-avoidance conflict
Conflicto de evitación y evitación

Awfulize   Hacer detestable

Axon   Axón

B

Behavioral approach   Método de comportamiento

Behavioral therapy   Terapia de comportamiento

Behaviorism   Behaviorismo

Behaviorists   Adeptos de la teoría del behaviorismo

Belongingness needs
Necesidades de estar en su ambiente

Beta waves   Ondas beta

Binocular disparity   Disparidad binocular

Biofeedback
Biorretroalimentación

Biological clocks   Mecanismos biológicos que determinan las funciones periódicas

Bipolar disorder   Trastorno bipolar

Blind spot   Punto ciego

Blood-sugar level   Nivel del azucar en la sangre

Borderline personality disorder
Trastorno de la personalidad dudosa

Break set   Discontinuar lo fijo

Brightness constancy
Invariabilidad de intensidad luminosa

Bulimia nervosa   Bulimia nerviosa

C

California Psychological Inventory   Inventario Psicológico de California

Cannon-Bard theory   Teoría de
Cannon-Bard

Case study method   Método de
monografía sobre un problema
médico o social

Catatonic schizophrenia
Esquizofrenia catatónica

Catharsis   Catarsis

Cerebellum   Cerebelo

Cerebral arteriosclerosis
Arteriosclerosis cerebral

Cerebral cortex   Corteza cerebral

Chaining   Encadenando

Chemical dependence
Dependencia química

Chemotherapy   Quimioterapia

Chromosomes   Cromosomas

Chronobiology   Cronobiología

Chunking   Agrupar; poner en
grupos

Cilia   Cilio

Circadian rhythm   Ritmos circa-
dianos

Clang associations   Asociaciones
con sonidos

Classical conditioning
Acondicionamiento clásico

Client-centered therapy   Terapia
concentrada en el cliente

Clinical psychologists
Psicólogo clínico

Clique   Cuadrilla

Closure   Cierre

Cochlea   Cóclea

Cognition   Cognición

Cognitive   Cognoscitivo

Cognitive approach   Enfoque
cognoscitivo

Cognitive approach (to learning)
Método cognoscitivo

Cognitive behavior therapy
Terapia de conducta cognoscitiva

Cognitive development

Desarrollo cognoscitivo

Cognitive dissonance
Disonancia cognoscitiva

Cognitive map   Mapa cognoscitivo

Cognitive strategy   Estrategia
cognoscitiva

Cognitive theory (Schachter)
Teoría cognoscitiva (Schachter)

Collective unconscious
Inconsciente colectivo

Color blindness   Daltonismo

Color constancy   Invariabilidad
de color

Compulsion   Compulsión

Concrete operations stage   Etapa
de operaciones concretas

Conditioned response
Respuesta condicionada

Conditioned stimulus   Estímulo
condicionado

Conditioning
Acondicionamiento

Cone   Cono

Conflict   Conflicto

Consciousness   Conciencia;
conocimiento

Consequences   Consecuencias

Conservation   Conservación

Consolidation   Consolidación

Construct   Constructo

Contact comfort   Comodidad
por contacto

Continuous reinforcement
Refuerzo continuo

Control group   Grupo de control

Conventional level   Nivel con-
vencional

Conversion disorder   Trastorno
de conversión

Cornea   Córnea

Corpus callosum   Cuerpo cal-
loso

Counseling psychologists
Psicólogos de consejo

Creativity   Facultad creadora;
originalidad

Critical period   Período crítico

Cross-sectional method   Método
de muestra representativa

Crowding   Apiñamiento

Crowds   Gentíos

Culture   Cultura

Curiosity motive   Motivo de
curiosidad

Cutaneous receptors   Receptores
cutáneo

D

Decibels   Decibeles

Defense mechanisms
Mecanismos de defensa

Deindividuation   Perder la indi-
vidualidad

Delta waves   Ondas delta

Delusion   Falso creencia
patológica

Dendrite   Dendrita

Denial   Negación

Density   Densidad

Dependent variable   Variable
dependiente

Depth perception   Visión pro-
funda; Percepción de la profundi-
dad

***Diagnostic and Statistical
Manual of Mental Disorders IV***
(Manual Diagnóstico y Estadístico
de Trastornos Mentales IV)

**Dictatorial (authoritarian) par-
enting style**   Estilo dictatorial de
criar niños

Diffusion   Difusión

Diffusion of responsibility
Difusión de respon-sabilidad

Discrimination   Discriminación

Discrimination learning

Aprendizaje por distinción

Displacement Desplazamiento

Dissociative disorders Trastornos disociativos

Dissociative identity disorder Trastorno de la personalidad múltiple

Distraction Distracción

Distress Aflicción

Dizygotic twins Gemelos fraternos

Dominance Dominación

Dopamine Dopamina

Double approach-avoidance conflict Conflicto de atracción y evitación doble

Double-blind study Estudio doble ciego

Drive Instinto

Dysthymic disorder Trastorno dysthymic (inglés)

E

Eardrum Tímpano

Early adolescence Adolescencia temprano

Early maturer Madurador temprano; Uno que madura temprano

Eating disorder Trastorno de comer

Eclecticism Eclectisismo

Ego Ego; (el) yo

Eidetic imagery Imaginación eidética

Elaboration Elaboración

Electroconvulsive therapy (ECT) Terapia electroconvulsiva

Emotion Emoción

Empty-nest period Período de casa vacía

Encounter groups Grupos de encuentro

Endocrine system Sistema endocrino

Endorphins Endorfinas

Entrainment Entrainment (inglés) - "arrastramiento"

Environment Medio ambiente

Estrogen Estrógeno

Ethnic group Grupo étnico

Eustress Tensión que motiva

Evaluation apprehension Aprensión por la evaluación

Experimental group Grupo experimental

Extended family Familia extendida

Extinction Extinción

Extrasensory perception Percepción por medios extrasensibles

Extrinsic motivation Motivación extrínseca

F

Feral children Niños salvajes

Fidelity Fidelidad

Field experiments Experimentos hechos en el campo

Fight or flight reaction Reacción de lucha o escape

Fissure Fisura

Fixed interval schedule Programa de intervalo fijo

Fixed ratio schedule Programa de razón fija

Flight of ideas Vuelo de ideas

Foreclosure Foreclosure (inglés)

Forgetting Olvidar

Forgetting curve Curva de olvidar

Formal operations Operaciones formales

Formal operations stage Etapa de operaciones formales

Free association Asociación libre

Free-running cycles Ciclos libremente en marcha

Frontal association area Área de asociación frontal

Frontal lobe Lóbulo frontal

Frustration Frustración

Fugue Fuga psicogénica

Fully functioning individual Individuo completamente funcionando

G

Gang Pandilla

Gender Género

Gender role behavior Conducta conformándose al papel del género

General adaptation syndrome Síndrome general de adaptación

Generalization Generalización

Genes Genes

Gerontology Gerontología

Gestalt Gestalt

Genital stage Etapa genital

Glands Glándulas

Glucose Glucosa

Gonads Gónadas

Group identity versus alienation Identidad de grupo contra alienación

Group intelligence tests Pruebas de inteligencia tomadas en grupo

Group therapy Terapia de grupo

Growth cycles Ciclos de crecimiento

Growth hormone Hormona del crecimiento

Growth spurt Aumento rápido de crecimiento

H

Hair cells Células del pelo

Hallucinations   Alucinaciones

Hallucinogen   Alucinógeno

Halo effect   Efecto de halo

Hemisphere   Hemisferio

Heredity   Herencia

Hierarchy of needs   Jerarquía de
necesidades

Hormones   Hormonas

Hospices   Hospicios

Humanism   Humanismo

Humanistic approach   Método
humanístico

Humanistic therapy   Terapia
humanística

Hypochodriasis   Hipocondría
(hipocondriasis)

Hypnosis   Hipnosis

Hypothalamus   Hipotálamo

Hypothesis   Hipótesis

I

Iconic memory   Memoria iconic
(inglés)

Id   Id

Ideal self   El yo (uno mismo)
ideal

Identical twins   Gemelos idénticos

Identification   Identificación

Identification with the aggressor
Identificación con el agresor

Identity   Identidad

Identity achievement   Lograr la
identidad

Identity confusion   Confusión
de identidad

Illusion   Ilusión

Illusory correlations
Correlaciones ilusorias

Imitation learning   Apredizaje
por imitación

Immune system   Sistema

inmune

Immunization   Inmunización

Imprinting   Improntación

Incubus attack   Ataque de
pesadilla

Independent variable   Variable
independiente

Individual intelligence tests
Pruebas de inteligencia individ-
uales

Information processing
Procesamiento de información

Insomnia   Insomnio

Intellectualization
Intelectualización

Intelligence   Inteligencia

Intelligence quotient   Cociente
de inteligencia

Intensity   Intensidad

Interference theory   Teoría de la
interferencia

Internalize   Adoptar conceptos o
ideas

Internalized sentences
Oraciones inherentes

Interview   Entrevistar

Intrinsic motivation   Motivación
intrínseca

Introspection   Introspección

Iris   Iris

Irrational ideas   Ideas irra-
cionales

J

James-Lange theory   Teoría de
James-Lange

Juvenile delinquency
Delincuencia juvenil

L

Late adolescence   Adolescencia
avanzada

Late maturer   Madurador atrasa-
do; Uno que madura tarde

Latency stage   Etapa latente

Learning curve   Curva de aprendizaje

Lens   Cristalino

Libido   Libido

Lobe   Lóbulo

Longitudinal method   Método
longitudinal

Long-term memory   Memoria a
largo plazo

Lower brain   Cerebro inferior

M

Mainstreaming   Mantener en la
corriente principal

Major depression   Depresión
mayor

Mania   Manía

Manipulation motive   Motivo
de manipulación

Maturation   Maduración

Mediation   Meditación

Menopause   Menopausia

Menstrual cycles   Ciclos men-
struales

Mental age   Edad mental

Mental retardation   Retardo
mental; retraso mental

Metabolism   Metabolismo

Middle adolescence
Adolescencia mediana

Migraine headache   Dolor de
cabeza migraña

MMPI-2   Inventario Multifásico
de Personalidad de Minnesota-2
(IMPM-2)

Mnemonic devices
Estratagemas mnemotécnicas;
Estratagemas nemónicas

Modeling   Modelamiento; seguir
el modelo de

Monozygotic twins   Gemelos
idénticos

Mood disorders   Trastornos del estado de ánimo

Moratorium   Moratoria

Motivation   Motivación

Motor strip   Tira motor

Müller-Lyer illusion   Ilusión de Müller-Lyer

Muscle contraction headaches   Dolores de cabeza causados por contracción del músculo

N

Narcolepsy   Narcolepsia

Naturalistic observation   Observación naturalista

Nature/nurture   Naturaleza/crianza (educación)

Negative identity   Identidad negativa

Negative reinforcement   Refuerzo negativo

Negative transfer   Transferencia negativa

Neo-Freudians   Neofreudianos

Neurobiological approach   Método neurobiológico

Neuron   Neurona

Neurotransmitters   Neurotransmisores

Nightmare   Pesadilla

Nondirective therapy   Terapia no directiva

Norms   Normas

NREM sleep   Sueño NREM; Sueño no REM

Nuclear family   Familia nuclear

O

Object permanence   Permanencia del objeto

Observational learning   Aprendizaje por observación

Obsession   Obsesión

Obsessive-compulsive disorder   Trastorno obsesivocompulsivo

Occipital lobe   Lóbulo occipital

Olfaction   Olfación

Olfactory bulbs   Bulbos olfatorios

Operant conditioning   Acondicionamiento operante

Opiates   Opiatos

Oral stage   Etapa oral

Ovaries   Ovarios

Overlearning   Sobreaprendizaje

P

Panic disorder   Trastorno de pánico

Paranoid   Paranoia

Paranoia schizophrenia   Esquizofrenia paranoia

Parietal lobe   Lóbulo parietal

Partial reinforcement schedule   Programa de refuerzo parcial

Perception   Percepción

Performance scale   Escala de ejecución

Permissive parenting style   Estilo permisivo de criar niños

Persona   Persona

Personal space   Espacio personal

Personality   Personalidad

Personality disorder   Trastorno de la personalidad

Personality inventory   Inventario de la personalidad

Personality traits   Características de la personalidad

Phallic stage   Etapa fálica

Phantom-limb pain   Dolor de un miembro fantasma (que no existe)

Pheromones   Pheromones (inglés)

Phobic disorder   Trastorno fóbico

Physical dependence   Dependencia física

Physiological needs   Necesidades fisiológicas

Pitch   Tono

Pituitary gland   Glándula pituitaria

Placebo   Placebo

Placebo effect   Efecto placebo

Polygraph   Polígrafo

Positive reinforcement   Refuerzo positivo

Positive transfer   Transferencia positiva

Postconventional level   Nivel posconvencional

Preconventional level   Nivel preconvencional

Prejudice   Prejuicio

Premenstrual syndrome (PMS)   Síndrome premenstrual

Preoperational stage   Etapa prefuncional

Primary reinforcement   Refuerzo primario

Principle learning   Aprendizaje principio

Projection   Proyección

Projective tests   Pruebas proyectivas

Proximity   Proximidad

Psychedelic   Psicodélico

Psychiatric nurses   Enfermeras psiquiátricas

Psychiatric social workers   Trabajador social psiquiátrico

Psychiatrists   Psiquiatras

Psychoanalysis   Psicoanálisis

Psychological dependence   Dependencia psicológica

Psychological tests   Pruebas psicológicas

Psychology   Psicología

Psychosis/psychotic disorders
Psicosis/Trastornos psicóticos

Psychosurgery   Psicocirugía

Psychotherapies   Psicoterapias

Psychotic disorders

Psychotic episodes   Episodios
psicóticos

Puberty   Pubertad

Punishment   Castigo

Pupil   Pupila

R

Race   Raza

Rational emotive therapy
Terapia emotiva racional

Rationalization   Racionalización

Reaction formation   Formación
reactiva

Recall   Recordar; traer a la
memoria

Recognition   Reconocimiento

Redefinition   Redefinición

Reinforcement   Refuerzo

Reference group   Grupo de referencia

Reflex   Reflejo

Regression   Regresión

Reliability   Seriedad

REM rebound   Rebote REM

REM sleep   Sueño REM

Repression   Represión

Research psychologists
Psicólogos que hacen investigaciones

Response   Respuesta

Reticular activating system/reticular formation   Sistema activo
reticular/formación reticular

Retina   Retina

Reverse halo   Halo reverso

Reversibility   Reversibilidad

Reversible figure   Figura
reversible

Risky shift phenomenon
Fenómeno arriesgado cambiado

Rite of passage   Rito de transición

Rod   Bastón

Rorschach test   Prueba de
Rorschach

S

Safety needs   Necesidades de
seguridad

Sample   Muestra

Scapegoating   Echando la culpa
a alguien por sus propios problemas; chivo expiatorio

Schedules of reinforcement
Programas de refuerzo

Schema   Esquema; plan

Schizophrenia   Esquizofrenia

Secondary Reinforcement
Refuerzo secundario

Selective forgetting
Selectivamente olvidando

Self-actualization   Realización
personal

Self-concept   Concepto de sí
mismo

Self-esteem   Amor propio

Self-esteem needs   Necesidades
del amor propio

Senile Dementia   Demencia
senil

Sensation   Sensación

Sensorimotor stage   Etapa motor
sensorial

Sensory deprivation   Privación
sensorial

Sensory memory system
Sistema de memoria sensorial

Sensory strip   Tira sensorial

Separation anxiety   Ansiedad de
separación

Serotonin   Serotonin (inglés)

Set   "Fijo"

Set point   Punto fijo

Shaping   Moldeamiento; concibiendo

Short-term memory   Memoria a
corto plazo

Similarity   Similitud; semejanza

Situational assessment
Avaluación de una situación;
Avaluación situacional

Size constancy   Constancia de
un tamaño

Sleep apnea   Apnea del sueño

Social contracts   Contratos
sociales

**Social entrainment (of the sleep
cycle)**   "Arrastramiento" social
(del ciclo de sueño)

Social learning   Aprendizaje
social

Sociocultural approach   Método
sociocultural

Sociopath   Sociópata

Somatoform disorder   Trastorno
somatoforme

Space constancy   Constancia
espacial

Spatial skills   Habilidades espaciales

Specific phobia   Fobia simple

Spinal cord   Médula espinal

Standardization
Estandardización

Standoutishness   Persona que se
destaca (en un sentido negativo)

Stanford-Binet Intelligence Test
Prueba de inteligencia Stanford-
Binet

State-dependent learning
Aprendizaje dependiente de una
condición

Stereotype   Estereotipo

Steroids   Esteroides

Stimulus   Estímulo

Stimulus generalization
Generalización de estímulo

Strategies   Estrategias

Stress   Tensión; estrés

Stress hormone   Hormona de tensión

Strong-Campbell Interest Inventory   Inventario de interés Strong-Campbell

Subconscious   Subconsciente

Subjects   Sujetos

Sublimation   Sublimación

Subliminal perception
Percepción subconsciente

Substance abuse   Abuso de sustancias tóxicas

Sudden death phenomenon
Fenómeno de la muerte súbita

Superego   Superego; superyo

Survey   Hacer una encuesta; encuesta

Synapse   Sinapsis

Synergistic effect   Efecto sinergístico

Systematic desensitization
Desensibilización sistemática

T

Taste receptors   Receptores del gusto

Temporal lobe   Lóbulo temporal

Territoriality   Territorialidad

Testes   Testículos

Thalamus   Tálamo

Thanatology   Tanatología

**Thematic Apperception Test
TAT**   Prueba de apercepción temática

Theory   Teoría

Theory of multiple intelligences
Teoría de inteligencias múltiples

Thought disorder   Trastorno del pensamiento

Thyroid gland   Glándula tiroides

Timbre   Timbre

Token economy   Economía ficha

Tolerance   Tolerancia

Trance   Trance; estado hipnótico

Transfer of training
Transferencia de aprendizaje; transferencia de entrenamiento

Transference   Transferencia

Type A personality
Personalidad tipo A

Type B personality
Personalidad tipo B

Twilight state   Estado de ocaso

U

Ulcer   Úlcera

Unconditional positive regard
Consideración positiva incondicional

Unconditioned response
Respuesta incondicional

Unconditioned stimulus
Estímulo incondicionado

Unconscious   Inconsciente

Undifferentiated schizophrenia
Esquizofrenia indiferenciada

Universal ethical principles
Principios éticos universales

V

Validity   Validez

Variable interval schedule
Programa de intervalo variable

Variable ratio schedule
Programa de razón variable

Variables   Variables

Verbal scale   Escala verbal

Visual area   Área visual

Visual cliff   Acantilado visual

Visual texture   Textura visual

Vocational interest test   Prueba de interés vocacional

W

Wechsler Adult Intelligence Scale-Revised (WAIS-R)   Escala de inteligencia Wechsler para adultos/revisada

Wechsler Intelligence Scale for Children-Revised (WISC-R)
Escala de inteligencia Wechsler para niños/revisada

White light   Luz blanca

Word salad   Ensalada de palabras

Z

Zygote   Zigoto

REFERENCES

A

Aaronson, B.S. (1972). Color perception and effect. *Amer. J. Clin. Hyp., 14,* 38–43.

Adams, A. B. (1969). *Eternal quest: The story of the great naturalists.* New York: Putnam's.

Adams, H. E., Feuerstein M., & Fowler, J. L. (1980). Migraine headache: Review of parameters, etiology, and intervention. *Psychol. Bull., 87,* 217–237.

Alcock, J. E. (1990). *Science and supernature: A critical appraisal of parapsychology.* Buffalo, NY: Prometheus.

American Psychiatric Association. (1994). *Diagnostic and statistical manual of mental disorders, 4th ed.* Washington, D.C.: Author.

American Psychological Association. (1992). *Ethical standards of psychologists and code of conduct.* Washington, D.C.: Author.

Anastasi, A. (1988). *Psychological testing* (6th ed.). New York: Macmillan.

Anderson, J. R. (1983). *The architecture of cognition.* Cambridge, MA: Harvard University Press.

Anderson, R. D. (1970). The history of witchcraft: A review with some psychiatric comments. *Amer. J. Psychiat., 126,* 1727–1735.

Andrewartha, H. G. (1961). *Introduction to the study of animal populations.* Chicago: University of Chicago Press.

Annett, M. (1978). Throwing loaded and unloaded dice. *Beh. Brain Sci., 1,* 278–279.

Arkes, H. R., & Garske, J. P. (1982). *Psychological theory of motivation* (2d ed.). Monterey, CA: Brooks/Cole.

Asch, S. E. (1952). *Social psychology.* Englewood Cliffs, NJ: Prentice-Hall.

Asher, L. (1980, August). Genetic alcoholism? *Psychol. Today.*

Axelrod, J., & Reisine, T. D. (1984). Stress hormones: Their interaction and regulation. *Science, 224,* 452–459.

B

Bagby, J. W. (1968). Quoted in J. D. Frank, The face of the enemy. *Psychol. Today, 2,* 24–29.

Bahrick, H. P., Bahrick, P. O., & Wittlinger, R. P. (1974). Long-term memory: Those unforgettable high school days. *Psychol. Today, 8*(7).

Balay, J., & Shevrin, H. (1988). The subliminal psychodynamic activation method. *Amer. Psychol., 43,* 161–174.

Baltes, P. B., & Kliegl, R. (1992). Further testing of limits of cognitive plasticity: Negative age differences in a mnemonic skill are robust. *Develop. Psychol., 28,* 121–125.

Baltes, R. B, Reese, H. W., & Lipsitt, L. P. (1980). Life-span developmental psychology. *Ann. Rev. Psychol., 31,* 65–110.

Bandura, A., Ross, D., & Ross, S. (1963). Imitation of film-mediated aggressive models. *J. Abnor. Soc. Psychol., 66,* 3–11.

Bandura, A., & Walters, R. (1963). *Social learning and personality development.* New York: Holt, Rinehart and Winston.

Barber, B., & Eccles, J. (1992). Long-term influence of divorce and single parenting on adolescent family- and work-related values, behaviors, and aspirations. *Psychol. Bull., 111,* 108–126.

Barber, T. X. (1969). An empirically based foundation of hypnotism. *Amer. J. Clin. Hypn., 12,* 100–130.

Barker, J. C., & Miller, M. B. (1969). Quoted in T. Wolpe, *The Practice of Behavior Theory.* New York: Pergamon Press.

Barron, F., & Harrington, D. M. (1981). Creativity, intelligence, and personality. *Ann. Rev. Psychol., 32,* 439–476.

Barton, E. M., Baltes, M. M., & Orzech, M. J. (1980). Etiology of dependence in older nursing home residents during morning care: The role of staff behavior. *J. Pers. Soc. Psychol., 38*, 423–431.

Bartoshuk, L. (1978). Gustatory system. In B. Masterton (Ed.), *The handbook of behavioral neurobiology* (Vol. 1). New York: Plenum.

Bauer, D. H. (1976). An exploratory study of developmental changes in children's fears. *J. Child. Psychol. Psychiat., 17*, 69–74.

Beauchamp, G. K. (1987). The human preference for excess salt. *Amer. Sci., 75*(1).

Beck, A. T. (1967). *Depression*. New York: Harper & Row.

_____. (1972). *Depression: Causes and treatment*. Philadelphia: University of Pennsylvania Press.

Beck, J. (1975). The perception of surface color. *Sci. Amer., 233*(2).

Beckwith, J., & Woodruff, M. (1984). Achievement in mathematics. *Science, 223*, 1247.

Beecher, H. K. (1956). Relationship of significance of wound to the pain experienced. *J. Amer. Med. Assn., 161*, 1609–1613.

Beilin, H. (1992). Piaget's enduring contribution to developmental psychology. *Developmental Psychology, 28*, 191–204.

Bell, R. Q. (1979). Parent, child, and reciprocal influences. *Amer. Psychol., 34*, 821–826.

Bell, R. R. (1983). *Marriage and family interaction* (6th ed.). Homewood, IL: Dorsey Press.

Bellack, A. J., Rozensky, R., & Schwartz, J. (1973). Self-monitoring as an adjunct to a behavioral weight reduction program. *Proceed. 81st Ann. Conv. Amer. Psychol. Assn.*

Belsky, J. (1990). Parental and nonparental child care and children's socioemotional development: A decade in review. *J. Marr. and Fam., 52*, 885–903.

_____. (1992). The research findings on gender issues in aging men and women. In B. R. Wainrib (Ed.) *Gender issues across the life cycle*. New York: Springer Publishing Co.

Bem, S. L. (1975). Sex role adaptability: One consequence of psychological androgyny. *J. Pers. Soc. Psychol., 31*, 634–643.

Benbow, C. P., & Stanley, J. C. (1983). Sex differences in mathematical reasoning ability: More facts. *Science, 222*, 1029–1031.

_____. (1985). Quoted in "The left hand of math and verbal talent." *Sci. News, 127*, 263.

Benedict, R. (1934). *Patterns of culture*. Boston: Houghton Mifflin.

Benjamin, Jr., L. T., Durkin, M., Link, M., Vestal, M., & Acord, J. (1992). Wundt's American doctoral students. *American Psychologist, 47*, 123–131.

Benjaminsen, S. (1981). Stressful life events preceding the onset of neurotic depression. *Psychol. Med., 11*, 369–378.

Bennett, W., & Gurin, J. (1982). *The Dieter's Dilemma*. New York: Basic Books.

Bergland, R. (1985). *The fabric of mind*. New York: Viking Press.

Berkowitz, L., & Green, R. G. (1967). Stimulus qualities of the target of aggression: A further study. *J. Personal. Soc. Psychol., 5*, 364–368.

Berman, P. W. (1980). Are women more responsive than men to the young? A review of developmental and situational variables. *Psychol. Bull., 88*, 668–695.

Bernard, J. (1981). The good-provider role: Its rise and fall. *Amer. Psychologist, 36*, 1–12.

Bernard, L. C. (1980). Multivariate analysis of new sex role formulations and personality. *J. Pers. and Soc. Psychol., 38*, 323–336.

Bickerton, D. (1984). The language bioprogram hypotheses. *Brain Beh. Sci., 7*, 173–221.

Biller, H. B. (1970). Father absence and the personality development of the male child. *Develop. Psychol., 2*, 181–201.

Birren, J. E. (1983). Aging in America: Roles for psychology. *Amer. Psychol., 38*, 298–299.

Blackman, S., & Catalina, D. (1973). The moon and the emergency room. *Percept. Mot. Skills, 37*, 624–626.

Blasi, A. (1980). Bridging moral cognition and moral action: A critical review of the literature. *Psychol. Bull., 88*, 1–45.

Block, J. M. (1973). Conceptions of sex role: Some cross-cultural and longitudinal perspectives. *Amer. Psychol., 28*, 512–526.

References

Blum, K. (1984). *Handbook of abusable drugs.* New York: Gardner Press.

Blum, K. (1988). Personal communication.

Bolles, R. D. (1969). The role of eye movements in Müller-Lyer illusion. *Percept. Psychophy., 6,* 175–176.

Bond, E. A. (1960). Tenth-grade abilities and achievements. Quoted in L. J. Cronbach, *Essentials of psychological testing* (2d ed.). New York: Harper & Row.

Boorstin, D. J. (1983). *The discoverers.* New York: Random House.

Bouchard, T. J., Jr. (1983). Twins. *Yrbk. Sci. and the Future.* Encyclopedia Britannica.

Bower, B. (1985). Neuroleptic backlash. *Sci. News, 128*(3).

Bower, G. H. (1981). Mood and memory. *Amer. Psychol., 36,* 129–148.

Bower, G. H., & Karlin, M. B. (1974). Depth of processing of faces and recognition memory. *J. Exper. Psychol., 103,* 751–759.

Bower, G. H., & Winzenz, D. (1969). Group structure, coding, and memory for digit series. *J. Exp. Psychol. Monogr., 80*(2), pt. 2.

Bozarth, M. A., & Wise, R. A. (1984). Anatomically distinct opiate receptor fields mediate reward and physical dependence. *Science, 229,* 516–517.

Brasch, R. (1967). *How did it begin?* New York: McKay.

Braudel, F. (1981). *The structures of everyday life* (Vol. 1). (S. Reynolds, Trans.). New York: Harper & Row.

Breggin, P. R. (1983) *Psychiatric drugs: Hazards to the brain.* New York: Springer.

_____. (1984). Electroshock therapy and brain damage: The acute organic brain syndrome as treatment. *Brain Beh. Sci., 7,* 24–25.

Bringmann, W. G., & Tweney, R. D. (Eds.). (1980). *Wundt studies: A centennial collection.* Toronto, Canada: Hogrefe.

Brislin, R. W. (1983). Cross-cultural research is psychology. *Ann. Rev. Psychol., 34,* 363–400.

Brody, E. M. (1974). Aging and family personality: A developmental view. *Fam. Process, 3,* 23–27.

Brody, J. E. (1988). Studies unmask origins of brutal migraines. *New York Times,* October 11.

Brody, M. S. (1962). Prognosis and results of psychoanalysis. In J. H. Nodine and J. H. Moyer (Eds.), *Psychosomatic medicine.* Philadelphia: Lea and Febiger.

Brome, V. (1967). *Freud and his early circle.* New York: William Morrow.

Bromley, D. B. (1974). *The psychology of human aging* (2d ed.). Baltimore: Penguin Books.

Brown, H. (1976). *Brain and behavior.* New York: Oxford University Press.

Brown, J. M., & Chaves, J. F. (1980). *Cognitive activity, pain perception, and hypnotic susceptibility in chronic pain patients.* Paper Amer. Psychol. Anns., Montreal.

Brown, R. (1973). *A first language.* Cambridge, MA: Harvard University Press.

Brownell, K. (1984). Quoted in "Physical factors explored in dieting, type A behavior." *APA Monitor, 15*(2).

Bruner, J. S. (1968). Foreword. In A. R. Luria, *The mind of a mnemonist.* New York: Basic Books.

Bryan, J. H., & Test, M. A. (1969). Models and helping: Naturalistic studies in aiding behavior. Quoted in P. H. Mussen and M. R. Rosensweig (Eds.), *Annual review of psychology.* Palo Alto, CA: Annual Review.

Bryer, K. B. (1979). The Amish way of death: A study of family support systems. *Amer. Psychol., 34,* 255–261.

Buchanan, C., Eccles, J., & Becker, J. (1992). Are adolescents the victims of raging hormones: Evidence for activational effects of hormones on moods and behavior at adolescence. *Psychol. Bull., 111,* 62–107.

Buckhout, R. Figueroa, D., & Hoff, E. (1972, November). *Psychology and eyewitness identification: A preliminary report.* Ctr. Responsive Psychol. Rep. (CR–1).

Budzynski, T. H. (1976). Biofeedback and the twilight states of consciousness. In G. E. Schwartz and D. Shapiro (Eds.), *Consciousness and self-regulation I.* New York: Plenum.

Bullock, A. (1953) *Hitler: A study in tyranny.* New York: Harper & Row.

Bureau of Census. (1983). *Current population reports.* P-25, no. 949.

_____. (1984). *Current population reports.* P-23, no. 128.

Burger, J. M., & Arkin, R. M. (1980). Prediction, control, and learned helplessness. *J. Pers. Soc. Psychol., 38,* 483–491.

Burros, M. (1988, February 23). Women: Out of the house but not out of the kitchen. *New York Times,* 1, 18.

Buss, A. H. (1966). *Psychopathology.* New York: Wiley.

C

Calhoun, J. B. (1962). Population density and social pathology. *Sci. Amer., 206,* 139–148.

Campbell, A. (1975). *Measuring the perceived quality of life.* New York: Russell Sage Foundation.

Campbell, D. E., & Beets, J. L. (1980). Lunacy and the moon. *Psychol. Bull., 85,* 1123–1129.

Cannon, W. B. (1939). *The wisdom of the body.* New York: Norton.

_____. (1942). Voodoo death. *Amer. Anthropol., 44,* 169.

Caplan, P. J. (1984). The myth of women's masochism. *Amer. Psychol., 40,* 786–799.

Carrington, P. (1972). Dreams and schizophrenia. *Arch. Gen. Psychiat., 26,* 343–350.

Carskadon, M. A., Harvey, K., Duke, P., Anders, T. F., Litt, I. F., & Dement, W. C. (1980). Pubertal changes in daytime sleepiness. *Sleep, 2,* 453–460.

Carver, R. P. (1971). *Sense and nonsense in speed reading.* Silver Springs, MD: Revrac Publications.

Case, R. B. (1985). Quoted in "Type A's maybe now you can relax." *Science 85,* 6(5).

Cash, T. F., & Janda, L. H. (1984). The eye of the beholder. *Psychology Today,* 18(12).

Casler, L. (1976). The "consciousness problem" is not the problem. *Percep. Mot. Skills, 42,* 227–232.

Chaves, J. F., & Barber, T. X. (1974). Acupuncture analgesia: A six-factor theory. *Psychoenergetic Syst., 1,* 11–21.

Chertkoff, J. M., & Conley, M. (1967). Opening offer and frequency of concession as bargaining strategies. *J. Pers. Soc. Psychol., 7,* 181–185.

Chomsky, N. (1980). Rules and representations. *Beh. Brain Sci., 3,* 1–15.

Cialdini, R. B., Petty, R. E., & Cacioppo, J. T. (1981). Attitude and attitude change. *Ann. Rev. Psychol., 32,* 357–404.

Clausen, J. (1975). The social meaning of differential physical and sexual maturation. In S. Dragastin and G.

Elder, Jr. (Eds.), *Adolescence and the life cycle.* New York: Halsted Press.

Clark, R. W. (1980). *Freud: The man and the cause.* New York: Random House.

Cleland, C. C., Case, J., & Manaster, G. J. (1980). IQs and etiologies: The two-group approach to mental retardation. *Bull. Psychon. Soc., 15,* 413–415.

Coates, B., Anderson, E., & Hartup, W. (1972). Interrelations in the attachment behavior of human infants. *Develop. Psychol., 6,* 218–230.

Coe, W. C., & Ryken, K. (1979). Hypnosis and risks to human subjects. *Amer. Psychol., 34,* 673–681.

Cohen, D. B. (1979). Remembering and forgetting dreaming. In J. F. Kihlstrom and F. J. Evans (Eds.), *Functional disorders of memory.* Hillsdale, NJ: Erlbaum.

_____. (1980a). REM dreaming as an adaptive process. Mimeographed paper, revised from APSS address. Received 1980.

_____. (1980b). Adaptive capabilities of the nervous system. In P. S. McConnell, G. J. Boer, H. J. Romijin, N. E. van de Poll, and M. A. Corner (Eds.), *Progress in brain research.* New York: Elsevier/North Holland Biomedical Press.

Cohen, S. (1980). Aftereffects of stress on human performance and social behavior: A review of research and theory. *Psychol. Bull., 88,* 82–108.

Cohen, S., & Williamson, G. (1991). Stress and infectious disease in humans. *Psychol. Bull., 109,* 5–24.

Cohn, L. (1991). Sex differences in the course of personality development: A meta-analysis. *Psychol. Bull., 109,* 252–266.

Coile, D. C., & Miller, N. E. (1984). How radical animal activists try to mislead humane people. *Amer. Psychol., 39,* 700–701.

Coleman, R. M. (1986). *Wide awake at 3:00 A.M.,* New York: W. H. Freeman.

Collette-Pratt, C. (1976). Attitudinal predictors of devaluation of old age in a multigenerational sample. *J. Geron., 31,* 193–197.

Collins, W. A., & Zimmerman, S. A. (1975). Convergent and divergent social cues: Effects of televised aggression on children. *Comm. Res., 2,* 331–346.

Colombo, J. (1982). The critical period concept: Research, methodology, and theoretical issues. *Psychol. Bull., 91,* 260–275.

References

Comstock, G., Chaffee, S., Katzman, N., McCombs, M., & Roberts, D. (1978). *Television and human behavior.* New York: Columbia University Press.

Conger, J. C., Conger, A. J., Costanzo, P. R., Wright, K. L., & Matter, J. A. (1980). The effect of social cues on the eating behavior of obese and normal subjects. *J. Pers., 48,* 258–271.

Conger, J. J., & Peterson, A. C. (1984). *Adolescents and youth.* New York: Harper & Row.

Cooper, E., & Tahoda, M. (1964). Quoted in W. W. Lambert and W. E. Lambert, *Social psychology.* Englewood Cliffs, NJ: Prentice-Hall.

Corballis, M. C., & Morgan, M. J. (1978). On the biological basis of human laterality: Evidence for a maturational left-right gradient. *Behav. Brain Sci., 1,* 261–269.

Cosse, W. J. (1992). Who's who and what's what? The effects of gender on development in adolescence. In B. R. Wainrib (Ed.). *Gender issues across the life cycle.* New York: Springer Publishing Co.

Costa, P. T., Jr., & McCrae, R. R. (1986). Cross-sectional studies of personality in a national sample: 1. Development and validation of survey measures. *Psychol. Aging, 1,* 140–143.

Costa, P. T., Jr., Zonderman, A. B., McCrae, R. R., Cornoni-Huntley, Locke, B. Z., & Barbano, H. E. (1987). Longitudinal analysis of psychological well-being in a national sample: Stability of mean levels. *J. Gerontol., 42,* 50–55.

Cowan, N. (1984). On short and long auditory stores. *Psychol. Bull., 96,* 341–370.

Cowart, B. J. (1981). Development of taste perception in humans: Sensitivity and preference throughout the life span. *Psychol. Bull., 90,* 43–73.

Cox, V. C., Paulus, P. B., & McCain, G. (1984). Prison crowding research: The relevance for prison housing standards and a general approach regarding crowding phenomena. *Amer. Psychol., 30,* 1148–1160.

Craik, F. I. M. (1979). Human memory. *Ann. Rev. Psychol., 30,* 63–102.

Crick, F. H. C. (1983). Thinking about the brain. *The brain.* San Francisco: W. H. Freeman.

Cronbach, L. J. (1989). *Essentials of psychological testing* (5th ed.). New York: Harper & Row.

Crosby, F., Bromley, S., & Saxe, L. (1980). Recent unobtrusive studies of black and white discrimination and prejudice: A literature review. *Psychol. Bull., 87,* 546–563.

Curtiss, S. (1977). *Genie: A psycholinguistic study of a modern-day "wild child."* New York: Academic Press.

D

Daniels, D. (1986). Differential experiences of siblings in the same family as predictors of adolescent sibling personality differences. *J. Pers. Soc. Psychol., 51,* 339–346.

Davenport, H. W. (1982). Why the stomach does not digest itself. *Sci. Amer., 226*(1).

Davis, K. (1972). The American family in relation to demographic change. In C. R. Westoff and R. Parke (Eds.), *Demographic and social aspects of population growth:* 1. Washington, DC: Bureau of Census.

Davis, K. E. (1985). Near and dear: Friendship and love compared. *Psychology Today, 19*(2).

Dean, S. J., Martin, R. B., & Steiner, D. (1968). Mediational control of the GSR. *J. Exp. Res. Personal, 3,* 71–76.

Deaux, K. (1985). Sex and gender. *Ann. Rev. Psychol., 36,* 49–81.

DeBold, J. F. (1983). Quoted in "Masculine/feminine behavior: New views." *Sci. News, 124,* 326.

Degler, C. N. (1980). *At Odds.* New York: Oxford University Press.

Delgado, J. M. R. (1969). *Physical control of the mind.* New York: Harper & Row.

Dement, W. C. (1974). *Some must watch while some must sleep.* San Francisco: W. H. Freeman.

_____. (1979). Normal sleep and sleep disorders. In G. Usdin and J. M. Lewis (Eds.), *Psychiatry in general practice.* New York: McGraw-Hill.

Denmark, F. (1992). The thirty-something woman: To career or not to career. In B. R. Wainrib (Ed.), *Gender issues across the life cycle.* New York: Springer Publishing Co.

Denton, D. (1983). *The hunger for salt.* New York: Springer-Verlag.

Depue, R. A., Slater, J. F., Wolfstetter-Kausch, H., Klein, D., Goplerud, E., & Farr, D. (1981). A behavioral paradigm for identifying persons at risk for bipolar depressive disorder: A conceptual framework and five validation studies. *J. Abn. Psychol. Monog., 90,* 381–437.

Derryberry, J. S. (1983). Quoted in "Scientists give nod to sleeping pills." *Sci. News., 124,* 342.

Deutsch, A. (1946). *The mentally ill in America* (2d ed.). New York: Columbia University Press.

Deutsch, J. A. (1973). *Physiological psychology* (2d ed.). Homewood, IL: Dorsey Press.

Diagnostic and Statistical Manual of Mental Disorders (4th ed.). (1994). Washington, DC: American Psychiatric Association.

Diener, E. (1976). Effects of prior destructive behavior, anonymity, and group presence on deindividuation and aggression. *J. Pers. Soc. Psychol., 33,* 497–507.

Diener, E., Fraser, S. C., Beaman, A. L., & Kelem, R. T. (1976). Effects of deindividuation variables on stealing among Halloween trick-or-treaters. *J. Pers. Soc. Psychol., 33,* 178–183.

Diener, E., & Woody, L. W. (1981). Television violence, conflict, realism, and action. *Comm. Res., 8,* 281–306.

Dindia, K., & Allen, M. (1992). Sex differences in self-disclosure: A meta-analysis. *Psychol. Bull., 112,* 106–124.

Dohrenwend, B. S., Dohrenwend, B. P., Link, B., & Neugebauer, R. (1979). Epidemiology and genetics of schizophrenia. *Soc. Biol., 26,* 142–153.

Doob, A. N., & Climie, J. R. (1972). Delay of measurement and the effects of film violence. *J. Exp. Soc. Psychol., 8,* 136–142.

Duckitt, J. (1992). Psychology and prejudice. *Amer. Psychol., 47,* 1182–1193.

Dunlop, R. (1965). *Doctors of the American frontier.* Garden City, NY: Doubleday.

Dunn, A. J. (1980). Neurochemistry of learning and memory: An evaluation of recent data. *Ann. Rev. Psychol., 31,* 343–390.

Dunn-Rankin, E. D. (1978). The visual characteristics of words. *Sci. Amer., 238*(1).

Dweck, C. S., Goets, T. E., & Strauss, N. L. (1980). Sex differences in learned helplessness: 4. An experimental and naturalistic study of failure generalization and its mediators. *J. Pers. Soc. Psychol., 38,* 441–452.

E

Eagly, A. H. (1978). Sex differences in influencibility. *Psychol. Bull., 85,* 86–116.

Eagly, A. H., & Himmelfarb, S. (1978). Attitudes and opinions. *Ann. Rev. Psychol, 29,* 517–554.

Edinger, J. A., & Paterson, M. L. (1983). Nonverbal involvement and social control. *Psychol. Bull., 93,* 30–56.

Ehrhardt, A. (1979). Biological sex differences: A developmental perspective. *Master lectures on issues of sex and gender in psychology.* (Tape 15/12). Washington, DC: American Psychological Association.

Eisdorfer, C. (1983). Conceptual models of aging. *Amer. Psychol., 38,* 197–202.

Eisenberg, N., & Lennon, R. (1983). Sex differences in empathy and related capacities. *Psychol. Bull., 94,* 100–131.

Eisenberger, R. (1972). Explanation of rewards that do not reduce tissue needs. *Psychol. Bull., 77,* 319–339.

Eisler, R. M., & Williams, W. V. (1972). A comparison of preadmission characteristics of patients selected for long- or short-term psychiatric treatment. *J. Clin. Psychol., 28,* 209–213.

Elkind, D. (1978). *The child's reality: Three developmental themes.* Hillsdale, NJ: Erlbaum.

Ellenberger, H. F. (1970). *The discovery of the unconscious.* New York: Basic Books.

Ellis, A. (1980). Rational-emotive theory and cognitive behavior therapy: Similarities and differences. *Cog. Ther. Res., 4,* 325–340.

Emery, R. E. (1982). Interparental conflict and the children of discord and divorce. *Psychol. Bull., 92,* 310–330.

Emlen, S. T. (1975). The stellar-orientation system of a migratory bird. *Sci. Amer., 233*(2).

Engen, T. (1987). Remembering odors and their names. *Amer. Sci., 75*(5).

Erikson, E. H. (1968). *Identity: Youth and crisis.* New York: Norton.

Erikson, E. H., Erikson, J. M., & Kivnick, H. Q. (1986). *Vital involvement in old age.* New York: W. W. Norton.

References

Eron, L. D. (1980). Prescriptions for reduction of aggression. *Amer. Psychol., 35,* 244–252.

_____. (1983). Quoted in "Parental behavior, TV habits, IQ predict aggression." *Sci News, 124,* 148.

Eron, L. D., & Huesman, L. R. (1985). Quoted in "Once a bully, always. . . ." *Psychology Today, 19*(7).

Evans, C., & Evans, P. (Eds.), *Landscapes of the night.* New York: Viking Press.

Evans, G. W. (1980). Environmental cognition. *Psychol. Bull., 88,* 259–287.

Evans, G. W., & Howard, R. B. (1973). Personal space. *Psychol. Bull., 80,* 334–344.

F

Falbo, T., & Peplau, L. A. (1980). Power strategies in intimate relationships. *J. Pers. Soc. Psychol., 38,* 618–628.

Falbo, T., & Polit, D. F. (1986). Quantitative review of the only child literature: Research evidence and theory development. *Psychological Bulletin, 100,* 176–189.

Fancher, R. E. (1979). *Pioneers of psychology.* New York: Norton.

Farber, M. L. (1968). *Theory of suicide.* New York: Funk & Wagnalls.

Farley, J., & Alkon, D. J. (1985). Cellular mechanisms of learning, memory, and information storage. *Ann. Rev. Psychol., 36,* 419–494.

Farr, L. (1975). Peddling the pedestal. *New Times, 5*(8).

Feingold, A. (1988). Cognitive gender differences are disappearing. *Amer. Psychol., 43,* 95–103.

_____. (1992). Gender differences in mate selection preferences: A test of the parental investment model. *Psychol. Bull., 112,* 125–139.

Festinger, L. (1957). *A theory of cognitive dissonance.* Stanford, CA: Stanford University Press.

Fingarett, H. (1988). *Heavy drinking.* Berkeley: University of California Press.

Fishman, S. M., & Sheehan, D. W. (1985). Anxiety and panic: Their cause and treatment. *Psychology Today, 19*(4).

Flexner, J. T. (1974). *Washington: The indispensable man.*

New York: New American Library.

Fobes, J. C., & Smock, C. C. (1981). Sensory capacities of marine mammals. *Psychol. Bull., 89,* 288–307.

Folkman, S., & Lazarus, R. (1988). Coping as a mediator of emotion. *J. Pers. Soc. Psychol., 54,* 466–475.

Fox, M. W. (Ed.), (1968). *Abnormal behavior in animals.* Philadelphia: Saunders.

_____. (1980a, July 27). Animal bulletin. In "Animal doctor." *St. Louis Post Dispatch.*

_____. (1980b). *The soul of the wolf.* Boston: Little, Brown.

_____. (1983). Humane ethics and animal rights. *Int. J. Stud. Anim. Prob., 4,* 286–289.

Frank G. (1966). *The Boston strangler.* New York: New American Library.

Frank, J. D. (1968). The face of the enemy. *Psychology Today, 2,* 24–29.

_____. (1971). Therapeutic factors is psychotherapy. *Amer. J. of Psychother., 25,* 350–361.

_____. (1974). *Persuasion and healing: A comparative study of psychotherapy.* Baltimore, MD: Johns Hopkins University Press.

Franzoi, S. L. (1985). Quoted in "The things they do for love." *Sci. News, 127,* 398.

Freedman, D. A., & Brown, S. L. (1968). On the role of somasthetic stimulation in the development of psychic structure. *Psychoanal. Quart., 37,* 418–438.

Freedman, J. L. (1984). Effect of television violence on aggressiveness. *Psychol. Bull., 96,* 227–246.

Freedman, J. L., & Fraser, S. C. (1966). Compliance without pressure. *J. Pers. Soc. Psychol., 4,* 196–202.

Freeman, C. (1985). Quoted in "The patients' perspective on ECT." *Sci. News, 127,* 74.

Freud, S. (1895). *Freud-Fleiss.* In Gay, P. (1988). *Freud: A life for our time.* New York: W. W. Norton.

_____. (1938). The history of the psychoanalytic movement. In A. A. Brill (Ed.), *The basic writings of Sigmund Freud.* New York: Random House.

Friedman, H. S., & Booth-Kewley, S. (1987). The "disease-prone" personality. *Amer. Psychol., 42,* 539–555.

Friedman, M. (1984). Quoted in "Type A: A change of heart and mind." *Sci. News, 126,* 109.

Friedman, M., & Rosenman, R. (1974). *Type A behavior and your heart.* New York: Knopf.

Frumkin, R. M. (1961). Beauty. In A. Ellis and A. Abarbanal (Eds.), *The encyclopedia of sexual behavior.* New York: Hawthorne Books.

Furst, C. J. (1979). The inside and outside of eidetic imagery. *Beh. Brain Sci., 2,* 602–603.

G

Gagnon, D. (1986). *Videogames and special skills.* Mimeograph from author.

Gardner, H. (1983). *Frames of mind: The theory of multiple intelligences.* New York: Basic Books.

Garfield, S. L. (1981). Psychotherapy: A 40-year appraisal. *Amer. Psychol., 36,* 174–183.

Gazzaniga, M. S. (1970). *The bisected brain.* Englewood Cliffs, NJ: Prentice-Hall.

Geddes, L. A., & Newberg, D. C. (1977). Cuff pressure oscillations in the measurement of relative blood pressure. *Psychophysio., 14,* 198–202.

Geen, R. (1977). The catharsis of aggression: An evaluation of a hypothesis. In L. Berkowitz (Ed.), *Advances in experimental social psychology.* New York: Academic Press.

Geschwind, N. (1983). Quoted in Kolata, G. Math genius may have hormonal basis. *Science, 222,* 1312.

Getzels, J. W., & Jackson, P. W. (1962). *Creativity and intelligence.* New York: Wiley.

Gibson, E. J., & Walk, R. D. (1960). The visual cliff. *Sci. Amer., 202*(4).

Gilbert, S. (1985). Noise pollution. *Sci. Dig., 93*(3).

Gill, R., & Keats, D. (1980). Elements of intellectual competence. Judgements by Australian and Malay university students. *J. Cross-Cult. Psychol., 11,* 233–243.

Glick, P. C. (1977). Updating the life cycle of the family. *J. Marr. Fam., 39,* 5–13.

Gold, M. S. (1985). Quoted in "Multiple drug use: A dangerous trend." *Sci. News, 128,* 6.

Goleman, D. (1980, February). 1,528 little geniuses and how they grew. *Psychology Today,* 28–53.

Goldfried, M. R. (1980). Toward the delineation of therapeutic change principles. *Amer. Psychol., 35,* 991–999.

Goodall, J. (1971). *In the shadow of man.* Boston, MA: Houghton Mifflin.

Goodwin, J. S., Goodwin, J. M., & Garry, P. J. (1984). Quoted in "Food for thought in the elderly." *Sci. News, 123,* 358.

Gough, H. G. (1960). *Manual for the California Psychological Inventory* (rev. ed.). Palo Alto, CA: Consulting Psychologists Press.

_____. (1976). Studying creativity by means of word association tests. *J. Appl. Psychol., 61,* 348–353.

_____. (1979). A creative personality scale for the Adjective Check List. *J. Pers. Soc. Psychol., 37,* 1398–1405.

Gould, J. (1985). Quoted in "To honeybees, a picture is worth a thousand line angles." *Sci. News, 127,* 196.

Gould, J. L. (1984). Quoted in "Mind maps." *Sci. News, 125,* 62–63.

Gould, R. (1975). Adult life stages: Growth toward self-tolerance. *Psychology Today, 8*(9).

Graber, E. (1988). Personal communication.

Graf, P., Squire, L. R., & Mandler, G. (1984). The information that amnesiac patients do not forget. *J. Exp. Psychol.: Lrn. Mem. Cog., 10,* 164–178.

Graham, K., LaRocque, L., Yetman, R., Ross, J. G., & Guistra, E. (1980). Aggression and barroom environments. *J. Stud. Alcoh., 41,* 277–292.

Graham, P. A. (1984). Wanting it all. *Wilson Quart., 7*(1).

Graham, S., (1992). "Most of the subjects were white and middle class." *Amer. Psychol., 47,* 629–639.

Grant, I., Sweetwood, H. L., Yager, J., & Gerst, M. (1981). Quality of life events in relation to psychiatric symptoms. *Arch. Gen. Psychiatr., 38,* 335–339.

Green, B. F. (1978). In defense of measurement. *Amer. Psychol., 33,* 664–670.

Green, R. (1974). *Sexual identity conflict in children and adults.* New York: Basic Books.

Greenough, W. (1985). Quoted in "The brain branches out." *Science 85, 6*(5).

References

Greenwald, A. G. (1992). New Look 3: Unconscious cognition reclaimed. *American Psychologist, 47,* 766–779.

Gregory, R. L. (1968). Visual illusions. *Sci. Amer., 219*(5).

_____. (1981). *Mind in science.* New York: Cambridge University Press.

Griffin, D. R. (1976). *The question of animal awareness.* New York: Rockefeller University Press.

Grinspoon, L. (1969). Marihuana. Sci. Amer., *221*(6).

Gripp, R. F., & Magaro, P. A. (1971). A token economy program evaluation with untreated control ward comparisons. *Beh. Res. Ther., 9,* 137–149.

Gruenewald, D. (1971). Hypnotic techniques without hypnosis in the treatment of dual personality. *J. New Ment. Dis., 153,* 41–46.

Guilleminault, C., Pedley, T., & Dement, W. C. (1977). Sleepwalking and epilepsy. *Sleep Res., 6,* 170.

Gutmann, D. (1975). Parenthood: A key to the comparative study of the life cycle. In N. Datan and L. Ginsberg (Eds.), *Lifespan developmental psychology: Normative life crises.* New York: Academic Press.

_____. (1987). *Reclaimed power: Towards a psychology of later life.* New York: Basic Books.

H

Haaga, D., Dyck, M., & Ernst, D. (1991). Empirical status of cognitive theory of depression. *Psychol. Bull., 110,* 215–236.

Haber, R. N. (1970). How we remember what we were. *Sci. Amer., 222*(5).

Hall, C. S., Lindzey, G., Loehlin, J. C., & Manosevitz, M. (1985). *Introduction to theories of personality.* New York: Wiley.

Hall, G. (1980). Exposure learning in animals. *Psychol. Bull., 88,* 535–550.

Halpert, H. P. (1969). Public acceptance of the mentally ill. *Public Health Rep., 84,* 59–64.

Hamilton, D. L. (1979). A cognitive-attributional analysis of stereotyping. In L. Berkowitz (Ed.), *Advances in experimental social psychology.* New York: Academic Press.

Hamilton, D. L., & Rose, T. L. (1980). Illusory correlation and the maintenance of stereotypic beliefs. *J. Pers. Soc. Psychol., 39,* 832–845.

Hamilton, E. (1942). *The Greek way.* New York: Norton.

Harlow, H. F. (1959). Love in infant monkeys. *Sci. Amer., 22*(6).

Harlow, H. F., Blazek, N., & McClearn, G. (1956). Manipulatory motivation in the infant rhesus monkey. *J. Comp. Physiol. Psychol., 49,* 444–448.

Harmon, L. D. (1973). The recognition of faces. *Sci. Amer., 229*(5).

Harper, R. A. (1968). *Psychoanalysis and psychotherapy: 36 systems.* Englewood Cliffs, NJ: Prentice-Hall.

Hartmann, E. (1973). *The functions of sleep.* New Haven, CT: Yale University Press.

_____. (1984). *The nightmare.* New York: Basic Books.

Hartmann, E., & Brewer, V. (1976). When is more or less sleep required? A study of variable sleepers. *Comp. Pschiatr., 17,* 275–284.

Haugeland, J. (1978). The nature and plausibility of cognitivism. *Behav. Brain Sci., 1,* 215–225.

Hawgood, J. A. (1967). *America's western frontiers.* New York: Knopf.

Hawkins, J. D., Catalano, R., & Miller, J. (1992). Risk and protective factors for alcohol and other drug problems in adolescence and early adulthood: Implications for substance abuse prevention. *Psychol. Bull., 112,* 64–105.

Hayflick, L. (1979). The cell biology of human aging. *Sci. Amer., 242*(1), 58–65.

Hearn, C. B., & Seeman, J. (1971). Personality integration and perception of interpersonal relationships. *J. Pers. Soc. Psychol., 2,* 138–143.

Heatherton, T., & Baumeister, R. (1991). Binge eating as escape from self-awareness. *Psychol. Bull., 110,* 86–108.

Hebb, D. O., & Donderi, D. C. (1987). *Textbook of Psychology.* Hillsdale, NJ: Erlbaum.

Heide, F. J. (1985). Relaxation: The storm before the calm. *Psychology Today, 19*(4).

Heilman, M. E. (1984). Information as a deterrent against sex discrimination: The effects of applicant sex and information type on preliminary employment decisions. *Organizational Behavior and Human Performance, 33,* 174–186.

Heinemann, L. G. (1970). Visual phenomena in a long sensory deprivation. *Percept. Mot. Skills, 30,* 563–570.

Hellige, J. B. (1990). Hemispheric asymmetry. *Ann. Rev. Psychol., 41,* 55–60.

Helms, J. (1992). Why is there no study of cultural equivalence in standardized cognitive ability testing? *Amer. Psychol., 47,* 1083–1101.

Hetherington, E. M. (1965). A developmental study of the effects of sex on the dominant parent on sex-role preference, identification, and imitation in children. *J. Pers. Soc. Psychol., 2,* 188–194.

Hilgard, E. R. (1974). Weapon against pain. *Psychology. Today, 8*(6).

_____. (1980). Consciousness in contemporary psychology. *Ann. Rev. Psychol., 31,* 1–26.

Hilgard, E. R., & Hilgard, J. R. (1975). *Hypnosis in the relief of pain.* Los Angeles: Daufmann.

Hinshaw, S. P. (1992). Externalizing behavior problems and academic underachievement in childhood and adolescence: Causal relationships and underlying mechanisms. *Psychological Bulletin, 111,* 127–155.

Hoffman, L. W. (1977). Changes in family roles, socialization, and sex differences. *Amer. Psychol., 32,* 644–657.

Hofling, C. K., Brotzman, E., Dalrymple, S., Graves, N., & Pierce, C. M. (1966). An experimental study in nurse-physician relationships. *J. Nerv. Ment. Dis., 143,* 171–180.

Holden, C. (1980). Twins reunited. *Science 80,* 55–59.

Hollingsworth, H. L. (1922). *Judging human character.* New York: Appleton-Century-Crofts.

Holmes, D. S. (1984). Meditation and somatic arousal reduction. *Amer. Psychol., 39,* 1–10.

Holmes, T. H., & Rahe, R. H. (1967). The social readjustment rating scale. *J. Psychosom. Res., 11,* 213–218.

Honts, C., Hodes, R., & Raskin, D. (1985). Quoted in "Beat that lie detector!" *Psychology Today, 19*(6).

Horney, K. (1950). *Neurosis and human growth.* New York: Norton.

Horton, D. L., & Mills, C. B. (1984). Human learning and memory. *Ann. Rev. Psychol., 35,* 361–394.

Horton, P., & Miller, D. (1972). The etiology of multiple personality. *Comp. Psychiatr., 13*(2).

Howells, W. (1962). *The heathens: Primitive man and his religions.* New York: Doubleday.

Hulicka, I. M. (1978). Cognitive functioning of older adults. *Master lectures on the psychology of aging.* Tape 14/15. Washington, DC: American Psychological Association.

Hurvich, L. M. (1974). Opponent processes as a model of neural organization. *Amer. Psychol., 29,* 88–102.

Hyde, J. S. (1990). *Understanding human sexuality.* New York: McGraw-Hill.

I

Imara, M. (1975). Dying as the last stage of growth. In E. Kübler-Ross (Ed.), *Death, the final stage of growth.* Englewood Cliffs, NJ: Prentice-Hall.

Institute for Social Research. (1984). University of Michigan.

Isaacson, R. L., & Pribram, K. H. (1975). *The hippocampus.* New York: Plenum.

Isner, J. M. (1987). Interviewed in "Cocaine cardiology: Problems, mysteries." *Sci. News, 131*(5).

Itard, J. M. G. (1932). *The wild boy of Aveyron.* New York: Appleton-Century-Crofts.

J

Jackson, D. D. (1984). If women needed a quick pick-me-up, Lydia provided one. *Smithsonian, 15*(4).

Jacobs, B. L. (1987). How hallucinogenic drugs work. *Amer. Sci., 75,* 386–392.

Jacobson, W. J., & Doran, R. L. (1985). Quoted in "Girls and science: The gap remains." *Psychology Today, 19*(6).

James, T. M. (1985). The trade. *Wilson Quart., 9*(1).

James, W. (1890). *Principles of psychology.* 2 vols. NY: Holt.

Jansen, D. G., & Nickles, L. A. (1973). Variables that differentiate between single and multiple admission psychiatric patients at a state hospital over a five-year

References

period. *J. Clin. Psychol., 29*, 83–85.

Jarvik, L. F. (1975). Thoughts on the psychobiology of aging. *Amer. Psychol., 30*, 576–583.

Jarvik, L. F., & Cohen, D. (1973). A biobehavioral approach to intellectual changes with aging. In C. E. Eisdorfer and M. P. Lawton (Eds.), *The psychology of adult development and aging.* Washington, DC: American Psychological Association.

Jay, R. (1987). *Learned pigs & fireproof women.* New York: Villard Books.

Jaynes, J. (1976). *The origin of consciousness in the breakdown of the bicameral mind.* Boston: Houghton Mifflin.

Jemmott, J. B., III, & Locke, S. E. (1984). Psychosocial factors, immunologic mediation, and human susceptibility to infectious diseases: How much do we know? *Psychol. Bull., 95*, 79–108.

Jensen, R. A., Martinez, J. L., McGaugh, J. L., Messing, R. B., & Vasquez, B. J. (1980). The psychobiology of aging. In G. J. Maletta and F. J. Pirossolo (Eds.), *The aging nervous system.* New York: Praeger.

Jerison, H. J. (1976). Paleoneurology and the evolution of mind. *Sci. Amer., 234*(1).

Jones, M. C. (1924). A laboratory study of fear: The case of Peter. *Pedagog. Semin., 31*, 308–315.

_____. (1974). Albert, Peter, and John B. Watson. *Amer. Psychol., 29*, 581–583.

Jones, R. M. (1970). *The new psychology of dreaming.* New York: Grune & Stratton.

Jouandet, M., & Gazzaniga, M. S. (1979). The frontal lobes. In M. S. Gazzaniga (Ed.), *Handbook of behavioral neurobiology.* New York: Plenum.

Jung, C. G. (1933). *Modern man in search of a soul.* New York: Harcourt Brace Jovanovich.

_____. (1958). Transformation symbolism in the mass. In V. S. deLaszio (Ed.), *Psyche and symbol: A selection of writings of C. G. Jung.* New York: Doubleday.

K

Kagan, J. (1975). Resilience in cognitive development. *Ethos, 3*, 231–247.

_____. (1979). Family experience and the child's development. *Amer. Psychol., 34*, 886–891.

_____. (1984). *The nature of the child.* New York: Basic Books.

Kahn, E., Fisher, C., Edwards, A., & Davis, D. (1972). Psychophysiology of night terrors and nightmares. *Proceed. 80th Annual Conv. Amer. Psychol. Assn.*

Kahn, L. S. (1980). The dynamics of scapegoating: The expulsion of evil. *Psychother. Theory Res. Pract., 17*, 79–84.

Kaluger, G., & Kaluger, M. F. (1984). *Human development.* St. Louis: Times Mirror/Mosby.

Kamin, L. J. (1978). Comment on Munsinger's review of adoption studies. *Psychol. Bull., 85*, 194–201.

_____. Inbreeding depression and I. Q. *Psychol. Bull., 87*, 469–478.

Kamil, A. C., & Roitblat, H. L. (1985). The ecology of foraging behavior: Implications for animal learning and memory. *Ann. Rev. Psychol., 36*, 141–169.

Kammerman, M. (Ed.). (1977). *Sensory isolation and personality change.* Springfield, IL: Thomas.

Kamerman, S. (1986, February). *Infant care usage in the United States.* Report to the National Academy of Sciences Ad Hoc committee on policy issues in child care for infants and toddlers. Washington, DC.

Kanfer, F. H., Karoly, P., & Newman, A. (1975). Reduction in children's fear of the dark by competence-related and situational threat-related verbal cues. *J. Clin. Psychol., 43*, 251–258.

Kapatos, G., & Gold, R. M. (1972). Tongue cooling during drinking: A regulator of water intake in rats. *Science, 176*, 685–686.

Kaplan, R. M. (1982). Nader's raid on the testing industry. *Amer. Psychol., 37*, 15–23.

Kary, S. (1984). Personal communication. (My thanks to Dr. Kary for his suggestion.)

Kaslow, F. (1992). Thirty-plus and not married. In B. R. Wainrib (Ed.), *Gender issues across the life cycle.* New York: Springer Publishing Co.

Kassin, S. M., Ellsworth, P. C., & Smith, V. L. (1989). The "general acceptance" of psychological research on eyewitness testimony. *Amer. Psychol., 44*, 1089–1098.

Kastenbaum, R., & Costa, P. T. (1977). Psychological perspectives on death. *Ann. Rev. Psychol., 28*, 225–249.

Katkin, E. S. (1985). Polygraph testing, psychological research and public policy. *Amer. Psychol., 40,* 346–347.

Katz, D., & Braley, K. (1958). Verbal stereotypes and racial prejudice. In E. Maccoby, T. Newcomb, and E. Hautley (Eds.), *Readings in social psychology.* New York: Holt, Rinehart and Winston.

Kavanaugh, R. E. (1974). *Facing death.* Baltimore: Penguin Books.

Keeton, W. T. (1974). The mystery of pigeon homing. *Sci. Amer., 231*(6).

Kellogg, R. T. (1980). Is conscious attention necessary for long-term storage? *J. Exp. Psychol. Hum. Lrn. Mem., 6,* 379–390.

Kellogg, W. N., & Kellogg, L. A. (1933). *The ape and the child.* New York: McGraw-Hill.

Kelton, E. (1993). Visions of a lost world. *American History Illustrated,* January-February, 50–59.

Kernberg, O. F., Bernstein, C. S., Coyne, R., Applebaum, D. A., Horwitz, H., & Voth, T. J. (1972). Psychotherapy and psychoanalysis: Final report of the Menninger Foundation's psychotherapy research project. *Bull. Menninger Clin., 36,* 1–276.

Kesner, R. P., & Conner, H. S. (1972). Independence of short- and long-term memory: A neural system analysis. *Science, 176,* 432–434.

Kidd, K. K. (1985). Quoted in "Depression and the family." *Sci. News, 127,* 360.

Kihlstrom, J. F., Barnhardt, T. M., & Tataryn, D. J. (1992). The psychological unconscious: Found, lost, and regained. *Amer. Psychol., 47,* 788–791.

Kimble, D. P. (1990). Functional effects of neural grafting in the mammalian central nervous system. *Psychol. Bull., 108,* 462–479.

Kinsbourne, M., & Wood, F. (1975). Short-term memory processes and the amnesia syndrome. In D. Deutsch and J. Deutsch (Eds.), *Short-term memory.* New York: Academic Press.

Klatzky, R. L. (1980). *Human memory: Structures and processes* (2d ed.). San Francisco: W. H. Freeman.

_____. (1984). *Memory and awareness: An information processing perspective.* New York: W. H. Freeman.

Kline, M. V. (1972). The production of antisocial behavior through hypnosis: New clinical data. *Int. J. Clin. Exp. Hyp., 2,* 80–94.

Kluft, R. (1991). Multiple personality disorder. In A. Tasnan, & S. Goldfinger, Eds. *Review of psychiatry, vol. 10.* Washington, DC: American Psychiatric Press.

Kobasa, S. C., Hilker, R. R., & Maddi, S. R. (1979). Who stays healthy under stress? *J. Occ. Med., 21,* 595–598.

Kobasa, S. C., Maddi, S. R., & Kahn, S. (1980). Intrinsic motivation and health. In H. I. Day (Ed.), *Advances in intrinsic motivation and aesthetics.* New York: Plenum.

_____. (1981) *Hardiness and health: A prospective study.* Mimeograph received from authors.

Kohlberg, L. (1963). Moral development and identification. In H. W. Stevenson (Ed.), *Yearbook of the national society for the study of education: 1. Child psychology.* Chicago: University of Chicago Press.

Kokkinidis, L. K., & Anisman, H. (1980). Amphetamine models of paranoid schizophrenia: An overview and elaboration of animal experimentation. *Psychol. Bull., 88,* 551–579.

Kolata, G. (1983). Math genius may have hormonal basis. *Science, 222,* 1312.

Kolodny, R. C., Masters, W. H., Kolodner, R. M., & Toro, G. (1974). Depression of plasma testosterone levels after chronic intensive marijuana use. *New Eng. J. Med., 290,* 872–874.

Kovacs, A. L. (1992). Helping men at midlife: Can the blind ever see? In B. R. Wainrib (Ed.), *Gender issues across the life cycle.* New York: Springer Publishing Co.

Krantz, D. S., & Manuck, S. B. (1985). Acute psychophysiologic reactivity and risk of cardiovascular disease: A review and methodologic critique. *Psychol. Bull., 96,* 435–464.

Krasnoff, A. G. (1981). The sex difference in self-assessed fears. *Sex Roles, 7,* 19–23.

Kübler-Ross, E. (1969). *On death and dying.* New York: Macmillan.

_____. (1975). *Death: The final stage of growth.* Englewood Cliffs, NJ: Prentice-Hall.

Kuehn, J. L., & Crinella, F. M. (1969). Sensitivity training: Interpersonal "overkill" and other problems. *Amer. J. Psychiat., 126,* 840–845.

L

Lachman, S. J. (1983). Psychophysiological interpretation of voodoo illness and voodoo death. *Omega, 13,* 345–360.

References

Lamb, M. E. (1979). Paternal influences and the father's role. *Amer. Psychol., 34,* 938–943.

Lambert, N. M., Hartsough, C. S., & Zimmerman, I. L. (1976). The comparative predictive efficiency of intellectual and nonintellectual components of high school functioning. *Amer. J. Orthopsychiat., 46,* 109–122.

Lambert, W. W., & Lambert, W. E. (1964). *Social psychology.* Englewood Cliffs, NJ: Prentice-Hall.

Land, E. H. (1977). The retinex theory of color vision. *Sci. Amer., 237*(6).

Lang, P. J., & Melamed, B. G. (1969). Case report: Avoidance conditioning therapy of an infant with chronic rumative vomiting. *J. Abnorm. Psychol., 74,* 1–8.

Latané, B., & Darley, J. M. (1970). *The unresponsive bystander: Why doesn't he help?* Englewood Cliffs, NJ: Prentice-Hall.

Laurence, J. R. (1983). Hypnotically created memory among highly hypnotizable subjects. *Science, 222,* 523–524.

Lazarus, R. S. (1974). *The riddle of man.* Englewood Cliffs, NJ: Prentice-Hall.

Lazarus, R. S., & Folkman, S. (1984). *Stress, appraisal, and coping.* New York: Springer.

Leary, D. E. (1992). William James and the art of human understanding. *Amer. Psychol., 47,* 152–160.

Lebovitz, P. S. (1972). Feminine behavior in boys: Aspects of its outcome. *Amer. J. Psychiat., 128,* 1283–1289.

Lerner, R. M., & Frank, P. (1974). Relations of race and sex to supermarket helping behavior. *J. Soc. Psychol., 94,* 201–203.

Lerner, R. M., & Hultsch, D. E. (1983). *Human development: A life-span perspective.* New York: McGraw-Hill.

Levant, R. (1992). The new father roles. In B. R. Wainrib (Ed.), *Gender issues across the life cycle.* New York: Springer Publishing Co.

Levanthal-Belfer, L., Cowan, P., & Cowan, C. (1992). Satisfaction with child care arrangements: Effects on adaptation to parenthood. *American Journal of Orthopsychiatry, 62,* 165–177.

Levine, J. D., & Gordon, N. C. (1985). Quoted in "The subtle strength of placebos." *Sci. News, 127,* 25.

Levine, R. V., West, L. J., & Reiss, H. T. (1980). Perceptions of time and punctuality in the United States and Brazil. *J. Pers. Soc. Psychol., 38,* 541–550.

Levinson, D., Vaillant, G., & Gould, R. (1975). Adult life cycles. *APA Monitor, 6*(9 & 10).

Levinson, D. J. (1978). *The seasons of a man's life.* New York: Knopf.

Lewinsohn, P. M., Mischel, W., Chaplin, W., & Barton, R. (1980). Social competence and depression: The role of illusory self-perceptions. *J. Abn. Psychol., 89,* 203–212.

Libet, B., Gleason, C. A., Wright, W. W., & Pearl, D. K. (1983). Time of conscious intention to act in relation to onset of cerebral activity (readiness-potential). *Brain, 106,* 623–642.

Lifton, R. (1961). *Thought reform and the psychology of totalism.* New York: Norton.

Liljefors, I., & Rahe, R. H. (1970). An identical twin study of psychosocial factors in coronary heart disease in Sweden. *Psychosom. Med., 32,* 523–542.

Linville, P. W., & Jones, E. E. (1980). Polarized appraisals of out-group members. *J. Pers. Soc. Psychol., 38,* 689–703.

Lipton, D. S., & Marel, R. (1980). The white adolescent's drug odyssey. *Youth and Society, 11,* 397–413.

Livson, F. B. (1976). Patterns of personality development in middle-aged women: A longitudinal study. *Int'l. J. Aging & Human Devel., 7,* 107–115.

Llinas, R., & Pellionisa, A. (1979). Brain modeling by tensor networks theory and computer simulation. The cerebellum: Distributed processor for predictive coordination, *Neuroscience, 4.*

Lloyd, M. (1985). *Adolescence.* New York: Harper & Row.

Loeb, G. E. (1985). The functional replacement of the ear. *Sci. Amer., 252*(2).

Loeber, R. (1990). Development and risk factors of juvenile antisocial behavior and delinquency. *Child Psychology Review, 10,* 1–41.

Loftus, E. F. (1980). The malleability of human memory. *Amer. Sci., 67,* 312–320.

_____. (1984). Eyewitnesses; Essential but unreliable. *Psychology Today, 181*(2).

Loftus, E. F., & Klinger, M. R. (1992). Is the unconscious smart or dumb? *American Psychologist, 47*, 761–765.

Lombroso-Ferrero, G. (1911). *Criminal man.* New York: Putnam's.

Lopez, B. H. (1978). *Of wolves and men.* New York: Scribner's.

Loque, A. W. (1986). *The psychology of eating and drinking.* New York: W. H. Freeman.

Lore, R., & Schultz, L. (1993). Control of human aggression. *Amer. Psychol., 48*, 16–25

Lorenz, K. (1952). *King Solomon's ring.* New York: Crowell.

_____. (1963). *On aggression.* New York: Harcourt Brace Jovanovich.

Lorenz, M. (1961). Problems posed by schizophrenic language. *Arch. Gen. Psychiat., 4*, 603–610.

Luce, G. G. (1971). *Body time.* New York: Random House.

Luria, A. R. (1968). *The mind of a mnemonist.* New York: Basic Books.

Lyell, R. G. (1984). Personal communication.

Lykken, D. T. (1981). *A tremor in the blood.* New York: McGraw-Hill.

_____. (1987). An alternate explanation for low or zero sib correlations. *Beh. Brain Sci., 10*, 31.

Lynch, G., & Baudry, M. (1984). The biochemistry of memory: A new and specific hypothesis. *Science, 225*, 1057–1063.

Lytton, H., & Romney, D. (1991). Parents' differential socialization of boys and girls: A meta-analysis. *Psychol. Bull., 109*, 267–296.

M

Maccoby, E. E., & Jacklin, C. N. (1974). *The psychology of sex differences.* Stanford, CA: Stanford University Press.

Mackenzie, B. (1984). Explaining race differences in IQ. *Amer. Psychol., 39*, 1214–1233.

Madden, N., & Slavin, R. (1983). Mainstreaming students with mild handicaps: Academic and social outcomes. *Review of Educational Research, 53*, 519–569.

Maddison, S., Wood, R. J., Rolls, E. T., Rolls, B. J., & Gibbs, J. (1980). Drinking in the rhesus monkey: Peripheral factors. *J. Comp. Physiol. Psychol., 94*, 365–374.

Malinowski, B. (1929). *The sexual life of savages in northwestern Melanesia.* New York: Harcourt Brace Jovanovich.

Mandler, G. (1984). *Mind and body: Psychology of emotion and stress.* New York: Norton.

Mandler, J. M., & Ritchey, G. H. (1977). Long-term memory for pictures. *J. Exp. Psychol.: Hum. Lrn. Mem., 3*, 386–396.

Manning, A. (1967). *An introduction to animal behavior.* Reading, MA: Addison-Wesley.

Marcia, J. E. (1980). Identity in adolescence. In J. Adelson (Ed.), *Handbook of adolescent psychology.* New York: Wiley.

Margules, D. L., & Olds, J. (1962). Identical "feeding" and "rewarding" systems in the lateral hypothalamus of rats. *Science, 135*, 374–375.

Marks, I. (1979). Conditioning models for clinical syndromes are out of date. *Beh. Brain Sci., 2*, 175–176.

Martinez, J. L., Jr., Jensen, R. A., Messing, R. B., Vasquez, B. J., Soumireau-Mourat, S., Geddes, D., Laing, K. C., & McGaugh, J. L. (1980). Central and peripheral actions of amphetamine on memory storage. *Brain Res., 182*, 157–166.

Martinez, J. L., Jr., Jensen, R. A., Vasquez, B. J., Lacob, J. S., McGaugh, J. L., & Purdy, R. E. (1979). Acquisition deficits induced by sodium nitrite in rats and mice. *Psychopharm., 60*, 221–228.

Martinko, M. J., & Gardner, W. L. (1983). A methodological review of sex-related access discrimination problems. *Sex Roles, 9*, 825–839.

Maslow, A. H. (1954). *Motivation and personality.* New York: Harper & Row.

_____. (1968). *Toward a psychology of being* (2d ed.). New York: D. Van Nostrand.

Massaro, D. W. (1970). Forgetting: Interference or decay? *J. Exp. Psychol., 83*, 238–243.

Matarazzo, J. D. (1985). Psychotherapy. In G. A. Kimble and K. Schlesinger (Eds.), *Topics in the history of psychology.* Hillsdale, NJ: Erlbaum.

References

_____. (1990). Psychological assessment versus psychological testing: Validation from Binet to the school, clinic, and courtroom. *Amer. Psychol., 45*, 999–1017.

Matson, F. W. (1964). *The broken image.* New York: Braziller.

Maxwell, J. (1969). *Skimming and scanning improvement.* New York: McGraw-Hill.

McCaul, K. D., & Malott, J. M. (1984). Distraction and coping with pain. *Psychol. Bull., 95*, 516–533.

McClelland, D. C. (1973). Testing for competence rather than for "intelligence." *Amer. Psychol., 28*, 1–14.

McClelland, D. C., Atkinson, J. W., Clark, R. A., & Lowell, E. L. (1953). *The achievement motive.* New York: Appleton-Century-Crofts.

McCloskey, M., & Zaragonza, M. (1985). Quoted in "How malleable are eyewitness memories?" *Sci. News, 127*, 164.

McConnell, J. V. (1989). Reinvention of subliminal perception. *The Skeptical Inquirer, 13*, 427–428.

McConnell, J. V., Cutler, R. L., & McNeil, E. B. (1958). Subliminal stimulation: An overview. *Amer. Psychol., 13*, 229–242.

McCullough, D. (1982). *The great bridge.* New York: Simon & Schuster.

McFarland, D. (Ed.). (1981). *The Oxford companion to animal behaviour.* New York: Oxford University Press.

McGaugh, J. L. (1983). Hormonal influences on memory. *Ann. Rev. Psychol., 34*, 297–324.

McGee, M. (1980). Faith, fantasy, and flowers: A content analysis of the American sympathy card. *Omega, 11*, 25–35.

McGill, M. E. (1980). *The 40- to 60-year-old male.* New York: Simon & Schuster.

McGlynn, F. D., & O'Brien, L. (1972). The semiautomated treatment of a phobia: A case study. *J. Clin. Psychol., 28*, 228–230.

McGrath, E. (1992). New treatment strategies for women in the middle. In B. R., Wainrib (Ed.), *Gender issues across the life cycle.* New York: Springer Publishing Co.

McGrath, R. D. (1985, February 26–28). The myth of frontier violence. *Harpers.*

McGuire, W. J. (1964). Inducing resistance to persuasion: Some contemporary approaches. In L. Berkowitz (Ed.), *Advances in experimental social psychology.* New York: Academic Press.

McMahon, F. B., & McMahon, J. W. (1983). *Abnormal behavior: Psychology's view.* Homewood, IL: Dorsey Press.

McMahon, J. (1987). [Untitled John Wesley Hardin poem.]

McWilliams, N. (1992). The worst of both worlds: Dilemmas of contemporary young women. In B. R. Wainrib (Ed.), *Gender issues across the life cycle.* New York: Springer Publishing Co.

Meador, B. D., & Rogers, C. R. (1973). Client-centered therapy. In R. Corsini (Ed.), *Current psychotherapy.* Itasca, IL: Peacock.

Meece, J. L., Parsons, J. E., Kaczala, C. M., Goff, S. B., & Futterman, R. (1982). Sex differences in math achievement: Toward a model of academic choice. *Psychol. Bull., 91*, 324–348.

Meehl, P. E. (1956). Wanted—a good cookbook. *Amer. Psychol., 11*, 262–272.

Melnechuk, T. (1983). The dream machine. *Psychology Today, 17*(11).

Melzack, R. (1987). Interview in "Pain's Gatekeeper." *Psychol. Today, 21*(8).

Melzack, R., & Wall, P. D. (1982). *The challenge of pain.* New York: Basic Books.

Merz, W. R., & Rutherford, B. M. (1972). Differential teacher regard for creative students and achieving students. *Calif. J. Educ. Res., 23*, 83–90.

Mesquita, B., & Frijda, N. H. (1992). Cultural variations in emotions: A review. *Psychol. Bull., 112*, 179–204.

Milgram, S. (1977). *The individual in a social world.* Reading, MA: Addison-Wesley.

Miller, G. A. (1962). *Psychology: The science of mental life.* New York: Harper & Row.

Miller, G. S. (1956). The magical number seven plus or minus two: Some limits on our capacity for processing information. *Psychol. Rev., 63*, 81–96.

Miller, J. A. (1983). Lessons from the lab. *Sci. News, 124*, 394–396.

Miller, N. E. (1985). Rx: Biofeedback. *Psychology Today, 19*(2).

Miller, R. C., & Berman, J. S. (1983). The efficacy of cognitive behavior therapies: A quantitative review of the research evidence. *Psychol. Bull., 9*, 39–53.

Miller, T., Turner, C., Tindale, R. S., Posavac, E., & Dugoni, B. (1991). Reasons for the trend toward null findings in research on Type A behavior. *Psychol. Bull., 110*, 409–485.

Miller, W. R., & Orr, J. (1980). Nature and sequence of neuro-psychological deficits in alcoholics. *J. Stud. Alco., 41*, 325–337.

Millodot, M. (1982). Accommodation and refraction of the eye. In H. B. Barlow and J. D. Mollon (Eds.), *The senses.* New York: Cambridge University Press.

Millon, T. (1981). *Disorders of personality.* New York: John Wiley & Sons.

Mollon, J. D. (1982). Colour vision and colour blindness. In H. B. Barlow and J. D. Mollon (Eds.), *The senses.* New York: Cambridge University Press.

Money, J. (1974). Differentiation of gender identity. *Master lectures on physiological psychology.* Tape. Washington, DC: American Psychological Association.

_____. (1980). *Love and love sickness.* Baltimore: Johns Hopkins University Press.

Monk, T. H. (1983). Quoted in "Clocks for mind and body." *Sci. News, 10*, 154.

Montagu, A. (1964). *Man's most dangerous myth: The fallacy of race* (4th ed.). New York: World.

_____. (1974). Aggression and the evolution of man. In R. E. Whalen (Ed.), *The neuropsychology of aggression.* New York: Plenum.

Moore, T. E. (1984). Subliminal delusion. *Psychology Today, 19*(7).

Moore-Ede, M. C. (1986, December 26). [Interview.] *New York Times.*

Moore-Ede, M. C., Sulzman, F. M., & Fuller, C. A. (1982). *The clocks that time us.* Cambridge, MA: Harvard University Press.

Morgan, D. (1984, February 20). If you want good schools, stop doting on a test like the SAT. *Washington Post Nat. Week. Edition.*

Moroney, W. F., & Zenhausern, R. J. (1972). Detection of deception as a function of galvanic skin response recording methodology. *J. Psychol., 80*, 255–262.

Mosher, L. R., Gunderson, J. G., & Buchsbaum, S. (1973). Special report: Schizophrenia, 1972. *Schiz. Bull., 7.*

Moss, C. S. (1965). *Hypnosis in perspective.* New York: Macmillan.

Mossip, C. E. (1977, April). *Hemispheric specialization as seen in children's perception of faces.* Paper presented at meeting of Eastern Psychological Association, Boston.

Moyer, K. E. (1975). *The psychobiology of aggression.* New York: Harper & Row.

Mueller, C. G. (1979). Some origins of psychology as science. *Ann. Rev. Psychol., 30*, 9–29.

Munroe, R. L., & Munroe, R. H. (1971). Male pregnancy symptoms and cross identity in three societies. *J. Soc. Psychol., 84*, 11–25.

Munsinger, H. (1975). The adopted child's IQ: A critical review. *Psychol. Bull., 82*, 623–659.

Muntz, W. (1981). Color vision. In D. McFarland (Ed.), *The Oxford companion to animal behaviour.* New York: Oxford University Press.

Murphy, G., & Kovach, J. (1972). *Historical introduction to modern psychology.* New York: Harcourt Brace Jovanovich.

Muse, K. (1985). Quoted in "Medical root for PMS found." *Sci. News, 127*, 24.

Musto, D. (1989). America's first cocaine epidemic. *The Wilson Quarterly, Summer*, 59–64.

Muuss, R. E. (1975). *Theories of adolescence* (3d ed.). New York: Random House.

Myers, D. G. (1983). *Social psychology.* New York: McGraw-Hill.

Myers, J. J. (1984). Right hemisphere language: Science or fiction? *Amer. Psychol., 39*, 315–319.

N

Nassau, K. (1980). The causes of color. *Sci. Amer., 243*(4).

Neal, A., & Turner, S. (1991). Anxiety disorders research with African Americans: Current status. *Psychol. Bull., 109*, 400–410.

References

Neufeld, R. W. J., & Davidson, P. O. (1971). The effects of various and cognitive rehearsals on pain tolerance. *J. Psychosom. Res., 15,* 329–335.

Neugarten, B. L. (1976). Adaptation and the life cycle. *Coun. Psychol., 6,* 16–20.

_____. (1977). Personality changes in adulthood. *Master lectures on brain-behavior relationships.* Tape 14/16. Washington, DC: American Psychological Association.

_____. (1980, June). Must everything be a midlife crisis? *Prime Times.*

Newcomb, T. (1963). Persistence and repression of changed attitudes: Long-range studies. *J. Soc. Issues, 19,* 3–14.

Newman, B. M., & Newman, P. R. (1984). *Development through life: A psychosocial approach.* Homewood, IL: Dorsey Press.

Newton, I. (1952). Optics, book 3. In R. M. Hutchins (Ed.), *Great books of the Western world,* no. 34. Chicago: Encyclopaedia Britannica.

Nias, D. K. (1979). Marital choice: Matching or complementation? In M. Cook and G. Wilson (Eds.), *Love and attraction.* New York: Pergamon Press.

Nicholson, J. (1984). *Men and women: How different are they?* New York: Oxford University Press.

Nicholson, R. A., & Berman, J. S. (1983). Is follow-up necessary in evaluating psychotherapy? *Psychol. Bull., 93,* 261–278.

Nielsen, A. C. (1985, February 18). Survey quoted in *U.S. News & World Report.*

Nizer, L. (1966). *The jury returns.* New York: Doubleday.

Normann, R. A., Perlman, I., Kolb, K., Jones, J., & Daly, S. J. (1984). Direct excitory interactions between cones of different spectral types in the turtle retina. *Science, 224,* 625–627.

Nourse, A. E. (1964). *The body.* New York: Time.

O

O'Kelly, L. I., & Muckler, F. A. (1955). *Introduction to psychopathology.* Englewood Cliffs, NJ: Prentice-Hall.

Olds, J. (1956). Pleasure centers in the brain. *Sci. Amer., 195*(4).

Olton, D. S. (1978). Characteristics of spatial memory. In S. H. Hulse, H. F. Fowler, and W. K. Honig (Eds.), *Cognitive aspects of animal behavior.* Hillsdale, NJ: Erlbaum.

_____. (1979). Mazes, maps and memory. *Amer. Psychol., 34,* 583–596.

Opton, E., Jr. (1979). A psychologist takes a closer look at the recent landmark *Larry P.* opinion. *APA Monitor, 10*(12).

Orlinsky, D. E., Howard, K. I., & Hill, J. A. (1970). The patient's concerns in psychotherapy. *J. Clin. Psychol., 26,* 104–111.

Ornstein, R. E. (1977). *The psychology of consciousness* (2d ed.). New York: Harcourt Brace Jovanovich.

Ornstein, R., & Sobel, D. (1987). *The healing brain: A new perspective on the brain and health.* New York: Simon & Schuster.

Oster, G. (1970). Phosphenes. *Sci. Amer., 222*(2).

Oswald, I. (1966). *Sleep.* Baltimore: Penguin Books.

Owen, D. (1983, May). The last days of ETS. *Harper's,* 21–37.

Owens, J., Bower, G. H., & Black, J. B. (1979). The "soap opera" effect in story recall. *Mem. Cogn., 7,* 185–191.

P

Paikoff, R. L., & Brooks-Gunn, J. (1991). Do parent-child relationships change during puberty? *Psychol. Bull., 110,* 47–66.

Parke, R. (1983). Quoted in "Researchers make room for father." *APA Monitor, 14*(12).

Parkin, A. J. (1987). *Memory and Amnesia: An introduction.* New York: Blackwell.

Patterson, K. E., & Baddeley, A. D. (1977). When face recognition fails. *J. Exper. Psychol.: Hum. Lrn. Mem., 3,* 406–417.

Pazy, A. (1992). Sex-linked bias in promotion decisions: The role of candidate's career relevance and respondent's prior experience. *Psychology of Women Quarterly, 16,* 209–228.

Pearce, P. L. (1980). Strangers, travelers, and Greyhound terminals: A study of small-scale helping behaviors. *J. Pers. Soc. Psychol., 38,* 935–940.

Pearlin, L. I. (1975). Sex roles and depression. In N. Datan and L. Ginsberg (Eds.), *Life-span developmental psychology: Normative life crises.* New York: Academic Press.

Pederson, P. B. (1991). Multiculturism as a generic approach to counseling. *J. Couns. Devel., 70,* 6–12.

Penfield, W. (1959). The interpretive cortex. *Science, 129*(6).

Pengelley, E. T., & Asmundson, S. J. (1971). Annual biological clocks. *Sci. Amer., 224*(4).

Perry, J. S., & Slemp, S. R. (1980). Differences among three adult age groups in their attitudes toward self and others. *J. Genetic Psychol., 136,* 275–279.

Peskin, H. (1973). Influence of the developmental schedule of puberty and early development. *J. Youth Adol., 2,* 273–290.

Peters, J. (1971). *A class divided.* Garden City, NY: Doubleday.

Petersen, A. (1987). Those gangly years. *Psychology Today, 21*(9), 28–34.

Phares, V. (1992). Where's Poppa? The relative lack of attention to the role of fathers in child and adolescent psychopathology. *Amer. Psychol., 47,* 656–664.

Phares, V., & Compas, B. (1992). The role of fathers in child and adolescent psychopathology: Make room for Daddy. *Psychol. Bull., 111,* 387–412.

Phillips, J. L., Jr. (1969). *The origins of intellect: Piaget's theory.* San Francisco: W. H. Freeman.

Phillips, J. S., & Bierman, K. L. (1981). Clinical psychology: Individual methods. *Ann. Rev. Psychol., 32,* 405–438.

Piaget, J. (1929). *The child's conception of the world.* New York: Harcourt, Brace Jovanovich.

Pittner, M. S., & Houston, B. K. (1980). Response to stress, cognitive coping strategies, and the type A behavior pattern. *J. Pers. Soc. Psychol., 39,* 147–157.

Plomin, R., & Daniels, D. (1987). Why are children in the same family so different from one another? *Beh. Brain Sci., 10,* 1–16.

Plomin, R., De Fries, J. C., & McClearn, G. E. (1980). *Behavioral genetics: A primer.* San Francisco: W. H. Freeman.

Poggio, G. F., & Fischer, B. (1977). Binocular interaction and depth sensitivity of striate and prestriate cortical neurons of behaving rhesus monkeys. *J. Neurophysiol., 40,* 39–145.

Poggio, T. (1984). Vision by man and machine. *Sci. Amer., 250*(4).

Pokorny, A. D., & Mefferd, R. B. (1966). Geomagnetic fluctuation and disturbed behavior. *J. Nerv. Ment. Dis., 143,* 140–151.

Poole, D. A., & White, L. T. (1991). Effects of question repetition on the eyewitness testimony of children and adults. *Developmental Psychology, 27,* 975–986.

Pope, H. G., Jr., & Katz, D. L. (1987). Of muscles and mania. *Psychology Today, 21*(9).

Posner, M., Klein, R., Summers, J., & Buggie, S. (1973). On the selection of signals. *Mem. Cogn., 1,* 2–12.

Pratkanis, A. R., & Greenwold, A. G. (1988). Recent perspectives on unconscious processing: Still no marketing applications. *Psychology and Marketing, 5,* 337–353.

Premack, D., & Woodruff, G. (1978). Does the chimpanzee have a theory of mind? *Beh. Brain Sci., 1,* 515–526.

Prescott, J. W. (1979, December). Alienation of affection. *Psychology Today,* p. 124.

Preston, S. H. (1984). Children and the elderly in the U.S. *Sci. Amer., 10*(13).

Pribram, K. H. (1971). *Languages of the brain: Experimental paradoxes and principles in neuropsychology.* Englewood Cliffs, NJ: Prentice-Hall.

Probst, T., Krafczyk, S., & Brandt, T. (1984). Interaction between perceived self-motion and object motion impairs vehicle guidance. *Science, 225,* 536–538.

Prochaska, J., DiClemente, C., & Norcross, J. (1992). In search of how people change: Applications to addictive behaviors. *Amer. Psychol., 47,* 1102–1114.

Q

Quattrone, G. A. (1985). On the congruity between internal states and action. *Psychol. Bull., 98,* 3–40.

R

Rachlin, H. (1985). Pain and behavior. *Beh. Brain Sci., 8,* 42–53.

References

Ransford, H. E., & Palisi, B. (1992). Has there been a resurgence of racist attitudes in the general population? *Sociological Spectrum, 12,* 231–255.

Rapoport, J. L. (1989). *The boy who couldn't stop washing: The experience and treatment of obsessive-compulsive disorders.* New York: Dutton.

Reedy, M. N. (1983). Personality and aging. In D. S. Woodruff and J. E. Birren (Eds.), *Aging: Scientific perspectives and social issues* (2d ed.). Monterey, CA: Brooks/Cole.

Reis, H. T., Nezlek, J., & Wheeler, L. (1980). Physical attractiveness in social interaction. *J. Pers. Soc. Psychol., 38,* 604–617.

Reisman, J. M. (1966). *The development of clinical psychology.* Englewood Cliffs, NJ: Prentice-Hall.

Rennie, T. (1972). Prognosis in manic depressive psychosis. *Amer. J. Psychiat., 98,* 801–814.

Restak, R. (1984). *The brain.* New York: Bantam Books.

Richardson, D., Vinsel, A., & Taylor, S. P. (1980). Female aggression as a function of attitudes toward women. *Sex Roles, 6,* 265–271.

Rivlin, R., & Gravelle, K. (1984). *Deciphering the senses.* New York: Simon & Schuster.

Rhodes, N., & Wood, W. (1992). Self-esteem and intelligence affect influenceability: The mediating role of message reception. *Psychol. Bull., 111,* 156–171.

Roberts, D. F., & Backen, D. M. (1981). Mass communication effects. *Amer. Rev. Psychol., 32,* 307–356.

Robinson, F. P. (1941). *Effective behavior.* New York: Harper & Row.

Robinson, H., & Robinson, N. (1970). Mental retardation. In P. H. Mussen (Ed.), *Carmichael's manual of child psychology* (3d ed.). New York: Wiley.

Rodin, J. (1984). A sense of control. *Psychology Today, 18*(12).

Rogers, C. R. (1951). *Client-centered therapy: Its current practice, implications and theory.* Boston: Houghton Mifflin.

———. (1961). *On becoming a person—A therapist's view of psychotherapy.* Boston: Houghton Mifflin.

———. (1986). Client-centered therapy. In I. L. Kutash and A. Wolf (Eds.), *Psychotherapist's casebook: Therapy and technique in practice.* San Francisco: Jossey-Bass.

Rogers, R. W., & Thistlethwaite, D. L. (1969). An analysis of active and passive denses inducing resistance to persuasion. *J. Per. Soc. Psychol., 11,* 301–308.

Romagnano, M. A., & Hamill, R. W. (1984). Spinal sympathetic pathway: An enkephalin ladder. *Science, 225,* 737–739.

Rorabaugh, W. J. (1979). *The alcoholic republic.* New York: Oxford University Press.

Rosenfeld, A. (1985). Stretching the span. *Wilson Quart., 9*(1).

Rosenzweig, M. (1962). The mechanisms of hunger and thirst. In L. Postman (Ed.), *Psychology in the making.* New York: Knopf.

Rosenzweig, M. R. (1984). Experience, memory, and the brain. *Amer. Psychol., 39,* 365–376.

Rosenzweig, M. R., Bennett, E. L., & Diamond, M. C. (1972). Brain changes in response to experience. *Sci. Amer., 226*(2).

Rotton, J., & Kelly, I. W. (1985). Much ado about the full moon: A meta-analysis of lunar-lunacy research. *Psychol. Bull., 97,* 286–306.

Rubenstein, A. (1992). Clinical issues in the treatment of adolescent girls. In B. R. Wainrib (Ed.), *Gender issues across the life cycle.* New York: Springer Publishing Co.

Rugg, M. (1985). Quoted in "Does the brain trigger an immune response?" *Science 85, 6*(2).

Rule, B. G., & Nesdale, A. R. (1976). Emotional arousal and aggressive behavior. *Psychol. Bull., 83,* 851–863.

Russell, J. A., & Ward, L. M. (1984). Environmental psychology. *Ann. Rev. Psychol., 33,* 651–688.

Russell, M. J., Switz, G. M., & Thompson, K. (1977, June). Olfactory influences on the human menstrual cycle. Paper. Amer. Assn. Advan. Sci.

Rust, S. M., & Black, K. A. (1972). The application of two mnemonic techniques following rote memorization of a free recall task. *J. Psychol., 80,* 247–253.

Rust, V. D. (1984). What can we learn from others? *Wilson Quart., 7*(1).

Ruttenber, A. J., & Luke, J. L. (1984). Heroin-related deaths: New epidemiologic insights. *Science, 226,* 14–20.

S

Sadker, M., & Sadker, D. (1985). Sexism in the schoolroom of the '80s. *Psychology Today, 19*(3).

Sagan, C. (1977). *The dragons of Eden.* New York: Random House.

Sagar, H. A., & Schofield, J. W. (1980). Racial and behavioral cues in black and white children's perceptions of ambiguously aggressive acts. *J. Pers. Soc. Psychol., 39,* 590–598.

Samuelson, F. (1980). J. B. Watson's Little Albert, Cyril Burt's twins, and the need for a critical science. *Amer. Psychol., 35,* 619–625.

Sarason, I., & Sarason, B. (1993). *Abnormal psychology.* Englewood Cliffs, NJ: Prentice-Hall, Inc.

Sarason, S. B., Mandler, G., & Craighill, P. G. (1952). The effect of differential instructions on anxiety and learning. *J. Abnorm. Soc. Psychol., 47,* 561.

Scarf, M. (1977). Husbands in crisis. In L. Allman and D. Jaffe (Eds.), *Readings in adult psychology: Contemporary perspectives.* New York: Harper & Row.

Schachter, S., & Rodin, J. (Eds.). (1974). *Obese humans and rats.* Potomac, MD: Erlbaum.

Schachter, S., & Singer, J. (1962). Cognitive, social, and psychological determinants of emotional state. *Psychol. Rev., 29,* 379–399.

Schaie, K. W. (Ed.). (1983). *Longitudinal studies of adult psychological development.* New York: Adult Development and Aging.

Schein, E. H., Schneider, I., & Barker, C. H. (1961). *Coercive persuasion.* New York: Norton.

Schettino, A. P., & Borden, R. J. (1976). Sex differences in response to naturalistic crowding: Affective reactions to group size and group density. *Pers. Soc. Psychol. Bull., 2,* 67–70.

Schleifer, S. J. (1985). Quoted in "Severe depression depresses immunity." *Sci. News, 127,* 100.

Schuckit, M. A. (1980, August). Cited in L. Asher, Genetic alcoholism? *Psychol. Today.*

Schulman, R. E., & London, P. (1963). Hypnosis and verbal learning. *J. Abnorm. Soc. Psychol., 67,* 363.

Schultz, D. P. (1969). *A history of modern psychology.* New York: Academic Press.

Schwartz, G. E. (1979). The brain as a health care system. In G. Stone, N. Adler, and F. Cohen (Eds.), *Health psychology.* San Francisco: Jossey-Bass.

Schwartz, J. C. (1979b). Childhood origins of psychopathology. *Amer. Psychol., 34,* 879–885.

Schwartz, R. (1980). How rich a theory of mind? *Beh. Brain Sci., 3,* 616–618.

Schwartz, S. H., & Gottlieb, A. (1980). Bystander anonymity and reactions to emergencies. *J. Pers. Soc. Psychol., 39,* 418–430.

Schwartz, W. J. (1984). Quoted in "Fetuses watch the clock." *Sci. News, 126,* 266.

Scovern, A. W., & Kilmann, P. R. (1980). Status of electroconvulsive therapy: Review of the outcome literature. *Psychol. Bull., 87,* 260–303.

Scruggs, T., & Mastropieri, A. (1992). Classroom applications of mnemonic instruction: Acquisition, maintenance, and generalization. *Exceptional Children, 58,* 219–229.

Sears, R. R., Maccoby, E. E., & Levin, H. (1966). Development of the gender role. In F. A. Beach (Ed.), *Sex and behavior.* New York: Wiley.

Seedman, A., & Hellman, P., (1974). *Chief!* New York: Arthur Fields Books.

Seevers, M. (1968). Use, misuse, and abuse of amphetamine-type drugs from the medical viewpoint. In J. Russo (Ed.), *Amphetamine abuse.* Springfield, IL: Thomas.

Segall, M., Dasen, P., Berry, J., & Poortinga, Y. (1990). *Human behavior in global perspective.* Boston: Allyn & Bacon.

Selcer, R. U., & Hilton, I. R. (1972). Cultural differences in the acquisition of sex roles. *Proceed. 80th Ann. Conv. Amer. Psychol. Assn.*

Seligman, M. E. P. (1971). Phobias and preparedness. *Beh. Ther., 2,* 307–320.

Selye, J. (1956). *The stress of life.* New York: McGraw-Hill.

Senk, S., & Usiskin, Z. (1984). Quoted in "Inventing gender differences." *Science 85, 6*(5).

Sheldon, W. H. (1936). *The varieties of temperament: A psychology of constitutional differences.* New York: Harper & Row.

References

Sheridan, C. L., & King, R. G., Jr. (1972). Obedience to authority with an authentic victim. *Proceed. 80th Ann. Conv. Amer. Psychol. Assn.*

Sherif, C. W. (1982). Social and psychological bases of social psychology. In A. G. Kraut (Ed.), *The G. Stanley Hall lecture series* (Vol. 2). Washington, DC: American Psychological Association.

Sherman, M. (1938). Verbalization and language symbols in personality adjustment. *Amer. J. Psychiat., 75,* 621–640.

Sherrod, D. (1982). *Social psychology.* New York: Random House.

Shinn, M. (1978). Father absence and children's cognitive development. *Psychol. Bull., 85,* 295–324.

Shotland, R. L. (1985). When bystanders just stand by. *Psychology Today, 19*(6).

Sidorowicz, L. S., & Lunney, G. S. (1980). Baby X revisited. *Sex Roles, 6,* 67–73.

Siegel, R. K. (1983). Quoted in "Natural highs in natural habitats." *Sci. News, 124,* 300–301.

_____. (1985). Quoted in "Cocaine use: Disturbing signs." *Sci. News, 128*(14).

Silverstein, L. (1991). Transforming the debate about child care and maternal employment. *Amer. Psychol., 46,* 1025–1032.

Simons, A. D. (1984). Quoted in "Changing ideas in depression." *Sci. News, 125,* 58.

Simons, M. (1987, February 13). Brazil's health crisis: The plague is just one part. *New York Times.*

Skinner, B. F. (1957). *Verbal behavior.* Englewood Cliffs, NJ: Prentice-Hall.

_____. (1967). Autobiography. In E. G. Boring and Lindzey (Eds.), *A history of psychology in autobiography.* Englewood Cliffs, NJ: Prentice-Hall.

_____. (1983). Intellectual self-management in old age. *Amer. Psychol., 38,* 239–254.

_____. (1990). Can psychology be a science of the mind? *Amer. Psychol., 45,* 1206–1210.

Sloane, B. (1983). Health care: Physical and mental. In D. S. Woodruff and J. E. Birren (Eds.), *Aging: Scientific perspectives and social issues* (2d ed.). Monterey, CA: Brooks/Cole.

Smith, D. O. (1984). Quoted in "Aging at the nerve-muscle junction." *Sci. News, 125,* 376.

Smith, R. J., Griffith, J. E., Griffith, H. K., & Steger, M. J. (1980). When is a stereotype a stereotype? *Psychol. Rep., 46,* 643–651.

Snarey, J. R. (1985). Cross-cultural universality of social-moral development: A critical review of Kohlbergian research. *Psychol. Bull., 97,* 202–232.

Snow, C. P. (1966). *Variety of men.* New York: Scribner's.

Snyder, S. (1980). *Biological aspects of mental disorder.* New York: Oxford University Press.

Snyder, S. H. (1984). Drug and neurotransmitter receptors in the brain. *Science, 224,* 22–31.

_____. (1986). *Drugs and the brain.* New York: W. H. Freeman.

Sommer, R. (1969). *Personal space: The behavioral basis of design.* Englewood Cliffs, NJ: Prentice-Hall.

Spain, D., and Bianchi, S. M. (1983, May). How women have changed. *Amer. Demogr.*

Spanos, N. P. (1986). Hypnotic behavior: A social-psychological interpretation. *Beh. Brain Sci., 9,* 449–467.

Spear, N. E. (1978). *The processes of memories: Forgetting and retention.* Hillsdale, NJ: Erlbaum.

Spitz, R. A. (1946). Hospitalism: A follow-up report. *Psychoanal. Study Child, 2,* 113–117.

Springer, S. P., & Deutsch, G. (1985). *Left brain, right brain.* New York: W. H. Freeman.

Squire, L. (1985). Quoted in "ECT: New studies on how, why, who." *APA Monitor, 16*(3).

Square, L. R. (1987). *Memory and brain.* New York: Oxford University Press.

Starr, R. H. (1979). Child abuse. *Amer. Psychol., 34,* 872–878.

Statistical Abstracts of the United States. (1986). Washington, DC: U.S. Government Printing Office.

Steinberg, L. (1987). Bound to bicker. *Psychol. Today, 21*(9).

Steinberg, L., Dornbusch, S., & Brown, R. (1992). Ethnic differences in adolescent achievement: An ecological perspective. *Amer. Psychol., 47,* 723–729.

Stephens, R., & Cottrell, E. (1972). A follow-up study of 200 narcotic addicts committed for treatment under the Narcotic Addict Rehabilitation act (NARA). *Brit. J. Addict., 67,* 45–53.

Stern, P. C. (1984, January). Saving energy: The human dimension. *Technology Rev.* (Mass. Inst. Technology).

Sternberg, R. J. (1984). Reinventing psychology. *Wilson Quart., 8*(5).

Stewart, A. J., & Winter, D. G. (1974). Self-definition and social definition in women. *J. Pers., 42,* 238–259.

Stewart, T. D. (1969). Fossil evidence of human violence. *Transaction, 6,* 48–53.

Stillings, N. A., Feinstein, M. H., Garfield, J. L., Rissland, E. L., Rosenbaum, D. A., Weisler, S. E., & Baker-Ward, L. (1987). *Cognitive science: An introduction.* Cambridge, MA: MIT Press.

Stokols, D. (1978). A typology of crowding experiences. In A. Baum and Y. Epstein (Eds.), *Human response to crowding.* Hillsdale, NJ: Erlbaum.

Stone, I. (1980). *The origin.* Franklin Center, PA: Franklin Library.

Strauss, J. S. (1979). Social and cultural influences on psychopathology. *Ann. Rev. Psychol., 30,* 397–415.

Sue, S., & Okazaki, S. (1990). Asian-American educational achievements: A phenomenon in search of an explanation. *Amer. Psychol., 45,* 913–920.

Suomi, S. J. (1983). Social development in rhesus monkeys: Consideration of individual differences. In A. Oliverio and M. Zappella (Eds.), *The behavior of human infants.* New York: Plenum Press.

Swaab, D. F., & Fliers, E. (1984). Quoted in "Sex differences found in human brains." *Sci. News, 127,* 341.

Swartz, K. B., & Rosenblum, L. A. (1980). Operant responding by bonnet macaques for color videotape recordings of a social stimuli. *Anim. Learn. Behav., 8,* 322–331.

Szasz, T. S. (1961). *The myth of mental illness: Foundations of a theory of personal conduct.* New York: Harper & Row.

T

Tabakoff, B., Melchoir, C. L., & Hoffman, P. (1984). Factors in ethanol tolerance. *Science, 224,* 523.

Tannen, D. (1990). *You just don't understand.* New York: Ballantine Books.

Taub, J. M., & Berger, R. J. (1976). Extended sleep and performance: The Rip Van Winkle effect. *Psychon. Sci., 16,* 204–265.

Taylor, M. C., & Hall, J. A. (1982). Psychological androgyny: Theories, methods, and conclusions. *Psychol. Bull., 92,* 347–366.

Tebbel, J. (1974). *The media in America.* New York: Crowell.

Tesser, A. (1978). Self-generated attitude change. *Adv. Exp. Soc. Psychol., 11,* 289–338.

Thomas, K. (1983). *Man and the natural world.* New York: Pantheon Books.

Thompson, J. K., Jarvie, G. J., Lahey, B. B., & Cureton, K. J. (1982). Exercise and obesity: Etiology, physiology, and intervention. *Psychol. Bull., 91,* 55–79.

Thompson, R. F. (1967). *Foundations of physiological psychology.* New York: Harper & Row.

Thorndike, E. L. (1920). A constant error in psychological testing. *J. Appl. Psychol., 4,* 25–29.

Tinbergen, N. (1969). *Herring gull's world.* New York: Basic Books.

Tolman, E. C., Ritchie, B. F., & Kalish, D. (1946). Studies in spatial learning. *J. Exp. Psychol., 36,* 221–229.

Torrance, E. P. (1979). Unique needs of the creative child and adult. *Nat. Soc. Study Educ. Yrbk., 78,* 352–371.

_____. (1980). Creativity and futurism in education: Retooling. *Education, 100,* 298–311.

Tosteson, D. C. (1981). Lithium and mania. *Sci. Amer., 244*(4).

Traxler, A. J. (1979). Let's get gerontologized: Developing a sensitivity to aging. In *The multipurpose senior center concept: A training manual for practitioners working with the aging.* Springfield, IL: Illinois Department on Aging.

Traxler, A. J., & Linksvayer, R. D. (1973). Attitudes and age-related stress periods in adulthood. *Proceedings, APA Convention,* 779–780.

Traxler, A. T. (1988). Personal communication.

References

Tulving, E., & Partay, J. E. (1962). Concurrent effects of contextual constraint and word frequency on immediate recall and learning of verbal material. *Canad. J. Psychol., 16*, 83–95.

Turkheimer, E. (1991). Individual and group differences in adoption studies of IQ. *Psychol. Bull., 110*, 392–405.

Turkington, C. (1984, January). Ideology affects approach taken to alleviate PMS. *APA Monitor.*

Turner, S. M., Beidel, D. C., & Nathan, R. S. (1985). Biological factors in obsessive-compulsive disorders. *Psychol. Bull., 97*, 430–450.

U

Ullmann, L., & Krasner, L. (1969, 1975). *A psychological approach to abnormal behavior.* Englewood Cliffs, NJ: Prentice-Hall.

V

Vaillant, G. E., & Milofsky, E. S. (1982). The etiology of alcoholism. *Amer. Psychol., 37*, 494–503.

Valenstein, E. S. (1973). *Brain control: A critical examination of brain stimulation and psychosurgery.* New York: Wiley.

Vetter, H. (1969). *Language behavior and psychopathology.* Chicago: Rand McNally.

Von Frisch, K. (1963). *Man and the living world.* New York: Harcourt Brace Jovanovich.

W

Wade, C., & Tavris, C. (1993). *Psychology.* NY: HarperCollins College Publishers.

Wadden, T. A., & Anderson, C. H. (1982). The clinical use of hypnosis. *Psychol. Bull., 91*, 215–243.

Wainrib, B. (1992a). The aging female client: Developmental or disorder issues. In B. R. Wainrib (Ed.), *Gender issues across the life cycle.* New York: Springer Publishing Co.

_____. (1992b). Introduction: Gender issues in the aging population. In B. R. Wainrib (Ed.), *Gender issues across the life cycle.* New York: Springer Publishing Co.

Wakefield, J. (1992). The concept of mental disorder: On the boundary between biological facts and social values. *Amer. Psychol., 47*, 373–388.

Wallace, R. K., & Benson, H. (1972). The physiology of meditation. *Sci. Amer., 225*(2).

Wallach, M., Kogan, N., & Bem, O. (1962). Group influence on individual risk taking. *J. Abnor. Soc. Psychol., 9*, 101–106.

Waller, M. B., McBride, W. J., Gatto, G. J., Lumeng, L., & Li, Ting-Kai. (1984). Intragastric self-infusion of ethanol by ethanol-preferring and -nonpreferring lines of rats. *Science, 225*, 78–79.

Walsh, W. B., & Betz, N. E. (1985). *Tests and assessment.* Englewood Cliffs, NJ: Prentice-Hall.

Watson, J. B. (1928). *Psychological care of infant and child.* NY: W. W. Norton.

Webb, W. B. (1982). Quoted in "Staying up." *Psychology Today, 16*(3).

Webb, W. B., & Agnew, H. W. (1974). Sleep and waking in a time-free environment. *Aerosp. Med., 45*, 617–622.

Webb, W. B., & Cartwright, R. D. (1978). Sleep and dreams. *Ann. Rev. Psychol., 29*, 223–252.

Weber, A. L., Cary, M. S., Conner, N., & Keyes, P. (1980). Human non-24-hour sleep-wake cycles in an everyday environment. *Sleep, 2*, 347–354.

Wechsler, D. (1975). Intelligence defined and undefined: A relativistic appraisal. *Amer. Psychol., 30*, 135–139.

_____. (1981). *WAIS-R manual.* New York: Psychological Corporation and Harcourt Brace Jovanovich.

Weinberger, D. A., Schwartz, G. E., & Davidson, R. J. (1979). Low-anxious, high-anxious, and repressive coping styles: Psychometric patterns and behavioral and physiological responses to stress. *J. Abn. Psychol., 88*, 369–380.

Weiner, B. (1985). "Spontaneous" causal thinking. *Psychol. Bull., 97*, 74–84.

Weiner, R. D. (1984). Does electroconvulsive therapy cause brain damage? *Brain Beh. Sci., 7*, 1–47.

Weisberg, P., & Waldrop, P. B. (1972). Fixed-interval work habits of Congress. *J. Appl. Behav. Anal., 5*, 93–97.

Weisberg, R. W. (1986). *Creativity: Genius and other myths.* New York: W. H. Freeman.

Weisenberg, M. (1977). Cultural and racial reactions to pain. In M. Weisenberg (Ed.), *The control of pain.* New York: Psychological Dimensions.

Weiss, D. J., & Davidson, M. L. (1981). Test theory and methods. *Ann. Rev. Psychol., 32,* 629–658.

Weiss, J. M. (1972). Psychological factors in stress and disease. *Sci. Amer., 226*(6).

Weissman, M. M. (1985). Quoted in "Growing up with depression." *Sci. News, 127,* 344.

Wells, G. L. (1984). Do the eyes have it? More on expert eyewitness testimony. *Amer. Psychol, 39,* 1064–1065.

Whalen, R. E., & Simon, N. G. (1984). Biological motivation. *Ann. Rev. Psychol., 35,* 257–276.

White, G. L. (1980). Physical attractiveness and courtship. *J. Pers. Soc. Psychol., 39,* 660–668.

White, R. D., & John, K. E. (1984, April 16). Teenagers agree with parents on drugs, politics, and sex. *Washington Post National Weekly.*

Williams, G. (1987). *The age of miracles.* Chicago: Academy Publishers.

Windholz, G. (1987). Pavlov as a psychologist. *Biol. Sci., 22*(3).

Winfree, A. T. (1987). *The timing of biological clocks.* New York: W. H. Freeman.

Winfrey, O. (1987, April 14). [Discussion.] "Oprah Winfrey Show."

Wolf, S. (1950). Effects of suggestion and conditioning on the action of chemical agents in human subjects. *J. Clin. Inves., 29,* 100–109.

Wolf, S., & Wolff, H. G. (1947). *Human gastric function.* London: Oxford University Press.

Wolfe, D. A. (1985). Child-abusive parents: An empirical review and analysis. *Psychol. Bull., 97,* 462–482.

Wolpe, J., & Lazarus, A. A. (1966). *Behavior therapy techniques: A guide to the treatment of neurosis.* Elmsford, NY: Pergamon Press.

Wong, D. F. (1985). Quoted in "Deciphering dopamine's decline." *Sci. News, 127*(1).

Wood, W., Wong, F., & Chachere, J. (1991). Effects of media violence on viewers' aggression in unconstrained social interaction. *Psychol. Bull., 109,* 371–383.

Woolfolk, R. L. (1985). What's at stake in the mental illness controversy? *Amer. Psychol., 40,* 468.

Worchel, S., & Cooper, J. (1983). *Understanding social psychology.* Homewood, IL: Dorsey Press.

Wormser, R. (1962). *The story of the law.* New York: Simon & Schuster.

Wright, B. J., & Isenstein, V. R. (1975). *Psychological tests and minorities.* Rockville, MD: Nat. Inst. Ment. Health.

Wundt, W. (1873). *Principles of physiological psychology.* (Vol. 1, translated by E. B. Titchener, 1904; author's preface to first edition). New York: Macmillan.

Wurtman, R. J. (1985). Alzheimer's disease. *Sci. Amer., 252*(1).

Y

Yalom, I. D., & Lieberman, M. A. (1971). A study of encounter group casualties. *Arch. Gen. Psychiat., 256,* 16–30.

Yarnold, P. R., & Grimm, L. G. (1982). Time urgency among coronary-prone individuals. *J. Abnorm. Psychol., 91,* 175–177.

Yates, A. (1989). Current perspectives on the eating disorders: I. History, psychological and biological aspects. *J. Amer. Acad. Child Adoles. Psychiat., 28,* 813–828.

Yetman, N. (Ed.). (1991). *Majority and minority: The dynamics of race and ethnicity in American life.* Boston: Allyn & Bacon.

Young, J. Z. (1978). *Programs of the brain.* New York: Oxford University Press.

Youtz, R. P. (1968). Can fingers "see" color? *Psychol. Today, 1*(9).

Z

Zeichner, A., & Pihl, R. O. (1979). Effects of alcohol and behavior contingencies on human aggression. *J. Abn. Psychol., 88,* 153–160.

Zelazo, P. R., Zelazo, N. A., & Kolb, S. (1972). "Walking" in the newborn. *Science, 176,* 314–315.

Zigler, E., Taussig, C., & Black, K. (1992). Early childhood intervention: A promising preventative for juvenile delinquency. *Amer. Psychol., 47,* 997–1006.

References

Zimbardo, P. G. (1972, April). Pathology of imprisonment. *Society*, 3–8.

Zubek, J. P., Hughes, G. R., & Shepard, J. M. (1971). A comparison of the effects of prolonged sensory deprivation and perceptual deprivation. *Can. J. Behav. Sci. Rev. Can. Sci. Comp., 3,* 282–290.

Zuckerman, M., Larrance, D. T., Porac, J. F. A., & Blanck, P. D. (1980). Effects of fear of success on intrinsic motivation, causal attribution, and choice behavior. *J. Pers. Soc. Psychol., 39,* 503–513.

Zuckerman, M., & Wheeler, L. (1975). To dispel fantasies about the fantasy-based measure of fear of success. *Psychol. Bull., 82,* 932–946.

Zung, W. W. K., & Green, F. L., Jr. (1974). Seasonal variation of suicide and depression. *Arch. Gen. Psychiat., 30,* 89–91.

INDEX

Z

Credits

p. xxviii Eric Meola, The Image Bank; **p. 6** Richard Laird; FPG International; **p. 7** FPG International; **p. 8** The Bettman Archive; **p. 9** The Bettman Archive; **p. 10** FPG International; **p. 10** Brown Brothers; **p. 13** The Bettman Archive; **p. 13** © Myrleen Ferguson, Photo Edit; **p. 14** The Bettman Archive; **p. 18** © Vossar, FPG International; **p. 21** © Rogers, Monkmeyer; **p. 28** © Mimi Forsyth, Monkmeyer; **p. 31** The Bettman Archive; **p. 37** The Bettman Archive; **p. 37** © Rob Crandall, Stock Boston; **p. 39** Oscar Burriel/Latin Stock/Science Photo Library, Photo Researchers; **p. 42** © Michael Hart, FPG International; **p. 48** © Rogers, Monkmeyer; **p. 56** © Richard Gaul, FPG International; **p. 58** J. Croyle, Custom Stock Medical; **p. 63** © duomo; **p. 63** © Howard Sochurek, Woodfin Camp; **p. 66** © T. Orban; **p. 73** © J. Zimmerman, FPG International; **p. 76** © Lennart Nilsson, *Beyond Man*, Little, Brown & Co.; **p. 81** © Michael Serino, The Picture Cube; **p. 90** Charles Krebs, The Stock Market; **p. 97** © Lennart Nilsson, *Beyond Man*, Little Brown & Co.; **p. 107** © Owen Franken, Stock Boston; **p. 109** © Ben Rose Photography; **p. 110** © Enrico Feroelli, DOT; **p. 111** The Bettman Archive; **p. 112** © Peter Menzel, Stock Boston; **p. 115** Kaiser Porcelain Ltd.; **p. 117** The Bettman Archive; **p. 124** © Ron Chapple, FPG International; **p. 126** © Michael Grecco, Stock Boston; **p. 128** Courtesy of Dr. Neal Miller; **p. 130** © St. Louis Post-Dispatch; **p. 131** © Anthony Bannister, Animals, Animals; **p. 135** AP/World Wide Photos; **p. 137, 138, 139** Harry F. Harlow, University of Wisconsin, Primate Laboratory; **p. 140** © Ted Polumbaum; **p. 143** © Jeff Isaac Greenberg, Photo Researchers; © Bill Stanton, Int'l Stock; **p. 144** © Bruce Byers, FPG International; **p. 147** © J. Schultz, Alaska Stock; **p. 147** © Tony Freeman, Photo Edit; **p. 154** © Charles Krebs, The Stock Market; **p. 158** © 1984 James R. Fisher, Photo Researchers; **p. 164** © J. Allan Hobson and Hoffman-LaRoche, Inc; **p. 166** Historical Picture Services; **p. 168** The Bettman Archive; **p. 173** The Bettman Archive; **p. 174** © Daemmrich, Stock Boston; **p. 175** © Arlene Collins, Monkmeyer; **p. 182** © Darrell Gulin, Allstock; **p. 184** Superstock; **p. 186** From "Case Report: Avoidance Conditioning Therapy of an Infant with Chronic Ruminative Vomiting" by P. J. Lang and B. G. Melamed, 1969 Journal of Abnormal Psychology; **p. 191** Courtesy Debbi Allman; **p. 194** © Will Rapport, B. F. Skinner; **p. 199** © G. Goodwin; © Frank Siteman, Monkmeyer Press; **p. 203** Courtesy of Alfred Bandura, Stanford; **p. 204** A. Bandura, D. Ross, and S. A. Ross, "Imitation of Film-mediated Aggressive Models," Journal of Abnormal and Social Psychology 68 (1963) 3–11. Copyright by the American Psychological Association Reprinted by permission; **p. 205** © Tony Freeman, Photo Edit; **p. 206** © Kagen, Monkmeyer; **p. 207** © Myrleen Ferguson, Photo Edit; **p. 214** Stewart Cohen, Index Stock Photography; **p. 220** © 1988 Tony Freeman, Photo Edit; **p. 221** © Richard Hutchings, Info Edit; **p. 230** © Robert Brenner, Photo Edit; **p. 233** © CRNI Science Photo Library, Photo Researchers; **p. 235** AP/Wide World; **p. 237** © Alan Odie, Photo Edit; **p. 246** © Bill Losh, FPG International; **p. 249** © Richard Hutchings, InfoEdit; Historical Pictures Services, Inc.; **p. 253** © Peter Vandermark, Stock Boston; **p. 257** Comstock; **p. 259** From the work of Conel (A) 1947; (b) 1955; (c) 1959. From *Language of the Brain* by K. Pribram, Prentice-Hall, Inc., 1971. Reprinted by permission; **p. 260** Smithsonian Institution; **p. 262** Courtesy of California Special Olympics; **p. 266** AP/Wide World; **p. 274** Gianalberto Cigolini, The Image Bank; **p. 276** © Gaillard/Jerrican, Photo Researchers; **p. 280** © Nicholas DeSciose, Photo Researchers; **p. 281** © Lionel Delevingne, Stock Boston; **p. 282** © Gerry Cranham, Rapho/Photo Researchers; **p. 284** Rina Leen, Life Magazine, Time, Inc.; **p. 285**

© Arthur Tilley, FPG International; **p. 287** © Jerry Berndt, Stock Boston; **p. 290** © Jeffry W. Myers, FPG International; **p. 293** © Mimi Forsyth, Monkmeyer; **p. 298** Photo Edit; **p. 299** © 1988 Tony Freeman, Photo Edit; **p. 301** © Sally Cassidy, The Picture Cube; **p. 308** © Richard Hutchings, Photo Researchers; **p. 311** © Michael Newman, Photo Edit; **p. 314** From Bachrach et al., "The Control of Eating Behavior in an Anorexic by Operant Conditioning Techniques" in Ullman & Krasner, Case Studies in Behavior Modification. Holt, Tinehart & Winston, 1965. Photos courtesy of A. E. Bachrach; **p. 316** © Bill Gillette, Stock Boston; **p. 318** © Michael Hart, © Ken Chernus, FPG International; **p. 319** © Sybil Shackman, Monkmeyer; **p. 324** The Museum of Modern Art/Film Stills Archive; **p. 325** © Mark Scott, FPG International; **p. 328** © David Young-Wolff; **p. 329** © Howard Grey, Tony Stone Images; **p. 336** © Ariel Skeiley, The Stock Market; **p. 338** © Richard Hutchings, Photo Edit; **p. 340** © 1989 Robert Brenner, Photo Edit; **p. 340** © Laine Enkelis, Stock Boston; **p. 341** © 1988 Tony Freeman, Photo Edit; **p. 342** © Arlene Collins, Monkmeyer; **p. 344** © Mary Kate Denny, Photo Edit; **p. 346** © Spencer Grant, Stock Boston; **p. 349** © Richard Sobol, Stock Boston; **p. 351** © Michael Grecco, Stock Boston; **p. 353** © Spencer Grant, Stock Boston; **p. 360** © E. Lettau, FPG International; **p. 363** Historical Pictures Services; **p. 366** © Gary Conner, Photo Edit; **p. 368** © Laima Druskis, © Bruce Roberts, Photo Researchers; **p. 370** © L.O.L. Inc., © J. Pickerell, FPG International; **p. 373** © Billy E. Barnes; **p. 374** © David Young-Wolff, Photo Edit; **p. 377** © Billy E. Barnes, Jeroboam, Inc.; **p. 379** © Susan Kuklin, Photo Researchers; **p. 386** © Paul Steel, The Image Bank; **p. 388** © Joe Viesti, Viesti Associates, Inc.; **p. 391** National Library of Medicine, Photo Edit; **p. 394** Stock Boston; **p. 396** Art Resources; **p. 400** Courtesy of the Harvard University News Office; **p. 401** © Billy E. Barnes, © Myrleen Ferguson, Photo Edit; **p. 404** © 1988 David Lissy, The Picture Cube; **p. 404** © Richard Hutchings, InfoEdit; **p. 404** Judith Canty, Stock Boston; **p. 409** © Dave Gleiter, FPG International; **p. 418** © Bob Shaw, The Stock Market; **p. 423** © G. Goodwin, Monkmeyer; **p. 431** © Richard Hutchings, InfoEdit; **p. 431** © George Zimbel, Monkmeyer; **p. 442** © Michael Newman, Photo Edit; **p. 448** © R. Maiman, Sygma; **p. 456** Courtesy Lester Grinspoon; **p. 459** FPG International; **p. 462** © Arlene Collins, Monkmeyer; **p. 465** © Charles Kenard, Stock Boston; **p. 474** Superstock; **p. 483** © Lew Merrim, Monkmeyer; **p. 484** © Richard Hutchings, Photo Researchers; **p. 489** © Don Helms, Duomo; **p. 489** Elizebeth Zuckerman, Photo Edit; **p. 491** © Ron Chapple, FPG International; **p. 500** © Michael Davidson, Florida State University; **p. 502** Superstock; **p.505** © Owen Franken, Stock Boston; **p. 511** © Bob Burch, Bruce Coleman, Inc.; **p. 512** © Cary Wolinsky, Stock Boston; **p. 517** © Bill Bridges, Globe Photos; **p. 517** © Myrleen Ferguson, Photo Edit; **p. 524** Derek Bayes, © Times, Inc.; **p. 534** Tom McCarthy Photos, Photo Edit; **p. 538** Reuters/Bettman Newsphotos; **p. 540** © Billy E. Barnes, Jeroboam; **p. 543** Courtesy of Albert Bandura; **p. 550** © J. Pickerell, FPG International; **p. 553** © Will McIntyre, Photo Researchers; **p. 562** Alberto Incrocci, The Image Bank; **p. 564** Photo Edit; **p. 569** © Richard Hutchings, Photo Edit; **p. 571** © Patrick Roberts, Sygma; **p. 578** © Robert Brenner, Photo Edit; **p. 582** © Robert Brenner, Photo Edit; **p. 592** © Tony Freeman, Photo Edit; **p. 594** © Michael Krasowitz, FPG International; **p. 597** © Elena Rooraid, Photo Edit; **p. 598** News Service, Stanford University; **p. 600** © Kindra Clineff, The Picture Cube; **p. 603** © R. Bossu, Sygma; **p. 605** From "Opinions and Social Pressure" by Solomon E. Asch. In Scientific American, Nov. 1955; **p. 607** © 1965 by Stanley Milgram. From the film OBEDIENCE, distributed by the New York University Film Division and The Pennylvania State University, PCR.